Whitman Encyclopedia of Obsolete Paper Money

Whitman Encyclopedia of Obsolete Paper Money

Notes Issued by United States Banks, 1782–1866

Q. David Bowers

States, districts, and territories covered in this series, in order:

Connecticut, Maine, New Hampshire, Massachusetts, Rhode Island, Vermont, Florida, Georgia, North Carolina, South Carolina, Alabama, Arkansas, Kentucky, Louisiana, Mississippi, Tennessee, Texas, Delaware, District of Columbia, Maryland, Virginia, New Jersey, Pennsylvania, New York, Illinois, Indiana, Michigan, Ohio, California, Colorado, Iowa, Kansas, Minnesota, Missouri, Nebraska, Utah, and Wisconsin

Also see volume 1, *An Introduction for Collectors and Historians.*

For news (or announcements) and more information, refer to www.Whitman.com.

Volume 7

South Atlantic Region, Part 2

Alabama, Arkansas, Kentucky, Louisiana, Mississippi, Tennessee, and Texas

Edited by
Q. David Bowers (State of Alabama),
Rodney Kelley (State of Arkansas),
Tony Swicer (State of Kentucky),
Randy Haynie (State of Louisiana),
Justin McClure (State of Mississippi),
Gary Burhop (State of Tennessee),
and Michael Marotta (State of Texas)

WHITMAN ENCYCLOPEDIA OF OBSOLETE PAPER MONEY

NOTES ISSUED BY UNITED STATES BANKS, 1782–1866

VOLUME 7: SOUTH ATLANTIC REGION, PART 2

ALABAMA, ARKANSAS, KENTUCKY, LOUISIANA, MISSISSIPPI, TENNESSEE, AND TEXAS

© 2016 Whitman Publishing, LLC
3101 Clairmont Road • Suite G • Atlanta, GA 30329

ISBN: 0794843964
Printed in China

All rights reserved, including duplication of any kind or storage in electronic or visual retrieval systems. Permission is granted for writers to use a limited number of brief excerpts and quotations in printed reviews, magazine articles, and numismatic catalogs, provided credit is given to the title of the work and the author. Written permission is required for other uses, including in books, any use of illustrations, and any use of any information or illustrations in electronic or other media.

The Whitman numbering system and rarity ratings published herein may be used in advertisements or price lists, for the limited purpose of offering notes for sale, or for editorial purposes in print-format research articles or commentary. For use of the numbering system and rarity ratings in reference works or other publications (print, electronic, or otherwise), request permission from the publisher: Whitman Publishing, Rights and Permissions, 3101 Clairmont Road, Suite G, Atlanta, GA 30329.

Disclaimer: No warranty or representation of any kind is made concerning the accuracy or completeness of the information presented, or its usefulness in purchases or sales. The opinions of others may vary. The author and consultants may buy, sell, and sometimes hold certain of the items discussed in this book.

Caveat: This book is designed to provide accurate and authoritative information with regard to the subject matters covered. Some information is necessarily incomplete, and some entries may be modified with new or corrected information in the future. It is distributed with the understanding that Whitman Publishing and the author are not engaged in rendering legal, financial, or other professional services. If financial or tax advice or other expert professional assistance is required, the services of a competent professional should be sought. The guidance herein is subject to differences of opinion. Before making decisions to buy or sell numismatic collectibles, consult the latest information, including current market conditions. Past performance of the paper-money market, or any series or note within that market, is not necessarily an indication of future performance, as the future is unknown. Such factors as changing demand, popularity, grading interpretations, strength of the overall market, and national and international economic conditions will continue to be influences.

If you have new information about any banks or notes listed in this volume, contact Whitman Publishing, Attn: Obsolete Paper Money, 3101 Clairmont Road, Suite G, Atlanta, GA 30329.

Whitman Publishing is a leader in the antiques and collectibles field.
For a catalog of related books, supplies, and storage products,
visit Whitman Publishing online at www.Whitman.com.

OCG™ COLLECTING GUIDE WHITMAN®

Contents

FOREWORD

For far too long, collectors of obsolete bank notes have languished without an up-to-date, easy-to-use, detailed guide to help them in their labor of love. Since the first time these fascinating notes began to be collected, many, many decades ago, the most difficult task confronting collectors or owners has always been identifying, cataloging, and valuing the myriad notes which present themselves. There exist literally thousands upon thousands of different obsolete bank notes issued by the many banks located within the boundaries of the United States. Attempts to categorize, illustrate, and value these notes in an updated medium since the publication of the pivotal 1988 Haxby *Standard Catalog of United States Obsolete Bank Notes* were deemed insurmountable, impractical, and even impossible, until Q. David Bowers and those so ably assisting him set about assembling the collection of work we now have at our fingertips.

Those problems which have plagued enthusiasts in the past have now been resoundingly resolved. Meticulously discussed within this work are every city, town, and locality that issued obsolete bank notes from the states under study. Furthermore, color photographs of hundreds of these marvelous notes, coupled with bank histories, rarity ratings, values, and much more are found within these pages to guide us upon our journey. Very easy to use, and certainly easy on the eyes, these books near-effortlessly aid collectors, researchers, and historians, eliminating the complex issues often presented in previous works. While those prior works were beneficial, they pale in comparison to the literal mountain of useful data contained within the pages of this incredible publication.

Obsolete bank notes provide us with a very real glimpse into this great nation's past. Through the lens of this old paper money, we are able to travel back in time to gain a vivid look at what life was like in the United States before, during, and in some cases after the Civil War. Other volumes in this series have gracefully and accurately conveyed beautiful illustrations to stimulate the imagination while at the same time supplying much-needed information relative to each bank note. Widening this lens, upon these works of art exist hundreds of vignettes, ranging from agrarian scenes to Greek mythological figures to some scenes we would rather not think about—but would do well to remember.

Our banking system has changed, although our history has not. The beauty, appeal, allure, and value of obsolete bank notes is almost unimaginably captured by Bowers within these pages. An amazing feat . . . to say the least.

Randy Shipley
Mooresburg, Tennessee

Credits and Acknowledgements

For global and general credits for the *Whitman Encyclopedia of Obsolete Paper Money*, see volume 1. For volume 7's study of Alabama, Arkansas, Kentucky, Louisiana, Mississippi, Tennessee, and Texas, specific credit goes to:

American Bank Note Co.; American Numismatic Association; American Numismatic Society; Wynn Bowers; Gary Burhop; Charles Cataldo; Ashley Clark; Phil Darby; DeGolyer Library; C. John Ferreri; Jeffrey M. Feuerman; Robert Gill; Bruce Hagen; James A. Haxby; Randy Haynie; Heritage Auctions (HA.com); Historical Society of Phoenixville, Pennsylvania; Wayne Homren; Michael Keane; Rodney Kelley; Lyn Knight Auctions; Russell L. Martin III; Justin McClure; Eric P. Newman; Phillips Library at the Peabody-Essex Museum; Michael Rocco; John Rowe; Neil Shafer; Randy Shipley; Smithsonian Institution; Southern Methodist University; Stack's Bowers Galleries; Tony Swicer; Harry Warren; and John and Nancy Wilson.

Valuations editors for volume 7: Gary Burhop; Randy Haynie; Rodney Kelley; Justin McClure; Tony Swicer.

Special valuations contributors: Phil Darby; Bruce Hagen; John Rowe; Randy Shipley.

Image Credits

ANS	American Numismatic Society, New York City, New York
CC	Caine Collection
ChasC	Charles Cataldo Collection
DG	DeGolyer Library, Southern Methodist University, Rowe-Barr Collection of Texas Currency
GB	Gary Burhop Collection
HA	Heritage Auction Archives
HSPA	Historical Society of Phoenixville, Pennsylvania
HW	Harry Warren Collection
JF	Jeffrey M. Feuerman Collection
JM	Justin McClure Collection
LK	Lyn Knight Auctions
MR	Michael Rocco Collection
NJW	Nancy and John Wilson Collection
NS	Neil Shafer Collection
QDB	Q. David Bowers Archives
RG	Robert Gill Collection
RH	Randy Haynie Collection
RS	Randy Shipley
SBG	Stack's Bowers Galleries
SI	Smithsonian Institution, National Numismatic Collection
TS	Tony Swicer Collection

How to Use This Book

When considering the purchase or sale of a note, two main considerations are grade and price. Beyond that, there are other aspects that are important in study and set one note apart from another. In certain aspects the study of notes is different from that of coins. Notes that are spurious (not official) can have significant value, as can counterfeits of standard notes. In some instances, a note in Extremely Fine-40 (EF-40) grade can be more valuable than an Uncirculated or unused note.

This guide explains the different aspects of typical bank listings in this book—covering the states of Alabama, Arkansas, Kentucky, Louisiana, Mississippi, Tennessee, and Texas. Volume 1 of this series contains a thoroughly detailed study of the entire field of obsolete state bank notes issued from 1782 to 1866, including a glossary of bank-note engravers, information on how currency was designed, printed, and distributed, and much more. If read even casually, volume 1 will set you on your way to becoming an expert. In the meantime, "How to Use This Book" will explain the current listings in the volume at hand.

Types of Notes

There are several classes of collectible notes in this series. Their status affects their collectability and desirability.

Valid Issues

Valid issues are notes that were printed from plates made by skilled engravers and produced by bank-note companies or other authorized sources. In their time, they were paid out at face value by banks. Such bills were often later redeemed for face value and replaced by new issues. If a bank failed and its notes could not be redeemed, today its notes are still considered to be valid issues by collectors. Valid notes form the main focus of collecting obsolete currency.

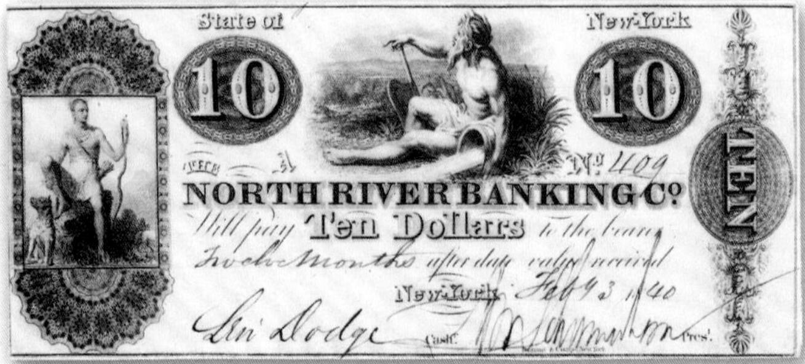

A valid issue from the North River Banking Co., New York.

Non-Valid Issues

These exist in several categories:

Counterfeit notes: Illegally issued notes from false plates that imitated genuine bills. They are collectible as "fillers" in some instances but generally sell for low prices. They are collectible mainly as curiosities.

Note counterfeited to be passed as an issue from the Bank of Cumberland, Maine.

Raised notes: It was a common deceptive practice to raise the value of a low-denomination note to a higher one by chemically removing the counters (as they are called) or denomination ornaments and altering them to read as a higher value. Such notes have nominal values as collectibles today.

Original note of the Merchants & Manufacturers Bank.

Raised note.

Altered notes: Notes that were valid or spurious when first printed but then fell into the hands of criminals who altered them. When a bank failed, its notes became worthless and could not be redeemed for face value. There was a market for such, often at 2 percent or 3 percent of face value. Criminals bought them and, by the use of chemicals, removed certain information such as the town, state, and sometimes even the name of the bank. New information was then printed in the blank spaces. As an example, quantities of worthless $10 notes of the Egg Harbor Bank, Egg Harbor, New Jersey, were altered to appear as $10 notes of the active and strong Valley Bank, Hillsborough, New Hampshire. Altered notes are collectible, but their values are considerably less than the genuine.

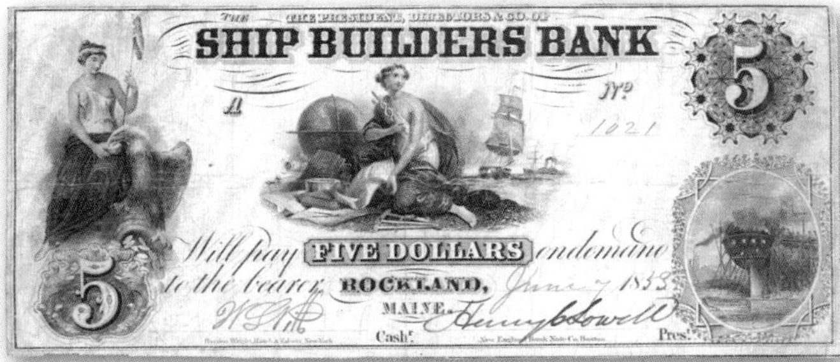

Original note of the Ship Builders Bank.

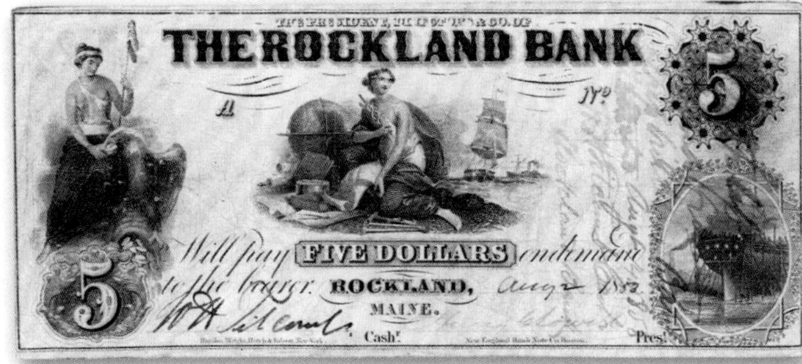

Altered note.

Spurious Issues

Spurious issues are notes from established engravers and printers that were delivered to banks that never opened their doors or to fraudsters who issued notes bearing the names of banks that never existed. Often these have fascinating stories. These are a basic part of collecting and in many instances are valued for as much as, or higher than, valid issues.

In this text Spurious issues are located in one of two places—under Valid Issues if the bank as a whole never opened or was fraudulently run, but the notes were genuinely printed, or under Non-Valid issues if notes from a genuine bank were taken into the hands of fraudsters and illegally distributed in a similar fashion to other Non-Valid notes such as counterfeits and altered notes.

Spurious note from a non-existent bank in a non-existent town. Fraudsters intended to alter it to represent the BOSTON bank of the same name.

Signed and Issued Notes

Banks typically received notes from the printer in sheets, most often a four-subject sheet bearing one to four denominations. Certain features needed to be added once the notes were received. Law cases affirmed that a bill was monetized only after the cashier affixed his signature. It was standard practice in small banks for the cashier to prepare the sheets in advance and then sign them only when the sheets were cut apart and ready to be issued. These features were added to prepare a note for distribution:

Date: Each note needed to bear a year, month, and day of when it was issued. Some notes had printed dates, such as *Jan.y 1st, 1854*, and did not require hand entry. Sometimes these referred to the charter date or were an annual date. It was not unusual for a note to be issued later than the date shown. Accordingly, if a note with a printed date of *Jan.y 1st, 1854*, was signed by cashier John Doe, who was named to that office on May 6, 1856, this was not an extraordinary situation. Many other notes had the number partially printed, such as 18__ or 185_, with the remainder to be inked in.

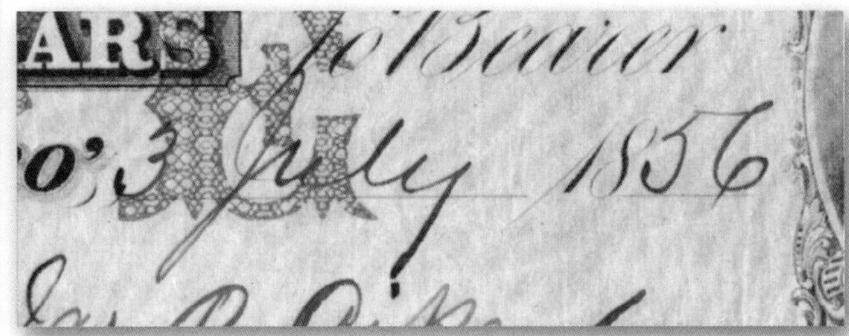

Partially printed date with the remainder inked in by hand.

Serial number: Serial numbers were usually added by hand in ink. Some notes had the same serial number twice on a note. The combination of the serial number, the date, and the plate letter defines a note as one of a kind.

To cut down on the work involved, serial-number sequences were often started anew when the date changed. This kept the numbers low. Unlike the situation for federal paper money, it is not unusual for an obsolete note to have a serial number below 100. Very few were higher than four digits. Sometimes colored ink was used for serial numbers. Certain notes of larger banks have the serial numbers printed by machine, but these are unusual.

Printed serial number.

President's signature: The primary duty of the president was to conduct meetings of the board of directors and the annual meeting of stockholders. Many directors lived at a distance from the bank and visited it infrequently. Accordingly, it was the custom of the president to sign large quantities of notes far in advance. The president of a small bank usually received a nominal salary, say $100 or $200 per year, or none at all.

Cashier's signature on the left. President's signature on the right.

Cashier's signature: The cashier was the person in charge. Often, for small banks, he was the only employee. It was not unusual for banks in small villages to be kept in the house of the cashier or, if the bank had its own building, for the cashier and his family to live on the premises. Security systems usually consisted only of locks and bolts. The cashier could keep watch at all times, including when the bank was closed.

The cashier was the highest-paid person, often $1,000 per year, more or less. The cashier opened the bank and closed it, kept the books, and took charge of money receipts and payments. Loans were usually arranged with another person on hand, such as one or two directors. Loans were given on "discount days," usually one or two days a week. This made it easier for one or more directors to attend. The discount day schedule was published in local papers. When the cashier affixed his signature to a note, it was officially monetized. That way, if notes were stolen but lacked the signature, the bank could simply declare them to be worthless.

Cashier's signature *D. Holmes*.

Notes in Circulation

Most bills circulated at face value locally or regionally. A $10 bill issued in New Haven, Connecticut, by a sound bank would be received at par with a slight discount for handling in Providence, Boston, or New York City. In Pittsburgh, Richmond, or another distant place, it would be taken in at a discount. Many earned extra profits by selling notes at a discount to brokers or runners who put them into circulation in distant places. The Hillsborough Bank of Amherst, New Hampshire, shipped bundles of notes to Marietta, Ohio, where they were placed into circulation easily. Storekeepers would buy them at a discount. The recipients would spend them, as would others. Hardly anyone went back to New Hampshire to exchange them for coins. Brokers in New York City handled large quantities of discounted notes.

Printed bank-note reporters and counterfeit detectors, as they were called, were published in many forms. These usually told of new counterfeits as well as of banks that had failed or were in financial difficulty. Long lists were presented by state, town, and bank, rating the notes and stating the discount from par at which banks and merchants should be valued.

Grading of Notes

There are no hard and fast rules for grading obsolete currency. Interpretations can vary, sometimes widely. Most old-time dealers and experienced auction houses tend to be more conservative than many who list in Internet sales or who are otherwise not part of the profession. A "Fine" note to one dealer may be another's "Very Fine." Similar to the situation for coins, grading has become looser over the years. A bill bought in the 1960s as Fine will easily be Very Fine today. Years ago, a bill with even a slight trace of a fold or crease was automatically excluded from the Uncirculated category. Today, bills described as such can have these traces, and, perhaps, one without such traces would be given a loftier designation such as Choice Uncirculated or Gem Uncirculated. And so it goes. The methodology is not as consistent or as well developed as is the grading of coins. Two commercial grading services are prominent in grading notes. PCGS Currency, once a part of the Professional Coin Grading Service but now independently owned, and PMG (Paper Money Grading), a division of the Numismatic Guaranty Corporation, have found wide acceptance in the marketplace. As of today they have published no standards, but they seem to more or less follow the guidelines given below.

These categories reflect the author's observations of current grading methods by many dealers and collectors. Beginning in the early 21st century, numbers have been attached to grades by some sellers based on the American Numismatic Association Grading Standards for United States Coins. However, as bills were printed, not minted, the term "Mint State" is not used for paper money.

Grading System

Choice or Gem Uncirculated

Unc-63 and 64 (Choice), Unc-65 (Gem).

A crisp, bright bill with no evidence of creases, folds, or stains. Tom Denly commented in 2004: "I consider centering to be a most important part of grade. For instance, a poorly centered note possibly cut into the design can never be called Gem or even Choice, no matter how nice it otherwise is." Most notes in this category are remainders.

Uncirculated

Unc-60.

A new, never circulated bill, but perhaps with slight evidences of a fold, a crease, or smudges from handling (presumably by bank officers). If part of the margin is trimmed away, this should be mentioned, but often is not. Most notes in this category are remainders.

About Uncirculated

AU-53, 55, and 58.

A bright, attractive note, with some creases, folds, or light discoloration, but with only slight evidences of use in commerce or, in the case of remainders, numismatic or bank handling. If signed and issued for circulation, this is a top-of-the-line grade in great demand.

Extremely Fine

EF-40 and 45.

Bright and attractive but with some slight stains or discoloration, perhaps with a pinhole or two or some small defect. Overall excellent appearance. A bill in this grade saw limited service in circulation.

Very Fine

VF-20 and 30.

This is a widely used grade for a "nice" note, worn but with nice features. Such a bill may be somewhat faded, but the printing and vignettes will be clear and with an attractive overall appearance. There may be an edge chip or two or perhaps a tiny piece off of a corner (but not into the printed part of the note). As most bank tellers and users were right-handed, the right side of a note usually has some discoloration from everyday handling.

Fine

Fine-12.

A note with even more wear, often limp or flimsy from extended use in commerce, but with all printed areas intact and most of them sharply defined. May be stained or discolored in areas.

Very Good

VG-8.

Well circulated, usually with some problems, tears, perhaps a small piece missing from the border, etc. Flimsy and often faded or discolored.

Good

G-4.

Extensively circulated and with evidence of such, including small tears, perhaps edge pieces missing, areas of the printing and vignettes indistinct, and, often, old writing on the face of the note.

Poor, Fair, and About Good

Poor-1, Fair-2, AG-3.

Notes that have been in circulation for a very long time, now with ragged edges or pieces missing and often with significant areas of the note faded or otherwise indiscernible. A filler note. There are quite a few very early bills from the late 18th and early 19th century for which these grades may represent the finest known.

Grade as a Determinant of Value

Remainder notes: Surprise! In the field of bank notes, a well-worn example is often worth more than an Uncirculated bill of the same variety! However, the explanation is simple: most Uncirculated bills are remainders that were never distributed. Most have no officers' signatures. Years after certain banks closed, large quantities of their unissued notes became available. In most instances, a nice Very Fine bill of the same denomination and design, signed and serially numbered, is worth more. Remainder notes of this kind are designated as Unc-Rem. A signed and dated Uncirculated note is designated as Unc-S&D.

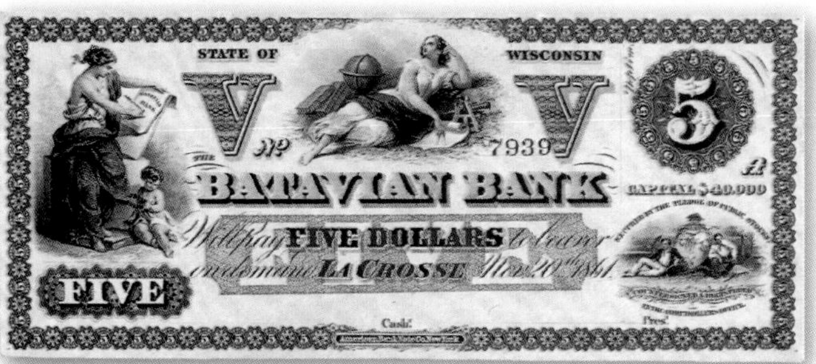

An Uncirculated remainder note.

Circulated notes: Among signed and numbered notes, higher-grade examples are more desirable than those in lower levels of preservation. In all instances, an About Uncirculated bill is worth more than an Extremely Fine one, and an EF is worth more than a Very Fine, and on down the line. Among the most desirable of circulated notes are those that are serially numbered, dated, and signed in ink by the cashier and president and which are in a high grade today.

A signed, dated, circulated note.

Cancelled notes: When worn notes were redeemed to be exchanged for others, banks often destroyed them. In many instances, however, they were saved but "canceled" to prevent them from being placed into circulation again. Several small, circular punch holes will either not affect the value of a note or will affect it only slightly, unless uncancelled notes are readily available. Large holes, notches cut out from the border, signatures cut off, and other cancellations that are unattractive are viewed negatively, as are stamped overprints, such as the common WORTHLESS and COUNTERFEIT.

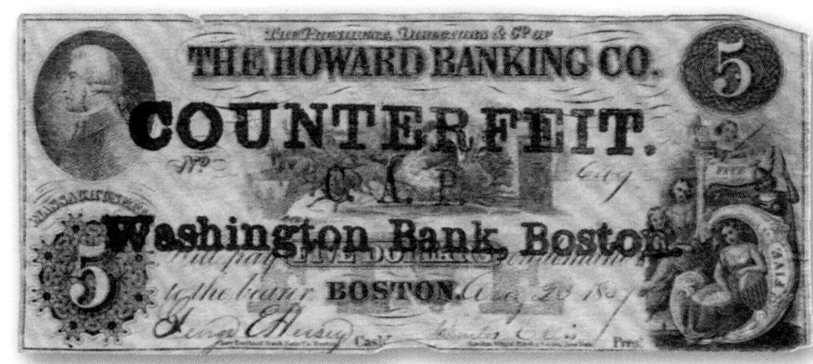

A note cancelled to prevent further circulation.

Proof notes: Proof notes are special printings on special paper or light card stock, are usually found Uncirculated, and can be very valuable, if they are contemporary (made in the 19th century). Modern Proof reprints are worth varying lesser amounts. Beware of scanned or photographic modern copies.

A Proof note, without signatures, printed on special stock.

Proprietary Proofs: Now and then Proprietary Proofs or modern reprints are made of existing genuine notes. These are often given brightly colored tints or overprints and are crisp and clean, but they were never seen during the bank-note–issuing era. Collectors should be aware that these notes are nearly always worth less than genuine notes. For more information, see page 12 of volume 1.

A genuine Northfield Bank note, Northfield, Vermont.

A Proprietary Proof note made from the same plates as the above genuine note. The tint is on a separate plate from the engraving.

Valuation of Notes

Explanation of Values

Values assigned to notes in given grades have been compiled by consulting with dealers and collectors and by studying listed prices and auction results. Unlike coins, which often have values determined by "bid" prices and, for some such as gold, trade on close margins, the valuation of paper currency is much more subjective. In a way, the pricing can be compared to that in the fields of tokens and medals.

Many notes are infrequently traded. This is especially true for rare early issues. Sometimes, years can elapse between offerings. In such instances the values here are "educated guesses." Actual sale results such as an offering at auction may differ widely. For that reason values in this book should be considered as estimates compiled at the time of publication. Although the future is unknown, in past decades the price trends have been upward. Many notes valued at $100 a decade ago may be valued at $125 to $175 or more now. Few if any valid-issue notes have decreased in value. When contemplating a purchase or sale it is recommended that you check with experts and other sources for current values.

Even for common remainder notes and for certain common circulated bills in a given grade, prices can vary in the same time frame. One note might be priced at $200, another at $175, and a third at $250. It may be worthwhile to say that the same variations are seen in many other collectibles markets—such as Currier & Ives prints, postcards, colonial coins, ancient coins, antique furniture, tokens and medals, and more. The point here is that federal coins of the past 200 years are often quite common, trade frequently, and have bid and ask prices—a situation not comparable to other collectible specialties as mentioned.

To aid in current valuation we recommend subscribing to publications about paper money and checking auction and sale listings, often available on the Internet.

If a long-sought rarity is offered, many if not most experienced dealers and collectors will "reach" for it. A rarity listed for $1,000 may be a good buy for $2,000 if it is the only one to be offered in recent years.

With some experience, you will get a grasp for pricing—just as collectors of tokens, medals, prints, and other things have. What starts as being esoteric will in time become familiar.

Factors Affecting Values

Grade or condition: Among notes that were signed, numbered, dated, and placed into circulation, the higher the grade, the more valuable the note is. Uncirculated notes or remainders can be worth less than a circulated signed note.

Location: Notes of certain states or territories can be worth a premium. Western notes of a given rarity, such as from Utah, Kansas Territory, or Arkansas can be worth more than notes from New York, Pennsylvania, or New Jersey.

Rarity: In a given series, a rare note is worth more a common one.

Demand and popularity: Notes of certain towns and states can be worth more if there are more collectors desiring to buy them. Notes from Florida are more widely collected than are those of Vermont. Accordingly, a note of a given rarity can be worth more if from Florida. Such popularity may change over a period of time. If two or three well-financed buyers each seek to build a collection of a state, there will be great competition for rarities, and prices will be much higher than if this competition were not present. In addition, the publication of a new reference work on a particular state or category can serve to increase the number of people desiring such notes.

Denomination: Within a given rarity, an unusual denomination such as $4, $6, $7, $8, or $9 will be worth more than a $1, $2, $3, $5, $10, or $20 (these being the most often seen). On their own, $3 notes have always attracted a following; once common in circulation, the denomination is considered unusual today. It has not been used since the federal government began issuing notes in quantity in 1861, despite being very popular with state-chartered banks. $50 and $100 notes are scarce for most banks, and with relatively few exceptions, $500 and $1,000 notes are great rarities.

Vignette topic: The illustration or vignette of a note can add value. A Connecticut note showing Iranistan, the palatial home of P.T. Barnum, or "the Battle of the Frogs" is worth more than one showing a train or buildings. Notes showing Santa Claus are extremely popular and often sell for much more than what a comparable-rarity bill of a miscellaneous subject might command.

"Battle of the Frogs."

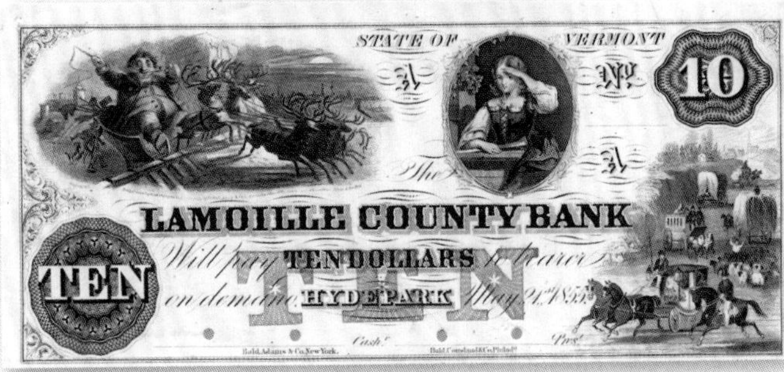

Santa Claus at upper left.

Proofs: Proof notes printed on special paper and intended as samples or for reference are usually found in Uncirculated preservation and will sell for many multiples of the price of common remainder notes.

Market and economic trends: The general market for obsolete paper money has been quite strong in recent decades. However, it was rather quiet before then. Market strength is based on the number of buyers at a given time and how much money they have to spend.

Imaging of Notes

Given their age and extensive circulation, obsolete bank notes are sometimes found with a high level of wear and tear. Within this encyclopedia, some images have been digitally enhanced to mitigate the effects of rust, water damage, stains, age, circulation wear, color fading, and other environmental stresses. Where necessary, they have been conceptually restored to more closely resemble their original form in an attempt to aid collectors and historians in identifying and analyzing the various issues, vignettes, engravings, and styles of the bank notes.

Printed Features of Note Designs

A typical note includes these printed features:

Name of bank: The name of the bank is usually the most prominently printed figure and can be found either high on the center of the note face or in a position about half way down. New Haven Bank, Derby Bank, Cochituate Bank, Bank of Commerce, Warner Bank, and Butchers and Drovers Bank are examples. Such titles often reflect the location of the bank, an industry such as farming or manufacturing, a geographical feature such as an ocean or river, or a proper name from history. Among the latter there are banks named Franklin, Washington, Lafayette, and Indian names such as Amoskeag, Oneida, Quinnipiack, and Mohawk. At any given time there was only one bank of a certain name in operation in a given state.

Location of bank: Every note gives the town and state. The town often appears near the bank name or is sometimes tagged on to it, such as the Tradesmens Bank of New Haven. The name of the state often appears away from the town name, perhaps in the field of the note or at a border.

Denomination: This is the face value of a note. The most popular values were $1, $2, $3, $5, and $10 among the lower denominations and were made in the largest quantities. $20, $50, and $100 values were made in smaller quantities. Only a few banks issued $500 or $1,000 notes. There are also fractional notes such as 25¢, 50¢, and 75¢ in existence, issued by banks as part of a series that included higher denominations. The more times a denomination was printed on a note, the harder it was to alter by raising. Many notes have the denomination given dozens of times in micro-letters in addition to larger digits. Odd-value notes such as $1.25, $1.50, $1.75, $4, and $6 to $9 were issued by a few banks.

Scattered small notes denominated in cents were sometimes issued, usually but not always privately, in times of economic distress and are called scrip. Scrip notes were usually made by local printers. They are not studied herein.

Denomination counters: While the denominations of many notes, especially early ones, were lettered or in script, most bills after about 1810 had the value as a number surrounded with an oval, circle, or fancy engraving. These are referred to as counters. Volume 1 gives many examples.

Main vignette: Most notes have a large vignette at the center or to one side extending to the center. These are often scenic in nature—a seated figure, laborers at work, a train and cars, capitols and commercial buildings, figures from mythology, seascapes, and more. After 1820 vignettes became increasingly ornate.

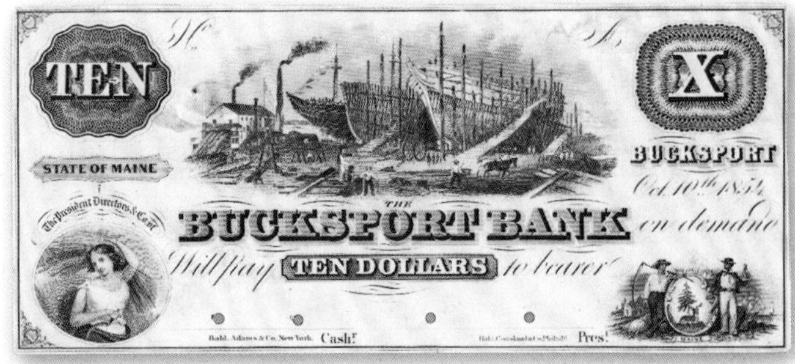

Other vignettes: Most notes also had two or more smaller vignettes. Portraits of people ranging from well-known, such as a national president, to obscure, such as a bank president, were popular. Others show standing or seated figures, people in various activities, etc. Medallion vignettes reproduce medals, cameos, or plaques by means of a medal-ruling machine.

Ornaments and borders: Various geometric figures and engraved ornaments add to the complexity of many notes, as do ornamental borders.

Seals and arms: State arms, seals stating that a note was backed by securities or liens on real estate, etc., were added to many notes.

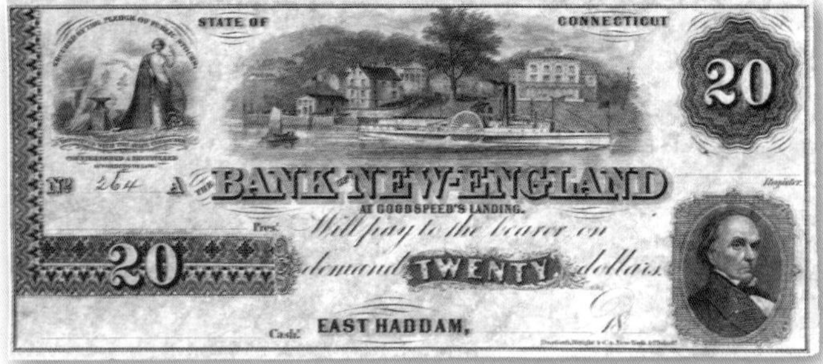

The state arms of Connecticut can be seen in the upper left corner.

Plate letter: It was common practice to assign a letter such as A, B, or C to the face of a note. A sheet of four notes might include, as an example, $1-$1-$1-$2. The three $1 notes would bear letters A, B, and C, and the $2 note would start again with A.

Engraver's imprint: The name of the bank-note printing company was nearly always stated in the face, usually in tiny letters at the bottom border but sometimes elsewhere. On some occasions ornamental vignettes were signed in micro-letters by engravers.

Place of redemption: While most bank notes could be redeemed over the counter of the banks that issued them, some others gave distant places where they could be redeemed, as at an office in another state, often in New York City. Such notes were frequently of questionable value.

Time of redemption: Most notes could be redeemed on demand, but many had a printed inscription stating that they could be redeemed only at a specified time later than the date on the note—six months, a year, or some other interval. Later-payment bills are called post notes, a term printed on some of them. Confederate States of America notes were redeemable two years after a peace treaty was signed with the United States, which, of course, never happened.

Overprints: Many notes, especially those after the 1820s, have overprints in color. These often give the denomination, such as ONE, FIVE, or TWENTY. Some later notes have grillwork, the denomination in micro-printing, or other features added in panels of color printing. On some the entire face can be overprinted in color.

Most engravers used the basic colors of red, blue, and green (with some rare yellows appearing infrequently). Over time, these colors can degrade into variously differing shades, such as ochre, orange, red-brown, etc. for red. For consistency and clarity these colors have been summed up with red, red-orange, and red-brown to indicate the color seen on the physical note.

Backs of notes: With only scattered exceptions, the backs of notes have not been discussed in reference books or auction catalogs. Hence, there are many notes listed in this book that have ornate backs not described.

Security features: Security features to deter counterfeiting or altering are seen on many notes. The most common is the "Canada green" or "Patent Green Tint" used on notes of Rawdon, Wright, Hatch & Edson in 1857 and by the American Bank Note Co. from 1858 onward. This color was said to deter copying by photographic means. Jacob Perkins's Patented Stereotype Steel Plate (PSSP) used micro-lettering to deter counterfeiting.

Other information: Ruled spaces and lettering were provided to indicate where the bank officers should sign and where the serial number should be placed. Various inscriptions, monograms, and other elements were sometimes added.

Listings of Notes

There are various elements to each bank and note in this book. Not every note will have the same or all of these characteristics. For ease of communication, description, and inventory, "Whitman numbers" have been assigned to the various notes.

Town / Town information: The name of and a brief historical sketch of the city or town in which the bank was located.

Bank name: The name of the bank. This is usually the name as imprinted on notes. Often on a note "The" will be the preface. "And" in a bank title is used in bank charters and is used here, as in Farmers and Merchants Bank. However, some notes and many numismatic listings use an ampersand (&) instead. It is numismatic practice to drop punctuation, to use Citizens instead of Citizens', for example. On some notes the name of the town is added to the title, such as the Farmers Bank of River City or the Farmers Bank in River City. Some notes of a given bank have such suffixes and others do not. They are not used here unless they are a main part of the title as boldly printed on a note, such as Smithville Bank of Commerce or Greenville Grocers Bank.

Date of operation: Years of existence, from the bank's charter date until it ceased operations, such as 1851–1865. Sometimes a bank did not begin operations until a year or two after it was chartered.

History: A synopsis of the history of the bank during its note-issuing period. Often much additional information can be found in historical texts or on the Internet and makes an interesting pursuit.

Numismatic commentary: Comments on the bank, the notes' overall availability, and more. In this volume Rodney Kelley, Tony Swicer, Randy Haynie, Justin McClure, Gary Burhop, and Michael Marotta were among those who assisted with this content.

Note listing: Divided into sections by Valid Issues (genuine notes from functioning banks), Issues (spurious notes from non-functioning or fraudulent banks), and Non-Valid Issues (notes from genuine banks that were later counterfeited, raised, made spurious by fraudsters, altered, etc.). The sample listing following is from the Bank of the State of Alabama, Cahawba, Alabama.

$1 • W-AL-010-001-G010 CC

Engraver: A.B. & C. Durand & Wright. ***Comments:*** H-AL-5-G2. 18__. 1820s.

Rarity: URS-2
Proof $2,600

$1: Denomination of the note shown.

W-AL-010-001-G010

W: Whitman number. This number is a sortable code unique to each bank and note.

AL: Abbreviation for the state under study.

010: Numerical designation for the Bank of the State of Alabama, Cahawba. Other banks have different numbers.

001: The denomination in dollars.

G010: G indicates a good or valid note. Other categories are indicated thus: C (counterfeit); R (raised); S (spurious); N (not-attributed); A (altered). 010 is the specific note shown. Notes are listed in a bank-series by increments of 10 in order of denomination—a "porous" system so new discoveries can be added if needed. Terminal letters following the numerical designation indicate variations of a note: a series of different colored overprints, tints, payees, etc., all on the same design of note. Thus the first type of a note will have no letter, the second an "a," the third a "b," the fourth a "c," and so on as necessary.

CC: Photographic image of an actual note in a collection, museum, or other location. Each photograph shown identifies its original source, when known, by an abbreviation at the upper right-hand corner of the image. A list of these creditors can be found at the front of the volume.

Vignette description: Primarily divided into Left, Center, Bottom center, and Right, these describe what is seen on the face of the note. Other descriptors include Overprint, Tint, Back, Payee, Engraver, and Comments, which includes other details about the note. For notes that are not illustrated, descriptions are given—based on information, when available, from contemporary bank-note reporters, counterfeit detectors, and other listings. Some are partial or may even prove to be inaccurate if an actual note is discovered. PSSP refers to a note of the Patent Stereotype Steel Plate by Jacob Perkins or his successor, the New England Bank Note Co. (see volume 1 for details). Illustrated notes will not have the primary descriptions included.

Rarity and Value: Estimate of the number of notes in existence today and the typical market value of a note at the time of publication. The figure indicates the center of a range. As an example, $400 suggests a range of about $350 to $450. Included as available.

Rarity (URS) Ratings

The Universal Rarity Scale

The Universal Rarity Scale uses a simple geometric progression of numbers by doubling the preceding value for each successive "rank": 1, 2, 4, 8, 16, 32, etc. (see the rightmost of each number pair), with the higher numbers rounded off for simplicity. Introduced in 1993, this has been widely used in various publications since that time. It is not copyrighted.

URS-1 = 1 known, unique
URS-2 = 2 known
URS-3 = 3 or 4
URS-4 = 5 to 8
URS-5 = 9 to 16
URS-6 = 17 to 32
URS-7 = 33 to 64
URS-8 = 65 to 124
URS-9 = 125 to 249
URS-10 = 250 to 499
URS-11 = 500 to 999
URS-12 = 1,000 to 1,999
URS-13 = 2,000 to 3,999
URS-14 = 4,000 to 7,999

Population Estimates

Drawing from authoritative catalogs, input from dealers and collectors, and other sources, rarity estimates have been given for many notes. In the past there have been many instances in which additional examples of previously rare notes have been found or new information has been learned. This will continue to be the case. Accordingly, some notes may become more plentiful than now listed. Many estates and other holdings with notes have not as of yet been examined or surveyed. To paraphrase an old comment, if Jones was not seen at a football game, he still might have been there.

Factors Affecting Present-Day Rarity

Some obsolete notes are very common. Others are so rare that only one or two exist. In some cases, a note may have been described in a bank-note reporter or other early reference, but no physical examples are known to exist. Such notes are assigned a Rarity listing of *None known*. Still others are so intangible that a guess has not been made as to their rarity; these are given a dash (—) as their Rarity listing.

If a bank was well-run and had no difficulties, its notes were usually redeemed at par. Sometimes these were burned—as mandated for banks in the state of Maine. There are many Maine notes that were once in circulation by the thousand but for which few are known today. In other states, notes were burned or were canceled at the option of the directors. In many instances quantities of canceled notes were saved, and later generations of collectors and dealers obtained them.

Many banks failed or otherwise could not redeem their notes. Spurious banks did not redeem any currency. Bills of such banks can be very common today. Quantities of unissued remainder notes, often as original sheets, exist for some banks. With increasing demand, many of the sheets have been cut apart. Notes of certain banks are extremely common as Uncirculated remainders, but signed and issued notes are rare and much more valuable. Original sheets can be collected as a specialty and are listed in this book. However, as they are not convenient to display and as the four notes to a sheet have been worth more individually in the past, most have been cut apart, as noted.

Learning More

Collecting obsolete bank notes can be a fascinating pursuit. Scarce and rare bills can often be obtained for fractions of the cost of comparably rare coins. With modest financial means it is often possible to build a first-class collection of notes from a particular area or with a particular theme.

As you have read to this point, you know that notes can be complex—and to an enthusiast, wonderfully so. Your enjoyment can be enriched by learning more. Whitman Publishing offers three key volumes that are guaranteed to please:

Volume 1 of the *Whitman Encyclopedia of Obsolete Paper Money* series is an in-depth study of obsolete paper money, how it was conceived, created, and distributed. Chapters go into great detail concerning engravers, vignettes, counterfeiting, and more. It is probably correct to say that if you spend a few evenings with your copy, you will be well on your way to becoming an expert. This book is a companion to the volume you are now holding and has been designed to complement it with much additional information.

Obsolete Paper Money Issued by Banks in the United States 1782–1866, published in 2006, is another essential volume on your way to becoming an expert and smart buyer.

The third book in the Whitman suite is *100 Greatest American Currency Notes*, a "for fun" volume that includes many different types of paper money with many obsolete bills featured.

Bank Note Reporter, issued monthly by Krause Publications, is filled with news and offerings. *Paper Money*, the journal of the Society of Paper Money Collectors, has much valuable information and many research articles.

The Professional Currency Dealers Association (PCDA) has dozens of members and opens the door to buying notes. It is strongly recommended that unless you are aware of special qualifications, you avoid buying notes on the Internet or other nonprofessional sources without an iron-clad money-back guarantee.

Obsolete notes are meant to be enjoyed. With some study of historical books and newspapers on the Internet or in a library, a single note can be your passport to a lot of ownership pleasure.

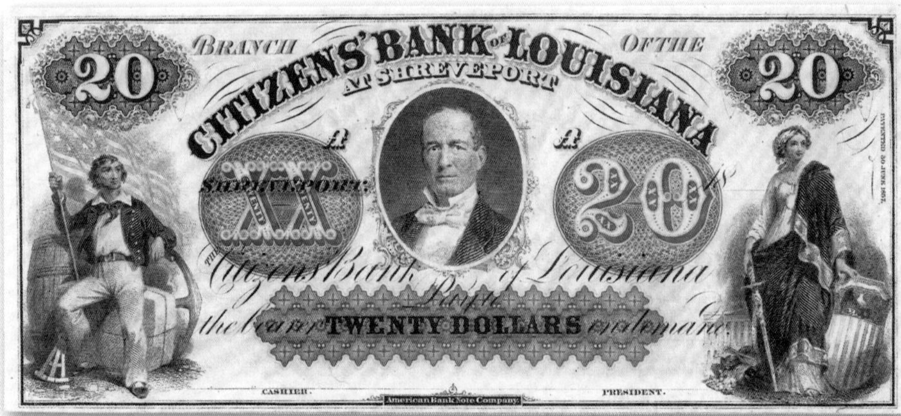

The Obsolete Bank Notes of Alabama

State Banking in Alabama

Currency of Alabama

Although Alabama did not achieve statehood until December 14, 1819, limited banking took place earlier in the district when it was still a part of the Mississippi Territory. Alabama achieved territorial status of its own in 1817.

Alabama has had five capitals, the first being Saint Stephens, which served as the seat of government for the territory. In 1820, a year after Alabama achieved statehood, the legislature first met in Cahawba, which had been chosen as capital of the state. The legislative session of 1825 and 1826 voted to leave Cahawba, however, due to the fact that it was considered to be an unhealthy place subject to flooding. The capital was relocated to Tuscaloosa, where it remained until the General Assembly in 1846 moved it to Montgomery. Andrew Dexter Jr., erstwhile fraudster of the notorious Farmers Exchange Bank of Gloucester, Rhode Island, held a large tract of land there. The new Capitol building was dedicated on December 6, 1847. On December 14, 1849, the building burned, after which a new structure was erected. With expansions and modifications, this is the Capitol still in use today.

The Planters and Mechanics (later known as the Planters and Merchants) Bank at Huntsville was chartered in 1816, followed in 1818 by the Bank of Mobile and the Tombeckbe Bank at Saint Stephens, the last earning many mentions in Eastern newspapers and financial journals of the era, including when it sustained a $35,000 robbery in 1819. The Huntsville Bank opened soon afterward. By 1823 both banks in Huntsville had closed, causing a loss to the Treasury Department which had deposited special funds in each. In its issue of July 7, 1827, *Niles' Weekly Register* printed this:

> We learn from the *Alabama Sentinel*, that the Tombeckbe Bank has stopped payment. It seems to have had a large amount of paper in circulation. A good deal of excitement prevailed among the people. The paper had fallen from 2% to 25%, and even to 50% percent below par. A letter from the president of the bank gives but little encouragement as to a recovery from its present embarrassments.

The Tombeckbe Bank did not recover, and in 1830 it earned the doubtful distinction of being the only failed bank in Alabama to be listed in the inaugural issue of *Bicknell's Counterfeit Detector*, the two other defunct banks at Huntsville having been overlooked by the compiler.

The Bank of the State of Alabama

The rationale for a state-owned bank and a commentary on conditions in Alabama at the time were given by John Jay Knox in his *History of Banking*, 1900:

> The Constitution expressly provided that the State might embark in the banking business for the benefit of the citizens. At this period the opinion prevailed that a bank was a great engine for developing the resources of a new country. The example of Mississippi, admitted to the Union in 1817, was before the eyes of the first Legislature, and was implicitly believed that it only required the enactment of suitable laws to make money abundant and easy to obtain. The success of the Second Bank of the United States and of many chartered corporations in the several states in paying large dividends to their private stockholders inspired confidence that if the business were controlled by the state the benefits would be equally divided among all the citizens instead of being absorbed by a favored few. It was the instinctive democratic opposition to monopolies of every kind that in the simplicity of inexperience hit upon this method.
>
> At the very first session of the General Assembly a law was enacted and approved on December 21, 1820, "To incorporate the subscribers to the Bank of the State of Alabama." At this time Cahawba was the capital of the State, and as long as it continued to be the capital it was to be the seat of the central bank. The limit of capital was fixed at $2,000,000, two-fifths of which ($800,000) were reserved for the State, and three-fifths to be raised by the subscriptions of citizens.
>
> At this date the population of Alabama was 127,901, of which number about 85,000 were whites and the remainder mostly slaves. The principal industry of the state was

> agriculture, and cotton was the chief staple . . . The hope of great returns from the development of the cotton industry and other collateral pursuits was as sanguine as that excited in California by the discoveries of gold, and the necessity of a circulating medium and of credit to turn the land and its products into lasting wealth pressed heavily upon a most energetic white population.

As stated above, the Bank of the State of Alabama was anticipated to be a very profitable venture for the state. However, the project failed when investors did not materialize. On December 20, 1823, another act provided for a bank under the same title, "to provide for the safe and profitable investment of the funds of the state, and to secure an extended and undepreciating currency."

As the prospect of selling stock subscriptions was uncertain, the bank was given no specific capital amount. Instead, the state was to provide the entire necessary funding, from rents on lands, sale of real estate, and the issuance of bonds bearing not more than six-percent interest. This money was mostly theoretical, based on the expectation that all would work out well, that citizens would enjoy a sound currency, and that the state would profit.

The bank was to be managed by 12 directors appointed annually by the legislature. There was no limit placed on the amount of notes that could be issued other than what the directors considered to be "most expedient and safe."

The Bank of the State of Alabama commenced business in 1825, first at its headquarters in Cahawba, then in Tuscaloosa in 1826 when the capital was relocated there. Branches were operated in Decatur, Huntsville, Mobile, Montgomery, and Tuscumbia. When these branches were in place, each had a president and a set of directors. Eventually the legislature granted between 60 and 70 such appointments each year.

William Garrett, in *Reminiscences of Public Men in Alabama for Thirty Years*, 1872, told of many curious and amusing incidents involving the bank. In one instance, a member of the legislature died during the annual election of bank directors. Following usual procedure, all of his fellows wore a badge of black crape on their arms for 30 days. The legislators so marked were treated to endless free cigars, dinners, and other courtesies by local restaurants, hotels, and various businesses, many of which had favorite candidates for the banking position. One out-of-town stranger noticed this, put crape on his arm, and was treated royally!

All seemed to develop as hoped for, and a capital of $15,859,420 was raised from public and related funds (such as transferring $500,000 from the State University of Alabama to the bank). This was considered a generous sum. During the next decade, cotton crops were excellent, and the economy of the state flourished. Real estate rose dramatically in price, adding to the feeling of prosperity.

There was no limit placed on the amount of money the bank presidents and directors of the main office and branches could personally borrow, and there were no requirements as to the security or collateral they had to furnish. As might be expected, the bank was thus poorly managed and was laced with, if not legal fraud, many highly questionable loans and other transactions. A statement of June 1, 1837, showed the bank's capital to be $7,889,886, bills in circulation totaling $4,600,000, and deposits of $6,700,000 from citizens and others. To service these liabilities the bank had a respectable $492,000 in specie, discounted notes (loans receivable) of $17,694,000, and $1,200,000 due from branches. Nevertheless, the unforeseen Hard Times era of that year soon caused problems, and it was found that there was $6,300,000 in bad debts in the discount portfolio. There was a shortage of cash, and in December 1837 the state of Alabama issued $7,500,000 in bonds to make up the deficiency. The directors of the bank were appointed politically, despite woeful lack of banking experience. These officials granted large loans at favored rates to the legislators who had made their selection. Members of the General Assembly continued to use the bank as an electioneering tool, offering favorable discounts to those who could help secure their reelection. The directors tapped the bank for personal loans, amounting in 1839 to nearly $780,000.

The bank was mentioned often in newspaper accounts in connection with such activities as non-redemption of bills, allowing only a small amount of currency to be exchanged each day, issuing post notes, and refusing perfectly good bills of other banks (stating that to do so in each instance required the approval of three directors). In 1841 the House and Senate branches of the state legislature each passed resolutions to investigate the bank, which had become the subject of many rumors. A subsequent report of the committee of inquiry included this:

> They have discovered the existence of a disgraceful league to plunder the banks and swindle the people of the state. Men high in office, members of the Legislature, and bank directors are supposed to be implicated. . . . With all these facts before them the Senate has seen fit to dissolve their portion of the committee. This renders it impossible for us to act efficiently and we therefore tender our resignation.[1]

It was learned that very little specie (silver and gold coins) was on hand to redeem notes. In 1842 and 1843 the state closed the branches, and after the bank's charter expired on January 1, 1845, it was liquidated. The papers and the journal of the joint committee were given to the governor. In 1849 the Capitol building in Montgomery was destroyed by fire, and the journals were allegedly consumed, apparently to the great relief of the many politicians mentioned in them. When matters were settled, the state recorded a debt of $14,000,000 to the state of Alabama's creditors. Including interest, the amount eventually totaled about $35,000,000, an unmitigated financial disaster.

The 1830s and Later

The second Bank of the United States (charter period 1816 to 1836) had a branch in the coastal city of Mobile which opened in 1826. After the branch closed at the expiration of the bank's charter, the Planters and Merchants Bank of Mobile was chartered by the state with $500,000 capitalization. It was permitted to issue paper money up to twice its paid-in capital. Launched into the Hard Times era, it failed in 1842. In 1849 and 1850 an unsuccessful effort was mounted to establish a "State Bank" in Mobile, with branches in Montgomery, Huntsville, Tuscaloosa, and Tuscumbia. This however never came to pass. The Bank of Montgomery was also proposed and later went into operation.

In 1850 a free-banking law was passed that enabled groups of citizens to form a bank in a simpler manner than before. It did not attract much interest from Alabama investors, quite unlike the situation in some other states that saw a rush of new banking activity. In 1854 a new law prohibited the circulation of bank notes of face values below $5. Related legislation was also passed over the years in certain other states. The object was to force citizens to use "hard money," silver and gold coins.

In the 1850s and early 1860s, new banks were chartered and operated with varying degrees of success, with most surviving into at least the early years of the Civil War.

Numismatic Comments

Bills of state-chartered banks in Alabama comprise an interesting specialty, but a rather short one in the context of obsolete currency. In comparison to states in the Northeast which boast many banks, Alabama has very few. Especially tantalizing among these are bills of the headquarters and branches of the Bank of the State of Alabama, so common in their day but which are elusive now, with many being unknown to present-day numismatists. Helping fill the need are some, but not many, Proof examples released from the paper archives of the American Bank Note Co.

Beyond these rarities, there are many available issues, including from the Hard Times era of banking difficulty as well as those dated from the 1850s onward, the latter being colorful and frequently overprinted. Among later bills are many that were redeemed but not destroyed. For other banks that burned their notes there are some incredible rarities—with just two or three examples of their bills known today.

Some Alabama banks continued operation into the Civil War, a collecting specialty in itself. A latecomer was the Farmers Bank of Alabama in Montgomery, established during the war by James Farley, a Confederate official. This particular institution did not last very long, and today its notes are readily available as a result.

Scrip notes (which are beyond the purview of this text) or fractional-denomination notes are enthusiastically collected as well. Many of these were payable in or exchangeable for Confederate States of America bills. Most were printed regionally and issued during the Civil War at a time when there were no silver or gold coins in circulation. Dealers report that obsolete Alabama notes of all kinds enjoy a very active market.

The standard reference on Alabama paper money is *Alabama Obsolete Notes and Scrip*, by Walter Rosene Jr. and published in 1984. For any scholar of Alabama's complex banking history, this is a great book to have.

Cahawba, Alabama

Located at the convergence of the Alabama and Cahawba rivers, Cahawba (also spelled Cahaba) was originally an undeveloped town site selected to be the state capital. On November 21, 1818, this was approved; however, the constitutional convention had to find different accommodations, as the area was still little more than wilderness.

By October 1819 the town had been laid out and lots were being auctioned. Similar to other towns in the south, Cahawba was built on a grid system. By 1820 the city was a thriving capital with a two-story brick statehouse. Unfortunately, the rivers often flooded, giving Cahawba a reputation of having an unsafe and unhealthy environment. In 1825 a massive flood caused the state house to collapse, and the capital was moved to Tuscaloosa in January 1826.

Cahawba remained the county seat of Dallas for many years after and eventually recovered from the loss of its prestige as the state capital. It became a central area for cotton production and distribution. In 1859 the railroad came to town, giving rise to an economic boom. By the 1860s the population totaled 3,000.

The Civil War brought difficulty to Cahawba, with military occupations causing the seizure of materials. In 1865 the rivers flooded again, and the Union prisoners and citizens of Cahawba suffered.

Bank of the State of Alabama

1820–1826

W-AL-010

History: On December 21, 1820, the Bank of the State of Alabama was incorporated. The authorized capital was limited to $2,000,000, of which $800,000 was to be reserved for the state.

The bank ended up being a failure and was unable to raise the appropriate stock that would encourage a successful enterprise. On December 20, 1823, the bank was reincorporated in order to provide safe investment in state funds. Where the first entity had placed its hope of success in the accrual of actual monetary subscriptions, the second entity had no limited capital and was financed by credit of the state. The capital would be made up of sales and rents in lands occupied by universities, land sales by acreage, and the lease of certain springs. In addition, stock in the state itself was sold at an amount of $100,000. John J. Knox, in his *History of Banking*, states that this was "the entering wedge for a reckless use of the credit of the State that caused much subsequent disaster."

In 1825 the bank commenced business. In 1826 the capital of the state of Alabama was moved to Tuscaloosa, and the Bank of the State of Alabama, W-AL-340, moved along with it.

Numismatic Commentary: Notes of the Bank of the State of Alabama are very rare, despite the many branches of the bank which would seem to indicate that there would be notes in plenty for today's collector. The short-lived nature of this particular location only increases the elusiveness of notes bearing the Cahawba imprint.

Valid Issues

$1 • W-AL-010-001-G010

CC

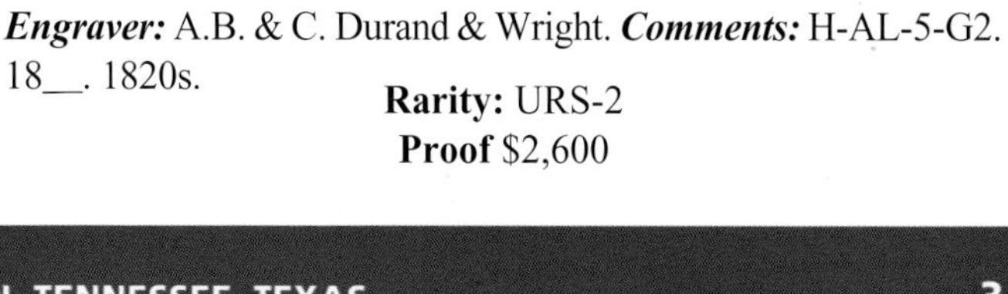

Engraver: A.B. & C. Durand & Wright. ***Comments:*** H-AL-5-G2. 18__. 1820s.

Rarity: URS-2
Proof $2,600

$2 • **W-AL-010-002-G020**

Left: Portrait of George Washington. ***Center:*** TWO / Man on horse / 2. ***Right:*** TWO vertically. ***Engraver:*** A.B. & C. Durand & Wright. ***Comments:*** H-AL-5-G4, Rosene-1-1. 18__. 1820s.

Rarity: URS-2
Proof $2,600

$3 • **W-AL-010-003-G030**

Left: Portrait of Benjamin Franklin. ***Center:*** 3 / Man on horse. ***Right:*** THREE vertically. ***Engraver:*** A.B. & C. Durand & Wright. ***Comments:*** H-AL-5-G6, Rosene-1-2. 18__. 1820s.

Rarity: URS-1
Proof $3,500

$5 • **W-AL-010-005-G040**

CC

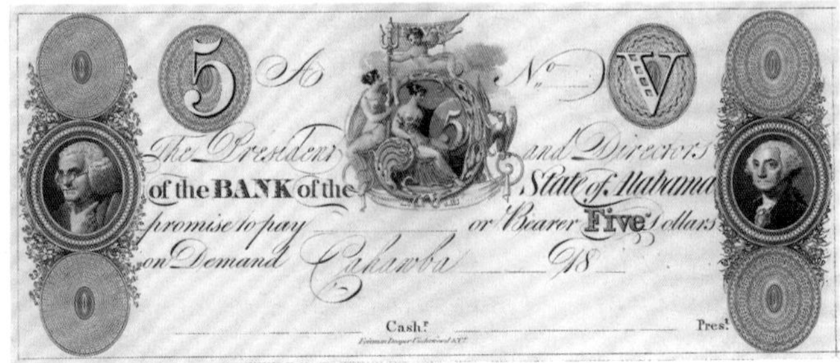

Engraver: Fairman, Draper, Underwood & Co. ***Comments:*** H-AL-5-G8. 18__. 1820s.

Rarity: URS-3
Proof $2,200

$10 • **W-AL-010-010-G050**

CC

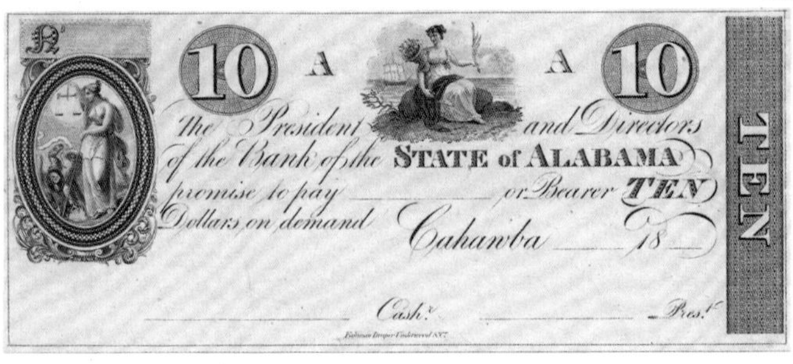

Engraver: Fairman, Draper, Underwood & Co. ***Comments:*** H-AL-5-G10. 18__. 1820s.

Rarity: URS-3
Proof $2,200

$20 • **W-AL-010-020-G060**

Comments: H-AL-5-G12. No description available. 18__. 1820s.

Rarity: *None known*

$50 • **W-AL-010-050-G070**

CC

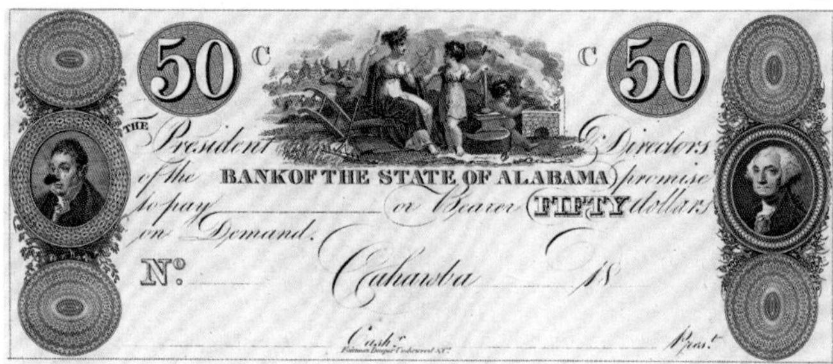

Engraver: Fairman, Draper, Underwood & Co. ***Comments:*** H-AL-5-G14. 18__. 1820s.

Rarity: URS-3
Proof $2,500

$100 • **W-AL-010-100-G080**

Comments: H-AL-5-G16. No description available. 18__. 1820s.

Rarity: *None known*

Non-Valid Issues

$100 • **W-AL-010-100-C080**

Comments: H-AL-5-C16. Counterfeit of W-AL-010-100-G080. 18__. 1820s.

Rarity: URS-3
F $350

Decatur, Alabama

Decatur was originally called "Rhodes Ferry Landing" after Dr. Henry W. Rhodes, who was a landowner and operated a ferry across the Tennessee River during the 1810s. The city was officially incorporated as Decatur in 1821 in order to honor military-hero Stephen Decatur, who was killed in 1820 in a duel. President James Monroe decreed that the town be named in his honor.

In the 1830s the Tuscumbia, Courtland and Decatur Railroad had its eastern terminus in Decatur. It was the first railway to be built west of the Appalachian Mountain range. The connection to the railroad and Decatur's location on the Tennessee River made the city a strategic position during the Civil War, and it was occupied by Union soldiers early in the conflict. Many buildings were destroyed, and in 1864 the Battle of Decatur earned the town the nickname of "A Tough Nut to Crack."

Bank of the State of Alabama (branch)

1833–1845

W-AL-020

History: The Bank of the State of Alabama moved from Cahawba, W-AL-010, to Tuscaloosa when the state capital was relocated there in 1826. The bank was able to raise $15,859,420 from various sources, including land sales, funds from university rents, and the sale of state stocks. Unfortunately, however, this amount was mostly used to keep the bank from failing during the Panic of 1837.

The branch at Decatur opened in 1833. In 1836 the cashier was James Dunro. Capital totaled $2,060,000, and circulation was as high as $1,551,054 in 1841.

The bank and its branches were poorly managed and engaged in many questionable and fraudulent activities. Finally, the bank was liquidated on January 1, 1845. The entity left the state with a debt of $14,000,000.

The Bank of the State of Alabama had its parent banks located first in Cahawba, W-AL-010, and later in Tuscaloosa, W-AL-340, and branches located in Huntsville, W-AL-090, Mobile, W-AL-190, Montgomery, W-AL-270, and Tuscumbia, W-AL-350.

Valid Issues

$1 • W-AL-020-001-G010

Left: ONE / Ceres with sheaf / ONE. ***Center:*** 1 / Ship / 1. ***Right:*** ONE / Woman standing with eagle / ONE. ***Back:*** Plain. ***Engraver:*** Rawdon, Wright & Hatch. ***Comments:*** H-AL-5-G56, Rosene-2-6. Possibly made only as Proofs. 18__. 1820s–1830s.

Rarity: —

$1 • W-AL-020-001-G010a

Back: Red-orange ONE. ***Engraver:*** Rawdon, Wright & Hatch. ***Comments:*** H-AL-5-G56a. Similar to W-AL-020-001-G010. 18__. 1830s.

Rarity: —

$2 • W-AL-020-002-G020

Left: TWO / Indian standing / TWO. ***Center:*** 2 / Eagle on rock in ocean / TWO. ***Right:*** 2 / Justice and Ceres flanking shield bearing 2 / TWO. ***Back:*** Plain. ***Engraver:*** Rawdon, Wright & Hatch. ***Comments:*** H-AL-5-G58, Rosene-2-7. Possibly made only as Proofs. 18__. 1820s–1830s.

Rarity: —

$2 • W-AL-020-002-G020a

Back: Red-orange. ***Engraver:*** Rawdon, Wright & Hatch. ***Comments:*** H-AL-5-G58a. Similar to W-AL-020-002-G020. 18__. 1830s.

Rarity: —

$3 • W-AL-020-003-G030

Left: 3 / Male portrait / 3. ***Center:*** 3 / Ceres / 3. ***Right:*** THREE / Woman standing / THREE. ***Back:*** Plain. ***Engraver:*** Rawdon, Wright & Hatch. ***Comments:*** H-AL-5-G60, Rosene-2-8. Possibly made only as Proofs. 18__. 1820s–1830s.

Rarity: —

$3 • W-AL-020-003-G030a

Back: Red-orange. ***Engraver:*** Rawdon, Wright & Hatch. ***Comments:*** H-AL-5-G60a. Similar to W-AL-020-003-G030. 18__. 1830s.

Rarity: —

$4 • W-AL-020-004-G040

CC

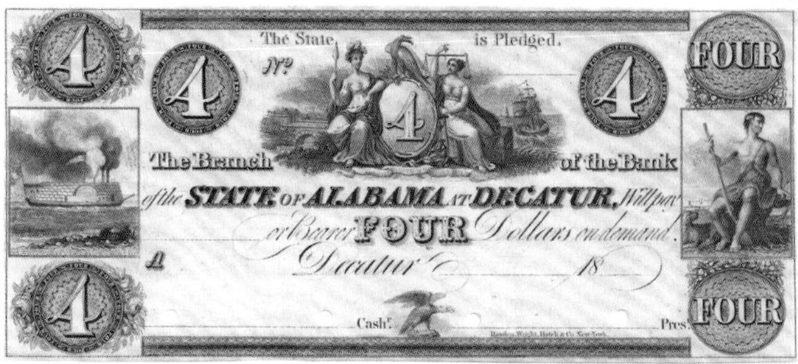

Back: Plain. ***Engraver:*** Rawdon, Wright, Hatch & Co. ***Comments:*** H-AL-5-G62, Rosene-2-9. Possibly made only as Proofs. 18__. 1820s–1830s.

Rarity: URS-2
F $4,100; **Proof** $2,500

$4 • W-AL-020-004-G040a

Left: 4 / Riverboat / 4. ***Center:*** 4 / Liberty and Justice flanking shield bearing 4, Ship / 4. ***Right:*** FOUR / Indian seated with dog and gun / FOUR. ***Back:*** Red-orange. ***Engraver:*** Rawdon, Wright & Hatch. ***Comments:*** H-AL-5-G62a. Similar to W-AL-020-004-G040. 18__. 1830s.

Rarity: —

$5 • W-AL-020-005-G050

SI

Back: Plain. ***Engraver:*** Rawdon, Wright, Hatch & Co. ***Comments:*** H-AL-5-G64, Rosene-2-10. 18__. 1830s.

Rarity: URS-3
VF $2,000; **Proof** $2,200

$10 • W-AL-020-010-G060

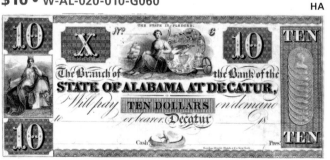

HA

Back: Plain. ***Engraver:*** Rawdon, Wright & Hatch. ***Comments:*** H-AL-5-G66, Rosene-2-13. 18__. 1830s.

Rarity: URS-3
Proof $2,200

$20 • **W-AL-020-020-G070**

Comments: H-AL-5-G68. No description available. 18__. 1820s.

Rarity: *None known*

$50 • **W-AL-020-050-G080**

Left: FIFTY vertically / 50. ***Center:*** 50 / Hebe watering eagle / 50. ***Right:*** FIFTY vertically / 50. ***Engraver:*** Rawdon, Wright & Hatch. ***Comments:*** H-AL-5-G70. 18__. 1830s.

Rarity: URS-2
Proof $3,500

$100 • **W-AL-020-100-G090**

Comments: H-AL-5-G72. No description available. 18__. 1820s.

Rarity: *None known*

Post Notes

$5 • **W-AL-020-005-G100**

CC

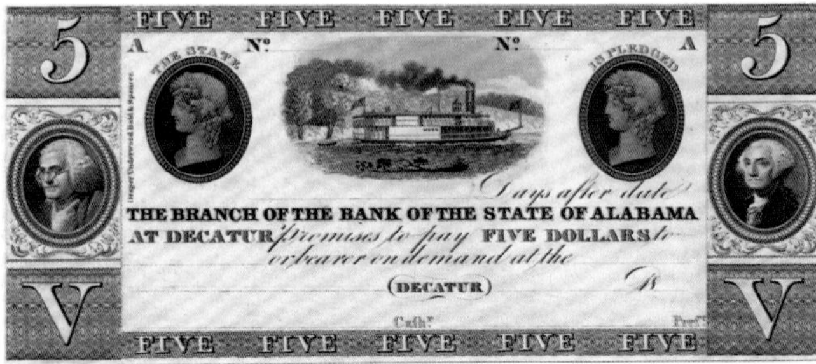

Engraver: Draper, Underwood, Bald & Spencer. ***Comments:*** H-AL-5-G76, Rosene-2-11. 18__. 1830s.

Rarity: URS-3
Proof $2,000
Selected auction price: Heritage Auctions, January 2010, Lot 12313, Proof $1,955

$10 • **W-AL-020-010-G110**

CC

Engraver: Draper, Underwood, Bald & Spencer. ***Comments:*** H-AL-5-G78, Rosene-2-12. 18__. 1830s.

Rarity: URS-3
Proof $2,000

$20 • **W-AL-020-020-G120**

Left: 20 / Woman seated / XX. ***Center:*** Female portrait / Lovers kissing / Female portrait. ***Right:*** 20 / Woman with sickle and wheat / XX. ***Engraver:*** Draper, Underwood, Bald & Spencer. ***Comments:*** H-AL-5-G80, Rosene-2-14. 18__. 1830s.

Rarity: URS-2
Proof $2,500

$50 • **W-AL-020-050-G130**

Left: Minerva / 50. ***Center:*** Woman seated with shield, Ship. ***Right:*** 50 on medallion head / Portrait of George Washington vertically / 50 on medallion head. ***Engraver:*** Draper, Underwood, Bald & Spencer. ***Comments:*** H-AL-5-G82, Rosene-2-17. 18__. 1830s.

Rarity: URS-2
Proof $2,500

$100 • **W-AL-020-100-G140**

Left: 100 on medallion head vertically / Portrait of Charles Carroll / 100 on medallion head vertically. ***Center:*** Three women seated, Ship. ***Right:*** 100 / C / 100 vertically. ***Engraver:*** Draper, Underwood, Bald & Spencer. ***Comments:*** H-AL-5-G84, Rosene-2-18. 18__. 1830s.

Rarity: URS-2
Proof $2,500

Post Notes Payable at the Citizens Bank in New Orleans

$5 • **W-AL-020-005-G150**

Left: 5 / Portrait of Benjamin Franklin / V. ***Center:*** Medallion head / Ship / Medallion head. ***Right:*** 5 / Portrait of George Washington / V. ***Engraver:*** Draper, Underwood, Bald & Spencer. ***Comments:*** H-AL-5-G90. 18__. 1830s.

Rarity: *None known*

$10 • **W-AL-020-010-G160**

Left: Portrait of Charles Carroll / TEN / Medallion head. ***Center:*** 10 / Hebe watering eagle / 10. ***Right:*** Portrait of Thomas Jefferson / TEN / Medallion head. ***Engraver:*** Draper, Underwood, Bald & Spencer. ***Comments:*** H-AL-5-G92. 18__. 1830s.

Rarity: *None known*

$20 • **W-AL-020-020-G170**

Left: 20 / Woman seated / XX. ***Center:*** Female portrait / Lovers kissing / Female portrait. ***Right:*** 20 / Woman with sickle and wheat / XX. ***Engraver:*** Draper, Underwood, Bald & Spencer. ***Comments:*** H-AL-5-G94. 18__. 1830s.

Rarity: *None known*

$50 • **W-AL-020-050-G180**

Left: Minerva / 50. ***Center:*** Woman seated with shield, Ship. ***Right:*** 50 on medallion head / Portrait of George Washington vertically / 50 on medallion head. ***Engraver:*** Draper, Underwood, Bald & Spencer. ***Comments:*** H-AL-5-G96. 18__. 1830s.

Rarity: *None known*

$100 • **W-AL-020-100-G190**

Left: 100 on medallion head vertically / Portrait of Charles Carroll / 100 on medallion head vertically. ***Center:*** Three women seated, Ship. ***Right:*** 100 / C / 100 vertically. ***Engraver:*** Draper, Underwood, Bald & Spencer. ***Comments:*** H-AL-5-G98. 18__. 1830s.

Rarity: *None known*

Post Notes Payable at the Bank of Louisiana in New Orleans

$5 • W-AL-020-005-G200

Left: 5 / Portrait of Benjamin Franklin / V. ***Center:*** Medallion head / Ship / Medallion head. ***Right:*** 5 / Portrait of George Washington / V. ***Engraver:*** Draper, Underwood, Bald & Spencer. ***Comments:*** H-AL-5-G100. 18__. 1830s.

Rarity: URS-2
Proof $3,000

$10 • W-AL-020-010-G210

Left: Portrait of Charles Carroll / TEN / Medallion head. ***Center:*** 10 / Hebe watering eagle / 10. ***Right:*** Portrait of Thomas Jefferson / TEN / Medallion head. ***Engraver:*** Draper, Underwood, Bald & Spencer. ***Comments:*** H-AL-5-G102. 18__. 1830s.

Rarity: URS-2
Proof $3,000

$20 • W-AL-020-020-G220

Left: 20 / Woman seated / XX. ***Center:*** Female portrait / Lovers kissing / Female portrait. ***Right:*** 20 / Woman with sickle and wheat / XX. ***Engraver:*** Draper, Underwood, Bald & Spencer. ***Comments:*** H-AL-5-G104. 18__. 1830s.

Rarity: *None known*

$50 • W-AL-020-050-G230

Left: Minerva / 50. ***Center:*** Woman seated with shield, Ship. ***Right:*** 50 on medallion head / Portrait of George Washington vertically / 50 on medallion head. ***Engraver:*** Draper, Underwood, Bald & Spencer. ***Comments:*** H-AL-5-G106. 18__. 1830s.

Rarity: *None known*

$100 • W-AL-020-100-G240

Left: 100 on medallion head vertically / Portrait of Charles Carroll / 100 on medallion head vertically. ***Center:*** Three women seated, Ship. ***Right:*** 100 / C / 100 vertically. ***Engraver:*** Draper, Underwood, Bald & Spencer. ***Comments:*** H-AL-5-G108. 18__. 1830s.

Rarity: *None known*

Post Notes Payable at the Phenix Bank in New York

$5 • W-AL-020-005-G250

Left: 5 / Portrait of Benjamin Franklin / V. ***Center:*** Medallion head / Ship / Medallion head. ***Right:*** 5 / Portrait of George Washington / V. ***Engraver:*** Draper, Underwood, Bald & Spencer. ***Comments:*** H-AL-5-G110. 18__. 1830s.

Rarity: *None known*

$10 • W-AL-020-010-G260

Left: Portrait of Charles Carroll / TEN / Medallion head. ***Center:*** 10 / Hebe watering eagle / 10. ***Right:*** Portrait of Thomas Jefferson / TEN / Medallion head. ***Engraver:*** Draper, Underwood, Bald & Spencer. ***Comments:*** H-AL-5-G112. 18__. 1830s.

Rarity: *None known*

$20 • W-AL-020-020-G270

Left: 20 / Woman seated / XX. ***Center:*** Female portrait / Lovers kissing / Female portrait. ***Right:*** 20 / Woman with sickle and wheat / XX. ***Engraver:*** Draper, Underwood, Bald & Spencer. ***Comments:*** H-AL-5-G114. 18__. 1830s.

Rarity: *None known*

$50 • W-AL-020-050-G280

Left: Minerva / 50. ***Center:*** Woman seated with shield, Ship. ***Right:*** 50 on medallion head / Portrait of George Washington vertically / 50 on medallion head. ***Engraver:*** Draper, Underwood, Bald & Spencer. ***Comments:*** H-AL-5-G116. 18__. 1830s.

Rarity: *None known*

$100 • W-AL-020-100-G290

Left: 100 on medallion head vertically / Portrait of Charles Carroll / 100 on medallion head vertically. ***Center:*** Three women seated, Ship. ***Right:*** 100 / C / 100 vertically. ***Engraver:*** Draper, Underwood, Bald & Spencer. ***Comments:*** H-AL-5-G118. 18__. 1830s.

Rarity: *None known*

Post Notes Payable at the Phenix Bank in New York or at the Union Bank in New Orleans

$5 • W-AL-020-005-G300

HSPA

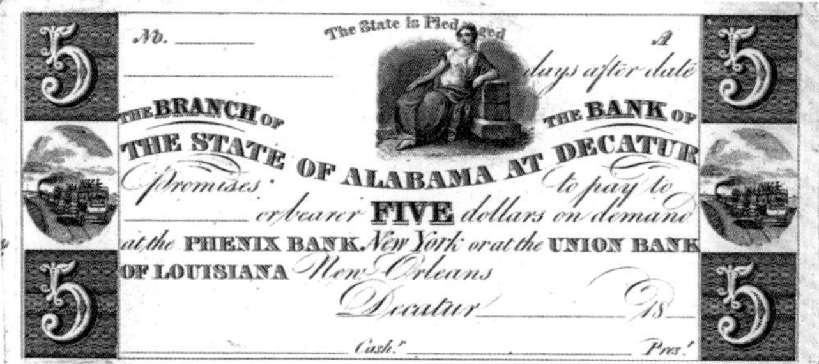

Engraver: Underwood, Bald & Spencer. ***Comments:*** H-Unlisted. 18__. 1830s.

Rarity: URS-2
Proof $2,000

$10 • W-AL-020-010-G310

HSPA

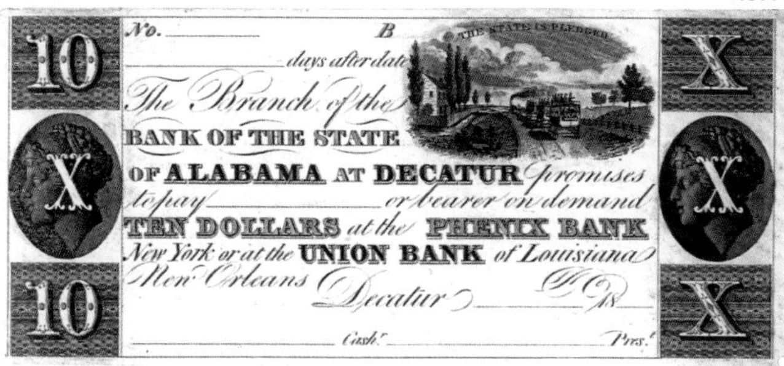

Engraver: Underwood, Bald & Spencer. ***Comments:*** H-Unlisted. 18__. 1830s.

Rarity: URS-2
Proof $2,000

Post Notes on Which the Place Payable is Blank

$5 • W-AL-020-005-G320

Left: 5 / Portrait of Benjamin Franklin / V. ***Center:*** Medallion head / Ship / Medallion head. ***Right:*** 5 / Portrait of George Washington / V. ***Engraver:*** Draper, Underwood, Bald & Spencer. ***Comments:*** H-AL-5-G120. 18__. 1830s.

Rarity: URS-3
Proof $1,000

$10 • W-AL-020-010-G330

Left: Portrait of Charles Carroll / TEN / Medallion head. ***Center:*** 10 / Hebe watering eagle / 10. ***Right:*** Portrait of Thomas Jefferson / TEN / Medallion head. ***Engraver:*** Draper, Underwood, Bald & Spencer. ***Comments:*** H-AL-5-G122. 18__. 1830s.

Rarity: URS-3
Proof $1,000

$20 • W-AL-020-020-G340

Left: 20 / Woman seated / XX. ***Center:*** Female portrait / Lovers kissing / Female portrait. ***Right:*** 20 / Woman with sickle and wheat / XX. ***Engraver:*** Draper, Underwood, Bald & Spencer. ***Comments:*** H-AL-5-G124. 18__. 1830s.

Rarity: *None known*

$50 • W-AL-020-050-G350

Left: Minerva / 50. ***Center:*** Woman seated with shield, Ship. ***Right:*** 50 on medallion head / Portrait of George Washington vertically / 50 on medallion head. ***Engraver:*** Draper, Underwood, Bald & Spencer. ***Comments:*** H-AL-5-G126. 18__. 1830s.

Rarity: *None known*

$100 • W-AL-020-100-G360

Left: 100 on medallion head vertically / Portrait of Charles Carroll / 100 on medallion head vertically. ***Center:*** Three women seated, Ship. ***Right:*** 100 / C / 100 vertically. ***Engraver:*** Draper, Underwood, Bald & Spencer. ***Comments:*** H-AL-5-G128. 18__. 1830s.

Rarity: *None known*

Non-Valid Issues

$50 • W-AL-020-050-R010

Comments: H-AL-5-R20. Raised from W-AL-020-005-G050. 18__. 1830s–1840s.

Rarity: *None known*

$100 • W-AL-020-100-R020

Comments: H-AL-5-R25. Raised from W-AL-020-005-G050. 18__. 1830s–1840s.

Rarity: *None known*

Planters and Merchants Bank (branch)

1836–1842

W-AL-030

History: In 1836 the Planters and Merchants Bank was chartered for a duration of 20 years with an authorized capital of $500,000. It was permissible for the bank to issue notes amounting to twice its capital. There was wide expansion in both circulation and capital, to the extent that the bank could not sustain it. In 1842 the bank suspended specie payments and later failed.

The Planters and Merchants Bank had its parent bank located in Mobile, W-AL-230.

There was an earlier, unrelated Planters and Merchants Bank, W-AL-140, located in Huntsville.

Valid Issues

$1 • W-AL-030-001-G010

Comments: H-AL-50-G30. No description available. 18__. 1830s.

Rarity: *None known*

$2 • W-AL-030-002-G020

Comments: H-AL-50-G32. No description available. 18__. 1830s.

Rarity: *None known*

$3 • W-AL-030-003-G030

Comments: H-AL-50-G34. No description available. 18__. 1830s.

Rarity: *None known*

$5 • W-AL-030-005-G040

Comments: H-AL-50-G36. No description available. 18__. 1830s.

Rarity: *None known*

$10 • W-AL-030-010-G050

Comments: H-AL-50-G38. No description available. 18__. 1830s.

Rarity: *None known*

$20 • W-AL-030-020-G060

Comments: H-AL-50-G40. No description available. 18__. 1830s.

Rarity: *None known*

Demopolis, Alabama

Demopolis was originally founded by French expatriates, many of whom lived in Philadelphia and who were granted the land by the U.S. Congress on the condition that they cultivate grape and olive crops. On July 14, 1817, the small group of pioneers settled on the Tombigbee River north of Mobile and founded the Vine and Olive Colony. However, many of the pioneers had little actual interest in farming and remained in Philadelphia, selling their shares of the colony. Adversities caused difficulties for the would-be settlers, including a forced move and the abandonment of the settlement. Two other towns, Aigleville and Arcola, were established in the district as a result.

American settlers came to fill the gap that the French pioneers had left, and in 1819 a company was formed with the goal of turning the land into a thriving river port. The Town Square was established in 1819, and the rise of Demopolis quickly followed. The river brought craftsmen and merchants from all over the country. Plantation owners established town homes in the community. There was also a healthy crowd of travelers who frequented taverns, giving Demopolis a rather decadent repute. Furthering this reputation, there was no church built in Demopolis until 1840, and a group of ministers went so far as to call Demopolis "wholly irreligious."

By the 1850s there were several steamboats coming to town regularly, either for the cotton trade or for passenger travel. In 1853 a yellow-fever epidemic caused many fatalities. Nevertheless, by 1860 the population of Demopolis was 1,200. The Civil War brought an end to many traditional trades and pursuits in Demopolis, and Confederate forces drew heavily from local men. Later, Demopolis became a key center of offices and warehouses, with its location on the river and access to the railroad.

Farmers Banking Association
1838
W-AL-040

History: The Farmers Banking Association was incorporated in 1838 with an authorized capital up to $1,000,000. John B. Cook, the former cashier of the Bank of the State of Alabama, W-AL-340, was the organizer of this entity.[2] However, there is some question as to whether the bank was ever officially chartered.

Numismatic Commentary: It is possible that some notes may have been printed in anticipation.

Valid Issues

12-1/2¢ • W-AL-040-00.12.50-G003
CC

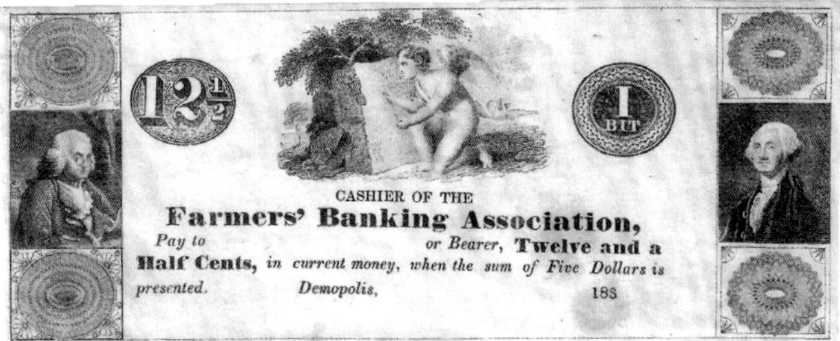

Comments: H-Unlisted, Rosene-Unlisted. 183_. 1830s.
Rarity: URS-1
Proof $1,500

12-1/2¢ • W-AL-040-00.12.50-G004
CC

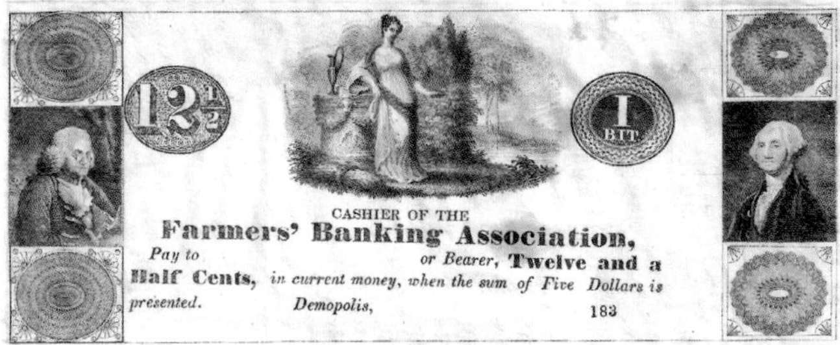

Comments: H-Unlisted, Rosene-Unlisted. 183_. 1830s.
Rarity: URS-1
Proof $1,500

25¢ • W-AL-040-00.25-G005
CC

Comments: H-Unlisted, Rosene-Unlisted. 183_. 1830s.
Rarity: URS-1
Proof $1,500

Post Notes

$5 • W-AL-040-005-G010
CC

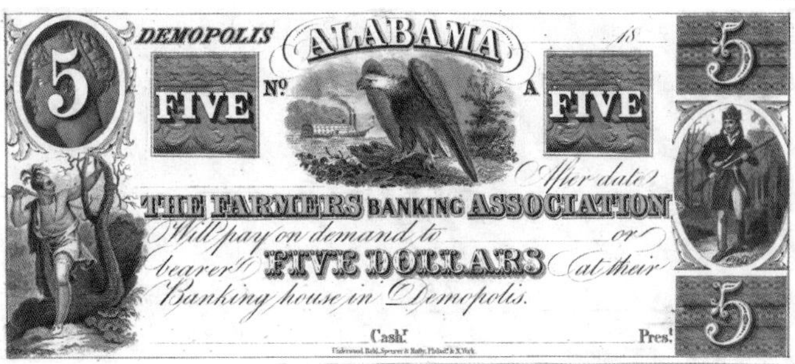

Engraver: Underwood, Bald, Spencer & Hufty. ***Comments:*** H-AL-10-G8, Rosene-60-6. 18__. 1830s.
Rarity: URS-3
Proof $2,000

$10 • W-AL-040-010-G020
CC

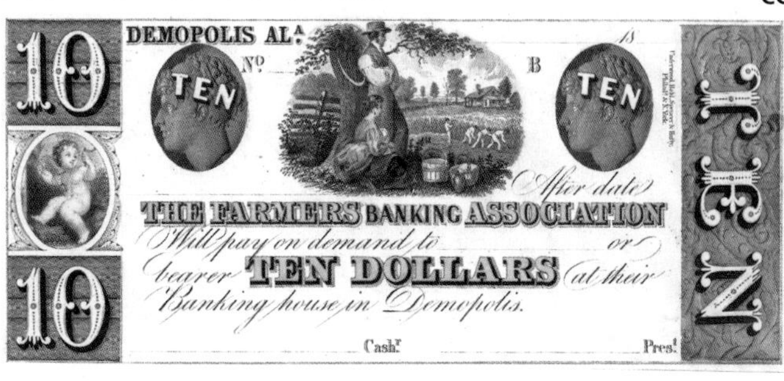

Engraver: Underwood, Bald, Spencer & Hufty. ***Comments:*** H-Unlisted. 18__. 1830s.
Rarity: URS-3
Proof $2,000
Selected auction price: Heritage Auctions, January 6, 2016, Lot 18421, F $1,057

$20 • W-AL-040-020-G030
CC

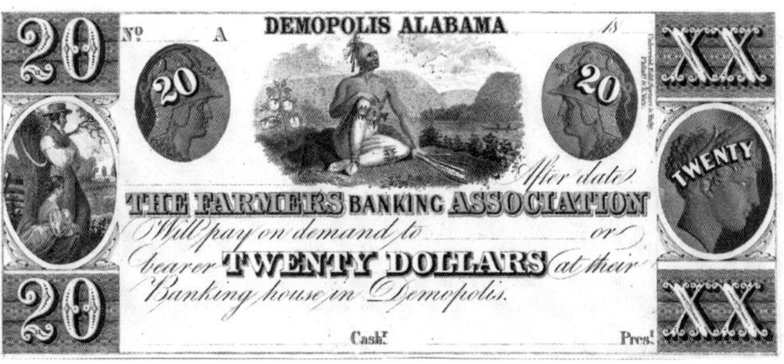

Engraver: Underwood, Bald, Spencer & Hufty. ***Comments:*** H-Unlisted. 18__. 1830s.
Rarity: URS-1
Proof $3,000

$50 • W-AL-040-050-G040 CC

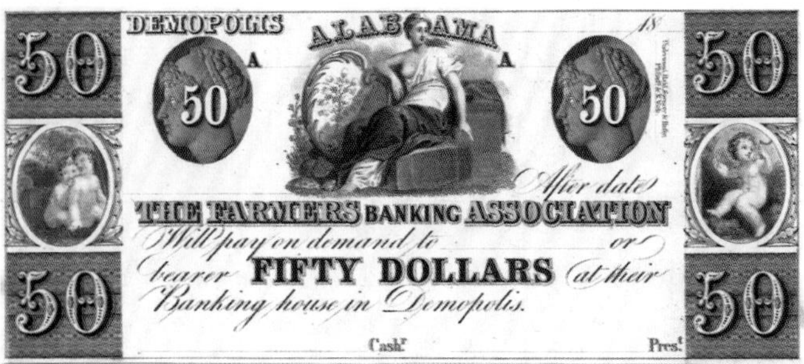

Engraver: Underwood, Bald, Spencer & Hufty. ***Comments:*** H-Unlisted. 18__. 1830s.

Rarity: URS-1
Proof $4,000

$100 • W-AL-040-100-G050 CC

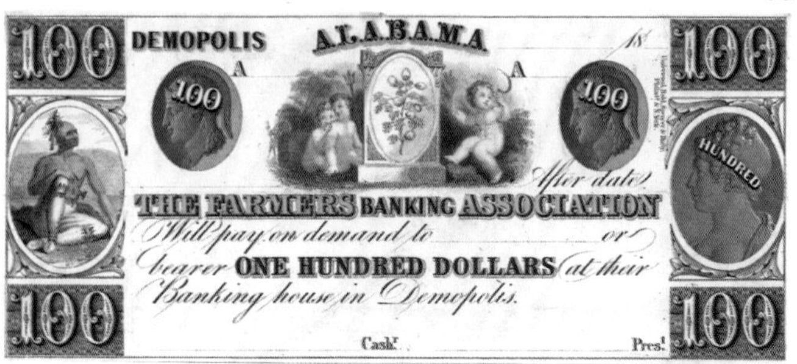

Engraver: Underwood, Bald, Spencer & Hufty. ***Comments:*** H-Unlisted. 18__. 1830s.

Rarity: URS-1
Proof $5,000

Uncut Sheets

12-1/2¢-12-1/2¢-25¢ • W-AL-040-00.12.50.00.12.50.00.25-US010 CC

Comments: All unlisted in Haxby. 183_. 1830s.

Rarity: URS-1
Proof $1,500

Eufaula, Alabama

The land that later included the town of Eufaula was originally occupied by Creek Indians, including the tribe of the Eufaulas. In the 1820s the district was still considered Creek Territory, but many settlers arrived and set up homesteads illegally. In 1827 the Creeks went to the government to protest their property rights, and federal troops removed the settlers by force. In 1832 the Treaty of Cusseta forced the Creeks to cede all of their land east of the Mississippi River to the United States, and settlers were at last legally allowed to purchase land, such action being all too typical of the relationship between the federal government and Native Americans at the time—a sad chapter in American history. By 1835 the land was mostly settled by American citizens, and the initial area was dubbed Irwinton.

Collectors and Researchers:

If you have new information about any banks or notes listed in this volume, contact Whitman Publishing, Attn: Obsolete Paper Money, 3101 Clairmont Road, Suite G, Atlanta, GA 30329.

In 1842 Irwinton was renamed Eufaula, taking its name from Native American tradition. The change was precipitated in part by postal and other confusion with Irwinton, Georgia. In 1857 Eufaula was officially incorporated. The town's advantageous position on the Chattahoochee River made it a central shipping port for cargo travelling to Apalachicola, Florida, connecting as far as New York City and Liverpool. A railroad was in the planning stage when the Civil War commenced, and the project was suspended. As to activities in Eufaula during the Civil War, little is known today. The records and newspapers of the time were destroyed or lost. There was a military encampment located at Eufaula, as well as a military hospital, and the town's location on the river fed the naval component of the war.

See also Irwinton, Alabama.

Eastern Bank of Alabama

1858–1867

W-AL-050

History: The Eastern Bank of Alabama was incorporated on February 8, 1858. John McNab was the first president, and J. Hardy was the first cashier. Among the stockholders were leading local citizens of the time such as future Alabama governor John Gill Shorter, Confederate hero-to-be Colonel E.C. Bullock, and Alabama frontiersman John Horry Dent. The bank building was erected on the corner of Broad and Randolph streets and cost $50,000. Soon the capital of the bank was $300,000, and $652,110 worth of bills was circulating. Specie totaled $224,670.

In 1867, past the note-issuing era under study, the bank's name was changed to the John McNab Bank, and finally it was closed by the Hanover National Bank on March 31, 1891.[3]

Numismatic Commentary: Uncut sheets of this bank are very rare, with the "peach-colored" $5 sheet being the most uncommon. These late Alabama issues bear colorful overprints and tints, making them especially pleasing for collectors.

Remaining at the American Bank Note Co. archives as of 2003 was a $1-$1-$2-$3 face plate and a $1-$1-$2-$3 tint plate.

Valid Issues

$1 • W-AL-050-001-G010 CC

Tint: Red-orange dies bearing white 1s, panel of microlettering, and panel. ***Engraver:*** American Bank Note Co. ***Comments:*** H-AL-15-G2a, Rosene-68-1. Handwritten serial number. March 15th, 1860.

Rarity: URS-6; URS-2
F $250
Proof $3,800

$1 • W-AL-050-001-G010a

Left: 1 / Cotton boll. ***Center:*** Man standing with boy and merchandise. ***Right:*** 1 / Eagle. ***Tint:*** Red-orange dies bearing white 1s, panel of microlettering, and panel. ***Engraver:*** American Bank Note Co. ***Comments:*** H-AL-15-G2b. Similar to W-AL-050-001-G010 but with printed serial number. March 15th, 1860.

Rarity: URS-6
F $250

$1 • W-AL-050-001-G010b HA

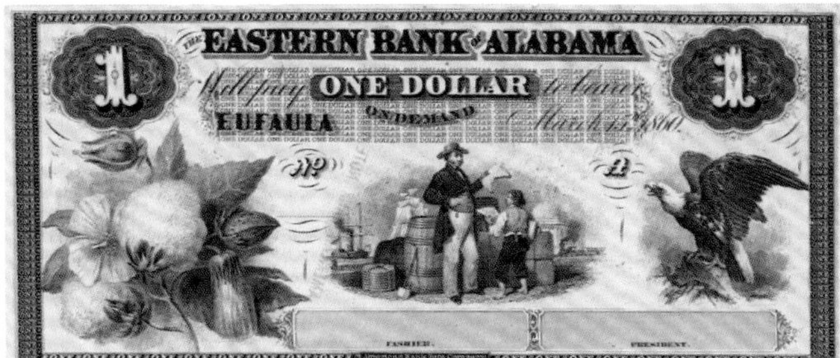

Tint: Fuchsia dies bearing white 1s, panel of microlettering, and panel. ***Engraver:*** American Bank Note Co. ***Comments:*** H-Unlisted. Similar to W-AL-050-001-G010. Proprietary Proof. March 15th, 1860.

Rarity: URS-4
Prop. Proof $550

$2 • W-AL-050-002-G020 CC

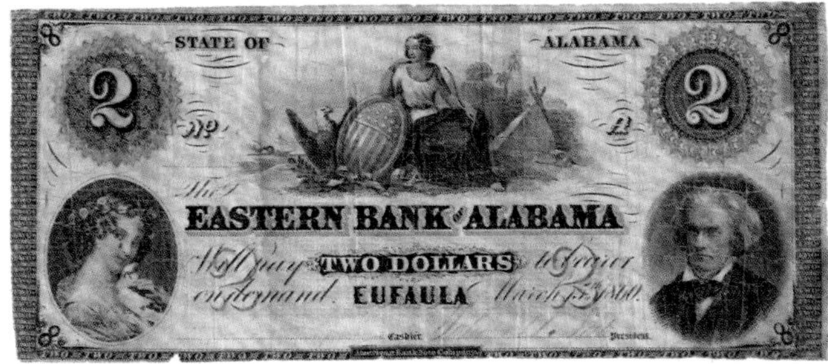

Tint: Red-orange dies bearing white 2s and panel of microlettering outlining white 2 / 2. ***Engraver:*** American Bank Note Co. ***Comments:*** H-AL-15-G4a, Rosene-68-2. Handwritten serial number. March 15th, 1860.

Rarity: URS-5
F $350

$2 • W-AL-050-002-G020a HA

Tint: Red-orange dies bearing white 2s and panel of microlettering outlining white 2 / 2. ***Engraver:*** American Bank Note Co. ***Comments:*** H-AL-15-G4b. Similar to W-AL-050-002-G020 but with printed serial number. March 15th, 1860.

Rarity: URS-5
F $350

$2 • **W-AL-050-002-G020b** HA

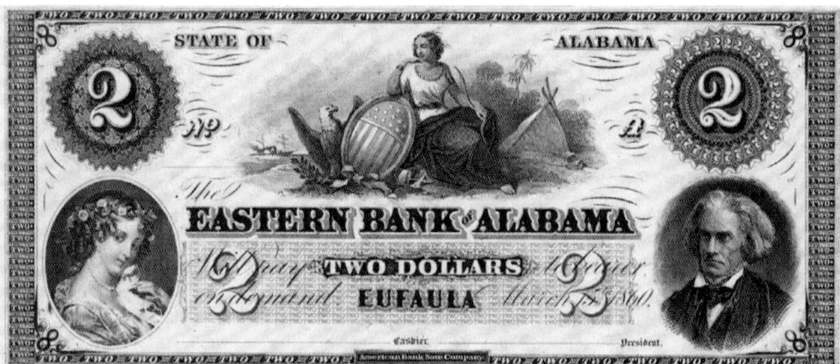

Tint: Fuchsia dies bearing white 2s and panel of microlettering outlining white 2 / 2. ***Engraver:*** American Bank Note Co. ***Comments:*** H-Unlisted. Similar to W-AL-050-002-G020. Proprietary Proof. March 15th, 1860.

Rarity: URS-4
Prop. Proof $400

$3 • **W-AL-050-003-G030** CC

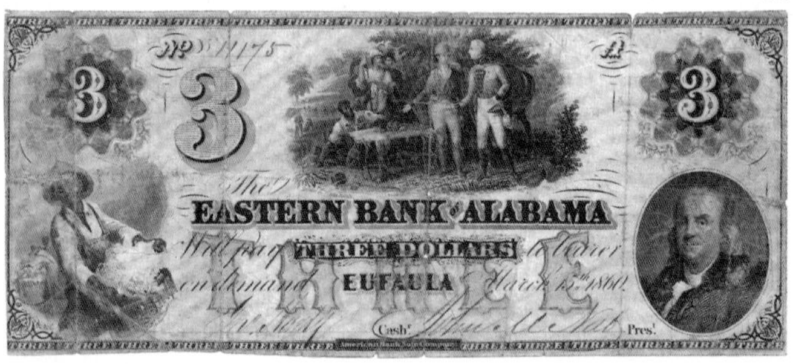

Tint: Red-orange THREE and dies bearing white 3s. ***Engraver:*** American Bank Note Co. ***Comments:*** H-AL-15-G6a, Rosene-68-3. Handwritten serial number. March 15th, 1860.

Rarity: URS-4
F $500

$3 • **W-AL-050-003-G030a**

Left: 3 / Man with cotton. ***Center:*** 3 / "General Marion's Sweet Potato Dinner." ***Right:*** 3 / Portrait of Benjamin Franklin. ***Tint:*** Red-orange THREE and dies bearing white 3s. ***Engraver:*** American Bank Note Co. ***Comments:*** H-AL-15-G6b. Similar to W-AL-050-003-G030 but with printed serial number. March 15th, 1860.

Rarity: URS-4
F $500

$3 • **W-AL-050-003-G030b** HA

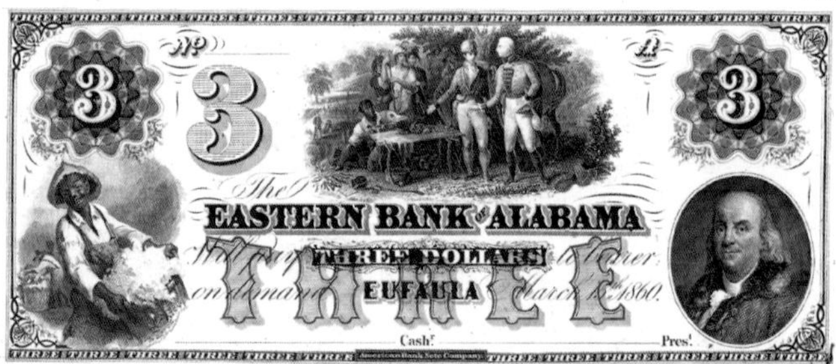

Tint: Fuchsia THREE and dies bearing white 3s. ***Engraver:*** American Bank Note Co. ***Comments:*** H-Unlisted. Similar to W-AL-050-003-G030. Proprietary Proof. March 15th, 1860.

Rarity: URS-4
Prop. Proof $500

$5 • **W-AL-050-005-G040** CC

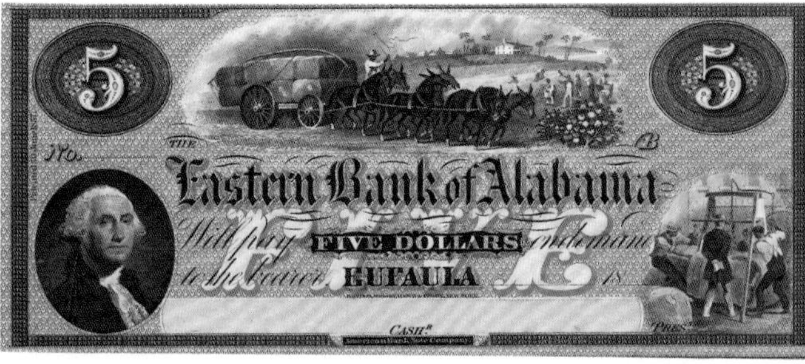

Tint: Green lathework outlining white FIVE and panel. ***Engraver:*** Rawdon, Wright, Hatch & Edson / American Bank Note Co. ***Comments:*** H-AL-15-G8a, Rosene-68-5. 18__. 1858.

Rarity: URS-10
F $200; **Unc-Rem** $400

$5 • **W-AL-050-005-G040a** HA

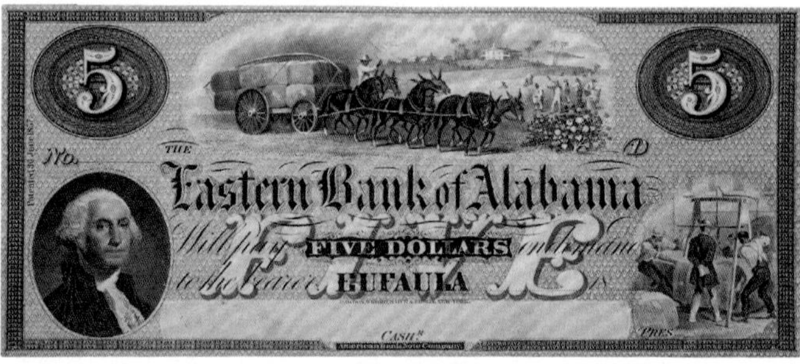

Tint: Red-orange lathework outlining white FIVE and panel. ***Engraver:*** Rawdon, Wright, Hatch & Edson / American Bank Note Co. ***Comments:*** H-AL-15-G8b. Similar to W-AL-050-005-G040. 18__. 1859.

Rarity: URS-8
VF $1,100; **Unc-Rem** $400
Selected auction price: Heritage Auctions, January 5, 2012, Lot 15728, VF $1,035

$10 • **W-AL-050-010-G050** HA

Tint: Green lathework outlining white TEN and panel. ***Engraver:*** Rawdon, Wright, Hatch & Edson / American Bank Note Co. ***Comments:*** H-AL-15-G10a, Rosene-68-7. 18__. 1858.

Rarity: URS-6
F $400

$10 • W-AL-050-010-G050a

CC

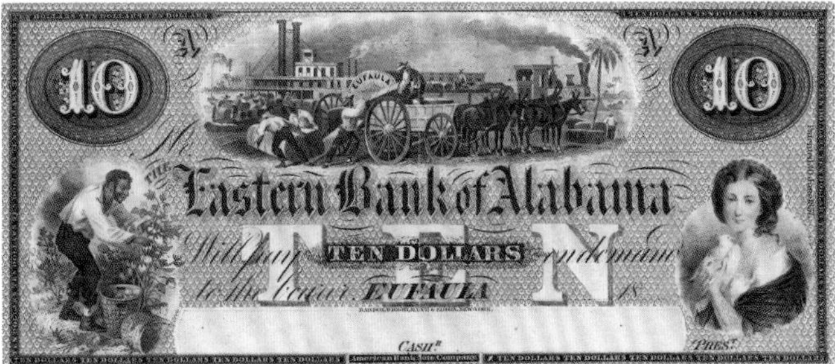

Tint: Red-orange lathework outlining white TEN and panel. ***Engraver:*** Rawdon, Wright, Hatch & Edson / American Bank Note Co. ***Comments:*** H-AL-15-G10b. Similar to W-AL-050-010-G050. 18__. 1859.

Rarity: URS-10

Unc-Rem $600

Selected auction price: Heritage Auctions, January 7, 2015, Lot 18006, Unc $763

$20 • W-AL-050-020-G060

HA

Tint: Green lathework outlining white TWENTY and panel. ***Engraver:*** Rawdon, Wright, Hatch & Edson / American Bank Note Co. ***Comments:*** H-AL-15-G12a, Rosene-68-8. 18__. 1858.

Rarity: URS-4

F $500

$20 • W-AL-050-020-G060a

CC

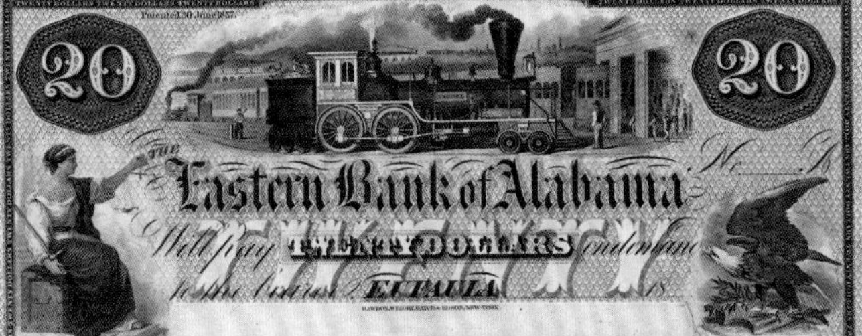

Tint: Red-orange lathework outlining white TWENTY and panel. ***Engraver:*** Rawdon, Wright, Hatch & Edson / American Bank Note Co. ***Comments:*** H-AL-15-G12b. Similar to W-AL-050-020-G060. 18__. 1859.

Rarity: URS-7

Unc-Rem $600

$50 • W-AL-050-050-G070

CC

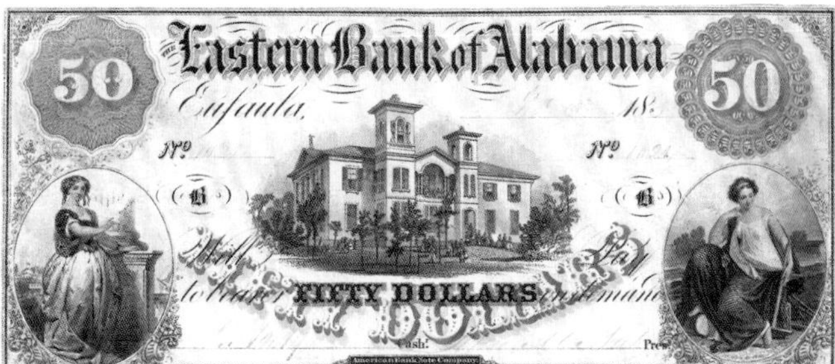

Tint: Red-orange FIFTY DOLLARS and dies outlining white 50s. ***Engraver:*** American Bank Note Co. ***Comments:*** H-AL-15-G14a, Rosene-68-9. 18__. 1860s.

Rarity: URS-2

VF $2,500; **Proof** $7,500

Uncut Sheets

$5-$5-$5-$5 • W-AL-050-005.005.005.005-US010

RG

Tint(s): Green lathework outlining white FIVE and panel. ***Engraver:*** Rawdon, Wright, Hatch & Edson / American Bank Note Co. ***Comments:*** H-AL-15-G8a, G8a, G8a, G8a. All four notes identical. 18__. 1858.

Rarity: URS-5

Unc-Rem $1,000

$5-$5-$5-$5 •

W-AL-050-005.005.005.005-US010a RG

Tint(s): Red-orange lathework outlining white FIVE and panel. ***Engraver:*** Rawdon, Wright, Hatch & Edson / American Bank Note Co. ***Comments:*** H-AL-15-G8b, G8b, G8b, G8b. Similar to W-AL-050-005.005.005.005-US010. All four notes identical. This sheet is considered to be the rarest of the three known from the Eastern Bank of Alabama. The red-orange tint is also described as "peach" in color. 18__. 1859.

Rarity: URS-4
Unc-Rem $1,500

$10-$10-$10-$20 •

W-AL-050-010.010.010.020-US020 RG

Tint(s): Red-orange. ***Engraver:*** Rawdon, Wright, Hatch & Edson / American Bank Note Co. ***Comments:*** H-AL-15-G10b, G10b, G10b, G12b. First three notes identical. 18__. 1859.

Rarity: URS-5
Unc-Rem $1,500

FLORENCE, ALABAMA

The land that became Florence was originally surveyed for the Cypress Land Company by Ferdinand Sannoner in 1818. He named it after Florence, Italy, the capital of the Tuscany region. In 1826 the area was incorporated as a town. LaGrange College was founded here in 1830, later becoming University of North Alabama.

Planters Bank of Alabama
1830s–1840s
W-AL-060

History: The Planters Bank of Alabama was a fraudulent bank, as there was no corporation under this name at this time or in this city.

There was an unrelated Planters Bank of Alabama located in Gainesville a few decades later, W-AL-080.

Numismatic Commentary: Notes with the Florence imprint bear the name of a Cincinnati-based engraving firm. The notes themselves were circulated at places distant from this Alabama town.

Issues

$5 • W-AL-060-005-G010

Engraver: Western Bank Note Co. / Woodruff, Tucker & Co.
Comments: H-AL-20-G8. No description available. 18__. 1830s.
Rarity: *None known*

$10 • W-AL-060-010-G020 CC

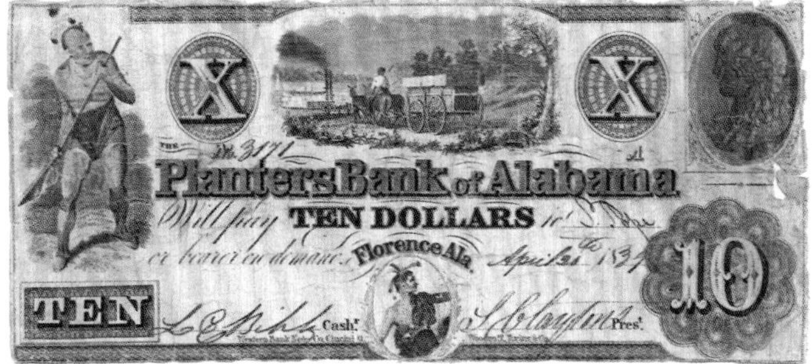

Engraver: Western Bank Note Co. / Woodruff, Tucker & Co.
Comments: H-AL-20-G10, Rosene-90-1. 18__. 1830s.
Rarity: URS-3
F $2,500; **Proof** $2,000
Selected auction price(s): Heritage Auctions, January 6, 2016, Lot 18463, Proof $1,057; Heritage Auctions, April 23, 2015, Lot 19002, F $1,057; Heritage Auctions, April 22, 2015, Lot 18393, F $1,762

$20 • W-AL-060-020-G030

Engraver: Western Bank Note Co. / Woodruff, Tucker & Co.
Comments: H-AL-20-G12. No description available. 18__. 1830s.
Rarity: *None known*

$50 • W-AL-060-050-G040 CC

Engraver: Western Bank Note Co. / Woodruff, Tucker & Co.
Comments: H-AL-20-G14, Rosene-90-2. 18__. 1830s.
Rarity: URS-2
F $4,500

Gainesville, Alabama

The land that later included Gainesville was originally owned by John Coleman, who was married to a Choctaw Indian woman. He sold the land in 1831 to Colonel Moses Lewis. The land was divided into lots, and Gainesville was laid out. It was first known as Eaton, after John H. Eaton, the Secretary of War serving President Andrew Jackson (whose wife Peggy, a *femme fatale* of the era, precipitated "the Petticoat Affair" that caused a rearrangement of the Cabinet). The town's name was later changed to Gainesville in honor of Colonel George Strother Gaines.

The first settlers traveled from Virginia, North Carolina, and South Carolina. By 1840 Gainesville was a substantial town, boasting a population of more than 4,000 residents. The river also allowed a port to be established, and soon 6,000 bales of cotton were shipped to Mobile annually via steamboat. In 1855 a fire struck the town, and 30 buildings were burned to the ground.

Gainesville Bank
1845
W-AL-070

History: Mention of the Gainesville Bank of 1845 is found in a reference of the history of Gainesville, Alabama, but it may have been a generic note referring to another financial entity. No record has been found of a bank authorized under this name.

Planters Bank of Alabama
1861
W-AL-080

History: The Planters Bank of Alabama was incorporated on November 28, 1861, with an authorized capital of $600,000 to be divided into shares of $100 each. The charter was to expire on June 1, 1892. The bank was also prohibited from issuing bills of any value less than $1.

It is not known if this bank, incorporated during the Civil War, ever went into operation.

There was an unrelated, fraudulent Planters Bank of Alabama located in Florence a few decades before, W-AL-060.

Huntsville, Alabama

Originally inhabited by the Chickasaw Indians, the area that later became Huntsville was ceded to the United States in 1805 and 1806 after a spate of land disputes, disease, and settler pressure. Leroy Pope, later associated with the Planters and Mechanics Bank, W-AL-130, named the area Twickenham.

In 1812 Twickenham was renamed Huntsville. The town was carefully planned and laid out, the first to be incorporated in Alabama. The cotton industry generated wealth in the area, and planters came from Virginia, Georgia, and the Carolinas to settle. In 1819 a constitutional convention was held in Huntsville for the purpose of discussing a state constitution. The temporary capital was established here before moving to Cahawba, then to Tuscaloosa, and finally to Montgomery, where it remains today. In 1855 the Memphis and Charleston Railroad was constructed with a pass through Huntsville, and further growth came to the town.

Huntsville initially opposed secession. Nevertheless, once the Confederacy was formed, many local men became soldiers. On April 11, 1862, Huntsville was seized by the Union army. Some buildings and homes were burned in the surrounding countryside, but Huntsville itself was, for the most part, unharmed.

Huntsville was the location imprinted on Civil War tokens of White & Swann, a partnership whose business specialty is not known to modern students of the series. Perhaps they were sutlers, as the Union forces were located in the area from 1862 onward.

Bank of the State of Alabama (branch)

1833–1845

W-AL-090

History: The Bank of the State of Alabama moved from Cahawba, W-AL-010, to Tuscaloosa when the state capital was relocated there in 1826. The bank was able to raise $15,859,420 from various sources, including land sales, funds from university rents, and the sale of state stocks. Unfortunately, however, this amount was mostly used to keep the bank from failing during the Panic of 1837.

The branch at Huntsville opened in 1833. In 1841 the capital totaled $1,860,060, and circulation was $977,158.

The bank and its branches were poorly managed and engaged in many questionable and fraudulent activities. Finally, the bank was liquidated on January 1, 1845. The entity left the state with a debt of $14,000,000.

The Bank of the State of Alabama had its parent banks located first in Cahawba, W-AL-010, and later in Tuscaloosa, W-AL-340, and branches located in Decatur, W-AL-020, Mobile, W-AL-190, Montgomery, W-AL-270, and Tuscumbia, W-AL-350.

Valid Issues

$1 • W-AL-090-001-G010

CC

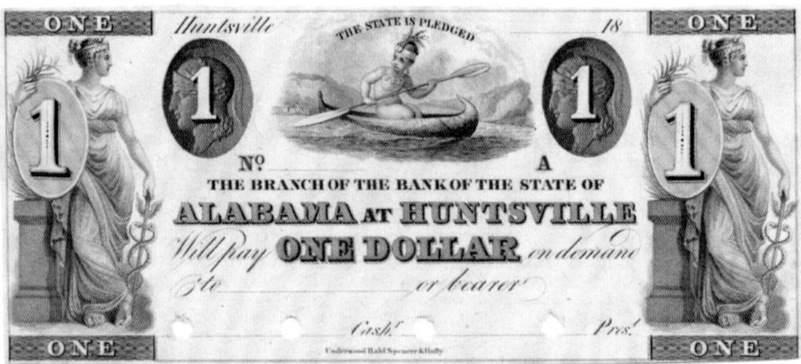

Engraver: Underwood, Bald, Spencer & Hufty. ***Comments:*** H-Unlisted. 18__. 1830s.

Rarity: URS-3

F $1,500; **Proof** $2,000

$2 • W-AL-090-002-G013

ChasC

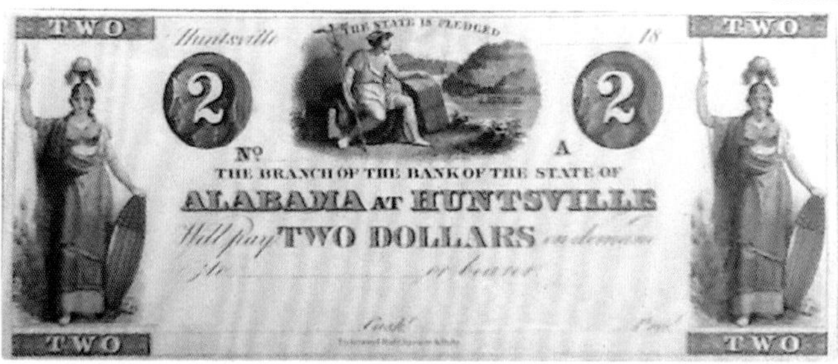

Engraver: Underwood, Bald, Spencer & Hufty. ***Comments:*** H-Unlisted, Rosene-Unlisted. 18__. 1830s.

Rarity: URS-1

Proof $3,000

$3 • W-AL-090-003-G015

ChasC

Engraver: Underwood, Bald, Spencer & Hufty. ***Comments:*** H-Unlisted, Rosene-Unlisted. 18__. 1830s.

Rarity: URS-1

Proof $3,000

$5 • W-AL-090-005-G020

CC

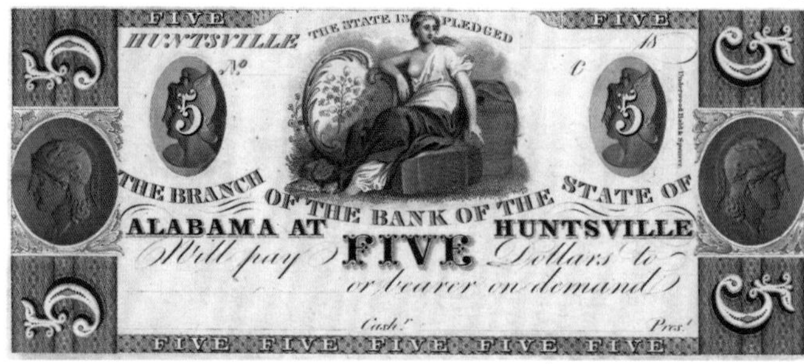

Engraver: Underwood, Bald & Spencer. ***Comments:*** H-AL-5-G130, Rosene-3-10. 18__. 1830s.

Rarity: URS-4

Proof $1,500

$5 • W-AL-090-005-G025

ChasC

Engraver: Draper, Toppan, Longacre & Co. ***Comments:*** H-Unlisted, Rosene-Unlisted. 18__. 1830s.

Rarity: URS-2

Proof $3,200

$10 • W-AL-090-010-G030

ChasC

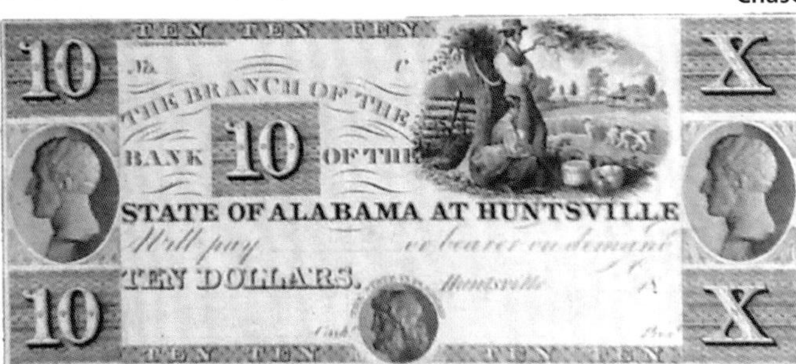

Engraver: Underwood, Bald & Spencer. ***Comments:*** H-AL-5-G132, Rosene-3-11. 18__. 1830s.

Rarity: URS-3

Proof $2,000

$10 • W-AL-090-010-G035

ChasC

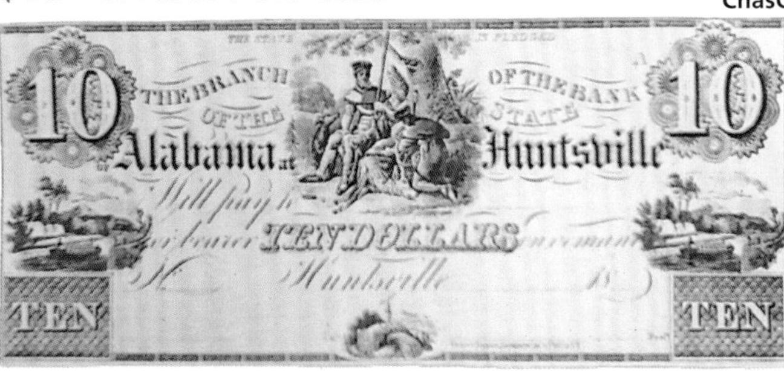

Engraver: Draper, Toppan, Longacre & Co. ***Comments:*** H-Unlisted, Rosene-Unlisted. 18__. 1830s.

Rarity: URS-1

$20 • W-AL-090-020-G040

ChasC

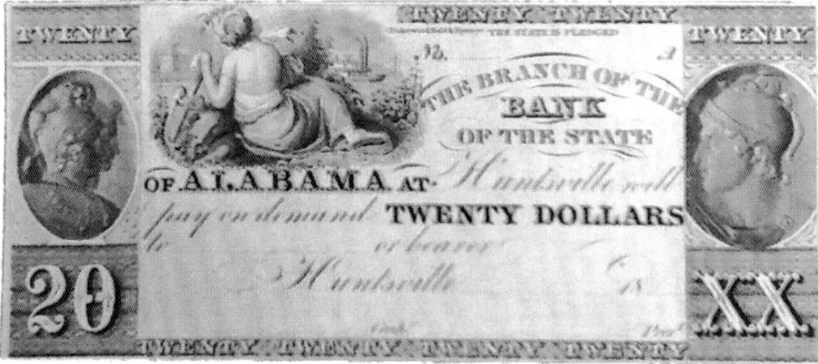

Engraver: Underwood, Bald & Spencer. ***Comments:*** H-AL-5-G134, Rosene-3-12. 18__. 1830s.

Rarity: URS-1

Proof $3,500

$20 • W-AL-090-020-G045

ChasC

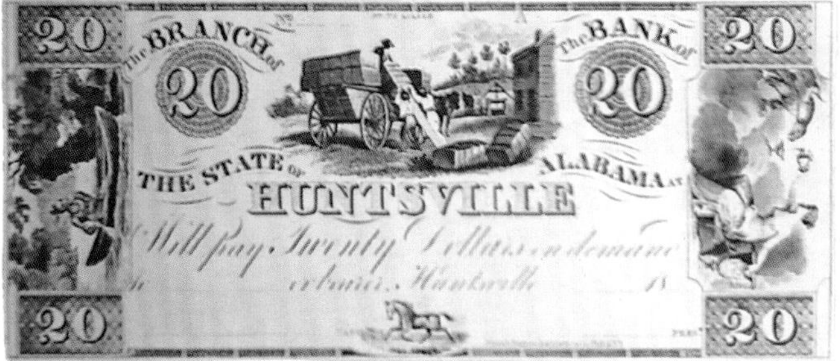

Engraver: Draper, Toppan, Longacre & Co. ***Comments:*** H-Unlisted, Rosene-Unlisted. 18__. 1830s.

Rarity: URS-1

$50 • W-AL-090-050-G050

Engraver: Underwood, Bald, Spencer & Hufty. ***Comments:*** H-AL-5-G136. No description available. 18__. 1830s.

Rarity: *None known*

$50 • W-AL-090-050-G055

ChasC

Engraver: Draper, Toppan, Longacre & Co. ***Comments:*** H-Unlisted, Rosene-Unlisted. 18__. 1830s.

Rarity: URS-1

$100 • W-AL-090-100-G060

ChasC

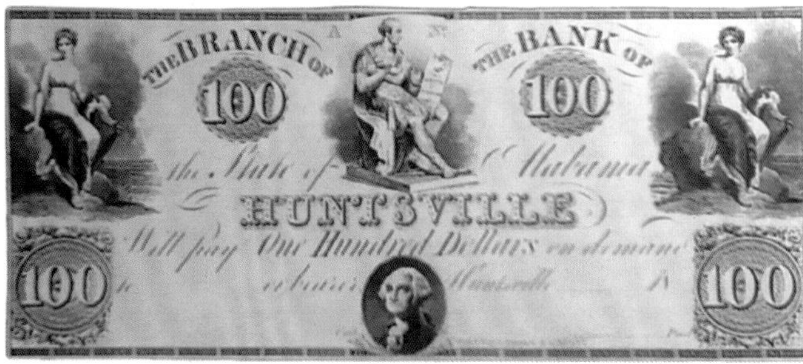

Engraver: Underwood, Bald, Spencer & Hufty. ***Comments:*** H-AL-5-G138. 18__. 1830s.

Rarity: URS-1

Proof $3,700

Post Notes

$10 • W-AL-090-010-G070

CC

Engraver: Draper, Toppan, Longacre & Co. ***Comments:*** H-Unlisted. 18__. 1830s.

Rarity: URS-2

Proof $2,500

$20 • W-AL-090-020-G080

Engraver: Underwood, Bald, Spencer & Hufty. ***Comments:*** H-AL-5-G146. No description available. 18__. 1830s.

Rarity: *None known*

$50 • W-AL-090-050-G090

Engraver: Underwood, Bald, Spencer & Hufty. ***Comments:*** H-AL-5-G148. No description available. 18__. 1830s.

Rarity: *None known*

$100 • W-AL-090-100-G100
Engraver: Underwood, Bald, Spencer & Hufty. ***Comments:*** H-AL-5-G150. No description available. 18__. 1830s.
Rarity: *None known*

Post Notes Payable at the Bank of Louisiana in New Orleans

$5 • W-AL-090-005-G110 HA

Engraver: Draper, Toppan, Longacre & Co. ***Comments:*** H-AL-5-G152. 18__. 1830s.
Rarity: —

$10 • W-AL-090-010-G120
Engraver: Underwood, Bald, Spencer & Hufty. ***Comments:*** H-AL-5-G154. No description available. 18__. 1830s.
Rarity: *None known*

$20 • W-AL-090-020-G130 RH

Engraver: Underwood, Bald, Spencer & Hufty. ***Comments:*** H-AL-5-G156. 18__. 1830s.
Rarity: URS-1
Proof $4,500

$50 • W-AL-090-050-G140 ChasC

Engraver: Underwood, Bald, Spencer & Hufty. ***Comments:*** H-AL-5-G158. 18__. 1830s.
Rarity: URS-1
Proof $5,500

$100 • W-AL-090-100-G150 RH

Engraver: Underwood, Bald, Spencer & Hufty. ***Comments:*** H-AL-5-G160. 18__. 1830s.
Rarity: URS-1
Proof $6,000

Farmers and Mechanics Bank
1820s
W-AL-100

History: Although scattered mentions of such a bank appear in print, nothing has been learned of a bank under this name that would indicate it was ever an entity being seriously planned or formed.

Numismatic Commentary: No notes with this imprint are known.

Huntsville Bank
1823
W-AL-110

History: In 1823, with notes circulating in bad credit, the Huntsville Bank closed. No further information about the bank's inception has been discovered.

Numismatic Commentary: No notes with this imprint have been found. Perhaps a loan office or some other enterprise was the original intention.

Northern Bank of Alabama
1852–1865
W-AL-120

History: The Northern Bank of Alabama was incorporated on February 10, 1852. J.J. Donegan was the first president, and T. Lacy was the first cashier. On February 8, 1854, the bank was approved to issue bills of denominations under $5. During the Panic of 1857, it was the only Alabama bank outside of Mobile to keep paying out specie.[4] By 1860 the capital was worth $500,000, bills in circulation totaled $205,704, specie was $108,787, and real estate was worth $16,342.

In 1865 the Northern Bank of Alabama closed.

Numismatic Commentary: Notes of this sought-after bank are extremely scarce, with most notes showing wear from circulation.

Valid Issues

$1 • W-AL-120-001-G010

ChasC

Engraver: Toppan, Carpenter, Casilear & Co. ***Comments:*** H-AL-25-G2, Rosene-134-1. 18__. 1850s.

Rarity: URS-6
G $200; **F** $350

$1 • W-AL-120-001-G010a

ChasC

Overprint: Red ONE. ***Engraver:*** Toppan, Carpenter, Casilear & Co. ***Comments:*** H-AL-25-G2a. Similar to W-AL-120-001-G010. 18__. 1850s.

Rarity: URS-4
F $350; **Proof** $3,000

$2 • W-AL-120-002-G020

ChasC

Engraver: Toppan, Carpenter, Casilear & Co. ***Comments:*** H-AL-25-G4, Rosene-134-3. 185_. 1850s.

Rarity: URS-4; URS-1
F $300
Proof $2,500

$2 • W-AL-120-002-G020a

HA

Overprint: Red TWO. ***Engraver:*** Toppan, Carpenter, Casilear & Co. ***Comments:*** H-AL-25-G4a. Similar to W-AL-120-002-G020. 185_. 1850s.

Rarity: URS-4
F $750

$5 • W-AL-120-005-G030

ChasC

Engraver: Toppan, Carpenter, Casilear & Co. ***Comments:*** H-AL-25-G6, Rosene-134-4. 18__. 1850s.

Rarity: URS-1
Proof $3,500

How to Read the Whitman Numbering System

$1 • W-AL-020-001-G010a

Denomination: Face value of the note shown.

W: Whitman number. This number is a sortable code unique to each bank and note.

AL: Abbreviation for the state under study.

020: Numerical designation specific to each bank.

001: The denomination in dollars.

G010a: G indicates a good or valid note. Other categories are indicated thus: C (counterfeit); R (raised); S (spurious); N (not-attributed); A (altered). Numbers are assigned starting with 010, 020, et seq. Terminal letters following the number indicate variations of a note: a series of different colored overprints, tints, payees, etc., all on the same design of note. For more information, see the "How to Use This Book" section at the front of the volume, page xiv.

$5 • W-AL-120-005-G030a

CC

Overprint: Red 5 / 5. ***Engraver:*** Toppan, Carpenter, Casilear & Co. ***Comments:*** H-AL-25-G6a. Similar to W-AL-120-005-G030. 18__. 1850s.

Rarity: URS-4
F $400; **VF** $650

$10 • W-AL-120-010-G040

Left: 10 / Portrait of Henry Clay / TEN. ***Center:*** Train. ***Right:*** 10 / Portrait of Daniel Webster / TEN. ***Engraver:*** Toppan, Carpenter, Casilear & Co. ***Comments:*** H-AL-25-G8, Rosene-134-5. 18__. 1850s.

Rarity: —

$10 • W-AL-120-010-G040a

CC

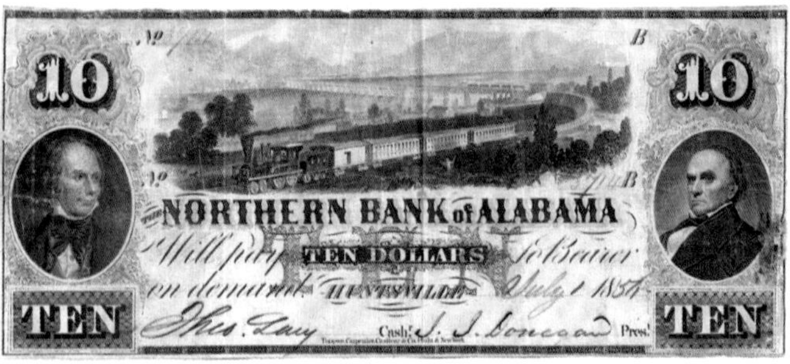

Overprint: Red TEN. ***Engraver:*** Toppan, Carpenter, Casilear & Co. ***Comments:*** H-AL-25-G8a. Similar to W-AL-120-010-G040. 18__. 1850s.

Rarity: URS-4
F $500; **Proof** $1,500

$20 • W-AL-120-020-G050

CC

Engraver: Toppan, Carpenter, Casilear & Co. ***Comments:*** H-AL-25-G10, Rosene-134-7. 18__. 1850s.

Rarity: URS-3
VG $450; **F** $1,100
Selected auction price(s): Heritage Auctions, April 27, 2015, Lot 22602, F $822; Heritage Auctions, October 23, 2015, Lot 19086, F $1,116

$20 • W-AL-120-020-G060

HA

Engraver: Toppan, Carpenter, Casilear & Co. ***Comments:*** H-Unlisted. 18__. 1850s.

Rarity: URS-4
F $1,300
Selected auction price: Heritage Auctions, October 23, 2015, Lot 19087, F $1,305

$50 • W-AL-120-050-G070

ChasC

Engraver: Toppan, Carpenter, Casilear & Co. ***Comments:*** H-AL-25-G12, Rosene-134-8. 18__. 1850s.

Rarity: URS-1
Proof $6,500

$100 • W-AL-120-100-G080

Left: Portrait of Benjamin Franklin / 100. ***Center:*** U.S. Capitol. ***Right:*** 100 / Portrait of George Washington. ***Engraver:*** Toppan, Carpenter, Casilear & Co. ***Comments:*** H-AL-25-G14, Rosene-134-9. 18__. 1850s.

Rarity: —

Planters and Mechanics Bank

1816–1818

W-AL-130

History: The Planters and Mechanics Bank was chartered on December 11, 1816. It was the first bank to be established in the state. It had an authorized capital of $500,000 and a duration limited to 21 years.[5] Business could begin once $50,000 had been subscribed to. The first president was Leroy Pope, one of the pioneer settlers of the area. The bank opened for business on October 17, 1817.

The institution as it stood under that name was short lived, and in January 1818, the Planters and Mechanics Bank became the Planters and Merchants Bank, W-AL-140.

Numismatic Commentary: Due to the brevity of this bank's nature, surviving issues bearing the Planters and Mechanics Bank imprint are practically unknown.

Valid Issues

$1 • W-AL-130-001-G010

Left: 1 / HUNTSVILLE vertically. ***Center:*** Woman, eagle, shield. ***Right:*** 1 / ALABAMA vertically. ***Engraver:*** Murray, Draper, Fairman & Co. ***Comments:*** H-AL-30-G2. 18__. 1817.

Rarity: —

$2 • W-AL-130-002-G020

Left: 2 / HUNTSVILLE vertically. ***Right:*** 2 / ALABAMA vertically. ***Engraver:*** Murray, Draper, Fairman & Co. ***Comments:*** H-AL-30-G4. 18__. 1817.

Rarity: —

$3 • W-AL-130-003-G030

Left: 3 / HUNTSVILLE vertically. ***Right:*** 3 / ALABAMA vertically. ***Engraver:*** Murray, Draper, Fairman & Co. ***Comments:*** H-AL-30-G6. 18__. 1817.

Rarity: —

$5 • W-AL-130-005-G040

Left: 5 / HUNTSVILLE vertically. ***Right:*** 5 / ALABAMA vertically. ***Engraver:*** Murray, Draper, Fairman & Co. ***Comments:*** H-AL-30-G8. 18__. 1817.

Rarity: —

$10 • W-AL-130-010-G050

Left: HUNTSVILLE vertically. ***Right:*** ALABAMA vertically. ***Engraver:*** Murray, Draper, Fairman & Co. ***Comments:*** H-AL-30-G10. 18__. 1817.

Rarity: —

$20 • W-AL-130-020-G060

Left: HUNTSVILLE vertically. ***Right:*** ALABAMA vertically. ***Engraver:*** Murray, Draper, Fairman & Co. ***Comments:*** H-AL-30-G12. 18__. 1817.

Rarity: —

$50 • W-AL-130-050-G070

Left: HUNTSVILLE vertically. ***Right:*** ALABAMA vertically. ***Engraver:*** Murray, Draper, Fairman & Co. ***Comments:*** H-AL-30-G14. 18__. 1817.

Rarity: —

Planters and Merchants Bank

1818–1825

W-AL-140

History: In January 1818 the Planters and Mechanics Bank, W-AL-130, became the Planters and Merchants Bank. The bank suspended specie payments on June 16, 1820, continued to experience difficulties, and closed its doors on February 1, 1825.

There was a later, unrelated Planters and Merchants Bank, W-AL-230, located in Mobile.

Numismatic Commentary: Only one note of this bank had been reported as of press time. The signature of Leroy Pope, one of the primary settlers of the area, can be found on the issue (and presumably on other notes issued).

Valid Issues

$1 • W-AL-140-001-G010

HA

Engraver: Murray, Draper, Fairman & Co. ***Comments:*** H-AL-32-G2. 18__. 1818–1820s.

Rarity: URS-1

F $3,900

$2 • W-AL-140-002-G020

Left: 2 / HUNTSVILLE vertically. ***Right:*** 2 / ALABAMA vertically. ***Engraver:*** Murray, Draper, Fairman & Co. ***Comments:*** H-AL-32-G4. 18__. 1818–1820s.

Rarity: —

$3 • W-AL-140-003-G030

HA

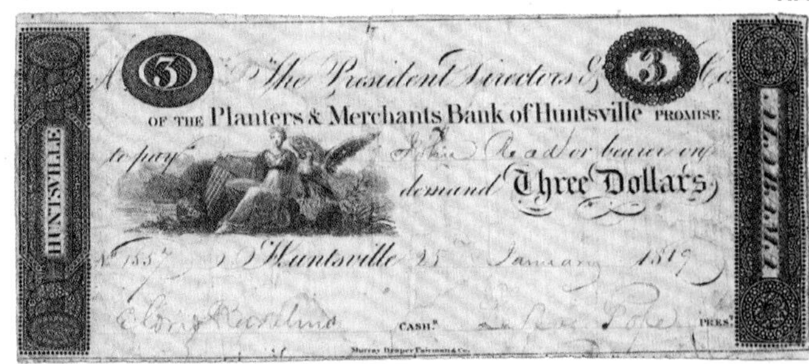

Engraver: Murray, Draper, Fairman & Co. ***Comments:*** H-AL-32-G6. 18__. 1818–1820s.

Rarity: URS-1

VF $3,000; **Proof** $3,000

Selected auction price(s): Heritage Auctions, January 6, 2016, Lot 18446, VF $3,055; Heritage Auctions, January 6, 2016, Lot 18445, Proof $2,350

$5 • W-AL-140-005-G040

Left: 5 / HUNTSVILLE vertically. ***Right:*** 5 / ALABAMA vertically. ***Engraver:*** Murray, Draper, Fairman & Co. ***Comments:*** H-AL-32-G8. 18__. 1818–1820s.

Rarity: *None known*

$10 • W-AL-140-010-G050

Left: HUNTSVILLE vertically. ***Right:*** ALABAMA vertically. ***Engraver:*** Murray, Draper, Fairman & Co. ***Comments:*** H-AL-32-G10. 18__. 1818–1820s.

Rarity: *None known*

$20 • W-AL-140-020-G060

Left: HUNTSVILLE vertically. ***Right:*** ALABAMA vertically. ***Engraver:*** Murray, Draper, Fairman & Co. ***Comments:*** H-AL-32-G12. 18__. 1818–1820s.

Rarity: *None known*

Non-Valid Issues

$50 • W-AL-140-050-R010 HA

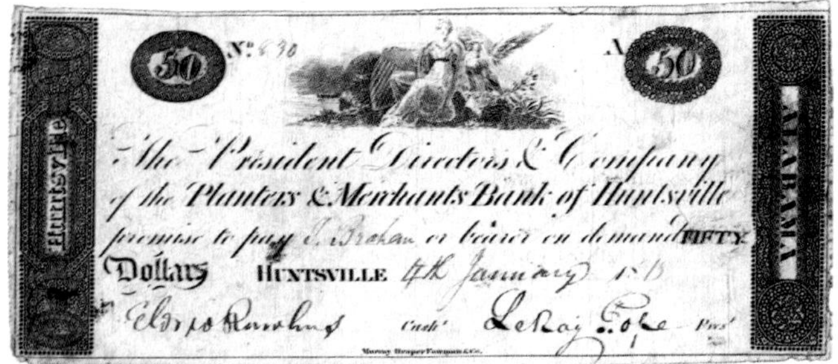

Engraver: Murray, Draper, Fairman & Co. ***Comments:*** H-AL-32-G14. Raised from $1. No original $50 notes are known to exist. 18__. 1818–1820s.

Rarity: URS-1
F $3,700
Selected auction price: Heritage Auctions, January 6, 2016, Lot 18447, F $3,760

Irwinton, Alabama

The land that became Irwinton was granted to General William Irwin, who served as the first state senator of Alabama. Irwin was able to use his wealth and influence to promote the area's development, and a steamboat wharf was established, paving the way for the growth and prominence of the trading center in town.

In 1843 Irwinton was renamed Eufaula, partly due to the fact that mail was frequently being misplaced in distant Irwinton, Georgia.

See also Eufaula, Alabama.

Irwinton Bridge Bank
1839
W-AL-150

History: The Irwinton Bridge Bank was established in 1839 by Edward B. Young. Later the name was changed to Young & Woods, which evolved into the Eufaula National Bank. The Irwinton Bridge Company was associated with this bank, which likely was formed to allow the corporation to raise stock for the purpose of conducting business.[6]

Numismatic Commentary: No notes of this bank are known to exist.

LaFayette, Alabama

Developed within Chambers County, the town of LaFayette was first called Chambersville. When it was incorporated on January 7, 1835, it was renamed Lafayette after the Marquis de Lafayette. Later the capitalization of the spelling was changed to LaFayette.

Rail Road Bank
1850s
W-AL-160

History: A non-existent bank represented only by notes altered from other banks.

Issues

$2 • W-AL-160-002-A010

Left: 2 / Man with scythe. ***Center:*** Man on horseback, Train. ***Right:*** 2 / Portrait of Lewis Cass. ***Overprint:*** Red TWO. ***Engraver:*** Toppan, Carpenter, Casilear & Co. ***Comments:*** H-AL-35-A5, Rosene-155-1. Altered from $2 Erie & Kalamazoo Rail Road Bank, Adrian, Michigan. Aug. 1, 1853.

Rarity: URS-3
F $400

Mobile, Alabama

Mobile was founded in 1702 as the capital of French Louisiana. It did not become a part of the United States until 1813, when it was seized and added to the Mississippi Territory. It became part of the Alabama Territory in 1817. On December 14, 1819, Mobile became a part of the state of Alabama. Cotton was a huge crop for the town, heralding in a new era of growth and commerce. Mobile's location as a seaport also brought it prosperity, and soon it was the second-largest international seaport on the Gulf Coast.

In 1827 a fire destroyed much of the city, and in 1839 another fire decimated the rebuilt town. It rose again from the ashes and became one of the busiest Gulf ports during the 1850s. Its wealth made the city a cultural pinnacle for the area and beyond. During the Civil War, Mobile saw much naval activity, including the Battle of Mobile Bay. After the war was over, an explosion of ammunition killed over 300 people and destroyed much of the city.

Bank in Mobile of the St. Stephens Steamboat Company
1818–1829
W-AL-170

History: The Bank in Mobile of the St. Stephens Steamboat Company was chartered in February 1818. Russell Stebbins was the first president, and Charles C. Hazzard was the first cashier. Hazzard was also previously the cashier of the Tombeckbe Bank, W-AL-300. The bank was fraudulently operated with the result that certain of the directors and officers were jailed until they agreed to stop issuing notes. In 1829 the charter was forfeited.

Numismatic Commentary: Notes bearing the Bank in Mobile of the St. Stephens Steamboat Company imprint are scarce. The limited issues and denominations make attaining an example extremely difficult. As is true with any currency from Alabama, the pleasure of ownership can be increased by learning more about an issuer's history. The Internet beckons in this regard.

Valid Issues

$1 • W-AL-170-001-G010

CC

Engraver: Fairman, Draper, Underwood & Co. ***Comments:*** H-AL-55-G2, Rosene-215-1. 18__. 1826.

Rarity: URS-4
F $600

$2 • W-AL-170-002-G020

CC

Engraver: Fairman, Draper, Underwood & Co. ***Comments:*** H-AL-55-G4, Rosene-215-2. 18__. 1826.

Rarity: URS-4
F $700

$3 • W-AL-170-003-G030

Engraver: Fairman, Draper, Underwood & Co. ***Comments:*** H-Unlisted, Rosene-215-3. No description available. 18__. 1826.

Rarity: *None known*

$5 • W-AL-170-005-G040

CC

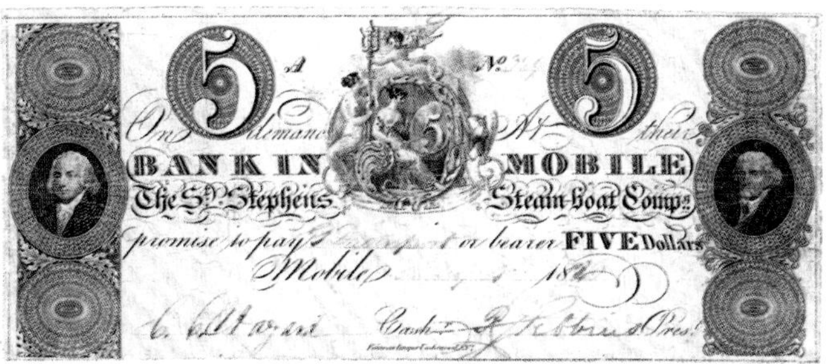

Engraver: Fairman, Draper, Underwood & Co. ***Comments:*** H-AL-55-G6, Rosene-215-4. 18__. 1826.

Rarity: URS-4
F $650

Bank of Mobile

1818–1866

W-AL-180

History: The Bank of Mobile was chartered in November 1818 with an authorized capital of $500,000. Lewis Judson was the first president. The bank opened for business on January 5, 1820.

In 1836 William R. Hallett became president. During the Panic of 1837, the bank suspended specie payments. In 1841 the capital amounted to $1,500,000, and circulation was $25,137. Thomas M. English became the cashier in 1848. On April 22 of that year, there was a run on the bank. Nevertheless, the officers met the challenge and paid the specie demanded "till 5 o'clock in the evening, and until the demand for it had entirely ceased. The circulation of the bank in November last was $2,300,000, and coin on hand $1,100,000."[7]

On February 27, 1852, cashier English passed away. He was replaced by Jonathan Emanuel. In 1857 the capital was $1,500,000, and bills in circulation totaled $1,460,334. Specie at the time was $716,879, and real estate was valued at $32,000. Although the bank survived the Panic of 1857 and remained in business, it collapsed during the Reconstruction Period after the Civil War.

Numismatic Commentary: Notes from this bank range from scarce to very rare. The spurious $100 issue is considered an uncommon prize.

Remaining at the American Bank Note Co. archives as of 2003 was a $20-$20-$100-$100 face plate, a $500-$500-$1,000-$1,000 face plate, a $50-$50 face plate, and a $5-$5-$10-$10 face plate.

Valid Issues

$1 • W-AL-180-001-G010

Left: ONE vertically. ***Center:*** Two women standing. ***Right:*** 1 / Running deer. ***Engraver:*** N. & S.S. Jocelyn. ***Comments:*** H-AL-45-G2, Rosene-183-1. 18__. 1820s–1830s.

Rarity: URS-2
Proof $2,250

$2 • W-AL-180-002-G020

Engraver: N. & S.S. Jocelyn. ***Comments:*** H-AL-45-G6. No description available. 18__. 1820s–1830s.

Rarity: *None known*

$5 • W-AL-180-005-G030

Left: FIVE / 5. ***Center:*** Ships, Woman, House. ***Right:*** FIVE / 5. ***Engraver:*** Murray, Draper, Fairman & Co. ***Comments:*** H-AL-45-G10, Rosene-183-4. 18__. 1820s–1830s.

Rarity: *None known*

$5 • W-AL-180-005-G040

Left: 5 / Woman / 5. ***Center:*** 5 / Hebe watering eagle / 5. ***Right:*** FIVE vertically. ***Engraver:*** Rawdon, Wright, Hatch & Co. ***Comments:*** H-AL-45-G12, Rosene-183-2. 18__. 1830s–1840s.

Rarity: URS-2
Proof $2,500

$5 • W-AL-180-005-G050

Left: 5 / Portrait of George Washington. ***Center:*** Portrait of James Madison / Two women seated on dock / Portrait of James Monroe. ***Right:*** 5 / Medallion head. ***Engraver:*** Toppan, Carpenter & Co. ***Comments:*** H-AL-45-G14, Rosene-183-5. 18__. 1840s–1850s.

Rarity: URS-3
Proof $2,000

$5 • W-AL-180-005-G060

Left: 5 / Portrait of George Washington. ***Center:*** Two women seated on dock. ***Right:*** 5 / Riverboat. ***Engraver:*** Toppan, Carpenter & Co. ***Comments:*** H-Unlisted, Rosene-183-3. 18__. 1840s–1850s.

Rarity: *None known*

$10 • W-AL-180-010-G070

Comments: H-AL-45-G16. No description available. 18__. 1820s–1830s.

Rarity: *None known*

$10 • W-AL-180-010-G080

Left: Zeus holding thunderbolt / 10. ***Center:*** 10 / Woman seated with eagle. ***Right:*** 10 / Ship / 10. ***Engraver:*** Rawdon, Wright, Hatch & Co. ***Comments:*** H-AL-45-G18, Rosene-183-7. 18__. 1830s–1850s.

Rarity: URS-2
Proof $2,500

$10 • W-AL-180-010-G090

Left: 10 / Female portrait. ***Center:*** Portrait of George Washington / Sailor seated against bale with flag / Portrait of Thomas Jefferson. ***Right:*** 10 / Justice seated with scales. ***Engraver:*** Toppan, Carpenter & Co. ***Comments:*** H-AL-45-G20, Rosene-183-6. 18__. 1840s–1850s.

Rarity: URS-2
Proof $2,500

$10 • W-AL-180-010-G100

Left: 10 / Female portrait. ***Center:*** Portrait of George Washington / Sailor seated against bale with flag / Portrait of Thomas Jefferson. ***Right:*** 10 / Woman with eagle and shield. ***Engraver:*** Toppan, Carpenter & Co. ***Comments:*** H-Unlisted, Rosene-183-8. 18__. 1840s–1850s.

Rarity: *None known*

$20 • W-AL-180-020-G110

Comments: H-AL-45-G24. No description available. 18__. 1820s–1830s.

Rarity: *None known*

$20 • W-AL-180-020-G120

Left: TWENTY vertically. ***Center:*** XX / Woman standing, Lion / XX. ***Right:*** TWENTY vertically. ***Engraver:*** Unverified, but likely Rawdon, Wright, Hatch & Co. ***Comments:*** H-AL-45-G26, Rosene-183-11. 18__. 1830s–1850s.

Rarity: *None known*

$20 • W-AL-180-020-G130

Left: 20 / Two ships. ***Center:*** Steamboat, ships, harbor, dock. ***Right:*** 20 / Cotton plant. ***Engraver:*** Unverified, but likely Toppan, Carpenter & Co. ***Comments:*** H-AL-45-G28, Rosene-183-10. 18__. 1840s–1850s.

Rarity: *None known*

$50 • W-AL-180-050-G140

Comments: H-AL-45-G30. No description available. 18__. 1820s–1830s.

Rarity: *None known*

$50 • W-AL-180-050-G150

Left: 50 / Woman standing / 50. ***Center:*** L / Woman, eagle, cornucopia / L. ***Right:*** FIFTY vertically. ***Engraver:*** Unverified, but likely Rawdon, Wright, Hatch & Co. ***Comments:*** H-AL-45-G32, Rosene-183-13. 18__. 1830s–1850s.

Rarity: *None known*

$50 • W-AL-180-050-G160

SBG

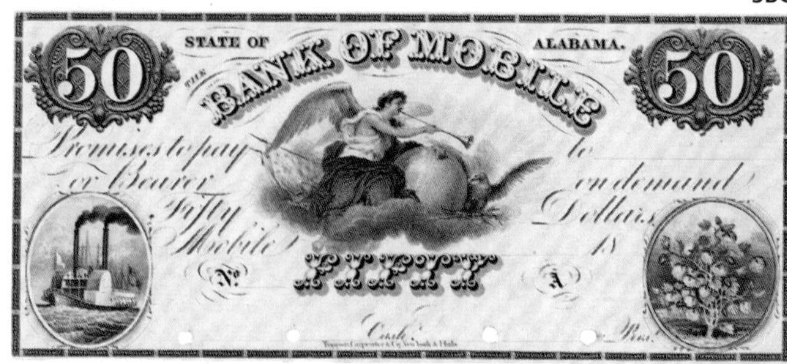

Engraver: Toppan, Carpenter & Co. ***Comments:*** H-AL-45-G34, Rosene-183-12. 18__. 1840s–1850s.

Rarity: URS-2
Proof $3,000

$100 • W-AL-180-100-G170

Comments: H-AL-45-G36. No description available. 18__. 1820s–1830s.

Rarity: *None known*

$100 • W-AL-180-100-G180

Left: Indian / 100. ***Center:*** 100 / Woman standing with scales / 100. ***Right:*** Man standing. ***Engraver:*** Unverified, but likely Rawdon, Wright, Hatch & Co. ***Comments:*** H-AL-45-G38, Rosene-183-14. 18__. 1830s–1850s.

Rarity: *None known*

$100 • W-AL-180-100-G190

CC

BANK OF MOBILE
ONE HUNDRED
100
100

Engraver: Toppan, Carpenter & Co. ***Comments:*** H-AL-45-G40, Rosene-183-15. 18__. 1840s–1850s.

Rarity: URS-3
VF $1,100
Selected auction price: Heritage Auctions, April 22, 2015, Lot 18401, VF $1,057

$500 • W-AL-180-500-G200

CC

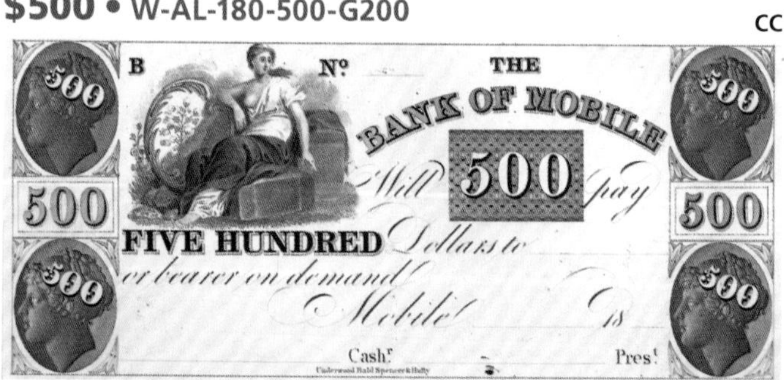

Engraver: Underwood, Bald, Spencer & Hufty. ***Comments:*** H-AL-45-G42, Rosene-183-16. 18__. 1830s–1850s.

Rarity: URS-3
Proof $2,500

$1,000 • **W-AL-180-1000-G210** CC

Engraver: Underwood, Bald, Spencer & Hufty. ***Comments:*** H-AL-45-G44, Rosene-183-17. 18__. 1830s–1850s.

Rarity: URS-3
Proof $2,500

Note Payable at the Merchants Bank in New York

$5 • **W-AL-180-005-G220** CC

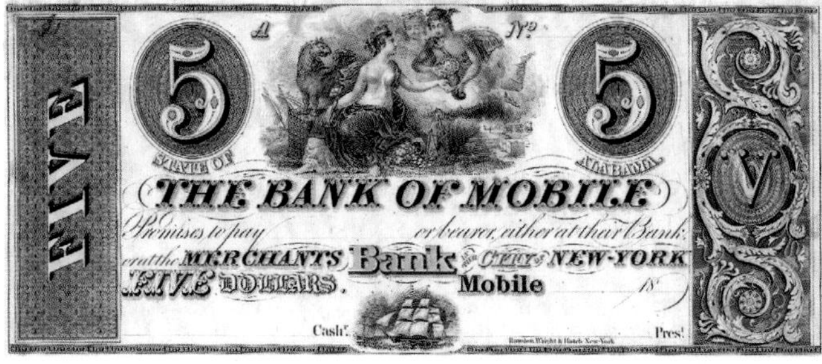

Engraver: Rawdon, Wright & Hatch. ***Comments:*** H-Unlisted. 18__. 1830s–1850s.

Rarity: URS-2
Proof $2,500

Uncut Sheets

$50-$50 • **W-AL-180-050.050-US010**

Vignette(s): ($50) Ship / Angel blowing trumpet, Globe, Eagle / Cotton plant. ***Engraver:*** Toppan, Carpenter & Co. ***Comments:*** H-AL-45-G34, G34. Both notes identical. 18__. 1840s–1850s.

Rarity: *None known*

Non-Valid Issues

$10 • **W-AL-180-010-C080**

Engraver: Rawdon, Wright, Hatch & Co. ***Comments:*** H-AL-45-C18. Counterfeit of W-AL-180-010-G080. 18__. 1843.

Rarity: *None known*

$10 • **W-AL-180-010-C090**

Engraver: Toppan, Carpenter & Co. ***Comments:*** H-AL-45-C20. Counterfeit of W-AL-180-010-G090. 18__. 1850s.

Rarity: *None known*

$10 • **W-AL-180-010-R010**

Comments: H-AL-45-R5. Raised from $1. 18__. 1830s.

Rarity: *None known*

$100 • **W-AL-180-100-R020**

Comments: H-AL-45-R10. Raised from $1. 18__. 1840s.

Rarity: *None known*

$100 • **W-AL-180-100-S010** CC

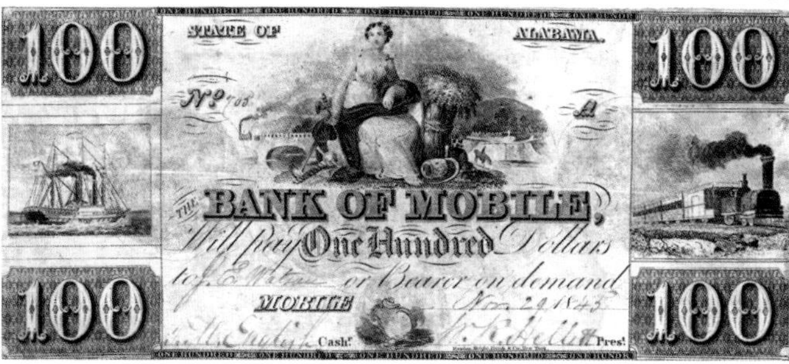

Engraver: Rawdon, Wright, Hatch & Co. ***Comments:*** H-AL-45-S5. 18__. 1830s–1840s.

Rarity: URS-3
VF $1,000

$100 • **W-AL-180-100-N010**

Center: Cherub riding on lion. ***Comments:*** H-AL-45-N20. 18__. 1850s.

Rarity: —

Bank of the State of Alabama (branch)

1835–1845

W-AL-190

History: The Bank of the State of Alabama moved from Cahawba, W-AL-010, to Tuscaloosa when the state capital was relocated there in 1826. The bank was able to raise $15,859,420 from various sources, including land sales, funds from university rents, and the sale of state stocks. Unfortunately, however, this amount was mostly used to keep the bank from failing during the Panic of 1837.

The branch at Mobile opened in 1835 with a capital of $2,000,000 and circulation of $1,440,575. The cashier was Andrew Strong.

The bank and its branches were poorly managed and engaged in many questionable and fraudulent activities. Finally, the bank was liquidated on January 1, 1845. The entity left the state with a debt of $14,000,000.

The Bank of the State of Alabama had its parent banks located first in Cahawba, W-AL-010, and later in Tuscaloosa, W-AL-340, and branches located in Decatur, W-AL-020, Huntsville, W-AL-090, Montgomery, W-AL-270, and Tuscumbia, W-AL-350.

Numismatic Commentary: In addition to regular notes, post notes of unknown description and denomination were issued payable at the Phenix Bank in New York.

Remaining at the American Bank Note Co. archives as of 2003 was a $5-$10 face plate.

Valid Issues

$1 • **W-AL-190-001-G010**

Left: 1. ***Center:*** 1 / Two women standing, Ship / 1. ***Right:*** ONE / Sailing ship / ONE. ***Engraver:*** Rawdon, Wright & Hatch. ***Comments:*** H-AL-5-G162, Rosene-4-6. 18__. 1830s–1840s.

Rarity: *None known*

$2 • **W-AL-190-002-G020**

Left: II / 2 / II. ***Center:*** 2 / Archimedes lifting world with lever / 2. ***Right:*** Portrait of cherub. ***Engraver:*** Rawdon, Wright & Hatch. ***Comments:*** H-AL-5-G164, Rosene-4-7. 18__. 1830s–1840s.

Rarity: *None known*

$3 • **W-AL-190-003-G030**

Left: III / 3 / III. ***Center:*** 3 / Indian and settler flanking shield bearing 3 surmounted by eagle. ***Right:*** Portrait of cherub. ***Engraver:*** Rawdon, Wright & Hatch. ***Comments:*** H-AL-5-G166, Rosene-4-8. 18__. 1830s–1840s.

Rarity: *None known*

$5 • **W-AL-190-005-G040**

Left: FIVE / Woman standing beside map and cotton plant / V. ***Center:*** 5 / Ship / 5. ***Right:*** FIVE / Mercury with cornucopia, map, and cotton plant / V. ***Engraver:*** Rawdon, Wright & Hatch. ***Comments:*** H-AL-5-G168, Rosene-4-9. 18__. 1830s–1840s.

Rarity: *None known*

$10 • **W-AL-190-010-G050**

Left: 10. ***Center:*** TEN / Woman and man flanking shield / TEN. ***Right:*** X / Male portrait / 10. ***Engraver:*** Rawdon, Wright & Hatch. ***Comments:*** H-AL-5-G170, Rosene-4-10. 18__. 1830s–1840s.

Rarity: *None known*

$20 • **W-AL-190-020-G060** HA

Engraver: Rawdon, Wright, Hatch & Co. ***Comments:*** H-AL-5-G172, Rosene-4-11. 18__. 1830s–1840s.

Rarity: URS-2

Proof $2,500

$50 • **W-AL-190-050-G070** CC

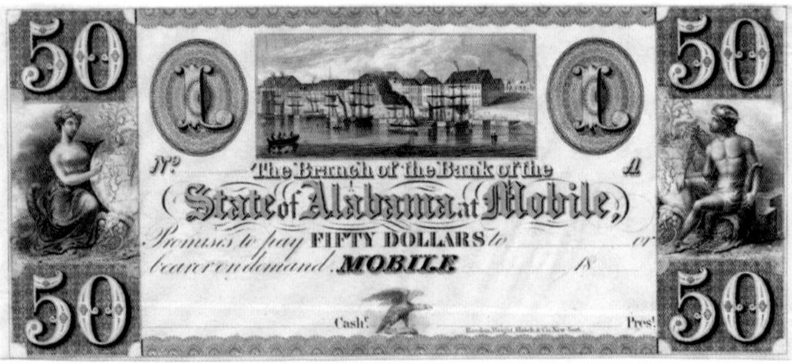

Engraver: Rawdon, Wright, Hatch & Co. ***Comments:*** H-AL-5-G174, Rosene-4-12. 18__. 1830s–1840s.

Rarity: URS-1

Proof $3,500

$100 • **W-AL-190-100-G080**

Engraver: Rawdon, Wright & Hatch. ***Comments:*** H-AL-5-G176. No description available. 18__. 1830s–1840s.

Rarity: *None known*

$500 • **W-AL-190-500-G090**

Left: 500 / Woman seated. ***Center:*** Ship / 500. ***Right:*** 500 / Man seated. ***Engraver:*** Rawdon, Wright & Hatch. ***Comments:*** H-AL-5-G178, Rosene-4-14. 18__. 1830s.

Rarity: *None known*

$1,000 • **W-AL-190-1000-G100**

Left: Ship / 1000. ***Center:*** 1000 / Man seated / 1000. ***Right:*** Ship / 1000. ***Engraver:*** Rawdon, Wright & Hatch. ***Comments:*** H-AL-5-G180, Rosene-4-15. 18__. 1830s.

Rarity: *None known*

Note Payable at the Phoenix Bank in Columbus, Georgia

$5 • **W-AL-190-005-G110** HA

Comments: H-Unlisted. 18__. 1850s.

Rarity: URS-2

F $1,250

Post Notes Payable at the Phenix Bank in New York

$20 • **W-AL-190-020-G120**

Engraver: Rawdon, Wright & Hatch. ***Comments:*** H-AL-5-G190. No description available. 18__. 1830s.

Rarity: *None known*

$50 • **W-AL-190-050-G130**

Engraver: Rawdon, Wright & Hatch. ***Comments:*** H-AL-5-G192. No description available. 18__. 1830s.

Rarity: *None known*

$100 • **W-AL-190-100-G140**

Left: 100. ***Center:*** Woman and man flanking shield / 100. ***Right:*** 100 / Male portrait / 100. ***Engraver:*** Rawdon, Wright & Hatch. ***Comments:*** H-AL-5-G194, Rosene-4-13. 18__. 1830s.

Rarity: *None known*

Post Notes Payable in New York

$20 • **W-AL-190-020-G150**

Engraver: Rawdon, Wright & Hatch. ***Comments:*** H-AL-5-G200. No description available. 18__. 1830s.

Rarity: *None known*

$50 • **W-AL-190-050-G160**

Engraver: Rawdon, Wright & Hatch. ***Comments:*** H-AL-5-G202. No description available. 18__. 1830s.

Rarity: *None known*

$100 • W-AL-190-100-G170
Left: 100. *Center:* Woman and man flanking shield / 100. *Right:* 100 / Male portrait / 100. *Engraver:* Rawdon, Wright & Hatch. *Comments:* H-AL-5-G204. 18__. 1830s.
Rarity: *None known*

Bank of the United States {2nd} (branch)
1826–1836
W-AL-200

History: The second Bank of the United States was chartered in 1816 for a duration of 20 years. Its capital was $35,000,000, of which the United States owned $7,000,000. Branch banks in several large cities were opened in direct competition with state banks, which caused continuing problems.

In 1832 President Andrew Jackson vetoed the 1836 renewal of the Bank of the United States which had been brought up before Congress. This instituted a period of great debate and political turmoil. In late 1833 and early 1834 there was a depression in some areas of business which only served to strengthen the bank, as it was backed by the government. The branches began closing and selling their buildings. In 1852 the properties of what used to be the Mobile branch of the Bank of the United States were offered at auction, bringing in more than $255,000.

Numismatic Commentary: Genuine notes are so rare as to be virtually non-collectible. The same can be said for bills of other branches. Most notes that come on the market are contemporary counterfeits, although they are not often recognized as such.

Valid Issues

$5 • W-AL-200-005-G010
Left: Eagle with shield / FIVE D. *Center:* 5. *Right:* FIVE. *Engraver:* Murray, Draper, Fairman & Co. *Comments:* H-US-2-G476. 18__. 1820s.
Rarity: *None known*

$5 • W-AL-200-005-G020 CC

Engraver: Fairman, Draper, Underwood & Co. *Comments:* H-US-2-G478, Rosene-184-1. 18__. 1820s.
Rarity: URS-4
F $500

$10 • W-AL-200-010-G030
Left: Eagle with shield / TEN D. *Center:* 10. *Right:* TEN. *Engraver:* Murray, Draper, Fairman & Co. *Comments:* H-US-2-G482. 18__. 1820s–1830s.
Rarity: *None known*

$10 • W-AL-200-010-G040
Left: 10. *Center:* Eagle with shield. *Right:* 10. *Engraver:* Fairman, Draper, Underwood & Co. *Comments:* H-US-2-G484, Rosene-184-2. 18__. 1820s.
Rarity: *None known*

$20 • W-AL-200-020-G050
Left: Eagle with shield / TWENTY D. *Center:* 20. *Right:* TWENTY. *Engraver:* Murray, Draper, Fairman & Co. *Comments:* H-US-2-G488. 18__. 1820s.
Rarity: *None known*

$20 • W-AL-200-020-G060
Left: 20. *Center:* Eagle with shield. *Right:* 20. *Engraver:* Fairman, Draper, Underwood & Co. *Comments:* H-US-2-G490, Rosene-184-3. 18__. 1820s–1830s.
Rarity: *None known*

$20 • W-AL-200-020-G070
Left: Eagle with shield. *Center:* 20 / TWENTY. *Right:* 20. *Engraver:* Draper, Underwood, Bald & Spencer. *Comments:* H-US-2-G492. 18__. 1820s.
Rarity: *None known*

$50 • W-AL-200-050-G080
Left: Eagle with shield / FIFTY D. *Center:* 50. *Right:* FIFTY. *Engraver:* Murray, Draper, Fairman & Co. *Comments:* H-US-2-G496. 18__. 1820s.
Rarity: *None known*

$50 • W-AL-200-050-G090
Left: 50. *Center:* Eagle with shield. *Right:* 50. *Engraver:* Fairman, Draper, Underwood & Co. *Comments:* H-US-2-G498. 18__. 1830s–1840s.
Rarity: *None known*

$50 • W-AL-200-050-G100
Left: 50. *Center:* Eagle with shield. *Right:* 50. *Engraver:* Draper, Underwood, Bald & Spencer. *Comments:* H-US-2-G500. 18__. 1830s–1840s.
Rarity: *None known*

$100 • W-AL-200-100-G110
Left: Eagle with shield / HUNDRED D. *Center:* 100. *Right:* HUNDRED. *Engraver:* Murray, Draper, Fairman & Co. *Comments:* H-US-2-G504. 18__. 1830s–1840s.
Rarity: *None known*

$100 • W-AL-200-100-G120
Center: Eagle with shield / 100. *Engraver:* Fairman, Draper, Underwood & Co. *Comments:* H-US-2-G506, Rosene-184-4. 18__. 1830s–1840s.
Rarity: *None known*

$100 • W-AL-200-100-G130
Left: Eagle with shield. *Center:* 100 / HUNDRED. *Right:* 100. *Engraver:* Draper, Underwood, Bald & Spencer. *Comments:* H-US-2-G508. 18__. 1830s–1840s.
Rarity: *None known*

Non-Valid Issues

$5 • W-AL-200-005-C010

Engraver: Murray, Draper, Fairman & Co. ***Comments:*** H-US-2-C476. Counterfeit of W-AL-200-005-G010. 18__. 1820s.

Rarity: *None known*

$10 • W-AL-200-010-C030

Engraver: Murray, Draper, Fairman & Co. ***Comments:*** H-US-2-C482. Counterfeit of W-AL-200-010-G030. 18__. 1820s.

Rarity: *None known*

$20 • W-AL-200-020-C050

Engraver: Murray, Draper, Fairman & Co. ***Comments:*** H-US-2-C488. Counterfeit of W-AL-200-020-G050. 18__. 1820s.

Rarity: *None known*

$50 • W-AL-200-050-C090

Engraver: Fairman, Draper, Underwood & Co. ***Comments:*** H-US-2-C498. Counterfeit of W-AL-200-050-G090. 18__. 1830s.

Rarity: *None known*

$100 • W-AL-200-100-C110

Engraver: Murray, Draper, Fairman & Co. ***Comments:*** H-US-2-C504. Counterfeit of W-AL-200-100-G110. 18__. 1820s.

Rarity: *None known*

$100 • W-AL-200-100-C120

Engraver: Draper, Underwood, Bald & Spencer. ***Comments:*** H-US-2-C506. Counterfeit of W-AL-200-100-G120. 18__. 1830s.

Rarity: *None known*

City Bank of Mobile

1830s–1840s

W-AL-210

History: No entity is known to have been chartered under this name. All notes are fantasies issued for the purpose of circulating in areas distant from Mobile. In 1842 news accounts warned the public to be wary of such counterfeits.

Issues

$50 • W-AL-210-050-G010 HA

Engraver: Western Bank Note Co. / Woodruff, Tucker & Co. ***Comments:*** H-Unlisted. 18__. 1830s–1840s.

Rarity: —
VF $1,500

Mechanics Aid Association Deposit Bank

1861 and 1862

W-AL-220

History: The Mechanics Aid Association of Mobile was incorporated on February 24, 1860. On November 11, 1861, the act was amended, allowing the entity to function as a Deposit Bank and thus pay out funds as deposited by its investors.

Numismatic Commentary: Notes of this bank are considered to be rare, with most issues appearing in Very Good to Very Fine condition, showing evidence of extensive use in their time.

Valid Issues

$2 • W-AL-220-002-G010 CC

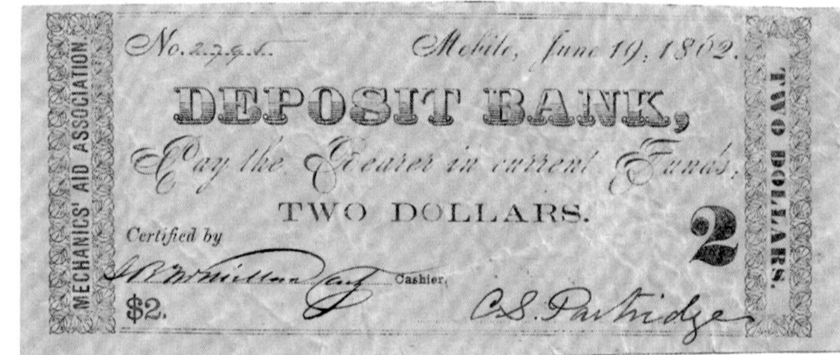

Engraver: W.R. Robertson. ***Comments:*** H-Unlisted. Aug. 19th, 1862.

Rarity: URS-8
VF $200

$2 • W-AL-220-002-G020 CC

MECHANICS' AID ASSOCIATION

DEPOSIT BANK,

Pay the Bearer in current Funds,

TWO DOLLARS.

Certified by

Cashier.

$2.

2

TWO DOLLARS.

Comments: H-Unlisted. June 19, 1862.

Rarity: URS-8
F $150

$3 • W-AL-220-003-G030 ANS

Comments: H-Unlisted. May 13, 1862.

Rarity: URS-8
F $150

$3 • W-AL-220-003-G030a CC

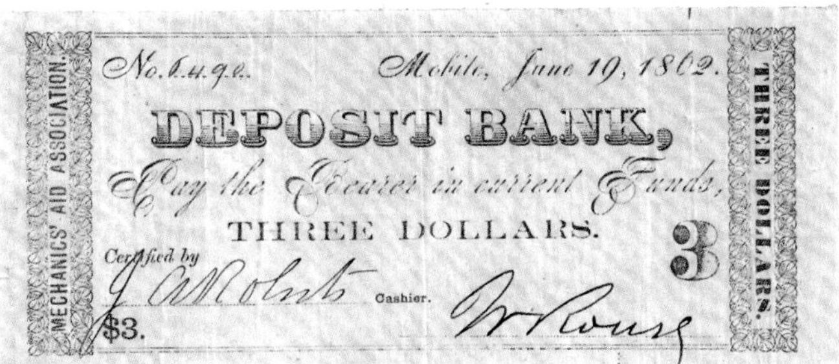

Comments: H-Unlisted. Similar to W-AL-220-003-G030 but with different date. June 19, 1862.

Rarity: URS-8
F $150

$3 • W-AL-220-003-G040 CC

Engraver: W.R. Robertson. ***Comments:*** H-Unlisted. Aug. 19th, 1862.

Rarity: URS-7
F $200

$5 • W-AL-220-005-G050 CC

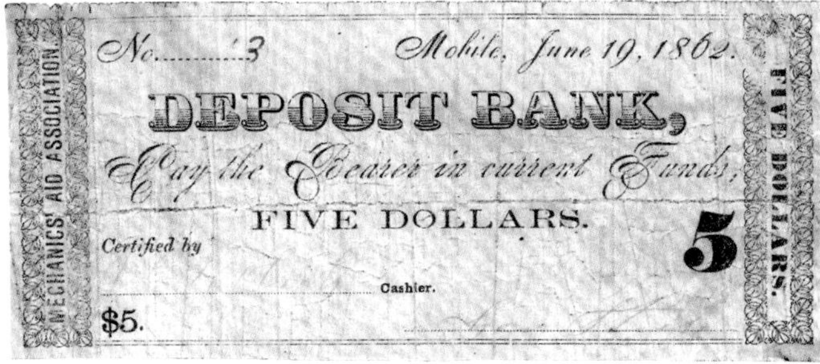

Comments: H-Unlisted. June 19, 1862.

Rarity: URS-8
F $150

Mobile Savings Bank

1852–1860s

W-AL-225

History: The Mobile Savings Bank was originally the Mobile Savings Company, which was originally the Mechanics Savings Company of Mobile, incorporated on February 7, 1852. On November 23, 1854, the name was changed to the Mobile Savings Company. On February 6, 1858, the Mobile Savings Company was legally authorized to suspend specie payments, as long as payments were resumed on or before February 15, 1858.

On February 10, 1860, the name of the company was changed to the Mobile Savings Bank. On December 9, 1861, the charter of the Mobile Savings Bank was amended to allow the savings bank to deposit bonds of the Confederate States of America or of the state of Alabama with the state. The Mobile Savings Bank had the National Park Bank (also seen as the Park Bank) as its New York correspondent.

Numismatic Commentary: Notes bearing the imprint of the Mechanics Savings Company of Mobile or the Mobile Savings Company have not been seen.

Valid Issues

Notes Payable in Current Funds

5¢ • W-AL-225-00.05-G010 HA

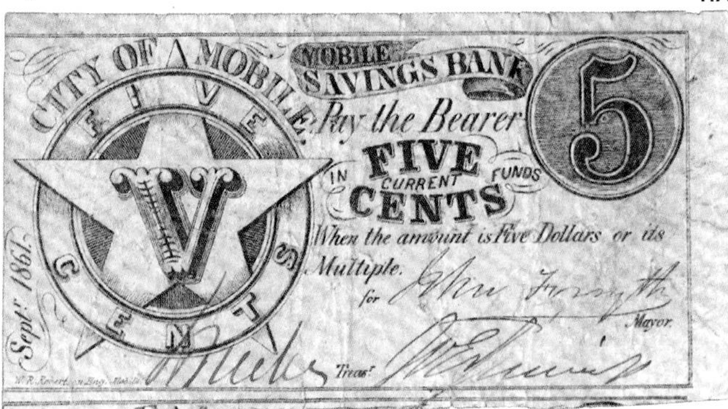

Engraver: W.R. Robertson. ***Comments:*** H-Unlisted. Septr. 1861.

Rarity: URS-5
F $75

10¢ • W-AL-225-00.10-G020 HA

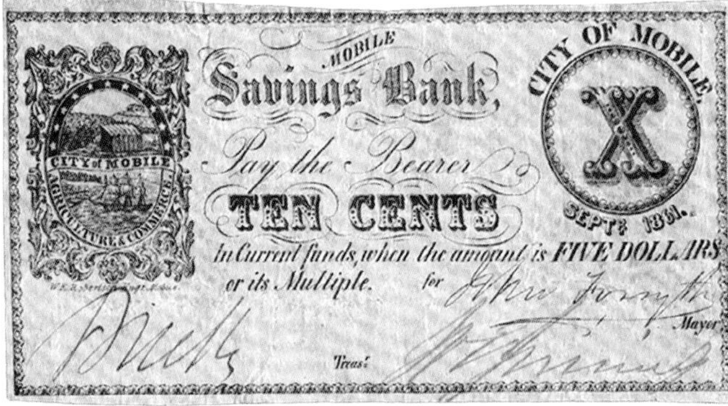

Engraver: W.R. Robertson. ***Comments:*** H-Unlisted. Septr. 1861.

Rarity: URS-5
F $75

50¢ • W-AL-225-00.50-G030 HA

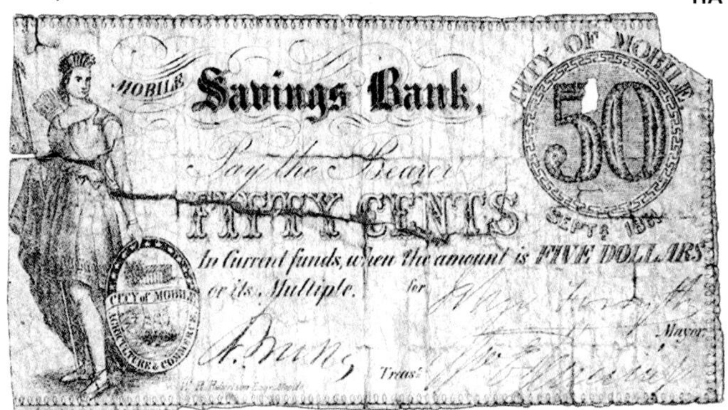

Engraver: W.R. Robertson. ***Comments:*** H-Unlisted. Septr. 1861.

Rarity: URS-5
F $100

Notes Payable in Confederate Notes

$1 • W-AL-225-001-G040

HA

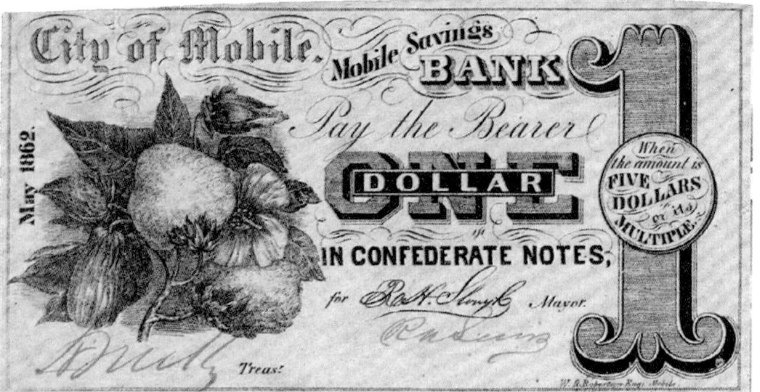

Engraver: W.R. Robertson. ***Comments:*** H-Unlisted. May 1862.

Rarity: URS-4

F $200

$2 • W-AL-225-002-G050

CC

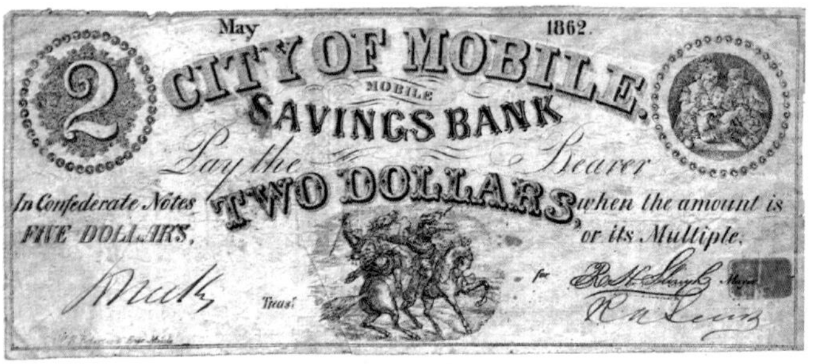

Engraver: W.R. Robertson. ***Comments:*** H-Unlisted. May 1862.

Rarity: URS-4

F $225

$3 • W-AL-225-003-G060

HA

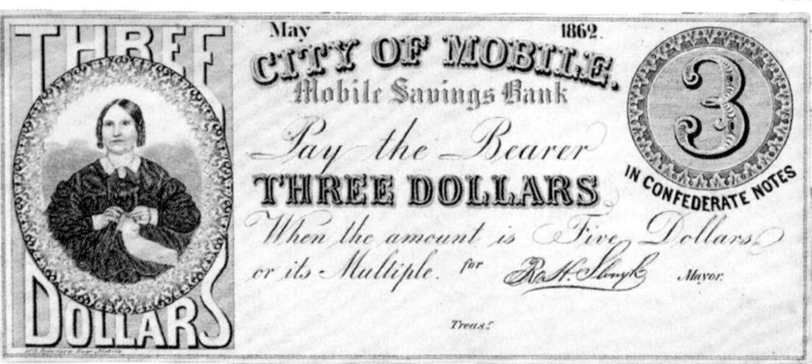

Engraver: W.R. Robertson. ***Comments:*** H-Unlisted. May 1862.

Rarity: URS-4

F $225

Planters and Merchants Bank

1836–1842

W-AL-230

History: In 1836 the Planters and Merchants bank was chartered for a duration of 20 years, with an authorized capital of $500,000. It was permissible for the bank to issue notes amounting to twice its capital. There was wide expansion in both circulation and capital, to the extent that the bank could not sustain it. In 1842 the bank suspended specie payments and later failed.

There was an earlier, unrelated Planters and Merchants Bank located in Huntsville, W-AL-140.

The Planters and Merchants Bank had a branch bank located in Decatur, W-AL-030.

Numismatic Commentary: Most notes of the Planters and Merchants Bank at Mobile are unknown today, with the $10 issue being the only one reported. There were no Proofs in the American Bank Note Company archives sale of 1990.

In addition to regular notes, post notes of unknown denominations and description were issued.

Valid Issues

$1 • W-AL-230-001-G010

Comments: H-AL-50-G2. No description available. 18__. 1830s.

Rarity: *None known*

$2 • W-AL-230-002-G020

Comments: H-AL-50-G4. No description available. 18__. 1830s.

Rarity: *None known*

$3 • W-AL-230-003-G030

Comments: H-AL-50-G6. No description available. 18__. 1830s.

Rarity: *None known*

$5 • W-AL-230-005-G040

Comments: H-AL-50-G8. No description available. 18__. 1830s.

Rarity: *None known*

$10 • W-AL-230-010-G050

CC

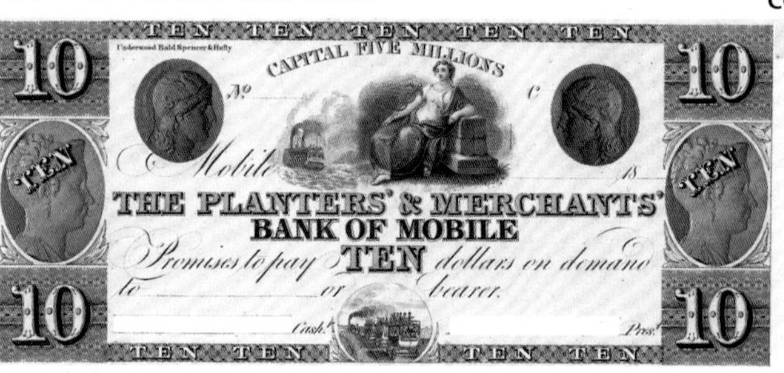

Engraver: Underwood, Bald, Spencer & Hufty. ***Comments:*** H-AL-50-G10. 18__. 1830s.

Rarity: URS-3

Proof $2,000

$20 • W-AL-230-020-G060

Comments: H-AL-50-G12. No description available. 18__. 1830s.

Rarity: *None known*

$50 • W-AL-230-050-G070

Comments: H-AL-50-G14. No description available. 18__. 1830s.

Rarity: *None known*

$100 • W-AL-230-100-G080

Comments: H-AL-50-G16. No description available. 18__. 1830s.

Rarity: *None known*

Collectors and Researchers:

If you have new information about any banks or notes listed in this volume, contact Whitman Publishing, Attn: Obsolete Paper Money, 3101 Clairmont Road, Suite G, Atlanta, GA 30329.

Southern Bank of Alabama

1850–1866

W-AL-240

History: In April 1850 the books of subscription for the Southern Bank of Alabama were opened. The first president elected was H.A. Schroeder, and he was accompanied in 1852 by Daniel C. Sampson as cashier. The authorized capital was $500,000.

In 1857 the capital of the bank had risen to $1,000,000. Bills in circulation totaled $2,028,270, and specie was worth $661,232. By 1866 the bank had closed.

Numismatic Commentary: Notes of this bank are rare. Some have unique blue overprints on the faces. Collectors can expect lively competition in trying to acquire one of these issues.

Remaining at the American Bank Note Co. archives as of 2003 was a $5-$5-$10-$10 face plate.

Valid Issues

$5 • W-AL-240-005-G010 HA

Engraver: Toppan, Carpenter, Casilear & Co. ***Comments:*** H-AL-60-G2, Rosene-214-1. 18__. 1850s.

Rarity: URS-5
F $400

$5 • W-AL-240-005-G010a HA

Overprint: Blue FIVE. ***Engraver:*** Toppan, Carpenter, Casilear & Co. ***Comments:*** H-AL-60-G2a. Similar to W-AL-240-005-G010. 18__. 1850s.

Rarity: URS-3
F $1,100
Selected auction price: Heritage Auctions, September 25, 2013, Lot 15766, VF $1,175

$10 • W-AL-240-010-G020

Left: Three women with anchor / TEN. ***Center:*** 10 / Eagle on shield. ***Right:*** 10 / Sailing ship. ***Engraver:*** Toppan, Carpenter, Casilear & Co. ***Comments:*** H-AL-60-G4, Rosene-214-2. 18__. 1850s.

Rarity: —

$10 • W-AL-240-010-G020a CC

Overprint: Blue TEN. ***Engraver:*** Toppan, Carpenter, Casilear & Co. ***Comments:*** H-AL-60-G4a. Similar to W-AL-240-010-G020. 18__. 1850s.

Rarity: URS-4
F $450

$20 • W-AL-240-020-G030

Left: 20 / Allegorical woman. ***Center:*** Steamship and ships. ***Right:*** 20 / Allegorical woman. ***Engraver:*** Toppan, Carpenter, Casilear & Co. ***Comments:*** H-AL-60-G6, Rosene-214-3. 18__. 1850s.

Rarity: URS-2
Proof $2,000

$50 • W-AL-240-050-G040

Left: 50 / Ships. ***Center:*** Three allegorical women. ***Right:*** 50 / Sailor seated with bales. ***Engraver:*** Toppan, Carpenter, Casilear & Co. ***Comments:*** H-AL-60-G8, Rosene-214-4. 18__. 1850s.

Rarity: URS-2
Proof $2,500

$100 • W-AL-240-100-G050

Left: 100 / Woman seated. ***Center:*** Woman seated with parcels. ***Right:*** 100 / Mechanic standing with sledge and cog wheel. ***Engraver:*** Toppan, Carpenter, Casilear & Co. ***Comments:*** H-AL-60-G10, Rosene-214-5. 18__. 1850s.

Rarity: URS-2
Proof $2,500

$500 • W-AL-240-500-G060

Left: Woman with eagle and globe / 500. ***Right:*** 500 / George Washington on horseback. ***Engraver:*** Toppan, Carpenter, Casilear & Co. ***Comments:*** H-AL-60-G12, Rosene-214-6. 18__. 1850s.

Rarity: URS-1
Proof $6,000

Non-Valid Issues

$50 • W-AL-240-050-N010

Center: 50 / Allegorical man, Building / 50. ***Bottom center:*** Beehive. ***Right:*** Woman and globe. ***Comments:*** H-AL-60-N10. 18__. 1850s.

Rarity: *None known*

$50 • W-AL-240-050-N020

Bottom center: Steamboat. ***Right:*** FIFTY vertically. ***Comments:*** H-AL-60-N15. 18__. 1850s.

Rarity: *None known*

Montgomery, Alabama

Montgomery lies on the Alabama River and was previously inhabited by the Alibamu Indians. Hernando de Soto and his group of explorers came to the area in 1540. In 1816 the county of Montgomery was formed, and in 1817 the first settlers arrived with General John Scott. They called the land they settled Alabama Town. Not long after, Andrew Dexter Jr., notorious schemer and fraudster of the Farmers Exchange Bank of Gloucester, Rhode Island, founded New Philadelphia in what is present-day downtown. On December 3, 1819, the two towns merged and were incorporated as the city of Montgomery, named after General Richard Montgomery. Montgomery County, on the other hand, was named after Major Lemuel P. Montgomery.

The cotton trade saw swift growth in Montgomery, and in 1821 the steamboat *Harriet* began running up and down the Alabama River between Montgomery and Mobile. In 1822 Montgomery became the county seat, and a courthouse was built at the foot of Market Street. In April 1825 the Marquis de Lafayette visited Montgomery. The Montgomery Railroad was laid out in 1832. The state legislature moved the capital location from Tuscaloosa to Montgomery on January 28, 1846. In 1849 the new Capitol building burned down, but it was rebuilt in 1851.

Although it was the first capital of the Confederate States of America, Montgomery was virtually untouched during the Civil War. The famous "Montgomery Notes," in denominations of $50, $100, $500, and $1,000, printed in New York City, bear the city's imprint. Montgomery was occupied by Union forces on April 12, 1865.

Alabama Savings Bank

1864–1867

W-AL-250

History: The Alabama Savings Bank was incorporated on December 12, 1864, with an authorized capital of $100,000. It was reincorporated on February 12, 1867, outside of the bank-note–issuing period under study.

Numismatic Commentary: This bank issued certificates of deposit, not bank notes.

Remaining at the American Bank Note Co. archives as of 2003 was a $1-$1-$2-$5 tint plate and a $1-$1-$2-$5 face plate.

Valid Issues

$1 • W-AL-250-001-G010

Comments: H-Unlisted. No description available. 18__. 1860s.

Rarity: *None known*

$2 • W-AL-250-002-G020

Comments: H-Unlisted. No description available. 18__. 1860s.

Rarity: *None known*

$5 • W-AL-250-005-G030

Comments: H-Unlisted. No description available. 18__. 1860s.

Rarity: *None known*

Bank of Montgomery

1852–1860s

W-AL-260

History: The Bank of Montgomery was chartered in 1852. By 1855 the capital amounted to $300,000. The president was William Poe, and the cashier was J.N. Norvell. By 1857 the capital had dropped to $100,000; bills in circulation were worth $96,382; and specie totaled $30,036. That year the president was E.C. Hannon, and the cashier was E.M. Burton.

Sometime during the 1860s, the Bank of Montgomery was closed.

Numismatic Commentary: Notes from this bank are considered extremely rare in all grades.

Remaining at the American Bank Note Co. archives as of 2003 was a $10-$20 face plate and a $10-$20 tint plate.

Valid Issues

$1 • W-AL-260-001-G010 HA

Engraver: Danforth, Wright & Co. ***Comments:*** H-AL-75-G2, Rosene-230-1. 18__. 1850s.

Rarity: URS-3

F $1,000

$2 • W-AL-260-002-G020 CC

Engraver: Danforth, Bald & Co. ***Comments:*** H-AL-75-G4, Rosene-230-2. 18__. 1850s.

Rarity: URS-2

Proof $2,000

$3 • W-AL-260-003-G030

Left: 3 / State arms. ***Center:*** Farmer, Sailor, Mechanic. ***Right:*** 3 / Cotton plant. ***Engraver:*** Danforth, Bald & Co. ***Comments:*** H-AL-75-G6, Rosene-230-3. 18__. 1850s.

Rarity: URS-4

F $750

$5 • W-AL-260-005-G040 CC

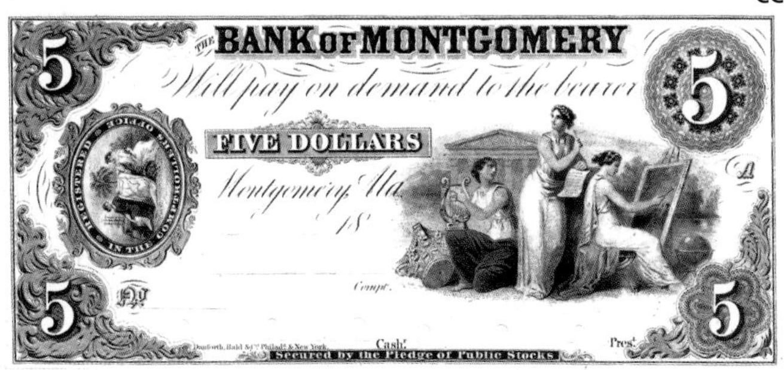

Engraver: Danforth, Bald & Co. ***Comments:*** H-AL-75-G8, Rosene-230-4. 18__. 1850s.

Rarity: URS-3
Proof $2,000

$10 • W-AL-260-010-G050

Left: TEN on X / Farmer. ***Center:*** State arms / 10. ***Right:*** 10 / Female portrait. ***Tint:*** Red-orange die outlining white 10. ***Engraver:*** Danforth, Wright & Co. ***Comments:*** H-AL-75-G10a, Rosene-230-5. 185_. 1850s–1860s.

Rarity: URS-1
Proof $3,000

$20 • W-AL-260-020-G060

Left: XX / Justice standing, Basket, Cotton plant / TWENTY. ***Center:*** State arms. ***Right:*** 20 / Woman standing, Two mechanics. ***Tint:*** Red-orange die outlining white 20. ***Engraver:*** Danforth, Wright & Co. ***Comments:*** H-AL-75-G12a, Rosene-230-6. 185_. 1850s–1860s.

Rarity: URS-1
Proof $3,500

Non-Valid Issues

$2 • W-AL-260-002-S010

Left: Woman standing in niche. ***Center:*** 2 / Mechanic seated / 2. ***Right:*** TWO DOLLARS vertically. ***Engraver:*** I. Bonar. ***Comments:*** H-AL-75-S5. Feb. 29, 185_. 1850s.

Rarity: URS-4
EF $300

$2 • W-AL-260-002-S010a

Engraver: I. Bonar. ***Comments:*** H-AL-75-S5a. Similar to W-AL-260-002-S010 but with engraved serial space. Feb. 29, 1853.

Rarity: *None known*

$3 • W-AL-260-003-S020

Left: THREE DOLLARS vertically. ***Center:*** 3 / Hebe watering eagle / 3. ***Right:*** Cherub / Cattle for sale / Cherub. ***Engraver:*** I. Bonar. ***Comments:*** H-AL-75-S10. Feb. 29, 185_. 1850s.

Rarity: URS-4
EF $400

$3 • W-AL-260-003-S020a

Engraver: I. Bonar. ***Comments:*** H-AL-75-S10a. Similar to W-AL-260-003-S020 but with engraved serial space. Feb. 29, 1853.

Rarity: *None known*

Bank of the State of Alabama (branch)

1833–1845

W-AL-270

History: The Bank of the State of Alabama moved from Cahawba, W-AL-010, to Tuscaloosa when the state capital was relocated there in 1826. The bank was able to raise $15,859,420 from various sources, including land sales, funds from university rents, and the sale of state stocks. Unfortunately, however, this amount was mostly used to keep the bank from failing during the Panic of 1837.

The branch at Montgomery opened in 1833. In 1841 capital was worth $1,818,917, and circulation was $1,079,518. The president was John Martin, and in 1844 the capital reached a peak of $1,818,917.

The bank and its branches were poorly managed and engaged in many questionable and fraudulent activities. Finally, the bank was liquidated on January 1, 1845. The entity left the state with a debt of $14,000,000.

The Bank of the State of Alabama had its parent banks located first in Cahawba, W-AL-010, and later in Tuscaloosa, W-AL-340, and branches located in Decatur, W-AL-020, Huntsville, W-AL-090, Mobile, W-AL-190, and Tuscumbia, W-AL-350.

Valid Issues

$1 • W-AL-270-001-G010 CC

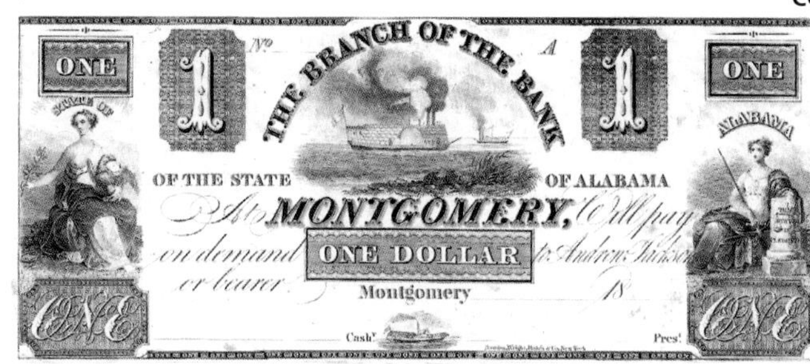

Engraver: Rawdon, Wright, Hatch & Co. ***Comments:*** H-Unlisted. 18__. 1830s.

Rarity: URS-3
Proof $1,500

$3 • W-AL-270-003-G020 CC

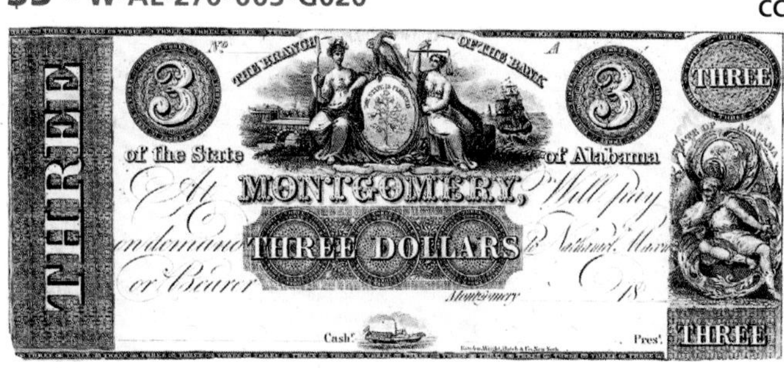

Engraver: Rawdon, Wright, Hatch & Co. ***Comments:*** H-Unlisted. 18__. 1830s.

Rarity: URS-2
Proof $2,000

$5 • **W-AL-270-005-G030**

CC

Engraver: Rawdon, Wright, Hatch & Co. ***Comments:*** H-AL-5-G210. 18__. 1830s.

Rarity: URS-3
Proof $2,000

$10 • **W-AL-270-010-G040**

CC

Engraver: Rawdon, Wright, Hatch & Co. ***Comments:*** H-AL-5-G212, Rosene-5-11. 18__. 1830s.

Rarity: URS-2
Proof $3,000

$20 • **W-AL-270-020-G050**

CC

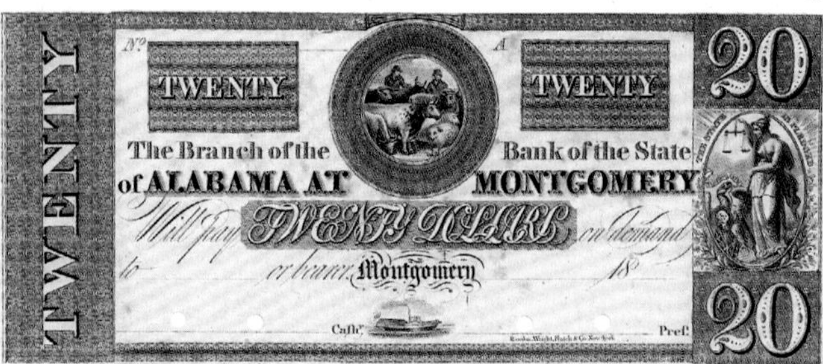

Engraver: Rawdon, Wright, Hatch & Co. ***Comments:*** H-AL-5-G214. 18__. 1830s.

Rarity: URS-1
Proof $4,500

$50 • **W-AL-270-050-G060**

Left: THE STATE OF ALABAMA IS PLEDGED / Indian / 50. ***Center:*** 50 / Liberty with angel and shield / 50. ***Right:*** FIFTY vertically. ***Engraver:*** Rawdon, Wright & Hatch. ***Comments:*** H-AL-5-G216, Rosene-5-14. 18__. 1830s.

Rarity: *None known*

$100 • **W-AL-270-100-G070**

Engraver: Rawdon, Wright & Hatch. ***Comments:*** H-AL-5-G218. No description available. 18__. 1830s.

Rarity: *None known*

Post Notes Payable at the Phenix Bank in New York

$20 • **W-AL-270-020-G080**

Engraver: Rawdon, Wright & Hatch. ***Comments:*** H-AL-5-G230. No description available. 18__. 1830s.

Rarity: *None known*

$50 • **W-AL-270-050-G090**

Left: FIFTY vertically. ***Center:*** 50 / Hebe watering eagle / 50. ***Right:*** POST NOTE vertically. ***Engraver:*** Rawdon, Wright & Hatch. ***Comments:*** H-AL-5-G232, Rosene-5-13. 18__. 1830s.

Rarity: URS-1
Proof $3,000

$100 • **W-AL-270-100-G100**

Engraver: Rawdon, Wright & Hatch. ***Comments:*** H-AL-5-G234. No description available. 18__. 1830s.

Rarity: *None known*

Post Notes Payable by the Montgomery Rail Road Company

$10 • **W-AL-270-010-G110**

CC

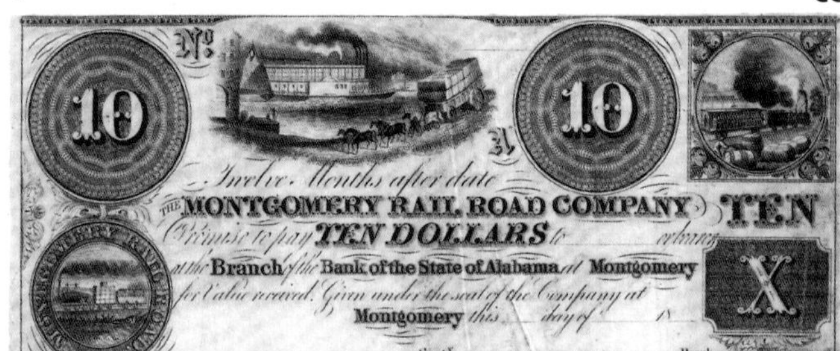

Engraver: Rawdon, Wright & Hatch. ***Comments:*** H-Unlisted. 18__. 1830s.

Rarity: —
Proof $3,000
Selected auction price: Stack's Bowers Galleries, January 2008, Lot 4009, Proof $3,046

Central Bank of Alabama

1854–1865

W-AL-280

History: The Central Bank of Alabama was incorporated on February 17, 1854, with an authorized capital of $1,500,000. William Knox was the first president, and H.W. Cater was the cashier. The books of subscription to the capital stock were opened on July 3 of that year. By 1857 the capital was worth $900,000, with bills in circulation totaling $1,702,509, specie amounting to $569,010, and real estate worth $55,000.

By 1865 the Central Bank of Alabama had closed.

Numismatic Commentary: The Central Bank of Alabama was one of the few banks that survived into the Civil War, although it closed during the conflict. As such notes from that era of the bank's history are especially rare. Issues of this bank are attractive, with large center vignettes and, often, bold red overprints.

Remaining at the American Bank Note Co. archives as of 2003 was a $1-$1-$1-$2 face plate, a $1-$1-$2-$3 face plate, a $20-$20-$50-$100 face plate, and a $5-$5-$10-$10 face plate.

Valid Issues

$1 • W-AL-280-001-G010

CC

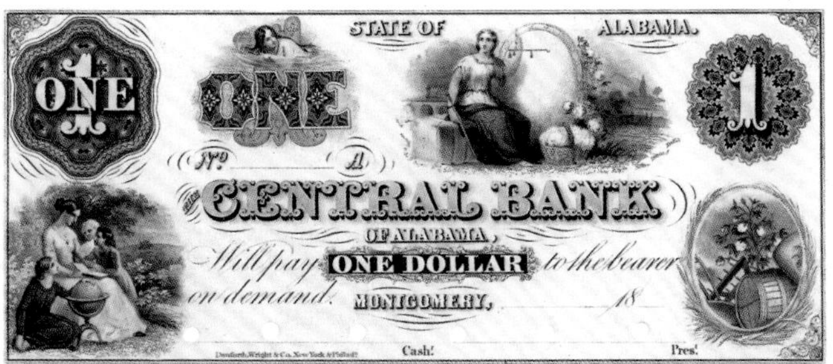

Engraver: Danforth, Wright & Co. ***Comments:*** H-AL-65-G2, Rosene-231-1. 18__. 1850s–1860s.

Rarity: URS-7; URS-3
F $100
Proof $1,200

$1 • W-AL-280-001-G020

Left: 1 / Girl shading eyes with hand. ***Center:*** Horses drawing carriage, Man. ***Right:*** 1 / ONE. ***Engraver:*** Bald, Cousland & Co. / Baldwin, Bald & Cousland. ***Comments:*** H-AL-65-G4, Rosene-231-3. Possibly made only as Proofs. 18__. 1850s–1860s.

Rarity: *None known*

$1 • W-AL-280-001-G020a

HA

Overprint: Red ONE. ***Engraver:*** Bald, Cousland & Co. / Baldwin, Bald & Cousland. ***Comments:*** H-AL-65-G4a. Similar to W-AL-280-001-G020. 18__. 1850s–1860s.

Rarity: URS-8; URS-2
F $75
Proof $1,200

$1 • W-AL-280-001-G030

Left: 1 / ONE / Cotton plant. ***Center:*** Justice. ***Right:*** 1 / Agriculture with implements. ***Engraver:*** Danforth, Wright & Co. ***Comments:*** H-Unlisted, Rosene-231-2. 18__. 1850s–1860s.

Rarity: *None known*

$2 • W-AL-280-002-G040

HA

Engraver: Danforth, Wright & Co. ***Comments:*** H-AL-65-G6, Rosene-231-6. 18__. 1850s–1860s.

Rarity: URS-7
VF $150

$2 • W-AL-280-002-G050

Left: TWO vertically. ***Center:*** Train. ***Right:*** 2 / TWO. ***Engraver:*** Bald, Cousland & Co. / Baldwin, Bald & Cousland. ***Comments:*** H-AL-65-G8, Rosene-231-4. Possibly made only as Proofs. 18__. 1850s–1860s.

Rarity: URS-3
Proof $750

$2 • W-AL-280-002-G050a

ANS

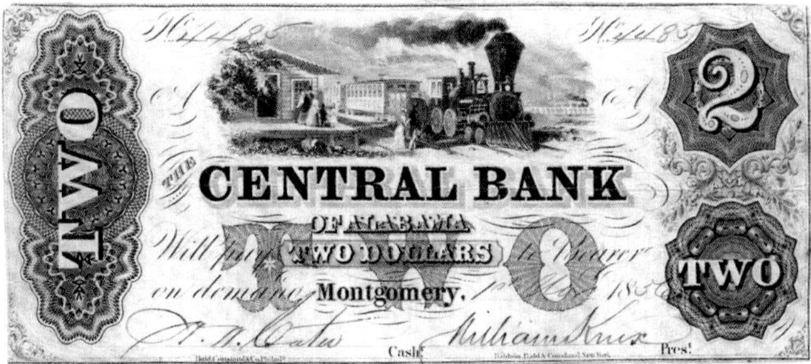

Overprint: Red TWO. ***Engraver:*** Bald, Cousland & Co. / Baldwin, Bald & Cousland. ***Comments:*** H-AL-65-G8a. Similar to W-AL-280-002-G050. 18__. 1850s–1860s.

Rarity: URS-8
F $125

$2 • W-AL-280-002-G060

Left: 2 / Farmer plowing. ***Center:*** Covered wagon, Bales. ***Right:*** 2 / Sailor. ***Engraver:*** Danforth, Wright & Co. ***Comments:*** H-Unlisted, Rosene-231-5. 18__. 1850s–1860s.

Rarity: URS-2
F $450

$2 • W-AL-280-002-G070

HA

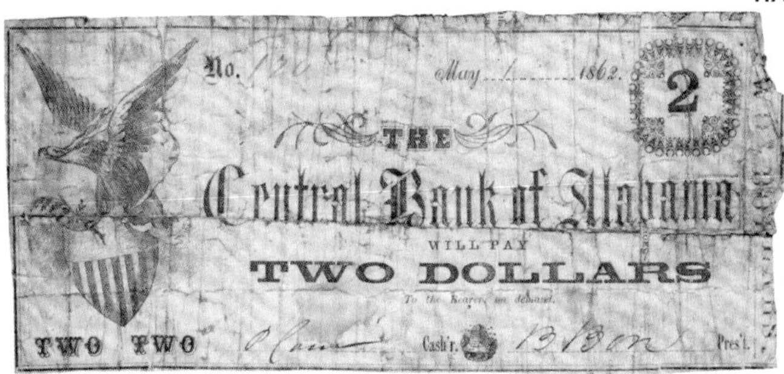

Comments: H-Unlisted. May __, 1862.

Rarity: URS-3
G $400

$3 • W-AL-280-003-G080

Left: THREE vertically. ***Center:*** Portrait of Andrew Jackson / Indian hunting deer. ***Right:*** 3 / THREE / 3. ***Engraver:*** Bald, Cousland & Co. / Baldwin, Bald & Cousland. ***Comments:*** H-AL-65-G10, Rosene-231-8. Possibly made only as Proofs. 18__. 1850s–1860s.

Rarity: URS-3
Proof $1,200

$3 • **W-AL-280-003-G080a** CC

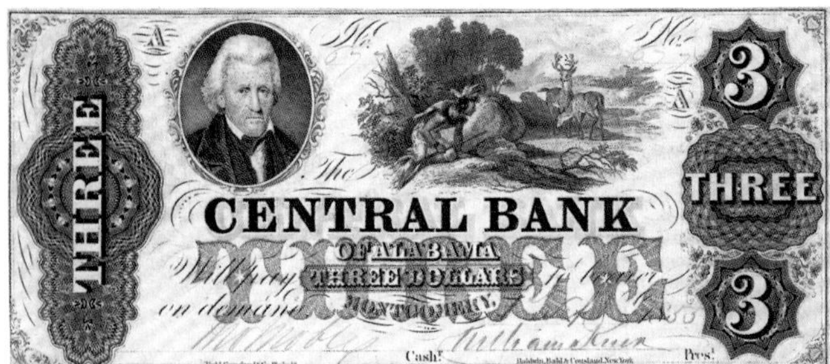

Overprint: Red THREE. ***Engraver:*** Bald, Cousland & Co. / Baldwin, Bald & Cousland. ***Comments:*** H-AL-65-G10a. Similar to W-AL-280-003-G080. 18__. 1850s–1860s.

Rarity: URS-8
F $150; **VF** $250

$3 • **W-AL-280-003-G090** SI

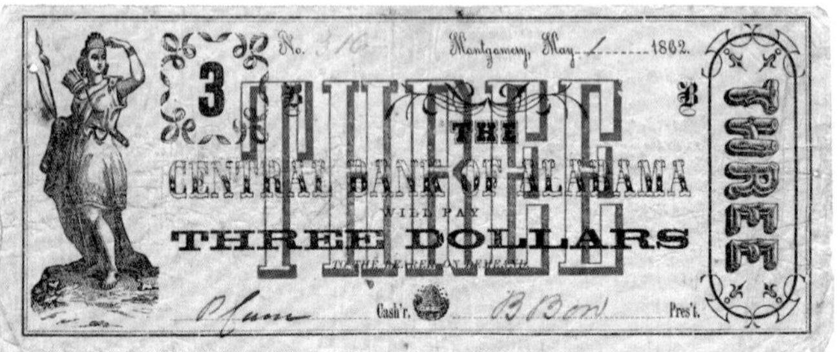

Overprint: Red THREE. ***Comments:*** H-Unlisted, Rosene-231-7. May __, 1862.

Rarity: URS-3
VF $1,250

$4 • **W-AL-280-004-G100** HA

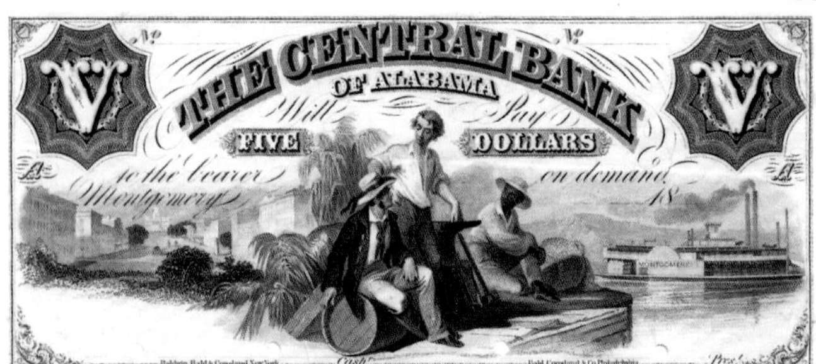

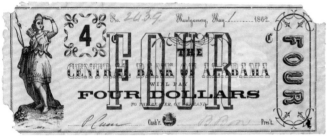

Overprint: Red FOUR. ***Comments:*** H-Unlisted, Rosene-231-9. May __, 1862.

Rarity: URS-3
G $500

$5 • **W-AL-280-005-G110** CC

Engraver: Bald, Cousland & Co. / Baldwin, Bald & Cousland. ***Comments:*** H-AL-65-G12, Rosene-231-10. Possibly made only as Proofs. 18__. 1850s–1860s.

Rarity: URS-3
Proof $1,200

$5 • **W-AL-280-005-G110a** CC

Overprint: Red 5 / 5. ***Engraver:*** Bald, Cousland & Co. / Baldwin, Bald & Cousland. ***Comments:*** H-AL-65-G12a. Similar to W-AL-280-005-G110. 18__. 1850s–1860s.

Rarity: URS-9
F $100

$5 • **W-AL-280-005-G110b** CC

Overprint: Red large 5 / 5. ***Engraver:*** Bald, Cousland & Co. / Baldwin, Bald & Cousland / ABNCo. monogram. ***Comments:*** H-AL-65-G12b. Similar to W-AL-280-005-G110 but with additional engraver imprint. 18__. 1850s–1860s.

Rarity: URS-9
F $150

$5 • **W-AL-280-005-G120** CC

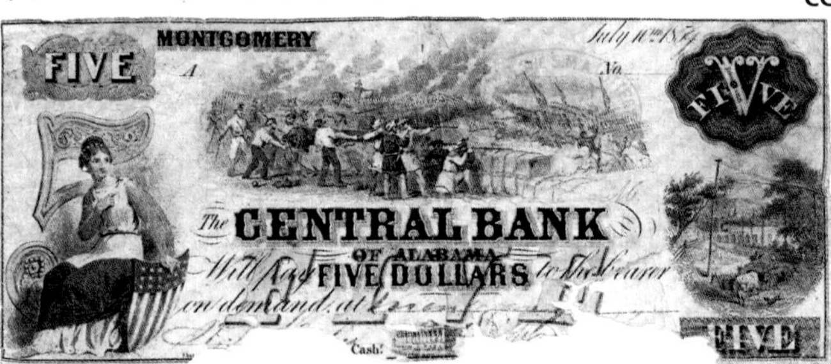

Overprint: Red FIVE. ***Engraver:*** Bald, Cousland & Co. ***Comments:*** H-Unlisted, Rosene-231-11. July 10th, 185_. 1850s.

Rarity: URS-4
F $200; **Proof** $1,000
Selected auction price: Heritage Auctions, January 6, 2016, Lot 18466, Proof $969

$10 • W-AL-280-010-G130

Left: X / Cotton harvest / TEN. ***Center:*** Field scene. ***Right:*** 10 / Portrait of George Washington. ***Engraver:*** Bald, Cousland & Co. / Baldwin, Bald & Cousland. ***Comments:*** H-AL-65-G16, Rosene-231-12. Possibly made only as Proofs. 18__. 1850s–1860s.

Rarity: URS-3
Proof $500

$10 • W-AL-280-010-G130a

CC

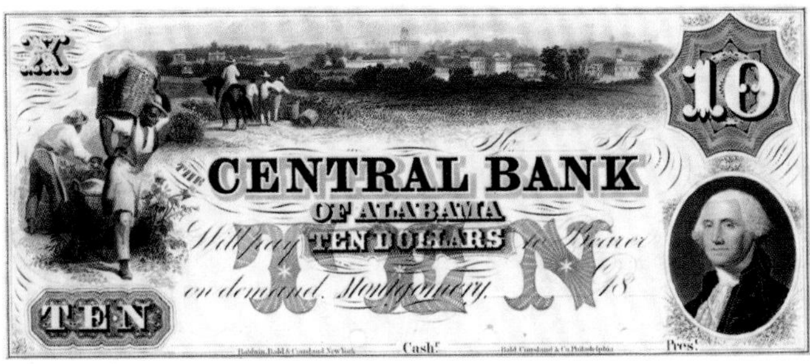

Overprint: Red TEN. ***Engraver:*** Bald, Cousland & Co. / Baldwin, Bald & Cousland. ***Comments:*** H-AL-65-G16a. Similar to W-AL-280-010-G130. 18__. 1850s–1860s.

Rarity: URS-10
F $100; **Proof** $1,200

$10 • W-AL-280-010-G130b

CC

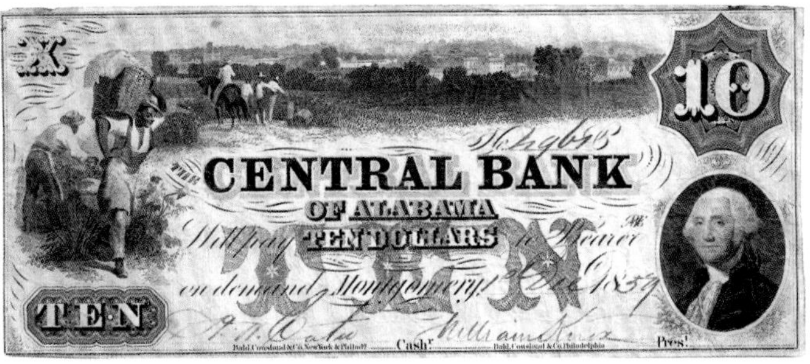

Overprint: Red TEN. ***Engraver:*** Bald, Cousland & Co. / Baldwin, Bald & Cousland / ABNCo. monogram. ***Comments:*** H-AL-65-G16b. Similar to W-AL-280-010-G130 but with additional engraver imprint. 18__. 1850s–1860s.

Rarity: URS-10
F $100

$10 • W-AL-280-010-G140

Left: Eagle, Train on bridge. ***Center:*** Woman seated. ***Engraver:*** Bald, Cousland & Co. ***Comments:*** H-Unlisted, Rosene-231-13. 18__. 1850s–1860s.

Rarity: *None known*

$20 • W-AL-280-020-G150

Left: 20 / Portrait of Benjamin Franklin. ***Center:*** Eagle with flag. ***Right:*** XX / Indian in teepee / XX. ***Engraver:*** Bald, Cousland & Co. / Baldwin, Bald & Cousland. ***Comments:*** H-AL-65-G18, Rosene-231-14. Possibly made only as Proofs. 18__. 1850s–1860s.

Rarity: URS-3
Proof $1,200

$20 • W-AL-280-020-G150a

CC

Overprint: Red XX. ***Engraver:*** Bald, Cousland & Co. / Baldwin, Bald & Cousland. ***Comments:*** H-AL-65-G18a. Similar to W-AL-280-020-G150. 18__. 1850s–1860s.

Rarity: URS-10
F $100

$20 • W-AL-280-020-G150b

Overprint: Red XX. ***Engraver:*** Bald, Cousland & Co. / Baldwin, Bald & Cousland / ABNCo. monogram. ***Comments:*** H-AL-65-G18b. Similar to W-AL-280-020-G150 but with additional engraver imprint. 18__. 1850s–1860s.

Rarity: *None known*

$20 • W-AL-280-020-G160

Left: Woman artist. ***Center:*** Liberty, Eagle. ***Right:*** Train. ***Engraver:*** Bald, Cousland & Co. ***Comments:*** H-Unlisted, Rosene-231-15. 18__. 1850s–1860s.

Rarity: *None known*

$50 • W-AL-280-050-G170

Left: L / Man with basket of cotton. ***Center:*** Woman seated with shield. ***Right:*** 50 / Woman seated. ***Engraver:*** Bald, Cousland & Co. / Baldwin, Bald & Cousland. ***Comments:*** H-AL-65-G20, Rosene-231-16. Possibly made only as Proofs. 18__. 1850s–1860s.

Rarity: URS-3
Proof $1,200

$50 • W-AL-280-050-G170a

CC

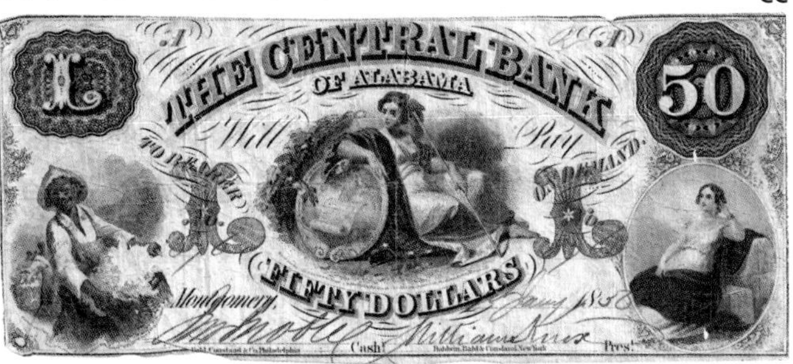

Overprint: Red L / L. ***Engraver:*** Bald, Cousland & Co. / Baldwin, Bald & Cousland. ***Comments:*** H-AL-65-G20a. Similar to W-AL-280-050-G170. 18__. 1850s–1860s.

Rarity: URS-7
F $200

$50 • W-AL-280-050-G170b

Overprint: Red L / L. ***Engraver:*** Bald, Cousland & Co. / Baldwin, Bald & Cousland / ABNCo. monogram. ***Comments:*** H-AL-65-G20b. Similar to W-AL-280-050-G170 but with additional engraver imprint. 18__. 1850s–1860s.

Rarity: *None known*

$100 • W-AL-280-100-G180

Left: C / 100 / C. ***Center:*** Indian and family in canoe. ***Right:*** ONE / C / HUNDRED. ***Engraver:*** Bald, Cousland & Co. / Baldwin, Bald & Cousland. ***Comments:*** H-AL-65-G22, Rosene-231-17. Possibly made only as Proofs. 18__. 1850s–1860s.

Rarity: URS-3
Proof $1,400

$100 • W-AL-280-100-G180a

CC

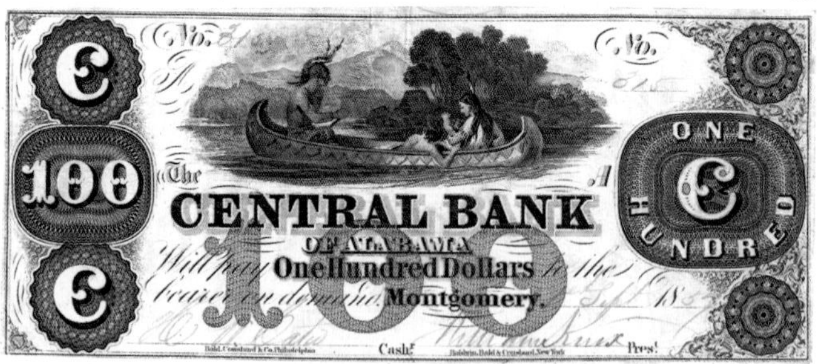

Overprint: Red 100. ***Engraver:*** Bald, Cousland & Co. / Baldwin, Bald & Cousland. ***Comments:*** H-AL-65-G22a. Similar to W-AL-280-100-G180. 18__. 1850s–1860s.

Rarity: URS-6
F $400

$100 • W-AL-280-100-G180b

Overprint: Red 100. ***Engraver:*** Bald, Cousland & Co. / Baldwin, Bald & Cousland / ABNCo. monogram. ***Comments:*** H-AL-65-G22b. Similar to W-AL-280-100-G180 but with additional engraver imprint. 18__. 1850s–1860s.

Rarity: —

$500 • W-AL-280-500-G190

CC

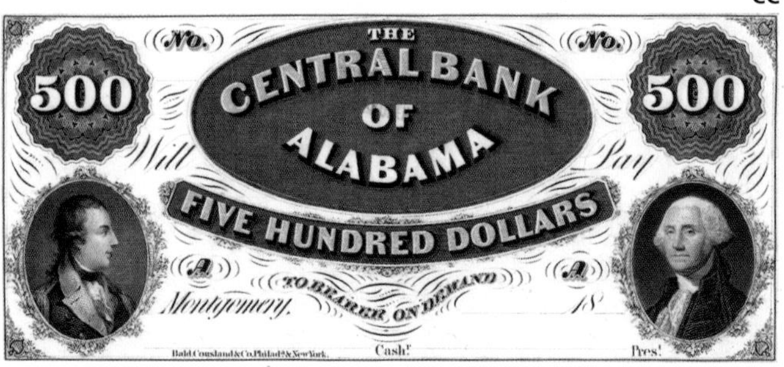

Engraver: Bald, Cousland & Co. ***Comments:*** H-Unlisted. 18__. 1850s–1860s.

Rarity: URS-5
Proof $1,200
Selected auction price: Heritage Auctions, September 25, 2013, Lot 15767, Proof $1,057

$500 • W-AL-280-500-G190a

CC

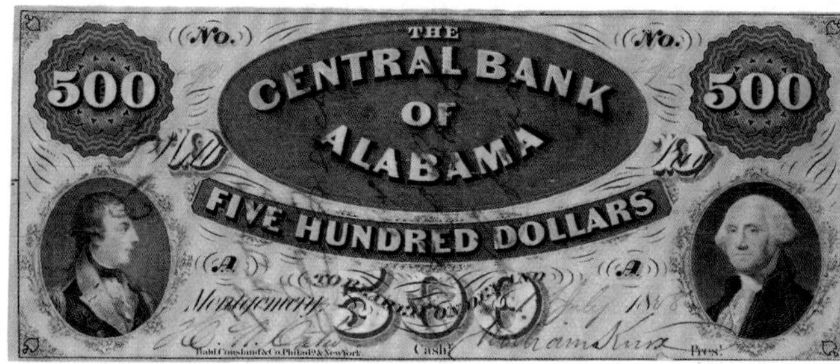

Tint: Red-orange lathework outlining white D / D / 500. ***Engraver:*** Bald, Cousland & Co. ***Comments:*** H-AL-65-G28a, Rosene-231-18. Similar to W-AL-280-500-G190. 18__. 1850s–1860s.

Rarity: URS-6
F $950; **VF** $1,400; **Proof** $900
Selected auction price: Heritage Auctions, October 23, 2015, Lot 19095, VF $1,410

Non-Valid Issues

$1 • W-AL-280-001-A010

Left: 1 on ONE / Horse-drawn wagon / ONE. ***Center:*** Harvest scene, Horses drawing cart. ***Right:*** 1 / Farmers walking. ***Engraver:*** Danforth, Wright & Co. ***Comments:*** H-AL-65-A5. Altered from $1 Central Bank of Tennessee, Nashville, Tennessee. Aug. 1, 1855.

Rarity: *None known*

$2 • W-AL-280-002-A020

CC

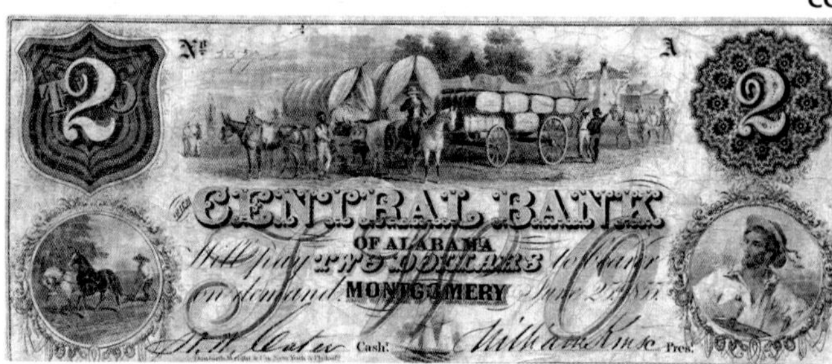

Overprint: Red TWO. ***Engraver:*** Danforth, Wright & Co. ***Comments:*** H-AL-65-A6. Altered from $2 Central Bank of Tennessee, Nashville, Tennessee. June 25th, 1855.

Rarity: URS-7
F $200

How to Read the Whitman Numbering System

$1 • W-AL-020-001-G010a

Denomination: Face value of the note shown.

W: Whitman number. This number is a sortable code unique to each bank and note.

AL: Abbreviation for the state under study.

020: Numerical designation specific to each bank.

001: The denomination in dollars.

G010a: G indicates a good or valid note. Other categories are indicated thus: C (counterfeit); R (raised); S (spurious); N (not-attributed); A (altered). Numbers are assigned starting with 010, 020, et seq. Terminal letters following the number indicate variations of a note: a series of different colored overprints, tints, payees, etc., all on the same design of note. For more information, see the "How to Use This Book" section at the front of the volume, page xiv.

$5 • W-AL-280-005-A030

Left: FIVE / Liberty seated in 5 with shield. ***Center:*** Port scene. ***Right:*** V on FIVE / Cattle on road / FIVE. ***Engraver:*** Danforth, Wright & Co. ***Comments:*** H-AL-65-A9. Altered from $5 Central Bank of Tennessee, Nashville, Tennessee. July 10, 1855.

Rarity: *None known*

$10 • W-AL-280-010-A040

Left: 10 / X / 10. ***Center:*** Woman standing with eagle, Bridge and train. ***Right:*** 10 / X / 10. ***Engraver:*** Danforth, Wright & Co. ***Comments:*** H-AL-65-A12. Altered from $5 Central Bank of Tennessee, Nashville, Tennessee. July 10, 1855.

Rarity: *None known*

$20 • W-AL-280-020-A050

Left: 20 / Woman standing with U.S. shield. ***Center:*** XX / Liberty standing, Eagle. ***Right:*** 20 / Train. ***Engraver:*** Danforth, Wright & Co. ***Comments:*** H-AL-65-A15. Altered from $5 Central Bank of Tennessee, Nashville, Tennessee. July 10, 1855.

Rarity: *None known*

Farmers Bank of Alabama

1861 and 1862

W-AL-290

History: On November 30, 1861, the Farmers Bank of Alabama was organized under the Free Banking Law of Alabama with the same privileges as other banks of the state. This bank was established during the Civil War by James Farley, a Confederate official. The institution did not last long.

Numismatic Commentary: Due to its short duration, notes of this bank are readily available.

Valid Issues

$1 • W-AL-290-001-G010 NS

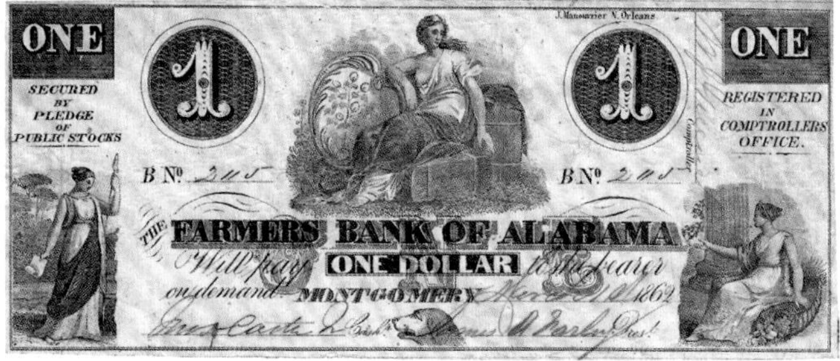

Overprint: Blue ONE. ***Engraver:*** J. Manouvrier. ***Comments:*** H-AL-70-G2a, Rosene-237-1. 1862.

Rarity: URS-8

VF $200

$5 • W-AL-290-005-G020 CC

Overprint: Green FIVE. ***Engraver:*** J. Manouvrier. ***Comments:*** H-AL-70-G8a, Rosene-237-2. 1862.

Rarity: URS-8

F $125

$20 • W-AL-290-020-G030 CC

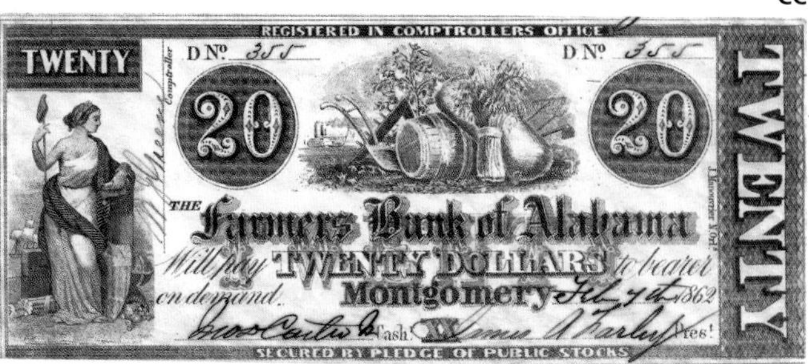

Overprint: Red TWENTY. ***Engraver:*** J. Manouvrier. ***Comments:*** H-AL-70-G12a, Rosene-237-3. 1862.

Rarity: URS-3

EF $1,000

Saint Stephens, Alabama

The Native American inhabitants of the land that would become Saint Stephens called the area Hobucakintopa. In 1772 surveyor Bernard Romans examined the land and dubbed it worthy of settlement. As of 1796 there were over 190 pioneers in residence. In 1803 the Choctaw Trading House was established, and in 1811 the first brick building—thought to be the first in Alabama—was built to serve as a warehouse.

On January 8, 1807, the town was incorporated as *St.* Stephens. The spelling was changed on December 18, 1811, to *Saint* Stephens. In 1817 the town became officially located in Alabama when Mississippi's statehood altered the state boundaries. For the next few years the town experienced massive growth, including the establishment of over 500 homes, 20 stores, 2 hotels, medical offices, legal agencies, and a theater.

When the state capital was moved to Cahawba, Saint Stephens experienced a decline. Yellow-fever outbreaks only worsened the situation, and soon New Saint Stephens was settled. The old town site was reduced to nothing more than a village by 1833, and during the Civil War it was almost entirely eclipsed by the new town.

Tombeckbe Bank
1818–1827
W-AL-300

History: The Tombeckbe Bank was chartered in February 1818. It opened for business on September 12 of that same year. Israel Pickens was the first president. He later became the governor of Alabama, as well as the organizer of the Bank of the State of Alabama, W-AL-340. On June 8, 1827, the bank suspended specie payments, and it failed the following November.

Numismatic Commentary: Notes from this bank are supremely rare, with the issues imaged below possibly being unique.

Valid Issues

$1 • W-AL-300-001-G010

Left: ONE / dollar. ***Center:*** I / ALABAMA, Woman reclining with shield, Ship / 1. ***Right:*** TOMBECKBE BANK vertically. ***Engraver:*** Murray, Draper, Fairman & Co. ***Comments:*** H-AL-80-G2. 18__. 1810s–1820s.

Rarity: —

$2 • W-AL-300-002-G020

Left: TWO / dollars. ***Center:*** II / ALABAMA, Woman reclining with shield, Ship / 2. ***Right:*** TOMBECKBE BANK vertically. ***Engraver:*** Murray, Draper, Fairman & Co. ***Comments:*** H-AL-80-G4. 18__. 1810s–1820s.

Rarity: —

$3 • W-AL-300-003-G030

HA

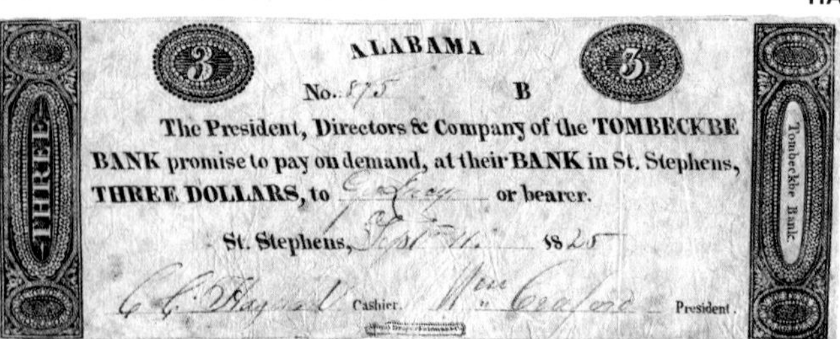

Engraver: Murray, Draper, Fairman & Co. ***Comments:*** H-AL-80-G6, Rosene-306-1. 18__. 1810s–1820s.

Rarity: URS-1
VF $3,500

$5 • W-AL-300-005-G040

HA

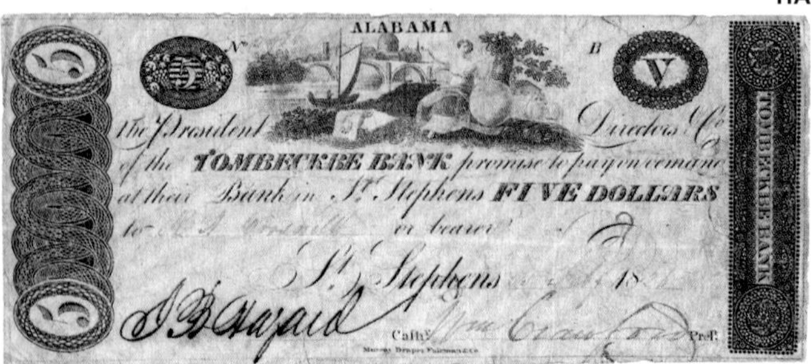

Engraver: Murray, Draper, Fairman & Co. ***Comments:*** H-AL-80-G8, Rosene-306-2. 18__. 1810s–1820s.

Rarity: URS-2
F $2,300

Selected auction price: Heritage Auctions, January 6, 2016, Lot 18487, F $2,232

$10 • W-AL-300-010-G050

Left: TEN / dollars. ***Center:*** X / ALABAMA, Woman reclining with shield, Ship / 10. ***Right:*** TOMBECKBE BANK vertically. ***Engraver:*** Murray, Draper, Fairman & Co. ***Comments:*** H-AL-80-G10, Rosene-306-3. 18__. 1810s–1820s.

Rarity: URS-1
F $4,700; **Proof** $3,000

$20 • W-AL-300-020-G060

HA

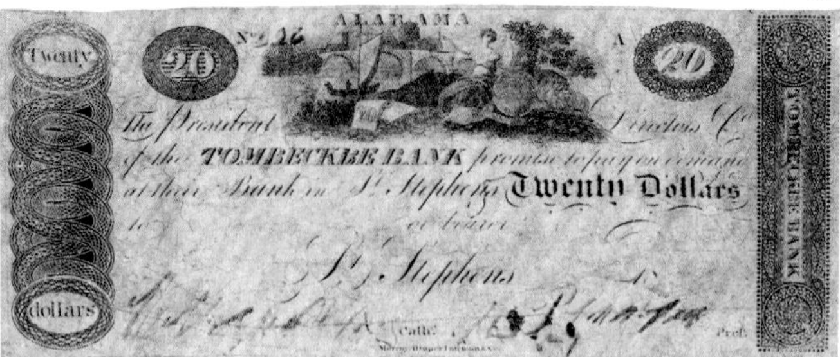

Engraver: Murray, Draper, Fairman & Co. ***Comments:*** H-AL-80-G12. 18__. 1810s–1820s.

Rarity: URS-1
F $3,000

Selected auction price: Heritage Auctions, April 22, 2015, Lot 18413, F $4,700

Selma, Alabama

The Muscogee Indians were the original inhabitants of the land that later became Selma. European settlers arrived, and in 1820 the area was incorporated as a town. William R. King planned the city and named it after the Ossianic poem *The Songs of Selma.*

During the Civil War, Selma was one of the primary manufacturing centers of military goods in the South, and supplies, munitions, and warships came out of Selma in quantities. An ironworks and a foundry were established in the town. Unfortunately this made Selma a prime target for raids. In defense, huge earth works abutting the river and surrounding the city were constructed, rising 8 to 12 feet in height. Artillery was placed in strategic locations among the mounds. Many attempts to take Selma were made by Union forces, but they did not succeed.

Bank of Selma
1859–1868
W-AL-310

History: The Bank of Selma was incorporated in 1859. W.M. Smith was the first president, and R. Lapsley was the cashier. Capital was $101,000, bills in circulation totaled $101,000, specie on hand equaled $25,360, and real estate was worth $7,958.

Most of the bank's notes were burned by the president on April 20, 1865, in an attempt to prevent their capture in the Civil War.[8] On August 11, 1868, the bank was closed.

Numismatic Commentary: Notes of the Bank of Selma are very beautiful, with bright red overprints and detailed vignettes. All range from scarce to rare. With patience, some varieties can be collected in high grades.

Remaining at the American Bank Note Co. archives as of 2003 was a $10-$100 tint plate, a $50-$100 face plate, a $5-$5-$10-$20 tint plate, and a $5-$5-$10-$20 face plate.

VALID ISSUES

$5 • W-AL-310-005-G010

CC

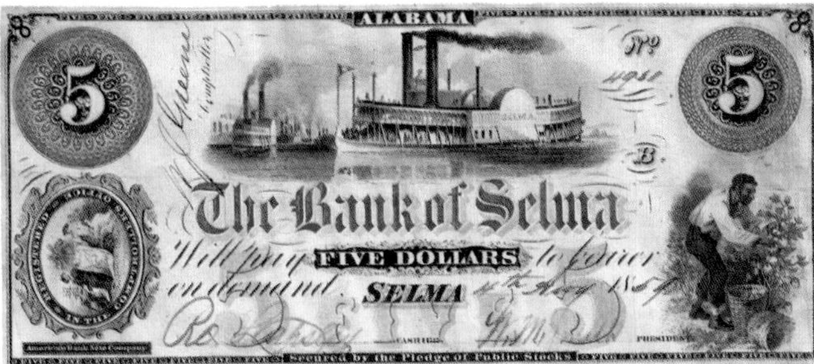

Tint: Red-orange. *Engraver:* American Bank Note Co. *Comments:* H-AL-95-G2a, Rosene-292-1. 18__. 1859–1862.

Rarity: URS-9

VF $300; **Unc-Rem** $800

Selected auction price: Heritage Auctions, October 21, 2015, Lot 18265, Choice New $822

$10 • W-AL-310-010-G020

CC

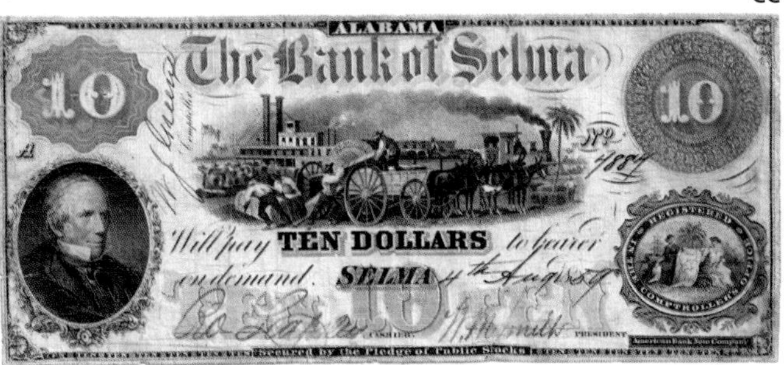

Tint: Red-orange. *Engraver:* American Bank Note Co. *Comments:* H-AL-95-G4a, Rosene-292-2. 18__. 1859–1862.

Rarity: URS-8

VF $750; **Proof** $1,750

Selected auction price(s): Heritage Auctions, January 6, 2016, Lot 18483, Unc $1,821; Heritage Auctions, April 27, 2015, Lot 22641, VF $763; Heritage Auctions, October 23, 2015, Lot 19097, Choice About New $1,762

$20 • W-AL-310-020-G030

CC

Tint: Red-orange. *Engraver:* American Bank Note Co. *Comments:* H-AL-95-G6a, Rosene-292-3. 18__. 1859–1862.

Rarity: URS-6

VF $1,200

Selected auction price(s): Heritage Auctions, April 27, 2015, Lot 22642, VF $1,292; Heritage Auctions, October 23, 2015, Lot 19098, VF $822; Heritage Auctions, January 5, 2012, Lot 15733, VF $1,035

$50 • W-AL-310-050-G040

Left: Woman reclining with globe / 50. *Center:* State arms. *Right:* FIFTY / Portrait of Jefferson Davis. *Tint:* Red-orange. *Engraver:* American Bank Note Co. *Comments:* H-AL-95-G8a, Rosene-292-4. 18__. 1860s.

Rarity: *None known*

$50 • W-AL-310-050-G040a

HA

Tint: Green die outlining white FIFTY and panels. *Engraver:* American Bank Note Co. *Comments:* H-Unlisted. Similar to W-AL-310-050-G040. Special Proof. 18__. 1860s.

Rarity: URS-5

Prop. Proof $1,100

Selected auction price: Heritage Auctions, April 22, 2015, Lot 18411, Proof $1,175

$100 • W-AL-310-100-G050

Left: Woman writing on tablet / 100. *Center:* 100 / State arms. *Right:* 100. *Tint:* Green. *Engraver:* American Bank Note Co. *Comments:* H-AL-95-G10a, Rosene-292-5. 18__. 1860s.

Rarity: *None known*

$100 • W-AL-310-100-G060

HA

Tint: Red-orange HUNDRED and dies outlining white 100s. ***Comments:*** H-Unlisted. 186_. 1860s.

Rarity: URS-3

F $4,000

Selected auction price(s): Heritage Auctions, April 23, 2015, Lot 19008, VF $4,700; Heritage Auctions, January 5, 2012, Lot 15734, VF $4,600

NON-VALID ISSUES

$5 • W-AL-310-005-C010

HA

Tint: Green bank title and dies outlining white 5s. ***Comments:*** H-Unlisted. Counterfeit of W-AL-310-005-G010. 18__. 1859–1862.

Rarity: URS-7

F $200

$5 • W-AL-310-005-C010a

HA

Tint: Red bank title and dies outlining white 5s. ***Comments:*** H-Unlisted. Counterfeit of W-AL-310-005-G010. 18__. 1859–1862.

Rarity: URS-6

F $150

Commercial Bank of Alabama

1856–1867

W-AL-320

History: In August 1856 the Commercial Bank of Alabama was chartered to begin operations in October. The first president was W.J. Norris, and the cashier was William T. Hatchett. In 1857 the capital amounted to $500,000. Bills in circulation amounted to $1,231,667, and specie totaled $411,200. The same year the bank's real estate was worth $35,000. In 1860 the cashier was Thomas C. Daniel.

By 1867 the Commercial Bank of Alabama had closed.

Numismatic Commentary: William R. King, who served as vice-president of the United States for only a brief period of time, is depicted on notes of the Commercial Bank of Alabama. King is distinctive in that he took his oath of office outside of the United States by a Special Act of Congress—being in Havana, Cuba, at the time for his health. Upon returning to the United States, he died of tuberculosis. He was in office for just over a month.

Remaining at the American Bank Note Co. archives as of 2003 was a $20-$50-$100 back plate and a $5-$5-$5-$10 back plate.

VALID ISSUES

$1 • W-AL-320-001-G010

CC

Overprint: Red 1 / 1. ***Engraver:*** Toppan, Carpenter & Co. ***Comments:*** H-AL-85-G2a, Rosene-294-1. 18__. 1850s–1860s.

Rarity: URS-9

F $125

$2 • W-AL-320-002-G020

CC

Overprint: Red 2 / 2. ***Engraver:*** Toppan, Carpenter & Co. ***Comments:*** H-AL-85-G4a. 18__. 1850s–1860s.

Rarity: URS-8

F $150

$3 • W-AL-320-003-G030 HA

Overprint: Red 3 / 3. ***Engraver:*** Toppan, Carpenter & Co. ***Comments:*** H-AL-85-G6a, Rosene-294-2. 18__. 1850s–1860s.

Rarity: URS-8
F $200; **EF** $600

$5 • W-AL-320-005-G040 CC, CC

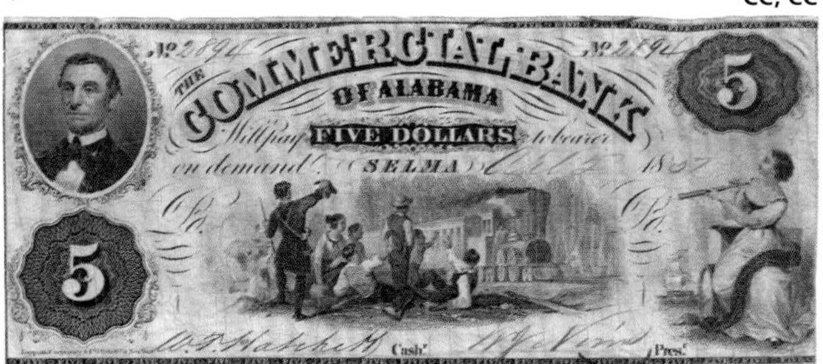

Back: Red-orange. ***Engraver:*** Toppan, Carpenter & Co. ***Comments:*** H-AL-85-G8a, Rosene-294-3. 18__. 1850s.

Rarity: URS-9
F $100; **VF** $150

$5 • W-AL-320-005-G040a

Left: Male portrait / 5. ***Center:*** Men and women pointing to oncoming train. ***Right:*** 5 / Woman seated with spyglass. ***Back:*** Red-orange. ***Engraver:*** Toppan, Carpenter & Co. / ABNCo. monogram. ***Comments:*** H-AL-85-G8b. Similar to W-AL-320-005-G040 but with additional engraver imprint. 18__. 1850s–1860s.

Rarity: *None known*

$10 • W-AL-320-010-G050 HA

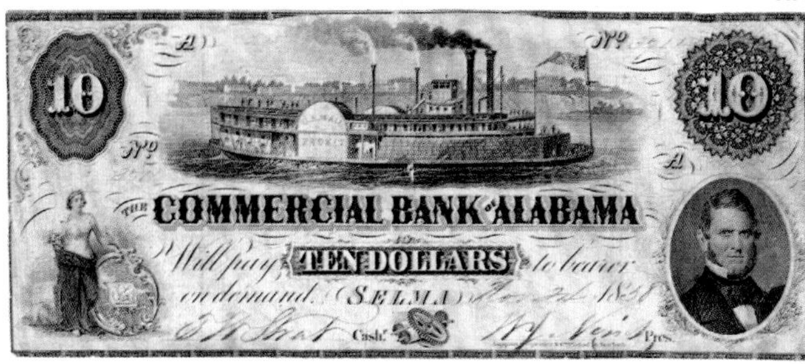

Back: Red-orange. ***Engraver:*** Toppan, Carpenter & Co. ***Comments:*** H-AL-85-G10a, Rosene-294-4. 18__. 1850s.

Rarity: URS-9
F $200

$10 • W-AL-320-010-G050a CC, CC

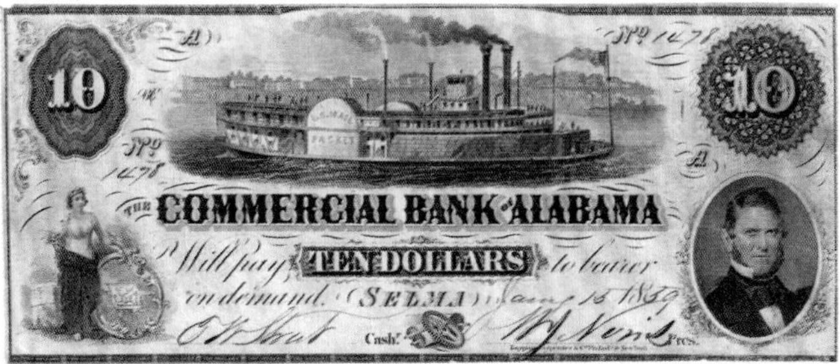

Back: Red-orange. ***Engraver:*** Toppan, Carpenter & Co. / ABNCo. monogram. ***Comments:*** H-AL-85-G10b. Similar to W-AL-320-010-G050 but with additional engraver imprint. 18__. 1850s–1860s.

Rarity: URS-9
F $200

$20 • W-AL-320-020-G060 HA

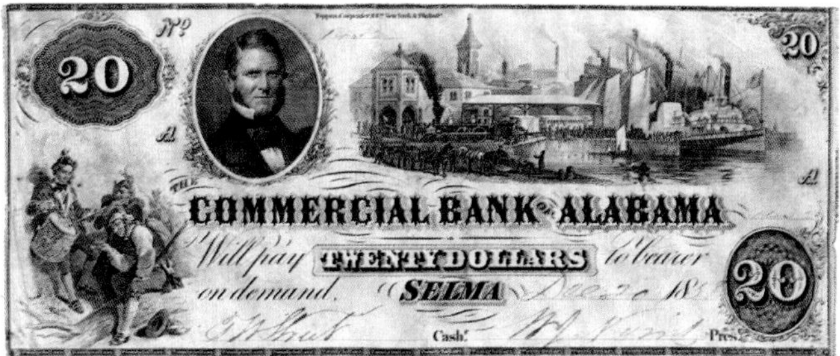

Back: Red-orange. ***Engraver:*** Toppan, Carpenter & Co. ***Comments:*** H-AL-85-G12a, Rosene-294-5. 18__. 1850s.

Rarity: URS-8
F $250

$20 • **W-AL-320-020-G060a** CC, CC

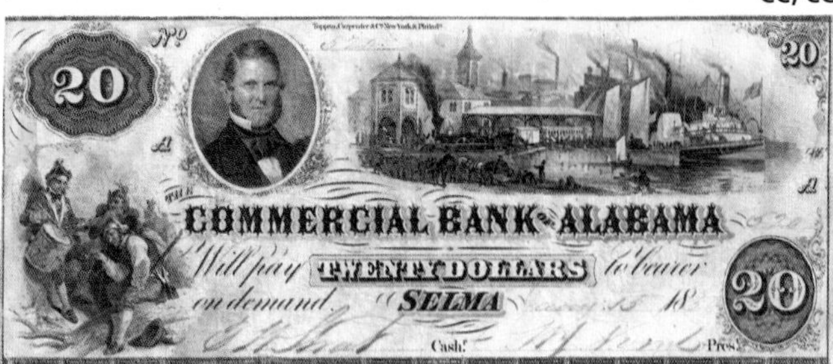

Back: Red-orange. ***Engraver:*** Toppan, Carpenter & Co. / ABNCo. monogram. ***Comments:*** H-AL-85-G12b. Similar to W-AL-320-020-G060 but with additional engraver imprint. 18__. 1850s–1860s.

Rarity: URS-8
F $250

$50 • **W-AL-320-050-G070** CC

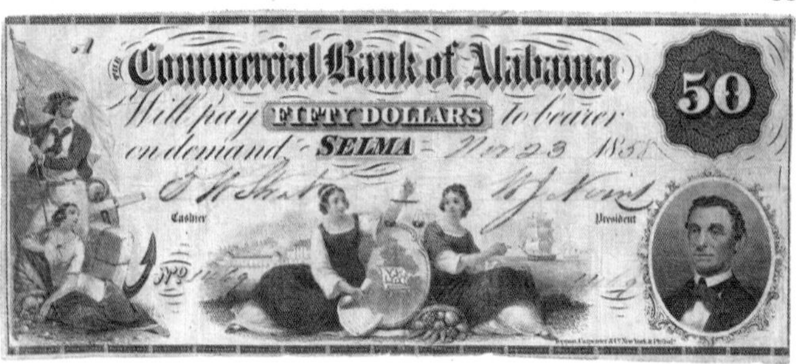

Back: Red-orange. ***Engraver:*** Toppan, Carpenter & Co. ***Comments:*** H-AL-85-G14a, Rosene-294-6. 18__. 1850s.

Rarity: URS-8
F $300

$50 • **W-AL-320-050-G070a**

Left: Sailor and woman with flag and anchor. ***Center:*** Two women flanking shield, Ship. ***Right:*** 50 / Male portrait. ***Back:*** Red-orange. ***Engraver:*** Toppan, Carpenter & Co. / ABNCo. monogram. ***Comments:*** H-AL-85-G14b. Similar to W-AL-320-050-G070 but with additional engraver imprint. 18__. 1850s–1860s.

Rarity: *None known*

$100 • **W-AL-320-100-G080** ANS, ANS

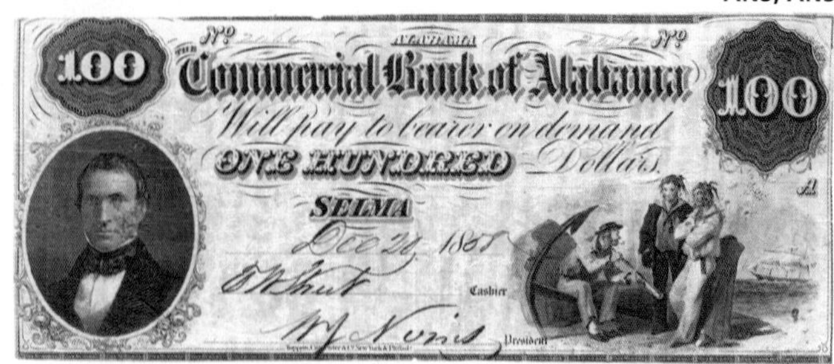

Back: Red-orange. ***Engraver:*** Toppan, Carpenter & Co. ***Comments:*** H-AL-85-G16a, Rosene-294-7. 18__. 1850s.

Rarity: URS-7
VF $700

$100 • **W-AL-320-100-G080a** HA

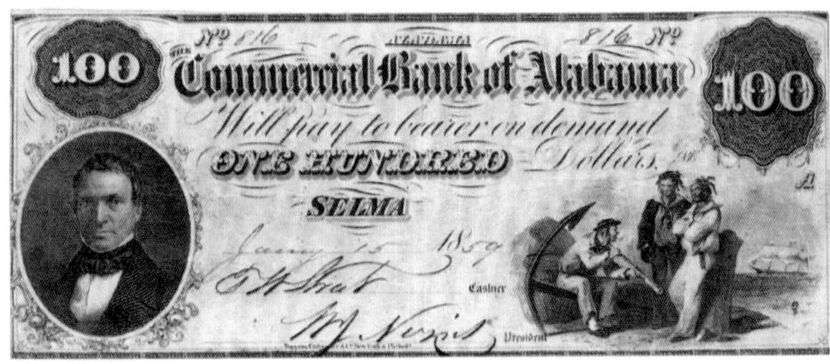

Back: Red-orange. ***Engraver:*** Toppan, Carpenter & Co. / ABNCo. monogram. ***Comments:*** H-AL-85-G16b. Similar to W-AL-320-100-G080 but with additional engraver imprint. 18__. 1850s–1860s.

Rarity: URS-7
F $400

Real Estate Banking Company of South Alabama

1838–1841

W-AL-330

History: This was a fraudulent operation related to the Real Estate Banking Company of Wetumpka, W-AL-370. The bank illegally speculated in cotton.

Issues

$1 • W-AL-330-001-G010

CC

Engraver: Rawdon, Wright & Hatch. ***Comments:*** H-AL-90-G2, Rosene-300-1. 18__. 1830s.

Rarity: URS-8

F $150; **Unc-Rem** $250

$2 • W-AL-330-002-G020

CC

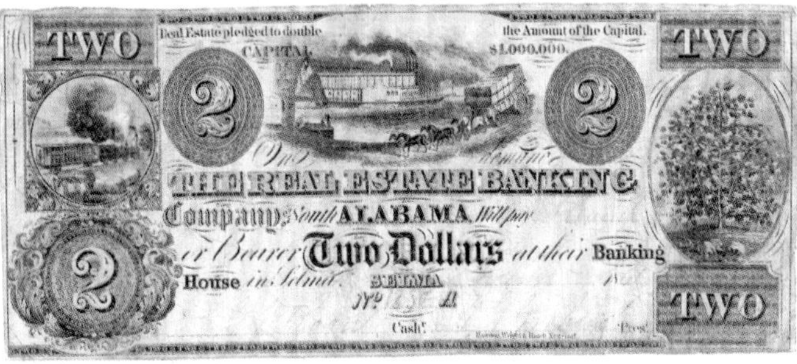

Engraver: Rawdon, Wright & Hatch ***Comments:*** H-AL-90-G4, Rosene-300-2. 18__. 1830s.

Rarity: URS-8

F $150; **Unc-Rem** $250

$3 • W-AL-330-003-G030

CC

Engraver: Rawdon, Wright & Hatch. ***Comments:*** H-AL-90-G6, Rosene-300-3. 18__. 1830s.

Rarity: URS-8

F $225

$5 • W-AL-330-005-G040

Engraver: Rawdon, Wright & Hatch. ***Comments:*** H-AL-90-G8. No description available. 18__. 1830s.

Rarity: *None known*

$10 • W-AL-330-010-G050

Left: 10 / Oxen pulling bales / 10. ***Center:*** X / Ship and cotton mill / X. ***Right:*** 10 / Farmer picking corn. ***Engraver:*** Rawdon, Wright & Hatch. ***Comments:*** H-AL-90-G10, Rosene-300-4. 18__. 1830s.

Rarity: *None known*

$20 • W-AL-330-020-G060

Left: Steamboats, Cherub. ***Center:*** 20 / Eagle / 20. ***Right:*** TWENTY / Cotton plant / TWENTY. ***Engraver:*** Rawdon, Wright & Hatch. ***Comments:*** H-Unlisted, Rosene-300-5. 18__. 1830s.

Rarity: *None known*

Uncut Sheets

$1-$1-$2-$3 • W-AL-330-001.001.002.003-US010

RG

Engraver: Rawdon, Wright & Hatch. ***Comments:*** H-AL-90-G2, G2, G4, G6. First two notes identical. 18__. 1830s.

Rarity: URS-5

EF $1,200

Tuscaloosa, Alabama

Tuscaloosa was named after Chief Tuskaloosa of a Muskogean-speaking Native American tribe. The town was incorporated on December 13, 1819, the day before Alabama was admitted as a state.

Tuscaloosa served as the capital of Alabama from 1826 to 1846, when the capital was moved to Montgomery. During that period, Tuscaloosa experienced rapid growth and a strong economy. After the capital was relocated, the economy declined. In the 1850s the Bryce State Hospital for the Insane was established, later becoming important.

Thousands of men from Tuscaloosa joined the Confederate army during the Civil War. The city was badly damaged by fire and raiding, and Reconstruction saw much suffering in the area.

Bank of the State of Alabama

1826–1845

W-AL-340

History: The Bank of the State of Alabama moved from Cahawba, W-AL-010, to Tuscaloosa when the state capital was relocated there in 1826. At the time the capital was $253,000, notes in circulation totaled $273,000, specie was valued at $141,000, and deposits in the bank equaled $164,000.

The bank was able to raise $15,859,420 from various sources, including land sales, funds from university rents, and the sale of state stocks. Unfortunately, however, this amount was mostly used to keep the bank from failing during the Panic of 1837. During that time the capital of the bank was $7,889,886, notes in circulation totaled $4,600,000, and deposits placed in the bank were valued at $6,700,000. $492,000 in specie was held in the bank vaults to cover all of this, and later $6,300,000 of discounted notes was found to be insolvent debts.

The bank and its branches were poorly managed and engaged in many questionable and fraudulent activities. In 1841 the House and Senate branches of the state legislature passed resolutions to investigate the bank. Finally, the bank was liquidated on January 1, 1845. The entity left the state with a debt of $14,000,000. The state restored taxation in order to recover this loss, and the final accounts of the bank were wound up in 1868.

The Bank of the State of Alabama had branches located in Decatur, W-AL-020, Huntsville, W-AL-090, Mobile, W-AL-190, Montgomery, W-AL-270, and Tuscumbia, W-AL-350.

Numismatic Commentary: These early Alabama notes are especially tantalizing to collectors, for while common in their day, the notes of this issuer are extremely rare today. Many are unknown to present-day numismatists, despite the many branches of the bank which would seem to indicate that notes would still be available. Some Proof examples from the American Bank Note Co. archives fill the need.

Remaining at the American Bank Note Co. archives as of 2003 was a 6-1/4¢-12-1/2¢-12-1/2¢-25¢-50¢-75¢ face plate and a 6-1/4¢-12-1/2¢-25¢-25¢-50¢-75¢ face plate.

Valid Issues

6-1/4¢ • W-AL-340-00.06.25-G010 CC

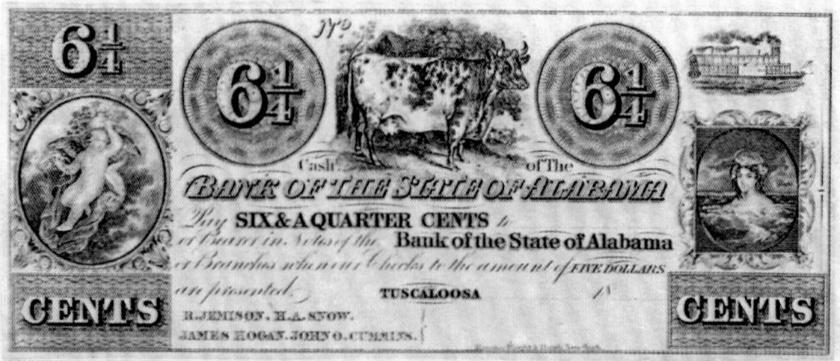

Engraver: Rawdon, Wright & Hatch. ***Comments:*** H-Unlisted. 18__. 1826–1840s.

Rarity: URS-3

Proof $1,200

12-1/2¢ • W-AL-340-00.12.50-G020 CC

Engraver: Rawdon, Wright & Hatch. ***Comments:*** H-Unlisted. 18__. 1826–1840s.

Rarity: URS-3

Proof $1,200

25¢ • W-AL-340-00.25-G030 CC

Engraver: Rawdon, Wright & Hatch. ***Comments:*** H-Unlisted. 18__. 1826–1840s.

Rarity: URS-3

Proof $1,300

Selected auction price: Stack's Bowers Galleries, January 2008, Lot 4013, Proof $1,300

50¢ • W-AL-340-00.50-G040

CC

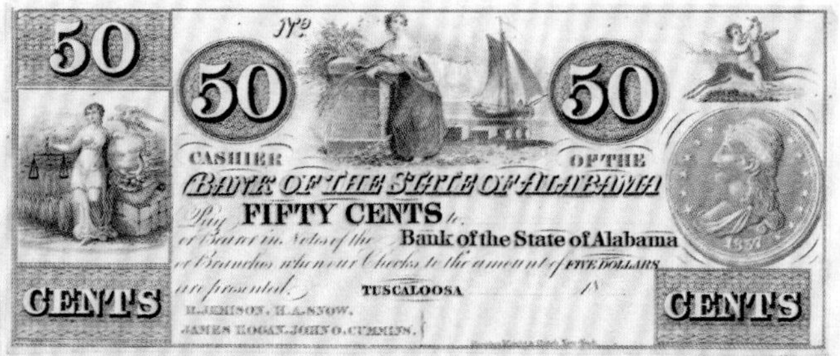

Engraver: Rawdon, Wright & Hatch. ***Comments:*** H-Unlisted. 18__. 1826–1840s.

Rarity: URS-3
Proof $1,300
Selected auction price: Stack's Bowers Galleries, January 2008, Lot 4014, Proof $1,300

75¢ • W-AL-340-00.75-G050

CC

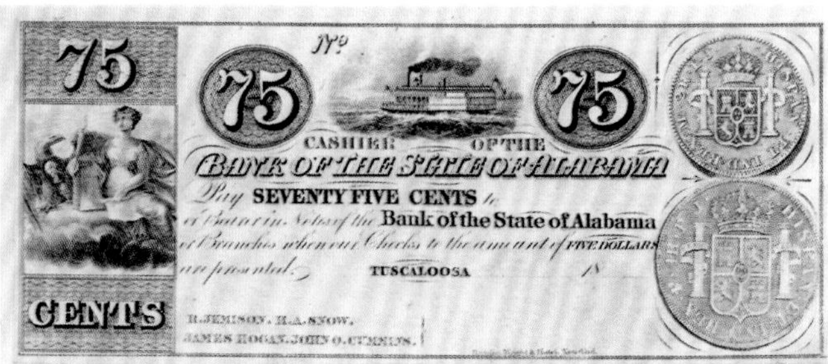

Engraver: Rawdon, Wright & Hatch. ***Comments:*** H-Unlisted. 18__. 1826–1840s.

Rarity: URS-3
Proof $1,300
Selected auction price: Stack's Bowers Galleries, January 2008, Lot 4016, Proof $1,200

$1 • W-AL-340-001-G060

Engraver: Fairman, Draper, Underwood & Co. ***Comments:*** H-AL-5-G26. No description available. 18__. 1826–1840s.

Rarity: *None known*

$2 • W-AL-340-002-G070

HA

Engraver: Fairman, Draper, Underwood & Co. ***Comments:*** H-AL-5-G28. 18__. 1826–1840s.

Rarity: —

$3 • W-AL-340-003-G080

CC

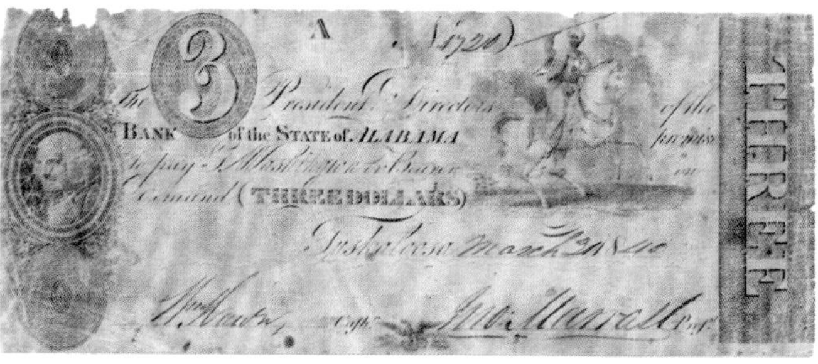

Engraver: Fairman, Draper, Underwood & Co. ***Comments:*** H-AL-5-G32, Rosene-6-8. 18__. 1826–1840s.

Rarity: URS-1
VG $2,000

$5 • W-AL-340-005-G090

Comments: H-AL-5-G34. No description available. 18__. 1826–1840s.

Rarity: *None known*

$10 • W-AL-340-010-G100

Comments: H-AL-5-G36. No description available. 18__. 1826–1840s.

Rarity: *None known*

$20 • W-AL-340-020-G110

Comments: H-AL-5-G38. No description available. 18__. 1826–1840s.

Rarity: *None known*

$50 • W-AL-340-050-G120

Comments: H-AL-5-G40. No description available. 18__. 1826–1840s.

Rarity: *None known*

$100 • W-AL-340-100-G130

Comments: H-AL-5-G42. No description available. 18__. 1826–1840s.

Rarity: *None known*

$500 • W-AL-340-500-G140

HA

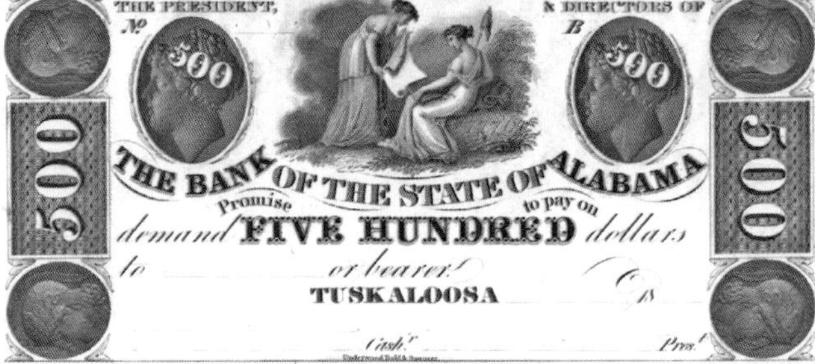

Engraver: Underwood, Bald & Spencer. ***Comments:*** H-AL-5-G44, Rosene-6-15. 18__. 1830s–1840s.

Rarity: URS-2
Proof $4,000

$1,000 • W-AL-340-1000-G150

Left: Medallion head / 1000 / Medallion head vertically. ***Center:*** 1000 on medallion head / Woman standing with corn / 1000 on medallion head. ***Right:*** Medallion head / 1000 / Medallion head vertically. ***Engraver:*** Underwood, Bald & Spencer. ***Comments:*** H-AL-5-G46, Rosene-6-16. 18__. 1830s–1840s.

Rarity: URS-2
Proof $5,000

Non-Valid Issues

$20 • W-AL-340-020-R010
Engraver: Fairman, Draper, Underwood & Co. ***Comments:*** H-AL-5-R5. Raised from $2. 18__. 1830s.
Rarity: —

$50 • W-AL-340-050-R020
Engraver: Fairman, Draper, Underwood & Co. ***Comments:*** H-AL-5-R10. Raised from $2. 18__. 1830s.
Rarity: —

$100 • W-AL-340-100-C100
Comments: H-AL-5-C36. Counterfeit of W-AL-340-010-G100. 18__. 1841.
Rarity: —

$100 • W-AL-340-100-R030
Engraver: Fairman, Draper, Underwood & Co. ***Comments:*** H-AL-5-R15. Raised from $2. 18__. 1830s.
Rarity: —

Tuscumbia, Alabama

In 1816 the first settlers arrived in the area that would later become Tuscumbia. A village arose that was called the Big Spring Community. In 1820 the town was incorporated as Ococoposa. In 1821 the name was changed to the familiar Big Spring, and on December 22, 1822, it was changed again to Tuscumbia.

In 1820 a federal highway was completed to Tuscumbia, and soon the town became a rich agricultural center. A railroad was completed in 1832, and in 1850 a major railroad hub ran through Tuscumbia to the South. In 1867 Tuscumbia became the seat for Colbert County.

Much of the town of Tuscumbia, including the railroad shops, was destroyed during the Civil War.

Bank of the State of Alabama (branch)

1833–1845

W-AL-350

History: The Bank of the State of Alabama moved from Cahawba, W-AL-010, to Tuscaloosa when the state capital was relocated there in 1826. The bank was able to raise $15,859,420 from various sources, including land sales, funds from university rents, and the sale of state stocks. Unfortunately, however, this amount was mostly used to keep the bank from failing during the Panic of 1837.

The branch at Tuscumbia opened in 1833. The bank and its branches were poorly managed and engaged in many questionable and fraudulent activities. Finally, the bank was liquidated on January 1, 1845. The entity left the state with a debt of $14,000,000.

The Bank of the State of Alabama had its parent banks located first in Cahawba, W-AL-010, and later in Tuscaloosa, W-AL-340, and branches located in Decatur, W-AL-020, Huntsville, W-AL-090, Mobile, W-AL-190, and Montgomery, W-AL-270.

Wetumpka, Alabama

Settlers from Georgia and the Carolinas arrived in abandoned lands that had originally been inhabited by the Creeks. Wetumpka located at the confluence of two rivers, was part of these lands. After settlement, the area swiftly became an important agricultural center. In 1834 the town was officially incorporated. Cotton was the primary crop, with plantations and fields covering the surrounding lands. A port on the Coosa River allowed the goods to be shipped via steamboat out of the area downriver to Mobile.

Wetumpka became a cotton-boom town, and the city was halved, with the eastern section becoming purely commercial and the western section becoming residential. When the decision to move the state capital was in progress, Wetumpka was a contender. Montgomery won the vote in 1845, and in the same year a fire decimated warehouses and commercial buildings in Wetumpka. Ironically, salvaged bricks and charcoal were shipped to Montgomery to help in building up the new capital.

Wetumpka escaped harm during the Civil War, as Union troops did not enter the area until 1865. Nevertheless, soldiers returning to Wetumpka found an economy that had been utterly decimated. In 1866 Wetumpka became the county seat of Elmore in an effort at Reconstruction.

Planters Bank of Alabama

1840s

W-AL-360

History: No such bank ever existed. It was represented by notes altered from genuine plates fraudulently obtained from the engraver.

Issues

$10 • W-AL-360-010-A010
Left: 10 / Justice standing. ***Center:*** X bearing cherubs / Two women standing, Ships, Cornucopia, plow. ***Right:*** 10 / Justice standing. ***Engraver:*** Rawdon, Wright & Hatch. ***Comments:*** H-AL-100-G2. Altered from $10 of the Planters Bank of Tennessee, Nashville, Tennessee. 18__. 1840s.
Rarity: *None known*

$20 • W-AL-360-020-A020
Left: 20 / Ceres with sickle / XX. ***Center:*** Woman with spear, Shield, Ribbon. ***Right:*** 20 / Woman with wheat / XX. ***Engraver:*** Rawdon, Wright & Hatch. ***Comments:*** H-AL-100-G4. Altered from $20 of the Planters Bank of Tennessee, Nashville, Tennessee. 18__. 1840s.
Rarity: *None known*

$50 • W-AL-360-050-A030
Left: FIFTY DOLLARS vertically. ***Center:*** 50 / Eagle on bale / 50. ***Right:*** STATE OF TENNESSEE vertically. ***Engraver:*** Rawdon, Wright & Hatch. ***Comments:*** H-AL-100-G6. Altered from $50 of the Planters Bank of Tennessee, Nashville, Tennessee. 18__. 1841.
Rarity: *None known*

$100 • **W-AL-360-100-A040**

Left: HUNDRED vertically. ***Center:*** Herd of deer, River. ***Right:*** Portrait of George Washington. ***Engraver:*** Rawdon, Wright & Hatch. ***Comments:*** H-AL-100-G8. Altered from $100 of the Planters Bank of Tennessee, Nashville, Tennessee. 18__. 1840s.

Rarity: *None known*

Real Estate Banking Company of Wetumpka

1838 and 1839

W-AL-370

History: This was a fraudulent operation related to the Real Estate Banking Company of South Alabama, W-AL-330.

Issues

$5 • **W-AL-370-005-G010** CC

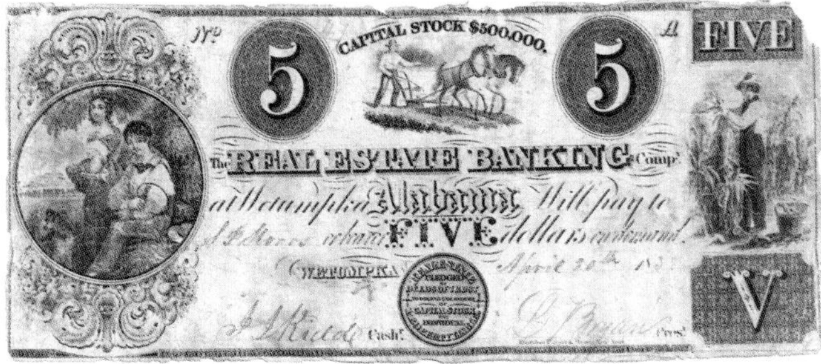

Engraver: Rawdon, Wright & Hatch. ***Comments:*** H-AL-105-G8. 18__. 1830s.

Rarity: URS-8
F $125

$10 • **W-AL-370-010-G020**

Left: Train, Bales, Parcels. ***Center:*** 10 / Mercury scattering coins out of cornucopia / 10. ***Right:*** 10 / Female portrait / 10. ***Engraver:*** Rawdon, Wright & Hatch. ***Comments:*** H-AL-105-G10. 18__. 1830s.

Rarity: URS-7
F $200

$20 • **W-AL-370-020-G030**

Left: TWENTY vertically. ***Center:*** 20 / Train, Bales, Parcels / 20. ***Right:*** XX / Woman seated with eagle and shield / 20. ***Engraver:*** Rawdon, Wright & Hatch. ***Comments:*** H-AL-105-G12. 18__. 1830s.

Rarity: URS-7
F $200

Wetumpka Trading Company

1830s–1860s

W-AL-380

History: The *Boston Weekly Magazine* reported this on May 11, 1839:

> The Wetumpka Trading Company, a banking association in Alabama, after cheating the public of about $140,000, have decamped as a body.

As of February 11, 1860, the bank was reported by the *Metropolitan Bank Note Reporter*, New York, to be broken.

Valid Issues

$3 • **W-AL-380-003-G010** 
HA

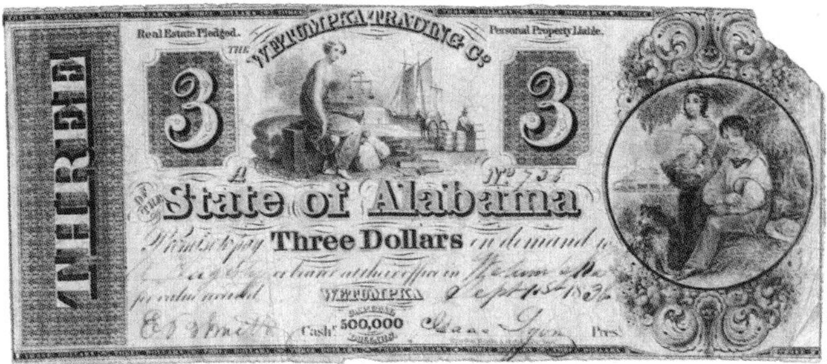

Engraver: Rawdon, Wright & Hatch. ***Comments:*** H-Unlisted. 18__. 1830s.

Rarity: URS-5
F $250; **VF** $350

$5 • **W-AL-380-005-G020** HA

Engraver: Rawdon, Wright & Hatch. ***Comments:*** H-Unlisted. 18__. 1830s.

Rarity: URS-6
F $150; **VF** $200

$10 • **W-AL-380-010-G030** HA

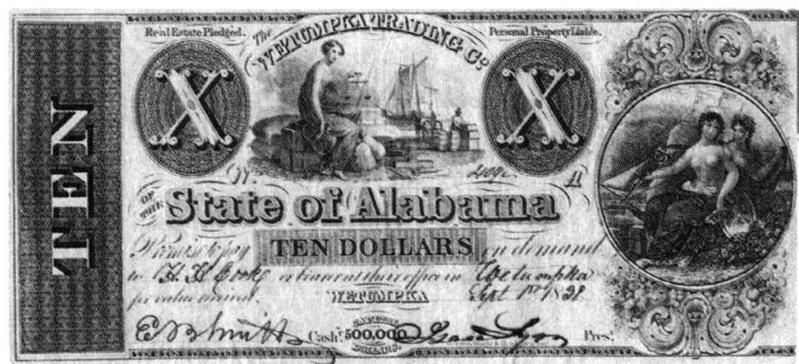

Engraver: Rawdon, Wright & Hatch. ***Comments:*** H-Unlisted. 18__. 1830s.

Rarity: URS-5
F $150; **VF** $300

$20 • **W-AL-380-020-G040** HA

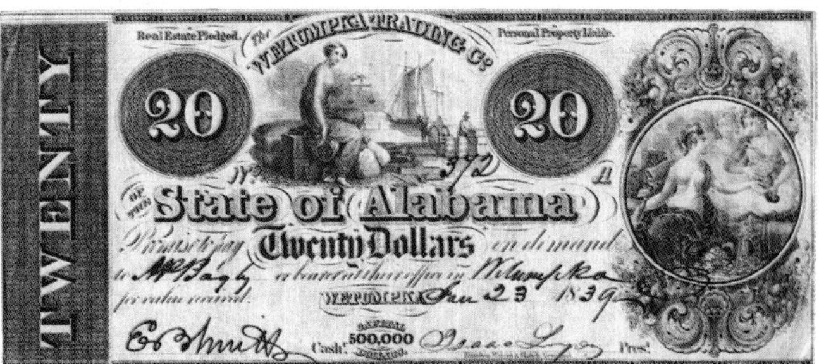

Engraver: Rawdon, Wright & Hatch. ***Comments:*** H-Unlisted. 18__. 1830s.

Rarity: URS-5
F $200; **VF** $300

Post Notes

$5 • W-AL-380-005-G050

HA

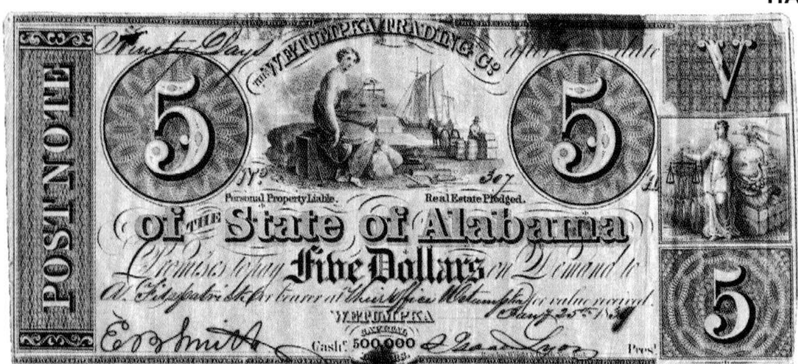

Engraver: Rawdon, Wright & Hatch. ***Comments:*** H-Unlisted. 18__. 1830s.

Rarity: URS-5
F $150; **VF** $200

$10 • W-AL-380-010-G060

HA

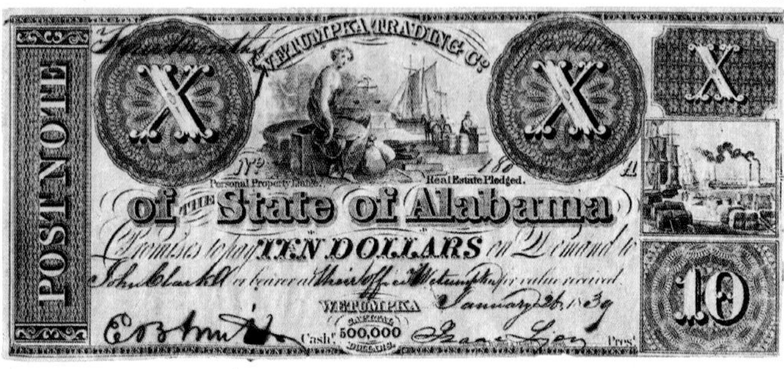

Engraver: Rawdon, Wright & Hatch. ***Comments:*** H-Unlisted. 18__. 1830s.

Rarity: URS-5

$20 • W-AL-380-020-G070

HA

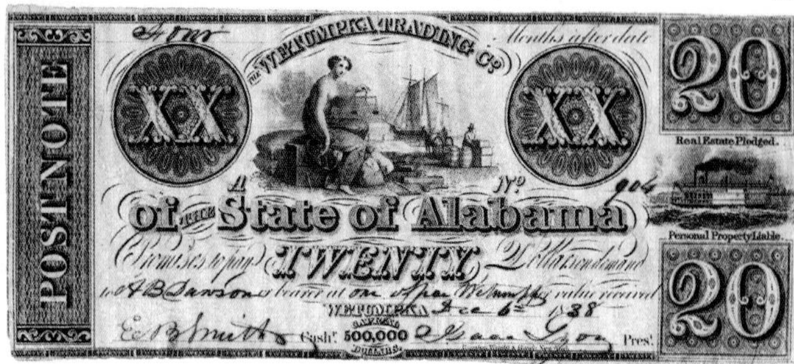

Engraver: Rawdon, Wright & Hatch. ***Comments:*** H-Unlisted. 18__. 1830s.

Rarity: URS-4
F $300; **VF** $400

$50 • W-AL-380-050-G080

HA

Engraver: Rawdon, Wright & Hatch. ***Comments:*** H-Unlisted. 18__. 1830s.

Rarity: URS-3
F $400; **VF** $500

Collectors and Researchers:

If you have new information about any banks or notes listed in this volume, contact Whitman Publishing, Attn: Obsolete Paper Money, 3101 Clairmont Road, Suite G, Atlanta, GA 30329.

The Obsolete Bank Notes of Arkansas

State Banking in Arkansas

Currency of Arkansas

The first recorded action involving a bank in the state of Arkansas took place in 1836 at the inaugural session of the state legislature. The Arkansas Constitution had the unusual requirement that only two banks could be established—one, the Bank of the State of Arkansas, and the other "to aid and promote the agriculture interests of the state." Governor James S. Conway proposed that these be set up right away. The legislature promptly replied by granting charters.

The Real Estate Bank of the State of Arkansas was to be capitalized at $2,250,000, financed by bonds guaranteed by the state. Branches were to be opened in Columbia, Helena, and Washington, with headquarters in Little Rock. The theory was that this bank would benefit from the value of land and that real estate represented permanent wealth. Several other Southern states had institutions established on the same basis. Subscriptions for stock, backed by the value of real estate held by the purchasers, were accepted at offices in the four cities where banking was to take place. At each office a board of 3 supervisors oversaw the operations for a period of 40 days commencing on March 1, 1837. Despite economic problems in the distant East, the program was well received and the stock was oversubscribed. A 5-person board of managers met in Little Rock and awarded 22,500 shares of $100 each to 184 subscribers in 14 counties. The members of the board of managers were allowed to buy stock prior to the distribution.

John W. Wilson, speaker of the state House of Representatives, was elected president of the main office in Little Rock. Thomas T. Williamson and later David T. Witter became the presidents of the Washington branch, Sanford Faulkner the Columbia office, and H.L. Briscoe the Helena branch.

In practice, the stated value of certain lands backing bonds was subject to variations. Appraisals could be high and buyers could be scarce. In November 1837 the state issued $2,000,000 worth of five-percent bonds to augment the capital. That December a major feud erupted on the floor of the state House of Representatives. Bank-president Wilson engaged in a fight with bowie knives and killed Representative Joseph J. Anthony, a long-time foe of the bank, who had charged that real estate had been inflated in value and that gross favoritism had taken place in the distribution of shares. Wilson was charged, acquitted, and in 1840 was reelected to the legislature. Later he moved to Texas. A.H. Davis succeeded him as president.

The bank opened the doors of its main office in Little Rock on December 10, 1838. The branch in Helena opened on February 15, 1839, the Columbia branch on March 4, 1839, and the Washington branch in April 1839. In 1840 a branch was opened in Van Buren, but no notes were printed there. The problems attending the operation of the bank and branches could make a book-length study. In 1842 the institution went into receivership and its assets were assigned. Liquidation took many years. Along the way many instances of fraud were uncovered.

Next, the Bank of the State of Arkansas was incorporated, capitalized at $1,000,000, and headquartered in Little Rock with branches in Batesville and Fayetteville. The authorization permitted the bank to do a general banking business, which included dealing in bullion and silver and gold coins. The Bank of the State of Arkansas was intended to help the interests of citizens and businesses in the upland regions in the northern and western districts of the state—in contrast to the agricultural emphasis of the other bank.

The charter provided that each office of the Bank of the State of Arkansas could open only after $50,000 in specie (gold and silver coins) was in the vaults. This was a mixture of federal coins as well as foreign coins, primarily Spanish-American issues, that Congress had made legal tender. Delays ensued as capital was raised. The main office in Little Rock opened on August 15, 1837, and the branches in Batesville and Fayetteville opened the following January. To guard the specie from being paid out in redemption for bank notes, one series of bills was payable in specie on demand, but the others were post notes with a date and payable interest to be filled in by the issuer. Such notes were filled out in various ways, not at all standard.

Success attended the Bank of the State of Arkansas, and a branch was opened at Arkansas Post at the confluence of the

Mississippi and Arkansas rivers. Another branch was planned for the town of Washington, but it never materialized, possibly because the Real Estate Bank of the State of Arkansas already operated there and opposed any competition. On October 31, 1839, all offices of the bank suspended specie payments. The Little Rock office later resumed payments on a limited basis for a time. Matters went from bad to worse, and in 1843 the legislature placed the bank in receivership.

Niles' National Register included this on March 2, 1842:

> The *Little Rock Gazette* of the 16th March says, "Few persons now receive Arkansas bank paper except at a discount of one-half."
>
> A review of the condition of the banks of that state which appears in the same paper, over the signature of *R.C. Byrd*, strongly urges the whole of the banks of the state to go into a state of liquidation. He says, "It is not right to disguise the true condition of our banks; and I assert, without fear of successful contradiction, that not a suspended bank in the state is able to pay her interest and resume the payment of specie on her notes, or will be in the next five years to come, if ever.
>
> Count all their specie, their bills receivable, bad and doubtful debts, banking houses, &c., and you will find, (taking all to be money) that the state has made nothing, or but a very small amount, by her banking operations. But deduct the bad, and half the doubtful debts, and she will be $150,000 minus. To arrive at this delectable state of bank prosperity, has required four years only, with a specie capital to begin on of $1,500,000. What are our prospects for the next four years, with neither specie, nor credit at home nor abroad, if we must still bank?

Thus state banking in Arkansas, short-lived, came to an undesirable end. A *cause célèbre* later arose and lingered for a long time, after $1,000,000 in Arkansas state bonds issued to fund the Bank of the State of Arkansas were used as security for a loan of $250,000 with the Ohio Valley Trust Co. in Cincinnati. The bonds changed hands at a deep discount and eventually were acquired by Holford's, an English firm, which demanded the full face value from the state. After the Civil War the state legislature repudiated any amount of the bonds beyond the actual cash benefit derived from them when they were pledged.

In 1846 an amendment to the State Constitution outlawed banks in the state. Years later in 1874, after the note-issuing era had ended, this provision was nullified by the new State Constitution.

Numismatic Comments

Collecting bank notes of Arkansas is a quick study, at least so far as reviewing the history of the two banks goes. However, acquiring actual currency can be a challenge. Bills of the Real Estate Bank of the State of Arkansas and Bank of the State of Arkansas, and their branches range from rare to unknown.

Although there were a few private banks and other businesses that engaged in finance, these two were the only issuers of bank notes. From the mid-1840s through the Civil War, no Arkansas state-chartered–bank bills were current in the state, a remarkable situation. Scrip issues, not studied here, were abundant and are popular to collect today.

The standard reference on Arkansas paper money is *Arkansas Obsolete Notes and Scrip*, by Matt Rothert Sr. and published in 1985. For any scholar of Arkansas' complex banking history, this is a great book to have.

Arkansas Post, Arkansas

Arkansas Post was established by the French in June 1686, the first settlement by foreigners in Arkansas. During the Civil War, Confederate forces established Fort Hindman, which was garrisoned with 5,000 troops. Union forces attacked with over 33,000 men and a heavy force of gunboats. After a bombardment, the fort surrendered and was destroyed.

Bank of the State of Arkansas (branch)

1839–1843

W-AR-010

History: The Bank of the State of Arkansas was incorporated on August 15, 1837. The authorized capital stock of the bank was approved at $1,000,000, to be gathered by selling state bonds and loans, $50,000 of which was required to be paid in before the bank could open for business. On January 3, 1839, the branch at Arkansas Post commenced business.

On October 31, 1839, the bank and all of its branches suspended specie payments. However, the bank never fully recovered, and in January 1843 the bank was placed in liquidation, in heavy debt to the state. It was considered a total loss and complete failure.

The Bank of the State of Arkansas had its parent bank located in Little Rock, W-AR-070, and branch banks located in Batesville, W-AR-020, and Fayetteville, W-AR-040. A branch was planned for Washington but never opened.

Numismatic Commentary: The branch at Arkansas Post never issued post notes. In June 1843 the branch had $56,020 outstanding in circulating bank notes. Nevertheless, notes of this bank and branch are still extremely rare.

Valid Issues

$5 • W-AR-010-005-G010 HA

Engraver: Draper, Toppan, Longacre & Co. ***Comments:*** H-AR-10-G62, Rothert-18-2. 18__. 1830s.

Rarity: URS-4

VF $800

$5 • W-AR-010-005-G020 HA

Engraver: Draper, Toppan, Longacre & Co. ***Comments:*** H-AR-10-G64, Rothert-18-1. 18__. 1830s.

Rarity: URS-4
VF $800

$10 • W-AR-010-010-G030

Left: 10 / Train / X. ***Center:*** Goddess with treasure. ***Right:*** 10 / Cow / X. ***Engraver:*** Draper, Toppan, Longacre & Co. ***Comments:*** H-AR-10-G66, Rothert-18-3. 18__. 1830s.

Rarity: URS-3
VF $1,000

$20 • W-AR-010-020-G040 HA

Engraver: Draper, Toppan, Longacre & Co. ***Comments:*** H-AR-10-G68, Rothert-18-5. 18__. 1830s.

Rarity: URS-3
VF $1,000

$50 • W-AR-010-050-G050

Engraver: Draper, Toppan, Longacre & Co. ***Comments:*** H-AR-10-G70. No description available. 18__. 1830s.

Rarity: *None known*

$100 • W-AR-010-100-G060

Engraver: Draper, Toppan, Longacre & Co. ***Comments:*** H-AR-10-G72. No description available. 18__. 1830s.

Rarity: *None known*

Batesville, Arkansas

After Georgetown, Batesville is the second-oldest municipality in Arkansas. James Woodson Bates was the first settler to arrive in 1810, and the town was named for him. The area was originally known as Poke Bayou.

Located on the White River, Batesville became an important port town and served as an entry point into northern Arkansas. Batesville also served as a land office during the settling of the Ozark Mountains. In 1819 a ferry was established across the White River, and a dozen houses were constructed. On March 3, 1822, the town was officially laid out. A post office was established that year, and on September 25, 1836, the Batesville Academy was incorporated. This was the state's first academy.

Batesville is located in an area rich in manganese ore, phosphate rock, sandstone, limestone, and marble. As a result, quarrying made up most of the town's economy.

Bank of the State of Arkansas (branch)

1838–1843

W-AR-020

History: The Bank of the State of Arkansas was incorporated on August 15, 1837. The authorized capital stock of the bank was approved at $1,000,000, to be gathered by selling state bonds and loans, $50,000 of which was required to be paid in before the bank could open for business. In January 1838 the branch in Batesville opened.

On October 31, 1839, the bank and all of its branches suspended specie payments. However, the bank never fully recovered, and in January 1843 the bank was placed in liquidation, in heavy debt to the state. It was considered a total loss and complete failure.

The Bank of the State of Arkansas had its parent bank located in Little Rock, W-AR-070, and branch banks located in Arkansas Post, W-AR-010, and Fayetteville, W-AR-040. A branch was planned for Washington but never opened.

Numismatic Commentary: The Batesville branch had $55,250 in circulation in June 1843. Nevertheless, notes of this bank and branch are still extremely rare.

Valid Issues

$5 • W-AR-020-005-G010 CC

Engraver: Rawdon, Wright & Hatch. ***Comments:*** H-AR-10-G120, Rothert-31-1. 18__. 1830s.

Rarity: URS-3
VG $800; **F** $1,000

$10 • W-AR-020-010-G020 CC

Engraver: Rawdon, Wright & Hatch. ***Comments:*** H-AR-10-G122, Rothert-31-2. 18__. 1830s.

Rarity: URS-3
F $1,000; **VF** $1,300; **Proof** $1,200

$20 • W-AR-020-020-G030 HA

Engraver: Rawdon, Wright & Hatch. ***Comments:*** H-AR-10-G124, Rothert-31-3. 18__. 1830s.

Rarity: URS-3
F $1,200

$50 • W-AR-020-050-G040

Engraver: Rawdon, Wright & Hatch. ***Comments:*** H-AR-10-G126. No description available. 18__. 1830s.

Rarity: *None known*

$100 • W-AR-020-100-G050

Left: 100 / Sheaves, Plow, implements / 100. ***Center:*** C / Cherub / C. ***Right:*** Venus / 100. ***Engraver:*** Rawdon, Wright & Hatch. ***Comments:*** H-AR-10-G128, Rothert-31-5. 18__. 1830s.

Rarity: *None known*

Post Notes

$10 • W-AR-020-010-G053 HA

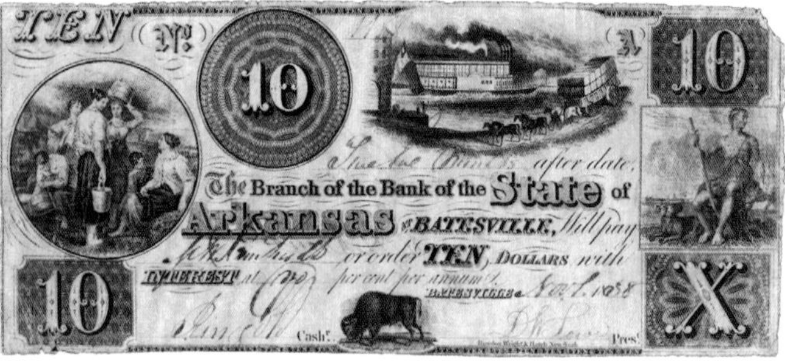

Engraver: Rawdon, Wright & Hatch. ***Comments:*** H-Unlisted, Rothert-31-7. 18__. 1830s.

Rarity: URS-1
VF $850

$20 • W-AR-020-020-G055

Left: Wheat harvest. ***Center:*** Buffalo. ***Right:*** Three allegorical figures. ***Engraver:*** Rawdon, Wright & Hatch. ***Comments:*** H-Unlisted, Rothert-31-8. 18__. 1830s.

Rarity: URS-1
G $600

$100 • W-AR-020-100-G060 HA

Engraver: Rawdon, Wright & Hatch. ***Comments:*** H-AR-10-G140. Handwritten "after 12 months." 18__. 1830s.

Rarity: URS-1
F $850

COLUMBIA, ARKANSAS

Columbia was founded in the early 1830s on the western bank of the Mississippi River in southeastern Arkansas. In 1833 it was established as the seat of Chicot County. By 1855 the population of the area was about 500. The town provided soldiers to Confederate ranks during the Civil War, but the coming of the railroad diminished the town's importance. During the 1870s the town's remains were washed away by the Mississippi River.

Real Estate Bank of the State of Arkansas (branch)

1839–1843

W-AR-030

History: On October 26, 1836, the Real Estate Bank of the State of Arkansas was chartered and approved by Governor James S. Conway. The capital was authorized at $2,250,000, with the amount to be raised by bonds, loans, and real-estate security.[1] The Columbia branch opened its doors for business on March 5, 1839. However, soon the bank was in disastrous order. In 1842 the bank went into receivership, and in 1843 the state put the bank in liquidation, heavily in debt. Many instances of fraud were soon discovered.

The Real Estate Bank of the State of Arkansas had its parent bank located in Little Rock, W-AR-080, and branch banks located in Helena, W-AR-060, Van Buren, W-AR-090, and Washington, W-AR-100.

Numismatic Commentary: On October 1, 1856, the Columbia branch had $3,115 in unredeemed bank notes outstanding. Chances of locating a note from this branch are extremely low.

Valid Issues

$5 • W-AR-030-005-G010

HA

Engraver: Rawdon, Wright & Hatch. ***Comments:*** H-AR-5-G30, Rothert-130-1. 18__. 1830s.

Rarity: URS-3
F $1,000

$10 • W-AR-030-010-G020

HA

Engraver: Rawdon, Wright & Hatch. ***Comments:*** H-AR-5-G32, Rothert-130-2. 18__. 1830s.

Rarity: URS-1
F $1,500

$20 • W-AR-030-020-G030

Engraver: Rawdon, Wright & Hatch. ***Comments:*** H-AR-5-G34. No description available. 18__. 1830s.

Rarity: *None known*

$50 • W-AR-030-050-G040

Left: FIFTY vertically. ***Center:*** L / State arms. ***Bottom center:*** Male portrait. ***Right:*** L / Shield. ***Engraver:*** Rawdon, Wright & Hatch. ***Comments:*** H-AR-5-G36, Rothert-130-9. Only the post note is known (W-AR-030-050-G090). 18__. 1830s.

Rarity: *None known*

$100 • W-AR-030-100-G050

Engraver: Rawdon, Wright & Hatch. ***Comments:*** H-AR-5-G38. No description available. 18__. 1830s.

Rarity: *None known*

Post Notes

$5 • W-AR-030-005-G060

Engraver: Rawdon, Wright & Hatch. ***Comments:*** H-AR-5-G40. No description available. 18__. 1830s.

Rarity: *None known*

$10 • W-AR-030-010-G070

Engraver: Rawdon, Wright & Hatch. ***Comments:*** H-AR-5-G42. No description available. 18__. 1830s.

Rarity: *None known*

$20 • W-AR-030-020-G080

Engraver: Rawdon, Wright & Hatch. ***Comments:*** H-AR-5-G44. No description available. 18__. 1830s.

Rarity: *None known*

$50 • W-AR-030-050-G090

Left: FIFTY vertically. ***Center:*** L / Woman seated on dock / L. ***Bottom center:*** Male portrait. ***Right:*** Shield. ***Engraver:*** Rawdon, Wright & Hatch. ***Comments:*** H-AR-5-G46. 18__. 1830s.

Rarity: URS-1
F $1,500

$100 • W-AR-030-100-G100

Engraver: Rawdon, Wright & Hatch. ***Comments:*** H-AR-5-G48. No description available. 18__. 1830s.

Rarity: *None known*

Fayetteville, Arkansas

George McGarrah settled at Big Spring in 1828 and founded the town of Washington. There was some confusion with a similarly named Washington nearby, and the name was changed to Fayetteville. This name came from Fayetteville, Tennessee, which was named after Fayetteville, North Carolina. The original Fayetteville was named in honor of the Marquis de Lafayette.

The first stores and homes in Fayetteville were built during the 1830s, and on November 3, 1836, the town was incorporated. In 1859 the town was chartered as a city. The Civil War caused the municipal government to be suspended, and it did not reinstate until 1867.

Bank of the State of Arkansas (branch)

1838–1843

W-AR-040

History: The Bank of the State of Arkansas was incorporated on August 15, 1837. The authorized capital stock of the bank was approved at $1,000,000, to be gathered by selling state bonds and loans, $50,000 of which was required to be paid in before the bank could open for business.

In January 1838 the branch in Fayetteville was opened. The Fayetteville branch was described by the *Arkansas Gazette* on October 30, 1839:

> It is a superb building, both the outside and the interior, and is the work of mechanics settled in our city. The banking room is large and splendidly furnished, and the semicircular counter is one of the best specimens of painting we have ever seen. It is done in a style to represent the grain of several kinds of wood, with a base of imitation marble. The wall has a heavy cornice of moulding, in plaster, with a beautiful ornament in the center of the ceiling. The doors are of handsomely finished wrought iron, with locks which would baffle the most expert burglar; and the vaults are massive and substantial, a sure defense against fire or robbery.

On October 31, 1839, the bank and all of its branches suspended specie payments. However, the bank never fully recovered, and in

January 1843 the bank was placed in liquidation, in heavy debt to the state. It was considered a total loss and complete failure.

The Bank of the State of Arkansas had its parent bank located in Little Rock, W-AR-070, and branch banks located in Arkansas Post, W-AR-010, and Batesville, W-AR-020. A branch was planned for Washington but never opened.

Numismatic Commentary: The Fayetteville branch had $164,350 of outstanding bank notes in June 1843, making its notes the most common branch notes of the series. Lower-denomination notes are still scarce, with higher-denomination notes being rare.

Valid Issues

$5 • W-AR-040-005-G010

HA

Engraver: Rawdon, Wright & Hatch. ***Comments:*** H-AR-10-G142, Rothert-186-1. 18__. 1838–1840.

Rarity: URS-4
F $500; **VF** $750

$10 • W-AR-040-010-G020

CC

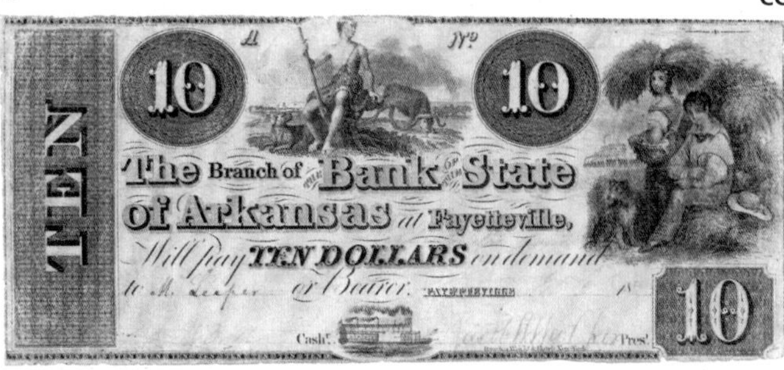

Engraver: Rawdon, Wright & Hatch. ***Comments:*** H-AR-10-G144, Rothert-186-2. 18__. 1838–1840.

Rarity: URS-4
F $600; **VF** $750

$20 • W-AR-040-020-G030

HA

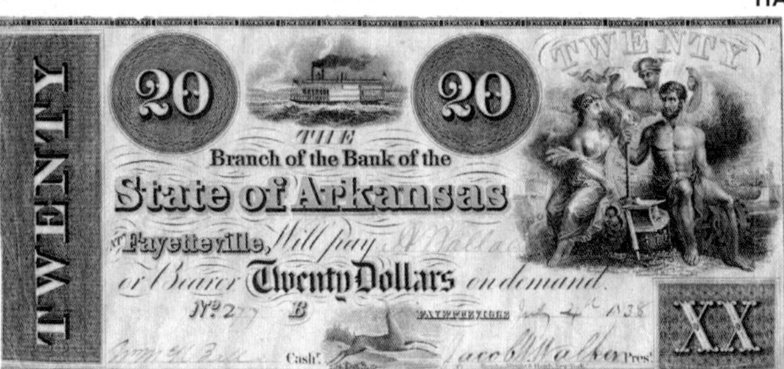

Engraver: Rawdon, Wright & Hatch. ***Comments:*** H-AR-10-G146, Rothert-186-3. 18__. 1838–1840.

Rarity: URS-4
F $500; **VF** $750; **EF** $1,000

$50 • W-AR-040-050-G040

HA

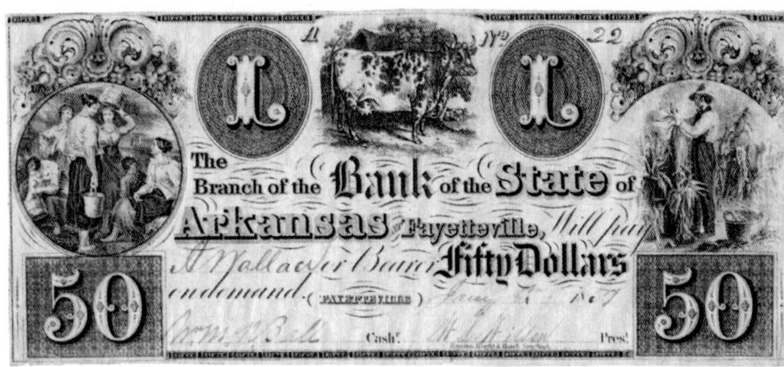

Engraver: Rawdon, Wright & Hatch. ***Comments:*** H-AR-10-G148, Rothert-186-4. 18__. 1838–1840.

Rarity: URS-3
F $1,100; **VF** $1,400

$100 • W-AR-040-100-G050

Engraver: Rawdon, Wright & Hatch. ***Comments:*** H-AR-10-G150. No description available. 18__. 1838–1840.

Rarity: *None known*

Post Notes

$5 • W-AR-040-005-G060

HA

Engraver: Rawdon, Wright & Hatch. ***Comments:*** H-AR-10-G152, Rothert-186-6. 18__. 1838.

Rarity: URS-4
F $500; **VF** $750

$10 • W-AR-040-010-G070

Left: TEN vertically. ***Center:*** 10 / Indian seated with dog, Cattle / 10. ***Right:*** Woman and man with dog and sheaves / 10. ***Engraver:*** Rawdon, Wright & Hatch. ***Comments:*** H-AR-10-G156. Handwritten "After Twelve Months." 18__. 1838–1840.

Rarity: URS-4
F $500; **VF** $750

$10 • W-AR-040-010-G080

HA

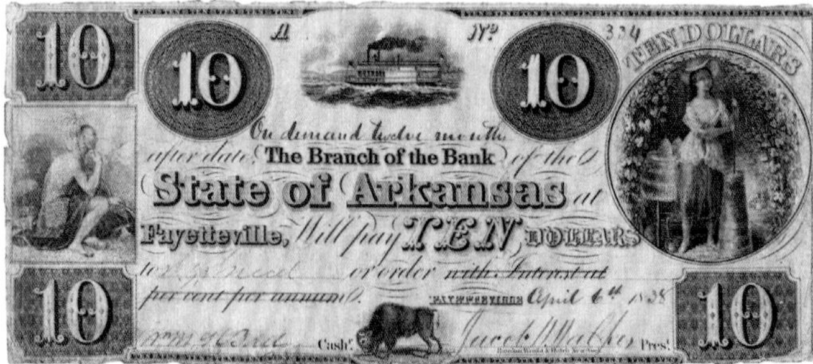

Engraver: Rawdon, Wright & Hatch. ***Comments:*** H-AR-10-G158. 18__. 1838.

Rarity: URS-4
F $500; **VF** $750

$20 • **W-AR-040-020-G090** HA

Engraver: Rawdon, Wright & Hatch. ***Comments:*** H-AR-10-G162. 18__. 1838.

Rarity: URS-4
F $500; **VF** $750

$50 • **W-AR-040-050-G100** HA

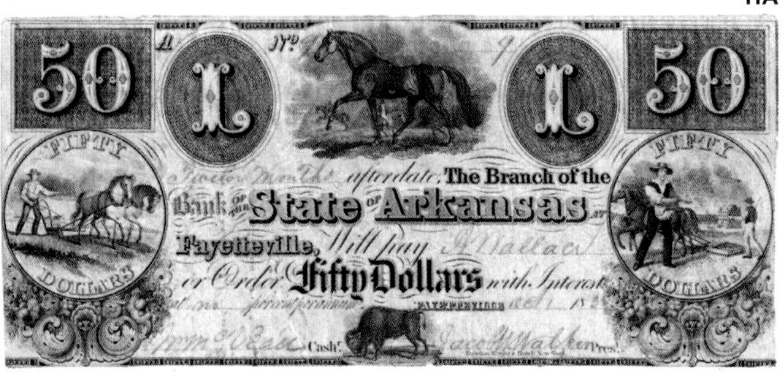

Engraver: Rawdon, Wright & Hatch. ***Comments:*** H-AR-10-G166. 18__. 1838.

Rarity: URS-3
F $1,000; **VF** $1,300

$100 • **W-AR-040-100-G110**

Engraver: Rawdon, Wright & Hatch. ***Comments:*** H-AR-10-G170. No description available. 18__. 1838.

Rarity: *None known*

HELENA, ARKANSAS

Helena was founded in 1833 along the Mississippi River. It was settled on a piece of land known as Crowley's Ridge, which was elevated away from the river and thus protected against flooding—a common and dangerous occurrence.

The Union army occupied Helena during the Civil War, leading up to the Battle of Helena in 1863.

Exchange Bank of Helena

1850s–1860s

W-AR-050

History: Following the star-crossed history of the two main banking institutions in the state, further banks were outlawed by the State Constitution in 1846. Therefore, the Exchange Bank of Helena was a private bank that operated without a charter. These notes are considered to be "drafts" in a strict sense but are listed for collector continuity.

Numismatic Commentary: Only remainder notes or notes that have been falsely filled in (probably by Union troops once Helena was occupied) have been found.

Remaining at the American Bank Note Co. archives as of 2003 was a $5-$5-$10-$20 face plate.

ISSUES

$5 • **W-AR-050-005-G010** QDB, QDB

Engraver: Rawdon, Wright, Hatch & Edson. ***Comments:*** H-Unlisted, Rothert-279-1. Printed on the backs of other notes. 18__. 1850s–1860s.

Rarity: URS-5
VG $100; **F** $150; **VF** $250; **Proof** $600

$10 • **W-AR-050-010-G020** CC

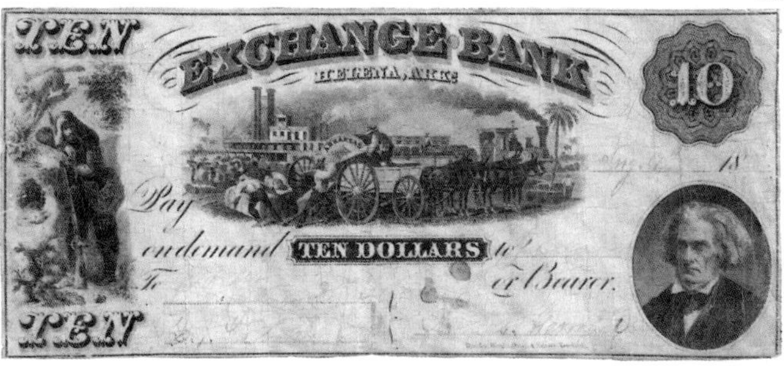

Engraver: Rawdon, Wright, Hatch & Edson. ***Comments:*** H-Unlisted, Rothert-279-2. 1850s.

Rarity: URS-5
VG $100; **F** $150; **VF** $250; **Proof** $600

$20 • **W-AR-050-020-G030** HA

Engraver: Rawdon, Wright, Hatch & Edson. ***Comments:*** H-Unlisted, Rothert-279-3. 18__. 1850s.

Rarity: URS-4
VG $125; **F** $175; **VF** $350

Real Estate Bank of the State of Arkansas (branch)

1839–1843

W-AR-060

History: On October 26, 1836, the Real Estate Bank of the State of Arkansas was chartered and approved by Governor James S. Conway. The capital was authorized at $2,250,000, with the amount to be raised by bonds, loans, and real-estate security.[2] The Helena branch opened its doors for business on February 15, 1839. H.L. Briscoe was the president. However, soon the bank was in disastrous order. In 1842 the bank went into receivership, and in 1843 the state put the bank in liquidation, heavily in debt. Many instances of fraud were soon discovered.

The Real Estate Bank of the State of Arkansas had its parent bank located in Little Rock, W-AR-080, and branch banks located in Columbia, W-AR-030, Van Buren, W-AR-090, and Washington, W-AR-100.

Numismatic Commentary: On October 1, 1856, the Helena branch had $4,815 in unredeemed bank notes outstanding. Only the $5 has turned up in the past, making issues from this branch extremely rare.

Valid Issues

$5 • W-AR-060-005-G010

Left: Maiden. ***Center:*** Shield bearing cotton. ***Right:*** Eagle, Shield. ***Engraver:*** Rawdon, Wright & Hatch. ***Comments:*** H-AR-5-G60. 18__. 1830s.

Rarity: URS-1
VF $1,500

$10 • W-AR-060-010-G020

Engraver: Rawdon, Wright & Hatch. ***Comments:*** H-AR-5-G62. No description available. 18__. 1830s.

Rarity: *None known*

$20 • W-AR-060-020-G030

Engraver: Rawdon, Wright & Hatch. ***Comments:*** H-AR-5-G64. No description available. 18__. 1830s.

Rarity: *None known*

$50 • W-AR-060-050-G040

Engraver: Rawdon, Wright & Hatch. ***Comments:*** H-AR-5-G66. No description available. 18__. 1830s.

Rarity: *None known*

$100 • W-AR-060-100-G050

Engraver: Rawdon, Wright & Hatch. ***Comments:*** H-AR-5-G68. No description available. 18__. 1830s.

Rarity: *None known*

Post Notes

$5 • W-AR-060-005-G060

Left: FIVE. ***Center:*** 5 / Standing figure next to two seated men / Female portrait / 5. ***Right:*** Shield. ***Engraver:*** Rawdon, Wright & Hatch. ***Comments:*** H-AR-5-G70. 18__. 1830s.

Rarity: URS-3
VF $1,000

$10 • W-AR-060-010-G070

Engraver: Rawdon, Wright & Hatch. ***Comments:*** H-AR-5-G72. No description available. 18__. 1830s.

Rarity: *None known*

$20 • W-AR-060-020-G080

Engraver: Rawdon, Wright & Hatch. ***Comments:*** H-AR-5-G74. No description available. 18__. 1830s.

Rarity: *None known*

$50 • W-AR-060-050-G090

Engraver: Rawdon, Wright & Hatch. ***Comments:*** H-AR-5-G76. No description available. 18__. 1830s.

Rarity: *None known*

$100 • W-AR-060-100-G100

Engraver: Rawdon, Wright & Hatch. ***Comments:*** H-AR-5-G78. No description available. 18__. 1830s.

Rarity: *None known*

Little Rock, Arkansas

The area that later became Little Rock, the state capital, was initially inhabited by various Native American tribes, including the Caddo, Osage, Choctaw, Quapaw, and Cherokee. Little Rock was named after a stone outcropping on the Arkansas River which was used as a landmark by early settlers.

Bank of the State of Arkansas

1837–1843

W-AR-070

History: The Bank of the State of Arkansas was incorporated on August 15, 1837, with Captain Jacob Brown as the president. However, he was also the Army Chief's disbursing officer to the Cherokees, who were in the process of migrating to the Western Territories. Due to the controversy regarding his holding two public offices, Brown resigned as president before the bank opened. He was replaced by William Field, and John H. Crease became the cashier.[3]

The authorized capital stock of the bank was approved at $1,000,000, to be gathered by selling state bonds and loans, $50,000 of which was required to be paid in before the bank could open for business. On October 31, 1839, the bank and all of its branches suspended specie payments. The parent bank resumed payments for a limited time. However, the bank never fully recovered, and in January 1843 the bank was placed in liquidation, in heavy debt to the state. It was considered a total loss and complete failure.

The Bank of the State of Arkansas had branch banks located in Arkansas Post, W-AR-010, Batesville, W-AR-020, and Fayetteville, W-AR-040. A branch was planned for Washington but never opened.

Numismatic Commentary: In June 1843 the bank in Little Rock had $2,230 in unredeemed bank notes. Only an issued $5 note has turned up, along with Proofs from the Longacre collection and the American Bank Note Co. archives, making issues from this branch extremely rare.

Valid Issues

$5 • W-AR-070-005-G010

CC

Engraver: Underwood, Bald, Spencer & Hufty. ***Comments:*** H-AR-10-G4, Rothert-400-1. 18__. 1830s.

Rarity: URS-3

Proof $1,100

Selected auction price: Heritage Auctions, January 2010, Lot 12510, Proof $1,092; R.M. Smythe, September 20, 1996, Lot 154, Proof $1,000

$10 • W-AR-070-010-G020

Left: 10 / Boy reclining under sheaf / 10. ***Center:*** Indian throwing tomahawk. ***Right:*** TEN on three medallion heads vertically. ***Engraver:*** Underwood, Bald, Spencer & Hufty. ***Comments:*** H-AR-10-G6, Rothert-400-2. 18__. 1830s.

Rarity: URS-3

Proof $1,800

$20 • W-AR-070-020-G030

SI

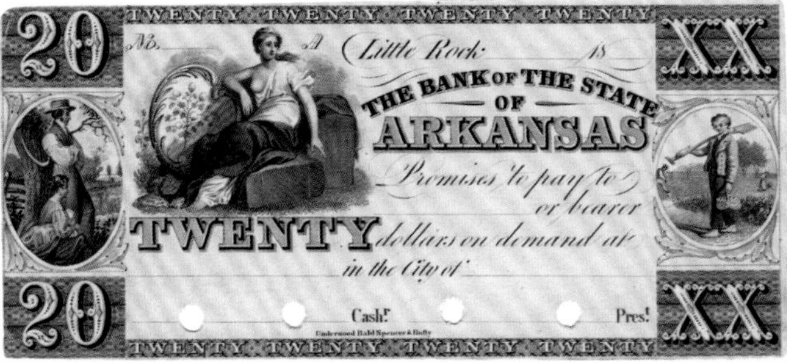

Engraver: Underwood, Bald, Spencer & Hufty. ***Comments:*** H-AR-10-G8, Rothert-400-3. 18__. 1830s.

Rarity: URS-3

Proof $1,200

$50 • W-AR-070-050-G040

LK

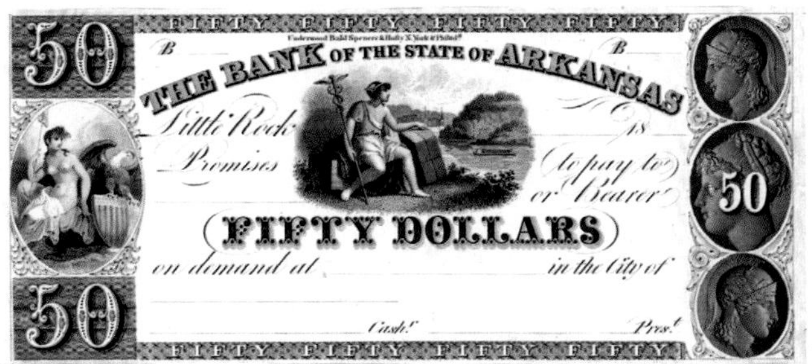

Engraver: Underwood, Bald, Spencer & Hufty. ***Comments:*** H-AR-10-G10, Rothert-400-4. 18__. 1830s.

Rarity: URS-2

Proof $3,000

$100 • W-AR-070-100-G050

CC

Engraver: Underwood, Bald, Spencer & Hufty. ***Comments:*** H-AR-10-G12, Rothert-400-5. 18__. 1830s.

Rarity: URS-3

Proof $1,200

Notes on Which the Place Payable is Blank

$5 • W-AR-070-005-G060

Left: 5 / Indian seated / V. ***Center:*** Medallion head bearing 5 / Goddess facing river. ***Right:*** FIVE vertically. ***Engraver:*** Underwood, Bald, Spencer & Hufty. ***Comments:*** H-AR-10-G40, Rothert-400-1. 18__. 1830s.

Rarity: URS-3

Proof $1,000

$10 • W-AR-070-010-G070

HA

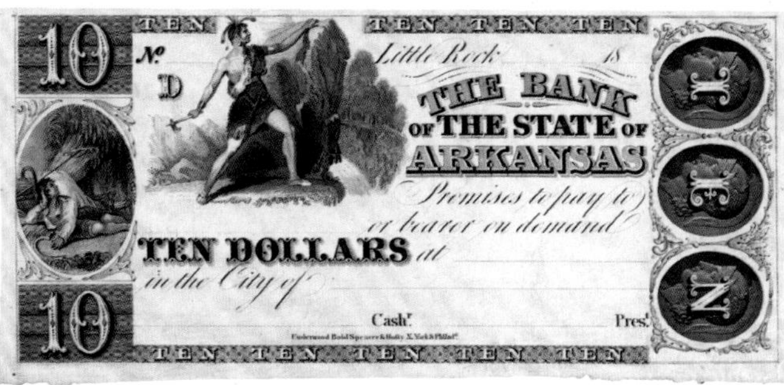

Engraver: Underwood, Bald, Spencer & Hufty. ***Comments:*** H-AR-10-G42, Rothert-400-2. 18__. 1830s.

Rarity: URS-2

Proof $2,000

$20 • W-AR-070-020-G080

Left: 20 / Man and woman / 20. ***Center:*** Goddess and shield. ***Right:*** XX / Farmer / XX. ***Engraver:*** Underwood, Bald, Spencer & Hufty. ***Comments:*** H-AR-10-G46, Rothert-400-3. 18__. 1830s.

Rarity: URS-3

Proof $1,200

$50 • W-AR-070-050-G090

Left: 50 / Woman seated / 50. ***Center:*** Mercury seated with bale next to river. ***Right:*** Medallion head / 50 on medallion head / Medallion head. ***Engraver:*** Underwood, Bald, Spencer & Hufty. ***Comments:*** H-AR-10-G48, Rothert-400-4. 18__. 1830s.

Rarity: URS-3

Proof $1,200

$100 • W-AR-070-100-G100

Left: 100 / HUNDRED on medallion head / 100. *Center:* Indian in canoe. *Right:* 100 / HUNDRED on medallion head / 100. *Engraver:* Underwood, Bald, Spencer & Hufty. *Comments:* H-AR-10-G50, Rothert-400-5. 18__. 1830s.

Rarity: URS-3
Proof $1,200

Post Notes

$10 • W-AR-070-010-G110

HA

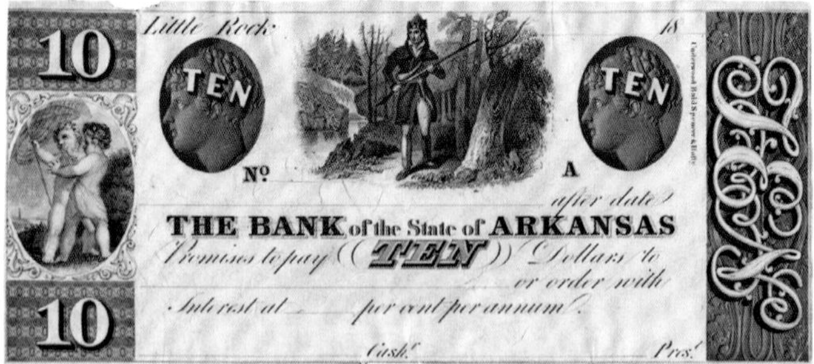

Engraver: Underwood, Bald, Spencer & Hufty. *Comments:* H-AR-10-G54. 18__. 1830s.

Rarity: URS-3
Proof $1,200

$20 • W-AR-070-020-G120

HA

Engraver: Underwood, Bald, Spencer & Hufty. *Comments:* H-AR-10-G56. 18__. 1830s.

Rarity: URS-3
Proof $1,200

$50 • W-AR-070-050-G130

LK

Engraver: Underwood, Bald, Spencer & Hufty. *Comments:* H-Unlisted. Partial note. 18__. 1830s.

Rarity: URS-1
Proof $2,200

$100 • W-AR-070-100-G140

LK

Engraver: Underwood, Bald, Spencer & Hufty. *Comments:* H-Unlisted. 18__. 1830s.

Rarity: URS-1
Proof $2,500

Post Notes on Which the Place Payable is Blank

$5 • W-AR-070-005-G150

Left: 5 / Horse / FIVE. *Center:* Goddess instructing Youth, Beehive. *Right:* 5 / Steamboat / FIVE. *Engraver:* Draper, Toppan, Longacre & Co. *Comments:* H-AR-10-G100, Rothert-18-1. 18__. 1830s.

Rarity: *None known*

$10 • W-AR-070-010-G160

Left: 10 / Train / X. *Center:* Goddess with treasure. *Right:* 10 / Cow / X. *Engraver:* Draper, Toppan, Longacre & Co. *Comments:* H-AR-10-G102, Rothert-18-3. 18__. 1830s.

Rarity: *None known*

$20 • W-AR-070-020-G170

Left: 20 / Train / 20. *Center:* Herd of sheep and cattle with drover. *Right:* 20 / Portrait of Thomas Jefferson / 20. *Engraver:* Draper, Toppan, Longacre & Co. *Comments:* H-AR-10-G104, Rothert-18-5. 18__. 1830s.

Rarity: *None known*

$50 • W-AR-070-050-G180

Engraver: Draper, Toppan, Longacre & Co. *Comments:* H-AR-10-G106. No description available. 18__. 1830s.

Rarity: *None known*

$100 • W-AR-070-100-G190

Engraver: Draper, Toppan, Longacre & Co. *Comments:* H-AR-10-G108. No description available. 18__. 1830s.

Rarity: *None known*

Uncut Sheets

$5-$5-$5-$5 •

W-AR-070-005.005.005.005-US010

LK

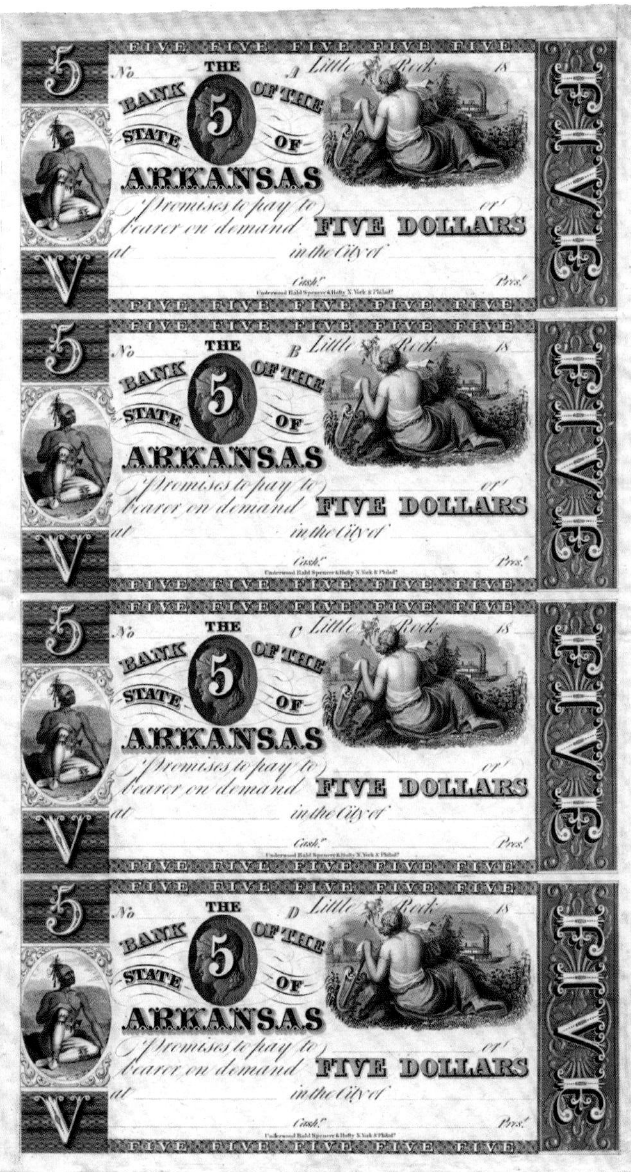

Engraver: Underwood, Bald, Spencer & Hufty. ***Comments:*** H-AR-10-G4, G4, G4, G4. All four notes identical. 18__. 1830s.

Rarity: URS-1

Proof $3,000

$10-$10-$10-$10 •

W-AR-070-010.010.010.010-US020

LK

Engraver: Underwood, Bald, Spencer & Hufty. ***Comments:*** H-AR-10-G6, G6, G6, G6. All four notes identical. 18__. 1830s.

Rarity: URS-1

Proof $2,500

How to Read the Whitman Numbering System

$1 • W-AL-020-001-G010a

Denomination: Face value of the note shown.

W: Whitman number. This number is a sortable code unique to each bank and note.

AL: Abbreviation for the state under study.

020: Numerical designation specific to each bank.

001: The denomination in dollars.

G010a: G indicates a good or valid note. Other categories are indicated thus: C (counterfeit); R (raised); S (spurious); N (not-attributed); A (altered). Numbers are assigned starting with 010, 020, et seq. Terminal letters following the number indicate variations of a note: a series of different colored overprints, tints, payees, etc., all on the same design of note. For more information, see the "How to Use This Book" section at the front of the volume, page xiv.

$20-$20-$20-$20 •
W-AR-070-020.020.020.020-US030 LK

Engraver: Underwood, Bald, Spencer & Hufty. ***Comments:*** H-AR-10-G8, G8, G8, G8. All four notes identical. 18__. 1830s.

Rarity: URS-1
Proof $3,000

$50-$50-$100-$100 •
W-AR-070-050-050-100-100-US040 LK

Engraver: Underwood, Bald, Spencer & Hufty. ***Comments:*** H-AR-10-G10, G10, G12, G12. First two notes identical; last two notes identical. 18__. 1830s.

Rarity: URS-1
Proof $6,000

Uncut Post-Note Sheets

$10-$10-$10-$20 • W-AR-070-010.010.010.020-US050

LK

Engraver: Underwood, Bald, Spencer & Hufty. ***Comments:*** H-AR-10-G54, G54, G54, G56. First three notes identical. 18__. 1830s.

Rarity: URS-1
Proof $6,000

$100-$50 • W-AR-070-100.050-US060

LK

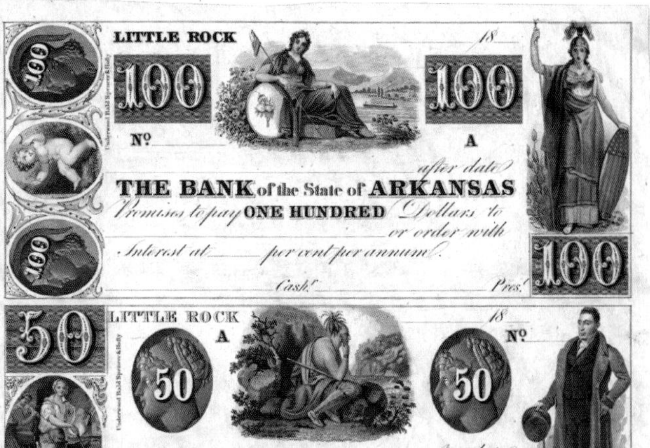

Engraver: Underwood, Bald, Spencer & Hufty. ***Comments:*** All unlisted in Haxby. Last note partial note. 18__. 1830s.

Rarity: URS-1
Proof $1,750

Real Estate Bank of the State of Arkansas

1836–1843

W-AR-080

History: On October 26, 1836, the Real Estate Bank of the State of Arkansas was chartered and approved by Governor James S. Conway. The capital was authorized at $2,250,000, with the amount to be raised by bonds, loans, and real-estate security.[4] The bank was constructed for the purpose of lending its funds to farm lands as security. 127,500 acres of land were mortgaged.[5] In November 1837 $2,000,000 worth of bonds was issued by the state in order to augment the bank's capital. John W. Wilson, a speaker of the state House of Representatives, was elected the president. He was later replaced by A.H. Davis.

The bank opened its doors for business on December 10, 1838. However, soon the bank was in disastrous order. In 1842 the bank went into receivership, and in 1843 the state put the bank in liquidation, heavily in debt. Many instances of fraud were soon discovered.

The Real Estate Bank of the State of Arkansas had branch banks located in Columbia, W-AR-030, Helena, W-AR-060, Van Buren, W-AR-090, and Washington, W-AR-100.

Numismatic Commentary: As of October 1, 1856, the bank in Little Rock had $1,805 in unredeemed bank notes. Only a $5 and a $100 note have turned up from this bank and location, making any notes of this bank extremely rare.

Valid Issues

$5 • W-AR-080-005-G010

Left: 5 / Cotton plant. ***Center:*** State arms flanked by Justice and Indian / V. ***Right:*** 5 / Farmer harvesting corn. ***Engraver:*** Rawdon, Wright & Hatch. ***Comments:*** H-AR-5-G2, Rothert-401-1. 18__. 1830s.

Rarity: URS-1
F $2,500

$10 • W-AR-080-010-G020
Engraver: Rawdon, Wright & Hatch. ***Comments:*** H-AR-5-G4. No description available. 18__. 1830s.

Rarity: *None known*

$20 • W-AR-080-020-G030
Engraver: Rawdon, Wright & Hatch. ***Comments:*** H-AR-5-G6. No description available. 18__. 1830s.

Rarity: *None known*

$50 • W-AR-080-050-G040
Engraver: Rawdon, Wright & Hatch. ***Comments:*** H-AR-5-G8. No description available. 18__. 1830s.

Rarity: *None known*

$100 • W-AR-080-100-G050
Left: 100 / Farmer plowing / C. ***Center:*** Justice and Indian flanking state arms. ***Right:*** 100 / Steamboat / C. ***Engraver:*** Rawdon, Wright & Hatch. ***Comments:*** H-AR-5-G10, Rothert-401-5. 18__. 1830s.

Rarity: URS-1
F $2,500

Post Notes

$5 • W-AR-080-005-G060
Engraver: Rawdon, Wright & Hatch. ***Comments:*** H-AR-5-G12. No description available. 18__. 1830s.

Rarity: *None known*

$10 • W-AR-080-010-G070
Engraver: Rawdon, Wright & Hatch. ***Comments:*** H-AR-5-G14. No description available. 18__. 1830s.

Rarity: *None known*

$20 • W-AR-080-020-G080
Engraver: Rawdon, Wright & Hatch. ***Comments:*** H-AR-5-G16. No description available. 18__. 1830s.

Rarity: *None known*

$50 • W-AR-080-050-G090
Engraver: Rawdon, Wright & Hatch. ***Comments:*** H-AR-5-G18. No description available. 18__. 1830s.

Rarity: *None known*

$100 • W-AR-080-100-G100
Engraver: Rawdon, Wright & Hatch. ***Comments:*** H-AR-5-G20. No description available. 18__. 1830s.

Rarity: *None known*

Van Buren, Arkansas

Van Buren was settled by David Boyd and Thomas Martin in 1818. A lumber yard was built there by the two pioneers in order to fuel traffic along the Arkansas River. In 1831 a post office followed; it soon became known as Phillips Landing. Not long after, it was named after Secretary of State Martin Van Buren (who later became president in 1837). The town was incorporated on December 24, 1842.

Real Estate Bank of the State of Arkansas (branch)
1840–1843
W-AR-090

History: On October 26, 1836, the Real Estate Bank of the State of Arkansas was chartered and approved by Governor James S. Conway. In 1840 the branch in Van Buren was opened. However, soon the bank was in disastrous order. In 1842 the bank went into receivership, and in 1843 the state put the bank in liquidation, heavily in debt. Many instances of fraud were soon discovered.

The Real Estate Bank of the State of Arkansas had its parent bank located in Little Rock, W-AR-080, and branch banks located in Columbia, W-AR-030, Helena, W-AR-060, and Washington, W-AR-100.

Numismatic Commentary: No bank notes were printed for the Van Buren branch location. However, some notes dated at other branches were made payable there. Only the note listed below has been seen of this issue, making it unique and extremely rare.

Valid Issues

Post Note Dated at Columbia and Payable in Van Buren

$50 • W-AR-090-050-G010
Left: FIFTY vertically. ***Center:*** L / Woman seated on dock. ***Right:*** L / Shield. ***Engraver:*** Rawdon, Wright & Hatch. ***Comments:*** H-AR-5-G56. 18__. 1830s.

Rarity: URS-1
F $1,500

Washington, Arkansas

Washington was established in 1826 and was an important place of rest for pioneers on their way to Texas. In 1825 the county courthouse was established there, and during the 1830s thousands of Native Americans passed through Washington on their journey to Indian Territories.

Washington was the capital of Arkansas from 1863 to 1865, but the town experienced a slow decline when the railway bypassed it.

Real Estate Bank of the State of Arkansas (branch)
1839–1843
W-AR-100

History: On October 26, 1836, the Real Estate Bank of the State of Arkansas was chartered and approved by Governor James S. Conway. The capital was authorized at $2,250,000, with the amount to be raised by bonds, loans, and real-estate security.[6] The branch in Washington was opened on April 1, 1839, with E. Brittin as cashier. Both Thomas T. Williamson and David T. Witter served as president in their time, being prominent landholders in Hempstead County. However, soon the bank was in disastrous order. In 1842 the bank went into receivership, and in 1843 the state put the bank in liquidation, heavily in debt. Many instances of fraud were soon discovered.

The Real Estate Bank of the State of Arkansas had its parent bank located in Little Rock, W-AR-080, and branch banks located in Columbia, W-AR-030, Helena, W-AR-060, and Van Buren, W-AR-090.

Numismatic Commentary: The branch at Washington had $5,045 in unredeemed bank notes as of October 1, 1856. Notes from this branch therefore turn up more often than any other branch of the bank. They are, however, still extremely rare.

Valid Issues

$5 • W-AR-100-005-G010

HA

Engraver: Rawdon, Wright & Hatch. ***Comments:*** H-AR-5-G90, Rothert-680-1. 18__. 1830s.

Rarity: URS-4
F $800

$10 • W-AR-100-010-G020

SI

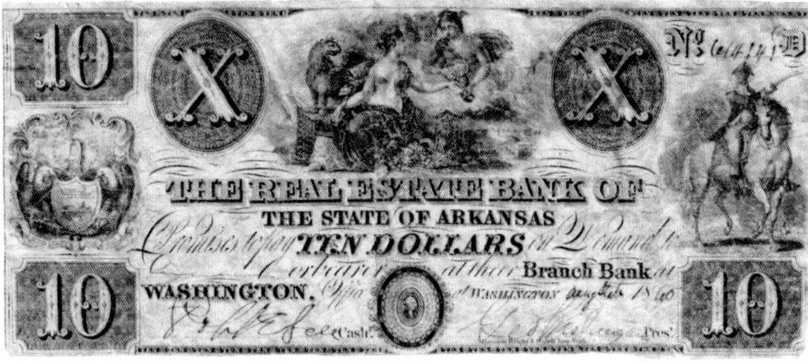

Engraver: Rawdon, Wright & Hatch. ***Comments:*** H-AR-5-G92, Rothert-680-2. 18__. 1830s.

Rarity: URS-3
F $1,000

$20 • W-AR-100-020-G030

HA

Engraver: Rawdon, Wright & Hatch. ***Comments:*** H-AR-5-G94, Rothert-680-3. 18__. 1830s.

Rarity: URS-3
F $1,200

$50 • W-AR-100-050-G040

Engraver: Rawdon, Wright & Hatch. ***Comments:*** H-AR-5-G96. No description available. 18__. 1830s.

Rarity: *None known*

$100 • W-AR-100-100-G050

Engraver: Rawdon, Wright & Hatch. ***Comments:*** H-AR-5-G98. No description available. 18__. 1830s.

Rarity: *None known*

Post Notes

$5 • W-AR-100-005-G060

Engraver: Rawdon, Wright & Hatch. ***Comments:*** H-AR-5-G100. No description available. 18__. 1830s.

Rarity: *None known*

$10 • W-AR-100-010-G070

Engraver: Rawdon, Wright & Hatch. ***Comments:*** H-AR-5-G102. No description available. 18__. 1830s.

Rarity: *None known*

$20 • W-AR-100-020-G080

Engraver: Rawdon, Wright & Hatch. ***Comments:*** H-AR-5-G104. No description available. 18__. 1830s.

Rarity: *None known*

$50 • W-AR-100-050-G090

Engraver: Rawdon, Wright & Hatch. ***Comments:*** H-AR-5-G106. No description available. 18__. 1830s.

Rarity: *None known*

$100 • W-AR-100-100-G100

Engraver: Rawdon, Wright & Hatch. ***Comments:*** H-AR-5-G108. No description available. 18__. 1830s.

Rarity: *None known*

The Obsolete Bank Notes of Kentucky

State Banking in Kentucky

Currency of Kentucky

Dominating the field of note-issuing banks in Kentucky are institutions that operated various branches, commencing alphabetically with the Bank of Ashland, which operated from the late 1850s through the 1860s. It was established in the city of that name but also had branches in Mayfield and Shelbyville. The Peoples Bank of Kentucky, which was in business during the same period, commenced in Bowling Green, later moved the head bank to Louisville, and had branches in Hartford and Paducah.

The Bank of the Commonwealth of Kentucky, early in the game and active in the 1820s, was headquartered in Frankfort and had branches in Bowling Green, Falmouth, Flemingsburg, Greensburg, Harrodsburg, Hartford, Lexington, Louisville, Mount Sterling, Princeton, Somerset, and Winchester. The Farmers Bank of Kentucky, operating in the 1850s and 1860s, had its head office in Frankfort but also did business in Bardstown, Covington, George Town, Henderson, Maysville, Mount Sterling, Princeton, and Somerset.

Chartered in 1806 and also headquartered in Frankfort, the "first" (sometimes seen as the "Old") Bank of Kentucky operated branches in Bardstown, Danville, Glasgow, Hopkinsville, Lexington, Louisville, Paris, Richmond, Russellville, Shelbyville, Springfield, Washington, and Winchester. This bank was especially prominent in its time and was central to commerce in the early years of the state. In early 1816 a report stated that it had $1,308,129.47 worth of bills in circulation.[1]

The Northern Bank of Kentucky, headquartered in Lexington, also did business in Barbourville, Covington, Glasgow, Louisville, Paris, and Richmond. The Bank of Louisville operated from the 1830s to the 1860s and had branches in Burksville (known today as *Burkesville*), Flemingsburg, and Paducah. The "second" Bank of Kentucky, centered in Louisville, had branches in Bowling Green, Burksville, Columbus, Danville, Flemingsburg, Frankfort, Glasgow, Greensburg, Hopkinsville, Lexington, Maysville, Mount Sterling, and Paducah. The Commercial Bank of Kentucky, operating in Paducah in the 1850s and 1860s, had branches in Cynthiana, Harrodsburg, Lebanon, Louisville, Monticello, Newport, and Versailles. The Southern Bank of Kentucky, in Russellville, branched out to Bowling Green, Carrolton, Hickman, Lebanon, Louisville, Owensboro, and Smithland.

Early Banking

The above being said, the *first* bank in the state was established on December 16, 1802, under the name of the Kentucky Insurance Company. It was capitalized at $150,000 with authorization to issue paper money through a clause not studied carefully by the legislators. On December 27, 1806, the "first" Bank of Kentucky was chartered (as stated above), the earliest institution to be established with the word *Bank* as part of its name.

In 1817 there were 40 new banks incorporated in the state. This was at the onset of the difficult economic years of 1818 and 1819, and there were many bank failures. *Niles' Weekly Register*, the nationally read news and financial journal, observed this on October 9, 1819:

> Kentucky Litter: It is believed unsafe, even in Kentucky, to receive the notes of more than two or three of the independent banks. Many of them have forfeited their charters, and others are wisely preparing to wind up their affairs. It will require many years of industry and economy to repair the depredations which these institutions have caused in Kentucky—but the severe lesson received, may give future safety to the people. Experience is a dear school.

In the same year a man giving his name as Hunter (really a Mr. Morse, a graduate of Rhode Island College), was arrested in Savannah, Georgia, with $50 and $100 bills and post notes of the Newport Bank worth a face value of hundreds of thousands of dollars. By some devious method he had obtained these from Murray, Draper, Fairman & Co. in Philadelphia. Authorities dubbed him the "classical scoundrel" in view of his education.[2]

On January 26, 1818, many banks were simultaneously chartered, most with a capital of $100,000. These were generally referred to as independent banks. The charters for *all* of these were revoked effective May 1, 1820. Three of these chartered banks did not have the word *Bank* in their names, but all were governed under a lengthy set of rules. It seems that some never opened for business, and many others failed by the summer of 1819 and were liquidated after that time. A notice in the *Daily National Intelligencer*, Washington, D.C., of November 19, 1819, related that recently formed banks had issued paper money but were "dead" now in these locations: Barbourville, Burlington, Carlisle, Columbia, George Town, Glasgow, Greenville, Morgantown, Nicholasville, Petersburg, Russellville, Shelbyville, and Springfield. Banks in Burksville were "either dead or deserve to die." Banks in Port William, Sanders, and Richmond never opened. Bills of Campbell, Cynthiana, Bardstown, Elizabethtown, Flemingsburg, Frankfort, Harrodsburg, Hopkinsville (Christian Bank), Lexington (Farmers and Mechanics Bank), Maysville (Bank of Limestone), Millersburg, Mount Sterling, and Versailles were current, but for some there were "suspicious reports afloat." The Kentucky Exporting Company (which failed in 1820) may have been unique in that its bills were received by the Bank of the United States in 1819.

Over a period of time, many other banks and branches were established, with mixed results. Commerce was flooded with paper money. On May 25, 1828, an article in *Niles' Weekly Register* remarked on the progress in eliminating at least some worthless currency from commerce:

> In Kentucky the people of that state, relieved of the leeches, are returning to the good old fashion of paying their debts as fast as they can and, rapidly recovering from the demoralizing and ruinous effects of the miserable expedients resorted to obstruct the ordinary course of the laws—which lost to the state 100,000 inhabitants and many millions of wealth. Bills of the banks of Kentucky are now simple articles of trade, among men of business, like hemp or hogs—so much for so much; and every now and then large quantities are burned. There is nothing like fire to purify a currency.

The 1830s and Later

Notwithstanding such commentary, the amount of paper money in commerce continued to grow. In 1830 the banks in the state had $61,000,000 in bills, a figure which soared to $149,000,000 by 1837. The Panic of 1837, which started in a large way with the suspension of specie payments in Eastern cities on March 10, spread westward and soon involved the financial institutions of Kentucky. Bank notes were no longer redeemable at par in silver and gold coins, but only in exchange for other paper. Nearly all banks experienced difficulty, and many failed. It was not until June 15, 1842, that all solvent banks in the state were again redeeming bills with coins.

For a long time the "second" Bank of Kentucky had the Schuylkill Bank in Philadelphia as its stock-transfer agent. On July 30, 1839, the agent was changed to Nicholas Biddle's Bank of the United States of Pennsylvania, which was later to be recognized as a star-crossed venture. After the switch it was learned that the Schuylkill Bank had passed off $1,300,000 in phony stock certificates of the Bank of Kentucky. The matter was thrashed out in the courts for a long time, after which the Bank of Kentucky was awarded $1,343,000, but the victory was Pyrrhic, as the defendant had assets of only $45,000 at the time.

Bankers' Magazine reported this in July 1852:

> A few weeks ago the plates of the Bank of Kentucky were abstracted from the engraver's possession, and a large amount of their bills were issued fraudulently by parties who are not yet detected.

The same magazine told this in its issue of April 1855:

> One or two banks on a limited scale have been established in Kentucky [in recent times], with the privilege of issuing bills on a deposit of state stocks. These were located at Newport and Covington. Both failed in 1854, and the redemption of their bills is a matter of uncertainty.
>
> The chartered banks at the same time were abundantly strong in coin and in Eastern funds, and their paper circulated (as it has for twenty years or more) with perfect confidence among the people. The notes of the Newport Bank are selling at ten cents per dollar. The banks of that state, chartered many years since, have sustained themselves ever since their resumption in 1842. . . .

In November 1856 *Bankers' Magazine* told of the earlier days, back to 1852, then brought readers up to date:

> Since then, charters have been granted to the Farmers Bank, with $2,300,000 capital; the Commercial Bank, with $400,000; the Kentucky Trust Company, with an *unlimited* capital; and the Newport Safety Fund Bank, with $300,000 capital. Both of these institutions failed in 1854, and their notes are now selling at 50 percent discount, and the small notes of the latter bank at 90 percent.
>
> With the exception of the charters of these two last banks, the legislation of Kentucky has been of a fixed character, and her circulation has ever been esteemed in the Western states as of the highest character. There are now 34 banks and branches in the state, but aggregate of whose capital is $11,730,000, and circulation about $13,300,000. In the session of 1854, it was proposed to charter six new banks, with capitals amounting to $6,100,000; but the governor having vetoed one of the bills of incorporation, the bills all failed to pass, and there for the present the matter rests.

Numismatic Comments

All of the many bank branches in the Bluegrass State unfortunately do not translate into a great opportunity to buy hundreds of varieties of notes in the marketplace, for as a general rule bills are quite scarce, and for many there are no surviving examples. Among those that do survive, the names of branches are often added in ink, with the result that the designs of the notes issued by many branches are the same. The portrait of Henry Clay, Kentucky's most famous politician for much of the note-issuing era, is found on several notes. John J. Crittenden, also popular in politics for a long time, is also seen on various issues.

Beyond the dizzying array of branch banks, throughout different towns and cities there were also several single-office locations, many of which were active during the earlier years of the 19th century. A majority used bills printed by Murray, Draper, Fairman & Co. in Philadelphia. As many early institutions failed and their bills became worthless, their notes can be found without difficulty today, although the condition of these is apt to be low, mostly from Fair to Very Good, reflecting their intense use in circulation. There were only a few standalone banks (not affiliated with branches) in business in the later years of the bank-note–issuing period.

The release of long-hidden Proofs from the American Bank Note Co. paper archives in 1990 and 1991 was a boon to specialists, and many rarities and previously unknown bills became available. By now most of these Proofs are very widely dispersed.

The standard reference on Kentucky paper money is *Kentucky Obsolete Notes and Scrip*, by Earl Hughes and published in 1998. For any scholar of Kentucky's complex banking history, this is a great book to have.

Ashland, Kentucky

Ashland started out as Poage Landing and was settled by the Poage family from Virginia. They established farms on the Ohio River and set up a sawmill in 1799. The next year, Richard Deering discovered iron ore in his land. In 1815 he began to create iron farm and kitchen utensils. By 1818 the business had grown enough to establish Argillite Furnace—considered to be the inception of the iron industry in Kentucky.

Further furnaces were built, and iron tools and ore were shipped on the Ohio River to markets in Pittsburgh and Cincinnati, contributing to the wealth and fame of the area. It wasn't long before Poage's Landing became an industrial center, and in 1847 a post office was opened. In 1854 the town was incorporated and renamed Ashland in honor of Henry Clay's estate in Lexington. The same year the Kentucky Iron, Coal and Manufacturing Company was chartered, and the company hired Martin Toby Hilton to lay out the streets of the new town, which would be an improvement on the few businesses and residential homes along the Ohio River that made up the settlement.

The first baby to be born in Ashland was named Ashland Poage—a combination of the old and new towns.

Bank of Ashland

1856–1872

W-KY-010

History: The Bank of Ashland was chartered on February 15, 1856, with an authorized capital of $400,000, $100,000 of which had to be paid in before the bank could open for business. In 1857 the president of the bank was Hugh Means, and the cashier was E.W. Martin. The capital by 1863 was worth $300,000. Circulation was $562,074.

On April 2, 1861, the charter of the bank was amended to allow it to issue notes with denominations less than $5. The bank operated successfully for a time, and in 1872 it wound up its affairs and was succeeded by the Ashland National Bank.

The Bank of Ashland had branches located in Mayfield, W-KY-1010, and Shelbyville, W-KY-1420.

Numismatic Commentary: Genuine notes from this bank, both circulated and Proof, are seldom seen. Proofs from this bank with the colorful green overprint are even more uncommon.

Remaining at the American Bank Note Co. archives as of 2003 was a $10-$10-$10-$20 face plate, a $10-$10-$10-$20 tint plate, a $1-$1-$1-$1 face plate, a $1-$1-$1-$1 tint plate, a $5-$5-$5-$5 face plate, and a $5-$5-$5-$5 tint plate.

Valid Issues

$1 • W-KY-010-001-G010 HA

Tint: Green panel of microlettering outlining white ONE and dies outlining white 1s. ***Engraver:*** American Bank Note Co. ***Comments:*** H-KY-5-G2a, Hughes-1. 18__. 1860s.

Rarity: URS-3

VG $325; **Proof** $1,175

Selected auction price: Heritage Auctions, October 21, 2015, Lot 18315, Proof $1,175

$5 • W-KY-010-005-G020

Left: 5 / Soldier charging with bayonet. ***Center:*** Portrait of girl / Five men at work in iron foundry / Portrait of girl. ***Right:*** 5 / Female portrait. ***Tint:*** Yellow. ***Back:*** Machinery. ***Engraver:*** Toppan, Carpenter & Co. ***Comments:*** H-KY-5-G4a, Hughes-3. 18__. 1857.

Rarity: URS-3

VF $500

$10 • W-KY-010-010-G030 CC

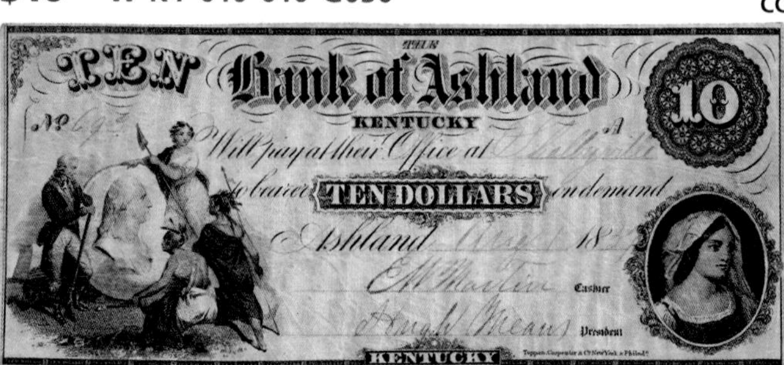

Tint: Yellow panel of microlettering outlining white TEN on white 10 outlined by lathework. ***Engraver:*** Toppan, Carpenter & Co. ***Comments:*** H-KY-5-G6a, Hughes-4. 18__. 1857.

Rarity: URS-4

G $100; **VG** $150; **F** $225

$20 • W-KY-010-020-G040 CC

Tint: Yellow lathework and panel of microlettering outlining white TWENTY. ***Engraver:*** Toppan, Carpenter & Co. ***Comments:*** H-KY-5-G8a, Hughes-6. 18__. 1857.

Rarity: URS-4
G $100; **F** $250

Non-Valid Issues

$1 • W-KY-010-001-C010

Tint: Green panel of microlettering outlining white ONE and dies outlining white 1s. ***Engraver:*** American Bank Note Co. ***Comments:*** H-KY-5-C2a, Hughes-2. Counterfeit of W-KY-010-001-G010. 18__. 1860s.

Rarity: URS-4
F $250

Augusta, Kentucky

Founded in 1786 by Philip Buckner, Augusta started as a trading post settled on the Ohio River. It was named after Augusta County, Virginia, and the area grew rapidly due to its prime riverside location. Upon the formation of Bracken County in 1796, Augusta became the seat. In 1839 the seat was transferred to Brooksville when the county courthouse was built there, due to its more central location. Augusta was incorporated as a city in 1850. Several schools were built, including the Augusta College, which provided education to the county until 1887.

Augusta Exporting Company

1818

W-KY-020

History: "A bank to be denominated the Augusta Exporting Company, to be established at the town of Augusta, in Bracken County," per the enabling text, was chartered on January 26, 1818. The authorized capital of $100,000 was divided into 1,000 shares of $100 par value each. Francis Well, James Armstrong, Nathaniel Patterson, and Arthur Thomas were appointed to take stock subscriptions. This was one of several official banks in Kentucky that did not have the word *Bank* in their names.

Numismatic Commentary: No notes with this imprint have been found.

Barbourville, Kentucky

In 1800 Barbourville was established as the county seat of Knox and was settled on the Cumberland River. Hilly country surrounding the town protected it from the most damaging storms, but the location made the city susceptible to flooding, which was sometimes disastrous.

Regardless of dangers and damages, Barbourville was the most populous and advanced city in the south of Kentucky. It became a stopping point for travelers crossing the Cumberland Gap. There was even a Barbourville Debating Society during the 1830s and 1840s which was able to influence the state government considerably, and through the society, many political careers were made. For that reason Barbourville bears the nickname "Home of Governors."

During the Civil War, the first armed battle in Kentucky occurred in Barbourville, and the first deaths for the state were experienced here on both sides. The town hosted both Confederate and Union troops in turn, with General Ulysses S. Grant using Barbourville as a rest stop while evaluating the Wilderness Road.

Bank of Barbourville

1818–1820

W-KY-030

History: The Bank of Barbourville (sometimes also seen as *Barboursville*) was chartered on January 26, 1818, with an authorized capital of $100,000 to be divided into 1,000 shares of $100 each. Joseph Eve, Richard Herndon, Richard Ballinger, Thomas Tuggle, William Hudson, and John Patton were appointed to take stock subscriptions. The bank operated only for a short time in the summer of 1819 and then stopped redeeming its notes. The charters of all independent banks authorized on January 26, 1818, were revoked effective May 1, 1820.

Numismatic Commentary: The short duration of this bank makes finding notes difficult.

Valid Issues

25¢ • W-KY-030-00.25-G010 CC

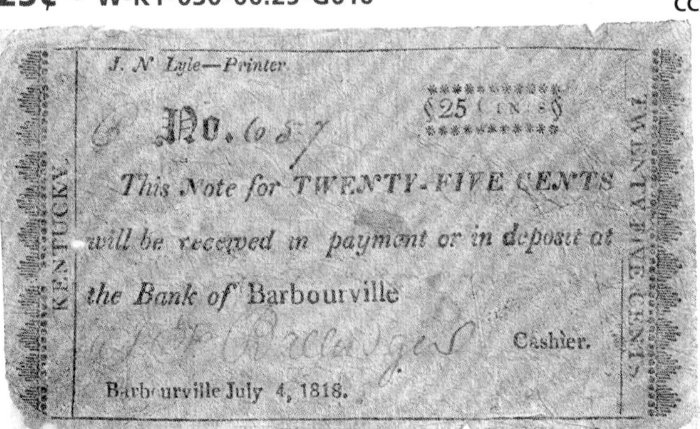

Comments: H-Unlisted, Hughes-Unlisted. July 4, 1818.

Rarity: URS-3
VG $250

$1 • **W-KY-030-001-G020**

Left: 1 / ONE DOLLAR / 1 vertically. ***Center:*** 1 / Woman standing beside plow / 1. ***Right:*** KENTUCKY vertically. ***Engraver:*** Murray, Draper, Fairman & Co. ***Comments:*** H-KY-15-G12, Hughes-8. 181_. 1810s.

Rarity: URS-3
VG $200; **F** $350

$2 • **W-KY-030-002-G030**

Left: 2 / TWO DOLLARS / 2 vertically. ***Center:*** II / Woman standing beside plow / 2. ***Right:*** KENTUCKY vertically. ***Engraver:*** Murray, Draper, Fairman & Co. ***Comments:*** H-Unlisted, Hughes-9. 181_. 1810s.

Rarity: URS-3
F $350

$3 • **W-KY-030-003-G040**

QDB

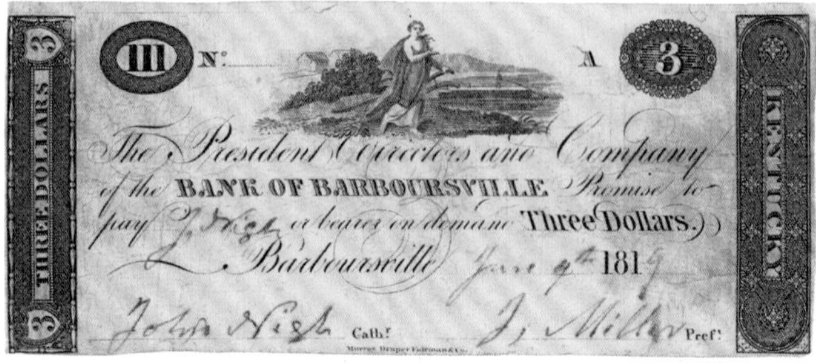

Engraver: Murray, Draper, Fairman & Co. ***Comments:*** H-KY-15-G16, Hughes-10. 181_. 1810s.

Rarity: URS-3
F $400; **EF** $600

$5 • **W-KY-030-005-G050**

QDB

Engraver: Murray, Draper, Fairman & Co. ***Comments:*** H-KY-15-G18, Hughes-11. 18__. 1810s.

Rarity: URS-3
VF $450; **EF** $600; **Unc-Rem** $600

$10 • **W-KY-030-010-G060**

CC

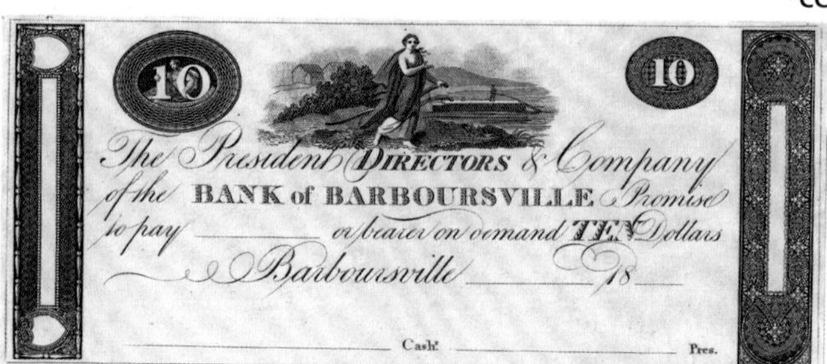

Engraver: Murray, Draper, Fairman & Co. ***Comments:*** H-KY-15-G20, Hughes-12. 181_. 1810s.

Rarity: URS-3
F $300; **Proof** $3,100

$20 • **W-KY-030-020-G070**

Left: 20 / TWENTY DOLLARS / 20 vertically. ***Center:*** 20 / Woman standing beside plow / 20. ***Right:*** KENTUCKY vertically. ***Engraver:*** Murray, Draper, Fairman & Co. ***Comments:*** H-Unlisted, Hughes-13. 181_. 1810s.

Rarity: URS-3
F $350

Northern Bank of Kentucky (branch)

1835–1860s

W-KY-040

History: The Northern Bank of Kentucky was chartered in 1835 with an authorized capital of $3,000,000. The Barbourville (sometimes also seen as *Barboursville*) branch had a capital of $100,000 in 1857. The president was George M. Adams, and the cashier was William McClanahan. Sometime during the 1860s the Northern Bank of Kentucky was converted to a bank of discount and deposit.

The Northern Bank of Kentucky had its parent bank located in Lexington, W-KY-830, and branch banks located in Covington, W-KY-260, Cynthiana, W-KY-305, Glasgow, W-KY-520, Louisville, W-KY-960, Paris, W-KY-1280, and Richmond, W-KY-1360.

Numismatic Commentary: Notes of this branch are scarce.

Valid Issues

$1 • **W-KY-040-001-G010**

CC

Engraver: Toppan, Carpenter, Casilear & Co. ***Comments:*** H-KY-175-G66, Hughes-433. 18__. 1850s.

Rarity: URS-4
F $300

$1 • **W-KY-040-001-G020**

Left: 1 / Portrait of boy. ***Center:*** Men with cattle, Sheep. ***Right:*** 1 / Portrait of girl. ***Tint:*** Red-orange. ***Engraver:*** American Bank Note Co. ***Comments:*** H-KY-175-G68, Hughes-436. 18__. 1850s.

Rarity: URS-4
VG $100; **F** $275

$5 • **W-KY-040-005-G030**

Left: 5 / Portrait of Henry Clay / 5. ***Center:*** 5 / Woman seated against bales, Cattle, Train / 5. ***Right:*** 5 / Portrait of George Washington / 5. ***Engraver:*** Toppan, Carpenter & Co. ***Comments:*** H-KY-175-G70, Hughes-Unlisted. 18__. 1850s.

Rarity: URS-1
F $600

$5 • W-KY-040-005-G040
Left: 5 / FIVE vertically. ***Center:*** Portrait of Henry Clay / Woman seated against bales, Cattle, Train / Male portrait. ***Right:*** 5 / FIVE vertically. ***Tint:*** Red-orange. ***Engraver:*** American Bank Note Co. ***Comments:*** H-KY-175-G72, Hughes-445. 18__. 1850s.
Rarity: URS-3
F $300

$10 • W-KY-040-010-G050
Left: Portrait of George Washington / 10. ***Center:*** Portrait of George Washington / Woman seated against bales, Cattle, Train / Portrait of Henry Clay. ***Right:*** 10 / Portrait of Daniel Webster. ***Engraver:*** Toppan, Carpenter, Casilear & Co. ***Comments:*** H-KY-175-G74, Hughes-450. 18__. 1850s.
Rarity: URS-3
F $300

$10 • W-KY-040-010-G060 CC

Engraver: Toppan, Carpenter, Casilear & Co. ***Comments:*** H-KY-175-G76, Hughes-452. 18__. 1850s.
Rarity: URS-3
F $300

$20 • W-KY-040-020-G070
Left: 20 / Portrait of George Washington / 20. ***Center:*** 20 / Woman seated against bales, Cattle, Train / 20. ***Right:*** 20 / Portrait of Henry Clay / 20. ***Engraver:*** Toppan, Carpenter & Co. ***Comments:*** H-KY-175-G78, Hughes-457. 18__. 1850s.
Rarity: URS-3
F $300

$20 • W-KY-040-020-G080
Left: 20 / 20. ***Center:*** Portrait of Henry Clay / Woman seated against bales, Cattle, Train / Male portrait. ***Right:*** 20 / 20. ***Tint:*** Red-orange. ***Engraver:*** American Bank Note Co. ***Comments:*** H-KY-175-G80, Hughes-458. 18__. 1850s.
Rarity: URS-3
VG $350

$50 • W-KY-040-050-G090
Left: 50 / Portrait of George Washington / 50. ***Center:*** 50 / Woman seated against bales, Cattle, Train. ***Right:*** 50 / Portrait of Henry Clay / 50. ***Engraver:*** Toppan, Carpenter & Co. ***Comments:*** H-KY-175-G82, Hughes-463. 18__. 1850s.
Rarity: URS-2
F $500

$50 • W-KY-040-050-G100
Left: 50 / 50. ***Center:*** Portrait of Henry Clay / Woman seated against bales, Cattle, Train. ***Right:*** 50 / Male portrait. ***Tint:*** Red-orange. ***Engraver:*** American Bank Note Co. ***Comments:*** H-KY-175-G84, Hughes-464. 18__. 1850s.
Rarity: URS-2
F $500

$100 • W-KY-040-100-G110
Left: 100 / Portrait of George Washington / 100. ***Center:*** Woman seated against bales, Cattle, Train / 100. ***Right:*** 100 / Portrait of Henry Clay / 100. ***Engraver:*** Toppan, Carpenter & Co. ***Comments:*** H-KY-175-G86, Hughes-466. 18__. 1850s.
Rarity: URS-2
F $600

$100 • W-KY-040-100-G120
Left: 100 / Portrait of Henry Clay / 100. ***Center:*** Woman seated against bales, Cattle, Train. ***Right:*** 100 / Male portrait / 100. ***Tint:*** Red-orange. ***Engraver:*** American Bank Note Co. ***Comments:*** H-KY-175-G88, Hughes-468. 18__. 1850s.
Rarity: URS-2
F $600

Non-Valid Issues

$1 • W-KY-040-001-C020 HA

Tint: Red-orange bank title and 1 / ONE / 1. ***Engraver:*** American Bank Note Co. ***Comments:*** H-Unlisted, Hughes-437. Counterfeit of W-KY-040-001-G020. 18__. 1850s.
Rarity: URS-4
VG $100; **F** $150

Bardstown, Kentucky

Bardstown was settled in 1780 and is considered to be the second-oldest city in Kentucky. It was dedicated as the county seat of Nelson in 1784 and established officially four years later in 1788. In 1838 it was incorporated.

Built in 1779, the Old Talbott Tavern of Bardstown has hosted many famous Americans, Daniel Boone, Abraham Lincoln, and Jesse James among them. The distillation of bourbon also became a large source of renown and commerce for the city, and due to this Bardstown is known as the "Bourbon Capital of the World."

Bank of Kentucky {1st} (branch)

1815–1822

W-KY-050

History: The Bank of Kentucky (sometimes seen later in print as the "Old" Bank of Kentucky) was incorporated on December 27, 1806, with an authorized capital of $1,000,000. Half of the capital was subscribed to by the state.

The Bardstown branch was opened in 1815. On January 21, 1822, the bank was ordered to start closing up its branches. This was to be completed by May 1, 1824. This act essentially shut down the bank. Curiously, all of the paperwork was not completed until the 1870s.

The first Bank of Kentucky had its parent bank located in Frankfort, W-KY-420, and branch banks located in Danville, W-KY-320, Glasgow, W-KY-500, Hopkinsville, W-KY-660, Lexington, W-KY-760, Louisville, W-KY-840, Paris, W-KY-1260, Richmond, W-KY-1350, Russellville, W-KY-1380, Shelbyville, W-KY-1430, Springfield, W-KY-1500, Washington, W-KY-1570, and Winchester, W-KY-1580.

Numismatic Commentary: Notes of this bank bearing the Bardstown location are almost unknown today.

Valid Issues

$1 • W-KY-050-001-G010

Comments: H-KY-110-G24, Hughes-Unlisted. No description available. 18__. 1815.

Rarity: *None known*

$1 • W-KY-050-001-G020

Left: BRANCH BANK vertically. ***Center:*** 1 / Running deer, plow, ax / 1. ***Right:*** 1 / ONE / 1 vertically. ***Engraver:*** Unverified, but likely Murray, Draper, Fairman & Co. ***Comments:*** H-KY-110-G26, Hughes-283. 18__. 1816.

Rarity: URS-3

F $300

$1 • W-KY-050-001-G030

Engraver: Murray, Draper, Fairman & Co. ***Comments:*** H-KY-110-G28, Hughes-Unlisted. No description available. 18__. 1821.

Rarity: *None known*

$5 • W-KY-050-005-G040

Engraver: Unverified, but likely W. Harrison. ***Comments:*** H-KY-110-G30, Hughes-Unlisted. No description available. 18__. 1810s.

Rarity: *None known*

$10 • W-KY-050-010-G050

Engraver: Unverified, but likely W. Harrison. ***Comments:*** H-KY-110-G32, Hughes-Unlisted. No description available. 18__. 1815.

Rarity: *None known*

$20 • W-KY-050-020-G060

Engraver: Unverified, but likely W. Harrison. ***Comments:*** H-KY-110-G34, Hughes-Unlisted. No description available. 18__. 1815–1817.

Rarity: *None known*

$50 • W-KY-050-050-G070

Engraver: Unverified, but likely W. Harrison. ***Comments:*** H-KY-110-G36, Hughes-Unlisted. No description available. 18__. 1815–1818.

Rarity: *None known*

$100 • W-KY-050-100-G080

Engraver: Unverified, but likely W. Harrison. ***Comments:*** H-KY-110-G38, Hughes-295. No description available. 18__. 1815–1818.

Rarity: *None known*

Post Notes

$__ • W-KY-050-__-G090

Left: POST NOTE vertically. ***Center:*** __ / Cherub riding leaping deer / __. ***Right:*** POST NOTE vertically. ***Engraver:*** Murray, Draper, Fairman & Co. ***Comments:*** H-KY-110-G40. 18__. 1810s.

Rarity: *None known*

Centre Bank of Kentucky

1818–1820

W-KY-060

History: The Centre Bank of Kentucky was chartered on January 26, 1818. The authorized capital of $200,000 was divided into 2,000 shares of $100 each. James Smiley, Martin H. Wickliff, Samuel T. Beall, Thomas Hite, Samuel McLean, Daniel S. Hawell, Thomas Q. Roberts, and Samuel Smiley Jr. were appointed to take stock subscriptions. The bank operated only for a short time. Its bills were current in 1819 but are believed to have become worthless in 1820. The charters of all independent banks authorized on January 26, 1818, were revoked effective May 1, 1820.

Numismatic Commentary: Three notes of this bank have been uncovered for collectors.

Valid Issues

$1 • W-KY-060-001-G010

Left: ONE / DOL. ***Center:*** 1 / Woman at plow / 1. ***Right:*** KENTUCKY vertically. ***Engraver:*** Murray, Draper, Fairman & Co. ***Comments:*** H-KY-20-G12, Hughes-14. 18__. 1810s.

Rarity: URS-1

Unc-Rem $400

$5 • W-KY-060-005-G020

Left: FIVE / DOL. ***Center:*** 5 / Woman at plow / 5. ***Right:*** KENTUCKY vertically. ***Engraver:*** Murray, Draper, Fairman & Co. ***Comments:*** H-KY-20-G14, Hughes-15. 18__. 1810s.

Rarity: *None known*

$10 • W-KY-060-010-G030

Left: TEN / DOL. ***Center:*** 10 / Woman at plow / 10. ***Right:*** KENTUCKY vertically. ***Engraver:*** Murray, Draper, Fairman & Co. ***Comments:*** H-KY-20-G16, Hughes-16. 18__. 1810s.

Rarity: *None known*

$20 • W-KY-060-020-G040 CC

Engraver: Murray, Draper, Fairman & Co. ***Comments:*** H-KY-20-G18, Hughes-17. 18__. 1810s.

Rarity: URS-2
VG $400; **F** $600

Farmers Bank of Kentucky (branch)

1850–1860s

W-KY-070

History: The Farmers Bank of Kentucky was chartered on February 15, 1850, with an authorized capital of $2,300,000. By September 1852 the bank had opened for business. On February 11, 1860, the charter for the bank was amended, allowing it to increase its capital. The branch located in Bardstown had a capital of $150,000. The bank wound down its business during the Civil War.

The Farmers Bank of Kentucky had its parent bank located in Frankfort, W-KY-450, and branch banks located in Covington, W-KY-240, George Town, W-KY-480, Henderson, W-KY-640, Maysville, W-KY-1050, Mount Sterling, W-KY-1130, Princeton, W-KY-1340, and Somerset, W-KY-1480.

Bowling Green, Kentucky

Robert and George Moore, along with Elijah Covington, came to the area in the 1790s, laid out tracts, and erected houses and homesteads in the area that would later become Bowling Green. On March 6, 1798, the town was officially incorporated.

Reports on the source of the town name vary, with some stating that it was named after the Bowling Green in New York City. Others state that the town was named after Bowling Green, Virginia. Some records list the town with various spellings, such as Bolin Green or Bowlingreen.

In 1810 Bowling Green supported a population of 154. Steamboats brought commerce and trade to the town, and canal locks and dams only enhanced this method of transportation. A mule-drawn railway connected the river and the courthouse in 1832. From that time the city experienced tremendous growth through the 1830s. The Louisville and Nashville Railroad was laid through Bowling Green in 1859, connecting the town with markets to the north and the south. Agriculture still remained a primary source of income.

Bowling Green attempted to remain neutral at the onset of the Civil War, but because of its prime location and assets, it became an immediate target for both sides. On September 18, 1861, the Confederate army occupied the city; in November 1861 Bowling Green was chosen to be the capital of the Confederate government in Kentucky.

The Confederate forces evacuated Bowling Green on February 14, 1862. In their wake they destroyed the bridges spanning the Barren River as well as the railroad-depot building and other key structures. Other raids disrupted the city for the rest of the war.

Bank of Kentucky {2nd} (branch)

1834–1866

W-KY-080

History: The second Bank of Kentucky (sometimes seen in print as the "New" Bank of Kentucky) was chartered in 1834 in order to assume the business of the first Bank of Kentucky, W-KY-420, which had recently closed. The capital of the bank was $5,000,000. The branch in Bowling Green was established in 1834. In 1848 the president was John H. Graham, and the cashier was Richard Curd. Capital was $175,000. By 1852 the officers had changed, and J. Hines was the president. In 1855 the cashier was Thomas C. Calvert, and the president was J.R. Underwood. In January 1866 almost all branches of the Bank of Kentucky were closed down, and the parent bank began winding up its business.

The second Bank of Kentucky had its parent bank located in Louisville, W-KY-850, and branch banks located in Burksville, W-KY-140, Columbus, W-KY-220, Danville, W-KY-330, Flemingsburg, W-KY-390, Frankfort, W-KY-430, Glasgow, W-KY-510, Greensburg, W-KY-540, Hopkinsville, W-KY-670, Lexington, W-KY-770, Maysville, W-KY-1020, Mount Sterling, W-KY-1100, and Paducah, W-KY-1220.

Numismatic Commentary: Contemporary counterfeits of this bank are sometimes seen, especially of the $1. Due to the scarcity of this branch bank's notes, these are also eagerly collected.

Collectors and Researchers:

If you have new information about any banks or notes listed in this volume, contact Whitman Publishing, Attn: Obsolete Paper Money, 3101 Clairmont Road, Suite G, Atlanta, GA 30329.

Valid Issues

$1 • W-KY-080-001-G010

CC

Engraver: Danforth, Bald & Co. ***Comments:*** H-KY-195-G48, Hughes-53. 18__. 1850s.

Rarity: URS-3
F $200; **Proof** $650

$5 • W-KY-080-005-G020

Left: FIVE / Liberty standing / V. ***Center:*** 5 / Horse / 5. ***Right:*** FIVE / Liberty standing / V. ***Engraver:*** Casilear, Durand, Burton & Evans. ***Comments:*** H-KY-195-G54, Hughes-55. 18__. 1830s–1840s.

Rarity: URS-3
F $300

$5 • W-KY-080-005-G030

Left: 5 / Portrait of Henry Clay / FIVE. ***Center:*** Portrait of John Q. Adams / Woman seated against bales, Train, Harvesting scene / Portrait of Thomas Jefferson. ***Right:*** 5 / Portrait of George Washington / FIVE. ***Engraver:*** Toppan, Carpenter & Co. ***Comments:*** H-KY-195-G58, Hughes-57. 18__. 1840s–1850s.

Rarity: URS-3
F $250

$10 • W-KY-080-010-G040

Left: 10 / Woman seated / X. ***Center:*** X / Three women seated / X. ***Right:*** 10 / Woman standing / X. ***Engraver:*** Casilear, Durand, Burton & Evans. ***Comments:*** H-KY-195-G62, Hughes-58. 18__. 1830s–1840s.

Rarity: URS-3
F $250

$10 • W-KY-080-010-G050

Left: 10 / Portrait of George Washington / 10. ***Center:*** Portrait of Andrew Jackson / Indian man and woman flanking shield bearing 10 surmounted by eagle / Portrait of Isaac Shelby. ***Right:*** 10 / Portrait of Henry Clay / 10. ***Engraver:*** Toppan, Carpenter & Co. ***Comments:*** H-KY-195-G66, Hughes-59. 18__. 1840s–1850s.

Rarity: URS-3
F $250

$20 • W-KY-080-020-G060

Left: 20 / Woman standing / 20. ***Center:*** XX / Woman seated with plow and bales, Cattle / XX. ***Right:*** 20 / Indian man standing / XX. ***Engraver:*** Casilear, Durand, Burton & Evans. ***Comments:*** H-KY-195-G70, Hughes-61. 18__. 1830s–1840s.

Rarity: URS-3
F $300

$20 • W-KY-080-020-G070

Left: Woman holding male portrait aloft / Male portrait. ***Center:*** 20 / Woman flying / 20. ***Right:*** Three women holding medallion head aloft. ***Engraver:*** Draper, Toppan & Co. ***Comments:*** H-KY-195-G72, Hughes-62. 18__. 1840s.

Rarity: URS-3
F $300

$20 • W-KY-080-020-G080

CC

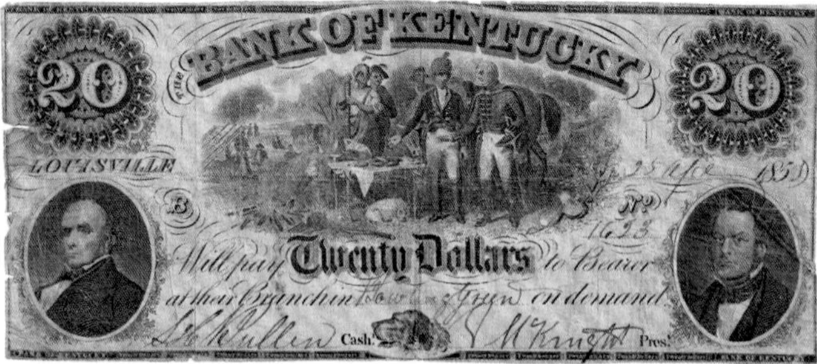

Engraver: Toppan, Carpenter & Co. ***Comments:*** H-KY-195-G74, Hughes-511. 185_. 1850s.

Rarity: URS-3
F $300

$50 • W-KY-080-050-G090

Left: Woman standing. ***Center:*** 50 / Steamboat *Henry Clay* / 50. ***Right:*** Woman standing. ***Engraver:*** Casilear, Durand, Burton & Evans. ***Comments:*** H-KY-195-G78, Hughes-66. 18__. 1830s–1840s.

Rarity: URS-2
F $400

Non-Valid Issues

$1 • W-KY-080-001-C010

HA

Engraver: Danforth, Bald & Co. ***Comments:*** H-Unlisted, Hughes-54. Counterfeit of W-KY-080-001-G010. August 15th, 1856.

Rarity: URS-4
EF $100

$5 • W-KY-080-005-C020

Engraver: Casilear, Durand, Burton & Evans. ***Comments:*** H-KY-195-C54, Hughes-56. Counterfeit of W-KY-080-005-G020. 18__. 1830s–1840s.

Rarity: URS-4
EF $100

$10 • W-KY-080-010-C050

Engraver: Toppan, Carpenter & Co. ***Comments:*** H-KY-195-C66, Hughes-60. Counterfeit of W-KY-080-010-G050. 18__. 1840s–1850s.

Rarity: URS-4
EF $100

$20 • **W-KY-080-020-C070**

Engraver: Draper, Toppan & Co. ***Comments:*** H-KY-195-C72, Hughes-509. Counterfeit of W-KY-080-020-G070. 18__. 1840s.

Rarity: URS-4
EF $100

$20 • **W-KY-080-020-C080**

Engraver: Toppan, Carpenter & Co. ***Comments:*** H-KY-195-C74, Hughes-512. Counterfeit of W-KY-080-020-G080. 18__. 1850s.

Rarity: URS-4
EF $100

Bank of the Commonwealth of Kentucky (branch)

1820–1830

W-KY-090

History: The Bank of the Commonwealth of Kentucky was chartered on November 29, 1820, with an authorized capital of $2,000,000. The local name for the bank was the "Peoples Bank," as it was chartered for the purpose of bringing relief to the population in a time of economic uncertainty. The later Peoples Bank, W-KY-100, in the same city had no connection. On December 22, 1820, an act was passed authorizing the bank to issue $3,000,000 in bills. The establishment of the Bank of the Commonwealth of Kentucky inadvertently caused the failure of the first Bank of Kentucky, W-KY-420.

In 1830 the bank lost its authorization to loan money, and it was instructed to close up its branches. Around that time the bank ceased new business, but the winding up of its affairs took until 1855.

The Bank of the Commonwealth of Kentucky had its parent bank located in Frankfort, W-KY-440, and branch banks located in Falmouth, W-KY-360, Flemingsburg, W-KY-410, Greensburg, W-KY-550, Harrodsburg, W-KY-580, Hartford, W-KY-610, Lexington, W-KY-780, Louisville, W-KY-870, Mount Sterling, W-KY-1120, Princeton, W-KY-1330, Somerset, W-KY-1470, and Winchester, W-KY-1590.

Numismatic Commentary: Almost all notes from this bank and its branches are unknown today.

Valid Issues

6-1/4¢ • **W-KY-090-00.06.25-G010**

Left: 6-1/4 CENTS. ***Center:*** 6-1/4 / 6-1/4 on die / 6-1/4. ***Right:*** KENTUCKY vertically. ***Comments:*** H-KY-95-G26, Hughes-Unlisted. 1822.

Rarity: URS-1
F $300

12-1/2¢ • **W-KY-090-00.12.50-G020**

Left: 12-1/2 CENTS. ***Center:*** 12-1/2 / 12-1/2 on die / 12-1/2. ***Right:*** KENTUCKY vertically. ***Comments:*** H-KY-95-G28, Hughes-239. 1822.

Rarity: URS-1
F $300

25¢ • **W-KY-090-00.25-G030**

Left: 25 CENTS. ***Center:*** 25 / 25 on die / 25. ***Right:*** KENTUCKY vertically. ***Comments:*** H-KY-95-G30, Hughes-239. 1822.

Rarity: URS-1
F $300

50¢ • **W-KY-090-00.50-G040**

Left: 50 CENTS. ***Center:*** 50 / 50 on die / 50. ***Right:*** KENTUCKY vertically. ***Comments:*** H-KY-95-G32, Hughes-241. 1822.

Rarity: URS-1
F $300

75¢ • **W-KY-090-00.75-G045**

Comments: H-Unlisted, Hughes-242. No description available. 1822.

Rarity: *None known*

$1 • **W-KY-090-001-G050**

Left: KENTUCKY vertically. ***Center:*** 1 / 1. ***Right:*** CAMPBELL COUNTY vertically. ***Engraver:*** Murray, Draper, Fairman & Co. ***Comments:*** H-KY-95-G36, Hughes-241. 18__. 1820s.

Rarity: URS-2
F $400

$1 • **W-KY-090-001-G060** HA

Comments: H-Unlisted, Hughes-243. 182_. 1820s.

Rarity: URS-3
VF $600

$3 • **W-KY-090-003-G070**

Left: KENTUCKY vertically. ***Center:*** 3 / 3. ***Right:*** CAMPBELL COUNTY vertically. ***Engraver:*** Murray, Draper, Fairman & Co. ***Comments:*** H-KY-95-G38, Hughes-242. 18__. 1820s.

Rarity: *None known*

$5 • **W-KY-090-005-G080**

Left: Woman holding staff. ***Center:*** 5 / Minerva standing with owl, shield, staff / 5. ***Right:*** Woman holding staff. ***Engraver:*** Murray, Draper, Fairman & Co. ***Comments:*** H-KY-95-G40, Hughes-243. 18__. 1820s.

Rarity: *None known*

$10 • **W-KY-090-010-G090**

Left: Woman holding staff. ***Center:*** 10 / Woman standing with staff, shield, Four cherubs / 10. ***Right:*** Woman holding staff. ***Engraver:*** Murray, Draper, Fairman & Co. ***Comments:*** H-KY-95-G42, Hughes-244. 18__. 1820s.

Rarity: *None known*

$20 • **W-KY-090-020-G100**

Engraver: Murray, Draper, Fairman & Co. ***Comments:*** H-KY-95-G44, Hughes-245. No description available. 18__. 1820s.

Rarity: *None known*

$50 • **W-KY-090-050-G110**

Engraver: Murray, Draper, Fairman & Co. ***Comments:*** H-KY-95-G46, Hughes-246. No description available. 18__. 1820s.

Rarity: *None known*

$100 • **W-KY-090-100-G120**

Engraver: Murray, Draper, Fairman & Co. ***Comments:*** H-KY-95-G48, Hughes-247. No description available. 18__. 1820s.

Rarity: *None known*

Peoples Bank of Kentucky

1856–1860s

W-KY-100

History: The Peoples Bank of Kentucky was chartered on February 15, 1856, with an authorized capital of $250,000. In 1861 the capital dropped to $168,000. A.G. Hobson was the cashier, and B.C. Brider was the president. In 1863 the capital was back at its full amount, and circulation was worth $322,887.

Later the bank moved to Louisville, W-KY-970, and the old location at Bowling Green became a branch, W-KY-110. The bank closed up sometime in the 1860s.

The Peoples Bank of Kentucky had branch banks located in Bowling Green, W-KY-110, Hartford, W-KY-620, and Paducah, W-KY-970.

Numismatic Commentary: Many notes of this bank have vivid red tints. With both a parent and a branch bank located in the town of Bowling Green, collectors have twice the opportunity to discover rare and interesting notes.

Valid Issues

$1 • **W-KY-100-001-G010**

Left: 1 / Man with hat seated. ***Center:*** Two men with barrels. ***Right:*** 1 / 1. ***Engraver:*** Danforth, Wright & Co. ***Comments:*** H-KY-25-G2, Hughes-70. 18__. 1850s.

Rarity: URS-3

F $300; **Proof** $750

$2 • **W-KY-100-002-G020**

Left: 2 / Female portrait. ***Center:*** Woman seated in 2. ***Right:*** 2 / Two girls. ***Engraver:*** Danforth, Wright & Co. ***Comments:*** H-KY-25-G4, Hughes-72. 18__. 1850s.

Rarity: URS-3

F $300

$3 • **W-KY-100-003-G030**

Left: THREE / Female portrait / THREE. ***Center:*** Woman seated with plow and sheaf. ***Right:*** 3 / Female portrait. ***Engraver:*** Danforth, Wright & Co. ***Comments:*** H-KY-25-G6, Hughes-74. 18__. 1850s.

Rarity: URS-3

F $300

$5 • **W-KY-100-005-G040**

Left: 5 / V. ***Center:*** Men with horses, cattle, and sheep. ***Right:*** 5 / Female portrait. ***Engraver:*** Danforth, Wright & Co. ***Comments:*** H-KY-25-G8, Hughes-76. 18__. 1850s.

Rarity: URS-3

F $300

$10 • **W-KY-100-010-G050**

Left: X / Female portrait. ***Center:*** Woman seated in 10 draped with flowers. ***Right:*** 10 / Farmer plowing with horses. ***Engraver:*** Danforth, Wright & Co. ***Comments:*** H-KY-25-G10. 18__. 1850s.

Rarity: URS-2

F $300

$20 • **W-KY-100-020-G060**

Left: 20 / Girl with dove. ***Center:*** Woman reclining with eagle. ***Right:*** 20 / Portrait of Henry Clay. ***Engraver:*** Danforth, Wright & Co. ***Comments:*** H-KY-25-G12, Hughes-79. 18__. 1850s.

Rarity: URS-3

F $300

Notes on Which the Place Payable is Blank

$1 • **W-KY-100-001-G070** SBG

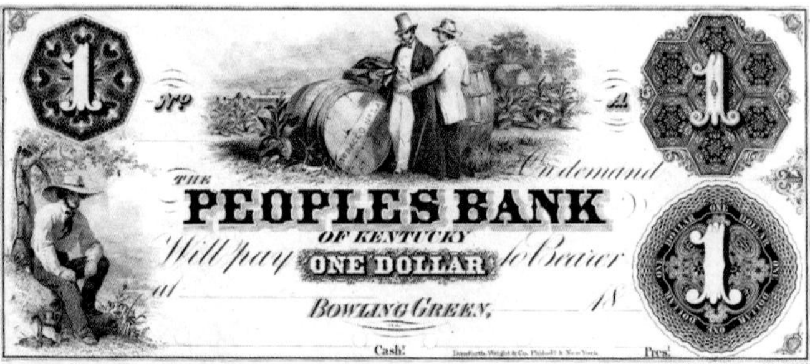

Engraver: Danforth, Wright & Co. ***Comments:*** H-KY-25-G32, Hughes-70. 18__. 1850s.

Rarity: URS-3

Proof $750

$1 • **W-KY-100-001-G070a** CC, CC

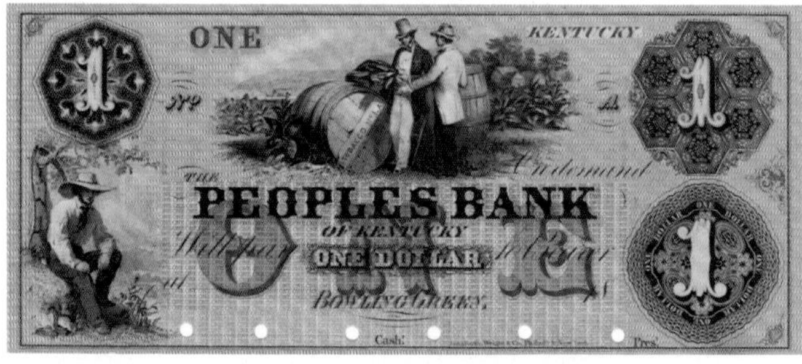

Tint: Red-orange. ***Back:*** Red-orange. ***Engraver:*** Danforth, Wright & Co. ***Comments:*** H-KY-25-G32a. Similar to W-KY-100-001-G070. 18__. 1850s.

Rarity: URS-2

F $500; **Proof** $3,200

Selected auction price: Stack's Bowers Galleries, March 2015, Proof $3,200

$2 • W-KY-100-002-G080

Left: 2 / Female portrait. ***Center:*** Woman seated in 2. ***Right:*** 2 / Two girls. ***Engraver:*** Danforth, Wright & Co. ***Comments:*** H-KY-25-G34, Hughes-72. 18__. 1850s.

Rarity: URS-3
F $300

$2 • W-KY-100-002-G080a

SBG, SBG

Tint: Red-orange. ***Back:*** Red-orange. ***Engraver:*** Danforth, Wright & Co. ***Comments:*** H-KY-25-G34a. Similar to W-KY-100-002-G080. 18__. 1850s.

Rarity: URS-2
F $600; **Proof** $2,500

$3 • W-KY-100-003-G090

Left: THREE / Female portrait / THREE. ***Center:*** Woman seated with plow and sheaf. ***Right:*** 3 / Female portrait. ***Engraver:*** Danforth, Wright & Co. ***Comments:*** H-KY-25-G36, Hughes-74. 18__. 1850s.

Rarity: URS-2
F $575

$3 • W-KY-100-003-G090a

SBG, SBG

Tint: Red-orange. ***Back:*** Red-orange. ***Engraver:*** Danforth, Wright & Co. ***Comments:*** H-KY-25-G36a. Similar to W-KY-100-003-G090. 18__. 1850s.

Rarity: URS-2
Proof $2,500

$5 • W-KY-100-005-G100

CC

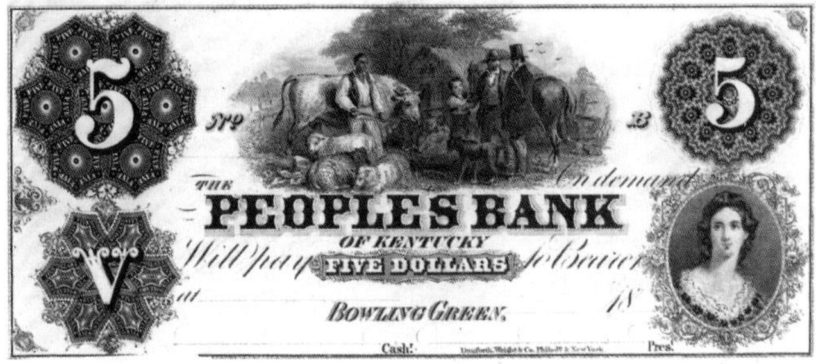

Engraver: Danforth, Wright & Co. ***Comments:*** H-KY-25-G38, Hughes-76. 18__. 1850s.

Rarity: URS-2
F $350; **Proof** $900

How to Read the Whitman Numbering System

$1 • W-AL-020-001-G010a

Denomination: Face value of the note shown.

W: Whitman number. This number is a sortable code unique to each bank and note.

AL: Abbreviation for the state under study.

020: Numerical designation specific to each bank.

001: The denomination in dollars.

G010a: G indicates a good or valid note. Other categories are indicated thus: C (counterfeit); R (raised); S (spurious); N (not-attributed); A (altered). Numbers are assigned starting with 010, 020, et seq. Terminal letters following the number indicate variations of a note: a series of different colored overprints, tints, payees, etc., all on the same design of note. For more information, see the "How to Use This Book" section at the front of the volume, page xiv.

$5 • W-KY-100-005-G100a

HA

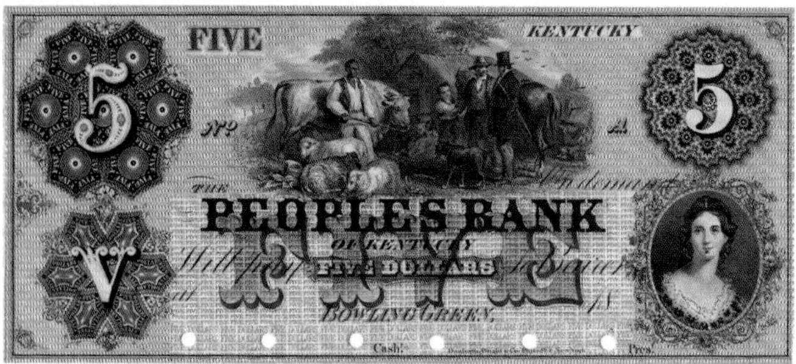

Tint: Red-orange. ***Back:*** Red-orange. ***Engraver:*** Danforth, Wright & Co. ***Comments:*** H-KY-25-G38a. Similar to W-KY-100-005-G100. 18__. 1850s.

Rarity: URS-2
Proof $2,500

$10 • W-KY-100-010-G110

Left: X / Female portrait. ***Center:*** Woman seated in 10 draped with flowers. ***Right:*** 10 / Farmer plowing with horses. ***Engraver:*** Danforth, Wright & Co. ***Comments:*** H-KY-25-G40. 18__. 1850s.

Rarity: URS-2
F $350

$10 • W-KY-100-010-G110a

SBG, SBG

Tint: Red-orange. ***Back:*** Red-orange. ***Engraver:*** Danforth, Wright & Co. ***Comments:*** H-KY-25-G40a. Similar to W-KY-100-010-G110. 18__. 1850s.

Rarity: URS-2
Proof $2,500

$20 • W-KY-100-020-G120

Left: 20 / Girl with dove. ***Center:*** Woman reclining with eagle. ***Right:*** 20 / Portrait of Henry Clay. ***Engraver:*** Danforth, Wright & Co. ***Comments:*** H-KY-25-G42, Hughes-79. 18__. 1850s.

Rarity: URS-3
F $300

$20 • W-KY-100-020-G120a

Tint: Red-orange. ***Back:*** Red-orange. ***Engraver:*** Danforth, Wright & Co. ***Comments:*** H-KY-25-G42a. Similar to W-KY-100-020-G120. 18__. 1850s.

Rarity: URS-2
VG $400

Peoples Bank of Kentucky (branch)

1860s

W-KY-110

History: The Peoples Bank of Kentucky was chartered on February 15, 1856, with an authorized capital of $250,000. Later the bank moved to Louisville, W-KY-970, and the old parent location at Bowling Green, W-KY-100, became a branch. The bank closed up sometime in the 1860s.

The Peoples Bank of Kentucky had its parent banks located first in Bowling Green, W-KY-100, then in Louisville, W-KY-970, and branch banks located in Hartford, W-KY-620, and Paducah, W-KY-1250.

Valid Issues

$3 • W-KY-110-003-G010

HA

Tint: Red-orange. ***Back:*** Red-orange. ***Engraver:*** Danforth, Wright & Co. ***Comments:*** H-Unlisted, Hughes-75. 18__. 1860s.

Rarity: URS-3
VF $200

$10 • W-KY-110-010-G020

HA

Tint: Red-orange. ***Back:*** Red-orange. ***Engraver:*** Danforth, Wright & Co. ***Comments:*** H-Unlisted, Hughes-78. 18__. 1860s.

Rarity: URS-3
VF $800

$20 • W-KY-110-020-G030 CC, SBG

Tint: Red-orange. ***Back:*** Red-orange. ***Engraver:*** Danforth, Wright & Co. ***Comments:*** H-Unlisted, Hughes-Unlisted. 18__. 1850s.

Rarity: URS-2

F $1,500

Southern Bank of Kentucky
1818–1820
W-KY-120

History: The Southern Bank of Kentucky was chartered on January 26, 1818, with an authorized capital of $300,000 to be divided into 3,000 shares of $100 apiece. Elijah M. Covington, Alexander Graham, Samuel I. McDowell, William R. Payne, John W. Powell, John Hines, James M. Blakey, and John Loving were appointed to take stock subscriptions. The bank operated only for a short time in the summer of 1819 before it stopped redeeming its notes. The charters of all independent banks authorized on January 26, 1818, were revoked effective May 1, 1820.

There was an unrelated Southern Bank of Kentucky, W-KY-130, in the same city at a later date.

Numismatic Commentary: The brief lifespan of this bank makes finding notes difficult.

Valid Issues

$1 • W-KY-120-001-G010 HA

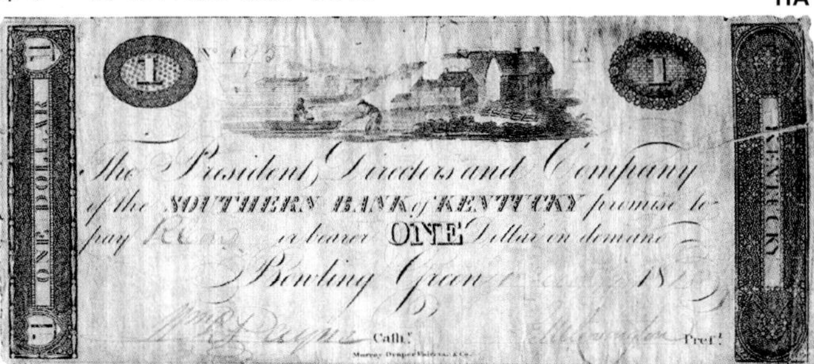

Engraver: Murray, Draper, Fairman & Co. ***Comments:*** H-KY-30-G12, Hughes-81. 18__. 1810s.

Rarity: URS-3

F $600; **Proof** $900

$2 • W-KY-120-002-G020 CC

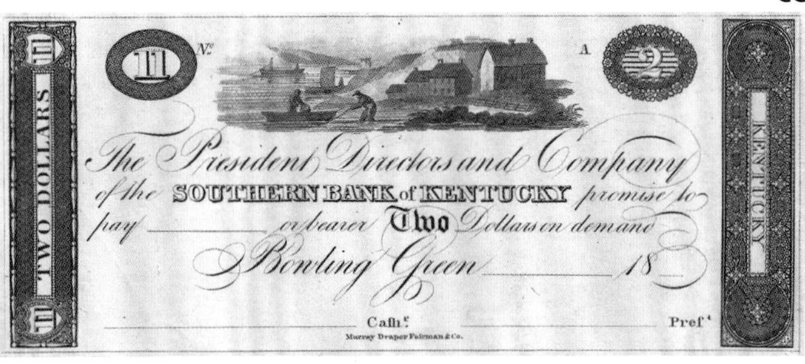

Engraver: Murray, Draper, Fairman & Co. ***Comments:*** H-Unlisted, Hughes-82. 18__. 1810s.

Rarity: URS-3

F $300; **Proof** $750

$5 • W-KY-120-005-G030 CC

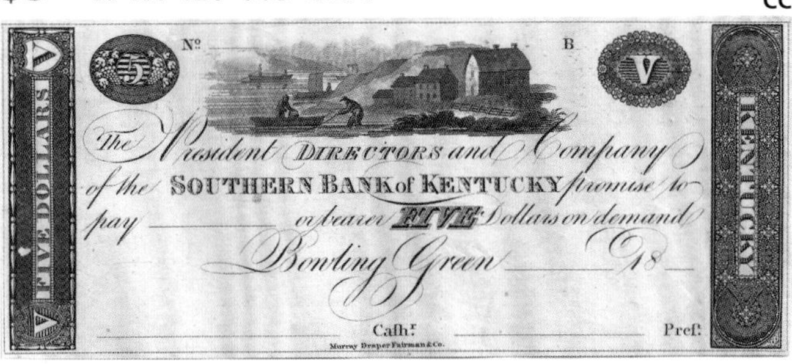

Engraver: Murray, Draper, Fairman & Co. ***Comments:*** H-KY-30-G18, Hughes-83. 18__. 1810s.

Rarity: URS-3

F $300; **Proof** $750

$10 • W-KY-120-010-G040 CC

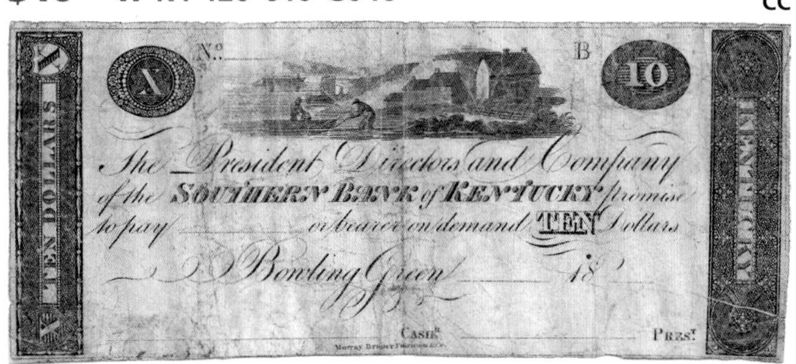

Engraver: Murray, Draper, Fairman & Co. ***Comments:*** H-KY-30-G20, Hughes-84. 18__. 1810s.

Rarity: URS-3

F $350

$20 • **W-KY-120-020-G050** CC

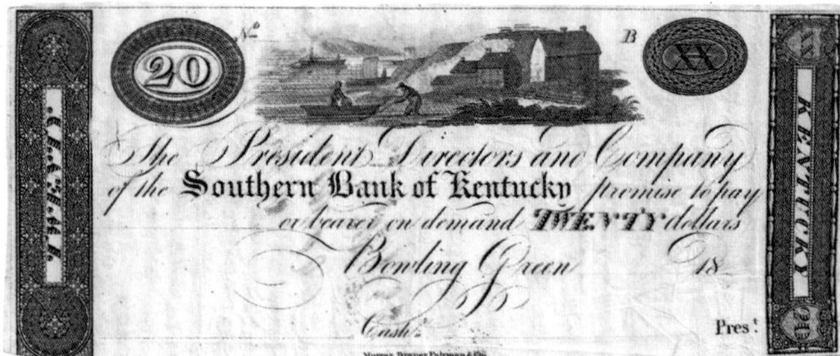

Engraver: Murray, Draper, Fairman & Co. ***Comments:*** H-KY-30-G22, Hughes-85. 18__. 1810s.

Rarity: URS-3
F $675

$50 • **W-KY-120-050-G060** CC

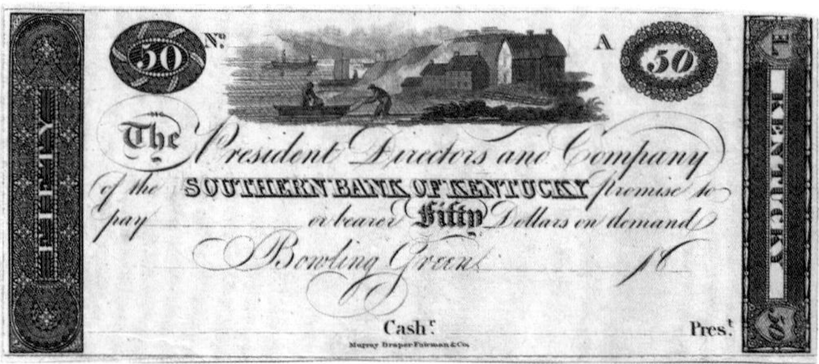

Engraver: Murray, Draper, Fairman & Co. ***Comments:*** H-KY-30-G24, Hughes-86. 18__. 1810s.

Rarity: URS-2
F $500; **Proof** $1,500

$100 • **W-KY-120-100-G070** CC

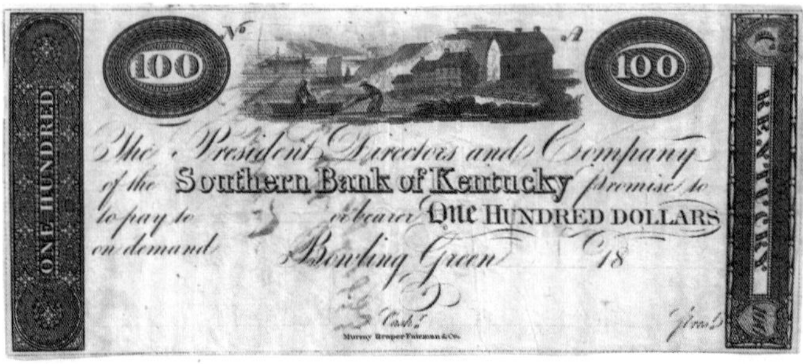

Engraver: Murray, Draper, Fairman & Co. ***Comments:*** H-Unlisted, Hughes-Unlisted. 18__. 1810s.

Rarity: URS-2
F $500; **Proof** $1,700

Southern Bank of Kentucky (branch)
1839–1865
W-KY-130

History: On February 20, 1839, the Southern Bank of Kentucky was chartered with an authorized capital of $2,000,000, of which the state subscribed to half. On February 15, 1850, the charter was extended to last until 1880.

By 1865 the bank had been put into liquidation. On March 4, 1865, an act was passed ordering the treatment of the bank's bills to be as promissory notes rather than as currency. On January 8, 1867, the bank issued its last report regarding the closing up of its affairs. The bank building was later occupied by Nimrod, Long & Co.

There was an unrelated Southern Bank of Kentucky, W-KY-120, in the same city at an earlier date.

The Southern Bank of Kentucky had its parent bank located in Russellville, W-KY-1400, and branch banks located in Carrollton, W-KY-200, Hickman, W-KY-650, Lebanon, W-KY-740, Louisville, W-KY-1000, Owensboro, W-KY-1200, and Smithland, W-KY-1460.

Numismatic Commentary: No notes with this imprint have been found.

Burksville, Kentucky

Burksville (known today as *Burkesville*) was settled before 1768, when the Iroquois Indians sold the land to the United States. It was first known as Cumberland Crossing, but in 1846 it was incorporated and renamed Burksville in honor of Isham Burk.

Burksville was a prime target for both Confederate and Union troops during the war. The Cumberland River split the opposing armies, and skirmishes occurred up and down the countryside. The Burksville courthouse was burned late in the war.

Bank of Kentucky {2nd} (branch)
1834–1866
W-KY-140

History: The second Bank of Kentucky (sometimes seen in print as the "New" Bank of Kentucky) was chartered in 1834 in order to assume the business of the first Bank of Kentucky, W-KY-420, which had recently closed. The capital of the bank was $5,000,000.

The branch in Burksville was established in 1834. In January 1866 almost all branches of the Bank of Kentucky were closed down, and the parent bank began winding up its business.

The second Bank of Kentucky had its parent bank located in Louisville, W-KY-850, and branch banks located in Bowling Green, W-KY-080, Columbus, W-KY-220, Danville, W-KY-330, Flemingsburg, W-KY-390, Frankfort, W-KY-430, Glasgow, W-KY-510, Greensburg, W-KY-540, Hopkinsville, W-KY-670, Lexington, W-KY-770, Maysville, W-KY-1020, Mount Sterling, W-KY-1100, and Paducah, W-KY-1220.

Numismatic Commentary: Notes of this bank and its branches are very rare.

Valid Issues

$5 • **W-KY-140-005-G010**

Left: 5 / Portrait of Henry Clay / FIVE. ***Center:*** Portrait of John Q. Adams / Woman seated against bales, Train, Harvesting scene / Portrait of Thomas Jefferson. ***Right:*** 5 / Portrait of George Washington / FIVE. ***Engraver:*** Toppan, Carpenter & Co. ***Comments:*** H-KY-195-G90, Hughes-494. 185_. 1850s.

Rarity: URS-3
F $400

$10 • W-KY-140-010-G020

Left: 10 / Portrait of George Washington / 10. ***Center:*** Portrait of Andrew Jackson / Indian man and woman flanking shield bearing 10 surmounted by eagle / Portrait of Isaac Shelby. ***Right:*** 10 / Portrait of Henry Clay / 10. ***Engraver:*** Toppan, Carpenter & Co. ***Comments:*** H-KY-195-G94, Hughes-499. 185_. 1850s.

Rarity: URS-3
F $400

$20 • W-KY-140-020-G030

Left: 20 / Portrait of Daniel Webster. ***Center:*** "General Marion's Sweet Potato Dinner." ***Right:*** 20 / Male portrait. ***Engraver:*** Toppan, Carpenter & Co. ***Comments:*** H-KY-195-G98, Hughes-511. 185_. 1850s.

Rarity: URS-3
F $450

Non-Valid Issues

$10 • W-KY-140-010-C020

Engraver: Toppan, Carpenter & Co. ***Comments:*** H-KY-195-C94, Hughes-501. Counterfeit of W-KY-140-010-G020. 185_. 1850s.

Rarity: URS-4
F $200

Bank of Louisville (branch)

1858–1860s

W-KY-150

History: In 1833 the Bank of Louisville was chartered with an authorized capital of $5,000,000. The branch located in Burksville (known today as *Burkesville*) was authorized in 1858. In 1863 the capital was $150,000. W.F. Owsley was the cashier, and F.W. Alexander was the president.

During the 1860s the Bank of Louisville closed its doors. Later it was absorbed by the Southern National Bank in 1899.

The Bank of Louisville had its parent bank located in Louisville, W-KY-860, and branch banks located in Flemingsburg, W-KY-400, and Paducah, W-KY-1230.

Numismatic Commentary: Contemporary counterfeits of the $10 note of this bank are known and collected from this rare bank.

Valid Issues

$5 • W-KY-150-005-G010

Left: 5 / V. ***Center:*** 5 / Woman, boy, and girl / 5. ***Right:*** 5 / V. ***Tint:*** Yellow. ***Engraver:*** American Bank Note Co. ***Comments:*** H-KY-190-G40, Hughes-536. 18__. 1850s–1860s.

Rarity: URS-3
EF $300

$10 • W-KY-150-010-G020

CC

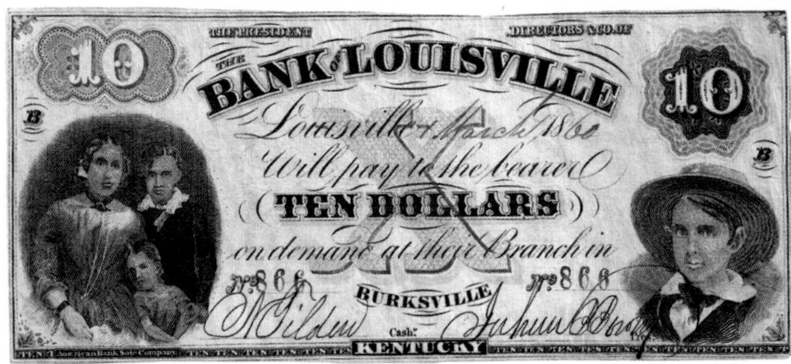

Tint: Red-orange X, die outlining white 10, and die bearing white 10. ***Engraver:*** American Bank Note Co. ***Comments:*** H-KY-190-G44, Hughes-542. 18__. 1850s–1860s.

Rarity: URS-3
F $350

Non-Valid Issues

$10 • W-KY-150-010-C020

HA

Tint: Red-orange X, die outlining white 10, and die bearing white 10. ***Engraver:*** American Bank Note Co. ***Comments:*** H-KY-190-C44, Hughes-543. Counterfeit of W-KY-150-010-G020. 18__. 1860.

Rarity: URS-3
F $150; **VF** $220

Cumberland Bank of Burksville

1818–1820

W-KY-160

History: The Cumberland Bank of Burksville (known today as *Burkesville*) was incorporated on January 26, 1818. The authorized capital of $100,000 was divided into 1,000 shares of $100 par value each. Peter Simmerman, James W. Taylor, William Smith, John M. Alexander, Isaac Taylor, John M. Emerson, and Joseph Alexander were appointed to take stock subscriptions. The bank operated only for a short time. In the summer of 1819 it was reported as being in precarious condition. The charters of all independent banks authorized on January 26, 1818, were revoked effective May 1, 1820.

Numismatic Commentary: The $10 note of this bank is the rarest and most coveted of the series. Due to the brief period of time the bank was in operation, all notes are considered to be scarce.

Valid Issues

$1 • W-KY-160-001-G010

CC

Engraver: Murray, Draper, Fairman & Co. ***Comments:*** H-KY-35-G12, Hughes-90. 18__. 1810s.

Rarity: URS-3
VG $200; **F** $350

$3 • W-KY-160-003-G020

CC

Engraver: Murray, Draper, Fairman & Co. ***Comments:*** H-KY-35-G16, Hughes-91. 18__. 1810s.

Rarity: URS-3
VF $450

$5 • W-KY-160-005-G030

Left: FIVE vertically. ***Center:*** River scene, Two men pushing barrels. ***Right:*** KENTUCKY vertically. ***Engraver:*** Murray, Draper, Fairman & Co. ***Comments:*** H-KY-35-G18, Hughes-92. 18__. 1810s.

Rarity: URS-3
F $300

$10 • W-KY-160-010-G040

HA

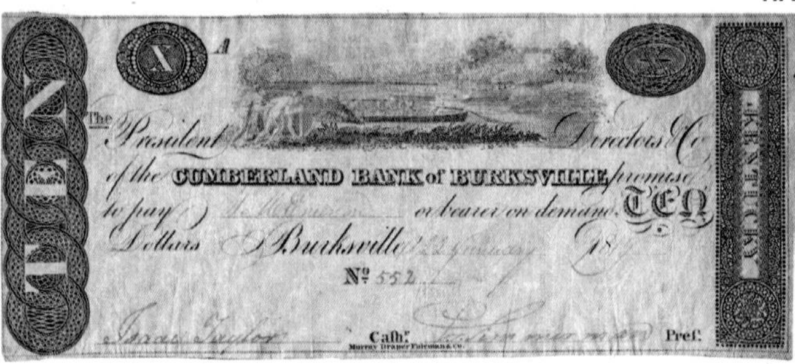

Engraver: Murray, Draper, Fairman & Co. ***Comments:*** H-KY-35-G20, Hughes-93. 18__. 1810s.

Rarity: URS-2
VF $350

$20 • W-KY-160-020-G050

CC

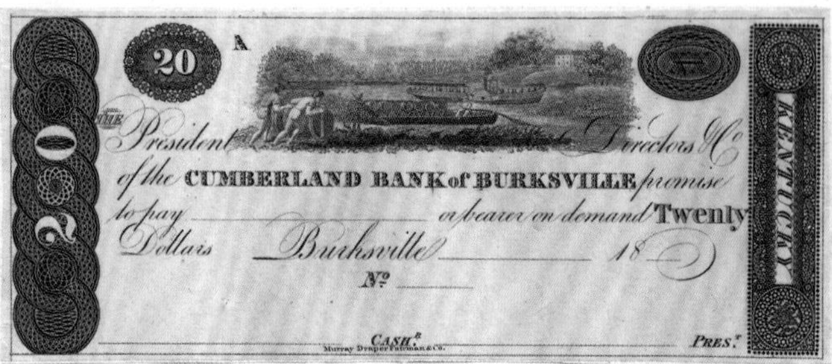

Engraver: Murray, Draper, Fairman & Co. ***Comments:*** H-KY-35-G22, Hughes-94. 18__. 1810s.

Rarity: URS-3
F $300; **Proof** $1,500

$50 • W-KY-160-050-G060

Left: 50 vertically. ***Center:*** River scene, Two men pushing barrels. ***Right:*** KENTUCKY vertically. ***Engraver:*** Murray, Draper, Fairman & Co. ***Comments:*** H-Unlisted, Hughes-95. 18__. 1810s.

Rarity: URS-2
F $400

Burlington, Kentucky

The area that later became Burlington was settled in 1799 as Craigs Camp. The next year it was renamed Wilmington, and in 1816 the name was changed again to Burlington. It became the county seat of Boone that year. In 1824 Burlington was officially incorporated as a town.

Bank of Burlington

1818–1820

W-KY-170

History: The Bank of Burlington was chartered on January 26, 1818, with an authorized capital of $100,000 to be divided into 1,000 shares of $100 apiece. William Vawter, Elijah Kirtley, Benjamin Johnson, and Willis Graves were appointed to take stock subscriptions. The bank operated only for a short time. In the summer of 1819 it stopped redeeming its notes. The charters of all independent banks authorized on January 26, 1818, were revoked effective May 1, 1820.

Numismatic Commentary: Notes from this short-lived bank are uncommon to unknown.

Valid Issues

50¢ • W-KY-170-00.50-G010

Left: Panel. ***Center:*** Legend. ***Right:*** FIFTY CENTS vertically. ***Comments:*** H-Unlisted, Hughes-96. 18__. 1810s.

Rarity: URS-2
F $300

$1 • W-KY-170-001-G020 HA

Engraver: Murray, Draper, Fairman & Co. ***Comments:*** H-KY-40-G12, Hughes-97. 18__. 1810s.

Rarity: URS-2
VG $300; **F** $400

$2 • W-KY-170-002-G030

Left: 2 / TWO DOLLARS / II vertically. ***Center:*** Man with horses and plow. ***Right:*** KENTUCKY vertically. ***Engraver:*** Murray, Draper, Fairman & Co. ***Comments:*** H-KY-40-G14, Hughes-98. 18__. 1810s.

Rarity: URS-1
F $600

$3 • W-KY-170-003-G040 NJW

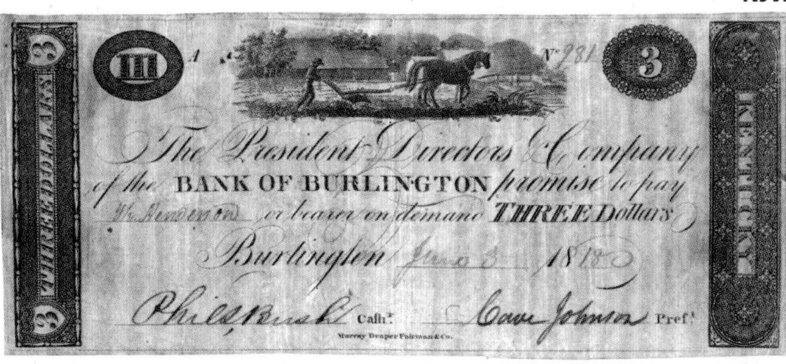

Engraver: Murray, Draper, Fairman & Co. ***Comments:*** H-KY-40-G16, Hughes-99. 18__. 1810s.

Rarity: URS-1
F $600

$5 • W-KY-170-005-G050

Left: 5 / FIVE DOLLARS / V vertically. ***Center:*** 5 / Man with horses and plow / 5. ***Right:*** KENTUCKY vertically. ***Engraver:*** Murray, Draper, Fairman & Co. ***Comments:*** H-KY-40-G18, Hughes-100. 18__. 1810s.

Rarity: URS-1
F $600

$10 • W-KY-170-010-G060

Left: 10 / TEN DOLLARS / X vertically. ***Center:*** 10 / Man with horses and plow / X. ***Right:*** KENTUCKY vertically. ***Engraver:*** Murray, Draper, Fairman & Co. ***Comments:*** H-KY-40-G20, Hughes-101. 18__. 1810s.

Rarity: *None known*

Canton, Kentucky

Abraham Boyd settled at a shipping point on the Cumberland River in 1799. It was known as Boyd's Landing for many years, with river commerce and a hotel known as the Brick Inn making up the majority of the settlement. In 1823 Boyd laid out the town and renamed it Canton. In 1825 General Marquis de Lafayette was given a reception in town, and the famous Jenny Lind sang from the inn's balcony in 1851.

Tobacco and other freight moved through Canton's port, and the town was also a major stopping point for coach lines making the trek from Nashville, Tennessee, to Evansville, Indiana. Warehouses, three schools, and a main hall were also a part of the town. After the Civil War, five hotels opened in Canton, and many railways connected through the city.

Traders and Mechanics Bank

1839

W-KY-180

History: No information as to the origin, operations, or fate of this bank is known. John Muscalus listed the $10 note in 1942, and Earl Hughes listed the same note in 1998, but no further record of such an institution has been found.

Valid Issues

$10 • W-KY-180-010-G010

Left: TEN vertically. ***Center:*** X / Ships, men, and merchandise at landing, Eagle perched on bales / X. ***Right:*** 10 / 10. ***Comments:*** H-KY-45-G10, Hughes-104. 18__. 1839.

Rarity: URS-1
VG $600

Carlisle, Kentucky

In 1816 John Kincart donated land to be used for the county seat of Ellisville. The same year Carlisle was founded; a courthouse was built in 1818. The town name came from Carlisle, Pennsylvania.

The population had peaked at 600 by 1830, but fires, cholera, and poor location slowly ate away at the growth of the town.

Farming and Commercial Bank of Carlisle

1818–1820

W-KY-190

History: The Farming and Commercial Bank of Carlisle was chartered on January 26, 1818. The authorized capital of $100,000 was divided into 1,000 shares valued at $100 each. I. Morriss, James Hughes, John G. Parks, Samuel M. Waugh, and James Baker were appointed to take stock subscriptions. The bank operated only for a short time, and in the summer of 1819 was reported as "dead." The charters of all independent banks authorized on January 26, 1818, were revoked effective May 1, 1820.

Numismatic Commentary: Some notes of this brief bank were printed on pink paper, adding an interesting feature for collectors.

Valid Issues

25¢ • W-KY-190-00.25-G010

CC

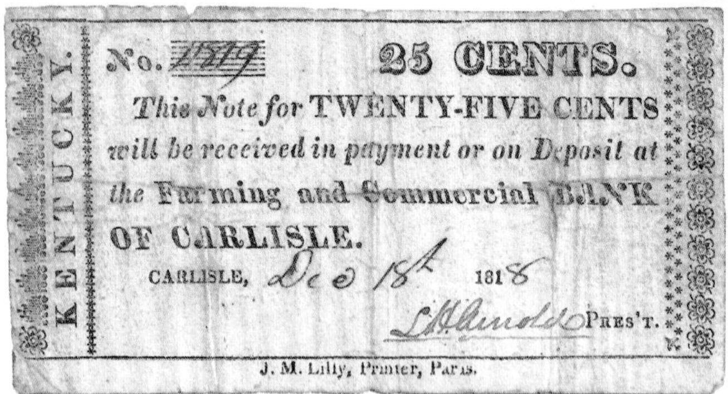

Comments: H-Unlisted, Hughes-Unlisted. 181_. 1810s.

Rarity: URS-3
F $275

50¢ • W-KY-190-00.50-G020

CC

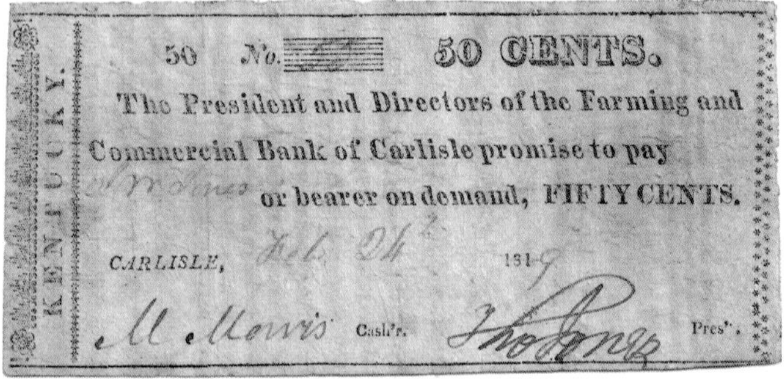

Comments: H-KY-50-G6, Hughes-106. 181_. 1810s.

Rarity: URS-3
VF $350

$1 • W-KY-190-001-G030

CC

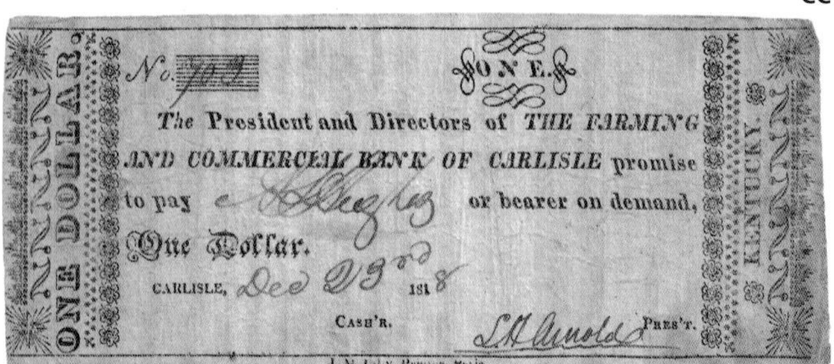

Comments: H-KY-50-G8, Hughes-107. 181_. 1810s.

Rarity: URS-3
F $700

$1 • W-KY-190-001-G040

CC

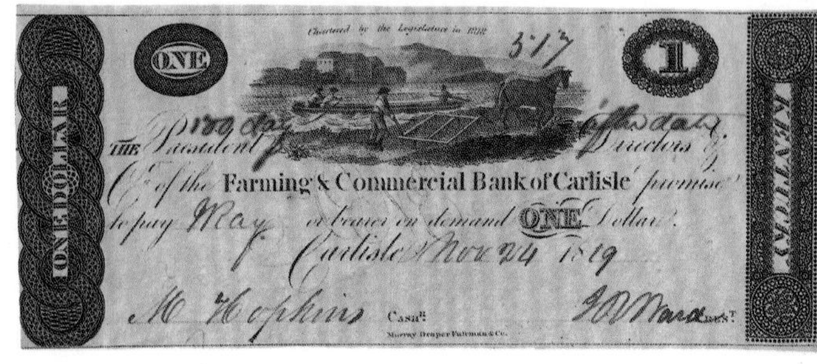

Engraver: Murray, Draper, Fairman & Co. ***Comments:*** H-KY-50-G12a, Hughes-108. Printed on pink paper. 18__. 1810s.

Rarity: URS-4
VF $350

$3 • W-KY-190-003-G050

CC

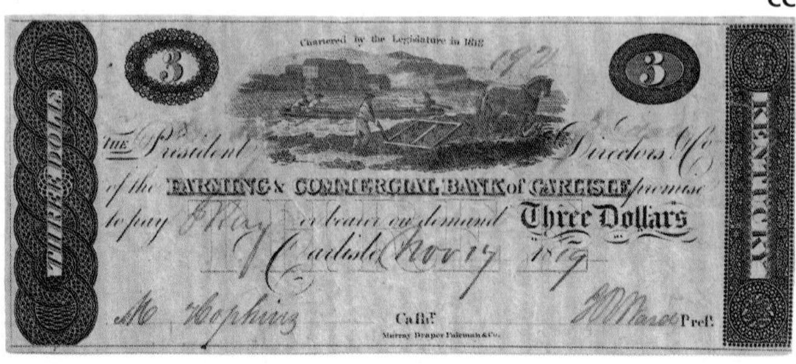

Engraver: Murray, Draper, Fairman & Co. ***Comments:*** H-KY-50-G14a, Hughes-109. Printed on pink paper. 18__. 1810s.

Rarity: URS-4
EF $350

$5 • W-KY-190-005-G060

CC

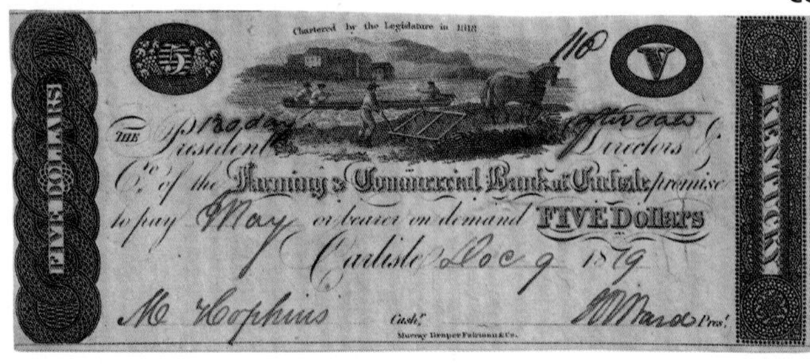

Engraver: Murray, Draper, Fairman & Co. ***Comments:*** H-KY-50-G16a, Hughes-110. Printed on pink paper. 18__. 1810s.

Rarity: URS-4
EF $350

Post Notes

$__ • W-KY-190-__-G070

Left: POST NOTE vertically. ***Center:*** Man in field next to river with horse and plow. ***Right:*** KENTUCKY vertically. ***Engraver:*** Murray, Draper, Fairman & Co. ***Comments:*** H-KY-50-G26a, Hughes-114. Printed on pink paper. Handwritten 130 days after date. 18__. 1819.

Rarity: URS-3
VG $75

$1 • W-KY-190-001-G080
Left: ONE DOLLAR vertically. *Center:* ONE / Man in field next to river with horse and plow / 1. *Right:* KENTUCKY vertically. *Engraver:* Murray, Draper, Fairman & Co. *Comments:* H-KY-50-G20a, Hughes-111. Printed on pink paper. Handwritten 130 days after date. 18__. 1819.

Rarity: URS-3
EF $150

$3 • W-KY-190-003-G090
Left: THREE DOLLS vertically. *Center:* 3 / Man in field next to river with horse and plow / 3. *Right:* KENTUCKY vertically. *Engraver:* Murray, Draper, Fairman & Co. *Comments:* H-KY-50-G22a, Hughes-112. Printed on pink paper. Handwritten 130 days after date. 18__. 1819.

Rarity: URS-3
EF $150; **Unc-Rem** $175

$5 • W-KY-190-005-G100
Left: FIVE DOLLARS vertically. *Center:* 5 / Man in field next to river with horse and plow / V. *Right:* KENTUCKY vertically. *Engraver:* Murray, Draper, Fairman & Co. *Comments:* H-KY-50-G24a, Hughes-113. Printed on pink paper. Handwritten 130 days after date. 18__. 1819.

Rarity: URS-3
Unc-Rem $125

CARROLLTON, KENTUCKY

In 1792 the area that would later become Carrollton was established and named Port William. It was laid out as the county seat of Gallatin until 1838, when the county split. Carrollton was then renamed and became the seat of the new Carroll County.

The Louisville and Nashville Railroad was laid near Carrollton in 1861, bringing new commerce and a thriving economy that sharply reduced the river shipping of the town.

See also Port William, Kentucky.

Southern Bank of Kentucky (branch)

1850–1864

W-KY-200

History: On February 20, 1839, the Southern Bank of Kentucky was chartered with an authorized capital of $2,000,000, of which the state subscribed to half. On February 15, 1850, the charter was extended to last until 1880.

The Carrollton branch opened in 1850. By 1855 the capital was $200,000. John A. Crawford was the cashier, and W.B. Winslow was the president. In 1864 the branch was closed. By 1865 the bank had been put into liquidation. On March 4, 1865, an act was passed ordering the treatment of the bank's bills to be as promissory notes rather than as currency. On January 8, 1867, the bank issued its last report regarding the closing up of its affairs. The bank building was occupied by Nimrod, Long & Co.

The Southern Bank of Kentucky had its parent bank located in Russellville, W-KY-1400, and branch banks located in Bowling Green, W-KY-130, Hickman, W-KY-650, Lebanon, W-KY-740, Louisville, W-KY-1000, Owensboro, W-KY-1200, and Smithland, W-KY-1460.

Numismatic Commentary: No validly issued notes of this branch bank have been found.

VALID ISSUES

$1 • W-KY-200-001-G010
Left: 1 / Woman reclining / ONE. *Center:* 1 / Female portrait surrounded by implements / 1. *Right:* 1 / Indian man reclining / ONE. *Engraver:* Toppan, Carpenter, Casilear & Co. *Comments:* H-KY-285-G50, Hughes-Unlisted. 18__. 1850s.

Rarity: *None known*

$1 • W-KY-200-001-G020
Left: Man with children and horse / ONE. *Center:* Portrait of young girl. *Right:* 1 / Flock of sheep. *Engraver:* Toppan, Carpenter & Co. *Comments:* H-KY-285-G52, Hughes-Unlisted. 18__. 1850s.

Rarity: *None known*

$1 • W-KY-200-001-G020a
Engraver: Toppan, Carpenter & Co. / ABNCo. monogram. *Comments:* H-KY-285-G52a, Hughes-Unlisted. Similar to W-KY-200-001-G020 but with additional engraver imprint. 18__. 1850s–1860s.

Rarity: *None known*

$2 • W-KY-200-002-G030
Left: 2 / Woman with basket / TWO. *Center:* Spread eagle / 2. *Bottom center:* Eagle. *Right:* Justice seated with scales and sword / TWO. *Engraver:* Toppan, Carpenter, Casilear & Co. *Comments:* H-KY-285-G56, Hughes-Unlisted. 18__. 1850s.

Rarity: *None known*

$2 • W-KY-200-002-G040
Left: 2 / Woman seated / TWO. *Center:* Female portrait. *Right:* 2 / Man with children and horse. *Engraver:* Toppan, Carpenter & Co. *Comments:* H-KY-285-G58, Hughes-Unlisted. 18__. 1850s.

Rarity: *None known*

$2 • W-KY-200-002-G040a
Engraver: Toppan, Carpenter & Co. / ABNCo. monogram. *Comments:* H-KY-285-G58a, Hughes-Unlisted. Similar to W-KY-200-002-G040 but with additional engraver imprint. 18__. 1850s–1860s.

Rarity: *None known*

$3 • W-KY-200-003-G050
Left: 3 / Female portrait / 3. *Center:* Woman with eagle. *Bottom center:* Steamboat. *Right:* 3 / Three women standing / THREE. *Engraver:* Toppan, Carpenter, Casilear & Co. *Comments:* H-KY-285-G62, Hughes-Unlisted. 18__. 1850s.

Rarity: *None known*

$3 • W-KY-200-003-G060
Left: 3 / Portrait of George Washington. *Center:* Portrait of young girl / Man with children and horse. *Right:* 3 / 3. *Engraver:* Toppan, Carpenter & Co. *Comments:* H-KY-285-G64, Hughes-Unlisted. 18__. 1850s.

Rarity: *None known*

$3 • W-KY-200-003-G060a
Engraver: Toppan, Carpenter & Co. / ABNCo. monogram. *Comments:* H-KY-285-G64a, Hughes-Unlisted. Similar to W-KY-200-003-G060 but with additional engraver imprint. 18__. 1850s–1860s.

Rarity: *None known*

$5 • W-KY-200-005-G070

Left: 5 / Female portrait / 5. ***Center:*** Man on horse. ***Right:*** 5 / Woman standing with flag. ***Engraver:*** Toppan, Carpenter, Casilear & Co. ***Comments:*** H-KY-285-G68, Hughes-Unlisted. 18__. 1850s.

Rarity: *None known*

$5 • W-KY-200-005-G080

Left: 5 / Portrait of boy. ***Center:*** Man on horse in farmyard. ***Right:*** V / Portrait of young girl. ***Overprint:*** Red FIVE. ***Engraver:*** Bald, Cousland & Co. / Baldwin, Bald & Cousland. ***Comments:*** H-KY-285-G70a, Hughes-Unlisted. 18__. 1850s.

Rarity: *None known*

$10 • W-KY-200-010-G090

Left: 10. ***Center:*** Woman reclining among farm implements. ***Bottom center:*** Female portrait. ***Right:*** 10. ***Engraver:*** Toppan, Carpenter, Casilear & Co. ***Comments:*** H-KY-285-G74, Hughes-Unlisted. 18__. 1850s.

Rarity: *None known*

$10 • W-KY-200-010-G100

Left: 10 / Woman seated. ***Center:*** Man, woman, child, dog, Haying scene. ***Right:*** 10 / Woman seated. ***Overprint:*** Red TEN. ***Engraver:*** Bald, Cousland & Co. / Baldwin, Bald & Cousland. ***Comments:*** H-KY-285-G76a, Hughes-Unlisted. 18__. 1850s.

Rarity: *None known*

Non-Valid Issues

$1 • W-KY-200-001-C010

Engraver: Toppan, Carpenter, Casilear & Co. ***Comments:*** H-KY-285-C50, Hughes-Unlisted. Counterfeit of W-KY-200-001-G010. 18__. 1850s.

Rarity: URS-2
F $100

$1 • W-KY-200-001-C020a

Engraver: Toppan, Carpenter & Co. / ABNCo. monogram. ***Comments:*** H-KY-285-C52a, Hughes-Unlisted. Counterfeit of W-KY-200-001-G020a. 18__. 1860s.

Rarity: URS-2
F $100

$3 • W-KY-200-003-C050

Engraver: Toppan, Carpenter, Casilear & Co. ***Comments:*** H-KY-285-C62, Hughes-Unlisted. Counterfeit of W-KY-200-003-G050. 18__. 1850s.

Rarity: URS-1
F $250

$3 • W-KY-200-003-C060a

Engraver: Toppan, Carpenter & Co. / ABNCo. monogram. ***Comments:*** H-KY-285-C64a, Hughes-Unlisted. Counterfeit of W-KY-200-003-G060a. 18__. 1860s.

Rarity: URS-1
F $250

Columbia, Kentucky

Columbia was settled in 1802 by Daniel Trabue. On April 1, 1806, the post office was established, along with a local store.

Bank of Columbia
1818–1820
W-KY-210

History: The Bank of Columbia was chartered on January 26, 1818, with an authorized capital of $100,000 to be divided into 1,000 shares of $100 apiece. William Caldwell, John Field, Benjamin Lampton, John Montgomery, Elijah Creel, William Patterson, and Benjamin Selby were appointed to take stock subscriptions. The bank operated only for a short time, and by the summer of 1819 it was no longer redeeming its notes. The charters of all independent banks authorized on January 26, 1818, were revoked effective May 1, 1820.

Numismatic Commentary: Notes of this early and transitory bank are scarce.

Valid Issues

$1 • W-KY-210-001-G010

CC

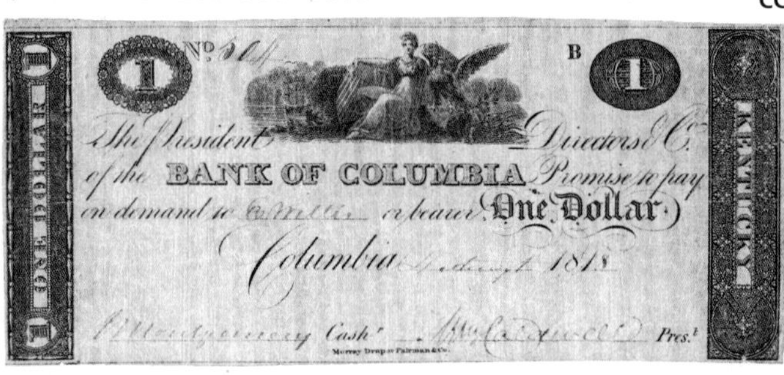

Engraver: Murray, Draper, Fairman & Co. ***Comments:*** H-KY-55-G12, Hughes-117. 18__. 1810s.

Rarity: URS-3
G $100; **F** $300

$2 • W-KY-210-002-G020

CC

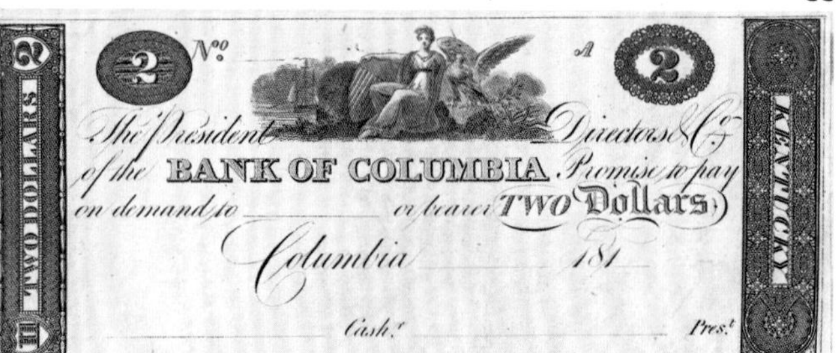

Engraver: Murray, Draper, Fairman & Co. ***Comments:*** H-KY-55-G14, Hughes-118. 181_. 1810s.

Rarity: URS-2
F $400; **Proof** $1,100

$5 • **W-KY-210-005-G030** CC

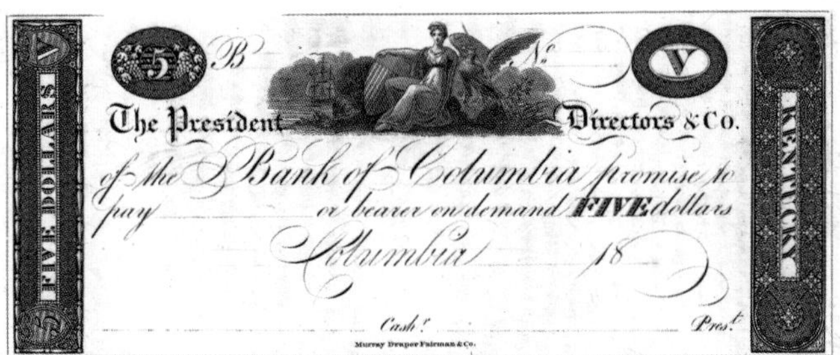

Engraver: Murray, Draper, Fairman & Co. ***Comments:*** H-KY-55-G18, Hughes-119. 18__. 1810s.

Rarity: URS-2

F $200; **Proof** $500

$10 • **W-KY-210-010-G040** HA

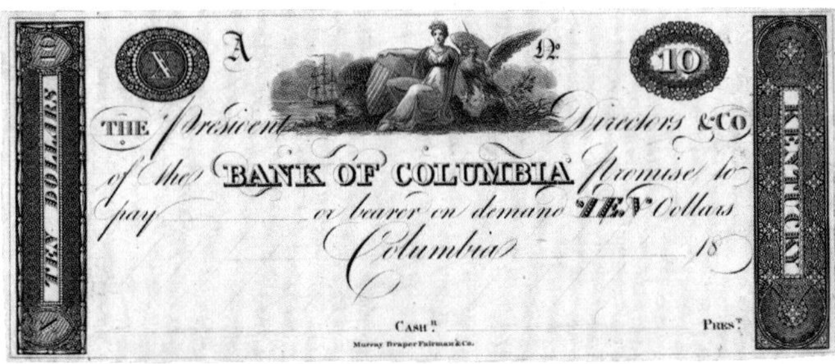

Engraver: Murray, Draper, Fairman & Co. ***Comments:*** H-KY-55-G20, Hughes-120. 181_. 1810s.

Rarity: URS-2

F $300; **Proof** $750

$20 • **W-KY-210-020-G050** CC

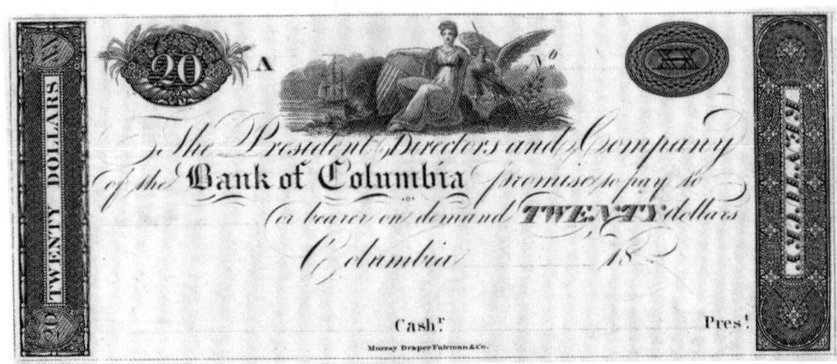

Engraver: Murray, Draper, Fairman & Co. ***Comments:*** H-KY-55-G22, Hughes-121. 18__. 1810s.

Rarity: URS-2

EF $400; **Proof** $1,000

$50 • **W-KY-210-050-G060** CC

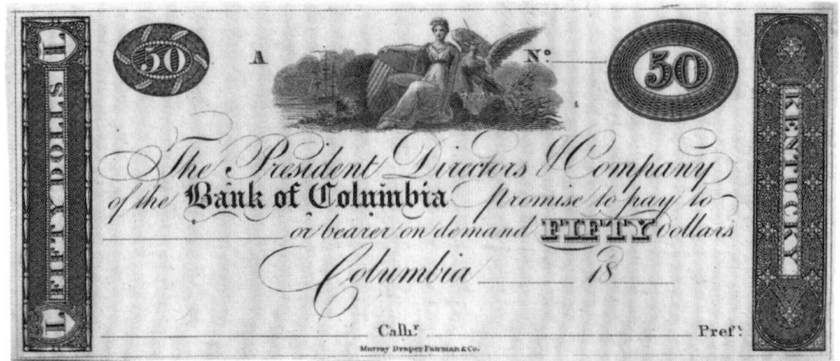

Engraver: Murray, Draper, Fairman & Co. ***Comments:*** H-KY-55-G24, Hughes-122. 181_. 1810s.

Rarity: URS-2

F $450; **Proof** $3,000

$100 • **W-KY-210-100-G070** CC

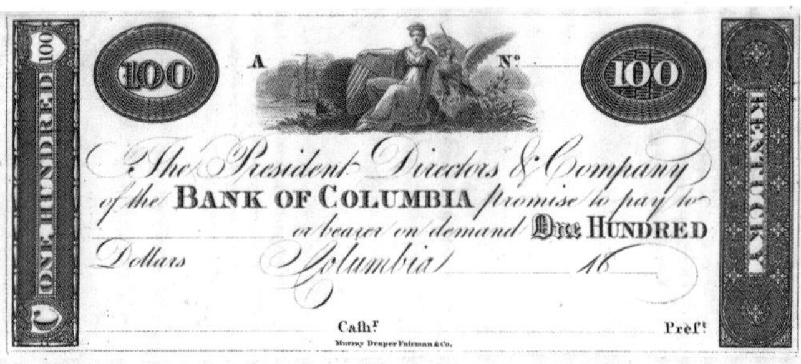

Engraver: Murray, Draper, Fairman & Co. ***Comments:*** H-KY-55-G26, Hughes-123. 18__. 1810s.

Rarity: URS-2

F $500; **Proof** $1,200

Post Notes

$100 • **W-KY-210-100-G080**

Engraver: Murray, Draper, Fairman & Co. ***Comments:*** H-Unlisted, Hughes-124. 18__. 1810s.

Rarity: URS-2

VF $500

Columbus, Kentucky

Columbus was settled in 1804 under the name of Iron Banks. In 1820 the name was changed to Columbus in honor of Christopher Columbus. The same year a post office was opened, and the town became the seat of Hickman County. Later the court was transferred to Clinton.

In 1860 the town was officially incorporated. It was later seized by the Confederate army.

Bank of Kentucky {2nd} (branch)

1834–1866

W-KY-220

History: The second Bank of Kentucky (sometimes seen in print as the "New" Bank of Kentucky) was chartered in 1834 in order to assume the business of the first Bank of Kentucky, W-KY-420, which had recently closed. The capital of the bank was $5,000,000.

The branch in Columbus was established in 1834. In 1863 the capital was $150,000. William Owens Jr. was the cashier, and J.M. Moore was the president. In January 1866 almost all branches of the Bank of Kentucky were closed down, and the parent bank began winding up its business.

The second Bank of Kentucky had its parent bank located in Louisville, W-KY-850, and branch banks located in Bowling Green, W-KY-080, Burksville, W-KY-140, Danville, W-KY-330, Flemingsburg, W-KY-390, Frankfort, W-KY-430, Glasgow, W-KY-510, Greensburg, W-KY-540, Hopkinsville, W-KY-670, Lexington, W-KY-770, Maysville, W-KY-1020, Mount Sterling, W-KY-1100, and Paducah, W-KY-1220.

Numismatic Commentary: No validly issued notes with this branch location have been found.

Valid Issues

$5 • W-KY-220-005-G010

Left: 5 / Portrait of Henry Clay / FIVE. ***Center:*** Portrait of John Q. Adams / Woman seated against bales, Train, Harvesting scene / Portrait of Thomas Jefferson. ***Right:*** 5 / Portrait of George Washington / FIVE. ***Engraver:*** Toppan, Carpenter & Co. ***Comments:*** H-KY-195-G100, Hughes-494. 185_. 1850s.

Rarity: *None known*

$10 • W-KY-220-010-G020

Left: 10 / Portrait of George Washington / 10. ***Center:*** Portrait of Andrew Jackson / Indian man and woman flanking shield bearing 10 surmounted by eagle / Portrait of Isaac Shelby. ***Right:*** 10 / Portrait of Henry Clay / 10. ***Engraver:*** Toppan, Carpenter & Co. ***Comments:*** H-KY-195-G104, Hughes-499. 185_. 1850s.

Rarity: *None known*

$20 • W-KY-220-020-G030

Left: 20 / Portrait of Daniel Webster. ***Center:*** "General Marion's Sweet Potato Dinner." ***Right:*** 20 / Male portrait. ***Engraver:*** Toppan, Carpenter & Co. ***Comments:*** H-KY-195-G108, Hughes-511. 185_. 1850s.

Rarity: *None known*

Non-Valid Issues

$10 • W-KY-220-010-C020

Engraver: Toppan, Carpenter & Co. ***Comments:*** H-KY-195-C104, Hughes-500. Counterfeit of W-KY-220-010-G020. 185_. 1850s.

Rarity: URS-2

F $300

Covington, Kentucky

Covington was established in 1814 when John and Richard Gano, along with Thomas Carneal, bought land along the Licking River at its confluence with the Ohio River. The town was officially incorporated in 1815. In 1862 the Stewart Iron Works was founded. This company grew to become the world's largest iron-fence maker.

Bank of the Commonwealth of Kentucky (agency)

1820s

W-KY-230

History: The Bank of the Commonwealth of Kentucky was chartered on November 29, 1820, with an authorized capital of $2,000,000. Notes issued by the branch at Falmouth, W-KY-360, were also imprinted Covington, where the bank may have had a facility.

Numismatic Commentary: Almost all notes from this bank and its branches are unknown today.

Valid Issues

$1 • W-KY-230-001-G010

HA

Engraver: Murray, Draper, Fairman & Co. ***Comments:*** H-KY-95-G62, Hughes-214. 182_. 1820s.

Rarity: URS-1

VG $500

Farmers Bank of Kentucky (branch)

1850–1871

W-KY-240

History: The Farmers Bank of Kentucky was chartered on February 15, 1850, with an authorized capital of $2,300,000. By September 1852 the bank had opened for business. On February 11, 1860, the charter for the bank was amended, allowing it to increase its capital.

The branch located in Covington had a capital of $600,000. The books of subscription were opened on March 25, 1850. The cashier was Cassius B. Sandford, and the president was C.A. Withers. In 1857 Withers resigned and was replaced by Thomas B. Page. The branch at Covington was closed and succeeded by the Covington City National Bank in 1871.

The Farmers Bank of Kentucky had its parent bank located in Frankfort, W-KY-450, and branch banks located in Bardstown, W-KY-070, George Town, W-KY-480, Henderson, W-KY-640, Maysville, W-KY-1050, Mount Sterling, W-KY-1130, Princeton, W-KY-1340, and Somerset, W-KY-1480.

Valid Issues

$1 • W-KY-240-001-G010

Left: 1 / Portrait of John Crittenden / ONE. ***Center:*** Man with dog, Running horses, Donkey. ***Right:*** 1 / Female portrait / ONE. ***Engraver:*** Toppan, Carpenter, Casilear & Co. ***Comments:*** H-KY-100-G26, Hughes-250. 18__. 1850s.

Rarity: URS-4

VG $110

$1 • W-KY-240-001-G010a

Back: Red-orange. ***Engraver:*** Toppan, Carpenter, Casilear & Co. / ABNCo. monogram. ***Comments:*** H-KY-100-G26b, Hughes-Unlisted. Similar to W-KY-240-001-G010 but with additional engraver imprint. 185_. 1850s.

Rarity: URS-3

F $200

$1 • W-KY-240-001-G020
Left: 1 / Man, wagon, and horses / 1. ***Center:*** Portraits of Mr. and Mrs. John Crittenden. ***Right:*** 1 / 1 on die / 1. ***Tint:*** Red-orange. ***Back:*** Red-orange. ***Engraver:*** American Bank Note Co. ***Comments:*** H-KY-100-G28a, Hughes-249. 18__. 1860s.
Rarity: URS-4
F $150

$2 • W-KY-240-002-G030
Left: 2 / Portrait of Mrs. John Crittenden. ***Center:*** 2 / Man on horse / 2. ***Right:*** 2 / Portrait of John Crittenden. ***Engraver:*** Toppan, Carpenter, Casilear & Co. ***Comments:*** H-KY-100-G30, Hughes-252. 18__. 1850s.
Rarity: URS-3
F $150

$2 • W-KY-240-002-G030a
Back: Red-orange. ***Engraver:*** Toppan, Carpenter, Casilear & Co. / ABNCo. monogram. ***Comments:*** H-KY-100-G30b, Hughes-Unlisted. Similar to W-KY-240-002-G030 but with additional engraver imprint. 185_. 1850s.
Rarity: URS-2
VF $200

$5 • W-KY-240-005-G040
Left: 5 / Portrait of John Crittenden / 5. ***Center:*** Cattle and sheep, Herders. ***Right:*** 5 / Portrait of Mrs. John Crittenden / 5. ***Engraver:*** Toppan, Carpenter, Casilear & Co. ***Comments:*** H-KY-100-G32, Hughes-256. 18__. 1850s.
Rarity: URS-3
F $150

$5 • W-KY-240-005-G040a
Overprint: Red FIVE. ***Engraver:*** Toppan, Carpenter, Casilear & Co. ***Comments:*** H-KY-100-G32a, Hughes-257. Similar to W-KY-240-005-G040. 18__. 1850s.
Rarity: URS-3
VF $200

$5 • W-KY-240-005-G050
Left: Men plowing with horse / V. ***Center:*** Portraits of Mr. and Mrs. John Crittenden. ***Right:*** 5 / 5. ***Tint:*** Red-orange. ***Back:*** Red-orange. ***Engraver:*** American Bank Note Co. ***Comments:*** H-KY-100-G34a, Hughes-255. 18__. 1859.
Rarity: URS-4
Unc-Rem $350

$10 • W-KY-240-010-G060
Left: 10 / Portrait of John Crittenden. ***Center:*** Portraits of Mr. and Mrs. John Crittenden. ***Engraver:*** Toppan, Carpenter, Casilear & Co. ***Comments:*** H-KY-100-G36, Hughes-Unlisted. 18__. 1850s.
Rarity: URS-3
F $200

$10 • W-KY-240-010-G060a
Tint: Red-orange outlining white TEN. ***Engraver:*** Toppan, Carpenter, Casilear & Co. ***Comments:*** H-KY-100-G36b, Hughes-Unlisted. Similar to W-KY-240-010-G060. 18__. 1850s.
Rarity: URS-3
F $200

$10 • W-KY-240-010-G070
Left: 10 / Portrait of John Crittenden. ***Center:*** Woman reclining against barrel, Harvest scene / Portrait of Mrs. John Crittenden. ***Right:*** 10 / Men harvesting corn. ***Tint:*** Red-orange. ***Back:*** Red-orange. ***Engraver:*** American Bank Note Co. ***Comments:*** H-KY-100-G38a, Hughes-259. 18__. 1859.
Rarity: URS-4
F $175

$20 • W-KY-240-020-G080
Left: Portrait of Mrs. John Crittenden / Portrait of John Crittenden. ***Center:*** 20 / Horses plowing. ***Right:*** 20. ***Engraver:*** Toppan, Carpenter, Casilear & Co. ***Comments:*** H-KY-100-G40, Hughes-Unlisted. 18__. 1850s.
Rarity: URS-3
F $250

$20 • W-KY-240-020-G080a
Tint: Red-orange. ***Back:*** Red-orange. ***Engraver:*** American Bank Note Co. ***Comments:*** H-KY-100-G42a, Hughes-261. Similar to W-KY-240-020-G080 but with different engraver imprint. 18__. 1859.
Rarity: URS-3
F $250

$50 • W-KY-240-050-G090
Left: Three women with anchor. ***Center:*** 50 / Portrait of Mrs. John Crittenden. ***Right:*** 50 / Portrait of John Crittenden / 50. ***Engraver:*** Toppan, Carpenter, Casilear & Co. ***Comments:*** H-KY-100-G44, Hughes-263. 18__. 1850s.
Rarity: URS-3
F $350

$100 • W-KY-240-100-G100
Left: 100 / Portrait of John Crittenden / 100. ***Center:*** Three women reclining / Portrait of Mrs. John Crittenden. ***Right:*** ONE HUNDRED vertically. ***Engraver:*** Toppan, Carpenter, Casilear & Co. ***Comments:*** H-KY-100-G46, Hughes-265. 18__. 1850s.
Rarity: URS-2
F $450

Non-Valid Issues

$3 • W-KY-240-003-N010
Comments: H-Unlisted, Hughes-254. 18__. 1850s.
Rarity: URS-3
VG $100

$5 • W-KY-240-005-C040
Engraver: Toppan, Carpenter, Casilear & Co. ***Comments:*** H-KY-100-C32. Counterfeit of W-KY-240-005-G040. 18__. 1850s.
Rarity: URS-4
F $150

$5 • W-KY-240-005-C040a
Overprint: Red FIVE. ***Engraver:*** Toppan, Carpenter, Casilear & Co. ***Comments:*** H-KY-100-C32a, Hughes-Unlisted. Counterfeit of W-KY-240-005-G040a. 18__. 1850s.
Rarity: URS-4
F $150

$10 • W-KY-240-010-C060a

Tint: Red-orange outlining white TEN. ***Engraver:*** Toppan, Carpenter, Casilear & Co. ***Comments:*** H-KY-100-G36a, Hughes-Unlisted. Counterfeit of W-KY-240-010-G060a. 18__. 1858.

Rarity: URS-4
F $150

Kentucky Trust Company Bank
1850–1854
W-KY-250

History: The Kentucky Trust Company Bank was chartered on November 18, 1850. On October 16, 1854, it failed. In April 1855 *Bankers' Magazine* reported: "*The Cincinnati Commercial* says that the affairs of the Kentucky Trust Company Bank, at Covington, will wind up much better than was generally anticipated."

Valid Issues

$1 • W-KY-250-001-G010

CC

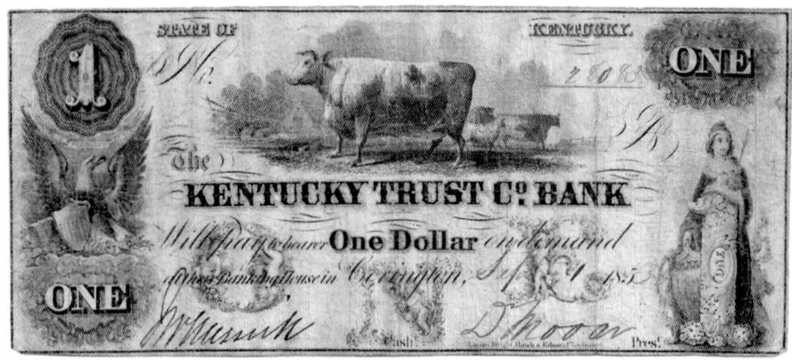

Engraver: Rawdon, Wright, Hatch & Edson. ***Comments:*** H-KY-60-G2, Hughes-161. 185_. 1850s.

Rarity: URS-5
VG $100; **F** $250

$2 • W-KY-250-002-G020

CC

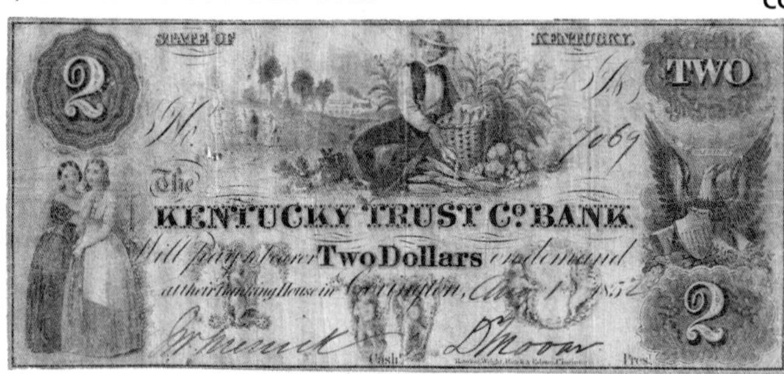

Engraver: Rawdon, Wright, Hatch & Edson. ***Comments:*** H-KY-60-G4, Hughes-162. 185_. 1850s.

Rarity: URS-5
F $200

$3 • W-KY-250-003-G030

NJW

Engraver: Rawdon, Wright, Hatch & Edson. ***Comments:*** H-KY-60-G6, Hughes-163. 185_. 1850s.

Rarity: URS-4
F $150

$5 • W-KY-250-005-G040

SI

Engraver: Rawdon, Wright, Hatch & Edson. ***Comments:*** H-KY-60-G8, Hughes-164. 185_. 1850s.

Rarity: URS-5
F $150

$10 • W-KY-250-010-G050

HA

Engraver: Rawdon, Wright, Hatch & Edson. ***Comments:*** H-KY-60-G10, Hughes-165. 185_. 1850s.

Rarity: URS-4
F $250

$20 • W-KY-250-020-G060

Right: 20 / Man / XX. ***Back:*** State arms. ***Engraver:*** Rawdon, Wright, Hatch & Edson. ***Comments:*** H-KY-60-G12, Hughes-166. 185_. 1850s.

Rarity: URS-4
F $350

Northern Bank of Kentucky (branch)

1835–1860s

W-KY-260

History: The Northern Bank of Kentucky was chartered in 1835 with an authorized capital of $3,000,000. The Covington branch was established immediately. In 1848 the president was James M. Preston, and the cashier was Phillip S. Bush. Capital was $250,000. In 1850 William Ernst took the place of cashier, as Phillip Bush had resigned. In 1855 the capital was $400,000. By 1864 it had risen to $450,000.

Sometime during the 1860s the Northern Bank of Kentucky was converted to a bank of discount and deposit, after which time no notes were issued.

The Northern Bank of Kentucky had its parent bank located in Lexington, W-KY-830, and branch banks located in Barbourville, W-KY-040, Cynthiana, W-KY-305, Glasgow, W-KY-520, Louisville, W-KY-960, Paris, W-KY-1280, and Richmond, W-KY-1360.

Valid Issues

$1 • W-KY-260-001-G010

Left: Portrait of George Washington / ONE / Portrait of Henry Clay. ***Center:*** 1 / Woman seated against bales, Cattle, Train. ***Right:*** 1 / Portrait of Rachel Jackson / 1. ***Engraver:*** Toppan, Carpenter & Co. ***Comments:*** H-KY-175-G94, Hughes-435. 18__. 1840s.

Rarity: URS-4
F $125

$1 • W-KY-260-001-G020

Left: Portrait of Henry Clay / 1. ***Center:*** Woman seated against bales, Cattle, Train / Female portrait. ***Right:*** 1 / Portrait of George Washington. ***Engraver:*** Toppan, Carpenter, Casilear & Co. ***Comments:*** H-KY-175-G96, Hughes-433. 18__. 1850s.

Rarity: URS-4
F $125

$1 • W-KY-260-001-G030

Left: 1 / Portrait of boy. ***Center:*** Men with cattle, Sheep. ***Right:*** 1 / Portrait of girl. ***Tint:*** Red-orange. ***Engraver:*** American Bank Note Co. ***Comments:*** H-KY-175-G98, Hughes-437. 18__. 1850s–1860s.

Rarity: URS-6
F $125

$3 • W-KY-260-003-G035

CC

Engraver: Draper, Toppan, Longacre & Co. ***Comments:*** H-Unlisted, Hughes-Unlisted. 18__. 1830s.

Rarity: URS-4
G $350

$5 • W-KY-260-005-G040

Left: FIVE vertically. ***Center:*** 5 / Train / 5. ***Right:*** FIVE vertically. ***Engraver:*** Casilear, Durand, Burton & Edmonds. ***Comments:*** H-KY-175-G104, Hughes-442. 18__. 1830s.

Rarity: URS-4
F $125

$5 • W-KY-260-005-G050

Left: FIVE vertically. ***Center:*** 5 / Woman standing, Train / 5. ***Right:*** FIVE vertically. ***Engraver:*** Draper, Toppan & Co. ***Comments:*** H-KY-175-G106, Hughes-Unlisted. 18__. 1840s.

Rarity: URS-3
F $150

$5 • W-KY-260-005-G060

Left: 5 / Portrait of Henry Clay / 5. ***Center:*** 5 / Woman seated against bales, Cattle, Train / 5. ***Right:*** 5 / Portrait of George Washington / 5. ***Engraver:*** Toppan, Carpenter & Co. ***Comments:*** H-KY-175-G108, Hughes-444. 18__. 1840s–1850s.

Rarity: URS-4
F $125

$5 • W-KY-260-005-G070

Left: 5 / FIVE vertically. ***Center:*** Portrait of Henry Clay / Woman seated against bales, Cattle, Train / Male portrait. ***Right:*** 5 / FIVE vertically. ***Tint:*** Red-orange. ***Engraver:*** American Bank Note Co. ***Comments:*** H-KY-175-G110, Hughes-445. 18__. 1850s–1860s.

Rarity: URS-4
F $125

$10 • W-KY-260-010-G080

Left: TEN vertically. ***Center:*** 10 / Train / 10. ***Right:*** TEN vertically. ***Engraver:*** Casilear, Durand, Burton & Edmonds. ***Comments:*** H-KY-175-G114, Hughes-446. 18__. 1830s.

Rarity: URS-4
F $150

Collectors and Researchers:

If you have new information about any banks or notes listed in this volume, contact Whitman Publishing, Attn: Obsolete Paper Money, 3101 Clairmont Road, Suite G, Atlanta, GA 30329.

$10 • **W-KY-260-010-G090**

Left: 10 / TEN vertically / 10. ***Center:*** Female portrait / Train, Woman seated / Female portrait. ***Right:*** 10 / TEN vertically / 10. ***Engraver:*** Draper, Toppan & Co. ***Comments:*** H-KY-175-G116, Hughes-Unlisted. 18__. 1840s.

Rarity: URS-3
F $150

$10 • **W-KY-260-010-G100**

Left: X / 10 / X. ***Center:*** Portrait of George Washington / Woman seated against bales, Cattle, Train / Portrait of Henry Clay. ***Right:*** X / 10 / X. ***Engraver:*** Toppan, Carpenter & Co. ***Comments:*** H-KY-175-G118, Hughes-447. 18__. 1840s–1850s.

Rarity: URS-4
F $125

$10 • **W-KY-260-010-G110** CC

Engraver: Toppan, Carpenter, Casilear & Co. ***Comments:*** H-KY-175-G120, Hughes-450. 18__. 1850s.

Rarity: URS-4
F $150

$10 • **W-KY-260-010-G120**

Left: 10 / Portrait of Henry Clay. ***Center:*** Woman seated against bales, Cattle, Train. ***Right:*** 10 / Male portrait. ***Tint:*** Red-orange. ***Engraver:*** American Bank Note Co. ***Comments:*** H-KY-175-G122, Hughes-452. 18__. 1850s–1860s.

Rarity: URS-4
F $125

$20 • **W-KY-260-020-G130**

Left: TWENTY vertically. ***Center:*** 20 / Train / 20. ***Right:*** TWENTY vertically. ***Engraver:*** Casilear, Durand, Burton & Edmonds. ***Comments:*** H-KY-175-G124, Hughes-453. 18__. 1830s.

Rarity: URS-4
F $125

$20 • **W-KY-260-020-G140**

Left: 20 / TWENTY vertically / 20. ***Center:*** Female portrait / Train, Woman seated / Female portrait. ***Right:*** 20 / TWENTY vertically / 20. ***Engraver:*** Draper, Toppan & Co. ***Comments:*** H-KY-175-G126, Hughes-455. 18__. 1840s.

Rarity: URS-4
F $125

$20 • **W-KY-260-020-G150**

Left: 20 / Portrait of George Washington / 20. ***Center:*** 20 / Woman seated against bales, Cattle, Train / 20. ***Right:*** 20 / Portrait of Henry Clay / 20. ***Engraver:*** Toppan, Carpenter & Co. ***Comments:*** H-KY-175-G128, Hughes-457. 18__. 1840s–1850s.

Rarity: URS-4
F $125

$20 • **W-KY-260-020-G160**

Left: 20 / 20. ***Center:*** Portrait of Henry Clay / Woman seated against bales, Cattle, Train / Male portrait. ***Right:*** 20 / 20. ***Tint:*** Red-orange. ***Engraver:*** American Bank Note Co. ***Comments:*** H-KY-175-G130, Hughes-458. 18__. 1850s–1860s.

Rarity: URS-4
F $125

$50 • **W-KY-260-050-G170**

Left: FIFTY vertically. ***Center:*** 50 / Train / 50. ***Right:*** FIFTY vertically. ***Engraver:*** Casilear, Durand, Burton & Edmonds. ***Comments:*** H-KY-175-G132, Hughes-460. 18__. 1830s.

Rarity: URS-3
F $200

$50 • **W-KY-260-050-G180**

Left: 50 / FIFTY vertically / 50. ***Center:*** Female portrait / Woman seated against bales, Cattle / Female portrait. ***Right:*** 50 / FIFTY vertically / 50. ***Engraver:*** Draper, Toppan & Co. ***Comments:*** H-KY-175-G134, Hughes-461. 18__. 1840s.

Rarity: URS-3
F $200

$50 • **W-KY-260-050-G190**

Left: 50 / Portrait of George Washington / 50. ***Center:*** 50 / Woman seated against bales, Cattle, Train. ***Right:*** 50 / Portrait of Henry Clay / 50. ***Engraver:*** Toppan, Carpenter & Co. ***Comments:*** H-KY-175-G136, Hughes-463. 18__. 1840s–1850s.

Rarity: URS-3
F $200

$50 • **W-KY-260-050-G200**

Left: 50 / 50. ***Center:*** Portrait of Henry Clay / Woman seated against bales, Cattle, Train. ***Right:*** 50 / Male portrait. ***Tint:*** Red-orange. ***Engraver:*** American Bank Note Co. ***Comments:*** H-KY-175-G138, Hughes-464. 18__. 1850s–1860s.

Rarity: URS-3
F $200

$100 • **W-KY-260-100-G210**

Left: ONE HUNDRED vertically. ***Center:*** C / Train / C. ***Right:*** ONE HUNDRED vertically. ***Tint:*** Red-orange. ***Engraver:*** Casilear, Durand, Burton & Edmonds. ***Comments:*** H-KY-175-G140, Hughes-465. 18__. 1830s.

Rarity: URS-3
F $700

$100 • **W-KY-260-100-G220**

Left: 100 / HUNDRED vertically / 100. ***Center:*** Female portrait / Woman seated against bales, Cattle, Train / Female portrait. ***Right:*** 100 / HUNDRED vertically / 100. ***Engraver:*** Draper, Toppan & Co. ***Comments:*** H-KY-175-G142, Hughes-Unlisted. 18__. 1840s.

Rarity: URS-2
F $700

$100 • W-KY-260-100-G230

CC

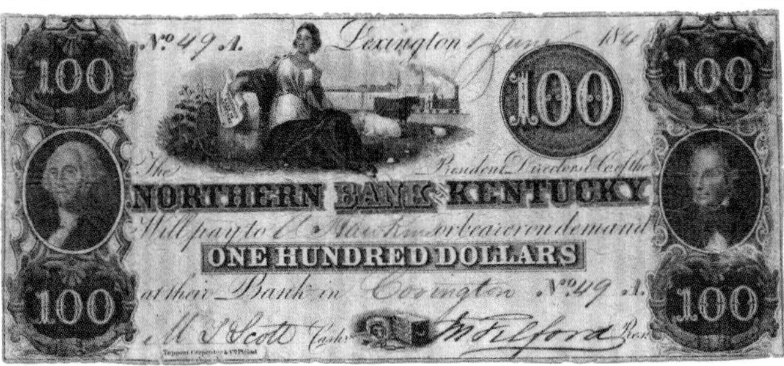

Engraver: Toppan, Carpenter & Co. ***Comments:*** H-KY-175-G144, Hughes-466. 18__. 1840s–1850s.

Rarity: URS-3
F $700

$100 • W-KY-260-100-G240

Left: 100 / Portrait of Henry Clay / 100. ***Center:*** Woman seated against bales, Cattle, Train. ***Right:*** 100 / Male portrait / 100. ***Tint:*** Red-orange. ***Engraver:*** American Bank Note Co. ***Comments:*** H-KY-175-G146, Hughes-468. 18__. 1850s–1860s.

Rarity: URS-3
F $700

Non-Valid Issues

$5 • W-KY-260-005-C040

Engraver: Casilear, Durand, Burton & Evans. ***Comments:*** H-KY-175-C104, Hughes-443. Counterfeit of W-KY-260-005-G040. 18__. Circa 1838.

Rarity: URS-5
F $100

$10 • W-KY-260-010-C100

Engraver: Toppan, Carpenter & Co. ***Comments:*** H-KY-175-C118, Hughes-Unlisted. Counterfeit of W-KY-260-010-G100. 18__. 1850s.

Rarity: URS-4
F $100

$20 • W-KY-260-020-C130

Engraver: Casilear, Durand, Burton & Evans. ***Comments:*** H-KY-175-C124, Hughes-454. Counterfeit of W-KY-260-020-G130. 18__. Circa 1838.

Rarity: URS-4
F $100

$20 • W-KY-260-020-C140

Engraver: Draper, Toppan & Co. ***Comments:*** H-KY-175-C126, Hughes-456. Counterfeit of W-KY-260-020-G140. 18__. 1840s.

Rarity: URS-4
VF $250

$50 • W-KY-260-050-C180

Engraver: Draper, Toppan & Co. ***Comments:*** H-KY-175-C134, Hughes-462. Counterfeit of W-KY-260-050-G180. 18__. 1840s.

Rarity: URS-3
F $150

Real Estate Bank of Covington

1818–1820

W-KY-270

History: The Real Estate Bank of Covington was chartered on January 26, 1818. It operated only for a short time and then failed within a year or two, along with many others with the same charter date. The charters of all independent banks authorized on January 26, 1818, were revoked effective May 1, 1820.

Numismatic Commentary: One note of this bank has been found.

Valid Issues

50¢ • W-KY-270-00.50-G010

Left: FIFTY CENTS. ***Center:*** FIFTY CENTS. ***Right:*** FIFTY CENTS. ***Engraver:*** Gridley. ***Comments:*** H-KY-65-G8, Hughes-176. 18__. 1819.

Rarity: URS-1
F $350

Cynthiana, Kentucky

Cynthiana was established by Robert Harrison, who donated the land and named it after his daughters, Cynthia and Anna. It became the seat of Harrison County, which was named after Colonel Benjamin Harrison.

During the Civil War there were two battles fought in Cynthiana. One was a Confederate raid that occurred July 17, 1862; the second resulted in a Confederate defeat on June 12, 1864.

Bank of Cynthiana

1818–1820

W-KY-280

History: The Bank of Cynthiana was chartered on January 26, 1818. William Brown, Isaac Miller, James Finley, James Kelly, Alexander Downing, Henry O. Brown, and Joseph Ward were appointed to take stock subscriptions. In autumn 1819 the bank's notes were circulating but were viewed with suspicion. The charters of all independent banks authorized on January 26, 1818, were revoked effective May 1, 1820.

Numismatic Commentary: Notes of this bank are considered to be very scarce due to the short duration of the charter.

Valid Issues

$1 • W-KY-280-001-G010

Left: One Dollar vertically. ***Center:*** 1 / Man with horse and plow / 1. ***Right:*** 1 / KENTUCKY / 1 vertically. ***Engraver:*** Murray, Draper, Fairman & Co. ***Comments:*** H-KY-70-G12, Hughes-184. 18__. 1810s.

Rarity: URS-3
VF $350

$2 • W-KY-280-002-G020 QDB

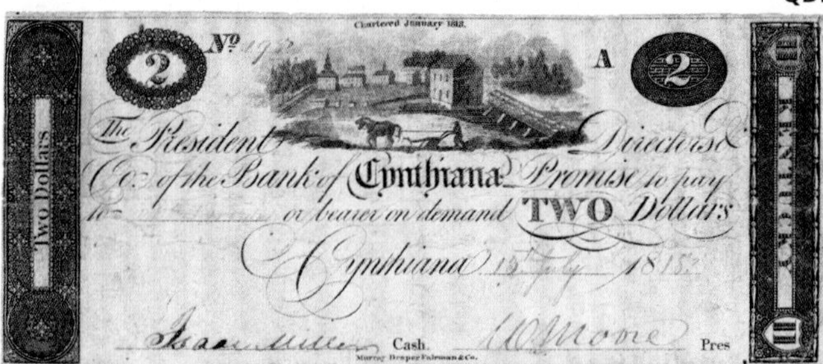

Engraver: Murray, Draper, Fairman & Co. ***Comments:*** H-KY-70-G14, Hughes-185. 18__. 1810s.

Rarity: URS-3
VF $400

$3 • W-KY-280-003-G030 NJW

Engraver: Murray, Draper, Fairman & Co. ***Comments:*** H-KY-70-G16, Hughes-186. 18__. 1810s.

Rarity: URS-3
VF $400

$5 • W-KY-280-005-G040

Left: Five Dollars vertically. ***Center:*** Man with horse and plow. ***Right:*** KENTUCKY vertically. ***Engraver:*** Murray, Draper, Fairman & Co. ***Comments:*** H-KY-70-G18, Hughes-187. 18__. 1810s.

Rarity: URS-3
VF $400

$10 • W-KY-280-010-G050

Left: Ten Dollars vertically. ***Center:*** Man with horse and plow. ***Right:*** KENTUCKY vertically. ***Engraver:*** Murray, Draper, Fairman & Co. ***Comments:*** H-KY-70-G20, Hughes-188. 18__. 1810s.

Rarity: URS-3
VF $400

$20 • W-KY-280-020-G060

Left: TWENTY vertically. ***Center:*** 20 / Man with horse and plow / XX. ***Right:*** KENTUCKY vertically. ***Comments:*** H-Unlisted, Hughes-189. 18__. 1810s.

Rarity: URS-2
VF $450

Post Notes

$20 • W-KY-280-020-G070

Left: TWENTY vertically. ***Center:*** 20 / Man with horse and plow / XX. ***Right:*** KENTUCKY vertically. ***Comments:*** H-Unlisted, Hughes-190. 18__. 1810s.

Rarity: URS-2
F $200

Commercial Bank of Kentucky (branch)

1852–1871

W-KY-290

History: On January 3, 1852, the Commercial Bank of Kentucky was chartered. In 1861 the capital of the Cynthiana branch was $100,000. On May 1, 1862, the assets of the Deposit Bank of Cynthiana, W-KY-300, were transferred to the local branch of the Commercial Bank of Kentucky. The bank was succeeded by the National Bank of Cynthiana in 1871.

The Commercial Bank of Kentucky had its parent bank located in Paducah, W-KY-1240, and branch banks located in Harrodsburg, W-KY-590, Lebanon, W-KY-720, Louisville, W-KY-900, Monticello, W-KY-1070, Newport, W-KY-1150, and Versailles, W-KY-1560.

Valid Issues

$1 • W-KY-290-001-G010

Left: ONE on 1 / ONE vertically / ONE on 1. ***Center:*** Woman seated with map, Two men in canoe. ***Right:*** 1 / Female portrait. ***Tint:*** Green. ***Engraver:*** American Bank Note Co. ***Comments:*** H-KY-255-G30a, Hughes-668. 18__. 1860s.

Rarity: URS-3
F $250

$2 • W-KY-290-002-G020

Left: 2 / Female portrait. ***Center:*** Woman seated with map, Two men in canoe. ***Right:*** TWO / TWO vertically / TWO. ***Tint:*** Green. ***Engraver:*** American Bank Note Co. ***Comments:*** H-KY-255-G32a, Hughes-673. 18__. 1860s.

Rarity: URS-3
F $250

$3 • W-KY-290-003-G030

Left: 3 / Boy with rabbits. ***Center:*** Woman seated with map, Two men in canoe. ***Right:*** 3 / Portrait of girl. ***Tint:*** Green. ***Engraver:*** American Bank Note Co. ***Comments:*** H-KY-255-G34a, Hughes-673. 18__. 1860s.

Rarity: URS-3
F $250

$5 • W-KY-290-005-G040

Left: FIVE / Men and women in and around V. ***Center:*** 5 / Women in and around 5, Dock. ***Right:*** FIVE / Portrait of Franklin Pierce. ***Tint:*** Red-orange. ***Engraver:*** Rawdon, Wright, Hatch & Edson / ABNCo. monogram. ***Comments:*** H-KY-255-G36a, Hughes-Unlisted. 18__. 1850s–1860s.

Rarity: URS-3
F $250

$10 • W-KY-290-010-G050

Left: 10 / Male portrait / TEN. ***Center:*** Steamboats. ***Right:*** TEN / Harrodsburg Springs / TEN. ***Engraver:*** Unverified, but likely Rawdon, Wright, Hatch & Edson. ***Comments:*** H-KY-255-G38, Hughes-Unlisted. 18__. 1850s.

Rarity: URS-3
F $300

Deposit Bank of Cynthiana

1856–1862

W-KY-300

History: The Deposit Bank of Cynthiana was chartered on February 27, 1856, with an authorized capital of $50,000. J.S. Withers was the cashier, and J.W. Peck was the president. In July 1858 it was reported that a dividend of six percent had been paid to stockholders. On May 1, 1862, the bank's assets were transferred to the local branch of the Commercial Bank of Kentucky, W-KY-290.

Northern Bank of Kentucky (branch)

1835–1860s

W-KY-305

History: The Northern Bank of Kentucky was chartered in 1835 with an authorized capital of $3,000,000. Sometime during the 1860s the Northern Bank of Kentucky was converted to a bank of discount and deposit, after which time no notes were issued.

The Northern Bank of Kentucky had its parent bank located in Lexington, W-KY-830, and branch banks located in Barbourville, W-KY-040, Covington, W-KY-260, Louisville, W-KY-960, Paris, W-KY-1280, and Richmond, W-KY-1360.

Valid Issues

6-1/4¢ • W-KY-305-00.06.25-G010 CC

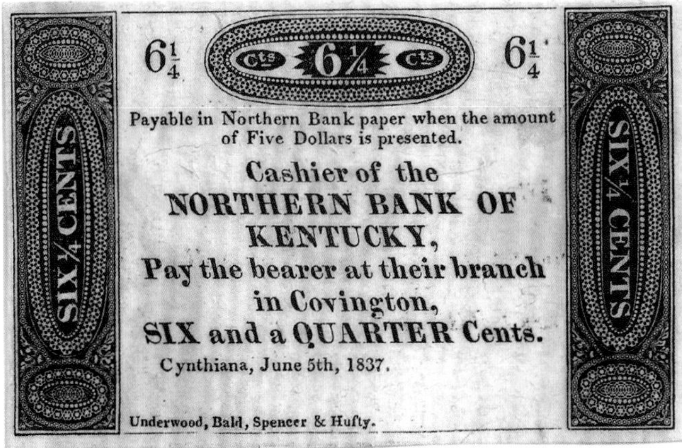

Comments: H-Unlisted, Hughes-Unlisted. 18__. June 5th, 1837.

Rarity: —

Unc-Rem $250

25¢ • W-KY-305-00.25-G020 CC

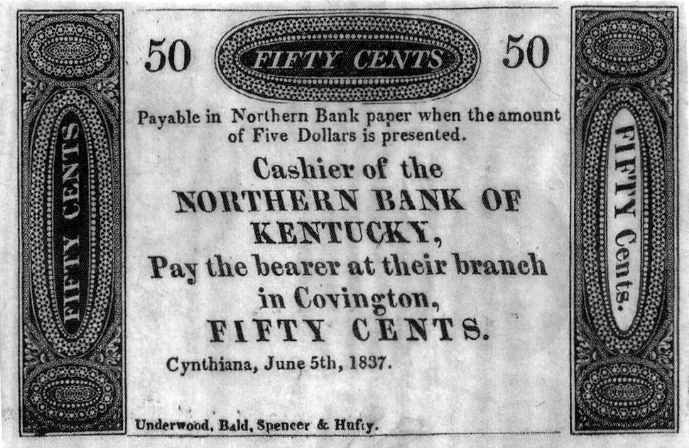

Comments: H-Unlisted, Hughes-Unlisted. 18__. June 5th, 1837.

Rarity: —

Unc-Rem $250

50¢ • W-KY-305-00.50-G030 CC

Comments: H-Unlisted, Hughes-Unlisted. 18__. June 5th, 1837.

Rarity: —

Unc-Rem $250

75¢ • W-KY-305-00.75-G040 CC

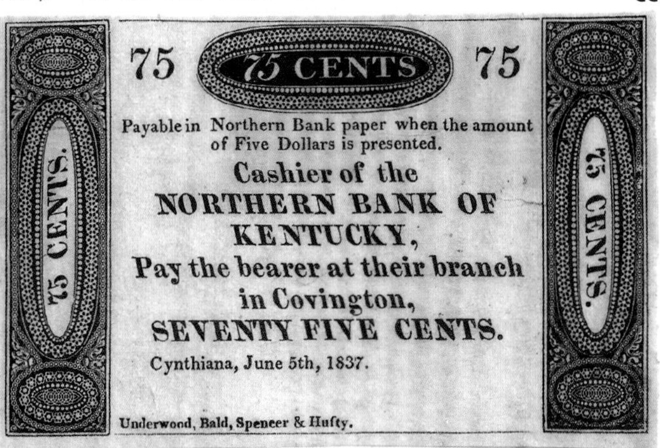

Comments: H-Unlisted, Hughes-Unlisted. June 5th, 1837.

Rarity: —

Unc-Rem $250

$1 • **W-KY-305-001-G050** CC

Comments: H-Unlisted, Hughes-Unlisted. 18__. 1850s–1860s.

Rarity: —

Proof $300

Danville, Kentucky

Danville was originally known as Crow's Station, after John Crow who settled the area in 1774. The town was ultimately named after Walker Daniel, however, who surveyed and plotted the town proper. On December 4, 1787, Danville was established.

To residents of Kentucky, Danville is known as the "City of Firsts." The first courthouse in Kentucky was built here; the first post office to the west of the Allegheny Mountains was established here; the first state-funded school for the deaf was constructed here; and the first (and today oldest) collegiate building exists here from Centre College, founded in 1819.

In 1842 Danville became the seat of the newly formed Boyle County. In 1850 the Lexington and Danville Railroad was formed, but funds were difficult to come by and the project halted. In 1860 a fire destroyed much of the city. The town suffered even further damage during the Civil War.

Bank of Danville

1818–1820

W-KY-310

History: The Bank of Danville was chartered on January 26, 1818. The authorized capital of $150,000 was divided into 1,500 shares of $100 apiece. Joshua Barbee, William Akin, John Calhoon, Charles Henderson, David Bell, Richard Davenport, Jeremiah Clemens, and James G. Birney were appointed to take stock subscriptions. The bank operated only for a short time. The charters of all independent banks authorized on January 26, 1818, were revoked effective May 1, 1820.

Numismatic Commentary: Few notes of this bank have been found.

Valid Issues

$1 • **W-KY-310-001-G010**

Left: KENTUCKY vertically. ***Center:*** 1 / Woman seated / 1. ***Right:*** ONE DOLLAR vertically. ***Engraver:*** Unverified, but likely Murray, Draper, Fairman & Co. ***Comments:*** H-KY-75-G12, Hughes-191. 18__. 1810s.

Rarity: *None known*

$3 • **W-KY-310-003-G020**

Left: KENTUCKY vertically. ***Center:*** 3 / Woman seated / 3. ***Right:*** THREE DOLLARS vertically. ***Engraver:*** Unverified, but likely Murray, Draper, Fairman & Co. ***Comments:*** H-KY-75-G16, Hughes-192. 18__. 1810s.

Rarity: *None known*

$5 • **W-KY-310-005-G030**

Left: KENTUCKY vertically. ***Center:*** 5 / Woman seated / 5. ***Right:*** FIVE DOLLARS vertically. ***Engraver:*** Unverified, but likely Murray, Draper, Fairman & Co. ***Comments:*** H-KY-75-G18, Hughes-193. 18__. 1810s.

Rarity: *None known*

$10 • **W-KY-310-010-G040**

Left: KENTUCKY vertically. ***Center:*** 10 / Woman seated / 10. ***Right:*** TEN DOLLARS vertically. ***Engraver:*** Unverified, but likely Murray, Draper, Fairman & Co. ***Comments:*** H-KY-75-G20, Hughes-194. 18__. 1810s.

Rarity: *None known*

$20 • **W-KY-310-020-G050**

Left: KENTUCKY vertically. ***Center:*** 20 / Woman seated / 20. ***Right:*** TWENTY vertically. ***Engraver:*** Unverified, but likely Murray, Draper, Fairman & Co. ***Comments:*** H-KY-75-G22, Hughes-195. 18__. 1810s.

Rarity: URS-2

F $400

Bank of Kentucky {1st} (branch)

1815–1822

W-KY-320

History: The Bank of Kentucky (sometimes seen later in print as the "Old" Bank of Kentucky) was incorporated on December 27, 1806, with an authorized capital of $1,000,000. Half of the capital was subscribed to by the state. The Danville branch was opened in 1815. On January 21, 1822, the bank was ordered to start closing up its branches. This was to be completed by May 1, 1824. This act essentially shut down the bank. Curiously, all of the paperwork was not completed until the 1870s.

The first Bank of Kentucky had its parent bank located in Frankfort, W-KY-420, and branch banks located in Bardstown, W-KY-050, Glasgow, W-KY-500, Hopkinsville, W-KY-660, Lexington, W-KY-760, Louisville, W-KY-840, Paris, W-KY-1260, Richmond, W-KY-1350, Russellville, W-KY-1380, Shelbyville, W-KY-1430, Springfield, W-KY-1500, Washington, W-KY-1570, and Winchester, W-KY-1580.

Valid Issues

$1 • **W-KY-320-001-G010**

Comments: H-KY-110-G42, Hughes-283. No description available. 18__. 1816–1821.

Rarity: *None known*

$1 • **W-KY-320-001-G020**

Engraver: Murray, Draper, Fairman & Co. ***Comments:*** H-KY-110-G44, Hughes-Unlisted. No description available. 18__. 1821.

Rarity: *None known*

$5 • W-KY-320-005-G030
Engraver: Unverified, but likely W. Harrison. ***Comments:*** H-KY-110-G46, Hughes-Unlisted. No description available. 18__. 1815.

Rarity: *None known*

$10 • W-KY-320-010-G040
Engraver: Unverified, but likely W. Harrison. ***Comments:*** H-KY-110-G48, Hughes-Unlisted. No description available. 18__. 1815.

Rarity: *None known*

$20 • W-KY-320-020-G050
Engraver: Unverified, but likely W. Harrison. ***Comments:*** H-KY-110-G50, Hughes-Unlisted. No description available. 18__. 1815.

Rarity: *None known*

$50 • W-KY-320-050-G060
Engraver: Unverified, but likely W. Harrison. ***Comments:*** H-KY-110-G52, Hughes-Unlisted. No description available. 18__. 1815–1817.

Rarity: *None known*

$100 • W-KY-320-100-G070
Engraver: Unverified, but likely W. Harrison. ***Comments:*** H-KY-110-G54, Hughes-295. No description available. 18__. 1815–1817.

Rarity: *None known*

Post Notes

$__ • W-KY-320-__-G080
Left: POST NOTE vertically. ***Right:*** POST NOTE. ***Engraver:*** W. Harrison. ***Comments:*** H-KY-110-G56. 18__. 1815–1822.

Rarity: URS-2
F $300

Bank of Kentucky {2nd} (branch)
1837–1866
W-KY-330

History: The second Bank of Kentucky (sometimes seen in print as the "New" Bank of Kentucky) was chartered in 1834 in order to assume the business of the first Bank of Kentucky, W-KY-420, which had recently closed. The capital of the bank was $5,000,000.

The branch in Danville was established in 1837. In 1848 the president was William Craig, and Thomas Mitchell was the cashier. Capital was $220,000. By 1855 James Kinnaird had taken the position of president. In January 1866 almost all branches of the Bank of Kentucky were closed down, and the parent bank began winding up its business.

The second Bank of Kentucky had its parent bank located in Louisville, W-KY-850, and branch banks located in Bowling Green, W-KY-080, Burksville, W-KY-140, Columbus, W-KY-220, Flemingsburg, W-KY-390, Frankfort, W-KY-430, Glasgow, W-KY-510, Greensburg, W-KY-540, Hopkinsville, W-KY-670, Lexington, W-KY-770, Maysville, W-KY-1020, Mount Sterling, W-KY-1100, and Paducah, W-KY-1220.

Numismatic Commentary: Notes of this bank and its branches are very rare.

Valid Issues

$1 • W-KY-330-001-G010 CC

Engraver: Danforth, Bald & Co. ***Comments:*** H-KY-195-G110, Hughes-484. 18__. 1850s.

Rarity: URS-3
F $300; **Proof** $500

$5 • W-KY-330-005-G020
Left: FIVE / Liberty standing / V. ***Center:*** 5 / Horse / 5. ***Right:*** FIVE / Liberty standing / V. ***Engraver:*** Casilear, Durand, Burton & Evans. ***Comments:*** H-KY-195-G114, Hughes-495. 18__. 1830s–1840s.

Rarity: URS-3
Proof $500

$5 • W-KY-330-005-G030
Left: 5 / Portrait of Henry Clay / FIVE. ***Center:*** Portrait of John Q. Adams / Woman seated against bales, Train, Harvesting scene / Portrait of Thomas Jefferson. ***Right:*** 5 / Portrait of George Washington / FIVE. ***Engraver:*** Toppan, Carpenter & Co. ***Comments:*** H-KY-195-G118, Hughes-494. 18__. 1840s–1850s.

Rarity: URS-3
F $250

$10 • W-KY-330-010-G040
Left: 10 / Woman seated / X. ***Center:*** X / Three women seated / X. ***Right:*** 10 / Woman standing / X. ***Engraver:*** Casilear, Durand, Burton & Evans. ***Comments:*** H-KY-195-G122, Hughes-497. 18__. 1830s–1840s.

Rarity: URS-3
F $250

$10 • W-KY-330-010-G050
Left: 10 / Portrait of George Washington / 10. ***Center:*** Portrait of Andrew Jackson / Indian man and woman flanking shield bearing 10 surmounted by eagle / Portrait of Isaac Shelby. ***Right:*** 10 / Portrait of Henry Clay / 10. ***Engraver:*** Toppan, Carpenter & Co. ***Comments:*** H-KY-195-G126, Hughes-499. 18__. 1840s–1850s.

Rarity: URS-3
F $250

$20 • W-KY-330-020-G060
Left: 20 / Woman standing / 20. ***Center:*** XX / Woman seated with plow and bales, Cattle / XX. ***Right:*** 20 / Indian man standing / XX. ***Engraver:*** Casilear, Durand, Burton & Evans. ***Comments:*** H-KY-195-G130, Hughes-506. 18__. 1830s–1840s.

Rarity: URS-3
F $250

$20 • W-KY-330-020-G070

Left: Woman holding male portrait aloft / Male portrait. ***Center:*** 20 / Woman flying / 20. ***Right:*** Three women holding medallion head aloft. ***Engraver:*** Draper, Toppan & Co. ***Comments:*** H-KY-195-G132, Hughes-508. 18__. 1840s.

Rarity: URS-3
F $250

$20 • W-KY-330-020-G080

Left: 20 / Portrait of Daniel Webster. ***Center:*** "General Marion's Sweet Potato Dinner." ***Right:*** 20 / Male portrait. ***Engraver:*** Toppan, Carpenter & Co. ***Comments:*** H-KY-195-G134, Hughes-511. 185_. 1850s.

Rarity: URS-3
F $250

$50 • W-KY-330-050-G090

Left: Woman standing. ***Center:*** 50 / Steamboat *Henry Clay* / 50. ***Right:*** Woman standing. ***Engraver:*** Casilear, Durand, Burton & Evans. ***Comments:*** H-KY-195-G138, Hughes-513. 18__. 1830s–1840s.

Rarity: URS-2
F $350

Post Notes

$__ • W-KY-330-__-G100

Left: Woman seated with plow, sheaves, Cattle / POST NOTE. ***Center:*** $__. ***Right:*** Three women seated / POST NOTE. ***Engraver:*** Casilear, Durand, Burton & Evans. ***Comments:*** H-KY-195-G142. 18__. 1830s.

Rarity: URS-2
F $85

Non-Valid Issues

$10 • W-KY-330-010-C050

Engraver: Toppan, Carpenter & Co. ***Comments:*** H-KY-195-C126, Hughes-500. Counterfeit of W-KY-330-010-G050. 18__. 1840s–1850s.

Rarity: URS-4
F $100

$20 • W-KY-330-020-C070

Engraver: Toppan, Carpenter & Co. ***Comments:*** H-KY-195-C132, Hughes-509. Counterfeit of W-KY-330-020-G070. 18__. 1840s.

Rarity: URS-4
F $100

$20 • W-KY-330-020-C080

Engraver: Toppan, Carpenter & Co. ***Comments:*** H-KY-195-C134, Hughes-512. Counterfeit of W-KY-330-020-G080. 185_. 1850s.

Rarity: URS-4
F $100

$500 • W-KY-330-500-S010

Left: Woman standing. ***Center:*** 500 / Woman gesturing to train / 500. ***Right:*** Woman standing. ***Engraver:*** Casilear, Durand, Burton & Evans. ***Comments:*** H-KY-195-S15, Hughes-522. 18__. 1839.

Rarity: URS-2
VF $345

Central Bank
Circa 1860s
W-KY-340

History: A congressional report of 1860 stated that this bank did not issue paper money. In 1861 the Central Bank had a capital of $100,000. The cashier was G. Rice, and the president was Clifton Rhodes. By 1863 the capital of the bank had dropped to $50,000. In 1865 E.W. Proctor took the place of cashier.

Numismatic Commentary: It seems that no bills were issued for circulation. If any Proofs were made, no record of them has been found.

Elizabethtown, Kentucky

Colonel John Hardin settled the area that would become Elizabethtown in 1793. The land was surveyed, laid off into lots, and named in honor of his wife. In 1797 Elizabethtown was officially established.

Abraham Lincoln's parents, Thomas and Nancy Lincoln, lived in Elizabethtown from 1806 to 1809. On March 5, 1850, the Louisville and Nashville Railroad Company was chartered, and the main line of the railway was laid through Elizabethtown. It was completed in 1858, opening a new era of economic growth. Elizabethtown became a significant trade center as well as a strategic location during the Civil War. Elizabethtown was attacked on December 27, 1862, by Confederate forces. The town was successfully seized, and the railway was burned and destroyed. The name of the town also appears as both Elizabeth and Elizabeth Town in certain early citations.

Union Bank of Elizabethtown
1818–1820
W-KY-350

History: The Union Bank of Elizabethtown was chartered on January 26, 1818, with an authorized capital of $100,000 to be divided into 1,000 shares of $100 par value each. James Crutcher, Benjamin Helm, Horatio G. Wintersmith, Charles Helm, William S. Young, James Larae, and James Perceval were appointed to take stock subscriptions. On April 13, 1819, the bank went into operation. Horatio G. Wintersmith was the cashier of the bank. On December 4, 1819, he verified that a report of the bank and its condition was true—that there was $4,400 of specie in the vaults of the bank, while the bank was owed debts to the total of $40,000. The charters of all independent banks authorized on January 26, 1818, were revoked effective May 1, 1820.

Numismatic Commentary: Only the rare $5 note of this bank is known.

Valid Issues

$1 • W-KY-350-001-G010

Left: 1 / 1. ***Center:*** Farm scene with horse, cow, farmers. ***Right:*** KENTUCKY vertically. ***Engraver:*** Murray, Draper, Fairman & Co. ***Comments:*** H-KY-80-G12, Hughes-205. 18__. 1810s.

Rarity: *None known*

$3 • W-KY-350-003-G020
Left: 3 / 3. ***Center:*** Farm scene with horse, cow, farmers. ***Right:*** KENTUCKY vertically. ***Engraver:*** Murray, Draper, Fairman & Co. ***Comments:*** H-KY-80-G16, Hughes-206. 18__. 1810s.

Rarity: *None known*

$5 • W-KY-350-005-G030 

HA

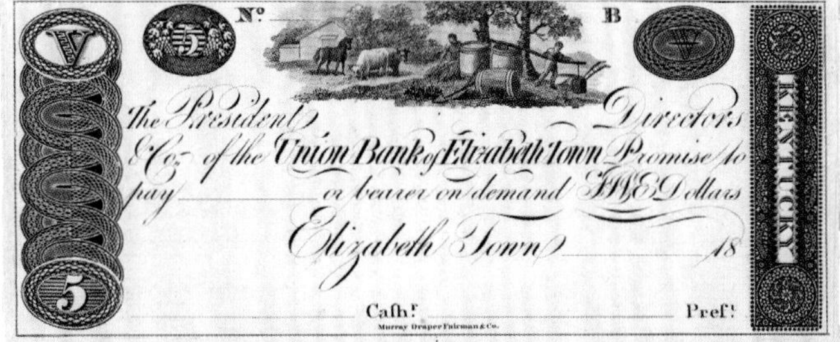

Engraver: Murray, Draper, Fairman & Co. ***Comments:*** H-KY-80-G18, Hughes-207. 18__. 1810s.

Rarity: URS-1
Proof $1,650
Selected auction price: Heritage Auctions, September 25, 2013, Lot 15823, Proof $1,645

$10 • W-KY-350-010-G040
Left: X / 10. ***Center:*** Farm scene with horse, cow, farmers. ***Right:*** KENTUCKY vertically. ***Engraver:*** Murray, Draper, Fairman & Co. ***Comments:*** H-KY-80-G20, Hughes-208. 18__. 1810s.

Rarity: *None known*

$20 • W-KY-350-020-G050
Left: XX / 20. ***Center:*** Farm scene with horse, cow, farmers. ***Right:*** KENTUCKY vertically. ***Engraver:*** Murray, Draper, Fairman & Co. ***Comments:*** H-KY-80-G22, Hughes-209. 18__. 1810s.

Rarity: *None known*

Falmouth, Kentucky

Falmouth was settled in 1780 and laid out by John Waller when it was officially established in 1793. The town was named after Waller's hometown of Falmouth, Virginia. In 1856 it was incorporated as a city.

Bank of the Commonwealth of Kentucky (branch)

1820–1830

W-KY-360

History: The Bank of the Commonwealth of Kentucky was chartered on November 29, 1820, with an authorized capital of $2,000,000. A local name for the bank was the "Peoples Bank," as it was chartered for the purpose of bringing relief to the population in a time of economic uncertainty. On December 22, 1820, an act was passed authorizing the bank to issue $3,000,000 in bills. The establishment of the Bank of the Commonwealth of Kentucky inadvertently caused the failure of the first Bank of Kentucky, W-KY-420.

In 1830 the bank lost its authorization to loan money, and it was instructed to close up its branches. Around that time the bank ceased new business, but the winding up of its affairs took until 1855.

Notes issued by the branch at Falmouth were also imprinted Covington, W-KY-230, where the bank may have had a facility.

The Bank of the Commonwealth of Kentucky had its parent bank located in Frankfort, W-KY-440, and branch banks located in Bowling Green, W-KY-090, Flemingsburg, W-KY-410, Greensburg, W-KY-550, Harrodsburg, W-KY-580, Hartford, W-KY-610, Lexington, W-KY-780, Louisville, W-KY-870, Mount Sterling, W-KY-1120, Princeton, W-KY-1330, Somerset, W-KY-1470, and Winchester, W-KY-1590.

Numismatic Commentary: Almost all notes from this bank and its branches are unknown today.

Valid Issues

6-1/4¢ • W-KY-360-00.06.25-G010

CC

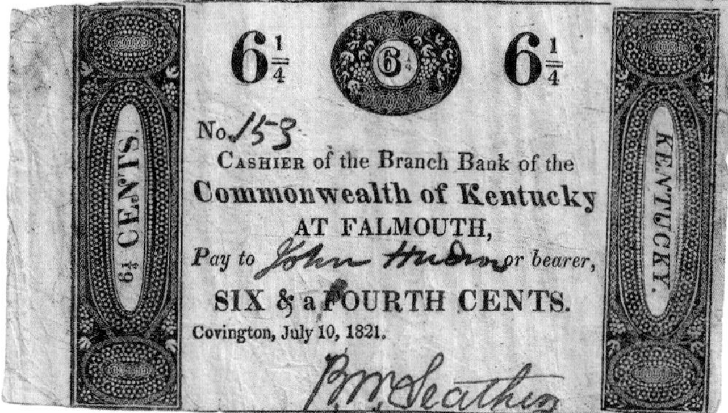

Comments: H-KY-95-G52, Hughes-210. 1822.

Rarity: URS-1
VF $275

12-1/2¢ • W-KY-360-00.12.50-G020
Left: 12-1/2 CENTS. ***Center:*** 12-1/2 / 12-1/2 on die / 12-1/2. ***Right:*** KENTUCKY. ***Comments:*** H-KY-95-G54, Hughes-211. 1822.

Rarity: URS-2
VG $200

25¢ • W-KY-360-00.25-G030
Left: 25 CENTS. ***Center:*** 25 / 25 on die / 25. ***Right:*** KENTUCKY. ***Comments:*** H-KY-95-G56, Hughes-212. 1822.

Rarity: URS-1
F $225

50¢ • W-KY-360-00.50-G040
Left: 50 CENTS. ***Center:*** 50 / 50 on die / 50. ***Right:*** KENTUCKY. ***Comments:*** H-KY-95-G58, Hughes-213. 1822.

Rarity: URS-1
F $225

$1 • W-KY-360-001-G050 SBG

Engraver: Murray, Draper, Fairman & Co. ***Comments:*** H-KY-95-G62, Hughes-214. 182_. 1820s.

Rarity: URS-2
F $350

$3 • W-KY-360-003-G060

Left: KENTUCKY vertically. ***Center:*** 3 / 3. ***Right:*** CAMPBELL COUNTY vertically. ***Engraver:*** Murray, Draper, Fairman & Co. ***Comments:*** H-Unlisted, Hughes-215. 18__. 1820s.

Rarity: URS-2
F $350

$5 • W-KY-360-005-G070

Left: Woman holding staff. ***Center:*** 5 / Minerva standing with owl, shield, staff / 5. ***Right:*** Woman holding staff. ***Engraver:*** Murray, Draper, Fairman & Co. ***Comments:*** H-KY-95-G66, Hughes-216. 18__. 1820s.

Rarity: URS-2
F $350

$10 • W-KY-360-010-G080

Left: Woman holding staff. ***Center:*** 10 / Woman standing with staff, shield, Four cherubs / 10. ***Right:*** Woman holding staff. ***Engraver:*** Murray, Draper, Fairman & Co. ***Comments:*** H-KY-95-G68, Hughes-217. 18__. 1820s.

Rarity: URS-2
F $350

$20 • W-KY-360-020-G090

Engraver: Murray, Draper, Fairman & Co. ***Comments:*** H-KY-95-G70, Hughes-218. No description available. 18__. 1820s.

Rarity: *None known*

$50 • W-KY-360-050-G100

Engraver: Murray, Draper, Fairman & Co. ***Comments:*** H-KY-95-G72, Hughes-219. No description available. 18__. 1820s.

Rarity: *None known*

$100 • W-KY-360-100-G110

Engraver: Murray, Draper, Fairman & Co. ***Comments:*** H-KY-95-G74, Hughes-220. No description available. 18__. 1820s.

Rarity: *None known*

Feliciana, Kentucky

Feliciana was settled in the 1820s. In 1829 the post office was opened.

South Western Real Estate Bank of Kentucky

Circa 1838

W-KY-370

History: This non-existent bank was a fraudulent operation. The name appears in print also as the *S.W. Real Estate Bank* and the *Real Estate Bank.*

From the *Daily Commercial Bulletin* in Saint Louis, November 21, 1838, this report on the bank was given:

> The Hopkinsville (Ky.) Gazette says that a splendid scheme of swindling is now in operation at a little place called Feliciana in that state, west of the Tennessee River. A large quantity of notes have been struck, purporting to be bank notes of the South Western Real Estate Bank of Kentucky, signed P. Cayce, Pres't., N. Moss, Cashier. Agents are said to be busily engaged in all directions, putting them in circulation upon the best terms they can.

Numismatic Commentary: All known notes of this bank are scarce.

Issues

$1 • W-KY-370-001-G003 CC

Engraver: Woodruff, Tucker & Co. ***Comments:*** H-Unlisted, Hughes-Unlisted. 18__. 1838.

Rarity: URS-3
F $225

$3 • W-KY-370-003-G005 CC

Engraver: Woodruff, Tucker & Co. ***Comments:*** H-Unlisted, Hughes-Unlisted. 18__. 1838.

Rarity: URS-3
F $400

$5 • W-KY-370-005-G010 CC

Engraver: Woodruff, Tucker & Co. ***Comments:*** H-KY-85-G8, Hughes-221. 18__. 1838.

Rarity: URS-3
VF $300; **EF** $475

$10 • W-KY-370-010-G020 HA

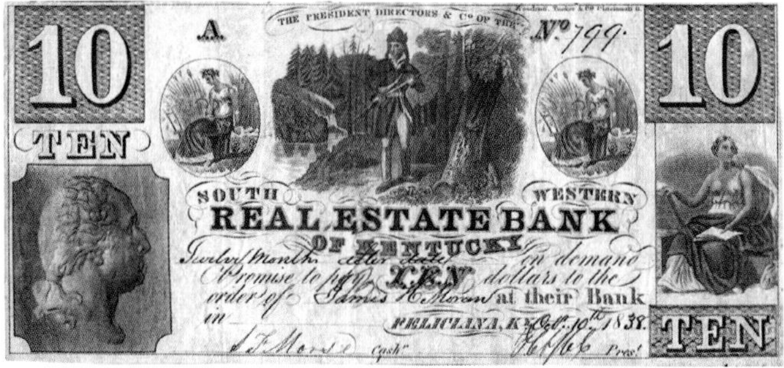

Engraver: Woodruff, Tucker & Co. ***Comments:*** H-KY-85-G10, Hughes-223. 18__. 1838.

Rarity: URS-3
F $350

$50 • W-KY-370-050-G030 QDB

Engraver: Woodruff, Tucker & Co. ***Comments:*** H-KY-85-G14, Hughes-225. 18__. 1838.

Rarity: URS-3
F $400

Post Notes

$5 • W-KY-370-005-G040

Left: 5. ***Center:*** 5 / Spread eagle on rock by river / Seated woman. ***Right:*** 5 / Ram / FIVE. ***Engraver:*** Woodruff, Tucker & Co. ***Comments:*** H-KY-85-G22, Hughes-222. 18__. 1830s.

Rarity: URS-3
F $250

$10 • W-KY-370-010-G050 HA

Engraver: Woodruff, Tucker & Co. ***Comments:*** H-KY-85-G24, Hughes-224. 18__. 1830s.

Rarity: URS-2
VF $250

$50 • W-KY-370-050-G060

Left: L / FIFTY / Woman seated with sheaf of grain. ***Center:*** Covered wagon, Herd in circle. ***Right:*** Portrait of Marquis de Lafayette / L / FIFTY. ***Engraver:*** Woodruff, Tucker & Co. ***Comments:*** H-KY-G28, Hughes-226. 18__. 1830s.

Rarity: URS-1
EF $400

FLEMINGSBURG, KENTUCKY

Founded in 1797 by George S. Stockton, Flemingsburg was named after Colonel John Fleming and was incorporated in 1812. It was established the seat of Fleming County. The town had two churches, a store, a hotel, and mineral springs known for their medicinal properties. Guests came from all over the state to enjoy the springs and the hotel. Flemingsburg was also the only place in the area to vote.

The courthouse was built in 1829. In 1833 cholera swept the county, and many residents died. Nevertheless, more churches were built, and the community recovered. A drought caused problems in 1854, and in 1855 cholera came again.

Bank of Flemingsburg

1818–1820

W-KY-380

History: The Bank of Flemingsburg was chartered on January 26, 1818. The authorized capital of $150,000 was divided into 1,500 shares of $100 par value each. William P. Roper, Joshua Stockton, Thomas Wallace, James Alexander, and Thomas W. Fleming were appointed to take stock subscriptions. The bank operated only for a short time. By the summer of 1819 it was no longer redeeming its notes. The charters of all independent banks authorized on January 26, 1818, were revoked effective May 1, 1820.

Numismatic Commentary: Another bank which only lasted for a couple of years, the Bank of Flemingsburg has a few notes with a common central vignette.

Valid Issues

$1 • W-KY-380-001-G010

CC

Engraver: Murray, Draper, Fairman & Co. ***Comments:*** H-KY-90-G12, Hughes-227. 18__. 1810s.

Rarity: URS-2
Proof $850

$3 • W-KY-380-003-G020

HA

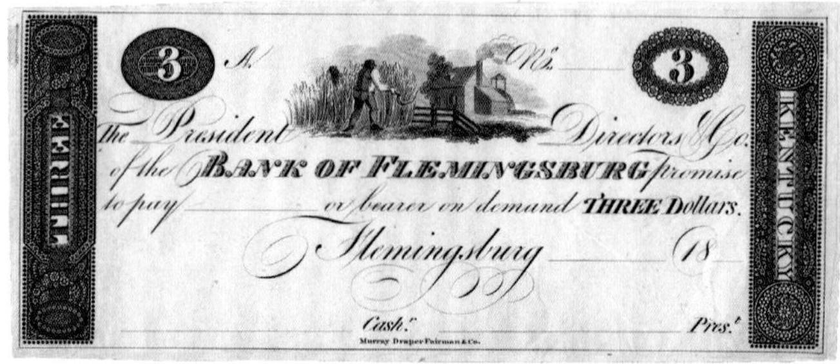

Engraver: Murray, Draper, Fairman & Co. ***Comments:*** H-KY-90-G16, Hughes-228. 18__. 1810s.

Rarity: URS-2
Proof $1,175
Selected auction price: Heritage Auctions, September 25, 2013, Lot 15824, Proof $1,175

$5 • W-KY-380-005-G030

HA

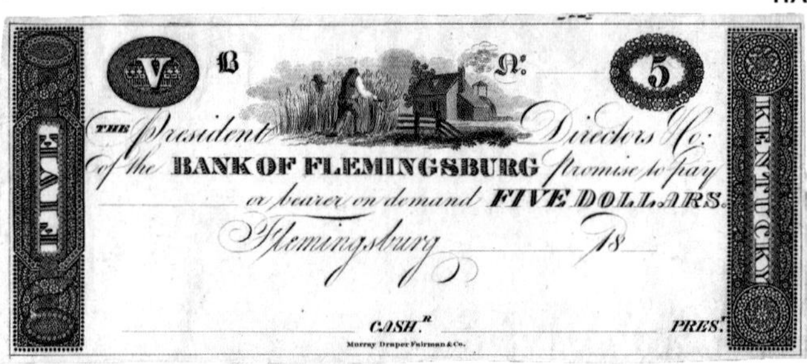

Engraver: Murray, Draper, Fairman & Co. ***Comments:*** H-KY-90-G18, Hughes-229. 18__. 1810s.

Rarity: URS-2
F $400; **Proof** $1,000
Selected auction price: Heritage Auctions, September 25, 2013, Lot 15825, Proof $998

$10 • W-KY-380-010-G040

Left: TEN vertically. ***Center:*** Man cutting grain, House. ***Right:*** KENTUCKY vertically. ***Engraver:*** Murray, Draper, Fairman & Co. ***Comments:*** H-KY-90-G20, Hughes-230. 18__. 1810s.

Rarity: URS-2
F $400

$20 • W-KY-380-020-G050

Left: TWENTY vertically. ***Center:*** Man cutting grain, House. ***Right:*** KENTUCKY vertically. ***Engraver:*** Murray, Draper, Fairman & Co. ***Comments:*** H-KY-90-G22, Hughes-231. 18__. 1810s.

Rarity: URS-2
F $450

$50 • W-KY-380-050-G060

CC

Engraver: Murray, Draper, Fairman & Co. ***Comments:*** H-Unlisted, Hughes-Unlisted. 18__. 1810s.

Rarity: URS-1
Proof $2,400

Bank of Kentucky {2nd} (branch)

1860s–1866

W-KY-390

History: The second Bank of Kentucky (sometimes seen in print as the "New" Bank of Kentucky) was chartered in 1834 in order to assume the business of the first Bank of Kentucky, W-KY-420, which had recently closed. The capital of the bank was $5,000,000.

The branch in Flemingsburg was established sometime in the 1860s. In January 1866 almost all branches of the Bank of Kentucky were closed down, and the parent bank began winding up its business.

The second Bank of Kentucky had its parent bank located in Louisville, W-KY-850, and branch banks located in Bowling Green, W-KY-080, Burksville, W-KY-140, Columbus, W-KY-220, Danville, W-KY-330, Frankfort, W-KY-430, Glasgow, W-KY-510, Greensburg, W-KY-540, Hopkinsville, W-KY-670, Lexington, W-KY-770, Maysville, W-KY-1020, Mount Sterling, W-KY-1100, and Paducah, W-KY-1220.

Numismatic Commentary: Notes of this bank and its branches are very rare.

Valid Issues

$5 • W-KY-390-005-G010

Left: 5 / Portrait of Henry Clay / FIVE. ***Center:*** Portrait of John Q. Adams / Woman seated against bales, Train, Harvesting scene / Portrait of Thomas Jefferson. ***Right:*** 5 / Portrait of George Washington / FIVE. ***Engraver:*** Toppan, Carpenter & Co. ***Comments:*** H-KY-195-G150, Hughes-494. 185_. 1850s.

Rarity: URS-2
F $400

$10 • W-KY-390-010-G020
Left: 10 / Portrait of George Washington / 10. *Center:* Portrait of Andrew Jackson / Indian man and woman flanking shield bearing 10 surmounted by eagle / Portrait of Isaac Shelby. *Right:* 10 / Portrait of Henry Clay / 10. *Engraver:* Toppan, Carpenter & Co. *Comments:* H-KY-195-G154, Hughes-499. 185_. 1850s.

Rarity: URS-2
F $400

$20 • W-KY-390-020-G030
Left: 20 / Portrait of Daniel Webster. *Center:* "General Marion's Sweet Potato Dinner." *Right:* 20 / Male portrait. *Engraver:* Toppan, Carpenter & Co. *Comments:* H-KY-195-G158, Hughes-511. 185_. 1850s.

Rarity: URS-2
F $400

Non-Valid Issues

$10 • W-KY-390-010-C020
Engraver: Toppan, Carpenter & Co. *Comments:* H-KY-195-C154, Hughes-500. Counterfeit of W-KY-390-010-G020. 185_. 1850s.

Rarity: URS-3
F $250

Bank of Louisville (branch)
1833–1860s
W-KY-400

History: The Bank of Louisville was chartered in 1833 with an authorized capital of $5,000,000. In 1848 the president of the Flemingsburg branch was Dorsey H. Stockton, and the cashier was H. Powers. Capital was $100,000. In 1861 S. Stockwell took the position of president. During the 1860s the Bank of Louisville closed its doors.

The Bank of Louisville had its parent bank located in Louisville, W-KY-860, and branch banks located in Burksville, W-KY-150, and Paducah, W-KY-1230.

Valid Issues

$1 • W-KY-400-001-G010
Left: ONE vertically. *Center:* 1 / 1. *Right:* ONE / Portrait of Henry Clay / ONE. *Engraver:* Draper, Toppan, Longacre & Co. *Comments:* H-KY-190-G50, Hughes-525. 18__. 1840s.

Rarity: URS-3
F $300

$2 • W-KY-400-002-G020
Left: 2. *Center:* 2 / 2 / Woman leaning on column. *Right:* TWO / Woman with shield / TWO. *Engraver:* Draper, Toppan, Longacre & Co. *Comments:* H-KY-190-G52, Hughes-529. 18__. 1840s.

Rarity: URS-3
F $300

$3 • W-KY-400-003-G030
Left: 3. *Center:* 3 / Steamboat / 3. *Right:* THREE / Woman standing / THREE. *Engraver:* Draper, Toppan, Longacre & Co. *Comments:* H-KY-190-G54, Hughes-530. 18__. 1840s.

Rarity: URS-3
F $300

$5 • W-KY-400-005-G040
Left: FIVE / Woman standing in V with wand, bale, and barrel. *Center:* 5 / Eagle standing on sheep, Wheel, Ships / 5. *Right:* FIVE / Woman standing in 5 / 5. *Back:* Train. *Engraver:* Unverified, but likely Draper, Toppan & Co. *Comments:* H-KY-190-G58, Hughes-533. 18__. 1840s.

Rarity: URS-3
F $300

$5 • W-KY-400-005-G050
Left: 5 / Woman seated with shield. *Center:* Portrait of Millard Fillmore. *Bottom center:* 5. *Right:* 5 / Woman seated with implements. *Engraver:* Toppan, Carpenter, Casilear & Co. *Comments:* H-KY-190-G60, Hughes-534. 18__. 1850s.

Rarity: URS-3
F $300

$5 • W-KY-400-005-G060 HA

Tint: Green 5 / 5, ornaments, and dies bearing white 5s. *Engraver:* American Bank Note Co. *Comments:* H-Unlisted, Hughes-Unlisted. 18__. 1850s–1860s.

Rarity: URS-2
Proof $250

$10 • W-KY-400-010-G070
Left: Woman holding up portrait of George Washington / Portrait of John Marshall. *Center:* 10 / Woman leaning on pillar / 10. *Right:* 10 / Female portrait / 10. *Engraver:* Draper, Toppan & Co. *Comments:* H-KY-190-G64, Hughes-539. 18__. 1840s.

Rarity: URS-3
F $250

$10 • W-KY-400-010-G075
Center: People / Boy with hat. *Tint:* Green 10 / X / 10. *Engraver:* American Bank Note Co. *Comments:* H-Unlisted, Hughes-Unlisted. 18__. 1840s.

Rarity: URS-2
Proof $200

$20 • W-KY-400-020-G080
Left: 20 / Indian men hunting buffalo. *Center:* Female portrait. *Right:* 20 / Man cutting down tree, Oxen, two children. *Engraver:* Unverified, but likely Draper, Toppan & Co. *Comments:* H-KY-190-G68, Hughes-547. 18__. 1840s.

Rarity: URS-3
F $250

$100 • W-KY-400-100-G090

CC

Engraver: Toppan, Carpenter & Co. ***Comments:*** H-Unlisted, Hughes-551. 18__. 1850s.

Rarity: URS-2
VF $500; **Proof** $1,000

Non-Valid Issues

$5 • W-KY-400-005-C050

Engraver: Toppan, Carpenter, Casilear & Co. ***Comments:*** H-KY-190-C60, Hughes-535. Counterfeit of W-KY-400-005-G050. 18__. 1850s.

Rarity: URS-4
F $150

$10 • W-KY-400-010-C070

Engraver: Draper, Toppan & Co. ***Comments:*** H-KY-190-C64, Hughes-540. Counterfeit of W-KY-400-010-G070. 18__. 1840s.

Rarity: URS-4
F $150

Bank of the Commonwealth of Kentucky (branch)

1820–1830

W-KY-410

History: The Bank of the Commonwealth of Kentucky was chartered on November 29, 1820, with an authorized capital of $2,000,000. A local name for the bank was the "Peoples Bank," as it was chartered for the purpose of bringing relief to the population in a time of economic uncertainty. On December 22, 1820, an act was passed authorizing the bank to issue $3,000,000 in bills. The establishment of the Bank of the Commonwealth of Kentucky inadvertently caused the failure of the first Bank of Kentucky, W-KY-420.

In 1830 the bank lost its authorization to loan money, and it was instructed to close up its branches. Around that time the bank ceased new business, but the winding up of its affairs took until 1855.

The Bank of the Commonwealth of Kentucky had its parent bank located in Frankfort, W-KY-440, and branch banks located in Bowling Green, W-KY-090, Falmouth, W-KY-360, Greensburg, W-KY-550, Harrodsburg, W-KY-580, Hartford, W-KY-610, Lexington, W-KY-780, Louisville, W-KY-870, Mount Sterling, W-KY-1120, Princeton, W-KY-1330, Somerset, W-KY-1470, and Winchester, W-KY-1590.

Numismatic Commentary: Almost all notes from this bank and its branches are unknown today.

Valid Issues

6-1/4¢ • W-KY-410-00.06.25-G010

Left: 6-1/4 CENTS. ***Center:*** 6-1/4 / 6-1/4 on die / 6-1/4. ***Right:*** KENTUCKY vertically. ***Comments:*** H-KY-95-G78, Hughes-237. 1822.

Rarity: *None known*

12-1/2¢ • W-KY-410-00.12.50-G020

Left: 12-1/2 CENTS. ***Center:*** 12-1/2 / 12-1/2 on die / 12-1/2. ***Right:*** KENTUCKY vertically. ***Comments:*** H-KY-95-G80, Hughes-238. 1822.

Rarity: *None known*

25¢ • W-KY-410-00.25-G030

Left: 25 CENTS. ***Center:*** 25 / 25 on die / 25. ***Right:*** KENTUCKY vertically. ***Comments:*** H-KY-95-G82, Hughes-239. 1822.

Rarity: URS-2
VG $250

25¢ • W-KY-410-00.25-G040

CC

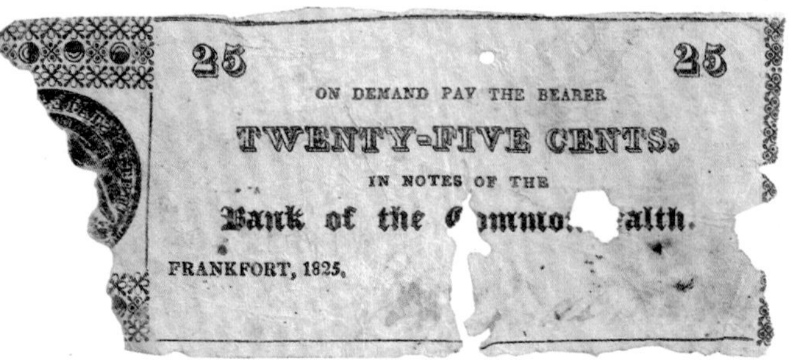

Comments: H-Unlisted, Hughes-Unlisted. 1825.

Rarity: URS-2
G $200

50¢ • W-KY-410-00.50-G050

CC

Comments: H-Unlisted, Hughes-Unlisted. 1821.

Rarity: URS-2
VG $250

50¢ • W-KY-410-00.50-G060 CC

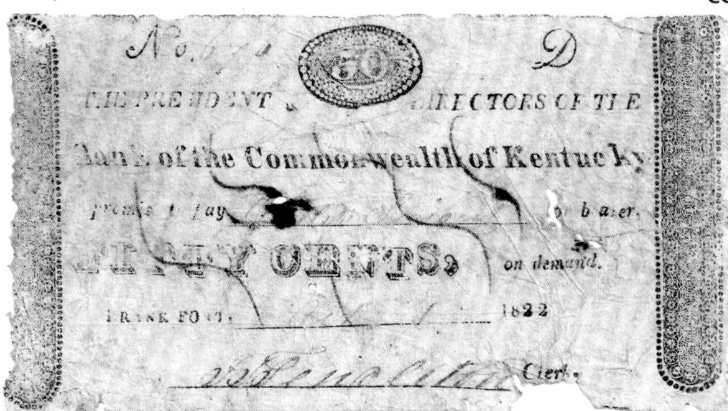

Comments: H-KY-95-G84, Hughes-240. 1822.

Rarity: URS-2
VG $250

$1 • W-KY-410-001-G070

Left: KENTUCKY vertically. ***Center:*** 1 / 1. ***Right:*** CAMPBELL COUNTY vertically. ***Engraver:*** Murray, Draper, Fairman & Co. ***Comments:*** H-KY-95-G88, Hughes-241. 18__. 1820s.

Rarity: URS-2
F $350

$3 • W-KY-410-003-G080

Left: KENTUCKY vertically. ***Center:*** 3 / 3. ***Right:*** CAMPBELL COUNTY vertically. ***Engraver:*** Murray, Draper, Fairman & Co. ***Comments:*** H-KY-95-G90, Hughes-242. 18__. 1820s.

Rarity: URS-2
F $350

$5 • W-KY-410-005-G090

Left: Woman holding staff. ***Center:*** 5 / Minerva standing with owl, shield, staff / 5. ***Right:*** Woman holding staff. ***Engraver:*** Murray, Draper, Fairman & Co. ***Comments:*** H-KY-95-G92, Hughes-243. 18__. 1820s.

Rarity: URS-1
F $600

$10 • W-KY-410-010-G100

Left: Woman holding staff. ***Center:*** 10 / Woman standing with staff, shield, Four cherubs / 10. ***Right:*** Woman holding staff. ***Engraver:*** Murray, Draper, Fairman & Co. ***Comments:*** H-KY-95-G94, Hughes-244. 18__. 1820s.

Rarity: URS-1
F $600

$20 • W-KY-410-020-G110

Engraver: Murray, Draper, Fairman & Co. ***Comments:*** H-KY-95-G96, Hughes-245. No description available. 18__. 1820s.

Rarity: *None known*

$50 • W-KY-410-050-G120

Engraver: Murray, Draper, Fairman & Co. ***Comments:*** H-KY-95-G98, Hughes-246. No description available. 18__. 1820s.

Rarity: *None known*

$100 • W-KY-410-100-G130

Engraver: Murray, Draper, Fairman & Co. ***Comments:*** H-KY-95-G100, Hughes-247. No description available. 18__. 1820s.

Rarity: *None known*

FRANKFORT, KENTUCKY

Frankfort was settled in 1786 by James Wilkinson. The name is thought to have come from a mispronunciation of Frank's Ford. A man named Stephen Frank was killed in an attack by Native Americans here, and the ford was named after him.

In 1792 Frankfort was selected to be the capital of the new state of Kentucky. In 1794 the post office was opened. In 1836 there was a fire at the post office that destroyed several documents and records.

Frankfort was occupied by both the Union army and the Confederate army at different times during the Civil War.

Bank of Kentucky {1st}

1806–1824

W-KY-420

History: The Bank of Kentucky (sometimes seen later in print as the "Old" Bank of Kentucky) was incorporated on December 27, 1806, with an authorized capital of $1,000,000. Half of the capital was subscribed to by the state. The president was John Pope, and the cashier was Benjamin Taylor. The War of 1812 caused a crisis for the bank, and it was forced to suspend specie payments. By 1815 it had resumed and was considered to be in good standing and credit. That same year the charter was increased to $3,000,000. In 1816 these values were given: capital $1,443,855; debts due the bank $3,098,106; deposits at the bank $1,178,789; bills in circulation $1,308,129; specie $989,347.

How to Read the Whitman Numbering System

$1 • W-AL-020-001-G010a

Denomination: Face value of the note shown.

W: Whitman number. This number is a sortable code unique to each bank and note.

AL: Abbreviation for the state under study.

020: Numerical designation specific to each bank.

001: The denomination in dollars.

G010a: G indicates a good or valid note. Other categories are indicated thus: C (counterfeit); R (raised); S (spurious); N (not-attributed); A (altered). Numbers are assigned starting with 010, 020, et seq. Terminal letters following the number indicate variations of a note: a series of different colored overprints, tints, payees, etc., all on the same design of note. For more information, see the "How to Use This Book" section at the front of the volume, page xiv.

In 1820 the bank suspended specie payments yet again. The bank's ability to make monetary loans was repealed, and on January 21, 1822, the bank was ordered to start closing up its branches. This was to be completed by May 1, 1824. This act essentially shut down the bank. Curiously, all of the paperwork was not completed until the 1870s.

The first Bank of Kentucky had branch banks located in Bardstown, W-KY-050, Danville, W-KY-320, Glasgow, W-KY-500, Hopkinsville, W-KY-660, Lexington, W-KY-760, Louisville, W-KY-840, Paris, W-KY-1260, Richmond, W-KY-1350, Russellville, W-KY-1380, Shelbyville, W-KY-1430, Springfield, W-KY-1500, Washington, W-KY-1570, and Winchester, W-KY-1580.

Numismatic Commentary: Notes of this bank are uncommon, despite the multiple branch banks located throughout the state.

Valid Issues

$1 • W-KY-420-001-G010

Left: 1 / BRANCH BANK vertically / 1. ***Center:*** Deer running through field, plow. ***Right:*** 1 / ONE / 1. ***Engraver:*** W. Harrison. ***Comments:*** H-Unlisted, Hughes-283. 18__. 1807–1812.

Rarity: URS-3
F $250

$1 • W-KY-420-001-G020

Left: ONE vertically. ***Center:*** 1 / 1. ***Right:*** FRANKFORT vertically. ***Engraver:*** Murray, Draper, Fairman & Co. ***Comments:*** H-KY-110-G2, Hughes-284. 18__. 1815–1821.

Rarity: URS-6
F $100

$3 • W-KY-420-003-G030

Center: 3 / Farm scene / 3. ***Engraver:*** Murray, Draper, Fairman & Co. ***Comments:*** H-KY-110-G4, Hughes-285. 18__. 1807–1812.

Rarity: URS-6
F $100

$5 • W-KY-420-005-G040

CC

Engraver: Murray, Draper, Fairman & Co. ***Comments:*** H-KY-110-G6, Hughes-Unlisted. 18__. 1807–1812.

Rarity: URS-3
F $525

$5 • W-KY-420-005-G050

HA

Engraver: Murray, Draper, Fairman & Co. ***Comments:*** H-KY-110-G8. 18__. 1813–1821.

Rarity: URS-4
G $125; **F** $150

$10 • W-KY-420-010-G060

Center: 10 / Farm scene / 10. ***Engraver:*** W. Harrison. ***Comments:*** H-KY-110-G10, Hughes-287. 18__. 1807–1812.

Rarity: URS-3
F $350

$10 • W-KY-420-010-G070

Left: TEN vertically. ***Center:*** Plow, trees, Deer. ***Right:*** FRANKFORT vertically. ***Engraver:*** Unverified, but likely Murray, Draper, Fairman & Co. ***Comments:*** H-KY-110-G12, Hughes-Unlisted. 18__. 1813–1816.

Rarity: URS-3
F $250

$20 • W-KY-420-020-G080

CC

Engraver: W. Harrison. ***Comments:*** H-KY-110-G14. 18__. 1807–1812.

Rarity: URS-3
VG $150; **F** $250

$20 • W-KY-420-020-G090

Left: TWENTY vertically. ***Center:*** Plow, trees, Deer. ***Right:*** FRANKFORT vertically. ***Engraver:*** Unverified, but like Murray, Draper, Fairman & Co. ***Comments:*** H-KY-110-G16, Hughes-Unlisted. 18__. 1813–1821.

Rarity: URS-2
F $250

$50 • W-KY-420-050-G100

Center: Plow, trees, Deer. ***Engraver:*** W. Harrison. ***Comments:*** H-KY-110-G17, Hughes-293. 18__. 1807–1812.

Rarity: URS-2
F $350

$50 • W-KY-420-050-G110
Left: FIFTY vertically. ***Center:*** Plow, trees, Deer. ***Right:*** FRANKFORT vertically. ***Engraver:*** Unverified, but likely Murray, Draper, Fairman & Co. ***Comments:*** H-KY-110-G18, Hughes-Unlisted. 18__. 1813–1821.

Rarity: URS-1
F $550

$100 • W-KY-420-100-G120
Center: 100 / Farm scene / 100. ***Engraver:*** W. Harrison. ***Comments:*** H-KY-110-G19, Hughes-Unlisted. 18__. 1800s–1810s.

Rarity: URS-1
F $550

$100 • W-KY-420-100-G130
Left: ONE HUNDRED vertically. ***Center:*** Plow, trees, Deer. ***Right:*** FRANKFORT vertically. ***Engraver:*** Murray, Draper, Fairman & Co. ***Comments:*** H-KY-110-G20, Hughes-Unlisted. 18__. 1810s–1820s.

Rarity: URS-1
F $550

Post Notes

$__ • W-KY-420-__-G140 CC

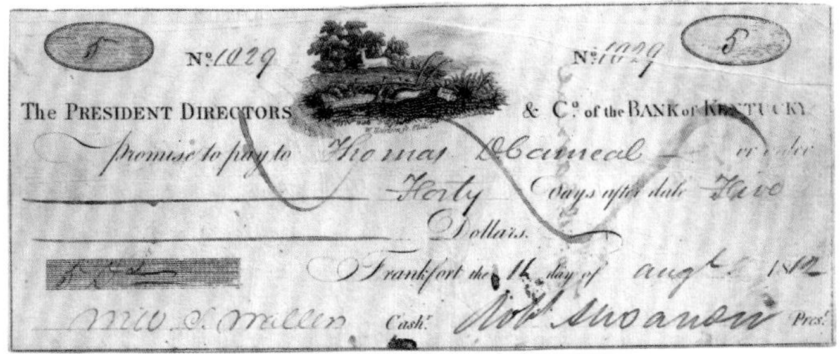

Engraver: W. Harrison. ***Comments:*** H-KY-110-G22, Hughes-Unlisted. 18__. 1810s.

Rarity: URS-4
F $250

$__ • W-KY-420-__-G150 CC

Engraver: Murray, Draper, Fairman & Co. ***Comments:*** H-KY-110-G23, Hughes-295. 18__. 1810s.

Rarity: URS-4
F $250; **EF** $500

$__ • W-KY-420-__-G160 CC

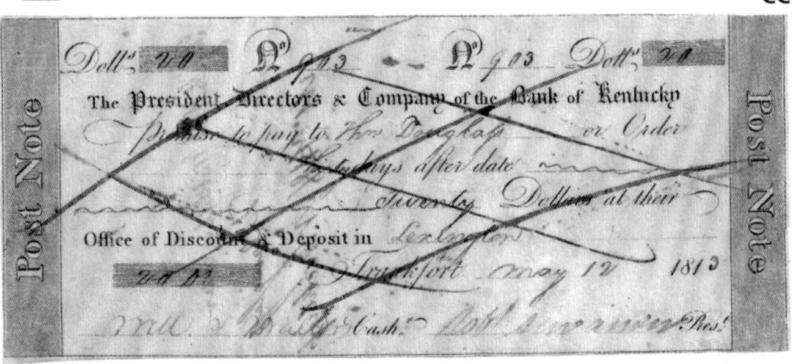

Comments: H-Unlisted, Hughes-Unlisted. 181_. 1810s.

Rarity: URS-4
F $250

$__ • W-KY-420-__-G170 CC

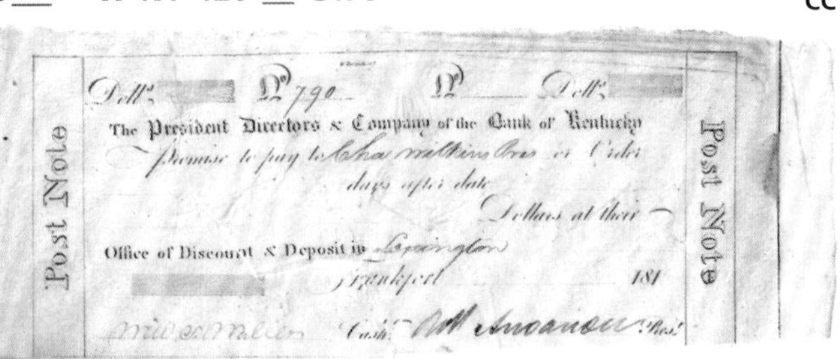

Comments: H-Unlisted, Hughes-Unlisted. 181_. 1810s.

Rarity: URS-3
F $300

$__ • W-KY-420-__-G180 CC

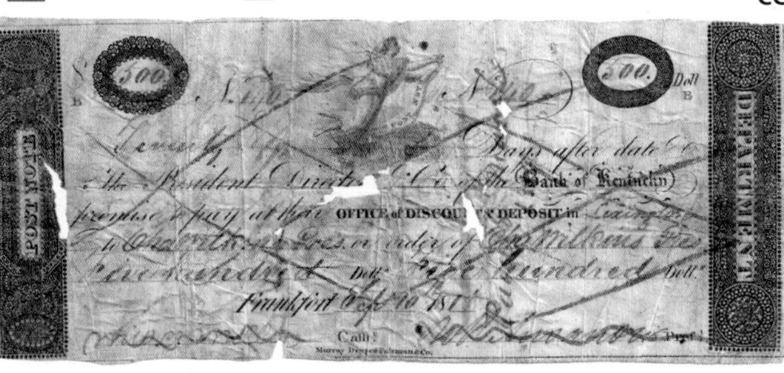

Engraver: Murray, Draper, Fairman & Co. ***Comments:*** H-Unlisted, Hughes-Unlisted. 18__. 1810s.

Rarity: URS-3
F $350

Non-Valid Issues

$10 • W-KY-420-010-C065
Left: DEPARTMENT vertically. ***Center:*** Plow, trees / TEN. ***Right:*** 10. ***Comments:*** H-Unlisted, Hughes-288. 18__. 1810s.

Rarity: URS-6
F $100

$10 • W-KY-420-010-C075
Center: Plow, Trees. ***Comments:*** H-Unlisted, Hughes-290. 18__. 1810s.

Rarity: URS-3
F $150

$20 • W-KY-420-020-C080

Engraver: W. Harrison. ***Comments:*** H-KY-110-C14, Hughes-292. Counterfeit of W-KY-420-020-G080. 18__. 1810s.

Rarity: URS-6
F $100

$50 • W-KY-420-050-C115

Center: Plow, Trees. ***Comments:*** H-Unlisted, Hughes-294. 18__. 1810s.

Rarity: URS-6
VF $225

Post Notes

$__ • W-KY-420-__-C140

Engraver: W. Harrison. ***Comments:*** H-KY-110-C22, Hughes-Unlisted. Counterfeit of W-KY-420-__-G140. 18__. 1810s.

Rarity: URS-4
F $100

Bank of Kentucky {2nd} (branch)

1835–1871

W-KY-430

History: The second Bank of Kentucky (sometimes seen in print as the "New" Bank of Kentucky) was chartered in 1834 in order to assume the business of the first Bank of Kentucky, W-KY-420, which had recently closed. The capital of the bank was $5,000,000. The branch in Frankfort was established in 1835. In January 1866 almost all branches of the Bank of Kentucky were closed down. The branch in Frankfort continued on until 1871, when its assets were assumed by the Kentucky National Bank.

The second Bank of Kentucky had its parent bank located in Louisville, W-KY-850, and branch banks located in Bowling Green, W-KY-080, Burksville, W-KY-140, Columbus, W-KY-220, Danville, W-KY-330, Flemingsburg, W-KY-390, Glasgow, W-KY-510, Greensburg, W-KY-540, Hopkinsville, W-KY-670, Lexington, W-KY-770, Maysville, W-KY-1020, Mount Sterling, W-KY-1100, and Paducah, W-KY-1220.

Numismatic Commentary: Notes of this bank and its branches are very rare.

Valid Issues

6-1/4¢ • W-KY-430-00.06.25-G001 CC

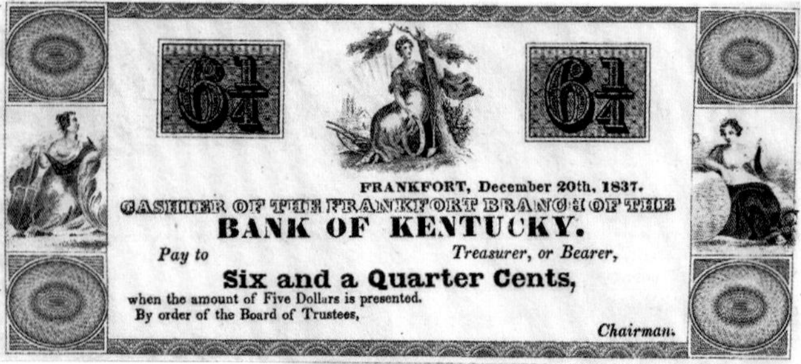

Comments: H-Unlisted, Hughes-Unlisted. December 20th, 1837.

Rarity: URS-2
Unc-Rem $250

6-1/4¢ • W-KY-430-00.06.25-G002 CC

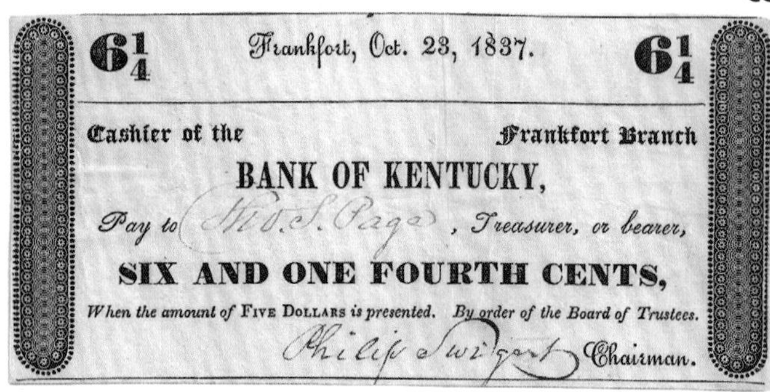

Comments: H-Unlisted, Hughes-Unlisted. Oct. 23, 1837.

Rarity: URS-1
Unc-Rem $450

12-1/2¢ • W-KY-430-00.12.50-G003 CC

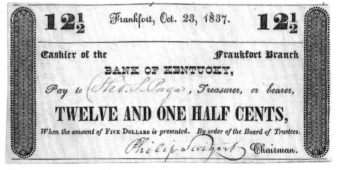

Comments: H-Unlisted, Hughes-Unlisted. December 20th, 1837.

Rarity: URS-2
Unc-Rem $250

12-1/2¢ • W-KY-430-00.12.50-G004 CC

Comments: H-Unlisted, Hughes-Unlisted. Oct. 23, 1837.

Rarity: URS-1
Unc-Rem $450

25¢ • W-KY-430-00.25-G005 CC

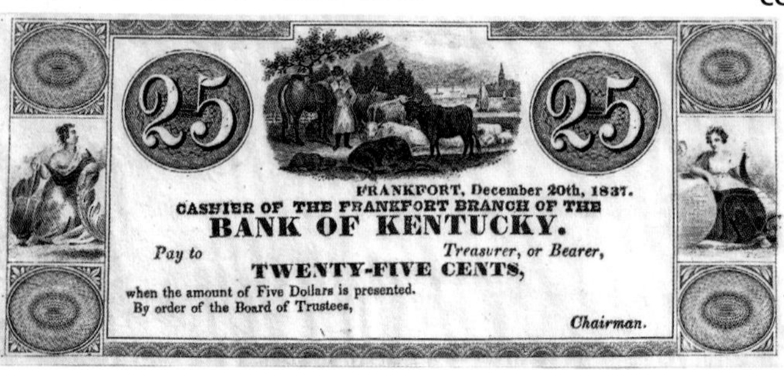

Comments: H-Unlisted, Hughes-Unlisted. December 20th, 1837.

Rarity: URS-2
VG $225; **Unc-Rem** $325

50¢ • W-KY-430-00.50-G006 CC

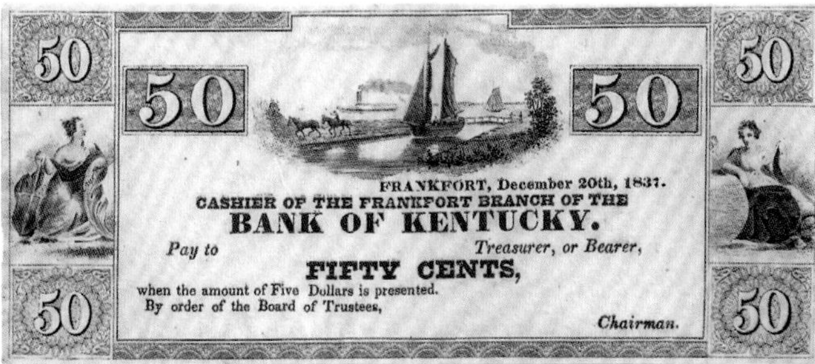

Comments: H-Unlisted, Hughes-Unlisted. December 20th, 1837.

Rarity: URS-2

VG $175; **Unc-Rem** $250

$1 • W-KY-430-001-G007 CC

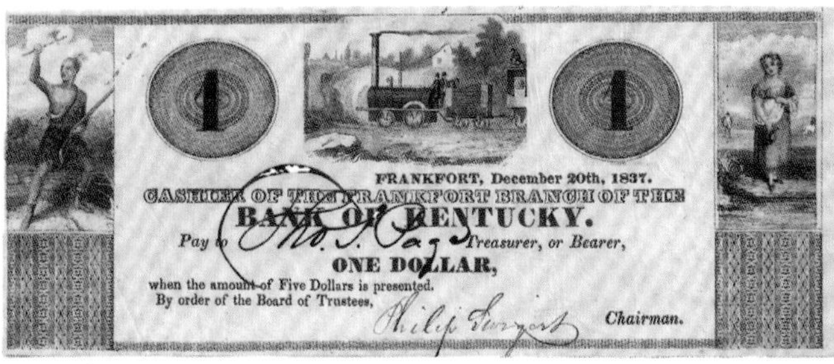

Comments: H-Unlisted, Hughes-Unlisted. December 20th, 1837.

Rarity: URS-2

VF $250

$1 • W-KY-430-001-G008 CC

Comments: H-Unlisted, Hughes-Unlisted. December 20th, 1837.

Rarity: URS-2

F $175

$1 • W-KY-430-001-G010

Left: ONE / Men and women. ***Center:*** Woman swimming / ONE / Portrait of Henry Clay / Woman swimming / ONE. ***Right:*** ONE / Man and women. ***Engraver:*** Danforth, Bald & Co. ***Comments:*** H-KY-195-G162, Hughes-484. 1850s.

Rarity: URS-3

F $350

$2 • W-KY-430-002-G015 CC

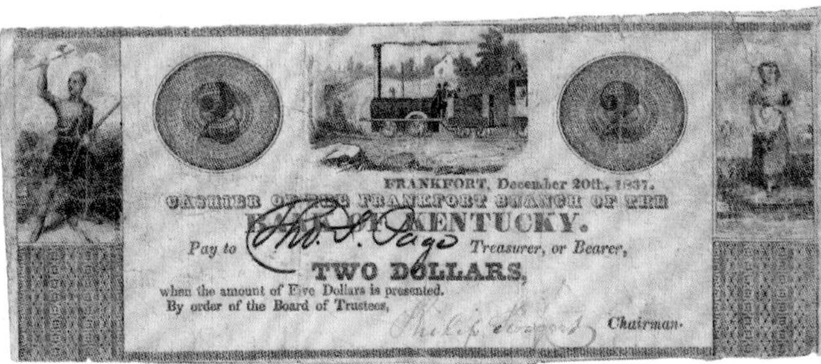

Comments: H-Unlisted, Hughes-Unlisted. December 20th, 1837.

Rarity: URS-2

VG $250

$5 • W-KY-430-005-G020

Left: FIVE / Liberty standing / V. ***Center:*** 5 / Horse / 5. ***Right:*** FIVE / Liberty standing / V. ***Engraver:*** Casilear, Durand, Burton & Evans. ***Comments:*** H-KY-195-G166, Hughes-495. 18__. 1830s–1840s.

Rarity: URS-3

F $350

$5 • W-KY-430-005-G030

Left: 5 / Portrait of Henry Clay / FIVE. ***Center:*** Portrait of John Q. Adams / Woman seated against bales, Train, Harvesting scene / Portrait of Thomas Jefferson. ***Right:*** 5 / Portrait of George Washington / FIVE. ***Engraver:*** Toppan, Carpenter & Co. ***Comments:*** H-KY-195-G170, Hughes-494. 18__. 1840s–1850s.

Rarity: URS-3

F $350

$10 • W-KY-430-010-G040

Left: 10 / Woman seated / X. ***Center:*** X / Three women seated / X. ***Right:*** 10 / Woman standing / X. ***Engraver:*** Casilear, Durand, Burton & Evans. ***Comments:*** H-KY-195-G174, Hughes-497. 18__. 1830s–1840s.

Rarity: URS-3

F $350

$10 • W-KY-430-010-G050

Left: 10 / Portrait of George Washington / 10. ***Center:*** Portrait of Andrew Jackson / Indian man and woman flanking shield bearing 10 surmounted by eagle / Portrait of Isaac Shelby. ***Right:*** 10 / Portrait of Henry Clay / 10. ***Engraver:*** Toppan, Carpenter & Co. ***Comments:*** H-KY-195-G178, Hughes-499. 18__. 1840s–1850s.

Rarity: URS-3

F $350

$20 • W-KY-430-020-G060

Left: 20 / Woman standing / 20. ***Center:*** XX / Woman seated with plow and bales, Cattle / XX. ***Right:*** 20 / Indian man standing / XX. ***Engraver:*** Casilear, Durand, Burton & Evans. ***Comments:*** H-KY-195-G182, Hughes-506. 18__. 1830s–1840s.

Rarity: URS-3

F $350

$20 • W-KY-430-020-G070

Left: Woman holding male portrait aloft / Male portrait. ***Center:*** 20 / Woman flying / 20. ***Right:*** Three women holding medallion head aloft. ***Engraver:*** Draper, Toppan & Co. ***Comments:*** H-KY-195-G184, Hughes-508. 18__. 1840s.

Rarity: URS-3

F $350

$20 • W-KY-430-020-G080

Left: 20 / Portrait of Daniel Webster. ***Center:*** "General Marion's Sweet Potato Dinner." ***Right:*** 20 / Male portrait. ***Engraver:*** Toppan, Carpenter & Co. ***Comments:*** H-KY-195-G186, Hughes-511. 18__. 1850s.

Rarity: URS-3
F $350

$50 • W-KY-430-050-G090

Left: Woman standing. ***Center:*** 50 / Steamboat *Henry Clay* / 50. ***Right:*** Woman standing. ***Engraver:*** Casilear, Durand, Burton & Evans. ***Comments:*** H-KY-195-G190, Hughes-513. 18__. 1830s–1840s.

Rarity: URS-2
F $500

Post Notes

$__ • W-KY-430-__-G100

Left: Woman seated with plow, sheaves, Cattle / POST NOTE. ***Center:*** $__. ***Right:*** Three women seated / POST NOTE. ***Engraver:*** Casilear, Durand, Burton & Evans. ***Comments:*** H-KY-195-G194, Hughes-523. 18__. 1830s.

Rarity: URS-3
F $300

Non-Valid Issues

$5 • W-KY-430-005-C020

Engraver: Casilear, Durand, Burton & Evans. ***Comments:*** H-KY-195-C166, Hughes-496. Counterfeit of W-KY-430-005-G020. 18__. 1840s.

Rarity: URS-4
F $100

$10 • W-KY-430-010-C050

Engraver: Toppan, Carpenter & Co. ***Comments:*** H-KY-195-C178, Hughes-500. Counterfeit of W-KY-430-010-G050. 18__. 1850s.

Rarity: URS-4
F $100

$20 • W-KY-430-020-C070

Engraver: Draper, Toppan & Co. ***Comments:*** H-KY-195-C184, Hughes-509. Counterfeit of W-KY-430-020-G070. 18__. 1840s.

Rarity: URS-4
F $100

$20 • W-KY-430-020-C080

Engraver: Toppan, Carpenter & Co. ***Comments:*** H-KY-195-C186, Hughes-512. Counterfeit of W-KY-430-020-G080. 185_. 1850s.

Rarity: URS-4
F $100

Bank of the Commonwealth of Kentucky

1820–1830

W-KY-440

History: The Bank of the Commonwealth of Kentucky was chartered on November 29, 1820, with an authorized capital of $2,000,000. A local name for the bank was the "Peoples Bank," as it was chartered for the purpose of bringing relief to the population in a time of economic uncertainty. On December 22, 1820, an act was passed authorizing the bank to issue $3,000,000 in bills. The establishment of the Bank of the Commonwealth of Kentucky inadvertently caused the failure of the first Bank of Kentucky, W-KY-420.

In 1825 these values were given: capital $334,368; bills in circulation $1,436,239; bills issued $2,943,620. In 1830 the bank lost its authorization to loan money, and it was instructed to close up its branches. Around that time the bank ceased new business, but the winding up of its affairs took until 1855.

The Bank of the Commonwealth of Kentucky had branch banks located in Bowling Green, W-KY-090, Falmouth, W-KY-360, Flemingsburg, W-KY-410, Greensburg, W-KY-550, Harrodsburg, W-KY-580, Hartford, W-KY-610, Lexington, W-KY-780, Louisville, W-KY-870, Mount Sterling, W-KY-1120, Princeton, W-KY-1330, Somerset, W-KY-1470, and Winchester, W-KY-1590.

Numismatic Commentary: Almost all notes from this bank and its branches are unknown today.

Valid Issues

6-1/4¢ • W-KY-440-00.06.25-G010

Comments: H-KY-95-G2, Hughes-237. No description available. 1820s–1830s.

Rarity: *None known*

12-1/2¢ • W-KY-440-00.12.50-G020

Comments: H-KY-95-G4, Hughes-238. No description available. 1820s–1830s.

Rarity: *None known*

25¢ • W-KY-440-00.25-G030

Comments: H-KY-95-G6, Hughes-239. No description available. 1820s–1830s.

Rarity: *None known*

50¢ • W-KY-440-00.50-G040

Comments: H-KY-95-G8, Hughes-240. No description available. 1820s–1830s.

Rarity: *None known*

$1 • W-KY-440-001-G050

Engraver: Murray, Draper, Fairman & Co. ***Comments:*** H-KY-95-G10, Hughes-241. No description available. 18__. 1820s.

Rarity: *None known*

$3 • W-KY-440-003-G060

Engraver: Murray, Draper, Fairman & Co. ***Comments:*** H-KY-95-G12, Hughes-242. No description available. 18__. 1820s.

Rarity: *None known*

$5 • W-KY-440-005-G070

Engraver: Murray, Draper, Fairman & Co. ***Comments:*** H-KY-95-G14, Hughes-243. No description available. 18__. 1820s.

Rarity: *None known*

$10 • W-KY-440-010-G080

Engraver: Murray, Draper, Fairman & Co. ***Comments:*** H-KY-95-G16, Hughes-244. No description available. 18__. 1820s.

Rarity: *None known*

$20 • W-KY-440-020-G090

Engraver: Murray, Draper, Fairman & Co. ***Comments:*** H-KY-95-G18, Hughes-245. No description available. 18__. 1820s.

Rarity: *None known*

$50 • W-KY-440-050-G100

Engraver: Murray, Draper, Fairman & Co. ***Comments:*** H-KY-95-G20, Hughes-246. No description available. 18__. 1820s.

Rarity: *None known*

$100 • W-KY-440-100-G110

Engraver: Murray, Draper, Fairman & Co. ***Comments:*** H-KY-95-G22, Hughes-247. No description available. 18__. 1820s.

Rarity: *None known*

Farmers Bank of Kentucky

1850–1860s

W-KY-450

History: The Farmers Bank of Kentucky was chartered on February 15, 1850, with an authorized capital of $2,300,000. On September 16, 1850, the bank opened for business. The cashier was J.B. Temple, and the president was J.H. Hanna. On February 11, 1860, the charter for the bank was amended, allowing it to increase its capital. In 1862 the bank's capital was $1,700,000, and circulation was $1,560,000. The bank wound down its business during the Civil War.

The Farmers Bank of Kentucky had branch banks located in Bardstown, W-KY-070, Covington, W-KY-240, George Town, W-KY-480, Henderson, W-KY-640, Maysville, W-KY-1050, Mount Sterling, W-KY-1130, Princeton, W-KY-1340, and Somerset, W-KY-1480.

Numismatic Commentary: Uncut sheets of this bank as well as single notes have shown up at auction since 2005.

Valid Issues

$1 • W-KY-450-001-G010 CC

Engraver: Toppan, Carpenter, Casilear & Co. ***Comments:*** H-KY-100-G2, Hughes-250. 185_. 1850s.

Rarity: URS-3

F $400

$1 • W-KY-450-001-G010a

Back: Red-orange. ***Engraver:*** Toppan, Carpenter, Casilear & Co. / ABNCo. monogram. ***Comments:*** H-KY-100-G2b. Similar to W-KY-450-001-G010 but with additional engraver imprint. 185_. 1850s.

Rarity: URS-2

F $500

$1 • W-KY-450-001-G020 CC

Tint: Red-orange bank title, 1, and die bearing white 1. ***Back:*** Red-orange. ***Engraver:*** American Bank Note Co. ***Comments:*** H-KY-100-G4, Hughes-249. 18__. 1859.

Rarity: URS-6

F $300; **Proof** $3,850

Selected auction price: Stack's Bowers Galleries, November 18, 2015, Lot 3849, Proof $3,850

$2 • W-KY-450-002-G030

Left: 2 / Portrait of Mrs. John Crittenden. ***Center:*** 2 / Man on horse / 2. ***Right:*** 2 / Portrait of John Crittenden. ***Engraver:*** Toppan, Carpenter, Casilear & Co. ***Comments:*** H-KY-100-G6, Hughes-252. 18__. 1850s.

Rarity: URS-3

F $250

$2 • W-KY-450-002-G030a

Back: Red-orange. ***Engraver:*** Toppan, Carpenter, Casilear & Co. / ABNCo. monogram. ***Comments:*** H-KY-100-G6b. Similar to W-KY-450-002-G030 but with additional engraver imprint. 185_. 1850s.

Rarity: URS-3

F $250

$5 • W-KY-450-005-G040 CC

Engraver: Toppan, Carpenter, Casilear & Co. ***Comments:*** H-KY-100-G8, Hughes-256. 18__. 1850s.

Rarity: URS-3

F $250

$5 • W-KY-450-005-G040a

Overprint: Red FIVE. ***Engraver:*** Toppan, Carpenter, Casilear & Co. ***Comments:*** H-KY-100-G8a. Similar to W-KY-450-005-G040. 18__. 1850s.

Rarity: URS-3

F $250

$5 • **W-KY-450-005-G050** CC, QDB

Tint: Red-orange bank title, FIVE / FIVE, and die bearing white 5. ***Back:*** Red-orange. ***Engraver:*** American Bank Note Co. ***Comments:*** H-KY-100-G10a, Hughes-255. 18__. 1860s.

Rarity: URS-6
EF $350; **Unc-Rem** $275

$5 • **W-KY-450-005-G060** NJW

Engraver: Cha. Toppan & Co. ***Comments:*** H-Unlisted, Hughes-Unlisted. 18__. 1850s.

Rarity: URS-2
F $200

$10 • **W-KY-450-010-G070**

Left: 10 / Portrait of John Crittenden. ***Center:*** Portraits of Mr. and Mrs. John Crittenden. ***Engraver:*** Toppan, Carpenter, Casilear & Co. ***Comments:*** H-KY-100-G12, Hughes-Unlisted. 18__. 1850s.

Rarity: URS-2
F $200

$10 • **W-KY-450-010-G070a**

Tint: Red-orange outlining white TEN. ***Engraver:*** Toppan, Carpenter, Casilear & Co. ***Comments:*** H-KY-100-G12b, Hughes-Unlisted. Similar to W-KY-450-010-G070. 18__. 1850s.

Rarity: URS-2
F $250

$10 • **W-KY-450-010-G080** CC, SBG

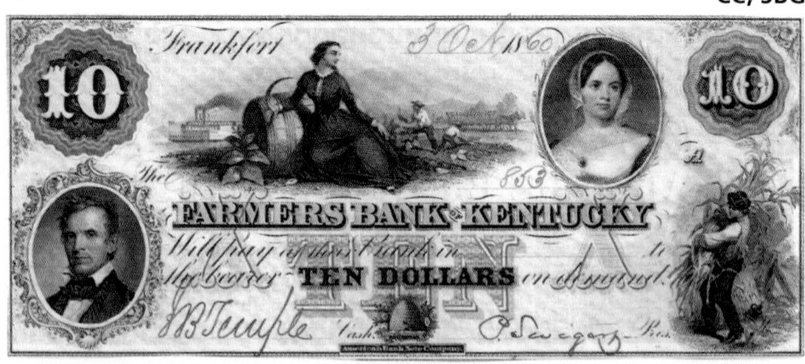

Tint: Red-orange X / TEN / X and dies bearing white 10s. ***Back:*** Red-orange. ***Engraver:*** American Bank Note Co. ***Comments:*** H-KY-100-G14a, Hughes-259. 18__. 1860s.

Rarity: URS-6
EF $350; **Unc-Rem** $275

$10 • **W-KY-450-010-G090**

Left: 10 / Portrait of John Crittenden. ***Center:*** Portraits of Mr. and Mrs. John Crittenden. ***Engraver:*** Toppan, Carpenter, Casilear & Co. ***Comments:*** H-Unlisted, Hughes-Unlisted. 18__. 1850s.

Rarity: URS-3
F $350

$20 • **W-KY-450-020-G100**

Left: Portrait of Mrs. John Crittenden / Portrait of John Crittenden. ***Center:*** 20 / Horses plowing. ***Right:*** 20. ***Engraver:*** Toppan, Carpenter, Casilear & Co. ***Comments:*** H-KY-100-G16, Hughes-261. 18__. 1850s.

Rarity: URS-2
F $350

Collectors and Researchers:

If you have new information about any banks or notes listed in this volume, contact Whitman Publishing, Attn: Obsolete Paper Money, 3101 Clairmont Road, Suite G, Atlanta, GA 30329.

$20 • **W-KY-450-020-G100a** NJW, NJW

Tint: Red-orange TWENTY and die bearing white 20. ***Back:*** Red-orange. ***Engraver:*** American Bank Note Co. ***Comments:*** H-KY-100-G18a. Similar to W-KY-450-020-G100 but with different engraver imprint. 18__. 1859.

Rarity: URS-5
VF $125; **Unc-Rem** $225

$50 • **W-KY-450-050-G110**

Left: Three women with anchor. ***Center:*** 50 / Portrait of Mrs. John Crittenden. ***Right:*** 50 / Portrait of John Crittenden / 50. ***Engraver:*** Toppan, Carpenter, Casilear & Co. ***Comments:*** H-KY-100-G20, Hughes-263. 18__. 1850s.

Rarity: URS-5
F $300

$100 • **W-KY-450-100-G120**

Left: 100 / Portrait of John Crittenden / 100. ***Center:*** Three women reclining / Portrait of Mrs. John Crittenden. ***Right:*** ONE HUNDRED vertically. ***Engraver:*** Toppan, Carpenter, Casilear & Co. ***Comments:*** H-KY-100-G22, Hughes-265. 18__. 1850s.

Rarity: URS-2
F $550

Notes on Which the Place Payable is Blank

$1 • **W-KY-450-001-G130**

Left: 1 / Portrait of John Crittenden / ONE. ***Center:*** Man with dog, Running horses, Donkey. ***Right:*** 1 / Female portrait / ONE. ***Engraver:*** Toppan, Carpenter, Casilear & Co. ***Comments:*** H-KY-100-G194. Proof. 18__. 1850s.

Rarity: —

$1 • **W-KY-450-001-G140**

Left: 1 / Man and wagon and horses / 1. ***Center:*** Portraits of Mr. and Mrs. John Crittenden. ***Right:*** 1 / 1 on die / 1. ***Tint:*** Red-orange. ***Back:*** Red-orange. ***Engraver:*** American Bank Note Co. ***Comments:*** H-KY-100-G196a. Proof. 18__. 1860s.

Rarity: —

$2 • **W-KY-450-002-G150**

Left: 2 / Portrait of Mrs. John Crittenden. ***Center:*** 2 / Man on horse / 2. ***Right:*** 2 / Portrait of John Crittenden. ***Engraver:*** Toppan, Carpenter, Casilear & Co. ***Comments:*** H-KY-100-G198. Proof. 18__. 1850s.

Rarity: —

$5 • **W-KY-450-005-G160**

Left: 5 / Portrait of John Crittenden / 5. ***Center:*** Cattle and sheep, Herders. ***Right:*** 5 / Portrait of Mrs. John Crittenden / 5. ***Engraver:*** Toppan, Carpenter, Casilear & Co. ***Comments:*** H-KY-100-G200. Proof. 18__. 1850s.

Rarity: —

$5 • **W-KY-450-005-G170**

Left: Men plowing with horse / V. ***Center:*** Portraits of Mr. and Mrs. John Crittenden. ***Right:*** 5 / 5. ***Tint:*** Red-orange. ***Back:*** Red-orange. ***Engraver:*** American Bank Note Co. ***Comments:*** H-KY-100-G202a. Proof. 18__. 1859.

Rarity: —

$10 • **W-KY-450-010-G180**

Left: 10 / Portrait of John Crittenden. ***Center:*** Portraits of Mr. and Mrs. John Crittenden. ***Engraver:*** Toppan, Carpenter, Casilear & Co. ***Comments:*** H-KY-100-G204. Proof. 18__. 1850s.

Rarity: —

$10 • **W-KY-450-010-G190**

Left: 10 / Portrait of John Crittenden. ***Center:*** Woman reclining against barrel, Harvest scene / Portrait of Mrs. John Crittenden. ***Right:*** 10 / Men harvesting corn. ***Tint:*** Red-orange. ***Back:*** Red-orange. ***Engraver:*** American Bank Note Co. ***Comments:*** H-KY-100-G206a. Proof. 18__. 1859.

Rarity: —

$20 • **W-KY-450-020-G200**

Left: Portrait of Mrs. John Crittenden / Portrait of John Crittenden. ***Center:*** 20 / Horses plowing. ***Right:*** 20. ***Engraver:*** Toppan, Carpenter, Casilear & Co. ***Comments:*** H-KY-100-G208. Proof. 18__. 1850s.

Rarity: —

$20 • **W-KY-450-020-G210**

Tint: Red-orange. ***Back:*** Red-orange. ***Engraver:*** American Bank Note Co. ***Comments:*** H-KY-100-G210a. Similar to W-KY-450-020-G200 but with different engraver imprint. Proof. 18__. 1859.

Rarity: —

$50 • **W-KY-450-050-G220**

Left: Three women with anchor. ***Center:*** 50 / Portrait of Mrs. John Crittenden. ***Right:*** 50 / Portrait of John Crittenden / 50. ***Engraver:*** Toppan, Carpenter, Casilear & Co. ***Comments:*** H-KY-100-G212. Proof. 18__. 1850s.

Rarity: —

$100 • **W-KY-450-100-G230**

Left: 100 / Portrait of John Crittenden / 100. ***Center:*** Three women reclining / Portrait of Mrs. John Crittenden. ***Right:*** ONE HUNDRED vertically. ***Engraver:*** Toppan, Carpenter, Casilear & Co. ***Comments:*** H-KY-100-G214. Proof. 18__. 1850s.

Rarity: —

Notes on Which the Place Payable is Unknown

$5 • W-KY-450-005-G240

HA

Tint: Red-orange bank title, FIVE / FIVE, and die bearing white 5. ***Back:*** Red-orange. ***Engraver:*** American Bank Note Co. ***Comments:*** H-KY-100-G220a. Signed remainder. 18__. 1859.

Rarity: URS-7
Unc-Rem $210

$10 • W-KY-450-010-G250

Left: 10 / Portrait of John Crittenden. ***Center:*** Woman reclining against barrel, Harvest scene / Portrait of Mrs. John Crittenden. ***Right:*** 10 / Men harvesting corn. ***Tint:*** Red-orange X / TEN / X and dies bearing white 10s. ***Back:*** Red-orange. ***Engraver:*** American Bank Note Co. ***Comments:*** H-KY-100-G224a. Signed remainder. 18__. 1859.

Rarity: URS-7
Unc-Rem $210

$20 • W-KY-450-020-G260

HA

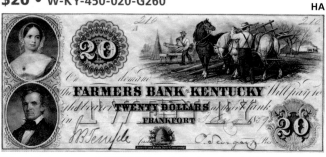

Tint: Red-orange TWENTY and die bearing white 20. ***Back:*** Red-orange. ***Engraver:*** American Bank Note Co. ***Comments:*** H-KY-100-G228a. Signed remainder. 18__. 1859.

Rarity: URS-7
Unc-Rem $250

Uncut Sheets

$5-$5-$5-$5 •
W-KY-450-005.005.005.005-US010

HA

Tint(s): Red-orange bank title, FIVE / FIVE, and die bearing white 5. ***Back(s):*** Red-orange. ***Engraver:*** American Bank Note Co. ***Comments:*** H-KY-100-G220a, G220a, G220a, G220a. All four notes identical. Signed remainder. 18__. 1859.

Rarity: URS-5
Unc-Rem $1,250

$10-$10-$10-$10 •
W-KY-450-010.010.010.010-US020

HA

Tint(s): Red-orange X / TEN / X and dies bearing white 10s. ***Back(s):*** Red-orange. ***Engraver:*** American Bank Note Co. ***Comments:*** H-KY-100-G224a, G224a, G224a, G224a. All four notes identical. Signed remainder. 18__. 1859.

Rarity: URS-5
Unc-Rem $1,250

$20-$20-$20-$20 •
W-KY-450-020.020.020.020-US030

HA

Tint(s): Red-orange TWENTY and die bearing white 20. ***Back(s):*** Red-orange. ***Engraver:*** American Bank Note Co. ***Comments:*** H-KY-100-G228a, G228a, G228a, G228a. All four notes identical. Signed remainder. 18__. 1859.

Rarity: URS-5
Unc-Rem $1,250
Selected auction price: Heritage Auctions, January 5, 2012, Lot 15862, Unc $805

Non-Valid Issues

$1 • W-KY-450-001-C010

Engraver: Toppan, Carpenter, Casilear & Co. ***Comments:*** H-Unlisted, Hughes-251. Counterfeit of W-KY-450-001-G010. 18__. 1850s.

Rarity: URS-4
F $150

$2 • W-KY-450-002-C030

Engraver: Toppan, Carpenter, Casilear & Co. ***Comments:*** H-KY-100-C6, Hughes-253. Counterfeit of W-KY-450-002-G030. 18__. 1850s.

Rarity: URS-4
F $150

$3 • W-KY-450-003-S010

Left: THREE. ***Center:*** 3 / Cattle. ***Right:*** 3 / Girl standing with basket and staff. ***Comments:*** H-Unlisted, Hughes-254. 18__. 1850s.

Rarity: URS-3
F $250

$5 • W-KY-450-005-C040

Engraver: Toppan, Carpenter, Casilear & Co. ***Comments:*** H-KY-100-C8, Hughes-256. Counterfeit of W-KY-450-005-G040. 18__. 1850s.

Rarity: URS-3
F $250

$5 • W-KY-450-005-C040a

Overprint: Red FIVE. ***Engraver:*** Toppan, Carpenter, Casilear & Co. ***Comments:*** H-KY-100-C8a, Hughes-257. Counterfeit of W-KY-450-005-G040a. 18__. 1850s.

Rarity: URS-3
F $250

$5 • W-KY-450-005-S020

Left: 5 / FIVE / Medallion head. ***Center:*** Cattle, Plow, Train. ***Right:*** 5 / FIVE / Medallion head. ***Engraver:*** Rawdon, Wright & Hatch. ***Comments:*** H-KY-100-S30, Hughes-Unlisted. 18__. 1850s.

Rarity: URS-3
F $250

$10 • W-KY-450-010-C080

Comments: H-Unlisted, Hughes-260. Counterfeit of W-KY-450-010-G080. 18__. 1860s.

Rarity: URS-3
F $250

$50 • W-KY-450-050-A010

Comments: H-Unlisted, Hughes-264. Altered from another bank. 18__. 1850s.

Rarity: URS-3
F $225

Frankfort Bank

1818–1830

W-KY-460

History: The Frankfort Bank was chartered in 1818 with an authorized capital of $500,000. This was to be divided into 5,000 shares of $100 each. John H. Hanna, Henry Crittenden, Samuel Lewis, William Hunter, and George Adams were appointed to take stock subscriptions. The bank was to be located between Ann and St. Clair streets. On December 31, 1830, an act was passed authorizing the stockholders to close up the affairs of the bank.

Numismatic Commentary: Quite a few uncut sheets of this bank have hit the market between 2006 and 2010.

Valid Issues

$1 • W-KY-460-001-G010

CC

Engraver: Tanner, Kearny & Tiebout. ***Comments:*** H-KY-105-G12, Hughes-267. 18__. 1810s.

Rarity: URS-8
EF $75; **Unc-Rem** $350

$3 • W-KY-460-003-G020

CC

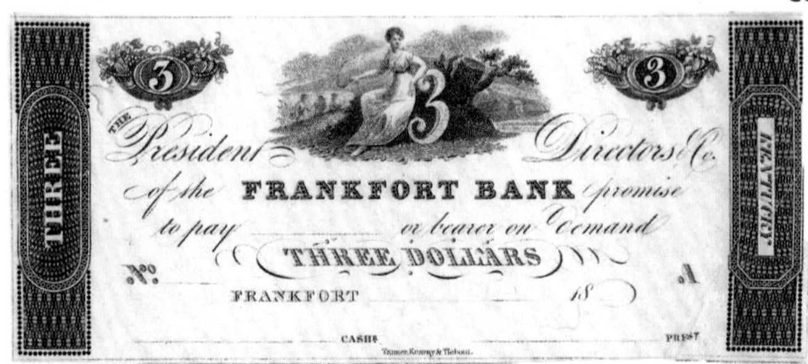

Engraver: Tanner, Kearny & Tiebout. ***Comments:*** H-KY-105-G14, Hughes-268. 18__. 1810s.

Rarity: URS-7
EF $75; **Unc-Rem** $350

$5 • **W-KY-460-005-G030** CC

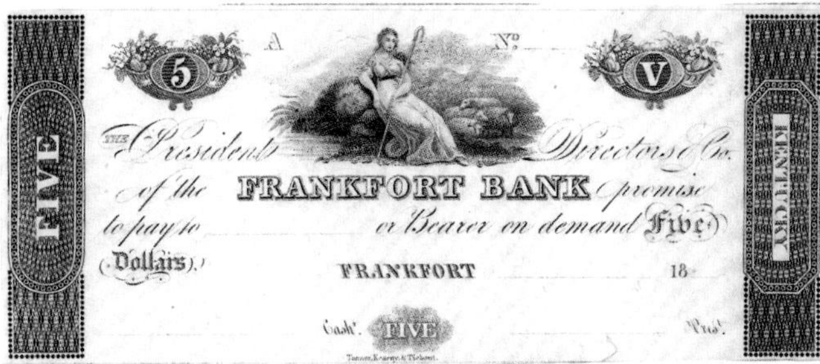

Engraver: Tanner, Kearny & Tiebout. ***Comments:*** H-KY-105-G16, Hughes-269. 18__. 1810s.

Rarity: URS-8

EF $75; **Unc-Rem** $150

$10 • **W-KY-460-010-G040** CC

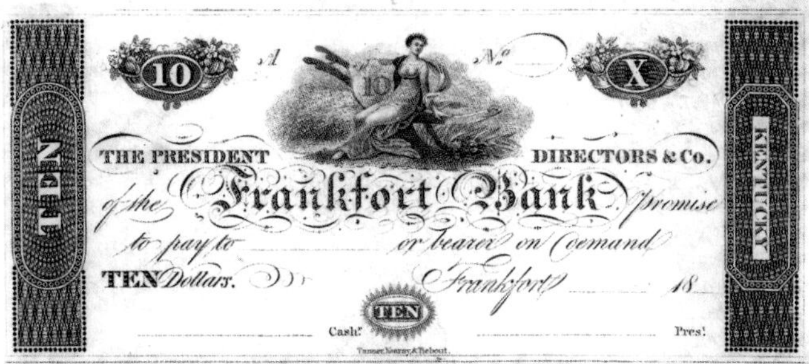

Engraver: Tanner, Kearny & Tiebout. ***Comments:*** H-KY-105-G18, Hughes-270. 18__. 1810s.

Rarity: URS-8

EF $75; **Unc-Rem** $150

$20 • **W-KY-460-020-G045** CC

Engraver: Tanner, Kearny & Tiebout. ***Comments:*** H-Unlisted, Hughes-Unlisted. 18__. 1810s.

Rarity: —

Post Notes

$__ • **W-KY-460-__-G050**

Engraver: Unverified, but likely Tanner, Kearny & Tiebout. ***Comments:*** H-KY-105-G26, Hughes-Unlisted. No description available. 18__. 1810s.

Rarity: *None known*

Uncut Sheets

$3-$3-$1-$1 •
W-KY-460-003.003.001.001-US010 RG

Engraver: Tanner, Kearny & Tiebout. ***Comments:*** H-KY-105-G14, G14, G12, G12. First two notes identical; last two notes identical. 18__. 1810s.

Rarity: URS-8

VF $750

$10-$5-$5-$5 •
W-KY-460-010.005.005.005-US020

CC

Engraver: Tanner, Kearny & Tiebout. ***Comments:*** H-KY-105-G18, G16, G16, G16. Last three notes identical. 18__. 1810s.

Rarity: URS-8
VF $750

George Town, Kentucky

Originally known as Lebanon in 1782, George Town was established in 1790 and named after George Washington. At that time there were already mills for the manufacturing of paper and cloth in existence, as well as a distillery and an academy. The city became the seat of Scott County in 1792, and in 1846 the spelling of the name was changed to Georgetown.

Confederate general John Hunt Morgan raided George Town on two occasions during the Civil War—once in 1862 and once in 1864.

Bank of George Town
1818–1820
W-KY-470

History: The Bank of George Town (also sometimes seen as George-Town on currency) was chartered on January 26, 1818. The authorized capital of $300,000 was divided into 3,000 shares of $100 apiece. James Johnson, Samuel Theobald, Philemon B. Brice, and William B. Keene were appointed to take stock subscriptions. In 1819 the institution was on a list of banks whose notes were redeemable at the Farmers and Mechanics Bank in Cincinnati.[3] The bank was defunct by the autumn of that year. The charters of all independent banks authorized on January 26, 1818, were revoked effective May 1, 1820.

Numismatic Commentary: Notes of this early bank have a simple design with a spread eagle at the center.

Valid Issues

$1 • W-KY-470-001-G010

CC

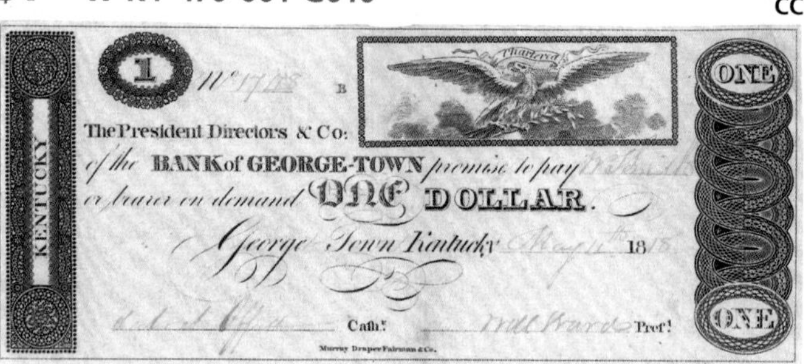

Engraver: Murray, Draper, Fairman & Co. ***Comments:*** H-KY-115-G12, Hughes-305. 18__. 1810s.

Rarity: URS-5
F $100; **VF** $175

$2 • W-KY-470-002-G020

CC

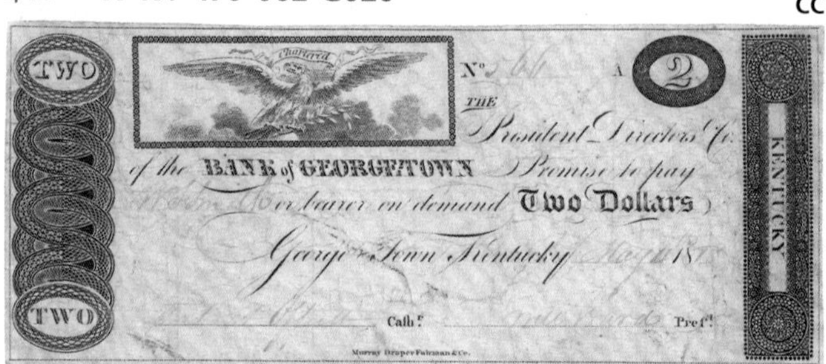

Engraver: Murray, Draper, Fairman & Co. ***Comments:*** H-KY-115-G14, Hughes-306. 18__. 1810s.

Rarity: URS-5
F $100; **VF** $175

$3 • W-KY-470-003-G030 CC

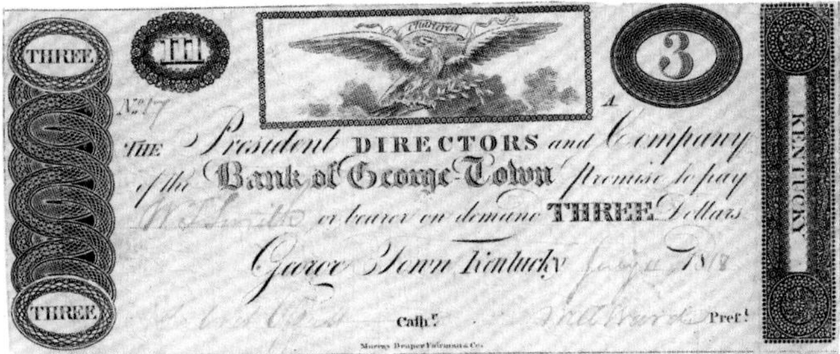

Engraver: Murray, Draper, Fairman & Co. ***Comments:*** H-KY-115-G16, Hughes-307. 18__. 1810s.

Rarity: URS-5
F $100; **VF** $175

$5 • W-KY-470-005-G040 CC

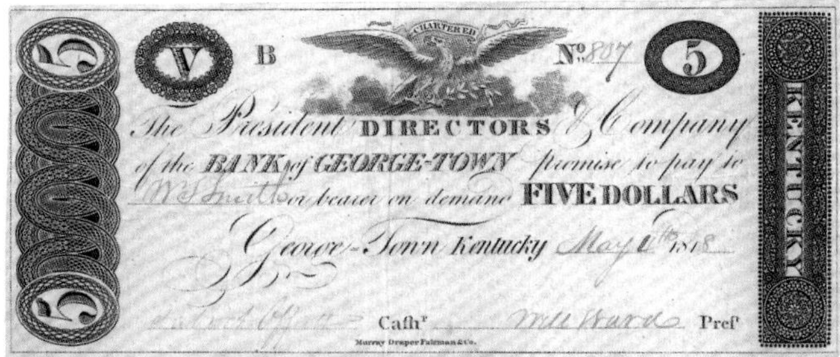

Engraver: Murray, Draper, Fairman & Co. ***Comments:*** H-KY-115-G18, Hughes-308. 181_. 1810s.

Rarity: URS-5
F $100; **VF** $175

$10 • W-KY-470-010-G050 CC

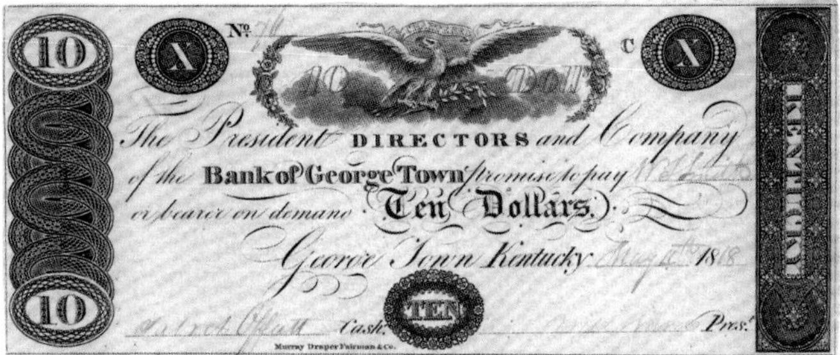

Engraver: Murray, Draper, Fairman & Co. ***Comments:*** H-KY-115-G20, Hughes-309. 18__. 1810s.

Rarity: URS-5
F $100; **VF** $175; **EF** $250; **Unc-Rem** $300

$20 • W-KY-470-020-G060 CC

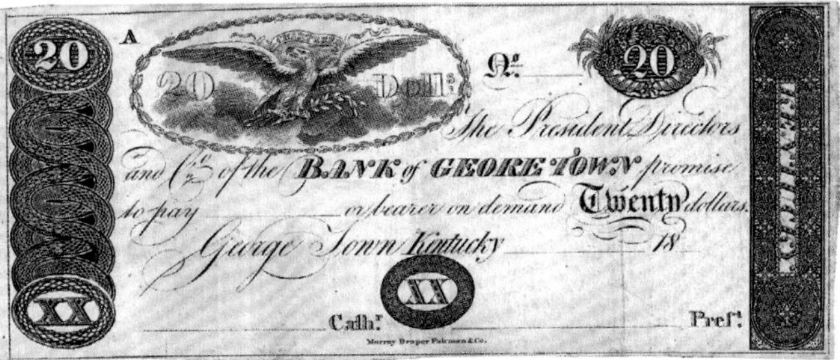

Engraver: Murray, Draper, Fairman & Co. ***Comments:*** H-KY-115-G22, Hughes-310. Bank title misspelled GEORETOWN. 18__. 1810s.

Rarity: URS-4
F $350; **VF** $500

Farmers Bank of Kentucky (branch)

1850–1860s

W-KY-480

History: The Farmers Bank of Kentucky was chartered on February 15, 1850, with an authorized capital of $2,300,000. By September 1852 the bank had opened for business. On February 11, 1860, the charter for the bank was amended, allowing it to increase its capital.

The branch located in George Town (spelled *Georgetown* at this time, but listed here as *George Town* for continuity) had a capital of $220,000. The cashier was P.S. Mitchell, and the president was J.T. Craig. In 1856 the cashier resigned to commence business ventures in Illinois, and J.T. Craig became the cashier. J.F. Robinson became the succeeding president. In 1863 the capital was $300,000. Fabricius C. McCalla was the cashier at that time.

As did many banks of the era, during the 1860s the Farmers Bank of Kentucky wound up its affairs and closed. The branch bank in George Town became the Farmers Bank and Trust Company.

The Farmers Bank of Kentucky had its parent bank located in Frankfort, W-KY-450, and branch banks located in Bardstown, W-KY-070, Covington, W-KY-240, Henderson, W-KY-640, Maysville, W-KY-1050, Mount Sterling, W-KY-1130, Princeton, W-KY-1340, and Somerset, W-KY-1480.

How to Read the Whitman Numbering System

$1 • W-AL-020-001-G010a

Denomination: Face value of the note shown.

W: Whitman number. This number is a sortable code unique to each bank and note.

AL: Abbreviation for the state under study.

020: Numerical designation specific to each bank.

001: The denomination in dollars.

G010a: G indicates a good or valid note. Other categories are indicated thus: C (counterfeit); R (raised); S (spurious); N (not-attributed); A (altered). Numbers are assigned starting with 010, 020, et seq. Terminal letters following the number indicate variations of a note: a series of different colored overprints, tints, payees, etc., all on the same design of note. For more information, see the "How to Use This Book" section at the front of the volume, page xiv.

Valid Issues

$1 • W-KY-480-001-G010

Left: 1 / Portrait of John Crittenden / ONE. ***Center:*** Man with dog, Running horses, Donkey. ***Right:*** 1 / Female portrait / ONE. ***Engraver:*** Toppan, Carpenter, Casilear & Co. ***Comments:*** H-KY-100-G50, Hughes-250. 18__. 1850s.

Rarity: URS-4
F $200

$1 • W-KY-480-001-G010a

Back: Red-orange. ***Engraver:*** Toppan, Carpenter, Casilear & Co. / ABNCo. monogram. ***Comments:*** H-KY-100-G50b, Hughes-Unlisted. Similar to W-KY-480-001-G010 but with additional engraver imprint. 185_. 1850s.

Rarity: URS-3
F $350

$1 • W-KY-480-001-G020

Left: 1 / Man and wagon and horses / 1. ***Center:*** Portraits of Mr. and Mrs. John Crittenden. ***Right:*** 1 / 1 on die / 1. ***Tint:*** Red-orange. ***Back:*** Red-orange. ***Engraver:*** American Bank Note Co. ***Comments:*** H-KY-100-G52a, Hughes-249. 18__. 1859.

Rarity: URS-4
F $200

$2 • W-KY-480-002-G030

Left: 2 / Portrait of Mrs. John Crittenden. ***Center:*** 2 / Man on horse / 2. ***Right:*** 2 / Portrait of John Crittenden. ***Engraver:*** Toppan, Carpenter, Casilear & Co. ***Comments:*** H-KY-100-G54, Hughes-252. 18__. 1850s.

Rarity: URS-3
F $350

$2 • W-KY-480-002-G030a

Back: Red-orange. ***Engraver:*** Toppan, Carpenter, Casilear & Co. / ABNCo. monogram. ***Comments:*** H-KY-100-G54b, Hughes-Unlisted. Similar to W-KY-480-002-G030 but with additional engraver imprint. 185_. 1850s.

Rarity: URS-3
F $350

$5 • W-KY-480-005-G040

Left: 5 / Portrait of John Crittenden / 5. ***Center:*** Cattle and sheep, Herders. ***Right:*** 5 / Portrait of Mrs. John Crittenden / 5. ***Engraver:*** Toppan, Carpenter, Casilear & Co. ***Comments:*** H-KY-100-G56, Hughes-256. 18__. 1850s.

Rarity: URS-3
F $350

$5 • W-KY-480-005-G040a

Overprint: Red FIVE. ***Engraver:*** Toppan, Carpenter, Casilear & Co. ***Comments:*** H-KY-100-G56a, Hughes-257. Similar to W-KY-480-005-G040. 18__. 1850s.

Rarity: URS-3
F $350

$5 • W-KY-480-005-G050

Left: Men plowing with horse / V. ***Center:*** Portraits of Mr. and Mrs. John Crittenden. ***Right:*** 5 / 5. ***Tint:*** Red-orange. ***Back:*** Red-orange. ***Engraver:*** American Bank Note Co. ***Comments:*** H-KY-100-G58a, Hughes-255. 18__. 1859.

Rarity: URS-3
F $350

$10 • W-KY-480-010-G060

Left: 10 / Portrait of John Crittenden. ***Center:*** Portraits of Mr. and Mrs. John Crittenden. ***Engraver:*** Toppan, Carpenter, Casilear & Co. ***Comments:*** H-KY-100-G60, Hughes-Unlisted. 18__. 1850s.

Rarity: URS-3
F $350

$10 • W-KY-480-010-G060a

Tint: Red-orange outlining white TEN. ***Engraver:*** Toppan, Carpenter, Casilear & Co. ***Comments:*** H-KY-100-G60b, Hughes-Unlisted. Similar to W-KY-480-010-G060. 18__. 1850s.

Rarity: URS-4
F $200

$10 • W-KY-480-010-G070

Left: 10 / Portrait of John Crittenden. ***Center:*** Woman reclining against barrel, Harvest scene / Portrait of Mrs. John Crittenden. ***Right:*** 10 / Men harvesting corn. ***Tint:*** Red-orange. ***Back:*** Red-orange. ***Engraver:*** American Bank Note Co. ***Comments:*** H-KY-100-G62a, Hughes-259. 18__. 1859.

Rarity: URS-5
F $175

$20 • W-KY-480-020-G080

Left: Portrait of Mrs. John Crittenden / Portrait of John Crittenden. ***Center:*** 20 / Horses plowing. ***Right:*** 20. ***Engraver:*** Toppan, Carpenter, Casilear & Co. ***Comments:*** H-KY-100-G64, Hughes-261. 18__. 1850s.

Rarity: URS-5
F $175

$20 • W-KY-480-020-G080a

Tint: Red-orange. ***Back:*** Red-orange. ***Engraver:*** American Bank Note Co. ***Comments:*** H-KY-100-G66a, Hughes-Unlisted. Similar to W-KY-480-020-G080 but with different engraver imprint. 18__. 1860s.

Rarity: URS-4
F $250

$50 • W-KY-480-050-G090

Left: Three women with anchor. ***Center:*** 50 / Portrait of Mrs. John Crittenden. ***Right:*** 50 / Portrait of John Crittenden / 50. ***Engraver:*** Toppan, Carpenter, Casilear & Co. ***Comments:*** H-KY-100-G68, Hughes-263. 18__. 1850s.

Rarity: URS-3
F $300

$100 • W-KY-480-100-G100

Left: 100 / Portrait of John Crittenden / 100. ***Center:*** Three women reclining / Portrait of Mrs. John Crittenden. ***Right:*** ONE HUNDRED vertically. ***Engraver:*** Toppan, Carpenter, Casilear & Co. ***Comments:*** H-KY-100-G70, Hughes-265. 18__. 1850s.

Rarity: URS-2
F $550

Non-Valid Issues

$5 • W-KY-480-005-C040

Engraver: Toppan, Carpenter, Casilear & Co. ***Comments:*** H-KY-100-C56, Hughes-Unlisted. Counterfeit of W-KY-480-005-G040. 18__. 1850s.

Rarity: URS-4
F $100

$5 • **W-KY-480-005-C040a**
Overprint: Red FIVE. *Engraver:* Toppan, Carpenter, Casilear & Co. *Comments:* H-KY-100-C56a, Hughes-Unlisted. Counterfeit of W-KY-480-005-G040a. 18__. 1850s.

Rarity: URS-4
F $100

$10 • **W-KY-480-010-C060**
Engraver: Toppan, Carpenter, Casilear & Co. *Comments:* H-KY-100-C60, Hughes-Unlisted. Counterfeit of W-KY-480-010-G060. 18__. 1850s.

Rarity: URS-4
F $100

Glasgow, Kentucky

Glasgow was settled in 1799 and became the seat of the county the same year. It was named after Glasgow, Scotland. A post office was opened in 1803. The town was incorporated as a city in 1809.

Glasgow was home to the Underground Railroad during the Civil War, with places like Big Spring Bottom where horses were kept as well as Spotswood House where slaves were hidden. Tunnels and underground rooms were dug underneath the Old Glasgow Seminary Home for the purpose of transporting escaped slaves toward the North.

Bank of Green River
1818–1820
W-KY-490

History: The Bank of Green River was chartered on January 26, 1818, with an authorized capital of $200,000 to be divided into 2,000 shares of $100 apiece. Samuel Murrell, Henry Crutcher, Braxton B. Winn, John Gyrin, William T. Bush, Alexander Adair, William Thompson, Richard Garnett, Joseph Winlock, Benjamin Monroe, and William Savage were appointed to take stock subscriptions. The bank issued paper money, but in the summer of 1819 stopped redeeming it. On February 12, 1820, an act was approved for the relief of the directors of the bank, allowing them to close up the affairs of the bank. The charters of all independent banks authorized on January 26, 1818, were revoked effective May 1, 1820.

Bank of Kentucky {1st} (branch)
1817–1822
W-KY-500

History: The Bank of Kentucky (sometimes seen later in print as the "Old" Bank of Kentucky) was incorporated on December 27, 1806, with an authorized capital of $1,000,000. Half of the capital was subscribed to by the state. The Glasgow branch was opened in 1817. On January 21, 1822, the bank was ordered to start closing up its branches. This was to be completed by May 1, 1824. This act essentially shut down the bank. Curiously, all of the paperwork was not completed until the 1870s.

The first Bank of Kentucky had its parent bank located in Frankfort, W-KY-420, and branch banks located in Bardstown, W-KY-050, Danville, W-KY-320, Hopkinsville, W-KY-660, Lexington, W-KY-760, Louisville, W-KY-840, Paris, W-KY-1260, Richmond, W-KY-1350, Russellville, W-KY-1380, Shelbyville, W-KY-1430, Springfield, W-KY-1500, Washington, W-KY-1570, and Winchester, W-KY-1580.

Valid Issues

$1 • **W-KY-500-001-G010**
Left: BRANCH BANK vertically. *Center:* 1 / Running deer, plow, ax / 1. *Right:* 1 / ONE / 1 vertically. *Engraver:* Unverified, but likely Murray, Draper, Fairman & Co. *Comments:* H-KY-110-G58, Hughes-283. 18__. 1820 and 1821.

Rarity: URS-3
F $225

$1 • **W-KY-500-001-G020**
Engraver: Murray, Draper, Fairman & Co. *Comments:* H-KY-110-G60, Hughes-Unlisted. No description available. 18__. 1821.

Rarity: *None known*

$5 • **W-KY-500-005-G030**
Engraver: Unverified, but likely W. Harrison. *Comments:* H-KY-110-G62, Hughes-Unlisted. No description available. 18__. 1817–1820.

Rarity: *None known*

$5 • **W-KY-500-005-G040**
Engraver: Unverified, but likely Murray, Draper, Fairman & Co. *Comments:* H-KY-110-G64, Hughes-Unlisted. No description available. 18__. 1820.

Rarity: *None known*

$10 • **W-KY-500-010-G050**
Engraver: Unverified, but likely W. Harrison. *Comments:* H-KY-110-G66, Hughes-Unlisted. No description available. 18__. 1817–1820.

Rarity: *None known*

$10 • **W-KY-500-010-G060**
Engraver: Unverified, but likely Murray, Draper, Fairman & Co. *Comments:* H-KY-110-G68, Hughes-Unlisted. No description available. 18__. 1820.

Rarity: *None known*

$20 • **W-KY-500-020-G070**
Engraver: Unverified, but likely W. Harrison. *Comments:* H-KY-110-G70, Hughes-Unlisted. No description available. 18__. 1817–1820.

Rarity: *None known*

$50 • **W-KY-500-050-G080**
Engraver: Unverified, but likely W. Harrison. *Comments:* H-KY-110-G72, Hughes-293. No description available. 18__. 1817–1820.

Rarity: *None known*

$100 • **W-KY-500-100-G090**
Engraver: Unverified, but likely W. Harrison. *Comments:* H-KY-110-G74, Hughes-295. No description available. 18__. 1817–1820.

Rarity: *None known*

Bank of Kentucky {2nd} (branch)

1860s–1866

W-KY-510

History: The second Bank of Kentucky (sometimes seen in print as the "New" Bank of Kentucky) was chartered in 1834 in order to assume the business of the first Bank of Kentucky, W-KY-420, which had recently closed. The capital of the bank was $5,000,000.

The branch in Glasgow was established in the 1860s. In January 1866 almost all branches of the Bank of Kentucky were closed down, and the parent bank began winding up its business.

The second Bank of Kentucky had its parent bank located in Louisville, W-KY-850, and branch banks located in Bowling Green, W-KY-080, Burksville, W-KY-140, Columbus, W-KY-220, Danville, W-KY-330, Flemingsburg, W-KY-390, Frankfort, W-KY-430, Greensburg, W-KY-540, Hopkinsville, W-KY-670, Lexington, W-KY-770, Maysville, W-KY-1020, Mount Sterling, W-KY-1100, and Paducah, W-KY-1220.

Numismatic Commentary: Notes of this bank and its branches are very rare.

Valid Issues

$5 • W-KY-510-005-G010

Left: 5 / Portrait of Henry Clay / FIVE. ***Center:*** Portrait of John Q. Adams / Woman seated against bales, Train, Harvesting scene / Portrait of Thomas Jefferson. ***Right:*** 5 / Portrait of George Washington / FIVE. ***Engraver:*** Toppan, Carpenter & Co. ***Comments:*** H-KY-195-G200, Hughes-494. 185_. 1850s.

Rarity: URS-2
F $450

$10 • W-KY-510-010-G020

Left: 10 / Portrait of George Washington / 10. ***Center:*** Portrait of Andrew Jackson / Indian man and woman flanking shield bearing 10 surmounted by eagle / Portrait of Isaac Shelby. ***Right:*** 10 / Portrait of Henry Clay / 10. ***Engraver:*** Toppan, Carpenter & Co. ***Comments:*** H-KY-195-G204, Hughes-499. 185_. 1850s.

Rarity: URS-2
F $450

$20 • W-KY-510-020-G030

Left: 20 / Portrait of Daniel Webster. ***Center:*** "General Marion's Sweet Potato Dinner." ***Right:*** 20 / Male portrait. ***Engraver:*** Toppan, Carpenter & Co. ***Comments:*** H-KY-195-G208, Hughes-511. 185_. 1850s.

Rarity: URS-2
F $450

Non-Valid Issues

$10 • W-KY-510-010-C020

Engraver: Toppan, Carpenter & Co. ***Comments:*** H-KY-195-C204, Hughes-500. Counterfeit of W-KY-510-010-G020. 185_. 1850s.

Rarity: URS-3
F $200

Northern Bank of Kentucky (branch)

1859 and 1860

W-KY-520

History: The Northern Bank of Kentucky was chartered in 1835 with an authorized capital of $3,000,000. The Glasgow branch was established in 1859. The capital was $150,000. Thomas J. Gorin was the cashier, and George W. Trabue was the president. In 1860 the branch bank closed.

Sometime during the 1860s the Northern Bank of Kentucky was converted to a bank of discount and deposit, after which time no notes were issued.

The Northern Bank of Kentucky had its parent bank located in Lexington, W-KY-830, and branch banks located in Barbourville, W-KY-040, Covington, W-KY-260, Cynthiana, W-KY-305, Louisville, W-KY-960, Paris, W-KY-1280, and Richmond, W-KY-1360.

Valid Issues

$1 • W-KY-520-001-G010

Left: 1 / Portrait of boy. ***Center:*** Men with cattle, Sheep. ***Right:*** 1 / Portrait of girl. ***Tint:*** Red-orange. ***Engraver:*** American Bank Note Co. ***Comments:*** H-KY-175-G150, Hughes-436. 18__. 1850s–1860s.

Rarity: URS-3
F $250

$5 • W-KY-520-005-G020

Left: 5 / FIVE vertically. ***Center:*** Portrait of Henry Clay / Woman seated against bales, Cattle, Train / Male portrait. ***Right:*** 5 / FIVE vertically. ***Tint:*** Red-orange. ***Engraver:*** American Bank Note Co. ***Comments:*** H-KY-175-G154, Hughes-445. 18__. 1850s–1860s.

Rarity: URS-3
F $250

$10 • W-KY-520-010-G030

Left: 10 / Portrait of Henry Clay. ***Center:*** Woman seated against bales, Cattle, Train. ***Right:*** 10 / Male portrait. ***Tint:*** Red-orange. ***Engraver:*** American Bank Note Co. ***Comments:*** H-KY-175-G158, Hughes-452. 18__. 1850s–1860s.

Rarity: URS-3
F $250

$20 • W-KY-520-020-G040

Left: 20 / 20. ***Center:*** Portrait of Henry Clay / Woman seated against bales, Cattle, Train / Male portrait. ***Right:*** 20 / 20. ***Tint:*** Red-orange. ***Engraver:*** American Bank Note Co. ***Comments:*** H-KY-175-G162, Hughes-458. 18__. 1850s–1860s.

Rarity: URS-3
F $250

$50 • W-KY-520-050-G050

Left: 50 / 50. ***Center:*** Portrait of Henry Clay / Woman seated against bales, Cattle, Train. ***Right:*** 50 / Male portrait. ***Tint:*** Red-orange. ***Engraver:*** American Bank Note Co. ***Comments:*** H-KY-175-G166, Hughes-464. 18__. 1850s–1860s.

Rarity: URS-2
F $550

$100 • W-KY-520-100-G060

Left: 100 / Portrait of Henry Clay / 100. ***Center:*** Woman seated against bales, Cattle, Train. ***Right:*** 100 / Male portrait / 100. ***Tint:*** Red-orange. ***Engraver:*** American Bank Note Co. ***Comments:*** H-KY-175-G170, Hughes-468. 18__. 1850s–1860s.

Rarity: URS-1
F $650

Greensburg, Kentucky

Greensburg was settled in 1780 as Glover's Station. It was named after John Glover, a soldier who received the land as a military grant. In 1792 the town was laid out to be the seat of Green County and was renamed Greensburg. It was incorporated as a city a year later.

In 1795 the public square was laid out. The post office was established in 1807.

Bank of Greensburgh
1818–1820
W-KY-530

History: The Bank of Greensburgh was chartered on January 26, 1818. The authorized capital of $100,000 was divided into 1,000 shares of $100 each. James Allen, Daniel Brown, Elias Barber, John Sandridge, and Nimrol H. Arnold were appointed to take stock subscriptions. The bank operated only for a short time. The charters of all independent banks authorized on January 26, 1818, were revoked effective May 1, 1820.

Numismatic Commentary: Notes of this bank are so scarce as to be collected in almost any grade.

Valid Issues

$1 • W-KY-530-001-G010 HA

Engraver: Murray, Draper, Fairman & Co. ***Comments:*** H-KY-125-G12, Hughes-318. 18__. 1810s.

Rarity: URS-3
F $300; **Proof** $600

$3 • W-KY-530-003-G020

Left: KENTUCKY vertically. ***Center:*** Spread eagle. ***Right:*** THREE DOLLARS vertically. ***Engraver:*** Murray, Draper, Fairman & Co. ***Comments:*** H-KY-125-G16, Hughes-319. 18__. 1810s.

Rarity: URS-3
F $300

$5 • W-KY-530-005-G030 CC

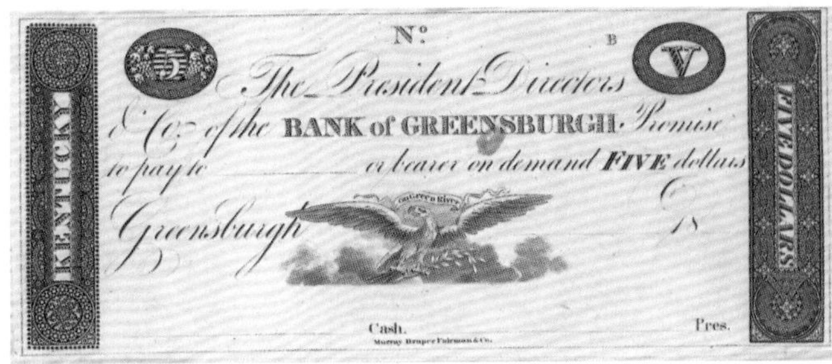

Engraver: Murray, Draper, Fairman & Co. ***Comments:*** H-KY-125-G18, Hughes-320. 18__. 1810s.

Rarity: URS-3
F $400; **Proof** $600

$10 • W-KY-530-010-G040 CC

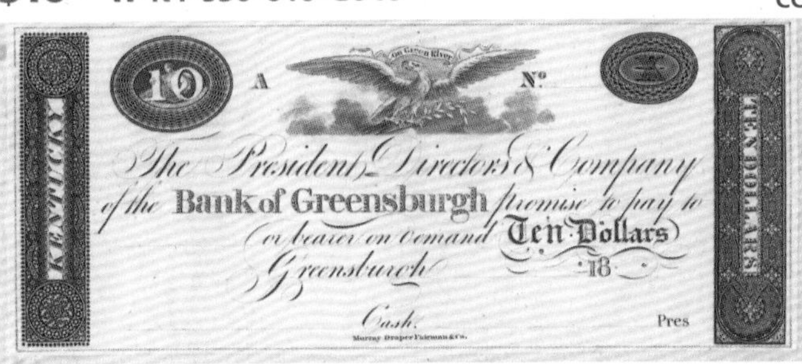

Engraver: Murray, Draper, Fairman & Co. ***Comments:*** H-KY-125-G20, Hughes-321. 18__. 1810s.

Rarity: URS-3
F $400; **Proof** $1,000
Selected auction price: Stack's Bowers Galleries, March 25, 2009, Proof $977

$20 • W-KY-530-020-G045 CC

Engraver: Murray, Draper, Fairman & Co. ***Comments:*** H-Unlisted, Hughes-Unlisted. 18__. 1810s.

Rarity: —
Proof $2,600
Selected auction price: Stack's Bowers Galleries, November 7, 2008, Proof $2,600

Post Notes

$__ • W-KY-530-__-G050

CC

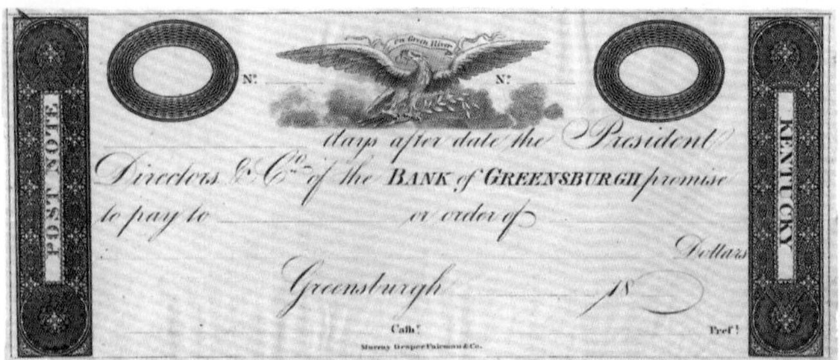

Engraver: Murray, Draper, Fairman & Co. ***Comments:*** H-Unlisted, Hughes-Unlisted. 18__. 1810s.

Rarity: URS-3
F $350

Bank of Kentucky {2nd} (branch)

1835–1866

W-KY-540

History: The second Bank of Kentucky (sometimes seen in print as the "New" Bank of Kentucky) was chartered in 1834 in order to assume the business of the first Bank of Kentucky, W-KY-420, which had recently closed. The capital of the bank was $5,000,000. The branch in Greensburg was established in 1835. In 1848 the president was Josiah Bromwell, and the cashier was William B. Allen. Capital was $125,000. In 1855 John Barrett took the presidency, and in 1860 he was replaced by E.H. Hobson, accompanied by William B. Fairman as cashier. In January 1866 almost all branches of the Bank of Kentucky were closed down, and the parent bank began winding up its business.

The second Bank of Kentucky had its parent bank located in Louisville, W-KY-850, and branch banks located in Bowling Green, W-KY-080, Burksville, W-KY-140, Columbus, W-KY-220, Danville, W-KY-330, Flemingsburg, W-KY-390, Frankfort, W-KY-430, Glasgow, W-KY-510, Hopkinsville, W-KY-670, Lexington, W-KY-770, Maysville, W-KY-1020, Mount Sterling, W-KY-1100, and Paducah, W-KY-1220.

Numismatic Commentary: Notes of this bank and its branches are very rare.

Valid Issues

$1 • W-KY-540-001-G010

Left: ONE / Men and women. ***Center:*** Woman swimming / ONE / Portrait of Henry Clay / Woman swimming / ONE. ***Right:*** ONE / Man and women. ***Engraver:*** Danforth, Bald & Co. ***Comments:*** H-KY-195-G212, Hughes-484. 18__. 1850s.

Rarity: URS-3
F $350

$5 • W-KY-540-005-G020

Left: FIVE / Liberty standing / V. ***Center:*** 5 / Horse / 5. ***Right:*** FIVE / Liberty standing / V. ***Engraver:*** Casilear, Durand, Burton & Evans. ***Comments:*** H-KY-195-G216, Hughes-495. 18__. 1830s–1840s.

Rarity: URS-3
F $350

$5 • W-KY-540-005-G030

Left: 5 / Portrait of Henry Clay / FIVE. ***Center:*** Portrait of John Q. Adams / Woman seated against bales, Train, Harvesting scene / Portrait of Thomas Jefferson. ***Right:*** 5 / Portrait of George Washington / FIVE. ***Engraver:*** Toppan, Carpenter & Co. ***Comments:*** H-KY-195-G220, Hughes-494. 18__. 1840s–1850s.

Rarity: URS-3
F $350

$10 • W-KY-540-010-G040

Left: 10 / Woman seated / X. ***Center:*** X / Three women seated / X. ***Right:*** 10 / Woman standing / X. ***Engraver:*** Casilear, Durand, Burton & Evans. ***Comments:*** H-KY-195-G224, Hughes-497. 18__. 1830s–1840s.

Rarity: URS-3
F $350

$10 • W-KY-540-010-G050

Left: 10 / Portrait of George Washington / 10. ***Center:*** Portrait of Andrew Jackson / Indian man and woman flanking shield bearing 10 surmounted by eagle / Portrait of Isaac Shelby. ***Right:*** 10 / Portrait of Henry Clay / 10. ***Engraver:*** Toppan, Carpenter & Co. ***Comments:*** H-KY-195-G228, Hughes-499. 18__. 1840s–1850s.

Rarity: URS-3
F $350

$20 • W-KY-540-020-G060

Left: 20 / Woman standing / 20. ***Center:*** XX / Woman seated with plow and bales, Cattle / XX. ***Right:*** 20 / Indian man standing / XX. ***Engraver:*** Casilear, Durand, Burton & Evans. ***Comments:*** H-KY-195-G232, Hughes-506. 18__. 1830s–1840s.

Rarity: URS-3
F $350

$20 • W-KY-540-020-G070

Left: Woman holding male portrait aloft / Male portrait. ***Center:*** 20 / Woman flying / 20. ***Right:*** Three women holding medallion head aloft. ***Engraver:*** Draper, Toppan & Co. ***Comments:*** H-KY-195-G234, Hughes-508. 18__. 1840s.

Rarity: URS-3
F $350

$20 • W-KY-540-020-G080

Left: 20 / Portrait of Daniel Webster. ***Center:*** "General Marion's Sweet Potato Dinner." ***Right:*** 20 / Male portrait. ***Engraver:*** Toppan, Carpenter & Co. ***Comments:*** H-KY-195-G236, Hughes-511. 18__. 1850s.

Rarity: URS-3
F $350

$50 • W-KY-540-050-G090

Left: Woman standing. ***Center:*** 50 / Steamboat *Henry Clay* / 50. ***Right:*** Woman standing. ***Engraver:*** Casilear, Durand, Burton & Evans. ***Comments:*** H-KY-195-G240, Hughes-513. 18__. 1830s–1840s.

Rarity: URS-2
F $600

Post Notes

$__ • W-KY-540-__-G100

Left: Woman seated with plow, sheaves, Cattle / POST NOTE. *Center:* $__. *Right:* Three women seated / POST NOTE. *Engraver:* Casilear, Durand, Burton & Evans. *Comments:* H-KY-195-G244, Hughes-523. 18__. 1830s.

Rarity: URS-3
F $350

Non-Valid Issues

$5 • W-KY-540-005-C020

Comments: H-KY-195-C216, Hughes-496. Counterfeit of W-KY-540-005-G020. 18__. 1830s–1840s.

Rarity: URS-3
F $100

$10 • W-KY-540-010-C050

Comments: H-KY-195-C228, Hughes-500. Counterfeit of W-KY-540-010-G050. 18__. 1840s–1850s.

Rarity: URS-3
F $100

$20 • W-KY-540-020-C070

Comments: H-KY-195-C234, Hughes-509. Counterfeit of W-KY-540-020-G070. 18__. 1840s.

Rarity: URS-3
F $100

$20 • W-KY-540-020-C080

Comments: H-KY-195-C236, Hughes-512. Counterfeit of W-KY-540-020-G080. 18__. 1850s.

Rarity: URS-3
F $100

Bank of the Commonwealth of Kentucky (branch)

1821–1830

W-KY-550

History: The Bank of the Commonwealth of Kentucky was chartered on November 29, 1820, with an authorized capital of $2,000,000. A local name for the bank was the "Peoples Bank," as it was chartered for the purpose of bringing relief to the population in a time of economic uncertainty. On December 22, 1820, an act was passed authorizing the bank to issue $3,000,000 in bills. The establishment of the Bank of the Commonwealth of Kentucky inadvertently caused the failure of the first Bank of Kentucky, W-KY-420.

The branch located at Greensburg opened for business in 1821. In 1830 the bank lost its authorization to loan money, and it was instructed to close up its branches. Around that time the bank cased new business, but the winding up of its affairs took until 1855.

The Bank of the Commonwealth of Kentucky had its parent bank located in Frankfort, W-KY-440, and branch banks located in Bowling Green, W-KY-090, Falmouth, W-KY-360, Flemingsburg, W-KY-410, Harrodsburg, W-KY-580, Hartford, W-KY-610, Lexington, W-KY-780, Louisville, W-KY-870, Mount Sterling, W-KY-1120, Princeton, W-KY-1330, Somerset, W-KY-1470, and Winchester, W-KY-1590.

Numismatic Commentary: Almost all notes from this bank and its branches are unknown today.

Valid Issues

6-1/4¢ • W-KY-550-00.06.25-G010

Left: 6-1/4 CENTS. *Center:* 6-1/4 / 6-1/4 on die / 6-1/4. *Right:* KENTUCKY vertically. *Comments:* H-KY-95-G104, Hughes-237. 1822.

Rarity: *None known*

12-1/2¢ • W-KY-550-00.12.50-G020

Left: 12-1/2 CENTS. *Center:* 12-1/2 / 12-1/2 on die / 12-1/2. *Right:* KENTUCKY vertically. *Comments:* H-KY-95-G106, Hughes-238. 1822.

Rarity: *None known*

25¢ • W-KY-550-00.25-G030

Left: 25 CENTS. *Center:* 25 / 25 on die / 25. *Right:* KENTUCKY vertically. *Comments:* H-KY-95-G108, Hughes-239. 1822.

Rarity: *None known*

50¢ • W-KY-550-00.50-G040

Left: 50 CENTS. *Center:* 50 / 50 on die / 50. *Right:* KENTUCKY vertically. *Comments:* H-KY-95-G110, Hughes-240. 1822.

Rarity: *None known*

$1 • W-KY-550-001-G050

Left: KENTUCKY vertically. *Center:* 1 / 1. *Right:* CAMPBELL COUNTY vertically. *Engraver:* Murray, Draper, Fairman & Co. *Comments:* H-KY-95-G114, Hughes-241. 18__. 1820s.

Rarity: URS-1
F $600

$3 • W-KY-550-003-G060

Left: KENTUCKY vertically. *Center:* 3 / 3. *Right:* CAMPBELL COUNTY vertically. *Engraver:* Murray, Draper, Fairman & Co. *Comments:* H-KY-95-G116, Hughes-242. 18__. 1820s.

Rarity: URS-1
F $600

$5 • W-KY-550-005-G070

Left: Woman holding staff. *Center:* 5 / Minerva standing with owl, shield, staff / 5. *Right:* Woman holding staff. *Engraver:* Murray, Draper, Fairman & Co. *Comments:* H-KY-95-G118, Hughes-243. 18__. 1820s.

Rarity: URS-1
F $600

$10 • W-KY-550-010-G080

Left: Woman holding staff. *Center:* 10 / Woman standing with staff, shield, Four cherubs / 10. *Right:* Woman holding staff. *Engraver:* Murray, Draper, Fairman & Co. *Comments:* H-KY-95-G120, Hughes-244. 18__. 1820s.

Rarity: *None known*

$20 • **W-KY-550-020-G090**

Engraver: Murray, Draper, Fairman & Co. ***Comments:*** H-KY-95-G122, Hughes-245. No description available. 18__. 1820s.

Rarity: *None known*

$50 • **W-KY-550-050-G100**

Engraver: Murray, Draper, Fairman & Co. ***Comments:*** H-KY-95-G124, Hughes-246. No description available. 18__. 1820s.

Rarity: *None known*

$100 • **W-KY-550-100-G110**

Engraver: Murray, Draper, Fairman & Co. ***Comments:*** H-KY-95-G126, Hughes-247. No description available. 18__. 1820s.

Rarity: *None known*

GREENVILLE, KENTUCKY

Greenville was settled on the estate of William Campbell in 1799. It was designated the seat of a new county, and in 1812 it was officially established. In 1848 it was incorporated as a city. The name likely comes from General Nathanael Greene.

Bank of Greenville

1818–1820

W-KY-560

History: The Bank of Greenville was chartered on January 26, 1818. James Weir, Alney McLean, William Campbell Sr., Charles F. Wing, Robert McLean, and John S. Eves were appointed to take stock subscriptions. The bank issued bills, but by autumn 1819 was no longer redeeming them. The charters of all independent banks authorized on January 26, 1818, were revoked effective May 1, 1820.

VALID ISSUES

$1 • **W-KY-560-001-G010**

Left: ONE. ***Center:*** 1 on die / 1 on die / 1 on die. ***Right:*** KENTUCKY vertically. ***Comments:*** H-Unlisted, Hughes-323. 1818.

Rarity: URS-1

F $600

$3 • **W-KY-560-003-G020**

Left: THREE. ***Center:*** 3 on die / 3 on die / 3 on die. ***Right:*** KENTUCKY vertically. ***Comments:*** H-Unlisted, Hughes-324. 1818.

Rarity: *None known*

$5 • **W-KY-560-005-G030**

Comments: H-Unlisted, Hughes-325. No description available. 1818.

Rarity: *None known*

$10 • **W-KY-560-010-G040**

CC

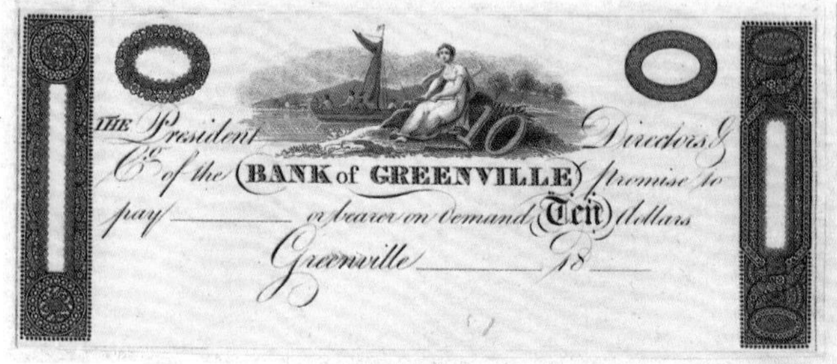

Comments: H-Unlisted, Hughes-326. 1818.

Rarity: URS-1

Proof $2,200

Selected auction price: Stack's Bowers Galleries, November 7, 2008, Proof $2,250

$20 • **W-KY-560-020-G050**

CC

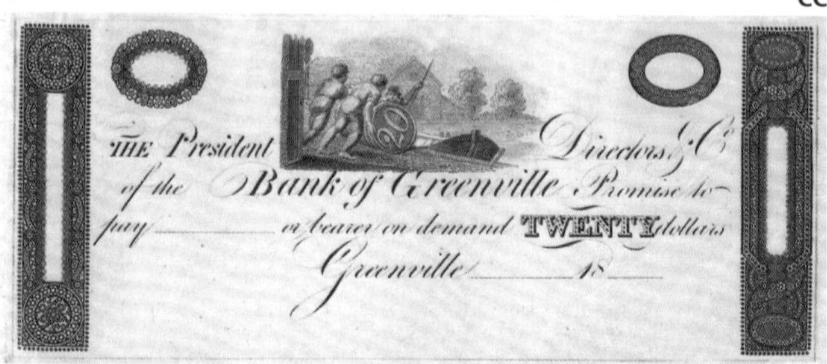

Comments: H-Unlisted, Hughes-327. 18__. 1818.

Rarity: URS-1

Proof $1,100

HARDINSBURG, KENTUCKY

Captain William Hardin formed an outpost in 1780 that was called Hardin's Fort. It was later referred to as Hardin's Station before being surveyed in 1784. The land was officially granted on June 21, 1786, and the settlement became Hardinsburg.

In 1800 Hardinsburg became the seat of Breckinridge County. The courthouse was built in 1801, and the post office opened in 1803.

Farmers Bank of Breckinridge

1818–1820

W-KY-570

History: The Farmers Bank of Breckinridge was chartered on January 26, 1818. The authorized capital of $100,000 was divided into 1,000 shares of $100 apiece. S. Shenault, David Murray, William Hardin, John P. Oldham, Joseph Allen, Nathan Anderson, and John Helm were appointed to take stock subscriptions. The charters of all independent banks authorized on January 26, 1818, were revoked effective May 1, 1820.

Harrodsburg, Kentucky

On June 16, 1774, James Harrod laid out and founded Harrodstown (also seen Harrod's Town). At an early time the settlement was abandoned due to Native American attacks, but it was reoccupied the next year. In 1785 the community was established as Harrodsburg, and in 1836 the town was incorporated. The city buildings were converted into hospitals for much of the duration of the Civil War.

Bank of the Commonwealth of Kentucky (branch)

1820–1830

W-KY-580

History: The Bank of the Commonwealth of Kentucky was chartered on November 29, 1820, with an authorized capital of $2,000,000. A local name for the bank was the "Peoples Bank," as it was chartered for the purpose of bringing relief to the population in a time of economic uncertainty. On December 22, 1820, an act was passed authorizing the bank to issue $3,000,000 in bills. The establishment of the Bank of the Commonwealth of Kentucky inadvertently caused the failure of the first Bank of Kentucky, W-KY-420.

The branch located at Harrodsburg experienced a burglary in 1830, and between $7,000 and $8,000 was stolen:

> In the fall of 1830, the Harrodsburg branch of the commonwealth's bank was robbed of a large sum in the notes of the bank. Four persons—John Banton, S.C. Banton, John Neal, and . . . [a man named] Harris, were suspected and arrested. Neal and Harris gave bail, left for Canada, and were not heard of afterwards. The Bantons were tried and acquitted, upon the ground that receiving stolen bank notes was not an offence punishable under our law. Neal had left the country, and the robbery had been almost forgotten, when a few days since, a carpenter by the name of Clinton Breese, who was engaged in covering the house occupied by Neal at the time of the robbery—now occupied by a Mrs. Watkins—found concealed in the house about six thousand dollars in commonwealth's bank paper. A nice legal question arises in settling the ownership of this treasure.[4]

In 1830 the bank lost its authorization to loan money, and it was instructed to close up its branches. Around that time the bank ceased new business, but the winding up of its affairs took until 1855.

The Bank of the Commonwealth of Kentucky had its parent bank located in Frankfort, W-KY-440, and branch banks located in Bowling Green, W-KY-090, Falmouth, W-KY-360, Flemingsburg, W-KY-410, Greensburg, W-KY-550, Hartford, W-KY-610, Lexington, W-KY-780, Louisville, W-KY-870, Mount Sterling, W-KY-1120, Princeton, W-KY-1330, Somerset, W-KY-1470, and Winchester, W-KY-1590.

Numismatic Commentary: Almost all notes from this bank and its branches are unknown today.

Valid Issues

6-1/4¢ • W-KY-580-00.06.25-G010

Left: 6-1/4 CENTS. ***Center:*** 6-1/4 / 6-1/4 on die / 6-1/4. ***Right:*** KENTUCKY vertically. ***Comments:*** H-KY-95-G130, Hughes-237. 1822.

Rarity: *None known*

12-1/2¢ • W-KY-580-00.12.50-G020

Left: 12-1/2 CENTS. ***Center:*** 12-1/2 / 12-1/2 on die / 12-1/2. ***Right:*** KENTUCKY vertically. ***Comments:*** H-KY-95-G132, Hughes-238. 1822.

Rarity: *None known*

25¢ • W-KY-580-00.25-G030

Left: 25 CENTS. ***Center:*** 25 / 25 on die / 25. ***Right:*** KENTUCKY vertically. ***Comments:*** H-KY-95-G134, Hughes-239. 1822.

Rarity: *None known*

50¢ • W-KY-580-00.50-G040

Left: 50 CENTS. ***Center:*** 50 / 50 on die / 50. ***Right:*** KENTUCKY vertically. ***Comments:*** H-KY-95-G136, Hughes-240. 1822.

Rarity: *None known*

$1 • W-KY-580-001-G050

Left: KENTUCKY vertically. ***Center:*** 1 / 1. ***Right:*** CAMPBELL COUNTY vertically. ***Engraver:*** Murray, Draper, Fairman & Co. ***Comments:*** H-KY-95-G140, Hughes-241. 18__. 1820s

Rarity: URS-1
F $600

$3 • W-KY-580-003-G060

Left: KENTUCKY vertically. ***Center:*** 3 / 3. ***Right:*** CAMPBELL COUNTY vertically. ***Engraver:*** Murray, Draper, Fairman & Co. ***Comments:*** H-KY-95-G142, Hughes-242. 18__. 1820s

Rarity: *None known*

$5 • W-KY-580-005-G070

Left: Woman holding staff. ***Center:*** 5 / Minerva standing with owl, shield, staff / 5. ***Right:*** Woman holding staff. ***Engraver:*** Murray, Draper, Fairman & Co. ***Comments:*** H-KY-95-G144, Hughes-243. 18__. 1820s

Rarity: *None known*

$10 • W-KY-580-010-G080

Left: Woman holding staff. ***Center:*** 10 / Woman standing with staff, shield, Four cherubs / 10. ***Right:*** Woman holding staff. ***Engraver:*** Murray, Draper, Fairman & Co. ***Comments:*** H-KY-95-G146, Hughes-244. 18__. 1820s

Rarity: *None known*

$20 • W-KY-580-020-G090

Engraver: Murray, Draper, Fairman & Co. ***Comments:*** H-KY-95-G148, Hughes-245. No description available. 18__. 1820s.

Rarity: *None known*

$50 • W-KY-580-050-G100

Engraver: Murray, Draper, Fairman & Co. ***Comments:*** H-KY-95-G150, Hughes-246. No description available. 18__. 1820s.

Rarity: *None known*

$100 • W-KY-580-100-G110

Engraver: Murray, Draper, Fairman & Co. ***Comments:*** H-KY-95-G152, Hughes-247. No description available. 18__. 1820s.

Rarity: *None known*

Commercial Bank of Kentucky (branch)

1852–1860s

W-KY-590

History: On January 3, 1852, the Commercial Bank of Kentucky was chartered. The Harrodsburg branch was established that year. The president was J. Hutchison, and the cashier was D.G. Hatch. In 1855 the capital was $100,000. By 1863 this had increased to $150,000. In 1864 the cashier was James A. Edwards, and the president was S. McBraver. The Commercial Bank of Kentucky closed sometime in the 1860s.

The Commercial Bank of Kentucky had its parent bank located in Paducah, W-KY-1240, and branch banks located in Cynthiana, W-KY-290, Lebanon, W-KY-720, Louisville, W-KY-900, Monticello, W-KY-1070, Newport, W-KY-1150, and Versailles, W-KY-1560.

Numismatic Commentary: Remaining at the American Bank Note Co. archives as of 2003 was a $1 face plate and a $100 face plate.

Valid Issues

$1 • W-KY-590-001-G010

Left: ONE / Steamboat vertically / ONE. ***Center:*** Coin, Man kneeling next to hewn log. ***Right:*** 1 / Male portrait / ONE. ***Engraver:*** Rawdon, Wright, Hatch & Edson. ***Comments:*** H-KY-255-G42, Hughes-664. 185_. 1850s.

Rarity: URS-3
G $100; **F** $350

$1 • W-KY-590-001-G020

CC

Tint: Green panel of microlettering outlining white ONE, die outlining white ONE, and ornaments. ***Engraver:*** American Bank Note Co. ***Comments:*** H-KY-255-G46a, Hughes-668. 185_. 1850s.

Rarity: URS-2; URS-1
VG $300
Proof $4,200

Selected auction price: Stack's Bowers Galleries, October 30, 2014, Lot 2076, Proof $4,200

$1 • W-KY-590-001-G030

CC

Overprint: Red ONE. ***Engraver:*** Toppan, Carpenter, Casilear & Co. ***Comments:*** H-Unlisted, Hughes-666. 185_. 1850s.

Rarity: URS-3
F $750

$2 • W-KY-590-002-G040

Left: 2 / Female portrait. ***Center:*** Woman seated with map, Two men in canoe. ***Right:*** TWO / TWO vertically / TWO. ***Tint:*** Green. ***Engraver:*** American Bank Note Co. ***Comments:*** H-KY-255-G48a, Hughes-670. 18__. 1860s.

Rarity: URS-3
F $350; **Proof** $1,100

$3 • W-KY-590-003-G050

Left: THREE / Male portrait / THREE. ***Center:*** Three gold dollars, Farmer with scythe, Blacksmith, Sailor. ***Right:*** 3 / Steamboat on stocks. ***Engraver:*** Rawdon, Wright, Hatch & Edson. ***Comments:*** H-KY-255-G50, Hughes-672. 185_. 1850s.

Rarity: URS-3
F $350

$3 • W-KY-590-003-G060

Left: 3 / Boy with rabbits. ***Center:*** Woman seated next to map, Two men in canoe. ***Right:*** 3 / Portrait of girl. ***Tint:*** Green. ***Engraver:*** American Bank Note Co. ***Comments:*** H-KY-255-G52a, Hughes-673. 18__. 1860s.

Rarity: URS-3
F $350; **Proof** $900

$5 • W-KY-590-005-G070

Left: 5 / Portrait of Millard Fillmore / FIVE. ***Center:*** Woman and man flanking three cherubs and five coins. ***Right:*** FIVE / Scene vertically / FIVE. ***Engraver:*** Rawdon, Wright, Hatch & Edson. ***Comments:*** H-KY-255-G54, Hughes-674. 185_. 1850s.

Rarity: URS-3
F $350

$5 • W-KY-590-005-G080

Left: FIVE / Men and women in and around V. ***Center:*** 5 / Women in and around 5, Dock. ***Right:*** FIVE / Portrait of Franklin Pierce. ***Engraver:*** Rawdon, Wright, Hatch & Edson / ABNCo. monogram. ***Comments:*** H-KY-255-G56, Hughes-Unlisted. 18__. 1850s–1860s.

Rarity: URS-2
F $600

$5 • W-KY-590-005-G080a

Tint: Red-orange. ***Engraver:*** Rawdon, Wright, Hatch & Edson / ABNCo. monogram. ***Comments:*** H-KY-255-G56a, Hughes-675. Similar to W-KY-590-005-G080 but with additional engraver imprint. 18__. 1850s–1860s.

Rarity: URS-3
F $350

$10 • W-KY-590-010-G090

Left: 10 / Male portrait / TEN. ***Center:*** Steamboats. ***Right:*** TEN / Harrodsburg Springs / TEN. ***Engraver:*** Unverified, but likely Rawdon, Wright, Hatch & Edson. ***Comments:*** H-KY-255-G58, Hughes-677. 185_. 1850s.

Rarity: URS-3
F $350

$100 • W-KY-590-100-G100

Comments: H-Unlisted, Hughes-Unlisted. No description available. 18__. 1850s.

Rarity: *None known*

Farmers Bank of Harrodsburg
1818–1820
W-KY-600

History: The Farmers Bank of Harrodsburg was chartered on January 26, 1818, with an authorized capital of $150,000 to be divided into 1,500 shares of $100 par value each. The bank operated only for a short time. The charters of all independent banks authorized on January 26, 1818, were revoked effective May 1, 1820.

Numismatic Commentary: One note of this bank is known today.

VALID ISSUES

$1 • W-KY-600-001-G010

Left: 1 / 1. ***Center:*** Farmer plowing. ***Right:*** 1 / KENTUCKY vertically / 1. ***Engraver:*** Murray, Draper, Fairman & Co. ***Comments:*** H-KY-140-G12, Hughes-328. 18__. 1810s.

Rarity: *None known*

$2 • W-KY-600-002-G020

Left: 2 / 2. ***Center:*** Farmer plowing. ***Right:*** 2 / KENTUCKY vertically / 2. ***Engraver:*** Murray, Draper, Fairman & Co. ***Comments:*** H-KY-140-G14, Hughes-329. 18__. 1810s.

Rarity: URS-1
F $700

$5 • W-KY-600-005-G030

Left: 5 / 5. ***Center:*** Farmer plowing. ***Right:*** 5 / KENTUCKY vertically / 5. ***Engraver:*** Murray, Draper, Fairman & Co. ***Comments:*** H-KY-140-G18, Hughes-330. 18__. 1810s.

Rarity: *None known*

$10 • W-KY-600-010-G040

Left: 10 / 10. ***Center:*** Farmer plowing. ***Right:*** 10 / KENTUCKY vertically / 10. ***Engraver:*** Murray, Draper, Fairman & Co. ***Comments:*** H-KY-140-G20, Hughes-331. 18__. 1810s.

Rarity: *None known*

$20 • W-KY-600-020-G050

Left: 20 / 20. ***Center:*** Farmer plowing. ***Right:*** 20 / KENTUCKY vertically / 20. ***Engraver:*** Murray, Draper, Fairman & Co. ***Comments:*** H-KY-140-G22, Hughes-332. 18__. 1810s.

Rarity: *None known*

HARTFORD, KENTUCKY

In 1782 the town of Hartford was surveyed, and in 1790 it was settled. It was known alternately as Fort Hartford and Hartford Station. In 1801 the post office was opened, and in 1808 the settlement was incorporated as Hartford. The town's courthouse was burned on December 20, 1864, during the Civil War.

Bank of the Commonwealth of Kentucky (branch)
1821–1830
W-KY-610

History: The Bank of the Commonwealth of Kentucky was chartered on November 29, 1820, with an authorized capital of $2,000,000. A local name for the bank was the "Peoples Bank," as it was chartered for the purpose of bringing relief to the population in a time of economic uncertainty. On December 22, 1820, an act was passed authorizing the bank to issue $3,000,000 in bills. The establishment of the Bank of the Commonwealth of Kentucky inadvertently caused the failure of the first Bank of Kentucky, W-KY-420. The branch located in Hartford opened in 1821.

In 1830 the bank lost its authorization to loan money, and it was instructed to close up its branches. Around that time the bank ceased new business, but the winding up of its affairs took until 1855.

The Bank of the Commonwealth of Kentucky had its parent bank located in Frankfort, W-KY-440, and branch banks located in Bowling Green, W-KY-090, Falmouth, W-KY-360, Flemingsburg, W-KY-410, Greensburg, W-KY-550, Harrodsburg, W-KY-580, Lexington, W-KY-780, Louisville, W-KY-870, Mount Sterling, W-KY-1120, Princeton, W-KY-1330, Somerset, W-KY-1470, and Winchester, W-KY-1590.

Numismatic Commentary: Almost all notes from this bank and its branches are unknown today.

VALID ISSUES

6-1/4¢ • W-KY-610-00.06.25-G010

Left: 6-1/4 CENTS. ***Center:*** 6-1/4 / 6-1/4 on die / 6-1/4. ***Right:*** KENTUCKY vertically. ***Comments:*** H-KY-95-G156, Hughes-237. 1822.

Rarity: *None known*

12-1/2¢ • W-KY-610-00.12.50-G020

Left: 12-1/2 CENTS. ***Center:*** 12-1/2 / 12-1/2 on die / 12-1/2. ***Right:*** KENTUCKY vertically. ***Comments:*** H-KY-95-G158, Hughes-238. 1822.

Rarity: *None known*

25¢ • W-KY-610-00.25-G030

Left: 25 CENTS. ***Center:*** 25 / 25 on die / 25. ***Right:*** KENTUCKY vertically. ***Comments:*** H-KY-95-G160, Hughes-239. 1822.

Rarity: *None known*

50¢ • W-KY-610-00.50-G040

Left: 50 CENTS. ***Center:*** 50 / 50 on die / 50. ***Right:*** KENTUCKY vertically. ***Comments:*** H-KY-95-G162, Hughes-240. 1822.

Rarity: *None known*

$1 • W-KY-610-001-G050
Left: KENTUCKY vertically. ***Center:*** 1 / 1. ***Right:*** CAMPBELL COUNTY vertically. ***Engraver:*** Murray, Draper, Fairman & Co. ***Comments:*** H-KY-95-G166, Hughes-241. 18__. 1820s.

Rarity: URS-1
F $600

$3 • W-KY-610-003-G060
Left: KENTUCKY vertically. ***Center:*** 3 / 3. ***Right:*** CAMPBELL COUNTY vertically. ***Engraver:*** Murray, Draper, Fairman & Co. ***Comments:*** H-KY-95-G168, Hughes-242. 18__. 1820s.

Rarity: URS-1
F $600

$5 • W-KY-610-005-G070
Left: Woman holding staff. ***Center:*** 5 / Minerva standing with owl, shield, staff / 5. ***Right:*** Woman holding staff. ***Engraver:*** Murray, Draper, Fairman & Co. ***Comments:*** H-KY-95-G170, Hughes-243. 18__. 1820s.

Rarity: URS-1
F $600

$10 • W-KY-610-010-G080
Left: Woman holding staff. ***Center:*** 10 / Woman standing with staff, shield, Four cherubs / 10. ***Right:*** Woman holding staff. ***Engraver:*** Murray, Draper, Fairman & Co. ***Comments:*** H-KY-95-G172, Hughes-244. 18__. 1820s.

Rarity: *None known*

$20 • W-KY-610-020-G090
Engraver: Murray, Draper, Fairman & Co. ***Comments:*** H-KY-95-G174, Hughes-245. No description available. 18__. 1820s.

Rarity: *None known*

$50 • W-KY-610-050-G100
Engraver: Murray, Draper, Fairman & Co. ***Comments:*** H-KY-95-G176, Hughes-246. No description available. 18__. 1820s.

Rarity: *None known*

$100 • W-KY-610-100-G110
Engraver: Murray, Draper, Fairman & Co. ***Comments:*** H-KY-95-G178, Hughes-247. No description available. 18__. 1820s.

Rarity: *None known*

Peoples Bank of Kentucky (branch)
1856–1860s
W-KY-620

History: The Peoples Bank of Kentucky was chartered on February 15, 1856, with an authorized capital of $250,000. In 1863 the president of the bank was L. Nall, and the cashier was J.W. Lewis. The branch was considered to be a successful enterprise.

Later the head office of the bank in Bowling Green, W-KY-100, moved to Louisville, W-KY-970, and the old parent location became a branch, W-KY-110. The bank closed up sometime in the 1860s.

The Peoples Bank of Kentucky had its parent banks located first in Bowling Green, W-KY-100, then in Louisville, W-KY-970, and branch banks located in Bowling Green, W-KY-110, and Paducah, W-KY-1250.

Numismatic Commentary: Remaining at the American Bank Note Co. archives as of 2003 was a $20-$50 face plate and a $20-$50 tint plate.

Valid Issues

Notes Dated at Parent Bank of Bowling Green Payable in Hartford

$1 • W-KY-620-001-G010
Left: 1 / Man with hat seated. ***Center:*** Two men with barrels. ***Right:*** 1 / 1. ***Tint:*** Red-orange. ***Engraver:*** Danforth, Wright & Co. ***Comments:*** H-KY-25-G14a, Hughes-71. 18__. 1850s.

Rarity: URS-2
F $500

$2 • W-KY-620-002-G020
Left: 2 / Female portrait. ***Center:*** TWO / Woman seated in 2 / TWO. ***Right:*** 2 / Two girls. ***Tint:*** Red-orange. ***Engraver:*** Danforth, Wright & Co. ***Comments:*** H-KY-25-G16a, Hughes-73. 18__. 1850s.

Rarity: URS-2
F $500

$3 • W-KY-620-003-G030 HA

Tint: Red-orange. ***Engraver:*** Danforth, Wright & Co. ***Comments:*** H-KY-25-G18a, Hughes-75. 18__. 1850s.

Rarity: URS-2
VF $750

$5 • W-KY-620-005-G040
Left: 5 / V. ***Center:*** Men with horses, cattle, and sheep. ***Right:*** 5 / Female portrait. ***Tint:*** Red-orange. ***Engraver:*** Danforth, Wright & Co. ***Comments:*** H-KY-25-G20a, Hughes-77. 18__. 1850s.

Rarity: URS-2
VF $750

Collectors and Researchers:
If you have new information about any banks or notes listed in this volume, contact Whitman Publishing, Attn: Obsolete Paper Money, 3101 Clairmont Road, Suite G, Atlanta, GA 30329.

$10 • **W-KY-620-010-G050**

HA

Tint: Red-orange. ***Engraver:*** Danforth, Wright & Co. ***Comments:*** H-KY-25-G22a, Hughes-78. 18__. 1850s.

Rarity: URS-2
F $900
Selected auction price: Heritage Auctions, October 23, 2015, Lot 19393, VF $881

$20 • **W-KY-620-020-G060**

HA

Tint: Red-orange. ***Back:*** Red-orange. ***Engraver:*** Danforth, Wright & Co. ***Comments:*** H-KY-25-G24a. 18__. 1850s.

Rarity: URS-2
F $1,500
Selected auction price: Heritage Auctions, April 18, 2012, Lot 15221, F $1,495

Notes Dated at Parent Bank of Louisville Payable in Hartford

$1 • **W-KY-620-001-G070**

CC

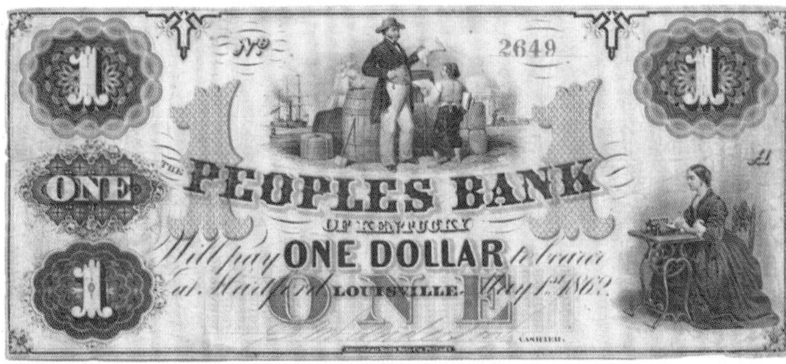

Tint: Green 1 / 1, panel of microlettering outlining ONE, and dies bearing white 1s. ***Engraver:*** American Bank Note Co. ***Comments:*** H-KY-25-G44a, Hughes-562. May 1st, 1862.

Rarity: URS-2
EF $800; **Proof** $1,500

$2 • **W-KY-620-002-G080**

CC

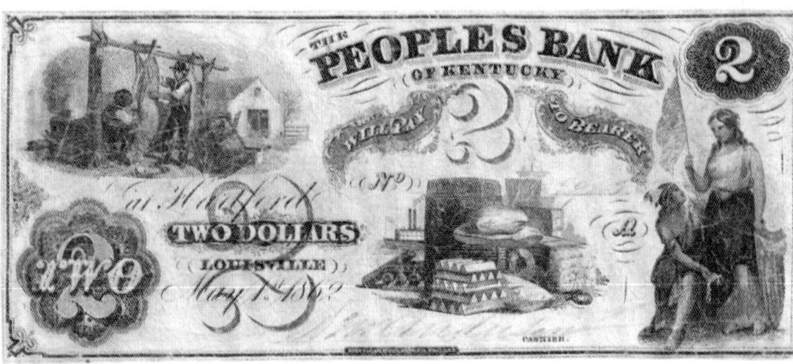

Tint: Green 2 / 2 and die bearing white TWO on 2. ***Engraver:*** American Bank Note Co. ***Comments:*** H-KY-25-G46a, Hughes-563. May 1st, 1862.

Rarity: URS-2
VG $400; **EF** $600; **Proof** $1,500

$5 • **W-KY-620-005-G090**

Left: Portrait of Henry Clay. ***Center:*** Girl with curls. ***Right:*** Farmer and horses at watering trough. ***Comments:*** H-KY-25-G48a, Hughes-565. Red and black print. 1862.

Rarity: URS-2
F $300; **Proof** $1,200

$5 • **W-KY-620-005-G090a**

Comments: H-KY-25-G48b, Hughes-566. Similar to W-KY-970-005-G090. Green and black print. 1862.

Rarity: URS-2
F $400; **Proof** $1,000

$10 • **W-KY-620-010-G100**

Left: X / 10. ***Center:*** Two men breaking hemp. ***Right:*** Two girls with sickle and flower basket. ***Comments:*** H-KY-25-G50a, Hughes-567. Green and black print. 1862.

Rarity: URS-2
F $400; **Proof** $1,000

$10 • **W-KY-620-010-G100a**

Comments: H-KY-25-G50b, Hughes-568. Similar to W-KY-970-010-G100. Red and black print. 1862.

Rarity: URS-2
F $400; **Proof** $1,000

$20 • **W-KY-620-020-G110**

HA

Tint: Red dies outlining white XX and dies bearing white 20s. ***Comments:*** H-KY-25-G52a, Hughes-569. Red and black print. 18__. 1862.

Rarity: URS-1
Proof $900

$50 • W-KY-620-050-G120

HA

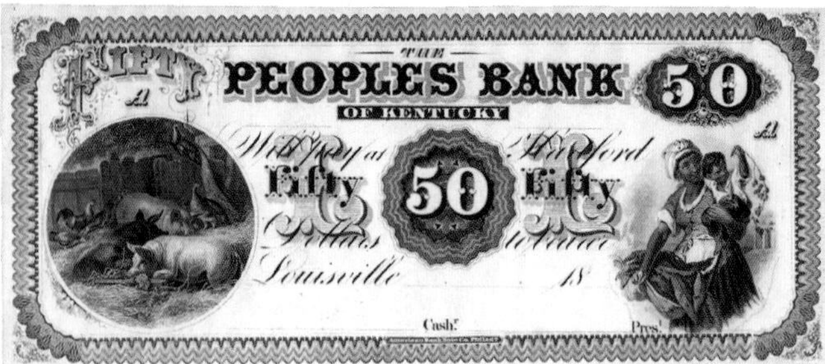

Tint: Red frame, L / L, and die bearing white 50. ***Engraver:*** American Bank Note Co. ***Comments:*** H-KY-25-G54a, Hughes-570. 18__. 1860s.

Rarity: URS-1
Proof $1,200

Non-Valid Issues

Notes Dated at Parent Bank of Bowling Green Payable in Hartford

$10 • W-KY-620-010-C050

Comments: H-KY-25-C22a, Hughes-5. Counterfeit of W-KY-620-010-G050. 18__. 1857.

Rarity: URS-3
F $150

$20 • W-KY-620-020-C060

Comments: H-KY-25-C24a, Hughes-7. Counterfeit of W-KY-620-010-G060. 18__. 1857.

Rarity: URS-3
F $150

Notes Dated at Parent Bank of Louisville Payable in Hartford

$2 • W-KY-970-002-C080

Comments: H-KY-25-C46a, Hughes-564. Counterfeit of W-KY-970-002-G080. May 1, 1862.

Rarity: URS-3
F $150

Henderson, Kentucky

Originally a village known as Red Banks, the land that included Henderson was purchased from Cherokee Indians by Colonel Richard Henderson on March 17, 1775. He bought over 17,000,000 acres in a sale known as the Transylvania Purchase. In the end the purchase was voided due to state-charter rights, but Henderson was granted 200,000 acres for development.

The town of Henderson was laid out in 1797 and formally established that year. By 1799 there was a population of 183, and the surrounding county had over 600 residents. A post office was opened in 1801, and the town was incorporated on January 21, 1840.

Tobacco became a major source of income for the county by the 1850s. Henderson was considered to be the largest producer of dark tobacco in the world.

Bank of Henderson
1818–1820
W-KY-630

History: The Bank of Henderson was chartered on January 26, 1818. The authorized capital of $150,000 was divided into 1,500 shares of $100 apiece. Samuel A. Bowen, James Wilson, James Hillyer, Walter Alves, Nicholas C. Horsley, Leonard Lyne, and Wiatt H. Ingram were appointed to take stock subscriptions. The bank operated only for a short time. The charters of all independent banks authorized on January 26, 1818, were revoked effective May 1, 1820.

Numismatic Commentary: Notes of this early bank are uncommon.

Valid Issues

$1 • W-KY-630-001-G010

HA

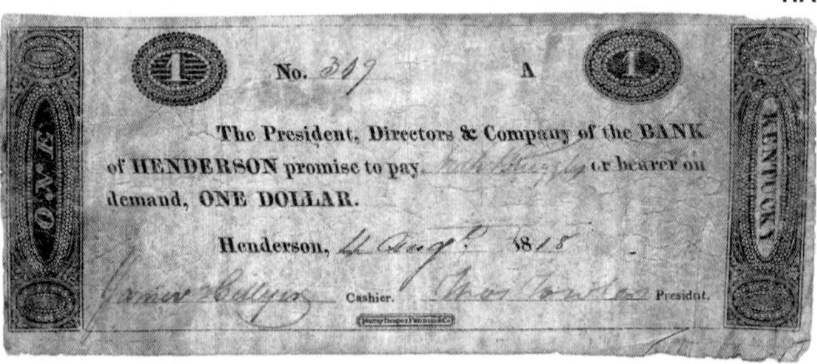

Engraver: Murray, Draper, Fairman & Co. ***Comments:*** H-KY-145-G12, Hughes-333. 18__. 1810s.

Rarity: URS-2
VG $250; **F** $400

$2 • W-KY-630-002-G020

Left: TWO vertically. ***Center:*** 2 / 2 / 2. ***Right:*** KENTUCKY vertically. ***Engraver:*** Murray, Draper, Fairman & Co. ***Comments:*** H-KY-145-G14, Hughes-334. 18__. 1810s.

Rarity: URS-2
F $450

$5 • W-KY-630-005-G030

CC

Engraver: Tanner, Kearney & Tiebout. ***Comments:*** H-KY-145-G18, Hughes-335. 18__. 1810s.

Rarity: URS-2
Proof $1,700
Selected auction price: Stack's Bowers Galleries, June 2010, Proof $1,700

$10 • **W-KY-630-010-G040** CC

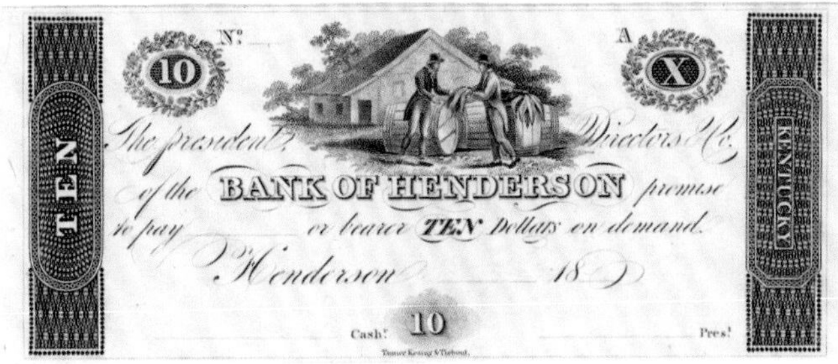

Engraver: Tanner, Kearney & Tiebout. ***Comments:*** H-KY-145-G20, Hughes-336. 18__. 1810s.

Rarity: URS-2
Proof $2,300

$20 • **W-KY-630-020-G050**

Left: TWENTY vertically. ***Center:*** 20 / Man with basket and 20 / XX. ***Right:*** KENTUCKY vertically. ***Engraver:*** Tanner, Kearney & Tiebout. ***Comments:*** H-KY-145-G22, Hughes-337. 18__. 1810s.

Rarity: URS-2
Proof $2,300
Selected auction price: Stack's Bowers Galleries, November 7, 2008, Proof $1,800

Farmers Bank of Kentucky (branch)

1850–1860s

W-KY-640

History: The Farmers Bank of Kentucky was chartered on February 15, 1850, with an authorized capital of $2,300,000. By September 1852 the bank had opened for business. On February 11, 1860, the charter for the bank was amended, allowing it to increase its capital.

The branch located in Henderson had a capital of $250,000. In 1855 the cashier was David Banks, and the president was Owen Class. In 1860 T.D. Tilford took over the position of cashier, and Joseph Adams was president. During the 1860s the Farmers Bank of Kentucky wound up its affairs and closed.

The Farmers Bank of Kentucky had its parent bank located in Frankfort, W-KY-450, and branch banks located in Bardstown, W-KY-070, Covington, W-KY-240, George Town, W-KY-480, Maysville, W-KY-1050, Mount Sterling, W-KY-1130, Princeton, W-KY-1340, and Somerset, W-KY-1480.

Valid Issues

$1 • **W-KY-640-001-G010** CC

Engraver: Toppan, Carpenter, Casilear & Co. ***Comments:*** H-KY-100-G74, Hughes-251. 185_. 1850s.

Rarity: URS-4
F $200

$1 • **W-KY-640-001-G010a** CC

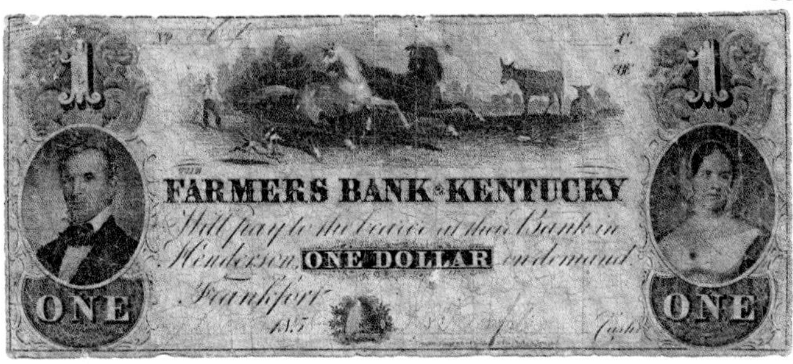

Back: Red-orange. ***Engraver:*** Toppan, Carpenter, Casilear & Co. / ABNCo. monogram. ***Comments:*** H-KY-100-G74b, Hughes-Unlisted. Similar to W-KY-640-001-G010 but with additional engraver imprint. 185_. 1850s.

Rarity: URS-3
VG $200; **F** $350

$1 • **W-KY-640-001-G020** CC

Tint: Red-orange bank title, 1, and die bearing white 1. ***Back:*** Red-orange. ***Engraver:*** American Bank Note Co. ***Comments:*** H-KY-100-G76a, Hughes-249. 18__. 1860s.

Rarity: URS-3
F $500

$2 • **W-KY-640-002-G030**

Left: 2 / Portrait of Mrs. John Crittenden. ***Center:*** 2 / Man on horse / 2. ***Right:*** 2 / Portrait of John Crittenden. ***Engraver:*** Toppan, Carpenter, Casilear & Co. ***Comments:*** H-KY-100-G78, Hughes-252. 18__. 1850s.

Rarity: URS-3
F $500

$2 • **W-KY-640-002-G030a**

Back: Red-orange. ***Engraver:*** Toppan, Carpenter, Casilear & Co. / ABNCo. monogram. ***Comments:*** H-KY-100-G78b, Hughes-Unlisted. Similar to W-KY-640-002-G030 but with additional engraver imprint. 185_. 1850s.

Rarity: URS-3
F $500

$5 • **W-KY-640-005-G040**

Left: 5 / Portrait of John Crittenden / 5. ***Center:*** Cattle and sheep, Herders. ***Right:*** 5 / Portrait of Mrs. John Crittenden / 5. ***Engraver:*** Toppan, Carpenter, Casilear & Co. ***Comments:*** H-KY-100-G80, Hughes-256. 18__. 1850s.

Rarity: URS-3
F $350

$5 • **W-KY-640-005-G040a**

Overprint: Red FIVE. ***Engraver:*** Toppan, Carpenter, Casilear & Co. ***Comments:*** H-KY-100-G80a, Hughes-257. Similar to W-KY-640-005-G040. 18__. 1850s.

Rarity: URS-3
F $350

$5 • **W-KY-640-005-G050**

Left: Men plowing with horse / V. ***Center:*** Portraits of Mr. and Mrs. John Crittenden. ***Right:*** 5 / 5. ***Tint:*** Red-orange. ***Back:*** Red-orange. ***Engraver:*** American Bank Note Co. ***Comments:*** H-KY-100-G82a, Hughes-255. 18__. 1859.

Rarity: URS-3
F $350

$10 • **W-KY-640-010-G060** CC

Engraver: Toppan, Carpenter, Casilear & Co. ***Comments:*** H-KY-100-G84, Hughes-Unlisted. 18__. 1850s.

Rarity: URS-3
F $350

$10 • **W-KY-640-010-G060a**

Tint: Red-orange outlining white TEN. ***Engraver:*** Toppan, Carpenter, Casilear & Co. ***Comments:*** H-KY-100-G84b, Hughes-Unlisted. Similar to W-KY-640-010-G060. 18__. 1850s.

Rarity: URS-3
F $350

$10 • **W-KY-640-010-G070**

Left: 10 / Portrait of John Crittenden. ***Center:*** Woman reclining against barrel, Harvest scene / Portrait of Mrs. John Crittenden. ***Right:*** 10 / Men harvesting corn. ***Tint:*** Red-orange. ***Back:*** Red-orange. ***Engraver:*** American Bank Note Co. ***Comments:*** H-KY-100-G86a, Hughes-259. 18__. 1859.

Rarity: URS-3
F $350

$20 • **W-KY-640-020-G080**

Left: Portrait of Mrs. John Crittenden / Portrait of John Crittenden. ***Center:*** 20 / Horses plowing. ***Right:*** 20. ***Engraver:*** Toppan, Carpenter, Casilear & Co. ***Comments:*** H-KY-100-G88, Hughes-261. 18__. 1850s.

Rarity: URS-2
F $550

$20 • **W-KY-640-020-G080a**

Tint: Red-orange. ***Back:*** Red-orange. ***Engraver:*** American Bank Note Co. ***Comments:*** H-KY-100-G90a, Hughes-Unlisted. Similar to W-KY-640-020-G080 but with different engraver imprint. 18__. 1859.

Rarity: URS-2
F $550

$50 • **W-KY-640-050-G090**

Left: Three women with anchor. ***Center:*** 50 / Portrait of Mrs. John Crittenden. ***Right:*** 50 / Portrait of John Crittenden / 50. ***Engraver:*** Toppan, Carpenter, Casilear & Co. ***Comments:*** H-KY-100-G92, Hughes-263. 18__. 1850s.

Rarity: URS-3
F $350

$100 • **W-KY-640-100-G100**

Left: 100 / Portrait of John Crittenden / 100. ***Center:*** Three women reclining / Portrait of Mrs. John Crittenden. ***Right:*** ONE HUNDRED vertically. ***Engraver:*** Toppan, Carpenter, Casilear & Co. ***Comments:*** H-KY-100-G94, Hughes-265. 18__. 1850s.

Rarity: URS-1
F $900

Non-Valid Issues

$5 • **W-KY-640-005-C040**

Comments: H-KY-100-C80, Hughes-257. Counterfeit of W-KY-640-005-G040. 18__. 1850s.

Rarity: URS-4
F $100

$5 • **W-KY-640-005-C040a**

Comments: H-KY-100-C80a, Hughes-Unlisted. Counterfeit of W-KY-640-005-G040a. 18__. 1850s.

Rarity: URS-4
F $100

$10 • **W-KY-640-010-C060**

Comments: H-KY-100-C84, Hughes-Unlisted. Counterfeit of W-KY-640-010-G060. 18__. 1850s.

Rarity: URS-4
F $100

Hickman, Kentucky

In 1819 the first cabin was built on the site of Hickman by James Mills. The community was called Mills Point, and in 1830 a post office was opened. In 1834 the surrounding area was purchased, and streets were laid out. In 1837 the area was renamed Hickman. It was incorporated as a town on February 18, 1841.

Southern Bank of Kentucky (branch)

1852–1865

W-KY-650

History: On February 20, 1839, the Southern Bank of Kentucky was chartered with an authorized capital of $2,000,000, of which the state subscribed to half. On February 15, 1850, the charter was extended to last until 1880.

The branch located at Hickman was established in 1852. William Owens Jr. was the cashier, and J.S. Hubbard was the president. In 1855 the capital was $150,000. By 1864 this had risen to $500,000. At that time John G. Barret was the cashier, and William B. Belknap was the president.

By 1865 the bank had been put into liquidation. On March 4, 1865, an act was passed ordering the treatment of the bank's bills to be as promissory notes rather than as currency. On January 8, 1867, the bank issued its last report regarding the closing up of its affairs. The bank building was later occupied by Nimrod, Long & Co.

The Southern Bank of Kentucky had its parent bank located in Russellville, W-KY-1400, and branch banks located in Bowling Green, W-KY-130, Carrollton, W-KY-200, Lebanon, W-KY-740, Louisville, W-KY-1000, Owensboro, W-KY-1200, and Smithland, W-KY-1460.

Valid Issues

$1 • W-KY-650-001-G010

Left: 1 / Woman reclining / ONE. ***Center:*** 1 / Female portrait surrounded by implements / 1. ***Right:*** 1 / Indian man reclining / ONE. ***Engraver:*** Toppan, Carpenter, Casilear & Co. ***Comments:*** H-KY-285-G92, Hughes-730. 18__. 1850s.

Rarity: URS-3
F $350

$1 • W-KY-650-001-G020

Left: Man with children and horse / ONE. ***Center:*** Portrait of young girl. ***Right:*** 1 / Flock of sheep. ***Engraver:*** Toppan, Carpenter & Co. ***Comments:*** H-KY-285-G94, Hughes-728. 18__. 1850s.

Rarity: URS-3
F $350

$1 • W-KY-650-001-G020a

Engraver: Toppan, Carpenter & Co. / ABNCo. monogram. ***Comments:*** H-KY-285-G94a, Hughes-Unlisted. Similar to W-KY-650-001-G020 but with additional engraver imprint. 18__. 1850s–1860s.

Rarity: URS-2
F $550

$2 • W-KY-650-002-G030

Left: 2 / Woman with basket / TWO. ***Center:*** Spread eagle / 2. ***Bottom center:*** Eagle. ***Right:*** Justice seated with scales and sword / TWO. ***Engraver:*** Toppan, Carpenter, Casilear & Co. ***Comments:*** H-KY-285-G98, Hughes-733. 18__. 1850s.

Rarity: URS-3
F $350

$2 • W-KY-650-002-G040

Left: 2 / Woman seated / TWO. ***Center:*** Female portrait. ***Right:*** 2 / Man with children and horse. ***Engraver:*** Toppan, Carpenter & Co. ***Comments:*** H-KY-285-G100, Hughes-735. 18__. 1850s.

Rarity: URS-3
F $350

$2 • W-KY-650-002-G040a

Engraver: Toppan, Carpenter & Co. / ABNCo. monogram. ***Comments:*** H-KY-285-G100a, Hughes-Unlisted. Similar to W-KY-650-002-G040 but with additional engraver imprint. 18__. 1850s–1860s.

Rarity: URS-2
F $550

$3 • W-KY-650-003-G050

Left: 3 / Female portrait / 3. ***Center:*** Woman with eagle. ***Bottom center:*** Steamboat. ***Right:*** 3 / Three women standing / THREE. ***Engraver:*** Toppan, Carpenter, Casilear & Co. ***Comments:*** H-KY-285-G104, Hughes-739. 18__. 1850s.

Rarity: URS-3
F $350

$3 • W-KY-650-003-G060

Left: 3 / Portrait of George Washington. ***Center:*** Portrait of young girl / Man with children and horse. ***Right:*** 3 / 3. ***Engraver:*** Toppan, Carpenter & Co. ***Comments:*** H-KY-285-G106, Hughes-737. 18__. 1850s–1860s.

Rarity: URS-3
F $350

$3 • W-KY-650-003-G060a

Engraver: Toppan, Carpenter & Co. / ABNCo. monogram. ***Comments:*** H-KY-285-G106a, Hughes-Unlisted. Similar to W-KY-650-003-G060 but with additional engraver imprint. 18__. 1850s–1860s.

Rarity: URS-2
F $550

$5 • W-KY-650-005-G070

Left: 5 / Female portrait / 5. ***Center:*** Man on horse. ***Right:*** 5 / Woman standing with flag. ***Engraver:*** Toppan, Carpenter, Casilear & Co. ***Comments:*** H-KY-285-G110, Hughes-742. 18__. 1850s.

Rarity: URS-3
F $350

$5 • W-KY-650-005-G080

Left: 5 / Portrait of boy. ***Center:*** Man on horse in farmyard. ***Right:*** V / Portrait of young girl. ***Overprint:*** Red FIVE. ***Engraver:*** Bald, Cousland & Co. / Baldwin, Bald & Cousland. ***Comments:*** H-KY-285-G112a, Hughes-744. 18__. 1850s.

Rarity: URS-3
F $350

$10 • W-KY-650-010-G090

Left: 10. ***Center:*** Woman reclining among farm implements. ***Bottom center:*** Female portrait. ***Right:*** 10. ***Engraver:*** Toppan, Carpenter, Casilear & Co. ***Comments:*** H-KY-285-G116, Hughes-749. 18__. 1850s.

Rarity: URS-3
F $350

$10 • W-KY-650-010-G100

Left: 10 / Woman seated. ***Center:*** Man, woman, child, dog, Haying scene. ***Right:*** 10 / Woman seated. ***Overprint:*** Red TEN. ***Engraver:*** Bald, Cousland & Co. / Baldwin, Bald & Cousland. ***Comments:*** H-KY-285-G118a, Hughes-750. 18__. 1850s.

Rarity: URS-3
F $350

Non-Valid Issues

$1 • W-KY-650-001-C010

Comments: H-KY-285-C92, Hughes-731. Counterfeit of W-KY-650-001-G010. 18__. 1850s.

Rarity: URS-4
F $100

$1 • W-KY-650-001-C020a

Comments: H-KY-285-C94a, Hughes-Unlisted. Counterfeit of W-KY-650-001-G020a. 18__. 1850s–1860s.

Rarity: URS-4
F $100

$3 • W-KY-650-003-C050

Comments: H-KY-185-C104, Hughes-740. Counterfeit of W-KY-650-003-G050. 18__. 1850s.

Rarity: URS-4
F $100

$3 • W-KY-650-003-C060a

Comments: H-KY-285-C106a, Hughes-738. Counterfeit of W-KY-650-003-G060a. 18__. 1850s–1860s.

Rarity: URS-4
F $100

Hopkinsville, Kentucky

Hopkinsville was originally part of a land grant to soldier Bartholomew Wood. In 1797 Christian County was established, and the area of Hopkinsville was selected to be its seat. A courthouse and jail were opened, and streets were laid out. In 1804 the town was named Hopkinsville after Samuel Hopkins.

In 1849 the South Kentucky College was established in Hopkinsville, followed by Bethel Female College in 1854. During the Civil War Hopkinsville was a center of Confederate support, but the town changed hands between the Confederate army and the Union army several times. The courthouse was burned by Confederate forces in 1864.

Bank of Kentucky {1st} (branch)

1816–1822

W-KY-660

History: The Bank of Kentucky (sometimes seen later in print as the "Old" Bank of Kentucky) was incorporated on December 27, 1806, with an authorized capital of $1,000,000. Half of the capital was subscribed to by the state.

The Hopkinsville branch was opened in 1816. On January 21, 1822, the bank was ordered to start closing up its branches. This was to be completed by May 1, 1824. This act essentially shut down the bank. Curiously, all of the paperwork was not completed until the 1870s.

The first Bank of Kentucky had its parent bank located in Frankfort, W-KY-420, and branch banks located in Bardstown, W-KY-050, Danville, W-KY-320, Glasgow, W-KY-500, Lexington, W-KY-760, Louisville, W-KY-840, Paris, W-KY-1260, Richmond, W-KY-1350, Russellville, W-KY-1380, Shelbyville, W-KY-1430, Springfield, W-KY-1500, Washington, W-KY-1570, and Winchester, W-KY-1580.

Valid Issues

$1 • W-KY-660-001-G010

Comments: H-KY-110-G76, Hughes-Unlisted. No description available. 18__. 1815.

Rarity: *None known*

$1 • W-KY-660-001-G020

Left: BRANCH BANK vertically. ***Center:*** 1 / Running deer, plow, ax / 1. ***Right:*** 1 / ONE / 1 vertically. ***Engraver:*** Unverified, but likely Murray, Draper, Fairman & Co. ***Comments:*** H-KY-110-G78, Hughes-283. 18__. 1816.

Rarity: URS-3
F $350

$1 • W-KY-660-001-G030

Engraver: Murray, Draper, Fairman & Co. ***Comments:*** H-KY-110-G80, Hughes-Unlisted. No description available. 18__. 1821.

Rarity: *None known*

$5 • W-KY-660-005-G040

Engraver: Unverified, but likely W. Harrison. ***Comments:*** H-KY-110-G82, Hughes-Unlisted. No description available. 18__. 1810s.

Rarity: *None known*

$10 • W-KY-660-010-G050

Engraver: Unverified, but likely W. Harrison. ***Comments:*** H-KY-110-G84, Hughes-Unlisted. No description available. 18__. 1810s–1820.

Rarity: *None known*

$20 • W-KY-660-020-G060

Engraver: Unverified, but likely W. Harrison. ***Comments:*** H-KY-110-G86, Hughes-291. No description available. 18__. 1810s.

Rarity: *None known*

$50 • W-KY-660-050-G070

Engraver: Unverified, but likely W. Harrison. ***Comments:*** H-KY-110-G88, Hughes-293. No description available. 18__. 1810s.

Rarity: *None known*

$100 • W-KY-660-100-G080

Engraver: Unverified, but likely W. Harrison. ***Comments:*** H-KY-110-G90, Hughes-295. No description available. 18__. 1810s.

Rarity: *None known*

Bank of Kentucky {2nd} (branch)

1834–1865

W-KY-670

History: The second Bank of Kentucky (sometimes seen in print as the "New" Bank of Kentucky) was chartered in 1834 in order to assume the business of the first Bank of Kentucky, W-KY-420, which had recently closed. The capital of the bank was $5,000,000.

The branch in Hopkinsville was established in 1834. The first president was John P. Campbell, and I.H. Caldwell was the first cashier. In 1848 Reuben Rowland took over the position as cashier. Capital was $250,000.

In 1865 the National Bank of Hopkinsville was chartered and purchased the branch of the Bank of Kentucky, assuming its assets.

The second Bank of Kentucky had its parent bank located in Louisville, W-KY-850, and branch banks located in Bowling Green, W-KY-080, Burksville, W-KY-140, Columbus, W-KY-220, Danville, W-KY-330, Flemingsburg, W-KY-390, Frankfort, W-KY-430, Glasgow, W-KY-510, Greensburg, W-KY-540, Lexington, W-KY-770, Maysville, W-KY-1020, Mount Sterling, W-KY-1100, and Paducah, W-KY-1220.

Numismatic Commentary: Notes of this bank and its branches are very rare.

Valid Issues

$1 • W-KY-670-001-G010

CC

Engraver: Danforth, Bald & Co. ***Comments:*** H-KY-195-G250, Hughes-484. 18__. 1850s.

Rarity: URS-4
F $350; **Proof** $1,800
Selected auction price: Heritage Auctions, April 18, 2012, Lot 15225, Proof $1,725

$5 • W-KY-670-005-G020

Left: FIVE / Liberty standing / V. ***Center:*** 5 / Horse / 5. ***Right:*** FIVE / Liberty standing / V. ***Engraver:*** Casilear, Durand, Burton & Evans. ***Comments:*** H-KY-195-G254, Hughes-495. 18__. 1830s–1840s.

Rarity: URS-3
F $350

$5 • W-KY-670-005-G030

Left: 5 / Portrait of Henry Clay / FIVE. ***Center:*** Portrait of John Q. Adams / Woman seated against bales, Train, Harvesting scene / Portrait of Thomas Jefferson. ***Right:*** 5 / Portrait of George Washington / FIVE. ***Engraver:*** Toppan, Carpenter & Co. ***Comments:*** H-KY-195-G258, Hughes-494. 18__. 1840s–1850s.

Rarity: URS-3
F $350

$10 • W-KY-670-010-G040

Left: 10 / Woman seated / X. ***Center:*** X / Three women seated / X. ***Right:*** 10 / Woman standing / X. ***Engraver:*** Casilear, Durand, Burton & Evans. ***Comments:*** H-KY-195-G262, Hughes-497. 18__. 1830s–1840s.

Rarity: URS-3
F $350

$10 • W-KY-670-010-G050

Left: 10 / Portrait of George Washington / 10. ***Center:*** Portrait of Andrew Jackson / Indian man and woman flanking shield bearing 10 surmounted by eagle / Portrait of Isaac Shelby. ***Right:*** 10 / Portrait of Henry Clay / 10. ***Engraver:*** Toppan, Carpenter & Co. ***Comments:*** H-KY-195-G266, Hughes-499. 18__. 1840s–1850s.

Rarity: URS-3
F $350

$20 • W-KY-670-020-G060

Left: 20 / Woman standing / 20. ***Center:*** XX / Woman seated with plow and bales, Cattle / XX. ***Right:*** 20 / Indian man standing / XX. ***Engraver:*** Casilear, Durand, Burton & Evans. ***Comments:*** H-KY-195-G270, Hughes-506. 18__. 1830s–1840s

Rarity: URS-3
F $350

$20 • W-KY-670-020-G070

Left: Woman holding male portrait aloft / Male portrait. ***Center:*** 20 / Woman flying / 20. ***Right:*** Three women holding medallion head aloft. ***Engraver:*** Draper, Toppan & Co. ***Comments:*** H-KY-195-G272, Hughes-508. 18__. 1840s.

Rarity: URS-3
F $350

$20 • W-KY-670-020-G080

CC

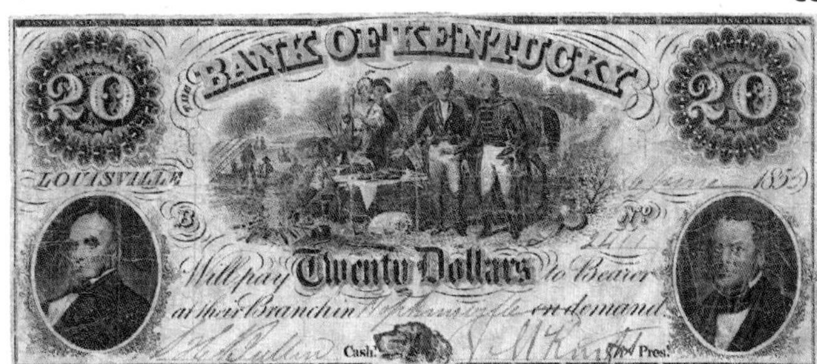

Engraver: Toppan, Carpenter & Co. ***Comments:*** H-KY-195-G274, Hughes-511. 185_. 1850s.

Rarity: URS-3
F $350

$50 • W-KY-670-050-G090

Left: Woman standing. ***Center:*** 50 / Steamboat *Henry Clay* / 50. ***Right:*** Woman standing. ***Engraver:*** Casilear, Durand, Burton & Evans. ***Comments:*** H-KY-195-G278, Hughes-513. 18__. 1830s–1860s.

Rarity: URS-3
F $350

Post Notes

$__ • W-KY-670-__-G100

Left: Woman seated with plow, sheaves, Cattle / POST NOTE. ***Center:*** $__. ***Right:*** Three women seated / POST NOTE. ***Engraver:*** Casilear, Durand, Burton & Evans. ***Comments:*** H-KY-195-G282, Hughes-523. 18__. 1830s.

Rarity: URS-2
F $250

Non-Valid Issues

$1 • W-KY-670-001-C010

CC

Comments: H-KY-195-C250, Hughes-485. Counterfeit of W-KY-670-001-G010. August 15th, 1856.

Rarity: URS-4
VG $50; **F** $100

$5 • W-KY-670-005-C020

Comments: H-KY-195-C254, Hughes-496. Counterfeit of W-KY-670-005-G020. 18__. 1830s–1840s.

Rarity: URS-3
F $100; **VF** $200

$10 • W-KY-670-010-C050

Comments: H-KY-195-C266, Hughes-500. Counterfeit of W-KY-670-010-G050. 18__. 1840s–1850s.

Rarity: URS-4
F $100

$10 • W-KY-670-010-R010

Comments: H-KY-195-R15, Hughes-502. Raised from W-KY-670-001-G010. 1830s–1850s.

Rarity: URS-4
F $100

$10 • W-KY-670-010-A010

Left: TEN / Two women and two men. ***Center:*** 10 / Male portrait / 10. ***Right:*** TEN / Man and woman with dog. ***Comments:*** H-Unlisted, Hughes-353. Altered from the main bank at Louisville. 1830s–1860s.

Rarity: URS-4
VF $150

$20 • W-KY-670-020-C070

Comments: H-KY-195-C272, Hughes-509. Counterfeit of W-KY-670-020-G070. 18__. 1840s.

Rarity: URS-4
F $90

$20 • W-KY-670-020-C080

Comments: H-KY-195-C274, Hughes-512. Counterfeit of W-KY-670-020-G080. 18__. 1850s.

Rarity: URS-4
F $100

$20 • W-KY-670-020-R020

Comments: H-KY-195-R20, Hughes-Unlisted. Raised from $1. 1830s–1850s.

Rarity: URS-4
F $125

Christian Bank

1818–1820

W-KY-680

History: The Christian Bank was chartered on January 26, 1818, with an authorized capital of $200,000. This was to be divided into 2,000 shares of $100 each. The bank operated for only a short time. In autumn 1819 it was reported that the bank "would hold out to the end," but the end was near. The charters of all independent banks authorized on January 26, 1818, were revoked effective May 1, 1820.

Numismatic Commentary: The series of notes from this early and short-lived bank are considered to be very rare. This is also thought to be the only use of "Christian" in a bank title in the era under study.

Valid Issues

$1 • W-KY-680-001-G010

QDB

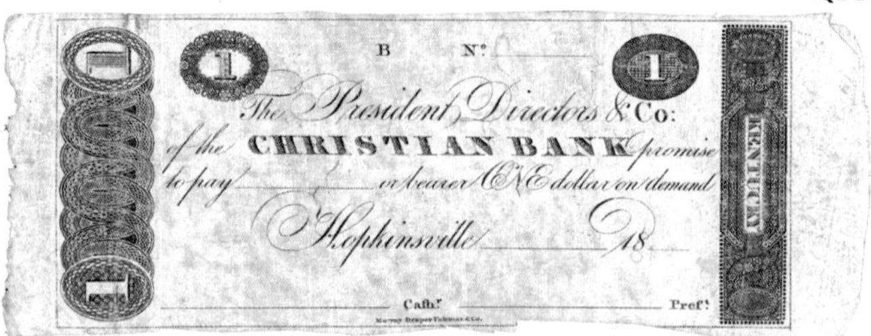

Engraver: Murray, Draper, Fairman & Co. ***Comments:*** H-KY-150-G12, Hughes-344. 18__. 1810s.

Rarity: URS-2
F $350; **VF** $900

$2 • W-KY-680-002-G020

Left: 2 / 2. ***Center:*** 2 / 2. ***Right:*** KENTUCKY vertically. ***Engraver:*** Murray, Draper, Fairman & Co. ***Comments:*** H-KY-150-G14, Hughes-345. 18__. 1810s.

Rarity: URS-2
F $500

$3 • W-KY-680-003-G030

CC

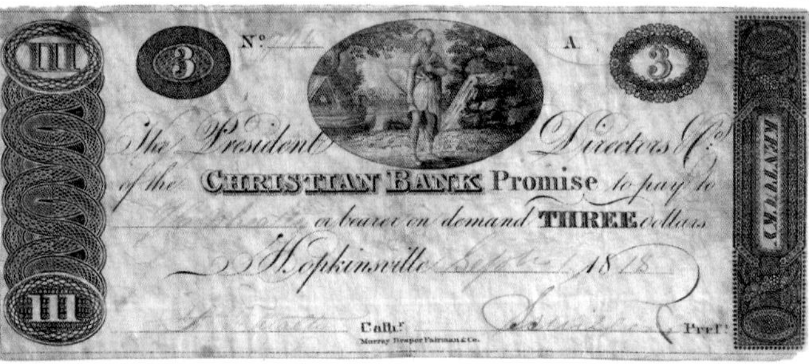

Engraver: Murray, Draper, Fairman & Co. ***Comments:*** H-KY-150-G16, Hughes-346. 18__. 1810s.

Rarity: URS-2
F $800
Selected auction price: R.M. Smythe, October 31, 2007, F $793

$5 • **W-KY-680-005-G040**

Left: 5 / 5. ***Center:*** V / Woman standing with pole and cap / V. ***Right:*** KENTUCKY vertically. ***Engraver:*** Murray, Draper, Fairman & Co. ***Comments:*** H-KY-150-G18, Hughes-347. 18__. 1810s.

Rarity: URS-2
VF $800

$10 • **W-KY-680-010-G050** CC

Engraver: Murray, Draper, Fairman & Co. ***Comments:*** H-KY-150-G20, Hughes-348. 18__. 1810s.

Rarity: URS-2
VF $600
Selected auction price: Heritage Auctions, January 2011, VF $592

$20 • **W-KY-680-020-G060** HA

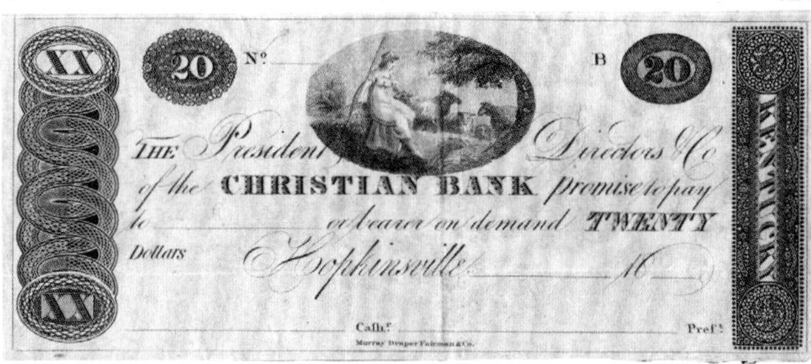

Engraver: Murray, Draper, Fairman & Co. ***Comments:*** H-KY-150-G22, Hughes-349. 18__. 1810s.

Rarity: URS-2
EF $700; **Proof** $1,200

$50 • **W-KY-680-050-G070**

Left: L / L. ***Center:*** 50 / Man plowing with horses, Buildings / 50. ***Right:*** KENTUCKY vertically. ***Engraver:*** Murray, Draper, Fairman & Co. ***Comments:*** H-KY-150-G24, Hughes-350. 18__. 1810s.

Rarity: URS-2
F $900

$100 • **W-KY-680-100-G080** HA

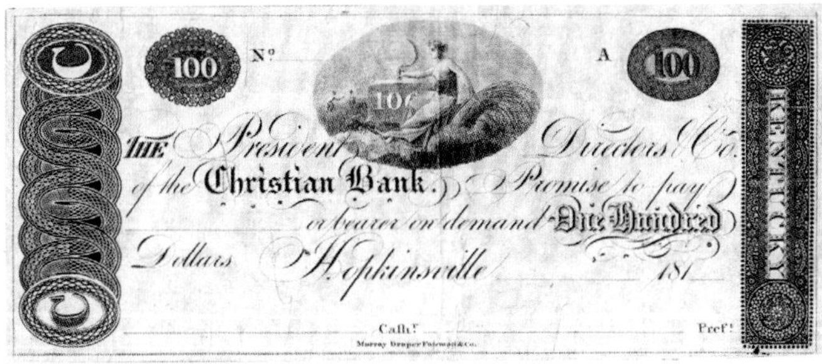

Engraver: Murray, Draper, Fairman & Co. ***Comments:*** H-KY-150-G26, Hughes-351. 181_. 1810s.

Rarity: URS-2
VG $650; **Proof** $1,200

Post Notes

$__ • **W-KY-680-__-G090**

Left: POST NOTE vertically. ***Center:*** Volant blowing trumpet. ***Right:*** KENTUCKY vertically. ***Comments:*** H-Unlisted, Hughes-352. 18__. 1810s.

Rarity: URS-2
F $300

LANCASTER, KENTUCKY

Captain William Buford donated the land that would become Lancaster in 1797. The surveying occurred the next year, and the town was named after Lancaster, Pennsylvania. The post office was opened in 1801, and in 1837 the town was officially incorporated.

Kentucky Exporting Company
1818–1820
W-KY-690

History: "A bank to be denominated the Kentucky Exporting Company, in the town of Lancaster," was chartered on January 26, 1818, per the wording in the legislative act. The authorized capital of $100,000 was divided into 1,000 shares of $100 apiece. Augustus A. Webber, Charles Caldwell, Charles W. Short, Samuel A. Miller, Joshua Hopson, Robert Patterson, Francis Wheatley, and John Burgess were appointed to take stock subscriptions. Although the word *Bank* was not in the title, this was indeed a chartered bank.

On November 19, 1819, the *Daily National Intelligencer* of Washington, D.C., stated that of the independent banks chartered in 1818, this one may have been unique in that its notes were received by the Bank of the United States. The charters of all independent banks authorized on January 26, 1818, were revoked effective May 1, 1820. From the *Reporter* of Lexington, Kentucky, July 12, 1820, this was reported: "The Kentucky Exporting Company, at Lancaster, has suspended its banking operations; funds are deposited with the merchants of Lancaster for the redemption of the notes in circulation."

VALID ISSUES

$20 • **W-KY-690-020-G010** CC

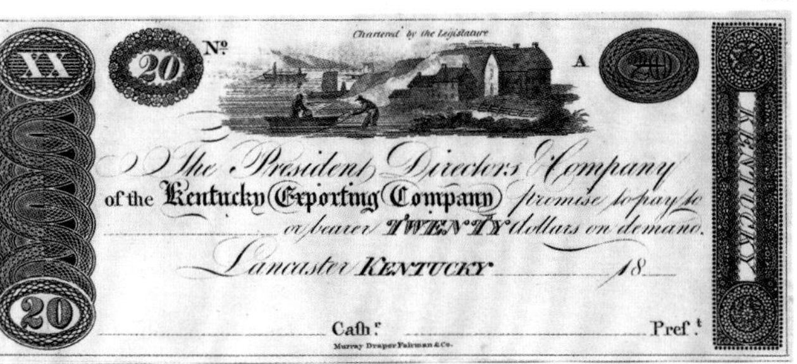

Comments: H-Unlisted, Hughes-Unlisted. 18__. 1810s.

Rarity: URS-1
Proof $1,200

$50 • **W-KY-690-050-G020** CC

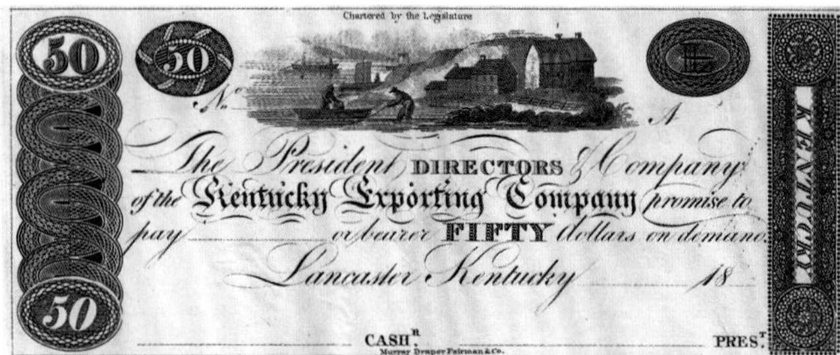

Comments: H-Unlisted, Hughes-Unlisted. 18__. 1810s.

Rarity: URS-1
Proof $1,400

Lancaster Deposit Bank
1860s
W-KY-700

History: The Lancaster Deposit Bank had a capital of $33,000 in 1861. The cashier was W.H. Kinnaird, and the president was J. Price. Kinnaird later went on to become the cashier of the National Bank of Lancaster.

LEBANON, KENTUCKY

Lebanon was settled in 1814 and named for the growth of cedar trees in the area. Neighboring George Town was called Lebanon in its early history, but the two towns are unrelated.

Lebanon was incorporated on January 28, 1815. It was selected to be the county seat of Marion in 1835. Andrew Jackson and Henry Clay met here in 1819, and in 1857 the Louisville and Nashville Railroad laid tracks through Lebanon. The Civil War halted the growth of the town, as three skirmishes took place in the area. The railroad, hotel, and residencies were burned in 1863.

Bank of Washington
1818–1820
W-KY-710

History: The Bank of Washington was chartered on January 26, 1818. The authorized capital of $100,000 was divided into 1,000 shares of $100 each. Benedict Spaulding, David Philips, Evan Young, Nathan H. Hall, Richard Forrest, Jeroboam Beauchamp, J. Paul, I. Booker, and William B. Booker were appointed to take stock subscriptions. The bank operated only for a short time in the summer of 1819, when it stopped redeeming its notes. The charters of all independent banks authorized on January 26, 1818, were revoked effective May 1, 1820.

VALID ISSUES

$1 • **W-KY-710-001-G010**

Left: ONE. ***Center:*** 1 / 1 / 1. ***Right:*** KENTUCKY vertically. ***Comments:*** H-Unlisted, Hughes-367. 1818.

Rarity: *None known*

$2 • **W-KY-710-002-G020**

Left: TWO. ***Center:*** 2 / 2 / 2. ***Right:*** KENTUCKY vertically. ***Comments:*** H-Unlisted, Hughes-368. 1818.

Rarity: URS-1
F $700

$5 • **W-KY-710-005-G030** CC

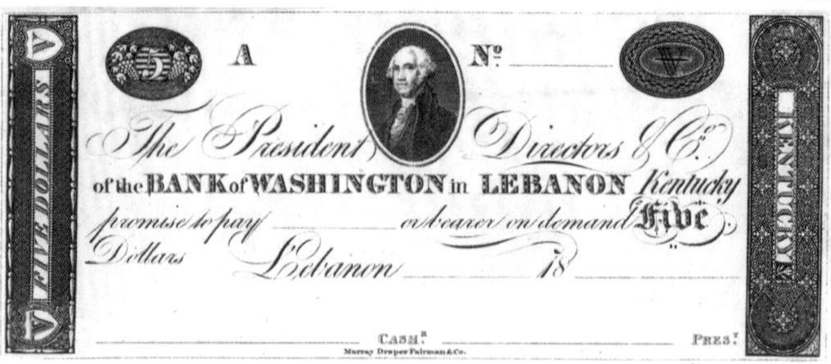

Engraver: Murray, Draper, Fairman & Co. ***Comments:*** H-Unlisted, Hughes-369. 18__. 1818.

Rarity: URS-1
Proof $1,200

$10 • **W-KY-710-010-G040** CC

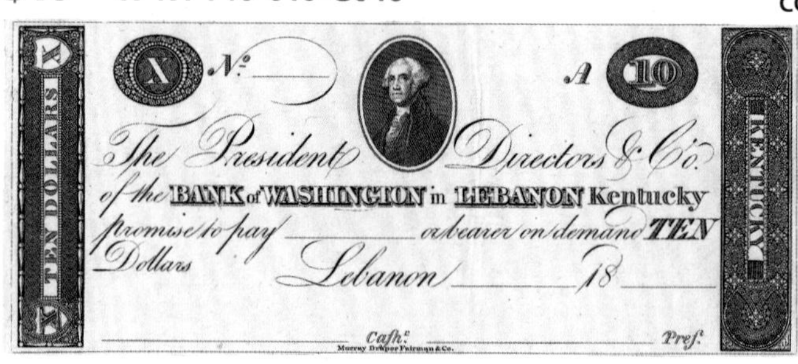

Comments: H-Unlisted, Hughes-370. 1818.

Rarity: URS-1
Proof $1,300

$20 • **W-KY-710-020-G050**

Comments: H-Unlisted, Hughes-371. No description available. 1818.

Rarity: *None known*

How to Read the Whitman Numbering System

$1 • **W-AL-020-001-G010a**

Denomination: Face value of the note shown.

W: Whitman number. This number is a sortable code unique to each bank and note.

AL: Abbreviation for the state under study.

020: Numerical designation specific to each bank.

001: The denomination in dollars.

G010a: G indicates a good or valid note. Other categories are indicated thus: C (counterfeit); R (raised); S (spurious); N (not-attributed); A (altered). Numbers are assigned starting with 010, 020, et seq. Terminal letters following the number indicate variations of a note: a series of different colored overprints, tints, payees, etc., all on the same design of note. For more information, see the "How to Use This Book" section at the front of the volume, page xiv.

$50 • W-KY-710-050-G060 CC

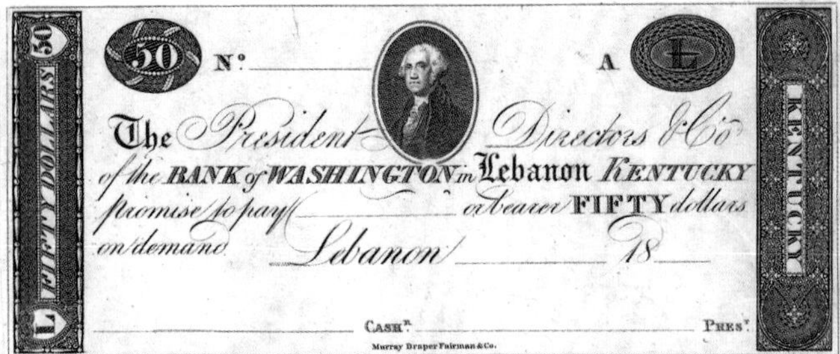

Comments: H-Unlisted, Hughes-372. 1818.

Rarity: URS-1
Proof $1,400

Commercial Bank of Kentucky (branch)

1852–1874

W-KY-720

History: On January 3, 1852, the Commercial Bank of Kentucky was chartered. In 1863 the capital of the Lebanon branch was $150,000. N.S. Ray was the cashier, and Benedict Spalding was the president. In 1874 the branch was succeeded by the Marion National Bank.

The Commercial Bank of Kentucky had its parent bank located in Paducah, W-KY-1240, and branch banks located in Cynthiana, W-KY-290, Harrodsburg, W-KY-590, Louisville, W-KY-900, Monticello, W-KY-1070, Newport, W-KY-1150, and Versailles, W-KY-1560.

Valid Issues

$1 • W-KY-720-001-G010

Left: ONE on 1 / ONE vertically / ONE on 1. ***Center:*** Woman seated with map, Two men in canoe. ***Right:*** 1 / Female portrait. ***Tint:*** Green. ***Engraver:*** American Bank Note Co. ***Comments:*** H-KY-255-G64a, Hughes-668. 185_. 1850s.

Rarity: URS-3
F $350

$2 • W-KY-720-002-G020

Left: 2 / Female portrait. ***Center:*** Woman seated with map, Two men in canoe. ***Right:*** TWO / TWO vertically / TWO. ***Tint:*** Green. ***Engraver:*** American Bank Note Co. ***Comments:*** H-KY-255-G66a, Hughes-670. 18__. 1860s.

Rarity: URS-3
F $350

$3 • W-KY-720-003-G030

Left: 3 / Boy with rabbits. ***Center:*** Woman seated with map, Two men in canoe. ***Right:*** 3 / Portrait of girl. ***Tint:*** Green. ***Engraver:*** American Bank Note Co. ***Comments:*** H-KY-255-G88a, Hughes-673. 18__. 1860s.

Rarity: URS-3
F $350

$5 • W-KY-720-005-G040

Left: FIVE / Men and women in and around V. ***Center:*** 5 / Women in and around 5, Dock. ***Right:*** FIVE / Portrait of Franklin Pierce. ***Tint:*** Red-orange. ***Engraver:*** Rawdon, Wright, Hatch & Edson / ABNCo. monogram. ***Comments:*** H-KY-255-G70a, Hughes-675. 18__. 1850s–1860s.

Rarity: URS-3
F $350

$10 • W-KY-720-010-G050

Left: 10 / Male portrait / TEN. ***Center:*** Steamboats. ***Right:*** TEN / Harrodsburg Springs / TEN. ***Engraver:*** Unverified, but likely Rawdon, Wright, Hatch & Edson. ***Comments:*** H-KY-255-G72, Hughes-677. 185_. 1850s.

Rarity: URS-3
F $350

Lebanon Deposit Bank

1856–1860s

W-KY-730

History: The Lebanon Deposit Bank (also seen as the Deposit Bank of Lebanon) was incorporated on March 5, 1856, with an authorized capital of $100,000. In 1861 the capital was $600,000.

Southern Bank of Kentucky (branch)

1858–1865

W-KY-740

History: On February 20, 1839, the Southern Bank of Kentucky was chartered with an authorized capital of $2,000,000, of which the state subscribed to half. On February 15, 1850, the charter was extended to last until 1880. The branch located in Lebanon was authorized on February 17, 1858.

By 1865 the bank had been put into liquidation. On March 4, 1865, an act was passed ordering the treatment of the bank's bills to be as promissory notes rather than as currency. On January 8, 1867, the bank issued its last report regarding the closing up of its affairs. The bank building was later occupied by Nimrod, Long & Co.

The Southern Bank of Kentucky had its parent bank located in Russellville, W-KY-1400, and branch banks located in Bowling Green, W-KY-130, Carrollton, W-KY-200, Hickman, W-KY-650, Louisville, W-KY-1000, Owensboro, W-KY-1200, and Smithland, W-KY-1460.

Valid Issues

$1 • W-KY-740-001-G010

Left: 1 / Woman reclining / ONE. ***Center:*** 1 / Female portrait surrounded by implements / 1. ***Right:*** 1 / Indian man reclining / ONE. ***Engraver:*** Toppan, Carpenter, Casilear & Co. ***Comments:*** H-KY-285-G136, Hughes-730. 18__. 1850s.

Rarity: URS-4
F $200

$1 • W-KY-740-001-G020

Left: Man with children and horse / ONE. ***Center:*** Portrait of young girl. ***Right:*** 1 / Flock of sheep. ***Engraver:*** Toppan, Carpenter & Co. ***Comments:*** H-KY-285-G138, Hughes-728. 18__. 1850s.

Rarity: URS-3
F $350

$1 • W-KY-740-001-G020a

Engraver: Toppan, Carpenter & Co. / ABNCo. monogram. ***Comments:*** H-KY-285-G138a, Hughes-Unlisted. Similar to W-KY-740-001-G020 but with additional engraver imprint. 18__. 1850s–1860s.

Rarity: URS-3
F $350

$2 • W-KY-740-002-G030

Left: 2 / Woman with basket / TWO. ***Center:*** Spread eagle / 2. ***Bottom center:*** Eagle. ***Right:*** Justice seated with scales and sword / TWO. ***Engraver:*** Toppan, Carpenter, Casilear & Co. ***Comments:*** H-KY-285-G142, Hughes-733. 18__. 1850s.

Rarity: URS-3
F $350

$2 • W-KY-740-002-G040

Left: 2 / Woman seated / TWO. ***Center:*** Female portrait. ***Right:*** 2 / Man with children and horse. ***Engraver:*** Toppan, Carpenter & Co. ***Comments:*** H-KY-285-G144, Hughes-735. 18__. 1850s.

Rarity: URS-3
F $350

$2 • W-KY-740-002-G040a

Engraver: Toppan, Carpenter & Co. / ABNCo. monogram. ***Comments:*** H-KY-285-G144a, Hughes-Unlisted. Similar to W-KY-740-002-G040 but with additional engraver imprint. 18__. 1850s–1860s.

Rarity: URS-2
F $350

$3 • W-KY-740-003-G050

Left: 3 / Female portrait / 3. ***Center:*** Woman with eagle. ***Bottom center:*** Steamboat. ***Right:*** 3 / Three women standing / THREE. ***Engraver:*** Toppan, Carpenter, Casilear & Co. ***Comments:*** H-KY-285-G148, Hughes-739. 18__. 1850s.

Rarity: URS-3
F $350

$3 • W-KY-740-003-G060

Left: 3 / Portrait of George Washington. ***Center:*** Portrait of young girl / Man with children and horse. ***Right:*** 3 / 3. ***Engraver:*** Toppan, Carpenter & Co. ***Comments:*** H-KY-285-G150, Hughes-737. 18__. 1850s–1860s.

Rarity: URS-3
F $350

$3 • W-KY-740-003-G060a

Engraver: Toppan, Carpenter & Co. / ABNCo. monogram. ***Comments:*** H-KY-285-G150a, Hughes-Unlisted. Similar to W-KY-740-003-G060 but with additional engraver imprint. 18__. 1850s–1860s.

Rarity: URS-2
F $350

$5 • W-KY-740-005-G070

Left: 5 / Female portrait / 5. ***Center:*** Man on horse. ***Right:*** 5 / Woman standing with flag. ***Engraver:*** Toppan, Carpenter, Casilear & Co. ***Comments:*** H-KY-285-G154, Hughes-742. 18__. 1850s.

Rarity: URS-3
F $350

$5 • W-KY-740-005-G080

Left: 5 / Portrait of boy. ***Center:*** Man on horse in farmyard. ***Right:*** V / Portrait of young girl. ***Overprint:*** Red FIVE. ***Engraver:*** Bald, Cousland & Co. / Baldwin, Bald & Cousland. ***Comments:*** H-KY-285-G156a, Hughes-744. 18__. 1850s.

Rarity: URS-3
F $350

$10 • W-KY-740-010-G090

Left: 10. ***Center:*** Woman reclining among farm implements. ***Bottom center:*** Female portrait. ***Right:*** 10. ***Engraver:*** Toppan, Carpenter, Casilear & Co. ***Comments:*** H-KY-285-G160, Hughes-747. 18__. 1850s.

Rarity: URS-3
F $350

$10 • W-KY-740-010-G100

Left: 10 / Woman seated. ***Center:*** Man, woman, child, dog, Haying scene. ***Right:*** 10 / Woman seated. ***Overprint:*** Red TEN. ***Engraver:*** Bald, Cousland & Co. / Baldwin, Bald & Cousland. ***Comments:*** H-KY-285-G162a, Hughes-750. 18__. 1850s.

Rarity: URS-3
F $350

Non-Valid Issues

$1 • W-KY-740-001-C010

Comments: H-KY-285-C136, Hughes-731. Counterfeit of W-KY-740-001-G010. 18__. 1850s.

Rarity: URS-4
F $100

$1 • W-KY-740-001-C020a

Comments: H-KY-285-C138a, Hughes-729. Counterfeit of W-KY-740-001-G020a. 18__. 1850s–1860s.

Rarity: URS-4
F $100

$3 • W-KY-740-003-C050

Comments: H-KY-185-C148, Hughes-740. Counterfeit of W-KY-740-003-G050. 18__. 1850s.

Rarity: URS-4
F $100

$3 • W-KY-740-003-C060a

Comments: H-KY-285-C150a, Hughes-738. Counterfeit of W-KY-740-003-G060a. 18__. 1850s–1860s.

Rarity: URS-4
F $100

Lexington, Kentucky

In 1775, 17 years before Kentucky became a state, Lexington was founded as a part of Virginia. The settlers named the town after Lexington, Massachusetts. In 1779 the first structures were built, delayed by the threat of attacks from Native Americans. In 1780 Lexington became the seat of Fayette County, and in 1782 the town was officially chartered.

As of 1820 Lexington was a large and wealthy town, earning it the nickname of "Athens of the West." In 1833 a cholera epidemic killed 500 residents. Further outbreaks hit the town in the late 1840s and early 1850s.

Agricultural Deposit Bank

1856–1860s

W-KY-750

History: The Agricultural Deposit Bank was incorporated on March 10, 1856, with an authorized capital of $300,000. In 1861 the capital was $99,500. J.S. Grinstead was the cashier, and J.G. James was the president.

Bank of Kentucky {1st} (branch)

1808–1822

W-KY-760

History: The Bank of Kentucky (sometimes seen later in print as the "Old" Bank of Kentucky) was incorporated on December 27, 1806, with an authorized capital of $1,000,000. Half of the capital was subscribed to by the state.

The Lexington branch was opened in 1808. On January 21, 1822, the bank was ordered to start closing up its branches. This was to be completed by May 1, 1824. This act essentially shut down the bank. Curiously, all of the paperwork was not completed until the 1870s.

The first Bank of Kentucky had its parent bank located in Frankfort, W-KY-420, and branch banks located in Bardstown, W-KY-050, Danville, W-KY-320, Glasgow, W-KY-500, Hopkinsville, W-KY-660, Louisville, W-KY-840, Paris, W-KY-1260, Richmond, W-KY-1350, Russellville, W-KY-1380, Shelbyville, W-KY-1430, Springfield, W-KY-1500, Washington, W-KY-1570, and Winchester, W-KY-1580.

Valid Issues

25¢ • W-KY-760-00.25-G010

Comments: H-KY-110-G92, Hughes-Unlisted. No description available. 18__. 1816.

Rarity: *None known*

50¢ • W-KY-760-00.50-G020

Comments: H-KY-110-G94, Hughes-Unlisted. No description available. 18__. 1816.

Rarity: *None known*

$1 • W-KY-760-001-G030

Comments: H-KY-110-G96, Hughes-Unlisted. No description available. 18__. 1815.

Rarity: *None known*

$1 • W-KY-760-001-G040

Engraver: Murray, Draper, Fairman & Co. ***Comments:*** H-KY-110-G98, Hughes-Unlisted. No description available. 18__. 1821.

Rarity: *None known*

$3 • W-KY-760-003-G050

Engraver: Murray, Draper, Fairman & Co. ***Comments:*** H-KY-110-G100, Hughes-285. No description available. 18__. 1821.

Rarity: *None known*

$5 • W-KY-760-005-G060

Engraver: Unverified, but likely W. Harrison. ***Comments:*** H-KY-110-G102, Hughes-Unlisted. No description available. 18__. 1810s.

Rarity: *None known*

$5 • W-KY-760-005-G070

Engraver: Unverified, but likely W. Harrison. ***Comments:*** H-KY-110-G104, Hughes-Unlisted. No description available. 18__. 1810s.

Rarity: *None known*

$5 • W-KY-760-005-G080

Engraver: Unverified, but likely Murray, Draper, Fairman & Co. ***Comments:*** H-KY-110-G106, Hughes-Unlisted. No description available. 18__. 1810s.

Rarity: *None known*

$10 • W-KY-760-010-G090

Left: DEPARMENT vertically. ***Center:*** Running deer, plow, ax / TEN. ***Right:*** 10. ***Engraver:*** W. Harrison. ***Comments:*** H-KY-110-G108, Hughes-287. 18__. 1808–1810s.

Rarity: URS-3

F $250

$10 • W-KY-760-010-G100

Engraver: Unverified, but likely W. Harrison. ***Comments:*** H-KY-110-G110, Hughes-Unlisted. No description available. 18__. 1810s–1820.

Rarity: *None known*

$10 • W-KY-760-010-G110　HA

Engraver: Murray, Draper, Fairman & Co. ***Comments:*** H-KY-110-G112, Hughes-Unlisted. 18__. 1810s.

Rarity: URS-3

F $250

$20 • W-KY-760-020-G120

Engraver: Unverified, but likely W. Harrison. ***Comments:*** H-KY-110-G114, Hughes-Unlisted. No description available. 18__. 1808–1810s.

Rarity: *None known*

$20 • **W-KY-760-020-G130**
Engraver: Unverified, but likely W. Harrison. ***Comments:*** H-KY-110-G116, Hughes-291. No description available. 18__. 1810s.
Rarity: *None known*

$50 • **W-KY-760-050-G140**
Engraver: Unverified, but likely W. Harrison. ***Comments:*** H-KY-110-G118, Hughes-Unlisted. No description available. 18__. 1808–1810s.
Rarity: *None known*

$50 • **W-KY-760-050-G150**
Engraver: Unverified, but likely W. Harrison. ***Comments:*** H-KY-110-G120, Hughes-Unlisted. No description available. 18__. 1810s.
Rarity: *None known*

$100 • **W-KY-760-100-G160**
Engraver: Unverified, but likely W. Harrison. ***Comments:*** H-KY-110-G122, Hughes-Unlisted. No description available. 18__. 1808–1810s.
Rarity: *None known*

$100 • **W-KY-760-100-G170**
Engraver: Unverified, but likely W. Harrison. ***Comments:*** H-KY-110-G124, Hughes-Unlisted. No description available. 18__. 1810s.
Rarity: *None known*

Post Notes

$__ • **W-KY-760-__-G180** CC

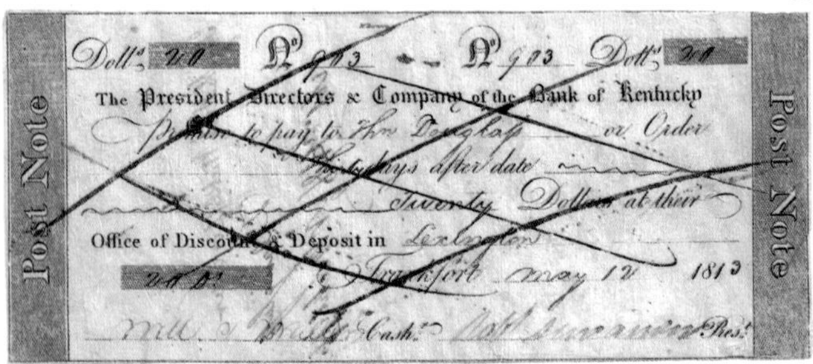

Engraver: W. Harrison. ***Comments:*** H-KY-110-G126, Hughes-Unlisted. 18__. 1810s.
Rarity: URS-2
F $550

$__ • **W-KY-760-__-G190** CC

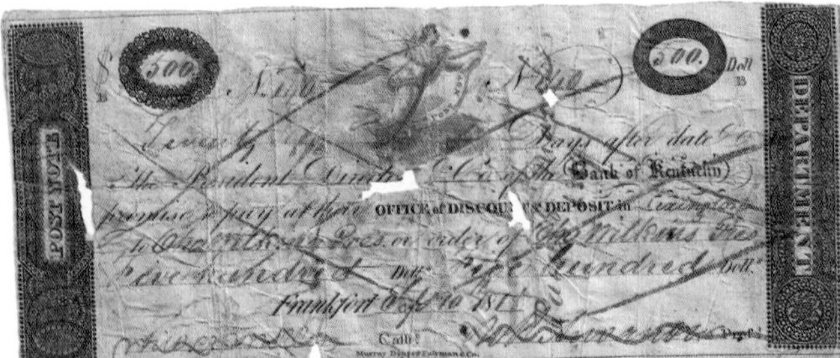

Engraver: Murray, Draper, Fairman & Co. ***Comments:*** H-KY-110-G128, Hughes-Unlisted. 18__. 1810s–1820s.
Rarity: URS-2
F $550

Bank of Kentucky {2nd} (branch)
1834–1866
W-KY-770

History: The second Bank of Kentucky (sometimes seen in print as the "New" Bank of Kentucky) was chartered in 1834 in order to assume the business of the first Bank of Kentucky, W-KY-420, which had recently closed. The capital of the bank was $5,000,000.

The branch in Lexington was established in 1834. In 1848 the president was Robert S. Todd, and the cashier was William S. Waller. Capital was $650,000. Upon the death of Todd in 1849, John B. Tilford became the president of the branch bank. As of 1855 Horace B. Hill became the cashier, and Henry Bell took the office of president. In 1864, with a capital of $550,000, the bank's officers remained the same.

On June 9, 1864, the Confederate cavalry seized $10,000 in funds from the Lexington branch. In January 1866 almost all branches of the Bank of Kentucky were closed down, and the parent bank began winding up its business. In 1870 the original branch building was purchased and occupied by the National Bank of Lexington.

The second Bank of Kentucky had its parent bank located in Louisville, W-KY-850, and branch banks located in Bowling Green, W-KY-080, Burksville, W-KY-140, Columbus, W-KY-220, Danville, W-KY-330, Flemingsburg, W-KY-390, Frankfort, W-KY-430, Glasgow, W-KY-510, Greensburg, W-KY-540, Hopkinsville, W-KY-670, Maysville, W-KY-1020, Mount Sterling, W-KY-1100, and Paducah, W-KY-1220.

Numismatic Commentary: Notes of this bank and its branches are very rare.

Valid Issues

6-1/4¢ • **W-KY-770-00.06.25-G003** CC

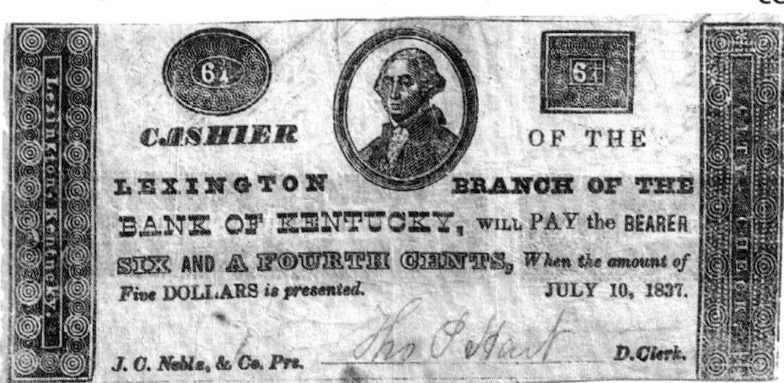

Comments: H-Unlisted, Hughes-Unlisted. July 10, 1837.
Rarity: URS-1
VF $600

12-1/2¢ • W-KY-770-00.06.25-G005

CC

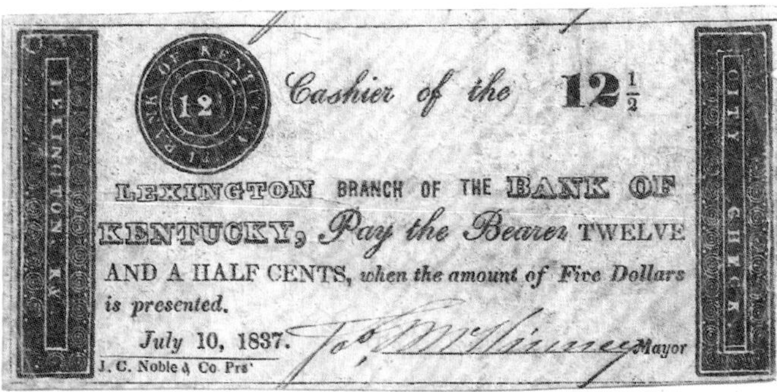

Comments: H-Unlisted, Hughes-Unlisted. July 10, 1837.

Rarity: URS-1
VF $600

$1 • W-KY-770-001-G007

CC

Comments: H-Unlisted, Hughes-Unlisted. 183_. 1830s.

Rarity: URS-1
VG $400

$1 • W-KY-770-001-G010

Left: ONE / Men and women. ***Center:*** Woman swimming / ONE / Portrait of Henry Clay / Woman swimming / ONE. ***Right:*** ONE / Man and women. ***Engraver:*** Danforth, Bald & Co. ***Comments:*** H-KY-195-G286, Hughes-484. 18__. 1850s.

Rarity: URS-3
F $350

$5 • W-KY-770-005-G020

Left: FIVE / Liberty standing / V. ***Center:*** 5 / Horse / 5. ***Right:*** FIVE / Liberty standing / V. ***Engraver:*** Casilear, Durand, Burton & Evans. ***Comments:*** H-KY-195-G290, Hughes-495. 18__. 1830s–1840s.

Rarity: URS-3
F $350

$5 • W-KY-770-005-G030

Left: 5 / Portrait of Henry Clay / FIVE. ***Center:*** Portrait of John Q. Adams / Woman seated against bales, Train, Harvesting scene / Portrait of Thomas Jefferson. ***Right:*** 5 / Portrait of George Washington / FIVE. ***Engraver:*** Toppan, Carpenter & Co. ***Comments:*** H-KY-195-G294, Hughes-494. 18__. 1840s–1850s.

Rarity: URS-3
F $350

$10 • W-KY-770-010-G040

Left: 10 / Woman seated / X. ***Center:*** X / Three women seated / X. ***Right:*** 10 / Woman standing / X. ***Engraver:*** Casilear, Durand, Burton & Evans. ***Comments:*** H-KY-195-G298, Hughes-497. 18__. 1830s–1840s.

Rarity: URS-3
F $350

$10 • W-KY-770-010-G050

Left: 10 / Portrait of George Washington / 10. ***Center:*** Portrait of Andrew Jackson / Indian man and woman flanking shield bearing 10 surmounted by eagle / Portrait of Isaac Shelby. ***Right:*** 10 / Portrait of Henry Clay / 10. ***Engraver:*** Toppan, Carpenter & Co. ***Comments:*** H-KY-195-G302, Hughes-499. 18__. 1840s–1850s.

Rarity: URS-3
F $350

$20 • W-KY-770-020-G060

Left: 20 / Woman standing / 20. ***Center:*** XX / Woman seated with plow and bales, Cattle / XX. ***Right:*** 20 / Indian man standing / XX. ***Engraver:*** Casilear, Durand, Burton & Evans. ***Comments:*** H-KY-195-G306, Hughes-506. 18__. 1830s–1840s.

Rarity: URS-3
F $350

$20 • W-KY-770-020-G070

Left: Woman holding male portrait aloft / Male portrait. ***Center:*** 20 / Woman flying / 20. ***Right:*** Three women holding medallion head aloft. ***Engraver:*** Draper, Toppan & Co. ***Comments:*** H-KY-195-G310, Hughes-508. 18__. 1840s.

Rarity: URS-3
F $350

$20 • W-KY-770-020-G080

Left: 20 / Portrait of Daniel Webster. ***Center:*** "General Marion's Sweet Potato Dinner." ***Right:*** 20 / Male portrait. ***Engraver:*** Toppan, Carpenter & Co. ***Comments:*** H-KY-195-G312, Hughes-511. 18__. 1850s.

Rarity: URS-3
F $350

$50 • W-KY-770-050-G090

Left: Woman standing. ***Center:*** 50 / Steamboat *Henry Clay* / 50. ***Right:*** Woman standing. ***Engraver:*** Casilear, Durand, Burton & Evans. ***Comments:*** H-KY-195-G316, Hughes-513. 18__. 1830s–1840s.

Rarity: URS-2
F $550

Post Notes

$__ • W-KY-770-__-G100

Left: Woman seated with plow, sheaves, Cattle / POST NOTE. ***Center:*** $__. ***Right:*** Three women seated / POST NOTE. ***Engraver:*** Casilear, Durand, Burton & Evans. ***Comments:*** H-KY-195-G320, Hughes-523. 18__. 1830s.

Rarity: URS-3
F $350

Non-Valid Issues

$5 • W-KY-770-005-C020

Comments: H-KY-195-C290, Hughes-496. Counterfeit of W-KY-770-005-G020. 18__. 1830s–1840s.

Rarity: URS-4
F $125

$10 • W-KY-770-010-C050

Comments: H-KY-195-C302, Hughes-500. Counterfeit of W-KY-770-010-G050. 18__. 1840s–1850s.

Rarity: URS-4
F $125

$20 • W-KY-770-020-C070
Comments: H-KY-195-C310, Hughes-509. Counterfeit of W-KY-770-020-G070. 18__. 1840s.
Rarity: URS-4
F $125

$20 • W-KY-770-020-C080
Comments: H-KY-195-C312, Hughes-512. Counterfeit of W-KY-770-020-G080. 18__. 1850s.
Rarity: URS-4
F $125

Bank of the Commonwealth of Kentucky (branch)
1821–1823
W-KY-780

History: The Bank of the Commonwealth of Kentucky was chartered on November 29, 1820, with an authorized capital of $2,000,000. A local name for the bank was the "Peoples Bank," as it was chartered for the purpose of bringing relief to the population in a time of economic uncertainty. On December 22, 1820, an act was passed authorizing the bank to issue $3,000,000 in bills. The establishment of the Bank of the Commonwealth of Kentucky inadvertently caused the failure of the first Bank of Kentucky, W-KY-420. The branch located in Lexington opened in 1821. It had closed by 1823.

In 1830 the bank lost its authorization to loan money, and it was instructed to close up its branches. Around that time the bank ceased new business, but the winding up of its affairs took until 1855.

The Bank of the Commonwealth of Kentucky had its parent bank located in Frankfort, W-KY-440, and branch banks located in Bowling Green, W-KY-090, Falmouth, W-KY-360, Flemingsburg, W-KY-410, Greensburg, W-KY-550, Harrodsburg, W-KY-580, Hartford, W-KY-610, Louisville, W-KY-870, Mount Sterling, W-KY-1120, Princeton, W-KY-1330, Somerset, W-KY-1470, and Winchester, W-KY-1590.

Numismatic Commentary: Almost all notes from this bank and its branches are unknown today.

Valid Issues

6-1/4¢ • W-KY-780-00.06.25-G010
Left: 6-1/4 CENTS. ***Center:*** 6-1/4 / 6-1/4 on die / 6-1/4. ***Right:*** KENTUCKY vertically. ***Comments:*** H-KY-95-G182, Hughes-237. 1822.
Rarity: *None known*

12-1/2¢ • W-KY-780-00.12.50-G020
Left: 12-1/2 CENTS. ***Center:*** 12-1/2 / 12-1/2 on die / 12-1/2. ***Right:*** KENTUCKY vertically. ***Comments:*** H-KY-95-G184, Hughes-238. 1822.
Rarity: *None known*

25¢ • W-KY-780-00.25-G030
Left: 25 CENTS. ***Center:*** 25 / 25 on die / 25. ***Right:*** KENTUCKY vertically. ***Comments:*** H-KY-95-G186, Hughes-239. 1822.
Rarity: *None known*

50¢ • W-KY-780-00.50-G040
Left: 50 CENTS. ***Center:*** 50 / 50 on die / 50. ***Right:*** KENTUCKY vertically. ***Comments:*** H-KY-95-G188, Hughes-240. 1822.
Rarity: *None known*

$1 • W-KY-780-001-G050
Left: KENTUCKY vertically. ***Center:*** 1 / 1. ***Right:*** CAMPBELL COUNTY vertically. ***Engraver:*** Murray, Draper, Fairman & Co. ***Comments:*** H-KY-95-G192, Hughes-241. 18__. 1820s
Rarity: URS-1
F $750

$3 • W-KY-780-003-G060
Left: KENTUCKY vertically. ***Center:*** 3 / 3. ***Right:*** CAMPBELL COUNTY vertically. ***Engraver:*** Murray, Draper, Fairman & Co. ***Comments:*** H-KY-95-G194, Hughes-242. 18__. 1820s
Rarity: URS-1
F $750

$5 • W-KY-780-005-G070
Left: Woman holding staff. ***Center:*** 5 / Minerva standing with owl, shield, staff / 5. ***Right:*** Woman holding staff. ***Engraver:*** Murray, Draper, Fairman & Co. ***Comments:*** H-KY-95-G196, Hughes-243. 18__. 1820s
Rarity: URS-1
F $750

$10 • W-KY-780-010-G080
Left: Woman holding staff. ***Center:*** 10 / Woman standing with staff, shield, Four cherubs / 10. ***Right:*** Woman holding staff. ***Engraver:*** Murray, Draper, Fairman & Co. ***Comments:*** H-KY-95-G198, Hughes-244. 18__. 1820s
Rarity: *None known*

$20 • W-KY-780-020-G090
Engraver: Murray, Draper, Fairman & Co. ***Comments:*** H-KY-95-G200, Hughes-245. No description available. 18__. 1820s.
Rarity: *None known*

$50 • W-KY-780-050-G100
Engraver: Murray, Draper, Fairman & Co. ***Comments:*** H-KY-95-G202, Hughes-246. No description available. 18__. 1820s.
Rarity: *None known*

$100 • W-KY-780-100-G110
Engraver: Murray, Draper, Fairman & Co. ***Comments:*** H-KY-95-G204, Hughes-247. No description available. 18__. 1820s.
Rarity: *None known*

Bank of the United States {2nd} (branch)
1817–1835
W-KY-790

History: The second Bank of the United States was chartered in 1816 for a duration of 20 years. Its authorized capital was $35,000,000, of which the United States owned $7,000,000. Branch banks in several large cities were opened during 1816 and 1817 in direct competition with state banks.

In 1817 the Bank of the United States opened a branch in Lexington. James Morrison was the president. In 1832 President Andrew Jackson vetoed the 1836 renewal of the Bank of the United States which had been brought up before Congress. This instituted a period of great debate and political turmoil. In late 1833 and early 1834 there was a depression in some areas of business which only served to temporarily strengthen the bank, as it was backed by the government. The branches began closing and selling their buildings.

In 1835 the charter of the Lexington branch was revoked. The Northern Bank of Kentucky, W-KY-830, bought the branch building and took over the affairs of the old bank.

The Bank of the United States had another branch bank located in Louisville, W-KY-880.

Numismatic Commentary: For all practical purposes, genuine notes of the second Bank of the United States are non-collectible. The vast majority appearing on the market are contemporary counterfeits, although in the past this aspect has been rarely mentioned.

VALID ISSUES

$5 • W-KY-790-005-G010

Left: Eagle with shield / FIVE D. ***Center:*** 5. ***Right:*** FIVE. ***Engraver:*** Murray, Draper, Fairman & Co. ***Comments:*** H-US-2-G372. 18__. 1820s.

Rarity: *None known*

$5 • W-KY-790-005-G020

Left: Portrait / Portrait. ***Center:*** Cherub with 5 / Eagle with shield / 5 / Cherub with 5. ***Right:*** Portrait / Portrait. ***Engraver:*** Fairman, Draper, Underwood & Co. ***Comments:*** H-US-2-G374. 18__. 1820s.

Rarity: *None known*

$5 • W-KY-790-005-G025

Left: FIVE vertically. ***Center:*** 5 / Eagle / V. ***Right:*** FIVE vertically. ***Comments:*** H-Unlisted, Hughes-375. Lexington handwritten. 1817–1830s.

Rarity: URS-2
F $750

$10 • W-KY-790-010-G030

Left: Eagle with shield / TEN D. ***Center:*** 10. ***Right:*** TEN. ***Engraver:*** Murray, Draper, Fairman & Co. ***Comments:*** H-US-2-G378. 18__. 1820s–1830s.

Rarity: *None known*

$10 • W-KY-790-010-G040

CC

Engraver: Fairman, Draper, Underwood & Co. ***Comments:*** H-US-2-G380. 18__. 1820s.

Rarity: URS-2
F $550

$10 • W-KY-790-010-G045

Comments: H-Unlisted, Hughes-376. No description available. 1817–1830s.

Rarity: *None known*

$20 • W-KY-790-020-G050

Left: Eagle with shield / TWENTY D. ***Center:*** 20. ***Right:*** TWENTY. ***Engraver:*** Murray, Draper, Fairman & Co. ***Comments:*** H-US-2-G384. 18__. 1820s.

Rarity: *None known*

$20 • W-KY-790-020-G060

Left: 20. ***Center:*** Eagle with shield. ***Right:*** 20. ***Engraver:*** Fairman, Draper, Underwood & Co. ***Comments:*** H-US-2-G386. 18__. 1820s–1830s.

Rarity: *None known*

$20 • W-KY-790-020-G070

Left: Eagle with shield. ***Center:*** 20 / TWENTY. ***Right:*** 20. ***Engraver:*** Draper, Underwood, Bald & Spencer. ***Comments:*** H-US-2-G388. 18__. 1820s.

Rarity: *None known*

$20 • W-KY-790-020-G075

Left: Female portraits vertically. ***Center:*** 20 / Eagle / 20. ***Right:*** Female portraits vertically. ***Engraver:*** Murray Draper Fairman & Co. ***Comments:*** H-Unlisted, Hughes-377. Lexington handwritten. 1817–1830s.

Rarity: URS-1
F $900

$50 • W-KY-790-050-G080

Left: Eagle with shield / FIFTY D. ***Center:*** 50. ***Right:*** FIFTY. ***Engraver:*** Murray, Draper, Fairman & Co. ***Comments:*** H-US-2-G392. 18__. 1820s.

Rarity: *None known*

$50 • W-KY-790-050-G090

Left: 50. ***Center:*** Eagle with shield. ***Right:*** 50. ***Engraver:*** Fairman, Draper, Underwood & Co. ***Comments:*** H-US-2-G394. 18__. 1830s–1840s.

Rarity: *None known*

$50 • W-KY-790-050-G100

Left: 50. ***Center:*** Eagle with shield. ***Right:*** 50. ***Engraver:*** Draper, Underwood, Bald & Spencer. ***Comments:*** H-US-2-G396. 18__. 1830s–1840s.

Rarity: *None known*

$100 • W-KY-790-100-G110

Left: Eagle with shield / HUNDRED D. ***Center:*** 100. ***Right:*** HUNDRED. ***Engraver:*** Murray, Draper, Fairman & Co. ***Comments:*** H-US-2-G400. 18__. 1830s–1840s.

Rarity: *None known*

$100 • W-KY-790-100-G120

Center: Eagle with shield / 100. ***Engraver:*** Fairman, Draper, Underwood & Co. ***Comments:*** H-US-2-G402. 18__. 1830s–1840s.

Rarity: *None known*

$100 • W-KY-790-100-G130

Left: Eagle with shield. ***Center:*** 100 / HUNDRED. ***Right:*** 100. ***Engraver:*** Draper, Underwood, Bald & Spencer. ***Comments:*** H-US-2-G404. 18__. 1830s–1840s.

Rarity: *None known*

Non-Valid Issues

$5 • W-KY-790-005-C010

Engraver: Murray, Draper, Fairman & Co. ***Comments:*** H-US-2-C372. Counterfeit of W-KY-790-005-G010. 18__. 1820s.

Rarity: URS-3
F $200

$10 • W-KY-790-010-C030

Engraver: Murray, Draper, Fairman & Co. ***Comments:*** H-US-2-C378. Counterfeit of W-KY-790-010-G030. 18__. 1820s.

Rarity: URS-3
F $200

$20 • W-KY-790-020-C050

Engraver: Murray, Draper, Fairman & Co. ***Comments:*** H-US-2-C384. Counterfeit of W-KY-790-020-G050. 18__. 1820s.

Rarity: URS-3
F $200

$50 • W-KY-790-050-C090

Engraver: Fairman, Draper, Underwood & Co. ***Comments:*** H-US-2-C394. Counterfeit of W-KY-790-050-G090. 18__. 1830s.

Rarity: URS-3
F $225

$100 • W-KY-790-100-C110

Engraver: Murray, Draper, Fairman & Co. ***Comments:*** H-US-2-C400. Counterfeit of W-KY-790-100-G110. 18__. 1820s.

Rarity: URS-2
F $250

$100 • W-KY-790-100-C120

Engraver: Draper, Underwood, Bald & Spencer. ***Comments:*** H-US-2-C402. Counterfeit of W-KY-790-100-G120. 18__. 1830s.

Rarity: URS-2
F $250

Exchange Deposit Bank

1850s

W-KY-800

History: Little is known about this banking entity. A congressional report of 1860 stated that this bank had not issued paper money by this time.

Farmers and Mechanics Bank

1818–1822

W-KY-810

History: The Farmers and Mechanics Bank was chartered on January 26, 1818. The authorized capital of $1,000,000 was divided into 10,000 shares of $100 par value each. Thomas Bodley, Asa Thompson, Thomas January, Elisha Warfield, Gabriel Tandy, Patterson Bain, and John T. Mason were appointed to take stock subscriptions. The president was R. Higgins, and the cashier was E. Warfield. The charters of all independent banks authorized on January 26, 1818, were revoked effective May 1, 1820. This bank may have operated unofficially for a short time afterward.

Numismatic Commentary: Notes of this bank are exceedingly rare, as are all from the many ephemeral entities that operated between 1818 and the 1820s.

Valid Issues

$1 • W-KY-810-001-G010

CC

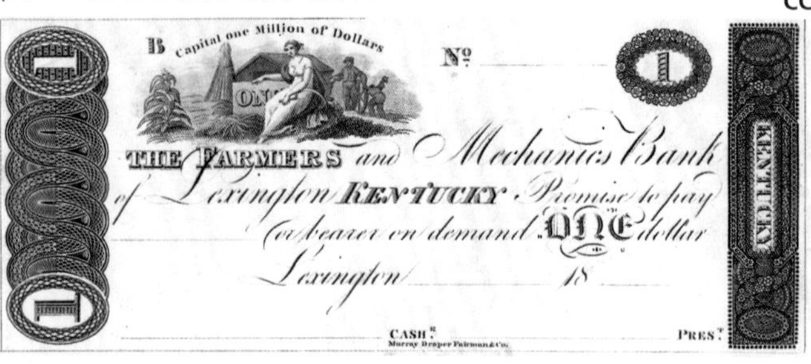

Engraver: Murray, Draper, Fairman & Co. ***Comments:*** H-Unlisted, Hughes-388. 18__. 1818.

Rarity: URS-2
Proof $1,100
Selected auction price: Stack's Bowers Galleries, March 2009, Proof $1,100

$3 • W-KY-810-003-G020

Comments: H-Unlisted, Hughes-389. 1818.

Rarity: URS-1
Proof $1,000
Selected auction price: Stack's Bowers Galleries, June 2010, Proof $1,000

$5 • W-KY-810-005-G030

Comments: H-Unlisted, Hughes-390. No description available. 1818.

Rarity: *None known*

$10 • W-KY-810-010-G040

CC

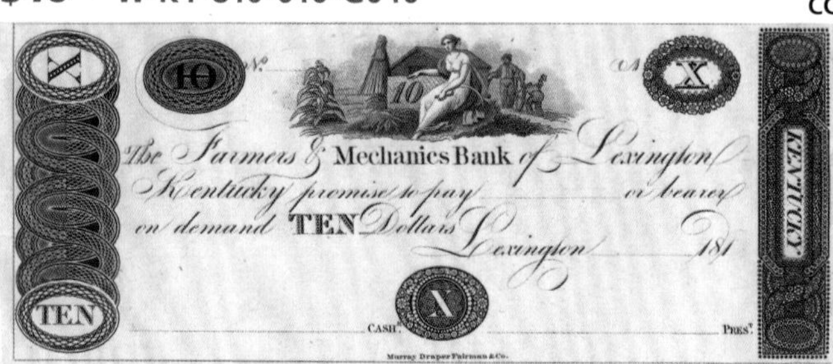

Engraver: Murray, Draper, Fairman & Co. ***Comments:*** H-Unlisted, Hughes-391. 181_. 1818.

Rarity: URS-1
Proof $1,800
Selected auction price: Stack's Bowers Galleries, March 25, 2009, Proof $1,777

$20 • W-KY-810-020-G050 CC

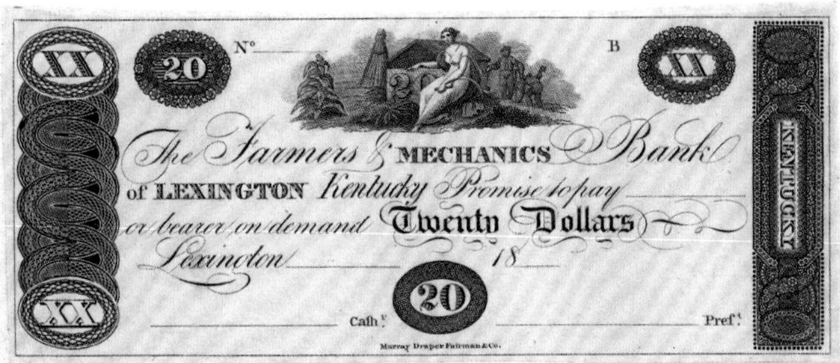

Comments: H-Unlisted, Hughes-392. 18__. 1818.
Rarity: URS-1
Proof $1,300

$50 • W-KY-810-050-G060 CC

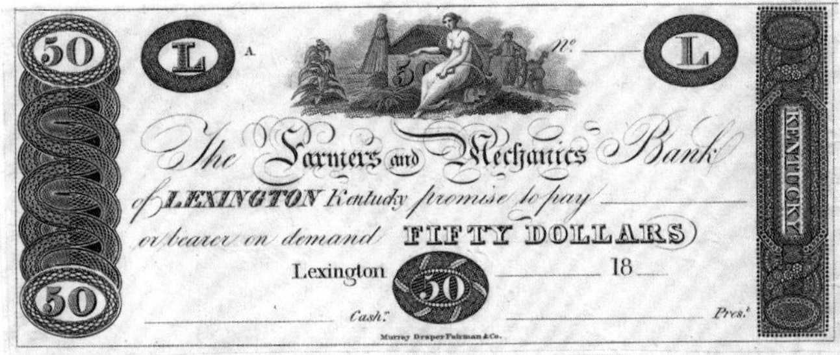

Comments: H-Unlisted, Hughes-393. 18__. 1818.
Rarity: URS-1
Proof $1,500

Kentucky Insurance Company
1802–1820
W-KY-820

History: The Kentucky Insurance Company was chartered on December 16, 1802, with an authorized capital of $150,000. "Banking privileges were surreptitiously obtained," making this the first entity west of the Allegheny Mountains to issue paper money as currency.[5] The company remained the only bank in Kentucky until the first Bank of Kentucky, W-KY-420, was incorporated in 1806.

The Kentucky Insurance Company was located on Main Street. William Morton was the first president. The bank "was widely criticized by the public for years" and was eventually purchased by a speculator in 1816.[6] This buyer, James Prentiss, distributed a flood of bank notes to the public, all of them worthless, and in 1817 the bank failed. Its charter expired in 1820, but it was not officially repealed until years later on March 9, 1868. It was often the case in Kentucky that the charters of insolvent banks were not officially canceled until years after they ceased doing business.

Numismatic Commentary: $1, $2, and $5 notes show up at auction regularly, usually in low grade.

Valid Issues

50¢ • W-KY-820-00.50-G010
Left: HALF DOLLAR. ***Comments:*** H-KY-170-G12, Hughes-395. 18__. 1810s.
Rarity: URS-3
F $250

50¢ • W-KY-820-00.50-G020
Left: 50. ***Center:*** FIFTY CENTS. ***Right:*** 50. ***Comments:*** H-Unlisted, Hughes-396. 18__. 1810s.
Rarity: URS-3
F $250

$1 • W-KY-820-001-G030 CC

Comments: H-KY-170-G20, Hughes-397. 18__. 1810s.
Rarity: URS-4
VF $275

$1 • W-KY-820-001-G040 CC

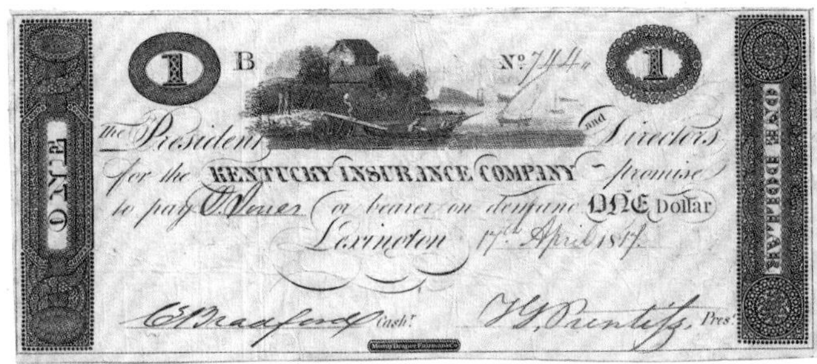

Engraver: Murray, Draper, Fairman & Co. ***Comments:*** H-KY-170-G24, Hughes-399. 18__. 1810s.
Rarity: URS-5
F $150; **VF** $250; **EF** $300

$2 • W-KY-820-002-G050
Left: TWO. ***Center:*** TWO / Sailing vessel / 2. ***Right:*** TWO DOLLS. ***Comments:*** H-KY-170-G28, Hughes-400. 18__. 1810s.
Rarity: URS-3
F $200

$2 • W-KY-820-002-G060 CC

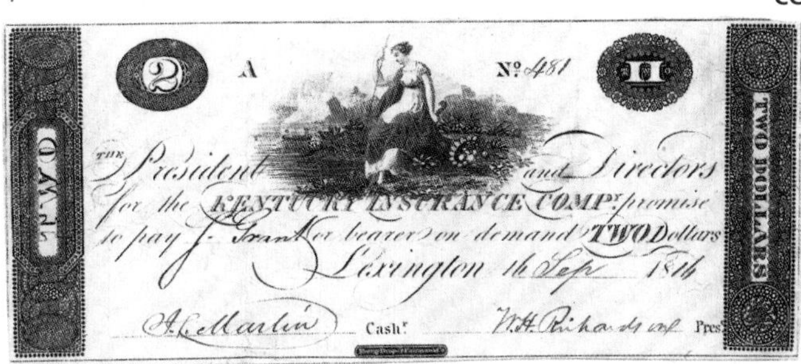

Engraver: Murray, Draper, Fairman & Co. ***Comments:*** H-KY-170-G32, Hughes-401. 18__. 1810s.
Rarity: URS-5
VG $150; **F** $200

$5 • W-KY-820-005-G070

Left: FIVE. *Center:* 5 / Anchor / 5. *Comments:* H-KY-170-G36, Hughes-402. 18__. 1800s.

Rarity: URS-5
F $100

$5 • W-KY-820-005-G080

CC

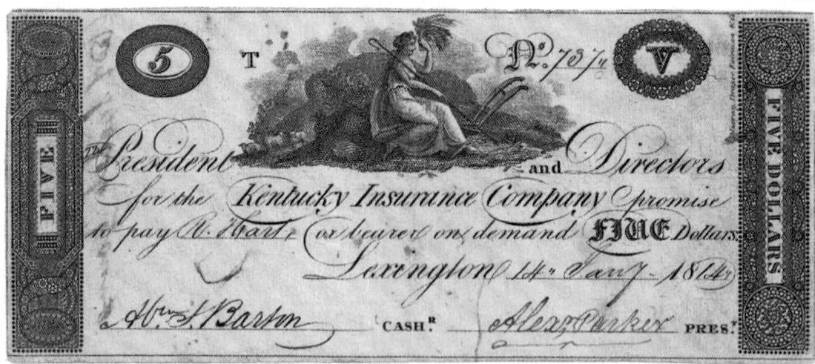

Engraver: Murray, Draper, Fairman & Co. *Comments:* H-KY-170-G40, Hughes-404. 18__. 1810s.

Rarity: URS-5
F $100; **VF** $200

$10 • W-KY-820-010-G090

Left: FIVE. *Center:* FIVE / Sailing vessel / 5. *Right:* FIVE DOLLS. *Comments:* H-KY-170-G44, Hughes-405. 18__. 1800s.

Rarity: URS-3
F $250

$10 • W-KY-820-010-G100

CC

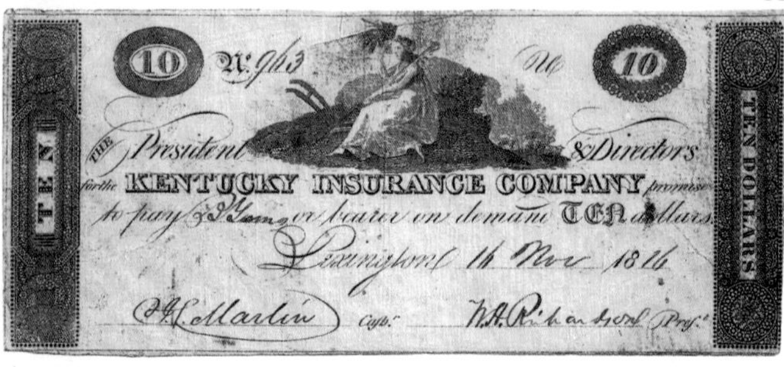

Engraver: Murray, Draper, Fairman & Co. *Comments:* H-KY-170-G48, Hughes-406. 18__. 1810s.

Rarity: URS-5
F $100; **VF** $150

$20 • W-KY-820-020-G110

Left: TWENTY. *Center:* TWENTY / Sailing vessel / 20. *Right:* TWENTY DOLLS. *Comments:* H-KY-170-G52, Hughes-407. 18__. 1800s.

Rarity: URS-3
F $100

$20 • W-KY-820-020-G120

HA

Engraver: Murray, Draper, Fairman & Co. *Comments:* H-KY-170-G56, Hughes-408. 18__. 1810s.

Rarity: URS-5
F $100; **VF** $200

$50 • W-KY-820-050-G130

CC

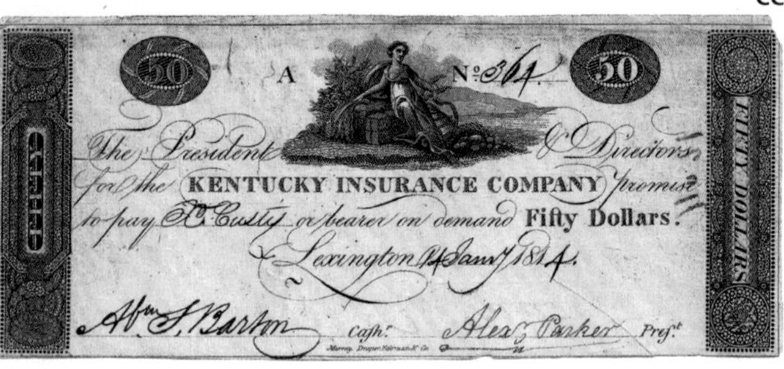

Comments: H-KY-170-G60, Hughes-409. 18__. 1800s.

Rarity: URS-3
F $500

$50 • W-KY-820-050-G140

Left: FIFTY. *Center:* FIFTY / Sailing vessel / 50. *Right:* FIFTY DOLLS. *Engraver:* Murray, Draper, Fairman & Co. *Comments:* H-KY-170-G64, Hughes-411. 18__. 1810s.

Rarity: URS-2
F $150

$100 • W-KY-820-100-G150

CC

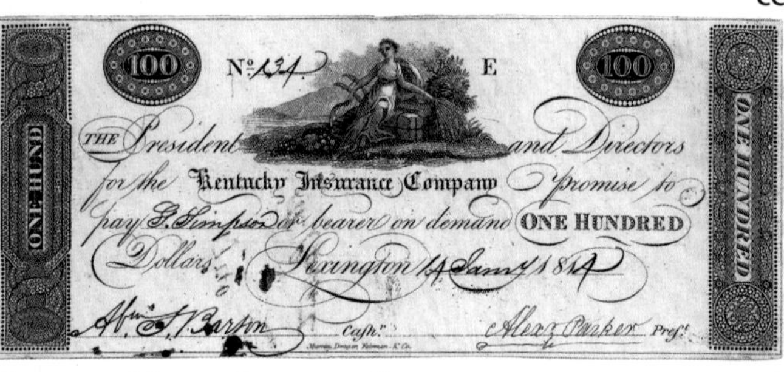

Engraver: Murray, Draper, Fairman & Co. *Comments:* H-KY-170-G72, Hughes-412. 18__. 1810s.

Rarity: URS-3
VG $100; **F** $200; **VF** $500

Post Notes

$__ • W-KY-820-__-G155

CC

Comments: H-Unlisted, Hughes-Unlisted. 18__. 1810s.

Rarity: URS-1
VF $700

Non-Valid Issues

$1 • W-KY-820-001-C030

Comments: H-KY-170-C20, Hughes-398. Counterfeit of W-KY-820-001-G030. 18__. 1810s.

Rarity: URS-4
F $75

$5 • W-KY-820-005-R010

Comments: H-KY-170-R36, Hughes-403. Raised from W-KY-820-005-G080. 18__. 1810s.

Rarity: URS-4
F $75

$50 • W-KY-820-050-N010

Comments: H-Unlisted, Hughes-410. Imitation of W-KY-820-050-G130. 18__. 1800s.

Rarity: URS-2
F $100

Northern Bank of Kentucky

1835–1860s

W-KY-830

History: The Northern Bank of Kentucky was chartered in 1835 with an authorized capital of $3,000,000. The president appointed was John Telford, and Matthew T. Scott was the cashier. On October 17, 1835, the bank purchased the branch office of the Bank of the United States, W-KY-790, which had recently closed in Lexington. The bank thus took over their debt, specie, and the building, and also became the agent for closing up the old entity's affairs.

Promptness in terms of collecting paid-in capital was not the bank's strong point, and it was not until 1837 that the bank reported a capital of 80-percent completion.[7] By 1841 the capital was $2,987,200, and circulation was $1,513,721. These values remained fairly steady until 1846, by which time the circulation had increased to $2,453,532. On May 18, 1846, $250,000 was forwarded to the governor of Kentucky to be used in the war with Mexico. From the late 1840s to the 1860s the capital of the bank only decreased. In 1848 it was worth $867,600; in 1855 it was $730,000; in 1857 $630,000; in 1861 $480,000. Sometime during the 1860s the Northern Bank of Kentucky was converted to a bank of discount and deposit, after which time no notes were issued.

The Northern Bank of Kentucky had branch banks located in Barbourville, W-KY-040, Covington, W-KY-260, Cynthiana, W-KY-305, Glasgow, W-KY-520, Louisville, W-KY-960, Paris, W-KY-1280, and Richmond, W-KY-1360.

Numismatic Commentary: Low-grade examples of this bank's notes show up regularly.

Remaining at the American Bank Note Co. archives as of 2003 was a $10-$10-$10-$10 face plate, a $10-$10-$10-$10 tint plate, two $1-$1-$1-$1 face plates, a $20-$20-$20-$20 tint plate, two $50-$100 face plates, a $50-$100 tint plate, a $5-$5-$5-$5 face plate, a $1-$1-$1-$1 tint plate, a $20-$20-$20-$20 face plate, and non-denominated back plates.

Valid Issues

$1 • W-KY-830-001-G010 CC

Engraver: Draper, Toppan, Longacre & Co. ***Comments:*** H-KY-175-G2, Hughes-431. 18__. 1830s–1840s.

Rarity: URS-4
F $200; **Proof** $1,200

$1 • W-KY-830-001-G020 CC

Engraver: Toppan, Carpenter & Co. ***Comments:*** H-KY-175-G6, Hughes-435. 18__. 1840s.

Rarity: URS-5
F $175

$1 • W-KY-830-001-G030

Left: Portrait of Henry Clay / 1. ***Center:*** Woman seated against bales, Cattle, Train / Female portrait. ***Right:*** 1 / Portrait of George Washington. ***Engraver:*** Toppan, Carpenter, Casilear & Co. ***Comments:*** H-KY-175-G8, Hughes-433. 18__. 1850s.

Rarity: URS-4
F $250

$1 • W-KY-830-001-G040 HA

Tint: Red-orange outlining bank title and 1 / ONE / 1. ***Engraver:*** American Bank Note Co. ***Comments:*** H-KY-175-G10, Hughes-436. 18__. 1850s–1860s.

Rarity: URS-4
F $175

$2 • W-KY-830-002-G050

NJW

Engraver: Draper, Toppan, Longacre & Co. ***Comments:*** H-KY-175-G12, Hughes-438. 18__. 1830s–1840s.

Rarity: URS-3

F $350

$3 • W-KY-830-003-G060

CC

Engraver: Draper, Toppan, Longacre & Co. ***Comments:*** H-KY-175-G14, Hughes-440. 18__. 1830s–1840s.

Rarity: URS-3

F $350

$5 • W-KY-830-005-G070

CC

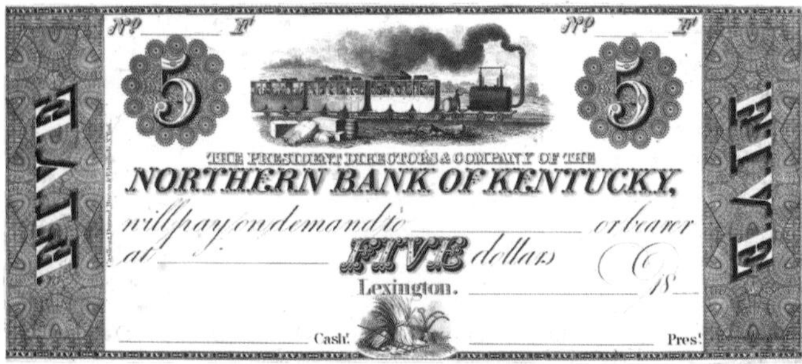

Engraver: Casilear, Durand, Burton & Edmonds. ***Comments:*** H-KY-175-G16, Hughes-442. 18__. 1830s.

Rarity: URS-2

Proof $1,100

Selected auction price: Stack's Bowers Galleries, March 25, 2009, Proof $1,007

$5 • W-KY-830-005-G080

ANS

Overprint: Red bank title and dies outlining white 5s. ***Engraver:*** Toppan, Carpenter & Co. ***Comments:*** H-KY-175-G20, Hughes-444. 18__. 1840s–1850s.

Rarity: URS-3

F $350

$5 • W-KY-830-005-G090

Left: 5 / FIVE vertically. ***Center:*** Portrait of Henry Clay / Woman seated against bales, Cattle, Train / Male portrait. ***Right:*** 5 / FIVE vertically. ***Tint:*** Red-orange. ***Engraver:*** American Bank Note Co. ***Comments:*** H-KY-175-G22, Hughes-445. 18__. 1850s–1860s.

Rarity: URS-3

F $350

$5 • W-KY-830-005-G100

HA

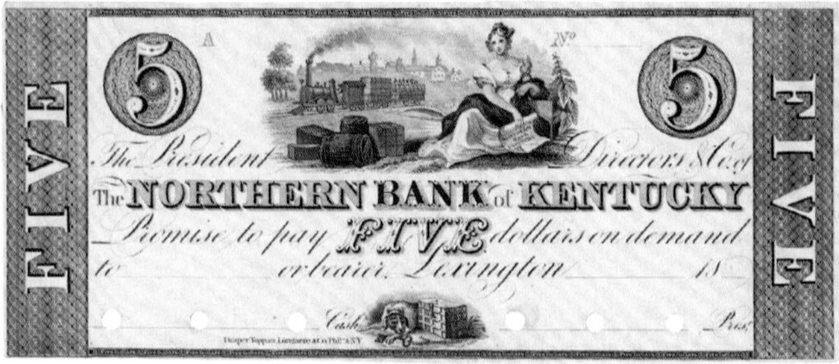

Engraver: Draper, Toppan, Longacre & Co. ***Comments:*** H-Unlisted, Hughes-Unlisted. 18__. 1840s.

Rarity: URS-2

Proof $1,100

$10 • W-KY-830-010-G110

CC

Engraver: Casilear, Durand, Burton & Edmonds. ***Comments:*** H-KY-175-G24, Hughes-446. 18__. 1830s–1840s.

Rarity: URS-3

F $250; **Unc-Rem** $300

Collectors and Researchers:

If you have new information about any banks or notes listed in this volume, contact Whitman Publishing, Attn: Obsolete Paper Money, 3101 Clairmont Road, Suite G, Atlanta, GA 30329.

$10 • **W-KY-830-010-G120** CC

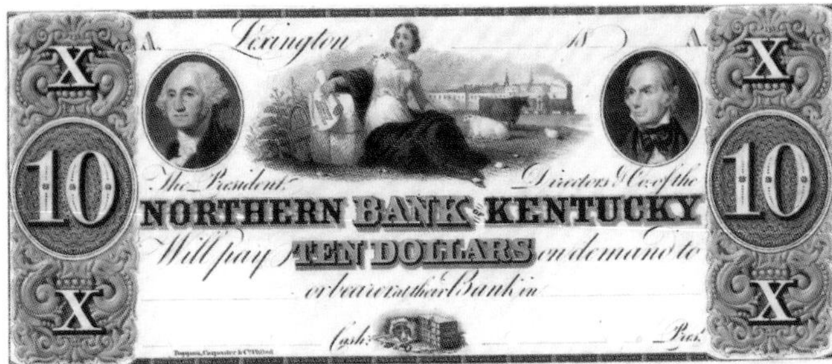

Engraver: Toppan, Carpenter & Co. ***Comments:*** H-KY-175-G28, Hughes-447. 18__. 1840s–1850s.

Rarity: URS-2
Proof $1,000

$10 • **W-KY-830-010-G130**

Left: Portrait of George Washington / 10. ***Center:*** Portrait of George Washington / Woman seated against bales, Cattle, Train / Portrait of Henry Clay. ***Right:*** 10 / Portrait of Daniel Webster. ***Engraver:*** Toppan, Carpenter, Casilear & Co. ***Comments:*** H-KY-175-G30, Hughes-450. 18__. 1850s.

Rarity: URS-3
F $350; **Proof** $1,300

$10 • **W-KY-830-010-G140**

Left: 10 / Portrait of Henry Clay. ***Center:*** Woman seated against bales, Cattle, Train. ***Right:*** 10 / Male portrait. ***Tint:*** Red-orange. ***Engraver:*** American Bank Note Co. ***Comments:*** H-KY-175-G32, Hughes-452. 18__. 1850s–1860s.

Rarity: URS-2
F $600

$10 • **W-KY-830-010-G150**

Left: 10 / Portrait of Henry Clay. ***Center:*** Woman seated against bales, Cattle, Train. ***Right:*** 10 / Male portrait. ***Engraver:*** Toppan, Carpenter, Casilear & Co. ***Comments:*** H-Unlisted, Hughes-Unlisted. 18__. 1850s–1860s.

Rarity: URS-3
F $350

$20 • **W-KY-830-020-G160**

Left: TWENTY vertically. ***Center:*** 20 / Train / 20. ***Right:*** TWENTY vertically. ***Engraver:*** Casilear, Durand, Burton & Edmonds. ***Comments:*** H-KY-175-G34, Hughes-453. 18__. 1830s.

Rarity: URS-3
F $350

$20 • **W-KY-830-020-G170** CC

Engraver: Draper, Toppan & Co. ***Comments:*** H-KY-175-G38, Hughes-455. 18__. 1840s.

Rarity: URS-3
F $350

$20 • **W-KY-830-020-G180** SBG

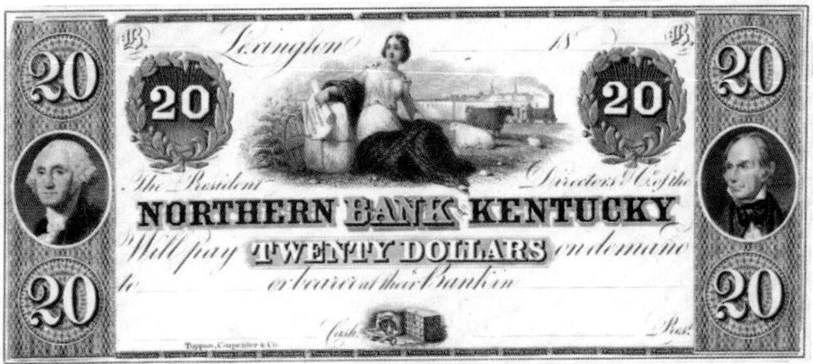

Engraver: Toppan, Carpenter & Co. ***Comments:*** H-KY-175-G40, Hughes-457. 18__. 1840s–1850s.

Rarity: URS-2
VF $450; **Proof** $950

$20 • **W-KY-830-020-G190** HA

Tint: Red-orange bank title and dies bearing white 20s. ***Engraver:*** American Bank Note Co. ***Comments:*** H-KY-175-G42, Hughes-458. 18__. 1850s–1860s.

Rarity: URS-3
F $350

$50 • **W-KY-830-050-G200** HA

Engraver: Casilear, Durand, Burton & Edmonds. ***Comments:*** H-KY-175-G44, Hughes-460. 18__. 1830s.

Rarity: URS-2
Proof $1,100

$50 • **W-KY-830-050-G210**

Left: 50 / FIFTY vertically / 50. ***Center:*** Female portrait / Woman seated against bales, Cattle / Female portrait. ***Right:*** 50 / FIFTY vertically / 50. ***Engraver:*** Draper, Toppan & Co. ***Comments:*** H-KY-175-G46, Hughes-461. 18__. 1840s.

Rarity: URS-2
F $450

$50 • W-KY-830-050-G220

Left: 50 / Portrait of George Washington / 50. *Center:* 50 / Woman seated against bales, Cattle, Train. *Right:* 50 / Portrait of Henry Clay / 50. *Engraver:* Toppan, Carpenter & Co. *Comments:* H-KY-175-G48, Hughes-463. 18__. 1840s–1850s.

Rarity: URS-2
F $450

$50 • W-KY-830-050-G230

Left: 50 / 50. *Center:* Portrait of Henry Clay / Woman seated against bales, Cattle, Train. *Right:* 50 / Male portrait. *Tint:* Red-orange. *Engraver:* American Bank Note Co. *Comments:* H-KY-175-G50, Hughes-464. 18__. 1850s–1860s.

Rarity: URS-2
F $450

$100 • W-KY-830-100-G240

CC

Engraver: Casilear, Durand, Burton & Edmonds. *Comments:* H-KY-175-G52, Hughes-465. 18__. 1830s.

Rarity: URS-2
F $450

$100 • W-KY-830-100-G250

Left: 100 / Portrait of George Washington / 100. *Center:* Woman seated against bales, Cattle, Train / 100. *Right:* 100 / Portrait of Henry Clay / 100. *Engraver:* Toppan, Carpenter & Co. *Comments:* H-KY-175-G56, Hughes-466. 18__. 1840s–1850s.

Rarity: URS-2
F $450

$100 • W-KY-830-100-G260

Left: 100 / Portrait of George Washington. *Center:* Woman seated with scroll and bale / Female portrait. *Right:* 100 / Male portrait. *Comments:* H-Unlisted, Hughes-467. 18__. 1840s–1850s.

Rarity: URS-2
F $450

$100 • W-KY-830-100-G270

Left: 100 / Portrait of Henry Clay / 100. *Center:* Woman seated against bales, Cattle, Train. *Right:* 100 / Male portrait / 100. *Tint:* Red-orange. *Engraver:* American Bank Note Co. *Comments:* H-KY-175-G58, Hughes-468. 18__. 1850s–1860s.

Rarity: URS-2
F $450

$100 • W-KY-830-100-G280

Left: 100 / Portrait / 100. *Center:* 100 / Indians trading with settlers. *Right:* 100 / Male portrait / 100. *Engraver:* Gwynne & Day. *Comments:* H-Unlisted, Hughes-469. 18__. 1850s–1860s.

Rarity: URS-2
F $450

Uncut Sheets

$20-$20-$20-$20 • W-KY-830-020.020.020.020-US010

Vignette(s): ($20) Portrait of George Washington / Woman seated against bales, Cattle, Train / Portrait of Henry Clay. *Engraver:* Toppan, Carpenter & Co. *Comments:* H-KY-175-G40, G40, G40, G40. All four notes identical. 18__. 1840s–1850s.

Rarity: URS-3
Unc-Rem $1,000

$50-$100 • W-KY-830-050.100-US020

Vignette(s): ($50) Portrait of George Washington / Woman seated against bales, Cattle, Train / Portrait of Henry Clay. *($100)* Portrait of George Washington / Woman seated against bales, Cattle, Train / Portrait of Henry Clay. *Engraver:* Toppan, Carpenter & Co. *Comments:* H-KY-175-G48, G56. 18__. 1840s–1850s.

Rarity: URS-2
Unc-Rem $1,500

Non-Valid Issues

$1 • W-KY-830-001-C010

Comments: H-KY-175-C2, Hughes-432. Counterfeit of W-KY-830-001-G010. 18__. 1830s–1840s.

Rarity: URS-3
G $20; **VG** $30; **F** $60

$1 • W-KY-830-001-C030

CC

Comments: H-Unlisted, Hughes-434. Counterfeit of W-KY-830-001-G030. 18__. 1850s.

Rarity: URS-6
F $80; **EF** $110

$1 • W-KY-830-001-C040

Comments: H-Unlisted, Hughes-437. Counterfeit of W-KY-830-001-G040. 18__. 1850s–1860s.

Rarity: URS-6
F $50

$2 • W-KY-830-002-C050

Comments: H-KY-175-C12, Hughes-439. Counterfeit of W-KY-830-002-G050. 18__. 1830s–1840s.

Rarity: URS-3
F $125

$3 • W-KY-830-003-C060

Comments: H-KY-175-C14, Hughes-441. Counterfeit of W-KY-830-003-G060. 18__. 1830s–1840s.

Rarity: URS-3
F $125

$5 • **W-KY-830-005-C070**

Comments: H-Unlisted, Hughes-443. Counterfeit of W-KY-830-005-G070. 18__. 1830s.

Rarity: URS-3
VG $30; **VF** $150

$10 • **W-KY-830-010-C110**

Comments: H-Unlisted, Hughes-448. Counterfeit of W-KY-830-010-G110. 18__. 1830s.

Rarity: URS-3
F $100

$10 • **W-KY-830-010-C120**

Comments: H-Unlisted, Hughes-449. Counterfeit of W-KY-830-010-G120. 18__. 1840s–1850s.

Rarity: URS-3
F $100

$10 • **W-KY-830-010-C130**

Comments: H-Unlisted, Hughes-451. Counterfeit of W-KY-830-010-G130. 18__. 1850s.

Rarity: URS-3
F $100

$20 • **W-KY-830-020-C160**

Comments: H-Unlisted, Hughes-454. Counterfeit of W-KY-830-020-G160. 18__. 1830s.

Rarity: URS-3
F $150

$20 • **W-KY-830-020-C170**

Comments: H-KY-175-C38, Hughes-456. Counterfeit of W-KY-830-020-G170. 18__. 1840s.

Rarity: URS-3
EF $200

$20 • **W-KY-830-020-S010**

Left: 20 / TWENTY / XX. ***Center:*** 20 / Man and woman / 20. ***Right:*** 20 / TWENTY / XX. ***Comments:*** H-Unlisted, Hughes-459. 18__. 1830s–1850s.

Rarity: URS-2
F $150

$50 • **W-KY-830-050-C210**

Comments: H-KY-175-C46, Hughes-462. Counterfeit of W-KY-830-050-G210. 18__. 1840s.

Rarity: URS-3
F $200

Notes on Which the Place Payable is Blank

$5 • **W-KY-830-005-R010**

Engraver: Unverified, but likely Toppan, Carpenter & Co. ***Comments:*** H-KY-175-R5. Raised from $1. 18__. 1840s.

Rarity: —

$10 • **W-KY-830-010-R020**

Engraver: Unverified, but likely Toppan, Carpenter & Co. ***Comments:*** H-KY-175-R10. Raised from $1. 18__. 1840s.

Rarity: —

$20 • **W-KY-830-020-R030**

Engraver: Unverified, but likely Toppan, Carpenter & Co. ***Comments:*** H-KY-175-R15. Raised from $1. 18__. 1840s.

Rarity: —

$20 • **W-KY-830-020-N010**

Center: Woman kneeling with flowers, Man standing. ***Comments:*** H-KY-175-N5. 18__. 1838.

Rarity: —

LOUISVILLE, KENTUCKY

Colonel George Rogers Clark is credited to be the founder of Louisville for settling on Corn Island in 1778. In 1780 the town was officially chartered and named after King Louis XVI of France. Louisville served as a transfer point for riverboats, and by 1828 the population was 7,000. The shipping industry prospered.

During the Civil War Louisville served as an escape point for many slaves on their journey to the North. The Union presence was strong in the town, and supplies, plans, recruiting, and transportation were organized here. Louisville was never attacked, though skirmishes occurred nearby, and thus the town escaped much damage.

Bank of Kentucky {1st} (branch)

1807–1822

W-KY-840

History: The Bank of Kentucky (sometimes seen later in print as the "Old" Bank of Kentucky) was incorporated on December 27, 1806, with an authorized capital of $1,000,000. Half of the capital was subscribed to by the state. The Louisville branch was opened in 1807. Only $400,000 of capital was allowed to be dedicated to this branch, the rest of the remaining capital being divvied up between the other branch banks.[8] On January 21, 1822, the bank was ordered to start closing up its branches. This was to be completed by May 1, 1824. This act essentially shut down the bank. Curiously, all of the paperwork was not completed until the 1870s.

The first Bank of Kentucky had its parent bank located in Frankfort, W-KY-420, and branch banks located in Bardstown, W-KY-050, Danville, W-KY-320, Glasgow, W-KY-500, Hopkinsville, W-KY-660, Lexington, W-KY-760, Paris, W-KY-1260, Richmond, W-KY-1350, Russellville, W-KY-1380, Shelbyville, W-KY-1430, Springfield, W-KY-1500, Washington, W-KY-1570, and Winchester, W-KY-1580.

Numismatic Commentary: In 1816, when coins were scarce in circulation, the Bank of Kentucky issued many fractional bills, some bearing the bank name imprinted as "Louisville Branch Bank."

Valid Issues

25¢ • W-KY-840-00.25-G010

CC

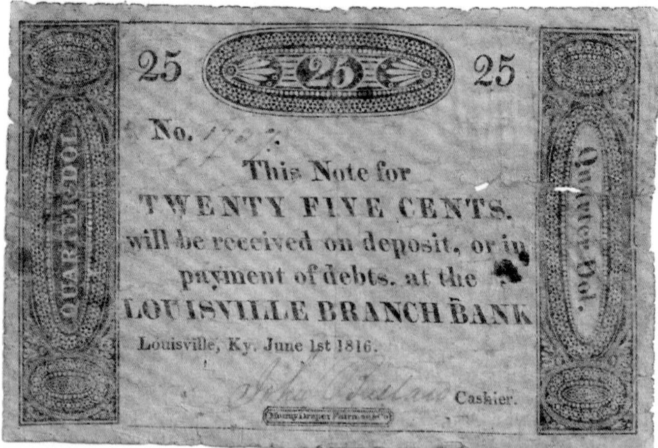

Engraver: Murray, Draper, Fairman & Co. ***Comments:*** H-KY-110-G130, Hughes-560. June 1st, 1816.

Rarity: URS-3
F $250

50¢ • W-KY-840-00.50-G020

CC

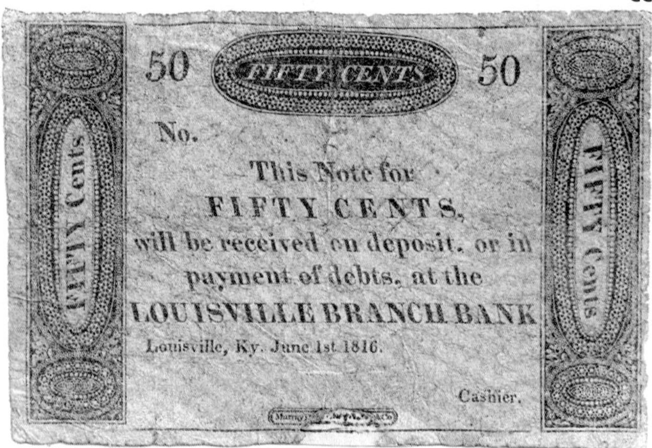

Engraver: Murray, Draper, Fairman & Co. ***Comments:*** H-KY-110-G132, Hughes-561. June 1st, 1816.

Rarity: URS-3
F $250

$1 • W-KY-840-001-G030

Comments: H-KY-110-G134, Hughes-Unlisted. No description available. 18__. 1815.

Rarity: *None known*

$1 • W-KY-840-001-G040

Left: BRANCH BANK vertically. ***Center:*** 1 / Running deer, plow, ax / 1. ***Right:*** 1 / ONE / 1 vertically. ***Engraver:*** Unverified, but likely Murray, Draper, Fairman & Co. ***Comments:*** H-KY-110-G136, Hughes-283. 18__. 1816.

Rarity: URS-3
F $350

$1 • W-KY-840-001-G050

Engraver: Murray, Draper, Fairman & Co. ***Comments:*** H-KY-110-G138, Hughes-Unlisted. No description available. 18__. 1821.

Rarity: *None known*

$3 • W-KY-840-003-G060

Engraver: Murray, Draper, Fairman & Co. ***Comments:*** H-KY-110-G140, Hughes-285. No description available. 18__. 1821.

Rarity: *None known*

$5 • W-KY-840-005-G070

Engraver: Unverified, but likely W. Harrison. ***Comments:*** H-KY-110-G142, Hughes-Unlisted. No description available. 18__. 1810s.

Rarity: *None known*

$5 • W-KY-840-005-G080

Engraver: Unverified, but likely W. Harrison. ***Comments:*** H-KY-110-G144, Hughes-Unlisted. No description available. 18__. 1810s.

Rarity: *None known*

$10 • W-KY-840-010-G090

Left: DEPARMENT vertically. ***Center:*** Running deer, plow, ax / TEN. ***Right:*** 10. ***Engraver:*** W. Harrison. ***Comments:*** H-KY-110-G146, Hughes-287. 18__. 1808–1810s.

Rarity: URS-3
F $350

$10 • W-KY-840-010-G100

Engraver: Unverified, but likely W. Harrison. ***Comments:*** H-KY-110-G148, Hughes-289. No description available. 18__. 1810s–1820.

Rarity: *None known*

$20 • W-KY-840-020-G110

Engraver: Unverified, but likely W. Harrison. ***Comments:*** H-KY-110-G150, Hughes-Unlisted. No description available. 18__. 1808–1810s.

Rarity: *None known*

$20 • W-KY-840-020-G120

Engraver: Unverified, but likely W. Harrison. ***Comments:*** H-KY-110-G152, Hughes-Unlisted. No description available. 18__. 1810s.

Rarity: *None known*

$50 • W-KY-840-050-G130

Engraver: Unverified, but likely W. Harrison. ***Comments:*** H-KY-110-G154, Hughes-Unlisted. No description available. 18__. 1808–1810s.

Rarity: *None known*

$50 • W-KY-840-050-G140

Engraver: Unverified, but likely W. Harrison. ***Comments:*** H-KY-110-G156, Hughes-Unlisted. No description available. 18__. 1810s.

Rarity: *None known*

$100 • W-KY-840-100-G150

Engraver: Unverified, but likely W. Harrison. ***Comments:*** H-KY-110-G158, Hughes-Unlisted. No description available. 18__. 1808–1810s.

Rarity: *None known*

$100 • W-KY-840-100-G160

Engraver: Unverified, but likely W. Harrison. ***Comments:*** H-KY-110-G160, Hughes-Unlisted. No description available. 18__. 1810s.

Rarity: *None known*

Post Notes

$__ • W-KY-840-__-G170

Left: Post Note vertically. ***Center:*** Dolls __ / Dolls __. ***Right:*** Post Note vertically. ***Engraver:*** W. Harrison. ***Comments:*** H-KY-110-G162, Hughes-Unlisted. 18__. 1810s–1820s.

Rarity: URS-3
F $350

Post Note Payable at the Bank of Pennsylvania, Philadelphia

$__ • W-KY-840-__-G180

Left: Post Note vertically. ***Center:*** Dolls __ / Dolls __. ***Right:*** Post Note vertically. ***Engraver:*** W. Harrison. ***Comments:*** H-KY-110-G164, Hughes-Unlisted. 18__. 1810s–1820s.

Rarity: URS-2
F $450

Post Note Payable at the Schuylkill Bank, Philadelphia

$__ • W-KY-840-__-G190

Left: Post Note vertically. ***Center:*** Dolls __ / Dolls __. ***Right:*** Post Note vertically. ***Engraver:*** W. Harrison. ***Comments:*** H-KY-110-G166, Hughes-Unlisted. 18__. 1810s–1820s.

Rarity: URS-2
F $450

Bank of Kentucky {2nd}

1834–1860s
W-KY-850

History: The second Bank of Kentucky (sometimes seen in print as the "New" Bank of Kentucky) was chartered in 1834 in order to assume the business of the first Bank of Kentucky, W-KY-420, which had recently closed. The capital of the bank was $5,000,000. Soon the bank had purchased the old building of the branch of the Bank of the United States, W-KY-880, located in Louisville.

In 1836 the bank "readily responded to demands for loans in behalf of public improvements. In 1836 it loaned $200,000 to the city of Louisville to pay its subscription to the stock of a railroad, and other similar loans were made."[9] In 1842 there was a scandal when the cashier of the Schuylkill Bank in Philadelphia, a man by the name of Lewis, spread spurious stock certificates of the Bank of Kentucky, amounting to $1,300,000. By 1849 the Schuylkill Bank had closed, and its banking properties were sold for $45,000, which amount was given to the Bank of Kentucky for its benefit.[10]

In 1848 the president of the bank was Thomas N. Lindsey, and the cashier was Edmund H. Taylor. In 1852 another fraud of the bank occurred, and *Bankers' Magazine* warned note holders that:

> The *Louisville Courier* of June 3rd states that the genuine plates of this bank, of the denomination of tens, have recently been stolen, and a large batch of new notes printed. Of course they will be put in circulation. The theft was managed so adroitly that no clue can be obtained to its discovery, or to lead to the detection of the perpetrator. The plates were stolen from the engraver in Cincinnati.

That year the president of the bank was Virgil McKnight, and the cashier was G.C. Gwathmey. Capital was $1,480,000. In 1862 capital had reached $3,666,000, and circulation was $1,185,000. In January 1866 almost all branches of the Bank of Kentucky were closed down, and the parent bank began winding up its business.

The second Bank of Kentucky had branch banks located in Bowling Green, W-KY-080, Burksville, W-KY-140, Columbus, W-KY-220, Danville, W-KY-330, Flemingsburg, W-KY-390, Frankfort, W-KY-430, Glasgow, W-KY-510, Greensburg, W-KY-540, Hopkinsville, W-KY-670, Lexington, W-KY-770, Maysville, W-KY-1020, Mount Sterling, W-KY-1100, and Paducah, W-KY-1220.

Numismatic Commentary: Notes of this bank and its branches are very rare.

Valid Issues

$1 • W-KY-850-001-G010

Left: Man / 1. ***Right:*** Woman standing / 1. ***Engraver:*** Draper, Toppan, Longacre & Co. ***Comments:*** H-KY-195-G4, Hughes-482. 18__. 1830s.

Rarity: URS-3
F $350

$2 • W-KY-850-002-G020 CC

Engraver: Draper, Toppan, Longacre & Co. ***Comments:*** H-KY-195-G8, Hughes-486. 18__. 1830s.

Rarity: URS-3
VG $250; **F** $350

$3 • W-KY-850-003-G030 CC

Engraver: Draper, Toppan, Longacre & Co. ***Engraver:*** Draper, Toppan, Longacre & Co. ***Comments:*** H-KY-195-G12, Hughes-489. 18__. 1830s–1840s.

Rarity: URS-3
F $350

$4 • **W-KY-850-004-G040**

Left: FOUR / FOUR. ***Center:*** 4 / Woman seated / 4. ***Right:*** FOUR / Woman standing / FOUR. ***Engraver:*** Draper, Toppan, Longacre & Co. ***Comments:*** H-KY-195-G16, Hughes-491. 18__. 1830s–1840s.

Rarity: URS-3
F $350

$5 • **W-KY-850-005-G050**

SBG

Engraver: Draper, Toppan, Longacre & Co. ***Comments:*** H-KY-195-G20, Hughes-493. 18__. 1830s–1840s.

Rarity: URS-3
Proof $1,000

$10 • **W-KY-850-010-G060**

SBG

Engraver: Draper, Toppan, Longacre & Co. ***Comments:*** H-KY-195-G24, Hughes-498. 18__. 1830s–1840s.

Rarity: URS-3
Proof $1,000

How to Read the Whitman Numbering System

$1 • **W-AL-020-001-G010a**

Denomination: Face value of the note shown.

W: Whitman number. This number is a sortable code unique to each bank and note.

AL: Abbreviation for the state under study.

020: Numerical designation specific to each bank.

001: The denomination in dollars.

G010a: G indicates a good or valid note. Other categories are indicated thus: C (counterfeit); R (raised); S (spurious); N (not-attributed); A (altered). Numbers are assigned starting with 010, 020, et seq. Terminal letters following the number indicate variations of a note: a series of different colored overprints, tints, payees, etc., all on the same design of note. For more information, see the "How to Use This Book" section at the front of the volume, page xiv.

$20 • **W-KY-850-020-G070**

Left: TWENTY / Woman with scythe / 20. ***Center:*** 20 / Cabin, Two drovers and a herd of cattle / XX. ***Right:*** TWENTY / Woman with scythe / 20. ***Engraver:*** Danforth, Underwood, Bald & Spencer. ***Comments:*** H-Unlisted, Hughes-507. 18__. 1830s–1840s.

Rarity: URS-3
F $350

$20 • **W-KY-850-020-G080**

CC

Engraver: Underwood, Bald & Spencer. ***Comments:*** H-KY-195-G28, Hughes-510. 18__. 1830s–1840s.

Rarity: URS-4
VF $100; **VF** $300; **Proof** $1,000

$20 • **W-KY-850-020-G090**

Comments: H-KY-195-G30, Hughes-Unlisted. No description available. 18__. 1840s.

Rarity: *None known*

$50 • **W-KY-850-050-G100**

QDB

Engraver: Casilear, Durand, Burton & Evans. ***Comments:*** H-KY-195-G32, Hughes-514. 18__. 1830s–1840s.

Rarity: URS-3
Unc-Rem $400; **Proof** $1,000

$100 • **W-KY-850-100-G105**

CC

Engraver: Casilear, Durand, Burton & Evans. ***Comments:*** H-Unlisted, Hughes-518. 18__. 1830s–1840s.

Rarity: —
F $600

$100 • **W-KY-850-100-G110** CC

Engraver: Casilear, Durand, Burton & Evans. ***Comments:*** H-KY-195-G36, Hughes-520. 18__. 1830s–1840s.

Rarity: URS-2
Proof $1,300

$500 • **W-KY-850-500-G120**

Left: FIVE HUNDRED vertically. ***Center:*** 500 / Indian woman surrounded by state arms, flags, drums / 500. ***Right:*** FIVE HUNDRED vertically. ***Comments:*** H-Unlisted, Hughes-521. 18__. 1830s–1840s.

Rarity: URS-2
F $750

$500 • **W-KY-850-500-G130**

Left: Woman standing. ***Center:*** 500 / Woman pointing to train / 500. ***Right:*** Woman standing. ***Engraver:*** Casilear, Durand, Burton & Evans. ***Comments:*** H-Unlisted, Hughes-522. 18__. 1830s–1840s.

Rarity: URS-2
F $750

Post Notes

$5 • **W-KY-850-005-G140**

Engraver: Rawdon, Wright & Hatch. ***Comments:*** H-KY-195-G40, Hughes-Unlisted. No description available. 18__. 1830s.

Rarity: *None known*

$10 • **W-KY-850-010-G150**

Engraver: Rawdon, Wright & Hatch. ***Comments:*** H-KY-195-G42, Hughes-Unlisted. No description available. 18__. 1830s.

Rarity: *None known*

Notes on Which the Place Payable is Blank

$1 • **W-KY-850-001-G160**

Comments: H-Unlisted, Hughes-483. No description available. 1830s–1860s.

Rarity: *None known*

$1 • **W-KY-850-001-G170**

Left: ONE / Two women seated, sailor and mechanic standing. ***Center:*** ONE on 1 / Portrait of Henry Clay / ONE on 1. ***Right:*** ONE / Two women seated, man and dog. ***Engraver:*** Danforth, Bald & Co. ***Comments:*** H-Unlisted, Hughes-484. 18__. 1830s–1840s.

Rarity: URS-3
F $350

$3 • **W-KY-850-003-G180** QDB

Comments: H-Unlisted, Hughes-488. 18__. 1830s–1840s.

Rarity: URS-3
F $350

$5 • **W-KY-850-005-G190** CC

Engraver: Casilear, Durand, Burton & Evans. ***Comments:*** H-KY-195-G400. 18__. 1830s–1840s.

Rarity: URS-3
F $350; **Proof** $1,000

$5 • **W-KY-850-005-G200** QDB

Engraver: Toppan, Carpenter & Co. ***Comments:*** H-KY-195-G404. 18__. 1840s–1850s.

Rarity: URS-2
Unc-Rem $550

$5 • **W-KY-850-005-G210**

Left: 5 on medallion head / Male portrait. ***Center:*** Ceres reclining. ***Right:*** 5 / Woman reaching for angel. ***Comments:*** H-Unlisted, Hughes-492. 18__. 1830s–1840s.

Rarity: URS-3
F $350

$10 • **W-KY-850-010-G220**

HA

Engraver: Casilear, Durand, Burton & Evans. ***Comments:*** H-KY-195-G408. 18__. 1830s–1840s.

Rarity: URS-2
Proof $1,000

$10 • **W-KY-850-010-G230**

CC

Engraver: Toppan, Carpenter & Co. ***Comments:*** H-KY-195-G412. 18__. 1840s–1850s.

Rarity: URS-3
EF $350

$10 • **W-KY-850-010-G235**

CC

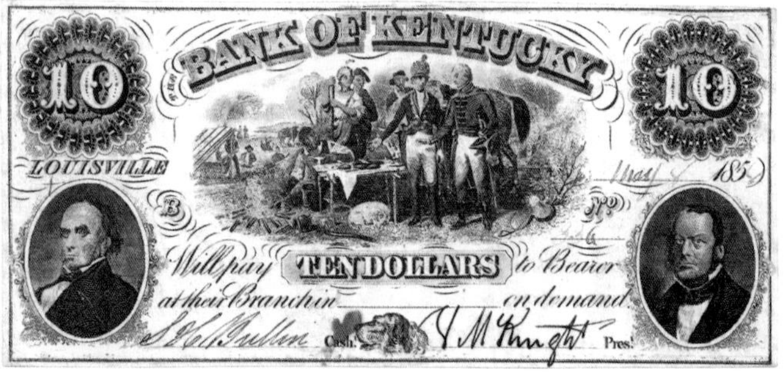

Comments: H-Unlisted, Hughes-Unlisted. 185_. 1850s.

Rarity: URS-3

$20 • **W-KY-850-020-G240**

CC

Engraver: Casilear, Durand, Burton & Evans. ***Comments:*** H-KY-195-G416. 18__. 1830s–1840s.

Rarity: URS-3
Proof $1,200

$20 • **W-KY-850-020-G250**

HA

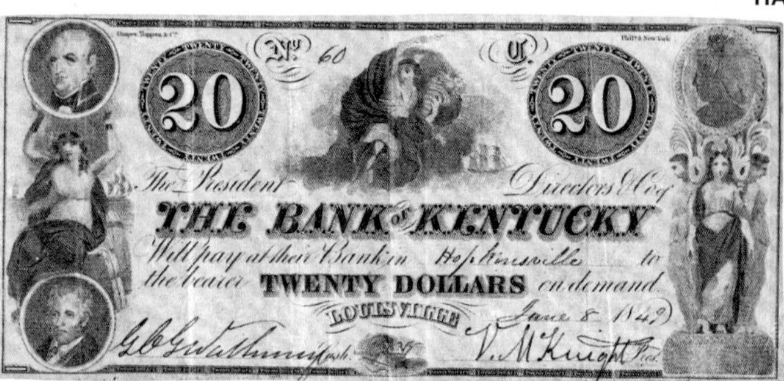

Engraver: Draper, Toppan & Co. ***Comments:*** H-KY-195-G420. 18__. 1840s.

Rarity: URS-3
VF $350

$20 • **W-KY-850-020-G260**

CC

Engraver: Toppan, Carpenter & Co. ***Comments:*** H-KY-195-G424. 185_. 1850s.

Rarity: URS-3
F $350

$50 • **W-KY-850-050-G270**

Left: Woman standing. ***Center:*** 50 / Steamboat *Henry Clay* / 50. ***Right:*** Woman standing. ***Engraver:*** Casilear, Durand, Burton & Evans. ***Comments:*** H-KY-195-G428. 18__. 1830s–1840s.

Rarity: URS-2
F $450

$50 • **W-KY-850-050-G280**

Left: Female portrait / 50. ***Center:*** "General Marion's Sweet Potato Dinner." ***Right:*** 50 / Male portrait. ***Engraver:*** Toppan, Carpenter & Co. ***Comments:*** H-KY-195-G432, Hughes-515. 18__. 1830s–1860s.

Rarity: URS-2
F $350

$100 • **W-KY-850-100-G290**

HA

Engraver: Casilear, Durand, Burton & Evans. ***Comments:*** H-KY-195-G436, Hughes-67. 18__. 1830s–1860s.

Rarity: URS-2
F $450

$100 • **W-KY-850-100-G300**
Left: 100 / Male portrait / 100. ***Center:*** Male portrait / Two women with anchor, barrels. ***Right:*** 100 / Portrait of Daniel Boone / Portrait of George Washington / 100. ***Engraver:*** Toppan, Carpenter & Co. ***Comments:*** H-KY-195-G440, Hughes-519. 18__. 1830s–1860s.
Rarity: URS-2
F $450

$500 • **W-KY-850-500-G310**
Left: FIVE HUNDRED vertically. ***Center:*** Indian woman surrounded by state arms, drums, flags. ***Right:*** FIVE HUNDRED vertically. ***Engraver:*** Toppan, Carpenter & Co. ***Comments:*** H-KY-195-G444, Hughes-521. 18__. 1830s–1860s.
Rarity: URS-2
F $500

Post Notes on Which the Place Payable is Blank

$__ • **W-KY-850-__-G320** CC

Engraver: Casilear, Durand, Burton & Evans. ***Comments:*** H-KY-195-G448, Hughes-523. 18__. 1830s.
Rarity: URS-2
F $450; **Proof** $1,350

Non-Valid Issues

$1 • **W-KY-850-001-C010**
Comments: H-KY-195-C4, Hughes-Unlisted. Counterfeit of W-KY-850-001-G010. 18__. 1830s.
Rarity: URS-3
F $200

$2 • **W-KY-850-002-C020** CC

Comments: H-KY-195-C8, Hughes-487. Counterfeit of W-KY-850-002-G020. 18__. 1830s.
Rarity: URS-4
F $150

$3 • **W-KY-850-003-C030**
Comments: H-KY-195-C12, Hughes-490. Counterfeit of W-KY-850-003-G030. 18__. 1830s–1840s.
Rarity: URS-3
F $175

$3 • **W-KY-850-003-N010**
Center: Woman, Farmhouse. ***Comments:*** H-KY-195-N5, Hughes-Unlisted. 18__. 1840s.
Rarity: URS-3
F $175

$3 • **W-KY-850-003-N020**
Left: Woman reclining / Portrait of Henry Clay. ***Right:*** Woman with goat. ***Comments:*** H-KY-195-N10, Hughes-Unlisted. 18__. 1840s.
Rarity: URS-3
F $175

$4 • **W-KY-850-004-C040**
Comments: H-KY-195-C16, Hughes-Unlisted. Counterfeit of W-KY-850-004-G040. 18__. 1830s–1840s.
Rarity: URS-3
F $150

$5 • **W-KY-850-005-R010**
Engraver: Casilear, Durand, Burton & Evans. ***Comments:*** H-KY-195-R25. Raised from $5. 18__. 1830s–1840s.
Rarity: URS-3
F $150

$10 • **W-KY-850-010-R020**
Comments: H-Unlisted, Hughes-503. Raised from W-KY-850-001-G010. 18__. 1830s–1840s.
Rarity: URS-3
VF $200

$10 • **W-KY-850-010-S010**
Left: 10 / Male portrait. ***Center:*** Men standing making deal. ***Right:*** 10 / Male portrait. ***Comments:*** H-KY-195-S25, Hughes-501. 18__. 1830s–1840s.
Rarity: URS-3
VF $250; **EF** $400

$20 • **W-KY-850-020-C080**
Comments: H-KY-195-C28, Hughes-505. Counterfeit of W-KY-850-020-G080. 18__. 1830s–1840s.
Rarity: URS-3
F $150

$50 • **W-KY-850-050-N030**
Left: Portrait of George Washington. ***Center:*** Scholar standing, Building. ***Comments:*** H-KY-195-N15. 18__. 1840s.
Rarity: URS-2
F $200

$50 • **W-KY-850-050-N040**
Center: Woman and two boys. ***Comments:*** H-KY-195-N20, Hughes-517. 18__. 1840s.
Rarity: URS-2
F $200

Notes on Which the Place Payable is Blank

$1 • W-KY-850-001-C170

Comments: H-Unlisted, Hughes-485. Counterfeit of W-KY-850-001-G170. 18__. 1830s–1840s.

Rarity: URS-3
F $150

$10 • W-KY-850-010-R030

Comments: H-Unlisted, Hughes-502. Raised from W-KY-850-001-G170. 18__. 1830s–1840s.

Rarity: URS-3
F $150

$50 • W-KY-850-050-C280

Comments: H-Unlisted, Hughes-516. Counterfeit of W-KY-850-050-G280. 18__. 1830s–1860s.

Rarity: URS-2
F $200

Bank of Louisville

1833–1860s

W-KY-860

History: In 1833 the Bank of Louisville was chartered with an authorized capital of $5,000,000. The bank building was located on Main Street, where it remained during the entirety of its existence. The building still stands today.

In 1840 the capital of the bank was $1,150,000, and circulation was $405,061. By 1845 this was $1,083,000 and $804,306, respectively. The president was Joshua B. Bowles, and the cashier was Alfred Thurston. In 1857 Charles Tilden took the position of cashier when Alfred Thurston resigned. On February 15, 1858, the charter of the bank was extended to last until 1888. At that time the capital was $880,000. In 1862 capital was back up to $1,930,000, and circulation was $824,000.

During the 1860s the Bank of Louisville closed its doors. Later it was absorbed by the Southern National Bank in 1899.

The Bank of Louisville had branch banks located in Burksville, W-KY-150, Flemingsburg, W-KY-400, and Paducah, W-KY-1230.

Numismatic Commentary: Notes of this bank are scarce, with even contemporary counterfeits and spurious issues drawing competitive attention.

Valid Issues

$1 • W-KY-860-001-G010

SI

Comments: H-Unlisted, Hughes-524. 1843.

Rarity: URS-3
F $350

$1 • W-KY-860-001-G020

CC

Engraver: Draper, Toppan, Longacre & Co. ***Comments:*** H-KY-190-G2, Hughes-525. 18__. 1840s.

Rarity: URS-3
F $350; **Proof** $1,900
Selected auction price: Stack's Bowers Galleries, Lot 5210, Proof $1,900

$2 • W-KY-860-002-G030

Left: 2. ***Center:*** 2 / 2 / Woman leaning on column. ***Right:*** TWO / Woman with shield / TWO. ***Engraver:*** Draper, Toppan, Longacre & Co. ***Comments:*** H-KY-190-G6, Hughes-529. 18__. 1840s.

Rarity: URS-3
F $350

$3 • W-KY-860-003-G040

NJW

Engraver: Draper, Toppan, Longacre & Co. ***Comments:*** H-KY-190-G10, Hughes-530. 18__. 1840s.

Rarity: URS-3
F $350

$5 • W-KY-860-005-G050

CC

Engraver: Danforth, Underwood, Bald & Spencer. ***Comments:*** H-KY-190-G12, Hughes-532. 18__. 1840s.

Rarity: URS-3
F $200; **Proof** $1,000

$10 • W-KY-860-010-G060 CC

Engraver: Danforth, Underwood, Bald & Spencer. ***Comments:*** H-KY-190-G16, Hughes-538. 18__. 1840s.

Rarity: URS-3
F $350; **Proof** $1,000

$10 • W-KY-860-010-G070

Left: 10 / 10. ***Center:*** Portrait of Henry Clay / Woman sitting in clouds with eagle, pole and cap, and fasces / Portrait of Daniel Webster. ***Right:*** 10 / 10. ***Engraver:*** Toppan, Carpenter, Casilear & Co. ***Comments:*** H-Unlisted, Hughes-541. 18__. 1840s–1850s.

Rarity: URS-3
F $350; **Proof** $1,000

$20 • W-KY-860-020-G080 CC

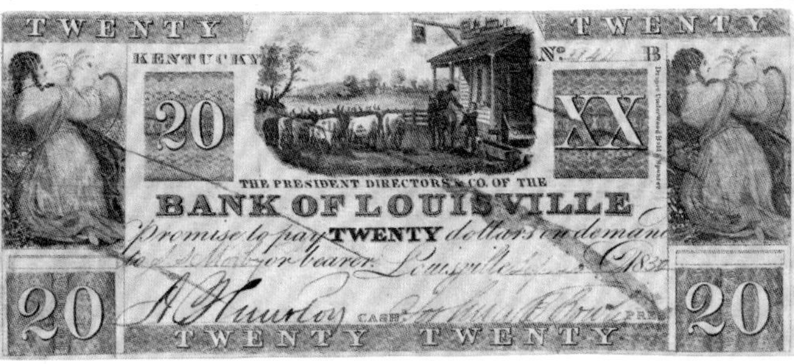

Engraver: Danforth, Underwood, Bald & Spencer. ***Comments:*** H-KY-190-G20, Hughes-544. 18__. 1830s–1840s.

Rarity: URS-3
F $350

$20 • W-KY-860-020-G090

Left: 20 / Portrait of George Washington. ***Center:*** Woman seated on a bale, Mercury, Ships, Buildings. ***Right:*** 20 / Medallion head. ***Engraver:*** Toppan, Carpenter & Co. ***Comments:*** H-KY-190-G24, Hughes-546. 18__. 1840s.

Rarity: URS-3
F $350

$50 • W-KY-860-050-G100

Left: 50 / Ceres seated with cornucopia / 50. ***Center:*** Women kneeling with sickle, Flowers. ***Right:*** 50 / Ceres seated with cornucopia / 50. ***Engraver:*** Danforth, Underwood, Bald & Spencer. ***Comments:*** H-KY-190-G28, Hughes-548. 18__. 1840s.

Rarity: URS-2
F $450

$100 • W-KY-860-100-G110

Left: 100 / Woman with rake. ***Center:*** Medallion head / Woman reclining on bale with spear, Steamboat / Medallion head. ***Right:*** C / Woman with rake. ***Engraver:*** Toppan, Carpenter & Co. ***Comments:*** H-KY-190-G32, Hughes-550. 18__. 1840s.

Rarity: URS-2
F $450

$100 • W-KY-860-100-G120

Left: HUNDRED / Medallion head / HUNDRED. ***Center:*** 100 / Angel blowing trumpet, Eagle and globe / 100. ***Right:*** HUNDRED / Medallion head / HUNDRED. ***Engraver:*** Toppan, Carpenter & Co. ***Comments:*** H-KY-190-G34, Hughes-551. 18__. 1840s.

Rarity: URS-2
F $300

Notes Payable at the Bank of North America, Philadelphia

$5 • W-KY-860-005-G130 CC

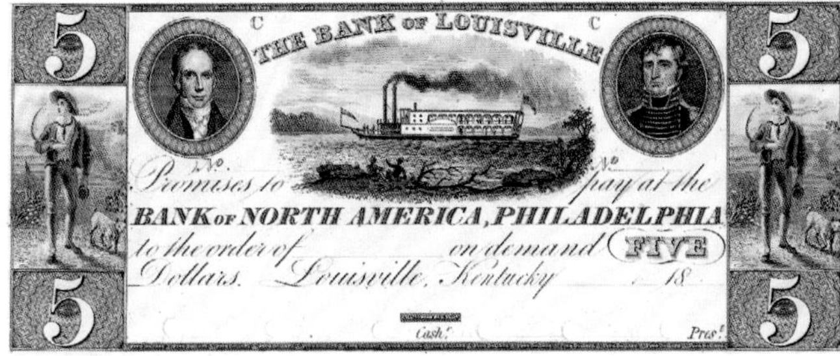

Engraver: Cha. Toppan & Co. ***Comments:*** H-Unlisted, Hughes-Unlisted. 18__. 1840s.

Rarity: URS-2
Proof $800

$10 • W-KY-860-010-G140 CC

Engraver: Cha. Toppan & Co. ***Comments:*** H-Unlisted, Hughes-Unlisted. 18__. 1840s.

Rarity: URS-2
Unc-Rem $500

Non-Valid Issues

$1 • W-KY-860-001-S010

Left: ONE / Woman leaning on pillar / 1. ***Center:*** Medallion head bearing ONE / Train, Factories / Medallion head bearing ONE. ***Right:*** 1 / Ship / ONE. ***Engraver:*** Underwood, Bald & Spencer. ***Comments:*** H-KY-190-S5. 18__. 1843.

Rarity: URS-4
VG $100

$3 • W-KY-860-003-C040

Comments: H-Unlisted, Hughes-531. Counterfeit of W-KY-860-003-G040. 18__. 1840s.

Rarity: URS-4
F $100

$5 • W-KY-860-005-C050

Comments: H-KY-190-C12, Hughes-535. Counterfeit of W-KY-860-005-G050. 18__. 1840s.

Rarity: URS-4
F $100

$20 • **W-KY-860-020-C080**
Comments: H-Unlisted, Hughes-545. Counterfeit of W-KY-860-020-G080. 18__. 1840s.

Rarity: URS-3
VG $40; **F** $100

$50 • **W-KY-860-050-C100**
Comments: H-KY-190-C28, Hughes-549. Counterfeit of W-KY-860-050-G100. 18__. 1840s.

Rarity: URS-3
F $150

Bank of the Commonwealth of Kentucky (branch)

1821–1830
W-KY-870

History: The Bank of the Commonwealth of Kentucky was chartered on November 29, 1820, with an authorized capital of $2,000,000. A local name for the bank was the "Peoples Bank," as it was chartered for the purpose of bringing relief to the population in a time of economic uncertainty. On December 22, 1820, an act was passed authorizing the bank to issue $3,000,000 in bills. The establishment of the Bank of the Commonwealth of Kentucky inadvertently caused the failure of the first Bank of Kentucky, W-KY-420. The branch located in Louisville opened in 1821. On September 17, 1829, the branch was broken into, and $25,000 of notes was stolen.

In 1830 the bank lost its authorization to loan money, and it was instructed to close up its branches. Around that time the bank ceased new business, but the winding up of its affairs took until 1855.

The Bank of the Commonwealth of Kentucky had its parent bank located in Frankfort, W-KY-440, and branch banks located in Bowling Green, W-KY-090, Falmouth, W-KY-360, Flemingsburg, W-KY-410, Greensburg, W-KY-550, Harrodsburg, W-KY-580, Hartford, W-KY-610, Lexington, W-KY-780, Mount Sterling, W-KY-1120, Princeton, W-KY-1330, Somerset, W-KY-1470, and Winchester, W-KY-1590.

Numismatic Commentary: Almost all notes from this bank and its branches are unknown today.

Valid Issues

6-1/4¢ • **W-KY-870-00.06.25-G010**
Left: 6-1/4 CENTS. ***Center:*** 6-1/4 / 6-1/4 on die / 6-1/4. ***Right:*** KENTUCKY vertically. ***Comments:*** H-KY-95-G208, Hughes-237. 1822.

Rarity: *None known*

12-1/2¢ • **W-KY-870-00.12.50-G020**
Left: 12-1/2 CENTS. ***Center:*** 12-1/2 / 12-1/2 on die / 12-1/2. ***Right:*** KENTUCKY vertically. ***Comments:*** H-KY-95-G210, Hughes-238. 1822.

Rarity: *None known*

25¢ • **W-KY-870-00.25-G030**
Left: 25 CENTS. ***Center:*** 25 / 25 on die / 25. ***Right:*** KENTUCKY vertically. ***Comments:*** H-KY-95-G212, Hughes-239. 1822.

Rarity: *None known*

50¢ • **W-KY-870-00.50-G040**
Left: 50 CENTS. ***Center:*** 50 / 50 on die / 50. ***Right:*** KENTUCKY vertically. ***Comments:*** H-KY-95-G214, Hughes-240. 1822.

Rarity: *None known*

$1 • **W-KY-870-001-G050**
Left: KENTUCKY vertically. ***Center:*** 1 / 1. ***Right:*** CAMPBELL COUNTY vertically. ***Engraver:*** Murray, Draper, Fairman & Co. ***Comments:*** H-KY-95-G218, Hughes-241. 18__. 1820s.

Rarity: URS-2
F $350

$3 • **W-KY-870-003-G060**
Left: KENTUCKY vertically. ***Center:*** 3 / 3. ***Right:*** CAMPBELL COUNTY vertically. ***Engraver:*** Murray, Draper, Fairman & Co. ***Comments:*** H-KY-95-G220, Hughes-242. 18__. 1820s.

Rarity: URS-2
F $350

$5 • **W-KY-870-005-G070**
Left: Woman holding staff. ***Center:*** 5 / Minerva standing with owl, shield, staff / 5. ***Right:*** Woman holding staff. ***Engraver:*** Murray, Draper, Fairman & Co. ***Comments:*** H-KY-95-G222, Hughes-243. 18__. 1820s.

Rarity: URS-2
F $350

$10 • **W-KY-870-010-G080**
Left: Woman holding staff. ***Center:*** 10 / Woman standing with staff, shield, Four cherubs / 10. ***Right:*** Woman holding staff. ***Engraver:*** Murray, Draper, Fairman & Co. ***Comments:*** H-KY-95-G224, Hughes-244. 18__. 1820s.

Rarity: URS-2
F $350

$20 • **W-KY-870-020-G090**
Engraver: Murray, Draper, Fairman & Co. ***Comments:*** H-KY-95-G226, Hughes-245. No description available. 18__. 1820s.

Rarity: *None known*

$50 • **W-KY-870-050-G100**
Engraver: Murray, Draper, Fairman & Co. ***Comments:*** H-KY-95-G228, Hughes-246. No description available. 18__. 1820s.

Rarity: *None known*

$100 • **W-KY-870-100-G110**
Engraver: Murray, Draper, Fairman & Co. ***Comments:*** H-KY-95-G230, Hughes-247. No description available. 18__. 1820s.

Rarity: *None known*

Bank of the United States {2nd} (branch)

1817–1835
W-KY-880

History: The second Bank of the United States was chartered in 1816 for a duration of 20 years. Its authorized capital was $35,000,000, of which the United States owned $7,000,000. Branch banks in several large cities were opened during 1816 and 1817 in direct competition with state banks.

In 1817 the Bank of the United States opened a branch in Louisville. John I. Jacob was the president, and John Bustard was the first cashier. In 1832 President Andrew Jackson vetoed the 1836 renewal of the Bank of the United States which had been brought up before Congress. This instituted a period of great debate and political turmoil. In late 1833 and early 1834 there was a depression in some areas of business which only served to temporarily strengthen the bank, as it was backed by the government. The branches began closing and selling their buildings.

In 1835 the charter of the Louisville branch was revoked. The second Bank of Kentucky, W-KY-850, bought the branch building and took over the affairs of the old bank.

The Bank of the United States had another branch bank located in Lexington, W-KY-790.

Numismatic Commentary: As is the case with notes from the Lexington branch, those issued in Louisville are essentially non-collectible today. Most offered in the past have been contemporary counterfeits.

Valid Issues

$5 • W-KY-880-005-G010

CC

Engraver: Murray, Draper, Fairman & Co. ***Comments:*** H-US-2-G412. 18__. 1820s.

Rarity: URS-1
F $400

$5 • W-KY-880-005-G020

Left: Portrait / Portrait. ***Center:*** Cherub with 5 / Eagle with shield / 5 / Cherub with 5. ***Right:*** Portrait / Portrait. ***Engraver:*** Fairman, Draper, Underwood & Co. ***Comments:*** H-US-2-G414. 18__. 1820s.

Rarity: URS-1
F $400

$5 • W-KY-880-005-G025

HA

Engraver: Murray, Draper, Fairman & Co. ***Comments:*** H-Unlisted, Hughes-476. Louisville handwritten. 18__. 1817–1830s.

Rarity: URS-2
VF $350

$10 • W-KY-880-010-G030

Left: Eagle with shield / TEN D. ***Center:*** 10. ***Right:*** TEN. ***Engraver:*** Murray, Draper, Fairman & Co. ***Comments:*** H-US-2-G418. 18__. 1820s–1830s.

Rarity: URS-1
F $400

$10 • W-KY-880-010-G040

Left: 10. ***Center:*** Eagle with shield. ***Right:*** 10. ***Engraver:*** Fairman, Draper, Underwood & Co. ***Comments:*** H-US-2-G420. 18__. 1820s.

Rarity: URS-1
F $400

$10 • W-KY-880-010-G045

Left: Female portraits vertically. ***Center:*** 10 / Spread eagle on shield, Ship / 10. ***Right:*** Female portraits vertically. ***Engraver:*** Fairman, Underwood & Co. ***Comments:*** H-Unlisted, Hughes-477. Louisville handwritten. 1817–1830s.

Rarity: URS-1
F $400

$20 • W-KY-880-020-G050

Left: Eagle with shield / TWENTY D. ***Center:*** 20. ***Right:*** TWENTY. ***Engraver:*** Murray, Draper, Fairman & Co. ***Comments:*** H-US-2-G424. 18__. 1820s.

Rarity: URS-1
VF $450

$20 • W-KY-880-020-G060

Left: 20. ***Center:*** Eagle with shield. ***Right:*** 20. ***Engraver:*** Fairman, Draper, Underwood & Co. ***Comments:*** H-US-2-G426. 18__. 1820s–1830s.

Rarity: URS-1
F $400

$20 • W-KY-880-020-G070

Left: Eagle with shield. ***Center:*** 20 / TWENTY. ***Right:*** 20. ***Engraver:*** Draper, Underwood, Bald & Spencer. ***Comments:*** H-US-2-G428. 18__. 1820s.

Rarity: URS-1
F $400

$20 • W-KY-880-020-G075

Left: Female portraits vertically. ***Center:*** 20 / Spread eagle on shield, Ship / 20. ***Right:*** Female portraits vertically. ***Engraver:*** Fairman, Underwood & Co. ***Comments:*** H-Unlisted, Hughes-478. Louisville handwritten. 1817–1830s.

Rarity: URS-1
EF $500

$50 • W-KY-880-050-G080

Left: Eagle with shield / FIFTY D. ***Center:*** 50. ***Right:*** FIFTY. ***Engraver:*** Murray, Draper, Fairman & Co. ***Comments:*** H-US-2-G432. 18__. 1820s.

Rarity: URS-1
F $500

$50 • W-KY-880-050-G090

Left: 50. ***Center:*** Eagle with shield. ***Right:*** 50. ***Engraver:*** Fairman, Draper, Underwood & Co. ***Comments:*** H-US-2-G434. 18__. 1830s–1840s.

Rarity: URS-1
F $500

$50 • **W-KY-880-050-G100**
Left: 50. ***Center:*** Eagle with shield. ***Right:*** 50. ***Engraver:*** Draper, Underwood, Bald & Spencer. ***Comments:*** H-US-2-G436. 18__. 1830s–1840s.
Rarity: URS-1
F $500

$100 • **W-KY-880-100-G110**
Left: Eagle with shield / HUNDRED D. ***Center:*** 100. ***Right:*** HUNDRED. ***Engraver:*** Murray, Draper, Fairman & Co. ***Comments:*** H-US-2-G440. 18__. 1830s–1840s.
Rarity: URS-1
F $550

$100 • **W-KY-880-100-G120**
Center: Eagle with shield / 100. ***Engraver:*** Fairman, Draper, Underwood & Co. ***Comments:*** H-US-2-G442. 18__. 1830s–1840s.
Rarity: URS-1
F $550

$100 • **W-KY-880-100-G130**
Left: Eagle with shield. ***Center:*** 100 / HUNDRED. ***Right:*** 100. ***Engraver:*** Draper, Underwood, Bald & Spencer. ***Comments:*** H-US-2-G444. 18__. 1830s–1840s.
Rarity: URS-1
F $550

Non-Valid Issues

$5 • **W-KY-880-005-C010**
Engraver: Murray, Draper, Fairman & Co. ***Comments:*** H-US-2-C412. Counterfeit of W-KY-880-005-G010. 18__. 1820s.
Rarity: URS-3
VF $240

$10 • **W-KY-880-010-C030**
Engraver: Murray, Draper, Fairman & Co. ***Comments:*** H-US-2-C418. Counterfeit of W-KY-880-010-G030. 18__. 1820s.
Rarity: URS-3
F $150

$20 • **W-KY-880-020-C050**
CC

Engraver: Murray, Draper, Fairman & Co. ***Comments:*** H-US-2-C424. Counterfeit of W-KY-880-020-G050. 18__. 1820s.
Rarity: URS-3
F $350

$50 • **W-KY-880-050-C090**
Engraver: Fairman, Draper, Underwood & Co. ***Comments:*** H-US-2-C434. Counterfeit of W-KY-880-050-G090. 18__. 1830s.
Rarity: URS-2
F $300

$100 • **W-KY-880-100-C110**
Engraver: Murray, Draper, Fairman & Co. ***Comments:*** H-US-2-C440. Counterfeit of W-KY-880-100-G110. 18__. 1820s.
Rarity: URS-2
F $300

$100 • **W-KY-880-100-C120**
Engraver: Draper, Underwood, Bald & Spencer. ***Comments:*** H-US-2-C442. Counterfeit of W-KY-880-100-G120. 18__. 1830s.
Rarity: URS-2
F $250

Commercial Bank of Louisville
1818–1820
W-KY-890

History: The Commercial Bank of Louisville was chartered on January 26, 1818. The authorized capital of $1,000,000 was divided into 10,000 shares of $100 apiece. John T. Gray, Levi Tyler, James McCrum, James H. Overstreet, John Gwathmey, Warren Pope Jr., and Thomas A. Pearce were appointed to take stock subscriptions. The president was Warren Pope Jr., and the cashier was A.L. Campbell. The bank operated only for a short time. The charters of all independent banks authorized on January 26, 1818, were revoked effective May 1, 1820.

Commercial Bank of Kentucky (branch)
1859–1860s
W-KY-900

History: On January 3, 1852, the Commercial Bank of Kentucky was chartered. The Louisville branch was established in 1859. In 1861 it had a capital of $350,000. William H. Davison was the cashier, and D.S. Benedict was the president. The Commercial Bank of Kentucky closed sometime in the 1860s.

The Commercial Bank of Kentucky had its parent bank located in Paducah, W-KY-1240, and branch banks located in Cynthiana, W-KY-290, Harrodsburg, W-KY-590, Lebanon, W-KY-720, Monticello, W-KY-1070, Newport, W-KY-1150, and Versailles, W-KY-1560.

Valid Issues

$1 • **W-KY-900-001-G010**
Left: ONE on 1 / ONE vertically / ONE on 1. ***Center:*** Woman seated with map, Two men in canoe. ***Right:*** 1 / Female portrait. ***Tint:*** Green. ***Engraver:*** American Bank Note Co. ***Comments:*** H-KY-255-G78a, Hughes-668. 18__. 1860s.
Rarity: URS-3
F $310

$2 • W-KY-900-002-G020

Left: 2 / Female portrait. ***Center:*** Woman seated with map, Two men in canoe. ***Right:*** TWO / TWO vertically / TWO. ***Tint:*** Green. ***Engraver:*** American Bank Note Co. ***Comments:*** H-KY-255-G80a, Hughes-670. 18__. 1860s.

Rarity: URS-3
F $350

$3 • W-KY-900-003-G030

Left: 3 / Boy with rabbits. ***Center:*** Woman seated with map, Two men in canoe. ***Right:*** 3 / Portrait of girl. ***Tint:*** Green. ***Engraver:*** American Bank Note Co. ***Comments:*** H-KY-255-G82a, Hughes-673. 18__. 1860s.

Rarity: URS-3
F $350

$5 • W-KY-900-005-G040

Left: FIVE / Men and women in and around V. ***Center:*** 5 / Women in and around 5, Dock. ***Right:*** FIVE / Portrait of Franklin Pierce. ***Tint:*** Red-orange. ***Engraver:*** Rawdon, Wright, Hatch & Edson / ABNCo. monogram. ***Comments:*** H-KY-255-G84a, Hughes-675. 18__. 1850s–1860s.

Rarity: URS-3
F $350; **Proof** $1,000

$10 • W-KY-900-010-G050

Left: 10 / Male portrait / TEN. ***Center:*** Steamboats. ***Right:*** TEN / Harrodsburg Springs / TEN. ***Engraver:*** Unverified, but likely Rawdon, Wright, Hatch & Edson. ***Comments:*** H-KY-255-G86, Hughes-677. 185_. 1850s.

Rarity: URS-3
F $350

Exchange Bank of Cincinnati
1837–1840
W-KY-910

History: No record has been discovered of this bank but for the spurious notes that were issued. Possibly connected to the Tennessee bank of the same name, W-TN-750.

Issues

$1 • W-KY-910-001-G010

Left: ONE / Train / ONE. ***Center:*** 1 / Two women flanking shield / 1. ***Right:*** ONE / Men with cattle / ONE. ***Comments:*** H-Unlisted, Hughes-480. 1840.

Rarity: *None known*

$5 • W-KY-910-005-G020

CC

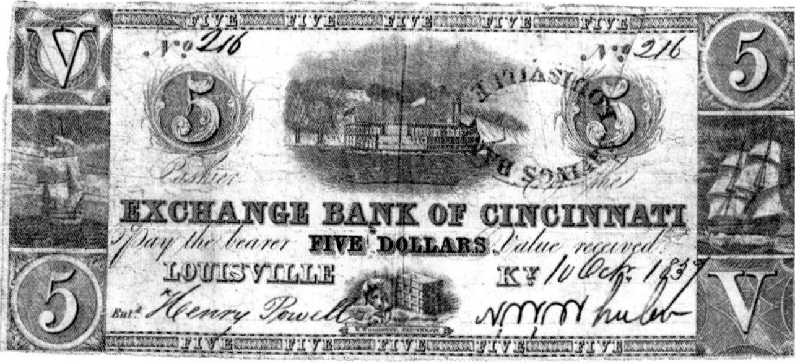

Engraver: W. Woodruff. ***Comments:*** H-Unlisted, Hughes-Unlisted. 1830s.

Rarity: URS-1
VF $750

Franklin Bank of Kentucky
1860s
W-KY-920

History: On March 3, 1860, an act was passed amending the charter of the Franklin Savings Institute to become the Franklin Bank of Kentucky, with all of the banking privileges therein. In 1861 the capital of the bank was $200,000. John D. O'Leary was the cashier, and James Marshall was the president.

Kentucky Savings Bank
1851–1860
W-KY-930

History: On February 25, 1851, the Kentucky Savings Bank (also seen as the Kentucky Savings Institution) was chartered. On March 3, 1860, the act was amended to change the name to the Merchants Bank of Kentucky, W-KY-950.

Mechanics Bank
1860s–1870
W-KY-940

History: In 1861 John M. Stokes was elected president of the Mechanics Bank in place of John P. Bull, who had recently passed away. The cashier at the time was H.S. Julian. The capital was worth $100,000.

In 1870, after being robbed of $71,000, the Mechanics Bank wound up its affairs. The rest of its liabilities and properties were sold to the Farmers and Drovers Bank.[11]

Collectors and Researchers:

If you have new information about any banks or notes listed in this volume, contact Whitman Publishing, Attn: Obsolete Paper Money, 3101 Clairmont Road, Suite G, Atlanta, GA 30329.

Issues

$10 • W-KY-940-010-A010

Left: 10 / Man at press. ***Center:*** X. ***Right:*** 10 / Men working in foundry. ***Comments:*** H-KY-200-A5, Hughes-559. Altered from the Mechanics Bank of Memphis, Memphis, Tennessee. 1860s.

Rarity: URS-3
EF $550

Merchants Bank of Kentucky

1860s

W-KY-950

History: On March 3, 1860, an act was passed authorizing the Kentucky Savings Bank, W-KY-930, to change its name to the Merchants Bank of Kentucky. In 1861 the capital was $500,000. H.C. Caruth was the president, and J.H. Lindenberger was the cashier.

Northern Bank of Kentucky (branch)

1835–1860s

W-KY-960

History: The Northern Bank of Kentucky was chartered in 1835 with an authorized capital of $3,000,000. The Louisville branch was established immediately. In 1848 the president was Chapman Coleman, and the cashier was William Richardson. The capital was $600,000, where it remained until 1864. That year it was $630,000. The president of the bank was L.L. Warren, and the cashier was Henry C. Pindell.

Sometime during the 1860s the Northern Bank of Kentucky was converted to a bank of discount and deposit, after which time no notes were issued.

The Northern Bank of Kentucky had its parent bank located in Lexington, W-KY-830, and branch banks located in Barbourville, W-KY-040, Covington, W-KY-260, Cynthiana, W-KY-305, Glasgow, W-KY-520, Paris, W-KY-1280, and Richmond, W-KY-1360.

Valid Issues

$1 • W-KY-960-001-G010

Left: Portrait of George Washington / ONE / Portrait of Henry Clay. ***Center:*** 1 / Woman seated against bales, Cattle, Train. ***Right:*** 1 / Portrait of Rachel Jackson / 1. ***Engraver:*** Toppan, Carpenter & Co. ***Comments:*** H-KY-175-G176, Hughes-435. 18__. 1830s–1840s.

Rarity: URS-3
F $350

$1 • W-KY-960-001-G020

Left: Portrait of Henry Clay / 1. ***Center:*** Woman seated against bales, Cattle, Train / Female portrait. ***Right:*** 1 / Portrait of George Washington. ***Engraver:*** Toppan, Carpenter, Casilear & Co. ***Comments:*** H-KY-175-G178, Hughes-433. 18__. 1850s.

Rarity: URS-3
F $550

$1 • W-KY-960-001-G030

Left: 1 / Portrait of boy. ***Center:*** Men with cattle, Sheep. ***Right:*** 1 / Portrait of girl. ***Tint:*** Red-orange. ***Engraver:*** American Bank Note Co. ***Comments:*** H-KY-175-G180, Hughes-436. 18__. 1850s–1860s.

Rarity: URS-3
F $350

$3 • W-KY-960-003-G035

CC

Engraver: Draper, Toppan, Longacre & Co. ***Comments:*** H-Unlisted, Hughes-440. 18__. 1830s.

Rarity: URS-2
VG $300

$5 • W-KY-960-005-G040

Left: FIVE vertically. ***Center:*** 5 / Train / 5. ***Right:*** FIVE vertically. ***Engraver:*** Casilear, Durand, Burton & Edmonds. ***Comments:*** H-KY-175-G184, Hughes-442. 18__. 1830s.

Rarity: URS-3
F $350

$5 • W-KY-960-005-G050

Left: FIVE vertically. ***Center:*** 5 / Woman standing, Train / 5. ***Right:*** FIVE vertically. ***Engraver:*** Draper, Toppan & Co. ***Comments:*** H-KY-175-G186, Hughes-Unlisted. 18__. 1840s.

Rarity: URS-3
F $350

$5 • W-KY-960-005-G060

Left: 5 / Portrait of Henry Clay / 5. ***Center:*** 5 / Woman seated against bales, Cattle, Train / 5. ***Right:*** 5 / Portrait of George Washington / 5. ***Engraver:*** Toppan, Carpenter & Co. ***Comments:*** H-KY-175-G188, Hughes-444. 18__. 1840s–1850s.

Rarity: URS-3
F $350

$5 • W-KY-960-005-G070

Left: 5 / FIVE vertically. ***Center:*** Portrait of Henry Clay / Woman seated against bales, Cattle, Train / Male portrait. ***Right:*** 5 / FIVE vertically. ***Tint:*** Red-orange. ***Engraver:*** American Bank Note Co. ***Comments:*** H-KY-175-G190, Hughes-445. 18__. 1850s–1860s.

Rarity: URS-3
F $350

$10 • W-KY-960-010-G080

Left: TEN vertically. ***Center:*** 10 / Train / 10. ***Right:*** TEN vertically. ***Engraver:*** Casilear, Durand, Burton & Edmonds. ***Comments:*** H-KY-175-G192, Hughes-446. 18__. 1830s.

Rarity: URS-3
F $350

$10 • W-KY-960-010-G090
Left: 10 / TEN vertically / 10. ***Center:*** Female portrait / Train, Woman seated / Female portrait. ***Right:*** 10 / TEN vertically / 10. ***Engraver:*** Draper, Toppan & Co. ***Comments:*** H-KY-175-G194, Hughes-447. 18__. 1840s.

Rarity: URS-3
F $350

$10 • W-KY-960-010-G100
Left: X / 10 / X. ***Center:*** Portrait of George Washington / Woman seated against bales, Cattle, Train / Portrait of Henry Clay. ***Right:*** X / 10 / X. ***Engraver:*** Toppan, Carpenter & Co. ***Comments:*** H-KY-175-G196, Hughes-Unlisted. 18__. 1840s–1850s.

Rarity: URS-3
F $350

$10 • W-KY-960-010-G110
Left: Portrait of George Washington / 10. ***Center:*** Portrait of George Washington / Woman seated against bales, Cattle, Train / Portrait of Henry Clay. ***Right:*** 10 / Portrait of Daniel Webster. ***Engraver:*** Toppan, Carpenter, Casilear & Co. ***Comments:*** H-KY-175-G198, Hughes-450. 18__. 1850s.

Rarity: URS-3
F $350

$10 • W-KY-960-010-G120
Left: 10 / Portrait of Henry Clay. ***Center:*** Woman seated against bales, Cattle, Train. ***Right:*** 10 / Male portrait. ***Tint:*** Red-orange. ***Engraver:*** American Bank Note Co. ***Comments:*** H-KY-175-G200, Hughes-452. 18__. 1850s–1860s.

Rarity: URS-3
F $350

$20 • W-KY-960-020-G130
Left: TWENTY vertically. ***Center:*** 20 / Train / 20. ***Right:*** TWENTY vertically. ***Engraver:*** Casilear, Durand, Burton & Edmonds. ***Comments:*** H-KY-175-G202, Hughes-453. 18__. 1830s.

Rarity: URS-3
F $350

$20 • W-KY-960-020-G140
Left: 20 / TWENTY vertically / 20. ***Center:*** Female portrait / Train, Woman seated / Female portrait. ***Right:*** 20 / TWENTY vertically / 20. ***Engraver:*** Draper, Toppan & Co. ***Comments:*** H-KY-175-G204, Hughes-455. 18__. 1840s.

Rarity: URS-3
F $350

$20 • W-KY-960-020-G150
Left: 20 / Portrait of George Washington / 20. ***Center:*** 20 / Woman seated against bales, Cattle, Train / 20. ***Right:*** 20 / Portrait of Henry Clay / 20. ***Engraver:*** Toppan, Carpenter & Co. ***Comments:*** H-KY-175-G206, Hughes-457. 18__. 1840s–1850s.

Rarity: URS-3
F $350

$20 • W-KY-960-020-G160
Left: 20 / 20. ***Center:*** Portrait of Henry Clay / Woman seated against bales, Cattle, Train / Male portrait. ***Right:*** 20 / 20. ***Tint:*** Red-orange. ***Engraver:*** American Bank Note Co. ***Comments:*** H-KY-175-G208, Hughes-458. 18__. 1850s–1860s.

Rarity: URS-3
F $350

$50 • W-KY-960-050-G170
Left: FIFTY vertically. ***Center:*** 50 / Train / 50. ***Right:*** FIFTY vertically. ***Engraver:*** Casilear, Durand, Burton & Edmonds. ***Comments:*** H-KY-175-G210, Hughes-Unlisted. 18__. 1830s.

Rarity: URS-2
F $450

$50 • W-KY-960-050-G180
Left: 50 / FIFTY vertically / 50. ***Center:*** Female portrait / Woman seated against bales, Cattle / Female portrait. ***Right:*** 50 / FIFTY vertically / 50. ***Engraver:*** Draper, Toppan & Co. ***Comments:*** H-KY-175-G212, Hughes-461. 18__. 1840s.

Rarity: URS-2
F $450

$50 • W-KY-960-050-G190
Left: 50 / Portrait of George Washington / 50. ***Center:*** 50 / Woman seated against bales, Cattle, Train. ***Right:*** 50 / Portrait of Henry Clay / 50. ***Engraver:*** Toppan, Carpenter & Co. ***Comments:*** H-KY-175-G214, Hughes-463. 18__. 1840s–1850s.

Rarity: URS-2
F $450

$50 • W-KY-960-050-G200
Left: 50 / 50. ***Center:*** Portrait of Henry Clay / Woman seated against bales, Cattle, Train. ***Right:*** 50 / Male portrait. ***Tint:*** Red-orange. ***Engraver:*** American Bank Note Co. ***Comments:*** H-KY-175-G216, Hughes-464. 18__. 1850s–1860s.

Rarity: URS-2
F $450

$100 • W-KY-960-100-G210
Left: ONE HUNDRED vertically. ***Center:*** C / Train / C. ***Right:*** ONE HUNDRED vertically. ***Tint:*** Red-orange. ***Engraver:*** Casilear, Durand, Burton & Edmonds. ***Comments:*** H-KY-175-G218, Hughes-465. 18__. 1830s.

Rarity: URS-2
F $450

$100 • W-KY-960-100-G220
Left: 100 / HUNDRED vertically / 100. ***Center:*** Female portrait / Woman seated against bales, Cattle, Train / Female portrait. ***Right:*** 100 / HUNDRED vertically / 100. ***Engraver:*** Draper, Toppan & Co. ***Comments:*** H-KY-175-G220, Hughes-Unlisted. 18__. 1840s.

Rarity: URS-2
F $450

$100 • W-KY-960-100-G230
Left: 100 / Portrait of George Washington / 100. ***Center:*** Woman seated against bales, Cattle, Train / 100. ***Right:*** 100 / Portrait of Henry Clay / 100. ***Engraver:*** Toppan, Carpenter & Co. ***Comments:*** H-KY-175-G222, Hughes-466. 18__. 1840s–1850s.

Rarity: URS-2
F $450

$100 • W-KY-960-100-G240
Left: 100 / Portrait of Henry Clay / 100. ***Center:*** Woman seated against bales, Cattle, Train. ***Right:*** 100 / Male portrait / 100. ***Tint:*** Red-orange. ***Engraver:*** American Bank Note Co. ***Comments:*** H-KY-175-G224, Hughes-468. 18__. 1850s–1860s.

Rarity: URS-2
F $450

Non-Valid Issues

$5 • W-KY-960-005-C040

Comments: H-KY-175-C184, Hughes-443. Counterfeit of W-KY-960-005-G040. 18__. 1830s.

Rarity: URS-4
F $90

$10 • W-KY-960-010-C100

Comments: H-KY-175-C196, Hughes-Unlisted. Counterfeit of W-KY-960-010-G100. 18__. 1840s–1850s.

Rarity: URS-4
F $90

$20 • W-KY-960-020-C130

Comments: H-KY-175-C202, Hughes-454. Counterfeit of W-KY-960-020-G130. 18__. 1830s.

Rarity: URS-3
F $125

$20 • W-KY-960-020-C140

Comments: H-KY-175-C204, Hughes-456. Counterfeit of W-KY-960-020-G140. 18__. 1840s.

Rarity: URS-3
F $125

$50 • W-KY-960-050-C180

Comments: H-KY-175-C212, Hughes-462. Counterfeit of W-KY-960-050-G180. 18__. 1840s.

Rarity: URS-3
F $125

Peoples Bank of Kentucky
1856–1860s
W-KY-970

History: The Peoples Bank of Kentucky was chartered on February 15, 1856, with an authorized capital of $250,000. In 1863 circulation was $322,887. J.H. Huber was the cashier, and W.B. Hamilton was the president. Later the head office of the bank in Bowling Green, W-KY-100, moved to Louisville, and the old parent location became a branch, W-KY-110. The bank closed up sometime in the 1860s.

The Peoples Bank of Kentucky had branch banks located in Bowling Green, W-KY-110, Hartford, W-KY-620, and Paducah, W-KY-1250.

Numismatic Commentary: A very scarce bank. No notes payable at the parent bank location in Louisville have been found—all notes are either payable at Bowling Green or Hartford.

Planters and Manufacturers Bank
1854
W-KY-980

History: The Planters and Manufacturers Bank was incorporated on February 21, 1854, with an authorized capital of $2,600,000. This was to be divided into shares of $100 apiece. The charter was authorized to continue until May 1, 1884.

On March 4, 1854, the House of Representatives took up the matter regarding the governor's rejection of the bank bill. The governor refused the bill due to the fact that the current overall bank debt was already high, and it was believed that further bank issues would only worsen the problem. On the matter of the bank, the governor wrote, "Heavy indebtedness ought to be avoided by individuals as well as states, if they wish to be free, prosperous and happy. . . . Do the commerce of our state, or the wants of our people, require such a large increase of bank capital? I think not."[12]

It was put to the vote whether the bank should be passed, "the Governor's objections to the contrary notwithstanding," and the House this time negated the bill. Thus it appears that the bank never went into operation at all.

The Planters and Manufacturers Bank had branch banks planned to be located in Barbourville, Catlettsburg, Cynthiana, Eddyville, Elizabethtown, Glasgow, Hawesville, Shelbyville, and Winchester.

Savings Bank of Louisville
1854
W-KY-990

History: The Savings Bank of Louisville (also seen as the Louisville Savings Bank) was incorporated on March 7, 1854. It was forbidden from issuing bank notes or bills payable on demand, but was allowed to deal in bills of exchange and issue certificates of deposit, as long as such bills and certificates did not exceed one-third of the capital stock. The permanent fund of the Savings Bank of Louisville was authorized at no more than $300,000.

Southern Bank of Kentucky (branch)
1839–1865
W-KY-1000

History: On February 20, 1839, the Southern Bank of Kentucky was chartered with an authorized capital of $2,000,000, of which the state subscribed to half. On February 15, 1850, the charter was extended to last until 1880.

The branch located in Louisville was opened in 1839. By 1853 the capital was $500,000. A.A. Gordon was the president, and J.B. Alexander was the cashier. In 1860 capital had dropped to $200,000. S.M. Wing took the position of president. In 1861 Will Garnett was the cashier. In 1863 the capital had regained its $500,000 value.

By 1865 the bank had been put into liquidation. On March 4, 1865, an act was passed ordering the treatment of the bank's bills to be as promissory notes rather than as currency. On January 8, 1867, the bank issued its last report regarding the closing up of its affairs. The bank building was later occupied by Nimrod, Long & Co.

The Southern Bank of Kentucky had its parent bank located in Russellville, W-KY-1400, and branch banks located in Bowling Green, W-KY-130, Carrollton, W-KY-200, Hickman, W-KY-650, Lebanon, W-KY-740, Owensboro, W-KY-1200, and Smithland, W-KY-1460.

Valid Issues

$1 • W-KY-1000-001-G010

Left: 1 / Woman reclining / ONE. ***Center:*** 1 / Female portrait surrounded by implements / 1. ***Right:*** 1 / Indian man reclining / ONE. ***Engraver:*** Toppan, Carpenter, Casilear & Co. ***Comments:*** H-KY-285-G190, Hughes-730. 18__. 1850s.

Rarity: URS-3
F $350

$1 • W-KY-1000-001-G020

Left: Man with children and horse / ONE. ***Center:*** Portrait of young girl. ***Right:*** 1 / Flock of sheep. ***Engraver:*** Toppan, Carpenter & Co. ***Comments:*** H-KY-285-G192, Hughes-728. 18__. 1850s.

Rarity: URS-3
F $350

$1 • W-KY-1000-001-G020a

Engraver: Toppan, Carpenter & Co. / ABNCo. monogram. ***Comments:*** H-KY-285-G192a, Hughes-Unlisted. Similar to W-KY-1000-001-G020 but with additional engraver imprint. 18__. 1850s–1860s.

Rarity: URS-3
F $350

$2 • W-KY-1000-002-G030

Left: 2 / Woman with basket / TWO. ***Center:*** Spread eagle / 2. ***Bottom center:*** Eagle. ***Right:*** Justice seated with scales and sword / TWO. ***Engraver:*** Toppan, Carpenter, Casilear & Co. ***Comments:*** H-KY-285-G196, Hughes-733. 18__. 1850s.

Rarity: URS-3
F $350

$2 • W-KY-1000-002-G040

Left: 2 / Woman seated / TWO. ***Center:*** Female portrait. ***Right:*** 2 / Man with children and horse. ***Engraver:*** Toppan, Carpenter & Co. ***Comments:*** H-KY-285-G198, Hughes-735. 18__. 1850s.

Rarity: URS-3
F $350

$2 • W-KY-1000-002-G040a

Engraver: Toppan, Carpenter & Co. / ABNCo. monogram. ***Comments:*** H-KY-285-G198a, Hughes-Unlisted. Similar to W-KY-1000-002-G040 but with additional engraver imprint. 18__. 1850s–1860s.

Rarity: URS-3
F $350

$3 • W-KY-1000-003-G050

Left: 3 / Female portrait / 3. ***Center:*** Woman with eagle. ***Bottom center:*** Steamboat. ***Right:*** 3 / Three women standing / THREE. ***Engraver:*** Toppan, Carpenter, Casilear & Co. ***Comments:*** H-KY-285-G202, Hughes-739. 18__. 1850s.

Rarity: URS-3
F $350

$3 • W-KY-1000-003-G060

Left: 3 / Portrait of George Washington. ***Center:*** Portrait of young girl / Man with children and horse. ***Right:*** 3 / 3. ***Engraver:*** Toppan, Carpenter & Co. ***Comments:*** H-KY-285-G204, Hughes-737. 18__. 1850s–1860s.

Rarity: URS-3
F $350

$3 • W-KY-1000-003-G060a

Engraver: Toppan, Carpenter & Co. / ABNCo. monogram. ***Comments:*** H-KY-285-G204a, Hughes-Unlisted. Similar to W-KY-1000-003-G060 but with additional engraver imprint. 18__. 1850s–1860s.

Rarity: URS-3
F $350

$5 • W-KY-1000-005-G070

Left: 5 / Female portrait / 5. ***Center:*** Man on horse. ***Right:*** 5 / Woman standing with flag. ***Engraver:*** Toppan, Carpenter, Casilear & Co. ***Comments:*** H-KY-285-G208, Hughes-742. 18__. 1850s.

Rarity: URS-3
F $350

$5 • W-KY-1000-005-G080

Left: 5 / Portrait of boy. ***Center:*** Man on horse in farmyard. ***Right:*** V / Portrait of young girl. ***Overprint:*** Red FIVE. ***Engraver:*** Bald, Cousland & Co. / Baldwin, Bald & Cousland. ***Comments:*** H-KY-285-G210a, Hughes-745. 18__. 1850s.

Rarity: URS-3
F $350

$10 • W-KY-1000-010-G090

Left: 10. ***Center:*** Woman reclining among farm implements. ***Bottom center:*** Female portrait. ***Right:*** 10. ***Engraver:*** Toppan, Carpenter, Casilear & Co. ***Comments:*** H-KY-285-G212, Hughes-747. 18__. 1850s.

Rarity: URS-3
F $350

$10 • W-KY-1000-010-G100

Left: 10 / Woman seated. ***Center:*** Man, woman, child, dog, Haying scene. ***Right:*** 10 / Woman seated. ***Overprint:*** Red TEN. ***Engraver:*** Bald, Cousland & Co. / Baldwin, Bald & Cousland. ***Comments:*** H-KY-285-G214a, Hughes-750. 18__. 1850s.

Rarity: URS-3
F $350

Non-Valid Issues

$1 • W-KY-1000-001-C010

Comments: H-KY-285-C190, Hughes-731. Counterfeit of W-KY-1000-001-G010. 18__. 1850s.

Rarity: URS-4
F $100

$1 • W-KY-1000-001-C020a

Comments: H-KY-285-C192a, Hughes-729. Counterfeit of W-KY-1000-001-G020a. 18__. 1850s–1860s.

Rarity: URS-4
F $100

$3 • W-KY-1000-003-C050

Comments: H-KY-185-C202, Hughes-740. Counterfeit of W-KY-1000-003-G050. 18__. 1850s.

Rarity: URS-4
F $100

$3 • W-KY-1000-003-C060a

Comments: H-KY-285-C204a, Hughes-738. Counterfeit of W-KY-1000-003-G060a. 18__. 1850s–1860s.

Rarity: URS-4
F $100

Mayfield, Kentucky

In 1818 Isaac Shelby and Andrew Jackson purchased Mayfield as well as eight other counties in what was called the Jackson Purchase. The town of Mayfield was established to be the county seat of Graves in 1821, and the county was organized in 1823. The town was named after Mayfield Creek.

In 1858 the Memphis, New Orleans, and Northern Railroad connected to Mayfield, and the Mayfield Woolen Mills followed in 1860. Manufacturing expanded in the town, with clothing becoming the main industry. Tobacco was also a strong product.

Bank of Ashland (branch)

1860–1872

W-KY-1010

History: The Bank of Ashland was chartered on February 15, 1856, with an authorized capital of $400,000, $100,000 of which had to be paid in before the bank could open for business. The Mayfield branch was authorized on January 27, 1860, and opened in 1861. By 1863 the capital was $100,000. J.N. Beadles was the cashier, and R.K. Williams was the president.

On April 2, 1861, the charter of the bank was amended to allow it to issue notes with denominations less than $5. The bank operated successfully for a time, and in 1872 it wound up its affairs and was succeeded by the Ashland National Bank.

The Bank of Ashland had its parent bank located in Ashland, W-KY-010, and a branch bank located in Shelbyville, W-KY-1420.

Valid Issues

$1 • W-KY-1010-001-G010

Left: ONE on 1 / Man husking corn. ***Center:*** Woman standing with pole and cap, foliage, bird. ***Right:*** ONE on 1 / Blacksmith. ***Tint:*** Green panel of microlettering outlining white ONE and dies outlining white 1s. ***Engraver:*** American Bank Note Co. ***Comments:*** H-KY-5-G10a. 18__. 1860s.

Rarity: —

$5 • W-KY-1010-005-G020

Left: 5 / Soldier charging with bayonet. ***Center:*** Portrait of girl / Five men at work in iron foundry / Portrait of girl. ***Right:*** 5 / Female portrait. ***Tint:*** Yellow. ***Back:*** Machinery. ***Engraver:*** Toppan, Carpenter & Co. ***Comments:*** H-KY-5-G12a. 18__. 1857.

Rarity: —

$10 • W-KY-1010-010-G030

Left: TEN / Soldier and Liberty flanking shield bearing portrait of George Washington, Two Indians. ***Right:*** 10 on die / Female portrait. ***Tint:*** Yellow panel of microlettering outlining white TEN on white 10 outlined by lathework. ***Engraver:*** Toppan, Carpenter & Co. ***Comments:*** H-KY-5-G14a. 18__. 1857.

Rarity: —

$20 • W-KY-1010-020-G040

Left: Train / 20 on die. ***Right:*** 20 on die / Male portrait. ***Tint:*** Yellow lathework and panel of microlettering outlining white TWENTY. ***Engraver:*** Toppan, Carpenter & Co. ***Comments:*** H-KY-5-G16a. 18__. 1857.

Rarity: —

Maysville, Kentucky

John May and Daniel Boone established a trading post and tavern in the area that would become Maysville. In 1787 the settlement, called Limestone, was incorporated as Maysville. The nearby town of Washington had far outstripped the settlement in terms of growth, but in 1795 the town began to expand. Ferry traffic across the river brought in traders and goods, and by 1807 Maysville was a prominent port. In 1811 the steamboat changed everything, and the population rose drastically.

As of 1830 Maysville had about 3,000 residents. The previously successful town of Washington had disintegrated after a fire in 1825 and several bouts of cholera. In 1848 Maysville replaced Washington as the county seat. In 1850 the Maysville and Lexington Railroad began to operate, but it failed in less than a decade.

Bank of Kentucky {2nd} (branch)

1834–1882

W-KY-1020

History: The second Bank of Kentucky (sometimes seen in print as the "New" Bank of Kentucky) was chartered in 1834 in order to assume the business of the first Bank of Kentucky, W-KY-420, which had recently closed. The capital of the bank was $5,000,000.

The branch in Maysville was established in 1834. In 1848 the president was Richard Henry Lee, and the cashier was H.B. Hill. By 1855 capital was worth $450,000. James Barbour had taken the office of cashier, and Andrew M. January was president.

In January 1866 almost all branches of the Bank of Kentucky were closed down, and the parent bank began winding up its business. In 1882, beyond the note-issuing period under study, the branch in Lexington became the Bank of Maysville.

The second Bank of Kentucky had its parent bank located in Louisville, W-KY-850, and branch banks located in Bowling Green, W-KY-080, Burksville, W-KY-140, Columbus, W-KY-220, Danville, W-KY-330, Flemingsburg, W-KY-390, Frankfort, W-KY-430, Glasgow, W-KY-510, Greensburg, W-KY-540, Hopkinsville, W-KY-670, Lexington, W-KY-770, Mount Sterling, W-KY-1100, and Paducah, W-KY-1220.

Numismatic Commentary: Notes of this bank and its branches are very rare.

Valid Issues

$1 • W-KY-1020-001-G010

Left: ONE / Men and women. ***Center:*** Woman swimming / ONE / Portrait of Henry Clay / Woman swimming / ONE. ***Right:*** ONE / Man and women. ***Engraver:*** Danforth, Bald & Co. ***Comments:*** H-KY-195-G326, Hughes-484. 18__. 1850s.

Rarity: URS-3

F $350

$5 • W-KY-1020-005-G020

Left: FIVE / Liberty standing / V. ***Center:*** 5 / Horse / 5. ***Right:*** FIVE / Liberty standing / V. ***Engraver:*** Casilear, Durand, Burton & Evans. ***Comments:*** H-KY-195-G330, Hughes-495. 18__. 1830s–1840s.

Rarity: URS-3
F $350

$5 • W-KY-1020-005-G030

Left: 5 / Portrait of Henry Clay / FIVE. ***Center:*** Portrait of John Q. Adams / Woman seated against bales, Train, Harvesting scene / Portrait of Thomas Jefferson. ***Right:*** 5 / Portrait of George Washington / FIVE. ***Engraver:*** Toppan, Carpenter & Co. ***Comments:*** H-KY-195-G334, Hughes-494. 18__. 1840s–1850s.

Rarity: URS-3
F $350

$10 • W-KY-1020-010-G040

Left: 10 / Woman seated / X. ***Center:*** X / Three women seated / X. ***Right:*** 10 / Woman standing / X. ***Engraver:*** Casilear, Durand, Burton & Evans. ***Comments:*** H-KY-195-G338, Hughes-497. 18__. 1830s–1840s.

Rarity: URS-3
F $350

$10 • W-KY-1020-010-G050 CC

Engraver: Toppan, Carpenter & Co. ***Comments:*** H-KY-195-G342, Hughes-499. 18__. 1840s–1850s.

Rarity: URS-3
F $350

$20 • W-KY-1020-020-G060

Left: 20 / Woman standing / 20. ***Center:*** XX / Woman seated with plow and bales, Cattle / XX. ***Right:*** 20 / Indian man standing / XX. ***Engraver:*** Casilear, Durand, Burton & Evans. ***Comments:*** H-KY-195-G346, Hughes-506. 18__. 1830s–1840s.

Rarity: URS-3
F $350

$20 • W-KY-1020-020-G070

Left: Woman holding male portrait aloft / Male portrait. ***Center:*** 20 / Woman flying / 20. ***Right:*** Three women holding medallion head aloft. ***Engraver:*** Draper, Toppan & Co. ***Comments:*** H-KY-195-G350, Hughes-508. 18__. 1840s.

Rarity: URS-3
F $350

$20 • W-KY-1020-020-G080

Left: 20 / Portrait of Daniel Webster. ***Center:*** "General Marion's Sweet Potato Dinner." ***Right:*** 20 / Male portrait. ***Engraver:*** Toppan, Carpenter & Co. ***Comments:*** H-KY-195-G352, Hughes-511. 18__. 1850s.

Rarity: URS-3
F $350

$50 • W-KY-1020-050-G090

Left: Woman standing. ***Center:*** 50 / Steamboat *Henry Clay* / 50. ***Right:*** Woman standing. ***Engraver:*** Casilear, Durand, Burton & Evans. ***Comments:*** H-KY-195-G356, Hughes-513. 18__. 1830s–1840s.

Rarity: URS-2
F $450

Post Notes

$__ • W-KY-1020-__-G100

Left: Woman seated with plow, sheaves, Cattle / POST NOTE. ***Center:*** $__. ***Right:*** Three women seated / POST NOTE. ***Engraver:*** Casilear, Durand, Burton & Evans. ***Comments:*** H-KY-195-G360, Hughes-523. 18__. 1830s.

Rarity: URS-3
F $350

Non-Valid Issues

$5 • W-KY-1020-005-C020

Comments: H-KY-195-C330, Hughes-496. Counterfeit of W-KY-1020-005-G020. 18__. 1830s–1840s.

Rarity: URS-4
F $100

$10 • W-KY-1020-010-C050

Comments: H-KY-195-C342, Hughes-500. Counterfeit of W-KY-1020-010-G050. 18__. 1840s–1850s.

Rarity: URS-4
F $100

$20 • W-KY-1020-020-C070

Comments: H-KY-195-C350, Hughes-509. Counterfeit of W-KY-1020-020-G070. 18__. 1840s.

Rarity: URS-4
F $100

$20 • W-KY-1020-020-C080

Comments: H-KY-195-C352, Hughes-512. Counterfeit of W-KY-1020-020-G080. 18__. 1850s.

Rarity: URS-4
F $100

Bank of Limestone

1818–1827

W-KY-1030

History: The Bank of Limestone was chartered on January 26, 1818. The authorized capital of $300,000 was divided into 3,000 shares of $100 each. The charters of all independent banks authorized on January 26, 1818, were revoked effective May 1, 1820. This bank seems to have lingered for a time, an exception to the general rule, as on December 29, 1827, an act was passed authorizing the stockholders of the bank to close up its affairs.

Valid Issues

$1 • **W-KY-1030-001-G010**

CC

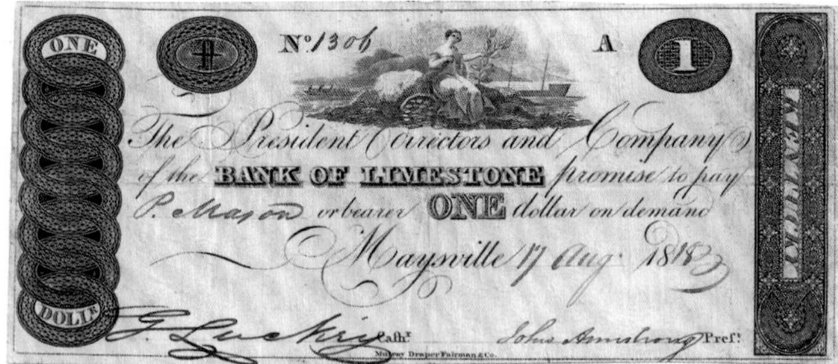

Engraver: Murray, Draper, Fairman & Co. ***Comments:*** H-KY-205-G12, Hughes-581. 181_. 1810s.

Rarity: URS-1
Proof $2,450

$2 • **W-KY-1030-002-G020**
Engraver: Murray, Draper, Fairman & Co. ***Comments:*** H-KY-205-G14, Hughes-582. No description available. 1810s.
Rarity: *None known*

$5 • **W-KY-1030-005-G030**
Engraver: Murray, Draper, Fairman & Co. ***Comments:*** H-KY-205-G18, Hughes-583. No description available. 1810s.
Rarity: *None known*

$10 • **W-KY-1030-010-G040**
Engraver: Murray, Draper, Fairman & Co. ***Comments:*** H-KY-205-G20, Hughes-584. No description available. 1810s.
Rarity: *None known*

$20 • **W-KY-1030-020-G050**
Engraver: Murray, Draper, Fairman & Co. ***Comments:*** H-KY-205-G22, Hughes-585. No description available. 1810s.
Rarity: *None known*

Bank of Maysville
1835
W-KY-1040

History: On February 3, 1834, a bill was proposed to incorporate the Bank of Maysville. The charter was given on January 3, 1835. The bank operated for only a short time.

Farmers Bank of Kentucky (branch)
1850–1867
W-KY-1050

History: The Farmers Bank of Kentucky was chartered on February 15, 1850, with an authorized capital of $2,300,000. By September 1852 the bank had opened for business. On February 11, 1860, the charter for the bank was amended, allowing it to increase its capital.

The branch located in Maysville had a capital of $400,000. In 1855 the cashier was James A. Johnson, and the president was J.P. Dobyns. In 1856 Harrison Taylor became the president. During the 1860s the Farmers Bank of Kentucky wound up its affairs and closed. The Maysville branch closed in 1867.

The Farmers Bank of Kentucky had its parent bank located in Frankfort, W-KY-450, and branch banks located in Bardstown, W-KY-070, Covington, W-KY-240, George Town, W-KY-480, Henderson, W-KY-640, Mount Sterling, W-KY-1130, Princeton, W-KY-1340, and Somerset, W-KY-1480.

Valid Issues

$1 • **W-KY-1050-001-G010**

CC

Engraver: Toppan, Carpenter, Casilear & Co. ***Comments:*** H-KY-100-G98, Hughes-250. 18__. 1850s.
Rarity: URS-3
F $350

$1 • **W-KY-1050-001-G010a**
Back: Red-orange. ***Engraver:*** Toppan, Carpenter, Casilear & Co. / ABNCo. monogram. ***Comments:*** H-KY-100-G98b, Hughes-Unlisted. Similar to W-KY-1050-001-G010 but with additional engraver imprint. 185_. 1850s.
Rarity: URS-3
F $350

$1 • **W-KY-1050-001-G020**
Left: 1 / Man and wagon and horses / 1. ***Center:*** Portraits of Mr. and Mrs. John Crittenden. ***Right:*** 1 / 1 on die / 1. ***Tint:*** Red-orange. ***Back:*** Red-orange. ***Engraver:*** American Bank Note Co. ***Comments:*** H-KY-100-G100a, Hughes-249. 18__. 1860s.
Rarity: URS-3
F $350

$2 • **W-KY-1050-002-G030**
Left: 2 / Portrait of Mrs. John Crittenden. ***Center:*** 2 / Man on horse / 2. ***Right:*** 2 / Portrait of John Crittenden. ***Engraver:*** Toppan, Carpenter, Casilear & Co. ***Comments:*** H-KY-100-G102, Hughes-252. 18__. 1850s.
Rarity: URS-3
F $350

$2 • **W-KY-1050-002-G030a**
Back: Red-orange. ***Engraver:*** Toppan, Carpenter, Casilear & Co. / ABNCo. monogram. ***Comments:*** H-KY-100-G102b, Hughes-Unlisted. Similar to W-KY-1050-002-G030 but with additional engraver imprint. 185_. 1850s.
Rarity: URS-3
F $350

$3 • W-KY-1050-003-G035

CC

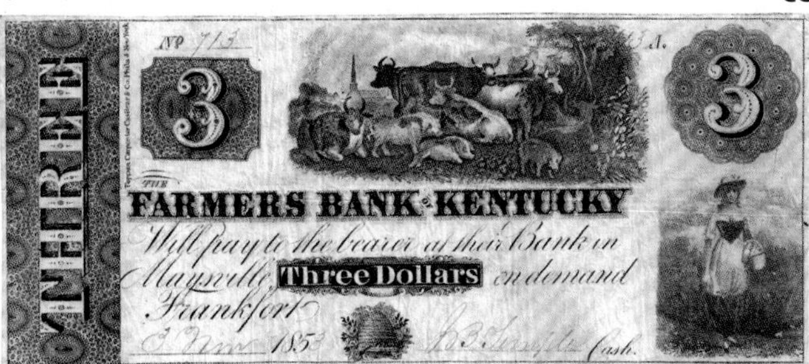

Engraver: Toppan, Carpenter, Casilear & Co. ***Comments:*** H-Unlisted, Hughes-Unlisted. 185_. 1850s.

Rarity: URS-3
F $350

$5 • W-KY-1050-005-G040

Left: 5 / Portrait of John Crittenden / 5. ***Center:*** Cattle and sheep, Herders. ***Right:*** 5 / Portrait of Mrs. John Crittenden / 5. ***Engraver:*** Toppan, Carpenter, Casilear & Co. ***Comments:*** H-KY-100-G104, Hughes-256. 18__. 1850s.

Rarity: URS-3
F $350

$5 • W-KY-1050-005-G040a

Overprint: Red FIVE. ***Engraver:*** Toppan, Carpenter, Casilear & Co. ***Comments:*** H-KY-100-G104a, Hughes-257. Similar to W-KY-1050-005-G040. 18__. 1850s.

Rarity: URS-3
F $350

$5 • W-KY-1050-005-G050

Left: Men plowing with horse / V. ***Center:*** Portraits of Mr. and Mrs. John Crittenden. ***Right:*** 5 / 5. ***Tint:*** Red-orange. ***Back:*** Red-orange. ***Engraver:*** American Bank Note Co. ***Comments:*** H-KY-100-G106a, Hughes-255. 18__. 1859.

Rarity: URS-4
F $250

$10 • W-KY-1050-010-G060

Left: 10 / Portrait of John Crittenden. ***Center:*** Portraits of Mr. and Mrs. John Crittenden. ***Engraver:*** Toppan, Carpenter, Casilear & Co. ***Comments:*** H-KY-100-G108, Hughes-Unlisted. 18__. 1850s.

Rarity: URS-2
F $450

$10 • W-KY-1050-010-G060a

Tint: Red-orange outlining white TEN. ***Engraver:*** Toppan, Carpenter, Casilear & Co. ***Comments:*** H-KY-100-G108b, Hughes-Unlisted. Similar to W-KY-1050-010-G060. 18__. 1850s.

Rarity: URS-2
F $450

$10 • W-KY-1050-010-G070

Left: 10 / Portrait of John Crittenden. ***Center:*** Woman reclining against barrel, Harvest scene / Portrait of Mrs. John Crittenden. ***Right:*** 10 / Men harvesting corn. ***Tint:*** Red-orange. ***Back:*** Red-orange. ***Engraver:*** American Bank Note Co. ***Comments:*** H-KY-100-G110a, Hughes-259. 18__. 1859.

Rarity: URS-4
F $200

$20 • W-KY-1050-020-G080

Left: Portrait of Mrs. John Crittenden / Portrait of John Crittenden. ***Center:*** 20 / Horses plowing. ***Right:*** 20. ***Engraver:*** Toppan, Carpenter, Casilear & Co. ***Comments:*** H-KY-100-G112, Hughes-Unlisted. 18__. 1850s.

Rarity: URS-2
F $450

$20 • W-KY-1050-020-G080a

Tint: Red-orange. ***Back:*** Red-orange. ***Engraver:*** American Bank Note Co. ***Comments:*** H-KY-100-G114a, Hughes-261. Similar to W-KY-1050-020-G080 but with different engraver imprint. 18__. 1859.

Rarity: URS-4
F $225

$50 • W-KY-1050-050-G090

Left: Three women with anchor. ***Center:*** 50 / Portrait of Mrs. John Crittenden. ***Right:*** 50 / Portrait of John Crittenden / 50. ***Engraver:*** Toppan, Carpenter, Casilear & Co. ***Comments:*** H-KY-100-G116, Hughes-263. 18__. 1850s.

Rarity: URS-4
F $225

$100 • W-KY-1050-100-G100

Left: 100 / Portrait of John Crittenden / 100. ***Center:*** Three women reclining / Portrait of Mrs. John Crittenden. ***Right:*** ONE HUNDRED vertically. ***Engraver:*** Toppan, Carpenter, Casilear & Co. ***Comments:*** H-KY-100-G118, Hughes-265. 18__. 1850s.

Rarity: URS-2
F $450

Post Notes

$1 • W-KY-1050-001-G110

Left: 1 / Portrait of John Crittenden / ONE. ***Center:*** Man with dog, Running horses, Donkey. ***Right:*** 1 / Female portrait / ONE. ***Engraver:*** Toppan, Carpenter, Casilear & Co. ***Comments:*** H-Unlisted, Hughes-Unlisted. 18__. 1850s.

Rarity: URS-3
F $225

Non-Valid Issues

$3 • W-KY-1050-003-S010

Left: THREE. ***Center:*** 3 / Cows. ***Right:*** 3 / Woman standing. ***Comments:*** H-Unlisted, Hughes-254. 18__. 1850s.

Rarity: URS-3
F $225

$5 • W-KY-1050-005-C040

Comments: H-KY-100-C104, Hughes-Unlisted. Counterfeit of W-KY-1050-005-G040. 18__. 1850s.

Rarity: URS-3
F $225

$5 • W-KY-1050-005-C040a

Comments: H-KY-100-C104a, Hughes-Unlisted. Counterfeit of W-KY-1050-005-G040a. 18__. 1850s.

Rarity: URS-3
F $225

Millersburg, Kentucky

Named after John Miller, Millersburg was founded in 1817.

Hinkston Exporting Company

1818–1820s

W-KY-1060

History: The Hinkston Exporting Company was given banking privileges in 1818. On November 8, 1819, it had $17,232 face value of notes in circulation. Robert E. Miller was the cashier, and in the early 1820s the capital was $50,120. The firm ceased business in this era.

Valid Issues

$1 • W-KY-1060-001-G010 CC

Engraver: Murray, Draper, Fairman & Co. ***Comments:*** H-KY-210-G12. 18__. 1810s.

Rarity: URS-1
Proof $1,100

$3 • W-KY-1060-003-G020

Left: KENTUCKY vertically. ***Center:*** 3 / Building / III. ***Right:*** THREE vertically. ***Engraver:*** Murray, Draper, Fairman & Co. ***Comments:*** H-KY-210-G16. 1810s.

Rarity: —

$5 • W-KY-1060-005-G030

Left: KENTUCKY vertically. ***Center:*** 5 / Building / V. ***Right:*** FIVE vertically. ***Engraver:*** Murray, Draper, Fairman & Co. ***Comments:*** H-KY-210-G18. 1810s.

Rarity: —

Monticello, Kentucky

John Smith was one of the first settlers to arrive in Monticello, where he built a log cabin that still stands today. In 1801 the town was officially established. The town's proximity to Lake Cumberland allowed fishing and boating to become primary industries. During the Civil War, several skirmishes took place near town, and the Brown-Lanier House was used as a hospital.

Commercial Bank of Kentucky (branch)

1852–1871

W-KY-1070

History: On January 3, 1852, the Commercial Bank of Kentucky was chartered. The Monticello branch had a capital of $50,000 in 1861. J.T. Sanders was the cashier, and William J. Kendrick was the president. In 1871 the branch was succeeded by the National Bank of Monticello.

The Commercial Bank of Kentucky had its parent bank located in Paducah, W-KY-1240, and branch banks located in Cynthiana, W-KY-290, Harrodsburg, W-KY-590, Lebanon, W-KY-720, Louisville, W-KY-900, Newport, W-KY-1150, and Versailles, W-KY-1560.

Valid Issues

$1 • W-KY-1070-001-G010

Left: ONE on 1 / ONE vertically / ONE on 1. ***Center:*** Woman seated with map, Two men in canoe. ***Right:*** 1 / Female portrait. ***Tint:*** Green. ***Engraver:*** American Bank Note Co. ***Comments:*** H-KY-255-G92a, Hughes-668. 185_. 1850s.

Rarity: URS-3
F $250; **Proof** $1,100

$2 • W-KY-1070-002-G020 CC

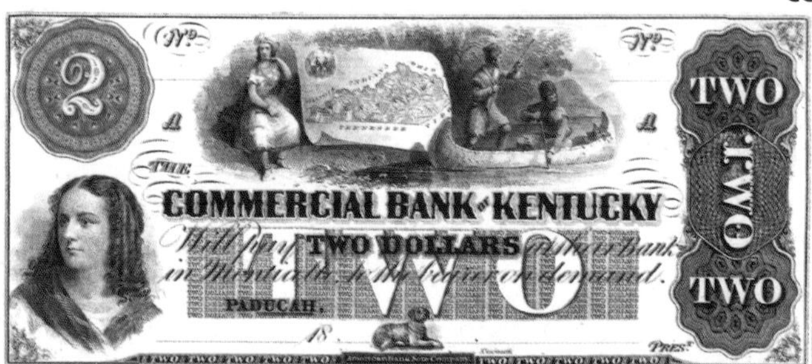

Tint: Green die outlining white 2 and panel of microlettering outlining white TWO. ***Engraver:*** American Bank Note Co. ***Comments:*** H-KY-255-G94a, Hughes-670. 18__. 1860s.

Rarity: URS-3
F $250; **Proof** $5,400
Selected auction price: Stack's Bowers Galleries, October 30, 2014, Lot 2060, Proof $5,400

$3 • W-KY-1070-003-G030 CC

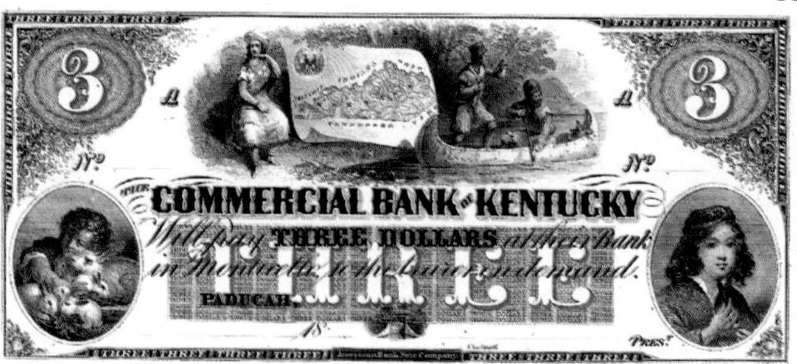

Tint: Green panel of microlettering outlining white THREE and dies outlining white 3s. ***Engraver:*** American Bank Note Co. ***Comments:*** H-KY-255-G96a, Hughes-673. 18__. 1860s.

Rarity: URS-3
F $350; **Proof** $2,900

$5 • W-KY-1070-005-G040

Left: FIVE / Men and women in and around V. ***Center:*** 5 / Women in and around 5, Dock. ***Right:*** FIVE / Portrait of Franklin Pierce. ***Tint:*** Red-orange. ***Engraver:*** Rawdon, Wright, Hatch & Edson / ABNCo. monogram. ***Comments:*** H-KY-255-G98a, Hughes-675. 18__. 1850s–1860s.

Rarity: URS-3
F $350

$10 • **W-KY-1070-010-G050**
Left: 10 / Male portrait / TEN. *Center:* Steamboats. *Right:* TEN / Harrodsburg Springs / TEN. *Engraver:* Unverified, but likely Rawdon, Wright, Hatch & Edson. *Comments:* H-KY-255-G100, Hughes-677. 185_. 1850s.

Rarity: URS-3
F $350

Monticello Bank
1818
W-KY-1080

History: The Monticello Bank was chartered in January 1818. It is unknown whether the bank ever opened for business.

Morgantown, Kentucky

In 1811 the land for Morgantown was donated to be the county seat of Butler. Originally the name was listed as Morgan Town, but in 1813 it was incorporated as Morgantown. The name is thought to have come from the first child born in the town, Daniel Morgan Smith.

Bank of Morgantown
1818–1820
W-KY-1090

History: The Bank of Morgantown was chartered on January 26, 1818. The authorized capital of $100,000 was divided into 1,000 shares of $100 each. Robert Morrison, Joel Suggs, John S. Waddle, Richard B. Dallam, John Harrill, Elisha Bennett, and James A. Porter were appointed to take stock subscriptions. The bank operated only for a short time, and in the summer of 1819 it stopped redeeming its notes. The charters of all independent banks authorized on January 26, 1818, were revoked effective May 1, 1820.

Numismatic Commentary: Notes of the Bank of Morgantown are extremely rare.

Valid Issues

$1 • **W-KY-1090-001-G010** QDB

Engraver: Murray, Draper, Fairman & Co. *Comments:* H-KY-220-G12, Hughes-599. 18__. 1810s.

Rarity: URS-2
F $500

$2 • **W-KY-1090-002-G020**
Left: TWO vertically. *Center:* 2 / 2. *Right:* KENTUCKY vertically. *Engraver:* Murray, Draper, Fairman & Co. *Comments:* H-KY-220-G14, Hughes-600. 181_. 1810s.

Rarity: URS-2
F $500

$5 • **W-KY-1090-005-G030**
Left: FIVE vertically. *Center:* 5 / 5. *Right:* KENTUCKY vertically. *Engraver:* Murray, Draper, Fairman & Co. *Comments:* H-KY-220-G18, Hughes-601. 181_. 1810s.

Rarity: URS-2
F $500

$10 • **W-KY-1090-010-G040**
Left: X / 10. *Center:* 10 / Farm scene, Houses. *Right:* KENTUCKY vertically. *Engraver:* Murray, Draper, Fairman & Co. *Comments:* H-KY-220-G20, Hughes-602. 181_. 1810s.

Rarity: URS-2
F $500

Mount Sterling, Kentucky

Hugh Forbes, the first settler to arrive on the land, named the area Mount Sterling after Stirling, Scotland. In 1792 the town was officially established, and in 1796 it became the county seat of Montgomery. The town was divided into 33 lots with 3 taverns and 4 stores. A courthouse was constructed along with a jail. Churches were built, and a market house was constructed which established Mount Sterling as a commercial center.

The town was occupied by both sides at different times during the Civil War.

Bank of Kentucky {2nd} (branch)
1860s–1866
W-KY-1100

History: The second Bank of Kentucky (sometimes seen in print as the "New" Bank of Kentucky) was chartered in 1834 in order to assume the business of the first Bank of Kentucky, W-KY-420, which had recently closed. The capital of the bank was $5,000,000.

The branch in Mount Sterling was established sometime in the 1860s. In January 1866 almost all branches of the Bank of Kentucky were closed down, and the parent bank began winding up its business.

The second Bank of Kentucky had its parent bank located in Louisville, W-KY-850, and branch banks located in Bowling Green, W-KY-080, Burksville, W-KY-140, Columbus, W-KY-220, Danville, W-KY-330, Flemingsburg, W-KY-390, Frankfort, W-KY-430, Glasgow, W-KY-510, Greensburg, W-KY-540, Hopkinsville, W-KY-670, Lexington, W-KY-770, Maysville, W-KY-1020, and Paducah, W-KY-1220.

Numismatic Commentary: Notes of this bank and its branches are very rare.

Valid Issues

$5 • W-KY-1100-005-G010

Left: 5 / Portrait of Henry Clay / FIVE. ***Center:*** Portrait of John Q. Adams / Woman seated against bales, Train, Harvesting scene / Portrait of Thomas Jefferson. ***Right:*** 5 / Portrait of George Washington / FIVE. ***Engraver:*** Toppan, Carpenter & Co. ***Comments:*** H-KY-195-G366, Hughes-494. 18__. 1840s–1850s.

Rarity: URS-2
F $450

$10 • W-KY-1100-010-G020

Left: 10 / Portrait of George Washington / 10. ***Center:*** Portrait of Andrew Jackson / Indian man and woman flanking shield bearing 10 surmounted by eagle / Portrait of Isaac Shelby. ***Right:*** 10 / Portrait of Henry Clay / 10. ***Engraver:*** Toppan, Carpenter & Co. ***Comments:*** H-KY-195-G370, Hughes-499. 18__. 1840s–1850s.

Rarity: URS-2
F $450

$20 • W-KY-1100-020-G030

Left: 20 / Portrait of Daniel Webster. ***Center:*** "General Marion's Sweet Potato Dinner." ***Right:*** 20 / Male portrait. ***Engraver:*** Toppan, Carpenter & Co. ***Comments:*** H-KY-195-G374, Hughes-511. 18__. 1850s.

Rarity: URS-2
F $450

Non-Valid Issues

$10 • W-KY-1100-010-C020

Comments: H-KY-195-C370, Hughes-500. Counterfeit of W-KY-1100-010-G020. 18__. 1840s–1850s.

Rarity: URS-3
F $150

Bank of Mount Sterling

1818–1820

W-KY-1110

History: The Bank of Mount Sterling was chartered on January 26, 1818, with an authorized capital of $100,000 to be divided into 1,000 shares of $100 each. The bank was in operation for a short time. Its bills were current in 1819, but not in 1820. The charters of all independent banks authorized on January 26, 1818, were revoked effective May 1, 1820.

Numismatic Commentary: Few notes of this bank are known to survive today.

Valid Issues

$1 • W-KY-1110-001-G010

Left: 1 / ONE DOLLAR / 1 vertically. ***Center:*** 1 / Man seated at table writing with quill / 1. ***Right:*** KENTUCKY vertically. ***Engraver:*** Murray, Draper, Fairman & Co. ***Comments:*** H-KY-225-G12, Hughes-615. 181_. 1810s.

Rarity: *None known*

$2 • W-KY-1110-002-G020

Left: 2 / TWO DOLLARS / 2 vertically. ***Center:*** 2 / Man seated at table writing with quill / 2. ***Right:*** KENTUCKY vertically. ***Engraver:*** Murray, Draper, Fairman & Co. ***Comments:*** H-KY-225-G14, Hughes-616. 181_. 1810s.

Rarity: *None known*

$3 • W-KY-1110-003-G030

CC

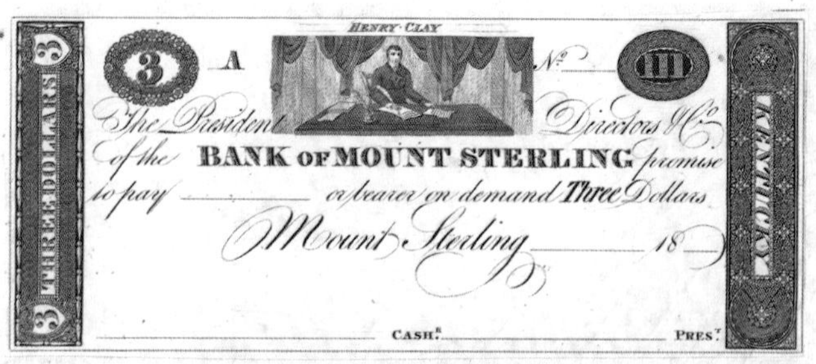

Engraver: Murray, Draper, Fairman & Co. ***Comments:*** H-KY-225-G16, Hughes-617. 181_. 1810s.

Rarity: URS-1
Proof $2,300

$5 • W-KY-1110-005-G040

Left: 5 / FIVE DOLLARS / 5 vertically. ***Center:*** 5 / Man seated at table writing with quill / 5. ***Right:*** KENTUCKY vertically. ***Engraver:*** Murray, Draper, Fairman & Co. ***Comments:*** H-KY-225-G18, Hughes-618. 181_. 1810s.

Rarity: *None known*

$10 • W-KY-1110-010-G050

Left: 10 / TEN DOLLARS / 10 vertically. ***Center:*** 10 / Man seated at table writing with quill / 10. ***Right:*** KENTUCKY vertically. ***Engraver:*** Murray, Draper, Fairman & Co. ***Comments:*** H-KY-225-G20, Hughes-619. 181_. 1810s.

Rarity: *None known*

Bank of the Commonwealth of Kentucky (branch)

1821–1824

W-KY-1120

History: The Bank of the Commonwealth of Kentucky was chartered on November 29, 1820, with an authorized capital of $2,000,000. A local name for the bank was the "Peoples Bank," as it was chartered for the purpose of bringing relief to the population in a time of economic uncertainty. On December 22, 1820, an act was passed authorizing the bank to issue $3,000,000 in bills. The establishment of the Bank of the Commonwealth of Kentucky inadvertently caused the failure of the first Bank of Kentucky, W-KY-420.

The branch located in Mount Sterling opened in 1821. It was established in the Captain Banks' Hotel, which was located on Main and Mayville streets. Edward Stockton was the first cashier, and George Howard was the president. Before it closed in 1824, the branch was relocated to West Main Street.

In 1830 the bank lost its authorization to loan money, and it was instructed to close up its branches. Around that time the bank ceased new business, but the winding up of its affairs took until 1855.

The Bank of the Commonwealth of Kentucky had its parent bank located in Frankfort, W-KY-440, and branch banks located in Bowling Green, W-KY-090, Falmouth, W-KY-360, Flemingsburg, W-KY-410, Greensburg, W-KY-550, Harrodsburg, W-KY-580, Hartford, W-KY-610, Lexington, W-KY-780, Louisville, W-KY-870, Princeton, W-KY-1330, Somerset, W-KY-1470, and Winchester, W-KY-1590.

Numismatic Commentary: Almost all notes from this bank and its branches are unknown today.

Valid Issues

6-1/4¢ • W-KY-1120-00.06.25-G010

Left: 6-1/4 CENTS. ***Center:*** 6-1/4 / 6-1/4 on die / 6-1/4. ***Right:*** KENTUCKY vertically. ***Comments:*** H-KY-95-G234, Hughes-237. 1822.

Rarity: *None known*

12-1/2¢ • W-KY-1120-00.12.50-G020

Left: 12-1/2 CENTS. ***Center:*** 12-1/2 / 12-1/2 on die / 12-1/2. ***Right:*** KENTUCKY vertically. ***Comments:*** H-KY-95-G236, Hughes-238. 1822.

Rarity: *None known*

25¢ • W-KY-1120-00.25-G030

Left: 25 CENTS. ***Center:*** 25 / 25 on die / 25. ***Right:*** KENTUCKY vertically. ***Comments:*** H-KY-95-G238, Hughes-239. 1822.

Rarity: *None known*

50¢ • W-KY-1120-00.50-G040

Left: 50 CENTS. ***Center:*** 50 / 50 on die / 50. ***Right:*** KENTUCKY vertically. ***Comments:*** H-KY-95-G240, Hughes-240. 1822.

Rarity: *None known*

$1 • W-KY-1120-001-G050

Left: KENTUCKY vertically. ***Center:*** 1 / 1. ***Right:*** CAMPBELL COUNTY vertically. ***Engraver:*** Murray, Draper, Fairman & Co. ***Comments:*** H-KY-95-G244, Hughes- 241. 18__. 1820s.

Rarity: URS-1
F $550

$3 • W-KY-1120-003-G060

Left: KENTUCKY vertically. ***Center:*** 3 / 3. ***Right:*** CAMPBELL COUNTY vertically. ***Engraver:*** Murray, Draper, Fairman & Co. ***Comments:*** H-KY-95-G246, Hughes-242. 18__. 1820s.

Rarity: URS-1
F $550

$5 • W-KY-1120-005-G070

Left: Woman holding staff. ***Center:*** 5 / Minerva standing with owl, shield, staff / 5. ***Right:*** Woman holding staff. ***Engraver:*** Murray, Draper, Fairman & Co. ***Comments:*** H-KY-95-G248, Hughes-243. 18__. 1820s.

Rarity: *None known*

$10 • W-KY-1120-010-G080

Left: Woman holding staff. ***Center:*** 10 / Woman standing with staff, shield, Four cherubs / 10. ***Right:*** Woman holding staff. ***Engraver:*** Murray, Draper, Fairman & Co. ***Comments:*** H-KY-95-G250, Hughes-244. 18__. 1820s.

Rarity: *None known*

$20 • W-KY-1120-020-G090

Engraver: Murray, Draper, Fairman & Co. ***Comments:*** H-KY-95-G252, Hughes-245. No description available. 18__. 1820s.

Rarity: *None known*

$50 • W-KY-1120-050-G100

Engraver: Murray, Draper, Fairman & Co. ***Comments:*** H-KY-95-G254, Hughes-246. No description available. 18__. 1820s.

Rarity: *None known*

$100 • W-KY-1120-100-G110

Engraver: Murray, Draper, Fairman & Co. ***Comments:*** H-KY-95-G256, Hughes-247. No description available. 18__. 1820s.

Rarity: *None known*

Exchange Bank of Barnes, White and Company

1860s

W-KY-1125

History: This is believed to have been an exchange house or office. No record has been found of a state charter for this bank. It is listed here for collector continuity.

Valid Issues

50¢ • W-KY-1125-00.50-G010

CC

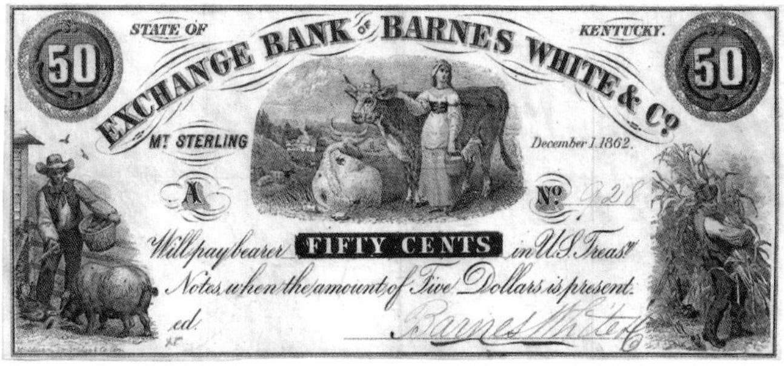

Comments: H-Unlisted, Hughes-Unlisted. December 1, 1862.

Rarity: URS-1
EF $600

50¢ • W-KY-1125-00.50-G020

CC

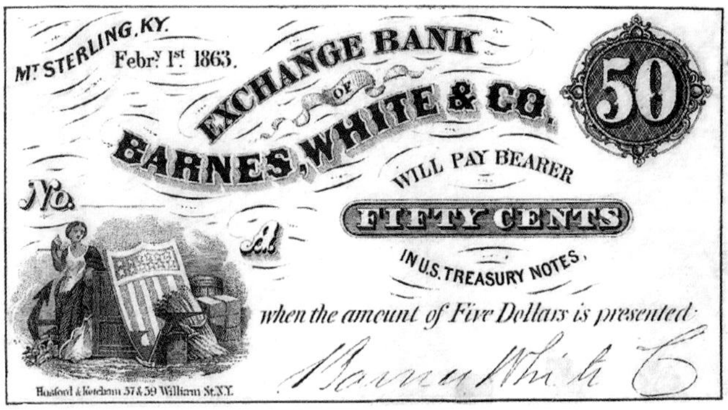

Comments: H-Unlisted, Hughes-Unlisted. Febry. 1st, 1863.

Rarity: URS-1
EF $600

Farmers Bank of Kentucky (branch)

1850–1875

W-KY-1130

History: The Farmers Bank of Kentucky was chartered on February 15, 1850, with an authorized capital of $2,300,000. By September 1852 the bank had opened for business. On February 11, 1860, the charter for the bank was amended, allowing it to increase its capital.

The branch located in Mount Sterling had a capital of $200,000. In 1854 the cashier, William Hoffman, resigned. He was replaced by William Mitchell. The president was Richard Apperson.

As did many banks of the era, during the 1860s the Farmers Bank of Kentucky wound up its affairs and closed. The Mount Sterling branch was closed and succeeded in interest by the Farmers National Bank in 1875.

The Farmers Bank of Kentucky had its parent bank located in Frankfort, W-KY-450, and branch banks located in Bardstown, W-KY-070, Covington, W-KY-240, George Town, W-KY-480, Henderson, W-KY-640, Maysville, W-KY-1050, Princeton, W-KY-1340, and Somerset, W-KY-1480.

Valid Issues

$1 • W-KY-1130-001-G010

Left: 1 / Portrait of John Crittenden / ONE. ***Center:*** Man with dog, Running horses, Donkey. ***Right:*** 1 / Female portrait / ONE. ***Engraver:*** Toppan, Carpenter, Casilear & Co. ***Comments:*** H-KY-100-G122, Hughes-250. 18__. 1850s.

Rarity: URS-3
F $350

$1 • W-KY-1130-001-G010a

Back: Red-orange. ***Engraver:*** Toppan, Carpenter, Casilear & Co. / ABNCo. monogram. ***Comments:*** H-KY-100-G122c, Hughes-Unlisted. Similar to W-KY-1130-001-G010 but with additional engraver imprint. 185_. 1850s.

Rarity: URS-3
F $350

$1 • W-KY-1130-001-G020

Left: 1 / Man and wagon and horses / 1. ***Center:*** Portraits of Mr. and Mrs. John Crittenden. ***Right:*** 1 / 1 on die / 1. ***Tint:*** Red-orange. ***Back:*** Red-orange. ***Engraver:*** American Bank Note Co. ***Comments:*** H-KY-100-G124a, Hughes-249. 18__. 1860s.

Rarity: URS-3
F $350

$2 • W-KY-1130-002-G030

Left: 2 / Portrait of Mrs. John Crittenden. ***Center:*** 2 / Man on horse / 2. ***Right:*** 2 / Portrait of John Crittenden. ***Engraver:*** Toppan, Carpenter, Casilear & Co. ***Comments:*** H-KY-100-G126, Hughes-252. 18__. 1850s.

Rarity: URS-3
F $350

$2 • W-KY-1130-002-G030a

Back: Red-orange. ***Engraver:*** Toppan, Carpenter, Casilear & Co. / ABNCo. monogram. ***Comments:*** H-KY-100-G126c Hughes-Unlisted. Similar to W-KY-1130-002-G030 but with additional engraver imprint. 185_. 1850s.

Rarity: URS-3
F $350

$5 • W-KY-1130-005-G040

Left: 5 / Portrait of John Crittenden / 5. ***Center:*** Cattle and sheep, Herders. ***Right:*** 5 / Portrait of Mrs. John Crittenden / 5. ***Engraver:*** Toppan, Carpenter, Casilear & Co. ***Comments:*** H-KY-100-G128, Hughes-256. 18__. 1850s.

Rarity: URS-3
F $350

$5 • W-KY-1130-005-G040a

Overprint: Red FIVE. ***Engraver:*** Toppan, Carpenter, Casilear & Co. ***Comments:*** H-KY-100-G128a, Hughes-257. Similar to W-KY-1130-005-G040. 18__. 1850s.

Rarity: URS-3
F $350

$5 • W-KY-1130-005-G050

Left: Men plowing with horse / V. ***Center:*** Portraits of Mr. and Mrs. John Crittenden. ***Right:*** 5 / 5. ***Tint:*** Red-orange. ***Back:*** Red-orange. ***Engraver:*** American Bank Note Co. ***Comments:*** H-KY-100-G130a, Hughes-255. 18__. 1859.

Rarity: URS-3
F $350

$10 • W-KY-1130-010-G060

Left: 10 / Portrait of John Crittenden. ***Center:*** Portraits of Mr. and Mrs. John Crittenden. ***Engraver:*** Toppan, Carpenter, Casilear & Co. ***Comments:*** H-KY-100-G132, Hughes-Unlisted. 18__. 1850s.

Rarity: URS-3
F $350

$10 • W-KY-1130-010-G060a

Tint: Red-orange outlining white TEN. ***Engraver:*** Toppan, Carpenter, Casilear & Co. ***Comments:*** H-KY-100-G132b, Hughes-Unlisted. Similar to W-KY-1130-010-G060. 18__. 1850s.

Rarity: URS-3
F $350

$10 • W-KY-1130-010-G070

Left: 10 / Portrait of John Crittenden. ***Center:*** Woman reclining against barrel, Harvest scene / Portrait of Mrs. John Crittenden. ***Right:*** 10 / Men harvesting corn. ***Tint:*** Red-orange. ***Back:*** Red-orange. ***Engraver:*** American Bank Note Co. ***Comments:*** H-KY-100-G134a, Hughes-259. 18__. 1859.

Rarity: URS-3
F $350

$20 • W-KY-1130-020-G080

Left: Portrait of Mrs. John Crittenden / Portrait of John Crittenden. ***Center:*** 20 / Horses plowing. ***Right:*** 20. ***Engraver:*** Toppan, Carpenter, Casilear & Co. ***Comments:*** H-KY-100-G136, Hughes-261. 18__. 1850s.

Rarity: URS-3
F $350

$20 • W-KY-1130-020-G080a

Tint: Red-orange. ***Back:*** Red-orange. ***Engraver:*** American Bank Note Co. ***Comments:*** H-KY-100-G138a, Hughes-Unlisted. Similar to W-KY-1130-020-G080 but with different engraver imprint. 18__. 1859.

Rarity: URS-3
F $350

$50 • W-KY-1130-050-G090

Left: Three women with anchor. ***Center:*** 50 / Portrait of Mrs. John Crittenden. ***Right:*** 50 / Portrait of John Crittenden / 50. ***Engraver:*** Toppan, Carpenter, Casilear & Co. ***Comments:*** H-KY-100-G140, Hughes-263. 18__. 1850s.

Rarity: URS-2
F $550

$100 • W-KY-1130-100-G100

Left: 100 / Portrait of John Crittenden / 100. ***Center:*** Three women reclining / Portrait of Mrs. John Crittenden. ***Right:*** ONE HUNDRED vertically. ***Engraver:*** Toppan, Carpenter, Casilear & Co. ***Comments:*** H-KY-100-G142, Hughes-265. 18__. 1850s.

Rarity: URS-2
F $550

Non-Valid Issues

$5 • W-KY-1130-005-C040

Comments: H-KY-100-C128, Hughes-Unlisted. Counterfeit of W-KY-1130-005-G040. 18__. 1850s.

Rarity: URS-3
F $125

$5 • W-KY-1130-005-C040a

Comments: H-KY-100-C128a, Hughes-Unlisted. Counterfeit of W-KY-1130-005-G040a. 18__. 1850s.

Rarity: URS-3
F $125

$10 • W-KY-1130-010-R010

Comments: H-KY-100-R10, Hughes-262. Raised from W-KY-1130-001-G010a. 185_. 1850s.

Rarity: URS-3
F $125

New Castle, Kentucky

In 1817 the city of New Castle was incorporated.

Bank of New Castle
1818–1820
W-KY-1140

History: The Bank of New Castle was chartered on January 26, 1818. The authorized capital of $100,000 was divided into 1,000 shares of $100 each. The bank was in operation for a short time. The charters of all independent banks authorized on January 26, 1818, were revoked effective May 1, 1820.

Numismatic Commentary: Notes of this bank are very rare, with only a handful of notes known on the market.

There was an unrelated Bank of New Castle chartered years later in 1870.

Valid Issues

25¢ • W-KY-1140-00.25-G010

Left: TWENTY FIVE CENTS vertically. ***Engraver:*** Unverified, but likely Earshell & Hosielt. ***Comments:*** H-Unlisted, Hughes-622. July 10, 1818.

Rarity: URS-2
F $300

50¢ • W-KY-1140-00.50-G020 CC

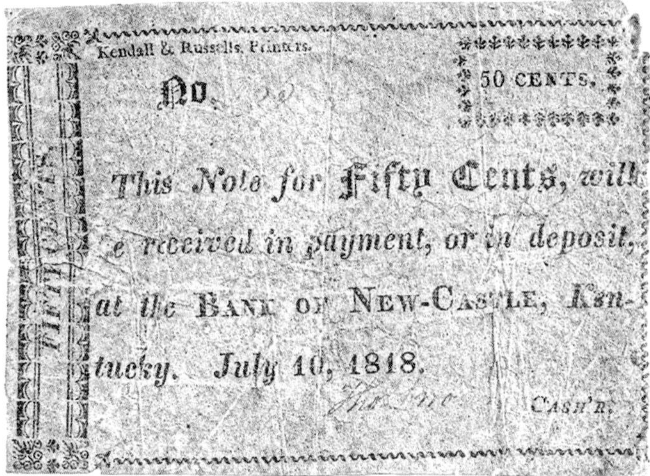

Comments: H-KY-230-G8, Hughes-623. July 10, 1818.

Rarity: URS-2
F $400

$1 • W-KY-1140-001-G030 HA

Engraver: Murray, Draper, Fairman & Co. ***Comments:*** H-KY-230-G12, Hughes-624. 181_. 1810s.

Rarity: URS-2
F $400; **Proof** $1,000
Selected auction price: Heritage Auctions, September 25, 2013, Lot 15831, Proof $998

$3 • W-KY-1140-003-G040

Left: 3 / THREE DOLLARS / 3 vertically. ***Center:*** 3 / Spread eagle with banner / 3. ***Right:*** KENTUCKY vertically. ***Engraver:*** Murray, Draper, Fairman & Co. ***Comments:*** H-KY-230-G16, Hughes-625. 181_. 1810s.

Rarity: *None known*

$5 • **W-KY-1140-005-G050** CC

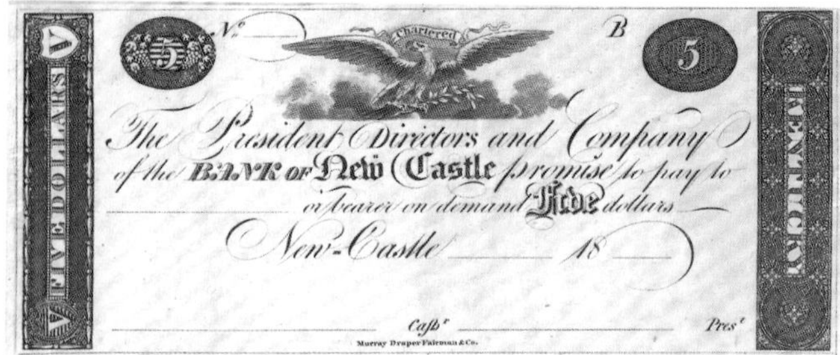

Engraver: Murray, Draper, Fairman & Co. ***Comments:*** H-KY-230-G18, Hughes-626. 18__. 1810s.

Rarity: URS-2

Proof $1,000

Selected auction price: Stack's Bowers Galleries, March 23, 2009, Proof $947

$10 • **W-KY-1140-010-G060** CC

Engraver: Murray, Draper, Fairman & Co. ***Comments:*** H-KY-230-G20, Hughes-627. 181_. 1810s.

Rarity: URS-1

Proof $1,200

NEWPORT, KENTUCKY

In 1791 James Taylor Jr. settled Newport. He named the area after Christopher Newport, who commanded the first ship to land in Jamestown, Virginia. The town was established on December 14, 1795. It was incorporated as a city on February 24, 1834.

In 1853 a bridge connected Covington and Newport. In 1866 the first bridge to span the Ohio River was built to Cincinnati.

Commercial Bank of Kentucky (branch)

1852–1860s

W-KY-1150

History: On January 3, 1852, the Commercial Bank of Kentucky was chartered. The bank closed sometime in the 1860s.

The Commercial Bank of Kentucky had its parent bank located in Paducah, W-KY-1240, and branch banks located in Cynthiana, W-KY-290, Harrodsburg, W-KY-590, Lebanon, W-KY-720, Louisville, W-KY-900, Monticello, W-KY-1070, and Versailles, W-KY-1560.

VALID ISSUES

$1 • **W-KY-1150-001-G010**

Left: ONE on 1 / ONE vertically / ONE on 1. ***Center:*** Woman seated with map, Two men in canoe. ***Right:*** 1 / Female portrait. ***Tint:*** Green. ***Engraver:*** American Bank Note Co. ***Comments:*** H-KY-255-G106a, Hughes-668. 185_. 1850s.

Rarity: URS-2

F $450

$2 • **W-KY-1150-002-G020**

Left: 2 / Female portrait. ***Center:*** Woman seated with map, Two men in canoe. ***Right:*** TWO / TWO vertically / TWO. ***Tint:*** Green. ***Engraver:*** American Bank Note Co. ***Comments:*** H-KY-255-G108a, Hughes-670. 18__. 1860s.

Rarity: URS-2

F $450

$3 • **W-KY-1150-003-G030**

Left: 3 / Boy with rabbits. ***Center:*** Woman seated with map, Two men in canoe. ***Right:*** 3 / Portrait of girl. ***Tint:*** Green. ***Engraver:*** American Bank Note Co. ***Comments:*** H-KY-255-G110a, Hughes-673. 18__. 1860s.

Rarity: URS-2

F $450

$5 • **W-KY-1150-005-G040**

Left: FIVE / Men and women in and around V. ***Center:*** 5 / Women in and around 5, Dock. ***Right:*** FIVE / Portrait of Franklin Pierce. ***Tint:*** Red-orange. ***Engraver:*** Rawdon, Wright, Hatch & Edson / ABNCo. monogram. ***Comments:*** H-KY-255-G112a, Hughes-675. 18__. 1850s–1860s.

Rarity: URS-2

F $450

$10 • **W-KY-1150-010-G050**

Left: 10 / Male portrait / TEN. ***Center:*** Steamboats. ***Right:*** TEN / Harrodsburg Springs / TEN. ***Engraver:*** Unverified, but likely Rawdon, Wright, Hatch & Edson. ***Comments:*** H-KY-255-G114, Hughes-677. 185_. 1850s.

Rarity: URS-2

F $450

Newport Bank

1818–1820

W-KY-1160

History: The Newport Bank (also sometimes seen in print as the Bank of Newport) was chartered on January 26, 1818, with an authorized capital of $200,000 to be divided into 2,000 shares of $100 each. James Taylor, Thomas D. Carneal, John McKinney, William Caldwell, and John B. Lindsey were appointed to take stock subscriptions. The bank was established by the town founder, James Taylor, and was located on the corner of Fourth and Monmouth streets. William Crawford was the cashier. The bank was in operation for a time short time only. The charters of all independent banks authorized on January 26, 1818, were revoked effective May 1, 1820.

Numismatic Commentary: James Taylor's signature appears on the $1 and $2 notes. All notes of the Newport Bank are fairly scarce, with between one and five known for each denomination.

Valid Issues

25¢ • W-KY-1160-00.25-G005

Center: 25 / 25. ***Comments:*** H-Unlisted, Hughes-Unlisted. October 14, 1818.

Rarity: URS-2
VG $450

50¢ • W-KY-1160-00.50-G010

TS

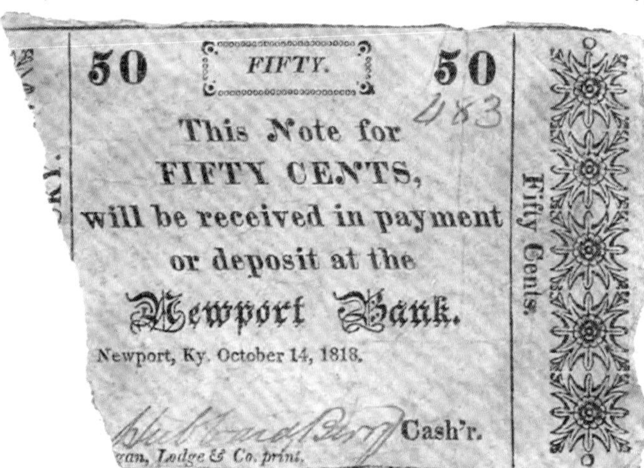

Comments: H-KY-235-G8, Hughes-630. October 14, 1818.

Rarity: URS-3
G $150; **VG** $350

$1 • W-KY-1160-001-G020

TS

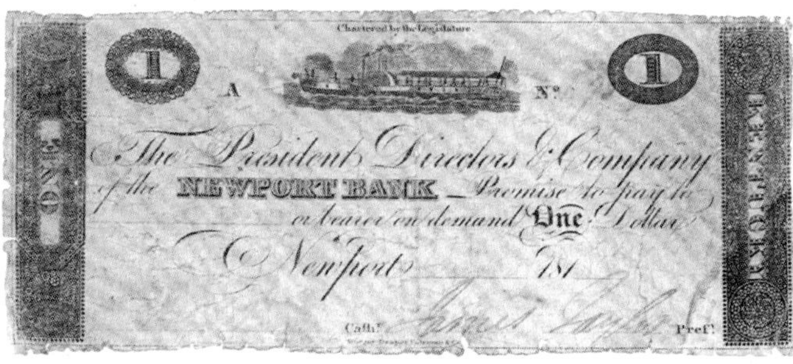

Engraver: Murray, Draper, Fairman & Co. ***Comments:*** H-KY-235-G12, Hughes-631. 181_. 1810s.

Rarity: URS-3
F $350

$2 • W-KY-1160-002-G030

TS

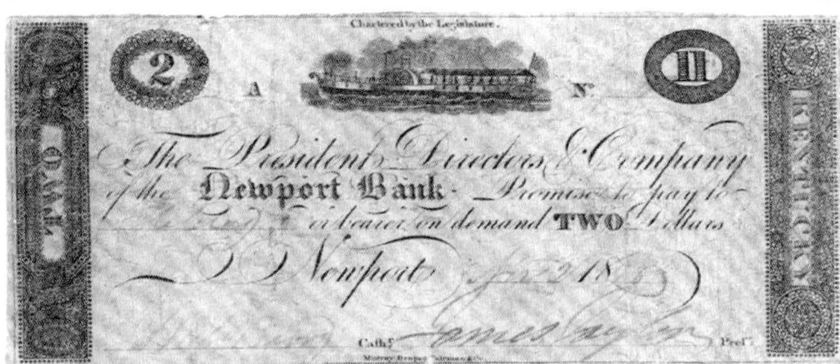

Engraver: Murray, Draper, Fairman & Co. ***Comments:*** H-KY-235-G14, Hughes-632. 18__. 1810s.

Rarity: URS-2
F $450

$5 • W-KY-1160-005-G040

TS

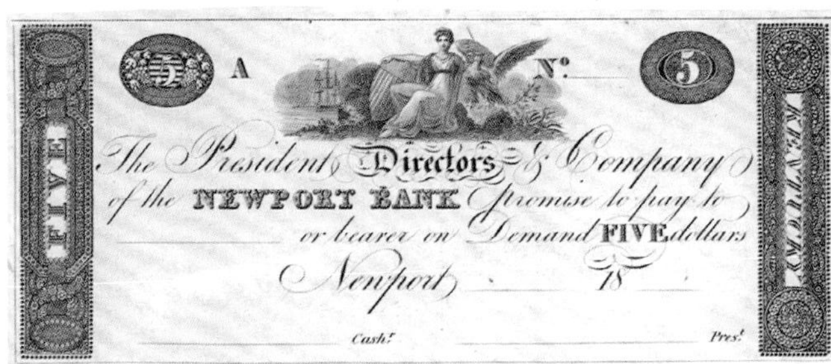

Engraver: Murray, Draper, Fairman & Co. ***Comments:*** H-KY-235-G18, Hughes-633. 18__. 1810s.

Rarity: URS-2
Proof $1,000

$10 • W-KY-1160-010-G050

TS

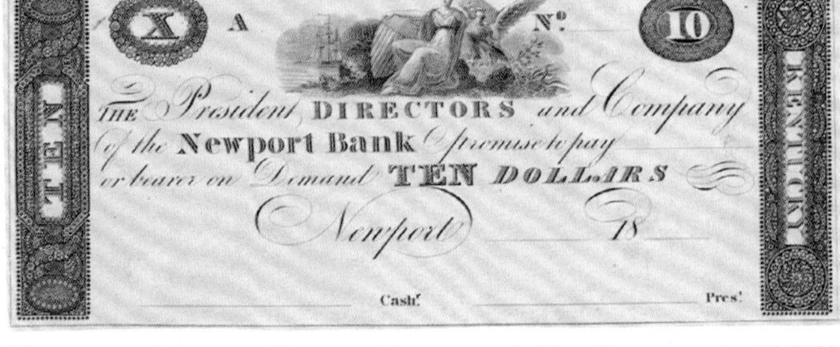

Engraver: Murray, Draper, Fairman & Co. ***Comments:*** H-KY-235-G20, Hughes-634. 18__. 1810s.

Rarity: URS-2
F $550; **Proof** $1,000

$20 • W-KY-1160-020-G060

Left: TWENTY vertically. ***Center:*** 20 / Liberty seated with eagle / 20. ***Right:*** KENTUCKY vertically. ***Engraver:*** Murray, Draper, Fairman & Co. ***Comments:*** H-KY-235-G22, Hughes-635. 18__. 1810s.

Rarity: URS-2
Proof $1,000

$50 • W-KY-1160-050-G070

Left: FIFTY vertically. ***Center:*** 50 / Liberty seated with eagle / 50. ***Right:*** KENTUCKY vertically. ***Engraver:*** Murray, Draper, Fairman & Co. ***Comments:*** H-Unlisted, Hughes-636. 18_. 1810s.

Rarity: URS-1
Proof $1,500

$100 • W-KY-1160-100-G080

TS

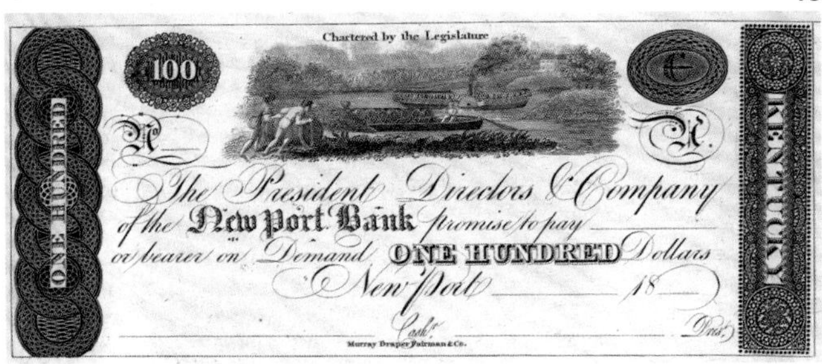

Engraver: Murray, Draper, Fairman & Co. ***Comments:*** H-Unlisted, Hughes-Unlisted. 18__. 1810s.

Rarity: URS-1
Proof $1,400

Post Notes

$__ • W-KY-1160-__-G090

TS

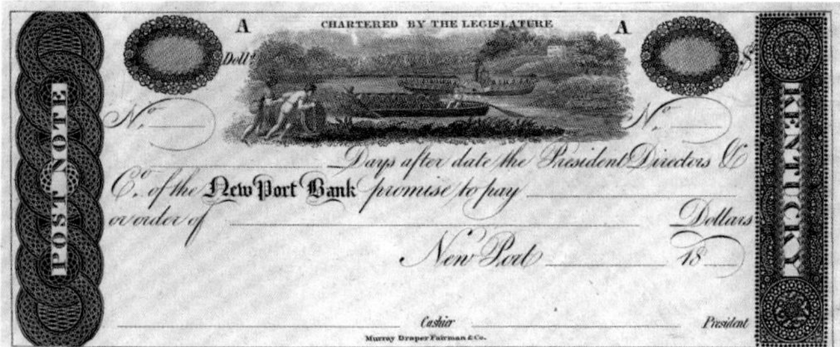

Engraver: Murray, Draper, Fairman & Co. ***Comments:*** H-Unlisted, Hughes-Unlisted. 18__. 1810s.

Rarity: URS-1
Proof $1,400

Non-Valid Issues

$20 • W-KY-1160-020-R010

CC

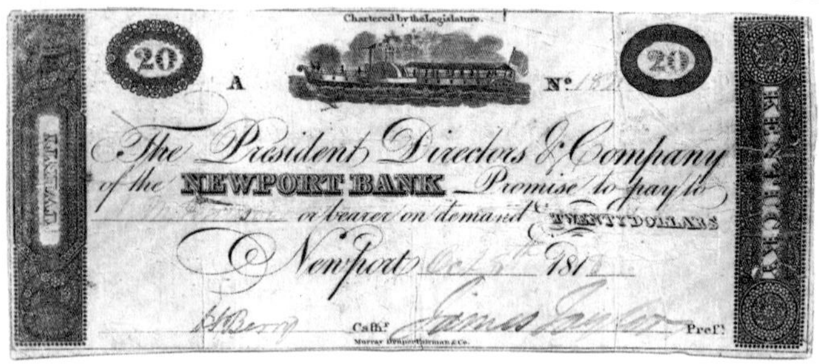

Comments: H-Unlisted, Hughes-Unlisted. Raised from $2. 1850s.

Rarity: —
Proof $300

Newport Safety Fund Bank of Kentucky

1851–1854

W-KY-1170

History: The Newport Safety Fund Bank of Kentucky was chartered on March 24, 1851, with an authorized capital of $100,000, increasable to $300,000. On January 2, 1852, the act was amended to allow the bank to issue notes of a denomination smaller than $5.

On October 17, 1854, the Newport Safety Fund Bank of Kentucky failed during a panic on all banks west of the Appalachian Mountains.

Numismatic Commentary: The notes of the Newport Safety Fund Bank of Kentucky appear from time to time in the marketplace.

Valid Issues

$1 • W-KY-1170-001-G010

TS

Engraver: Danforth, Bald & Co. ***Comments:*** H-KY-240-G2, Hughes-642. Feby. 2d, 1852.

Rarity: URS-6
VG $50; **F** $110; **VF** $150; **Proof** $600

$1 • W-KY-1170-001-G010a

CC

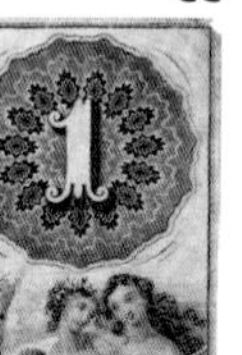

Engraver: Danforth, Bald & Co. ***Comments:*** H-KY-240-G2a. Similar to W-KY-1170-001-G010 but with different date. Feby. 2d, 185_. 1850s.

Rarity: URS-6
VG $50; **F** $100; **EF** $200; **VF** $150

$2 • W-KY-1170-002-G020

CC

Engraver: Danforth, Bald & Co. ***Comments:*** H-KY-240-G4, Hughes-643. Feby. 2d, 1852.

Rarity: URS-6
VG $50; **F** $110; **VF** $150; **Proof** $1,000
Selected auction price: Stack's Bowers Galleries, March 23, 2009, Proof $880

$2 • **W-KY-1170-002-G020a** CC

Engraver: Danforth, Bald & Co. ***Comments:*** H-KY-240-G4a. Similar to W-KY-1170-002-G020 but with different date. Feby. 2d, 185_. 1850s.

Rarity: URS-6
F $250; **EF** $300

$3 • **W-KY-1170-003-G030**

Left: 3 on medallion head / Male portrait. ***Center:*** Woman with cornucopia, Angel, Woman flying. ***Right:*** 3. ***Engraver:*** Danforth, Bald & Co. ***Comments:*** H-KY-240-G6, Hughes-644. Feby. 2d, 1852.

Rarity: URS-6
F $100; **VF** $250

$3 • **W-KY-1170-003-G030a** CC

Engraver: Danforth, Bald & Co. ***Comments:*** H-KY-240-G6a. Similar to W-KY-1170-003-G030 but with different date. Feb. 2, 185_. 1850s.

Rarity: URS-6
VG $100; **F** $150; **VF** $250; **Proof** $1,000

$5 • **W-KY-1170-005-G040** CC

Engraver: Danforth, Bald & Co. ***Comments:*** H-KY-240-G8, Hughes-645. 18__. 1850s.

Rarity: URS-6
VG $150; **F** $175; **VF** $250

$10 • **W-KY-1170-010-G050** CC

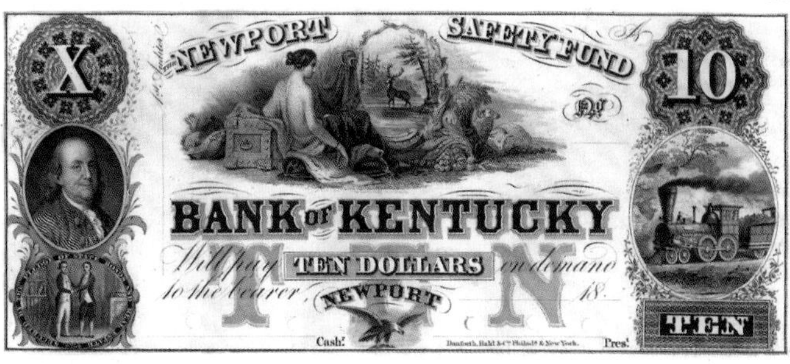

Engraver: Danforth, Bald & Co. ***Comments:*** H-KY-240-G10, Hughes-647. 18__. 1850s.

Rarity: URS-4
F $200; **Proof** $1,200
Selected auction price: Stack's Bowers Galleries, March 23, 2009, Proof $1,184

$20 • **W-KY-1170-020-G060**

Left: State arms / Portrait of Thomas Jefferson / TWENTY. ***Center:*** Wild horses running. ***Right:*** 20 / Medallion head / XX. ***Engraver:*** Danforth, Bald & Co. ***Comments:*** H-KY-240-G12, Hughes-648. 18__. 1850s.

Rarity: URS-5
F $200; **Proof** $1,200

How to Read the Whitman Numbering System

$1 • **W-AL-020-001-G010a**

Denomination: Face value of the note shown.

W: Whitman number. This number is a sortable code unique to each bank and note.

AL: Abbreviation for the state under study.

020: Numerical designation specific to each bank.

001: The denomination in dollars.

G010a: G indicates a good or valid note. Other categories are indicated thus: C (counterfeit); R (raised); S (spurious); N (not-attributed); A (altered). Numbers are assigned starting with 010, 020, et seq. Terminal letters following the number indicate variations of a note: a series of different colored overprints, tints, payees, etc., all on the same design of note. For more information, see the "How to Use This Book" section at the front of the volume, page xiv.

Uncut Sheets

$5-$5-$5-$5 • W-KY-1170-005.005.005.005-US010 RG

Engraver: Danforth, Bald & Co. ***Comments:*** H-KY-240-G8, G8, G8, G8. All four notes identical. 18__. 1850s.

Rarity: URS-3
Unc-Rem $1,500

Non-Valid Issues

$5 • W-KY-1170-005-R010

Comments: H-KY-240-R5, Hughes-646. Raised from W-KY-1170-001-G010. Feb. 2, 1852.

Rarity: URS-5
F $100

Nicholasville, Kentucky

Nicholasville was founded in 1798. It was named after Colonel George Nicholas and incorporated in 1837.

Farmers Bank of Jessamine

1818–1820

W-KY-1180

History: The Farmers Bank of Jessamine was chartered on January 26, 1818. The authorized capital of $100,000 was divided into 1,000 shares of $100 apiece. William Shreve, George Walker, Francis P. Hord, James Harvey, and Daniel B. Price were appointed to take stock subscriptions. The bank issued paper money, but by the summer of 1819 it was no longer redeeming bills. The charters of all independent banks authorized on January 26, 1818, were revoked effective May 1, 1820.

Numismatic Commentary: Only two denominations of this bank are known. It is possible low-denomination notes were also issued, but no evidence of such has appeared.

Valid Issues

$5 • W-KY-1180-005-G010 QDB

Engraver: Murray, Draper, Fairman & Co. ***Comments:*** H-Unlisted, Hughes-650. 18__. 1818.

Rarity: URS-2
Proof $1,400

$10 • W-KY-1180-010-G020 QDB

Engraver: Murray, Draper, Fairman & Co. ***Comments:*** H-Unlisted, Hughes-651. 18__. 1818.

Rarity: URS-2
Proof $1,400

Owensboro, Kentucky

William Smeathers was the first settler to arrive in Owensboro in 1797. The area was originally known as Yellow Banks. In 1817 the town was established as Owensborough, in honor of Colonel Abraham Owen. Later the name was shortened to Owensboro. Owensboro was raided in 1865 by Confederate troops.

Owensboro Deposit Bank
1860s
W-KY-1190

History: In 1861 the capital of the Owensboro Deposit Bank was $50,000. The cashier was W.B. Tyler, and the president was T.C. McCreery.

Southern Bank of Kentucky (branch)
1839–1865
W-KY-1200

History: On February 20, 1839, the Southern Bank of Kentucky was chartered with an authorized capital of $2,000,000, of which the state subscribed to half. On February 15, 1850, the charter was extended to last until 1880. The branch located in Owensboro had a capital of $300,000. James B. Anderson was the cashier, and William Bell was the president.

By 1865 the bank had been put into liquidation. On March 4, 1865, an act was passed ordering the treatment of the bank's bills to be as promissory notes rather than as currency. On January 8, 1867, the bank issued its last report regarding the closing up of its affairs. The bank building was later occupied by Nimrod, Long & Co.

The Southern Bank of Kentucky had its parent bank located in Russellville, W-KY-1400, and branch banks located in Bowling Green, W-KY-130, Carrollton, W-KY-200, Hickman, W-KY-650, Lebanon, W-KY-740, Louisville, W-KY-1000, and Smithland, W-KY-1460.

Valid Issues

$1 • W-KY-1200-001-G010

Left: 1 / Woman reclining / ONE. ***Center:*** 1 / Female portrait surrounded by implements / 1. ***Right:*** 1 / Indian man reclining / ONE. ***Engraver:*** Toppan, Carpenter, Casilear & Co. ***Comments:*** H-KY-285-G232, Hughes- 730. 18__. 1850s.

Rarity: URS-3
F $175

$1 • W-KY-1200-001-G020

Left: Man with children and horse / ONE. ***Center:*** Portrait of young girl. ***Right:*** 1 / Flock of sheep. ***Engraver:*** Toppan, Carpenter & Co. ***Comments:*** H-KY-285-G234, Hughes-728. 18__. 1850s.

Rarity: URS-3
F $175

$1 • W-KY-1200-001-G020a

Engraver: Toppan, Carpenter & Co. / ABNCo. monogram. ***Comments:*** H-KY-285-G234a, Hughes-Unlisted. Similar to W-KY-1200-001-G020 but with additional engraver imprint. 18__. 1850s–1860s.

Rarity: URS-3
F $200

$2 • W-KY-1200-002-G030

CC

Engraver: Toppan, Carpenter, Casilear & Co. ***Comments:*** H-KY-285-G238, Hughes-733. 18__. 1850s.

Rarity: URS-3
F $350

$2 • W-KY-1200-002-G040

Left: 2 / Woman seated / TWO. ***Center:*** Female portrait. ***Right:*** 2 / Man with children and horse. ***Engraver:*** Toppan, Carpenter & Co. ***Comments:*** H-KY-285-G240, Hughes-735. 18__. 1850s.

Rarity: URS-3
F $350

$2 • W-KY-1200-002-G040a

Engraver: Toppan, Carpenter & Co. / ABNCo. monogram. ***Comments:*** H-KY-285-G240a, Hughes-Unlisted. Similar to W-KY-1200-002-G040 but with additional engraver imprint. 18__. 1850s–1860s.

Rarity: URS-2
F $450

$3 • W-KY-1200-003-G050

Left: 3 / Female portrait / 3. ***Center:*** Woman with eagle. ***Bottom center:*** Steamboat. ***Right:*** 3 / Three women standing / THREE. ***Engraver:*** Toppan, Carpenter, Casilear & Co. ***Comments:*** H-KY-285-G244, Hughes-739. 18__. 1850s.

Rarity: URS-3
F $350

$3 • W-KY-1200-003-G060

Left: 3 / Portrait of George Washington. ***Center:*** Portrait of young girl / Man with children and horse. ***Right:*** 3 / 3. ***Engraver:*** Toppan, Carpenter & Co. ***Comments:*** H-KY-285-G246, Hughes-737. 18__. 1850s–1860s.

Rarity: URS-3
F $350

$3 • W-KY-1200-003-G060a

Engraver: Toppan, Carpenter & Co. / ABNCo. monogram. ***Comments:*** H-KY-285-G246a, Hughes-Unlisted. Similar to W-KY-1200-003-G060 but with additional engraver imprint. 18__. 1850s–1860s.

Rarity: URS-2
F $450

$5 • W-KY-1200-005-G070

Left: 5 / Female portrait / 5. ***Center:*** Man on horse. ***Right:*** 5 / Woman standing with flag. ***Engraver:*** Toppan, Carpenter, Casilear & Co. ***Comments:*** H-KY-285-G250, Hughes-742. 18__. 1850s.

Rarity: URS-3
F $350

$5 • W-KY-1200-005-G080

Left: 5 / Portrait of boy. ***Center:*** Man on horse in farmyard. ***Right:*** V / Portrait of young girl. ***Overprint:*** Red FIVE. ***Engraver:*** Bald, Cousland & Co. / Baldwin, Bald & Cousland. ***Comments:*** H-KY-285-G252a, Hughes-745. 18__. 1850s.

Rarity: URS-3
F $350

$10 • W-KY-1200-010-G090 CC

Engraver: Toppan, Carpenter, Casilear & Co. ***Comments:*** H-KY-285-G256, Hughes-747. 18__. 1850s.

Rarity: URS-3
F $250

$10 • W-KY-1200-010-G100

Left: 10 / Woman seated. ***Center:*** Man, woman, child, dog, Haying scene. ***Right:*** 10 / Woman seated. ***Overprint:*** Red TEN. ***Engraver:*** Bald, Cousland & Co. / Baldwin, Bald & Cousland. ***Comments:*** H-KY-285-G258a, Hughes-750. 18__. 1850s.

Rarity: URS-3
F $350

Non-Valid Issues

$1 • W-KY-1200-001-C010

Comments: H-KY-285-C232, Hughes-731. Counterfeit of W-KY-1200-001-G010. 18__. 1850s.

Rarity: URS-4
F $100

$1 • W-KY-1200-001-C020a

Comments: H-KY-285-C234a, Hughes-729. Counterfeit of W-KY-1200-001-G020a. 18__. 1850s–1860s.

Rarity: URS-4
F $100

$3 • W-KY-1200-003-C050

Comments: H-KY-185-C244, Hughes-740. Counterfeit of W-KY-1200-003-G050. 18__. 1850s.

Rarity: URS-4
F $100

$3 • W-KY-1200-003-C060a

Comments: H-KY-285-C246a, Hughes-738. Counterfeit of W-KY-1200-003-G060a. 18__. 1850s–1860s.

Rarity: URS-4
F $100

Owingsville, Kentucky

Owingsville was established in 1811 and incorporated in 1829. It was laid out on land donated by Richard Menefee and Thomas Dye Owings.

Bank of Owingsville

1818–1820

W-KY-1210

History: The Bank of Owingsville was chartered on January 26, 1818, with an authorized capital of $100,000 to be divided into 1,000 shares of $100 apiece. Thompson Ward, Thomas D. Owings, James McIlhaney, Daniel Connor, James M. Graham, Alexander Lackey, and James Sanders were appointed to take stock subscriptions. The bank was in operation for a short time, but the charters of all independent banks authorized on January 26, 1818, were revoked effective May 1, 1820.

Numismatic Commentary: Two notes of this bank are known today.

Valid Issues

25¢ • W-KY-1210-00.25-G010

Comments: H-KY-250-G8, Hughes-657. 1818–1820.

Rarity: URS-1
F $500

50¢ • W-KY-1210-00.50-G020

Comments: H-KY-250-G10, Hughes-658. No description available. 1818–1820.

Rarity: *None known*

$1 • W-KY-1210-001-G030

Left: I / I. ***Center:*** 1 / Three women holding shield bearing I, Buildings and boat / 1. ***Right:*** KENTUCKY vertically. ***Engraver:*** Murray, Draper, Fairman & Co. ***Comments:*** H-KY-250-G12, Hughes-659. 181_. 1818–1820.

Rarity: *None known*

$2 • W-KY-1210-002-G040

Left: II / II. ***Center:*** 2 / Three women holding shield bearing II, Buildings and boat / 2. ***Right:*** KENTUCKY vertically. ***Engraver:*** Murray, Draper, Fairman & Co. ***Comments:*** H-KY-250-G14, Hughes-660. 181_. 1818–1820.

Rarity: *None known*

$5 • W-KY-1210-005-G050

Left: V / V. ***Center:*** 5 / Three women holding shield bearing V, Buildings and boat / 5. ***Right:*** KENTUCKY vertically. ***Engraver:*** Murray, Draper, Fairman & Co. ***Comments:*** H-KY-250-G16, Hughes-661. 181_. 1818–1820.

Rarity: *None known*

$10 • W-KY-1210-010-G060
Left: X / X. ***Center:*** 10 / Three women holding shield bearing X, Buildings and boat / 10. ***Right:*** KENTUCKY vertically. ***Engraver:*** Murray, Draper, Fairman & Co. ***Comments:*** H-KY-250-G18, Hughes-662. 181_. 1818–1820.

Rarity: *None known*

$15 • W-KY-1210-015-G070
Left: XV / XV. ***Center:*** 15 / Three women holding shield bearing XV, Buildings and boat / 15. ***Right:*** KENTUCKY vertically. ***Engraver:*** Murray, Draper, Fairman & Co. ***Comments:*** H-KY-250-G20, Hughes-663. 181_. 1818–1820.

Rarity: URS-1
F $500

Paducah, Kentucky

First known and settled as Pekin, the town of Paducah was laid out by William Clark in 1827, when it was renamed Paducah. In 1830 it was incorporated as a town, and in 1838 it was established as a city. Steamboats used the rivers and ports to bring trade and commerce to the area, and railways began to be laid through the town. At this time there was a brick factory, a foundry, and facilities for steamboats, tow boats, and barges. Coalfields were also located nearby, making Paducah a hub for the Illinois Central Railroad.

Paducah remained under Union control for the majority of the Civil War, at which time it was an important supply depot for the Union army.

Bank of Kentucky {2nd} (branch)

1834–1866
W-KY-1220

History: The second Bank of Kentucky (sometimes seen in print as the "New" Bank of Kentucky) was chartered in 1834 in order to assume the business of the first Bank of Kentucky, W-KY-420, which had recently closed. The capital of the bank was $5,000,000. The branch in Paducah was established in 1834. In January 1866 almost all branches of the Bank of Kentucky were closed down, and the parent bank began winding up its business.

The second Bank of Kentucky had its parent bank located in Louisville, W-KY-850, and branch banks located in Bowling Green, W-KY-080, Burksville, W-KY-140, Columbus, W-KY-220, Danville, W-KY-330, Flemingsburg, W-KY-390, Frankfort, W-KY-430, Glasgow, W-KY-510, Greensburg, W-KY-540, Hopkinsville, W-KY-670, Lexington, W-KY-770, Maysville, W-KY-1020, and Mount Sterling, W-KY-1100.

Numismatic Commentary: Notes of this bank and its branches are very rare.

Valid Issues

$5 • W-KY-1220-005-G010
Left: 5 / Portrait of Henry Clay / FIVE. ***Center:*** Portrait of John Q. Adams / Woman seated against bales, Train, Harvesting scene / Portrait of Thomas Jefferson. ***Right:*** 5 / Portrait of George Washington / FIVE. ***Engraver:*** Toppan, Carpenter & Co. ***Comments:*** H-KY-195-G380, Hughes-494. 18__. 1840s–1850s.

Rarity: URS-3
F $350

$10 • W-KY-1220-010-G020
Left: 10 / Portrait of George Washington / 10. ***Center:*** Portrait of Andrew Jackson / Indian man and woman flanking shield bearing 10 surmounted by eagle / Portrait of Isaac Shelby. ***Right:*** 10 / Portrait of Henry Clay / 10. ***Engraver:*** Toppan, Carpenter & Co. ***Comments:*** H-KY-195-G384, Hughes-499. 18__. 1840s–1850s.

Rarity: URS-3
F $350

$20 • W-KY-1220-020-G030
Left: 20 / Portrait of Daniel Webster. ***Center:*** "General Marion's Sweet Potato Dinner." ***Right:*** 20 / Male portrait. ***Engraver:*** Toppan, Carpenter & Co. ***Comments:*** H-KY-195-G388, Hughes-511. 18__. 1850s.

Rarity: URS-3
F $350

Non-Valid Issues

$10 • W-KY-1220-010-C020
Comments: H-KY-195-C384, Hughes-500. Counterfeit of W-KY-1220-010-G020. 18__. 1840s–1850s.

Rarity: URS-4
F $250

Bank of Louisville (branch)

1845–1860s
W-KY-1230

History: In 1833 the Bank of Louisville was chartered with an authorized capital of $5,000,000. In 1845 the branch located in Paducah was opened with a capital of $200,000. Its building was established on First Street. James Campbell was the president, accompanied by Adam Rankin as cashier. In 1857 S.B. Hughes took the position of cashier after the death of Rankin.

During the 1860s the Bank of Louisville closed its doors. Later it was absorbed by the Southern National Bank in 1899.

The Bank of Louisville had its parent bank located in Louisville, W-KY-860, and branch banks located in Burksville, W-KY-150, and Flemingsburg, W-KY-400.

Valid Issues

$1 • W-KY-1230-001-G010
Left: ONE vertically. ***Center:*** 1 / 1. ***Right:*** ONE / Portrait of Henry Clay / ONE. ***Engraver:*** Draper, Toppan, Longacre & Co. ***Comments:*** H-KY-190-G80, Hughes-525. 18__. 1840s.

Rarity: URS-3
F $350

$1 • W-KY-1230-001-G015

CC

Tint: Yellow microlettering and panel outlining white ONE. ***Engraver:*** Wellstood, Hay & Whiting. ***Comments:*** H-KY-190-G82, Hughes-527. Printed with blue ink. 1840s–1850s.

Rarity: URS-2
F $550

Selected auction price: Stack's Bowers Galleries, November 18, 2011, Lot 7170, F $535

$2 • W-KY-1230-002-G020

Left: 2. ***Center:*** 2 / 2 / Woman leaning on column. ***Right:*** TWO / Woman with shield / TWO. ***Engraver:*** Draper, Toppan, Longacre & Co. ***Comments:*** H-KY-190-G84, Hughes-529. 18__. 1840s.

Rarity: URS-3
F $350

$3 • W-KY-1230-003-G030

Left: 3. ***Center:*** 3 / Steamboat / 3. ***Right:*** THREE / Woman standing / THREE. ***Engraver:*** Draper, Toppan, Longacre & Co. ***Comments:*** H-KY-190-G86, Hughes-530. 18__. 1840s.

Rarity: URS-3
F $350

$5 • W-KY-1230-005-G040

Left: FIVE / Woman standing in V with wand, bale, and barrel. ***Center:*** 5 / Eagle standing on sheep, Wheel, Ships / 5. ***Right:*** FIVE / Woman standing in 5 / 5. ***Back:*** Train. ***Engraver:*** Unverified, but likely Draper, Toppan & Co. ***Comments:*** H-KY-190-G90, Hughes-533. 18__. 1840s.

Rarity: URS-3
F $200

$5 • W-KY-1230-005-G050

CC

Engraver: Toppan, Carpenter, Casilear & Co. ***Comments:*** H-KY-190-G92, Hughes-534. 18__. 1850s.

Rarity: URS-3
F $350

$10 • W-KY-1230-010-G060

CC

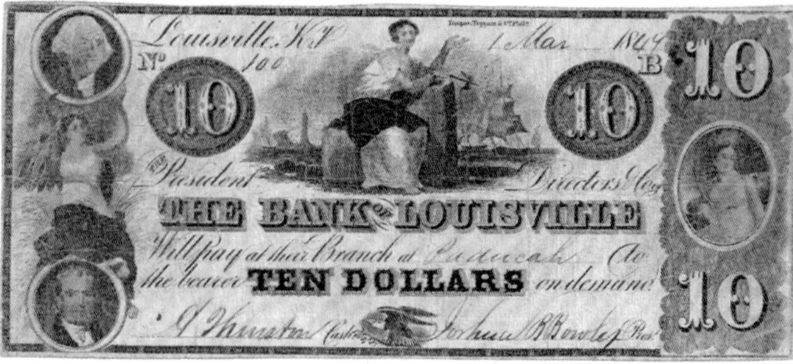

Engraver: Draper, Toppan & Co. ***Comments:*** H-KY-190-G96, Hughes-539. 18__. 1840s.

Rarity: URS-3
F $350

$20 • W-KY-1230-020-G070

Left: 20 / Indian men hunting buffalo. ***Center:*** Female portrait. ***Right:*** 20 / Man cutting down tree, Oxen, two children. ***Engraver:*** Unverified, but likely Draper, Toppan & Co. ***Comments:*** H-KY-190-G100, Hughes-547. 18__. 1840s.

Rarity: URS-3
F $350

Non-Valid Issues

$5 • W-KY-1230-005-C050

Comments: H-KY-190-C92, Hughes-535. Counterfeit of W-KY-1230-005-G050. 18__. 1850s.

Rarity: URS-3
F $350

$10 • W-KY-1230-010-C060

Comments: H-KY-190-C96, Hughes-540. Counterfeit of W-KY-1230-010-G060. 18__. 1840s.

Rarity: URS-3
F $350

Commercial Bank of Kentucky

1852–1860s

W-KY-1240

History: On January 3, 1852, the Commercial Bank of Kentucky was chartered. The bank building was established at the corner of Third and Broadway streets. L.M. Flournoy was the president, and James. M. Dallam was the cashier. In 1855 the authorized capital was $200,000. By 1860 this had increased to $400,000. In 1862 the total capital of the bank was $1,745,000, and circulation was $1,040,000. By 1863 the circulation had risen to $1,701,417.

The Commercial Bank of Kentucky closed sometime in the 1860s.

The Commercial Bank of Kentucky had branch banks located in Cynthiana, W-KY-290, Harrodsburg, W-KY-590, Lebanon, W-KY-720, Louisville, W-KY-900, Monticello, W-KY-1070, Newport, W-KY-1150, and Versailles, W-KY-1560.

Numismatic Commentary: It is rare indeed that notes of this bank come on the market.

Remaining at the American Bank Note Co. archives as of 2003 was a $1-$1 face plate, two $1-$1-$1-$1 face plates, a $1-$1-$2-$3 face plate, two $1-$1-$2-$3 tint plates, and a $5-$5-$10-$20 face plate.

VALID ISSUES

$1 • W-KY-1240-001-G010

Left: ONE / Steamboat vertically / ONE. ***Center:*** Coin, Man kneeling next to hewn log. ***Right:*** 1 / Male portrait / ONE. ***Engraver:*** Rawdon, Wright, Hatch & Edson. ***Comments:*** H-KY-255-G2, Hughes-664. 185_. 1850s.

Rarity: URS-3
F $350

$1 • W-KY-1240-001-G020

HA

Tint: Green dies outlining white 1s and ONE. ***Engraver:*** American Bank Note Co. ***Comments:*** H-KY-255-G6a, Hughes-667. 18__. 1850s.

Rarity: URS-3
VF $1,000

$2 • W-KY-1240-002-G030

Comments: H-Unlisted, Hughes-Unlisted. No description available. 18__. 1850s.

Rarity: *None known*

$3 • W-KY-1240-003-G040

HA

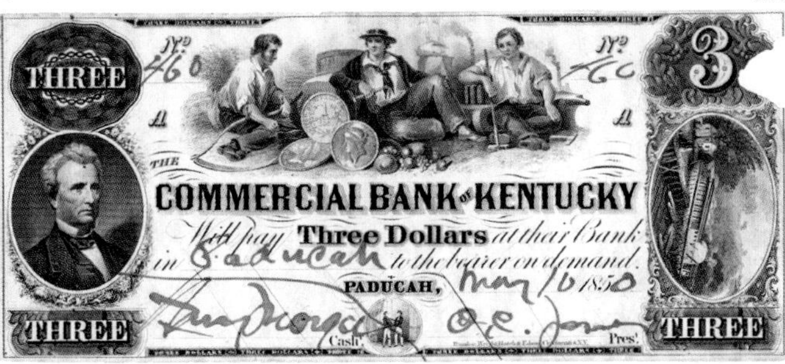

Engraver: Rawdon, Wright, Hatch & Edson. ***Comments:*** H-KY-255-G8, Hughes-672. 185_. 1850s.

Rarity: URS-3
VF $350

$5 • W-KY-1240-005-G050

Left: 5 / Portrait of Millard Fillmore / FIVE. ***Center:*** Woman and man flanking three cherubs and five coins. ***Right:*** FIVE / Scene vertically / FIVE. ***Engraver:*** Rawdon, Wright, Hatch & Edson. ***Comments:*** H-KY-255-G12, Hughes-674. 185_. 1850s.

Rarity: URS-3
F $200; **Proof** $1,100

$5 • W-KY-1240-005-G060

CC

Tint: Red lathework outlining white FIVE and panels. ***Engraver:*** Rawdon, Wright, Hatch & Edson / ABNCo. monogram. ***Comments:*** H-KY-255-G14a, Hughes-675. 185_. 1850s–1860s.

Rarity: URS-3
F $200; **Proof** $1,100

$10 • W-KY-1240-010-G070

Left: 10 / Male portrait / TEN. ***Center:*** Steamboats. ***Right:*** TEN / Harrodsburg Springs / TEN. ***Engraver:*** Unverified, but likely Rawdon, Wright, Hatch & Edson. ***Comments:*** H-KY-255-G16, Hughes-677. 185_. 1850s.

Rarity: URS-3
F $350

$20 • W-KY-1240-020-G080

Left: XX / Male portrait / TWENTY. ***Center:*** Woodcutter, stump, Men fishing, Oxen, horse. ***Right:*** XX / Steamboat on stocks / TWENTY. ***Engraver:*** Unverified, but likely Rawdon, Wright, Hatch & Edson. ***Comments:*** H-KY-255-G18, Hughes-678. 185_. 1850s.

Rarity: URS-3
F $350

$20 • W-KY-1240-020-G090

Left: 20 / Harrodsburg Springs / TWENTY. ***Center:*** Woman reclining with strongbox, Shield, Milkmaids, cattle, Train. ***Right:*** XX / Portrait of Henry Clay / TWENTY. ***Engraver:*** Unverified, but likely Rawdon, Wright, Hatch & Edson. ***Comments:*** H-KY-255-G20, Hughes-679. 185_. 1850s.

Rarity: URS-3
F $350

$50 • W-KY-1240-050-G100

Left: 50 / Portrait of Henry Clay / FIFTY. ***Center:*** 50 / Liberty with eagle, globe, Ships. ***Right:*** 50 / Portrait of John Crittenden / FIFTY. ***Engraver:*** Unverified, but likely Rawdon, Wright, Hatch & Edson. ***Comments:*** H-KY-255-G22, Hughes-681. 185_. 1850s.

Rarity: URS-2
F $450

$100 • W-KY-1240-100-G110

Left: 100 / Male portrait / 100. ***Center:*** 100 / Indians trading with settlers. ***Right:*** 100 / Male portrait / 100. ***Engraver:*** Unverified, but likely Rawdon, Wright, Hatch & Edson. ***Comments:*** H-KY-255-G24, Hughes-682. 185_. 1850s.

Rarity: URS-2
F $450

Notes on Which the Place Payable is Blank

$1 • W-KY-1240-001-G120

Left: ONE / Steamboat vertically / ONE. ***Center:*** Coin, Man kneeling next to hewn log. ***Right:*** 1 / Male portrait / ONE. ***Engraver:*** Rawdon, Wright, Hatch & Edson. ***Comments:*** H-KY-255-G136. 185_. 1850s.

Rarity: —

$3 • W-KY-1240-003-G130

Left: THREE / Male portrait / THREE. ***Center:*** Three gold dollars, Farmer with scythe, Blacksmith, Sailor. ***Right:*** 3 / Steamboat on stocks. ***Engraver:*** Rawdon, Wright, Hatch & Edson. ***Comments:*** H-KY-255-G138. 185_. 1850s.

Rarity: —

$5 • W-KY-1240-005-G140

Left: 5 / Portrait of Millard Fillmore / FIVE. ***Center:*** Woman and man flanking three cherubs and five coins. ***Right:*** FIVE / Scene vertically / FIVE. ***Engraver:*** Rawdon, Wright, Hatch & Edson. ***Comments:*** H-KY-255-G140. 185_. 1850s.

Rarity: —

$5 • W-KY-1240-005-G150

Left: FIVE / Men and women in and around V. ***Center:*** 5 / Women in and around 5, Dock. ***Right:*** FIVE / Portrait of Franklin Pierce. ***Tint:*** Red-orange. ***Engraver:*** Rawdon, Wright, Hatch & Edson / ABNCo. monogram. ***Comments:*** H-KY-255-G142a. 18__. 1850s–1860s.

Rarity: —

$10 • W-KY-1240-010-G160

Left: 10 / Male portrait / TEN. ***Center:*** Steamboats. ***Right:*** TEN / Harrodsburg Springs / TEN. ***Engraver:*** Unverified, but likely Rawdon, Wright, Hatch & Edson. ***Comments:*** H-KY-255-G204. 185_. 1850s.

Rarity: —

$20 • W-KY-1240-020-G170

Left: XX / Male portrait / TWENTY. ***Center:*** Woodcutter, stump, Men fishing, Oxen, horse. ***Right:*** XX / Steamboat on stocks / TWENTY. ***Engraver:*** Unverified, but likely Rawdon, Wright, Hatch & Edson. ***Comments:*** H-KY-255-G146. 185_. 1850s.

Rarity: —

$20 • W-KY-1240-020-G180

Left: 20 / Harrodsburg Springs / TWENTY. ***Center:*** Woman reclining with strongbox, Shield, Milkmaids, cattle, Train. ***Right:*** XX / Portrait of Henry Clay / TWENTY. ***Engraver:*** Unverified, but likely Rawdon, Wright, Hatch & Edson. ***Comments:*** H-KY-255-G148. 185_. 1850s.

Rarity: —

$50 • W-KY-1240-050-G190

Left: 50 / Portrait of Henry Clay / FIFTY. ***Center:*** 50 / Liberty with eagle, globe, Ships. ***Right:*** 50 / Portrait of John Crittenden / FIFTY. ***Engraver:*** Unverified, but likely Rawdon, Wright, Hatch & Edson. ***Comments:*** H-KY-255-G150. 185_. 1850s.

Rarity: —

$100 • W-KY-1240-100-G200

Left: 100 / Male portrait / 100. ***Center:*** 100 / Indians trading with settlers. ***Right:*** 100 / Male portrait / 100. ***Engraver:*** Unverified, but likely Rawdon, Wright, Hatch & Edson. ***Comments:*** H-KY-255-G152. 185_. 1850s.

Rarity: —

Non-Valid Issues

$2 • W-KY-1240-002-S010

Left: TWO / Portrait of Daniel Webster / TWO. ***Center:*** 2 / Sailing ship / 2. ***Right:*** TWO / Ship / TWO. ***Comments:*** H-KY-255-S5, Hughes-671. From a modified, fraudulent plate originally for a spurious $2 of the Merchants Bank, Newburyport, Massachusetts. 1850s.

Rarity: URS-3
F $100

$5 • W-KY-1240-005-A010

Left: FIVE / Woman standing. ***Center:*** 5 / Farm scene, Buildings / V. ***Right:*** FIVE / Woman. ***Comments:*** H-KY-255-A5, Hughes-676. Altered from $5 Commercial Bank of Millington, Millington, Maryland. 1850s.

Rarity: URS-3
VG $70; **F** $110

Peoples Bank of Kentucky (branch)

1856–1860s

W-KY-1250

History: The Peoples Bank of Kentucky was chartered on February 15, 1856, with an authorized capital of $250,000. Later, the bank in Bowling Green, W-KY-100, moved to Louisville, W-KY-970, and the old parent location became a branch, W-KY-110. The bank closed up sometime in the 1860s.

The Peoples Bank of Kentucky had its parent banks located first in Bowling Green, W-KY-100, then in Louisville, W-KY-970, and branch banks located in Bowling Green, W-KY-110, and Hartford, W-KY-620.

Paris, Kentucky

The first settler in the area that would later become Paris was Joseph Houston, who built a station in 1776. Land-grant issues forced him to depart, but in 1786 Lawrence Protzman purchased the area. He laid out the town and offered it for public use as long as the town became the seat of Bourbon County. In 1789 the town was officially established as Hopewell. The next year it was renamed Paris. It was incorporated as a town in 1839.

Bank of Kentucky {1st} (branch)

1815–1822

W-KY-1260

History: The Bank of Kentucky (sometimes seen later in print as the "Old" Bank of Kentucky) was incorporated on December 27, 1806, with an authorized capital of $1,000,000. Half of the capital was subscribed to by the state.

The Paris branch was opened in 1815. On January 21, 1822, the bank was ordered to start closing up its branches. This was to be completed by May 1, 1824. This act essentially shut down the bank. Curiously, all of the paperwork was not completed until the 1870s.

The first Bank of Kentucky had its parent bank located in Frankfort, W-KY-420, and branch banks located in Bardstown, W-KY-050, Danville, W-KY-320, Glasgow, W-KY-500, Hopkinsville, W-KY-660, Lexington, W-KY-760, Louisville, W-KY-840, Richmond, W-KY-1350, Russellville, W-KY-1380, Shelbyville, W-KY-1430, Springfield, W-KY-1500, Washington, W-KY-1570, and Winchester, W-KY-1580.

Valid Issues

$1 • W-KY-1260-001-G010

Left: BRANCH BANK vertically. *Center:* 1 / Running deer, plow, ax / 1. *Right:* 1 / ONE / 1 vertically. *Engraver:* Unverified, but likely Murray, Draper, Fairman & Co. *Comments:* H-KY-110-G168, Hughes-283. 18__. 1816.

Rarity: URS-2
F $550

$1 • W-KY-1260-001-G020

Engraver: Murray, Draper, Fairman & Co. *Comments:* H-KY-110-G170, Hughes-Unlisted. No description available. 18__. 1821.

Rarity: *None known*

$5 • W-KY-1260-005-G030

Engraver: Unverified, but likely W. Harrison. *Comments:* H-KY-110-G172, Hughes-Unlisted. No description available. 18__. 1810s.

Rarity: *None known*

$10 • W-KY-1260-010-G040

Engraver: Unverified, but likely W. Harrison. *Comments:* H-KY-110-G174, Hughes-Unlisted. No description available. 18__. 1810s–1820.

Rarity: *None known*

$20 • W-KY-1260-020-G050

Engraver: Unverified, but likely W. Harrison. *Comments:* H-KY-110-G176, Hughes-Unlisted. No description available. 18__. 1810s.

Rarity: *None known*

$50 • W-KY-1260-050-G060

Engraver: Unverified, but likely W. Harrison. *Comments:* H-KY-110-G178, Hughes-Unlisted. No description available. 18__. 1810s.

Rarity: *None known*

$100 • W-KY-1260-100-G070

Engraver: Unverified, but likely W. Harrison. *Comments:* H-KY-110-G180, Hughes-Unlisted. No description available. 18__. 1810s.

Rarity: *None known*

Post Notes

$__ • W-KY-1260-__-G080

Left: POST NOTE vertically. *Center:* __ / Cherub riding leaping deer / __. *Right:* POST NOTE vertically. *Engraver:* Murray, Draper, Fairman & Co. *Comments:* H-KY-110-G182. 18__. 1810s.

Rarity: URS-2
F $550

Deposit Bank

1860s

W-KY-1270

History: A congressional report of 1860 stated that the Deposit Bank had not issued paper money by that time. In 1861 the Deposit Bank had a capital of $50,000. The cashier was H.W. Rucker, and the president was George W. Williams. By 1863 circulation was $388,057. In 1864 the president was Charles V. Higgins.

Northern Bank of Kentucky (branch)

1835–1860s

W-KY-1280

History: The Northern Bank of Kentucky was chartered in 1835 with an authorized capital of $3,000,000. The Paris branch was established immediately. In 1848 the president was John B. Raine, and the cashier was Thomas Y. Brent. At that time the capital was $370,000. This value remained constant through the life of the branch. In 1860 the president of the bank was Charlton Alexander, and the cashier was Thomas Kelly. By 1864 the president was Robert T. Davis, and Alexander had taken the role of cashier.

Sometime during the 1860s the Northern Bank of Kentucky was converted to a bank of discount and deposit, after which time no notes were issued.

The Northern Bank of Kentucky had its parent bank located in Lexington, W-KY-830, and branch banks located in Barbourville, W-KY-040, Covington, W-KY-260, Cynthiana, W-KY-305, Glasgow, W-KY-520, Louisville, W-KY-960, and Richmond, W-KY-1360.

Valid Issues

$1 • W-KY-1280-001-G010

Left: Portrait of George Washington / ONE / Portrait of Henry Clay. *Center:* 1 / Woman seated against bales, Cattle, Train. *Right:* 1 / Portrait of Rachel Jackson / 1. *Engraver:* Toppan, Carpenter & Co. *Comments:* H-KY-175-G230, Hughes-435. 18__. 1840s.

Rarity: URS-3
F $150

$1 • W-KY-1280-001-G020

Left: Portrait of Henry Clay / 1. *Center:* Woman seated against bales, Cattle, Train / Female portrait. *Right:* 1 / Portrait of George Washington. *Engraver:* Toppan, Carpenter, Casilear & Co. *Comments:* H-KY-175-G232, Hughes-433. 18__. 1850s.

Rarity: URS-3
F $150

Collectors and Researchers:

If you have new information about any banks or notes listed in this volume, contact Whitman Publishing, Attn: Obsolete Paper Money, 3101 Clairmont Road, Suite G, Atlanta, GA 30329.

$1 • W-KY-1280-001-G030

Left: 1 / Portrait of boy. ***Center:*** Men with cattle, Sheep. ***Right:*** 1 / Portrait of girl. ***Tint:*** Red-orange. ***Engraver:*** American Bank Note Co. ***Comments:*** H-KY-175-G234, Hughes-436. 18__. 1850s–1860s.

Rarity: URS-3
F $150

$5 • W-KY-1280-005-G040

Left: FIVE vertically. ***Center:*** 5 / Train / 5. ***Right:*** FIVE vertically. ***Engraver:*** Casilear, Durand, Burton & Edmonds. ***Comments:*** H-KY-175-G238, Hughes-442. 18__. 1830s.

Rarity: URS-3
F $350

$5 • W-KY-1280-005-G050

Left: FIVE vertically. ***Center:*** 5 / Woman standing, Train / 5. ***Right:*** FIVE vertically. ***Engraver:*** Draper, Toppan & Co. ***Comments:*** H-KY-175-G240, Hughes-Unlisted. 18__. 1840s.

Rarity: URS-2
F $450

$5 • W-KY-1280-005-G060

CC

Tint: Red-orange bank title and dies outlining white 5 / 5. ***Engraver:*** Toppan, Carpenter & Co. ***Comments:*** H-KY-175-G242, Hughes-444. 18__. 1840s–1850s.

Rarity: URS-3
F $350

$5 • W-KY-1280-005-G070

Left: 5 / FIVE vertically. ***Center:*** Portrait of Henry Clay / Woman seated against bales, Cattle, Train / Male portrait. ***Right:*** 5 / FIVE vertically. ***Tint:*** Red-orange. ***Engraver:*** American Bank Note Co. ***Comments:*** H-KY-175-G244, Hughes-445. 18__. 1850s–1860s.

Rarity: URS-3
F $350

$10 • W-KY-1280-010-G080

CC

Engraver: Casilear, Durand, Burton & Edmonds. ***Comments:*** H-KY-175-G246, Hughes-446. 18__. 1830s.

Rarity: URS-3
F $350

$10 • W-KY-1280-010-G090

Left: 10 / TEN vertically / 10. ***Center:*** Female portrait / Train, Woman seated / Female portrait. ***Right:*** 10 / TEN vertically / 10. ***Engraver:*** Draper, Toppan & Co. ***Comments:*** H-KY-175-G248, Hughes-Unlisted. 18__. 1840s.

Rarity: URS-2
F $450

$10 • W-KY-1280-010-G100

Left: X / 10 / X. ***Center:*** Portrait of George Washington / Woman seated against bales, Cattle, Train / Portrait of Henry Clay. ***Right:*** X / 10 / X. ***Engraver:*** Toppan, Carpenter & Co. ***Comments:*** H-KY-175-G250, Hughes-447. 18__. 1840s–1850s.

Rarity: URS-3
F $350

$10 • W-KY-1280-010-G110

Left: Portrait of George Washington / 10. ***Center:*** Portrait of George Washington / Woman seated against bales, Cattle, Train / Portrait of Henry Clay. ***Right:*** 10 / Portrait of Daniel Webster. ***Engraver:*** Toppan, Carpenter, Casilear & Co. ***Comments:*** H-KY-175-G252, Hughes-450. 18__. 1850s.

Rarity: URS-3
F $350

$10 • W-KY-1280-010-G120

Left: 10 / Portrait of Henry Clay. ***Center:*** Woman seated against bales, Cattle, Train. ***Right:*** 10 / Male portrait. ***Tint:*** Red-orange. ***Engraver:*** American Bank Note Co. ***Comments:*** H-KY-175-G254, Hughes-452. 18__. 1850s–1860s.

Rarity: URS-3
F $350

$20 • W-KY-1280-020-G130

NJW

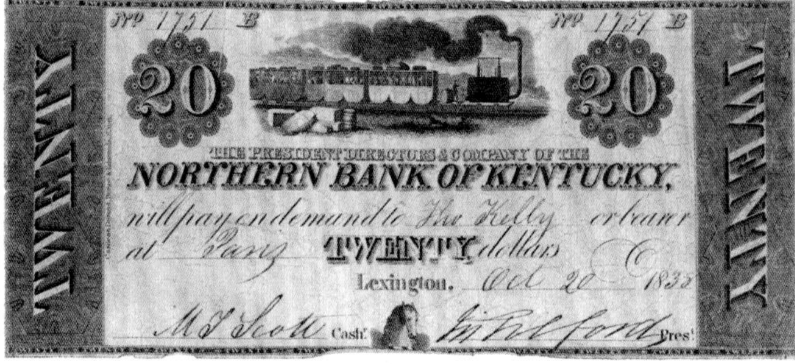

Engraver: Casilear, Durand, Burton & Edmonds. ***Comments:*** H-KY-175-G256, Hughes-453. 18__. 1830s.

Rarity: URS-3
F $350

$20 • W-KY-1280-020-G140

Left: 20 / TWENTY vertically / 20. ***Center:*** Female portrait / Train, Woman seated / Female portrait. ***Right:*** 20 / TWENTY vertically / 20. ***Engraver:*** Draper, Toppan & Co. ***Comments:*** H-KY-175-G258, Hughes-455. 18__. 1840s.

Rarity: URS-3
F $350

$20 • W-KY-1280-020-G150

Left: 20 / Portrait of George Washington / 20. ***Center:*** 20 / Woman seated against bales, Cattle, Train / 20. ***Right:*** 20 / Portrait of Henry Clay / 20. ***Engraver:*** Toppan, Carpenter & Co. ***Comments:*** H-KY-175-G260, Hughes-457. 18__. 1840s–1850s.

Rarity: URS-3
F $350

$20 • W-KY-1280-020-G160

Left: 20 / 20. ***Center:*** Portrait of Henry Clay / Woman seated against bales, Cattle, Train / Male portrait. ***Right:*** 20 / 20. ***Tint:*** Red-orange. ***Engraver:*** American Bank Note Co. ***Comments:*** H-KY-175-G262, Hughes-458. 18__. 1850s–1860s.

Rarity: URS-3
F $350

$50 • W-KY-1280-050-G170

Left: FIFTY vertically. ***Center:*** 50 / Train / 50. ***Right:*** FIFTY vertically. ***Engraver:*** Casilear, Durand, Burton & Edmonds. ***Comments:*** H-KY-175-G264, Hughes-Unlisted. 18__. 1830s.

Rarity: URS-2
F $450

$50 • W-KY-1280-050-G180

Left: 50 / FIFTY vertically / 50. ***Center:*** Female portrait / Woman seated against bales, Cattle / Female portrait. ***Right:*** 50 / FIFTY vertically / 50. ***Engraver:*** Draper, Toppan & Co. ***Comments:*** H-KY-175-G266, Hughes-461. 18__. 1840s.

Rarity: URS-2
F $450

$50 • W-KY-1280-050-G190

Left: 50 / Portrait of George Washington / 50. ***Center:*** 50 / Woman seated against bales, Cattle, Train. ***Right:*** 50 / Portrait of Henry Clay / 50. ***Engraver:*** Toppan, Carpenter & Co. ***Comments:*** H-KY-175-G268, Hughes-463. 18__. 1840s–1850s.

Rarity: URS-2
F $450

$50 • W-KY-1280-050-G200

Left: 50 / 50. ***Center:*** Portrait of Henry Clay / Woman seated against bales, Cattle, Train. ***Right:*** 50 / Male portrait. ***Tint:*** Red-orange. ***Engraver:*** American Bank Note Co. ***Comments:*** H-KY-175-G270, Hughes-464. 18__. 1850s–1860s.

Rarity: URS-2
F $450

$100 • W-KY-1280-100-G210

Left: ONE HUNDRED vertically. ***Center:*** C / Train / C. ***Right:*** ONE HUNDRED vertically. ***Tint:*** Red-orange. ***Engraver:*** Casilear, Durand, Burton & Edmonds. ***Comments:*** H-KY-175-G272, Hughes-465. 18__. 1830s.

Rarity: URS-2
F $450

$100 • W-KY-1280-100-G220

Left: 100 / HUNDRED vertically / 100. ***Center:*** Female portrait / Woman seated against bales, Cattle, Train / Female portrait. ***Right:*** 100 / HUNDRED vertically / 100. ***Engraver:*** Draper, Toppan & Co. ***Comments:*** H-KY-175-G274, Hughes-Unlisted. 18__. 1840s.

Rarity: URS-2
F $450

$100 • W-KY-1280-100-G230

Left: 100 / Portrait of George Washington / 100. ***Center:*** Woman seated against bales, Cattle, Train / 100. ***Right:*** 100 / Portrait of Henry Clay / 100. ***Engraver:*** Toppan, Carpenter & Co. ***Comments:*** H-KY-175-G276, Hughes-466. 18__. 1840s–1850s.

Rarity: URS-2
F $450

$100 • W-KY-1280-100-G240

Left: 100 / Portrait of Henry Clay / 100. ***Center:*** Woman seated against bales, Cattle, Train. ***Right:*** 100 / Male portrait / 100. ***Tint:*** Red-orange. ***Engraver:*** American Bank Note Co. ***Comments:*** H-KY-175-G278, Hughes-468. 18__. 1850s–1860s.

Rarity: URS-2
F $450

Non-Valid Issues

$5 • W-KY-1280-005-C040

Comments: H-KY-175-C238, Hughes-443. Counterfeit of W-KY-1280-005-G040. 18__. 1830s.

Rarity: URS-4
F $100

$10 • W-KY-1280-010-C100

Comments: H-KY-175-C250, Hughes-449. Counterfeit of W-KY-1280-010-G100. 18__. 1840s–1850s.

Rarity: URS-4
VG $100

$20 • W-KY-1280-020-C130

Comments: H-KY-175-C256, Hughes-454. Counterfeit of W-KY-1280-020-G130. 18__. 1830s.

Rarity: URS-4
F $100

$20 • W-KY-1280-020-C140

Comments: H-KY-175-C258, Hughes-456. Counterfeit of W-KY-1280-020-G140. 18__. 1840s.

Rarity: URS-4
F $100

$50 • W-KY-1280-050-C180

Comments: H-KY-175-C266, Hughes-462. Counterfeit of W-KY-1280-050-G180. 18__. 1840s.

Rarity: URS-4
F $150

Paris Bank

1818

W-KY-1290

History: The Paris Bank was chartered on January 26, 1818. The authorized capital of $300,000 was divided into 3,000 shares of $100 each. Henry Clay Jr. (son of the famous politician), Abraham Spears, Hugh Brent, William Scott, William Cockran, Samuel G. Mitchell, Hugh Talbot, and William Garrard were appointed to take stock subscriptions. It is uncertain whether the bank ever opened for business.

Petersburg, Kentucky

Petersburg (also sometimes seen as *Petersburgh* in contemporary accounts) was once known as Tanner's Station, which was settled prior to 1790.

Farmers Bank of Gallatin

1818–1820

W-KY-1300

History: The Farmers Bank of Gallatin was chartered on January 26, 1818. The authorized capital of $100,000 was divided into 1,000 shares of $100 each. Samuel Sanders, Thomas L. Butler, and Garland Bullock were appointed to take stock subscriptions. The bank operated for a short time, but by autumn 1819 it had stopped redeeming its notes. The charters of all independent banks authorized on January 26, 1818, were revoked effective May 1, 1820.

The Farmers Bank of Gallatin had a branch bank of the same name planned for Port William, W-KY-1320. The branch never opened for business.

Numismatic Commentary: One note from this bank exists for collectors today.

Valid Issues

$5 • W-KY-1300-005-G010

Left: 5 / 5 vertically. *Center:* 5 / Woman standing by water / 5. *Right:* KENTUCKY vertically. *Comments:* H-Unlisted, Hughes-704. 1818.

Rarity: URS-1
Proof $1,200

$10 • W-KY-1300-010-G020

Comments: H-Unlisted, Hughes-705. No description available. 1818.

Rarity: *None known*

Petersburg Steam Mill Company

1818–1820

W-KY-1310

History: "A bank to be denominated the Petersburg Steam Mill Company, in the town of Petersburg," per the wording of the legislation, was chartered on January 26, 1818. The authorized capital of $100,000 was divided into 1,000 shares of $100 each. Archibald Huston, Benjamin G. Willis, John Alloway Jr., John Terril, and Oliver Fairchild were appointed to take stock subscriptions. This is a rare instance of a chartered bank not having the word *Bank* in its name. The company issued paper money, but in the summer of 1819 it ceased to redeem bills. The charters of all independent banks authorized on January 26, 1818, were revoked effective May 1, 1820.

Port William, Kentucky

In 1792 the land that later became Carrollton was established and named Port William. It was laid out as the seat of Gallatin County until 1838, when the county split and the town was renamed Carrollton.

See also Carrollton, Kentucky.

Farmers Bank of Gallatin (branch)

1818

W-KY-1320

History: The Farmers Bank of Gallatin was chartered on January 26, 1818. The branch never opened for business.

The Farmers Bank of Gallatin had its parent bank located in Petersburg, W-KY-1300.

Valid Issues

$3 • W-KY-1320-003-G005

Left: 3 / 3 vertically. *Center:* 3 / Woman standing / 3. *Right:* KENTUCKY vertically. *Engraver:* Murray, Draper, Fairman & Co. *Comments:* H-Unlisted, Hughes-Unlisted. 18__. 1818.

Rarity: URS-2
G $800

$5 • W-KY-1320-005-G010 CC

Engraver: Murray, Draper, Fairman & Co. *Comments:* H-Unlisted, Hughes-704. 18__. 1818.

Rarity: URS-2
VF $850

$10 • W-KY-1320-010-G020

Comments: H-Unlisted, Hughes-705. No description available. 1818.

Rarity: *None known*

Princeton, Kentucky

Located at the source of Eddy Creek, the settlement that became Princeton was originally known as Eddy Grove. The land was granted to William Prince for time served during the Revolutionary War, and in 1799 he settled and built Shandy Hall. In 1817 the town was established and a courthouse was built. That same year the town was renamed Princetown, which was later shortened to Princeton.

In 1860 the construction of Princeton College was underway, but the Civil War put a halt on all plans. Part of the campus was used as a hospital during the war, and in 1864 the courthouse was burned and the town raided.

Bank of the Commonwealth of Kentucky (branch)

1821–1830

W-KY-1330

History: The Bank of the Commonwealth of Kentucky was chartered on November 29, 1820, with an authorized capital of $2,000,000. A local name for the bank was the "Peoples Bank," as it was chartered for the purpose of bringing relief to the population in a time of economic uncertainty. On December 22, 1820, an act was passed authorizing the bank to issue $3,000,000 in bills. The establishment of the Bank of the Commonwealth of Kentucky inadvertently caused the failure of the first Bank of Kentucky, W-KY-420. The branch located in Princeton opened in 1821. John Phelps was the president, and Reuben Rowland was the cashier.

In 1830 the bank lost its authorization to loan money, and it was instructed to close up its branches. Around that time the bank ceased new business, but the winding up of its affairs took until 1855.

The Bank of the Commonwealth of Kentucky had its parent bank located in Frankfort, W-KY-440, and branch banks located in Bowling Green, W-KY-090, Falmouth, W-KY-360, Flemingsburg, W-KY-410, Greensburg, W-KY-550, Harrodsburg, W-KY-580, Hartford, W-KY-610, Lexington, W-KY-780, Louisville, W-KY-870, Mount Sterling, W-KY-1120, Somerset, W-KY-1470, and Winchester, W-KY-1590.

Numismatic Commentary: Almost all notes from this bank and its branches are unknown today.

Valid Issues

6-1/4¢ • W-KY-1330-00.06.25-G010

Left: 6-1/4 CENTS. ***Center:*** 6-1/4 / 6-1/4 on die / 6-1/4. ***Right:*** KENTUCKY vertically. ***Comments:*** H-KY-95-G260, Hughes-237. 1822.

Rarity: *None known*

12-1/2¢ • W-KY-1330-00.12.50-G020

Left: 12-1/2 CENTS. ***Center:*** 12-1/2 / 12-1/2 on die / 12-1/2. ***Right:*** KENTUCKY vertically. ***Comments:*** H-KY-95-G262, Hughes-238. 1822.

Rarity: *None known*

25¢ • W-KY-1330-00.25-G030

Left: 25 CENTS. ***Center:*** 25 / 25 on die / 25. ***Right:*** KENTUCKY vertically. ***Comments:*** H-KY-95-G264, Hughes-239. 1822.

Rarity: *None known*

50¢ • W-KY-1330-00.50-G040

Left: 50 CENTS. ***Center:*** 50 / 50 on die / 50. ***Right:*** KENTUCKY vertically. ***Comments:*** H-KY-95-G266, Hughes-240. 1822.

Rarity: *None known*

$1 • W-KY-1330-001-G050

Left: KENTUCKY vertically. ***Center:*** 1 / 1. ***Right:*** CAMPBELL COUNTY vertically. ***Engraver:*** Murray, Draper, Fairman & Co. ***Comments:*** H-KY-95-G270, Hughes-241. 18__. 1820s.

Rarity: URS-1

F $750

$3 • W-KY-1330-003-G060

Left: KENTUCKY vertically. ***Center:*** 3 / 3. ***Right:*** CAMPBELL COUNTY vertically. ***Engraver:*** Murray, Draper, Fairman & Co. ***Comments:*** H-KY-95-G272, Hughes-242. 18__. 1820s.

Rarity: *None known*

$5 • W-KY-1330-005-G070

Left: Woman holding staff. ***Center:*** 5 / Minerva standing with owl, shield, staff / 5. ***Right:*** Woman holding staff. ***Engraver:*** Murray, Draper, Fairman & Co. ***Comments:*** H-KY-95-G274, Hughes-243. 18__. 1820s.

Rarity: URS-1

F $750

$10 • W-KY-1330-010-G080

Left: Woman holding staff. ***Center:*** 10 / Woman standing with staff, shield, Four cherubs / 10. ***Right:*** Woman holding staff. ***Engraver:*** Murray, Draper, Fairman & Co. ***Comments:*** H-KY-95-G276, Hughes-244. 18__. 1820s.

Rarity: *None known*

$20 • W-KY-1330-020-G090

Engraver: Murray, Draper, Fairman & Co. ***Comments:*** H-KY-95-G278, Hughes-245. No description available. 18__. 1820s.

Rarity: *None known*

$50 • W-KY-1330-050-G100

Engraver: Murray, Draper, Fairman & Co. ***Comments:*** H-KY-95-G280, Hughes-246. No description available. 18__. 1820s.

Rarity: *None known*

$100 • W-KY-1330-100-G110

Engraver: Murray, Draper, Fairman & Co. ***Comments:*** H-KY-95-G282, Hughes-247. No description available. 18__. 1820s.

Rarity: *None known*

Farmers Bank of Kentucky (branch)

1850–1865

W-KY-1340

History: The Farmers Bank of Kentucky was chartered on February 15, 1850, with an authorized capital of $2,300,000. By September 1852 the bank had opened for business. On February 11, 1860, the charter for the bank was amended, allowing it to increase its capital.

The branch located in Princeton had a capital of $300,000. In 1855 the cashier was Caleb B. Henry, and the president was W.W. Tinsley. In 1861 P.B. McGoodwin became the president.

As did many banks of the era, during the 1860s the Farmers Bank of Kentucky wound up its affairs and closed. The Princeton branch closed in 1865.

The Farmers Bank of Kentucky had its parent bank located in Frankfort, W-KY-450, and branch banks located in Bardstown, W-KY-070, Covington, W-KY-240, George Town, W-KY-480, Henderson, W-KY-640, Maysville, W-KY-1050, Mount Sterling, W-KY-1130, and Somerset, W-KY-1480.

Valid Issues

$1 • W-KY-1340-001-G010

Left: 1 / Portrait of John Crittenden / ONE. ***Center:*** Man with dog, Running horses, Donkey. ***Right:*** 1 / Female portrait / ONE. ***Engraver:*** Toppan, Carpenter, Casilear & Co. ***Comments:*** H-KY-100-G146, Hughes-250. 18__. 1850s.

Rarity: URS-3
F $350

$1 • W-KY-1340-001-G010a

Back: Red-orange. ***Engraver:*** Toppan, Carpenter, Casilear & Co. / ABNCo. monogram. ***Comments:*** H-KY-100-G146b, Hughes-Unlisted. Similar to W-KY-1340-001-G010 but with additional engraver imprint. 185_. 1850s.

Rarity: URS-3
F $350

$1 • W-KY-1340-001-G020

Left: 1 / Man and wagon and horses / 1. ***Center:*** Portraits of Mr. and Mrs. John Crittenden. ***Right:*** 1 / 1 on die / 1. ***Tint:*** Red-orange. ***Back:*** Red-orange. ***Engraver:*** American Bank Note Co. ***Comments:*** H-KY-100-G148a, Hughes-249. 18__. 1860s.

Rarity: URS-3
F $350

$2 • W-KY-1340-002-G030

Left: 2 / Portrait of Mrs. John Crittenden. ***Center:*** 2 / Man on horse / 2. ***Right:*** 2 / Portrait of John Crittenden. ***Engraver:*** Toppan, Carpenter, Casilear & Co. ***Comments:*** H-KY-100-G150, Hughes-252. 18__. 1850s.

Rarity: URS-3
F $350

$2 • W-KY-1340-002-G030a

Back: Red-orange. ***Engraver:*** Toppan, Carpenter, Casilear & Co. / ABNCo. monogram. ***Comments:*** H-KY-100-G150b, Hughes-Unlisted. Similar to W-KY-1340-002-G030 but with additional engraver imprint. 185_. 1850s.

Rarity: URS-3
F $350

$5 • W-KY-1340-005-G040

Left: 5 / Portrait of John Crittenden / 5. ***Center:*** Cattle and sheep, Herders. ***Right:*** 5 / Portrait of Mrs. John Crittenden / 5. ***Engraver:*** Toppan, Carpenter, Casilear & Co. ***Comments:*** H-KY-100-G152, Hughes-256. 18__. 1850s.

Rarity: URS-3
F $350

$5 • W-KY-1340-005-G040a

Overprint: Red FIVE. ***Engraver:*** Toppan, Carpenter, Casilear & Co. ***Comments:*** H-KY-100-G152a, Hughes-257. Similar to W-KY-1340-005-G040. 18__. 1850s.

Rarity: URS-3
F $350

$5 • W-KY-1340-005-G050

Left: Men plowing with horse / V. ***Center:*** Portraits of Mr. and Mrs. John Crittenden. ***Right:*** 5 / 5. ***Tint:*** Red-orange. ***Back:*** Red-orange. ***Engraver:*** American Bank Note Co. ***Comments:*** H-KY-100-G154a, Hughes-255. 18__. 1859.

Rarity: URS-3
F $350

$10 • W-KY-1340-010-G060

Left: 10 / Portrait of John Crittenden. ***Center:*** Portraits of Mr. and Mrs. John Crittenden. ***Engraver:*** Toppan, Carpenter, Casilear & Co. ***Comments:*** H-KY-100-G156, Hughes-Unlisted. 18__. 1850s.

Rarity: URS-3
F $350

$10 • W-KY-1340-010-G060a

Tint: Red-orange outlining white TEN. ***Engraver:*** Toppan, Carpenter, Casilear & Co. ***Comments:*** H-KY-100-G156b, Hughes-Unlisted. Similar to W-KY-1340-010-G060. 18__. 1850s.

Rarity: URS-3
F $350

$10 • W-KY-1340-010-G070

Left: 10 / Portrait of John Crittenden. ***Center:*** Woman reclining against barrel, Harvest scene / Portrait of Mrs. John Crittenden. ***Right:*** 10 / Men harvesting corn. ***Tint:*** Red-orange. ***Back:*** Red-orange. ***Engraver:*** American Bank Note Co. ***Comments:*** H-KY-100-G158a, Hughes-259. 18__. 1859.

Rarity: URS-3
F $350

$20 • W-KY-1340-020-G080

Left: Portrait of Mrs. John Crittenden / Portrait of John Crittenden. ***Center:*** 20 / Horses plowing. ***Right:*** 20. ***Engraver:*** Toppan, Carpenter, Casilear & Co. ***Comments:*** H-KY-100-G160, Hughes-261. 18__. 1850s.

Rarity: URS-2
F $450

$20 • W-KY-1340-020-G080a

Tint: Red-orange. ***Back:*** Red-orange. ***Engraver:*** American Bank Note Co. ***Comments:*** H-KY-100-G162a, Hughes-Unlisted. Similar to W-KY-1340-020-G080 but with different engraver imprint. 18__. 1859.

Rarity: URS-2
F $450

$50 • W-KY-1340-050-G090

Left: Three women with anchor. ***Center:*** 50 / Portrait of Mrs. John Crittenden. ***Right:*** 50 / Portrait of John Crittenden / 50. ***Engraver:*** Toppan, Carpenter, Casilear & Co. ***Comments:*** H-KY-100-G164, Hughes-263. 18__. 1850s.

Rarity: URS-1
F $550

$100 • W-KY-1340-100-G100

Left: 100 / Portrait of John Crittenden / 100. ***Center:*** Three women reclining / Portrait of Mrs. John Crittenden. ***Right:*** ONE HUNDRED vertically. ***Engraver:*** Toppan, Carpenter, Casilear & Co. ***Comments:*** H-KY-100-G166, Hughes-265. 18__. 1850s.

Rarity: URS-1
F $750

Non-Valid Issues

$5 • W-KY-1340-005-C040

Comments: H-KY-100-C152, Hughes-Unlisted. Counterfeit of W-KY-1340-005-G040. 18__. 1850s.

Rarity: URS-3
F $350

$5 • W-KY-1340-005-C040a
Comments: H-KY-100-C152a, Hughes-Unlisted. Counterfeit of W-KY-1340-005-G040a. 18__. 1850s.

Rarity: URS-3
F $350

Richmond, Kentucky

Richmond was founded in 1798 by Colonel John Miller. The town was named Richmond that year and became the county seat. In 1809 the town was officially incorporated. The Battle of Richmond took place on August 30, 1862, resulting in a definitive Confederate victory.

Bank of Kentucky {1st} (branch)
1807–1822
W-KY-1350

History: The Bank of Kentucky (sometimes seen later in print as the "Old" Bank of Kentucky) was incorporated on December 27, 1806, with an authorized capital of $1,000,000. Half of the capital was subscribed to by the state.

The Richmond branch was opened in 1807. On January 21, 1822, the bank was ordered to start closing up its branches. This was to be completed by May 1, 1824. This act essentially shut down the bank. Curiously, all of the paperwork was not completed until the 1870s.

The first Bank of Kentucky had its parent bank located in Frankfort, W-KY-420, and branch banks located in Bardstown, W-KY-050, Danville, W-KY-320, Glasgow, W-KY-500, Hopkinsville, W-KY-660, Lexington, W-KY-760, Louisville, W-KY-840, Paris, W-KY-1260, Russellville, W-KY-1380, Shelbyville, W-KY-1430, Springfield, W-KY-1500, Washington, W-KY-1570, and Winchester, W-KY-1580.

Valid Issues

$1 • W-KY-1350-001-G010
Comments: H-KY-110-G184, Hughes-Unlisted. No description available. 18__. 1815.

Rarity: *None known*

$1 • W-KY-1350-001-G020
Left: BRANCH BANK vertically. *Center:* 1 / Running deer, plow, ax / 1. *Right:* 1 / ONE / 1 vertically. *Engraver:* Unverified, but likely Murray, Draper, Fairman & Co. *Comments:* H-KY-110-G186, Hughes-283. 18__. 1816.

Rarity: URS-3
F $450

$1 • W-KY-1350-001-G030
Engraver: Murray, Draper, Fairman & Co. *Comments:* H-KY-110-G188, Hughes-Unlisted. No description available. 18__. 1821.

Rarity: *None known*

$5 • W-KY-1350-005-G040
Engraver: Unverified, but likely W. Harrison. *Comments:* H-KY-110-G190, Hughes-Unlisted. No description available. 18__. 1810s.

Rarity: *None known*

$5 • W-KY-1350-005-G050
Engraver: Unverified, but likely Murray, Draper, Fairman & Co. *Comments:* H-KY-110-G192, Hughes-Unlisted. No description available. 18__. 1810s.

Rarity: *None known*

$10 • W-KY-1350-010-G060
Engraver: Unverified, but likely W. Harrison. *Comments:* H-KY-110-G194, Hughes-Unlisted. No description available. 18__. 1810s–1820.

Rarity: *None known*

$20 • W-KY-1350-020-G070
Engraver: Unverified, but likely W. Harrison. *Comments:* H-KY-110-G196, Hughes-Unlisted. No description available. 18__. 1810s.

Rarity: *None known*

$50 • W-KY-1350-050-G080
Engraver: Unverified, but likely W. Harrison. *Comments:* H-KY-110-G198, Hughes-Unlisted. No description available. 18__. 1810s.

Rarity: *None known*

$100 • W-KY-1350-100-G090
Engraver: Unverified, but likely W. Harrison. *Comments:* H-KY-110-G200, Hughes-Unlisted. No description available. 18__. 1810s.

Rarity: *None known*

Post Notes

$__ • W-KY-1350-__-G100
Left: POST NOTE vertically. *Center:* __ / Cherub riding leaping deer / __. *Right:* POST NOTE vertically. *Engraver:* Murray, Draper, Fairman & Co. *Comments:* H-KY-110-G202, Hughes-Unlisted. 18__. 1810s.

Rarity: URS-2
F $550

Northern Bank of Kentucky (branch)
1835–1860s
W-KY-1360

History: The Northern Bank of Kentucky was chartered in 1835 with an authorized capital of $3,000,000. The Richmond branch was established immediately. In 1848 the president was William McClanahan, and the cashier was E.L. Shackelford. Capital was $150,000. In 1863 Daniel Breck took the presidency.

Sometime during the 1860s the Northern Bank of Kentucky was converted to a bank of discount and deposit, after which time no notes were issued.

The Northern Bank of Kentucky had its parent bank located in Lexington, W-KY-830, and branch banks located in Barbourville, W-KY-040, Covington, W-KY-260, Cynthiana, W-KY-305, Glasgow, W-KY-520, Louisville, W-KY-960, and Paris, W-KY-1280.

Valid Issues

$1 • W-KY-1360-001-G010

Left: Portrait of George Washington / ONE / Portrait of Henry Clay. ***Center:*** 1 / Woman seated against bales, Cattle, Train. ***Right:*** 1 / Portrait of Rachel Jackson / 1. ***Engraver:*** Toppan, Carpenter & Co. ***Comments:*** H-KY-175-G284, Hughes-435. 18__. 1840s.

Rarity: URS-3
F $200

$1 • W-KY-1360-001-G020

CC

Engraver: Toppan, Carpenter, Casilear & Co. ***Comments:*** H-KY-175-G286, Hughes-433. 18__. 1850s.

Rarity: URS-4
F $225

$1 • W-KY-1360-001-G030

Left: 1 / Portrait of boy. ***Center:*** Men with cattle, Sheep. ***Right:*** 1 / Portrait of girl. ***Tint:*** Red-orange. ***Engraver:*** American Bank Note Co. ***Comments:*** H-KY-175-G288, Hughes-436. 18__. 1850s–1860s.

Rarity: URS-3
F $100

$5 • W-KY-1360-005-G040

Left: FIVE vertically. ***Center:*** 5 / Train / 5. ***Right:*** FIVE vertically. ***Engraver:*** Casilear, Durand, Burton & Edmonds. ***Comments:*** H-KY-175-G294, Hughes-442. 18__. 1830s.

Rarity: URS-3
F $350

$5 • W-KY-1360-005-G050

Left: FIVE vertically. ***Center:*** 5 / Woman standing, Train / 5. ***Right:*** FIVE vertically. ***Engraver:*** Draper, Toppan & Co. ***Comments:*** H-KY-175-G296, Hughes-Unlisted. 18__. 1840s.

Rarity: URS-2
F $550

$5 • W-KY-1360-005-G060

Left: 5 / Portrait of Henry Clay / 5. ***Center:*** 5 / Woman seated against bales, Cattle, Train / 5. ***Right:*** 5 / Portrait of George Washington / 5. ***Engraver:*** Toppan, Carpenter & Co. ***Comments:*** H-KY-175-G298, Hughes-Unlisted. 18__. 1840s–1850s.

Rarity: URS-2
F $550

$5 • W-KY-1360-005-G070

Left: 5 / FIVE vertically. ***Center:*** Portrait of Henry Clay / Woman seated against bales, Cattle, Train / Male portrait. ***Right:*** 5 / FIVE vertically. ***Tint:*** Red-orange. ***Engraver:*** American Bank Note Co. ***Comments:*** H-KY-175-G300, Hughes-445. 18__. 1850s–1860s.

Rarity: URS-3
F $350

$10 • W-KY-1360-010-G085

Left: TEN vertically. ***Center:*** 10 / Train / 10. ***Right:*** TEN vertically. ***Engraver:*** Casilear, Durand, Burton & Edmonds. ***Comments:*** H-KY-175-G302, Hughes-446. 18__. 1830s.

Rarity: URS-3
VG $225; **F** $350

$10 • W-KY-1360-010-G100

Left: 10 / TEN vertically / 10. ***Center:*** Female portrait / Train, Woman seated / Female portrait. ***Right:*** 10 / TEN vertically / 10. ***Engraver:*** Draper, Toppan & Co. ***Comments:*** H-KY-175-G304, Hughes-Unlisted. 18__. 1840s.

Rarity: URS-2
F $550

$10 • W-KY-1360-010-G110

Left: X / 10 / X. ***Center:*** Portrait of George Washington / Woman seated against bales, Cattle, Train / Portrait of Henry Clay. ***Right:*** X / 10 / X. ***Engraver:*** Toppan, Carpenter & Co. ***Comments:*** H-KY-175-G306, Hughes-Unlisted. 18__. 1840s–1850s.

Rarity: URS-2
F $550

$10 • W-KY-1360-010-G120

Left: Portrait of George Washington / 10. ***Center:*** Portrait of George Washington / Woman seated against bales, Cattle, Train / Portrait of Henry Clay. ***Right:*** 10 / Portrait of Daniel Webster. ***Engraver:*** Toppan, Carpenter, Casilear & Co. ***Comments:*** H-KY-175-G308, Hughes-450. 18__. 1850s.

Rarity: URS-3
F $350

$10 • W-KY-1360-010-G130

Left: 10 / Portrait of Henry Clay. ***Center:*** Woman seated against bales, Cattle, Train. ***Right:*** 10 / Male portrait. ***Tint:*** Red-orange. ***Engraver:*** American Bank Note Co. ***Comments:*** H-KY-175-G310, Hughes-452. 18__. 1850s–1860s.

Rarity: URS-3
F $350

$20 • W-KY-1360-020-G140

Left: TWENTY vertically. ***Center:*** 20 / Train / 20. ***Right:*** TWENTY vertically. ***Engraver:*** Casilear, Durand, Burton & Edmonds. ***Comments:*** H-KY-175-G312, Hughes-453. 18__. 1830s.

Rarity: URS-3
F $350

$20 • W-KY-1360-020-G150

Left: 20 / TWENTY vertically / 20. ***Center:*** Female portrait / Train, Woman seated / Female portrait. ***Right:*** 20 / TWENTY vertically / 20. ***Engraver:*** Draper, Toppan & Co. ***Comments:*** H-KY-175-G314, Hughes-455. 18__. 1840s.

Rarity: URS-3
F $350

$20 • W-KY-1360-020-G160

Left: 20 / Portrait of George Washington / 20. ***Center:*** 20 / Woman seated against bales, Cattle, Train / 20. ***Right:*** 20 / Portrait of Henry Clay / 20. ***Engraver:*** Toppan, Carpenter & Co. ***Comments:*** H-KY-175-G316, Hughes-457. 18__. 1840s–1850s.

Rarity: URS-3
F $350

$20 • W-KY-1360-020-G170

Left: 20 / 20. ***Center:*** Portrait of Henry Clay / Woman seated against bales, Cattle, Train / Male portrait. ***Right:*** 20 / 20. ***Tint:*** Red-orange. ***Engraver:*** American Bank Note Co. ***Comments:*** H-KY-175-G318, Hughes-458. 18__. 1850s–1860s.

Rarity: URS-3
F $350

$50 • W-KY-1360-050-G185

Left: FIFTY vertically. ***Center:*** 50 / Train / 50. ***Right:*** FIFTY vertically. ***Engraver:*** Casilear, Durand, Burton & Edmonds. ***Comments:*** H-KY-175-G320, Hughes-461. 18__. 1830s.

Rarity: URS-2
F $550

$50 • W-KY-1360-050-G200

Left: 50 / FIFTY vertically / 50. ***Center:*** Female portrait / Woman seated against bales, Cattle / Female portrait. ***Right:*** 50 / FIFTY vertically / 50. ***Engraver:*** Draper, Toppan & Co. ***Comments:*** H-KY-175-G322, Hughes-Unlisted. 18__. 1840s.

Rarity: URS-1
F $750

$50 • W-KY-1360-050-G210

Left: 50 / Portrait of George Washington / 50. ***Center:*** 50 / Woman seated against bales, Cattle, Train. ***Right:*** 50 / Portrait of Henry Clay / 50. ***Engraver:*** Toppan, Carpenter & Co. ***Comments:*** H-KY-175-G324, Hughes-463. 18__. 1840s–1850s.

Rarity: URS-1
F $750

$50 • W-KY-1360-050-G220

Left: 50 / 50. ***Center:*** Portrait of Henry Clay / Woman seated against bales, Cattle, Train. ***Right:*** 50 / Male portrait. ***Tint:*** Red-orange. ***Engraver:*** American Bank Note Co. ***Comments:*** H-KY-175-G326, Hughes-464. 18__. 1850s–1860s.

Rarity: URS-1
F $750

$100 • W-KY-1360-100-G230

Left: ONE HUNDRED vertically. ***Center:*** C / Train / C. ***Right:*** ONE HUNDRED vertically. ***Tint:*** Red-orange. ***Engraver:*** Casilear, Durand, Burton & Edmonds. ***Comments:*** H-KY-175-G328, Hughes-465. 18__. 1830s.

Rarity: URS-1
F $850

$100 • W-KY-1360-100-G240

Left: 100 / HUNDRED vertically / 100. ***Center:*** Female portrait / Woman seated against bales, Cattle, Train / Female portrait. ***Right:*** 100 / HUNDRED vertically / 100. ***Engraver:*** Draper, Toppan & Co. ***Comments:*** H-KY-175-G330, Hughes-Unlisted. 18__. 1840s.

Rarity: URS-1
F $850

$100 • W-KY-1360-100-G250

Left: 100 / Portrait of George Washington / 100. ***Center:*** Woman seated against bales, Cattle, Train / 100. ***Right:*** 100 / Portrait of Henry Clay / 100. ***Engraver:*** Toppan, Carpenter & Co. ***Comments:*** H-KY-175-G332, Hughes-466. 18__. 1840s–1850s.

Rarity: URS-1
F $850

$100 • W-KY-1360-100-G260

Left: 100 / Portrait of Henry Clay / 100. ***Center:*** Woman seated against bales, Cattle, Train. ***Right:*** 100 / Male portrait / 100. ***Tint:*** Red-orange. ***Engraver:*** American Bank Note Co. ***Comments:*** H-KY-175-G334, Hughes-468. 18__. 1850s–1860s.

Rarity: URS-1
F $850

Non-Valid Issues

$1 • W-KY-1360-001-C020

HA

Comments: H-KY-175-C286, Hughes-434. Counterfeit of W-KY-1360-001-G020. 18__. 1850s.

Rarity: URS-4
F $75; **Unc-Rem** $100

$5 • W-KY-1360-005-C040

Comments: H-KY-175-C294, Hughes-443. Counterfeit of W-KY-1360-005-G040. 18__. 1830s.

Rarity: URS-4
F $75

$10 • W-KY-1360-010-C110

Comments: H-KY-175-C306 Hughes-Unlisted. Counterfeit of W-KY-1360-010-G110. 18__. 1840s–1850s.

Rarity: URS-4
F $75

How to Read the Whitman Numbering System

$1 • W-AL-020-001-G010a

Denomination: Face value of the note shown.

W: Whitman number. This number is a sortable code unique to each bank and note.

AL: Abbreviation for the state under study.

020: Numerical designation specific to each bank.

001: The denomination in dollars.

G010a: G indicates a good or valid note. Other categories are indicated thus: C (counterfeit); R (raised); S (spurious); N (not-attributed); A (altered). Numbers are assigned starting with 010, 020, et seq. Terminal letters following the number indicate variations of a note: a series of different colored overprints, tints, payees, etc., all on the same design of note. For more information, see the "How to Use This Book" section at the front of the volume, page xiv.

$20 • **W-KY-1360-020-C140**
Comments: H-KY-175-C312, Hughes-454. Counterfeit of W-KY-1360-020-G140. 18__. 1830s.
Rarity: URS-3
F $125

$20 • **W-KY-1360-020-C150**
Comments: H-KY-175-C314, Hughes-456. Counterfeit of W-KY-1360-020-G150. 18__. 1840s.
Rarity: URS-3
F $125

$50 • **W-KY-1360-050-C200**
Comments: H-KY-175-C322, Hughes-Unlisted. Counterfeit of W-KY-1360-050-G200. 18__. 1840s.
Rarity: URS-3
F $150

Richmond Bank
1818
W-KY-1370

History: The Richmond Bank was chartered on January 26, 1818, but never opened for business.

Valid Issues

$1 • **W-KY-1370-001-G010**
Left: KENTUCKY vertically. ***Center:*** I / Woman seated with spread eagle and flag / 1. ***Right:*** ONE. ***Engraver:*** Murray, Draper, Fairman & Co. ***Comments:*** H-KY-275-G12, Hughes-710. 18__. 1810s.
Rarity: *None known*

$3 • **W-KY-1370-003-G020**
Left: KENTUCKY vertically. ***Center:*** III / Woman seated with spread eagle and flag / 3. ***Right:*** THREE. ***Engraver:*** Murray, Draper, Fairman & Co. ***Comments:*** H-KY-275-G16, Hughes-711. 18__. 1810s.
Rarity: *None known*

$5 • **W-KY-1370-005-G030** CC

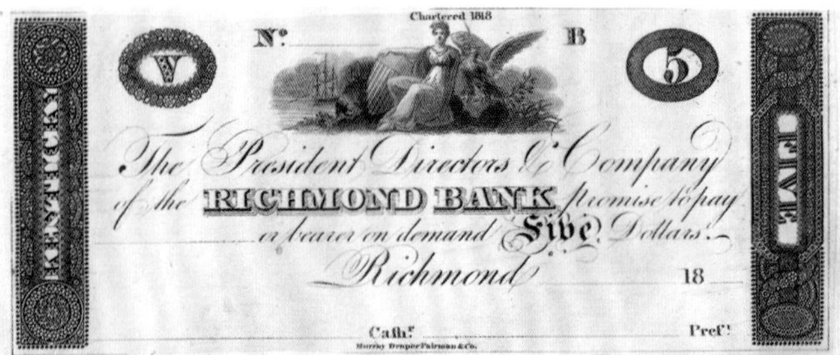

Engraver: Murray, Draper, Fairman & Co. ***Comments:*** H-KY-275-G18, Hughes-712. 18__. 1810s.
Rarity: URS-2
Proof $1,100

$10 • **W-KY-1370-010-G040** CC

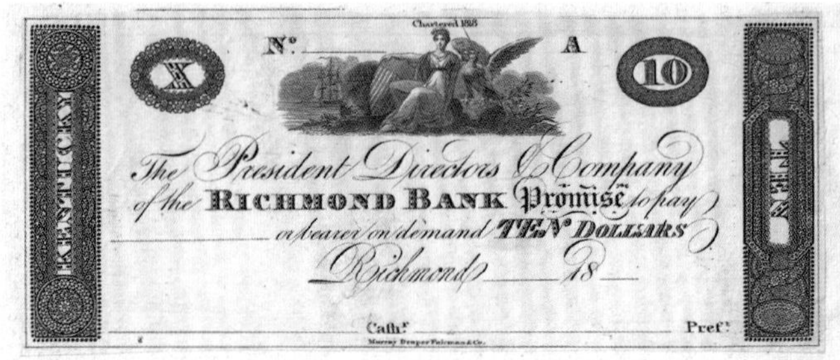

Engraver: Murray, Draper, Fairman & Co. ***Comments:*** H-KY-275-G20, Hughes-713. 18__. 1810s.
Rarity: URS-1
Proof $2,300

$20 • **W-KY-1370-020-G050** CC

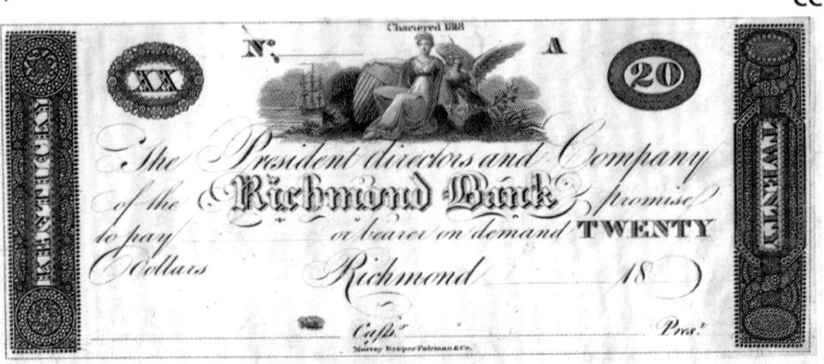

Engraver: Murray, Draper, Fairman & Co. ***Comments:*** H-KY-275-G22, Hughes-714. 18__. 1810s.
Rarity: URS-2
Proof $2,300

Russellville, Kentucky

Alternately called Big Boiling Spring, Gasper Butcher's Spring, and Butcher's Station in its early history, the land that became Russellville was first settled by William Cook and his family. In 1795 the land was granted to General William Russell and named after him. It was established on January 15, 1810, and incorporated as a city on February 19, 1840.

Four future governors of Kentucky came from Russellville, which was a prime area for politics. The city declared itself to be neutral at the onset of the Civil War. In 1862 a delegation of 43 counties gathered together at the Russellville Convention for the purpose of settling a separate Confederate Kentucky government. The government was recognized by the Confederacy, providing the source of the Confederate flag's 13th star.

Bank of Kentucky {1st} (branch)
1808–1822
W-KY-1380

History: The Bank of Kentucky (sometimes seen later in print as the "Old" Bank of Kentucky) was incorporated on December 27, 1806, with an authorized capital of $1,000,000. Half of the capital was subscribed to by the state.

The Russellville branch was opened in 1808. On January 21, 1822, the bank was ordered to start closing up its branches. This was to be completed by May 1, 1824. This act essentially shut down the bank. Curiously, all of the paperwork was not completed until the 1870s.

The first Bank of Kentucky had its parent bank located in Frankfort, W-KY-420, and branch banks located in Bardstown, W-KY-050, Danville, W-KY-320, Glasgow, W-KY-500, Hopkinsville, W-KY-660, Lexington, W-KY-760, Louisville, W-KY-840, Paris, W-KY-1260, Richmond, W-KY-1350, Shelbyville, W-KY-1430, Springfield, W-KY-1500, Washington, W-KY-1570, and Winchester, W-KY-1580.

Valid Issues

$1 • W-KY-1380-001-G010

Left: BRANCH BANK vertically. ***Center:*** 1 / Running deer, plow, ax / 1. ***Right:*** 1 / ONE / 1 vertically. ***Engraver:*** Unverified, but likely Murray, Draper, Fairman & Co. ***Comments:*** H-KY-110-G204, Hughes-283. 18__. 1816.

Rarity: URS-3
F $350

$1 • W-KY-1380-001-G020

Engraver: Murray, Draper, Fairman & Co. ***Comments:*** H-KY-110-G206, Hughes-Unlisted. No description available. 18__. 1821.

Rarity: *None known*

$3 • W-KY-1380-003-G030

Engraver: Murray, Draper, Fairman & Co. ***Comments:*** H-KY-110-G208, Hughes-Unlisted. No description available. 18__. 1821.

Rarity: *None known*

$5 • W-KY-1380-005-G040

Engraver: Unverified, but likely W. Harrison. ***Comments:*** H-KY-110-G210, Hughes-Unlisted. No description available. 18__. 1810s.

Rarity: *None known*

$5 • W-KY-1380-005-G050

Engraver: Unverified, but likely W. Harrison. ***Comments:*** H-KY-110-G212, Hughes-Unlisted. No description available. 18__. 1810s.

Rarity: *None known*

$10 • W-KY-1380-010-G060

Left: DEPARMENT vertically. ***Center:*** Running deer, plow, ax / TEN. ***Right:*** 10. ***Engraver:*** W. Harrison. ***Comments:*** H-KY-110-G214, Hughes-287. 18__. 1808–1810s.

Rarity: URS-2
F $550

$10 • W-KY-1380-010-G070

Engraver: Unverified, but likely W. Harrison. ***Comments:*** H-KY-110-G216, Hughes-Unlisted. No description available. 18__. 1810s–1820.

Rarity: *None known*

$10 • W-KY-1380-010-G080

Engraver: Unverified, but likely Murray, Draper, Fairman & Co. ***Comments:*** H-KY-110-G218, Hughes-Unlisted. No description available. 18__. 1810s.

Rarity: *None known*

$20 • W-KY-1380-020-G090

Engraver: Unverified, but likely W. Harrison. ***Comments:*** H-KY-110-G220, Hughes-Unlisted. No description available. 18__. 1808–1810s.

Rarity: *None known*

$20 • W-KY-1380-020-G100

Engraver: Unverified, but likely W. Harrison. ***Comments:*** H-KY-110-G222, Hughes-Unlisted. No description available. 18__. 1810s.

Rarity: *None known*

$50 • W-KY-1380-050-G110

Engraver: Unverified, but likely W. Harrison. ***Comments:*** H-KY-110-G224, Hughes-Unlisted. No description available. 18__. 1808–1810s.

Rarity: *None known*

$50 • W-KY-1380-050-G120

Engraver: Unverified, but likely W. Harrison. ***Comments:*** H-KY-110-G226, Hughes-Unlisted. No description available. 18__. 1810s.

Rarity: *None known*

$100 • W-KY-1380-100-G130

Engraver: Unverified, but likely W. Harrison. ***Comments:*** H-KY-110-G228, Hughes-Unlisted. No description available. 18__. 1808–1810s.

Rarity: *None known*

$100 • W-KY-1380-100-G140

Engraver: Unverified, but likely W. Harrison. ***Comments:*** H-KY-110-G230, Hughes-Unlisted. No description available. 18__. 1810s.

Rarity: *None known*

Farmers and Mechanics Bank of Logan

1818–1820

W-KY-1390

History: The Farmers and Mechanics Bank of Logan was chartered on January 26, 1818. The authorized capital of $200,000 was divided into 2,000 shares of $100 par value each. Amos Edwards, Jonathan Payne, David Caldwell, William I. Morton, and Joseph Gray were appointed to take stock subscriptions. The bank issued paper money, but by autumn 1819 it was no longer redeeming its bills. The charters of all independent banks authorized on January 26, 1818, were revoked effective May 1, 1820.

Numismatic Commentary: Notes of the branch bank in Logan are extremely rare.

Valid Issues

50¢ • W-KY-1390-00.50-G010

HA

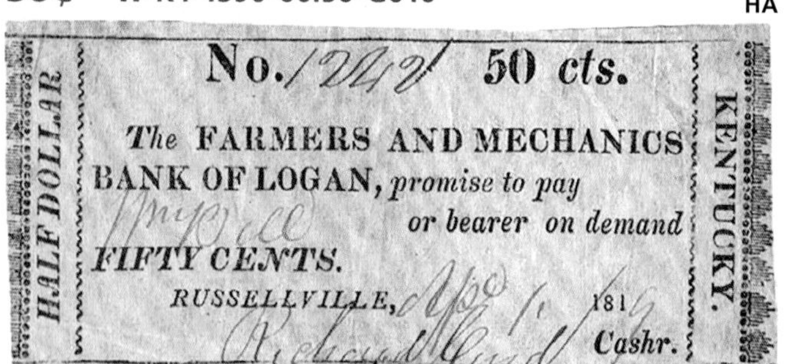

Comments: H-KY-280-G8, Hughes-720. 181_. 1810s.

Rarity: URS-2
F $550

$1 • W-KY-1390-001-G020

Left: ONE vertically. ***Center:*** ONE / ONE. ***Right:*** KENTUCKY vertically. ***Engraver:*** Murray, Draper, Fairman & Co. ***Comments:*** H-KY-280-G12, Hughes-721. 18__. 1810s.

Rarity: URS-2
F $550

$2 • W-KY-1390-002-G030

QDB

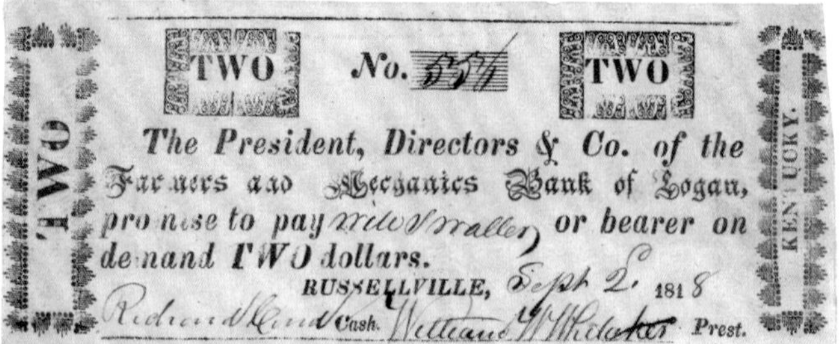

Engraver: Murray, Draper, Fairman & Co. ***Comments:*** H-Unlisted, Hughes-722. 181_. 1810s.

Rarity: URS-2
F $550

$3 • W-KY-1390-003-G040

CC

Engraver: Murray, Draper, Fairman & Co. ***Comments:*** H-KY-280-G16, Hughes-722. 18__. 1810s.

Rarity: URS-2
Proof $1,400

$5 • W-KY-1390-005-G050

Left: 5 / FIVE DOLLARS vertically. ***Center:*** V / Man and woman flanking shield bearing 5 / 5. ***Right:*** KENTUCKY vertically. ***Engraver:*** Murray, Draper, Fairman & Co. ***Comments:*** H-KY-280-G18, Hughes-723. 18__. 1810s.

Rarity: URS-2
Proof $1,400

$10 • W-KY-1390-010-G060

CC

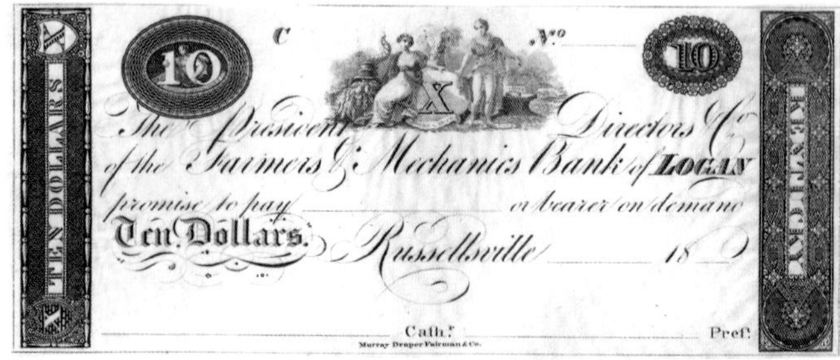

Engraver: Murray, Draper, Fairman & Co. ***Comments:*** H-KY-280-G20, Hughes-724. 18__. 1810s.

Rarity: URS-2
Proof $1,400

$20 • W-KY-1390-020-G070

CC

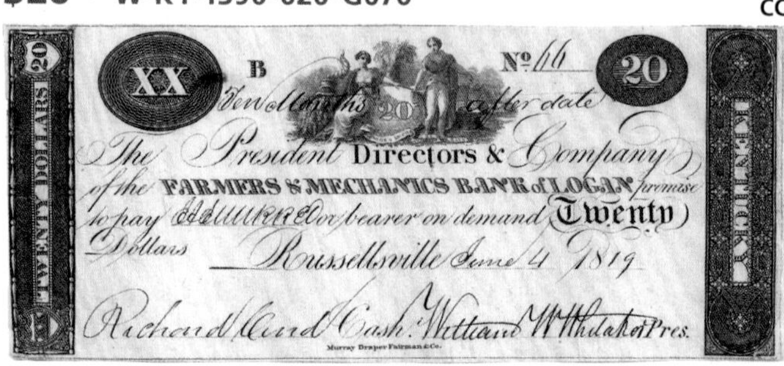

Engraver: Murray, Draper, Fairman & Co. ***Comments:*** H-KY-280-G22, Hughes-725. 18__. 1810s.

Rarity: URS-2
F $450

$50 • W-KY-1390-050-G080

Left: 50 / FIFTY DOLLARS vertically. ***Center:*** L / Man and woman flanking shield bearing 50 / 50. ***Right:*** KENTUCKY vertically. ***Engraver:*** Murray, Draper, Fairman & Co. ***Comments:*** H-KY-280-G26, Hughes-726. 18__. 1810s.

Rarity: URS-2
F $450

$100 • W-KY-1390-100-G090

CC

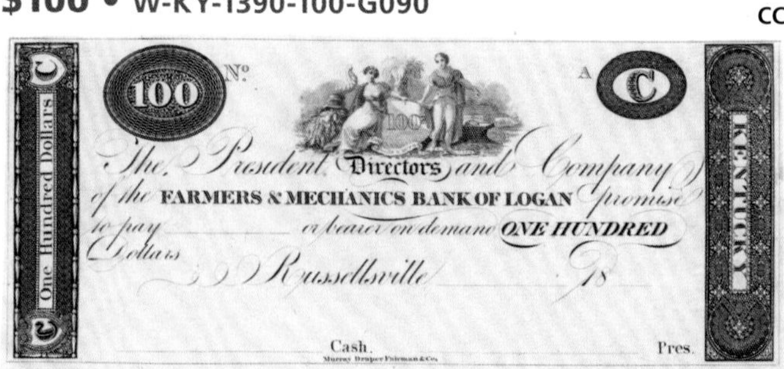

Engraver: Murray, Draper, Fairman & Co. ***Comments:*** H-Unlisted, Hughes-Unlisted. 18__. 1810s.

Rarity: URS-1
Proof $2,800

Post Notes

$__ • W-KY-1390-__-G100 CC

Engraver: Murray, Draper, Fairman & Co. ***Comments:*** H-KY-280-G26, Hughes-727. 18__. 1810s.

Rarity: URS-2

F $350

Southern Bank of Kentucky

1839–1865

W-KY-1400

History: On February 20, 1839, the Southern Bank of Kentucky was chartered with an authorized capital of $2,000,000, of which the state subscribed to half. On February 15, 1850, the charter was extended to last until 1880. The cashier of the bank in 1855 was M.B. Morton. The president at this time was George W. Norton. In 1862 the capital of the bank was $1,500,000 against a circulation of $1,042,000. By 1863 circulation had risen to $1,512,112, while the capital remained the same.

By 1865 the bank had been put into liquidation. On March 4, 1865, an act was passed ordering the treatment of the bank's bills to be as promissory notes rather than as currency. On January 8, 1867, the bank issued its last report regarding the closing up of its affairs. The bank building was later occupied by Nimrod, Long & Co.

The Southern Bank of Kentucky had branch banks located in Bowling Green, W-KY-130, Carrollton, W-KY-200, Hickman, W-KY-650, Lebanon, W-KY-740, Louisville, W-KY-1000, Owensboro, W-KY-1200, and Smithland, W-KY-1460.

Numismatic Commentary: More Proof notes from this bank have turned up in the 21st century than most other banks in Kentucky.

Valid Issues

$1 • W-KY-1400-001-G010 CC

Engraver: Toppan, Carpenter, Casilear & Co. ***Comments:*** H-KY-285-G4, Hughes-730. 18__. 1850s.

Rarity: URS-4

F $175

$1 • W-KY-1400-001-G020 NJW

Engraver: Toppan, Carpenter & Co. ***Comments:*** H-KY-285-G6, Hughes-728. 18__. 1850s.

Rarity: URS-4

VG $100; **VF** $150; **Unc-Rem** $200

$1 • W-KY-1400-001-G020a

Engraver: Toppan, Carpenter & Co. / ABNCo. monogram. ***Comments:*** H-KY-285-G6a, Hughes-Unlisted. Similar to W-KY-1400-001-G020 but with additional engraver imprint. 18__. 1850s–1860s.

Rarity: URS-3

F $250

$2 • W-KY-1400-002-G030 CC

Engraver: Toppan, Carpenter, Casilear & Co. ***Comments:*** H-KY-285-G10, Hughes-733. 18__. 1850s.

Rarity: URS-3

F $350

$2 • W-KY-1400-002-G040 NJW

Engraver: Toppan, Carpenter & Co. ***Comments:*** H-KY-285-G12, Hughes-735. 18__. 1850s.

Rarity: URS-3

F $350

$2 • W-KY-1400-002-G050

Left: Drover and cattle. ***Center:*** Milkmaid, cows, implements. ***Right:*** Two cherubs. ***Comments:*** H-Unlisted, Hughes-736. 18__. 1850s.

Rarity: URS-3

F $350

$3 • W-KY-1400-003-G060

CC

Engraver: Toppan, Carpenter & Co. ***Comments:*** H-KY-285-G18, Hughes-737. 18__. 1850s–1860s.

Rarity: URS-3
F $350

$3 • W-KY-1400-003-G060a

Engraver: Toppan, Carpenter & Co. / ABNCo. monogram. ***Comments:*** H-KY-285-G18a, Hughes-Unlisted. Similar to W-KY-1400-003-G060 but with additional engraver imprint. 18__. 1850s–1860s.

Rarity: URS-3
F $350

$3 • W-KY-1400-003-G070

CC

Engraver: Toppan, Carpenter, Casilear & Co. ***Comments:*** H-Unlisted, Hughes-739. 18__. 1850s.

Rarity: URS-3
F $350

$3 • W-KY-1400-003-G080

Left: Female portrait. ***Center:*** Steamboat. ***Right:*** Three women. ***Comments:*** H-Unlisted, Hughes-741. 18__. 1850s.

Rarity: URS-3
F $350

$5 • W-KY-1400-005-G090

CC

Engraver: Toppan, Carpenter, Casilear & Co. ***Comments:*** H-KY-285-G22, Hughes-742. 18__. 1850s.

Rarity: URS-3
F $350

$5 • W-KY-1400-005-G090a

Overprint: Red FIVE. ***Engraver:*** Toppan, Carpenter, Casilear & Co. ***Comments:*** H-Unlisted, Hughes-745. Similar to W-KY-1400-005-G090. 18__. 1850s.

Rarity: URS-2
F $200; **Proof** $1,000

$5 • W-KY-1400-005-G090b

Tint: Red-orange lathework outlining white V. ***Engraver:*** Toppan, Carpenter, Casilear & Co. ***Comments:*** H-Unlisted, Hughes-746. Similar to W-KY-1400-005-G090. 18__. 1850s.

Rarity: URS-3
F $200

$5 • W-KY-1400-005-G100

LK

Overprint: Red FIVE. ***Engraver:*** Bald, Cousland & Co. / Baldwin, Bald & Cousland. ***Comments:*** H-KY-285-G24a, Hughes-Unlisted. 18__. 1850s.

Rarity: URS-4
Proof $900
Selected auction price: R.M. Smythe, October 2007, Lot 3140, Proof $900

$10 • W-KY-1400-010-G110

CC

Engraver: Toppan, Carpenter, Casilear & Co. ***Comments:*** H-KY-285-G28, Hughes-747. 18__. 1850s.

Rarity: URS-3
F $350; **Proof** $1,150

$10 • W-KY-1400-010-G120

Left: 10 / Woman seated. ***Center:*** Man, woman, child, dog, Haying scene. ***Right:*** 10 / Woman seated. ***Engraver:*** Bald, Cousland & Co. / Baldwin, Bald & Cousland. ***Comments:*** H-Unlisted, Hughes-749. 18__. 1850s.

Rarity: URS-3
F $200

$10 • W-KY-1400-010-G120a SBG

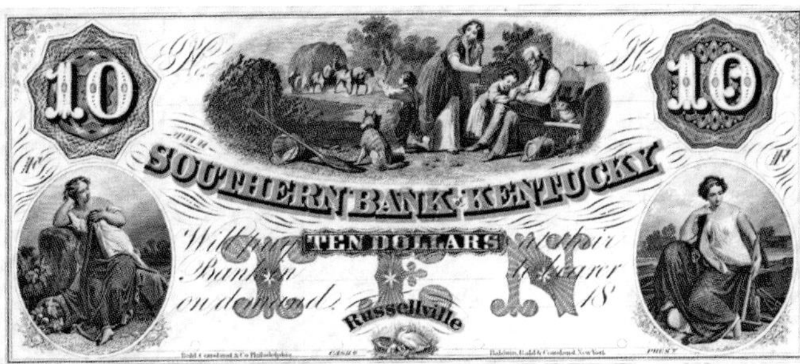

Overprint: Red TEN. ***Engraver:*** Bald, Cousland & Co. / Baldwin, Bald & Cousland. ***Comments:*** H-KY-285-G30a, Hughes-750. Similar to W-KY-1400-010-G120. 18__. 1850s.

Rarity: URS-5
Proof $750

$10 • W-KY-1400-010-G120b HA, SBG

Tint: Red-orange lathework outlining white X and TEN / TEN. ***Back:*** Red. ***Engraver:*** Bald, Cousland & Co. / Baldwin, Bald & Cousland. ***Comments:*** H-KY-285-G30b, Hughes-751. Similar to W-KY-1400-010-G120. 18__. 1850s.

Rarity: URS-3
Proof $800
Selected auction price: Heritage Auctions, October 17, 2012, Lot 15221, Proof $763

$10 • W-KY-1400-010-G130

Left: 10. ***Center:*** Agriculture holding ear of corn, Woman. ***Right:*** 10. ***Comments:*** H-Unlisted, Hughes-752. 18__. 1850s.

Rarity: URS-3
F $350

$20 • W-KY-1400-020-G140

Left: Man with flag, Woman, anchor. ***Center:*** 20 / Man seated by barrel. ***Right:*** 20 / Female portrait / 20. ***Engraver:*** Toppan, Carpenter, Casilear & Co. ***Comments:*** H-KY-285-G34, Hughes-753. 18__. 1850s.

Rarity: URS-3
F $350

$20 • W-KY-1400-020-G150

Left: Farmer stacking corn, Cherub seated on scroll. ***Center:*** 20 / Harvest scene / 20. ***Right:*** Female portrait, Cherub seated on scroll. ***Engraver:*** Toppan, Carpenter & Co. ***Comments:*** H-KY-285-G38, Hughes-754. 18__. 1850s.

Rarity: URS-3
F $350

$50 • W-KY-1400-050-G160 CC

Engraver: Toppan, Carpenter, Casilear & Co. ***Comments:*** H-KY-285-G42, Hughes-756. 18__. 1850s.

Rarity: URS-2
Proof $2,250
Selected auction price: R.M. Smythe, October 31, 2007, Lot 3142, Proof $2,248

$50 • W-KY-1400-050-G170 CC

Engraver: Draper, Toppan & Co. ***Comments:*** H-Unlisted, Hughes-757. 18__. 1850s.

Rarity: URS-2
F $450

$100 • W-KY-1400-100-G180

Left: 100 / George Washington on horseback. ***Center:*** Female portrait / 100. ***Right:*** ONE HUNDRED. ***Engraver:*** Toppan, Carpenter, Casilear & Co. ***Comments:*** H-KY-285-G46, Hughes-758. 18__. 1850s.

Rarity: URS-2
F $550

Notes on Which the Place Payable is Blank

$1 • W-KY-1400-001-G190

Left: 1 / Woman reclining / ONE. ***Center:*** 1 / Female portrait surrounded by implements / 1. ***Right:*** 1 / Indian man reclining / ONE. ***Engraver:*** Toppan, Carpenter, Casilear & Co. ***Comments:*** H-KY-285-G316. 18__. 1850s.

Rarity: —

$1 • **W-KY-1400-001-G200**
Left: Man with children and horse / ONE. ***Center:*** Portrait of young girl. ***Right:*** 1 / Flock of sheep. ***Engraver:*** Toppan, Carpenter & Co. ***Comments:*** H-KY-285-G318. 18__. 1850s.
Rarity: —

$2 • **W-KY-1400-002-G210**
Left: 2 / Woman with basket / TWO. ***Center:*** Spread eagle / 2. ***Bottom center:*** Eagle. ***Right:*** Justice seated with scales and sword / TWO. ***Engraver:*** Toppan, Carpenter, Casilear & Co. ***Comments:*** H-KY-285-G322. 18__. 1850s.
Rarity: URS-1
Proof $750

$2 • **W-KY-1400-002-G220**
Left: 2 / Woman seated / TWO. ***Center:*** Female portrait. ***Right:*** 2 / Man with children and horse. ***Engraver:*** Toppan, Carpenter & Co. ***Comments:*** H-KY-285-G324. 18__. 1850s.
Rarity: URS-1
Proof $1,000

$3 • **W-KY-1400-003-G230**
Left: 3 / Female portrait / 3. ***Center:*** Woman with eagle. ***Bottom center:*** Steamboat. ***Right:*** 3 / Three women standing / THREE. ***Engraver:*** Toppan, Carpenter, Casilear & Co. ***Comments:*** H-KY-285-G328. 18__. 1850s.
Rarity: URS-1
Proof $750

$3 • **W-KY-1400-003-G240**
Left: 3 / Portrait of George Washington. ***Center:*** Portrait of young girl / Man with children and horse. ***Right:*** 3 / 3. ***Engraver:*** Toppan, Carpenter & Co. ***Comments:*** H-KY-285-G330. 18__. 1850s–1860s.
Rarity: —

$5 • **W-KY-1400-005-G250**
Left: 5 / Female portrait / 5. ***Center:*** Man on horse. ***Right:*** 5 / Woman standing with flag. ***Engraver:*** Toppan, Carpenter, Casilear & Co. ***Comments:*** H-KY-285-G334. 18__. 1850s.
Rarity: URS-1
Proof $1,000

$5 • **W-KY-1400-005-G260** HA

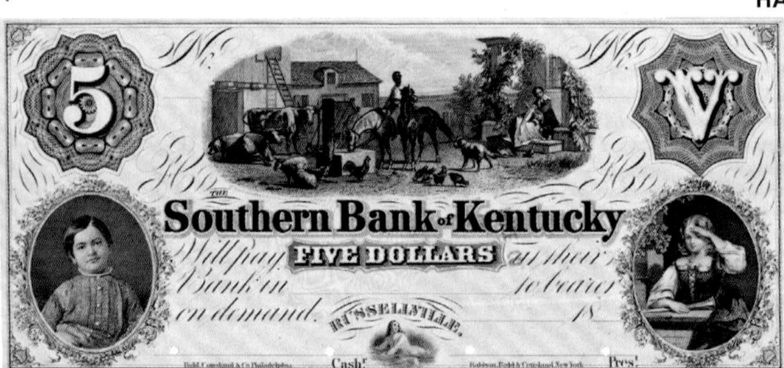

Engraver: Bald, Cousland & Co. / Baldwin, Bald & Cousland. ***Comments:*** H-KY-285-G336, Hughes-744. 18__. 1850s.
Rarity: URS-3
Proof $750

$5 • **W-KY-1400-005-G260a** HA

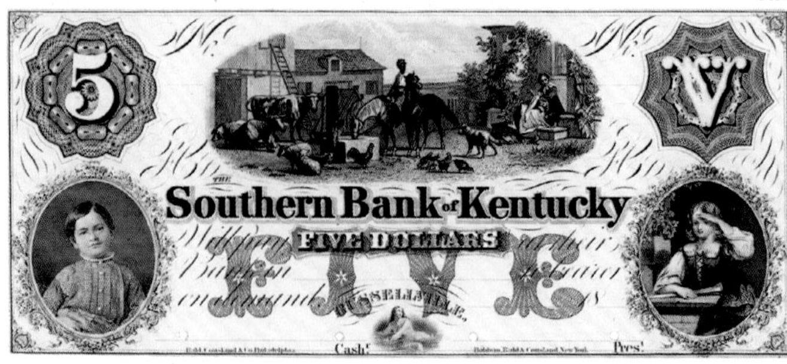

Overprint: Red FIVE. ***Engraver:*** Bald, Cousland & Co. / Baldwin, Bald & Cousland. ***Comments:*** H-KY-285-G336a. Similar to W-KY-1400-005-G260. 18__. 1850s.
Rarity: URS-1
Proof $1,000

$10 • **W-KY-1400-010-G270**
Left: 10. ***Center:*** Woman reclining among farm implements. ***Bottom center:*** Female portrait. ***Right:*** 10. ***Engraver:*** Toppan, Carpenter, Casilear & Co. ***Comments:*** H-KY-285-G340. 18__. 1850s.
Rarity: URS-1
Proof $1,000

$10 • **W-KY-1400-010-G280**
Left: 10 / Woman seated. ***Center:*** Man, woman, child, dog, Haying scene. ***Right:*** 10 / Woman seated. ***Engraver:*** Bald, Cousland & Co. / Baldwin, Bald & Cousland. ***Comments:*** H-KY-285-G342. 18__. 1850s.
Rarity: URS-1
Proof $1,000

$10 • **W-KY-1400-010-G280a** HA

Overprint: Red TEN. ***Engraver:*** Bald, Cousland & Co. / Baldwin, Bald & Cousland. ***Comments:*** H-KY-285-G342a. Similar to W-KY-1400-010-G280. 18__. 1850s.
Rarity: URS-3
Proof $750

$10 • **W-KY-1400-010-G280b**
Tint: Red-orange lathework outlining white X and TEN / TEN. ***Engraver:*** Bald, Cousland & Co. / Baldwin, Bald & Cousland. ***Comments:*** H-KY-285-G342b. Similar to W-KY-1400-010-G280. 18__. 1850s.
Rarity: —

$20 • **W-KY-1400-020-G290**
Left: Man with flag, Woman, anchor. ***Center:*** 20 / Man seated by barrel. ***Right:*** 20 / Female portrait / 20. ***Engraver:*** Toppan, Carpenter, Casilear & Co. ***Comments:*** H-KY-285-G346. 18__. 1850s.
Rarity: URS-1
Proof $1,000

$20 • W-KY-1400-020-G300
Left: Farmer stacking corn, Cherub seated on scroll. ***Center:*** 20 / Harvest scene / 20. ***Right:*** Female portrait, Cherub seated on scroll. ***Engraver:*** Toppan, Carpenter & Co. ***Comments:*** H-KY-285-G348. 18__. 1850s.

Rarity: URS-1
Proof $1,000

$50 • W-KY-1400-050-G310
Left: 50 / Daniel Boone and dog. ***Center:*** Female portrait. ***Right:*** 50 / Woman with flag and shield. ***Engraver:*** Toppan, Carpenter, Casilear & Co. ***Comments:*** H-KY-285-G352. 18__. 1850s.

Rarity: URS-1
Proof $1,000

$100 • W-KY-1400-100-G320
Left: 100 / George Washington on horseback. ***Center:*** Female portrait / 100. ***Right:*** ONE HUNDRED. ***Engraver:*** Toppan, Carpenter, Casilear & Co. ***Comments:*** H-KY-285-G356. 18__. 1850s.

Rarity: URS-1
Proof $1,000

Non-Valid Issues

$1 • W-KY-1400-001-C020a HA

Engraver: Toppan, Carpenter & Co. / ABNCo. monogram. ***Comments:*** H-Unlisted, Hughes-729. Counterfeit of W-KY-1400-001-G020a. 18__. 1850s–1860s.

Rarity: URS-4
VF $130

$1 • W-KY-1400-001-A010
Left: 1 / Cattle and telephone poles, Train on bridge. ***Center:*** Woman standing, Two calves, Trees and river. ***Right:*** 1 / Woman leaning elbow on fence. ***Tint:*** Red-orange. ***Comments:*** H-KY-285-A5, Hughes-732. Altered from $1 Southern Bank of Georgia, Bainbridge, Georgia. 18__. 1850s.

Rarity: URS-4
F $100

$2 • W-KY-1400-002-C030
Comments: H-Unlisted, Hughes-734. Counterfeit of W-KY-1400-002-G030. 18__. 1850s.

Rarity: URS-2
F $200

$3 • W-KY-1400-003-C060
Comments: H-KY-285-C18, Hughes-738. Counterfeit of W-KY-1400-003-G060. 18__. 1850s–1860s.

Rarity: URS-4
F $100

$3 • W-KY-1400-003-C070
Comments: H-Unlisted, Hughes-740. Counterfeit of W-KY-1400-003-G070. 18__. 1850s.

Rarity: URS-4
F $100

$5 • W-KY-1400-005-C090
Comments: H-KY-285-C22, Hughes-743. Counterfeit of W-KY-1400-005-G090. 18__. 1850s.

Rarity: URS-4
F $100

$10 • W-KY-1400-010-C110
Comments: H-Unlisted, Hughes-748. Counterfeit of W-KY-1400-010-G110. 18__. 1850s.

Rarity: URS-4
F $100

$20 • W-KY-1400-020-C150
Comments: H-Unlisted, Hughes-755. Counterfeit of W-KY-1400-020-G150. 18__. 1850s.

Rarity: URS-4
F $100

$50 • W-KY-1400-050-S010
Left: L / Portrait of George Washington / L. ***Center:*** 50 / Classical scholar standing with building / 50. ***Right:*** Woman with foot on globe. ***Comments:*** H-KY-285-S5, Hughes-757. June 15, 1862.

Rarity: URS-2
F $200

Notes on Which the Place Payable is Unknown

$3 • W-KY-1400-003-R010
Engraver: Toppan, Carpenter, Casilear & Co. ***Comments:*** H-KY-285-R5. Raised from $1. 18__. 1850s.

Rarity: —

$5 • W-KY-1400-005-R020
Engraver: Toppan, Carpenter & Co. ***Comments:*** H-KY-285-R10. Raised from $1. 18__. 1850s.

Rarity: —

$5 • W-KY-1400-005-R030
Comments: H-KY-285-R15. Raised from $2. 18__. 1850s.

Rarity: —

$10 • W-KY-1400-010-R040
Engraver: Toppan, Carpenter & Co. ***Comments:*** H-KY-285-R20. Raised from $1. 18__. 1850s.

Rarity: —

$10 • W-KY-1400-010-R050
Comments: H-KY-285-R25. Raised from $2. 18__. 1850s.

Rarity: —

$20 • W-KY-1400-020-R060
Comments: H-KY-285-R30. Raised from $2. 18__. 1850s.

Rarity: —

Sanders, Kentucky

The area that later became Sanders was established on a salt lick between Licking River and Drennon Springs. Originally settled as Rislerville, the community became known as Sanders Mill after Nathaniel Sanders, who opened a post office in 1816. At some point it was shortened to Sanders before changing again to Dixie when the Louisville, Cincinnati and Lexington Railroad arrived in 1867. The name changed yet again to Liberty Station, only to settle on the familiar Sanders in 1874, after State Senator Larkin Sanders.

Sanders Manufacturing Company

1818–1820

W-KY-1410

History: The Sanders Manufacturing Company was incorporated on January 31, 1818, and on February 3 of the same year it was awarded banking privileges. The capital was $300,000 divided into shares of $50 each, half of which were designated for the banking business. Notes issued for circulation were not to exceed $600,000. This privilege was repealed on February 10, 1820.

Shelbyville, Kentucky

Established in 1792, Shelbyville was designated the county seat of Shelby at its inception. The town was mainly agricultural in nature and located at the joining of the Clear and Mulberry creeks. By 1800 the town boasted 262 inhabitants, and expansion occurred through 1816.

During the 1830s the Louisville and Shelbyville Turnpike was constructed, followed by the Louisville and Frankfort Railroad in 1849. At the end of the Civil War a brief skirmish took place here.

Bank of Ashland (branch)

1856–1869

W-KY-1420

History: The Bank of Ashland was chartered on February 15, 1856, with an authorized capital of $400,000, $100,000 of which had to be paid in before the bank could open for business. The Shelbyville branch had a capital of $200,000. The president was Josephus H. Wilson, accompanied by James L. O'Neill as cashier. By 1861 O'Neill had been replaced by Shelby Vannatta.

On April 2, 1861, the charter of the bank was amended to allow it to issue notes with denominations less than $5. In 1869 the branch in Shelbyville was closed down and succeeded by the Bank of Shelbyville.

The Bank of Ashland had its parent bank located in Ashland, W-KY-010, and a branch bank located in Mayfield, W-KY-010.

Valid Issues

$1 • W-KY-1420-001-G010

Left: ONE on 1 / Man husking corn. ***Center:*** Woman standing with pole and cap, foliage, bird. ***Right:*** ONE on 1 / Blacksmith. ***Tint:*** Green panel of microlettering outlining white ONE and dies outlining white 1s. ***Engraver:*** American Bank Note Co. ***Comments:*** H-KY-5-G18a. 18__. 1860s.

Rarity: —

$5 • W-KY-1420-005-G020

Left: 5 / Soldier charging with bayonet. ***Center:*** Portrait of girl / Five men at work in iron foundry / Portrait of girl. ***Right:*** 5 / Female portrait. ***Tint:*** Yellow. ***Back:*** Machinery. ***Engraver:*** Toppan, Carpenter & Co. ***Comments:*** H-KY-5-G20a. 18__. 1857.

Rarity: —

$10 • W-KY-1420-010-G030 HA

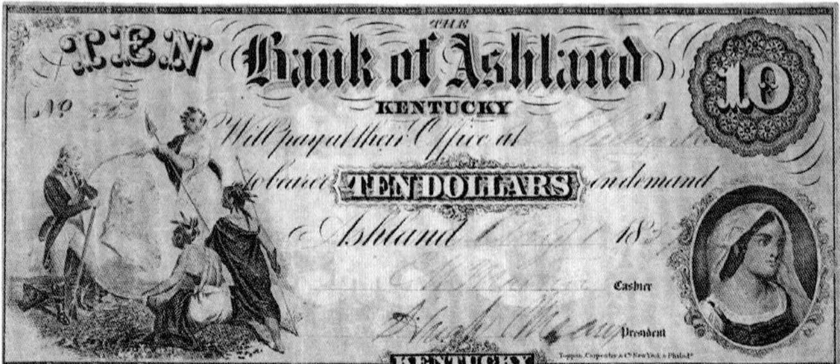

Tint: Yellow panel of microlettering outlining white TEN on white 10 outlined by lathework. ***Engraver:*** Toppan, Carpenter & Co. ***Comments:*** H-KY-5-G22a, Hughes-4. 18__. 1850s.

Rarity: URS-4
F $250; **VF** $350

$20 • W-KY-1420-020-G040

Left: Train / 20 on die. ***Right:*** 20 on die / Male portrait. ***Tint:*** Yellow lathework and panel of microlettering outlining white TWENTY. ***Engraver:*** Toppan, Carpenter & Co. ***Comments:*** H-KY-5-G24a. 18__. 1857.

Rarity: —

Non-Valid Issues

$10 • W-KY-1420-010-C030

Tint: Yellow panel of microlettering outlining white TEN on white 10 outlined by lathework. ***Engraver:*** Toppan, Carpenter & Co. ***Comments:*** H-KY-5-C22a. Counterfeit of W-KY-1420-010-G030. 18__. 1850s.

Rarity: URS-4
F $100; **VF** $150

$20 • W-KY-1420-020-C040

Tint: Yellow lathework and panel of microlettering outlining white TWENTY. ***Engraver:*** Toppan, Carpenter & Co. ***Comments:*** H-KY-5-C24a, Hughes-5. Counterfeit of W-KY-1420-020-G040. 18__. 1857.

Rarity: —

Bank of Kentucky {1st} (branch)

1816–1822

W-KY-1430

History: The Bank of Kentucky (sometimes seen later in print as the "Old" Bank of Kentucky) was incorporated on December 27, 1806, with an authorized capital of $1,000,000. Half of the capital was subscribed to by the state. The Shelbyville branch was opened in 1816. On January 21, 1822, the bank was ordered to start closing up its branches. This was to be completed by May 1, 1824. This act essentially shut down the bank. Curiously, all of the paperwork was not completed until the 1870s.

The first Bank of Kentucky had its parent bank located in Frankfort, W-KY-420, and branch banks located in Bardstown, W-KY-050, Danville, W-KY-320, Glasgow, W-KY-500, Hopkinsville, W-KY-660, Lexington, W-KY-760, Louisville, W-KY-840, Paris, W-KY-1260, Richmond, W-KY-1350, Russellville, W-KY-1380, Springfield, W-KY-1500, Washington, W-KY-1570, and Winchester, W-KY-1580.

Valid Issues

$1 • W-KY-1430-001-G010

Comments: H-KY-110-G234, Hughes-284. No description available. 18__. 1815.

Rarity: *None known*

$1 • W-KY-1430-001-G020

Left: BRANCH BANK vertically. ***Center:*** 1 / Running deer, plow, ax / 1. ***Right:*** 1 / ONE / 1 vertically. ***Engraver:*** Unverified, but likely Murray, Draper, Fairman & Co. ***Comments:*** H-KY-110-G236, Hughes-283. 18__. 1816.

Rarity: URS-3

F $350

$1 • W-KY-1430-001-G030

Engraver: Murray, Draper, Fairman & Co. ***Comments:*** H-KY-110-G238, Hughes-Unlisted. No description available. 18__. 1821.

Rarity: *None known*

$5 • W-KY-1430-005-G040

Engraver: Unverified, but likely W. Harrison. ***Comments:*** H-KY-110-G240, Hughes-Unlisted. No description available. 18__. 1810s.

Rarity: *None known*

$10 • W-KY-1430-010-G050

Engraver: Unverified, but likely W. Harrison. ***Comments:*** H-KY-110-G242, Hughes-Unlisted. No description available. 18__. 1810s–1820.

Rarity: *None known*

$20 • W-KY-1430-020-G060

Engraver: Unverified, but likely W. Harrison. ***Comments:*** H-KY-110-G244, Hughes-Unlisted. No description available. 18__. 1810s.

Rarity: *None known*

$50 • W-KY-1430-050-G070

Engraver: Unverified, but likely W. Harrison. ***Comments:*** H-KY-110-G246, Hughes-Unlisted. No description available. 18__. 1810s.

Rarity: *None known*

$100 • W-KY-1430-100-G080

Engraver: Unverified, but likely W. Harrison. ***Comments:*** H-KY-110-G248, Hughes-Unlisted. No description available. 18__. 1810s.

Rarity: *None known*

Farmers and Mechanics Bank of Shelbyville

1818–1820

W-KY-1440

History: The Farmers and Mechanics Bank of Shelbyville was chartered on January 26, 1818, with an authorized capital of $200,000 to be divided into 2,000 shares of $100 each. The bank issued paper money, but by autumn 1819 it was no longer redeeming its bills. The charters of all independent banks authorized on January 26, 1818, were revoked effective May 1, 1820.

Numismatic Commentary: Only a few issues from this bank are known today.

Valid Issues

$1 • W-KY-1440-001-G010 CC

Comments: H-Unlisted, Hughes-760. 18__. 1818.

Rarity: URS-3

Proof $900

$2 • W-KY-1440-002-G020 CC

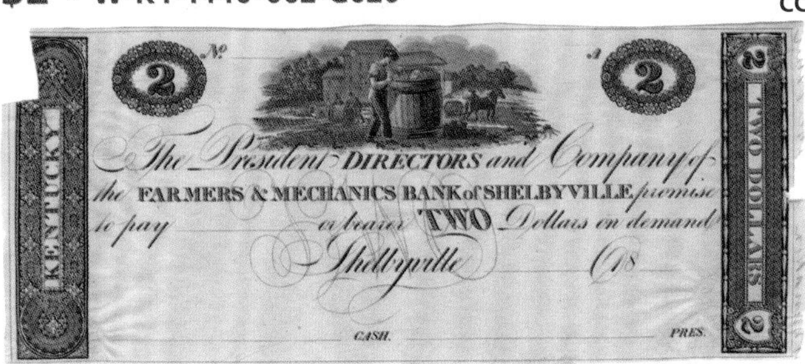

Comments: H-Unlisted, Hughes-761. 18__. 1818.

Rarity: URS-3

Proof $500

$4 • W-KY-1440-004-G030

Comments: H-Unlisted, Hughes-762. No description available. 1818.

Rarity: *None known*

$10 • **W-KY-1440-010-G040**

CC

Comments: H-Unlisted, Hughes-763. 18__. 1818.

Rarity: URS-3

Proof $750

$25 • **W-KY-1440-025-G050**

CC

Comments: H-Unlisted, Hughes-764. 18__. 1818.

Rarity: URS-2

Proof $4,200

Selected auction price: Stack's Bowers Galleries, March 2015, Lot 3101, Proof $4,235

$100 • **W-KY-1440-100-G060**

CC

Comments: H-Unlisted, Hughes-765. 18__. 1818.

Rarity: URS-2

Proof $4,200

Selected auction price: Stack's Bowers Galleries, January 1, 2010, Lot 2033, Proof $4,200

SHEPHERDSVILLE, KENTUCKY

In 1773 Captain Thomas Bullitt established the area known as Bullitt's Lick after the salt licks located on the land. These led to the first commercial salt works in Kentucky. A mill was built, and Shepherdsville expanded around it. It was named after Adam Shepherd and chartered in 1793. In 1796 the town became the county seat of Bullitt.

In 1806 the post office was opened, and in 1836 a spa fed by mineral water was established. The Louisville and Nashville Railroad arrived in the 1850s, serving as a prime target during the Civil War.

Bank of Shepherdsville

1818–1820

W-KY-1450

History: The Bank of Shepherdsville was chartered on January 26, 1818. The authorized capital of $100,000 was divided into 1,000 shares of $100 each. Wilfred Lee, George F. Pope, James Alexander, Daniel Drake, Guy Phelps, John Burks Jr., John Reid, William Simmons Sr., and Rodophus Buckey were appointed to take stock subscriptions. The bank operated for a short time. The charters of all independent banks authorized on January 26, 1818, were revoked effective May 1, 1820.

Numismatic Commentary: Notes of this bank are supremely scarce, with perhaps only a couple examples of each issue surviving.

VALID ISSUES

$1 • **W-KY-1450-001-G010**

CC

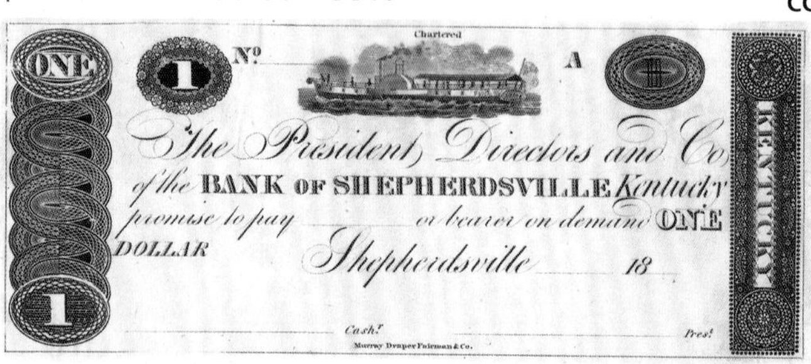

Engraver: Murray, Draper, Fairman & Co. ***Comments:*** H-KY-295-G12, Hughes-766. 18__. 1818–1820.

Rarity: URS-2

Proof $1,100

$3 • **W-KY-1450-003-G020**

Left: THREE / 3. ***Center:*** 3 / Riverboat / Die. ***Right:*** KENTUCKY vertically. ***Engraver:*** Murray, Draper, Fairman & Co. ***Comments:*** H-KY-295-G16, Hughes-767. 18__. 1818–1820.

Rarity: URS-2

F $550

$5 • **W-KY-1450-005-G030**

QDB

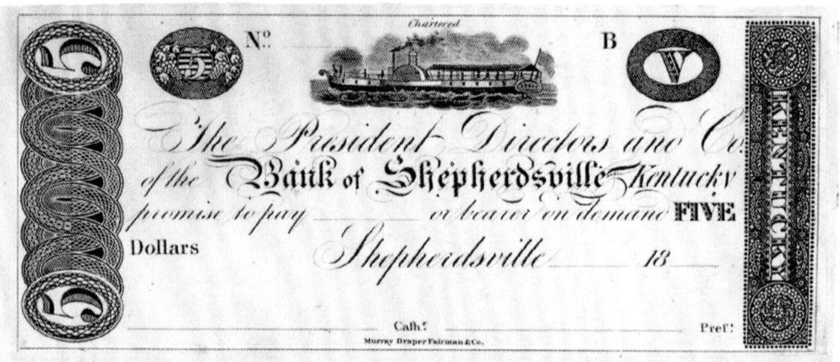

Engraver: Murray, Draper, Fairman & Co. ***Comments:*** H-KY-295-G18, Hughes-768. 18__. 1818–1820.

Rarity: URS-2

Proof $2,150

Selected auction price: Stack's Bowers Galleries, March 7, 2008, Lot 2037, Proof $2,130

$10 • W-KY-1450-010-G040 HA

Engraver: Murray, Draper, Fairman & Co. ***Comments:*** H-KY-295-G20, Hughes-769. 18__. 1818–1820.

Rarity: URS-2
Proof $1,100

Selected auction price: Heritage Auctions, September 25, 2013, Lot 15834, Proof $1,116

Smithland, Kentucky

John Smith was the first settler to arrive in the area, though with many delays and hardships. Eventually, the community grew and became a port along the Ohio and Cumberland rivers. It was laid out in 1805, but no records were officially made of it from then until 1837, when the town expanded.

Businesses and inns were built, and in 1800 a road was constructed connecting Smithland to Eddyville. In 1811 there was a significant earthquake that produced tremors in the area for months. Saw mills, a boat yard, a brickyard, a blacksmith shop, the Smithland Dock Company, an iron factory, a grocery store, and a dry goods store were all established during the 1830s. In 1840 Smithland became the county seat of Crittenden.

Southern Bank of Kentucky (branch)

1839–1865

W-KY-1460

History: On February 20, 1839, the Southern Bank of Kentucky was chartered with an authorized capital of $2,000,000, of which the state subscribed to half. On February 15, 1850, the charter was extended to last until 1880. The Smithland branch had a capital of $300,000. B. Barner was the cashier, and William Gordon was the president. In 1857 the president was T.M. Davis.

By 1865 the bank had been put into liquidation. On March 4, 1865, an act was passed ordering the treatment of the bank's bills to be as promissory notes rather than as currency. On January 8, 1867, the bank issued its last report regarding the closing up of its affairs. The bank building was later occupied by Nimrod, Long & Co.

The Southern Bank of Kentucky had its parent bank located in Russellville, W-KY-1400, and branch banks located in Bowling Green, W-KY-130, Carrollton, W-KY-200, Hickman, W-KY-650, Lebanon, W-KY-740, Louisville, W-KY-1000, and Owensboro, W-KY-1200.

Valid Issues

$1 • W-KY-1460-001-G010

Left: 1 / Woman reclining / ONE. ***Center:*** 1 / Female portrait surrounded by implements / 1. ***Right:*** 1 / Indian man reclining / ONE. ***Engraver:*** Toppan, Carpenter, Casilear & Co. ***Comments:*** H-KY-285-G274, Hughes-730. 18__. 1850s.

Rarity: URS-3
F $150

$1 • W-KY-1460-001-G020

Left: Man with children and horse / ONE. ***Center:*** Portrait of young girl. ***Right:*** 1 / Flock of sheep. ***Engraver:*** Toppan, Carpenter & Co. ***Comments:*** H-KY-285-G276, Hughes-728. 18__. 1850s.

Rarity: URS-3
F $150

$1 • W-KY-1460-001-G020a

Engraver: Toppan, Carpenter & Co. / ABNCo. monogram. ***Comments:*** H-KY-285-G276a, Hughes-Unlisted. Similar to W-KY-1460-001-G020 but with additional engraver imprint. 18__. 1850s–1860s.

Rarity: URS-3
F $150; **Unc-Rem** $200

$2 • W-KY-1460-002-G030

Left: 2 / Woman with basket / TWO. ***Center:*** Spread eagle / 2. ***Bottom center:*** Eagle. ***Right:*** Justice seated with scales and sword / TWO. ***Engraver:*** Toppan, Carpenter, Casilear & Co. ***Comments:*** H-KY-285-G280, Hughes-733. 18__. 1850s.

Rarity: URS-3
F $200

$2 • W-KY-1460-002-G040

Left: 2 / Woman seated / TWO. ***Center:*** Female portrait. ***Right:*** 2 / Man with children and horse. ***Engraver:*** Toppan, Carpenter & Co. ***Comments:*** H-KY-285-G282, Hughes-735. 18__. 1850s.

Rarity: URS-3
F $350

$2 • W-KY-1460-002-G040a

Engraver: Toppan, Carpenter & Co. / ABNCo. monogram. ***Comments:*** H-KY-285-G282a, Hughes-Unlisted. Similar to W-KY-1460-002-G040 but with additional engraver imprint. 18__. 1850s–1860s.

Rarity: URS-3
F $350

$3 • W-KY-1460-003-G050

Left: 3 / Female portrait / 3. ***Center:*** Woman with eagle. ***Bottom center:*** Steamboat. ***Right:*** 3 / Three women standing / THREE. ***Engraver:*** Toppan, Carpenter, Casilear & Co. ***Comments:*** H-KY-285-G286, Hughes-739. 18__. 1850s.

Rarity: URS-3
F $350

$3 • W-KY-1460-003-G060

Left: 3 / Portrait of George Washington. ***Center:*** Portrait of young girl / Man with children and horse. ***Right:*** 3 / 3. ***Engraver:*** Toppan, Carpenter & Co. ***Comments:*** H-KY-285-G288, Hughes-737. 18__. 1850s–1860s.

Rarity: URS-3
F $350

$3 • W-KY-1460-003-G060a

Engraver: Toppan, Carpenter & Co. / ABNCo. monogram. ***Comments:*** H-KY-285-G288a, Hughes-Unlisted. Similar to W-KY-1460-003-G060 but with additional engraver imprint. 18__. 1850s–1860s.

Rarity: URS-3
F $350

$5 • W-KY-1460-005-G070

Left: 5 / Female portrait / 5. ***Center:*** Man on horse. ***Right:*** 5 / Woman standing with flag. ***Engraver:*** Toppan, Carpenter, Casilear & Co. ***Comments:*** H-KY-285-G292, Hughes-742. 18__. 1850s.

Rarity: URS-3
F $350

$5 • W-KY-1460-005-G080

Left: 5 / Portrait of boy. ***Center:*** Man on horse in farmyard. ***Right:*** V / Portrait of young girl. ***Overprint:*** Red FIVE. ***Engraver:*** Bald, Cousland & Co. / Baldwin, Bald & Cousland. ***Comments:*** H-KY-285-G294a, Hughes-745.

Rarity: URS-3
F $350

$10 • W-KY-1460-010-G090

CC

Engraver: Toppan, Carpenter, Casilear & Co. ***Comments:*** H-KY-285-G298, Hughes-747. 18__. 1850s.

Rarity: URS-3
F $350

$10 • W-KY-1460-010-G100

Left: 10 / Woman seated. ***Center:*** Man, woman, child, dog, Haying scene. ***Right:*** 10 / Woman seated. ***Overprint:*** Red TEN. ***Engraver:*** Bald, Cousland & Co. / Baldwin, Bald & Cousland. ***Comments:*** H-KY-285-G300a, Hughes-750. 18__. 1850s.

Rarity: URS-3
F $350

Non-Valid Issues

$1 • W-KY-1460-001-C010

Comments: H-KY-285-C274, Hughes-731. Counterfeit of W-KY-1460-001-G010. 18__. 1850s.

Rarity: URS-4
F $175

$1 • W-KY-1460-001-C020a

CC

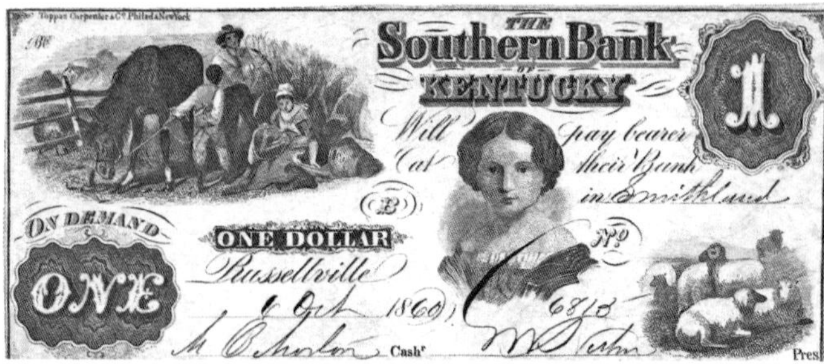

Comments: H-KY-285-C276a, Hughes-729. Counterfeit of W-KY-1460-001-G020a. 18__. 1850s–1860s.

Rarity: URS-4
F $250

$3 • W-KY-1460-003-C050

Comments: H-KY-185-C286, Hughes-740. Counterfeit of W-KY-1460-003-G050. 18__. 1850s.

Rarity: URS-4
F $200

$3 • W-KY-1460-003-C060a

Comments: H-KY-285-C288a, Hughes-738. Counterfeit of W-KY-1460-003-G060a. 18__. 1850s–1860s.

Rarity: URS-4
F $200

Somerset, Kentucky

Thomas Hansford was the first settler to arrive in Somerset in 1798. He named it after Somerset County, New Jersey. The town became the county seat of Pulaski in 1802, and it was officially incorporated in 1887. Somerset never saw battle directly during the Civil War, but two skirmishes took place close to its borders.

Bank of the Commonwealth of Kentucky (branch)

1820–1830

W-KY-1470

History: The Bank of the Commonwealth of Kentucky was chartered on November 29, 1820, with an authorized capital of $2,000,000. A local name for the bank was the "Peoples Bank," as it was chartered for the purpose of bringing relief to the population in a time of economic uncertainty. On December 22, 1820, an act was passed authorizing the bank to issue $3,000,000 in bills. The establishment of the Bank of the Commonwealth of Kentucky inadvertently caused the failure of the first Bank of Kentucky, W-KY-420.

The branch located in Somerset opened in November 1820. Its office was set on Main Street. The cashier was John B. Curd.

In 1830 the bank lost its authorization to loan money, and it was instructed to close up its branches. Around that time the bank ceased new business, but the winding up of its affairs took until 1855.

The Bank of the Commonwealth of Kentucky had its parent bank located in Frankfort, W-KY-440, and branch banks located in Bowling Green, W-KY-090, Falmouth, W-KY-360, Flemingsburg, W-KY-410, Greensburg, W-KY-550, Harrodsburg, W-KY-580, Hartford, W-KY-610, Lexington, W-KY-780, Louisville, W-KY-870, Mount Sterling, W-KY-1120, Princeton, W-KY-1330, and Winchester, W-KY-1590.

Numismatic Commentary: Almost all notes from this bank and its branches are unknown today.

Valid Issues

6-1/4¢ • W-KY-1470-00.06.25-G010

Left: 6-1/4 CENTS. ***Center:*** 6-1/4 / 6-1/4 on die / 6-1/4. ***Right:*** KENTUCKY vertically. ***Comments:*** H-KY-95-G286, Hughes-237. 1822.

Rarity: *None known*

12-1/2¢ • W-KY-1470-00.12.50-G020

Left: 12-1/2 CENTS. ***Center:*** 12-1/2 / 12-1/2 on die / 12-1/2. ***Right:*** KENTUCKY vertically. ***Comments:*** H-KY-95-G288, Hughes-238. 1822.

Rarity: *None known*

25¢ • W-KY-1470-00.25-G030

Left: 25 CENTS. ***Center:*** 25 / 25 on die / 25. ***Right:*** KENTUCKY vertically. ***Comments:*** H-KY-95-G290, Hughes-239. 1822.

Rarity: *None known*

50¢ • W-KY-1470-00.50-G040

Left: 50 CENTS. ***Center:*** 50 / 50 on die / 50. ***Right:*** KENTUCKY vertically. ***Comments:*** H-KY-95-G292, Hughes-240. 1822.

Rarity: *None known*

$1 • W-KY-1470-001-G050

Left: KENTUCKY vertically. ***Center:*** 1 / 1. ***Right:*** CAMPBELL COUNTY vertically. ***Engraver:*** Murray, Draper, Fairman & Co. ***Comments:*** H-KY-95-G296, Hughes-241. 18__. 1820s.

Rarity: *None known*

$3 • W-KY-1470-003-G060

Left: KENTUCKY vertically. ***Center:*** 3 / 3. ***Right:*** CAMPBELL COUNTY vertically. ***Engraver:*** Murray, Draper, Fairman & Co. ***Comments:*** H-KY-95-G298, Hughes-242. 18__. 1820s.

Rarity: *None known*

$5 • W-KY-1470-005-G070

Left: Woman holding staff. ***Center:*** 5 / Minerva standing with owl, shield, staff / 5. ***Right:*** Woman holding staff. ***Engraver:*** Murray, Draper, Fairman & Co. ***Comments:*** H-KY-95-G300, Hughes-243. 18__. 1820s.

Rarity: URS-1
F $550

$10 • W-KY-1470-010-G080

Left: Woman holding staff. ***Center:*** 10 / Woman standing with staff, shield, Four cherubs / 10. ***Right:*** Woman holding staff. ***Engraver:*** Murray, Draper, Fairman & Co. ***Comments:*** H-KY-95-G302, Hughes-244. 18__. 1820s.

Rarity: URS-1
F $550

$20 • W-KY-1470-020-G090

Engraver: Murray, Draper, Fairman & Co. ***Comments:*** H-KY-95-G304, Hughes-245. No description available. 18__. 1820s.

Rarity: *None known*

$50 • W-KY-1470-050-G100

Engraver: Murray, Draper, Fairman & Co. ***Comments:*** H-KY-95-G306, Hughes-246. No description available. 18__. 1820s.

Rarity: *None known*

$100 • W-KY-1470-100-G110

Engraver: Murray, Draper, Fairman & Co. ***Comments:*** H-KY-95-G308, Hughes-247. No description available. 18__. 1820s.

Rarity: *None known*

Farmers Bank of Kentucky (branch)

1850–1860s

W-KY-1480

History: The Farmers Bank of Kentucky was chartered on February 15, 1850, with an authorized capital of $2,300,000. By September 1852 the bank had opened for business. On February 11, 1860, the charter for the bank was amended, allowing it to increase its capital. The branch located in Somerset had a capital of $100,000. John G. Lair was the cashier in 1855, and Cyrenius Waite was the president. In 1863 Eben Milton was the cashier, and John M. Mail was the president.

As did many banks of the era, during the 1860s the Farmers Bank of Kentucky wound up its affairs and closed.

The Farmers Bank of Kentucky had its parent bank located in Frankfort, W-KY-450, and branch banks located in Bardstown, W-KY-070, Covington, W-KY-240, George Town, W-KY-480, Henderson, W-KY-640, Maysville, W-KY-1050, Mount Sterling, W-KY-1130, and Princeton, W-KY-1340.

Valid Issues

$1 • W-KY-1480-001-G010

Left: 1 / Portrait of John Crittenden / ONE. ***Center:*** Man with dog, Running horses, Donkey. ***Right:*** 1 / Female portrait / ONE. ***Engraver:*** Toppan, Carpenter, Casilear & Co. ***Comments:*** H-KY-100-G170, Hughes-250. 18__. 1850s.

Rarity: URS-3
F $350

$1 • W-KY-1480-001-G010a

Back: Red-orange. ***Engraver:*** Toppan, Carpenter, Casilear & Co. / ABNCo. monogram. ***Comments:*** H-KY-100-G170b, Hughes-Unlisted. Similar to W-KY-1480-001-G010 but with additional engraver imprint. 185_. 1850s.

Rarity: URS-3
F $350

$1 • W-KY-1480-001-G020

Left: 1 / Man and wagon and horses / 1. ***Center:*** Portraits of Mr. and Mrs. John Crittenden. ***Right:*** 1 / 1 on die / 1. ***Tint:*** Red-orange. ***Back:*** Red-orange. ***Engraver:*** American Bank Note Co. ***Comments:*** H-KY-100-G172a, Hughes-249. 18__. 1860s.

Rarity: URS-3
F $350

$2 • **W-KY-1480-002-G030**
Left: 2 / Portrait of Mrs. John Crittenden. ***Center:*** 2 / Man on horse / 2. ***Right:*** 2 / Portrait of John Crittenden. ***Engraver:*** Toppan, Carpenter, Casilear & Co. ***Comments:*** H-KY-100-G174, Hughes-252. 18__. 1850s.

Rarity: URS-3
F $350

$2 • **W-KY-1480-002-G030a**
Back: Red-orange. ***Engraver:*** Toppan, Carpenter, Casilear & Co. / ABNCo. monogram. ***Comments:*** H-KY-100-G174b, Hughes-Unlisted. Similar to W-KY-1480-002-G030 but with additional engraver imprint. 185_. 1850s.

Rarity: URS-3
F $350

$5 • **W-KY-1480-005-G040** CC

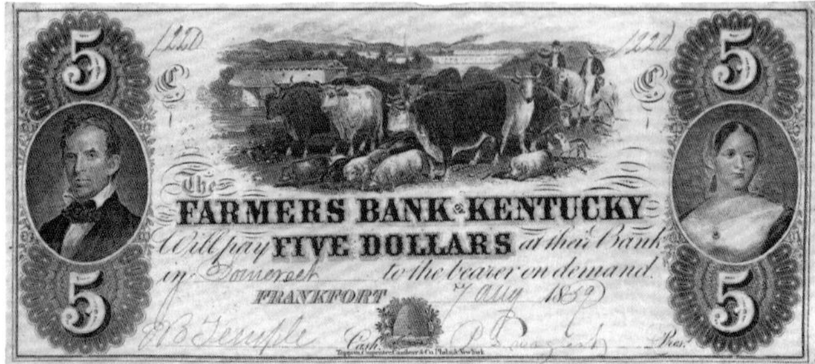

Engraver: Toppan, Carpenter, Casilear & Co. ***Comments:*** H-KY-100-G176, Hughes-256. 18__. 1850s.

Rarity: URS-3
F $200; **EF** $500

$5 • **W-KY-1480-005-G040a**
Overprint: Red FIVE. ***Engraver:*** Toppan, Carpenter, Casilear & Co. ***Comments:*** H-KY-100-G176a, Hughes-257. Similar to W-KY-1480-005-G040. 18__. 1850s.

Rarity: URS-3
F $350

$5 • **W-KY-1480-005-G050**
Left: Men plowing with horse / V. ***Center:*** Portraits of Mr. and Mrs. John Crittenden. ***Right:*** 5 / 5. ***Tint:*** Red-orange. ***Back:*** Red-orange. ***Engraver:*** American Bank Note Co. ***Comments:*** H-KY-100-G178a, Hughes-255. 18__. 1859.

Rarity: URS-3
F $350

$10 • **W-KY-1480-010-G060**
Left: 10 / Portrait of John Crittenden. ***Center:*** Portraits of Mr. and Mrs. John Crittenden. ***Engraver:*** Toppan, Carpenter, Casilear & Co. ***Comments:*** H-KY-100-G180, Hughes-Unlisted. 18__. 1850s.

Rarity: URS-3
F $350

$10 • **W-KY-1480-010-G060a**
Tint: Red-orange outlining white TEN. ***Engraver:*** Toppan, Carpenter, Casilear & Co. ***Comments:*** H-KY-100-G180b, Hughes-Unlisted. Similar to W-KY-1480-010-G060. 18__. 1850s.

Rarity: URS-3
F $350

$10 • **W-KY-1480-010-G070**
Left: 10 / Portrait of John Crittenden. ***Center:*** Woman reclining against barrel, Harvest scene / Portrait of Mrs. John Crittenden. ***Right:*** 10 / Men harvesting corn. ***Tint:*** Red-orange. ***Back:*** Red-orange. ***Engraver:*** American Bank Note Co. ***Comments:*** H-KY-100-G182a, Hughes-259. 18__. 1859.

Rarity: URS-3
F $350

$20 • **W-KY-1480-020-G080**
Left: Portrait of Mrs. John Crittenden / Portrait of John Crittenden. ***Center:*** 20 / Horses plowing. ***Right:*** 20. ***Engraver:*** Toppan, Carpenter, Casilear & Co. ***Comments:*** H-KY-100-G184, Hughes-261. 18__. 1850s.

Rarity: URS-3
F $350

$20 • **W-KY-1480-020-G080a**
Tint: Red-orange. ***Back:*** Red-orange. ***Engraver:*** American Bank Note Co. ***Comments:*** H-KY-100-G186a, Hughes-Unlisted. Similar to W-KY-1480-020-G080 but with different engraver imprint. 18__. 1859.

Rarity: URS-3
F $350

$50 • **W-KY-1480-050-G090**
Left: Three women with anchor. ***Center:*** 50 / Portrait of Mrs. John Crittenden. ***Right:*** 50 / Portrait of John Crittenden / 50. ***Engraver:*** Toppan, Carpenter, Casilear & Co. ***Comments:*** H-KY-100-G188, Hughes-263. 18__. 1850s.

Rarity: URS-2
F $550

$100 • **W-KY-1480-100-G100**
Left: 100 / Portrait of John Crittenden / 100. ***Center:*** Three women reclining / Portrait of Mrs. John Crittenden. ***Right:*** ONE HUNDRED vertically. ***Engraver:*** Toppan, Carpenter, Casilear & Co. ***Comments:*** H-KY-100-G190, Hughes-265. 18__. 1850s.

Rarity: URS-2
F $550

Non-Valid Issues

$5 • **W-KY-1480-005-C040**
Comments: H-KY-100-C176, Hughes-Unlisted. Counterfeit of W-KY-1480-005-G040. 18__. 1850s.

Rarity: URS-4
F $140

$5 • **W-KY-1480-005-C040a**
Comments: H-KY-100-C176a, Hughes-Unlisted. Counterfeit of W-KY-1480-005-G040a. 18__. 1850s.

Rarity: URS-4
F $200

Farmers Bank of Somerset
1818 and 1819
W-KY-1490

History: The Farmers Bank of Somerset was chartered on January 26, 1818. The authorized capital of $100,000 was divided into 1,000 shares of $100 each. William Fox, William C. Thurman, Daniel Clare, John Tammelson, and John Prather were appointed to take stock subscriptions. The bank operated only for a short time in the summer of 1819, when it stopped redeeming its notes. The charters of all independent banks authorized on January 26, 1818, were revoked effective May 1, 1820.

Valid Issues

$1 • W-KY-1490-001-G010

CC

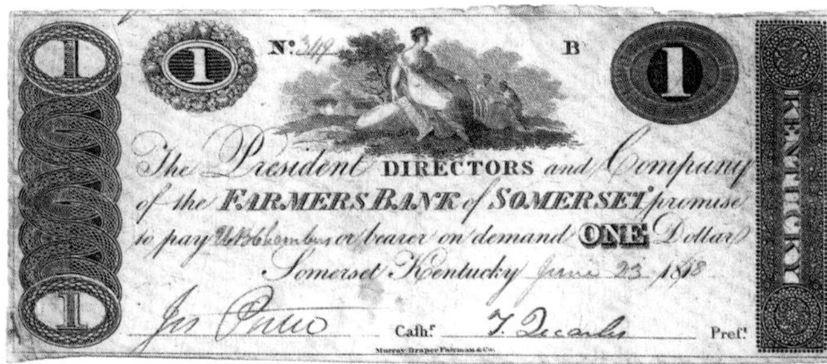

Engraver: Murray, Draper, Fairman & Co. ***Comments:*** H-KY-300-G12, Hughes-772. 181_. 1810s.

Rarity: URS-2
F $400

$3 • W-KY-1490-003-G020

Left: 3 / 3. ***Center:*** III / Woman / 3. ***Right:*** KENTUCKY vertically. ***Engraver:*** Murray, Draper, Fairman & Co. ***Comments:*** H-KY-300-G16, Hughes-773. 181_. 1810s.

Rarity: URS-1
F $550

$5 • W-KY-1490-005-G030

CC

Engraver: Murray, Draper, Fairman & Co. ***Comments:*** H-KY-300-G18, Hughes-774. 181_. 1810s.

Rarity: URS-1
Proof $3,000
Selected auction price: Stack's Bowers Galleries, November 7, 2008, Lot 2038, Proof $3,000

$10 • W-KY-1490-010-G040

CC

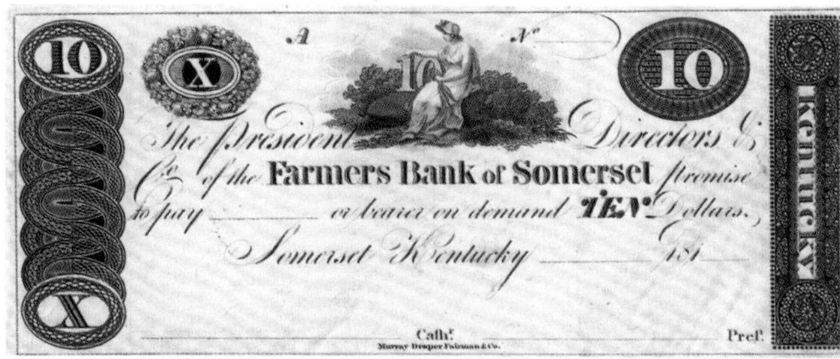

Engraver: Murray, Draper, Fairman & Co. ***Comments:*** H-KY-300-G20, Hughes-775. 181_. 1810s.

Rarity: URS-2
Proof $1,300

$20 • W-KY-1490-020-G050

Engraver: Murray, Draper, Fairman & Co. ***Comments:*** H-KY-300-G22, Hughes-776. No description available. 1810s.

Rarity: *None known*

Springfield, Kentucky

Established in 1793, Springfield was most likely named after springs found in the area. A ferry was established across the Beech Fork River in 1783 as a means of transportation for travelers coming to and from the settlement. Goods were also transported by flatboat up and down the waterway. The town became the county seat of Washington. In 1816 the courthouse was built.

Bank of Kentucky {1st} (branch)

1817–1822

W-KY-1500

History: The Bank of Kentucky (sometimes seen later in print as the "Old" Bank of Kentucky) was incorporated on December 27, 1806, with an authorized capital of $1,000,000. Half of the capital was subscribed to by the state.

The Springfield branch was opened in 1817. On January 21, 1822, the bank was ordered to start closing up its branches. This was to be completed by May 1, 1824. This act essentially shut down the bank. Curiously, all of the paperwork was not completed until the 1870s.

The first Bank of Kentucky had its parent bank located in Frankfort, W-KY-420, and branch banks located in Bardstown, W-KY-050, Danville, W-KY-320, Glasgow, W-KY-500, Hopkinsville, W-KY-660, Lexington, W-KY-760, Louisville, W-KY-840, Paris, W-KY-1260, Richmond, W-KY-1350, Russellville, W-KY-1380, Shelbyville, W-KY-1430, Washington, W-KY-1570, and Winchester, W-KY-1580.

Valid Issues

$1 • W-KY-1500-001-G010

Comments: H-KY-110-G250, Hughes-Unlisted. No description available. 18__. 1815.

Rarity: *None known*

Collectors and Researchers:

If you have new information about any banks or notes listed in this volume, contact Whitman Publishing, Attn: Obsolete Paper Money, 3101 Clairmont Road, Suite G, Atlanta, GA 30329.

$1 • **W-KY-1500-001-G020**
Left: BRANCH BANK vertically. ***Center:*** 1 / Running deer, plow, ax / 1. ***Right:*** 1 / ONE / 1 vertically. ***Engraver:*** Unverified, but likely Murray, Draper, Fairman & Co. ***Comments:*** H-KY-110-G252, Hughes-283. 18__. 1816.

Rarity: URS-3
F $450

$1 • **W-KY-1500-001-G030**
Engraver: Murray, Draper, Fairman & Co. ***Comments:*** H-KY-110-G254, Hughes-Unlisted. No description available. 18__. 1821.

Rarity: *None known*

$5 • **W-KY-1500-005-G040**
Engraver: Unverified, but likely W. Harrison. ***Comments:*** H-KY-110-G256, Hughes-Unlisted. No description available. 18__. 1810s.

Rarity: *None known*

$10 • **W-KY-1500-010-G050**
Engraver: Unverified, but likely W. Harrison. ***Comments:*** H-KY-110-G258, Hughes-Unlisted. No description available. 18__. 1810s–1820.

Rarity: *None known*

$20 • **W-KY-1500-020-G060**
Engraver: Unverified, but likely W. Harrison. ***Comments:*** H-KY-110-G260, Hughes-Unlisted. No description available. 18__. 1810s.

Rarity: *None known*

$50 • **W-KY-1500-050-G070**
Engraver: Unverified, but likely W. Harrison. ***Comments:*** H-KY-110-G262, Hughes-Unlisted. No description available. 18__. 1810s.

Rarity: *None known*

$100 • **W-KY-1500-100-G080**
Engraver: Unverified, but likely W. Harrison. ***Comments:*** H-KY-110-G264, Hughes-Unlisted. No description available. 18__. 1810s.

Rarity: *None known*

Post Notes

$__ • **W-KY-1500-__-G090**
Left: POST NOTE vertically. ***Center:*** __ / Cherub riding leaping deer / __. ***Right:*** POST NOTE vertically. ***Engraver:*** Murray, Draper, Fairman & Co. ***Comments:*** H-KY-110-G266, Hughes-295. 18__. 1810s.

Rarity: URS-2
F $450

Farmers and Mechanics Bank of Springfield
1818–1820
W-KY-1510

History: The Farmers and Mechanics Bank of Springfield was chartered on January 26, 1818. It operated briefly, but by autumn 1819 it was no longer redeeming its bills. The charters of all independent banks authorized on January 26, 1818, were revoked effective May 1, 1820.

Numismatic Commentary: Low-denomination notes probably exist but have not been verified.

Valid Issues

$50 • **W-KY-1510-050-G010** CC

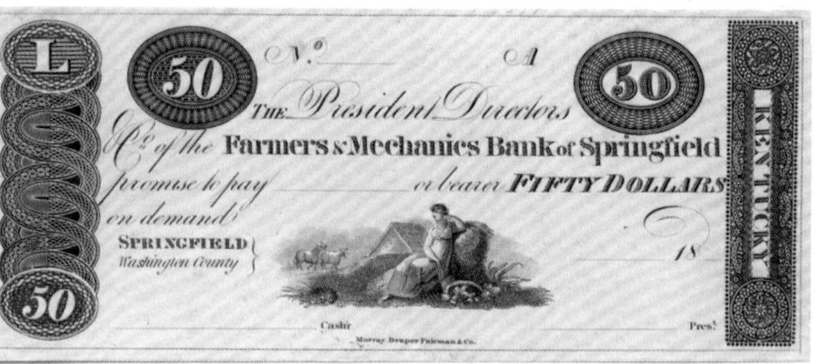

Engraver: Murray, Draper, Fairman & Co. ***Comments:*** H-Unlisted, Hughes-777. 18__. 1818.

Rarity: URS-1
Proof $2,500

$100 • **W-KY-1510-100-G020**
Comments: H-Unlisted, Hughes-778. No description available. 1818.

Rarity: *None known*

Springfield Deposit Bank
1860s
W-KY-1520

History: In 1861 the capital of the Springfield Deposit Bank was $50,000. The cashier was C.R. McElroy, and the president was H. McElroy. In 1863 the circulation of the bank was $32,027.

Stanford, Kentucky

Benjamin Logan founded Stanford in 1775 at a place called Logan's Fort. It was also known as Saint Asaph for a time, but the original name is thought to have come from "Standing Fort," another name by which Fort Logan was known. Another theory is that it was named after Stamford, England. The courthouse was built in 1781. In 1786 Stanford was chartered, and the first church was built in 1790. A library was built during the 1830s, and the first school followed in the 1850s.

Stanford was unaffected for the most part during the Civil War, with the closest battle taking place 20 miles away from the town's borders. This allowed the town to recover very quickly after the war had ended.

Stanford Bank
1818
W-KY-1530

History: The Stanford Bank was chartered in January 1818. It is unknown whether the bank ever opened for business.

Stanford Deposit Bank

1854–1860s

W-KY-1540

History: On March 1, 1854, the Stanford Deposit Bank was chartered. In 1861 the cashier was J.W. Proctor, and the president was Leo Hayden. Capital was $50,000, and circulation was $55,281.

Versailles, Kentucky

On June 23, 1792, the city of Versailles was founded and named after the town of the same name in France. The area became known for its healthy livestock and thoroughbred horses. The town was officially incorporated on February 13, 1837. During the Civil War, Versailles was occupied at various times by both the Confederacy and the Union.

Bank of Versailles

1818–1820

W-KY-1550

History: The Bank of Versailles was chartered on January 26, 1818, with an authorized capital of $200,000 to be divided into 2,000 shares of $100 apiece. Peter C. Buck, John McKinney Jr., William P. Long, William Mayo, Porter Clay, Norborn B. Cook, and John Buford were appointed to take stock subscriptions. The bank's bills were current in 1819, but the charters of all independent banks authorized on January 26, 1818, were revoked effective May 1, 1820.

Valid Issues

$1 • W-KY-1550-001-G010

CC

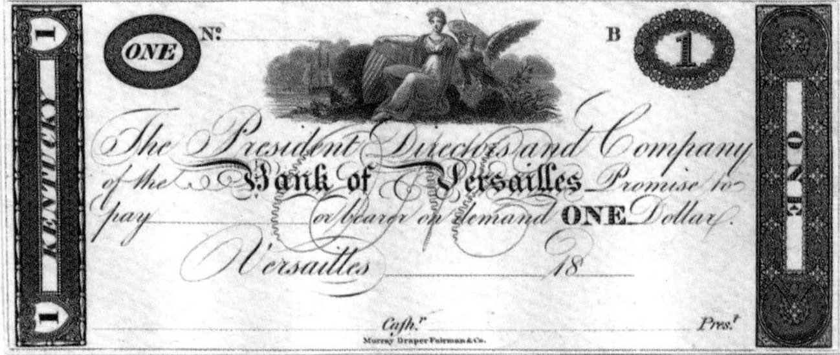

Engraver: Murray, Draper, Fairman & Co. ***Comments:*** H-KY-315-G12, Hughes-782. 181_. 1810s.

Rarity: URS-2

Proof $900

$3 • W-KY-1550-003-G020

CC

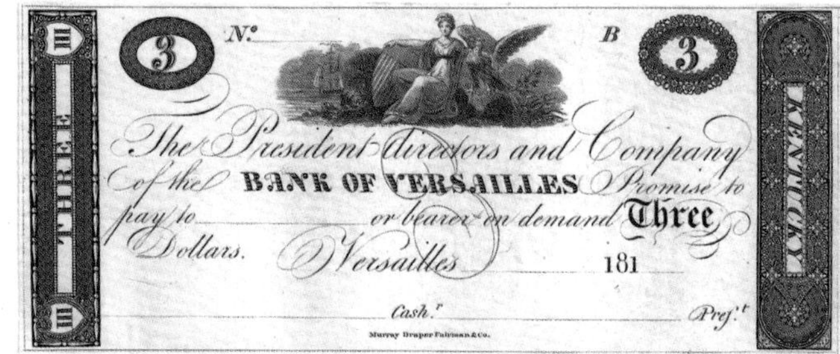

Engraver: Murray, Draper, Fairman & Co. ***Comments:*** H-KY-315-G16, Hughes-783. 181_. 1810s.

Rarity: URS-1

Proof $1,200

$5 • W-KY-1550-005-G030

HA

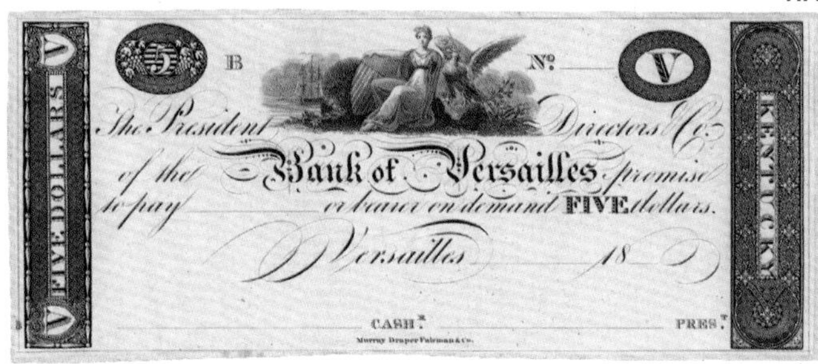

Engraver: Murray, Draper, Fairman & Co. ***Comments:*** H-KY-315-G18, Hughes-784. 18__. 1810s.

Rarity: URS-2

Proof $2,400

Selected auction price: Heritage Auctions, September 25, 2013, Lot 15835, Proof $2,350

$10 • W-KY-1550-010-G040

Left: X / TEN DOLL / X vertically. ***Center:*** 10 / Woman with eagle, Ship / X. ***Right:*** KENTUCKY vertically. ***Engraver:*** Murray, Draper, Fairman & Co. ***Comments:*** H-KY-315-G20, Hughes-785. 181_. 1810s.

Rarity: URS-1

Proof $2,300

$20 • W-KY-1550-020-G050

CC

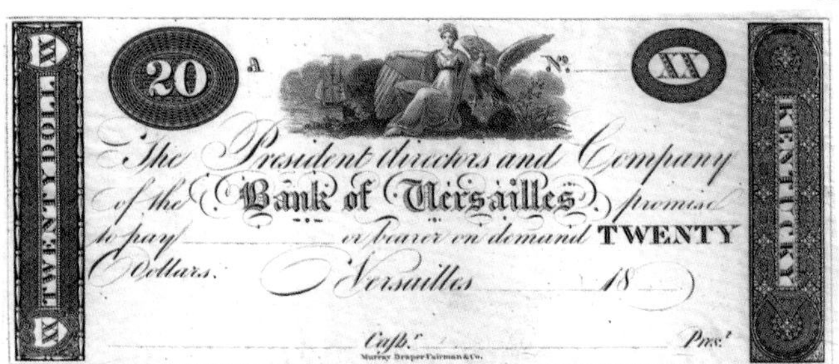

Engraver: Murray, Draper, Fairman & Co. ***Comments:*** H-KY-315-G22, Hughes-786. 181_. 1810s.

Rarity: URS-2

F $700; **Proof** $2,400

Post Notes

$__ • W-KY-1550-__-G060 CC

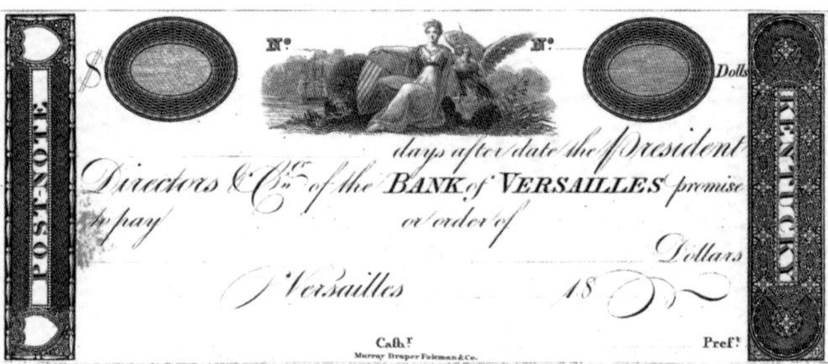

Engraver: Murray, Draper, Fairman & Co. ***Comments:*** H-Unlisted, Hughes-Unlisted. 18__. 1810s.

Rarity: URS-2
F $550

Commercial Bank of Kentucky (branch)

1852–1871

W-KY-1560

History: On January 3, 1852, the Commercial Bank of Kentucky was chartered. The Versailles branch was established the same year. The president was D. Thornton, and the cashier was E.H. Taylor Jr. In 1855 the capital was $100,000. Richard D. Shipp took the position of cashier. By 1861 the capital had risen to $150,000. In 1871 the branch was succeeded by the Commercial National Bank.

The Commercial Bank of Kentucky had its parent bank located in Paducah, W-KY-1240, and branch banks located in Cynthiana, W-KY-290, Harrodsburg, W-KY-590, Lebanon, W-KY-720, Louisville, W-KY-900, Monticello, W-KY-1070, and Newport, W-KY-1150.

Numismatic Commentary: Remaining at the American Bank Note Co. archives as of 2003 was a $1 face plate, two $1-$1-$1-$1 tint plates, a $5-$5-$10-$20 back plate, and two $5-$5-$10-$20 tint plates.

Valid Issues

$1 • W-KY-1560-001-G010 CC

Tint: Green panel of microlettering outlining white ONE, die outlining white ONE, and ornaments. ***Engraver:*** American Bank Note Co. ***Comments:*** H-Unlisted, Hughes-668. 18__. 1860s.

Rarity: URS-3
F $350; **Proof** $750

$1 • W-KY-1560-001-G020

Left: ONE / Steamboat vertically / ONE. ***Center:*** Coin, Man kneeling next to hewn log. ***Right:*** 1 / Male portrait / ONE. ***Engraver:*** Rawdon, Wright, Hatch & Edson. ***Comments:*** H-KY-255-G120, Hughes-664. 185_. 1850s.

Rarity: URS-3
F $350

$1 • W-KY-1560-001-G030

Left: Woman with 1 / 1. ***Center:*** Farmers, Woman seated. ***Right:*** Woman with 1 / 1. ***Engraver:*** Toppan, Carpenter, Casilear & Co. ***Comments:*** H-KY-255-G122, Hughes-665. 185_. 1850s.

Rarity: URS-3
F $350

$1 • W-KY-1560-001-G030a

Overprint: Red ONE. ***Engraver:*** Toppan, Carpenter, Casilear & Co. ***Comments:*** H-KY-G122a, Hughes-666. Similar to W-KY-1560-001-G030. 185_. 1850s.

Rarity: URS-3
F $350

$1 • W-KY-1560-001-G030b

Tint: Green. ***Engraver:*** Toppan, Carpenter, Casilear & Co. / ABNCo. monogram. ***Comments:*** H-KY-G122b, Hughes-Unlisted. Similar to W-KY-1560-001-G030 but with additional engraver imprint. 185_. 1850s.

Rarity: URS-3
F $550

How to Read the Whitman Numbering System

$1 • W-AL-020-001-G010a

Denomination: Face value of the note shown.

W: Whitman number. This number is a sortable code unique to each bank and note.

AL: Abbreviation for the state under study.

020: Numerical designation specific to each bank.

001: The denomination in dollars.

G010a: G indicates a good or valid note. Other categories are indicated thus: C (counterfeit); R (raised); S (spurious); N (not-attributed); A (altered). Numbers are assigned starting with 010, 020, et seq. Terminal letters following the number indicate variations of a note: a series of different colored overprints, tints, payees, etc., all on the same design of note. For more information, see the "How to Use This Book" section at the front of the volume, page xiv.

$3 • W-KY-1560-003-G040
Left: THREE / Male portrait / THREE. ***Center:*** Three gold dollars, Farmer with scythe, Blacksmith, Sailor. ***Right:*** 3 / Steamboat on stocks. ***Engraver:*** Rawdon, Wright, Hatch & Edson. ***Comments:*** H-KY-255-G124, Hughes-673. 185_. 1850s.
Rarity: URS-3
F $350

$5 • W-KY-1560-005-G050
Left: 5 / Portrait of Millard Fillmore / FIVE. ***Center:*** Woman and man flanking three cherubs and five coins. ***Right:*** FIVE / Scene vertically / FIVE. ***Engraver:*** Rawdon, Wright, Hatch & Edson. ***Comments:*** H-KY-255-G126, Hughes-674. 185_. 1850s.
Rarity: URS-3
F $200

$5 • W-KY-1560-005-G060
Left: FIVE / Men and women in and around V. ***Center:*** 5 / Women in and around 5, Dock. ***Right:*** FIVE / Portrait of Franklin Pierce. ***Engraver:*** Rawdon, Wright, Hatch & Edson / ABNCo. monogram. ***Comments:*** H-KY-255-G128. 18__. 1850s–1860s.
Rarity: URS-3
F $200

$5 • W-KY-1560-005-G060a
Tint: Red-orange. ***Engraver:*** Rawdon, Wright, Hatch & Edson / ABNCo. monogram. ***Comments:*** H-KY-255-G128a, Hughes-675. Similar to W-KY-1560-005-G060. 18__. 1850s–1860s.
Rarity: URS-3
F $200

$10 • W-KY-1560-010-G070
Left: 10 / Male portrait / TEN. ***Center:*** Steamboats. ***Right:*** TEN / Harrodsburg Springs / TEN. ***Engraver:*** Unverified, but likely Rawdon, Wright, Hatch & Edson. ***Comments:*** H-KY-255-G130, Hughes-677. 185_. 1850s.
Rarity: URS-3
F $250

$20 • W-KY-1560-020-G080
Comments: H-Unlisted, Hughes-Unlisted. No description available. 18__. 1850s.
Rarity: *None known*

Non-Valid Issues

$20 • W-KY-1560-020-R010
Overprint: Red-brown TWENTY. ***Comments:*** H-KY-255-R10, Hughes-680. Raised from W-KY-1560-001-G020. 185_. 1850s.
Rarity: URS-4
F $150

Washington, Kentucky

Arthur Fox founded Washington in 1786, along with a preacher by the name of William Wood. This area is thought to be the first namesake of George Washington. Most of the settlers were made up of discharged soldiers who had served in the Revolutionary War. With a population of 462 in 1790, Washington was the second-largest town in the future state of Kentucky, exceeded only by Lexington.

The post office of Washington was opened in 1789. In 1830 Andrew Jackson vetoed a law allowing the government to purchase stock of the Maysville-Washington-Lexington Turnpike Road Company. In 1833 Harriet Beecher (later Harriet Beecher Stowe) visited Washington, and many of the characters and locations in her novel *Uncle Tom's Cabin* are thought to be based on the people and places she saw there.

Washington began to decline during the 1840s. In 1848 Maysville replaced Washington as the county seat of Mason.

Bank of Kentucky {1st} (branch)

1813–1822

W-KY-1570

History: The Bank of Kentucky (sometimes seen later in print as the "Old" Bank of Kentucky) was incorporated on December 27, 1806, with an authorized capital of $1,000,000. Half of the capital was subscribed to by the state.

The Washington branch was opened in 1813. On January 21, 1822, the bank was ordered to start closing up its branches. This was to be completed by May 1, 1824. This act essentially shut down the bank. Curiously, all of the paperwork was not completed until the 1870s.

The first Bank of Kentucky had its parent bank located in Frankfort, W-KY-420, and branch banks located in Bardstown, W-KY-050, Danville, W-KY-320, Glasgow, W-KY-500, Hopkinsville, W-KY-660, Lexington, W-KY-760, Louisville, W-KY-840, Paris, W-KY-1260, Richmond, W-KY-1350, Russellville, W-KY-1380, Shelbyville, W-KY-1430, Springfield, W-KY-1500, and Winchester, W-KY-1580.

Valid Issues

50¢ • W-KY-1570-00.50-G010
Comments: H-KY-110-G268, Hughes-Unlisted. No description available. 18__. June 1, 1816.
Rarity: *None known*

$1 • W-KY-1570-001-G020
Left: BRANCH BANK vertically. ***Center:*** 1 / Running deer, plow, ax / 1. ***Right:*** 1 / ONE / 1 vertically. ***Engraver:*** Unverified, but likely Murray, Draper, Fairman & Co. ***Comments:*** H-KY-110-G270, Hughes-283. 18__. 1816.
Rarity: URS-2
F $300

$1 • W-KY-1570-001-G030
Engraver: Murray, Draper, Fairman & Co. ***Comments:*** H-KY-110-G272, Hughes-Unlisted. No description available. 18__. 1821.
Rarity: *None known*

$3 • W-KY-1570-003-G040
Engraver: Murray, Draper, Fairman & Co. ***Comments:*** H-KY-110-G274, Hughes-Unlisted. No description available. 18__. 1821.
Rarity: *None known*

$5 • W-KY-1570-005-G050
Engraver: Unverified, but likely W. Harrison. ***Comments:*** H-KY-110-G276, Hughes-Unlisted. No description available. 18__. 1810s.

Rarity: *None known*

$5 • W-KY-1570-005-G060
Engraver: Unverified, but likely W. Harrison. ***Comments:*** H-KY-110-G278, Hughes-Unlisted. No description available. 18__. 1810s.

Rarity: *None known*

$10 • W-KY-1570-010-G070
Left: DEPARMENT vertically. ***Center:*** Running deer, plow, ax / TEN. ***Right:*** 10. ***Engraver:*** W. Harrison. ***Comments:*** H-KY-110-G280, Hughes-287. 18__. 1808–1810s.

Rarity: URS-2
F $550

$10 • W-KY-1570-010-G080
Engraver: Unverified, but likely W. Harrison. ***Comments:*** H-KY-110-G282, Hughes-Unlisted. No description available. 18__. 1810s–1820.

Rarity: *None known*

$20 • W-KY-1570-020-G090
Engraver: Unverified, but likely W. Harrison. ***Comments:*** H-KY-110-G284, Hughes-Unlisted. No description available. 18__. 1808–1810s.

Rarity: *None known*

$20 • W-KY-1570-020-G100
Engraver: Unverified, but likely W. Harrison. ***Comments:*** H-KY-110-G286, Hughes-Unlisted. No description available. 18__. 1810s.

Rarity: *None known*

$50 • W-KY-1570-050-G110
Engraver: Unverified, but likely W. Harrison. ***Comments:*** H-KY-110-G288, Hughes-Unlisted. No description available. 18__. 1808–1810s.

Rarity: *None known*

$50 • W-KY-1570-050-G120
Engraver: Unverified, but likely W. Harrison. ***Comments:*** H-KY-110-G290, Hughes-Unlisted. No description available. 18__. 1810s.

Rarity: *None known*

$100 • W-KY-1570-100-G130
Engraver: Unverified, but likely W. Harrison. ***Comments:*** H-KY-110-G292, Hughes-Unlisted. No description available. 18__. 1808–1810s.

Rarity: *None known*

$100 • W-KY-1570-100-G140
Engraver: Unverified, but likely W. Harrison. ***Comments:*** H-KY-110-G294, Hughes-Unlisted. No description available. 18__. 1810s.

Rarity: *None known*

Post Notes

$__ • W-KY-1570-__-G150
Left: Post Note vertically. ***Center:*** Dolls __ / Dolls __. ***Right:*** Post Note vertically. ***Engraver:*** W. Harrison. ***Comments:*** H-KY-110-G296, Hughes-Unlisted. 18__. 1810s–1820s.

Rarity: URS-2
F $550

$__ • W-KY-1570-__-G160
Left: POST NOTE vertically. ***Center:*** __ / Cherub riding leaping deer / __. ***Right:*** POST NOTE vertically. ***Engraver:*** Murray, Draper, Fairman & Co. ***Comments:*** H-KY-110-G298, Hughes-295. 18__. 1810s.

Rarity: URS-2
F $550

WINCHESTER, KENTUCKY

Winchester was named after Winchester, Virginia, and was established in 1793. It was chosen to be the county seat of Clark.

Bank of Kentucky {1st} (branch)
1816–1822
W-KY-1580

History: The Bank of Kentucky (sometimes seen later in print as the "Old" Bank of Kentucky) was incorporated on December 27, 1806, with an authorized capital of $1,000,000. Half of the capital was subscribed to by the state.

The Winchester branch was opened in 1816. On January 21, 1822, the bank was ordered to start closing up its branches. This was to be completed by May 1, 1824. This act essentially shut down the bank. Curiously, all of the paperwork was not completed until the 1870s.

The first Bank of Kentucky had its parent bank located in Frankfort, W-KY-420, and branch banks located in Bardstown, W-KY-050, Danville, W-KY-320, Glasgow, W-KY-500, Hopkinsville, W-KY-660, Lexington, W-KY-760, Louisville, W-KY-840, Paris, W-KY-1260, Richmond, W-KY-1350, Russellville, W-KY-1380, Shelbyville, W-KY-1430, Springfield, W-KY-1500, and Washington, W-KY-1570.

VALID ISSUES

25¢ • W-KY-1580-00.25-G010
Left: QUARTER DOLLAR. ***Center:*** 25 CENTS. ***Comments:*** H-KY-110-G300, Hughes-787. July 10, 1816.

Rarity: URS-2
F $550

50¢ • W-KY-1580-00.50-G020
Comments: H-KY-110-G302, Hughes-Unlisted. No description available. 1816.

Rarity: *None known*

$1 • W-KY-1580-001-G030
Comments: H-KY-110-G304, Hughes-Unlisted. No description available. 18__. 1815.

Rarity: *None known*

$1 • W-KY-1580-001-G040
Left: BRANCH BANK vertically. ***Center:*** 1 / Running deer, plow, ax / 1. ***Right:*** 1 / ONE / 1 vertically. ***Engraver:*** Unverified, but likely Murray, Draper, Fairman & Co. ***Comments:*** H-KY-110-G306, Hughes-283. 18__. 1816.

Rarity: URS-3
F $350

$1 • W-KY-1580-001-G050
Engraver: Murray, Draper, Fairman & Co. ***Comments:*** H-KY-110-G308, Hughes-Unlisted. No description available. 18__. 1821.
Rarity: *None known*

$5 • W-KY-1580-005-G060
Engraver: Unverified, but likely W. Harrison. ***Comments:*** H-KY-110-G310, Hughes-Unlisted. No description available. 18__. 1810s.
Rarity: *None known*

$5 • W-KY-1580-005-G070
Engraver: Unverified, but likely Murray, Draper, Fairman & Co. ***Comments:*** H-KY-110-G312, Hughes-Unlisted. No description available. 18__. 1810s.
Rarity: *None known*

$10 • W-KY-1580-010-G080
Engraver: Unverified, but likely W. Harrison. ***Comments:*** H-KY-110-G314, Hughes-Unlisted. No description available. 18__. 1810s–1820.
Rarity: *None known*

$20 • W-KY-1580-020-G090
Engraver: Unverified, but likely W. Harrison. ***Comments:*** H-KY-110-G316, Hughes-Unlisted. No description available. 18__. 1810s.
Rarity: *None known*

$50 • W-KY-1580-050-G100
Engraver: Unverified, but likely W. Harrison. ***Comments:*** H-KY-110-G318, Hughes-Unlisted. No description available. 18__. 1810s.
Rarity: *None known*

$100 • W-KY-1580-100-G110
Engraver: Unverified, but likely W. Harrison. ***Comments:*** H-KY-110-G320, Hughes-Unlisted. No description available. 18__. 1810s.
Rarity: *None known*

Bank of the Commonwealth of Kentucky (branch)
1821–1830
W-KY-1590

History: The Bank of the Commonwealth of Kentucky was chartered on November 29, 1820, with an authorized capital of $2,000,000. A local name for the bank was the "Peoples Bank," as it was chartered for the purpose of bringing relief to the population in a time of economic uncertainty. On December 22, 1820, an act was passed authorizing the bank to issue $3,000,000 in bills. The establishment of the Bank of the Commonwealth of Kentucky inadvertently caused the failure of the first Bank of Kentucky, W-KY-420. The branch located in Winchester opened in 1821.

In 1830 the bank lost its authorization to loan money, and it was instructed to close up its branches. Around that time the bank ceased new business, but the winding up of its affairs took until 1855.

The Bank of the Commonwealth of Kentucky had its parent bank located in Frankfort, W-KY-440, and branch banks located in Bowling Green, W-KY-090, Falmouth, W-KY-360, Flemingsburg, W-KY-410, Greensburg, W-KY-550, Harrodsburg, W-KY-580, Hartford, W-KY-610, Lexington, W-KY-780, Louisville, W-KY-870, Mount Sterling, W-KY-1120, Princeton, W-KY-1330, and Somerset, W-KY-1470.

Numismatic Commentary: Almost all notes from this bank and its branches are unknown today.

Valid Issues

6-1/4¢ • W-KY-1590-00.06.25-G010
Left: 6-1/4 CENTS. ***Center:*** 6-1/4 / 6-1/4 on die / 6-1/4. ***Right:*** KENTUCKY vertically. ***Comments:*** H-KY-95-G312, Hughes-237. 1822.
Rarity: *None known*

12-1/2¢ • W-KY-1590-00.12.50-G020
Left: 12-1/2 CENTS. ***Center:*** 12-1/2 / 12-1/2 on die / 12-1/2. ***Right:*** KENTUCKY vertically. ***Comments:*** H-KY-95-G314, Hughes-238. 1822.
Rarity: *None known*

25¢ • W-KY-1590-00.25-G030
Left: 25 CENTS. ***Center:*** 25 / 25 on die / 25. ***Right:*** KENTUCKY vertically. ***Comments:*** H-KY-95-G316, Hughes-239. 1822.
Rarity: *None known*

50¢ • W-KY-1590-00.50-G040
Left: 50 CENTS. ***Center:*** 50 / 50 on die / 50. ***Right:*** KENTUCKY vertically. ***Comments:*** H-KY-95-G318, Hughes-240. 1822.
Rarity: *None known*

$1 • W-KY-1590-001-G050
Left: KENTUCKY vertically. ***Center:*** 1 / 1. ***Right:*** CAMPBELL COUNTY vertically. ***Engraver:*** Murray, Draper, Fairman & Co. ***Comments:*** H-KY-95-G322, Hughes-241. 18__. 1820s.
Rarity: URS-2
F $550

$3 • W-KY-1590-003-G060
Left: KENTUCKY vertically. ***Center:*** 3 / 3. ***Right:*** CAMPBELL COUNTY vertically. ***Engraver:*** Murray, Draper, Fairman & Co. ***Comments:*** H-KY-95-G324, Hughes-242. 18__. 1820s.
Rarity: *None known*

$5 • W-KY-1590-005-G070
Left: Woman holding staff. ***Center:*** 5 / Minerva standing with owl, shield, staff / 5. ***Right:*** Woman holding staff. ***Engraver:*** Murray, Draper, Fairman & Co. ***Comments:*** H-KY-95-G326, Hughes-243. 18__. 1820s.
Rarity: *None known*

$10 • W-KY-1590-010-G080
Left: Woman holding staff. ***Center:*** 10 / Woman standing with staff, shield, Four cherubs / 10. ***Right:*** Woman holding staff. ***Engraver:*** Murray, Draper, Fairman & Co. ***Comments:*** H-KY-95-G328, Hughes-244. 18__. 1820s.
Rarity: *None known*

$20 • W-KY-1590-020-G090
Engraver: Murray, Draper, Fairman & Co. ***Comments:*** H-KY-95-G330, Hughes-245. No description available. 18__. 1820s.
Rarity: *None known*

$50 • W-KY-1590-050-G100
Engraver: Murray, Draper, Fairman & Co. ***Comments:*** H-KY-95-G332, Hughes-246. No description available. 18__. 1820s.
Rarity: *None known*

$100 • W-KY-1590-100-G110
Engraver: Murray, Draper, Fairman & Co. ***Comments:*** H-KY-95-G334, Hughes-247. No description available. 18__. 1820s.
Rarity: *None known*

Winchester Commercial Bank
1818–1820
W-KY-1600

History: The Winchester Commercial Bank was chartered in 1818 with an authorized capital of $200,000. It was in operation for a short time before closing in 1820.

Numismatic Commentary: Few notes of this bank have been found.

Valid Issues

$1 • W-KY-1600-001-G010
Left: ONE vertically. ***Center:*** ONE / Woman gazing at river, Boat / ONE. ***Right:*** KENTUCKY vertically. ***Engraver:*** Murray, Draper, Fairman & Co. ***Comments:*** H-KY-320-G12, Hughes-788. 18__. 1810s.
Rarity: *None known*

$3 • W-KY-1600-003-G020
Left: THREE vertically. ***Center:*** THREE / Woman gazing at river, Boat / THREE. ***Right:*** KENTUCKY vertically. ***Engraver:*** Murray, Draper, Fairman & Co. ***Comments:*** H-KY-320-G16, Hughes-789. 18__. 1810s.
Rarity: *None known*

$5 • W-KY-1600-005-G030
Left: FIVE vertically. ***Center:*** FIVE / Woman gazing at river, Boat / FIVE. ***Right:*** KENTUCKY vertically. ***Engraver:*** Murray, Draper, Fairman & Co. ***Comments:*** H-KY-320-G18, Hughes-790. 18__. 1810s.
Rarity: *None known*

$10 • W-KY-1600-010-G040
Left: TEN vertically. ***Center:*** TEN / Woman gazing at river, Boat / TEN. ***Right:*** KENTUCKY vertically. ***Engraver:*** Murray, Draper, Fairman & Co. ***Comments:*** H-KY-320-G20, Hughes-791. 18__. 1810s.
Rarity: *None known*

$20 • W-KY-1600-020-G050
Left: TWENTY vertically. ***Center:*** TWENTY / Woman gazing at river, Boat / TWENTY. ***Right:*** KENTUCKY vertically. ***Engraver:*** Murray, Draper, Fairman & Co. ***Comments:*** H-KY-320-G22, Hughes-792. 18__. 1810s.
Rarity: *None known*

$50 • W-KY-1600-050-G060
Left: FIFTY vertically. ***Center:*** FIFTY / Woman gazing at river, Boat / FIFTY. ***Right:*** KENTUCKY vertically. ***Engraver:*** Murray, Draper, Fairman & Co. ***Comments:*** H-KY-320-G24, Hughes-793. 18__. 1810s.
Rarity: URS-1
Proof $1,000

Post Notes

$__ • W-KY-1600-__-G070
Center: Woman gazing at river, Boat. ***Right:*** KENTUCKY vertically. ***Comments:*** H-Unlisted, Hughes-795. 18__. 1810s.
Rarity: URS-2
F $400

$100 • W-KY-1600-100-G080
Left: HUNDRED vertically. ***Center:*** HUNDRED / Woman gazing at river, Boat / HUNDRED. ***Right:*** KENTUCKY vertically. ***Comments:*** H-Unlisted, Hughes-794. 18__. 1810s.
Rarity: —

THE OBSOLETE BANK NOTES OF LOUISIANA

STATE BANKING IN LOUISIANA

Early Banking

The first bank in the Louisiana Territory, part of a vast expanse that was to become a state in 1812, was established in 1804 with a capital of $500,000. The Louisiana Bank, as it was called, was based in New Orleans and did business until the early 1820s. By 1815 there were a total of three banks operating in Louisiana with a combined capital of $1,432,300. The Commercial Bank, an entity of which little is known today (and different from the later Commercial Bank established in 1833), was set up to supply water to New Orleans but pursued banking and issued paper money. The Planters Bank is numismatically remembered for counterstamping cut sections of Spanish dollars in the 1810s. In 1819 the cashier of the bank, B. Blanchard, disappeared, and it was rumored that he had decamped with a large sum of money. Hurried examination of the bank's assets revealed that all was in good order. Blanchard's body was later found in the Mississippi River, the victim of thugs.

On March 14, 1818, the state proposed to enter the banking business for its own account by subscribing to $500,000 of the proposed $2,000,000 capital of the Louisiana State Bank; only $100,000 was eventually paid in. Headquartered in New Orleans and with branches in Alexandria, Baton Rouge, Donaldsonville, New Orleans (second municipality), Saint Francisville, Saint Martinville, and Shreveport, the bank remained in business through the Civil War and later became the State National Bank of New Orleans. Although it was named *State Bank* during the obsolete-currency era, most stock was held by private entities.

On April 7, 1824, the Bank of Louisiana was capitalized at $4,000,000, with the state having half interest. The head office was in New Orleans, and five branches were required to be established. This bank also operated for a long time, later evolving into the National Bank of New Orleans. The Union Bank of Louisiana, incorporated in New Orleans for $7,000,000 in 1832, failed in 1842. The bank was financed by state bonds, and subscribers to the stock pledged mortgages as surety. A decade later another bank opened with this name and eventually became the Union National Bank.

Among the southernmost states studied in the present text, Louisiana is the only one that was under control of the Confederate States of America for a short time. After the Civil War ended in 1865, many soundly based banks in operation transitioned to become national banks, in contrast to the other southernmost states where nearly all of the banks failed by the end of the Civil War. National banks later established there were unrelated to the earlier state-chartered banks in terms of officers, shareholders, and business.

The Hard Times Era

During the era under study, many other banks were set up in Louisiana, with New Orleans being their primary location. The New Orleans Canal and Banking Company, known as the Canal Bank, went into operation in 1831 and soon did an extensive business. The New Orleans Gas Light and Banking Company, called the "Gas Bank" in popular accounts, was chartered in 1835 with an authorized capital of $6,000,000, and in the same year purchased the facilities but not the business of the branch of the second Bank of the United States. Branches for this bank were planned for Alexandria, Harrisonburg, Napoleonville, Port Hudson, and Springfield, with the expectation that similar gas-light systems would be put into place in those towns. However, these never went into operation, and in 1845 the banking privileges of the company were surrendered. By January 1, 1837, there were 16 banks in Louisiana doing business through 31 offices, these in addition to brokers and other businesses trading as banks and often issuing bills. The Panic of 1837 took hold full force across America beginning in May of that year, two months after Martin Van Buren was inaugurated as president. All banks in Louisiana suffered to an extent, and specie payments (redemption of bank notes with gold and silver coins) were suspended by most institutions nationwide.

In the twilight of the Hard Times period, banking conditions precipitated anarchy in New Orleans. *Niles' National Register*, June 18, 1842, reported:

> The attempt of the banks of New Orleans to resume specie payments has proved unavailing. They resumed on the 18th and 19th of May, but an immediate depreciation of

> the municipality notes ensued, and on the 20th a mob destroyed several brokers' shops, but was soon quelled with the arrest of the ringleaders. In a few days, more than $600,000 was drained from them.
>
> Some disagreement amongst themselves led to distrust; a panic and a severe run ensued, which some of them maintained for several days, and finally all had to suspend. The Citizens Bank and Louisiana State Bank on the 31st ult. announced that they suspend until the 5th of December. The Consolidated Bank, the Commercial Bank, and the Canal Bank were overwhelmed on the 1st inst. The crowd was tremendous and some lives were lost. The City Bank held out until the 2d inst. but then gave in. The Mechanics and Traders bank, the Carrollton Bank, and Union Bank and the Bank of Louisiana continue to pay specie, but except the latter, they are said to have no notes out, and to be doing but little business.

In July 1842 conditions improved, and four banks in New Orleans were able to resume specie payments: the Gas Bank, the Bank of Louisiana, the Union Bank, and the Mechanics and Traders Bank. However, these banks had very few bills in circulation. Those that did saw their currency trading at deep discounts, as much as 30% to 35% for the Canal, Commercial, and Consolidated banks, and up to 40% for the Citizens Bank. This wreaked havoc on the holders of such bills who held them as assets and sought to use them in everyday transactions and commerce.

In the pivotal year of 1842, following difficult times and bank failures, the state enacted a law requiring banks to maintain a reserve in specie equal to one-third of their public debts, to place restrictions on loans, and to subject to quarterly examinations, among other features. This legislation was widely regarded as a model of excellence. However, it was not foolproof.

The Free Banking Era

In July 1851 this advertisement appeared in various New Orleans newspapers:

> *Free Banking.* The subscriber will commence banking on his individual account at No. 107 Gravier Street, on the 26th instant, under the name and title of the "Bank of Commerce," associating others with him as soon as the existing tax laws shall be modified as to render an association of individuals for banking practicable; for which purpose arrangements have been made. No revision or enactment of other laws is necessary to give full scope to free banking. The funds of the savings bank department will be kept separate from the other concerns of the bank. Manager and trustees to be elected by the stockholders as soon as the association shall be formed.
>
> *Jacob Barker. New Orleans, July 24th, 1851.*

Readers of this account had no way of knowing that this was the notorious Barker who was implicated in bank frauds in New York during the 1820s. In April 1853 the state enacted the Free Banking Law, also with strict requirements. *Bankers' Magazine*, June 1853, included this:

> LOUISIANA FREE BANKING LAW. The principal feature which distinguishes this law from those of the other States, is that which requires the banker to keep on hand one dollar in coin for every three dollars of liabilities, exclusive of circulation. The Bank of New Orleans, (or any other new bank under the law) with a capital of $1,000,000, and with deposits, bank balances, &c., to the amount of three millions of dollars, must keep one million of dollars in coin on hand. It may be remarked, however, that the incorporated Banks of that city have for some years kept up that proportion of coin, and generally a much larger sum. . . .

The first to organize under this law was the Bank of New Orleans. In due course Jacob Barker's Bank of Commerce opened and issued a flood of bills.

An update was provided by *Bankers' Magazine* in April 1855:

> The general banking law of this State was adopted in April 1853; authorizing any five or more persons to associate as a banking corporation, with a capital not less than $100,000. Bonds of the United States, and of the State of Louisiana, and of the consolidated city of New-Orleans, are receivable by the Auditor of State, in exchange for circulating notes. Each bank is required to keep on hand specie to the amount of one third of its liabilities, (circulation excluded.) On a failure to redeem its notes, the Auditor is required to sell the securities after three days' notice. Three banks have been organized under this law with an aggregate capital of $6,000,000.

Due in large part to these well-crafted laws, during the next major financial crisis, the Panic of 1857, not a single bank in Louisiana suspended specie payments, not even the Bank of Commerce, a remarkable record. In contrast, in New York City all but one bank (the Chemical Bank) suspended during the panic. However, Barker's bank failed several years later. The Canal Bank, the largest issuer of paper money in the state, continued in business long beyond the era under study here.

During the secession and subsequent Confederate occupation of New Orleans, a period from January 26, 1861, to May 1, 1862, banks continued to operate, as they did afterward. Certain currency under the repatriation of the city bore special overprints relating to "Forced Issue."

Numismatic Comments

Over two dozen different banks were established in the state of Louisiana, to which number many branches can be added. New Orleans was the focal point of banking, and nearly all institutions were headquartered there. Contemporary newspaper and financial accounts reveal that private banks and many other entities issued bills in New Orleans, but their nature and extent is not known today beyond those studied here.

Louisiana notes in the numismatic marketplace are dominated by New Orleans bills, punctuated by relatively few from the branches. Large quantities of unissued bills remained from the Canal Bank of New Orleans, in particular, and were extremely plentiful on the market (including sheets) in the mid-20th century.

They are still easy enough to find now. Certain bills used during the Confederate occupation form an interesting study in themselves, as do bills issued after the repatriation of New Orleans in 1862, some of the latter having special overprints such as "Forced Issue" relating to General Benjamin "Beast" Butler and the demands he made on banks.

Certain bills of the Citizens Bank of Louisiana, in New Orleans, are bilingual and have the French word *dix* in addition to the English *ten*. At least two other banks in the same city issued bilingual notes with the *dix* imprint as well. It is said that early *dix* bills, and perhaps similar bills of other institutions, were a familiar sight to rivermen who came down the Mississippi to the "land of the dix notes," which evolved into the "land of Dixie" or "Dixieland."

Many articles and comments to this effect have appeared over the years, such as "The Bank Notes that Named Dixie Land" in *The Numismatist* of July 1917, which noted in part:

> Back in ante-bellum days, when counterfeiting was in wide circulation and the country was flooded with wild-cat currency of all sorts, the Citizens Bank, of New Orleans, had power to issue money notes in denominations of $10 and $20 to the extent of a few millions. Backed by a sound and strong institution, they came to be a very popular form of currency, being honored throughout the Mississippi Valley, and, in fact, throughout the country.
>
> These notes were engraved in French, and the $10 bills bore on the reverse side the word "dix," prominently printed. Ignorant Americans living along the river knew little or nothing of the niceties of French pronunciation, and consequently to them the word was simply "d-i-x." So when they went to trade in the Southern metropolis, they said they were going south to collect some "dixies."
>
> Thus it came about that the stretch of country above New Orleans became known as the land of the dixies, and later as Dixie Land.

This is the generally accepted origin of *Dixieland* and remains unchallenged, unless someone can come up with a use prior to the 1830s when the banks started issuing these notes.

Many surviving Louisiana bills are from the 1850s and 1860s and have bright colors and ornate vignettes. It is easier to form a large collection of Louisiana bills than for any other state among those studied in the present volume. These are relatively inexpensive to collect and yield what is perhaps an ideal numismatic situation. If you are contemplating starting a general collection of obsolete bills, it might be well to buy a dozen or so common Louisiana notes, study their characteristics and enjoy their features, and then go on to other states.

Alexandria, Louisiana

The city of Alexandria is located in Rapides Parish on the Red River and was originally inhabited by settlers and the occupants of the adjacent Spanish outposts. Traders and merchants made up the majority of the community. In 1785 Alexander Fulton received a land grant from Spain and organized the first settlement. The town was laid out in 1805, and it was named initially in Fulton's honor. In 1819 Alexandria, as it is now known, was incorporated as a town, and it received a city charter in 1832.

In 1863 Alexandria was occupied by Union forces. An Admiral David Porter and a General Nathaniel Banks traded control over the city in the next year and ended up quarreling over cotton supplies. Porter presumably seized cotton from all sources—whether it belonged to Confederate forces or loyal citizens. Banks was furious at this abuse of authority; his response was to try and beat Porter to the rest of the cotton.

The city was set on fire on May 13, 1864, when the Union army departed Alexandria. A strong wind spread the flames, and soon the town was in utter disarray. The town struggled to rebuild in the last year of the war, and food, clothing, and shoes became extremely scarce.

Bank of Louisiana (branch)
1824–1863
W-LA-010

History: On April 7, 1824, the Bank of Louisiana was chartered with an authorized capital of $4,000,000. Half of this amount was subscribed to by the state. It was required that five branches be opened. The branch located in Alexandria was established to service the parishes of Rapides, Avoyelles, Catahoula, Concordia, Ouachita, and Natchitoches. The authorized capital was $200,000. On June 13, 1863, three commissioners were assigned to put the liquidation of the Bank of Louisiana into effect.

The Bank of Louisiana had its parent bank located in New Orleans, W-LA-140, and branch banks located in Baton Rouge, W-LA-030, Donaldsonville, W-LA-060, Saint Francisville, W-LA-440, and Saint Martinville, W-LA-460.

Numismatic Commentary: To date there are no known or reported Bank of Louisiana notes with the Alexandria location.

Louisiana State Bank (branch)
1818–1825
W-LA-020

History: The Louisiana State Bank was chartered in 1818. By March 14 of that year, the state had subscribed to $500,000 of the authorized $2,000,000 capital of the bank. A bonus of $100,000 was required to be paid to the state before the bank could commence operations. Of the capital stock, $150,000 was reserved for the branch at Alexandria. In 1825 a law was passed discontinuing the branch.

The Louisiana State Bank had its parent bank located in New Orleans, W-LA-280, and branch banks located in Baton Rouge, W-LA-040, Donaldsonville, W-LA-070, New Orleans (second municipality), W-LA-290, Saint Francisville, W-LA-450, Saint Martinville, W-LA-470, and Shreveport, W-LA-490.

Numismatic Commentary: No notes of this branch are known today.

Baton Rouge, Louisiana

The area where Baton Rouge was founded was visited in 1699 by French explorer Sieur d'Iberville, who led a party up the Mississippi River. The name for the area, as given by the Native

Americans in residence, was Istrouma. D'Iberville and his men stumbled upon the location when they found a red-cypress pole upon which several carcasses hung, marking the boundaries of the hunting grounds of the Houma and the Bayou Goula tribes. They named the area *le bâton rouge*, or "red stick."

The first settlers arrived in 1719, and a military post was established. Since its inception, Baton Rouge has been occupied by France, Britain, Louisiana, Spain, the Florida Republic, the Confederate States, and the United States—under seven flags. The city increased its growth by means of trade and transportation via steamboats. The city of Baton Rouge was incorporated in 1817 and became the state capital of Louisiana in 1849. James Dakin designed the Capitol building, a Gothic Revival structure overlooking the Mississippi River.

The population of Baton Rouge was 5,500 at the time of the Civil War, but the conflict brought a halt to all economic advancement. Everything but that which would serve the war effort stopped, and the Union army arrived to occupy the city in 1862. After that time it remained in Union control.

Bank of Louisiana (branch)

1824–1863

W-LA-030

History: On April 7, 1824, the Bank of Louisiana was chartered with an authorized capital of $4,000,000. Half of this amount was subscribed to by the state. It was required that five branches be opened. The branch located in Baton Rouge was established to service the parishes of East and West Baton Rouge, Washington, Saint Helena, and Saint Tammany. The authorized capital was $200,000. On June 13, 1863, three commissioners were assigned to put the liquidation of the Bank of Louisiana into effect.

The Bank of Louisiana had its parent bank located in New Orleans, W-LA-140, and branch banks located in Alexandria, W-LA-010, Donaldsonville, W-LA-060, Saint Francisville, W-LA-440, and Saint Martinville, W-LA-460.

Numismatic Commentary: There are no known or discovered Bank of Louisiana notes for this branch location.

Louisiana State Bank (branch)

1850–1870

W-LA-040

History: The Louisiana State Bank was chartered in 1818. By March 14 of that year, the state had subscribed to $500,000 of the authorized $2,000,000 capital of the bank. A bonus of $100,000 was required to be paid to the state before the bank could commence operations. The branch at Baton Rouge was not established until 1850. William S. Pike was appointed the cashier, and the president was J.B. Kleinpeter.

The Louisiana State Bank survived the Civil War—one of very few banks in the South to do so. In 1867 it dropped its capital down to $600,000, and in 1870 it closed its doors. It was succeeded in interest by the State National Bank.[1]

The Louisiana State Bank had its parent bank located in New Orleans, W-LA-280, and branch banks located in Alexandria, W-LA-020, Donaldsonville, W-LA-070, New Orleans (second municipality), W-LA-290, Saint Francisville, W-LA-450, Saint Martinville, W-LA-470, and Shreveport, W-LA-490.

Numismatic Commentary: Besides the bank notes listed below, City of Baton Rouge notes dated November 4, 1861, and January 2, 1862, have printed "Will pay at the Branch of the Louisiana State Bank, Baton Rouge."

VALID ISSUES

$5 • W-LA-040-005-G010 RH

Back: Red-orange. ***Engraver:*** Rawdon, Wright, Hatch & Edson. ***Comments:*** H-LA-80-G70a. 18__. 1840s–1850s.

Rarity: URS-2
Proof $5,000

$10 • W-LA-040-010-G020

Left: 10 / Minerva standing. ***Center:*** Three figures, Horse head / Portrait of boy. ***Right:*** 10 / Ship. ***Engraver:*** Rawdon, Wright, Hatch & Edson. ***Comments:*** H-LA-80-G72a. 18__. 1840s–1850s.

Rarity: *None known*

$20 • W-LA-040-020-G030

Left: View of Place d'Armes and Cathedral in New Orleans vertically. ***Engraver:*** Rawdon, Wright, Hatch & Edson. ***Comments:*** H-LA-80-G74a. 18__. 1840s–1850s.

Rarity: *None known*

NON-VALID ISSUES

$20 • W-LA-040-020-C030

Engraver: Rawdon, Wright, Hatch & Edson. ***Comments:*** H-LA-80-C74a. Counterfeit of W-LA-040-020-G030. 18__. 1850s.

Rarity: *None known*

CLINTON, LOUISIANA

Clinton became the seat of government for East Feliciana Parish after the Feliciana Parish split in two in 1824 (see also Saint Francisville, Louisiana). The city of Jackson was displaced from this position, and Clinton rose to prominence.

During the Civil War, several battles occurred in or near Clinton. The Union army occupied Clinton on June 7, 1863, lead by General Benjamin Grierson. Several buildings were burned, including some merchandise and supply establishments, a mill, ammunition, and a railroad depot. The town was raided a second time on September 5, 1864, when General Albert Lee left Baton Rouge. Clinton again saw action on March 5, 1865, as General Francis Herron pushed Confederate activities north of Clinton by 20 miles.

New Orleans and Carrollton Rail Road and Banking Company (branch)

1835–1844

W-LA-050

History: The New Orleans and Carrollton Rail Road and Banking Company (also seen as the Carrollton Bank and as the New Orleans Bank) was incorporated in April 1835 with an authorized capital of $3,000,000. On March 1, 1836, the act was amended, requiring the bank to pay $500 to a boys' orphanage annually for ten years.

The Clinton branch made news nationwide in 1835 when D.N. Babcock, the cashier of the branch, absconded with $30,000 worth of notes. He was apprehended in Baltimore and discovered to have between $7,000 and $8,000 on his person.

During a crisis in 1842, the bank was one of few in the city to continue paying out specie, but its circulation dropped to nearly nothing. By 1844 banking privileges had been surrendered, and in May 1845 it was reported that the bank was in liquidation.

The New Orleans and Carrollton Rail Road and Banking Company had its parent bank located in New Orleans, W-LA-340.

Numismatic Commentary: To date there are no known or reported Clinton-branch notes.

Union Bank of Louisiana {1st} (branch)

1832–1842

W-LA-055

History: The Union Bank of Louisiana was chartered in April 1832 with an authorized capital of $7,000,000 funded by bonds provided by the state. The bank was incredibly successful for the first five years it was in operation. It survived the Panic of 1837, but in 1842 the crisis of that time overtook it. It took over a decade for the affairs of the bank to be wound up.

The Union Bank of Louisiana had its parent bank located in New Orleans, W-LA-410.

Numismatic Commentary: Private scrip, which is beyond the purview of this study and thus not listed here, was issued on November 19, 1837, stating "Redeemable at the branch of the Union Bank in Clinton, Louisiana." Also, checks and drafts are known stating "Cashier of the Office of Discount and Deposit of the Union Bank of Louisiana, at Clinton." Bank notes from this location are not known today.

Donaldsonville, Louisiana

Donaldsonville is located along the Mississippi River and was originally inhabited by the Houma and Chitimacha Indians. Settlers and colonists brought disease and sickness with them, and the native peoples suffered great disruption.

French settlers arrived first in the area, naming the land Lafourche-des-Chitimachas in honor of the people living there. Agriculture was the principal industry at the time, primarily sugar-cane plantations worked by slaves. In 1803 the land was included in the Louisiana Purchase and officially became a part of the United States. American colonists began to arrive, including landowner and planter William Donaldson. He commissioned Barthelemy Lafon to plan a new town on the land, and it was named Donaldsonville in his honor.

Donaldsonville was the capital of Louisiana for a brief time in 1830 and 1831. Sugar and cotton brought great wealth to the area, and mansions and fine buildings were built. In 1862 the city was attacked by the Union army in an attempt to gain control of the Mississippi River. Gunboats were deployed, threatening total destruction of the town and surrounding farms. The city was occupied and became a base for Union forces, and the plantations were commandeered to supply the Union army.

Bank of Louisiana (branch)

1824–1863

W-LA-060

History: On April 7, 1824, the Bank of Louisiana was chartered with an authorized capital of $4,000,000. Half of this amount was subscribed to by the state. It was required that five branches be opened. The branch located in Donaldsonville was established to service the parishes of Saint James, Ascension, Assumption, Lafourche Interior, Iberville, and Terrebonne. The authorized capital was $200,000. On June 13, 1863, three commissioners were assigned to put the liquidation of the Bank of Louisiana into effect.

The Bank of Louisiana had its parent bank located in New Orleans, W-LA-140, and branch banks located in Alexandria, W-LA-010, Baton Rouge, W-LA-030, Saint Francisville, W-LA-440, and Saint Martinville, W-LA-460.

Numismatic Commentary: There are no known or reported Bank of Louisiana notes to date that bear "Redeemable at the branch in Donaldsonville, Louisiana."

Louisiana State Bank (branch)

1818–1825

W-LA-070

History: The Louisiana State Bank was chartered in 1818. By March 14 of that year, the state had subscribed to $500,000 of the authorized $2,000,000 capital of the bank. A bonus of $100,000 was required to be paid to the state before the bank could commence operations. Of the capital stock, $100,000 was reserved for the branch at Donaldsonville. In 1825 a law was passed discontinuing the branch.

The Louisiana State Bank had its parent bank located in New Orleans, W-LA-280, and branch banks located in Alexandria, W-LA-020, Baton Rouge, W-LA-040, New Orleans (second municipality), W-LA-290, Saint Francisville, W-LA-450, Saint Martinville, W-LA-470, and Shreveport, W-LA-490.

Numismatic Commentary: No notes of this branch are known today.

Jackson, Louisiana

Jackson was founded in 1815 to be the seat of justice for the Feliciana Parish. It remained the parish seat until 1824, when Feliciana was split into East and West. The town was a major commercial center and was called the "Athens of the South." It is thought the area was named after Andrew Jackson, who camped here after the 1815 Battle of New Orleans. In 1825 the College of Louisiana was established, lasting until 1845 and followed by the Centenary College, which remained until 1908.

Clinton and Port Hudson Rail Road Company

1833–1842

W-LA-080

History: The Clinton and Port Hudson Rail Road Company was chartered in 1833 with an authorized capital of $100,000, increasable to $200,000. In 1834 the capital was increased to $500,000, of which $250,000 was required to be secured by loan, with the remaining to be secured by stock subscriptions. However, the company forfeited its charter not long after, and on March 26, 1842, it was put into liquidation.

Numismatic Commentary: Proof and issued notes from this bank are extremely rare. Less than a dozen notes from this bank have been discovered to date.

Valid Issues

$5 • W-LA-080-005-G010 RH

Engraver: Draper, Toppan, Longacre & Co. ***Comments:*** H-LA-25-G2. 18__. 1830s.

Rarity: URS-4; URS-1
F $2,500
Proof $4,000

$5 • W-LA-080-005-G010a

Back: Black. ***Engraver:*** Draper, Toppan, Longacre & Co. ***Comments:*** H-LA-25-G2a. Similar to W-LA-080-005-G010. 18__. 1830s.

Rarity: URS-1
F $2,500

$10 • W-LA-080-010-G020 RH

Engraver: Draper, Toppan, Longacre & Co. ***Comments:*** H-LA-25-G4. 18__. 1830s.

Rarity: URS-5
F $2,000; **Proof** $3,500

$10 • W-LA-080-010-G020a

Back: Black. ***Engraver:*** Draper, Toppan, Longacre & Co. ***Comments:*** H-LA-25-G4a. Similar to W-LA-080-010-G020. 18__. 1830s.

Rarity: URS-3
F $2,000

$20 • W-LA-080-020-G030 RH

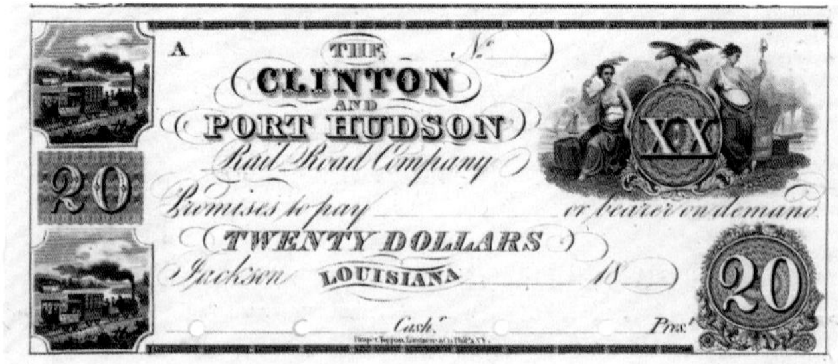

Engraver: Draper, Toppan, Longacre & Co. ***Comments:*** H-LA-25-G6. 18__. 1830s.

Rarity: URS-1
F $4,000

$50 • W-LA-080-050-G040 RH

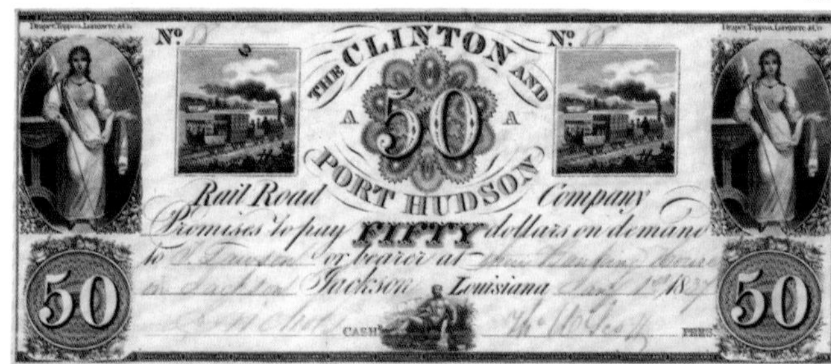

Engraver: Draper, Toppan, Longacre & Co. ***Comments:*** H-LA-25-G8. 18__. 1830s.

Rarity: URS-2; URS-1
F $5,000
Proof $5,500

$100 • **W-LA-080-100-G050** RH

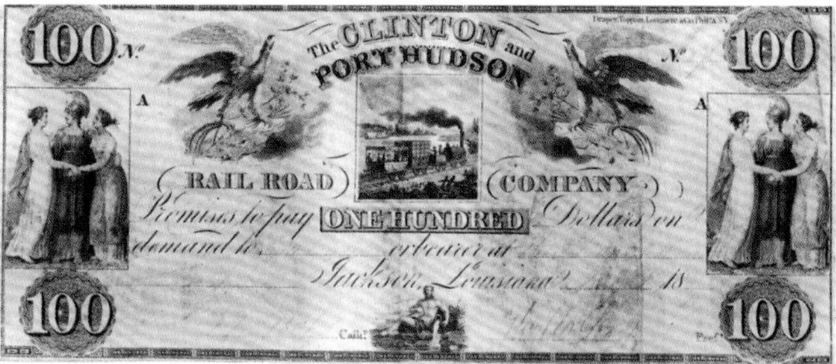

Engraver: Draper, Toppan, Longacre & Co. ***Comments:*** H-LA-25-G10. 18__. 1830s.

Rarity: URS-2
G $4,000

Notes Payable at the Citizens Bank of Louisiana, New Orleans

$5 • **W-LA-080-005-G060** RH

Engraver: Draper, Toppan, Longacre & Co. ***Comments:*** H-LA-25-G14. 18__. 1830s.

Rarity: URS-1
F $3,500

$5 • **W-LA-080-005-G060a** RH

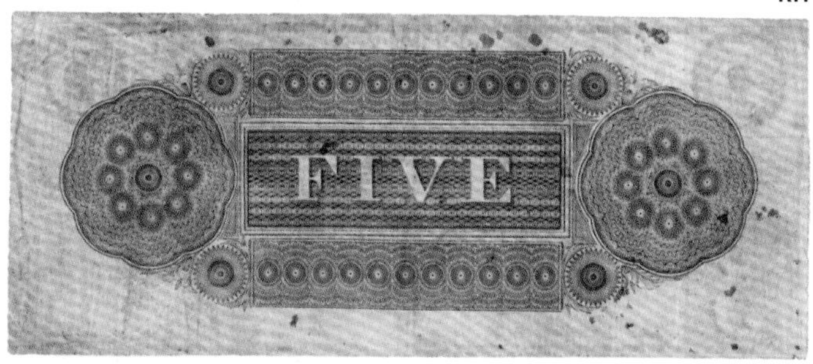

Back: Black. ***Engraver:*** Draper, Toppan, Longacre & Co. ***Comments:*** H-LA-25-G14a. Similar to W-LA-080-005-G060. Back of note shown. 18__. 1830s.

Rarity: URS-1
F $3,500

$10 • **W-LA-080-010-G070** RH

Engraver: Draper, Toppan, Longacre & Co. ***Comments:*** H-LA-25-G16. 18__. 1830s.

Rarity: URS-1
F $3,500

$10 • **W-LA-080-010-G070a** RH

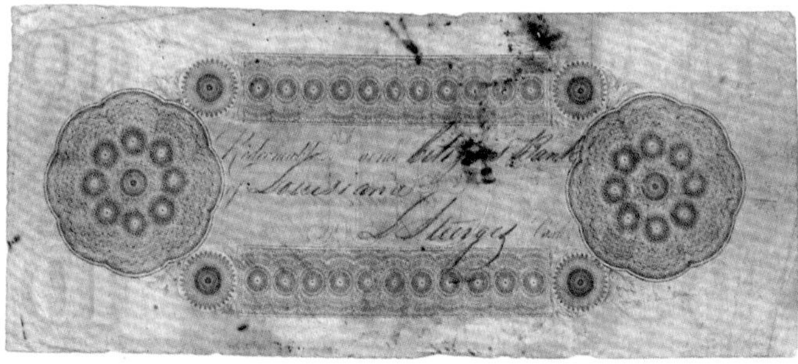

Back: Black. ***Engraver:*** Draper, Toppan, Longacre & Co. ***Comments:*** H-LA-25-G16a. Similar to W-LA-080-010-G070. Back of note shown. 18__. 1830s.

Rarity: URS-1
F $3,500

$20 • **W-LA-080-020-G080** RH

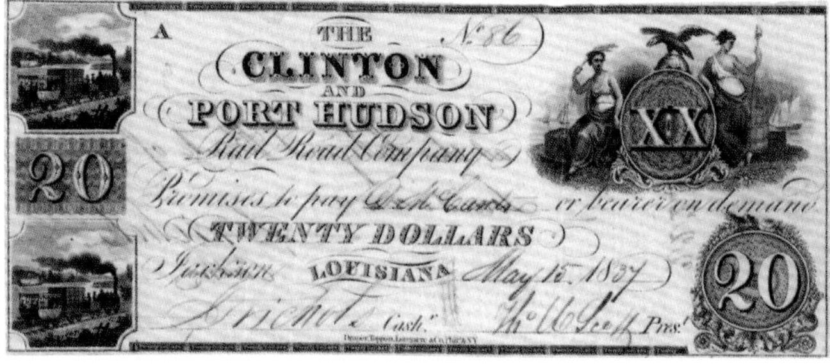

Engraver: Draper, Toppan, Longacre & Co. ***Comments:*** H-LA-25-G18. 18__. 1830s.

Rarity: URS-1
F $3,500

$50 • **W-LA-080-050-G090**

Left: Woman standing / 50. ***Center:*** Train / 50 / Train. ***Right:*** Woman standing / 50. ***Engraver:*** Draper, Toppan, Longacre & Co. ***Comments:*** H-LA-25-G20. 18__. 1830s.

Rarity: *None known*

$100 • **W-LA-080-100-G100**

Left: 100 / Three women standing / 100. ***Center:*** Eagle / Train / Eagle. ***Right:*** 100 / Three women standing / 100. ***Engraver:*** Draper, Toppan, Longacre & Co. ***Comments:*** H-LA-25-G22. 18__. 1830s.

Rarity: *None known*

New Orleans, Louisiana

In the 1690s fur trappers and traders arrived with French explorers, settling in and among the Native Americans who inhabited the land. In 1718 the city of Nouvelle-Orléans was founded under the guidance of Jean-Baptiste Le Moyne de Bienville. The area was chosen due to its elevation away from the river, which was prone to flooding, and also due to its proximity along the trading route of the Mississippi River and Lake Pontchartrain. The city was named in honor of the Duke of Orléans.

In 1722 a hurricane struck the city, destroying many of the buildings, and a grid plan was adopted afterwards. In 1763 the French colony (including New Orleans) was ceded to Spain. Napoleon then sold Louisiana in April 1803 to the United States as part of the Louisiana Purchase. The city was handed over officially to the United States on December 20.

In January 1815 General Andrew Jackson fought off an attempt by British troops to take the city, as part of the War of 1812. Unknown to the combatants, a peace treaty ending the war had been signed the month before. The encounter actually occurred down river from the city, but nevertheless it was known as the Battle of New Orleans.

During the 1830s many new settlers arrived, and the population increased sharply. Natural gas was introduced during this time, and the first steam cotton press followed. Foreign exports doubled, and soon New Orleans included a massive commercial district. In 1838 the New Orleans Mint opened in the city, one of three branch mints authorized by Congress in 1835 (the others were in Charlotte, North Carolina, and Dahlonega, Georgia). By 1840 New Orleans was one of the wealthiest and most populous cities in the entire nation, with 102,000 citizens. In 1849 a breach in the levee upriver from the city caused the worst flooding New Orleans had ever seen up to that time, leaving 12,000 people homeless. It was not until Hurricane Katrina in 2005 that a greater tragedy occurred.

New Orleans came under Union control on April 28, 1862, with General Benjamin Butler entering the city on May 1. After several meetings of the city's Committee of Public Safety, May 6 was chosen to be the date when the circulation of all private scrip was halted. These bills were to be redeemed in newly printed city notes dated May 6, 1862. All private-scrip printing plates and remaining notes were collected and destroyed. On May 19, an order was issued for the city's commercial and other banks to stop paying out Confederate notes as bankable funds. It is believed that this order precipitated the blue "forced issue" stamps commonly found on the Bank of Louisiana, W-LA140, notes. It is important to note that all currency issued in New Orleans after May 6, 1862, should be considered "occupation" notes.

As the city remained under Union control for the rest of the war, it was spared the destruction that many other Southern cities sustained.

Atchafalaya Rail Road and Banking Company

1836–1847

W-LA-090

History: The Atchafalaya Rail Road and Banking Company was incorporated on January 28, 1836. On March 3, 1837, the company was granted right of way through the public lands of the states for the purpose of laying roads.

On April 9, 1842, the Atchafalaya Rail Road and Banking Company was set into liquidation. Its notes were at a 50-percent discount. The liquidation process lasted through 1847.

Numismatic Commentary: Notes from this bank are rare, with an estimated total of only 20 from all denominations recorded to date.

Valid Issues

$5 • W-LA-090-005-G010 RH

Back: Plain. ***Engraver:*** Rawdon, Wright & Hatch. ***Comments:*** H-LA-10-G2. 18__. 1830s.

Rarity: URS-5

F $1,500

$5 • W-LA-090-005-G010a

Tint: Unknown. ***Back:*** Printed. ***Engraver:*** Rawdon, Wright & Hatch / Rawdon, Wright, Hatch & Edson. ***Comments:*** H-LA-10-G2b. Similar to W-LA-090-005-G010 but with additional engraver imprint. 18__. 1840s.

Rarity: *None known*

$10 • W-LA-090-010-G020 RH

Back: Plain. ***Engraver:*** Rawdon, Wright & Hatch. ***Comments:*** H-LA-10-G4. 18__. 1830s.

Rarity: URS-5

F $1,500

$10 • W-LA-090-010-G020a

Tint: Unknown. ***Back:*** Printed. ***Engraver:*** Rawdon, Wright & Hatch / Rawdon, Wright, Hatch & Edson. ***Comments:*** H-LA-10-G4b. Similar to W-LA-090-010-G020 but with additional engraver imprint. 18__. 1840s.

Rarity: *None known*

$20 • W-LA-090-020-G030

RH

Back: Plain. ***Engraver:*** Rawdon, Wright & Hatch. ***Comments:*** H-LA-10-G6. 18__. 1830s.

Rarity: URS-3

F $2,500

$20 • W-LA-090-020-G030a

Tint: Unknown. ***Back:*** Printed. ***Engraver:*** Rawdon, Wright & Hatch / Rawdon, Wright, Hatch & Edson. ***Comments:*** H-LA-10-G6b. Similar to W-LA-090-020-G030 but with additional engraver imprint. 18__. 1840s.

Rarity: *None known*

$50 • W-LA-090-050-G040

RH

Back: Plain. ***Engraver:*** Rawdon, Wright & Hatch. ***Comments:*** H-LA-10-G8. 18__. 1830s.

Rarity: URS-3

F $3,000

$50 • W-LA-090-050-G040a

RH, RH

Tint: Red-orange FIFTY. ***Back:*** Black. ***Engraver:*** Rawdon, Wright & Hatch / Rawdon, Wright, Hatch & Edson. ***Comments:*** H-LA-10-G8b. Similar to W-LA-090-050-G040 but with additional engraver imprint. 18__. 1840s.

Rarity: URS-2

F $3,500

$100 • W-LA-090-100-G050

HA

Back: Plain. ***Engraver:*** Rawdon, Wright & Hatch. ***Comments:*** H-LA-10-G10. 18__. 1830s.

Rarity: URS-5

F $1,500

Selected auction price(s): Heritage Auctions, October 21, 2015, Lot 18339, VF $1,997; Heritage Auctions, January 9, 2013, Lot 15794, F $910

Collectors and Researchers:

If you have new information about any banks or notes listed in this volume, contact Whitman Publishing, Attn: Obsolete Paper Money, 3101 Clairmont Road, Suite G, Atlanta, GA 30329.

$100 • **W-LA-090-100-G050a** RH, RH

Tint: Blue C. ***Back:*** Brown. ***Engraver:*** Rawdon, Wright & Hatch / Rawdon, Wright, Hatch & Edson. ***Comments:*** H-LA-10-G10b. Similar to W-LA-090-100-G050 but with additional engraver imprint. 18__. 1840s.

Rarity: URS-2
F $2,500

$500 • **W-LA-090-500-G060**

Left: 500 / Steamboat / 500. ***Center:*** Woman seated, Barrel, bales, and plow, Ships. ***Right:*** 500 / Train / 500. ***Back:*** Plain. ***Engraver:*** Rawdon, Wright & Hatch. ***Comments:*** H-LA-10-G12. 18__. 1830s.

Rarity: *None known*

$500 • **W-LA-090-500-G060a** HA, RH

Back: Blue. ***Engraver:*** Rawdon, Wright & Hatch / Rawdon, Wright, Hatch & Edson. ***Comments:*** H-LA-10-G12b. Similar to W-LA-090-500-G060 but with additional engraver imprint. 18__. 1840s.

Rarity: URS-2
VF $3,500
Selected auction price: Heritage Auctions, April 23, 2015, Lot 19079, VF $8,225

Post Notes

$5 • **W-LA-090-005-G070** RH

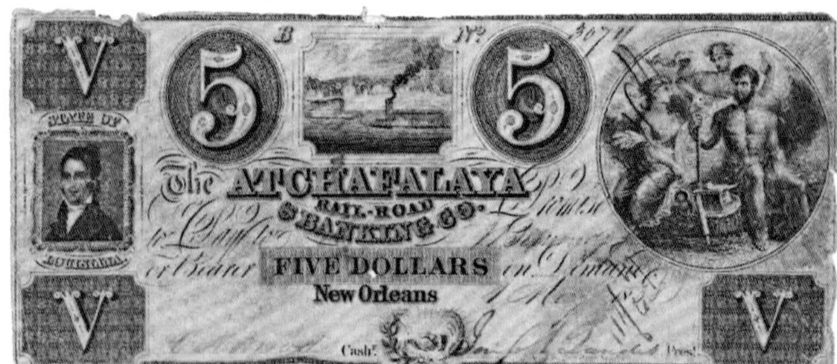

Back: Plain. ***Engraver:*** Rawdon, Wright & Hatch. ***Comments:*** H-LA-10-G20. 18__. 1830s.

Rarity: URS-3
F $1,500

$10 • **W-LA-090-010-G080**

Left: TEN DOLLARS / Two men and one woman / 10. ***Center:*** X / Train on bridge / X. ***Right:*** 10. ***Engraver:*** Rawdon, Wright & Hatch. ***Comments:*** H-LA-10-G22. 18__. 1830s.

Rarity: *None known*

$20 • **W-LA-090-020-G090**

Left: 20 / Train on bridge / 20. ***Center:*** XX / Cow / XX. ***Right:*** Two men and one woman / 20. ***Back:*** Plain. ***Engraver:*** Rawdon, Wright & Hatch. ***Comments:*** H-LA-10-G24. 18__. 1830s.

Rarity: *None known*

$50 • **W-LA-090-050-G100**

Left: Woman standing / 50. ***Center:*** L / Steamboat / L. ***Right:*** FIFTY DOLLARS / Two men and one woman / 50. ***Back:*** Plain. ***Engraver:*** Rawdon, Wright & Hatch. ***Comments:*** H-LA-10-G26. 18__. 1830s.

Rarity: *None known*

$100 • **W-LA-090-100-G110** RH

Back: Plain. ***Engraver:*** Rawdon, Wright & Hatch. ***Comments:*** H-LA-10-G28. 18__. 1830s.

Rarity: URS-2
F $2,500

Notes Payable at the Phenix Bank in New York City

$10 • W-LA-090-010-G120 RH

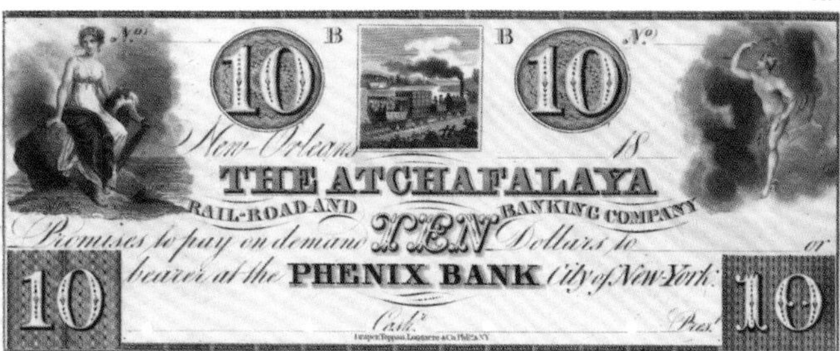

Engraver: Draper, Toppan, Longacre & Co. ***Comments:*** H-LA-10-G34. 18__. 1830s–1840s.

Rarity: URS-2
Proof $2,500

$20 • W-LA-090-020-G130 RH

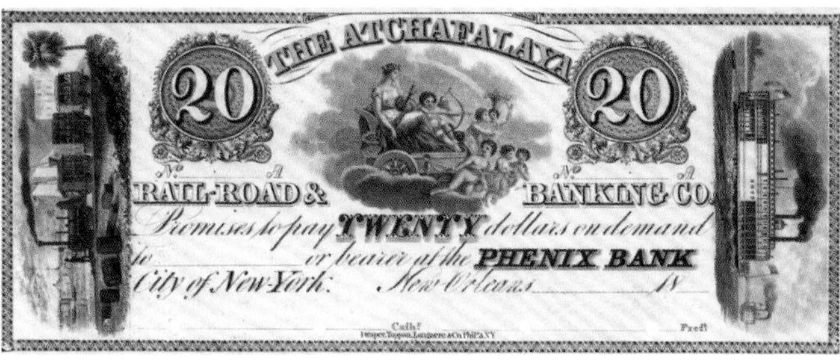

Engraver: Draper, Toppan, Longacre & Co. ***Comments:*** H-LA-10-G36. 18__. 1830s–1840s.

Rarity: URS-2
Proof $3,500

Banking House of Gray, Macmurdo and Company

1850s–1860s

W-LA-100

History: The Banking House of Gray, Macmurdo and Company was the trade of George E.H. Gray and J.R. Macmurdo, bankers or merchants.

Numismatic Commentary: Notes from this banking house are scarce but available to the collector in both issued and remainder forms.

Valid Issues

$1 • W-LA-100-001-G010 RH

Engraver: Rawdon, Wright, Hatch & Edson. ***Comments:*** H-Unlisted. 18__. 1850s–1860s.

Rarity: URS-4; URS-1
F $1,000
Unc-Rem $2,000

$2 • W-LA-100-002-G020 RH

Engraver: Rawdon, Wright, Hatch & Edson. ***Comments:*** H-Unlisted. 18__. 1850s–1860s.

Rarity: URS-4; URS-1
F $1,500
Unc-Rem $2,000

$5 • W-LA-100-005-G030 RH

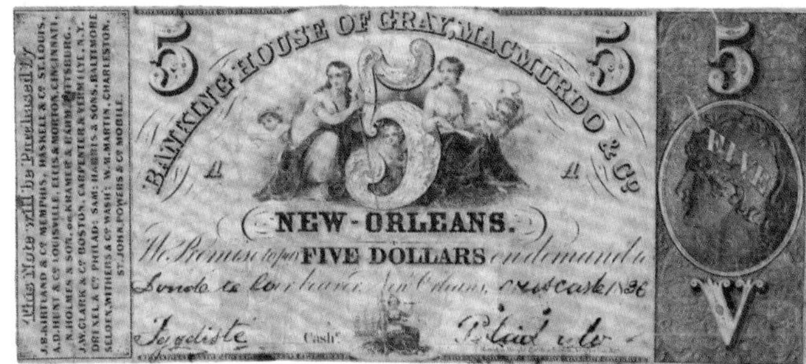

Engraver: Rawdon, Wright, Hatch & Edson. ***Comments:*** H-Unlisted. 18__. 1850s–1860s.

Rarity: URS-4; URS-1
F $1,500
Unc-Rem $2,000

Bank of America
1857–1862
W-LA-110

History: The Bank of America was chartered in 1857 with an authorized capital of $1,000,000. Later that year the paid-in capital was $507,800, and bills in circulation totaled $240,240. Specie totaled $578,387, and real estate was valued at $1,863. The cashier was A.M. Fortier, and the president was William G. Hewes. By 1862 the Bank of America had closed its doors.

Numismatic Commentary: Notes from this bank are extremely rare, with only four notes known to date.

Valid Issues

$5 • W-LA-110-005-G010 RH, RH

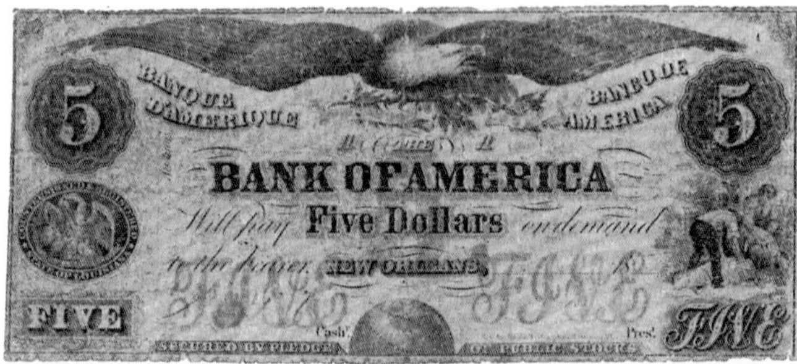

Tint: Red-orange FIVE FIVE. ***Back:*** Blue. ***Engraver:*** Rawdon, Wright, Hatch & Edson. ***Comments:*** H-LA-5-G2b. 18__. 1850s.

Rarity: URS-2
F $4,500

$5 • W-LA-110-005-G010a

Tint: Red-orange FIVE FIVE. ***Back:*** Blue. ***Engraver:*** Rawdon, Wright, Hatch & Edson / ABNCo. monogram. ***Comments:*** H-LA-5-G2c. Similar to W-LA-110-005-G010 but with additional engraver imprint. 18__. 1850s.

Rarity: URS-1
VF $5,500

$10 • W-LA-110-010-G020 HA, RH

Tint: Red-orange TEN / X / TEN. ***Back:*** Green. ***Engraver:*** Rawdon, Wright, Hatch & Edson. ***Comments:*** H-LA-5-G4b. 18__. 1850s.

Rarity: URS-2
F $4,500
Selected auction price: Heritage Auctions, April 23, 2015, Lot 19076, F $8,225

$10 • W-LA-110-010-G020a

Tint: Red-orange TEN TEN. ***Back:*** Blue. ***Engraver:*** Rawdon, Wright, Hatch & Edson / ABNCo. monogram. ***Comments:*** H-LA-5-G4c. Similar to W-LA-110-010-G020 but with additional engraver imprint. 18__. 1850s.

Rarity: URS-1
F $5,500

$20 • W-LA-110-020-G030

Left: TWENTY / State arms and 20 / TWENTY. ***Center:*** Eagle with wings spread, Globe. ***Right:*** TWENTY / 20 / Two women. ***Tint:*** Red-orange TWENTY. ***Back:*** Blue. ***Engraver:*** Rawdon, Wright, Hatch & Edson. ***Comments:*** H-LA-5-G6b. 18__. 1850s.

Rarity: *None known*

$20 • W-LA-110-020-G030a

Tint: Red-orange TWENTY. ***Back:*** Blue. ***Engraver:*** Rawdon, Wright, Hatch & Edson / ABNCo. monogram. ***Comments:*** H-LA-5-G6c. Similar to W-LA-110-020-G030 but with additional engraver imprint. 18__. 1850s.

Rarity: *None known*

$50 • W-LA-110-050-G040

Left: Cattle and sheep / 50 / State arms. ***Center:*** Eagle with wings spread, Globe. ***Right:*** Train / 50 / Two ships on stocks. ***Tint:*** Red-orange FIFTY. ***Back:*** Blue. ***Engraver:*** Rawdon, Wright, Hatch & Edson. ***Comments:*** H-LA-5-G8b. 18__. 1850s.

Rarity: *None known*

$50 • W-LA-110-050-G040a

Tint: Red-orange FIFTY. ***Back:*** Blue. ***Engraver:*** Rawdon, Wright, Hatch & Edson / ABNCo. monogram. ***Comments:*** H-LA-5-G8c. Similar to W-LA-110-050-G040 but with additional engraver imprint. 18__. 1850s.

Rarity: *None known*

$100 • W-LA-110-100-G050

Left: 100 / State arms / Boy and girl holding grapes. ***Center:*** Eagle with wings spread, Globe. ***Right:*** 100 / 100. ***Tint:*** Red-orange HUNDRED. ***Back:*** Blue. ***Engraver:*** Rawdon, Wright, Hatch & Edson. ***Comments:*** H-LA-5-G10b. 18__. 1850s.

Rarity: *None known*

$100 • W-LA-110-100-G050a

Tint: Red-orange HUNDRED. ***Back:*** Blue. ***Engraver:*** Rawdon, Wright, Hatch & Edson / ABNCo. monogram. ***Comments:*** H-LA-5-G10c. Similar to W-LA-110-100-G050 but with additional engraver imprint. 18__. 1850s.

Rarity: *None known*

Occupation Notes

$2 • W-LA-110-002-G060

HA

Overprint: Red TWO. ***Comments:*** H-Unlisted. 1860s.

Rarity: URS-1

VF $5,900

Selected auction price: Heritage Auctions, April 23, 2015, Lot 19077, VF $5,875

$5 • W-LA-110-005-G070

RH

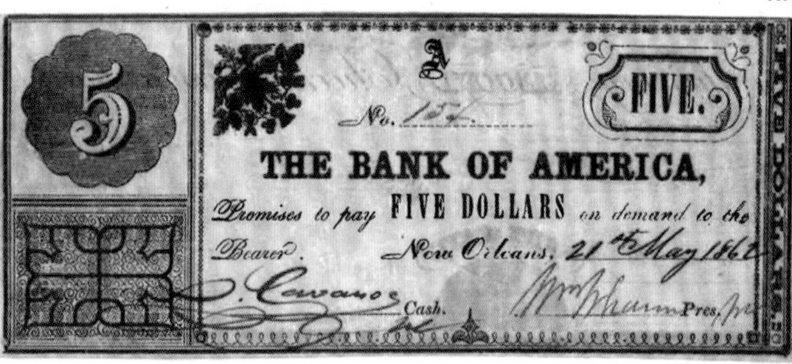

RH

Back: Black. ***Comments:*** H-Unlisted. ____. 1860s.

Rarity: URS-1

VF $5,900

Selected auction price: Heritage Auctions, April 23, 2015, Lot 19078, VF $5,875

Bank of Commerce

1853–1862

W-LA-120

History: In July 1851 the first advertisement for the Bank of Commerce was placed in various New Orleans newspapers by Jacob Barker, who was looking for subscriptions to his new banking corporation. Readers could have no way of knowing that Barker was a notorious fraudster from New York, and so once the Free Banking Law was passed in April 1853, Barker opened his bank and immediately issued a flood of bills. Although the Bank of Commerce did not fail during the Panic of 1857, as would have been expected for a fraudulent enterprise, the bank did fail several years later. By 1862 the Bank of Commerce had closed its doors.

Numismatic Commentary: Notes from this bank are scarce, with an estimated total of 30 known to date. The $1 and $2 post notes with the green overprints are more common.

Issues

$1 • W-LA-120-001-G010

RH

Engraver: Toppan, Carpenter, Casilear & Co. ***Comments:*** H-LA-30-G30. 18__. 1850s.

Rarity: URS-3

Proof $2,000

$2 • W-LA-120-002-G020

Left: 2 / Female portrait / TWO. ***Center:*** Ships. ***Right:*** 2 / Woman with spyglass / TWO. ***Engraver:*** Toppan, Carpenter, Casilear & Co. ***Comments:*** H-LA-30-G32. 18__. 1850s.

Rarity: —

$5 • **W-LA-120-005-G030**

RH

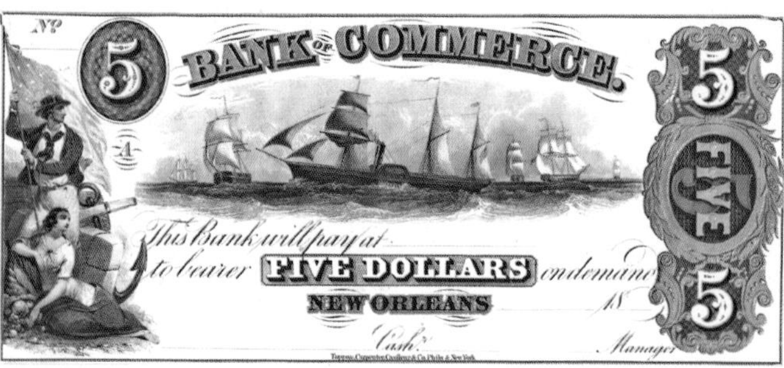

Back: Blue. ***Engraver:*** Toppan, Carpenter, Casilear & Co. ***Comments:*** H-LA-30-G34. 18__. 1850s.

Rarity: URS-3
Proof $2,000

$10 • **W-LA-120-010-G040**

RH

Engraver: Toppan, Carpenter, Casilear & Co. ***Comments:*** H-LA-30-G36. 18__. 1850s.

Rarity: URS-3
Proof $2,000

$20 • **W-LA-120-020-G050**

RH

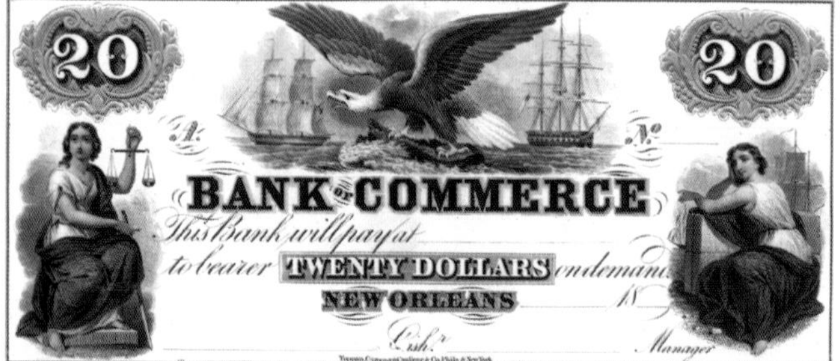

Back: Blue. ***Engraver:*** Toppan, Carpenter, Casilear & Co. ***Comments:*** H-LA-30-G38. 18__. 1850s.

Rarity: URS-2
Proof $2,500

Transitional Occupation Notes

$5 • **W-LA-120-005-G060**

Left: Man standing, Woman seated, Anchor, Flag. ***Center:*** 5 / Ships. ***Right:*** 5 / FIVE on 5 vertically / 5. ***Back:*** Blue. ***Engraver:*** Toppan, Carpenter, Casilear & Co. ***Comments:*** H-LA-30-G10a. 18__. 1850s.

Rarity: URS-1
F $4,500

$5 • **W-LA-120-005-G060a**

CC, CC

Back: Blue on parts of Saint Charles Parish notes. ***Engraver:*** Toppan, Carpenter, Casilear & Co. ***Comments:*** H-LA-30-G10b. Similar to W-LA-120-005-G060. 18__. 1862.

Rarity: URS-5
F $800

$10 • **W-LA-120-010-G070**

Left: 10 / Man standing with flag. ***Center:*** Three figures reclining / TEN DOLLARS. ***Right:*** X / TEN / 10. ***Back:*** Blue. ***Engraver:*** Toppan, Carpenter, Casilear & Co. ***Comments:*** H-LA-30-G12a. 18__. 1850s.

Rarity: —

$10 • **W-LA-120-010-G070a**

RH, RH

Back: Blue on parts of Saint Charles Parish notes. ***Engraver:*** Toppan, Carpenter, Casilear & Co. ***Comments:*** H-LA-30-G12b. Similar to W-LA-120-010-G070. 18__. 1862.

Rarity: URS-4
F $1,500; **Proof** $2,000

$20 • **W-LA-120-020-G080**

Left: 20 / Woman seated. ***Center:*** Eagle, Ships. ***Right:*** 20 / Woman seated. ***Back:*** Blue. ***Engraver:*** Toppan, Carpenter, Casilear & Co. ***Comments:*** H-LA-30-G14a. 18__. 1850s.

Rarity: —

$20 • **W-LA-120-020-G080a**

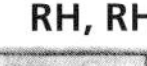

Back: Blue on parts of Saint Charles Parish notes. ***Engraver:*** Toppan, Carpenter, Casilear & Co. ***Comments:*** H-LA-30-G14b. Similar to W-LA-120-020-G080. 18__. 1862.

Rarity: URS-4
F $1,500; **Proof** $2,000

Occupation-Era Post Notes

$1 • **W-LA-120-001-G090**

Left: ONE vertically. ***Center:*** THE BANK OF COMMERCE / ONE DOLLAR. ***Right:*** ONE vertically. ***Back:*** Plain. ***Comments:*** H-LA-30-G44. May 5th, 1862.

Rarity: URS-1
F $2,500

$1 • **W-LA-120-001-G090a**

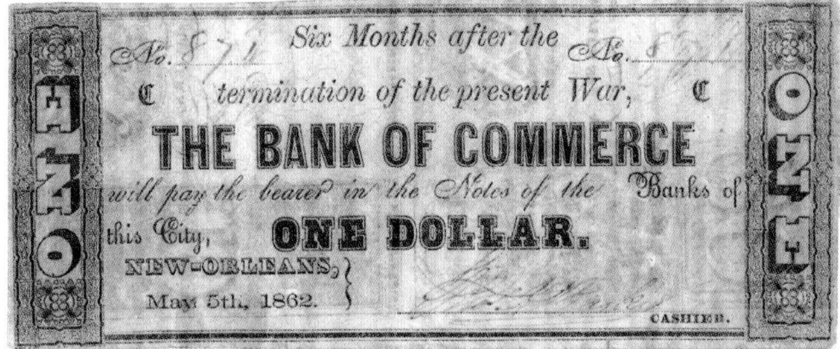

Back: Parts of other notes. ***Comments:*** H-LA-30-G44a. Similar to W-LA-120-001-G090. May 5th, 1862.

Rarity: URS-3
VF $2,500

$2 • **W-LA-120-002-G100**

Left: TWO. ***Center:*** THE BANK OF COMMERCE / TWO DOLLARS. ***Right:*** TWO. ***Back:*** Plain. ***Comments:*** H-LA-30-G46. May 5th, 1862.

Rarity: URS-2
F $2,500

$2 • **W-LA-120-002-G100a**

Back: Parts of other notes. ***Comments:*** H-LA-30-G46a. Similar to W-LA-120-002-G100. May 5th, 1862.

Rarity: URS-2
F $2,500

$3 • **W-LA-120-003-G110**

Left: THREE. ***Center:*** THE BANK OF COMMERCE / THREE DOLLARS. ***Right:*** THREE. ***Back:*** Plain. ***Comments:*** H-LA-30-G50. May 5th, 1862.

Rarity: URS-3
F $1,500

$3 • **W-LA-120-003-G110a**

Back: Parts of other notes. ***Comments:*** H-LA-30-G50a. Similar to W-LA-120-003-G110. May 5th, 1862.

Rarity: URS-3
F $1,500

$5 • **W-LA-120-005-G120**

RH, RH

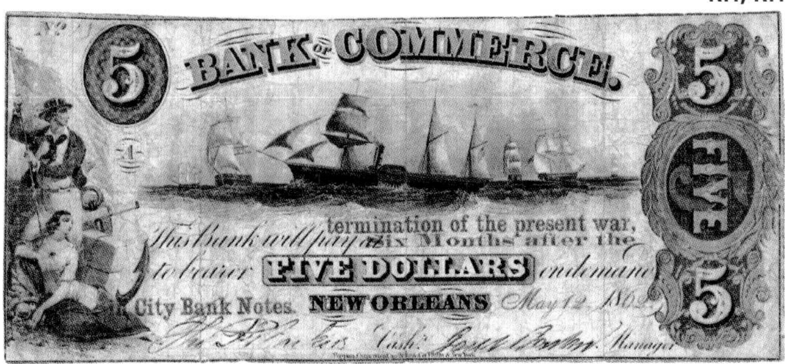

Overprint: Black stamp. ***Back:*** Blue. ***Engraver:*** Toppan, Carpenter, Casilear & Co. ***Comments:*** H-LA-30-G52. Converted to a post note via a black overprint on the face. 18__. 1860s.

Rarity: URS-4
F $1,500

Post-Occupation Post Notes

$1 • W-LA-120-001-G130

RH

Engraver: American Bank Note Co. ***Comments:*** H-Unlisted. May 5th, 1862.

Rarity: URS-3
Proof $1,500

$1 • W-LA-120-001-G130a

CC

Overprint: Green 1 1. ***Engraver:*** American Bank Note Co. ***Comments:*** H-LA-30-G42a. Similar to W-LA-120-001-G130. May 5th, 1862.

Rarity: URS-8
EF $275

$2 • W-LA-120-002-G140

RH

Engraver: American Bank Note Co. ***Comments:*** H-Unlisted. May 5th, 1862.

Rarity: URS-3
Proof $2,000

$2 • W-LA-120-002-G140a

CC

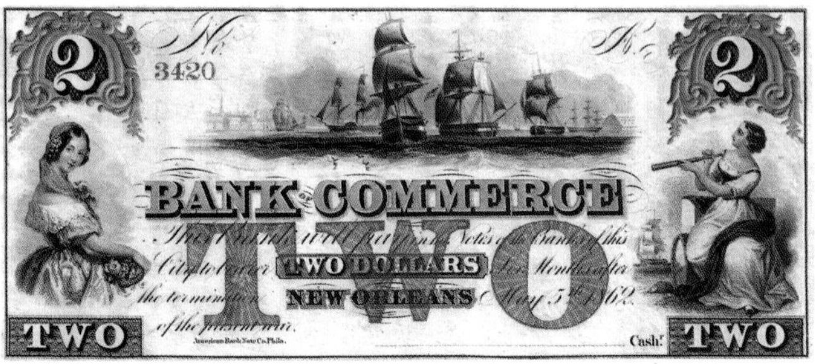

RH

Overprint: Green TWO. ***Back:*** Green. ***Engraver:*** American Bank Note Co. ***Comments:*** H-LA-30-G48a. Similar to W-LA-120-002-G140. May 5th, 1862.

Rarity: URS-7
EF $350; **Unc-Rem** $450

$5 • W-LA-120-005-G150

RH, RH

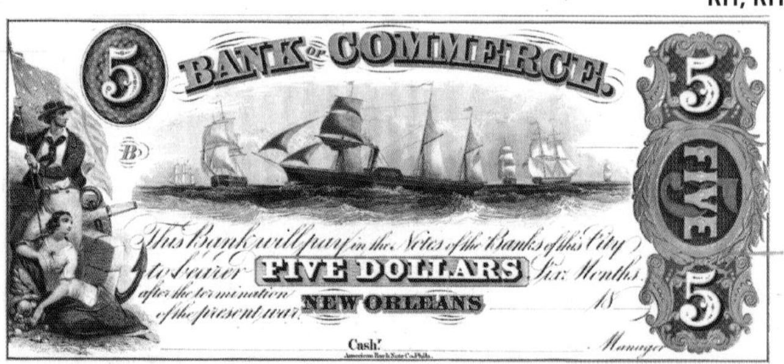

Back: Blue. ***Engraver:*** American Bank Note Co. ***Comments:*** H-Unlisted. 18__. 1860s.

Rarity: URS-5
F $350; **Proof** $1,500

$10 • W-LA-120-010-G160

RH

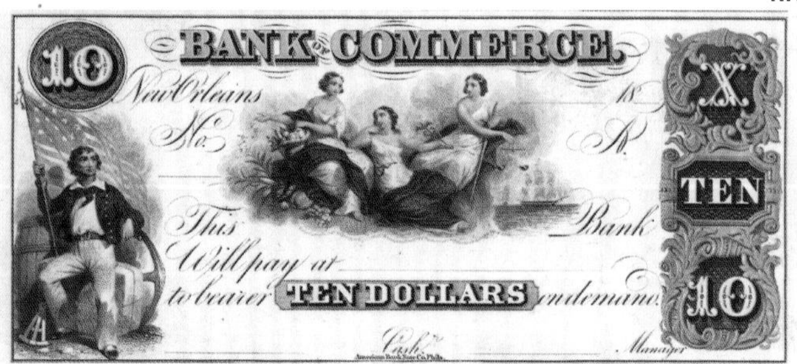

Back: Blue. ***Engraver:*** American Bank Note Co. ***Comments:*** H-Unlisted. Lacks termination verbiage. 18__. 1860s.

Rarity: —

$20 • W-LA-120-020-G170 RH

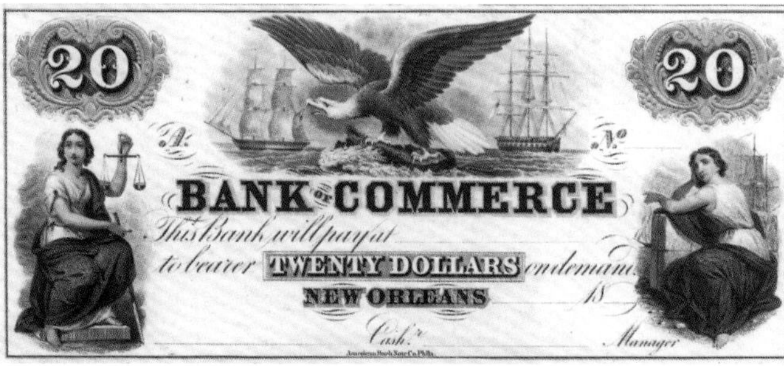

Back: Blue. ***Engraver:*** American Bank Note Co. ***Comments:*** H-Unlisted. Lacks termination verbiage. 18__. 1860s.

Rarity: —

Uncut Sheets

$1-$1-$2-$1 • W-LA-120-001.001.002.001-US010 RH

Engraver: American Bank Note Co. ***Comments:*** All unlisted in Haxby. First two notes and last note identical. May 5th, 1862.

Rarity: —

$1-$1-$2-$1 • W-LA-120-001.001.002.001-US010a RG

Overprint(s): Green. ***Engraver:*** American Bank Note Co. ***Comments:*** H-LA-30-G42a, G42a, G48a, G42a. Similar to W-LA-120-001.001.002.001-US010. First two notes and last note identical. May 5th, 1862.

Rarity: URS-4
EF $3,000
Selected auction price: Heritage Auctions, April 24, 2013, Lot 15222, EF $3,055

$5-$5-$10-$20 •
W-LA-120-005.005.010.020-US020 RH

Engraver: American Bank Note Co. ***Comments:*** All unlisted in Haxby. First two notes identical; last two notes lack termination verbiage. 18__. 1860s.
Rarity: —

Bank of James Robb
1857–1859
W-LA-130

History: The Bank of James Robb was chartered in March 1857. The Panic of 1857 took place that autumn, but the new bank did not suspend specie payments. In 1859 it evolved into the second Merchants Bank, W-LA-320.

Numismatic Commentary: Proof and issued notes from this bank are extremely rare, with only three notes recorded to date.

Valid Issues

$5 • W-LA-130-005-G010 RH, RH

Engraver: Rawdon, Wright, Hatch & Edson. ***Comments:*** H-LA-135-G2. 18__. 1850s.
Rarity: URS-2
VG $5,000

$10 • W-LA-130-010-G020 RH

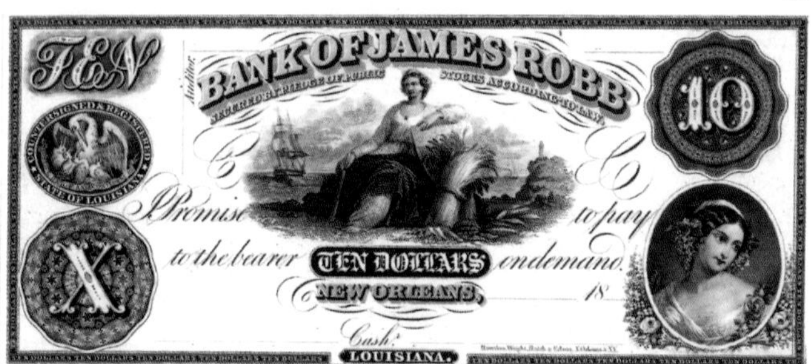

Engraver: Rawdon, Wright, Hatch & Edson. ***Comments:*** H-LA-135-G4. 18__. 1850s.
Rarity: URS-1
Proof $5,000

$20 • W-LA-130-020-G030 RH

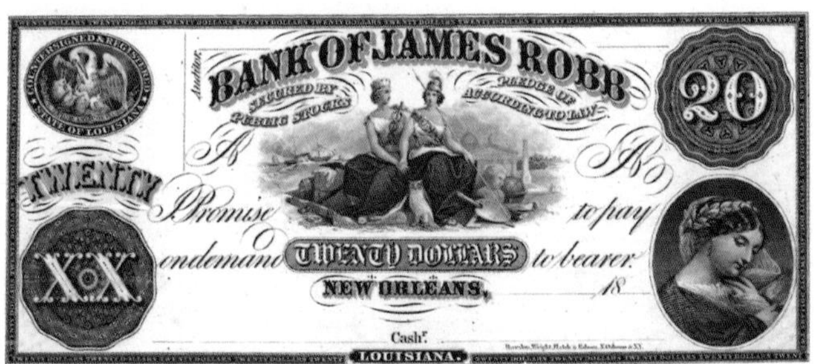

Engraver: Rawdon, Wright, Hatch & Edson. ***Comments:*** H-LA-135-G6. 18__. 1850s.
Rarity: URS-1
Proof $5,000

$50 • W-LA-130-050-G040

Left: State arms / Female portrait / FIFTY. ***Center:*** 50 / Woman leaning on shield and holding spear, Strongbox, barrels, Steamship. ***Right:*** FIFTY / Justice standing. ***Engraver:*** Rawdon, Wright, Hatch & Edson. ***Comments:*** H-LA-135-G8. 18__. 1850s.

Rarity: *None known*

$100 • W-LA-130-100-G050

Left: 100 / State arms / 100. ***Center:*** Three women seated, Cherubs, wheel, and anvil, Ship. ***Right:*** 100 / Two women. ***Engraver:*** Rawdon, Wright, Hatch & Edson. ***Comments:*** H-LA-135-G10. 18__. 1850s.

Rarity: *None known*

Bank of Louisiana

1824–1863

W-LA-140

History: On April 7, 1824, the Bank of Louisiana was chartered with an authorized capital of $4,000,000. Half of this amount was subscribed to by the state. It was required that five branches be opened. Through the 1820s and into 1830, the Bank of Louisiana did very well. It was reported in *Niles' Register* that "The Bank of Louisiana shows a handsome exhibit of its condition." At the time there was $576,332 in circulation compared to a large $420,880 worth of specie at the bank. Only $392,355 of credit to individuals had been paid out versus a $4,000,000 capital nearly all paid in.

Eventually, some losses did occur. In 1841 a few clerks absconded with an amount totaling $174,722. In 1842 there was a crisis, and the Bank of Louisiana was one of just a few banks in New Orleans to continue paying out specie. However, its circulation dropped significantly. By 1843 it was $1,000,726. In 1848 the long-time president of the Bank of Louisiana, Benjamin Story, passed away. He was replaced by William W. Montgomery, with Robert M. Davis as cashier. In 1849 the circulation rose again to $1,532,327. Capital was $599,603. By 1860 Robert M. Davis had taken the position of president, and his old position as cashier was filled by Auguste Montreuil. The capital was worth $3,993,500. Circulation was valued at $1,720,902. On June 13, 1863, three commissioners were assigned to put the liquidation of the Bank of Louisiana into effect.

The Bank of Louisiana had branch banks located in Alexandria, W-LA-010, Baton Rouge, W-LA-030, Donaldsonville, W-LA-060, Saint Francisville, W-LA-440, and Saint Martinville, W-LA-460.

Numismatic Commentary: Notes from this bank are available to collectors with almost all available as issued notes. There are many different variations of the ten denominations. Some are overstamped in blue ink as "registered" or "forced" issues. Some have a red-ink overstamp "Redeemable in Confederate notes."

Valid Issues

$1 • W-LA-140-001-G010

CC

Engraver: Rawdon, Wright, Hatch & Edson. ***Comments:*** H-LA-75-G2. 18__. 1861.

Rarity: URS-7
F $250

$1 • W-LA-140-001-G010a

RH

Overprint: Blue REGISTERED stamp. ***Engraver:*** Rawdon, Wright, Hatch & Edson. ***Comments:*** H-LA-75-G2a. Similar to W-LA-140-001-G010. 18__. 1861.

Rarity: URS-6
F $350

$1 • W-LA-140-001-G010b

HA

Overprint: Red REDEEMABLE IN CONFEDERATE NOTES stamp. ***Engraver:*** Rawdon, Wright, Hatch & Edson. ***Comments:*** H-LA-75-G2b. Similar to W-LA-140-001-G010. 18__. 1861.

Rarity: URS-5
F $250

$2 • **W-LA-140-002-G020** CC

Engraver: Rawdon, Wright, Hatch & Edson. ***Comments:*** H-LA-75-G4. 18__. 1861.

Rarity: URS-6
F $250; **VF** $350

$2 • **W-LA-140-002-G020a** RH

Overprint: Blue REGISTERED stamp. ***Engraver:*** Rawdon, Wright, Hatch & Edson. ***Comments:*** H-LA-75-G4a. Similar to W-LA-140-002-G020. 18__. 1861.

Rarity: URS-6
F $250

$2 • **W-LA-140-002-G020b** RH

Overprint: Red REDEEMABLE IN CONFEDERATE NOTES stamp. ***Engraver:*** Rawdon, Wright, Hatch & Edson. ***Comments:*** H-LA-75-G4b. Similar to W-LA-140-002-G020. 18__. 1861.

Rarity: URS-4
F $350

$2 • **W-LA-140-002-G020c** RH

Overprint: Blue REGISTERED stamp and red REDEEMABLE IN CONFEDERATE NOTES stamp. ***Engraver:*** Rawdon, Wright, Hatch & Edson. ***Comments:*** H-Unlisted. Similar to W-LA-140-002-G020. 18__. 1861.

Rarity: URS-2
F $1,500

$3 • **W-LA-140-003-G030** CC

Engraver: Rawdon, Wright, Hatch & Edson. ***Comments:*** H-LA-75-G6. 18__. 1861.

Rarity: URS-6
F $450

$3 • **W-LA-140-003-G030a** RH

Overprint: Blue REGISTERED stamp. ***Engraver:*** Rawdon, Wright, Hatch & Edson. ***Comments:*** H-LA-75-G6a. Similar to W-LA-140-003-G030. 18__. 1861.

Rarity: URS-6
F $350

$3 • W-LA-140-003-G030b

CC

Overprint: Red REDEEMABLE IN CONFEDERATE NOTES stamp. ***Engraver:*** Rawdon, Wright, Hatch & Edson. ***Comments:*** H-LA-75-G6b. Similar to W-LA-140-003-G030. 18__. 1861.

Rarity: URS-5

F $350

$5 • W-LA-140-005-G040

RH

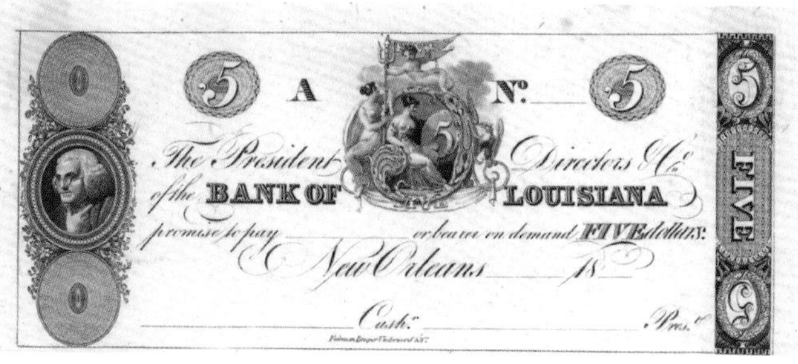

Engraver: Fairman, Draper, Underwood & Co. ***Comments:*** H-Unlisted. 18__. 1820s–1830s.

Rarity: URS-2

Proof $3,000

How to Read the Whitman Numbering System

$1 • W-AL-020-001-G010a

Denomination: Face value of the note shown.

W: Whitman number. This number is a sortable code unique to each bank and note.

AL: Abbreviation for the state under study.

020: Numerical designation specific to each bank.

001: The denomination in dollars.

G010a: G indicates a good or valid note. Other categories are indicated thus: C (counterfeit); R (raised); S (spurious); N (not-attributed); A (altered). Numbers are assigned starting with 010, 020, et seq. Terminal letters following the number indicate variations of a note: a series of different colored overprints, tints, payees, etc., all on the same design of note. For more information, see the "How to Use This Book" section at the front of the volume, page xiv.

$5 • W-LA-140-005-G050

RH, RH

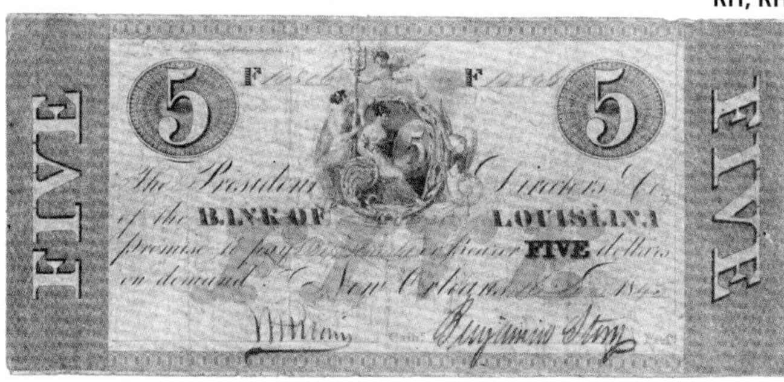

Tint: Red FIVE. ***Back:*** Blue. ***Engraver:*** Fairman, Draper, Underwood & Co. / Rawdon, Wright, Hatch & Edson. ***Comments:*** H-LA-75-G8a. 18__. 1840s–1850s.

Rarity: URS-4

F $400

$5 • W-LA-140-005-G050a

RH, RH

Overprint: Blue REGISTERED stamp. ***Tint:*** Red FIVE. ***Back:*** Blue. ***Engraver:*** Fairman, Draper, Underwood & Co. / Rawdon, Wright, Hatch & Edson. ***Comments:*** H-Unlisted. Similar to W-LA-140-005-G050. 18__. 1840s–1850s.

Rarity: URS-4

F $300

$5 • W-LA-140-005-G050b

QDB

Engraver: Fairman, Draper, Underwood & Co. / Rawdon, Wright, Hatch & Edson. ***Comments:*** H-LA-75-G8. Similar to W-LA-140-005-G050. 18__. 1820s–1830s.

Rarity: URS-4
F $1,500

$5 • W-LA-140-005-G050c

CC, RH

Overprint: Blue FORCED ISSUE stamp. ***Back:*** Red-orange. ***Engraver:*** Fairman, Draper, Underwood & Co. / Rawdon, Wright, Hatch & Edson. ***Comments:*** H-Unlisted. Similar to W-LA-140-005-G050. 18__. 1850s–1860s.

Rarity: URS-5
F $300

$5 • W-LA-140-005-G050d

RH

Tint: Blue FIVE. ***Back:*** Red-orange. ***Engraver:*** Fairman, Draper, Underwood & Co. / Rawdon, Wright, Hatch & Edson. ***Comments:*** H-LA-75-G8b. Similar to W-LA-140-005-G050. 18__. 1862.

Rarity: URS-6
F $300

$5 • W-LA-140-005-G050e

QDB, QDB

Overprint: Blue FORCED ISSUE stamp. ***Tint:*** Blue FIVE. ***Back:*** Red-orange. ***Engraver:*** Fairman, Draper, Underwood & Co. / Rawdon, Wright, Hatch & Edson. ***Comments:*** H-LA-75-G8e. Similar to W-LA-140-005-G050. 18__. 1850s–1860s.

Rarity: URS-6
F $300

$5 • W-LA-140-005-G050f

RH

Overprint: Blue REGISTERED stamp. ***Back:*** Red-orange. ***Engraver:*** Fairman, Draper, Underwood & Co. / Rawdon, Wright, Hatch & Edson. ***Comments:*** H-LA-75-G8d. Similar to W-LA-140-005-G050. Back of note shown. 18__. 1850s–1860s.

Rarity: URS-6
F $300

$5 • **W-LA-140-005-G060** RH

Back: Red-orange. ***Engraver:*** Rawdon, Wright, Hatch & Edson. ***Comments:*** H-Unlisted. Handwritten date in April. 18__. 1850s–1860s.

Rarity: URS-9
F $150

$5 • **W-LA-140-005-G060a** RH

Overprint: Blue REGISTERED stamp. ***Back:*** Red-orange. ***Engraver:*** Rawdon, Wright, Hatch & Edson. ***Comments:*** H-Unlisted. Similar to W-LA-140-005-G060. Handwritten date in April. 18__. 1850s–1860s.

Rarity: URS-9
F $125

$5 • **W-LA-140-005-G060b** RH, HA

Overprint: Blue REGISTERED stamp and red REDEEMABLE stamp. ***Back:*** Red-orange. ***Engraver:*** Rawdon, Wright, Hatch & Edson. ***Comments:*** H-LA-75-G10b. Similar to W-LA-140-005-G060. Handwritten date in April. 18__. 1860.

Rarity: URS-3
F $750

$5 • **W-LA-140-005-G060c** RH

Overprint: Red REDEEMABLE stamp. ***Back:*** Red-orange. ***Engraver:*** Rawdon, Wright, Hatch & Edson. ***Comments:*** H-Unlisted. Similar to W-LA-140-005-G060. Handwritten date in April. 18__. 1850s–1860s.

Rarity: URS-3
F $750

$5 • **W-LA-140-005-G060d** CC, SI

Back: Red-orange. ***Engraver:*** Rawdon, Wright, Hatch & Edson. ***Comments:*** H-LA-75-G10a. Similar to W-LA-140-005-G060. 18__. 1850s–1860s.

Rarity: URS-9
F $150

$5 • **W-LA-140-005-G060e** CC, CC

Overprint: Blue FORCED ISSUE stamp. ***Back:*** Red-orange. ***Engraver:*** Rawdon, Wright, Hatch & Edson. ***Comments:*** H-LA-75-G10c. Similar to W-LA-140-005-G060. 18__. 1862.

Rarity: URS-9
F $125

$10 • **W-LA-140-010-G070**

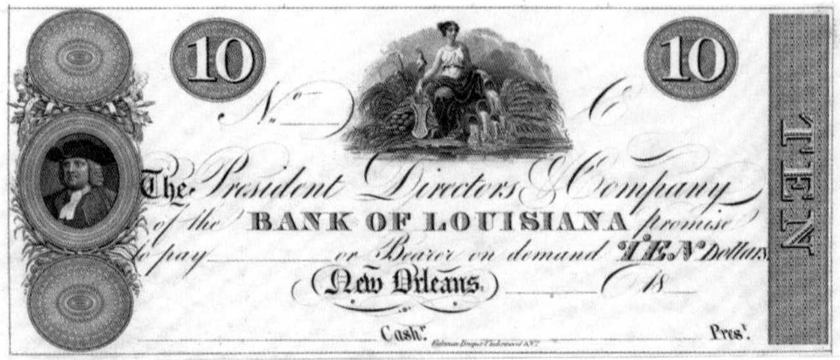

Engraver: Fairman, Draper, Underwood & Co. ***Comments:*** H-Unlisted. 18__. 1830s–1840s.

Rarity: URS-3
Proof $2,500

$10 • **W-LA-140-010-G080**

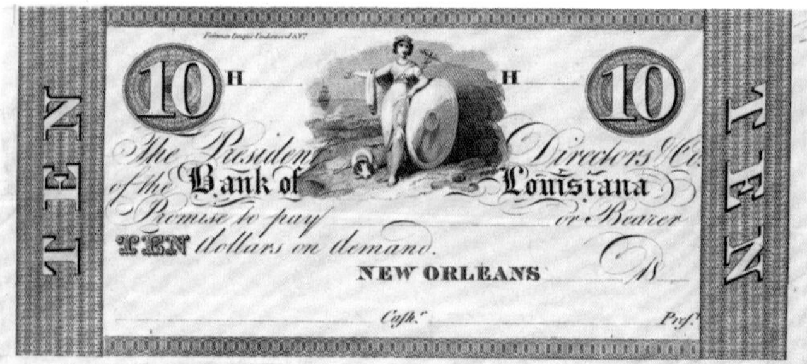

Engraver: Fairman, Draper, Underwood & Co. ***Comments:*** H-LA-75-G12. 18__. 1820s–1830s.

Rarity: URS-3
Proof $2,500

$10 • **W-LA-140-010-G080a**

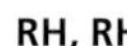

Tint: Blue TEN. ***Back:*** Red-orange. ***Engraver:*** Fairman, Draper, Underwood & Co. / Rawdon, Wright, Hatch & Edson. ***Comments:*** H-LA-75-G12a. Similar to W-LA-140-010-G080 but with additional engraver imprint. 18__. 1840s–1850s.

Rarity: URS-5
F $275

$10 • **W-LA-140-010-G080b** RH, RH

Overprint: Blue REGISTERED stamp. ***Tint:*** Blue TEN. ***Back:*** Red-orange. ***Engraver:*** Fairman, Draper, Underwood & Co. / Rawdon, Wright, Hatch & Edson. ***Comments:*** H-Unlisted. Similar to W-LA-140-010-G080 but with additional engraver imprint. 18__. 1840s–1850s.

Rarity: URS-5
F $275

$10 • W-LA-140-010-G080c CC, SI

Back: Red-orange. ***Engraver:*** Fairman, Draper, Underwood & Co. / Rawdon, Wright, Hatch & Edson. ***Comments:*** H-LA-75-G12b. Similar to W-LA-140-010-G080 but with additional engraver imprint. 18__. 1860s.

Rarity: URS-9
F $75; **VF** $125

$10 • W-LA-140-010-G080d

Overprint: Blue REGISTERED stamp. ***Back:*** Red-orange. ***Engraver:*** Fairman, Draper, Underwood & Co. / Rawdon, Wright, Hatch & Edson. ***Comments:*** H-LA-75-G12c. Similar to W-LA-140-010-G080 but with additional engraver imprint. 18__. 1860s.

Rarity: —

$10 • W-LA-140-010-G080e RH, RH

Overprint: Blue FORCED ISSUE stamp. ***Back:*** Red-orange. ***Engraver:*** Fairman, Draper, Underwood & Co. / Rawdon, Wright, Hatch & Edson. ***Comments:*** H-LA-75-G12d. Similar to W-LA-140-010-G080 but with additional engraver imprint. 18__. 1860s.

Rarity: URS-9
F $75

$10 • W-LA-140-010-G090 RH, RH

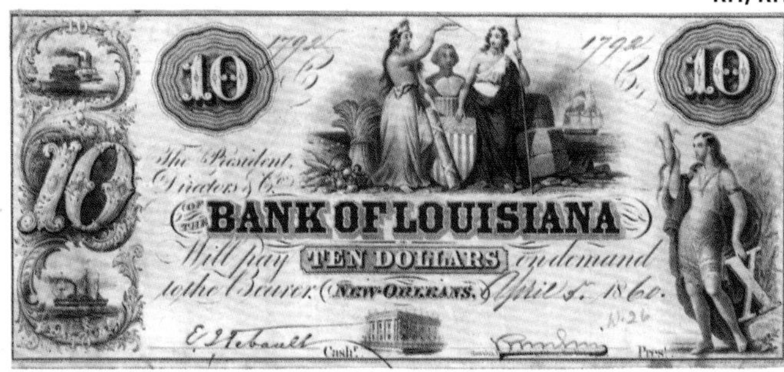

Back: Red-orange woman. ***Engraver:*** Rawdon, Wright, Hatch & Edson. ***Comments:*** H-Unlisted. Handwritten date in April. 18__. 1850s–1860s.

Rarity: URS-9
F $75

$10 • W-LA-140-010-G090a RH, RH

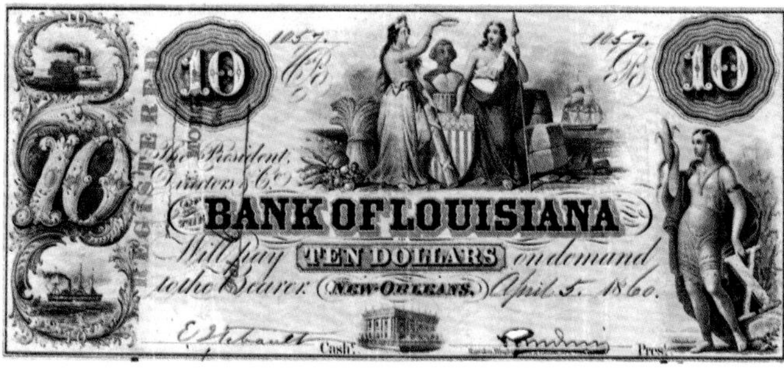

Overprint: Blue REGISTERED stamp. ***Back:*** Red-orange woman. ***Engraver:*** Rawdon, Wright, Hatch & Edson. ***Comments:*** H-LA-75-G14b. Similar to W-LA-140-010-G090. 18__. 1860s.

Rarity: URS-8
F $125

$10 • **W-LA-140-010-G090b** CC

Back: Red-orange woman. ***Engraver:*** Rawdon, Wright, Hatch & Edson. ***Comments:*** H-LA-75-G14a. Similar to W-LA-140-010-G090. 18__. 1850s–1860s.

Rarity: URS-9
F $125

$10 • **W-LA-140-010-G090c** QDB, QDB

Overprint: Blue FORCED ISSUE stamp. ***Back:*** Red-orange woman. ***Engraver:*** Rawdon, Wright, Hatch & Edson. ***Comments:*** H-LA-75-G14c. Similar to W-LA-140-010-G090. 18__. 1860s.

Rarity: URS-8
F $125

$20 • **W-LA-140-020-G100** RH

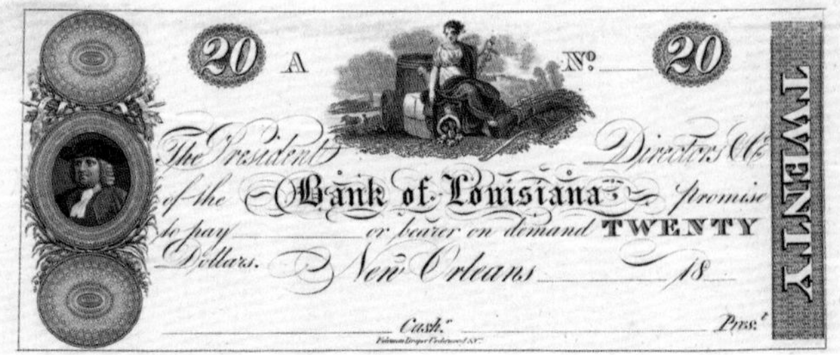

Engraver: Fairman, Draper, Underwood & Co. ***Comments:*** H-Unlisted. 18__. 1820s–1830s.

Rarity: URS-2
Proof $3,500

$20 • **W-LA-140-020-G110** RH

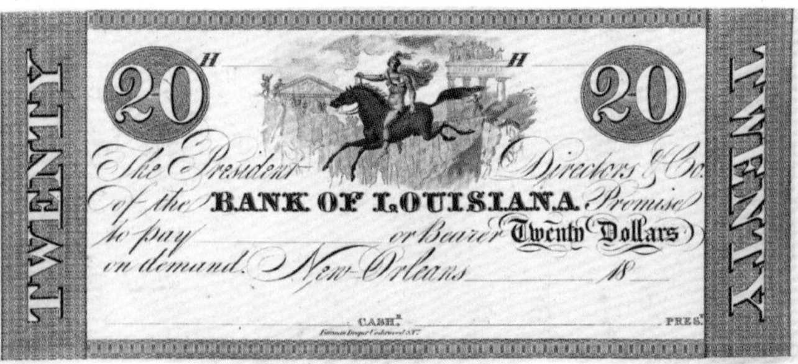

Engraver: Fairman, Draper, Underwood & Co. ***Comments:*** H-LA-75-G16. 18__. 1820s–1830s.

Rarity: URS-3
Proof $2,500

$20 • **W-LA-140-020-G110a** RH, RH

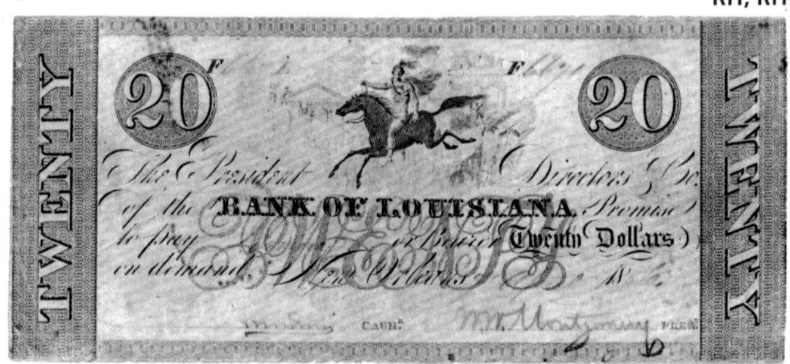

Tint: Green TWENTY. ***Back:*** Black. ***Engraver:*** Fairman, Draper, Underwood & Co. / Rawdon, Wright, Hatch & Edson. ***Comments:*** H-Unlisted. Similar to W-LA-140-020-G110 but with additional engraver imprint. Handwritten date in April. 18__. 1850s–1860s.

Rarity: URS-9
F $100

Collectors and Researchers:

If you have new information about any banks or notes listed in this volume, contact Whitman Publishing, Attn: Obsolete Paper Money, 3101 Clairmont Road, Suite G, Atlanta, GA 30329.

$20 • **W-LA-140-020-G110b** RH, RH

Overprint: Blue REGISTERED stamp. ***Tint:*** Green TWENTY. ***Back:*** Black. ***Engraver:*** Fairman, Draper, Underwood & Co. / Rawdon, Wright, Hatch & Edson. ***Comments:*** H-LA-75-G16c. Similar to W-LA-140-020-G110 but with additional engraver imprint. 18__. 1850s–1860s.

Rarity: URS-8
F $100

$20 • **W-LA-140-020-G110c** QDB, QDB

Tint: Green TWENTY. ***Back:*** Black. ***Engraver:*** Fairman, Draper, Underwood & Co. / Rawdon, Wright, Hatch & Edson. ***Comments:*** H-LA-75-G16b. Similar to W-LA-140-020-G110 but with additional engraver imprint. 18__. 1850s–1860s.

Rarity: URS-9
F $100

$20 • **W-LA-140-020-G110d** CC, SI

Overprint: Blue FORCED ISSUE stamp. ***Tint:*** Green TWENTY. ***Back:*** Black. ***Engraver:*** Fairman, Draper, Underwood & Co. / Rawdon, Wright, Hatch & Edson. ***Comments:*** H-LA-75-G16d. Similar to W-LA-140-020-G110 but with additional engraver imprint. 18__. 1850s–1860s.

Rarity: URS-8
F $150

$20 • **W-LA-140-020-G120** RH, RH

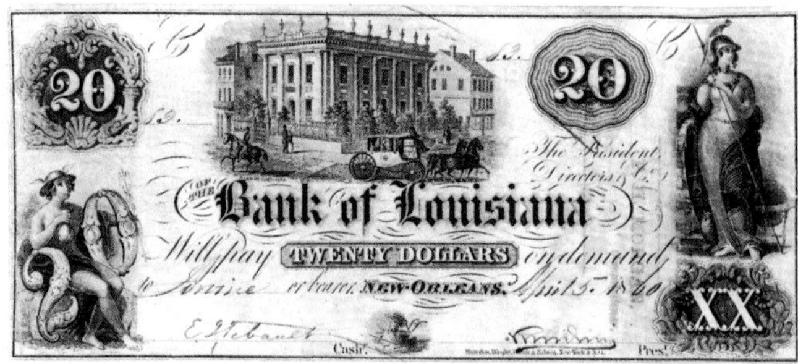

Overprint: Blue REGISTERED stamp. ***Back:*** Red-orange. ***Engraver:*** Rawdon, Wright, Hatch & Edson. ***Comments:*** H-LA-75-G18b. 18__. 1860s.

Rarity: URS-2
Proof $3,500

$20 • W-LA-140-020-G120a

QDB, QDB

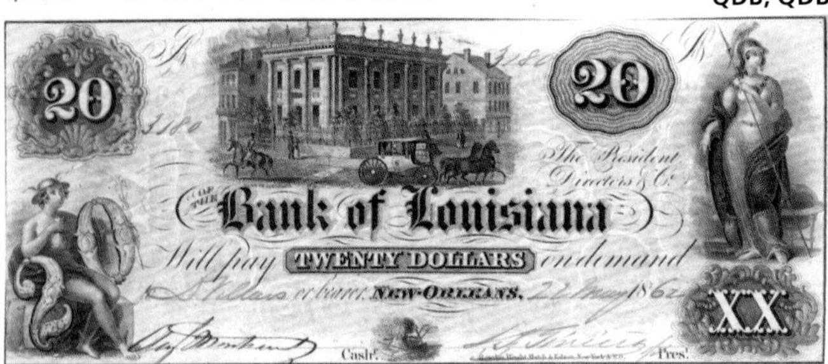

Back: Red-orange. ***Engraver:*** Rawdon, Wright, Hatch & Edson. ***Comments:*** H-LA-75-G18a. Similar to W-LA-140-020-G120. 18__. 1850s–1860s.

Rarity: URS-8
F $150

$20 • W-LA-140-020-G120b

CC, CC

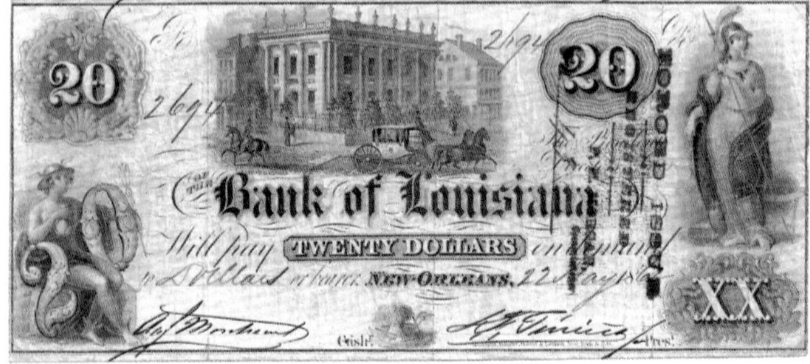

Overprint: Blue FORCED ISSUE stamp. ***Back:*** Red-orange. ***Engraver:*** Rawdon, Wright, Hatch & Edson. ***Comments:*** H-LA-75-G18c. Similar to W-LA-140-020-G120. 18__. 1860s.

Rarity: URS-8
F $150

$50 • W-LA-140-050-G130

RH

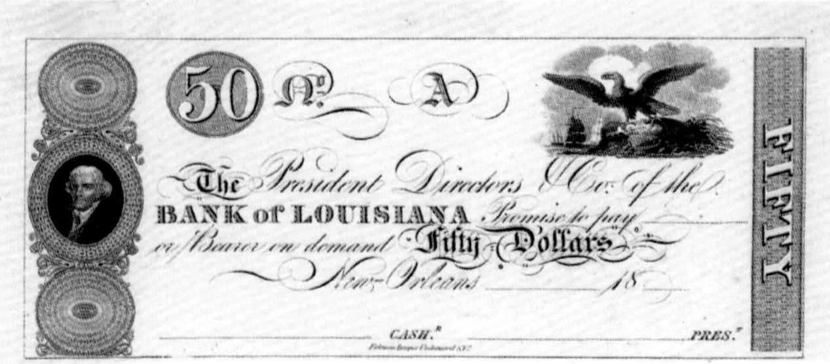

Engraver: Fairman, Draper, Underwood & Co. ***Comments:*** H-Unlisted. 18__. 1820s–1830s.

Rarity: URS-2
Proof $4,500

$50 • W-LA-140-050-G140

Left: FIFTY vertically. ***Center:*** 50 / Woman seated with scroll / 50. ***Right:*** FIFTY vertically. ***Engraver:*** Fairman, Draper, Underwood & Co. ***Comments:*** H-LA-75-G20. 18__. 1820s–1830s.

Rarity: *None known*

$50 • W-LA-140-050-G140a

RH, RH

Tint: Red-brown FIFTY. ***Back:*** Green. ***Engraver:*** Fairman, Draper, Underwood & Co. / Rawdon, Wright, Hatch & Edson. ***Comments:*** H-LA-75-G20a. Similar to W-LA-140-050-G140 but with additional engraver imprint. 18__. 1840s–1850s.

Rarity: URS-3
F $1,000

$50 • W-LA-140-050-G140b

RH, RH

Overprint: Red-brown FIFTY and blue REGISTERED stamp. ***Back:*** Green. ***Engraver:*** Fairman, Draper, Underwood & Co. / Rawdon, Wright, Hatch & Edson. ***Comments:*** H-LA-75-G20c. Similar to W-LA-140-050-G140 but with additional engraver imprint. 18__. 1860s.

Rarity: URS-3
F $600

$50 • W-LA-140-050-G140c

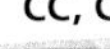

CC, CC

Tint: Blue FIFTY. ***Back:*** Red-orange. ***Engraver:*** Fairman, Draper, Underwood & Co. / Rawdon, Wright, Hatch & Edson. ***Comments:*** H-LA-75-G20b. Similar to W-LA-140-050-G140 but with additional engraver imprint. 18__. 1860s.

Rarity: URS-7
F $140

$50 • W-LA-140-050-G140d

RH, RH

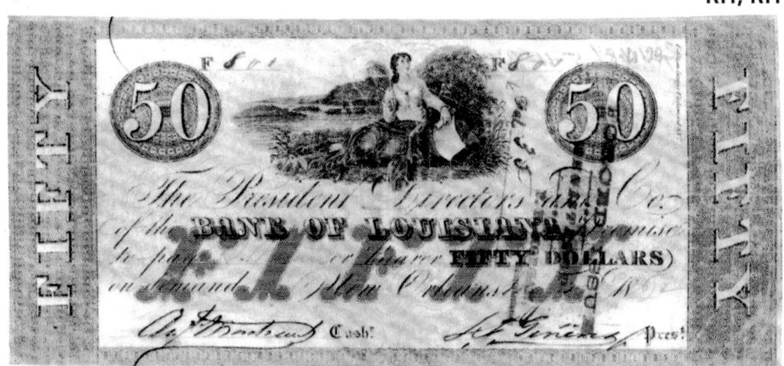

Overprint: Blue FIFTY and FORCED ISSUE stamp. ***Back:*** Red-orange. ***Engraver:*** Fairman, Draper, Underwood & Co. / Rawdon, Wright, Hatch & Edson. ***Comments:*** H-LA-75-G20d. Similar to W-LA-140-050-G140 but with additional engraver imprint.18__. 1860s.

Rarity: URS-8
F $100

$50 • W-LA-140-050-G150

RH, RH

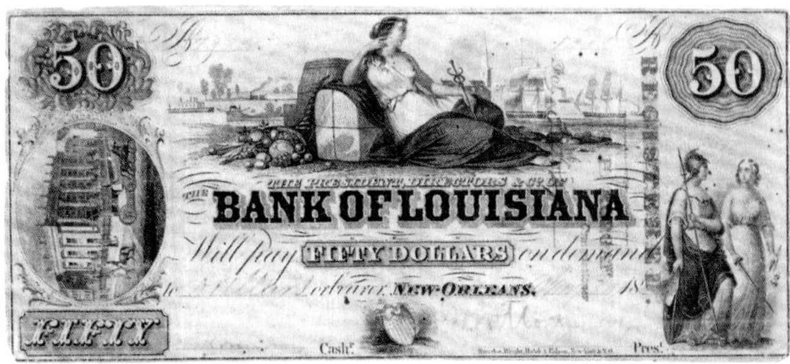

Overprint: Blue REGISTERED stamp. ***Back:*** Red-orange. ***Engraver:*** Rawdon, Wright, Hatch & Edson. ***Comments:*** H-LA-75-G22b. 18__. 1860s.

Rarity: URS-8
F $150

$50 • **W-LA-140-050-G150a** RH, RH

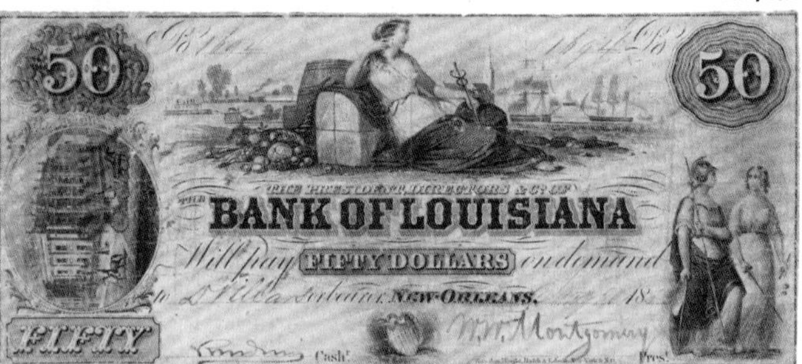

Back: Red-orange. ***Engraver:*** Rawdon, Wright, Hatch & Edson. ***Comments:*** H-LA-75-G22a. Similar to W-LA-140-050-G150. 18__. 1850s–1860s.

Rarity: URS-8
F $150

$50 • **W-LA-140-050-G150b** RH, RH

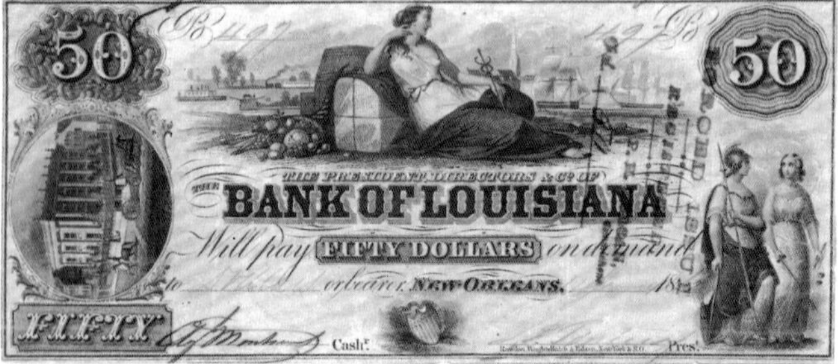

Overprint: Blue FORCED ISSUE stamp. ***Back:*** Red-orange. ***Engraver:*** Rawdon, Wright, Hatch & Edson. ***Comments:*** H-LA-75-G22c. Similar to W-LA-140-050-G150. 18__. 1860s.

Rarity: URS-7
F $200

$100 • **W-LA-140-100-G160** RH

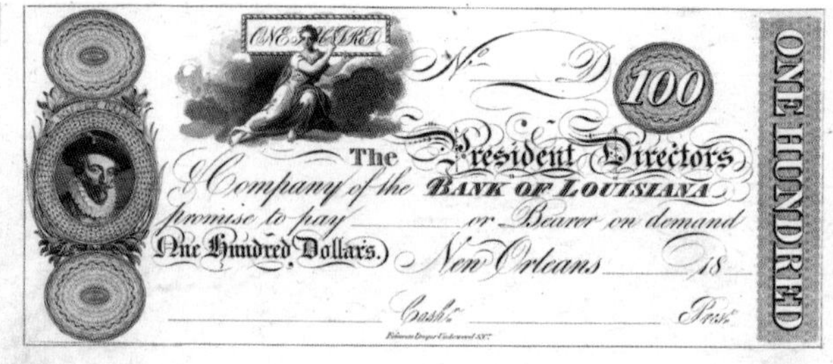

Engraver: Fairman, Draper, Underwood & Co. ***Comments:*** H-Unlisted. 18__. 1820s–1830s.

Rarity: URS-2
Proof $5,000

$100 • **W-LA-140-100-G170** RH

Engraver: Fairman, Draper, Underwood & Co. ***Comments:*** H-LA-75-G24. 18__. 1820s–1830s.

Rarity: URS-2
Proof $5,000

$100 • **W-LA-140-100-G170a** RH, RH

Tint: Black 100. ***Back:*** Green. ***Engraver:*** Fairman, Draper, Underwood & Co. / Rawdon, Wright, Hatch & Edson. ***Comments:*** H-LA-75-G24a. Similar to W-LA-140-100-G170 but with additional engraver imprint. 18__. 1840s–1850s.

Rarity: URS-3
F $1,500

$100 • **W-LA-140-100-G170b**

RH, RH

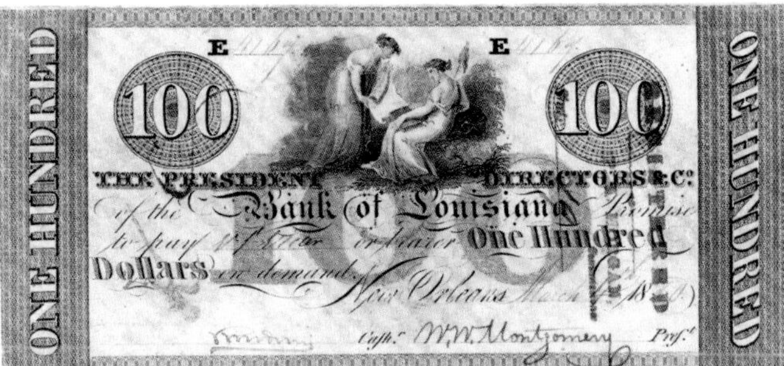

Overprint: Blue REGISTERED stamp. ***Tint:*** Black 100. ***Back:*** Green. ***Engraver:*** Fairman, Draper, Underwood & Co. / Rawdon, Wright, Hatch & Edson. ***Comments:*** H-Unlisted. Similar to W-LA-140-100-G170 but with additional engraver imprint. 18__. 1840s–1850s.

Rarity: URS-3
F $1,500

$100 • **W-LA-140-100-G170c**

RH, RH

Tint: Blue 100. ***Back:*** Red-orange. ***Engraver:*** Fairman, Draper, Underwood & Co. / Rawdon, Wright, Hatch & Edson. ***Comments:*** H-LA-75-G24b. Similar to W-LA-140-100-G170 but with additional engraver imprint. 18__. 1860s.

Rarity: URS-6
F $200

$100 • **W-LA-140-100-G170d**

Overprint: Blue REGISTERED stamp. ***Back:*** Red-orange. ***Engraver:*** Fairman, Draper, Underwood & Co. / Rawdon, Wright, Hatch & Edson. ***Comments:*** H-LA-75-G24c. Similar to W-LA-140-100-G170 but with additional engraver imprint. 18__. 1860s.

Rarity: —

$100 • **W-LA-140-100-G170e**

RH, RH

Overprint: Blue 100 and FORCED ISSUE stamp. ***Back:*** Red-orange. ***Engraver:*** Fairman, Draper, Underwood & Co. / Rawdon, Wright, Hatch & Edson. ***Comments:*** H-LA-75-G24d. Similar to W-LA-140-100-G170 but with additional engraver imprint. 18__. 1860s.

Rarity: URS-7
F $300

$100 • **W-LA-140-100-G180**

RH, RH

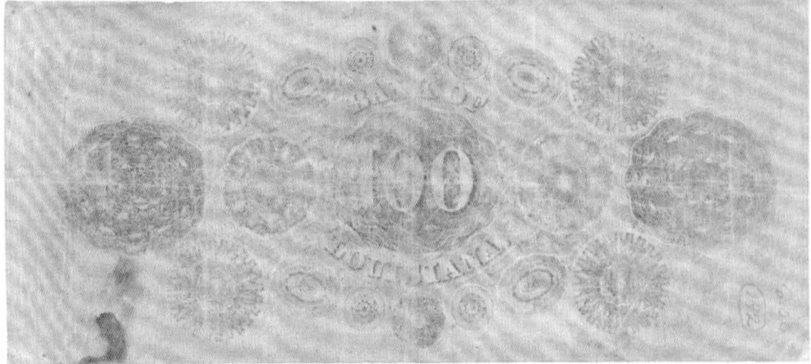

Overprint: Blue REGISTERED stamp. ***Back:*** Red-orange. ***Engraver:*** Rawdon, Wright, Hatch & Edson. ***Comments:*** H-LA-75-G26b. 18__. 1860s.

Rarity: URS-6
F $250

$100 • **W-LA-140-100-G180a**

RH, RH

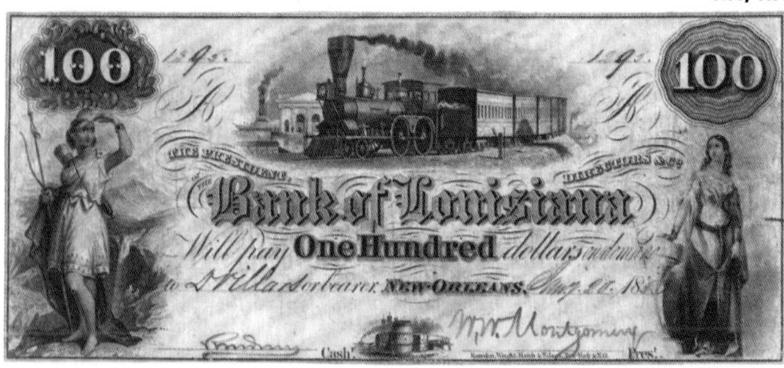

Back: Red-orange. ***Engraver:*** Rawdon, Wright, Hatch & Edson. ***Comments:*** H-LA-75-G26a. Similar to W-LA-140-100-G180. 18__. 1850s–1860s.

Rarity: URS-9
F $200

$100 • **W-LA-140-100-G180b**

QDB, QDB

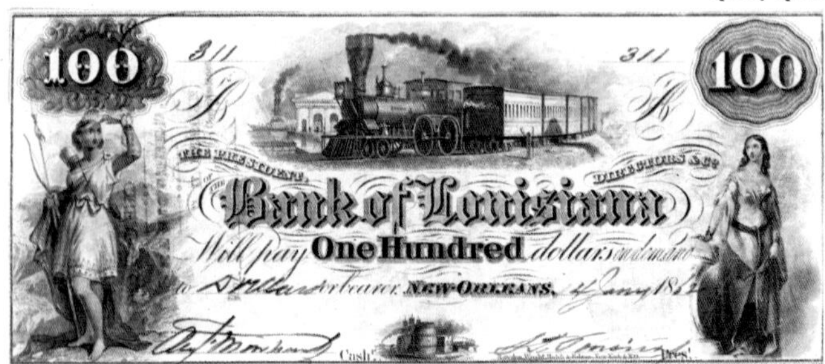

Overprint: Blue FORCED ISSUE stamp. ***Back:*** Red-orange. ***Engraver:*** Rawdon, Wright, Hatch & Edson. ***Comments:*** H-LA-75-G26c. Similar to W-LA-140-100-G180. 18__. 1860s.

Rarity: URS-8
F $200; **VF** $300

$500 • **W-LA-140-500-G190**

RH

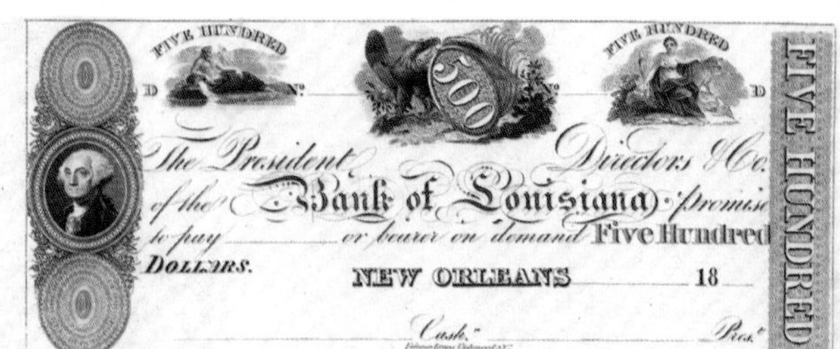

Engraver: Fairman, Draper, Underwood & Co. ***Comments:*** H-LA-75-G28. 18__. 1820s–1840s.

Rarity: URS-1
Proof $7,500

$500 • **W-LA-140-500-G190a**

RH

Overprint: Blue REGISTERED stamp. ***Engraver:*** Fairman, Draper, Underwood & Co. ***Comments:*** H-Unlisted. Similar to W-LA-140-500-G190. 18__. 1820s–1840s.

Rarity: URS-3
F $2,500

$500 • **W-LA-140-500-G190b**

RH, RH

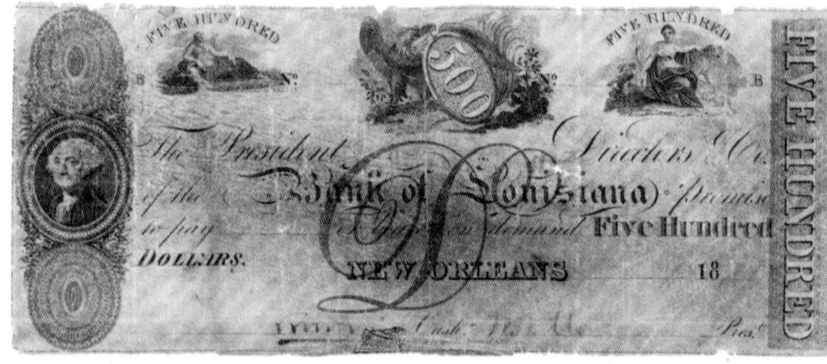

Tint: Blue D. ***Back:*** Brown. ***Engraver:*** Fairman, Draper, Underwood & Co. / Rawdon, Wright, Hatch & Edson. ***Comments:*** H-LA-75-G28a. Similar to W-LA-140-500-G190 but with additional engraver imprint. 18__. 1840s–1850s.

Rarity: URS-3
G $2,000

$500 • W-LA-140-500-G190c CC, CC

Overprint: Blue REGISTERED stamp. ***Back:*** Brown. ***Engraver:*** Fairman, Draper, Underwood & Co. / Rawdon, Wright, Hatch & Edson. ***Comments:*** H-LA-75-G28b. Similar to W-LA-140-500-G190 but with additional engraver imprint. 18__. 1840s–1850s.

Rarity: URS-4
F $2,500

$500 • W-LA-140-500-G200a QDB, QDB

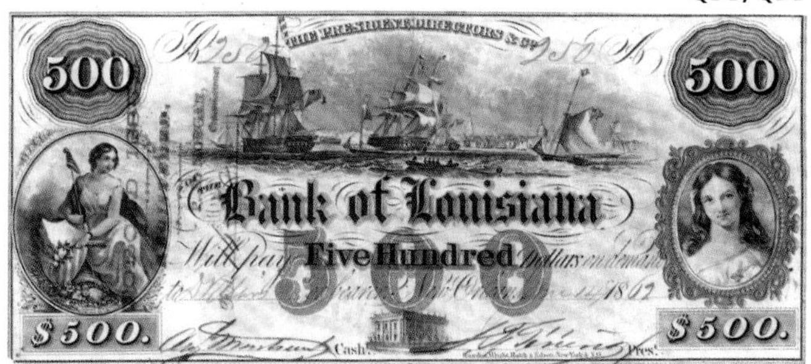

Overprint: Blue FORCED ISSUE stamp. ***Tint:*** Blue 500. ***Back:*** Red-orange. ***Engraver:*** Rawdon, Wright, Hatch & Edson. ***Comments:*** H-LA-75-G30c. Similar to W-LA-140-500-G200. 18__. 1860s.

Rarity: URS-6
F $400; **VF** $600

$500 • W-LA-140-500-G200 CC, CC

Tint: Blue 500. ***Back:*** Red-orange. ***Engraver:*** Rawdon, Wright, Hatch & Edson. ***Comments:*** H-LA-75-G30a. 18__. 1860s.

Rarity: URS-7
F $400; **VF** $750

$1,000 • W-LA-140-1000-G210 RH, RH

Tint: Blue 1000. ***Back:*** Red-orange. ***Engraver:*** Rawdon, Wright, Hatch & Edson. ***Comments:*** H-LA-75-G32a. 18__. 1860s.

Rarity: URS-4
F $750

$1,000 • **W-LA-140-1000-G210a** QDB, QDB

Overprint: Blue FORCED ISSUE stamp. ***Back:*** Red-orange. ***Engraver:*** Rawdon, Wright, Hatch & Edson. ***Comments:*** H-LA-75-G32c. Similar to W-LA-140-1000-G210. 18__. 1860s.

Rarity: URS-7
F $700; **VF** $900

Notes Payable at the Merchants Bank in New York

$5 • **W-LA-140-005-G220** QDB

Engraver: Underwood, Bald, & Spencer. ***Comments:*** H-LA-75-G40. 18__. 1830s–1840s.

Rarity: URS-3
Proof $2,500

$10 • **W-LA-140-010-G230** QDB

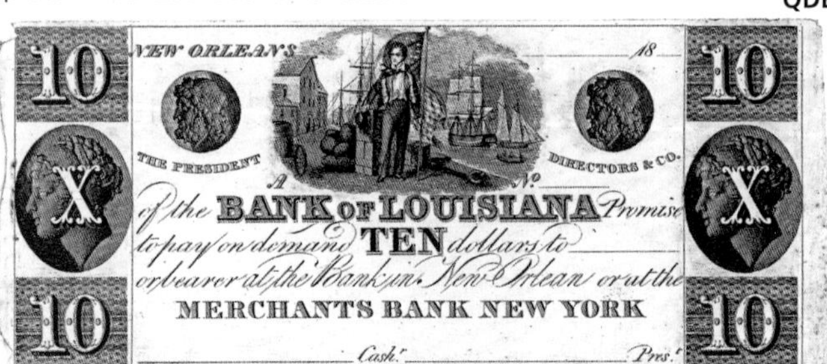

Engraver: Underwood, Bald, & Spencer. ***Comments:*** H-LA-75-G42. 18__. 1830s–1840s.

Rarity: URS-3
Proof $2,500

$20 • **W-LA-140-020-G240** HA

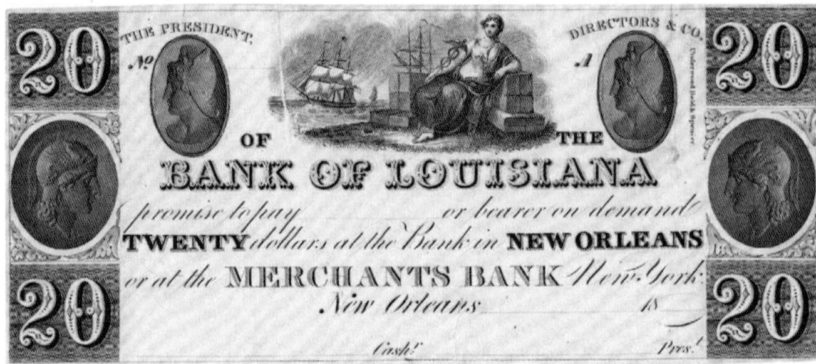

Engraver: Underwood, Bald, & Spencer. ***Comments:*** H-LA-75-G44. 18__. 1830s–1840s.

Rarity: URS-3
Proof $2,500

$50 • **W-LA-140-050-G250** RH

Engraver: Underwood, Bald, & Spencer. ***Comments:*** H-LA-75-G46. 18__. 1830s–1840s.

Rarity: URS-1
Proof $5,000

$100 • **W-LA-140-100-G260** RH

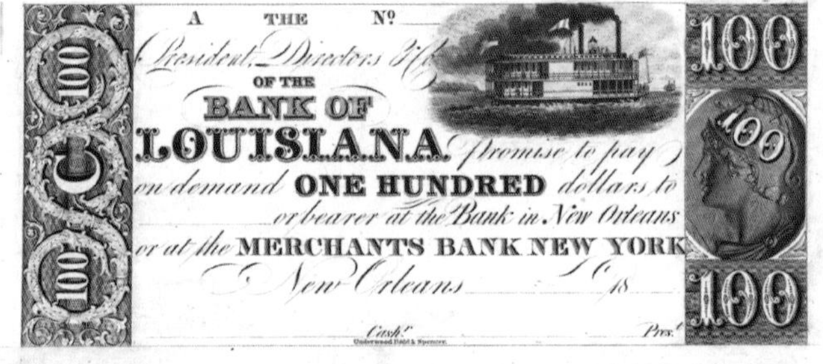

Engraver: Underwood, Bald, & Spencer. ***Comments:*** H-LA-75-G48. 18__. 1830s–1840s.

Rarity: URS-1
Proof $8,000

Bank of New Orleans {1st}

1811–1842

W-LA-150

History: In 1811 the first Bank of New Orleans was incorporated with an authorized capital of $500,000. The cashier, William F. Saul, committed suicide in 1829. In 1842 the bank went into liquidation.

Numismatic Commentary: Proof or issued bank notes from this first period have not yet been discovered or reported.

Bank of New Orleans {2nd}

1853–1870

W-LA-160

History: On May 5, 1853, the second Bank of New Orleans was chartered as the first bank to be incorporated under the Free Banking Law in Louisiana. Its authorized capital was $1,000,000, and it was allowed to circulate notes up to three times that amount, as long as the full capital was kept on hand in specie for the purpose of redeeming notes. W.P. Converse was elected president, and W.P. Grayson was cashier. The bank opened for business on October 1 of that year.

The bank established favorable reviews from the beginning, with the *Bankers' Magazine* reporting that:

> There is nothing lacking in all the preparatory externals of the bank; and with its admirable organization, chartered privileges and influential stockholders, it is bound to rank number one among our banking institutions, which are acknowledged to be, in credit and stability, equal to any in the Union.

As further proof that the bank was held in good standing and that the public had full confidence in the free-banking system, before 3 p.m. on the day the bank opened, over $1,150,000 was deposited with the cashier.[2] By 1857 the capital had risen to $2,000,000, with $630,975 in circulation and $629,641 of specie in the vault. Real estate was valued at $130,000.

By 1870 the Bank of New Orleans had closed.

Numismatic Commentary: Issued bank notes from this second period are scarce but available for collectors. The series was issued "countersigned and registered," with notes bearing red-orange backs, and also without "countersigned and registered" (blue backs).

Valid Issues

$5 • W-LA-160-005-G010

RH, RH

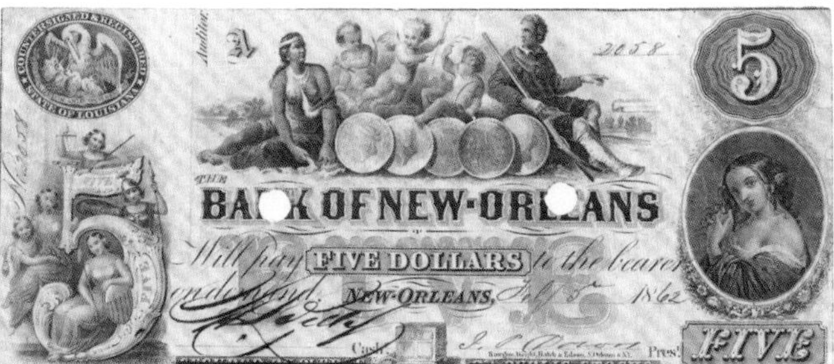

Back: Red-orange state arms. ***Engraver:*** Rawdon, Wright, Hatch & Edson. ***Comments:*** H-LA-100-G2a. Bears Auditor's signature and pledge. 18__. 1850s.

Rarity: URS-7
F $200

$5 • W-LA-160-005-G010a

RH

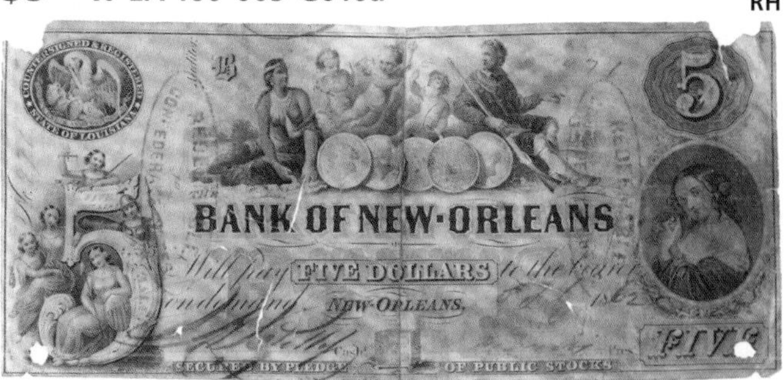

Overprint: Red REDEEMABLE IN CONFEDERATE NOTES stamp. ***Back:*** Red-orange state arms. ***Engraver:*** Rawdon, Wright, Hatch & Edson. ***Comments:*** H-Unlisted. Similar to W-LA-160-005-G010. 18__. 1850s.

Rarity: URS-4
G $400

$10 • W-LA-160-010-G020

Left: Woman standing / 10. ***Center:*** State arms / Woman seated. ***Right:*** 10 / Man standing / TEN. ***Back:*** Red-orange state arms. ***Engraver:*** Rawdon, Wright, Hatch & Edson. ***Comments:*** H-LA-100-G4a. Bears Auditor's signature and pledge. 18__. 1850s.

Rarity: URS-2
F $750

$10 • W-LA-160-010-G020a

RH

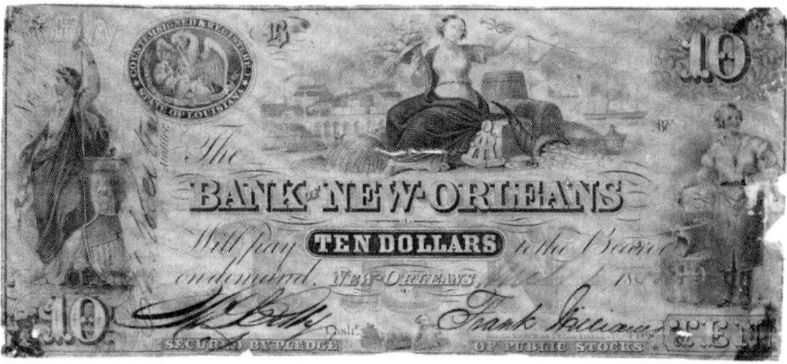

Back: Red-orange state arms. ***Engraver:*** Rawdon, Wright, Hatch & Edson / ABNCo. monogram. ***Comments:*** H-LA-100-G4b. Similar to W-LA-160-010-G020 but with additional engraver imprint. 18__. 1850s–1861.

Rarity: URS-3
G $500

$20 • W-LA-160-020-G030

Left: State arms / Mercury sitting in and holding 20 / TWENTY. ***Center:*** Train. ***Right:*** 20 / Woman standing / TWENTY. ***Back:*** Red-orange state arms. ***Engraver:*** Rawdon, Wright, Hatch & Edson. ***Comments:*** H-LA-100-G6a. Bears Auditor's signature and pledge. 18__. 1850s.

Rarity: URS-5
F $750

$20 • **W-LA-160-020-G030a**

HA, RH

Back: Red-orange state arms. ***Engraver:*** Rawdon, Wright, Hatch & Edson / ABNCo. monogram. ***Comments:*** H-LA-100-G6b. Similar to W-LA-160-020-G030 but with additional engraver imprint. 18__. 1850s–1861.

Rarity: URS-5
F $750
Selected auction price: Heritage Auctions, October 23, 2015, Lot 19467, VF $998

$50 • **W-LA-160-050-G040**

Left: 50 / Cherubs / State arms. ***Center:*** Two women with shield and horse head / FIFTY. ***Right:*** 50 / Male portrait / FIFTY. ***Back:*** Red-orange state arms. ***Engraver:*** Rawdon, Wright, Hatch & Edson. ***Comments:*** H-LA-100-G8a. Bears Auditor's signature and pledge. 18__. 1850s.

Rarity: *None known*

$50 • **W-LA-160-050-G040a**

Back: Red-orange state arms. ***Engraver:*** Rawdon, Wright, Hatch & Edson / ABNCo. monogram. ***Comments:*** H-LA-100-G8b. Similar to W-LA-160-050-G040 but with additional engraver imprint. 18__. 1850s–1861.

Rarity: *None known*

$100 • **W-LA-160-100-G050**

Left: 100 / Minerva / ONE HUNDRED. ***Center:*** Steamship / State arms vertically / 100. ***Right:*** 100 / Woman / ONE HUNDRED. ***Back:*** Red-orange state arms. ***Engraver:*** Rawdon, Wright, Hatch & Edson. ***Comments:*** H-LA-100-G10a. Bears Auditor's signature and pledge. 18__. 1850s.

Rarity: *None known*

$100 • **W-LA-160-100-G050a**

Back: Red-orange state arms. ***Engraver:*** Rawdon, Wright, Hatch & Edson / ABNCo. monogram. ***Comments:*** H-LA-100-G10b. Similar to W-LA-160-100-G050 but with additional engraver imprint. 18__. 1850s–1861.

Rarity: *None known*

$500 • **W-LA-160-500-G060**

Left: 500 / Woman standing. ***Center:*** State arms vertically / Woman seated with bird / 100. ***Right:*** 500 / Female portrait / 500. ***Back:*** Red-orange state arms. ***Engraver:*** Rawdon, Wright, Hatch & Edson. ***Comments:*** H-LA-100-G12a. Bears Auditor's signature and pledge. 18__. 1850s.

Rarity: *None known*

$500 • **W-LA-160-500-G060a**

Back: Red-orange state arms. ***Engraver:*** Rawdon, Wright, Hatch & Edson / ABNCo. monogram. ***Comments:*** H-LA-100-G12b. Similar to W-LA-160-500-G060 but with additional engraver imprint. 18__. 1850s–1861.

Rarity: *None known*

Unregistered Occupation Issues

$1 • **W-LA-160-001-G070**

Left: ONE. ***Center:*** Beehive. ***Right:*** ONE. ***Engraver:*** Douglas. ***Comments:*** H-LA-100-G14. Lithographed on the backs of drafts. April 16th, 1862.

Rarity: —

$2 • **W-LA-160-002-G080**

HA

Engraver: Douglas. ***Comments:*** H-LA-100-G16. Lithographed on the backs of drafts. April 16th, 1862.

Rarity: URS-6
F $250

$3 • **W-LA-160-003-G090**

RH

Engraver: Douglas. ***Comments:*** H-LA-100-G18. Lithographed on the backs of drafts. April 16th, 1862.

Rarity: URS-6
F $250

$5 • **W-LA-160-005-G100**

Left: State arms / 5. ***Center:*** Five cherubs with five coins. ***Right:*** 5 / Female portrait / FIVE. ***Back:*** Blue state arms. ***Engraver:*** Rawdon, Wright, Hatch & Edson. ***Comments:*** H-LA-100-G20a. Lacks Auditor's signature and pledge. 18__. 1862.

Rarity: —

$10 • **W-LA-160-010-G110** RH, RH

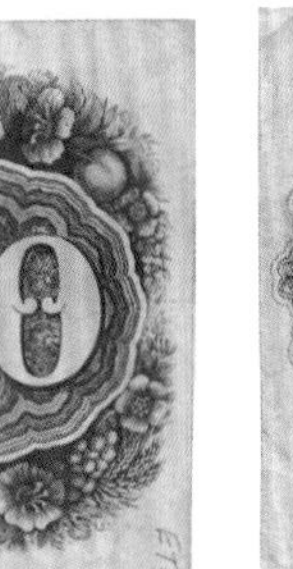

Back: Blue state arms. ***Engraver:*** Rawdon, Wright, Hatch & Edson / ABNCo. monogram. ***Comments:*** H-LA-100-G22b. Lacks Auditor's signature and pledge. 18__. 1862.

Rarity: URS-6

F $400

$20 • **W-LA-160-020-G120** CC, CC

Back: Blue state arms. ***Engraver:*** Rawdon, Wright, Hatch & Edson / ABNCo. monogram. ***Comments:*** H-LA-100-G24b. Lacks Auditor's signature and pledge. 18__. 1862.

Rarity: URS-8

F $200

$50 • **W-LA-160-050-G130** CC, CC

Back: Blue state arms. ***Engraver:*** Rawdon, Wright, Hatch & Edson / ABNCo. monogram. ***Comments:*** H-LA-100-G26b. Lacks Auditor's signature and pledge. 18__. 1862.

Rarity: URS-7

F $250

$100 • **W-LA-160-100-G140** CC, CC

Back: Blue state arms. ***Engraver:*** Rawdon, Wright, Hatch & Edson / ABNCo. monogram. ***Comments:*** H-LA-100-G28b. Lacks Auditor's signature and pledge. 18__. 1862.

Rarity: URS-6

F $500

$500 • **W-LA-160-500-G150**

HA, RH

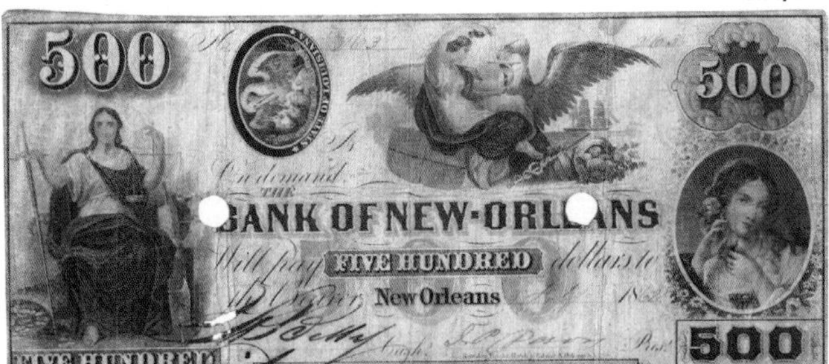

Back: Blue state arms. ***Engraver:*** Rawdon, Wright, Hatch & Edson / ABNCo. monogram. ***Comments:*** H-LA-100-G30b. Lacks Auditor's signature and pledge. 18__. 1862.

Rarity: URS-3
F $3,500
Selected auction price: Heritage Auctions, April 23, 2015, Lot 19092, F $3,525

Bank of Orleans
1811–1849
W-LA-170

History: The Bank of Orleans was incorporated on April 30, 1811, with an authorized capital of $500,000. In 1817 the president was Samuel Packwood. Later that same year Benjamin Morgan became the president, and the cashier elected was Joseph Saul. On March 26, 1823, the bank's charter was renewed to last until 1847. At this time a bonus of $25,000 was required to be paid to the state treasurer before the bank could continue.

On June 23, 1843, the state appointed a body of commissioners to liquidate the affairs of the Bank of Orleans. This lasted until 1849, when the bank was finally settled.

Numismatic Commentary: Proof and issued notes from this early period are extremely rare, as less than a dozen notes have been discovered and reported to date.

Valid Issues

$1 • **W-LA-170-001-G010**

RH

Engraver: Draper, Toppan, Longacre & Co. ***Comments:*** H-LA-125-G4. 18__. 1830s–1840s.

Rarity: URS-3
Proof $2,500

$1 • **W-LA-170-001-G020**

RH

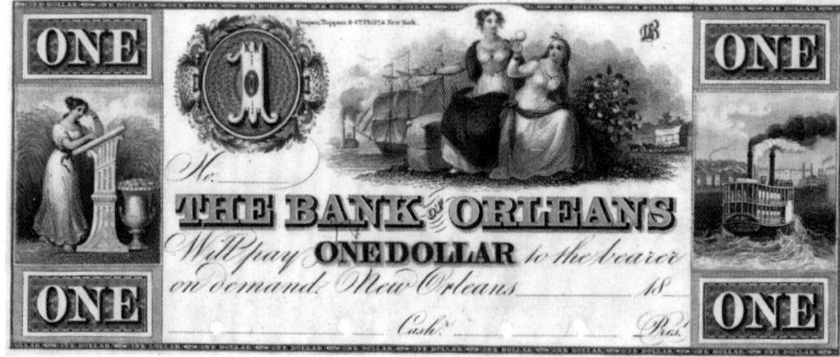

Engraver: Draper, Toppan & Co. ***Comments:*** H-LA-125-G6. 18__. 1840s.

Rarity: URS-3
Proof $2,500

$2 • **W-LA-170-002-G030**

RH

Engraver: Draper, Toppan, Longacre & Co. ***Comments:*** H-LA-125-G8. 18__. 1830s–1840s.

Rarity: URS-3
Proof $3,000

How to Read the Whitman Numbering System

$1 • **W-AL-020-001-G010a**

Denomination: Face value of the note shown.

W: Whitman number. This number is a sortable code unique to each bank and note.

AL: Abbreviation for the state under study.

020: Numerical designation specific to each bank.

001: The denomination in dollars.

G010a: G indicates a good or valid note. Other categories are indicated thus: C (counterfeit); R (raised); S (spurious); N (not-attributed); A (altered). Numbers are assigned starting with 010, 020, et seq. Terminal letters following the number indicate variations of a note: a series of different colored overprints, tints, payees, etc., all on the same design of note. For more information, see the "How to Use This Book" section at the front of the volume, page xiv.

$2 • W-LA-170-002-G040 RH

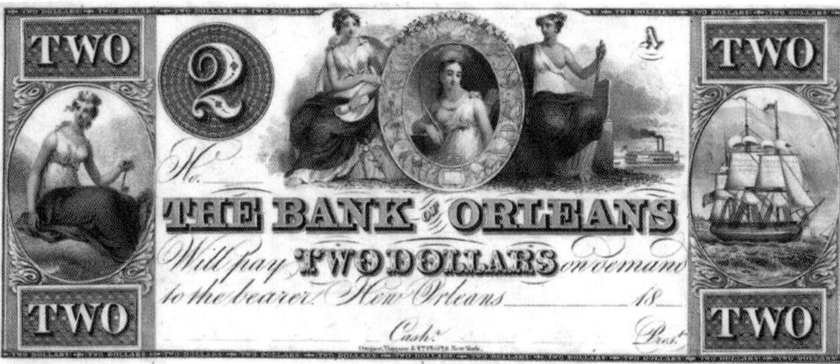

Engraver: Draper, Toppan & Co. ***Comments:*** H-LA-125-G10. 18__. 1840s.

Rarity: URS-3
Proof $3,000

$3 • W-LA-170-003-G050 RH

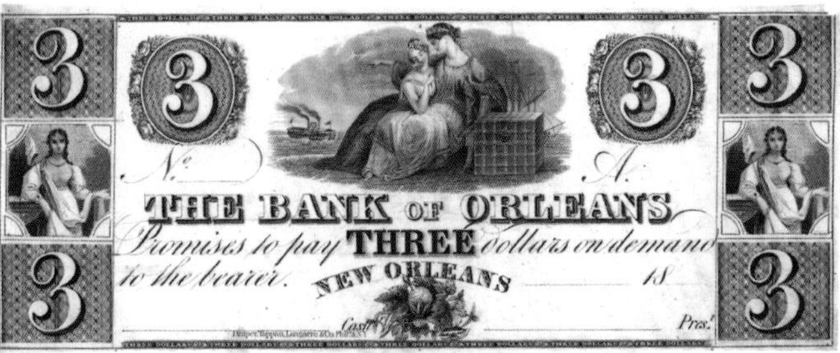

Engraver: Draper, Toppan, Longacre & Co. ***Comments:*** H-LA-125-G12. 18__. 1830s–1840s.

Rarity: URS-2
Proof $4,000

$3 • W-LA-170-003-G060 RH

Engraver: Draper, Toppan & Co. ***Comments:*** H-LA-125-G14. 18__. 1840s.

Rarity: URS-2
Proof $4,000

$5 • W-LA-170-005-G070

Left: BANK OF / FIVE / ORLEANS. ***Center:*** 5 / Eagle / 5. ***Engraver:*** Murray, Draper, Fairman & Co. ***Comments:*** H-LA-125-G16. 18__. 1810s.

Rarity: —

$5 • W-LA-170-005-G080 RH

Engraver: W. Harrison. ***Comments:*** H-LA-125-G18. 18__. 1810s.

Rarity: URS-3
F $5,000

$5 • W-LA-170-005-G090 RH

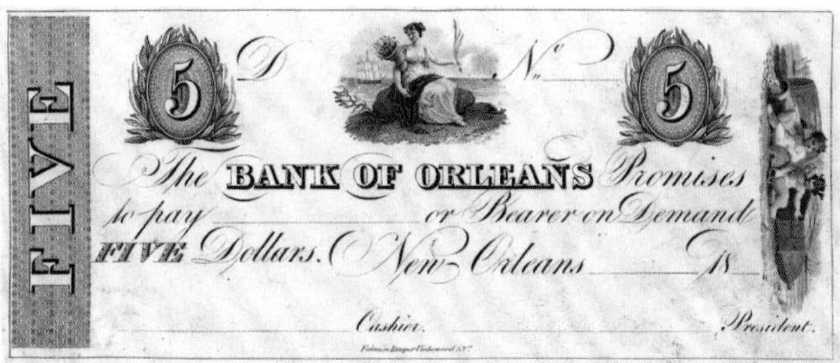

Engraver: Fairman, Draper, Underwood & Co. ***Comments:*** H-LA-125-G20. 18__. 1820s–1830s.

Rarity: URS-3
Proof $2,000

$5 • W-LA-170-005-G100 HA

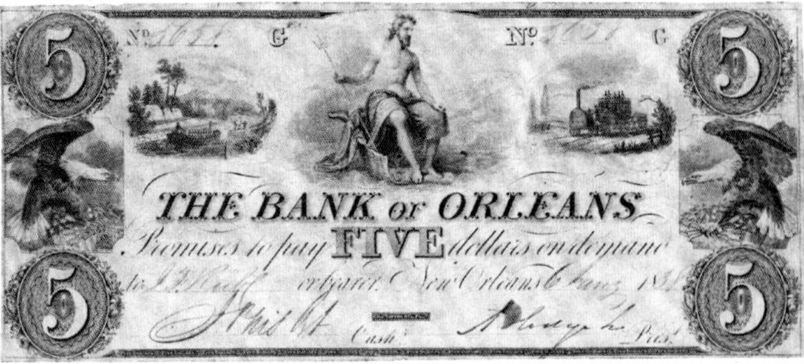

Engraver: Chas. Toppan. ***Comments:*** H-LA-125-G22. 18__. 1830s–1840s.

Rarity: URS-3
F $1,500; **Proof** $2,000
Selected auction price: Heritage Auctions, October 21, 2015, Lot 18353, VF $1,527

$10 • W-LA-170-010-G110 RH

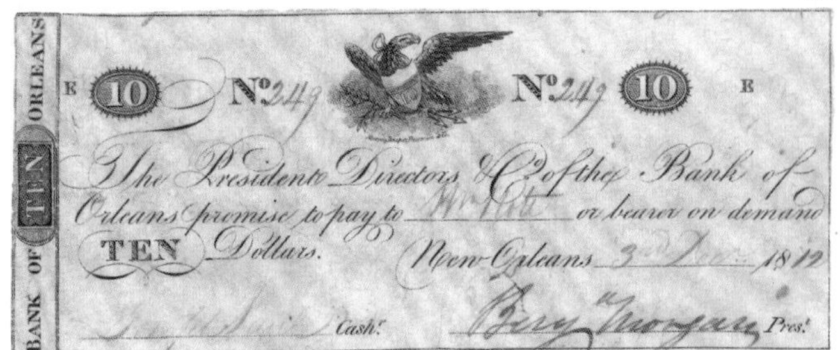

Engraver: Murray, Draper, Fairman & Co. ***Comments:*** H-LA-125-G24. 18__. 1810s.

Rarity: URS-2
F $4,000

$10 • **W-LA-170-010-G120** RH

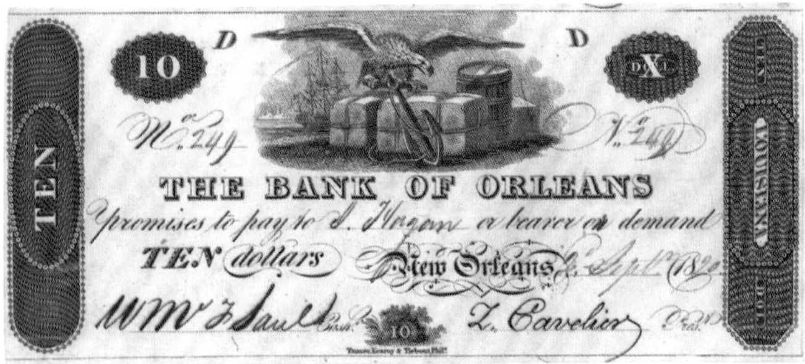

Engraver: Tanner, Kearny & Tiebout. ***Comments:*** H-LA-125-G26. 18__. 1810s–1820s.

Rarity: URS-2
VF $4,000

$10 • **W-LA-170-010-G130** RH

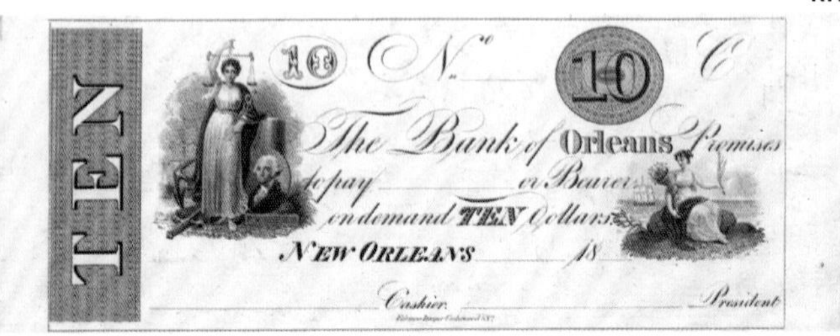

Engraver: Fairman, Draper, Underwood & Co. ***Comments:*** H-LA-125-G28. 18__. 1820s–1830s.

Rarity: URS-3
Proof $2,000

$10 • **W-LA-170-010-G140** RH

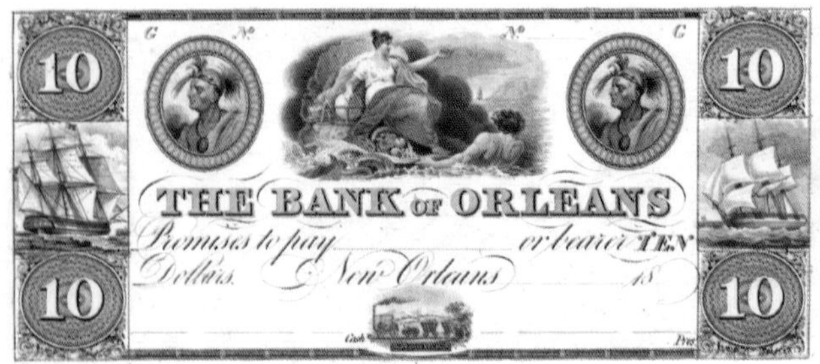

Engraver: Chas. Toppan. ***Comments:*** H-LA-125-G30. 18__. 1830s–1840s.

Rarity: URS-3
Proof $2,000

$20 • **W-LA-170-020-G150**

Left: BANK OF / TWENTY / ORLEANS. ***Center:*** 20 / Eagle / 20. ***Engraver:*** Murray, Draper, Fairman & Co. ***Comments:*** H-LA-125-G32. 18__. 1810s.

Rarity: *None known*

$20 • **W-LA-170-020-G160**

Engraver: W. Harrison. ***Comments:*** H-LA-125-G34. No description available. 18__. 1810s.

Rarity: *None known*

$20 • **W-LA-170-020-G170** RH

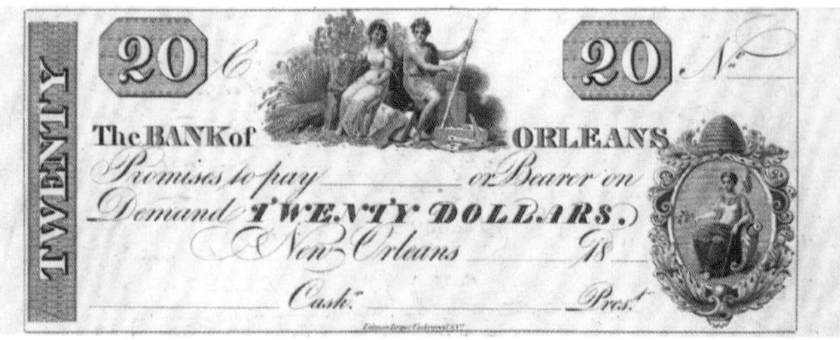

Engraver: Fairman, Draper, Underwood & Co. ***Comments:*** H-LA-125-G36. 18__. 1820s–1830s.

Rarity: URS-3
Proof $2,500

$20 • **W-LA-170-020-G180** RH

Engraver: Chas. Toppan. ***Comments:*** H-LA-125-G38. 18__. 1830s–1840s.

Rarity: URS-3
Proof $2,500

$50 • **W-LA-170-050-G190**

Left: BANK OF / FIFTY / ORLEANS. ***Center:*** 50 / Eagle / 50. ***Engraver:*** Murray, Draper, Fairman & Co. ***Comments:*** H-LA-125-G40. 18__. 1810s.

Rarity: *None known*

$50 • **W-LA-170-050-G200**

Engraver: W. Harrison. ***Comments:*** H-LA-125-G42. No description available. 18__. 1810s.

Rarity: *None known*

$50 • **W-LA-170-050-G210** RH

Engraver: Fairman, Draper, Underwood & Co. ***Comments:*** H-LA-125-G44. 18__. 1820s.

Rarity: URS-2
Proof $4,000

$50 • **W-LA-170-050-G220** RH

Engraver: Chas. Toppan. ***Comments:*** H-LA-125-G44. 18__. 1820s.

Rarity: URS-2
Proof $4,000

$100 • **W-LA-170-100-G230**

Left: BANK OF / HUNDRED / ORLEANS. ***Center:*** 100 / Eagle / 100. ***Engraver:*** Murray, Draper, Fairman & Co. ***Comments:*** H-LA-125-G46. 18__. 1810s.

Rarity: *None known*

$100 • **W-LA-170-100-G240** HA

Engraver: W. Harrison. ***Comments:*** H-LA-125-G48. 18__. 1810s.

Rarity: URS-1
Proof $7,000
Selected auction price: Heritage Auctions, April 23, 2015, Lot 19094, EF $7,050

$100 • **W-LA-170-100-G250** RH

Engraver: Fairman, Draper, Underwood & Co. ***Comments:*** H-LA-125-G50. 18__. 1820s.

Rarity: URS-3
Proof $3,500

$100 • **W-LA-170-100-G260** RH

Engraver: Chas. Toppan. ***Comments:*** H-Unlisted. 18__. 1820s.

Rarity: URS-2
Proof $4,000

$500 • **W-LA-170-500-G270** RH

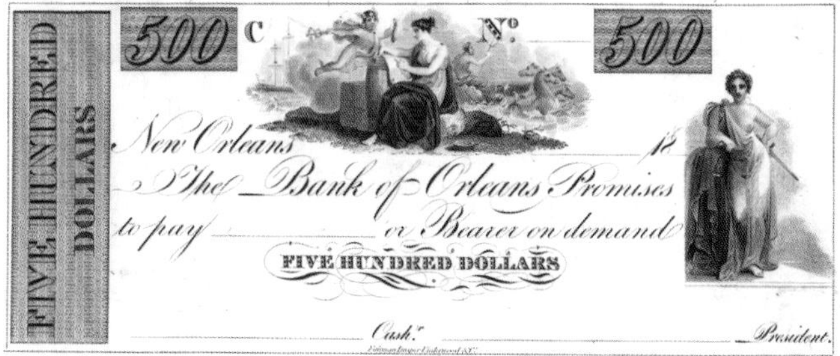

Engraver: Fairman, Draper, Underwood & Co. ***Comments:*** H-LA-125-G54. 18__. 1820s.

Rarity: URS-2
Proof $6,000

$500 • **W-LA-170-500-G280** RH

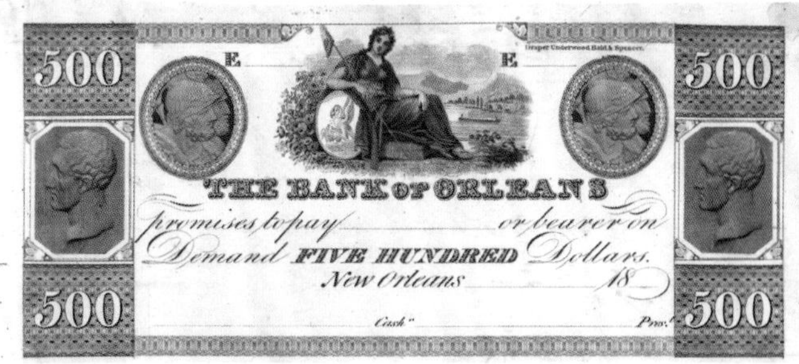

Engraver: Draper, Underwood, Bald & Spencer. ***Comments:*** H-LA-125-G56. 18__. 1830s–1840s.

Rarity: URS-2
Proof $6,000

$1,000 • **W-LA-170-1000-G290**

Engraver: Fairman, Draper, Underwood & Co. ***Comments:*** H-LA-125-G60. No description available. 18__. 1820s.

Rarity: *None known*

$1,000 • **W-LA-170-1000-G300** RH

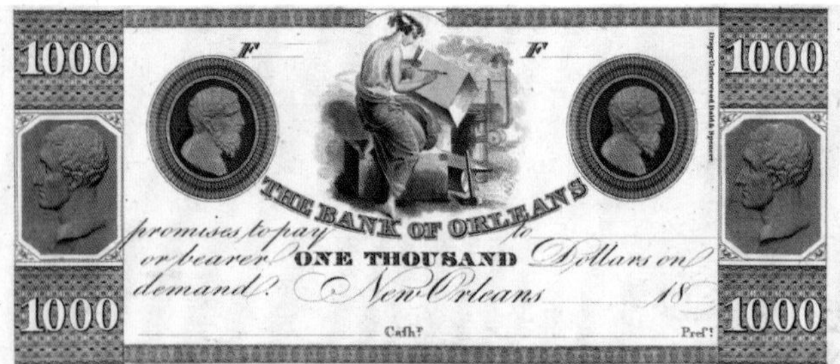

Engraver: Draper, Underwood, Bald & Spencer. ***Comments:*** H-LA-125-G62. 18__. 1830s–1840s.

Rarity: URS-2
Proof $7,500

Post Notes

$__ • **W-LA-170-__-G310** RH

Engraver: Draper, Underwood, Bald & Spencer. ***Comments:*** H-LA-125-G70. 18__. 1830s.

Rarity: URS-2
F $1,500

Post Notes Payable in Philadelphia

$5 • **W-LA-170-005-G320** RH

Engraver: Draper, Underwood, Bald & Spencer. ***Comments:*** H-LA-125-G72. 18__. 1830s.

Rarity: URS-2
Proof $1,500

$10 • **W-LA-170-010-G330** RH

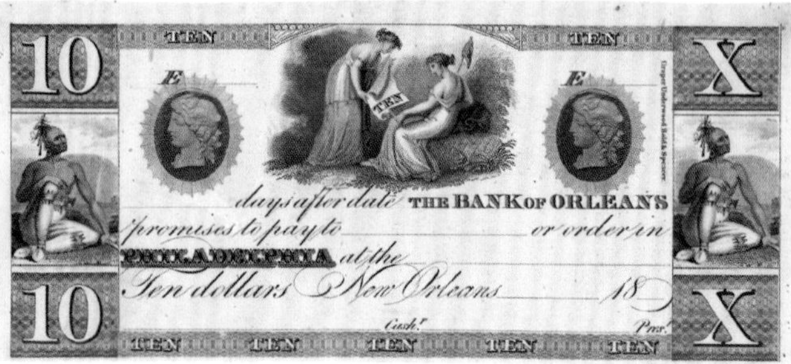

Engraver: Draper, Underwood, Bald & Spencer. ***Comments:*** H-LA-125-G74. 18__. 1830s.

Rarity: URS-3
F $1,500

$20 • **W-LA-170-020-G340** HSPA

Engraver: Draper, Underwood, Bald & Spencer. ***Comments:*** H-LA-125-G76. 18__. 1830s.

Rarity: URS-3
F $2,000

$50 • **W-LA-170-050-G350** RH

Engraver: Draper, Underwood, Bald & Spencer. ***Comments:*** H-LA-125-G78. 18__. 1830s.

Rarity: URS-2
F $3,500

$100 • **W-LA-170-100-G360** RH

Engraver: Draper, Underwood, Bald & Spencer. ***Comments:*** H-LA-125-G80. 18__. 1830s.

Rarity: URS-2

F $4,500

Non-Valid Issues

$1 • **W-LA-170-001-C020** RH

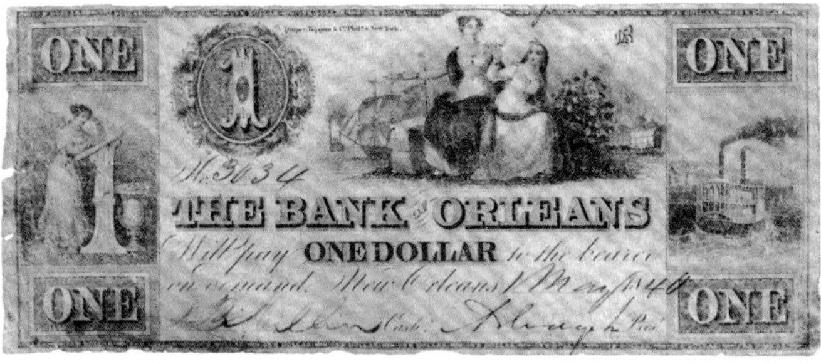

Engraver: Draper, Toppan & Co. ***Comments:*** H-Unlisted. Counterfeit of W-LA-170-001-G020. 18__. 1840s.

Rarity: URS-4

F $400

$3 • **W-LA-170-003-C050**

Engraver: Draper, Toppan, Longacre & Co. ***Comments:*** H-LA-125-C12. Counterfeit of W-LA-170-003-G050. 18__. 1839.

Rarity: *None known*

$5 • **W-LA-170-005-C080** HA

Engraver: W. Harrison. ***Comments:*** H-LA-125-C18. Counterfeit of W-LA-170-005-G080. 18__. 1810s–1820s.

Rarity: URS-4

F $750

$10 • **W-LA-170-010-C120**

Engraver: W. Harrison. ***Comments:*** H-LA-125-C26. Counterfeit of W-LA-170-010-G120. 18__. 1817.

Rarity: *None known*

$50 • **W-LA-170-050-R010**

Engraver: W. Harrison. ***Comments:*** H-LA-125-R5. Raised from W-LA-170-005-G080. 18__. 1810s–1820s.

Rarity: *None known*

$100 • **W-LA-170-100-C240** RH

Engraver: W. Harrison. ***Comments:*** H-LA-125-C48. Counterfeit of W-LA-170-100-G240. 18__. 1817–1823.

Rarity: URS-3

F $2,000

Bank of the United States {1st} (branch)

1791–1811

W-LA-175

History: The first Bank of the United States was chartered in 1791. In 1809 the bank began to wind down its affairs, as it seemed the charter would not be renewed. Various state-chartered banks, often with politically connected shareholders and officers, viewed the bank as a threat to their businesses and an unfair competitor due to the fact that it had government backing, even though most of the bank's shares were held by others.

The New Orleans branch closed out its affairs in 1811 when Congress failed to renew the charter for the Bank of the United States.

Numismatic Commentary: Only counterfeits are known of this branch, and they are exceedingly rare.

Valid Issues

$5 • **W-LA-175-005-G010**

Center: 5 / 5. ***Comments:*** H-US-1-G220. 1___. 1800s.

Rarity: *None known*

$5 • **W-LA-175-005-G020**

Center: 5 / Phoenix / 5. ***Comments:*** H-US-1-G222. 1___. 1800s.

Rarity: *None known*

$10 • **W-LA-175-010-G030**

Center: 10 / 10. ***Comments:*** H-US-1-G226. 1___. 1800s.

Rarity: *None known*

$10 • **W-LA-175-010-G040**

Center: 10 / Phoenix / 10. ***Comments:*** H-US-1-G228. 1___. 1800s.

Rarity: *None known*

$20 • **W-LA-175-020-G050**

Center: 20 / 20. ***Comments:*** H-US-1-G232. 1___. 1800s.

Rarity: *None known*

$20 • **W-LA-175-020-G060**
Center: 20 / Phoenix / 20. ***Comments:*** H-US-1-G234. 1___. 1800s.
Rarity: *None known*

$50 • **W-LA-175-050-G070**
Center: 50 / 50. ***Comments:*** H-US-1-G238. 1___. 1800s.
Rarity: *None known*

$50 • **W-LA-175-050-G080**
Center: 50 / Phoenix / 50. ***Comments:*** H-US-1-G240. 1___. 1800s.
Rarity: *None known*

$100 • **W-LA-175-100-G090**
Center: 100 / 100. ***Comments:*** H-US-1-G244. 1___. 1800s.
Rarity: *None known*

$100 • **W-LA-175-100-G100**
Center: 100 / Phoenix / 100. ***Comments:*** H-US-1-G246. 1___. 1800s.
Rarity: *None known*

Non-Valid Issues

$50 • **W-LA-175-050-C080**
Comments: H-US-1-C240. Counterfeit of W-LA-175-050-G080. 1___. 1800s.
Rarity: *None known*

Bank of the United States {2nd} (branch)
1817–1835
W-LA-180

History: The second Bank of the United States was chartered in 1816 for a duration of 20 years. Its capital was $35,000,000, of which the United States owned $7,000,000. Branch banks in several large cities were opened during 1816 and 1817 in direct competition with state banks.

In 1832 President Andrew Jackson vetoed the 1836 renewal of the Bank of the United States which had been brought up before Congress. This instituted a period of great debate and political turmoil. In late 1833 and early 1834 there was a depression in some areas of business which only served to strengthen the bank, as it was backed by the government. The branches began closing and selling their buildings. In November 1835 the New Orleans Gas Light and Banking Company, W-LA-360, purchased the office facilities of the Bank of the United States.

Numismatic Commentary: Genuine notes are almost non-collectible. Over a long period of years, nearly all that have appeared on the market for study (via clear illustrations) have been counterfeits, although rarely noted as such. Caution is urged when contemplating the purchase of such a note.

Valid Issues

$5 • **W-LA-180-005-G010**
Left: Medallion head / Medallion head. *Center:* Woman with 5 / Eagle on shield, 5 / Woman with 5. ***Right:*** Portrait / Portrait. ***Engraver:*** Fairman, Draper, Underwood & Co. ***Comments:*** H-US-2-G588. 18__. 1810–1820s.
Rarity: *None known*

$5 • **W-LA-180-005-G020**
Left: FIVE vertically. ***Center:*** 5 / Eagle on shield / V. ***Right:*** FIVE vertically. ***Engraver:*** Fairman, Draper, Underwood & Co. ***Comments:*** H-US-2-G590. 18__. 1820s–1830s.
Rarity: *None known*

$10 • **W-LA-180-010-G030**
Left: Medallion head / Medallion head. ***Center:*** 10 / Eagle on shield / 10. ***Right:*** Portrait / Portrait. ***Engraver:*** Fairman, Draper, Underwood & Co. ***Comments:*** H-US-2-G594. 18__. 1810–1820s.
Rarity: *None known*

$10 • **W-LA-180-010-G040**
Left: 10 vertically. ***Center:*** X / Eagle on shield / 10. ***Right:*** TEN vertically. ***Engraver:*** Fairman, Draper, Underwood & Co. ***Comments:*** H-US-2-G596. 18__. 1820s–1830s.
Rarity: *None known*

$20 • **W-LA-180-020-G050**
Left: Medallion head / Medallion head. ***Center:*** 20 / Eagle on shield / 20. ***Right:*** Portrait / Portrait. ***Engraver:*** Murray, Draper, Fairman & Co. ***Comments:*** H-US-2-G600. 18__. 1810–1820s.
Rarity: *None known*

$20 • **W-LA-180-020-G060**
Left: Eagle on shield / Portrait of George Washington / Medallion head. ***Center:*** 20 / Eagle on shield / 20. ***Right:*** Eagle on shield / Portrait of Benjamin Franklin / Female portrait. ***Engraver:*** Fairman, Draper, Underwood & Co. ***Comments:*** H-US-2-G602. 18__. 1820s–1830s.
Rarity: *None known*

$20 • **W-LA-180-020-G070**
Left: 20 vertically. ***Center:*** 20 / Eagle on shield / 20. ***Right:*** XX vertically. ***Engraver:*** Danforth, Underwood, Bald & Spencer. ***Comments:*** H-US-2-G604. 18__. 1830s.
Rarity: *None known*

$50 • **W-LA-180-050-G080**
Left: Medallion head / Medallion head. ***Center:*** 50 / Eagle on shield / 50. ***Right:*** Portrait / Portrait. ***Engraver:*** Murray, Draper, Fairman & Co. ***Comments:*** H-US-2-G608. 18__. 1810–1820s.
Rarity: *None known*

$50 • **W-LA-180-050-G090**
Left: Eagle on shield / Portrait of George Washington / Medallion head. ***Right:*** Eagle on shield / Portrait of Benjamin Franklin / Female portrait. ***Engraver:*** Fairman, Draper, Underwood & Co. ***Comments:*** H-US-2-G610. 18__. 1820s–1830s.
Rarity: *None known*

$50 • **W-LA-180-050-G100**
Left: L / Medallion head / 50. ***Center:*** FIFTY / 50 / Eagle on shield / FIFTY / L. ***Right:*** 50 / Medallion head / L. ***Engraver:*** Danforth, Underwood, Bald & Spencer. ***Comments:*** H-US-2-G612. 18__. 1830s.
Rarity: *None known*

$100 • **W-LA-180-100-G110**
Left: Medallion head / Medallion head. ***Center:*** 100 / Eagle on shield / 100. ***Right:*** Portrait / Portrait. ***Engraver:*** Murray, Draper, Fairman & Co. ***Comments:*** H-US-2-G616. 18__. 1810–1820s.
Rarity: *None known*

$100 • W-LA-180-100-G120

Left: Eagle on shield / Portrait of George Washington / Medallion head. ***Center:*** 100 / Eagle on shield / 100. ***Right:*** Eagle on shield / Portrait of Benjamin Franklin / Female portrait. ***Engraver:*** Fairman, Draper, Underwood & Co. ***Comments:*** H-US-2-G618. 18__. 1820s–1830s.

Rarity: *None known*

$100 • W-LA-180-100-G130

Left: 100 / Medallion head / C. ***Center:*** 100 / Eagle on shield / 100. ***Right:*** C / Medallion head / 100. ***Engraver:*** Danforth, Underwood, Bald & Spencer. ***Comments:*** H-US-2-G620. 18__. 1830s.

Rarity: *None known*

Non-Valid Issues

$5 • W-LA-180-005-C010

RH

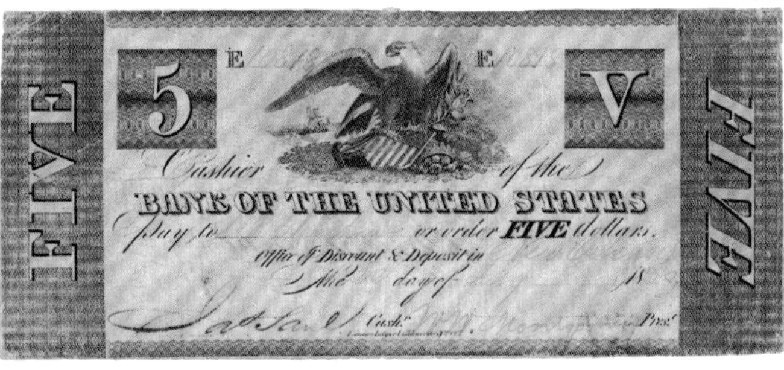

Engraver: Fairman, Draper, Underwood & Co. ***Comments:*** H-US-2-C588. Counterfeit of W-LA-180-005-G010. 18__. 1820s.

Rarity: URS-5

F $450

$5 • W-LA-180-005-C020

RH

Engraver: Fairman, Draper, Underwood & Co. ***Comments:*** H-Unlisted. Counterfeit of W-LA-180-005-G020. 18__. 1820s–1830s.

Rarity: URS-5

F $400

$10 • W-LA-180-010-C030

RH

Engraver: Fairman, Draper, Underwood & Co. ***Comments:*** H-US-2-C594. Counterfeit of W-LA-180-010-G030. 18__. 1820s.

Rarity: URS-5

F $400

$10 • W-LA-180-010-C040

RH

Engraver: Fairman, Draper, Underwood & Co. ***Comments:*** H-Unlisted. Counterfeit of W-LA-180-010-G040. 18__. 1820s–1830s.

Rarity: URS-3

F $1,000

$20 • W-LA-180-020-C050

RH

Engraver: Murray, Draper, Fairman & Co. ***Comments:*** H-US-2-C600. Counterfeit of W-LA-180-020-G050. 18__. 1820s.

Rarity: URS-4

F $750

$50 • W-LA-180-050-C090

Engraver: Fairman, Draper, Underwood & Co. ***Comments:*** H-US-2-C610. Counterfeit of W-LA-180-050-G090. 18__. 1820s.

Rarity: *None known*

$100 • W-LA-180-100-C110

RH

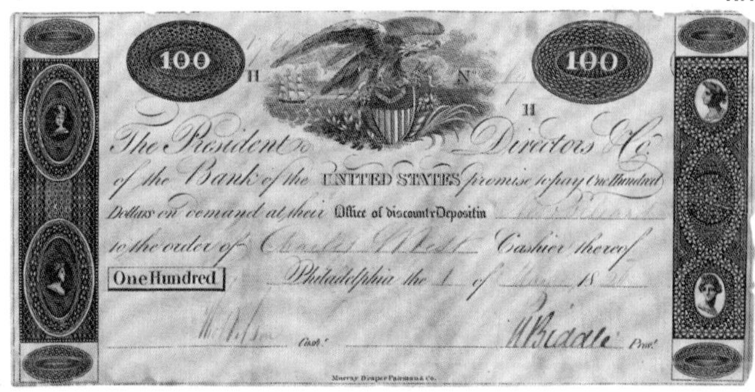

Engraver: Murray, Draper, Fairman & Co. ***Comments:*** H-US-2-C616. Counterfeit of W-LA-180-100-G110. 18__. 1820s.

Rarity: URS-3

F $2,000

$100 • **W-LA-180-100-C120**

RH

Engraver: Danforth, Underwood, Bald & Spencer. ***Comments:*** H-US-2-C618. Counterfeit of W-LA-180-100-G120. 18__. 1820s.

Rarity: URS-3

F $2,500

RH

Back: Red-orange male portrait. ***Engraver:*** Draper, Toppan, Longacre & Co. ***Comments:*** H-Unlisted. Octr. 1, 1838.

Rarity: URS-3

F $2,500

Bank of the United States of Pennsylvania

1838–1841

W-LA-190

History: The Bank of the United States of Pennsylvania was chartered by the Pennsylvania legislature and had no connection with the first Bank of the United States (1791–1811) or the second Bank of the United States, W-LA-180. These two entities, headquartered in Philadelphia, were chartered by Congress and had many branches. Nicholas Biddle, earlier the president of the second Bank of the United States, supervised the formation of the Bank of the United States of Pennsylvania in 1838, after the Bank of the United States had closed. He neglected to put "of Pennsylvania" on his notes in an attempt to deceive holders of the notes, who would then pass them at a distance. The bank failed in 1841. Biddle, a scion of Philadelphia society, died in disgrace not long after.

Numismatic Commentary: Genuine, issued notes from this period are extremely rare. New Orleans is handwritten in for the branch-bank locations.

Issues

Note Payable at the Merchants Bank, New Orleans

$5 • **W-LA-190-005-N010**

HA

Canal Bank

1831–1870

W-LA-195

History: The Canal Bank was a nickname for the New Orleans Canal and Banking Company which was chartered in March 1831 and went into operation in June with an authorized capital of $4,000,000.

See the New Orleans Canal and Banking Company, W-LA-350.

Citizens Bank of Louisiana

1833–1874

W-LA-200

History: The Citizens Bank of Louisiana was incorporated on April 1, 1833. The directors of the bank were authorized to issue $12,000,000 worth of bonds, secured by $14,400,000 in stock subscriptions. Of this amount, the state reserved a credit of $500,000, unless the bank would fund the digging of the Lake Borgne Canal by the Lake Borgne Navigation Company.

On January 30, 1836, the bank was reincorporated with an amended charter due to its inability to sell the initial amount of bonds. $3,000,000 worth of bonds was immediately set to be issued, the backing was secured, and the bank finally opened for business. In 1847 the Citizens Bank was doing well enough that it reorganized under the original charter, and it was stated in *The Numismatist* that the notes of the bank "came to be a very popular form of currency, being honored throughout the Mississippi Valley, and, in fact, throughout the country."

In 1852 the bank was reorganized again, splitting the company into a banking department and a mortgage department. The following year the president was James D. Denegre, and the cashier was Eugene Rousseau. In 1863 the capital of the bank was a large $6,930,666. Bills in circulation totaled $2,574,910.

In 1874 the Citizens Bank, the oldest bank in the city of New Orleans, suspended specie payments at last and went into bankruptcy. The bank was unable to recover from the Civil War and closed.

The Citizens Bank had a branch bank located in Shreveport, W-LA-480.

Numismatic Commentary: Considered to be one of the most popular notes issued by this bank, the $10 note of the Citizens Bank bears the French word *dix* on its face, meaning *ten*. Eventually this morphed into the word *Dixie*, which became a nickname for the South.

The $1,000 sheet (W-LA-200-1000-US090) has a partial, faded $500 note. The plate was initially engraved as a two-note plate. For whatever reason, the $500 note was never needed. When the $1,000 was printed, only that part of the plate was inked, and a smaller sheet of paper was used. Through progression, some ink did migrate to the $500 part of the plate. As a result, there is a shadow on some $1,000 sheets. This is called a "partially printed" sheet. The only $500 notes known exist as single Proofs.

Valid Issues

$1 • W-LA-200-001-G010

NJW

Engraver: American Bank Note Co. ***Comments:*** H-LA-15-G2. 18__. 1860s.

Rarity: URS-12
Unc-Rem $75

$2 • W-LA-200-002-G020

NJW

Engraver: American Bank Note Co. ***Comments:*** H-LA-15-G4. 18__. 1860s.

Rarity: URS-12
Unc-Rem $75

$3 • W-LA-200-003-G030

CC

Engraver: American Bank Note Co. ***Comments:*** H-LA-15-G6. 18__. 1860s.

Rarity: URS-9
F $90

$5 • W-LA-200-005-G040

HA

Engraver: Draper, Toppan, Longacre & Co. ***Comments:*** H-LA-15-G10. 18__. 1830s–1840s.

Rarity: URS-3
Proof $2,900
Selected auction price: Heritage Auctions, April 23, 2015, Lot 19080, Proof $2,820

$5 • W-LA-200-005-G050

Left: FIVE vertically. ***Center:*** 5 / Woman with shield, flag, and cornucopia of coins / 5. ***Right:*** CINQ vertically. ***Back:*** Blue. ***Engraver:*** Rawdon, Wright, Hatch & Edson. ***Comments:*** H-LA-15-G12b. 18__. 1840s–1850s.

Rarity: *None known*

$5 • W-LA-200-005-G050a

RH, RH

Tint: Red-orange FIVE. ***Back:*** Blue. ***Engraver:*** Rawdon, Wright, Hatch & Edson. ***Comments:*** H-Unlisted. Similar to W-LA-200-005-G050. 18__. 1840s–1850s.

Rarity: URS-3
F $900

Collectors and Researchers:

If you have new information about any banks or notes listed in this volume, contact Whitman Publishing, Attn: Obsolete Paper Money, 3101 Clairmont Road, Suite G, Atlanta, GA 30329.

$5 • W-LA-200-005-G050b LK, NS

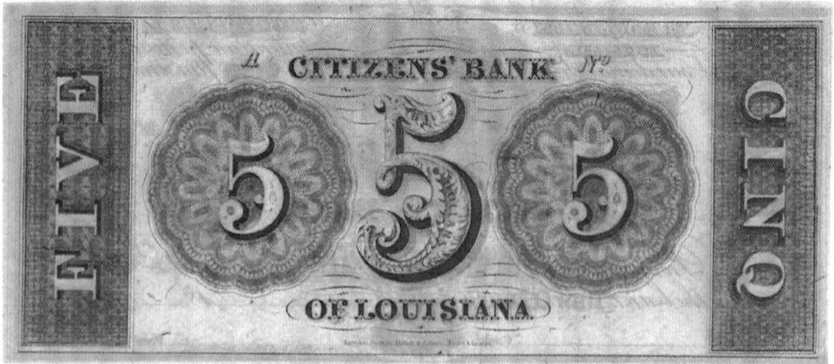

Tint: Red-orange FIVE. ***Back:*** Blue. ***Engraver:*** Rawdon, Wright, Hatch & Edson / ABNCo. monogram. ***Comments:*** H-LA-15-G12c. Similar to W-LA-200-005-G050 but with additional engraver imprint and back bears check letter and serial number. 18__. 1850s–1860s.

Rarity: URS-7
F $750

$5 • W-LA-200-005-G060 RH, QDB

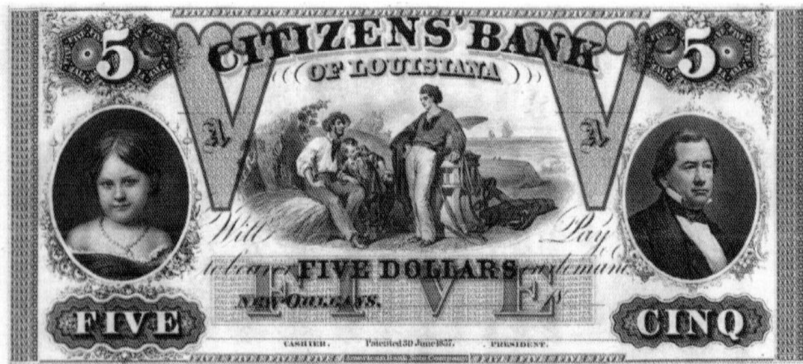

Tint: Green. ***Back:*** Red-orange. ***Engraver:*** American Bank Note Co. ***Comments:*** H-LA-15-G14a. 18__. 1860s.

Rarity: URS-4
Proof $1,000
Selected auction price: Heritage Auctions, October 21, 2015, Lot 18341, Proof $998

$5 • W-LA-200-005-G070

Left: Two steamboats at sea / FIVE on 5. ***Center:*** Portrait of child. ***Right:*** 5 / Man picking cotton. ***Tint:*** Green. ***Comments:*** H-LA-15-G16a. 18__. 1860s.

Rarity: —

$10 • W-LA-200-010-G080 RH

Engraver: Draper, Toppan, Longacre & Co. ***Comments:*** H-LA-15-G18. 18__. 1830s–1840s.

Rarity: URS-3
Proof $2,000

$10 • W-LA-200-010-G090 RH, RH

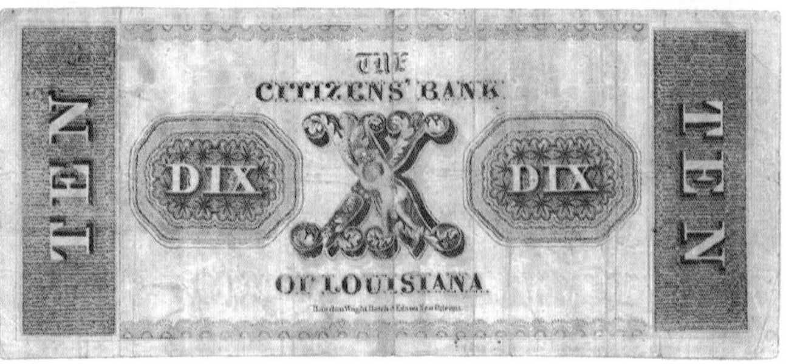

Tint: Blue TEN. ***Back:*** Red-brown. ***Engraver:*** Rawdon, Wright, Hatch & Edson. ***Comments:*** H-LA-15-G20a. 18__. 1840s–1850s.

Rarity: URS-4
F $3,000

$10 • W-LA-200-010-G090a

NJW, NJW

Tint: Blue TEN. ***Back:*** Red-brown. ***Engraver:*** Rawdon, Wright, Hatch & Edson. ***Comments:*** H-LA-15-G20b. Similar to W-LA-200-010-G090 but back bears check letter and serial number. 18__. 1850s.

Rarity: URS-5
F $2,000

$10 • W-LA-200-010-G100

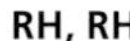
RH, RH

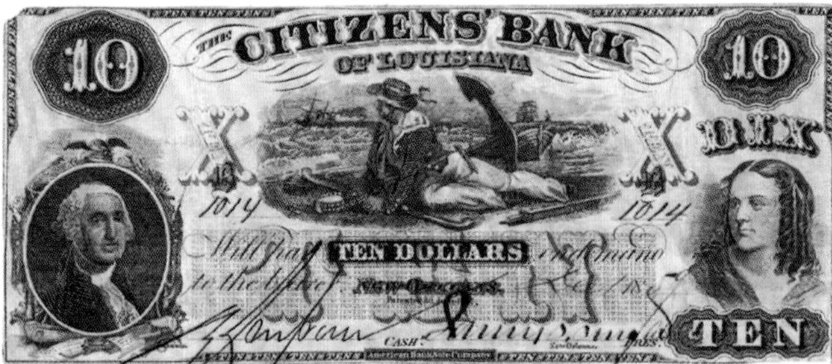

Tint: Green X / X and panel of microlettering bearing TEN. ***Back:*** Red-orange ship and implements. ***Engraver:*** American Bank Note Co. ***Comments:*** H-LA-15-G22a. 18__. 1859–1860s.

Rarity: URS-5
F $1,500

$10 • W-LA-200-010-G110

Left: 10 / Man buying newspaper from boy. ***Right:*** 10 / Woman with anchor, ropes, and machinery. ***Tint:*** Green TEN. ***Engraver:*** Unverified, but likely American Bank Note Co. ***Comments:*** H-LA-15-G24a. 18__. 1860s.

Rarity: *None known*

$10 • W-LA-200-010-G120

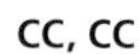
CC, CC

Tint: Red-orange. ***Back:*** Red-orange. ***Engraver:*** National Bank Note Co. ***Comments:*** H-LA-15-G26a. 186_. 1860s.

Rarity: URS-8
Unc-Rem $900; **Proof** $6,000
Selected auction price(s): Heritage Auctions, September 25, 2013, Lot 15839, Remainder $998; Heritage Auctions, October 17, 2012, Lot 15224, Remainder $1,880; Heritage Auctions, April 27, 2011, Lot 15217, Unc $1,955; Heritage Auctions, September 7, 2011, Lot 15758, Unc $1,265; Heritage Auctions, September 7, 2011, Lot 15759, Proof $920

$10 • W-LA-200-010-G120a

RH, RH

Tint: Red-orange. ***Back:*** Red-orange. ***Engraver:*** National Bank Note Co. ***Comments:*** H-Unlisted. Similar to W-LA-200-010-G120. Color-trial Proof. 186_. 1860s.

Rarity: URS-2
Proof $8,000

$10 • W-LA-200-010-G120b

RH, RH

Tint: Green. *Back:* Black. *Engraver:* National Bank Note Co. *Comments:* H-Unlisted. Similar to W-LA-200-010-G120. Color-trial Proof. 186_. 1860s.

Rarity: URS-2
Proof $3,000

$20 • W-LA-200-020-G130

Left: TWENTY. *Center:* 20 / 20 / Pelican feeding young. *Right:* VINGT PIASTRES. *Engraver:* Draper, Toppan, Longacre & Co. *Comments:* H-LA-15-G28. 18__. 1830s–1840s.

Rarity: —

$20 • W-LA-200-020-G140

Left: Woman with shield, flag, and cornucopia of coins / 20. *Center:* VIGNT. *Right:* 20 / Eagle / XX. *Engraver:* Rawdon, Wright, Hatch & Edson. *Comments:* H-LA-15-G30b. 18__. 1840s–1850s.

Rarity: *None known*

$20 • W-LA-200-020-G140a

NS, NS

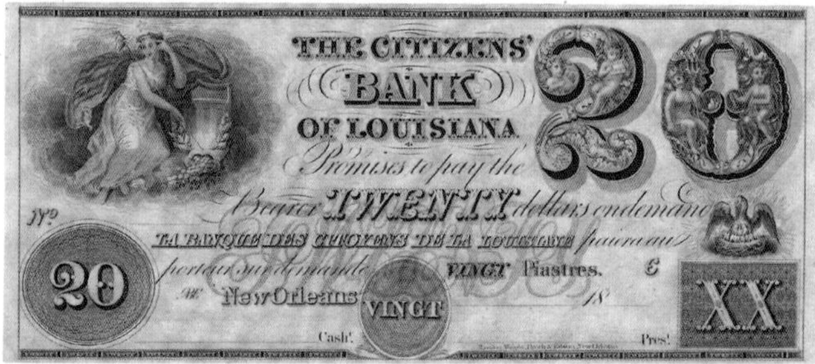

Tint: Green TWENTY. *Back:* Red-orange. *Engraver:* Rawdon, Wright, Hatch & Edson / ABNCo. monogram. *Comments:* H-LA-15-G30c. Similar to W-LA-200-020-G140 but with additional engraver imprint. 18__. 1850s–1860s.

Rarity: URS-8
Unc-Rem $100

$20 • W-LA-200-020-G150

RH, RH

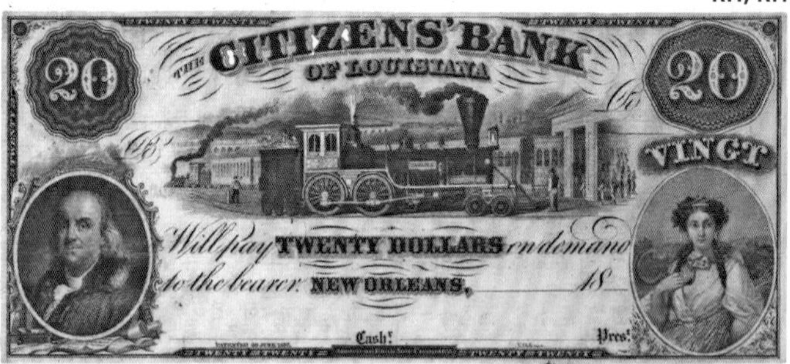

Back: Black portrait of George Washington. *Engraver:* American Bank Note Co. *Comments:* H-LA-15-G32a. 18__. 1860s.

Rarity: URS-3
Proof $2,500

$20 • W-LA-200-020-G150a

RH

Tint: Green panel of microlettering and die outlining white 20. *Back:* Red-orange portrait of George Washington. *Engraver:* American Bank Note Co. *Comments:* H-LA-15-G32b. Similar to W-LA-200-020-G150. 18__. 1860s.

Rarity: URS-2
Proof $4,000

$50 • **W-LA-200-050-G160** RH

Engraver: Draper, Toppan, Longacre & Co. ***Comments:*** H-LA-15-G36. 18__. 1830s–1840s.

Rarity: URS-3
F $4,000

$50 • **W-LA-200-050-G170** RH, RH

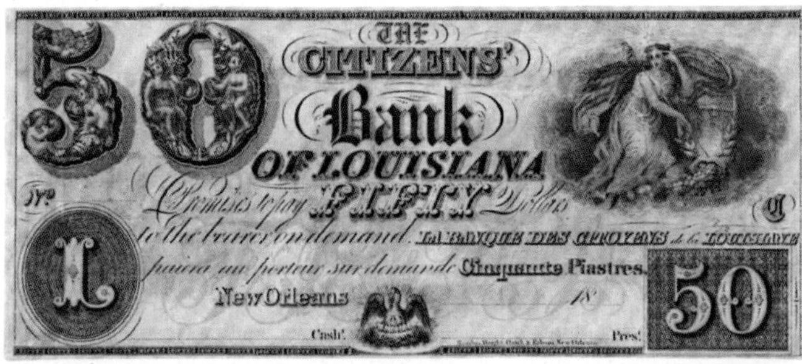

Tint: Grey FIFTY. ***Back:*** Green. ***Engraver:*** Rawdon, Wright, Hatch & Edson. ***Comments:*** H-LA-15-G38b. 18__. 1840s–1850s.

Rarity: URS-5
F $750

$50 • **W-LA-200-050-G180** CC, CC

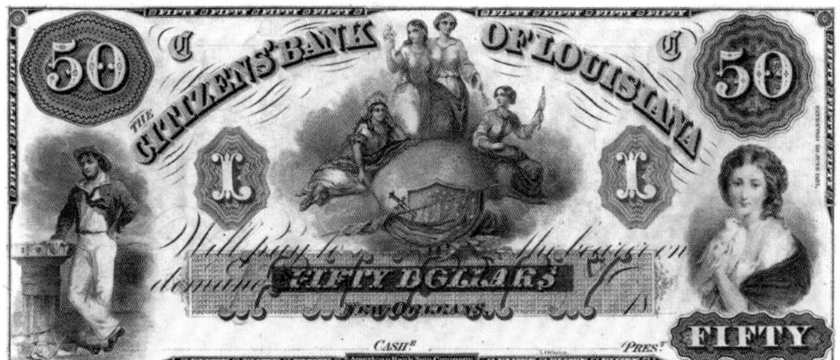

Tint: Green dies outlining white L / L and panel of microlettering bearing FIFTY. ***Back:*** Red-orange portrait of Marquis de Lafayette. ***Engraver:*** American Bank Note Co. ***Comments:*** H-LA-15-G40a. 18__. 1860s.

Rarity: URS-10
F $100

$100 • **W-LA-200-100-G190** HA

Engraver: Draper, Toppan, Longacre & Co. ***Comments:*** H-LA-15-G44. 18__. 1830s.

Rarity: URS-5
Proof $2,200
Selected auction price: Heritage Auctions, April 23, 2015, Lot 19081, Proof $2,115

$100 • **W-LA-200-100-G200** NJW, NJW

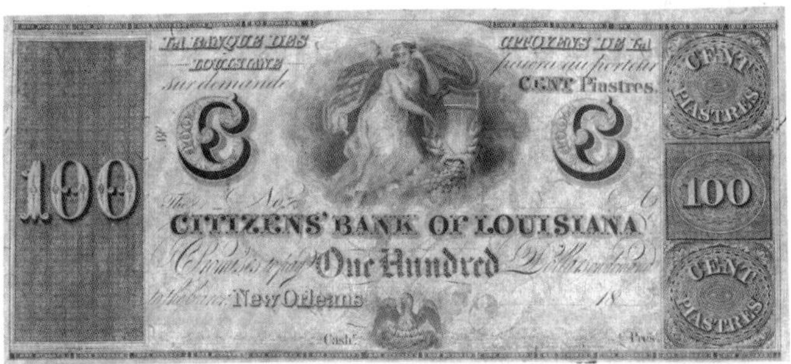

Tint: Orange C. ***Back:*** Red-brown. ***Engraver:*** Rawdon, Wright, Hatch & Edson. ***Comments:*** H-LA-15-G46b. 18__. 1840s.

Rarity: URS-10
Unc-Rem $90

$100 • **W-LA-200-100-G200a**

Engraver: Rawdon, Wright, Hatch & Edson / ABNCo. monogram. ***Comments:*** H-LA-15-G46c. Similar to W-LA-200-100-G200 but with additional engraver imprint. 18__. 1850s–1860s.

Rarity: —

$100 • W-LA-200-100-G210

CC, CC

Tint: Green C / C and panel of microlettering bearing HUNDRED. ***Back:*** Red-orange male portrait. ***Engraver:*** American Bank Note Co. ***Comments:*** H-LA-15-G48a. 18__. 1860s.

Rarity: URS-10
Unc-Rem $75

$500 • W-LA-200-500-G220

RH

Engraver: Draper, Toppan, Longacre & Co. ***Comments:*** H-Unlisted. 18__. 1830s.

Rarity: URS-1
Proof $8,000

$500 • W-LA-200-500-G230

Left: 500 / Pelican feeding young. ***Right:*** Liberty with pole and cap, U.S. shield, flag / 500. ***Tint:*** Red-orange. ***Back:*** Blue. ***Engraver:*** Rawdon, Wright, Hatch & Edson. ***Comments:*** H-LA-15-G50b. 18__. 1840s–1850s.

Rarity: —

$1,000 • W-LA-200-1000-G240

RH

Engraver: Draper, Toppan, Longacre & Co. ***Comments:*** H-Unlisted. 18__. 1830s.

Rarity: URS-1
Proof $10,000

$1,000 • W-LA-200-1000-G250

NJW, NJW

Tint: Red-brown M. ***Back:*** Red-orange. ***Engraver:*** Rawdon, Wright, Hatch & Edson. ***Comments:*** H-LA-15-G54b. 18__. 1840s–1850s.

Rarity: URS-7
Unc-Rem $400

Uncut Sheets

$1-$1-$2-$3 • W-LA-200-001.001.002.003-US010 RG

Engraver: American Bank Note Co. ***Comments:*** H-LA-15-G2, G2, G4, G6. First two notes identical. 18__. 1860s.

Rarity: URS-8
F $250

$5-$5-$5-$5 • W-LA-200-005.005.005.005-US020 RG

Tint(s): Red-orange. ***Back(s):*** Blue. ***Engraver:*** Rawdon, Wright, Hatch & Edson / ABNCo. monogram. ***Comments:*** H-LA-15-G12c, G12c, G12c, G12c. All four notes identical. 18__. 1850s–1860s.

Rarity: URS-10
F $200

$5-$5-$5-$5 • W-LA-200-005.005.005.005-US030 RG

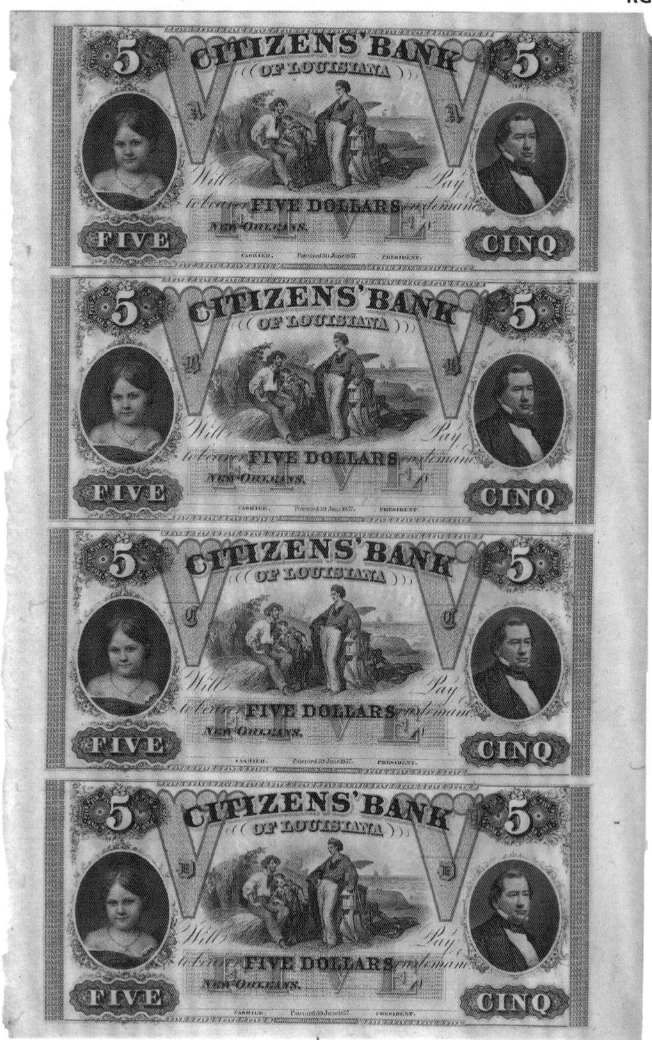

Tint(s): Green. ***Back(s):*** Red-orange. ***Engraver:*** American Bank Note Co. ***Comments:*** H-LA-15-G14a, G14a, G14a, G14a. All four notes identical. 18__. 1860s.

Rarity: URS-10
F $200

$10-$10-$10-$10 • W-LA-200-010.010.010.010-US040 RG

Tint(s): Red-orange. ***Back(s):*** Red-orange. ***Engraver:*** National Bank Note Co. ***Comments:*** H-LA-15-G26a, G26a, G26a, G26a. All four notes identical. 186_. 1860s.

Rarity: URS-6
F $3,000
Selected auction price(s): Heritage Auctions, September 16, 2015, Lot 18438, Unc $2,467; Heritage Auctions, April 24, 2013, Lot 15217, Remainder $2,820

$20-$20-$20-$20 •
W-LA-200-020.020.020.020-US050 RG

Tint(s): Green. ***Back(s):*** Red-orange. ***Engraver:*** Rawdon, Wright, Hatch & Edson. ***Comments:*** H-LA-15-G30c, G30c, G30c, G30c. All four notes identical. 18__. 1850s–1860s.

Rarity: URS-8
F $300

$50-$50-$50-$50 •
W-LA-200-050.050.050.050-US060 RG

Tint(s): Green. ***Back(s):*** Red-orange portrait of Marquis de Lafayette. ***Engraver:*** American Bank Note Co. ***Comments:*** H-LA-15-G40a, G40a, G40a, G40a. All four notes identical. 18__. 1860s.

Rarity: URS-8
F $300

$100-$100-$100-$100 •
W-LA-200-100.100.100.100-US070

RG

Tint(s): Orange C. ***Back(s):*** Red-brown. ***Engraver:*** Rawdon, Wright, Hatch & Edson. ***Comments:*** H-LA-15-G46b, G46b, G46b, G46b. All four notes identical. 18__. 1840s.

Rarity: URS-8
F $250

$100-$100-$100-$100 •
W-LA-200-100.100.100.100-US080

RG

Tint(s): Green. ***Back(s):*** Red-orange male portrait. ***Engraver:*** American Bank Note Co. ***Comments:*** H-LA-15-G48a, G48a, G48a, G48a. All four notes identical. 18__. 1860s.

Rarity: URS-8
F $250

$1,000 • W-LA-200-1000-US090 RG

Tint: Red-brown M. ***Back:*** Red-orange. ***Engraver:*** Rawdon, Wright, Hatch & Edson. ***Comments:*** H-LA-15-G54b. Sheet of one note. There is a partial, faded $500 note. See numismatic commentary. 18__. 1840s–1850s.

Rarity: URS-6
F $350

Non-Valid Issues

$5 • W-LA-200-005-C050b

Engraver: Rawdon, Wright, Hatch & Edson. ***Comments:*** H-LA-15-C12c. Counterfeit of W-LA-200-005-G050b. 18__. 1850s.

Rarity: —

$10 • W-LA-200-010-C080 RH

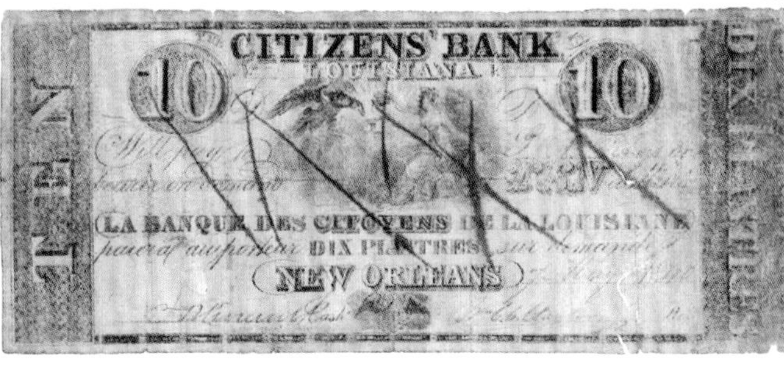

Engraver: Draper, Toppan, Longacre & Co. ***Comments:*** H-LA-15-C18. Counterfeit of W-LA-200-010-G080. 18__. 1840.

Rarity: URS-2
F $450

$10 • W-LA-200-010-C090

Engraver: Rawdon, Wright, Hatch & Edson. ***Comments:*** H-LA-15-C20a. Counterfeit of W-LA-200-010-G090. 18__. 1840s–1850s.

Rarity: —

$10 • W-LA-200-010-C090a HA

Tint: Blue TEN. ***Engraver:*** Rawdon, Wright, Hatch & Edson. ***Comments:*** H-LA-15-C20b. Counterfeit of W-LA-200-010-G090a. 18__. 1850s.

Rarity: URS-7
F $1,500
Selected auction price: Heritage Auctions, April 24, 2013, Lot 15219, VF $2,232

$10 • W-LA-200-010-C100 NJW, NJW

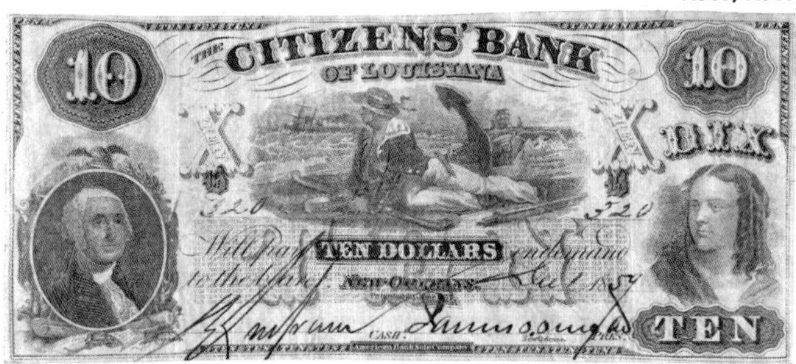

Tint: Green outlining white X / X and panel of microlettering bearing TEN. ***Back:*** Red-orange ship. ***Engraver:*** American Bank Note Co. ***Comments:*** H-LA-15-C22a. Counterfeit of W-LA-200-010-G100. 18__. 1859.

Rarity: URS-6
F $800

$50 • W-LA-200-050-C160 HA

Engraver: Draper, Toppan, Longacre & Co. ***Comments:*** H-LA-15-C36. Counterfeit of W-LA-200-050-G160. 18__. 1830s.

Rarity: URS-4
F $500

$50 • W-LA-200-050-R010

Engraver: Draper, Toppan, Longacre & Co. ***Comments:*** H-LA-15-R5. Raised from W-LA-200-005-G040. 18__. 1830s.

Rarity: —

City Bank of New Orleans

1831–1850

W-LA-210

History: The City Bank of New Orleans was chartered in March 1831 with an authorized capital of $2,000,000. By 1836 the paid-in capital was $400,000. In 1842 this amount spiked to the full $2,000,000. The circulation at this time was $644,050.

Following a crisis in the city, many banks suspended specie payment, and those that did not had very little currency in circulation. On June 2, 1842, after hanging on for a long time against suspending payments, the City Bank had to give in. Notes were at a discount and some banks failed.

In 1848 the president of the bank was Samuel J. Peters, and the cashier was Robert J. Palfrey. Capital was $1,888,600. In April of that year there was a bank robbery, when "some scoundrel entered the City Bank . . . and stole from the private vault of the cashier, Robert J. Palfrey . . . [an amount] valued at $4,320."[3] The money was apparently the property of the cashier's relatives. In 1849 it was observed that the City Bank was reducing its business affairs, and that year the stockholders were requested to surrender their stock certificates so that the bank could prepare to liquidate. At that time circulation had dropped to $322,785.

On May 1, 1850, the charter of the bank expired, and the assets were purchased by the Louisiana State Bank, W-LA-280.

Numismatic Commentary: Proof and issued notes from this bank are for the most part rare. There are an estimated three-dozen issued notes known.

Valid Issues

$1 • W-LA-210-001-G010

Left: ONE on 1 / Woman with anchor. ***Center:*** Dock scene, Men unloading canal boats. ***Right:*** ONE on 1 / Two women. ***Engraver:*** Unverified, but likely American Bank Note Co. ***Comments:*** H-LA-20-G4. 18__. 1860s.

Rarity: —

$2 • W-LA-210-002-G020

Left: 2 / Boy playing with dog. ***Center:*** 2 / Sailor / 2. ***Right:*** 2 / Female portrait. ***Engraver:*** Unverified, but likely American Bank Note Co. ***Comments:*** H-LA-20-G6. 18__. 1860s.

Rarity: —

$3 • W-LA-210-003-G030

Left: 3 / Sailor. ***Center:*** 3 / Liberty resting arm on pedestal / 3. ***Right:*** THREE / Sailing ship. ***Engraver:*** Unverified, but likely American Bank Note Co. ***Comments:*** H-LA-20-G8. 18__. 1860s.

Rarity: —

$5 • W-LA-210-005-G040

RH

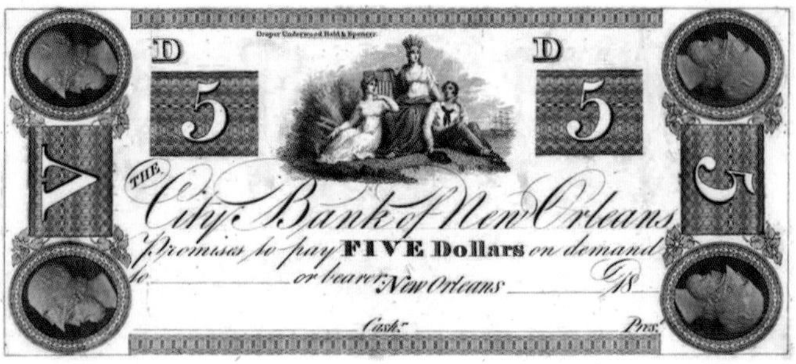

Engraver: Danforth, Underwood, Bald & Spencer. ***Comments:*** H-LA-20-G10. 18__. 1830s.

Rarity: URS-3

Proof $2,000

$5 • W-LA-210-005-G050

RH

Engraver: Rawdon, Wright & Hatch. ***Comments:*** H-LA-20-G12. 18__. 1830s.

Rarity: URS-2

VF $4,500

$5 • W-LA-210-005-G060

CC, CC

Tint: Blue FIVE. ***Back:*** Red-orange. ***Engraver:*** Rawdon, Wright, Hatch & Edson. ***Comments:*** H-LA-20-G14b. 184_. 1840s.

Rarity: URS-5

VG $200; **F** $300

$5 • W-LA-210-005-G060a SI, SI

Tint: Blue FIVE. ***Back:*** Red-orange. ***Engraver:*** Rawdon, Wright, Hatch & Edson. ***Comments:*** H-LA-20-G14c. Similar to W-LA-210-005-G060 but with second check letter. 184_. 1840s.

Rarity: URS-6
F $200

$5 • W-LA-210-005-G060b RH

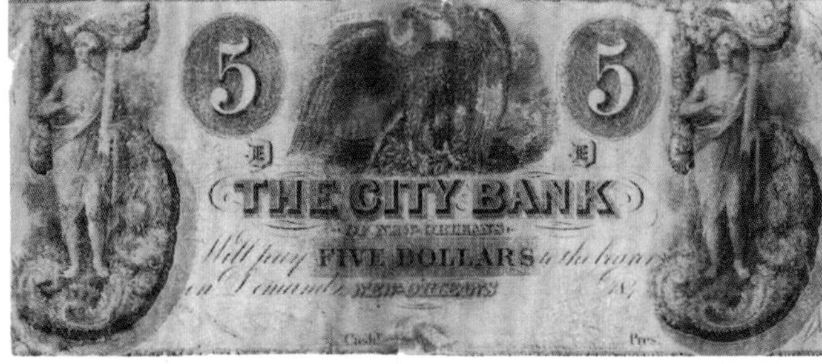

Tint: None. ***Back:*** Red-orange. ***Engraver:*** Rawdon, Wright, Hatch & Edson. ***Comments:*** H-Unlisted. Similar to W-LA-210-005-G060 but with second check letter. 184_. 1840s.

Rarity: URS-4
VG $150

$5 • W-LA-210-005-G070

Left: Steamboat. ***Center:*** Portrait of child. ***Right:*** 5 / Cotton picking scene. ***Engraver:*** Unverified, but likely American Bank Note Co. ***Comments:*** H-LA-20-G18. 18__. 1860s.

Rarity: *None known*

$10 • W-LA-210-010-G080

Center: TEN / Eagle / TEN. ***Engraver:*** Danforth, Underwood, Bald & Spencer. ***Comments:*** H-LA-20-G20. 18__. 1830s.

Rarity: *None known*

$10 • W-LA-210-010-G090 RH

Engraver: Danforth, Underwood, Bald & Spencer. ***Comments:*** H-LA-20-G22. 18__. 1830s.

Rarity: URS-3
Proof $2,000

$10 • W-LA-210-010-G100 RH, RH

Tint: Red-orange TEN. ***Back:*** Blue. ***Engraver:*** Rawdon, Wright, Hatch & Edson. ***Comments:*** H-LA-20-G26b. 184_. 1840s.

Rarity: URS-5
F $400

How to Read the Whitman Numbering System

$1 • W-AL-020-001-G010a

Denomination: Face value of the note shown.

W: Whitman number. This number is a sortable code unique to each bank and note.

AL: Abbreviation for the state under study.

020: Numerical designation specific to each bank.

001: The denomination in dollars.

G010a: G indicates a good or valid note. Other categories are indicated thus: C (counterfeit); R (raised); S (spurious); N (not-attributed); A (altered). Numbers are assigned starting with 010, 020, et seq. Terminal letters following the number indicate variations of a note: a series of different colored overprints, tints, payees, etc., all on the same design of note. For more information, see the "How to Use This Book" section at the front of the volume, page xiv.

$10 • W-LA-210-010-G100a

SI, SI

Tint: Red-orange TEN. ***Back:*** Blue. ***Engraver:*** Rawdon, Wright, Hatch & Edson. ***Comments:*** H-LA-20-G26c. Similar to W-LA-210-010-G100 but with second check letter. 184_. 1840s.

Rarity: URS-5
F $400

$10 • W-LA-210-010-G110

Left: 10 / Man buying newspaper from boy. ***Right:*** 10 / Woman, anchor, rope, factory. ***Engraver:*** Unverified, but likely American Bank Note Co. ***Comments:*** H-LA-20-G30. 18__. 1860s.

Rarity: —

$20 • W-LA-210-020-G120

RH

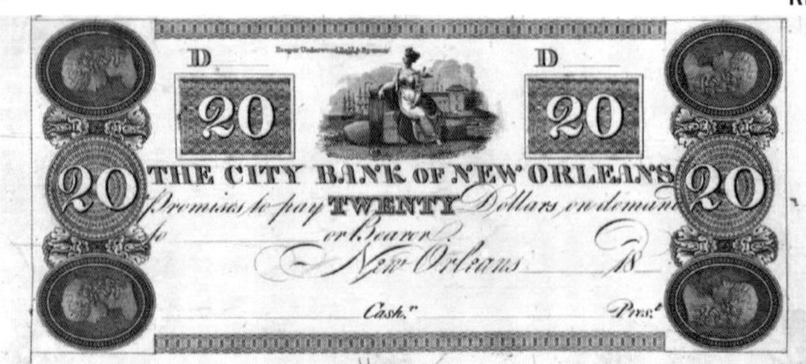

Engraver: Danforth, Underwood, Bald & Spencer. ***Comments:*** H-LA-20-G32. 18__. 1830s.

Rarity: URS-3
Proof $2,000

$20 • W-LA-210-020-G130

RH

Tint: Black TWENTY. ***Back:*** Green. ***Engraver:*** Rawdon, Wright, Hatch & Edson. ***Comments:*** H-LA-20-G36b. 184_. 1840s.

Rarity: URS-4
Fair $500

$20 • W-LA-210-020-G130a

SI, SI

Tint: Black TWENTY. ***Back:*** Green. ***Engraver:*** Rawdon, Wright, Hatch & Edson. ***Comments:*** H-LA-20-G36c. Similar to W-LA-210-020-G130 but with second check letter. 184_. 1840s.

Rarity: URS-4
Fair $500
Selected auction price: Heritage Auctions, April 24, 2013, Lot 15221, F $881

$50 • W-LA-210-050-G140

RH

Engraver: Danforth, Underwood, Bald & Spencer. ***Comments:*** H-LA-20-G40. 18__. 1830s.

Rarity: URS-2
Proof $3,500

$50 • **W-LA-210-050-G150** HA, RH

Tint: Green FIFTY. ***Back:*** Brown medallion head / medallion head. ***Engraver:*** Rawdon, Wright, Hatch & Edson. ***Comments:*** H-LA-20-G42b. 184_. 1840s.

Rarity: URS-5
VF $1,600
Selected auction price: Heritage Auctions, October 23, 2015, Lot 19430, VF $1,645

$50 • **W-LA-210-050-G150a** CC, CC

Tint: Green FIFTY. ***Back:*** Brown medallion head / medallion head. ***Engraver:*** Rawdon, Wright, Hatch & Edson. ***Comments:*** H-LA-20-G42c. Similar to W-LA-210-050-G150 but with second check letter. 184_. 1840s.

Rarity: URS-4
F $1,000
Selected auction price: Heritage Auctions, September 16, 2015, Lot 18439, F $1,057

$100 • **W-LA-210-100-G160** RH

Engraver: Danforth, Underwood, Bald & Spencer. ***Comments:*** H-LA-20-G46. 18__. 1830s.

Rarity: URS-3
Proof $4,500

$100 • **W-LA-210-100-G170** RH

Engraver: Danforth, Underwood, Bald & Spencer. ***Comments:*** H-Unlisted. 18__. 1830s.

Rarity: URS-3
Fair $1,000

$100 • **W-LA-210-100-G180** CC, CC

Tint: Blue C. ***Back:*** Yellow. ***Engraver:*** Rawdon, Wright, Hatch & Edson. ***Comments:*** H-LA-20-G48b. 184_. 1840s.

Rarity: URS-5
VG $300; **F** $500

$100 • W-LA-210-100-G180a

ANS, ANS

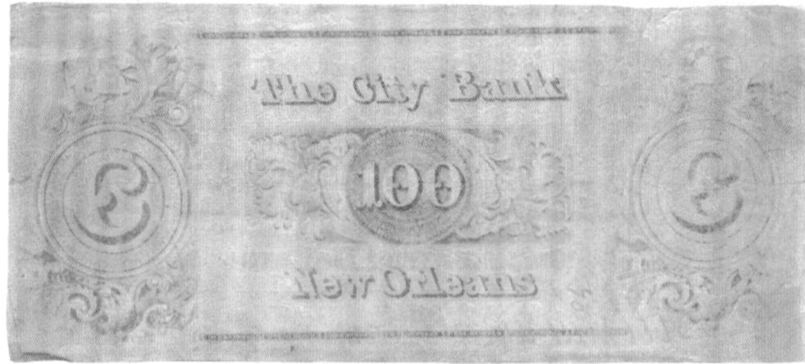

Tint: Blue C. ***Back:*** Yellow. ***Engraver:*** Rawdon, Wright, Hatch & Edson. ***Comments:*** H-LA-20-G48c. Similar to W-LA-210-100-G180 but with second check letter. 184_. 1840s.

Rarity: URS-5
F $500

$500 • W-LA-210-500-G190

RH

Back: Green. ***Engraver:*** Danforth, Underwood, Bald & Spencer. ***Comments:*** H-LA-20-G52. 18__. 1830s.

Rarity: URS-2
Proof $6,000

$500 • W-LA-210-500-G190a

RH

RH

Tint: Red D. ***Back:*** Green. ***Comments:*** H-LA-20-G52a. Similar to W-LA-210-500-G190 but with no engraver imprint. 18__. 1840s.

Rarity: *None known*

$1,000 • W-LA-210-1000-G200

RH

Back: Green. ***Engraver:*** Danforth, Underwood, Bald & Spencer. ***Comments:*** H-LA-20-G54. 18__. 1830s.

Rarity: URS-2
Proof $7,500

$1,000 • W-LA-210-1000-G200a

HA, RH

Tint: Red M. ***Back:*** Green. ***Comments:*** H-LA-20-G54a. Similar to W-LA-210-1000-G200 but with no engraver imprint. 18__. 1840s.

Rarity: URS-3
F $3,500
Selected auction price: Heritage Auctions, April 23, 2015, Lot 19082, F $4,230

Post Notes Payable at the Union Bank in New York

$5 • W-LA-210-005-G210

Engraver: Rawdon, Wright, Hatch & Co. ***Comments:*** H-LA-20-G70. No description available. 18__. 1830s.

Rarity: *None known*

$10 • W-LA-210-010-G220

Left: 10 / Two women flanking shield surmounted by eagle / 10. ***Center:*** 10 / Hebe watering eagle. ***Bottom center:*** Pelican and chicks. ***Right:*** 10 / Wharf with bales, Boats / 10. ***Engraver:*** Rawdon, Wright, Hatch & Co. ***Comments:*** H-LA-20-G72. 18__. 1830s.

Rarity: *None known*

Post Notes Payable at the City Bank, Baton Rouge

$1 • W-LA-210-001-G230

RH

Engraver: Rawdon, Wright & Hatch. ***Comments:*** H-Unlisted. January 1st, 1840.

Rarity: URS-2
F $4,000

$2 • W-LA-210-002-G240

RH

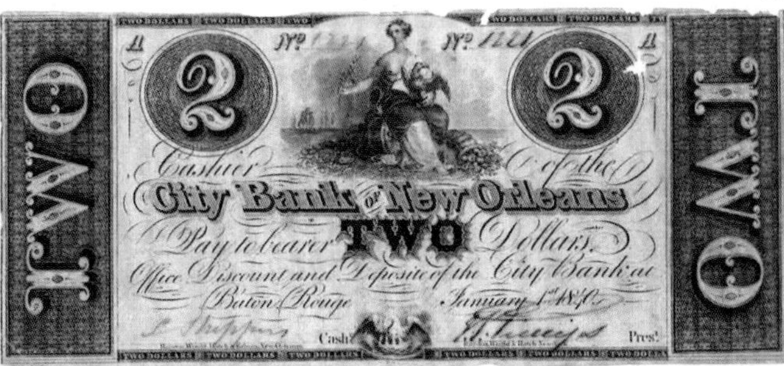

Engraver: Rawdon, Wright & Hatch. ***Comments:*** H-Unlisted. January 1st, 1840.

Rarity: URS-2
F $4,000

Non-Valid Issues

$1 • W-LA-210-001-S010

Left: ONE / Woman standing / 1. ***Center:*** Medallion head / Train / Medallion head. ***Right:*** ONE / Woman standing / 1. ***Comments:*** H-LA-20-G-S5. 18__. 1843.

Rarity: —

$20 • W-LA-210-020-R010

RH

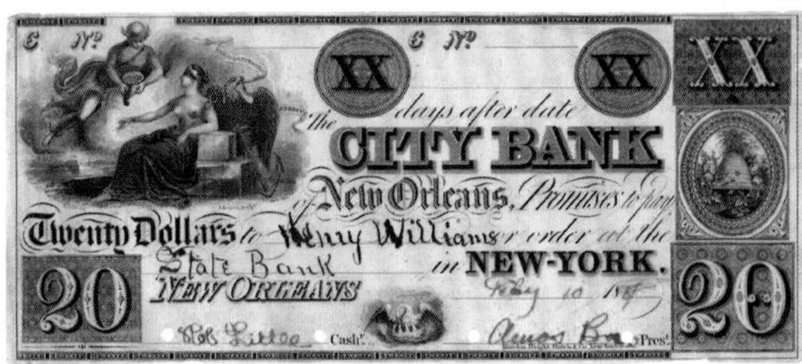

Engraver: Rawdon, Wright, Hatch & Co. ***Comments:*** H-Unlisted. 18__. 1850s.

Rarity: URS-1
Proof $4,000

$100 • W-LA-210-100-R020

Engraver: Rawdon, Wright, Hatch & Co. ***Comments:*** H-LA-20-R5. Raised from W-LA-210-005-G210. 18__. 1830s.

Rarity: *None known*

$100 • W-LA-210-100-R030

RH

Engraver: Rawdon, Wright, Hatch & Co. ***Comments:*** H-LA-20-R10. Raised from W-LA-210-010-G220. 18__. 1830s.

Rarity: URS-1
F $5,000

Commercial Bank

1833–1843

W-LA-220

History: The Commercial Bank was chartered in April 1833 with an authorized capital of $3,000,000. It was organized in order to construct a waterworks, alongside its banking business, and $500,000 of its capital was thus reserved by the state.[4] In 1835 the capital was $2,088,150, and circulation was $293,155.

In 1842 almost all of the banks in New Orleans were affected by a crisis, and many suspended specie payments. The Commercial Bank was one of the first banks to be hit by a severe run, and it was overwhelmed immediately. Notes of the bank fell to a 20-percent discount. To further the difficulties of the bank, in 1843 forgeries of the bank's notes were reported. That same year the bank was put into liquidation.

Numismatic Commentary: Proof and issued notes from this bank are extremely rare, with less than a dozen reported.

VALID ISSUES

$5 • W-LA-220-005-G010

ANS

Engraver: Rawdon, Wright, Hatch & Co. ***Comments:*** H-LA-35-G2. 18__. 1830s–1840s.

Rarity: URS-2
G $3,000

$10 • W-LA-220-010-G020

RH

Engraver: Rawdon, Wright, Hatch & Co. ***Comments:*** H-LA-35-G4. 18__. 1830s–1840s.

Rarity: URS-2
Proof $4,000

$20 • W-LA-220-020-G030

RH

Engraver: Rawdon, Wright, Hatch & Co. ***Comments:*** H-LA-35-G6. 18__. 1830s–1840s.

Rarity: URS-2
Proof $4,000

$50 • W-LA-220-050-G040

ANS

Engraver: Rawdon, Wright, Hatch & Co. ***Comments:*** H-LA-35-G8. 18__. 1830s–1840s.

Rarity: URS-2
Proof $4,500

$100 • W-LA-220-100-G050

ANS

Engraver: Rawdon, Wright, Hatch & Co. ***Comments:*** H-LA-35-G10. 18__. 1830s–1840s.

Rarity: URS-2
VG $3,000; **Proof** $5,500

Notes Payable at the Bank of America in New York

$20 • W-LA-220-020-G060

RH

Engraver: Rawdon, Wright, Hatch & Co. ***Comments:*** H-Unlisted. 18__. 1830s–1840s.

Rarity: URS-2
G $1,500

Collectors and Researchers:

If you have new information about any banks or notes listed in this volume, contact Whitman Publishing, Attn: Obsolete Paper Money, 3101 Clairmont Road, Suite G, Atlanta, GA 30329.

$50 • W-LA-220-050-G070 RH

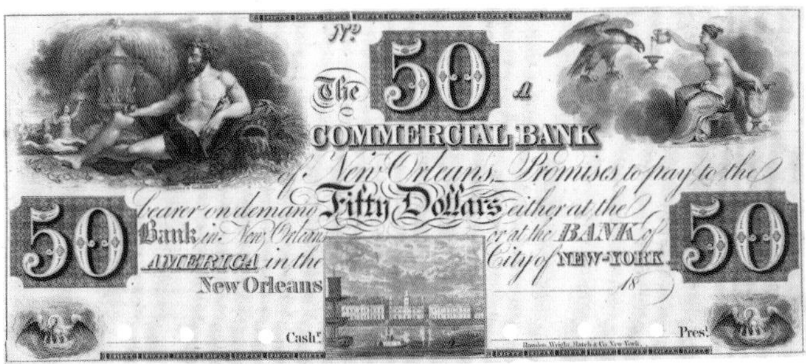

Engraver: Rawdon, Wright, Hatch & Co. ***Comments:*** H-LA-35-G8. 18__. 1830s–1840s.

Rarity: URS-1
Proof $6,000

NON-VALID ISSUES

$5 • W-LA-220-005-A010

Left: V / 5 / V. ***Center:*** 5 / Woman / 5. ***Right:*** V / 5 / V. ***Engraver:*** Rawdon, Wright & Hatch / Rawdon, Wright, Hatch & Edson. ***Comments:*** H-LA-35-A5. Altered from $5 Commercial Bank of Enterprise, Enterprise, Mississippi. 18__. 1840.

Rarity: —

$10 • W-LA-220-010-A020 ANS

Engraver: Rawdon, Wright & Hatch / Rawdon, Wright, Hatch & Edson. ***Comments:*** H-LA-35-A10. Altered from $10 Commercial Bank of Enterprise, Enterprise, Mississippi. 18__. 1840.

Rarity: URS-2
F $1,000

$20 • W-LA-220-020-C030

Engraver: Rawdon, Wright, Hatch & Co. ***Comments:*** H-LA-35-C6. Counterfeit of W-LA-220-020-G030. 18__. 1830s–1840s.

Rarity: —

$20 • W-LA-220-020-A030 SI

Engraver: Rawdon, Wright & Hatch / Rawdon, Wright, Hatch & Edson. ***Comments:*** H-LA-35-A15. Altered from $20 Commercial Bank of Enterprise, Enterprise, Mississippi. 18__. 1840.

Rarity: URS-3
F $1,000

$50 • W-LA-220-050-A040 CC

Engraver: Rawdon, Wright & Hatch / Rawdon, Wright, Hatch & Edson. ***Comments:*** H-LA-35-A20. Altered from $50 Commercial Bank of Enterprise, Enterprise, Mississippi. 18__. 1840.

Rarity: URS-3
F $900

Consolidated Association Bank of the Planters of Louisiana

1827–1842

W-LA-230

History: The Consolidated Association Bank of the Planters of Louisiana was established in 1827 after the failure of the Planters Bank, W-LA-390. The association was meant to replace the old bank. Unfortunately, the Panic of 1837 hit the institution hard, and the state of Louisiana was forced to bolster the organization with state bonds. In December 1842 the state bonds defaulted, leaving the bank defunct.

Numismatic Commentary: Proof and issued notes from this bank are extremely rare. Less than a dozen notes from this bank have been reported to date.

VALID ISSUES

$5 • W-LA-230-005-G010 RH

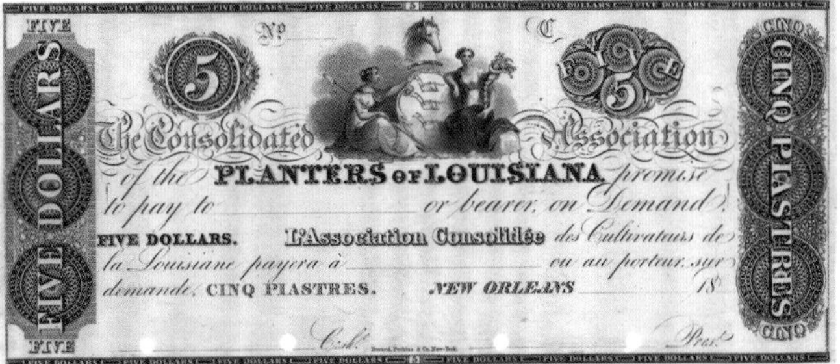

Engraver: Durand, Perkins & Co. ***Comments:*** H-LA-40-G2. 18__. 1820s–1830s.

Rarity: URS-2
Proof $4,000

$5 • W-LA-230-005-G020

RH, RH

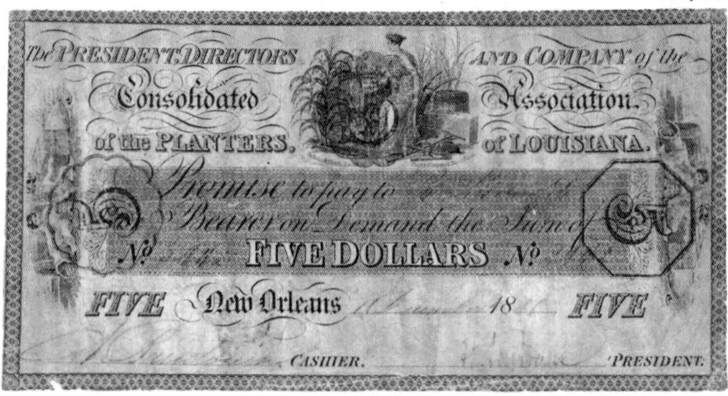

Overprint: Black. ***Back:*** Black three women seated. ***Engraver:*** Perkins & Heath. ***Comments:*** H-LA-40-G4. 18__. 1830s.

Rarity: URS-1
F $5,000

$10 • W-LA-230-010-G030

RH

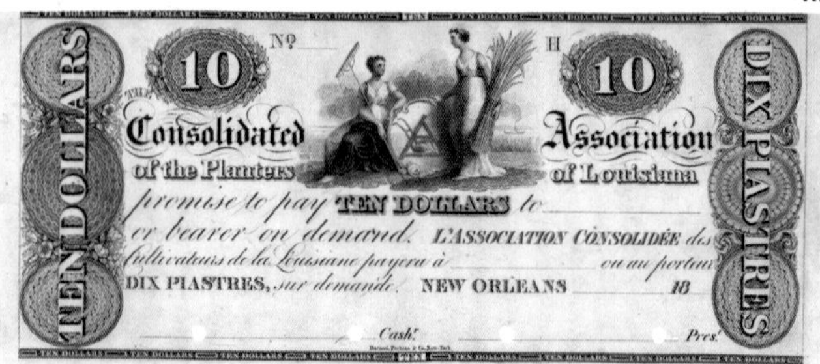

Engraver: Durand, Perkins & Co. ***Comments:*** H-LA-40-G6. 18__. 1820s–1830s.

Rarity: URS-2
Proof $4,000

$10 • W-LA-230-010-G040

Left: Cherubs seated vertically. ***Center:*** Woman standing in cornfield. ***Right:*** Cherubs seated vertically. ***Engraver:*** Perkins & Heath. ***Comments:*** H-LA-40-G8. 18__. 1830s.

Rarity: *None known*

$20 • W-LA-230-020-G050

Left: TWENTY DOLLARS vertically. ***Center:*** 20 / Man seated / 20. ***Engraver:*** Durand, Perkins & Co. ***Comments:*** H-LA-40-G10. 18__. 1820s–1830s.

Rarity: *None known*

$20 • W-LA-230-020-G060

RH, RH

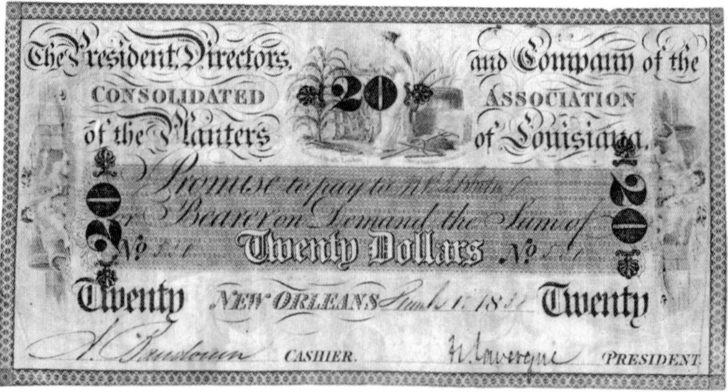

Overprint: Black. ***Back:*** Black three women seated. ***Engraver:*** Perkins & Heath. ***Comments:*** H-LA-40-G12. 18__. 1830s.

Rarity: URS-1
F $6,000

$50 • W-LA-230-050-G070

RH

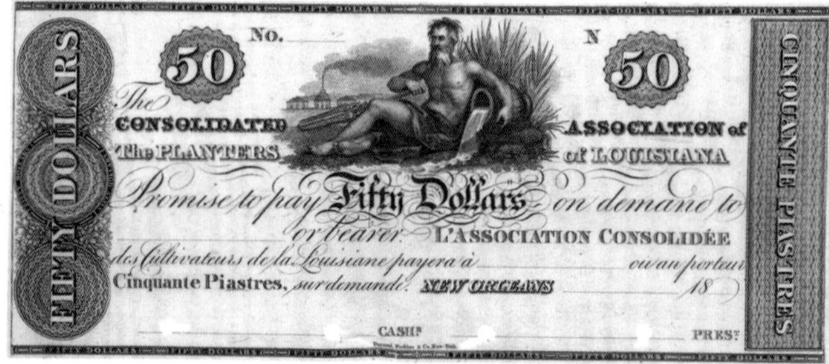

Engraver: Durand, Perkins & Co. ***Comments:*** H-LA-40-G14. 18__. 1820s–1830s.

Rarity: URS-2
Proof $5,000

$50 • W-LA-230-050-G070a

Engraver: Durand, Perkins & Co. ***Comments:*** H-LA-40-G14a. Similar to W-LA-230-050-G070 but printed on yellow paper. 18__. 1830s.

Rarity: *None known*

$100 • **W-LA-230-100-G080** RH

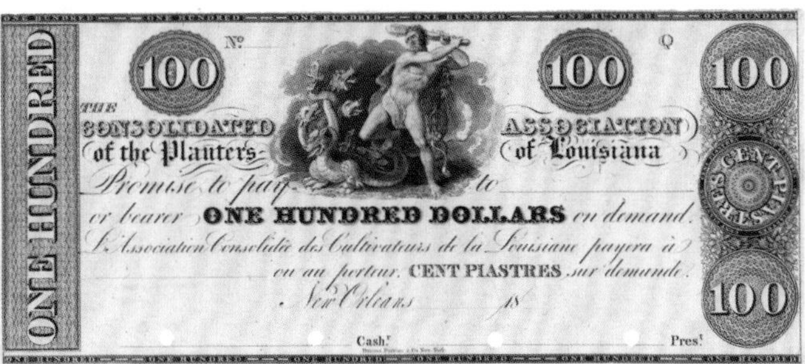

Engraver: Durand, Perkins & Co. ***Comments:*** H-LA-40-G18. 18__. 1820s–1830s.

Rarity: URS-2
Proof $6,000

$500 • **W-LA-230-500-G090** RH

Engraver: Durand, Perkins & Co. ***Comments:*** H-LA-40-G22. 18__. 1820s–1830s.

Rarity: URS-1
F $7,500

$500 • **W-LA-230-500-G090a**

Engraver: Durand, Perkins & Co. ***Comments:*** H-LA-40-G22a. Similar to W-LA-230-500-G090 but printed on pink paper. 18__. 1830s.

Rarity: *None known*

Non-Valid Issues

$50 • **W-LA-230-050-N010**

Center: Bank building. ***Comments:*** H-LA-40-N5. 18__. 1838.

Rarity: *None known*

$500 • **W-LA-230-500-R010**

Engraver: Durand, Perkins & Co. ***Comments:*** H-LA-40-R5. Raised from W-LA-230-050-G070a. Printed on yellow paper. 18__. 1830s.

Rarity: *None known*

Crescent City Bank

1857–1862

W-LA-240

History: The Crescent City Bank was chartered in 1857 with an authorized capital of $1,000,000. The nickname *Crescent City* given to New Orleans inspired the bank's title. Bills in circulation that year came to $282,224. Specie was valued at $261,049, and real estate was worth $35,376. In 1861 the cashier of the bank was Joseph Rau, and the president was J.J. Person. By 1862 the bank had closed its doors.

Numismatic Commentary: Issued notes from this bank are extremely rare, with less than a dozen notes known or reported.

Valid Issues

$5 • **W-LA-240-005-G010**

Left: 5 / Men and women surrounding V. ***Center:*** State arms / Indian men and women seated. ***Right:*** V / Women in and around 5. ***Tint:*** Red-orange FIVE. ***Back:*** Red-orange. ***Engraver:*** Rawdon, Wright, Hatch & Edson. ***Comments:*** H-LA-45-G2a. 18__. 1850s.

Rarity: URS-3
Fair $1,000

$5 • **W-LA-240-005-G010a** RH, SBG

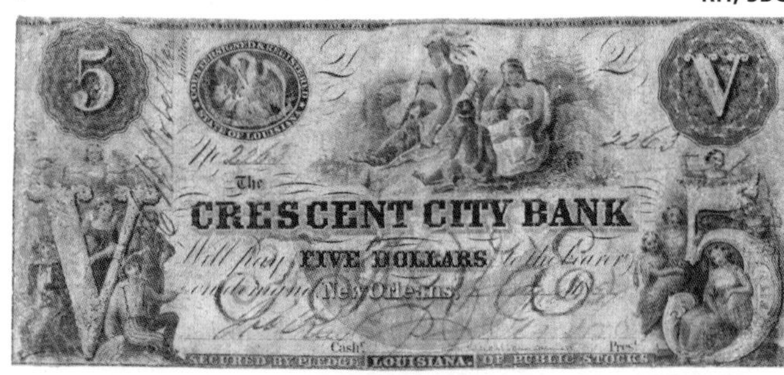

Tint: Red-orange FIVE. ***Back:*** Red-orange. ***Engraver:*** Rawdon, Wright, Hatch & Edson / ABNCo. monogram. ***Comments:*** H-LA-45-G2b. Similar to W-LA-240-005-G010 but with additional engraver imprint. 18__. 1850–1860s.

Rarity: URS-4
F $1,500

$10 • **W-LA-240-010-G020**

Left: 10 / Man standing. ***Center:*** State arms vertically / Woman and cherubs seated. ***Right:*** 10 / Female portrait / TEN. ***Tint:*** Red-orange TEN. ***Back:*** Red-orange. ***Engraver:*** Rawdon, Wright, Hatch & Edson. ***Comments:*** H-LA-45-G4a. 18__. 1850s.

Rarity: —

$10 • W-LA-240-010-G020a

RH, RH

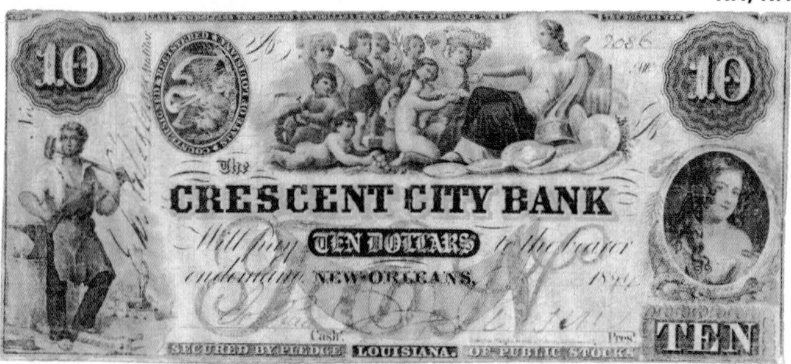

Tint: Red-orange TEN. ***Back:*** Red-orange. ***Engraver:*** Rawdon, Wright, Hatch & Edson / ABNCo. monogram. ***Comments:*** H-LA-45-G4b. Similar to W-LA-240-010-G020 but with additional engraver imprint. 18__. 1850–1860s.

Rarity: URS-4
F $1,500

$20 • W-LA-240-020-G030

RH, RH

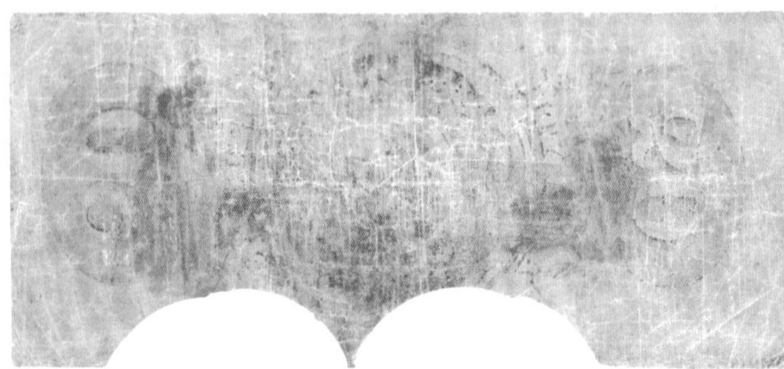

Tint: Red-orange TWENTY. ***Back:*** Red-orange. ***Engraver:*** Rawdon, Wright, Hatch & Edson. ***Comments:*** H-LA-45-G6a. Cancelled note. 18__. 1850s.

Rarity: URS-2
F $1,000

$50 • W-LA-240-050-G040

RH, RH

Tint: Red-orange FIFTY. ***Back:*** Red-orange. ***Engraver:*** Rawdon, Wright, Hatch & Edson. ***Comments:*** H-LA-45-G8a. 18__. 1850s.

Rarity: URS-2
F $2,500

$100 • W-LA-240-100-G050

Left: 100 / State arms / Two cherubs / 100. ***Center:*** Drove of wild horses. ***Right:*** 100 / Female portrait / 100. ***Tint:*** Red-orange. ***Back:*** Red-orange. ***Engraver:*** Rawdon, Wright, Hatch & Edson. ***Comments:*** H-LA-45-G10a. 18__. 1850s.

Rarity: *None known*

Unregistered Issues

$5 • W-LA-240-005-G060

RH, RH

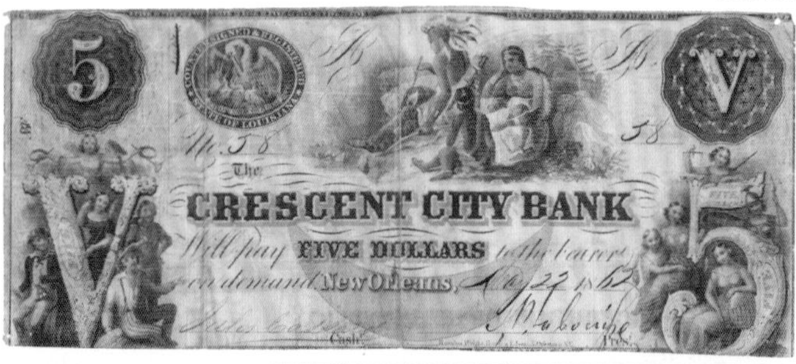

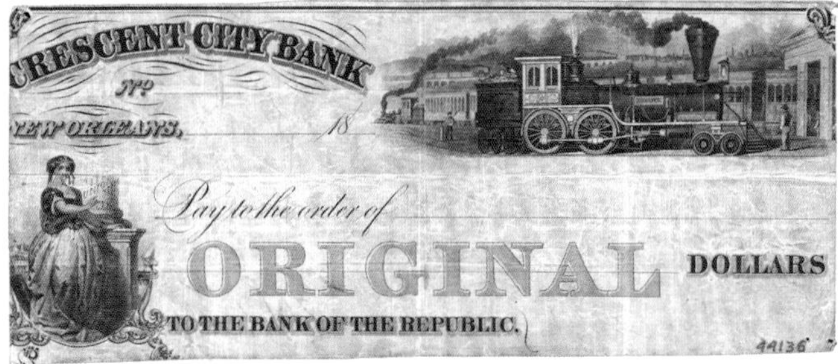

Back: Printed on remainder. ***Engraver:*** Rawdon, Wright, Hatch & Edson / ABNCo. monogram. ***Comments:*** H-Unlisted. Lacks Auditor's signature. 18__. 1862.

Rarity: URS-4
F $1,000

$5 • W-LA-240-005-G060a

Tint: Red-orange. ***Back:*** Green. ***Engraver:*** Rawdon, Wright, Hatch & Edson / ABNCo. monogram. ***Comments:*** H-LA-45-G12a. Similar to W-LA-240-005-G060. Lacks Auditor's signature. 18__. 1862.

Rarity: *None known*

$10 • W-LA-240-010-G070

RH

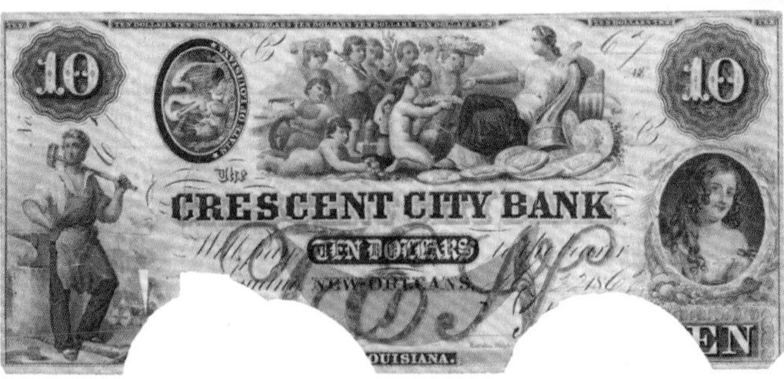

Tint: Green TEN. ***Back:*** Green. ***Engraver:*** Rawdon, Wright, Hatch & Edson / ABNCo. monogram. ***Comments:*** H-LA-45-G14a. Lacks Auditor's signature. Cancelled note. 18__. 1862.

Rarity: URS-3
F $1,000

$20 • W-LA-240-020-G080

Left: TWENTY / Woman feeding chickens. ***Center:*** State arms / 20 / Men picking cotton. ***Right:*** 20 / Portrait of Martha Washington / TWENTY. ***Tint:*** Red-orange. ***Back:*** Green. ***Engraver:*** Rawdon, Wright, Hatch & Edson. ***Comments:*** H-LA-45-G16a. Lacks Auditor's signature. 18__. 1862.

Rarity: *None known*

$50 • W-LA-240-050-G090

Left: State arms / Girl / FIFTY. ***Center:*** 50 / Two women flanking anvil. ***Right:*** 50 / Men weighing cotton / FIFTY. ***Tint:*** Red-orange. ***Back:*** Green. ***Engraver:*** Rawdon, Wright, Hatch & Edson. ***Comments:*** H-LA-45-G18a. Lacks Auditor's signature. 18__. 1862.

Rarity: *None known*

$100 • W-LA-240-100-G100

RH, RH

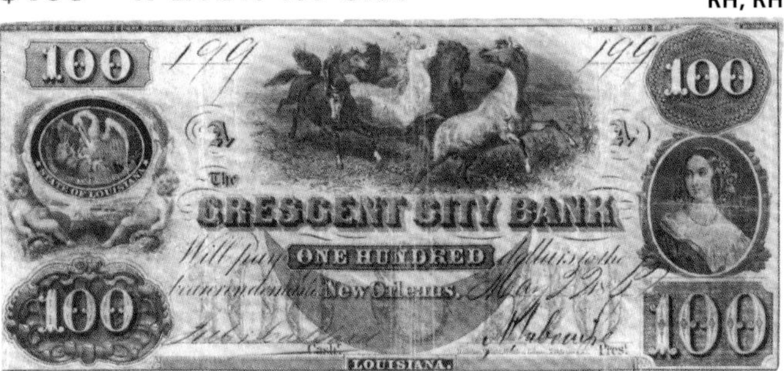

Tint: Red-orange 100 / C / 100. ***Back:*** Green. ***Engraver:*** Rawdon, Wright, Hatch & Edson. ***Comments:*** H-LA-45-G20a. Lacks Auditor's signature. 18__. 1862.

Rarity: URS-2
VF $5,000

Exchange Bank
1860s
W-LA-250

History: The Exchange Bank was a short-lived enterprise. Little is known of its history.

Numismatic Commentary: Notes from the Exchange Bank are very rare and have been observed from two similarly engraved series.

Valid Issues

$1 • W-LA-250-001-G010

RH

Overprint: Red ONE. ***Engraver:*** Rawdon, Wright, Hatch & Edson. ***Comments:*** H-LA-50-G2a. 18__. 1860s.

Rarity: URS-3
F $2,500

$2 • W-LA-250-002-G020

RH

Overprint: Red TWO. ***Engraver:*** Rawdon, Wright, Hatch & Edson. ***Comments:*** H-LA-50-G4a. 18__. 1860s.

Rarity: URS-2
F $4,500

$2 • W-LA-250-002-G020a

RH

Overprint: Red TWO. ***Engraver:*** Rawdon, Wright, Hatch & Edson. ***Comments:*** H-Unlisted. Similar to W-LA-250-002-G020 but countersigned and registered. 18__. 1860s.

Rarity: URS-2
F $4,000

$3 • W-LA-250-003-G030

RH

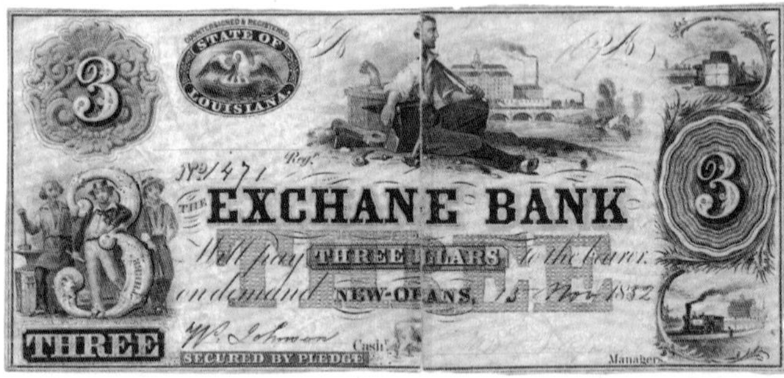

Overprint: Red THREE. ***Engraver:*** Rawdon, Wright, Hatch & Edson. ***Comments:*** H-Unlisted. Repaired note. 18__. 1860s.

Rarity: URS-2
F $4,000

$5 • W-LA-250-005-G040

HA

Overprint: Red FIVE. ***Engraver:*** Rawdon, Wright, Hatch & Edson. ***Comments:*** H-LA-50-G8a. 18__. 1860s.

Rarity: —

Exchange and Banking Company
1835–1842
W-LA-255

History: The Exchange and Banking Company was chartered in April 1835 with an authorized capital of $2,000,000. The bank was incorporated under the condition that it would construct a hotel. Following the requirements, the bank funded and built the St. Charles Hotel, which cost the bank $616,775.[5] In 1842 the bank went into liquidation.

Valid Issues

$5 • W-LA-255-005-G010

CC

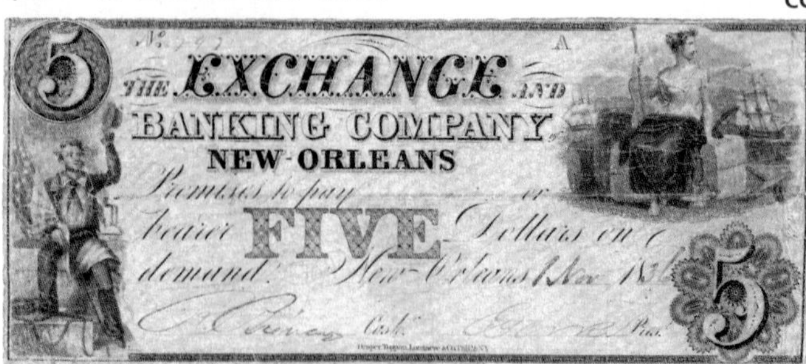

Engraver: Draper, Toppan, Longacre & Co. ***Comments:*** H-LA-55-G2. 18__. 1830s–1840s.

Rarity: URS-5
F $750

$5 • W-LA-255-005-G010a

RH

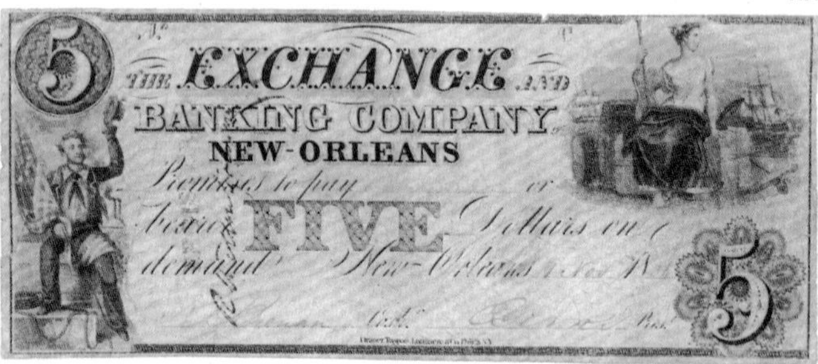

Overprint: Red REGISTERED stamp. ***Engraver:*** Draper, Toppan, Longacre & Co. ***Comments:*** H-Unlisted. Similar to W-LA-255-005-G010. 18__. 1830s–1840s.

Rarity: URS-5
F $750

$5 • W-LA-255-005-G020

HA

Engraver: Underwood, Bald, Spencer & Hufty / Danforth, Underwood & Co. ***Comments:*** H-LA-55-G4. 18__. 1840s.

Rarity: URS-6
F $250; **Proof** $750

$5 • W-LA-255-005-G020a

RH

Overprint: Red REGISTERED stamp. ***Engraver:*** Underwood, Bald, Spencer & Hufty / Danforth, Underwood & Co. ***Comments:*** H-Unlisted. Similar to W-LA-255-005-G020. 18__. 1840s.

Rarity: URS-6

F $250

$10 • W-LA-255-010-G030

CC

Engraver: Draper, Toppan, Longacre & Co. ***Comments:*** H-LA-55-G6. 18__. 1830s–1840s.

Rarity: URS-6

F $375; **Proof** $800

Selected auction price: Heritage Auctions, October 21, 2015, Lot 18343, Proof $763

$10 • W-LA-255-010-G030a

RH

Overprint: Red REGISTERED stamp. ***Engraver:*** Draper, Toppan, Longacre & Co. ***Comments:*** H-LA-55-G6a. Similar to W-LA-255-010-G030. 18__. 1840s.

Rarity: URS-6

F $375

$20 • W-LA-255-020-G040

Left: 20 / Portrait of George Washington / 20 vertically. ***Center:*** Woman seated / Man seated with urn / Woman seated. ***Right:*** 20 / Portrait of George Washington / 20. ***Engraver:*** Draper, Toppan, Longacre & Co. ***Comments:*** H-LA-55-G8. 18__. 1830s.

Rarity: URS-5

VG $700; **F** $1,000

$20 • W-LA-255-020-G040a

CC

Overprint: Red REGISTERED stamp. ***Engraver:*** Draper, Toppan, Longacre & Co. ***Comments:*** H-LA-55-G8a. Similar to W-LA-255-020-G040. 18__. 1840s.

Rarity: URS-5

F $1,000

$20 • W-LA-255-020-G040b

RH

Overprint: Black REGISTERED stamp. ***Engraver:*** Draper, Toppan, Longacre & Co. ***Comments:*** H-LA-55-G8a. Similar to W-LA-255-020-G040. 18__. 1840s.

Rarity: URS-5

F $1,000

$50 • W-LA-255-050-G050

Left: 50 / Ship / 50. ***Right:*** Woman seated in field with cornucopia, Ship / 50. ***Engraver:*** Draper, Toppan, Longacre & Co. ***Comments:*** H-LA-55-G10. 18__. 1830s.

Rarity: URS-5

Proof $2,000

$50 • W-LA-255-050-G050a

CC

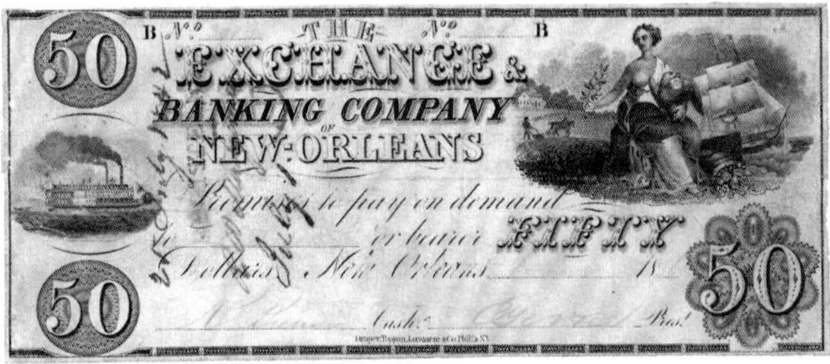

Overprint: Red REGISTERED stamp. ***Engraver:*** Draper, Toppan, Longacre & Co. ***Comments:*** H-LA-55-G10a. Similar to W-LA-255-050-G050. 18__. 1840s.

Rarity: URS-5

F $1,000

$100 • **W-LA-255-100-G060**

RH

Engraver: Draper, Toppan, Longacre & Co. ***Comments:*** H-LA-55-G12. 18__. 1830s.

Rarity: URS-5
F $1,000; **Proof** $2,000

$100 • **W-LA-255-100-G060a**

CC

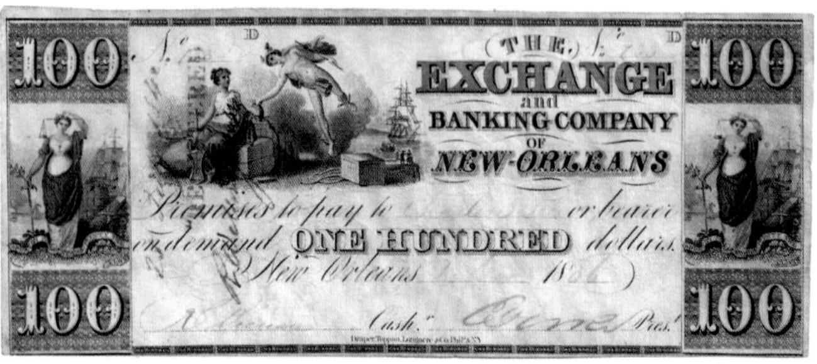

Overprint: Red REGISTERED stamp. ***Engraver:*** Draper, Toppan, Longacre & Co. ***Comments:*** H-LA-55-G12a. Similar to W-LA-255-100-G060. 18__. 1840s.

Rarity: URS-5
F $1,000

$100 • **W-LA-255-100-G060b**

CC

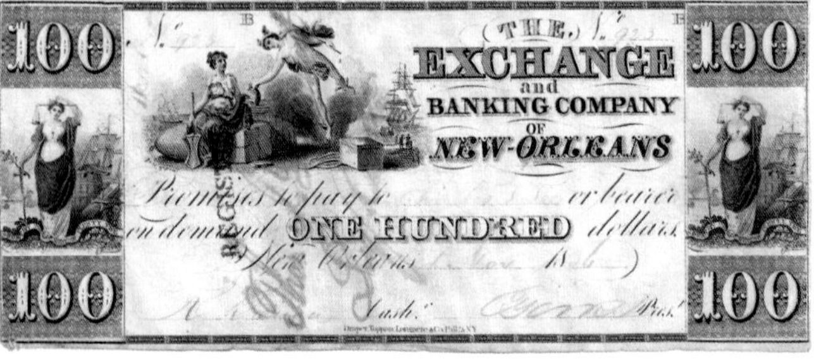

Overprint: Black REGISTERED stamp. ***Engraver:*** Draper, Toppan, Longacre & Co. ***Comments:*** H-Unlisted. Similar to W-LA-255-100-G060. 18__. 1840s.

Rarity: URS-6
F $900

$500 • **W-LA-255-500-G070**

Engraver: Draper, Toppan, Longacre & Co. ***Comments:*** H-LA-55-G14. No description available. 18__. 1830s–1840s.

Rarity: *None known*

$1,000 • **W-LA-255-1000-G080**

Engraver: Draper, Toppan, Longacre & Co. ***Comments:*** H-LA-55-G16. No description available. 18__. 1830s–1840s.

Rarity: *None known*

Non-Valid Issues

$100 • **W-LA-255-100-R010**

Engraver: Draper, Toppan, Longacre & Co. ***Comments:*** H-LA-55-R5. Raised from W-LA-255-010-G030. 18__. 1830s–1840s.

Rarity: *None known*

Insurance Bank of W.B. Partee and Company

1847–1851

W-LA-260

History: W.B. Partee and Company engaged in many ventures, including acting as an agency for banks. Their Insurance Bank issued small-denomination notes during the period under study. Some of these were printed on the backs of other notes.

Numismatic Commentary: Proofs from this banking house are extremely rare. Remainders are also rare, as they have been cut as singles from the backs of State of Louisiana $1-$2 sheets, issued in Baton Rouge and dated February 24, 1862.

Remaining at the American Bank Note Co. archives as of 2003 was a 10¢-10¢-25¢-25¢-50¢-50¢-$1-$2 face plate.

Valid Issues

10¢ • **W-LA-260-00.10-G010**

HA

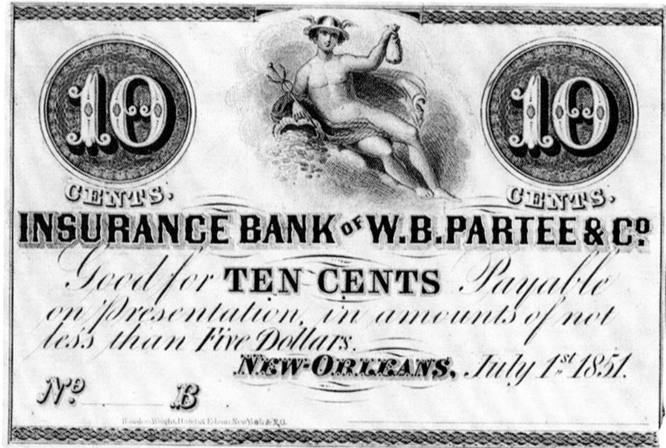

Engraver: Rawdon, Wright, Hatch & Edson. ***Comments:*** H-Unlisted. July 1st, 1851.

Rarity: URS-3
Proof $2,850
Selected auction price: Heritage Auctions, October 21, 2015, Lot 18345, Proof $2,820

25¢ • W-LA-260-00.25-G020 HA

Engraver: Rawdon, Wright, Hatch & Edson. ***Comments:*** H-Unlisted. July 1st, 1851.

Rarity: URS-1
Proof $10,000
Selected auction price: Heritage Auctions, October 21, 2015, Lot 18346, Proof $9,987

50¢ • W-LA-260-00.50-G030 HA

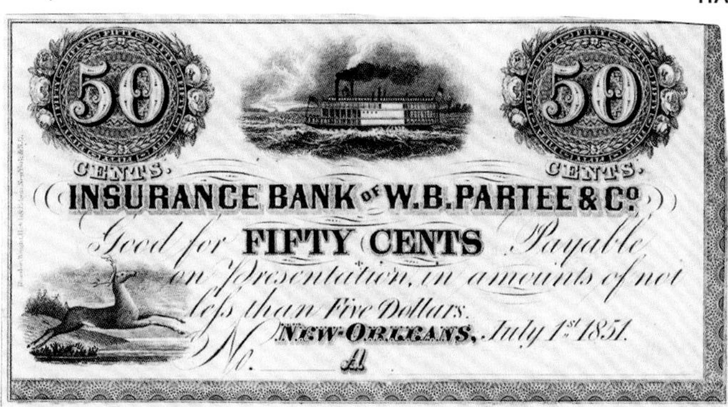

Engraver: Rawdon, Wright, Hatch & Edson. ***Comments:*** H-Unlisted. July 1st, 1851.

Rarity: URS-5; URS-1
Proof $4,700
Selected auction price: Heritage Auctions, October 21, 2015, Lot 18347, Proof $4,700

$1 • W-LA-260-001-G040 HA

Engraver: Rawdon, Wright, Hatch & Edson. ***Comments:*** H-Unlisted. 18__. 1800s–1810s.

Rarity: URS-5; URS-1
Proof $1,900
Selected auction price: Heritage Auctions, April 23, 2015, Lot 19085, Proof $1,880

$2 • W-LA-260-002-G050 HA

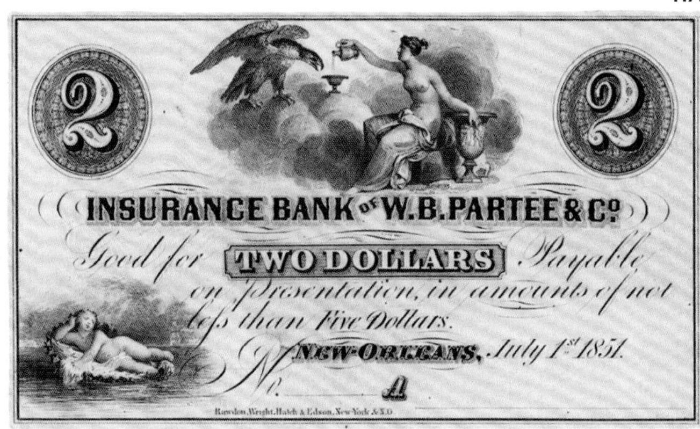

Engraver: Rawdon, Wright, Hatch & Edson. ***Comments:*** H-Unlisted. July 1st, 1851.

Rarity: URS-5; URS-1
Proof $2,900
Selected auction price: Heritage Auctions, April 23, 2015, Lot 19086, Proof $2,820

Louisiana Bank
1804–1819
W-LA-270

History: The Louisiana Bank was chartered in March 1804 with an authorized capital of $500,000. In 1819 the bank went into liquidation and closed up its affairs.

Numismatic Commentary: Proof and issued notes from this bank are extremely rare, with less than half a dozen known.

VALID ISSUES

$5 • W-LA-270-005-G010 RH

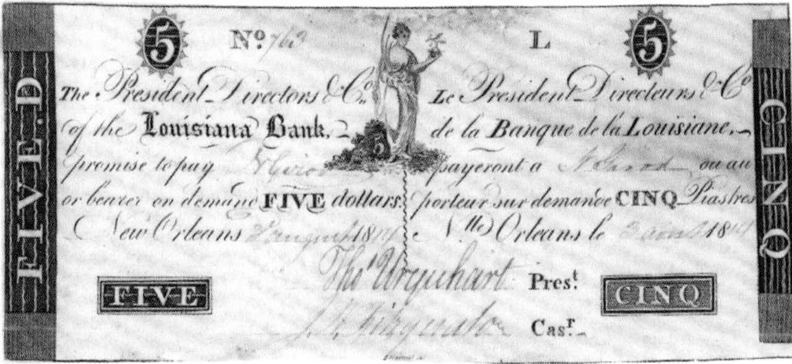

Engraver: P. Maverick. ***Comments:*** H-LA-70-G4. 18__. 1800s–1810s.

Rarity: URS-3
F $3,000

$10 • W-LA-270-010-G020

Engraver: P. Maverick. ***Comments:*** H-LA-70-G10. No description available. 18__. 1800s–1810s.

Rarity: *None known*

$20 • W-LA-270-020-G030

Engraver: P. Maverick. ***Comments:*** H-LA-70-G16. No description available. 18__. 1800s–1810s.

Rarity: *None known*

$50 • **W-LA-270-050-G040**

RH

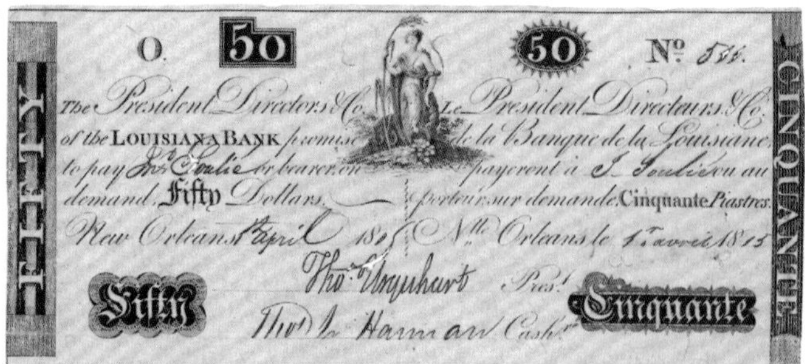

Engraver: P. Maverick. ***Comments:*** H-LA-70-G20. 18__. 1800s–1810s.

Rarity: URS-2
F $5,000

$100 • **W-LA-270-100-G050**

RH

Engraver: P. Maverick. ***Comments:*** H-LA-70-G24. 18__. 1800s.

Rarity: URS-3
F $2,000

$500 • **W-LA-270-500-G060**

Engraver: P. Maverick. ***Comments:*** H-LA-70-G28. No description available. 18__. 1800s.

Rarity: *None known*

$1,000 • **W-LA-270-1000-G070**

Left: ONE THOUSAND. ***Center:*** 1000 / Ship / 1000. ***Right:*** MILLE. ***Engraver:*** P. Maverick. ***Comments:*** H-LA-70-G32. 18__. 1800s.

Rarity: —

Non-Valid Issues

$5 • **W-LA-270-005-C010**

SI

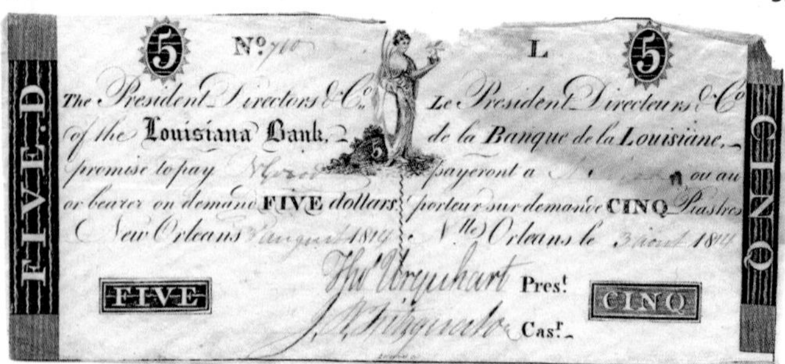

Engraver: P. Maverick. ***Comments:*** H-LA-70-C4. Counterfeit of W-LA-270-005-G010. 18__. 1800s–1810s.

Rarity: URS-3
F $950

Louisiana State Bank

1818–1870

W-LA-280

History: The Louisiana State Bank was chartered in 1818. By March 14 of that year, the state had subscribed to $500,000 of the authorized $2,000,000 capital of the bank. A bonus of $100,000 was required to be paid to the state before the bank could commence operations. In 1820 there was a case regarding the clever counterfeiting of several $100 bills of the Louisiana State Bank. In 1836 the capital was $1,000,000. By 1842 this had risen to $4,000,000. Circulation at that time was $988,565.[6] Later that year there was a crisis, and many of the New Orleans banks were forced to suspend specie payments. On June 31 the Louisiana State Bank suspended as well. By 1843 the circulation of the bank was as low as $79,341. Slowly, the bank began to recover, and in 1845 circulation was back up to $384,680.

In 1848 the president of the bank was John B.B. Vignie, and Richard Relf was the cashier. Capital was $1,775,000. By 1850 the capital had risen to $1,958,580, which was the largest of any bank in New Orleans, and the bank redeemed its notes in specie.[7] That year there was a robbery at the bank in broad daylight. A young man entering the bank to deposit funds was jostled upon entering, and when looking in his book, he found that the notes were gone. The thieves were arrested, but the notes had already been changed.[8] In 1857 the president of the bank was J.M. Lapeyre. The capital was $2,000,000. Bills in circulation totaled $2,593,775, and specie was worth $2,746,614. Real estate came to $121,753.

The Louisiana State Bank survived the Civil War—one of very few banks in the South to do so. In 1867 it dropped its capital down to $600,000, and in 1870 it closed its doors. It was succeeded in interest by the State National Bank.[9]

The Louisiana State Bank had branch banks located in Alexandria, W-LA-020, Baton Rouge, W-LA-040, Donaldsonville, W-LA-070, New Orleans (second municipality), W-LA-290, Saint Francisville, W-LA-450, Saint Martinville, W-LA-470, and Shreveport, W-LA-490.

Numismatic Commentary: Proof and most issued notes from this bank are extremely rare. More common remainders exist of the $1, $2, $3, $5, and $10 notes.

Valid Issues

$1 • **W-LA-280-001-G010**

CC

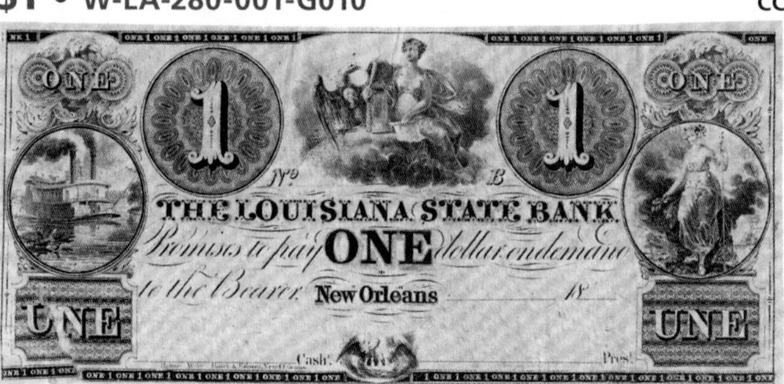

Engraver: Rawdon, Wright, Hatch & Edson. ***Comments:*** H-LA-80-G2. 18__. 1861.

Rarity: URS-4; URS-6
F $150
Unc-Rem $125

$1 • W-LA-280-001-G010a RG

Overprint: Red REDEEMABLE In Confederate Notes stamp. ***Engraver:*** Rawdon, Wright, Hatch & Edson. ***Comments:*** H-LA-80-G2a. Similar to W-LA-280-001-G010. 18__. 1861.

Rarity: URS-8
F $150; **Unc-Rem** $200

$2 • W-LA-280-002-G020 HA

Engraver: Rawdon, Wright, Hatch & Edson. ***Comments:*** H-LA-80-G4. 18__. 1861.

Rarity: URS-5
F $200

$2 • W-LA-280-002-G020a SBG

Overprint: Red REDEEMABLE In Confederate Notes stamp. ***Engraver:*** Rawdon, Wright, Hatch & Edson. ***Comments:*** H-LA-80-G4a. Similar to W-LA-280-002-G020. 18__. 1861.

Rarity: URS-6
F $200

$3 • W-LA-280-003-G030 RH

Engraver: Rawdon, Wright, Hatch & Edson. ***Comments:*** H-LA-80-G6. 18__. 1861.

Rarity: URS-5
F $350

$3 • W-LA-280-003-G030a RG

Overprint: Red REDEEMABLE in Confederate Notes stamp. ***Engraver:*** Rawdon, Wright, Hatch & Edson. ***Comments:*** H-LA-80-G6a. Similar to W-LA-280-003-G030. 18__. 1861.

Rarity: URS-6
F $750

$5 • W-LA-280-005-G040 RH

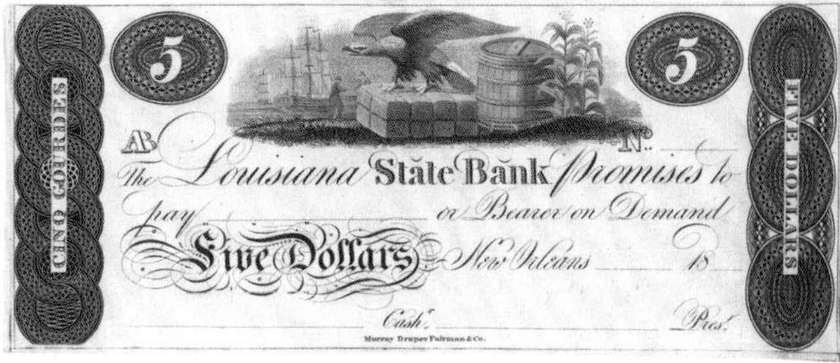

Engraver: Murray, Draper, Fairman & Co. ***Comments:*** H-LA-80-G8. 18__. 1861.

Rarity: URS-2
Proof $4,000

$5 • W-LA-280-005-G050

Left: 5 / Woman with sickle / FIVE. ***Center:*** Woman seated with eagle. ***Right:*** 5 / Eagle, vase, and shield. ***Comments:*** H-LA-80-G12. 18__. 1850s.

Rarity: *None known*

$5 • **W-LA-280-005-G060**

RH, RH

Back: Red-orange. ***Engraver:*** Rawdon, Wright, Hatch & Edson. ***Comments:*** H-LA-80-G14a. 18__. 1850s.

Rarity: URS-3
F $250; **Unc-Rem** $375

$5 • **W-LA-280-005-G060a**

Engraver: Rawdon, Wright, Hatch & Edson / ABNCo. monogram. ***Comments:*** H-LA-80-G14b. Similar to W-LA-280-005-G060 but with additional engraver imprint. 18__. 1860s.

Rarity: *None known*

$5 • **W-LA-280-005-G070**

RH

Tint: Red-orange. ***Engraver:*** National Bank Note Co. ***Comments:*** H-LA-80-G16a. 18__. 1860s.

Rarity: URS-3
F $5,000; **Proof** $8,000

$10 • **W-LA-280-010-G080**

Engraver: Murray, Draper, Fairman & Co. ***Comments:*** H-LA-80-G18. No description available. 18__. 1818–1830s.

Rarity: *None known*

$10 • **W-LA-280-010-G090**

Left: 10 / Male portrait / 10. ***Center:*** X / Woman seated with shield. ***Right:*** Roman senator with cask / 10. ***Comments:*** H-LA-80-G22. 18__. 1850s.

Rarity: *None known*

$10 • **W-LA-280-010-G100**

RH, RH

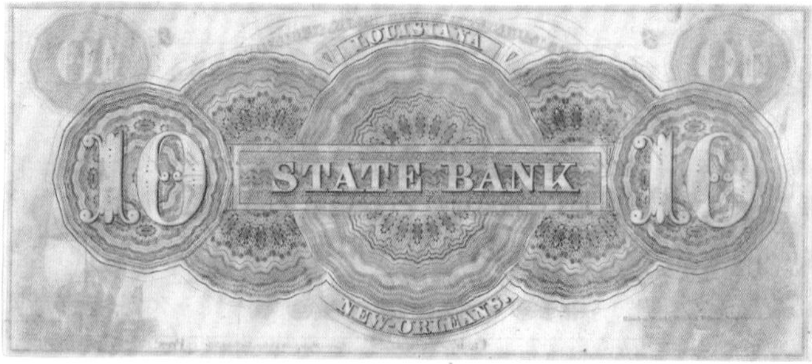

Back: Red-orange. ***Engraver:*** Rawdon, Wright, Hatch & Edson. ***Comments:*** H-LA-80-G24a. 18__. 1840s–1850s.

Rarity: URS-8
F $300

$10 • **W-LA-280-010-G100a**

RH, RH

Back: Red-orange. ***Engraver:*** Rawdon, Wright, Hatch & Edson / ABNCo. monogram. ***Comments:*** H-LA-80-G24b. Similar to W-LA-280-010-G100 but with additional engraver imprint. 18__. 1850s–1860s.

Rarity: URS-8
F $300

$10 • **W-LA-280-010-G110** RH

Tint: Red-orange. ***Engraver:*** National Bank Note Co. ***Comments:*** H-LA-80-G26. 18__. 1860s.

Rarity: URS-3
F $6,000; **Proof** $8,000

$20 • **W-LA-280-020-G120** RH

Engraver: Murray, Draper, Fairman & Co. ***Comments:*** H-LA-80-G28. 18__. 1818–1830s.

Rarity: URS-2
Proof $5,000

$20 • **W-LA-280-020-G130**

Left: 20 / Female portrait / 20. ***Center:*** Woman leaning on bale, Spinning wheel, City. ***Right:*** 20 / Woman seated with pail. ***Comments:*** H-LA-80-G32. 18__. 1850s.

Rarity: *None known*

$20 • **W-LA-280-020-G140** SI, SI

Back: Red-orange. ***Engraver:*** Rawdon, Wright, Hatch & Edson. ***Comments:*** H-LA-80-G34a. 18__. 1850s.

Rarity: URS-8
F $250

$50 • **W-LA-280-050-G150** RH

Engraver: Murray, Draper, Fairman & Co. ***Comments:*** H-LA-80-G38. 18__. 1818–1830s.

Rarity: URS-2
Proof $6,000

$50 • **W-LA-280-050-G160**

Left: FIFTY / Male portrait / 50. ***Center:*** L / Cherub holding shield, Coins. ***Right:*** FIFTY / Male portrait / 50. ***Comments:*** H-LA-80-G42. 18__. 1850s.

Rarity: *None known*

$50 • **W-LA-280-050-G170**

Left: 50 / Female portrait. ***Center:*** Woman seated. ***Right:*** 50 / Woman standing with cherubs. ***Back:*** Red-orange. ***Engraver:*** Rawdon, Wright, Hatch & Edson. ***Comments:*** H-LA-80-G44a. 18__. 1850s.

Rarity: *None known*

$50 • **W-LA-280-050-G170a** RH, RH

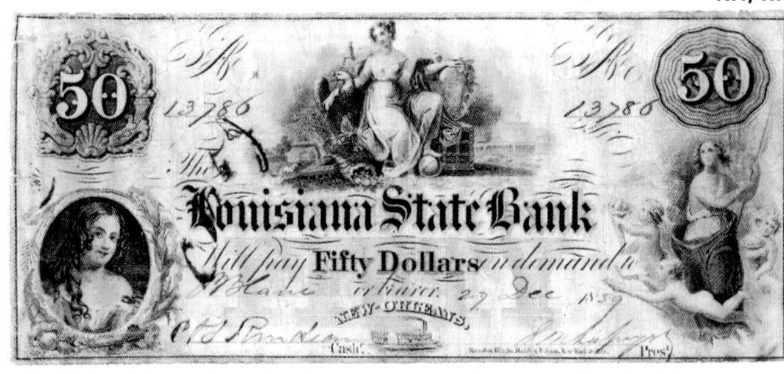

Back: Red-orange. ***Engraver:*** Rawdon, Wright, Hatch & Edson / ABNCo. monogram. ***Comments:*** H-LA-80-G44b. Similar to W-LA-280-050-G170 but with additional engraver imprint. 18__. 1850s.

Rarity: URS-4
F $350

$50 • W-LA-280-050-G180

RH, RH

Back: Red-orange. ***Engraver:*** American Bank Note Co. ***Comments:*** H-LA-80-G46a. 18__. 1860s.

Rarity: URS-2
VF $2,500

$100 • W-LA-280-100-G190

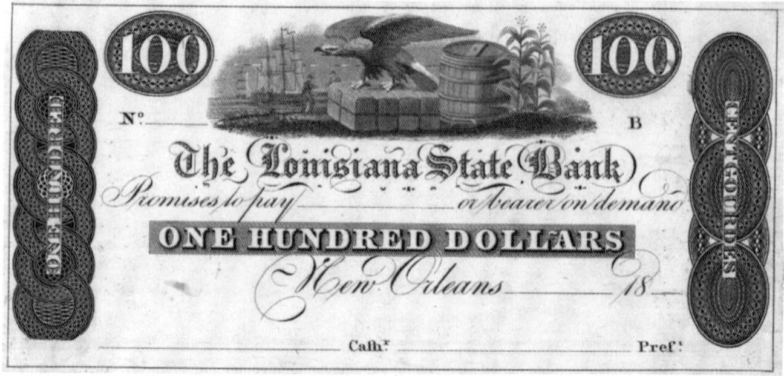

Engraver: Murray, Draper, Fairman & Co. ***Comments:*** H-LA-80-G48. 18__. 1818–1830s.

Rarity: URS-1
Proof $7,500

$100 • W-LA-280-100-G200

RH

Back: Inverted red-orange. ***Engraver:*** Toppan, Carpenter & Co. ***Comments:*** H-LA-80-G52. 18__. 1850s.

Rarity: URS-2
Fair $1,500

$100 • W-LA-280-100-G210

Left: 100 / Building / 100. ***Center:*** Two women flanking portrait of George Washington. ***Right:*** 100 / 100. ***Back:*** Red-orange. ***Engraver:*** Rawdon, Wright, Hatch & Edson. ***Comments:*** H-LA-80-G54a. 18__. 1850s.

Rarity: *None known*

$100 • W-LA-280-100-G210a

RH, RH

Back: Red-orange. ***Engraver:*** Rawdon, Wright, Hatch & Edson / ABNCo. monogram. ***Comments:*** H-LA-80-G54b. Similar to W-LA-280-100-G210 but with additional engraver imprint. 18__. 1850s–1860s.

Rarity: URS-3
F $1,500

$100 • W-LA-280-100-G220 RH

Back: Red-orange. ***Engraver:*** American Bank Note Co. ***Comments:*** H-LA-80-G56. 18__. 1860s.

Rarity: URS-2

Proof $3,500

$500 • W-LA-280-500-G230

Left: Two men carrying woman on their shoulders. ***Center:*** 500 / Portrait of Martha Washington / 500 / Pelican. ***Right:*** Woman seated with basket of flowers, D / 500. ***Back:*** Red-orange. ***Engraver:*** Rawdon, Wright, Hatch & Edson. ***Comments:*** H-LA-80-G60a. 18__. 1850s.

Rarity: *None known*

$1,000 • W-LA-280-1000-G240

Left: 1000 supported by two nymphs / Portrait of George Washington. ***Center:*** Steamship and three sailing ships / Pelican. ***Right:*** 1000. ***Back:*** Red-orange. ***Engraver:*** Rawdon, Wright, Hatch & Edson. ***Comments:*** H-LA-80-G64a. 18__. 1850s.

Rarity: —

Uncut Sheets

$1-$1-$2-$3 • W-LA-280-001.001.002.003-US010 RG

Overprint(s): Red REDEEMABLE In Confederate Notes stamp. ***Engraver:*** Rawdon, Wright, Hatch & Edson. ***Comments:*** H-LA-80-G2a, G2a, G4a, G6a. First two notes identical. 18__. 1861.

Rarity: URS-5

F $750

Non-Valid Issues

$5 • W-LA-280-005-C040

Engraver: Murray, Draper, Fairman & Co. ***Comments:*** H-LA-80-C8. Counterfeit of W-LA-280-005-G040. 18__. 1810s.

Rarity: *None known*

$10 • W-LA-280-010-C080

Engraver: Murray, Draper, Fairman & Co. ***Comments:*** H-LA-80-C18. Counterfeit of W-LA-280-010-G080. 18__. 1810s.

Rarity: *None known*

How to Read the Whitman Numbering System

$1 • W-AL-020-001-G010a

Denomination: Face value of the note shown.

W: Whitman number. This number is a sortable code unique to each bank and note.

AL: Abbreviation for the state under study.

020: Numerical designation specific to each bank.

001: The denomination in dollars.

G010a: G indicates a good or valid note. Other categories are indicated thus: C (counterfeit); R (raised); S (spurious); N (not-attributed); A (altered). Numbers are assigned starting with 010, 020, et seq. Terminal letters following the number indicate variations of a note: a series of different colored overprints, tints, payees, etc., all on the same design of note. For more information, see the "How to Use This Book" section at the front of the volume, page xiv.

$10 • W-LA-280-010-C100a

Back: Red-brown. ***Engraver:*** Rawdon, Wright, Hatch & Edson / ABNCo. monogram. ***Comments:*** H-LA-80-C24b. Counterfeit of W-LA-280-010-G100a. 18__. 1850s.

Rarity: *None known*

$10 • W-LA-280-010-N010

Engraver: Western Bank Note Co. ***Comments:*** H-LA-80-N5. No description available. 18__. 1830s–1840s.

Rarity: *None known*

$20 • W-LA-280-020-C140

HA, HA

Back: Red-orange. ***Engraver:*** Rawdon, Wright, Hatch & Edson. ***Comments:*** H-LA-80-C34a. Counterfeit of W-LA-280-020-G140. 18__. 1850s.

Rarity: URS-6
F $200

$50 • W-LA-280-050-R010

Engraver: Murray, Draper, Fairman & Co. ***Comments:*** H-LA-80-R5. Raised from W-LA-280-005-G040. 18__. 1810s.

Rarity: *None known*

$50 • W-LA-280-050-S010

Left: 50. ***Center:*** 50 / Woman seated / 50. ***Right:*** FIFTY. ***Engraver:*** Rawdon, Wright, Hatch & Edson. ***Comments:*** H-LA-80-S5. 18__. 1850.

Rarity: *None known*

$100 • W-LA-280-100-C190

Engraver: Murray, Draper, Fairman & Co. ***Comments:*** H-LA-80-C48. Counterfeit of W-LA-280-100-G190. 18__. 1810s.

Rarity: *None known*

$100 • W-LA-280-100-C210

Engraver: Rawdon, Wright, Hatch & Edson. ***Comments:*** H-LA-80-C54a. Counterfeit of W-LA-280-100-G210. 18__. 1850s.

Rarity: *None known*

$100 • W-LA-280-100-R020

Engraver: Murray, Draper, Fairman & Co. ***Comments:*** H-LA-80-R10. Raised from W-LA-280-005-G040. 18__. 1830.

Rarity: *None known*

$100 • W-LA-280-100-S020

Left: Medallion head. ***Center:*** Train. ***Right:*** Portrait of Benjamin Franklin. ***Comments:*** H-LA-80-S10. 18__. 1850s.

Rarity: *None known*

Louisiana State Bank (branch)

1836–1852

W-LA-290

History: The Louisiana State Bank was chartered in 1818. By March 14 of that year, the state had subscribed to $500,000 of the authorized $2,000,000 capital of the bank. A bonus of $100,000 was required to be paid to the state before the bank could commence operations. In 1836, due to strife building between the American and Creole inhabitants of New Orleans, the legislature repealed the charter of the city and divided it into a new municipal organization. This was to "prevent racial ill feeling," with each municipality providing its own separate government and power. A single mayor and council still presided over the city. At this time notes of the Louisiana State Bank were made payable in the second municipality of New Orleans. This continued until 1852, when the friction between the Americans and the Creoles had all but disappeared, and thus the municipalities were made obsolete.[10]

The Louisiana State Bank had its parent bank located in New Orleans, W-LA-280, and branch banks located in Alexandria, W-LA-020, Baton Rouge, W-LA-040, Donaldsonville, W-LA-070, Saint Francisville, W-LA-450, Saint Martinville, W-LA-470, and Shreveport, W-LA-490.

Valid Issues

$5 • W-LA-290-005-G010

SI, SI

Back: Red-orange. ***Engraver:*** Rawdon, Wright, Hatch & Edson. ***Comments:*** H-LA-80-G80a. 18__. 1840s–1850s.

Rarity: URS-7
F $250

$10 • W-LA-290-010-G020 CC, CC

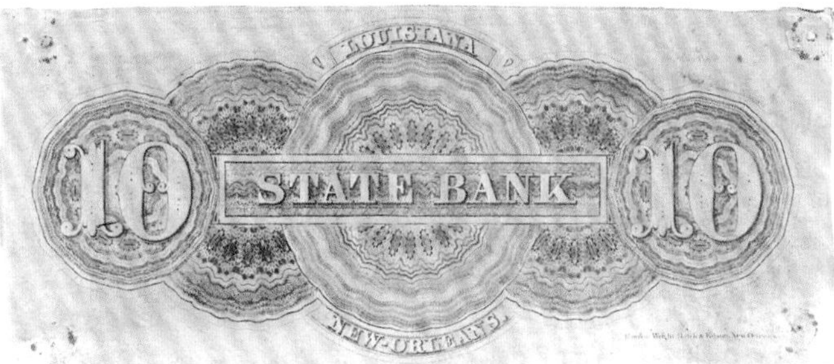

Back: Red-orange. ***Engraver:*** Rawdon, Wright, Hatch & Edson. ***Comments:*** H-LA-80-G82a. 18__. 1840s–1850s.

Rarity: URS-7
F $200

$20 • W-LA-290-020-G030

Left: 20 / View of Place d'Armes and Cathedral in New Orleans vertically / TWENTY. ***Center:*** 20 / Woman seated in 20. ***Right:*** 20 / Woman seated in 20. ***Engraver:*** Rawdon, Wright, Hatch & Edson. ***Comments:*** H-LA-80-G84a. 18__. 1840s–1850s.

Rarity: *None known*

Uncut Sheets

$5-$5-$5-$5 • W-LA-290-005.005.005.005-US010 RG

Back(s): Red-orange. ***Engraver:*** Rawdon, Wright, Hatch & Edson. ***Comments:*** H-LA-80-G80a, G80a, G80a, G80a. All four notes identical. 18__. 1840s–1850s.

Rarity: URS-5
VF $900

$10-$10-$10-$10 •
W-LA-290-010.010.010.010-US020

RH

Back(s): Red-orange. *Engraver:* Rawdon, Wright, Hatch & Edson. *Comments:* H-LA-80-G82a, G82a, G82a, G82a. All four notes identical. 18__. 1840s–1850s.

Rarity: URS-5
EF $1,000

Non-Valid Issues

$10 • W-LA-290-010-C020

Engraver: Rawdon, Wright, Hatch & Edson. *Comments:* H-LA-80-C82a. Counterfeit of W-LA-290-010-G020. 18__. 1850s.

Rarity: *None known*

Mechanics and Traders Bank

1833–1879

W-LA-300

History: The Mechanics and Traders Bank was chartered in April 1833 with an authorized capital of $2,000,000. By 1836 bills in circulation totaled $239,880. In 1842, during the crisis of that year in New Orleans, the Mechanics and Traders Bank was one of a few banks to continue paying out specie, though its bills were trading at a steep discount. By 1843 the circulation had risen again to $303,090. In 1845 it was $885,160. The president of the bank in 1848 was George Morgan, and the cashier was Samuel C. Bell. Bell resigned in 1849 and was replaced by Jackson Duplessis. Unfortunately, it was discovered that he was a defaulter (in an amount between $10,000 and $15,000) before he even took office. Later his deficit totaled $48,000.

In March 1850 the bank was authorized to begin its liquidation. However, in 1853 it was converted by the Free Banking Law, and by 1855 it had a capital of $1,689,600. The cashier was G. Cruzat, and the president was U.H. Dudley. In 1857 these values were given: capital $1,445,200; bills in circulation $412,505; specie $420,632; real estate $56,220.

The Mechanics and Traders Bank survived the Civil War and finally closed in 1879.

Numismatic Commentary: Proof and issued notes from this bank are extremely rare, with about a dozen known or reported. The Mechanics and Traders Bank also issued certificates of deposit in denominations of $1, $2, and $3, which are common.

Remaining at the American Bank Note Co. archives as of 2003 were two $1-$1-$2-$3 back plates (certificates of deposit and not listed below).

Valid Issues

$5 • W-LA-300-005-G010

Engraver: Rawdon, Wright, Hatch & Co. *Comments:* H-LA-85-G2. No description available. 18__. 1830s–1840s.

Rarity: *None known*

$10 • W-LA-300-010-G020

Engraver: Rawdon, Wright, Hatch & Co. *Comments:* H-LA-85-G6. No description available. 18__. 1830s–1840s.

Rarity: *None known*

$20 • W-LA-300-020-G030

RH

Engraver: Rawdon, Wright, Hatch & Co. *Comments:* H-LA-85-G10. 18__. 1830s–1840s.

Rarity: URS-2
Proof $3,000

$50 • W-LA-300-050-G040

Engraver: Rawdon, Wright, Hatch & Co. *Comments:* H-LA-85-G14. 18__. 1830s–1840s.

Rarity: URS-2
Proof $3,500

$100 • W-LA-300-100-G050

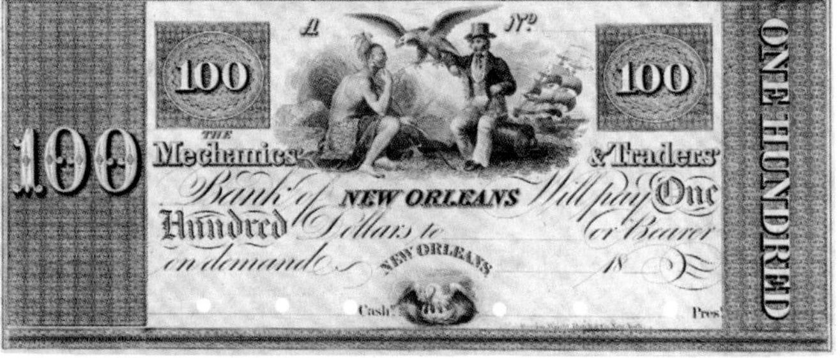

Engraver: Rawdon, Wright, Hatch & Co. *Comments:* H-LA-85-G18. 18__. 1830s–1840s.

Rarity: URS-1
Proof $7,000

Free-Bank Issues

$5 • W-LA-300-005-G060

Left: 5 / State arms / 5. *Center:* FIVE / Man seated with sledgehammer. *Right:* 5 / Woman with hat / V. *Back:* Red-orange. *Engraver:* Rawdon, Wright, Hatch & Edson. *Comments:* H-LA-85-G18a. 18__. 1850s.

Rarity: *None known*

$5 • W-LA-300-005-G060a

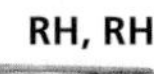

Back: Red-orange. *Engraver:* Rawdon, Wright, Hatch & Edson / ABNCo. monogram. *Comments:* H-LA-85-G18b. Similar to W-LA-300-005-G060 but with additional engraver imprint. 18__. 1850s–1860s.

Rarity: URS-2
F $2,500

$10 • W-LA-300-010-G070

Left: 10 / Train vertically / TEN. *Center:* State arms / Woman reclining with globe. *Right:* 10 / Woman seated / TEN. *Back:* Red-orange. *Engraver:* Rawdon, Wright, Hatch & Edson. *Comments:* H-LA-85-G20a. 18__. 1850s.

Rarity: *None known*

$10 • W-LA-300-010-G070a

RH, RH

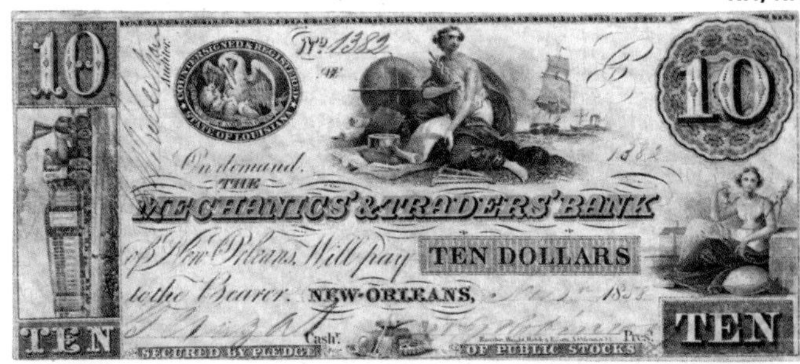

Back: Red-orange. *Engraver:* Rawdon, Wright, Hatch & Edson / ABNCo. monogram. *Comments:* H-LA-85-G20b. Similar to W-LA-300-010-G070 but with additional engraver imprint. 18__. 1850s–1860s.

Rarity: URS-3
F $2,000

$20 • **W-LA-300-020-G080**

Left: 20 / Sailor holding oar / XX. ***Center:*** State arms / Woman seated on rock, Cherubs playing with dolphin / Plow and sheaf. ***Right:*** 20 / Portrait of Benjamin Franklin / XX. ***Engraver:*** Rawdon, Wright, Hatch & Edson. ***Comments:*** H-LA-85-G22a. 18__. 1850s.

Rarity: *None known*

$20 • **W-LA-300-020-G080a**

Engraver: Rawdon, Wright, Hatch & Edson / ABNCo. monogram. ***Comments:*** H-LA-85-G22b. Similar to W-LA-300-020-G080 but with additional engraver imprint. 18__. 1850s–1860s.

Rarity: *None known*

$50 • **W-LA-300-050-G090**

Left: 50 / Sailor with telescope / FIFTY. ***Center:*** State arms / Mechanic holding hammer and chisel, Men working on boiler, Ship / Arm and hammer. ***Right:*** 50 / Woman seated / 50. ***Back:*** Red-orange. ***Engraver:*** Rawdon, Wright, Hatch & Edson. ***Comments:*** H-LA-85-G24a. 18__. 1850s.

Rarity: *None known*

$50 • **W-LA-300-050-G090a**

Engraver: Rawdon, Wright, Hatch & Edson / ABNCo. monogram. ***Comments:*** H-LA-85-G24b. Similar to W-LA-300-050-G090 but with additional engraver imprint. 18__. 1850s–1860s.

Rarity: *None known*

$100 • **W-LA-300-100-G100**

Back: Red-orange. ***Engraver:*** Rawdon, Wright, Hatch & Edson. ***Comments:*** H-LA-85-G26a. No description available. 18__. 1850s.

Rarity: *None known*

$100 • **W-LA-300-100-G100a**

Back: Red-orange. ***Engraver:*** Rawdon, Wright, Hatch & Edson / ABNCo. monogram. ***Comments:*** H-LA-85-G26b. Similar to W-LA-300-100-G100 but with additional engraver imprint. 18__. 1850s–1860s.

Rarity: *None known*

$1,000 • **W-LA-300-1000-G110**

RH

Engraver: Rawdon, Wright, Hatch & Co. ***Comments:*** H-Unlisted. 18__. 1850s–1860s.

Rarity: URS-1
Proof $10,000

Unregistered Issues

$1 • **W-LA-300-001-G120**

RH

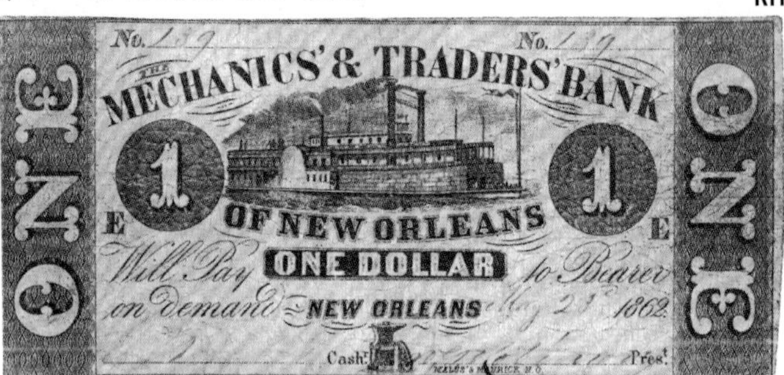

Comments: H-Unlisted. 18__. 1862.

Rarity: URS-2
F $1,500

$5 • **W-LA-300-005-G130**

Left: 5 / 5. ***Center:*** FIVE / Man seated with sledgehammer. ***Right:*** 5 / Woman with hat / V. ***Engraver:*** Rawdon, Wright, Hatch & Edson / ABNCo. monogram. ***Comments:*** H-LA-85-G30a. Lacks Auditor's signature. 18__. 1862.

Rarity: *None known*

$10 • **W-LA-300-010-G140**

RH

Engraver: Rawdon, Wright, Hatch & Edson / ABNCo. monogram. ***Comments:*** H-LA-85-G32a. Lacks Auditor's signature. 18__. 1862.

Rarity: URS-2
Prop. Proof $1,000

$20 • **W-LA-300-020-G150**

RH

Engraver: Rawdon, Wright, Hatch & Edson / ABNCo. monogram. ***Comments:*** H-LA-85-G34a. Lacks Auditor's signature. 18__. 1862.

Rarity: URS-2
Prop. Proof $1,000

$50 • **W-LA-300-050-G160** RH

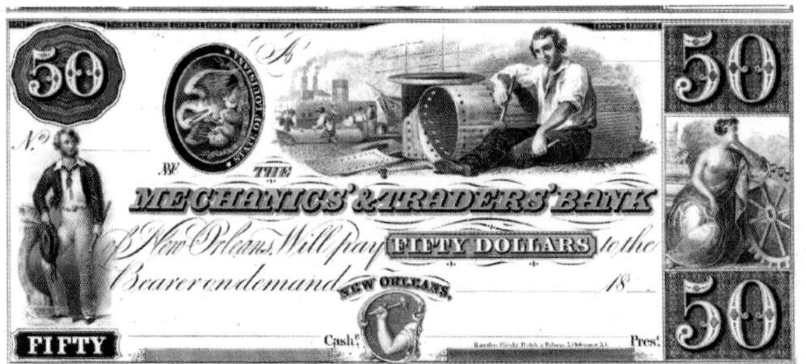

Engraver: Rawdon, Wright, Hatch & Edson / ABNCo. monogram. ***Comments:*** H-LA-85-G36a. Lacks Auditor's signature. 18__. 1862.

Rarity: URS-2
Prop. Proof $1,500

$100 • **W-LA-300-100-G170** RH

Engraver: Rawdon, Wright, Hatch & Edson / ABNCo. monogram. ***Comments:*** H-LA-85-G38a. Lacks Auditor's signature. 18__. 1862.

Rarity: URS-2
Prop. Proof $1,700

Non-Valid Issues

$3 • **W-LA-300-003-A010**
Left: Zeus seated with staff and thunderbolts / 3. ***Center:*** 3 / Two men cradling grain. ***Right:*** THREE / Portrait of George Washington / 3. ***Engraver:*** Rawdon, Wright & Hatch. ***Comments:*** H-LA-85-A5. Altered from $3 Chippeway County Bank, Sault De St. Mary, Michigan. 18__. 1830s–1840s.

Rarity: *None known*

$5 • **W-LA-300-005-N010**
Center: Steamboat. ***Comments:*** H-LA-85-N5. 18__. 1843.

Rarity: *None known*

$5 • **W-LA-300-005-A020**
Left: 5 / Woman seated on bale, Ship. ***Center:*** Moneta seated with key receiving bag of coins from Mercury in clouds, Griffin on strongbox / 5. ***Right:*** FIVE / Two allegorical women seated with caduceus, shield, and cornucopia. ***Engraver:*** Rawdon, Wright & Hatch. ***Comments:*** H-LA-85-A10. Altered from $5 Chippeway County Bank, Sault De St. Mary, Michigan. 18__. 1830s–1840s.

Rarity: *None known*

$10 • **W-LA-300-010-C020**
Engraver: Rawdon, Wright, Hatch & Co. ***Comments:*** H-LA-85-C6. Counterfeit of W-LA-300-010-G020. 18__. 1840s.

Rarity: *None known*

$10 • **W-LA-300-010-A030**
Left: 10 / Train / 10. ***Center:*** Amphitrite and Neptune in shell drawn by seahorses / X. ***Right:*** X / Farm produce and implements / 10. ***Engraver:*** Rawdon, Wright & Hatch. ***Comments:*** H-LA-85-A15. Altered from $10 Chippeway County Bank, Sault De St. Mary, Michigan. 18__. 1830s–1840s.

Rarity: *None known*

$50 • **W-LA-300-050-R010**
Engraver: Rawdon, Wright, Hatch & Co. ***Comments:*** H-LA-85-R5. Raised from W-LA-300-010-G020. 18__. 1840s.

Rarity: *None known*

$100 • **W-LA-300-100-R020**
Engraver: Rawdon, Wright, Hatch & Co. ***Comments:*** H-LA-85-R10. Raised from W-LA-300-010-G020. 18__. 1840s.

Rarity: *None known*

Merchants Bank of New Orleans {1st}

1836–1845

W-LA-310

History: The first Merchants Bank of New Orleans was chartered in February 1836 with an authorized capital of $1,000,000. The cashier was William S. Mount, and the president was Phoenix N. Wood. By 1845 the bank had gone into liquidation.

Numismatic Commentary: Proof and issued notes from this bank are extremely rare, with only half a dozen notes recorded to date.

Valid Issues

$5 • **W-LA-310-005-G010** HA

Engraver: Draper, Toppan, Longacre & Co. ***Comments:*** H-LA-90-G2. 18__. 1830s.

Rarity: URS-2
Proof $5,900
Selected auction price: Heritage Auctions, April 23, 2015, Lot 19088, Proof $5,875

$10 • W-LA-310-010-G020

HA

Engraver: Draper, Toppan, Longacre & Co. ***Comments:*** H-LA-90-G4. 18__. 1830s.

Rarity: URS-2
Proof $4,700
Selected auction price: Heritage Auctions, April 23, 2015, Lot 19089, Proof $4,700

$20 • W-LA-310-020-G030

RH

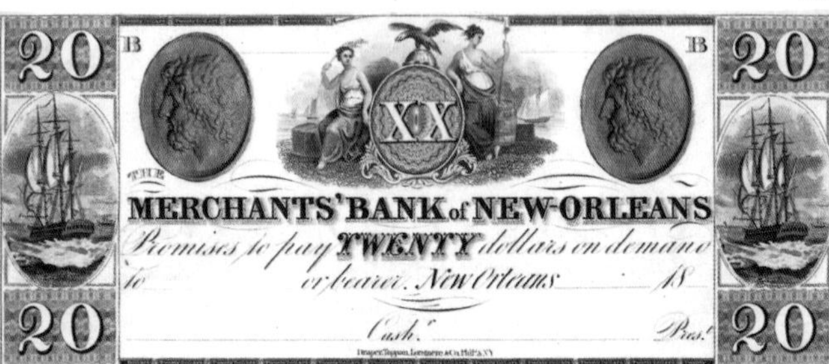

Engraver: Draper, Toppan, Longacre & Co. ***Comments:*** H-LA-90-G6. 18__. 1830s.

Rarity: URS-2
Proof $5,000

$50 • W-LA-310-050-G040

RH

Engraver: Draper, Toppan, Longacre & Co. ***Comments:*** H-LA-90-G8. 18__. 1830s.

Rarity: URS-2
Proof $5,000

$100 • W-LA-310-100-G050

RH

Engraver: Draper, Toppan, Longacre & Co. ***Comments:*** H-LA-90-G10. 18__. 1830s.

Rarity: URS-2
Proof $6,500

NON-VALID ISSUES

$50 • W-LA-310-050-R010

Engraver: Draper, Toppan, Longacre & Co. ***Comments:*** H-LA-90-R5. Raised from W-LA-310-005-G010. 18__. 1830s.

Rarity: —

Merchants Bank of New Orleans {2nd}

1859–1879

W-LA-320

History: In 1859 the Bank of James Robb, W-LA-130, became the second Merchants Bank of New Orleans under the Free Banking Law. The bank survived the Civil War and finally closed its doors in 1879.

Numismatic Commentary: Proof and issued notes from this bank are rare. There are about two-dozen notes known.

VALID ISSUES

Free-Bank Issues

$5 • W-LA-320-005-G010

RH, RH

Tint: Green 5 / V / FIVE. ***Back:*** Red-orange. ***Engraver:*** Rawdon, Wright, Hatch & Edson / ABNCo. monogram. ***Comments:*** H-LA-95-G4a. 18__. 1859–1861.

Rarity: URS-4
F $750

Collectors and Researchers:

If you have new information about any banks or notes listed in this volume, contact Whitman Publishing, Attn: Obsolete Paper Money, 3101 Clairmont Road, Suite G, Atlanta, GA 30329.

$10 • W-LA-320-010-G020 RH, RH

Tint: Green X / X and panel of microlettering bearing TEN. ***Back:*** Red-orange. ***Engraver:*** Rawdon, Wright, Hatch & Edson / ABNCo. monogram. ***Comments:*** H-LA-95-G6a. 18__. 1859–1861.

Rarity: URS-4
F $1,000

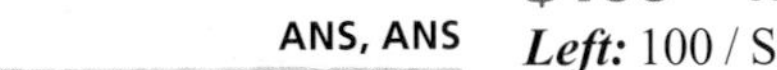

$20 • W-LA-320-020-G030 ANS, ANS

Tint: Green outlining white XX / XX and panel of microlettering bearing TWENTY. ***Back:*** Red-orange. ***Engraver:*** Rawdon, Wright, Hatch & Edson / ABNCo. monogram. ***Comments:*** H-LA-95-G8a. 18__. 1859–1861.

Rarity: URS-4
F $1,500

$50 • W-LA-320-050-G040 RH, RH

Tint: Green panel of microlettering bearing FIFTY. ***Back:*** Red-orange. ***Engraver:*** Rawdon, Wright, Hatch & Edson / ABNCo. monogram. ***Comments:*** H-LA-95-G10a. 18__. 1859–1861.

Rarity: URS-2
G $2,000

$100 • W-LA-320-100-G050

Left: 100 / State arms / 100. ***Center:*** Three women seated, Cherubs, wheel, and anvil, Ship. ***Right:*** 100 / Two women with staff. ***Tint:*** Green. ***Back:*** Red-orange. ***Engraver:*** Rawdon, Wright, Hatch & Edson / ABNCo. monogram. ***Comments:*** H-LA-95-G12a. 18__. 1859–1861.

Rarity: *None known*

Unregistered Issues

$1 • W-LA-320-001-G060 HA

Overprint: Red 1 / ONE / 1. ***Engraver:*** Douglas. ***Comments:*** H-LA-95-G14a. Lithographed. May 27th, 1862.

Rarity: URS-3
VF $1,900
Selected auction price: Heritage Auctions, January 8, 2014, Lot 15336, VF $1,880

$1.50 • W-LA-320-001.50-G070

RH

Overprint: Red ONE DOLLAR AND FIFTY CENTS. ***Engraver:*** Douglas. ***Comments:*** H-LA-95-G16a. Lithographed. May 27th, 1862.

Rarity: URS-3
VF $1,700

$1.50 • W-LA-320-001.50-G070a

RH

Overprint: Red 1 50/100 / ONE DOLLAR AND FIFTY CENTS / 1 50/100. ***Engraver:*** Douglas. ***Comments:*** H-Unlisted. Similar to W-LA-320-001.50-G070. Lithographed. May 27th, 1862.

Rarity: URS-3
VF $1,800

$2 • W-LA-320-002-G080

HA

Overprint: Red 2 / TWO / 2. ***Engraver:*** Douglas. ***Comments:*** H-Unlisted. Lithographed. May 27th, 1862.

Rarity: URS-2
VF $2,250
Selected auction price: Heritage Auctions, October 21, 2015, Lot 18351, VF $2,232

$5 • W-LA-320-005-G090

RH

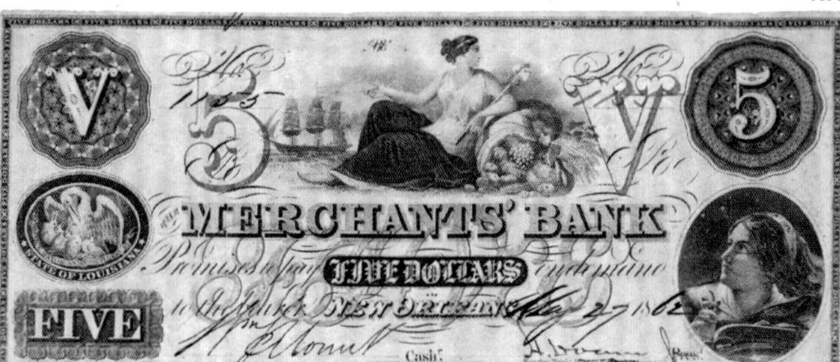

Tint: Red 5 / V / FIVE. ***Back:*** Red-orange. ***Engraver:*** Rawdon, Wright, Hatch & Edson / ABNCo. monogram. ***Comments:*** H-LA-95-G22a. Lacks Auditor's signature. 18__. 1862.

Rarity: URS-3
F $3,000

$5 • W-LA-320-005-G100

Left: FIVE. ***Center:*** 5 / Woman seated / 5. ***Right:*** FIVE. ***Overprint:*** Red 5 / FIVE / 5. ***Engraver:*** Douglas. ***Comments:*** H-LA-95-G24a. May 27th, 1862.

Rarity: *None known*

$10 • W-LA-320-010-G110

RH

Tint: Red X / X and panel of microlettering bearing TEN. ***Back:*** Red-orange. ***Engraver:*** Rawdon, Wright, Hatch & Edson / ABNCo. monogram. ***Comments:*** H-LA-95-G26a. Lacks Auditor's signature. 18__. 1862.

Rarity: URS-2
F $3,000

$20 • W-LA-320-020-G120

Left: State arms / TWENTY / XX. ***Center:*** XX / Two women seated / XX / TWENTY. ***Right:*** 20 / Female portrait. ***Tint:*** Green. ***Back:*** Red-orange. ***Engraver:*** Rawdon, Wright, Hatch & Edson / ABNCo. monogram. ***Comments:*** H-LA-95-G28a. Lacks Auditor's signature. 18__. 1862.

Rarity: *None known*

$50 • W-LA-320-050-G130

Left: State arms / Female portrait / FIFTY. ***Center:*** 50 / Minerva pointing to steamship, Shield, safe, and cornucopia. ***Right:*** FIFTY / Justice standing with sword and balance. ***Tint:*** Green. ***Back:*** Red-orange. ***Engraver:*** Rawdon, Wright, Hatch & Edson / ABNCo. monogram. ***Comments:*** H-LA-95-G30a. Lacks Auditor's signature. 18__. 1862.

Rarity: *None known*

$100 • W-LA-320-100-G140 HA

Tint: Red C / HUNDRED / C and panel of microlettering. ***Engraver:*** Rawdon, Wright, Hatch & Edson / ABNCo. monogram. ***Comments:*** H-Unlisted. Lacks Auditor's signature. Partial note. 18__. 1862.

Rarity: URS-1
VF $1,900
Selected auction price: Heritage Auctions, April 23, 2015, Lot 19090, VF $1,880

$100 • W-LA-320-100-G140a

Tint: Red C / HUNDRED / C and panel of microlettering. ***Back:*** Red-orange. ***Engraver:*** Rawdon, Wright, Hatch & Edson / ABNCo. monogram. ***Comments:*** H-LA-95-G32a. Similar to W-LA-320-100-G140. Lacks Auditor's signature. 18__. 1862.

Rarity: —

Non-Valid Issues

$20 • W-LA-320-020-C030

Engraver: Rawdon, Wright, Hatch & Edson / ABNCo. monogram. ***Comments:*** H-LA-95-C8a. Counterfeit of W-LA-320-020-G030. 18__. 1859.

Rarity: *None known*

Merchants and Traders Bank of New Orleans

1830s–1850

W-LA-330

History: The Merchants and Traders Bank of New Orleans had a circulation of $1,026,970 in February 1850. In March that year an act was passed authorizing the liquidation of the bank.

Numismatic Commentary: Proof and issued notes from this bank are extremely rare, with less than half a dozen notes known or recorded.

New Orleans and Carrollton Rail Road and Banking Company

1835–1844

W-LA-340

History: The New Orleans and Carrollton Rail Road and Banking Company (also seen as the Carrollton Bank and as the New Orleans Bank) was incorporated in April 1835 with an authorized capital of $3,000,000. On March 1, 1836, the act was amended, requiring the bank to pay $500 to a boys' orphanage annually for ten years. In May 1841 the real estate loans given by the bank totaled $37,793,798.[11] During a crisis in 1842, the bank was one of few in the city to continue paying out specie, but its circulation dropped to nearly nothing. By 1844 banking privileges had been surrendered, and in May 1845 it was reported that the bank was in liquidation.

The New Orleans and Carrollton Rail Road and Banking Company had a branch bank located in Clinton, W-LA-050.

Numismatic Commentary: Proof and issued notes from this bank are extremely rare, with less than half a dozen notes known. Featured on some notes is a portrait of Charles Carroll, one of the signers of the Declaration of Independence.

Valid Issues

$5 • W-LA-340-005-G010 RH

Engraver: Rawdon, Wright, Hatch & Edson. ***Comments:*** H-LA-110-G2. 18__. 1830s.

Rarity: URS-1
Fair $750

$10 • W-LA-340-010-G020

Engraver: Rawdon, Wright, Hatch & Edson. ***Comments:*** H-LA-110-G4. No description available. 18__. 1830s.

Rarity: *None known*

$20 • W-LA-340-020-G030

Engraver: Rawdon, Wright, Hatch & Edson. ***Comments:*** H-LA-110-G6. No description available. 18__. 1830s.

Rarity: *None known*

$50 • W-LA-340-050-G040

Engraver: Rawdon, Wright, Hatch & Edson. ***Comments:*** H-LA-110-G8. No description available. 18__. 1830s.

Rarity: *None known*

$100 • W-LA-340-100-G050

Engraver: Rawdon, Wright, Hatch & Edson. ***Comments:*** H-LA-110-G10. No description available. 18__. 1830s.

Rarity: *None known*

$1,000 • W-LA-340-1000-G055

RH

Engraver: Draper, Toppan, Longacre & Co. ***Comments:*** H-Unlisted. 18__. 1830s.

Rarity: URS-1
Proof $10,000

Notes Payable at the Commercial Bank of Pennsylvania

$5 • W-LA-340-005-G060

RH

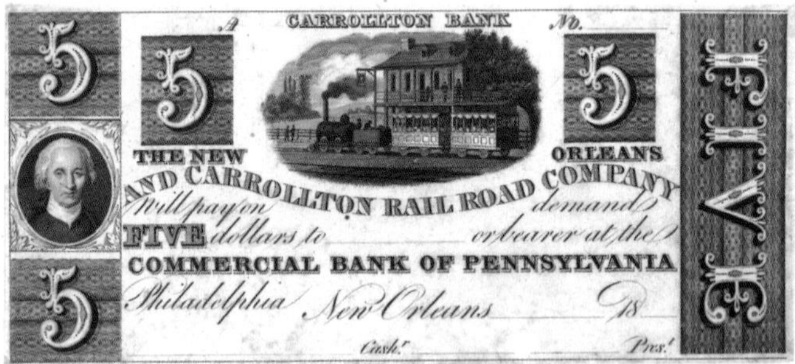

Engraver: Underwood, Bald & Spencer. ***Comments:*** H-LA-110-G12. Proofs lack imprint. 18__. 1830s.

Rarity: URS-2
Proof $3,500

$10 • W-LA-340-010-G070

RH

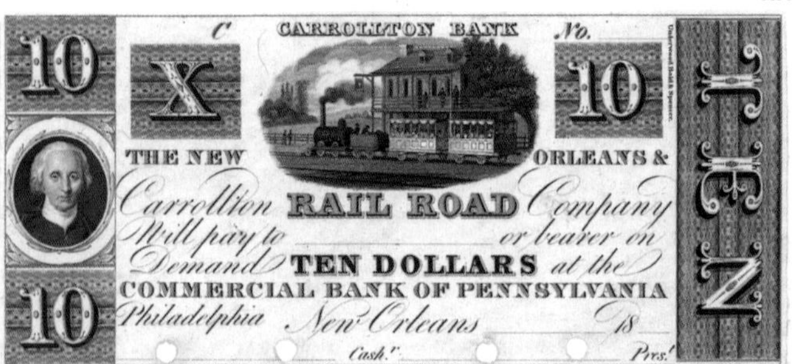

Engraver: Underwood, Bald & Spencer. ***Comments:*** H-LA-110-G14. Proofs lack imprint. 18__. 1830s.

Rarity: URS-2
Proof $3,500

$20 • W-LA-340-020-G080

RH

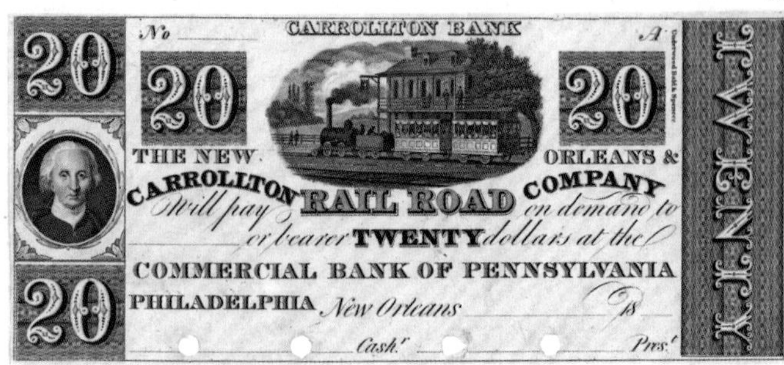

Engraver: Underwood, Bald & Spencer. ***Comments:*** H-LA-110-G16. Proofs lack imprint. 18__. 1830s.

Rarity: URS-2
Proof $3,500

$50 • W-LA-340-050-G090

RH

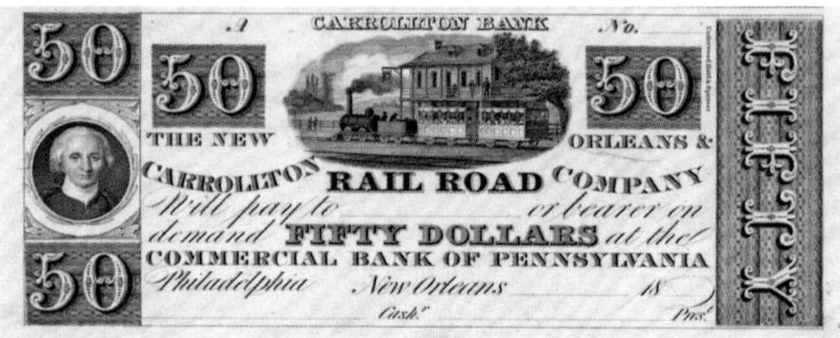

Engraver: Underwood, Bald & Spencer. ***Comments:*** H-LA-110-G18. Proofs lack imprint. 18__. 1830s.

Rarity: URS-2
Proof $3,500

$100 • W-LA-340-100-G100

Engraver: Underwood, Bald & Spencer. ***Comments:*** H-LA-110-G20. No description available. 18__. 1830s.

Rarity: *None known*

$500 • W-LA-340-500-G110

Engraver: Underwood, Bald & Spencer. ***Comments:*** H-LA-110-G22. No description available. 18__. 1830s.

Rarity: *None known*

$1,000 • W-LA-340-1000-G120

Engraver: Underwood, Bald & Spencer. ***Comments:*** H-LA-110-G24. No description available. 18__. 1830s.

Rarity: *None known*

New Orleans Canal and Banking Company

1831–1870

W-LA-350

History: The New Orleans Canal and Banking Company (also seen as the Canal and Banking Company and as the Canal Bank) was chartered in March 1831 and went into operation in June with an authorized capital of $4,000,000. The president elected was Archibald R. Taylor, and Beverly Chew was the cashier.

In 1848 there was an extensive fraud of counterfeit notes from the Canal Bank. Several $100 bills were floating with altered descriptions of a very cunning nature. Later that year a run was made on the bank, but it successfully redeemed all notes presented. The bank, at that time, had $1,877,117 in specie on hand to cover a circulation of $1,286,260. The amount presented to the bank, and successfully met, was $120,000.[12]

In 1855 the capital of the bank was $3,164,000. The cashier was Samuel C. Bell, and the president was H.A. Rathbone. Bell passed away in 1856, after a career of 30 years, and was replaced by Alfred H. Kernion. The bank's original charter expired in 1870, but the bank reorganized and continued on into the 20th century, well beyond the bank-note–issuing period under study.

Numismatic Commentary: As late as the 1950s, thousands of uncut sheets of this bank were available in the marketplace. Bundles of uncut sheets were found during the remodeling of a French Quarter building, tucked behind the walls and between the studs as a form of insulation. By now most have been dispersed, and many sheets have been cut apart. Today, notes of this bank are still by far the most common remainders of any bank of the early 19th century. A fine collection of different varieties can be assembled for modest cost.

Remaining at the American Bank Note Co. archives as of 2003 was a $10-$10-$10-$10 back plate and a $500-$1,000 back plate.

Valid Issues

$5 • W-LA-350-005-G010

RH

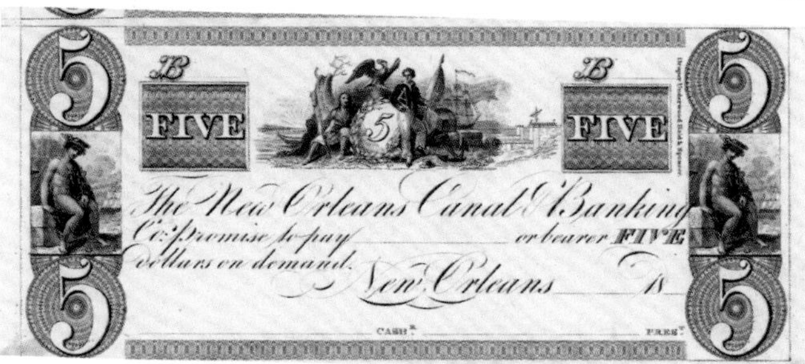

Engraver: Danforth, Underwood, Bald & Spencer. ***Comments:*** H-LA-105-G6. 18__. 1830s.

Rarity: URS-3
Proof $2,000

$5 • W-LA-350-005-G020

NS

Engraver: Rawdon, Wright, Hatch & Edson. ***Comments:*** H-LA-105-G10. 18__. 1840s.

Rarity: URS-12
Unc-Rem $50

$5 • W-LA-350-005-G030

NJW, NJW

Back: Red-brown woman seated in V. ***Engraver:*** Toppan, Carpenter & Co. ***Comments:*** H-LA-105-G12a. 18__. 1840s.

Rarity: URS-12
Unc-Rem $50

$5 • W-LA-350-005-G040

RH, RH

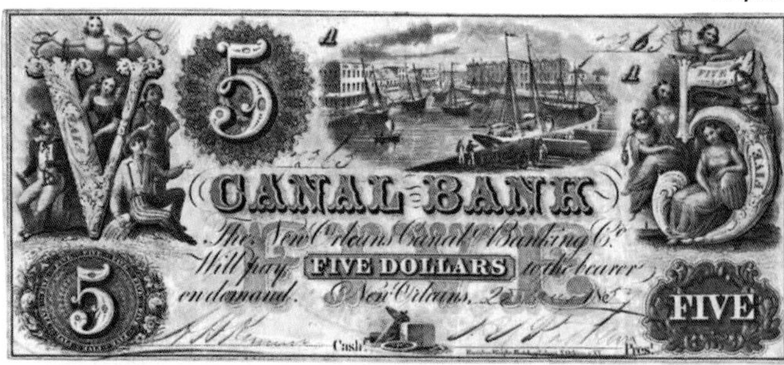

Back: Red-orange. ***Engraver:*** Rawdon, Wright, Hatch & Edson. ***Comments:*** H-LA-105-G14a. 18__. 1850s–1860s.

Rarity: URS-5
VF $1,500

$5 • W-LA-350-005-G050

RH

Engraver: Underwood, Bald, Spencer & Hufty. ***Comments:*** H-Unlisted. 18__. 1830s.

Rarity: URS-3
Proof $2,000

$10 • W-LA-350-010-G060

RH

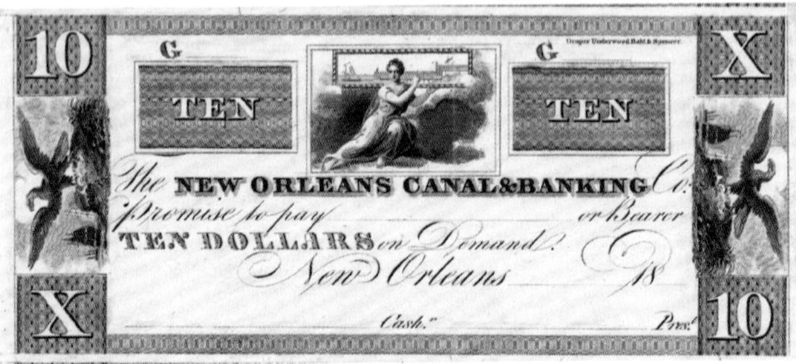

Engraver: Danforth, Underwood, Bald & Spencer. ***Comments:*** H-LA-105-G16. 18__. 1830s.

Rarity: URS-3
Proof $2,000

$10 • W-LA-350-010-G070

Engraver: Rawdon, Wright, Hatch & Edson. ***Comments:*** H-LA-105-G20. No description available. 18__. 1840s.

Rarity: *None known*

$10 • W-LA-350-010-G080

NJW, NJW

Back: Red-brown eagle. ***Engraver:*** Toppan, Carpenter & Co. ***Comments:*** H-LA-105-G22a. 18__. 1840s.

Rarity: URS-10
Unc-Rem $75

$10 • W-LA-350-010-G090

NJW, NJW

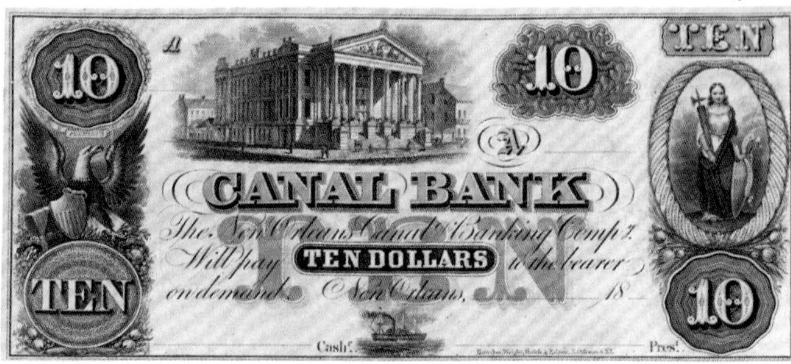

Back: Red-orange. ***Engraver:*** Rawdon, Wright, Hatch & Edson. ***Comments:*** H-LA-105-G24a. 18__. 1850s.

Rarity: URS-10
Unc-Rem $75

$10 • W-LA-350-010-G100

CC

Tint: Red-orange. ***Engraver:*** National Bank Note Co. ***Comments:*** H-LA-105-G26a. 1860s.

Rarity: URS-8
Unc-Rem $120

$20 • W-LA-350-020-G110

RH

Engraver: Danforth, Underwood, Bald & Spencer. ***Comments:*** H-LA-105-G28. 18__. 1830s.

Rarity: URS-3
Proof $2,500

$20 • W-LA-350-020-G120 CC

Engraver: Rawdon, Wright, Hatch & Edson. ***Comments:*** H-LA-105-G32. 18__. 1840s.

Rarity: URS-7
Unc-Rem $150

$20 • W-LA-350-020-G120a CC, CC

Tint: Blue 20. ***Back:*** Red-brown. ***Engraver:*** Rawdon, Wright, Hatch & Edson. ***Comments:*** H-LA-105-G32a. Similar to W-LA-350-020-G120. 18__. 1840s.

Rarity: URS-8
Unc-Rem $75

$20 • W-LA-350-020-G130 RH

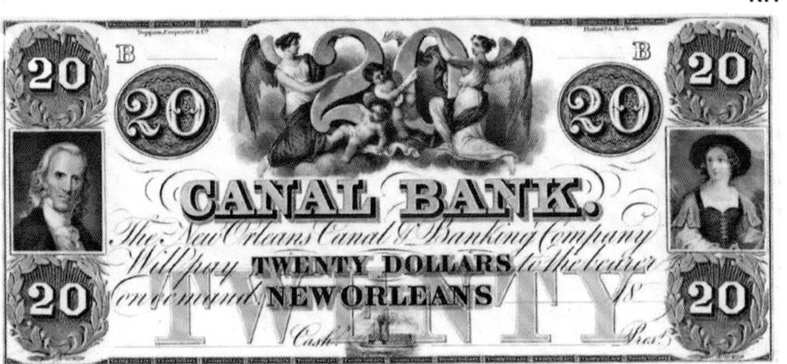

Engraver: Toppan, Carpenter & Co. ***Comments:*** H-Unlisted. 18__. 1840s.

Rarity: URS-3
Proof $2,000

$20 • W-LA-350-020-G130a CC, CC

Back: Red-brown. ***Engraver:*** Toppan, Carpenter & Co. / ABNCo. monogram. ***Comments:*** H-LA-105-G34a. Similar to W-LA-350-020-G130 but with additional engraver imprint. 18__. 1840s.

Rarity: URS-9
Unc-Rem $50

$20 • W-LA-350-020-G140 CC, CC

Back: Red-orange. ***Engraver:*** Rawdon, Wright, Hatch & Edson. ***Comments:*** H-LA-105-G36a. 18__. 1850s.

Rarity: URS-8
F $100

$50 • **W-LA-350-050-G150** RH

Engraver: Danforth, Underwood, Bald & Spencer. ***Comments:*** H-Unlisted. 18__. 1830s.

Rarity: URS-3
Proof $2,500

$50 • **W-LA-350-050-G160** CC

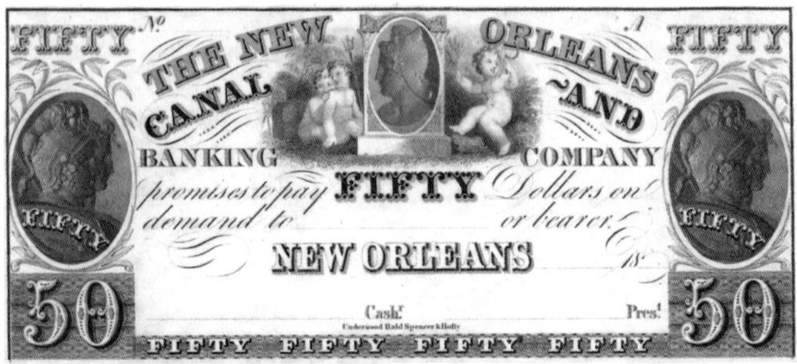

Engraver: Underwood, Bald, Spencer & Hufty. ***Comments:*** H-LA-105-G40. 18__. 1830s.

Rarity: URS-10
Unc-Rem $125; **Proof** $2,000

$50 • **W-LA-350-050-G170** CC

Engraver: Rawdon, Wright, Hatch & Edson. ***Comments:*** H-LA-105-G44. 18__. 1840s.

Rarity: URS-8
Unc-Rem $75

$50 • **W-LA-350-050-G170a** CC

CC

Tint: Blue 50. ***Back:*** Brown. ***Engraver:*** Rawdon, Wright, Hatch & Edson. ***Comments:*** H-LA-105-G44a. Similar to W-LA-350-050-G170. 18__. 1840s.

Rarity: URS-8
Unc-Rem $75

$50 • **W-LA-350-050-G180** LK, ANS

Back: Red-brown. ***Engraver:*** Toppan, Carpenter & Co. ***Comments:*** H-LA-105-G46a. 18__. 1840s.

Rarity: URS-9
Unc-Rem $50

How to Read the Whitman Numbering System

$1 • **W-AL-020-001-G010a**

Denomination: Face value of the note shown.

W: Whitman number. This number is a sortable code unique to each bank and note.

AL: Abbreviation for the state under study.

020: Numerical designation specific to each bank.

001: The denomination in dollars.

G010a: G indicates a good or valid note. Other categories are indicated thus: C (counterfeit); R (raised); S (spurious); N (not-attributed); A (altered). Numbers are assigned starting with 010, 020, et seq. Terminal letters following the number indicate variations of a note: a series of different colored overprints, tints, payees, etc., all on the same design of note. For more information, see the "How to Use This Book" section at the front of the volume, page xiv.

$50 • **W-LA-350-050-G190** CC, CC

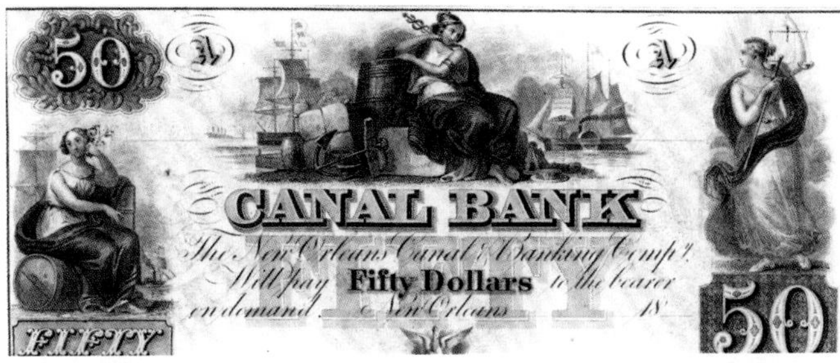

Back: Red-orange. ***Engraver:*** Rawdon, Wright, Hatch & Edson. ***Comments:*** H-LA-105-G48a. 18__. 1850s.

Rarity: URS-9
Unc-Rem $50

$100 • **W-LA-350-100-G200** RH

Engraver: Danforth, Underwood, Bald & Spencer. ***Comments:*** H-Unlisted. 18__. 1830s.

Rarity: URS-3
Proof $3,500

$100 • **W-LA-350-100-G210** CC

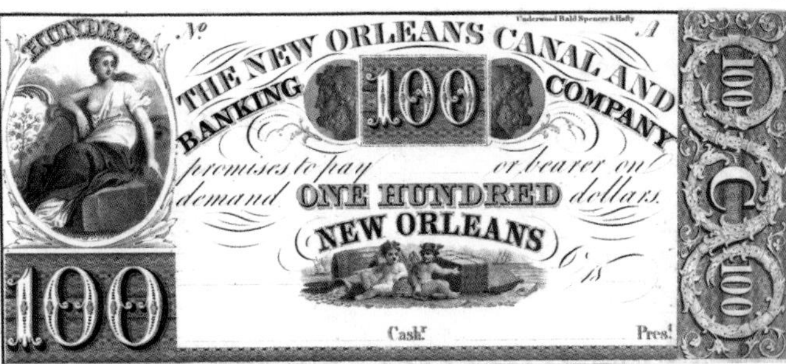

Engraver: Underwood, Bald, Spencer & Hufty. ***Comments:*** H-LA-105-G52. 18__. 1830s.

Rarity: URS-9
Unc-Rem $150; **Proof** $2,500

$100 • **W-LA-350-100-G220** RH, RH

Engraver: Rawdon, Wright, Hatch & Edson. ***Comments:*** H-Unlisted. 18__. 1840s.

Rarity: URS-2
F $1,500

$100 • **W-LA-350-100-G230** CC

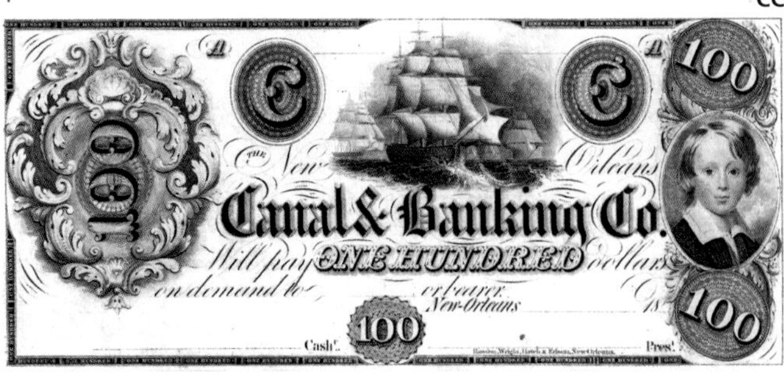

Engraver: Rawdon, Wright, Hatch & Edson. ***Comments:*** H-LA-105-G56. 18__. 1840s.

Rarity: URS-9
F $75

$100 • W-LA-350-100-G230a

CC, CC

Tint: Blue 100. *Back:* Brown. *Engraver:* Rawdon, Wright, Hatch & Edson. *Comments:* H-LA-105-G56a. Similar to W-LA-350-100-G230. 18__. 1840s.

Rarity: URS-8
Unc-Rem $100

$100 • W-LA-350-100-G240

CC

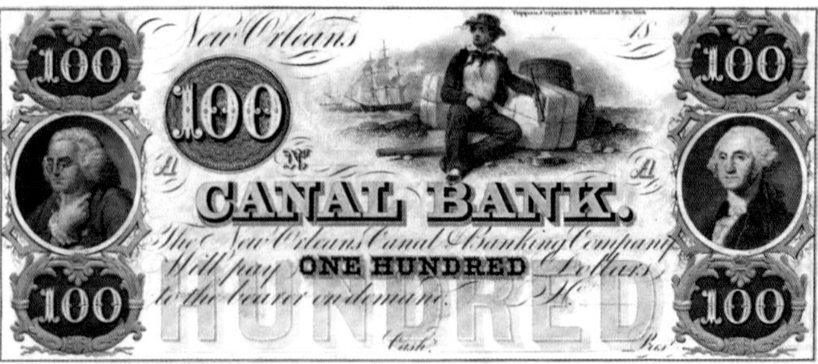

Engraver: Toppan, Carpenter & Co. *Comments:* H-LA-105-G58a. 18__. 1840s.

Rarity: URS-9
Unc-Rem $100

$100 • W-LA-350-100-G250

CC

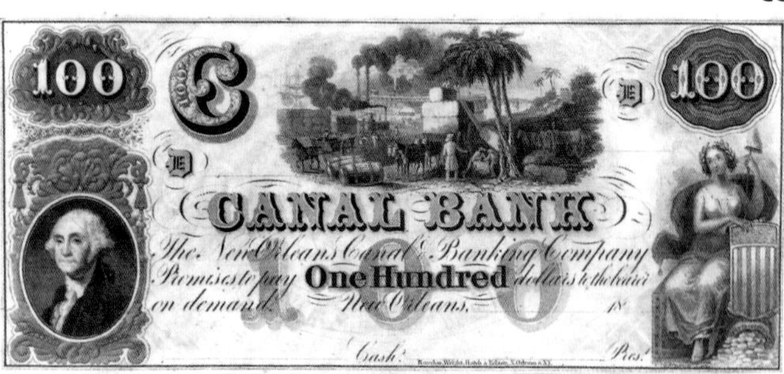

CC

Back: Red-orange. *Engraver:* Rawdon, Wright, Hatch & Edson. *Comments:* H-LA-105-G60a. 18__. 1850s.

Rarity: URS-9
Unc-Rem $75

$500 • W-LA-350-500-G260

RH

Engraver: Danforth, Underwood, Bald & Spencer. *Comments:* H-Unlisted. 18__. 1840s.

Rarity: URS-2
Proof $4,500

$500 • W-LA-350-500-G270

RH

Engraver: Underwood, Bald, Spencer & Hufty. *Comments:* H-Unlisted. 18__. 1840s.

Rarity: URS-1
Proof $6,000

$500 • W-LA-350-500-G280

Left: Medallion head. *Center:* 500 / Two griffins flanking shield bearing key. *Right:* 500 / Woman reclining / 500. *Engraver:* Rawdon, Wright, Hatch & Edson. *Comments:* H-LA-105-G66. 18__. 1840s.

Rarity: *None known*

$500 • **W-LA-350-500-G280a**

CC, CC

Tint: Blue D. ***Back:*** Brown. ***Engraver:*** Rawdon, Wright, Hatch & Edson. ***Comments:*** H-LA-105-G66a. Similar to W-LA-350-500-G280. 18__. 1840s.

Rarity: URS-7
Unc-Rem $300

$500 • **W-LA-350-500-G290**

RH, RH

Engraver: Toppan, Carpenter & Co. ***Comments:*** H-LA-105-G68a. 18__. 1840s.

Rarity: URS-1
Proof $8,000

$500 • **W-LA-350-500-G300**

CC, NJW

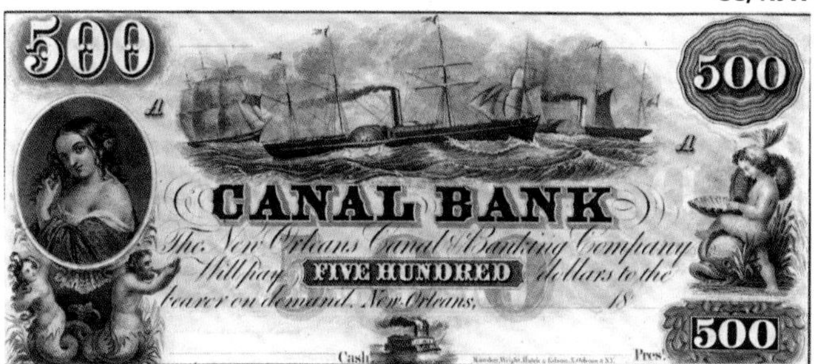

Back: Red-orange. ***Engraver:*** Rawdon, Wright, Hatch & Edson. ***Comments:*** H-LA-105-G70a. 18__. 1850s.

Rarity: URS-8
Unc-Rem $250

$1,000 • **W-LA-350-1000-G310**

Left: Medallion head. ***Center:*** 1000 / Ships / 1000. ***Right:*** Medallion head. ***Engraver:*** Rawdon, Wright, Hatch & Edson. ***Comments:*** H-LA-105-G76. 18__. 1840s.

Rarity: —

$1,000 • **W-LA-350-1000-G310a**

CC, CC

Tint: Blue M. ***Back:*** Brown. ***Engraver:*** Rawdon, Wright, Hatch & Edson. ***Comments:*** H-LA-105-G76a. Similar to W-LA-350-1000-G310. 18__. 1840s.

Rarity: URS-6
Unc-Rem $400

$1,000 • W-LA-350-1000-G320

RH, RH

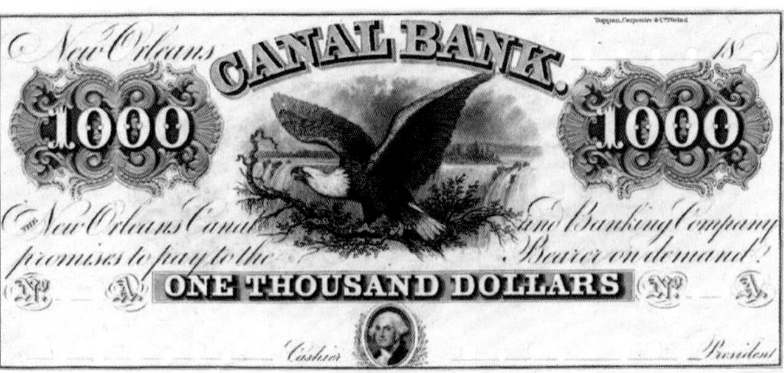

Back: Red-brown. ***Engraver:*** Toppan, Carpenter & Co. ***Comments:*** H-LA-105-G78a. 18__. 1840s–1850s.

Rarity: URS-1
Proof $10,000

$1,000 • W-LA-350-1000-G330

CC, CC

Back: Red-orange. ***Engraver:*** Rawdon, Wright, Hatch & Edson. ***Comments:*** H-LA-105-G80a. 18__. 1850s.

Rarity: URS-7
Unc-Rem $300

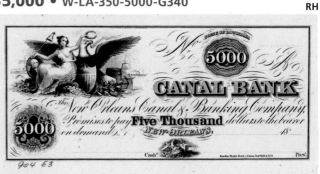

$5,000 • W-LA-350-5000-G340

RH

Engraver: Rawdon, Wright, Hatch & Edson. ***Comments:*** H-Unlisted. 18__. 1850s.

Rarity: URS-2
Proof $3,000

Notes Payable at the Bank of America in New York

$10 • W-LA-350-010-G350

HA

Engraver: Underwood, Bald & Spencer. ***Comments:*** H-LA-105-G84. 18__. 1830s.

Rarity: URS-9
Unc-Rem $60

$20 • W-LA-350-020-G360

CC

Engraver: Underwood, Bald & Spencer. ***Comments:*** H-LA-105-G86. 18__. 1830s.

Rarity: URS-8
Unc-Rem $75

Uncut Sheets

$5-$5-$5-$5 • W-LA-350-005.005.005.005-US010 RG

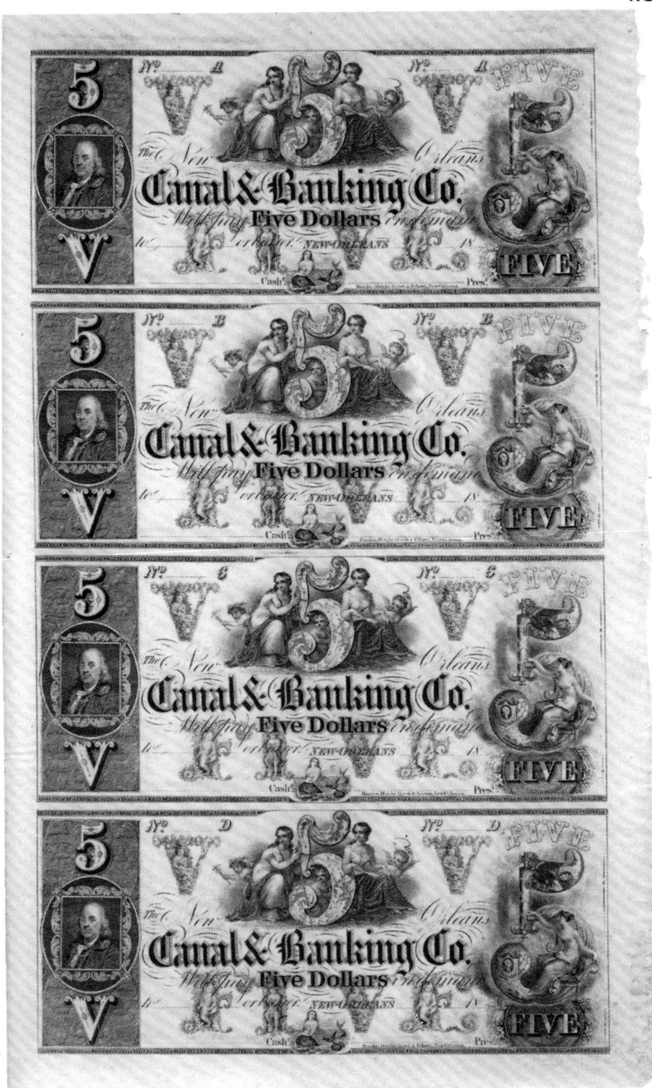

Engraver: Rawdon, Wright, Hatch & Edson. ***Comments:*** H-LA-105-G10, G10, G10, G10. All four notes identical. 18__. 1840s.

Rarity: URS-10
F $275

$5-$5-$5-$5 • W-LA-350-005.005.005.005-US020 RG

Back(s): Red-brown. ***Engraver:*** Toppan, Carpenter & Co. ***Comments:*** H-LA-105-G12a, G12a, G12a, G12a. All four notes identical. 18__. 1840s.

Rarity: URS-10
F $275

$10-$10-$10-$10 •

W-LA-350-010.010.010.010-US030

RG

Back(s): Red-brown. ***Engraver:*** Toppan, Carpenter & Co. ***Comments:*** H-LA-105-G22a, G22a, G22a, G22a. All four notes identical. 18__. 1840s.

Rarity: URS-9
F $275

$10-$10-$10-$10 •

W-LA-350-010.010.010.010-US040

RG

Back(s): Red-orange. ***Engraver:*** Rawdon, Wright, Hatch & Edson. ***Comments:*** H-LA-105-G24a, G24a, G24a, G24a. All four notes identical. 18__. 1850s.

Rarity: URS-10
F $275

$10-$10-$10-$10 •
W-LA-350-010.010.010.010-US050

RG

Tint(s): Red-orange. ***Engraver:*** National Bank Note Co. ***Comments:*** H-LA-105-G26a, G26a, G26a, G26a. All four notes identical. 1860s.

Rarity: URS-7
F $250

$20-$20 • W-LA-350-020.020-US060

RG

Engraver: Rawdon, Wright, Hatch & Edson. ***Comments:*** H-LA-105-G32, G32. Both notes identical. Partially printed plate. 18__. 1840s.

Rarity: URS-8
F $100

$20-$20-$20-$20 •
W-LA-350-020.020.020.020-US070

Engraver: Danforth, Underwood, Bald & Spencer. ***Comments:*** H-LA-105-G28, G28, G28, G28. All four notes identical. 18__. 1830s.

Rarity: URS-10
F $250

$20-$20-$20-$20 •

W-LA-350-020.020.020.020-US080

RG

Back(s): Red-brown. *Engraver:* Toppan, Carpenter & Co. *Comments:* H-LA-105-G34a, G34a, G34a, G34a. All four notes identical. 18__. 1840s.

Rarity: URS-10
F $175

$20-$20-$20-$20 •

W-LA-350-020.020.020.020-US090

Back(s): Red-orange. *Engraver:* Rawdon, Wright, Hatch & Edson. *Comments:* H-LA-105-G36a, G36a, G36a, G36a. All four notes identical. 18__. 1850s.

Rarity: URS-10
F $175

$20-$20-$50-$100 •

W-LA-350-020.020.050.100-US100

Vignette(s): ($20) Medallion head / Woman with shield and eagle / Female portrait. *($50)* Woman with shield and eagle / Medallion head. *($100)* Sailing ship / Portrait of boy. *Engraver:* Rawdon, Wright, Hatch & Edson. *Comments:* H-LA-105-G32, G32, G44, G56. First two notes identical. 18__. 1840s.

Rarity: URS-10
F $275

$20-$20-$50-$100 •

W-LA-350-020.020.050.100-US110

RG

HA

Tint(s): Blue. ***Back(s):*** Red-brown. ***Engraver:*** Rawdon, Wright, Hatch & Edson. ***Comments:*** H-LA-105-G32a, G32a, G44a, G56a. Similar to W-LA-350-020.020.050.100-US100. First two notes identical. 18__. 1840s.

Rarity: URS-8

F $350

$50-$50-$50-$50 •
W-LA-350-050.050.050.050-US120

RG

Back(s): Red-brown. ***Engraver:*** Toppan, Carpenter & Co. ***Comments:*** H-LA-105-G46a, G46a, G46a, G46a. All four notes identical. 18__. 1840s.

Rarity: URS-10
F $200

$50-$50-$50-$50 •
W-LA-350-050.050.050.050-US130

RG

Back(s): Red-orange. ***Engraver:*** Rawdon, Wright, Hatch & Edson. ***Comments:*** H-LA-105-G48a, G48a, G48a, G48a. All four notes identical. 18__. 1850s.

Rarity: URS-10
F $200

$50-$100 • W-LA-350-050.100-US140

RG

Engraver: Rawdon, Wright, Hatch & Edson. ***Comments:*** H-LA-105-G44, G56. Partially printed plate. 18__. 1840s.

Rarity: URS-7

F $250

$50-$100 • W-LA-350-050.100-US150

Vignette(s): ***($50)*** Woman seated / Woman seated with cargo on dock, Ships behind / Woman standing. ***($100)*** Portrait of George Washington / Palm trees and factories / Woman leaning on shield. ***Back(s):*** Red-orange. ***Engraver:*** Rawdon, Wright, Hatch & Edson. ***Comments:*** H-LA-105-G48a, G60a. 18__. 1850s.

Rarity: URS-7

F $250

$100-$100-$50-$50 • W-LA-350-100.100.050.050-US160

RG

Engraver: Underwood, Bald, Spencer & Hufty. ***Comments:*** H-LA-105-G52, G52, G40, G40. First two notes identical; last two notes identical. 18__. 1830s.

Rarity: URS-7

Proof $500

$100-$100-$100-$100 •
W-LA-350-100.100.100.100-US170

RG

Engraver: Toppan, Carpenter & Co. ***Comments:*** H-LA-105-G58a, G58a, G58a, G58a. All four notes identical. 18__. 1840s.

Rarity: URS-8

F $400

$100-$100-$100-$100 •
W-LA-350-100.100.100.100-US180

RG

Back(s): Red-orange. ***Engraver:*** Rawdon, Wright, Hatch & Edson. ***Comments:*** H-LA-105-G60a, G60a, G60a, G60a. All four notes identical. 18__. 1850s.

Rarity: URS-8

F $250

$500-$1,000 • W-LA-350-500.1000-US190

Vignette(s): ***($500)*** Two griffins / Woman reclining. ***($1,000)*** Medallion head / Ships / Helmeted medallion head. ***Tint(s):*** Blue. ***Back(s):*** Red-brown. ***Engraver:*** Rawdon, Wright, Hatch & Edson. ***Comments:*** H-LA-105-G66a, G76a. 18__. 1840s.

Rarity: URS-8

F $600

$500-$1,000 • W-LA-350-500.1000-US200

RG

Back(s): Red-orange. ***Engraver:*** Rawdon, Wright, Hatch & Edson. ***Comments:*** H-LA-105-G70a, G80a. 18__. 1850s.

Rarity: URS-8

F $500

Uncut Sheets Payable at the Bank of America in New York

$10-$10-$10-$20 • W-LA-350-010.010.010.020-US210

RG

Engraver: Underwood, Bald & Spencer. ***Comments:*** H-LA-105-G84, G84, G84, G86. First three notes identical. 18__. 1830s.

Rarity: URS-7

F $175

Non-Valid Issues

$5 • W-LA-350-005-C010

Engraver: Danforth, Underwood, Bald & Spencer. ***Comments:*** H-LA-105-C6. Counterfeit of W-LA-350-005-G010. 18__. 1830s.

Rarity: —

$10 • W-LA-350-010-C090

Engraver: Rawdon, Wright, Hatch & Edson. ***Comments:*** H-LA-105-C24a. Counterfeit of W-LA-350-010-G090. 18__. 1850s.

Rarity: —

$20 • W-LA-350-020-C120a

Engraver: Rawdon, Wright, Hatch & Edson. ***Comments:*** H-LA-105-C32a. Counterfeit of W-LA-350-020-G120a. 18__. 1840s.

Rarity: —

$20 • W-LA-350-020-C140

CC, CC

Engraver: Rawdon, Wright, Hatch & Edson. ***Comments:*** H-LA-105-C36a. Counterfeit of W-LA-350-020-G140. 18__. 1850s.

Rarity: URS-6

F $150

$50 • W-LA-350-050-C190

RH, RH

Back: Red-brown. ***Engraver:*** Rawdon, Wright, Hatch & Edson. ***Comments:*** H-LA-105-C48a. Counterfeit of W-LA-350-050-G190. 18__. 1850s.

Rarity: URS-4

G $200

$100 • W-LA-350-100-N010

Left: 100 / Medallion head / 100. ***Center:*** C / Train / C. ***Right:*** Portrait of Benjamin Franklin / Two women. ***Comments:*** H-LA-105-N5. 18__. 1847.

Rarity: —

New Orleans Gas Light and Banking Company

1835–1845

W-LA-360

History: The New Orleans Gas Light and Banking Company (also seen as the Gas Bank) was chartered in April 1835 with an authorized capital of $6,000,000. James H. Caldwell was the president of the bank, and with the banking privileges bestowed upon the company, he was able to complete a gas-light system in New Orleans, considered to be the best street lights in America to that time.[13] That same year the company bought the facilities of the branch bank of the closed second Bank of the United States, W-LA-180, located in New Orleans.

Branches for this bank were planned for Alexandria, Harrisonburg, Napoleonville, Port Hudson, and Springfield, with the expectation that similar gas-light systems would be put into place in those towns. However, this never occurred, and in 1845 the banking privileges of the company were surrendered.

Numismatic Commentary: Proof and issued notes from this bank are extremely rare, with less than half a dozen reported.

Valid Issues

$5 • W-LA-360-005-G010

Left: FIVE. ***Center:*** V / Woman seated next to eagle / V / Running deer. ***Right:*** Hercules / 5. ***Engraver:*** Rawdon, Wright, Hatch & Edson. ***Comments:*** H-LA-115-G2. 18__. 1830s–1840s.

Rarity: *None known*

$10 • W-LA-360-010-G020

Left: TEN. ***Center:*** X / Woman seated next to eagle / X / Running deer. ***Right:*** Hercules / 10. ***Engraver:*** Rawdon, Wright, Hatch & Edson. ***Comments:*** H-LA-115-G4. 18__. 1830s–1840s.

Rarity: *None known*

$20 • W-LA-360-020-G030

Left: TWENTY. ***Center:*** XX / Woman seated next to eagle / XX / Running deer. ***Right:*** Hercules / 20. ***Engraver:*** Rawdon, Wright, Hatch & Edson. ***Comments:*** H-LA-115-G6. 18__. 1830s–1840s.

Rarity: *None known*

Notes Payable at the Bank of America in New York

$10 • W-LA-360-010-G040

HA

Engraver: Underwood, Bald & Spencer. ***Comments:*** H-Unlisted. 18__. 1830s–1840s.

Rarity: URS-4
F $2,000
Selected auction price: Heritage Auctions, April 23, 2015, Lot 19091, Proof $1,410

$50 • W-LA-360-050-G050

CC

Engraver: Underwood, Bald & Spencer. ***Comments:*** H-LA-115-G16. 18__. 1830s–1840s.

Rarity: URS-2
Proof $3,500

$100 • W-LA-360-100-G060

Left: Medallion head / 100 / Medallion head vertically. ***Center:*** Medallion head bearing 100 / Woman / Medallion head bearing 100. ***Right:*** Medallion head / 100 / Medallion head vertically. ***Engraver:*** Underwood, Bald & Spencer. ***Comments:*** H-LA-115-G18. 18__. 1830s–1840s.

Rarity: URS-2
Proof $3,500

New Orleans Improvement and Banking Company

1836–1842

W-LA-370

History: The New Orleans Improvement and Banking Company was chartered in February 1836 with an authorized capital of $2,000,000. The company was granted banking privileges for the purpose of raising funds to construct the St. Louis Hotel. During the city banking crisis of 1842, the bank went into liquidation, but its affairs continued to be wrapped up until 1846.

Numismatic Commentary: Issued notes from this bank are scarce, but notes are collectible in the $5, $10, $20, and $100 denominations. The $50, $500, and $1,000 notes are rare.

Valid Issues

$5 • W-LA-370-005-G010

ANS

Engraver: Rawdon, Wright & Hatch. ***Comments:*** H-LA-120-G2. 18__. 1830s–1840s.

Rarity: URS-8
G $150; **F** $275

$10 • W-LA-370-010-G020

ANS

Engraver: Rawdon, Wright & Hatch. ***Comments:*** H-LA-120-G4. 18__. 1830s–1840s.

Rarity: URS-8
G $150; **F** $275

$20 • W-LA-370-020-G030

CC

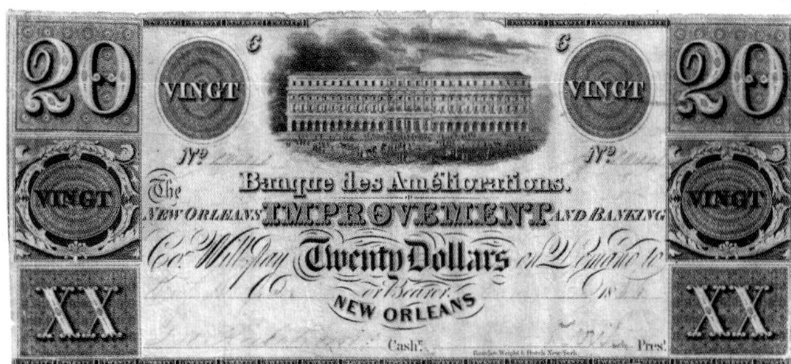

Engraver: Rawdon, Wright & Hatch. ***Comments:*** H-LA-120-G6. 18__. 1830s–1840s.

Rarity: URS-8
G $275

$50 • **W-LA-370-050-G040** RH

Engraver: Rawdon, Wright & Hatch. ***Comments:*** H-LA-120-G8. 18__. 1830s–1840s.

Rarity: URS-6
G $250; **F** $375

$100 • **W-LA-370-100-G050** HA

Engraver: Rawdon, Wright & Hatch. ***Comments:*** H-LA-120-G10. 18__. 1830s–1840s.

Rarity: URS-7
G $250; **F** $375

$500 • **W-LA-370-500-G060** HA

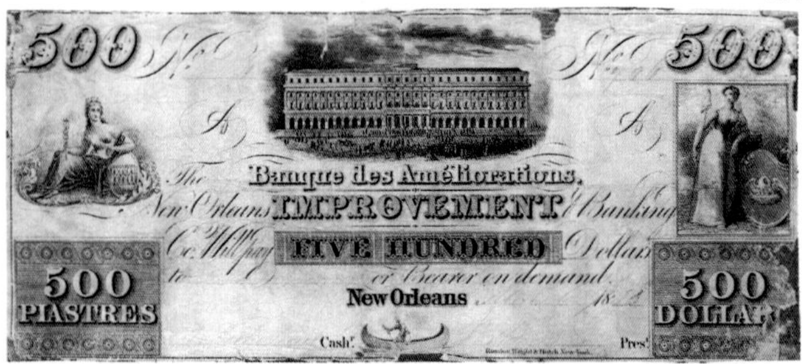

Engraver: Rawdon, Wright & Hatch. ***Comments:*** H-LA-120-G12. 18__. 1830s–1840s.

Rarity: URS-3
F $2,000
Selected auction price: Heritage Auctions, October 21, 2015, Lot 18354, F $1,762

$1,000 • **W-LA-370-1000-G070** HA

Engraver: Rawdon, Wright & Hatch. ***Comments:*** H-LA-120-G14. 18__. 1830s–1840s.

Rarity: URS-3
F $2,850
Selected auction price: Heritage Auctions, April 23, 2015, Lot 19093, F $2,820

New Orleans, Jackson and Great Northern Rail Road Company

1861 and 1862

W-LA-380

History: The New Orleans, Jackson and Great Northern Rail Road Company was authorized under acts of December 20, 1861, and January 22, 1862, "to issue notes for circulation to the amount of three hundred thousand dollars to be redeemable at their offices in Canton and New Orleans."

See also listing under Mississippi, W-MS-120.

Numismatic Commentary: Notes from this railroad company are common and available to collectors. After taking control of the city, Union general Benjamin Butler allowed this company to continue circulating its scrip, to put the railroad in service to the Union.

Valid Issues

$1 • **W-LA-380-001-G010** ANS

Comments: H-Unlisted. Nov. 16th, 1864.

Rarity: URS-8
F $100

Collectors and Researchers:

If you have new information about any banks or notes listed in this volume, contact Whitman Publishing, Attn: Obsolete Paper Money, 3101 Clairmont Road, Suite G, Atlanta, GA 30329.

$1 • **W-LA-380-001-G020** SI

Comments: H-Unlisted. Nov. 16th, 1864.

Rarity: URS-8

F $100

$1.50 • **W-LA-380-001.50-G030** SI

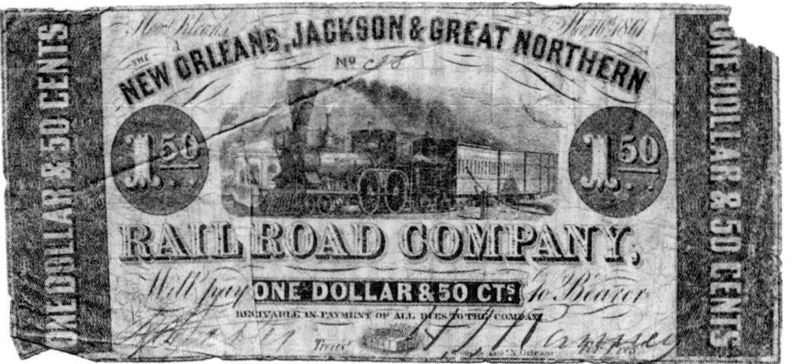

Comments: H-Unlisted. Nov. 16th, 1864.

Rarity: URS-8

F $100

$1.50 • **W-LA-380-001.50-G040** SI

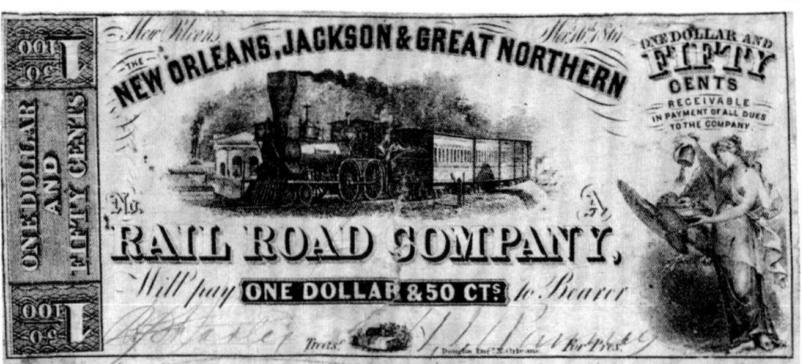

Comments: H-Unlisted. Nov. 16th, 1864.

Rarity: URS-8

F $100

$2 • **W-LA-380-002-G050** ANS

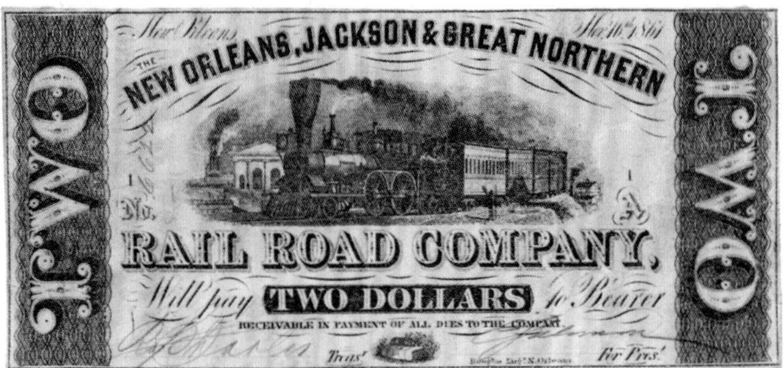

Comments: H-Unlisted. Nov. 16th, 1864.

Rarity: URS-9

F $75

$2 • **W-LA-380-002-G060** ANS

Comments: H-Unlisted. Nov. 16th, 1864.

Rarity: URS-8

F $100

$3 • **W-LA-380-003-G070** ANS

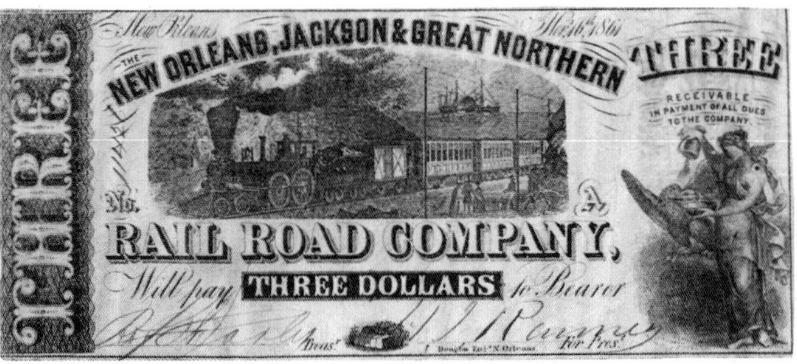

Comments: H-Unlisted. Nov. 16th, 1864.

Rarity: URS-8

F $100

$3 • **W-LA-380-003-G070a** ANS

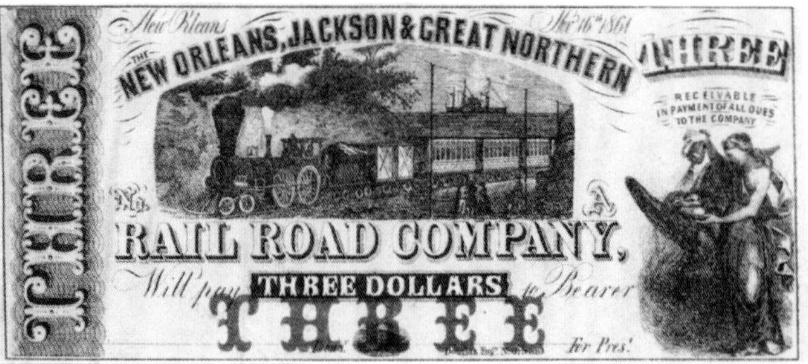

Overprint: Blue THREE. ***Comments:*** H-Unlisted. Similar to W-LA-380-003-G070. Nov. 16th, 1864.

Rarity: URS-8

F $100

$3 • **W-LA-380-003-G080** ANS

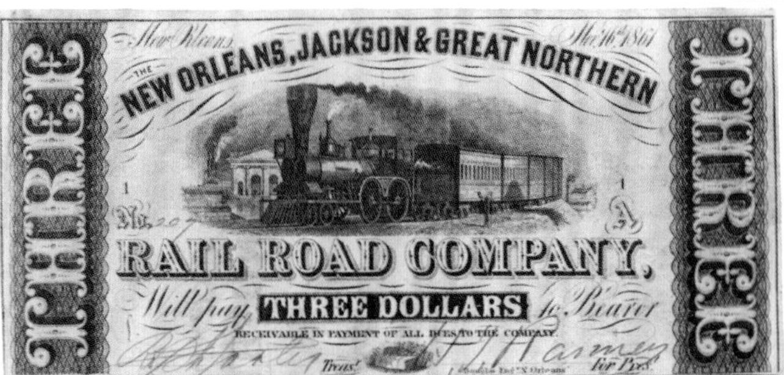

Comments: H-Unlisted. Nov. 16th, 1864.

Rarity: URS-9

F $75

Planters Bank

1811–1826

W-LA-390

History: The Planters Bank was chartered in April 1811 with an authorized capital of $600,000. The bank was considered to be a well-run institution. In 1819 there was a scandal when the cashier of the bank, B. Blanchard, disappeared, and it was thought that he had been assassinated. It was also rumored that he had absconded with sums of money. An investigation revealed the bank's affairs to be in order, but there was a run on the tellers. The bank was able to satisfy all presenters of currency at that time. It was eventually discovered that the late cashier Blanchard did indeed fall under foul play.

In 1820 the bank suspended operations, and the charter officially expired in 1826.

Numismatic Commentary: Issued notes are extremely rare with less than half a dozen known.

Valid Issues

$5 • W-LA-390-005-G010

RH

Engraver: W. Harrison. ***Comments:*** H-LA-130-G8. 18__. 1810s–1820s.

Rarity: URS-2

F $4,000

$10 • W-LA-390-010-G020

RH

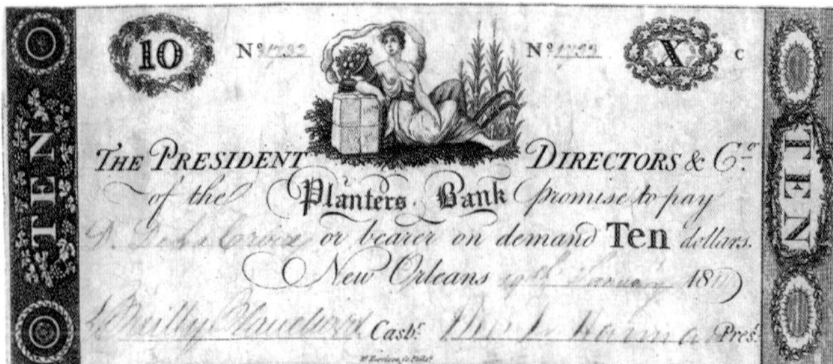

Engraver: W. Harrison. ***Comments:*** H-LA-130-G12. 18__. 1810s–1820s.

Rarity: URS-2

F $5,000

$20 • W-LA-390-020-G030

Engraver: W. Harrison. ***Comments:*** H-LA-130-G16. No description available. 18__. 1810s–1820s.

Rarity: *None known*

$50 • W-LA-390-050-G040

Engraver: W. Harrison. ***Comments:*** H-LA-130-G20. No description available. 18__. 1810s–1820s.

Rarity: *None known*

$100 • W-LA-390-100-G050

RH

Engraver: W. Harrison. ***Comments:*** H-LA-130-G24. 18__. 1810s–1820s.

Rarity: URS-1

F $6,000

Southern Bank

1854–1879

W-LA-400

History: The Southern Bank was chartered in 1854 with an authorized capital of $1,250,000. The first president was John Edgerton, and the first cashier was James L. Wibray. The first installment of the capital was due on July 1 of that year. On November 11, Edgerton retired and was replaced in the presidency by F. Rodewald.

In 1857 these values were given: capital $1,250,000; bills in circulation $305,575; specie $242,269; real estate $66,668. In 1860 Thomas Layton took on the position of cashier.

The Southern Bank survived the Civil War and finally closed in 1879.

Numismatic Commentary: Proof and issued notes of this bank are extremely rare, with less than a dozen known.

Valid Issues

$5 • W-LA-400-005-G010

RH

Back: Red-orange. ***Engraver:*** Rawdon, Wright, Hatch & Edson. ***Comments:*** H-LA-140-G2a. 18__. 1850s.

Rarity: URS-2

Proof $4,500

$5 • W-LA-400-005-G010a

RH, RH

Back: Green. ***Engraver:*** Rawdon, Wright, Hatch & Edson / ABNCo. monogram. ***Comments:*** H-LA-140-G2b. Similar to W-LA-400-005-G010 but with additional engraver imprint. 18__. 1850s.

Rarity: URS-3
G $1,500

$10 • W-LA-400-010-G020

HA, RH

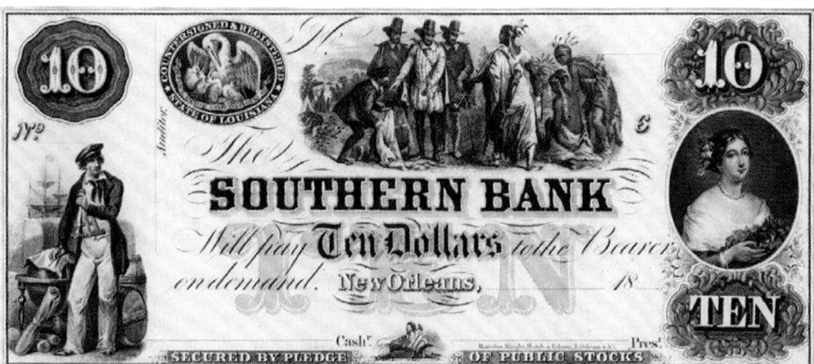

Back: Red-orange. ***Engraver:*** Rawdon, Wright, Hatch & Edson. ***Comments:*** H-LA-140-G4a. 18__. 1850s.

Rarity: URS-2
Proof $4,000
Selected auction price: Heritage Auctions, April 23, 2015, Lot 19095, Proof $3,290

$10 • W-LA-400-010-G020a

Engraver: Rawdon, Wright, Hatch & Edson / ABNCo. monogram. ***Comments:*** H-LA-140-G4b. Similar to W-LA-400-010-G020 but with additional engraver imprint. 18__. 1850s.

Rarity: *None known*

$20 • W-LA-400-020-G030

RH

Back: Red-orange. ***Engraver:*** Rawdon, Wright, Hatch & Edson. ***Comments:*** H-LA-140-G6a. 18__. 1850s.

Rarity: URS-2
Proof $2,000

$20 • W-LA-400-020-G030a

Engraver: Rawdon, Wright, Hatch & Edson / ABNCo. monogram. ***Comments:*** H-LA-140-G6b. Similar to W-LA-400-020-G030 but with additional engraver imprint. 18__. 1850s.

Rarity: *None known*

$50 • W-LA-400-050-G040

Left: FIFTY / State arms / Two sea horses. ***Center:*** 50 / Liberty reclining draped in flag, Globe, Eagle, Ships. ***Bottom center:*** Cogwheels, bales. ***Right:*** 50 / Portrait of George Washington / 50. ***Back:*** Red-orange. ***Engraver:*** Rawdon, Wright, Hatch & Edson. ***Comments:*** H-LA-140-G8a. 18__. 1850s.

Rarity: *None known*

$50 • W-LA-400-050-G040a

Engraver: Rawdon, Wright, Hatch & Edson / ABNCo. monogram. ***Comments:*** H-LA-140-G8b. Similar to W-LA-400-050-G040 but with additional engraver imprint. 18__. 1850s.

Rarity: *None known*

$100 • W-LA-400-100-G050

RH

Back: Red-orange. ***Engraver:*** Rawdon, Wright, Hatch & Edson. ***Comments:*** H-LA-140-G10a. Back of note shown. 18__. 1850s.

Rarity: URS-2
F $6,000

$100 • W-LA-400-100-G050a

Left: State arms / Male portrait / 100. ***Center:*** Train, Woman reclining with shield, strongbox, and bales, Factory and ship, Two milkmaids and two cows / Shield. ***Right:*** 100 / Indian woman seated on rock with baby / 100. ***Engraver:*** Rawdon, Wright, Hatch & Edson / ABNCo. monogram. ***Comments:*** H-LA-140-G10b. Similar to W-LA-400-100-G050 but with additional engraver imprint. 18__. 1850s.

Rarity: *None known*

$500 • **W-LA-400-500-G060**

Left: 500 / Female portrait. ***Center:*** State arms / Woman and eagle floating in clouds with cornucopia and shield. ***Right:*** 500 / Steamship, Sailing ship. ***Back:*** Red-orange. ***Engraver:*** Rawdon, Wright, Hatch & Edson. ***Comments:*** H-LA-140-G12a. 18__. 1850s.

Rarity: *None known*

Non-Valid Issues

$50 • **W-LA-400-050-S010** RH, RH

Back: Red-brown. ***Engraver:*** Draper, Toppan & Co. ***Comments:*** H-LA-140-S5. 18__. 1850s.

Rarity: URS-2
F $2,000

Union Bank of Louisiana {1st}

1832–1842

W-LA-410

History: The Union Bank of Louisiana was chartered in April 1832 with an authorized capital of $7,000,000 funded by bonds provided by the state. Throughout its duration, the Union Bank garnered much attention and admiration, shown in part by the fact that several institutions in the West copied the organization and makeup of the bank to create their own companies. This was done also in preparation for the closing of the Bank of the United States, in order "to prevent the damage which otherwise might result from the withdrawal of the funds of the United States Bank, should that institution fail to obtain a renewal of its charter."[14]

The subscription books were immediately overwhelmed. The bank was incredibly successful for the first five years it was in operation and was considered to be one of the most prosperous banks in the city. It survived the Panic of 1837, but in 1842 the crisis of that time overtook it, and it failed "with its assets in such shape that the collection of anything from them was a slow and difficult matter."[15] Its circulation slowly dropped from $477,170 in 1842 to $68,335 in 1844, and finally down to $25,935 in 1849. It took over a decade for the affairs of the bank to be wound up.

The Union Bank of Louisiana had its branch bank located in Clinton, W-LA-055.

Numismatic Commentary: Proofs from this bank are extremely rare, as only half a dozen are known to have been discovered.

Remaining at the American Bank Note Co. archives as of 2003 was a $10-$10-$10-$10 back plate, a $20-$20-$50-$100 back plate, and a $5-$5-$5-$5 back plate.

Valid Issues

$5 • **W-LA-410-005-G010** RH

Engraver: Rawdon, Wright, Hatch & Co. ***Comments:*** H-LA-145-G8. 18__. 1830s–1840s.

Rarity: URS-3
Proof $2,500

$5 • **W-LA-410-005-G010a** RH, RH

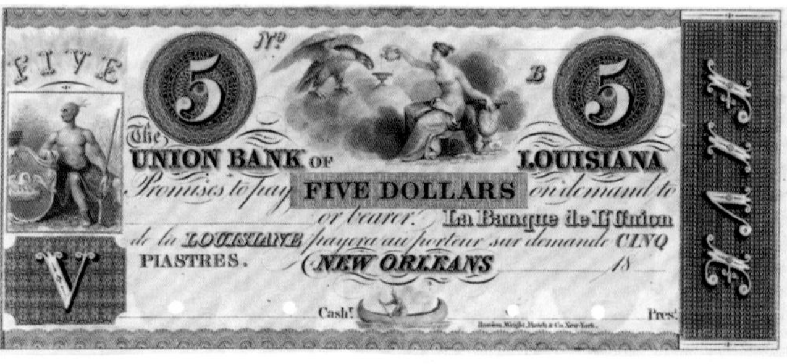

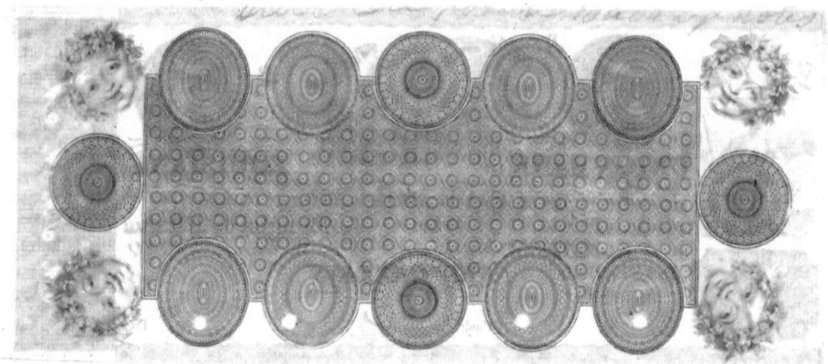

Back: Red-brown cherubs. ***Engraver:*** Rawdon, Wright, Hatch & Co. ***Comments:*** H-Unlisted. Similar to W-LA-410-005-G010. Trial Proof. 18__. 1830s–1840s.

Rarity: URS-2
Proof $3,000

$10 • **W-LA-410-010-G020** RH

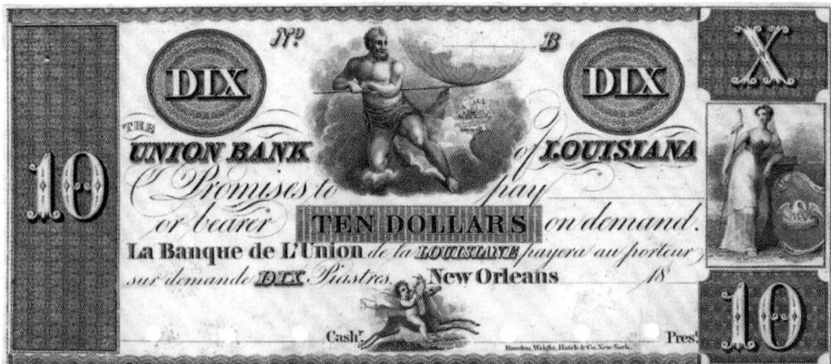

Engraver: Rawdon, Wright, Hatch & Co. ***Comments:*** H-LA-145-G10. 18__. 1830s–1840s.

Rarity: URS-2
Proof $4,500

$20 • **W-LA-410-020-G030** RH

Engraver: Rawdon, Wright, Hatch & Co. ***Comments:*** H-LA-145-G12. 18__. 1830s–1840s.

Rarity: URS-2
Proof $4,000

$50 • **W-LA-410-050-G040** RH

Engraver: Rawdon, Wright, Hatch & Co. ***Comments:*** H-LA-145-G14. 18__. 1830s–1840s.

Rarity: URS-1
Proof $4,500

$100 • **W-LA-410-100-G050** RH

Engraver: Rawdon, Wright, Hatch & Co. ***Comments:*** H-LA-145-G16. 18__. 1830s–1840s.

Rarity: URS-1
Proof $5,000

$500 • **W-LA-410-500-G060** RH

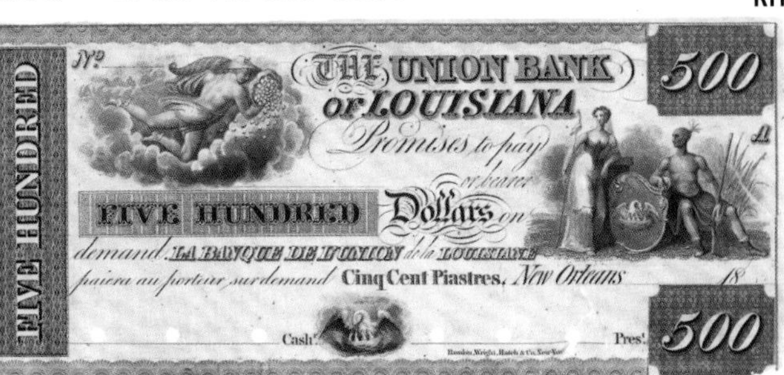

Engraver: Rawdon, Wright, Hatch & Co. ***Comments:*** H-LA-145-G18. 18__. 1830s–1840s.

Rarity: URS-1
Proof $7,500

$1,000 • **W-LA-410-1000-G070** RH

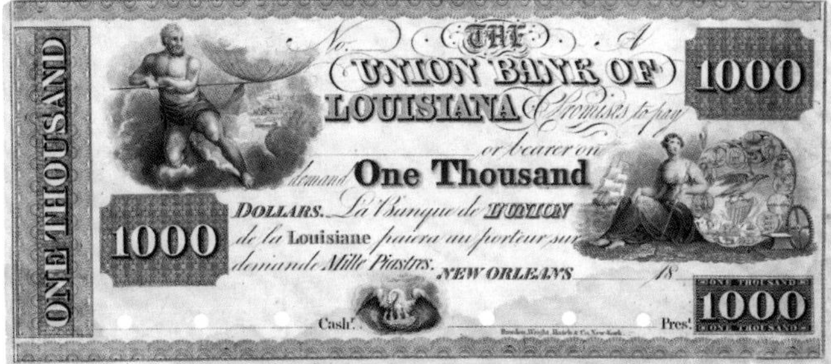

Engraver: Rawdon, Wright, Hatch & Co. ***Comments:*** H-LA-145-G18. 18__. 1830s–1840s.

Rarity: URS-1
Proof $10,000

Non-Valid Issues

$20 • **W-LA-410-020-C030**

Engraver: Rawdon, Wright, Hatch & Co. ***Comments:*** H-LA-145-C12. Counterfeit of W-LA-410-020-G030. 18__. 1839.

Rarity: —

Union Bank of Louisiana {2nd}

1854–1871

W-LA-420

History: After the failure of the first bank of the same name, a new bank was organized in 1853 and finally chartered in 1854. Phenix W. Wood was selected as cashier, and the bank was established at 121 Canal Street. In 1855 the capital was $1,370,000, and the president was Alfred Penn. In 1857 George A. Freret was the cashier. That year these values were given: capital $1,500,000; bills in circulation $558,200; specie $601,213; real estate $54,474.

The Union Bank finally closed in 1871.

Numismatic Commentary: Proof and issued notes from this series are extremely rare, with about a dozen notes known.

VALID ISSUES

$5 • W-LA-420-005-G010

HA

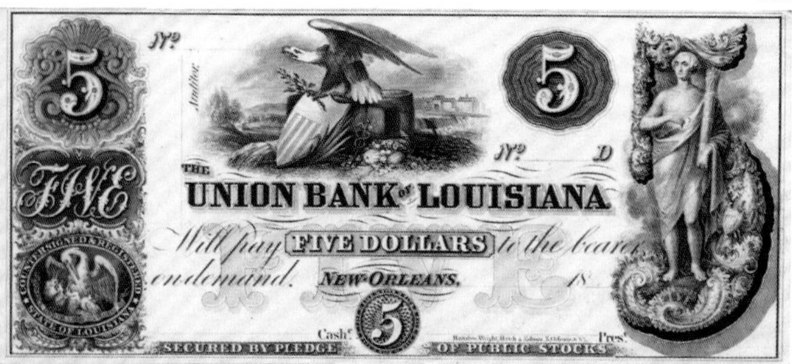

Back: Red-orange eagle. ***Engraver:*** Rawdon, Wright, Hatch & Edson. ***Comments:*** H-LA-150-G2a. 18__. 1850s.

Rarity: URS-2
Proof $4,500
Selected auction price: Heritage Auctions, October 21, 2015, Lot 18361, Choice About New $4,465

$5 • W-LA-420-005-G010a

RH

Back: Red-orange eagle. ***Engraver:*** Rawdon, Wright, Hatch & Edson / ABNCo. monogram. ***Comments:*** H-Unlisted. Similar to W-LA-420-005-G010 but with additional engraver imprint. 18__. 1850s.

Rarity: —

How to Read the Whitman Numbering System

$1 • W-AL-020-001-G010a

Denomination: Face value of the note shown.

W: Whitman number. This number is a sortable code unique to each bank and note.

AL: Abbreviation for the state under study.

020: Numerical designation specific to each bank.

001: The denomination in dollars.

G010a: G indicates a good or valid note. Other categories are indicated thus: C (counterfeit); R (raised); S (spurious); N (not-attributed); A (altered). Numbers are assigned starting with 010, 020, et seq. Terminal letters following the number indicate variations of a note: a series of different colored overprints, tints, payees, etc., all on the same design of note. For more information, see the "How to Use This Book" section at the front of the volume, page xiv.

$10 • W-LA-420-010-G020

HA

Back: Red-orange eagle. ***Engraver:*** Rawdon, Wright, Hatch & Edson. ***Comments:*** H-LA-150-G4a. 18__. 1850s.

Rarity: URS-2
F $1,200
Selected auction price(s): Heritage Auctions, January 6, 2016, Lot 18562, F $1,527; Heritage Auctions, April 23, 2015, Lot 19084, VF $3,290

$20 • W-LA-420-020-G030

Left: Minerva holding spear with shield, globe, pedestal / TWENTY. ***Center:*** State arms / "Signing of the Declaration of Independence." ***Right:*** XX / Female portrait / 20. ***Back:*** Red-orange eagle. ***Engraver:*** Rawdon, Wright, Hatch & Edson. ***Comments:*** H-LA-150-G6a. 18__. 1850s.

Rarity: *None known*

$50 • W-LA-420-050-G040

CC, CC

Back: Red-orange eagle. ***Engraver:*** Rawdon, Wright, Hatch & Edson. ***Comments:*** H-LA-150-G8a. 18__. 1850s.

Rarity: URS-3
F $2,500; **Prop. Proof** $1,000

$50 • **W-LA-420-050-G050** HA, RH

Back: Red-orange eagle. ***Engraver:*** Rawdon, Wright, Hatch & Edson / ABNCo. monogram. ***Comments:*** H-LA-150-G10a. 18__. 1850s–1860s.

Rarity: URS-2
VF $4,700
Selected auction price: Heritage Auctions, April 23, 2015, Lot 19096, VF $4,700

$100 • **W-LA-420-100-G060** RH, RH

Back: Red-orange eagle. ***Engraver:*** Rawdon, Wright, Hatch & Edson. ***Comments:*** H-LA-150-G12a. 18__. 1850s.

Rarity: URS-2
G $1,500

$500 • **W-LA-420-500-G070** RH

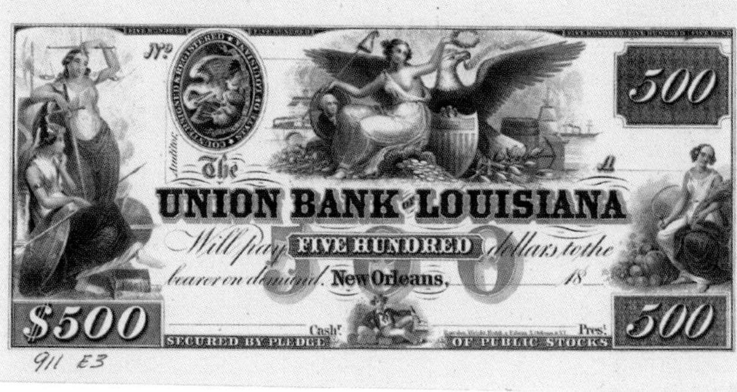

Back: Red-orange eagle. ***Engraver:*** Rawdon, Wright, Hatch & Edson. ***Comments:*** H-LA-150-G14a. 18__. 1850s.

Rarity: URS-2
Prop. Proof $2,000

Post-Occupation Notes

$5 • **W-LA-420-005-G080** RH

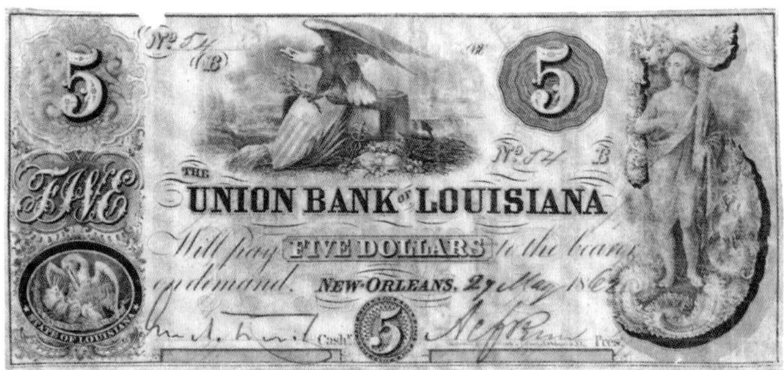

Back: Blue eagle. ***Engraver:*** Rawdon, Wright, Hatch & Edson / ABNCo. monogram. ***Comments:*** H-Unlisted. 18__. 1850s.

Rarity: URS-2
F $1,500

$20 • **W-LA-420-020-G090** RH, RH

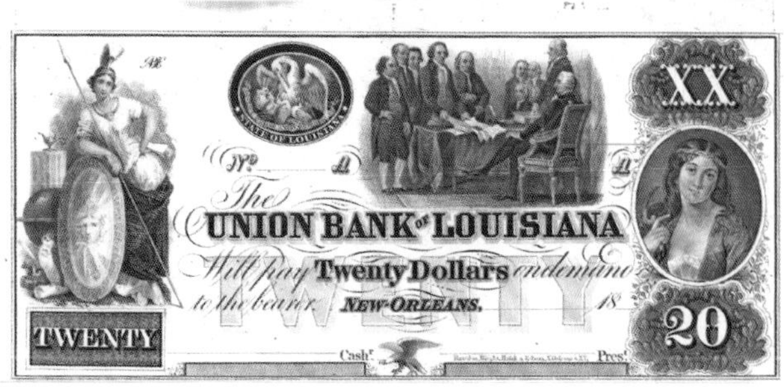

Back: Blue eagle. ***Engraver:*** Rawdon, Wright, Hatch & Edson / ABNCo. monogram. ***Comments:*** H-Unlisted. 18__. 1850s.

Rarity: URS-3
VG $2,000; **Prop. Proof** $1,000

$50 • **W-LA-420-050-G100** HA

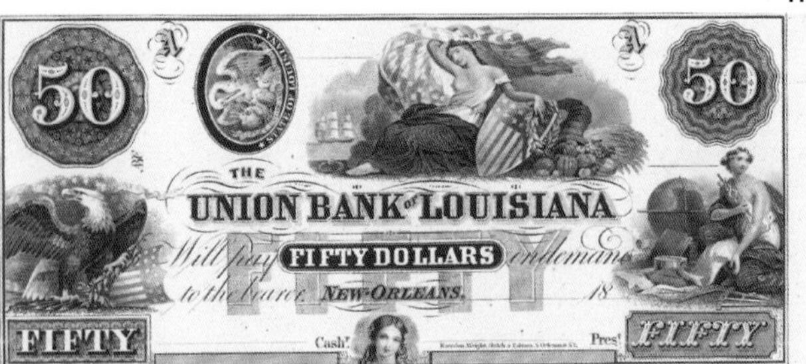

Back: Blue eagle. ***Engraver:*** Rawdon, Wright, Hatch & Edson / ABNCo. monogram. ***Comments:*** H-Unlisted. 18__. 1860s.

Rarity: —

$100 • **W-LA-420-100-G110** RH

Back: Blue eagle. ***Engraver:*** Rawdon, Wright, Hatch & Edson / ABNCo. monogram. ***Comments:*** H-Unlisted. 18__. 1850s.

Rarity: URS-3
Prop. Proof $1,000

Non-Valid Issues

$2 • **W-LA-420-002-N010**

Center: Mechanic with sledge, Train. ***Comments:*** H-LA-150-N5. 18__. 1850s.

Rarity: *None known*

$3 • **W-LA-420-003-N020**

Center: Mechanic with sledge, Train. ***Comments:*** H-LA-150-N10. 18__. 1850s.

Rarity: *None known*

$5 • **W-LA-420-005-N030**

Center: Mechanic with sledge, Train. ***Comments:*** H-LA-150-N15. 18__. 1850s.

Rarity: *None known*

$10 • **W-LA-420-010-N040**

Center: Mechanic with sledge, Train. ***Comments:*** H-LA-150-N20. 18__. 1850s.

Rarity: *None known*

$50 • **W-LA-420-050-C040** CC, CC

CC

Back: Red-brown eagle. ***Engraver:*** Rawdon, Wright, Hatch & Edson. ***Comments:*** H-LA-150-C8a. Counterfeit of W-LA-420-050-G040. 18__. 1850s.

Rarity: URS-3
F $650

$100 • **W-LA-420-100-S010** HA, RH

Back: Red-brown. ***Engraver:*** Toppan, Carpenter & Co. ***Comments:*** H-LA-150-S10. 18__. 1850s.

Rarity: URS-2
F $2,500
Selected auction price: Heritage Auctions, April 23, 2015, Lot 19097, F $2,467

W.A. Britton and Company Banking House

1835–1860s

W-LA-430

History: The W.A. Britton and Company Banking House was actually a brokerage and exchange business located in Natchez, Mississippi, and was not chartered as a bank of issue. It closed down during the Civil War.

See also listing under Mississippi, W-MS-680.

Numismatic Commentary: Issued $1, $2, and $3 notes from this banking house are available to the collector. Proofs are extremely rare.

Valid Issues

$1 • W-LA-430-001-G010

RH

Engraver: Underwood, Bald, Spencer & Hufty / Danforth, Underwood & Co. ***Comments:*** H-Unlisted. 184_. 1840s.

Rarity: URS-2
Proof $2,500

$2 • W-LA-430-002-G020

RH

Engraver: Underwood, Bald, Spencer & Hufty / Danforth, Underwood & Co. ***Comments:*** H-Unlisted. 184_. 1840s.

Rarity: URS-1
Proof $3,000

$3 • W-LA-430-003-G030

RH

Engraver: Underwood, Bald, Spencer & Hufty / Danforth, Underwood & Co. ***Comments:*** H-Unlisted. 184_. 1840s.

Rarity: URS-1
Proof $3,000

$5 • W-LA-430-005-G040

RH

Engraver: Underwood, Bald, Spencer & Hufty / Danforth, Underwood & Co. ***Comments:*** H-Unlisted. 184_. 1840s.

Rarity: URS-2
Proof $2,000

$10 • W-LA-430-010-G050

RH

Engraver: Underwood, Bald, Spencer & Hufty / Danforth, Underwood & Co. ***Comments:*** H-Unlisted. 18__. 1840s.

Rarity: URS-2
Proof $3,000

$20 • W-LA-430-020-G060

RH

Engraver: Underwood, Bald, Spencer & Hufty / Danforth, Underwood & Co. ***Comments:*** H-Unlisted. 18__. 1840s.

Rarity: URS-1
Proof $4,000

$50 • W-LA-430-050-G070

RH

Engraver: Underwood, Bald, Spencer & Hufty / Danforth, Underwood & Co. ***Comments:*** H-Unlisted. 18__. 1840s.

Rarity: URS-1
Proof $5,000

$100 • W-LA-430-100-G080 RH

Engraver: Underwood, Bald, Spencer & Hufty / Danforth, Underwood & Co. ***Comments:*** H-Unlisted. 18__. 1840s.

Rarity: URS-1
Proof $6,000

Saint Francisville, Louisiana

Established in 1809, Saint Francisville was developed along a ridge overlooking the Mississippi River. It became the center of the plantation countryside surrounding it, both culturally and commercially. In 1810 the city was the capital of the Republic of West Florida, part of an independent republic put together by local planters who ousted the Spanish government for 74 days. Later the land was annexed to the Territory of Orleans and became a possession of the United States (which had acquired the land as part of the Louisiana Purchase of 1803).

Saint Francisville became the seat of the West Feliciana Parish government in 1824 when the Feliciana Parish was split in two (see also Clinton, Louisiana). During the Civil War, Saint Francisville became the burial grounds of Union navy officer John Hart, who was buried by Confederate army officer William Leake. Leake arranged for the burial after Hart died on his ship in a Union blockade on the Mississippi River. The event is known as "The Day the War Stopped" (at least briefly) and is reenacted every year.

Bank of Louisiana (branch)

1824–1863

W-LA-440

History: On April 7, 1824, the Bank of Louisiana was chartered with an authorized capital of $4,000,000. Half of this amount was subscribed to by the state. It was required that five branches be opened. The branch located in Saint Francisville was established to service the parishes of East and West Feliciana and Pointe Coupee. The authorized capital was $200,000. On June 13, 1863, three commissioners were assigned to put the liquidation of the Bank of Louisiana into effect.

The Bank of Louisiana had its parent bank located in New Orleans, W-LA-140, and branch banks located in Alexandria, W-LA-010, Baton Rouge, W-LA-030, Donaldsonville, W-LA-060, and Saint Martinville, W-LA-460.

Numismatic Commentary: No bank notes for this branch have been discovered, but private scrip dated 1837 bears "Redeemable in current bank notes at the office of the Bank of Louisiana in St. Francisville."

Louisiana State Bank (branch)

1818–1825

W-LA-450

History: The Louisiana State Bank was chartered in 1818. By March 14 of that year, the state had subscribed to $500,000 of the authorized $2,000,000 capital of the bank. A bonus of $100,000 was required to be paid to the state before the bank could commence operations. Of the capital stock, $200,000 was reserved for the branch at Saint Francisville. In 1825 a law was passed discontinuing the branch.

The Louisiana State Bank had its parent bank located in New Orleans, W-LA-280, and branch banks located in Alexandria, W-LA-020, Baton Rouge, W-LA-040, Donaldsonville, W-LA-070, New Orleans (second municipality), W-LA-290, Saint Martinville, W-LA-470, and Shreveport, W-LA-490.

Numismatic Commentary: No bank notes for this branch have been reported.

Saint Martinville, Louisiana

The Attakapan people lived in the area that later made up Saint Martinville before colonists arrived. In 1699 French explorers began to travel through the territory, and soon a trading post was founded on the banks of the Bayou Teche. More French settlers arrived in 1765 and were assigned the area by Jean-Jacques Blaise d'Abbadie. Joseph Broussard led 15 families to settle in the land, and by 1767 the trading-post area had a population of 150 people. The population soon swelled to 409. After Louisiana became a state, the Saint Martin Parish was founded. The trading post was called Saint Martinville and designated the county seat of the parish.

Saint Martinville became what is known as the birthplace of the Cajun culture, made up of a multicultural community of Acadians, Cajuns, Creoles, French, Spaniards, Africans, and African Americans. New Orleans nearby suffered some epidemics, and residents of the city escaped for Saint Martinville. Also known as "Petit Paris" (Little Paris), the town had hotels, a French theater, and an opera house.

Bank of Louisiana (branch)

1824–1863

W-LA-460

History: On April 7, 1824, the Bank of Louisiana was chartered with an authorized capital of $4,000,000. Half of this amount was subscribed to by the state. It was required that five branches be opened. The branch located in Saint Martinville was established to service the parishes of Saint Mary, Saint Martin, Lafayette, and Saint Landry. The authorized capital was $200,000. On June 13, 1863, three commissioners were assigned to put the liquidation of the Bank of Louisiana into effect.

The Bank of Louisiana had its parent bank located in New Orleans, W-LA-140, and branch banks located in Alexandria, W-LA-010, Baton Rouge, W-LA-030, Donaldsonville, W-LA-060, and Saint Francisville, W-LA-440.

Numismatic Commentary: No bank notes for this branch have been discovered.

Louisiana State Bank (branch)

1818–1870

W-LA-470

History: The Louisiana State Bank was chartered in 1818. By March 14 of that year, the state had subscribed to $500,000 of the authorized $2,000,000 capital of the bank. A bonus of $100,000 was required to be paid to the state before the bank could commence operations. Of the capital stock, $150,000 was reserved for the branch at Saint Martinville. In 1825 a law was passed discontinuing all existing branches save this one, which continued on.

The Louisiana State Bank survived the Civil War—one of very few banks in the South to do so. In 1867 it dropped its capital down to $600,000, and in 1870 it closed its doors. It was succeeded in interest by the State National Bank.[16]

The Louisiana State Bank had its parent bank located in New Orleans, W-LA-280, and branch banks located in Alexandria, W-LA-020, Baton Rouge, W-LA-040, Donaldsonville, W-LA-070, New Orleans (second municipality), W-LA-290, Saint Francisville, W-LA-450, and Shreveport, W-LA-490.

Numismatic Commentary: No bank notes from this branch have been recorded.

Shreveport, Louisiana

Shreveport was a contrived town founded in 1836 by the Shreve Town Company. The corporation wanted to develop a town at the junction of the Red River and the Texas Trail. The town was originally known as Shreve Town and hosted riverboats and rafts for transportation and shipping.

On March 20, 1839, the town was incorporated as Shreveport. It consisted of 64 blocks and 16 streets running west and south. Soon the area became central for steamboat commerce, transporting cotton and agricultural crops along the river. A slave market was also in existence here, though the trade of such was not as widespread as it was elsewhere in Louisiana. The population of slaves was half as large as the population of free men, whereas in other parts of the country the inverse was true, with slaves outnumbering free men by nearly double.

Shreveport became a Confederate base during the Civil War. It was an ideal location due to its isolation from events in the East.

Citizens Bank of Louisiana (branch)

1860–1874

W-LA-480

History: The Citizens Bank of Louisiana was incorporated on April 1, 1833. The directors of the bank were authorized to issue $12,000,000 worth of bonds, secured by $14,400,000 in stock subscriptions. Of this the state reserved a credit of $500,000, unless the bank would fund the digging of the Lake Borgne Canal by the Lake Borgne Navigation Company.

On January 30, 1836, the bank was reincorporated with an amended charter due to its inability to sell the initial amount of bonds. $3,000,000 of bonds was immediately set to be issued, the backing was secured, and the bank finally opened for business. In January 1860 the branch in Shreveport was established, and the next year the capital was worth $1,250,000. The cashier was Ulger Lauve, and the president was Charles R. Griswold.

In 1874 the Citizens Bank suspended specie payments at last and went into bankruptcy. The bank was unable to recover from the Civil War and closed.

The Citizens Bank had a parent bank located in New Orleans, W-LA-200.

Numismatic Commentary: Remainder notes are plentiful for collectors of this bank. Proofs are extremely rare.

Valid Issues

$5 • W-LA-480-005-G010 CC, CC

Tint: Green. ***Back:*** Red-orange. ***Engraver:*** American Bank Note Co. ***Comments:*** H-LA-15-G60a. 18__. 1860s.

Rarity: URS-11

F $75

Selected auction price: Heritage Auctions, October 21, 2015, Lot 18364, Proof $998

$10 • W-LA-480-010-G020

NJW, NJW

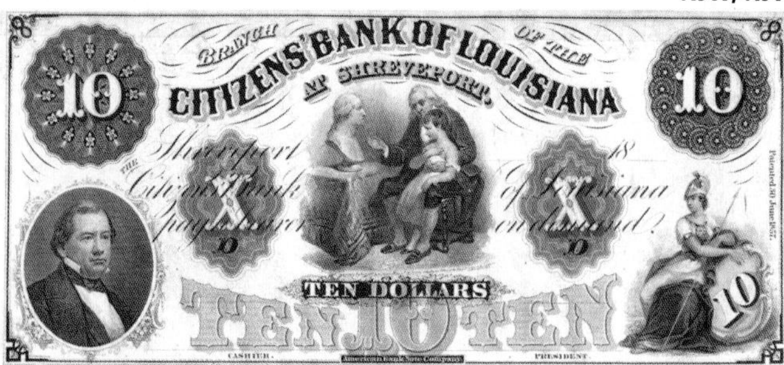

Tint: Green TEN / 10 / TEN and dies outlining white X / X. ***Back:*** Red-orange. ***Engraver:*** American Bank Note Co. ***Comments:*** H-LA-15-G64a. 18__. 1860s.

Rarity: URS-11
F $75

$20 • W-LA-480-020-G030

CC, CC

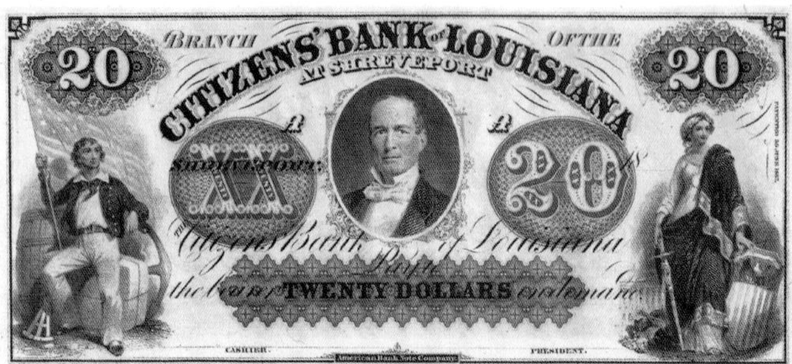

Tint: Green panel and dies bearing XX / 20. ***Back:*** Red-orange. ***Engraver:*** American Bank Note Co. ***Comments:*** H-LA-15-G68a. 18__. 1860s.

Rarity: URS-11
F $75

$50 • W-LA-480-050-G040

CC, CC

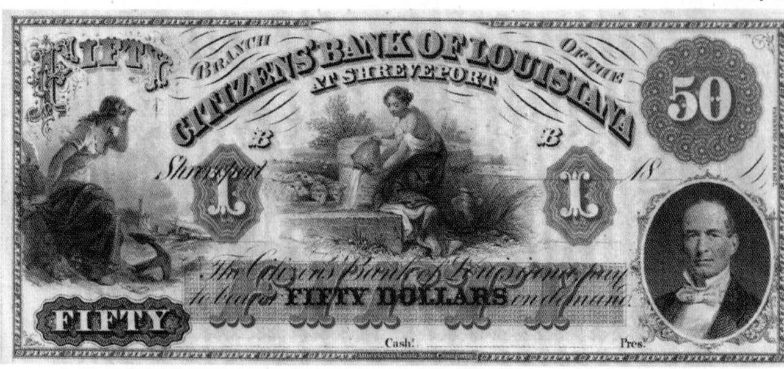

Tint: Green microlettering bearing FIFTY and dies outlining white L / L / 50. ***Back:*** Red-orange. ***Engraver:*** American Bank Note Co. ***Comments:*** H-LA-15-G72a. 18__. 1860s.

Rarity: URS-11
F $75

Uncut Sheets

$5-$5-$5-$5 •

W-LA-480-005.005.005.005-US010

RG

Tint(s): Green. ***Back(s):*** Red-orange. ***Engraver:*** American Bank Note Co. ***Comments:*** H-LA-15-G60a, G60a, G60a, G60a. All four notes identical. 18__. 1860s.

Rarity: URS-8

F $200

$10-$10-$10-$10 •

W-LA-480-010.010.010.010-US020

RG

Tint(s): Green. ***Back(s):*** Red-orange. ***Engraver:*** American Bank Note Co. ***Comments:*** H-LA-15-G64a, G64a, G64a, G64a. All four notes identical. 18__. 1860s.

Rarity: URS-8

F $200

$20-$20-$20-$20 •
W-LA-480-020.020.020.020-US030 RG

Tint(s): Green. ***Back(s):*** Red-orange. ***Engraver:*** American Bank Note Co. ***Comments:*** H-LA-15-G68a, G68a, G68a, G68a. All four notes identical. 18__. 1860s.

Rarity: URS-9
F $200

$50-$50-$50-$50 •
W-LA-480-050.050.050.050-US040 RG

Tint(s): Green. ***Back(s):*** Red-orange. ***Engraver:*** American Bank Note Co. ***Comments:*** H-LA-15-G72a, G72a, G72a, G72a. All four notes identical. 18__. 1860s.

Rarity: URS-9
F $200

Louisiana State Bank (branch)

1850–1870

W-LA-490

History: The Louisiana State Bank was chartered in 1818. By March 14 of that year, the state had subscribed to $500,000 of the authorized $2,000,000 capital of the bank. A bonus of $100,000 was required to be paid to the state before the bank could commence operations. The branch at Shreveport was not established until 1850.

The Louisiana State Bank survived the Civil War—one of very few banks in the South to do so. In 1867 it dropped its capital down to $600,000, and in 1870 it closed its doors. It was succeeded in interest by the State National Bank.[17]

The Louisiana State Bank had its parent bank located in New Orleans, W-LA-280, and branch banks located in Alexandria, W-LA-020, Baton Rouge, W-LA-040, Donaldsonville, W-LA-070, New Orleans (second municipality), W-LA-290, Saint Francisville, W-LA-450, and Saint Martinville, W-LA-470.

Numismatic Commentary: No bank notes for this branch have been reported.

The Obsolete Bank Notes of Mississippi

State Banking in Mississippi

Early Banking

Prior to Mississippi's statehood (December 1817), the Bank of *the* Mississippi, chartered by the territorial government in 1809, did an excellent business in Natchez under private ownership. The capital stock was $500,000, of which $100,000 was paid in, against which three times the amount could be issued in paper money. For any violation exceeding this, the directors were to be individually liable. The currency served well and was redeemed upon presentation. In 1818 it was reorganized under the state government as the Bank of the State of Mississippi, with a capital limited to $3,000,000. The state was to take a quarter interest. Still headquartered in Natchez, the bank set up branches in Port Gibson, Vicksburg, and Woodville. As part of the arrangement, the state legislature stated that no other bank would be authorized by the state until the bank's charter expired in 1840.

Notwithstanding this agreement, the state allowed the incorporation of the Planters Bank of the State of Mississippi in 1830, capital of $3,000,000, to be set up in the same city, with the state holding a two-thirds ownership interest. After this became known, the directors of the long-established Bank of the State of Mississippi contemplated the current rampant speculation in trading slaves and dealing in undeveloped land and decided to discontinue business in view of an uncertain future. The new Planters Bank started operation and became the depository for state funds. Branches were operated in Columbus, Jackson, Manchester (later Yazoo City), Monticello, Port Gibson, Vicksburg, and Woodville. After September 1839 the state transferred its deposits to the Mississippi Railroad Company. The Planters Bank closed down soon thereafter. The Railroad Company operated branches in Canton, Gallatin, and Raymond, and issued numerous bills, many of which were post notes bearing interest. The bank went out of business in the early 1840s.

The Hard Times Era

By 1837 there were 18 banks in the state with a combined capital of about $13,000,000 and a conservatively estimated bank-note circulation of about $5,000,000. On February 5, 1838, the state passed a special act to charter the gigantic Mississippi Union Bank, headquartered in Jackson and capitalized at $15,500,000. To finance the operation, the act authorized $15,000,000 worth of bonds to be loaned to the bank, the security for which was backed by the state's good faith and credit. Nicholas Biddle, president of the Bank of the United States of Pennsylvania, was given the agency for selling the bonds. These were difficult times, and holders of the bonds as well as the bank currency frequently made inquiry to the state offices to be sure all was well. In all instances the state replied that it stood fully behind these obligations.

The Mississippi Union Bank collapsed in 1840, carrying down with it a number of other banks in the state. Governor Alexander G. McNutt contemplated the damages, the difficulty of raising money at current high-interest rates, and other options. He sent a form letter to creditors on July 14, 1841, saying that the state "denies all obligation to pay the bonds" on the grounds of a clause in the State Constitution which provided that no loan of money should be made on the credit of the state for the payment or redemption of any loan or debt unless,

> such law be proposed in the Senate or House of Representatives and be agreed on by the majority of the members of each house and entered on their journals with the yeas and nays taken thereon, and be referred to the next succeeding Legislature, and published three months previous to the next regular election in three newspapers of the state, and unless the next Legislature duly passes the said law.

The state further claimed that the arrangement with Biddle was invalid, as no bonds were to be sold below par, making his operation of the commission an "intentional and willful fraud." The very institution of the Mississippi Union Bank was deemed to be illegal. Citing the records of George Washington, Benjamin

Franklin, James Madison, Thomas Jefferson, and other national leaders who repudiated amounts owed to mercenary foreigners, the citizens of Mississippi had no intention of paying the out-of-state, money-grubbing people who held these illegal bonds:

> Higher and holier motives than mere pecuniary considerations actuate [the citizens of Mississippi]. They have determined that they will never submit to an invasion of their constitution by either a foreign or domestic foe. The rights secured to them under that sacred instrument they will maintain at all hazards; and relying on the correctness of their principles and the justice of their cause they will, with confidence and cheerfulness, submit to the verdict of posterity.

So the argument went, repeated endlessly, while creditors and newspaper editors reacted with shock and disbelief. Courts in other states found that the 1838 act was indeed legal, despite Mississippi's attempt to illegitimatize it. To have the last word, the Mississippi state legislature passed a law forbidding the state to ever settle the debt, thereby canceling other court decisions.

In his message of January 1, 1844, Governor Tilghman Tucker, ignoring the nationwide revival of business resulting from the end of the Hard Times period, attributed new prosperity in Mississippi as "the natural result of industry, economy and time which have (aided by the bankrupt law), swept off a large portion of the debts and embarrassments of the people created by the disasters of past idleness, prodigality, gambling, and banking operations." Financial journals and newspapers across the United States continued to react in horror, but Mississippi ignored the outcry. For years, up to the Civil War, the financial reputation of the state was in shambles, and frequent mention of this was made in *Bankers' Magazine* and elsewhere.

The 1830s and Later

During the 1830s and 1840s many other banks were formed in Mississippi, nearly all with loose supervision and oversight. Results were mixed but generally unfavorable, and most eventually failed. Banking in the state was sharply diminished in the 1850s, leading into the Civil War in 1861. Few new banks were chartered. In 1856 the Commercial Bank at Yazoo City opened its doors. Capitalized at $200,000, it operated profitably into the early 1860s.

The Northern Bank of Mississippi, located in Holly Springs, was established in the unpropitious year of 1837 and went on to operate into the Civil War. It was far from being a local bank and issued paper payable in New Orleans. In the 1850s there were strict rules in Texas concerning the issuance of paper money, and partly for this reason scarcely any native banks issued bills. The banking house of R. & D.G. Mills in Houston, Texas, made an arrangement with the Northern Bank of Mississippi to acquire large quantities of its paper money. It circulated the bills with good effect in Texas, backed by the excellent reputation of the Mills enterprise. In early 1862 Mills could not redeem the notes, and a panic swept through the financial community. The scare was short lived, and soon the strength of Mills was regained.

During this era, scrip and other bills were issued by various merchants, railroads, and other commercial interests in Mississippi. In addition, large quantities of New Orleans bills were seen in commerce.

Numismatic Comments

The currency of Mississippi includes bank issues as well as certain bills issued by other entities, such as the Mississippi and Alabama Railroad Company and the Real Estate Banking Company of Clinton, Mississippi. Of the various railroads and real estate entities that issued paper money, some are documented and others are mainly known only from the currency that survives. The real estate offices issued notes to clients who pledged land as collateral. A particularly elaborate title is the Lake Washington and Deer Creek Railroad and Banking Company, located in Princeton and active in the 1830s. It evolved in the same decade to become the Bank of Mississippi, a bank unrelated to the other institution with a somewhat similar name.

Certain entities issued paper money despite the fact that they were not granted official banking privileges. Of these, the following have been of special interest to numismatists: the Brandon Savings Institution, the Cotton Planting and Shipping Company of Mississippi, the Grenada Savings Institution, the Hillsboro Change Company, the Joint Stock Bank, the Mississippi Central Rail Road Company, the Mobile and Ohio Railroad Company, the Madisonville and Pearl River Turnpike Company, the Manchester Insurance Company, the J.O. Pierson Exchange, and the Southern Railroad Company. Most issued paper money for only a short time. The railroads listed here operated during the Civil War and mostly issued fractional and low-denomination notes to make up for the shortage of coins at that time. The others operated during the 1830s when specie had almost entirely disappeared from the state. They too issued fractional and low-denomination notes.

Finally, several exchange houses operated in Mississippi and often had the word *bank* in their titles. These are listed here for collector continuity but often did not have state-chartered banking privileges. Instead they had newly opened Native American lands pledged as collateral by early speculators and landowners. Some attempted to be legitimate banking businesses, while others were fraudulent from the start. Others were change banks run most likely by private merchants that issued fractional currency to make up for the shortage of specie.

With so many issuers and so many denominations and vignettes, bills of Mississippi are widely collected today and are very interesting to view, although most date from before the colorful era of the 1850s. There are, to be sure, rarities, particularly among those of earlier dates. Currency of the Bank of the Mississippi, headquartered in Natchez and active in the 1820s, is uncollectible today. Certain other issues across the banking spectrum are known only through Proofs.

Rich vignettes, interesting bank titles, and many stories for those who enjoy history come together in the currency of this state. There is a lot to like.

The standard references on Mississippi paper money are *Mississippi Obsolete Notes and Scrip* by Guy Kraus, published in 1996, and *Mississippi Obsolete Paper Money and Scrip* by L. Chandler Leggett, published in 1975. For any scholar of Mississippi's complex banking history, these are excellent books to have.

Aberdeen, Mississippi

The first Europeans to arrive in Mississippi were led by Hernando DeSoto in 1540, who explored the land that would later become the town of Aberdeen. In 1834 Aberdeen was settled by Robert Gordon. He selected the site due to its elevated proximity to the Tombigbee River: its hilltop location would protect the area during flood season while still allowing the inhabitants to set up a port community. It was officially incorporated as a town in 1837. By 1849 it had become the county seat of Monroe.

During the 1850s, Aberdeen became the second-largest city in Mississippi, experiencing substantial growth. Its port on the Tombigbee River was the largest in the state, transporting cotton from northern and western towns and sending them on to Mobile. Large mansions were built by the merchants and landowners, with many products from Europe entering the town by steamboats.

Aberdeen and Pontotoc Rail Road and Banking Company

1836–1840

W-MS-010

History: The Aberdeen and Pontotoc Rail Road and Banking Company was incorporated on February 27, 1836, with an authorized capital of $1,000,000, for the direct purpose of raising funds to construct a railroad traversing the distance from Aberdeen to Pontotoc. The capital was divided into shares of $100 each. The bank had to raise $250,000 before it could go into business.

The charter of the bank was to expire on January 1, 1861, and a branch was authorized to be opened in Pontotoc. However, in February 1840 it was reported that the governor of Mississippi had declared the charter of the Aberdeen and Pontotoc Rail Road and Banking Company, along with various other banks, forfeited, due to the fact that it was believed they had failed to comply with banking law by not paying specie for their notes.[1]

Numismatic Commentary: Notes of this issuer are scarce, with $5 and $10 notes being common.

Valid Issues

$5 • W-MS-010-005-G010 JM

Engraver: Draper, Toppan, Longacre & Co. ***Comments:*** H-MS-10-G8, Kraus-10025. 18__. 1830s.

Rarity: URS-3

F $2,500

Selected auction price: Heritage Auctions, January 6, 2016, Lot 18585, F $881

$10 • W-MS-010-010-G020 JM

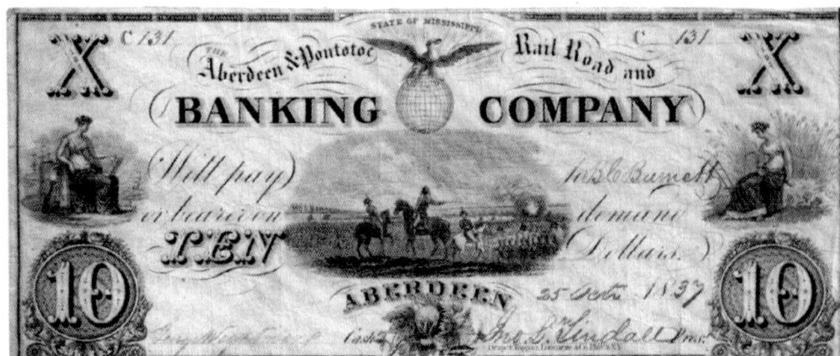

Engraver: Draper, Toppan, Longacre & Co. ***Comments:*** H-MS-10-G14, Kraus-10026. 18__. 1830s.

Rarity: URS-4

VF $2,500; **Proof** $4,000

Selected auction price: Heritage Auctions, January 11, 2016, Lot 23704, VG $763; Heritage Auctions, April 23, 2015, Lot 19196, VF $2,585

$20 • W-MS-010-020-G030 CC

Engraver: Draper, Toppan, Longacre & Co. ***Comments:*** H-MS-10-G16, Kraus-10027. 18__. 1830s.

Rarity: URS-3

F $2,500

Selected auction price: Heritage Auctions, April 23, 2015, Lot 19197, Proof $1,880

$50 • W-MS-010-050-G040 JM

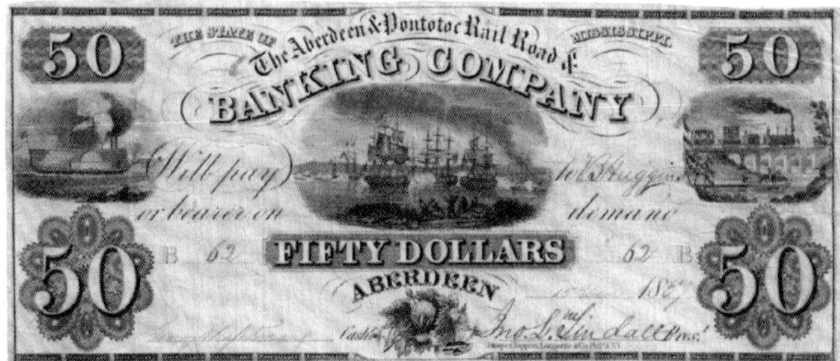

Engraver: Draper, Toppan, Longacre & Co. ***Comments:*** H-MS-10-G18, Kraus-10029. 18__. 1830s.

Rarity: URS-2

F $4,000

$100 • W-MS-010-100-G050 JM

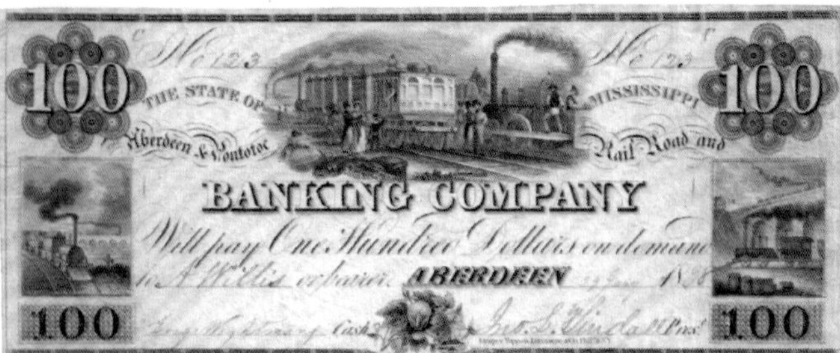

Engraver: Draper, Toppan, Longacre & Co. ***Comments:*** H-MS-10-G20, Kraus-Unlisted. 18__. 1830s.

Rarity: URS-3
F $4,000

Post Notes

$5 • W-MS-010-005-G060
Engraver: Draper, Toppan, Longacre & Co. ***Comments:*** H-Unlisted, Kraus-10040. No description available. ____ AFTER DATE. 1836–1840.
Rarity: *None known*

$10 • W-MS-010-010-G070
Engraver: Draper, Toppan, Longacre & Co. ***Comments:*** H-Unlisted, Kraus-10041. No description available. ____ AFTER DATE. 1836–1840.
Rarity: *None known*

$20 • W-MS-010-020-G080
Engraver: Draper, Toppan, Longacre & Co. ***Comments:*** H-Unlisted, Kraus-10042. No description available. ____ AFTER DATE. 1836–1840.
Rarity: *None known*

$50 • W-MS-010-050-G090
Left: 50. ***Right:*** Two women seated, Athena holding U.S. flag, Mirror, River. ***Engraver:*** Draper, Toppan, Longacre & Co. ***Comments:*** H-Unlisted, Kraus-10043. ____ AFTER DATE. 1836–1840.
Rarity: URS-1
Proof $4,000

$100 • W-MS-010-100-G100
Left: 100. ***Right:*** Clipper ship, Two schooners. ***Engraver:*** Draper, Toppan, Longacre & Co. ***Comments:*** H-Unlisted, Kraus-10044. ____ AFTER DATE. 1836–1840.
Rarity: URS-1
Proof $4,000

Bank of Aberdeen
1862
W-MS-020

History: On January 17, 1862, the Bank of Aberdeen was chartered with an authorized capital of $500,000. Its charter was to continue for 20 years.[2]

Valid Issues

$1 • W-MS-020-001-G010 CC

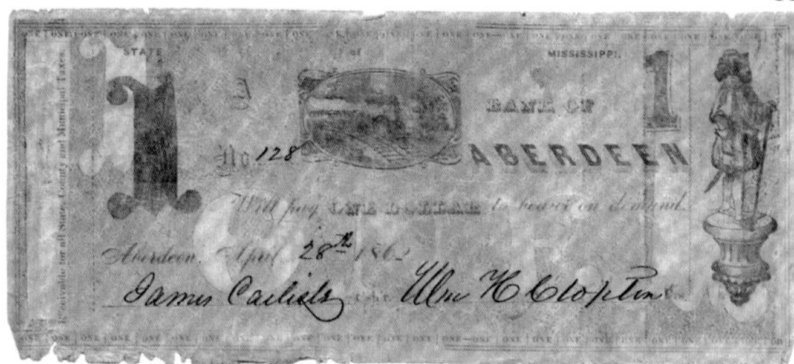

Tint: Red. ***Engraver:*** S.S.B. & J.O. ***Comments:*** H-Unlisted, Kraus-51110. April __ 1862.
Rarity: URS-6
F $250

$2 • W-MS-020-002-G020 CC

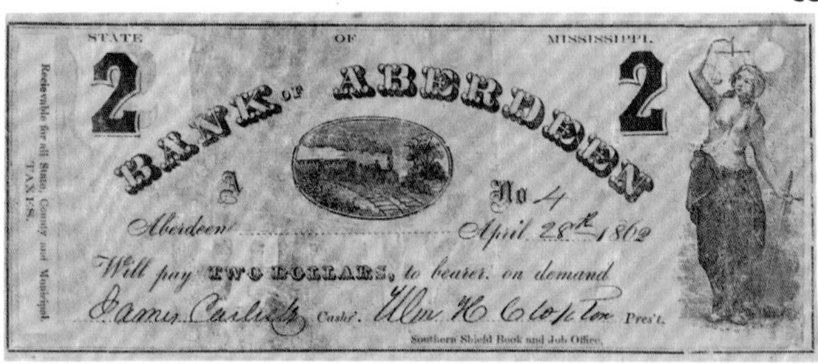

Tint: Red. ***Engraver:*** S.S.B. & J.O. ***Comments:*** H-Unlisted, Kraus-51111. April __ 1862.
Rarity: URS-6
F $400

$3 • W-MS-020-003-G030 CC

Tint: Red. ***Engraver:*** S.S.B. & J.O. ***Comments:*** H-Unlisted, Kraus-51132. April __ 1862.
Rarity: URS-5
F $350

$5 • W-MS-020-005-G040
Left: 5 / Two farmers walking. ***Center:*** Ship, Liberty and Ceres flanking shield bearing 5, Train. ***Right:*** Eagle with shield. ***Overprint:*** Green FIVE. ***Engraver:*** J.T. Paterson & Co. ***Comments:*** H-Unlisted, Kraus-51160r. July __, 186_.
Rarity: URS-1
F $1,500

$5 • **W-MS-020-005-G050** HA

Tint: Red. ***Engraver:*** S.S.B. & J.O. ***Comments:*** H-Unlisted, Kraus-51114. April __ 1862.

Rarity: URS-6
F $350

$5 • **W-MS-020-005-G050a** JM

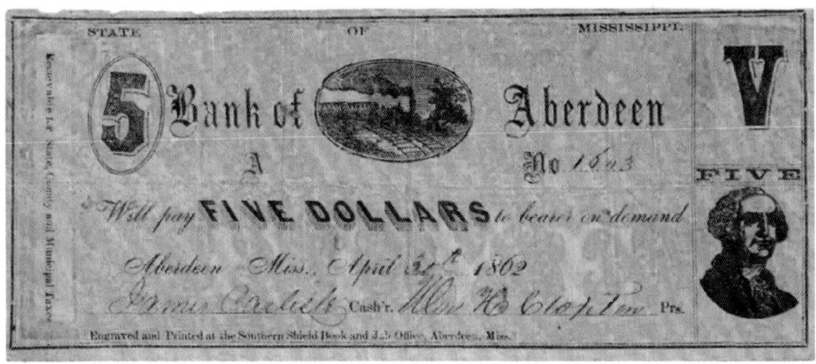

Tint: Red. ***Engraver:*** S.S.B. & J.O. ***Comments:*** H-Unlisted, Kraus-51113. Similar to W-MS-020-005-G050 but with V in upper-right corner. Text in left panel reads in the opposite direction from G050. April __ 1862.

Rarity: URS-6
F $350

$10 • **W-MS-020-010-G060** CC

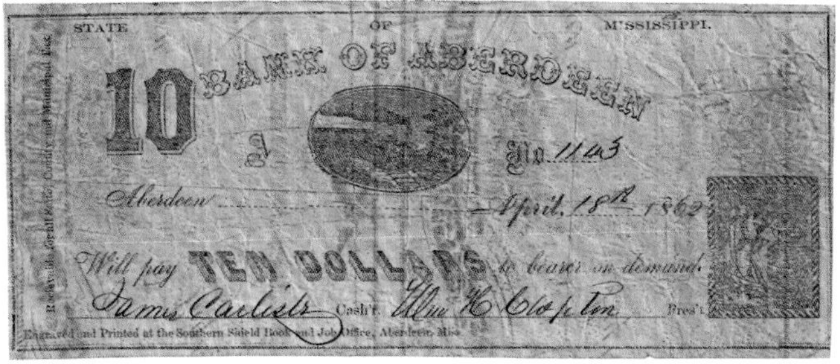

Tint: Red. ***Engraver:*** S.S.B. & J.O. ***Comments:*** H-Unlisted, Kraus-51115. April, __ 1862.

Rarity: URS-5
F $350

$20 • **W-MS-020-020-G070** JM

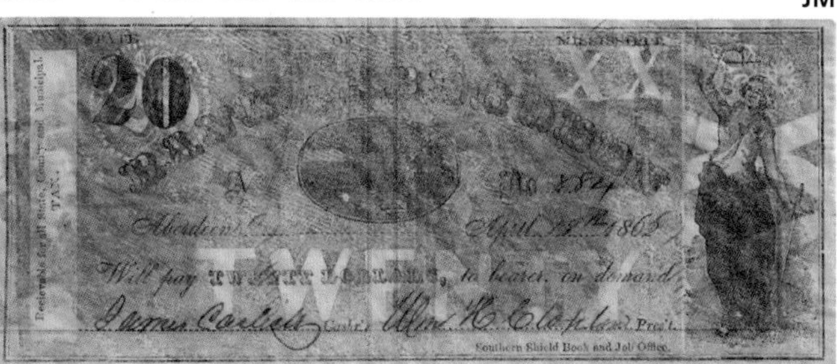

Tint: Red. ***Engraver:*** S.S.B. & J.O. ***Comments:*** H-Unlisted, Kraus-51116. April __ 1862.

Rarity: URS-5
F $400

$20 • **W-MS-020-020-G080**

Left: 20. ***Center:*** Men in field. ***Right:*** Justice with scales. ***Engraver:*** S.S.B. & J.O. ***Comments:*** H-Unlisted, Kraus-51135. April __ 1862.

Rarity: URS-6

Mississippi Mutual Insurance Company

1850–1860s

W-MS-030

History: The Mississippi Mutual Insurance Company was incorporated on February 8, 1850, under the name of "The Mutual Insurance Company of Mississippi." On February 24, 1854, the title was amended to the form shown on the notes featured here. On February 21, 1856, the act of incorporation was amended to change the number of directors in the company from 12 to 7. However, it was declared in the act "That nothing herein contained shall be so construed as to authorize said company to issue bills or certificates of any description calculated or intended to circulate as money within the limits of the State." In 1857 the president of the bank was W.A. Sykes, and the cashier was James Carlisle. In 1860 the capital was $100,000. H.D. Spratt was cashier at that time, and the president was T.W. Williams.

Complicating matters from the viewpoint of numismatic understanding, on January 25, 1862, the Mississippi Mutual Insurance Company, declared to be invested with all the rights and privileges of a banking business, was authorized to increase its capital to $200,000. On December 9, 1863, the corporation was authorized to issue and put in circulation bills not exceeding a total of $100,000, as long as the notes were change bills of a value less than $1 and that an equal amount of circulating currency of the bank was taken in at the time of issuance.

Sometime during the Civil War, the bank closed for business.

Collectors and Researchers:

If you have new information about any banks or notes listed in this volume, contact Whitman Publishing, Attn: Obsolete Paper Money, 3101 Clairmont Road, Suite G, Atlanta, GA 30329.

Valid Issues

$1 • W-MS-030-001-G010

JM

Overprint: Red ONE. ***Engraver:*** Danforth, Wright & Co. ***Comments:*** H-Unlisted, Kraus-46910. 18__. 1850s–1860s.

Rarity: URS-4

F $250; **Proof** $1,000

$2 • W-MS-030-002-G020

JM

Overprint: Red TWO. ***Engraver:*** Danforth, Wright & Co. ***Comments:*** H-Unlisted, Kraus-46911. 18__. 1850s–1860s.

Rarity: URS-5

F $350; **Proof** $1,000

$3 • W-MS-030-003-G030

JM

Overprint: Red THREE. ***Engraver:*** Danforth, Wright & Co. ***Comments:*** H-Unlisted, Kraus-46912. 18__. 1850s–1860s.

Rarity: URS-3

F $500; **Proof** $1,000

$5 • W-MS-030-005-G040

CC

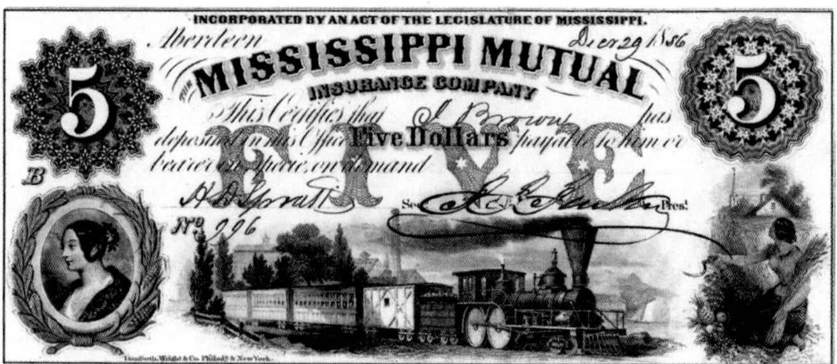

Overprint: Red FIVE. ***Engraver:*** Danforth, Wright & Co. ***Comments:*** H-Unlisted, Kraus-46913. 18__. 1850s–1860s.

Rarity: URS-5

F $400; **EF** $750; **Proof** $1,000

$10 • W-MS-030-010-G050

JM

Overprint: Red TEN. ***Engraver:*** Danforth, Wright & Co. ***Comments:*** H-Unlisted, Kraus-46914. 18__. 1850s–1860s.

Rarity: URS-5

F $500; **Proof** $1,000

$20 • W-MS-030-020-G060

Left: 20 / Woman with bucket. ***Center:*** Riverboat. ***Right:*** 20 / Train. ***Overprint:*** Red TWENTY. ***Engraver:*** Danforth, Wright & Co. ***Comments:*** H-Unlisted, Kraus-46915. 18__. 1850s–1860s.

Rarity: —

Planters Bank of Aberdeen

Circa 1838

W-MS-040

History: In the past it has been thought that the Planters Bank of Aberdeen had some connection with the Planters Bank of the State of Mississippi, W-MS-670, but this has not been confirmed. There is no Aberdeen branch reported for the Planters Bank of the State of Mississippi in the original legislature of the bank. Today it is presumed to be a separate entity, but nothing of its history is known.

Numismatic Commentary: Specific details concerning this bank's operation and issuance of paper money are elusive.

Valid Issues

$5 • W-MS-040-005-G010 CC

Engraver: Rawdon, Wright & Hatch. ***Comments:*** H-MS-15-G4, Kraus-3300. 18__. 1838.

Rarity: URS-7
F $275

$10 • W-MS-040-010-G020 CC

Engraver: Rawdon, Wright & Hatch. ***Comments:*** H-MS-15-G8, Kraus-3301. 18__. 1838.

Rarity: URS-5
F $350

$20 • W-MS-040-020-G030 CC

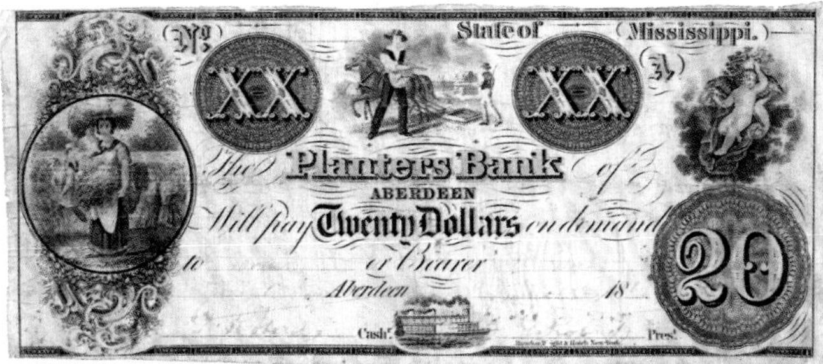

Engraver: Rawdon, Wright & Hatch. ***Comments:*** H-MS-15-G12, Kraus-3302. 18__. 1838.

Rarity: URS-5
F $350

Benton, Mississippi

Benton was settled in 1828 by William W. Gadberry, who built a log home that later housed the first county court. In 1829 Benton became the county seat, after which it developed quickly into a central trading town. In 1836 the city received its official charter, and in 1846 it was incorporated. By 1849 the county seat had moved to Yazoo City, and Benton began to decline. The population dwindled, stores faded, and the neighborhood commerce declined.

Benton and Manchester Rail Road and Banking Company

1836–1840

W-MS-050

History: The Benton and Manchester Rail Road and Banking Company was incorporated on February 26, 1836, with an authorized capital of $1,000,000. On May 12, 1837, the corporation was officially chartered, and the power to construct a railroad spanning from Benton to Manchester was conferred. The charter was to last until January 1, 1858, but in 1840 the bank forfeited its charter due to its failure to pay specie when its notes were presented for redemption.

Numismatic Commentary: Notes from the Benton and Manchester Rail Road and Banking Company are extremely rare.

Valid Issues

$5 • W-MS-050-005-G010 JM

Engraver: Draper, Toppan, Longacre & Co. ***Comments:*** H-Unlisted, Kraus-10070. 18__. 1838.

Rarity: URS-3
F $5,000
Selected auction price: Heritage Auctions, April 23, 2015, Lot 19198, VF $4,935

$10 • W-MS-050-010-G020 JM

Engraver: Draper, Toppan, Longacre & Co. ***Comments:*** H-MS-20-G10, Kraus-10071. 18__. 1838.

Rarity: URS-3
F $4,000

$10 • **W-MS-050-010-G020a**

Left: Woman leaning on column / X. ***Center:*** 10 / Woman seated at table with scales, Mill and falls / 10. ***Right:*** Liberty as Minerva standing with U.S. shield, Staff / X. ***Overprint:*** Black CRAFTS J. WRIGHT'S EXCHANGE OFFICE / CINCINNATI, OHIO stamp. ***Engraver:*** Draper, Toppan, Longacre & Co. ***Comments:*** H-MS-20-G10a, Kraus-Unlisted. Similar to W-MS-050-010-G020. 18__. 1838.

Rarity: URS-3
F $3,500

$20 • **W-MS-050-020-G030**

JM

Engraver: Draper, Toppan, Longacre & Co. ***Comments:*** H-MS-20-G12, Kraus-10072. 18__. 1838.

Rarity: URS-2
F $6,000

$20 • **W-MS-050-020-G030a**

Left: 20 / Train / 20. ***Center:*** Portrait of Henry Clay / Moneta seated with strongbox. ***Right:*** Portrait of George Washington / 20. ***Overprint:*** Black CRAFTS J. WRIGHT'S EXCHANGE OFFICE / CINCINNATI, OHIO stamp. ***Engraver:*** Draper, Toppan, Longacre & Co. ***Comments:*** H-MS-20-G12a, Kraus-Unlisted. Similar to W-MS-050-020-G030. 18__. 1838.

Rarity: URS-2
F $3,000

$50 • **W-MS-050-050-G040**

Left: Sailor with colonial flag. ***Right:*** Two women flanking XX surmounted by eagle / 20. ***Engraver:*** Draper, Toppan, Longacre & Co. ***Comments:*** H-Unlisted, Kraus-10073. 18__. 1838.

Rarity: URS-2
F $3,000

$100 • **W-MS-050-100-G050**

Left: 100 / Portrait of George Washington / 100. ***Center:*** 100 / Indian maiden seated with bow and arrows / 100. ***Right:*** 100 / Male portrait / 100. ***Engraver:*** Draper, Toppan, Longacre & Co. ***Comments:*** H-Unlisted, Kraus-10074. 18__. 1838.

Rarity: URS-2
F $3,000

Post Notes

$20 • **W-MS-050-020-G060**

CC

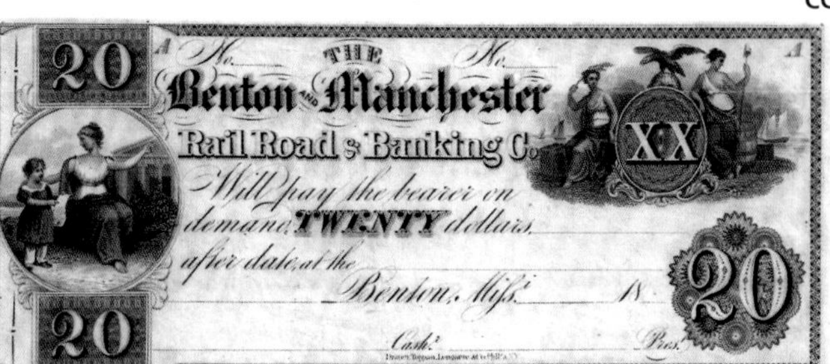

Engraver: Draper, Toppan, Longacre & Co. ***Comments:*** H-Unlisted. 18__. 1838.

Rarity: URS-2
EF $5,000
Selected auction price: Heritage Auctions, January 5, 2012, Lot 15929, About New $4,025

Brandon, Mississippi

Brandon was first settled by Europeans in the early 1800s. The area was named after Gerard C. Brandon, who was the first native-born governor of Mississippi. In 1829 the town was named the county seat of Rankin.

Commercial Bank of Natchez (branch)

1836–1856

W-MS-060

History: The Commercial Bank of Natchez was incorporated on February 27, 1836, with an authorized capital of $3,000,000. The bank was forbidden to distribute notes of a denomination lower than $5. The bank did not last long, and on February 6, 1841, an act was passed to close the branch banks and wind up the affairs of the parent bank. The closing of the bank was extended due to a battle with creditors that went all the way to the U.S. Supreme Court. Finally the bank went into liquidation in 1856.

The Commercial Bank of Natchez had its parent bank located in Natchez, W-MS-640, and branch banks located in Canton, W-MS-100, Holmesville, W-MS-420, and Shieldsboro, W-MS-830.

Numismatic Commentary: No notes with this branch location are known. The listings below are speculative, based on the parent bank.

Valid Issues

$5 • **W-MS-060-005-G010**

Left: FIVE vertically. ***Center:*** Two cherubs as Liberty and Commerce with U.S. flag, Ship. ***Right:*** FIVE vertically. ***Engraver:*** Underwood, Bald, Spencer & Hufty. ***Comments:*** H-Unlisted, Kraus-4020p. 18__. 1830s.

Rarity: *None known*

$10 • **W-MS-060-010-G020**

Left: TEN vertically. ***Center:*** 10 / Ships / 10. ***Right:*** TEN vertically. ***Engraver:*** Underwood, Bald, Spencer & Hufty. ***Comments:*** H-Unlisted, Kraus-4021p. 18__. 1830s.

Rarity: *None known*

$20 • **W-MS-060-020-G030**

Left: TWENTY vertically. ***Center:*** Medallion head bearing TWENTY / Mercury seated at river / Medallion head bearing TWENTY. ***Right:*** TWENTY vertically. ***Engraver:*** Underwood, Bald, Spencer & Hufty. ***Comments:*** H-Unlisted, Kraus-4022p. 18__. 1830s.

Rarity: *None known*

$50 • **W-MS-060-050-G040**

Left: Athena as Liberty with U.S. shield and spear / FIFTY. ***Center:*** Medallion head bearing FIFTY / Neptune seated on sea / Medallion head bearing FIFTY. ***Right:*** Minerva as Liberty with U.S. shield and spear / FIFTY. ***Engraver:*** Underwood, Bald, Spencer & Hufty. ***Comments:*** H-Unlisted, Kraus-4023p. 18__. 1830s.

Rarity: *None known*

$100 • **W-MS-060-100-G050**

Left: Woman standing with medallion head and caduceus / 100. ***Center:*** Medallion head bearing 100 / Indian in canoe / Medallion head bearing 100. ***Right:*** Woman standing with medallion head and caduceus / 100. ***Engraver:*** Underwood, Bald, Spencer & Hufty. ***Comments:*** H-Unlisted, Kraus-4024p. 18__. 1830s.

Rarity: *None known*

Mississippi and Alabama Rail Road Company

1836–1841

W-MS-070

History: The Mississippi and Alabama Rail Road Company was locally called the Brandon Bank and was chartered on February 9, 1836. The company was to lay a road from Brandon to Mobile. In 1838, with its circulation in need of redemption, the bank issued 70-day post notes payable in distant Philadelphia. It seemed the company was speculating in cotton, and by 1840 it was in trouble. The company evolved to become a bankrupt, fraudulent enterprise that ended poorly, so much so that it was referenced in 1842 in "Humbuggiana: A Poem, Volume 8," an epic rhyme by M. Deavenport:

> . . . From Biddle's Bubble, to the Brandon Bank![3]
> Come bankrupt thou who've seen a better day,
> Who, every body owes, yet ne'er can pay . . .
> for each and every man,
> May filch the funds, and swindle all he can,
> And almost beat that crew, far-famed and fled,
> That drained the "Brandon Bank" so dry and dead,
> When Shelton, scamp'ring, like a stall'd-steed, off,
> Left lean-limb'd Lynch to gnaw an empty trough!

It is noted by Deavenport later that Sheldon was the president of the bank at the height of its corruption. He was succeeded, after he fled his scandals, by Governor Lynch, who was considered to be a worthy man. Nevertheless, Lynch was unable to recover the bank, and it failed in 1841. Later it became a part of the Southern Railroad Company. The reference to Biddle is to Nicholas Biddle, notorious fraudster of the Bank of the United States of Pennsylvania, W-LA-190.

The Mississippi and Alabama Rail Road Company had a branch located in Paulding, W-MS-710.

Numismatic Commentary: This bank issued more varieties of notes than any other bank in Mississippi, and as a result issues are mostly common.

Just like the Northern Bank of Mississippi, W-MS-400, the Mississippi and Alabama Rail Road Company had endorsement in Texas by R. & D.G. Mills, a commercial house located in Galveston, Texas. The endorsements can sometimes be seen on the backs of the notes.

VALID ISSUES

$1 • **W-MS-070-001-G010**

Engraver: Draper, Toppan, Longacre & Co. ***Comments:*** H-MS-25-G2, Kraus-Unlisted. No description available. 18__. 1830s.

Rarity: *None known*

$1 • **W-MS-070-001-G020**

JM

Engraver: Draper, Toppan, Longacre & Co. ***Comments:*** H-Unlisted, Kraus-10100. 18__. 1830s.

Rarity: URS-3
F $1,500

$2 • **W-MS-070-002-G030**

JM

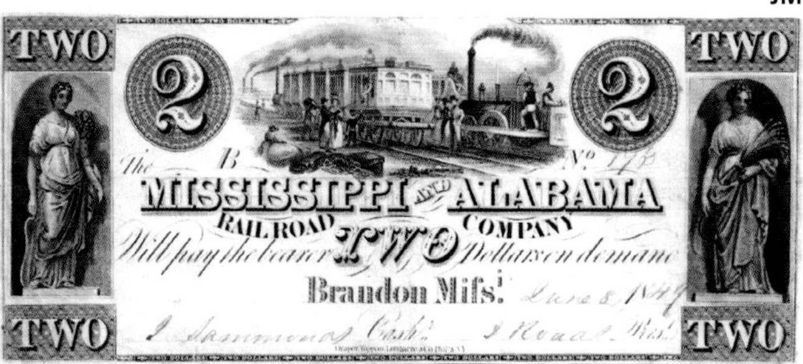

Engraver: Draper, Toppan, Longacre & Co. ***Comments:*** H-MS-25-G4, Kraus-10101. 18__. 1830s.

Rarity: URS-3
F $1,500

$3 • W-MS-070-003-G040

JM

Engraver: Draper, Toppan, Longacre & Co. ***Comments:*** H-MS-25-G6, Kraus-10102. 18__. 1830s.

Rarity: URS-3
F $1,500

$5 • W-MS-070-005-G050

JM

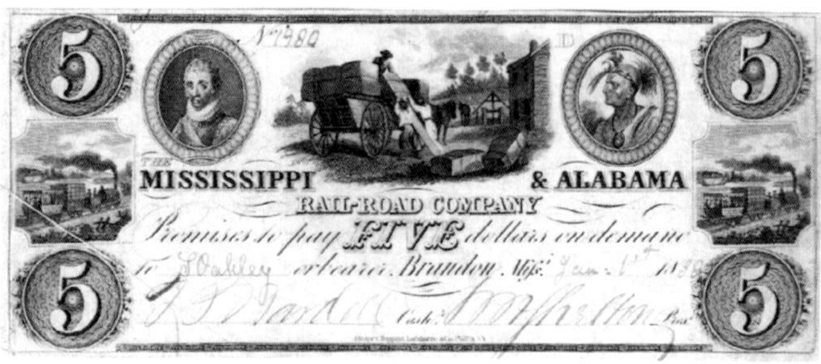

Back: Plain. ***Engraver:*** Draper, Toppan, Longacre & Co. ***Comments:*** H-MS-25-G8, Kraus-Unlisted. 18__. 1837 and 1838.

Rarity: URS-12
F $100

$5 • W-MS-070-005-G050a

Left: 5 / Train / 5. ***Center:*** Portrait of Fernando De Soto / Wagon / Portrait of Indian. ***Right:*** 5 / Train / 5. ***Back:*** Orange. ***Engraver:*** Draper, Toppan, Longacre & Co. ***Comments:*** H-MS-25-G8b, Kraus-Unlisted. Similar to W-MS-070-005-G050. 18__. 1838.

Rarity: *None known*

$5 • W-MS-070-005-G060

JM

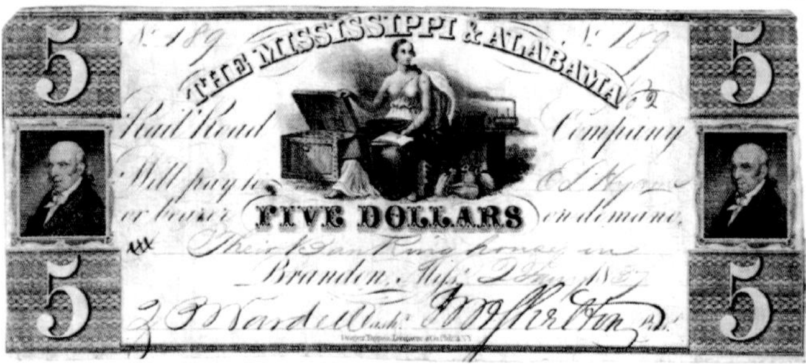

Engraver: Draper, Toppan, Longacre & Co. ***Comments:*** H-MS-25-G10, Kraus-10110. 18__. 1837.

Rarity: URS-10
F $150

$10 • W-MS-070-010-G070

CC

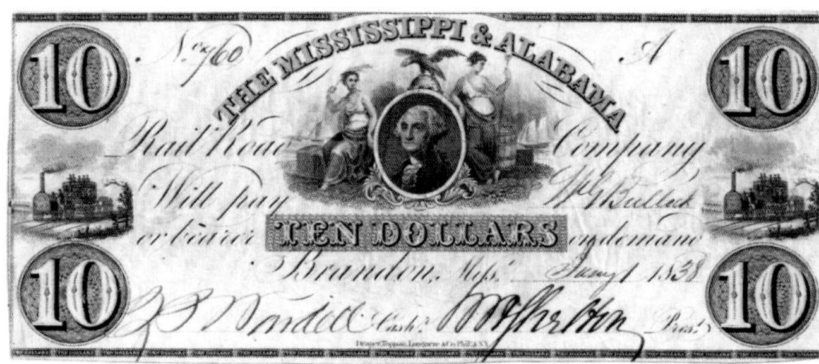

Back: Plain. ***Engraver:*** Draper, Toppan, Longacre & Co. ***Comments:*** H-MS-25-G12, Kraus-Unlisted. 18__. 1837 and 1838.

Rarity: URS-12
VF $125

$10 • W-MS-070-010-G070a

JM

Overprint: Black REISSUED stamp. ***Back:*** Plain. ***Engraver:*** Draper, Toppan, Longacre & Co. ***Comments:*** H-MS-25-G12a, Kraus-Unlisted. Similar to W-MS-070-010-G070. 18__. 1837 and 1838.

Rarity: URS-10
F $150

$10 • W-MS-070-010-G070b

JM

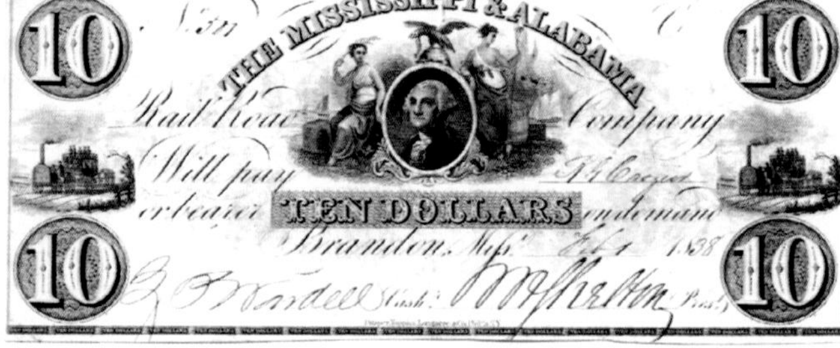

Back: Orange. ***Engraver:*** Draper, Toppan, Longacre & Co. ***Comments:*** H-MS-25-G12b, Kraus-Unlisted. Similar to W-MS-070-010-G070. 18__. 1838.

Rarity: URS-9
F $175

$10 • W-MS-070-010-G070c

JM

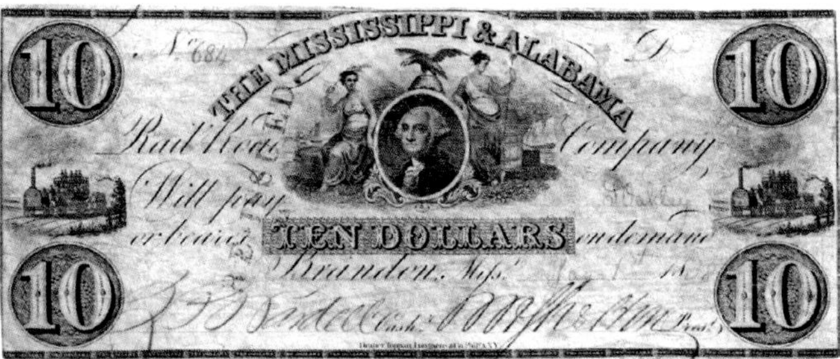

Overprint: Black REISSUED stamp. ***Back:*** Orange. ***Engraver:*** Draper, Toppan, Longacre & Co. ***Comments:*** H-MS-25-G12c, Kraus-Unlisted. Similar to W-MS-070-010-G070. 18__. 1838.

Rarity: URS-9

F $175

$10 • W-MS-070-010-G080

JM

Engraver: Draper, Toppan, Longacre & Co. ***Comments:*** H-MS-25-G14, Kraus-10111. 18__. 1837.

Rarity: URS-10

F $125

$10 • W-MS-070-010-G080a

JM

Overprint: Black REISSUED stamp. ***Engraver:*** Draper, Toppan, Longacre & Co. ***Comments:*** H-Unlisted, Kraus-Unlisted. Similar to W-MS-070-010-G080. 18__. 1837.

Rarity: URS-10

F $125

$20 • W-MS-070-020-G090

JM

Back: Plain. ***Engraver:*** Draper, Toppan, Longacre & Co. ***Comments:*** H-MS-25-G16, Kraus-Unlisted. 18__. 1837 and 1838.

Rarity: URS-10

F $125

$20 • W-MS-070-020-G090a

JM

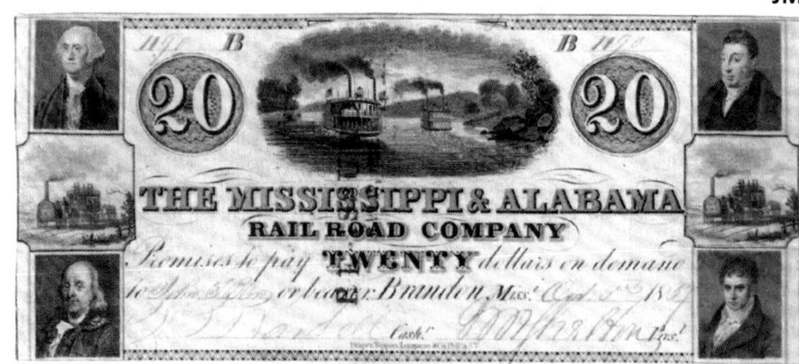

Overprint: Black REISSUED stamp. ***Back:*** Plain. ***Engraver:*** Draper, Toppan, Longacre & Co. ***Comments:*** H-MS-25-G16a, Kraus-Unlisted. Similar to W-MS-070-020-G090. 18__. 1837 and 1838.

Rarity: URS-7

F $200

How to Read the Whitman Numbering System

$1 • W-AL-020-001-G010a

Denomination: Face value of the note shown.

W: Whitman number. This number is a sortable code unique to each bank and note.

AL: Abbreviation for the state under study.

020: Numerical designation specific to each bank.

001: The denomination in dollars.

G010a: G indicates a good or valid note. Other categories are indicated thus: C (counterfeit); R (raised); S (spurious); N (not-attributed); A (altered). Numbers are assigned starting with 010, 020, et seq. Terminal letters following the number indicate variations of a note: a series of different colored overprints, tints, payees, etc., all on the same design of note. For more information, see the "How to Use This Book" section at the front of the volume, page xiv.

$20 • W-MS-070-020-G090b

CC, CC

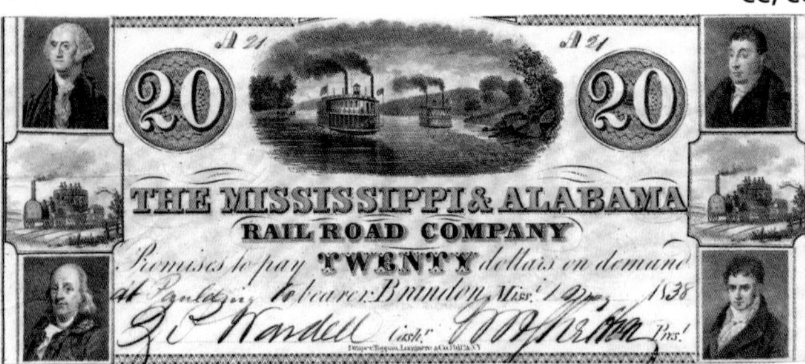

Back: Red-orange medallion head / Medallion head. ***Engraver:*** Draper, Toppan, Longacre & Co. ***Comments:*** H-MS-25-G16b, Kraus-Unlisted. Similar to W-MS-070-020-G090. 18__. 1838.

Rarity: URS-10
F $125

$20 • W-MS-070-020-G090c

Overprint: Black REISSUED stamp. ***Back:*** Red-orange medallion head / Medallion head. ***Engraver:*** Draper, Toppan, Longacre & Co. ***Comments:*** H-Unlisted, Kraus-Unlisted. Similar to W-MS-070-020-G090. 18__. 1830s.

Rarity: —

$20 • W-MS-070-020-G100

JM

Engraver: Draper, Toppan, Longacre & Co. ***Comments:*** H-MS-25-G18, Kraus-10122. 18__. 1837.

Rarity: URS-10
F $125

$25 • W-MS-070-025-G110

CC

Back: Plain. ***Engraver:*** Draper, Toppan, Longacre & Co. ***Comments:*** H-MS-25-G22, Kraus-Unlisted. 18__. 1837 and 1838.

Rarity: URS-10
F $125

$25 • W-MS-070-025-G110a

Left: Portrait of George Washington / Train / Portrait of Benjamin Franklin. ***Center:*** 25 / Three women seated / 25. ***Right:*** Portrait of Marquis de Lafayette / Train / Portrait of Robert Fulton. ***Overprint:*** Black REISSUED stamp. ***Back:*** Plain. ***Engraver:*** Draper, Toppan, Longacre & Co. ***Comments:*** H-MS-25-G22a, Kraus-Unlisted. Similar to W-MS-070-025-G110. 18__. 1837 and 1838.

Rarity: —

$25 • W-MS-070-025-G110b

JM

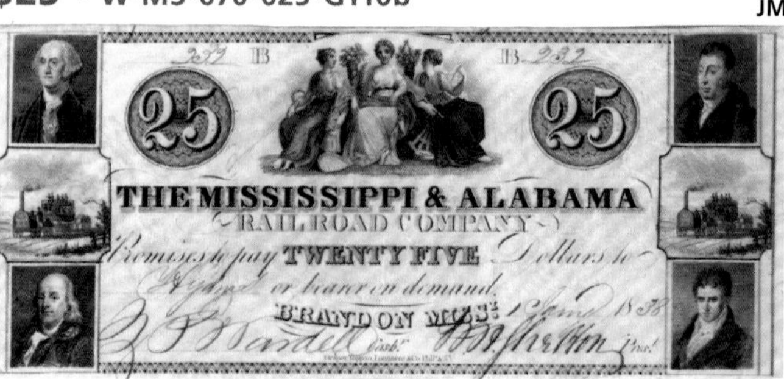

Back: Orange. ***Engraver:*** Draper, Toppan, Longacre & Co. ***Comments:*** H-MS-25-G22b, Kraus-Unlisted. Similar to W-MS-070-025-G110. 18__. 1838.

Rarity: URS-10
F $125

$25 • W-MS-070-025-G110c

JM

Overprint: Black stamp. ***Back:*** Orange. ***Engraver:*** Draper, Toppan, Longacre & Co. ***Comments:*** H-Unlisted, Kraus-Unlisted. Similar to W-MS-070-025-G110. 18__. 1830s.

Rarity: URS-9
F $150

$25 • W-MS-070-025-G120

CC

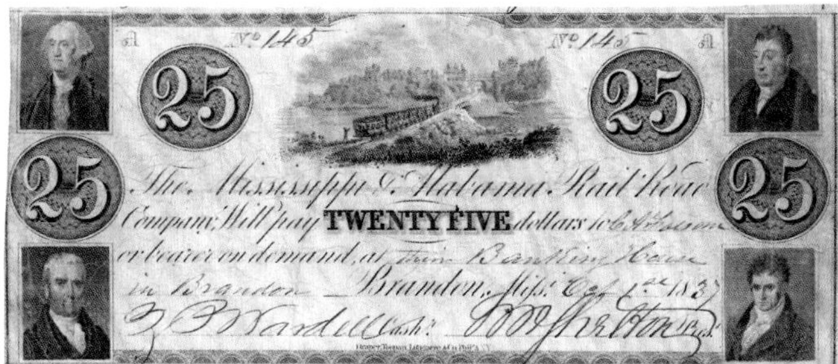

Engraver: Draper, Toppan, Longacre & Co. ***Comments:*** H-MS-25-G24, Kraus-10123. 18__. 1837.

Rarity: URS-10
F $125

$50 • W-MS-070-050-G130

JM

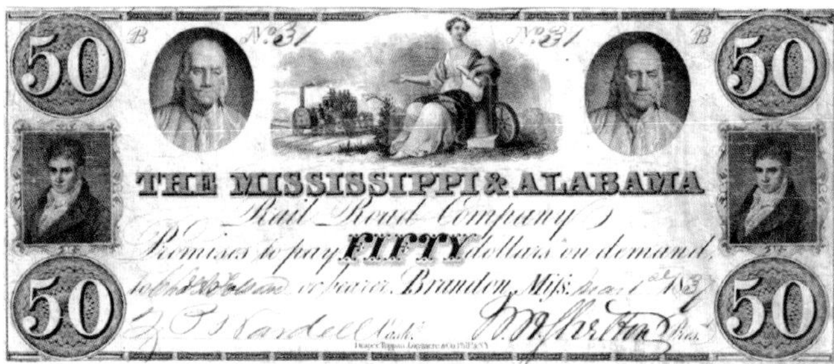

Back: Plain. ***Engraver:*** Draper, Toppan, Longacre & Co. ***Comments:*** H-MS-25-G26, Kraus-Unlisted. 18__. 1837 and 1838.

Rarity: URS-9
F $150

$50 • W-MS-070-050-G130a

JM

Overprint: Black REISSUED stamp. ***Back:*** Plain. ***Engraver:*** Draper, Toppan, Longacre & Co. ***Comments:*** H-MS-25-G26a, Kraus-Unlisted. Similar to W-MS-070-050-G130. 18__. 1837 and 1838.

Rarity: URS-8
F $175

$50 • W-MS-070-050-G130b

JM

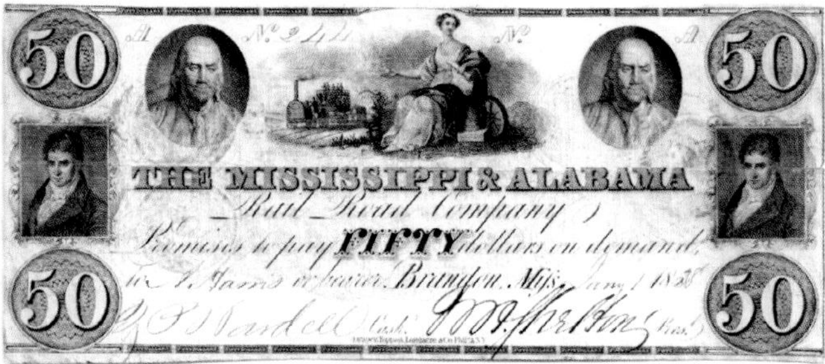

Back: Orange. ***Engraver:*** Draper, Toppan, Longacre & Co. ***Comments:*** H-MS-25-G26b, Kraus-Unlisted. Similar to W-MS-070-050-G130. 18__. 1838.

Rarity: URS-9
F $175

$50 • W-MS-070-050-G130c

Overprint: Black REISSUED stamp. ***Back:*** Orange. ***Engraver:*** Draper, Toppan, Longacre & Co. ***Comments:*** H-Unlisted, Kraus-Unlisted. Similar to W-MS-070-050-G130. 18__. 1830s.

Rarity: —

$50 • W-MS-070-050-G140

JM

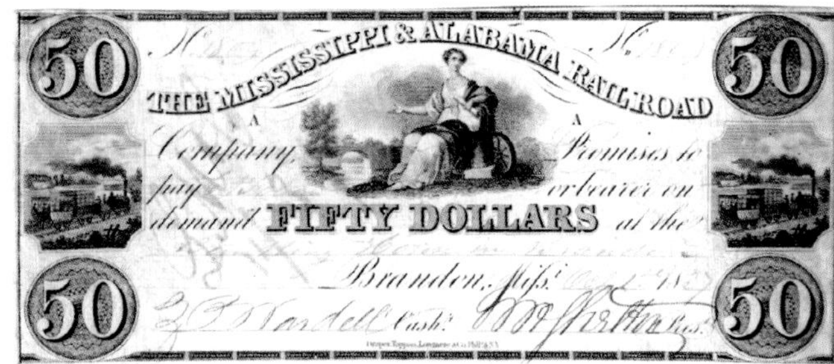

Engraver: Draper, Toppan, Longacre & Co. ***Comments:*** H-MS-25-G28, Kraus-10124. 18__. 1837.

Rarity: URS-3
F $1,200

$100 • W-MS-070-100-G150

JM

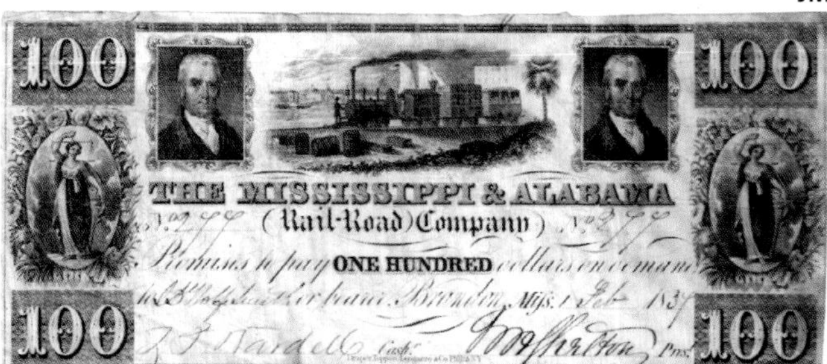

Back: Plain. ***Engraver:*** Draper, Toppan, Longacre & Co. ***Comments:*** H-MS-25-G30, Kraus-Unlisted. 18__. 1837 and 1838.

Rarity: URS-9
VF $275

$100 • W-MS-070-100-G150a

JM

Overprint: Black REISSUED stamp. ***Back:*** Plain. ***Engraver:*** Draper, Toppan, Longacre & Co. ***Comments:*** H-MS-25-G30a, Kraus-Unlisted. Similar to W-MS-070-100-G150. 18__. 1837 and 1838.

Rarity: URS-9
VF $250

$100 • W-MS-070-100-G150b

JM

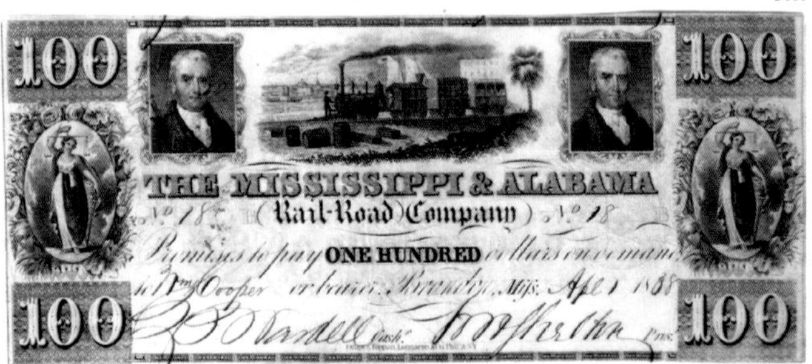

Back: Orange. ***Engraver:*** Draper, Toppan, Longacre & Co. ***Comments:*** H-MS-25-G30b, Kraus-Unlisted. Similar to W-MS-070-100-G150. 18__. 1838.

Rarity: URS-9
VF $250

$100 • W-MS-070-100-G150c

Overprint: Black REISSUED stamp. ***Back:*** Orange. ***Engraver:*** Draper, Toppan, Longacre & Co. ***Comments:*** H-Unlisted, Kraus-Unlisted. Similar to W-MS-070-100-G150. 18__. 1830s.

Rarity: —

$100 • W-MS-070-100-G160

CC

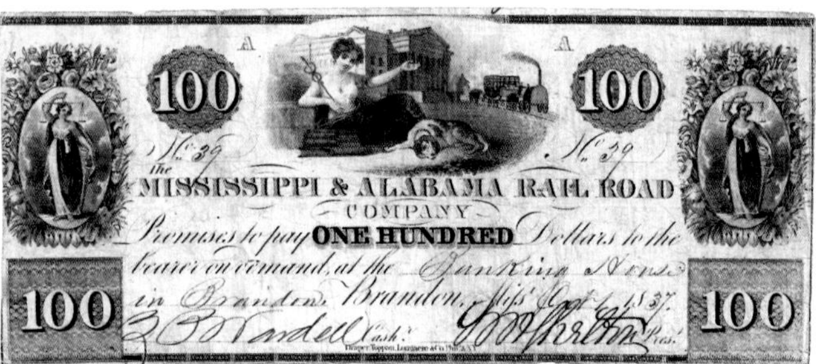

Engraver: Draper, Toppan, Longacre & Co. ***Comments:*** H-MS-25-G32, Kraus-10125. 18__. 1837.

Rarity: URS-6
F $250

$100 • W-MS-070-100-G160a

JM

Overprint: Black REISSUED stamp. ***Engraver:*** Draper, Toppan, Longacre & Co. ***Comments:*** H-Unlisted, Kraus-Unlisted. Similar to W-MS-070-100-G160. 18__. 1837.

Rarity: URS-5
F $300

$500 • W-MS-070-500-G170

CC

Engraver: Draper, Toppan, Longacre & Co. ***Comments:*** H-MS-25-G34, Kraus-10126. 18__. 1837.

Rarity: URS-5
F $550

$500 • W-MS-070-500-G170a

Left: Muse seated / 500. ***Center:*** 500 / Hebe watering eagle / 500. ***Right:*** Muse seated / 500. ***Overprint:*** Black REISSUED stamp. ***Engraver:*** Draper, Toppan, Longacre & Co. ***Comments:*** H-MS-25-G34a, Kraus-10126m. Similar to W-MS-070-500-G170. 18__. 1837.

Rarity: URS-4
F $650

$1,000 • W-MS-070-1000-G180

JM

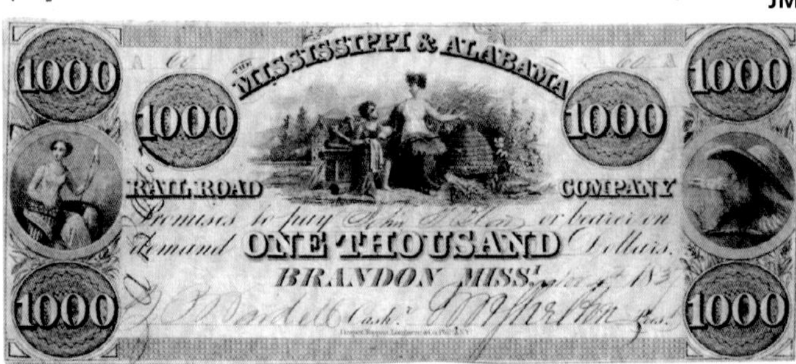

Engraver: Draper, Toppan, Longacre & Co. ***Comments:*** H-MS-25-G36, Kraus-10127. 18__. 1837.

Rarity: URS-4
F $500

$1,000 • W-MS-070-1000-G180a

Left: 1000 / Liberty with shield, pole and cap / 1000. ***Center:*** 1000 / Woman seated with child, Beehive / 1000. ***Right:*** 1000 / Eagle / 1000. ***Overprint:*** Black REISSUED stamp. ***Engraver:*** Draper, Toppan, Longacre & Co. ***Comments:*** H-MS-25-G36a, Kraus-10127n. Similar to W-MS-070-1000-G180. 18__. 1837.

Rarity: URS-3
F $600

Post Notes

$5 • W-MS-070-005-G190

JM

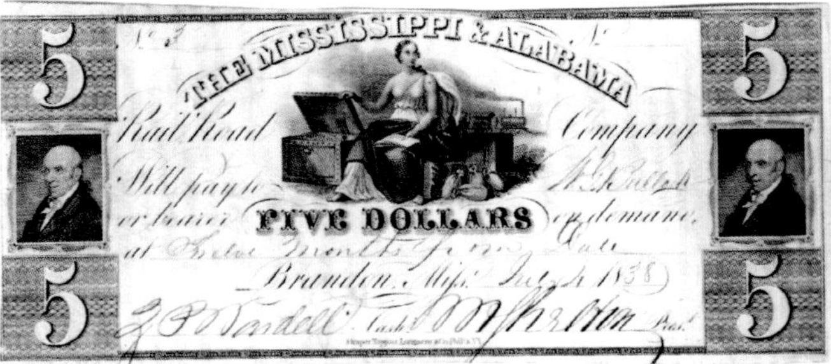

Engraver: Draper, Toppan, Longacre & Co. ***Comments:*** H-MS-25-G40, Kraus-10120t. 18__. 1838.

Rarity: URS-5
VF $400

$5 • W-MS-070-005-G190a

JM

Engraver: Draper, Toppan, Longacre & Co. ***Comments:*** H-MS-25-G40a, Kraus-10140s. Similar to W-MS-070-005-G190 but with handwritten "5% Int. Twelve months from date." 18__. 1838.

Rarity: URS-5
VF $400

$10 • W-MS-070-010-G200

JM

Engraver: Draper, Toppan, Longacre & Co. ***Comments:*** H-MS-25-G42, Kraus-10121t. 18__. 1838.

Rarity: URS-5
VF $400

$10 • W-MS-070-010-G200a

Left: 10 / Portrait of George Washington / 10. ***Center:*** Spread eagle. ***Right:*** 10 / Portrait of Marquis de Lafayette / 10. ***Engraver:*** Draper, Toppan, Longacre & Co. ***Comments:*** H-MS-25-G42a, Kraus-10121z. Similar to W-MS-070-010-G200 but with handwritten "5% Int. Twelve months from date." 18__. 1838.

Rarity: URS-5
VF $400

$10 • W-MS-070-010-G210

Left: 10 / Dog with key and strongbox / X. ***Right:*** Men and women in and around chariot drawn by horses, Cherub flying / 10. ***Engraver:*** Draper, Toppan, Longacre & Co. ***Comments:*** H-MS-25-G44, Kraus-10190. Handwritten "Their Banking House with 5% Interest." 18__. 1838.

Rarity: *None known*

$20 • W-MS-070-020-G220

JM

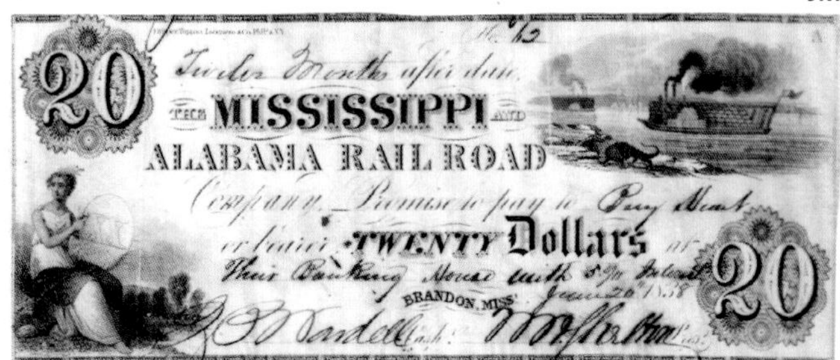

Engraver: Draper, Toppan, Longacre & Co. ***Comments:*** H-MS-25-G48, Kraus-Unlisted. Handwritten "Their Banking House with 5% Interest." 183_. 1838.

Rarity: URS-8
F $200

$20 • W-MS-070-020-G230

JM

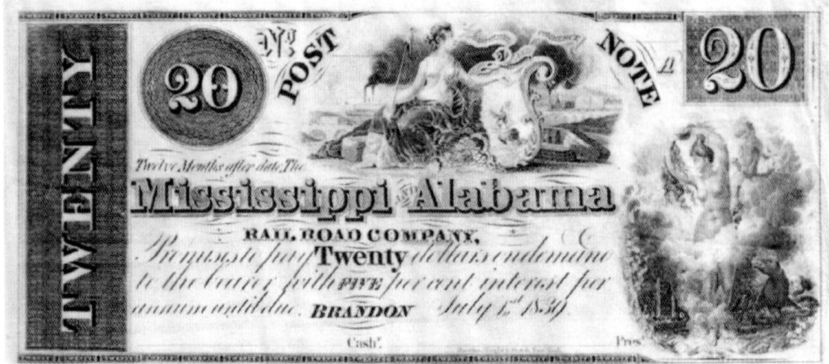

Engraver: Rawdon, Wright & Hatch. ***Comments:*** H-MS-25-G50, Kraus-10200. July 1st, 1839.

Rarity: URS-5
F $350

$50 • W-MS-070-050-G240

Left: 50 / Man seated with staff. ***Right:*** Ship, Eagle with shield, Woman seated with pole and cap / 50. ***Engraver:*** Draper, Toppan, Longacre & Co. ***Comments:*** H-MS-25-G54, Kraus-Unlisted. 18__. 1838.

Rarity: —

$50 • **W-MS-070-050-G250**

JM

Back: Orange. ***Engraver:*** Draper, Toppan, Longacre & Co. ***Comments:*** H-MS-25-G56b, Kraus-10145o. Handwritten "After 1 July 1839 with 5 per cent interest from date." 18__. 1838.

Rarity: URS-5
F $450

$50 • **W-MS-070-050-G260**

JM

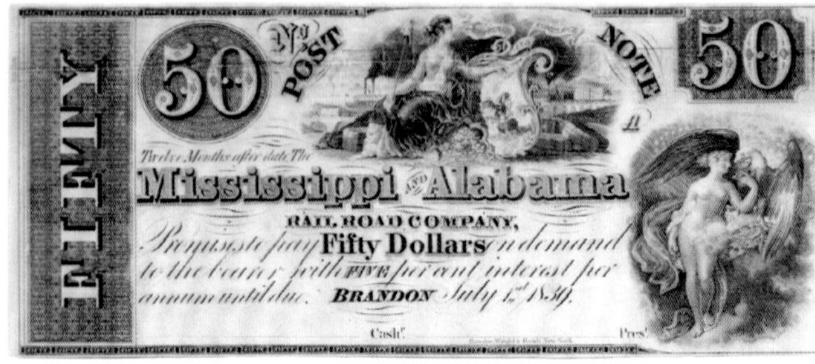

Engraver: Rawdon, Wright & Hatch. ***Comments:*** H-MS-25-G58, Kraus-10201. July 1st, 1839.

Rarity: URS-5
F $450

$100 • **W-MS-070-100-G270**

JM

Engraver: Draper, Toppan, Longacre & Co. ***Comments:*** H-MS-25-G62, Kraus-Unlisted. 183_. 1838.

Rarity: URS-2
F $750

$100 • **W-MS-070-100-G280**

JM

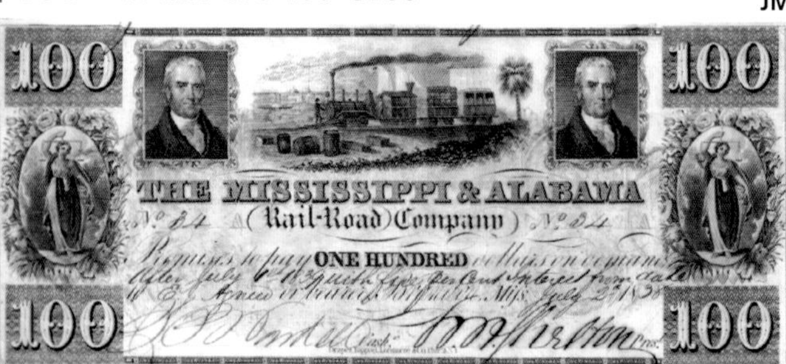

Back: Orange. ***Engraver:*** Draper, Toppan, Longacre & Co. ***Comments:*** H-MS-25-G64b, Kraus-10146q. Handwritten "After July 1st 1839 with five per cent interest from date." 18__. 1838.

Rarity: URS-5
F $450

$100 • **W-MS-070-100-G290**

JM

Engraver: Rawdon, Wright & Hatch. ***Comments:*** H-MS-25-G66, Kraus-10202. July 1st, 1839.

Rarity: URS-6
F $500

Notes Payable at the Girard Bank, Philadelphia

$5 • **W-MS-070-005-G300**

JM

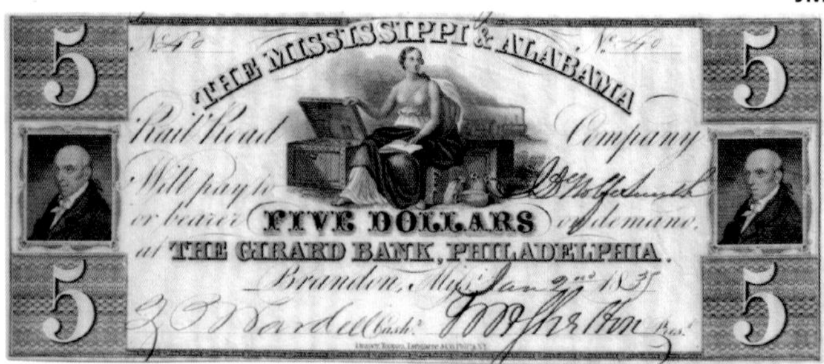

Engraver: Draper, Toppan, Longacre & Co. ***Comments:*** H-MS-25-G90, Kraus-10120. Engraved "The Girard Bank, Philadelphia." 18__. 1837.

Rarity: URS-8
F $100

$5 • **W-MS-070-005-G300a**

Engraver: Draper, Toppan, Longacre & Co. ***Comments:*** H-Unlisted, Kraus-Unlisted. Similar to W-MS-070-005-G300. Handwritten "The Girard Bank, Philadelphia." 18__. 1837.

Rarity: —

$10 • **W-MS-070-010-G310**

SI

Engraver: Draper, Toppan, Longacre & Co. ***Comments:*** H-MS-25-G92, Kraus-10121. Engraved "The Girard Bank, Philadelphia." 18__. 1837.

Rarity: URS-6
F $150

$10 • **W-MS-070-010-G310a**

Left: 10 / Portrait of George Washington / 10. ***Center:*** Spread eagle. ***Right:*** 10 / Portrait of Marquis de Lafayette / 10. ***Engraver:*** Draper, Toppan, Longacre & Co. ***Comments:*** H-MS-25-G92a, Kraus-1012c. Similar to W-MS-070-010-G310. Handwritten "The Girard Bank, Philadelphia." 18__. 1837.

Rarity: URS-5
F $450

$10 • **W-MS-070-010-G320**

JM

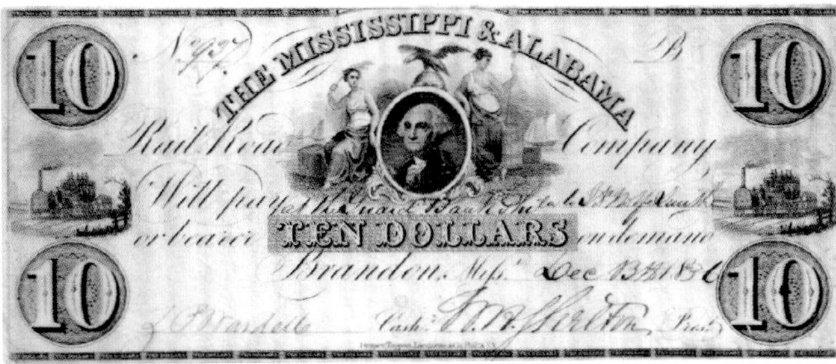

Back: Plain. ***Engraver:*** Draper, Toppan, Longacre & Co. ***Comments:*** H-MS-25-G94, Kraus-10141c. Handwritten "at the Girard Bank, Phila. to J. Harris." 18__. 1837.

Rarity: URS-5
F $250

$20 • **W-MS-070-020-G330**

Left: Portrait of George Washington / 20 / Portrait of John Marshall. ***Center:*** 20 / Woman seated with child and plow / 20. ***Right:*** Portrait of Marquis de Lafayette / 20 / Portrait of Robert Fulton. ***Engraver:*** Draper, Toppan, Longacre & Co. ***Comments:*** H-MS-25-G96, Kraus-Unlisted. Handwritten "The Girard Bank, Philadelphia." 18__. 1837.

Rarity: URS-3
F $450

$25 • **W-MS-070-025-G335**

Left: Portrait of George Washington / 25 / Portrait of John Marshall. ***Center:*** 25 / Train / 25. ***Right:*** Portrait of Marquis de Lafayette / 25 / Portrait of Robert Fulton. ***Engraver:*** Draper, Toppan, Longacre & Co. ***Comments:*** H-Unlisted, Kraus-Unlisted. Handwritten "The Girard Bank, Philadelphia." 18__. 1830s.

Rarity: —

$50 • **W-MS-070-050-G340**

Left: 50 / Train / 50. ***Center:*** Commerce seated, Bridge. ***Right:*** 50 / Train / 50. ***Engraver:*** Draper, Toppan, Longacre & Co. ***Comments:*** H-MS-25-G98, Kraus-Unlisted. Handwritten "The Girard Bank, Philadelphia." 18__. 1837.

Rarity: URS-3
F $450

$100 • **W-MS-070-100-G350**

JM

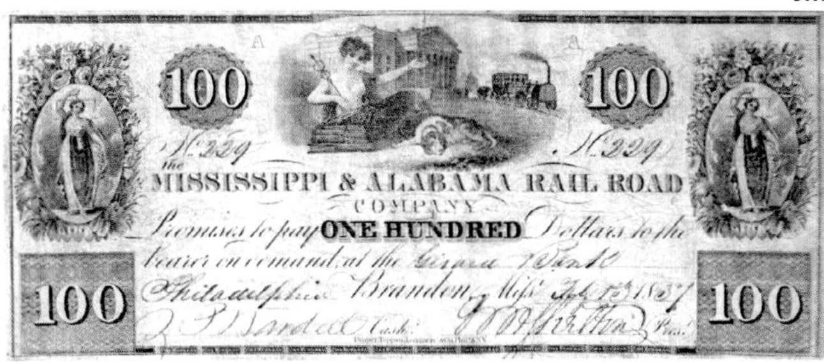

Engraver: Draper, Toppan, Longacre & Co. ***Comments:*** H-MS-25-G100, Kraus-Unlisted. Handwritten "The Girard Bank, Philadelphia." 18__. 1837.

Rarity: URS-5
F $350

Notes Payable "at the Girard Bank, Phila. & at New Orleans"

$10 • **W-MS-070-010-G360**

JM

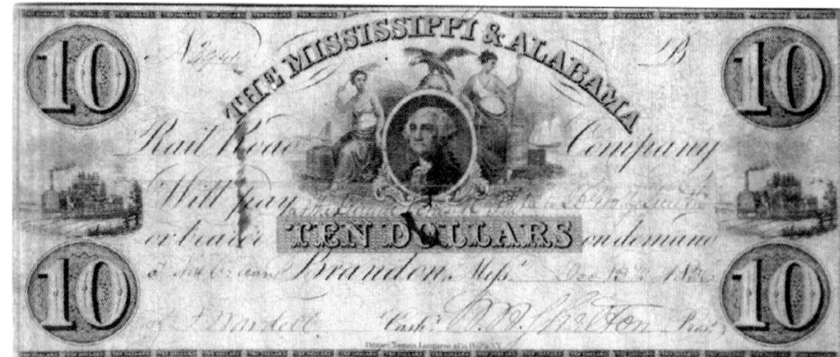

Back: Plain. ***Engraver:*** Draper, Toppan, Longacre & Co. ***Comments:*** H-MS-25-G104, Kraus-10141d. Handwritten "at the Girard Bank, Phila. & at New Orleans." 18__. 1837.

Rarity: URS-4
F $500

Notes Payable "at the Bank of J.L. & S. Joseph & Co., New York"

$5 • **W-MS-070-005-G370**

JM

Engraver: Draper, Toppan, Longacre & Co. ***Comments:*** H-MS-25-G110, Kraus-10120e. 18__. 1837.

Rarity: URS-10
F $200

$10 • **W-MS-070-010-G380**

Left: 10 / Portrait of George Washington / 10. ***Center:*** Spread eagle. ***Right:*** 10 / Portrait of Marquis de Lafayette / 10. ***Engraver:*** Draper, Toppan, Longacre & Co. ***Comments:*** H-MS-25-G112, Kraus-10121e. 18__. 1837.

Rarity: URS-5
F $350

$20 • **W-MS-070-020-G390**

JM

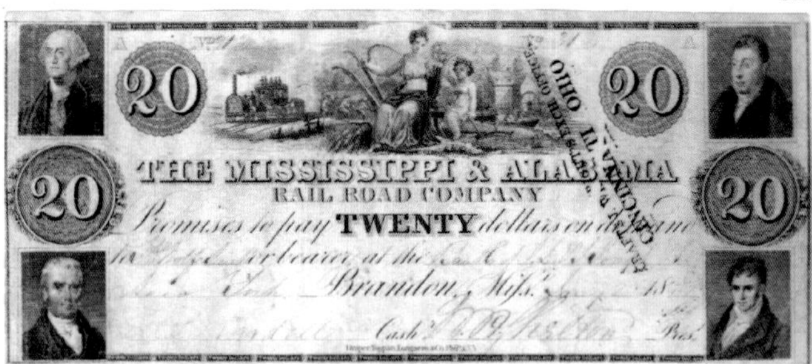

Engraver: Draper, Toppan, Longacre & Co. ***Comments:*** H-MS-25-G114, Kraus-10122e. 18__. 1837.

Rarity: URS-5
F $350

$25 • **W-MS-070-025-G400**

JM

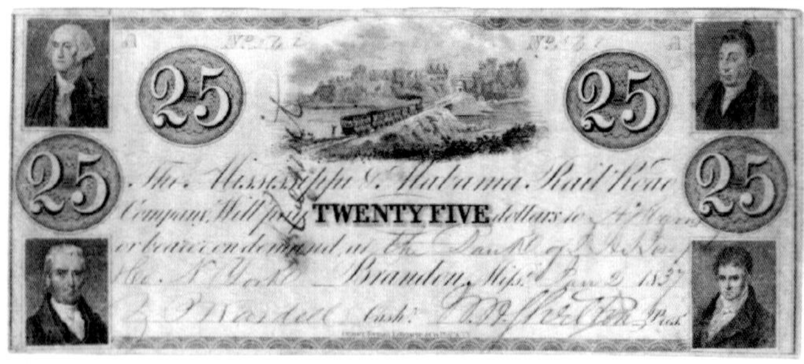

Engraver: Draper, Toppan, Longacre & Co. ***Comments:*** H-Unlisted, Kraus-10123e. 18__. 1837.

Rarity: URS-5
F $350

$50 • **W-MS-070-050-G410**

JM

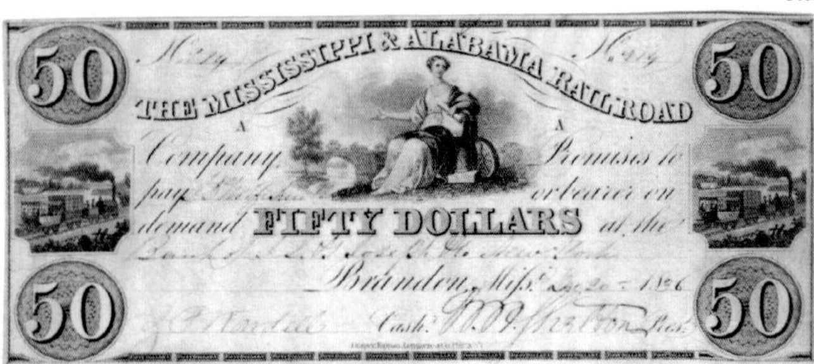

Engraver: Draper, Toppan, Longacre & Co. ***Comments:*** H-MS-25-G118, Kraus-10124e. 18__. 1837.

Rarity: URS-5
F $350

$100 • **W-MS-070-100-G420**

JM

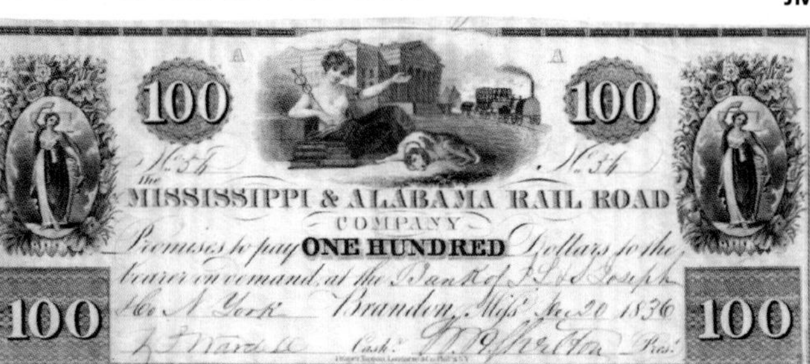

Engraver: Draper, Toppan, Longacre & Co. ***Comments:*** H-MS-25-G120, Kraus-10125e. 18__. 1837.

Rarity: URS-5
EF $350

Notes Payable at the Bank of Louisiana, New Orleans

$5 • **W-MS-070-005-G430**

JM

Engraver: Draper, Toppan, Longacre & Co. ***Comments:*** H-MS-25-G124, Kraus-Unlisted. 18__. 1837.

Rarity: URS-5
F $350

$5 • **W-MS-070-005-G435**

Left: 5 / Train / 5. ***Center:*** Portrait of Fernando De Soto / Wagon / Portrait of Indian. ***Right:*** 5 / Train / 5. ***Back:*** Plain. ***Engraver:*** Draper, Toppan, Longacre & Co. ***Comments:*** H-Unlisted, Kraus-Unlisted. 18__. 1830s.

Rarity: —

$10 • **W-MS-070-010-G440**

JM

Back: Plain. ***Engraver:*** Draper, Toppan, Longacre & Co. ***Comments:*** H-MS-25-G126, Kraus-10121f. Handwritten "at the Bank of La. New Orleans." 18__. 1837.

Rarity: URS-6
F $200

$10 • **W-MS-070-010-G445**

Left: 10 / Portrait of George Washington / 10. ***Center:*** Spread eagle. ***Right:*** 10 / Portrait of Marquis de Lafayette / 10. ***Engraver:*** Draper, Toppan, Longacre & Co. ***Comments:*** H-Unlisted, Kraus-Unlisted. 18__. 1830s.

Rarity: —

Notes Payable at the Merchants Bank, New York

$5 • **W-MS-070-005-G450**

JM

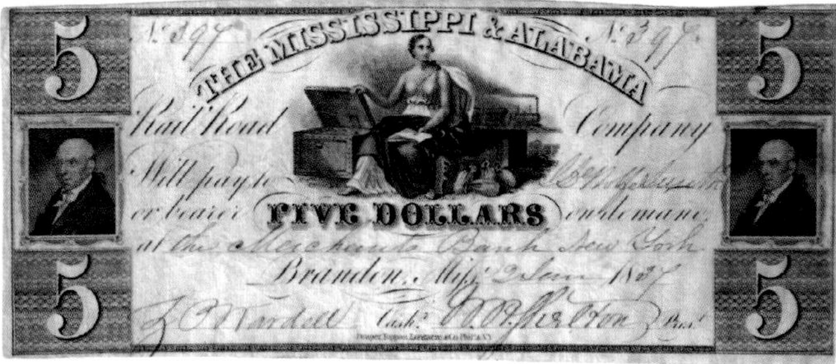

Engraver: Draper, Toppan, Longacre & Co. ***Comments:*** H-MS-25-G130, Kraus-10120g. 18__. 1837.

Rarity: URS-5
F $250

$10 • **W-MS-070-010-G460**

JM

Engraver: Draper, Toppan, Longacre & Co. ***Comments:*** H-MS-25-G132, Kraus-10121g. 18__. 1837.

Rarity: URS-5
F $250

$20 • **W-MS-070-020-G470**

JM

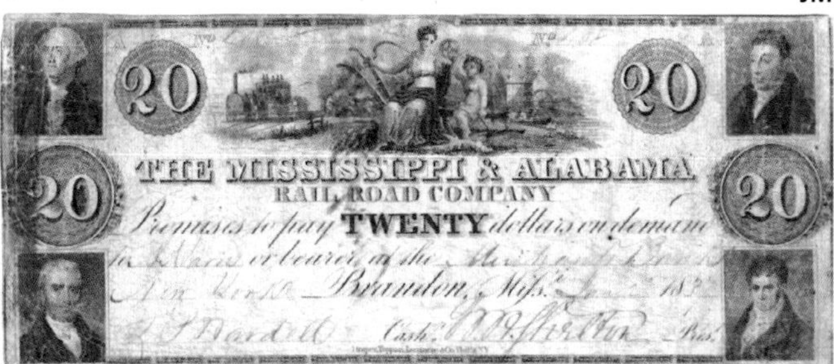

Engraver: Draper, Toppan, Longacre & Co. ***Comments:*** H-MS-25-G136, Kraus-10122g. 18__. 1837.

Rarity: URS-5
F $250

$25 • **W-MS-070-025-G480**

JM

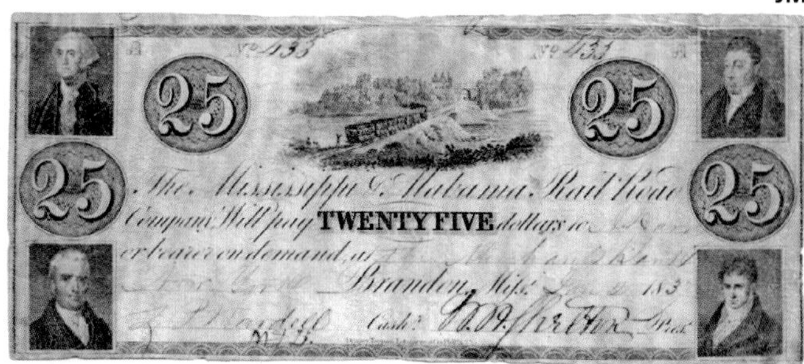

Engraver: Draper, Toppan, Longacre & Co. ***Comments:*** H-MS-25-G138, Kraus-10123g. 18__. 1837.

Rarity: URS-5
F $250

$50 • **W-MS-070-050-G485**

Left: 50 / Train / 50. ***Center:*** Commerce seated, Bridge. ***Right:*** 50 / Train / 50. ***Engraver:*** Draper, Toppan, Longacre & Co. ***Comments:*** H-Unlisted, Kraus-Unlisted. 18__. 1830s.

Rarity: —

$100 • **W-MS-070-100-G490**

Left: Justice standing / 100. ***Center:*** 100 / Commerce seated, Dog lying down, Train, Building / 100. ***Right:*** Justice standing / 100. ***Engraver:*** Draper, Toppan, Longacre & Co. ***Comments:*** H-Unlisted, Kraus-Unlisted. 18__. 1830s.

Rarity: —

Notes Payable at the Bank of the United States, Philadelphia

$5 • **W-MS-070-005-G495**

Left: 5 / Portrait of Stephen Girard / 5. ***Center:*** Moneta seated with treasure chest. ***Right:*** 5 / Portrait of Stephen Girard / 5. ***Engraver:*** Draper, Toppan, Longacre & Co. ***Comments:*** H-MS-25-G146, Kraus-10120h. 18__. 1837.

Rarity: URS-3
F $400

$10 • **W-MS-070-010-G500**

Left: 10 / Portrait of George Washington / 10. ***Center:*** Spread eagle. ***Right:*** 10 / Portrait of Marquis de Lafayette / 10. ***Engraver:*** Draper, Toppan, Longacre & Co. ***Comments:*** H-MS-25-G148, Kraus-10121h. 18__. 1837.

Rarity: URS-3
F $400

Post Notes Payable at the Bank of the United States, Philadelphia

$5 • W-MS-070-005-G510

JM

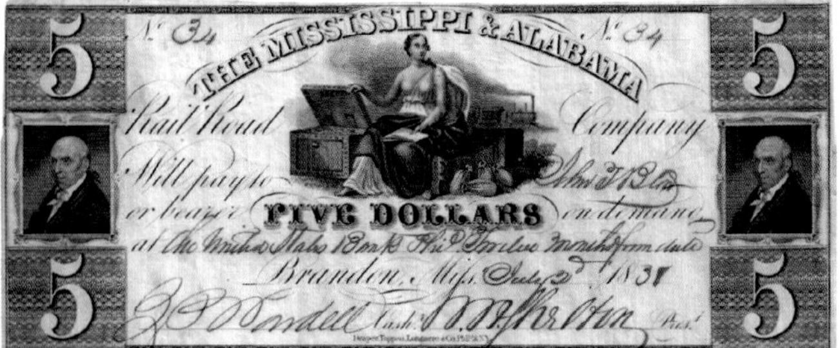

Engraver: Draper, Toppan, Longacre & Co. ***Comments:*** H-MS-25-G156, Kraus-10120w. 18__. 1837.

Rarity: URS-5
F $250

$10 • W-MS-070-010-G520

JM

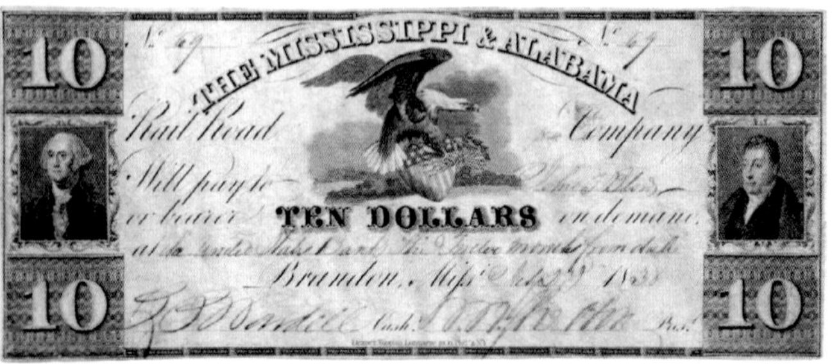

Engraver: Draper, Toppan, Longacre & Co. ***Comments:*** H-MS-25-G158, Kraus-10121v. 18__. 1837.

Rarity: URS-8
F $200

$10 • W-MS-070-010-G530

JM

Engraver: Draper, Toppan, Longacre & Co. ***Comments:*** H-MS-25-G160, Kraus-10190u. 183_. 1838.

Rarity: URS-8
F $200

$20 • W-MS-070-020-G540

JM

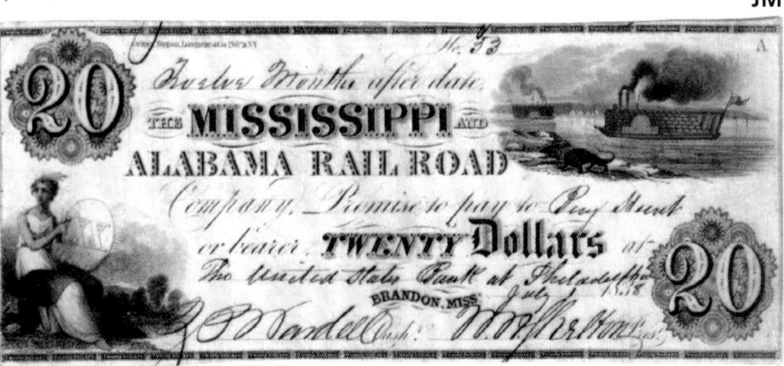

Engraver: Draper, Toppan, Longacre & Co. ***Comments:*** H-MS-25-G164, Kraus-10191w. 183_. 1838.

Rarity: URS-8
F $200

$25 • W-MS-070-025-G550

Left: Portrait of George Washington / Train / Portrait of Benjamin Franklin. ***Center:*** 25 / Three women seated / 25. ***Right:*** Portrait of Marquis de Lafayette / Train / Portrait of Robert Fulton. ***Back:*** Plain. ***Engraver:*** Draper, Toppan, Longacre & Co. ***Comments:*** H-MS-25-G166, Kraus-10157x. 18__. 1837 and 1838.

Rarity: URS-6
F $300

$25 • W-MS-070-025-G550a

JM

Back: Orange. ***Engraver:*** Draper, Toppan, Longacre & Co. ***Comments:*** H-Unlisted, Kraus-Unlisted. Similar to W-MS-070-025-G550. 18__. 1837 and 1838.

Rarity: URS-8
F $200

$50 • W-MS-070-050-G560

JM

Engraver: Draper, Toppan, Longacre & Co. ***Comments:*** H-MS-25-G170, Kraus-10192u. 183_. 1838.

Rarity: URS-6
F $275

$50 • W-MS-070-050-G560a

JM

Overprint: Black stamp. ***Engraver:*** Draper, Toppan, Longacre & Co. ***Comments:*** H-Unlisted, Kraus-Unlisted. Similar to W-MS-070-050-G560. 183_. 1838.

Rarity: URS-6
F $275

$100 • W-MS-070-100-G570 JM

Engraver: Draper, Toppan, Longacre & Co. ***Comments:*** H-MS-25-G174, Kraus-10193w. 183_. 1838.

Rarity: URS-4
F $450

Non-Valid Issues

$1 • W-MS-070-001-N010

Comments: H-Unlisted, Kraus-10100a. Fraudulent issue of W-MS-070-001-G020. Filled-in remainder. 18__. 1830s.

Rarity: *None known*

$2 • W-MS-070-002-N020

Comments: H-Unlisted, Kraus-10101a. Fraudulent issue of W-MS-070-002-G030. Filled-in remainder. 18__. 1830s.

Rarity: *None known*

$3 • W-MS-070-003-N030

Comments: H-Unlisted, Kraus-10102a. Fraudulent issue of W-MS-070-003-G040. Filled-in remainder. 18__. 1830s.

Rarity: *None known*

Brookhaven, Mississippi

Originally inhabited by Choctaw Indians, the area that became Brookhaven was founded in 1818 by Samuel Jayne. He named it after Brookhaven on Long Island. In 1858 the railroad reached Brookhaven, connecting it to New Orleans and Memphis. Unfortunately, during the Civil War this made the town a target, and on April 29, 1863, Union forces burned public buildings and destroyed the railway. Eventually the railroad was rebuilt.

Bank of Brookhaven

1862

W-MS-080

History: The Bank of Brookhaven was authorized on January 17, 1862, with a capital of $300,000.[4] The fate of this bank is unknown.

Numismatic Commentary: No notes of this bank are known.

Canton, Mississippi

In 1833 Madison County appointed John B. Peyton as surveyor in order to select a location for the county seat. The next year a site was chosen, and 40 acres were purchased. The land was divided into plots with a public square at the center, and in 1836 the town of Canton was incorporated with a population of 400. The origin of the name is uncertain, but the two possibilities are both Chinese in inspiration. One states that Canton, Mississippi, is exactly on the opposite side of the world from Canton, China. The other possibility claims that a girl from a Chinese family died in the area, and the community named the town after the family.

By 1838 Canton supported two banks, two hotels, a drug store, various dry-goods stores, grocery stores, a bakery, tailor shops, watchmakers, and a tin shop. A courthouse, jailhouse, church, and academy for girls were also established.

Citizens Bank of Madison County

1837–1840

W-MS-090

History: The Citizens Bank of Madison County was incorporated on May 3, 1837, with an authorized capital of $1,000,000. In 1840 an act was passed forcing the bank to forfeit its charter due to its failure to pay specie when its notes were presented for redemption.

The Citizens Bank of Madison County had branch banks located in Livingston, W-MS-500, and Utica, W-MS-850.

Numismatic Commentary: The 25¢ and 50¢ notes are known only as remainders or filled-in remainders and are fairly common. Validly issued notes are dated 1837 and 1838.

Valid Issues

Post Notes

25¢ • W-MS-090-00.25-G010 CC

Engraver: Rawdon, Wright & Hatch. ***Comments:*** H-MS-30-G20, Kraus-3341r. 18__. 1838.

Rarity: URS-7
F $200

50¢ • W-MS-090-00.50-G020 CC

Engraver: Rawdon, Wright & Hatch. ***Comments:*** H-MS-30-G22, Kraus-3342r. 18__. 1838.

Rarity: URS-6
F $250

$1 • **W-MS-090-001-G030**

JM

Engraver: Rawdon, Wright & Hatch. ***Comments:*** H-MS-30-G24, Kraus-3343. 18__. 1838.

Rarity: URS-5
F $300

$2 • **W-MS-090-002-G040**

CC

Engraver: Rawdon, Wright & Hatch. ***Comments:*** H-MS-30-G26, Kraus-3344. 18__. 1838.

Rarity: URS-5
F $300

$5 • **W-MS-090-005-G050**

JM

Engraver: Rawdon, Wright & Hatch. ***Comments:*** H-MS-30-G30, Kraus-3345. 18__. 1838.

Rarity: URS-7
F $200

$10 • **W-MS-090-010-G060**

JM

Engraver: Rawdon, Wright & Hatch. ***Comments:*** H-MS-30-G32, Kraus-3346. 18__. 1838.

Rarity: URS-7
F $250

$20 • **W-MS-090-020-G070**

CC

Engraver: Rawdon, Wright & Hatch. ***Comments:*** H-MS-30-G36, Kraus-3347. 18__. 1838.

Rarity: URS-6
VF $350

$50 • **W-MS-090-050-G080**

CC

Engraver: Rawdon, Wright & Hatch. ***Comments:*** H-MS-30-G38, Kraus-3348. 18__. 1838.

Rarity: URS-5
F $450

Collectors and Researchers:

If you have new information about any banks or notes listed in this volume, contact Whitman Publishing, Attn: Obsolete Paper Money, 3101 Clairmont Road, Suite G, Atlanta, GA 30329.

$100 • W-MS-090-100-G090

JM

Engraver: Rawdon, Wright & Hatch. ***Comments:*** H-MS-30-G40, Kraus-3349. 18__. 1838.

Rarity: URS-5
F $450

Uncut Post-Note Sheets

$1-$1-$2 • W-MS-090-001.001.002-US010

JM

Engraver: Rawdon, Wright & Hatch. ***Comments:*** H-MS-30-G24, G24, G26. First two notes identical. 18__. 1838.

Rarity: URS-2
F $1,500

Non-Valid Issues

$100 • W-MS-090-100-N010

Comments: H-Unlisted, Kraus-3349d. Fraudulently issued note during the Confederate period. Filled-in remainder. 18__. 1838.

Rarity: —

Commercial Bank of Natchez (branch)

1836–1856

W-MS-100

History: The Commercial Bank of Natchez was incorporated on February 27, 1836, with an authorized capital of $3,000,000. The bank was forbidden to distribute notes of a denomination lower than $5. The bank did not last long, and on February 6, 1841, an act was passed to close the branch banks and wind up the affairs of the parent bank. The closing of the bank was extended due to a battle with creditors that went all the way to the U.S. Supreme Court. Finally the bank went into liquidation in 1856.

The Commercial Bank of Natchez had its parent bank located in Natchez, W-MS-640, and branch banks located in Brandon, W-MS-060, Holmesville, W-MS-420, and Shieldsboro, W-MS-830.

Numismatic Commentary: No notes with this branch location are known. The listings below are speculative, based on the parent bank.

Valid Issues

$5 • W-MS-100-005-G010

Left: FIVE vertically. ***Center:*** Two cherubs as Liberty and Commerce with U.S. flag, Ship. ***Right:*** FIVE vertically. ***Engraver:*** Underwood, Bald, Spencer & Hufty. ***Comments:*** H-MS-160-G100, Kraus-4020p. 18__. 1830s.

Rarity: *None known*

$10 • W-MS-100-010-G020

Left: TEN vertically. ***Center:*** 10 / Ships / 10. ***Right:*** TEN vertically. ***Engraver:*** Underwood, Bald, Spencer & Hufty. ***Comments:*** H-MS-160-G106, Kraus-4021p. 18__. 1830s.

Rarity: *None known*

$20 • W-MS-100-020-G030

Left: TWENTY vertically. ***Center:*** Medallion head bearing TWENTY / Mercury seated at river / Medallion head bearing TWENTY. ***Right:*** TWENTY vertically. ***Engraver:*** Underwood, Bald, Spencer & Hufty. ***Comments:*** H-MS-160-G108, Kraus-4022p. 18__. 1830s.

Rarity: *None known*

$50 • W-MS-100-050-G040

Left: Athena as Liberty with U.S. shield and spear / FIFTY. ***Center:*** Medallion head bearing FIFTY / Neptune seated on sea / Medallion head bearing FIFTY. ***Right:*** Athena as Liberty with U.S. shield and spear / FIFTY. ***Engraver:*** Underwood, Bald, Spencer & Hufty. ***Comments:*** H-MS-160-G110, Kraus-4023p. 18__. 1830s.

Rarity: *None known*

$100 • W-MS-100-100-G050

Left: Woman standing with medallion head and caduceus / 100. ***Center:*** Medallion head bearing 100 / Indian in canoe / Medallion head bearing 100. ***Right:*** Woman standing with medallion head and caduceus / 100. ***Engraver:*** Underwood, Bald, Spencer & Hufty. ***Comments:*** H-MS-160-G112, Kraus-4024p. 18__. 1830s.

Rarity: *None known*

Mississippi Rail Road and Banking Company (branch)

1836–1841

W-MS-110

History: The Mississippi Rail Road and Banking Company (also seen as the Mississippi Rail Road Company on notes) was chartered on February 26, 1836. The bank had a positive net worth of $116,668.06 as of February 24, 1838. In 1840 it was reported that the bank could not redeem its notes, and in March 1841 this issuer, along with several others, had its charter revoked for this reason.

The Mississippi Rail Road and Banking Company had its parent bank located in Natchez, W-MS-650, and branches located in Gallatin, W-MS-320, and Raymond, W-MS-810.

Numismatic Commentary: No notes payable at the branch bank in Canton are known. Merchant scrip payable at the Mississippi Rail Road Company is known.

New Orleans, Jackson and Great Northern Rail Road Company

1861 and 1862

W-MS-120

History: The New Orleans, Jackson and Great Northern Rail Road Company was authorized under acts of December 20, 1861, and January 22, 1862, "to issue notes for circulation to the amount of three hundred thousand dollars to be redeemable at their offices in Canton and New Orleans."

See also listing under Louisiana, W-LA-380.

Valid Issues

10¢ • W-MS-120-00.10-G010

JM

Overprint: Red lathework panel. ***Comments:*** H-Unlisted, Kraus-51910. July 1st, 1862.

Rarity: URS-7
F $200

50¢ • W-MS-120-00.50-G020

JM

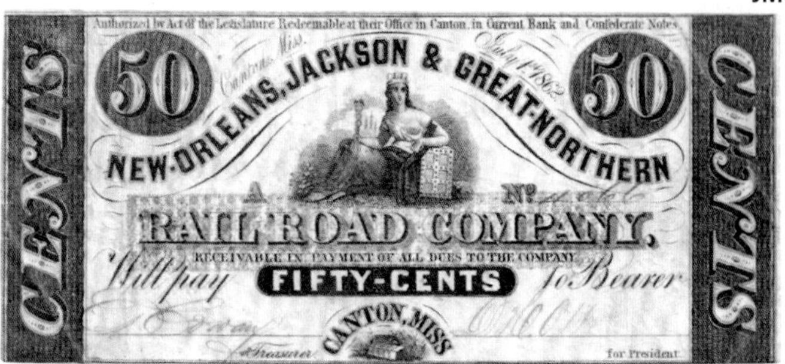

Overprint: Red lathework panel. ***Comments:*** H-Unlisted, Kraus-51911. July 1st, 1862.

Rarity: URS-7
F $200

75¢ • W-MS-120-00.75-G030

JM

Overprint: Red lathework panel. ***Comments:*** H-Unlisted, Kraus-51912. July 1st, 1862.

Rarity: URS-7
F $200

$1 • W-MS-120-001-G040

JM

Overprint: Red lathework panel. ***Comments:*** H-Unlisted, Kraus-51913. July 1t, 1862.

Rarity: URS-7
F $200

$1.50 • W-MS-120-001.50-G050

JM

Overprint: Red lathework panel. ***Comments:*** H-Unlisted, Kraus-51914. July 1t, 1862.

Rarity: URS-6
F $250

$2 • W-MS-120-002-G060 JM

Overprint: Red lathework panel. ***Comments:*** H-Unlisted, Kraus-51915. July 1t, 1862.

Rarity: URS-6
F $250

$3 • W-MS-120-003-G070 JM

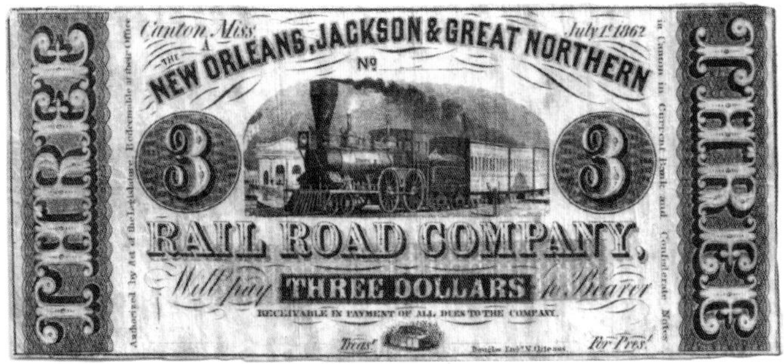

Overprint: Red lathework panel. ***Comments:*** H-Unlisted, Kraus-51916. July 1t, 1862.

Rarity: URS-3
F $400

$5 • W-MS-120-005-G080 JM

Overprint: Red lathework panel. ***Comments:*** H-Unlisted, Kraus-51917. July 1t, 1862.

Rarity: URS-4
F $400

CARTHAGE, MISSISSIPPI

On July 31, 1834, Carthage was established and became the seat of Leake County. The area was originally known as Leakesville, but soon it was renamed by the Harris family, who were the original settlers, after their hometown of Carthage, Tennessee. In 1836 a courthouse and a jail were built, and a post office followed in 1837.

In 1876 Carthage was incorporated as a town.

Planters Real Estate Banking Company of Leake County

CIRCA 1838
W-MS-130

History: This is believed to have been an exchange house or office that issued notes based on real estate holdings. No record has been found of a state charter for this bank, and it is presumed it was a private enterprise. It is listed here for collector continuity.

Numismatic Commentary: Notes from the Planters Real Estate Banking Company of Leake County are extremely rare.

VALID ISSUES

$1 • W-MS-130-001-G010

Left: Panel. ***Center:*** 1 / Train / 1. ***Right:*** Panel. ***Comments:*** H-MS-35-G2, Kraus-13851. 183_. Circa 1838.

Rarity: URS-1
VF $3,000

$5 • W-MS-130-005-G020 JM

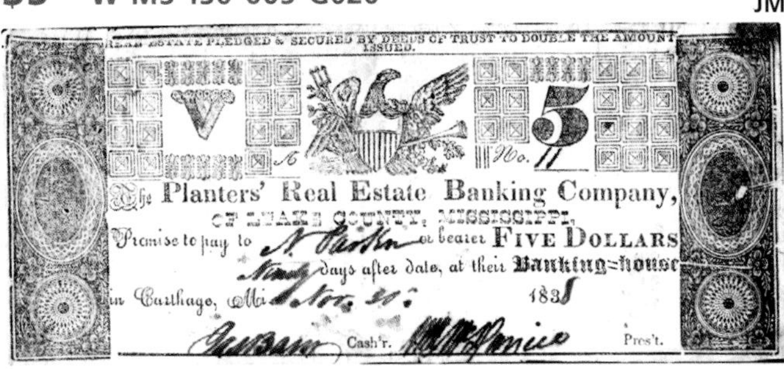

Comments: H-MS-35-G6, Kraus-13855. 183_. Circa 1838.

Rarity: URS-2
VF $2,300
Selected auction price: Heritage Auctions, October 21, 2015, Lot 18441, VF $2,232

CLINTON, MISSISSIPPI

The area that later became Clinton was founded in 1823 as Mount Salus, meaning "Mountain of Health." It was named after a nearby plantation belonging to Walter Leake, the third governor of Mississippi. In 1828 the town was renamed in honor of DeWitt Clinton.

The Natchez Trace, an improvement on an old Native American trail, was the first road to be laid through Clinton. On January 24, 1826, Mississippi College was founded under the name of Hampstead Academy. Today it is the oldest college in the state of Mississippi. In 1853 Central Female Institute was founded, later becoming known as Hillman College in 1891.

In 1831 the railroad came to Clinton, connecting the town with Vicksburg and becoming the second railway in the state. Cotton was exported and brought great prosperity to the area. During the Civil War, Clinton was briefly occupied in turn by both Confederate forces and Union generals Ulysses S. Grant and William T. Sherman.

Citizens Change Banking Company

1838

W-MS-140

History: This is believed to have been an exchange house or related business that issued notes used regionally. No record has been found of a state charter for this bank, and it is presumed it was a private enterprise. It is listed here for collector continuity.

Valid Issues

12-1/2¢ • W-MS-140-00.12.50-G010

JM

Comments: H-Unlisted, Kraus-20430. 183_. 1838.

Rarity: URS-2

F $2,500

25¢ • W-MS-140-00.25-G020

Comments: H-Unlisted, Kraus-20431. No description available. 183_. 1838. **Rarity:** *None known*

50¢ • W-MS-140-00.50-G030

JM

Comments: H-Unlisted, Kraus-20442. 183_. 1838.

Rarity: URS-4

F $400

50¢ • W-MS-140-00.50-G040

JM

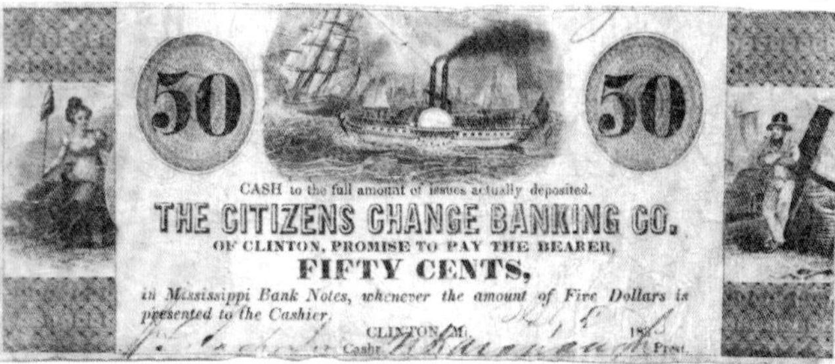

Comments: H-Unlisted, Kraus-20451. 183_. 1838.

Rarity: URS-4

F $400

50¢ • W-MS-140-00.50-G050

Center: Sheep. ***Comments:*** H-Unlisted, Kraus-20432. 183_. 1838.

Rarity: *None known*

75¢ • W-MS-140-00.75-G060

Center: Sheep. ***Comments:*** H-Unlisted, Kraus-20433. 183_. 1838.

Rarity: URS-1

F $1,200

$1 • W-MS-140-001-G070

JM

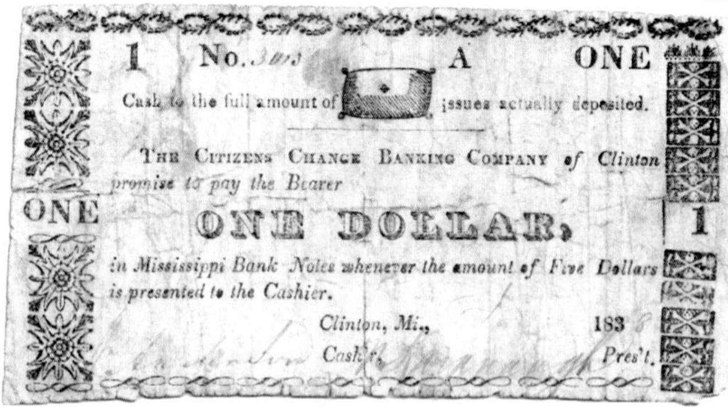

Comments: H-Unlisted, Kraus-20434. 183_. 1838.

Rarity: URS-1

F $2,000

$1 • W-MS-140-001-G080

JM

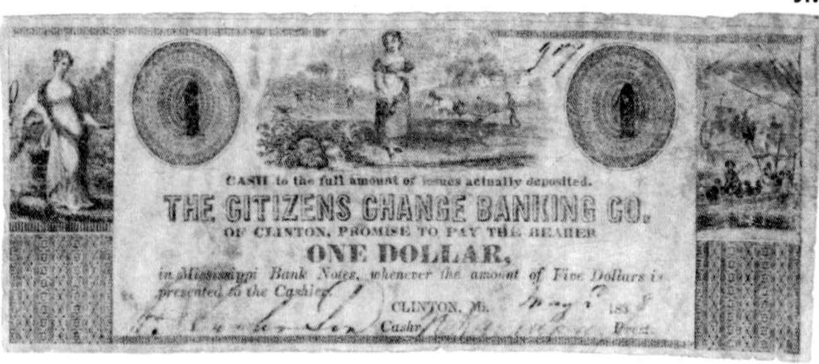

Comments: H-Unlisted, Kraus-20443. 183_. 1838.

Rarity: URS-4

F $400

$1 • W-MS-140-001-G090

JM

Comments: H-Unlisted, Kraus-20453. 183_. 1838.

Rarity: URS-4

F $400

$2 • W-MS-140-002-G100

JM

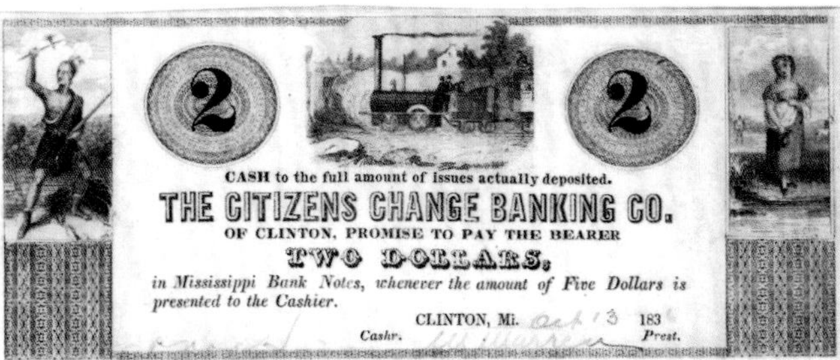

Comments: H-Unlisted, Kraus-20444. 183_. 1838.

Rarity: URS-4

F $400

$3 • W-MS-140-003-G110

JM

Comments: H-Unlisted, Kraus-20455. 183_. 1838.

Rarity: URS-4

F $400

$3 • W-MS-140-003-G120

JM

Comments: H-Unlisted, Kraus-20445. 183_. 1838.

Rarity: URS-4

F $400

Commercial and Rail Road Bank of Vicksburg (branch)

1836–1840

W-MS-150

History: The Commercial and Rail Road Bank of Vicksburg (also seen in print as the Commercial Railroad and Banking Company) was incorporated on December 19, 1831, under the name of the Clinton and Vicksburg Rail Road Company. It had an authorized capital of $4,000,000. On January 28, 1836, it was reincorporated with the name of Commercial and Rail Road Bank of Vicksburg. It was to lay a railway from Vicksburg to Clinton, and of the three other railroad and banking companies in the state and decade, it was the only one to complete its task. By 1840 the railroad was finished, stretching 54 miles.[5]

The year before the railway's completion, the company began winding up its banking affairs. In 1839 it was reported that the bank had suspended specie payments and that the stock held in New York and Philadelphia had been running down.[6] With the railroad finished, the bank finalized its affairs and closed.

The Commercial and Rail Road Bank of Vicksburg had its parent bank located in Vicksburg, W-MS-910, and branch banks located in Utica, W-MS-860, and Vernon, W-MS-870.

Numismatic Commentary: Notes from this branch have Clinton handwritten.

Valid Issues

$5 • W-MS-150-005-G010

Left: 5 / Medallion head / 5 ***Center:*** Medallion head bearing 5 / Ship, Woman seated with bales on dock / Medallion head bearing 5. ***Right:*** 5 / Medallion head / 5. ***Engraver:*** Underwood, Bald, Spencer & Hufty. ***Comments:*** H-MS-205-G24. 18__. 1830s.

Rarity: URS-3

F $500

$10 • W-MS-150-010-G020

Left: 10 / Medallion head / 10. ***Center:*** 10 / Neptune seated, Ship / X. ***Right:*** X / Medallion head / X. ***Engraver:*** Underwood, Bald, Spencer & Hufty. ***Comments:*** H-MS-205-G26. 18__. 1830s.

Rarity: URS-3

F $500

$20 • W-MS-150-020-G030

Left: 20 / Medallion head / 20. ***Center:*** 20 / Sailor standing on dock holding flag / 20. ***Right:*** 20 / Medallion head / 20. ***Engraver:*** Underwood, Bald, Spencer & Hufty. ***Comments:*** H-MS-205-G28. 18__. 1830s.

Rarity: URS-3

F $500

$50 • W-MS-150-050-G040

JM

Engraver: Rawdon, Wright, Hatch & Edson. ***Comments:*** H-MS-205-G30. 18__. 1830s.

Rarity: URS-3

F $1,000

$100 • W-MS-150-100-G050

Left: ONE HUNDRED vertically. ***Center:*** 100 / Liberty seated with shield, Ship / 100. ***Right:*** ONE HUNDRED vertically. ***Engraver:*** Rawdon, Wright, Hatch & Edson. ***Comments:*** H-MS-205-G32. 18__. 1830s.

Rarity: URS-3

Real Estate Banking Company of Hinds County

1839 and 1840

W-MS-160

History: This was an exchange house that issued notes used regionally. Real estate was pledged as collateral. No record has been found of a state charter for this bank, and it is presumed it was a private enterprise. It is listed here for collector continuity.

Valid Issues

$1 • W-MS-160-001-G010

CC

Engraver: Draper, Toppan, Longacre & Co. ***Comments:*** H-MS-40-G8a, Kraus-13880. 18__. 1837.

Rarity: URS-5
F $250

$2 • W-MS-160-002-G020

CC

Engraver: Draper, Toppan, Longacre & Co. ***Comments:*** H-MS-40-G10a, Kraus-13881. 18__. 1830s.

Rarity: URS-4
F $550

$3 • W-MS-160-003-G030

JM

Engraver: Draper, Toppan, Longacre & Co. ***Comments:*** H-MS-40-G14a, Kraus-13882. 18__. 1830s.

Rarity: URS-3
F $600

$10 • W-MS-160-010-G040

Left: TEN / Cotton plant / 10. ***Center:*** Ceres with wheat and sickle. ***Right:*** TEN / Cotton plant / 10. ***Engraver:*** Draper, Toppan, Longacre & Co. ***Comments:*** H-MS-40-G16a, Kraus-13884. 18__. 1830s.

Rarity: *None known*

$20 • W-MS-160-020-G050

Left: Liberty standing with U.S. shield. ***Center:*** Hope and Commerce seated. ***Right:*** 20 / Cotton plant / 20. ***Engraver:*** Draper, Toppan, Longacre & Co. ***Comments:*** H-MS-40-G18a, Kraus-13885. 18__. 1830s.

Rarity: *None known*

$50 • W-MS-160-050-G060

Left: Woman leaning against column / 50. ***Center:*** Minerva as Liberty with Muse and Commerce seated with U.S. shield, Ship. ***Right:*** 50 / Cotton plant / 50. ***Engraver:*** Draper, Toppan, Longacre & Co. ***Comments:*** H-MS-40-G20a, Kraus-13886. 18__. 1830s.

Rarity: *None known*

$100 • W-MS-160-100-G070

Left: Liberty with Commerce. ***Center:*** Liberty with Ceres, U.S. shield. ***Right:*** 100 / Cotton plant / 100. ***Engraver:*** Draper, Toppan, Longacre & Co. ***Comments:*** H-MS-40-G22a, Kraus-13887. 18__. 1830s.

Rarity: *None known*

Post Notes

$5 • W-MS-160-005-G080

CC

Engraver: Draper, Toppan, Longacre & Co. ***Comments:*** H-MS-40-G26, Kraus-13883. 18__. 1830s.

Rarity: URS-7
F $250

$5 • W-MS-160-005-G090

Left: 5 / Milkmaid / 5 ***Center:*** Five cupids with 5 in clouds. ***Right:*** 5 / Portrait of George Washington / 5. ***Engraver:*** Draper, Toppan, Longacre & Co. ***Comments:*** H-Unlisted, Kraus-14000. Known only as remainders. 18__. 1830s.

Rarity: URS-3
Unc-Rem $300

$5 • W-MS-160-005-G090a

JM

Back: Brown. ***Engraver:*** Draper, Toppan, Longacre & Co. ***Comments:*** H-Unlisted, Kraus-14010. Similar to W-MS-160-005-G090. 18__. 1830s.

Rarity: URS-4
G $300

$10 • W-MS-160-010-G100

Left: 10 / Milkmaid / 10. ***Center:*** Five cupids with 10 in clouds. ***Right:*** 10 / Portrait of George Washington / 10. ***Engraver:*** Draper, Toppan, Longacre & Co. ***Comments:*** H-Unlisted. 18__. 1830s.

Rarity: URS-4
F $400

$10 • W-MS-160-010-G100a

Back: Brown. ***Engraver:*** Draper, Toppan, Longacre & Co. ***Comments:*** H-Unlisted. Similar to W-MS-160-010-G100. 18__. 1830s.

Rarity: URS-4
F $400

$10 • W-MS-160-010-G110

CC

Engraver: Draper, Toppan, Longacre & Co. ***Comments:*** H-MS-40-G28, Kraus-13884b. 18__. 1830s.

Rarity: URS-6
F $250

$10 • W-MS-160-010-G120

Left: 10 / Ceres with eagle and U.S. shield / X. ***Center:*** Commerce with caduceus, Ceres with wheat, Cargo and cotton plant. ***Right:*** 10 / Ceres with eagle and U.S. shield / X. ***Engraver:*** Draper, Toppan, Longacre & Co. ***Comments:*** H-MS-40-G30. 18__. 1830s.

Rarity: URS-4
F $450

$10 • W-MS-160-010-G120a

Back: Brown. ***Engraver:*** Draper, Toppan, Longacre & Co. ***Comments:*** H-MS-40-G30a, Kraus-14001r. Similar to W-MS-160-010-G120. 18__. 1830s.

Rarity: URS-4
F $450

$20 • W-MS-160-020-G130

JM

Engraver: Draper, Toppan, Longacre & Co. ***Comments:*** H-MS-40-G32, Kraus-13885b. 18__. 1830s.

Rarity: URS-5
VF $500

$20 • W-MS-160-020-G140

Left: Indian / Eagle / Indian. ***Center:*** 20 / Female portrait framed by globe, scroll, harp / 20. ***Right:*** Liberty / Eagle / Moneta. ***Engraver:*** Draper, Toppan, Longacre & Co. ***Comments:*** H-MS-40-G34, Kraus-14011. 18__. 1830s.

Rarity: URS-5
VF $500

$20 • W-MS-160-020-G140a

CC, CC

Back: Brown. ***Engraver:*** Draper, Toppan, Longacre & Co. ***Comments:*** H-MS-40-G34a, Kraus-14011r. Similar to W-MS-160-020-G140. 18__. 1830s.

Rarity: URS-5
F $400

$20 • **W-MS-160-020-G140b** JM, JM

Back: Brown. ***Engraver:*** Draper, Toppan, Longacre & Co. ***Comments:*** H-MS-40-G34c. Similar to W-MS-160-020-G140 but with "at their Banking House in Clinton with interest at the rate of five per cent per annum until due." 18__. 1830s.

Rarity: URS-4
F $450

$50 • **W-MS-160-050-G150** JM

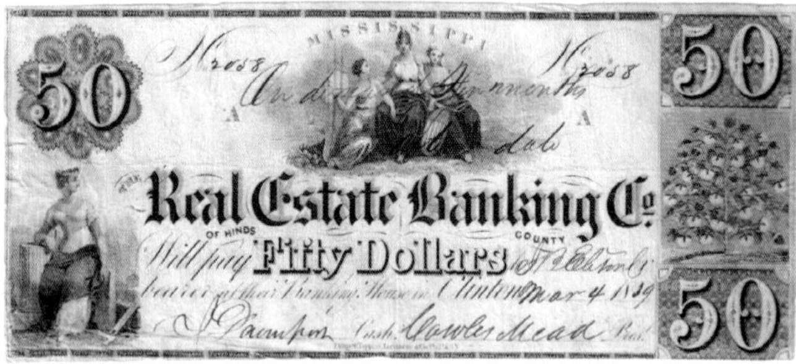

Engraver: Draper, Toppan, Longacre & Co. ***Comments:*** H-MS-40-G36a, Kraus-13886b. 18__. 1830s.

Rarity: URS-5
F $750

$50 • **W-MS-160-050-G160** HA

Engraver: Draper, Toppan, Longacre & Co. ***Comments:*** H-MS-40-G38, Kraus-14012. Proof. 18__. 1830s.

Rarity: URS-4
Proof $900
Selected auction price: Heritage Auctions, April 18, 2012, Lot 15250, Proof $862

$50 • **W-MS-160-050-G160a** CC, CC

Back: Brown. ***Engraver:*** Draper, Toppan, Longacre & Co. ***Comments:*** H-MS-40-G38a, Kraus-14012r. Similar to W-MS-160-050-G160. 18__. 1830s.

Rarity: URS-4
F $750

$50 • **W-MS-160-050-G160b** JM, JM

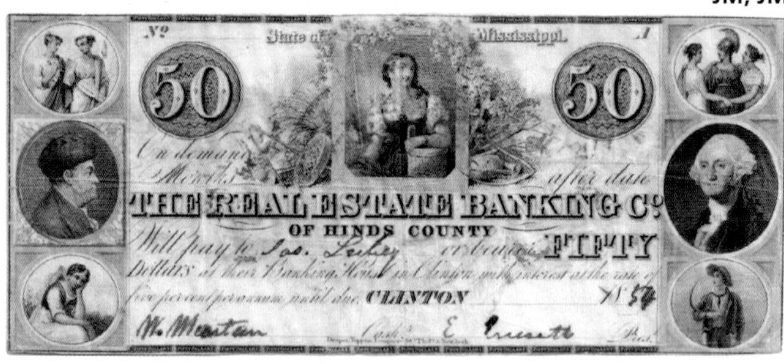

Back: Brown. ***Engraver:*** Draper, Toppan, Longacre & Co. ***Comments:*** H-MS-40-G38c. Similar to W-MS-160-050-G160 but with "at their Banking House in Clinton with interest at the rate of five per cent per annum until due." 18__. 1830s.

Rarity: URS-4
F $650

$100 • **W-MS-160-100-G170**

Left: Liberty with Commerce. ***Center:*** Liberty with Ceres, U.S. shield. ***Right:*** 100 / Cotton plant / 100. ***Engraver:*** Draper, Toppan, Longacre & Co. ***Comments:*** H-MS-40-G40a, Kraus-13887b. 18__. 1830s.

Rarity: URS-4
VF $700

$100 • W-MS-160-100-G180

Left: ONE HUNDRED vertically. ***Center:*** 100 / Farmer and soldier flanking shield bearing cotton plant, Ships / 100. ***Right:*** ONE HUNDRED vertically. ***Engraver:*** Draper, Toppan, Longacre & Co. ***Comments:*** H-MS-40-G42, Kraus-14012. 18__. 1830s.

Rarity: URS-4
Proof $1,000

$100 • W-MS-160-100-G180a

Back: Brown. ***Engraver:*** Draper, Toppan, Longacre & Co. ***Comments:*** H-MS-40-G42a, Kraus-14012r. Similar to W-MS-160-100-G180. Remainder. 18__. 1830s.

Rarity: URS-3
EF $500

$100 • W-MS-160-100-G180b JM, JM

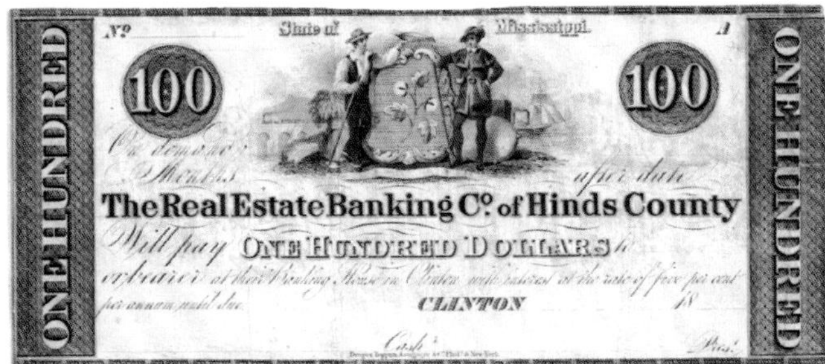

Back: Brown. ***Engraver:*** Draper, Toppan, Longacre & Co. ***Comments:*** H-MS-40-G42c, Kraus-14004. Similar to W-MS-160-100-G180 but with "at their Banking House in Clinton with interest at the rate of five per cent per annum until due." 18__. 1830s.

Rarity: URS-3
Unc-Rem $1,000

Non-Valid Issues

$20 • W-MS-160-020-N010

Comments: H-Unlisted, Kraus-14022d. Fraudulent issue. Filled-in remainder. 18__. 1830s.

Rarity: *None known*

$100 • W-MS-160-100-N020

Comments: H-Unlisted, Kraus-14025d. Fraudulent issue. Filled-in remainder. 18__. 1830s.

Rarity: *None known*

Colbert, Mississippi

The area known informally as Colbert was first visited by Europeans when French soldiers came through the area in 1736. That same year James Logan Colbert arrived with British traders to visit the Chickasaw Nation. He married one of the Chickasaw women, and his son Levi became acting chief sometime after 1750.

Much disruption occurred in this area as settlers arrived and expanded into Chickasaw lands, often illegally. On October 20, 1832, the Treaty of Pontotoc was signed, allowing the land to be surveyed. The Mississippi federal marshal attempted to control the "squatters" from invading the Chickasaw land before the survey was completed, but such actions were often ineffectual. From 1834 to 1837 the Chickasaw sold off their land, often at undervalued prices, and soon they began moving west.

Commercial Bank of Colbert

1830s

W-MS-170

History: This is believed to have been an exchange house or related business that issued notes used regionally. No record has been found of a state charter for this bank, and it is presumed it was a private enterprise. It is listed here for collector continuity.

Numismatic Commentary: Only one note of this bank is known to have survived.

Valid Issues

25¢ • W-MS-170-00.25-G010

Comments: H-Unlisted, Kraus-14120. No description available. 18__. 1830s.

Rarity: *None known*

50¢ • W-MS-170-00.50-G020

Left: Portrait of Benjamin Franklin. ***Center:*** "Victory on Lake Erie." ***Right:*** Portrait of George Washington. ***Comments:*** H-Unlisted, Kraus-14121. Center vignette depicting Captain Perry transferring his flag to the Niagara during the battle, September 10, 1813. From a painting by Thomas Birch. 18__. 1830s.

Rarity: *None known*

$1 • W-MS-170-001-G030

Comments: H-Unlisted, Kraus-14122. No description available. 18__. 1830s.

Rarity: *None known*

Columbus, Mississippi

Columbus was founded in 1821 on a site originally known by the local natives as Possum Town. The neighboring community of Plymouth, established in 1817, had failed due to flooding, and the settlers transferred across the river to Columbus. The name was suggested by Silas McBee, who in turn gave his name to a local creek.

A public school was one of the first buildings to be erected, and today it still stands as Mississippi's first public academy. Columbus' location was a bit nebulous at first due to the fact that the town sits right on the border between Mississippi and Alabama, which fluctuated during the years preceding Mississippi's entry into statehood. Therefore, Columbus was alternately seen as Columbus, Alabama, and Columbus, Mississippi, until the border was defined.

Columbus served as a hospital town during the Civil War and also provided gunpowder and cannons. The Union army tried to invade the town for this reason but was repulsed.

Bank of Columbus
1862
W-MS-180

History: The Bank of Columbus was authorized on January 17, 1862, with a capital of $500,000.[7] It is unknown if this bank ever went into operation.

Columbus and Tombigby Transportation Company
1839 and 1840
W-MS-190

History: The Columbus and Tombigby Transportation Company was incorporated on February 15, 1839, with an authorized capital of $500,000. Banking privileges were granted in order to allow the company to maintain steamboats on the Tombigby River. Bills that were issued were used in the vicinity and not handled by distant exchange offices.

Numismatic Commentary: The $50 and $100 denominations are most common.

Valid Issues

25¢ • W-MS-190-00.25-G010
Comments: H-Unlisted, Kraus-14150. No description available. 1830s–1840s.

Rarity: *None known*

50¢ • W-MS-190-00.50-G020
JM

Comments: H-Unlisted, Kraus-14151. 1838.

Rarity: URS-1
Fair $1,500

$1 • W-MS-190-001-G030
Comments: H-Unlisted, Kraus-14152. No description available. 1830s–1840s.

Rarity: *None known*

$5 • W-MS-190-005-G040
JM

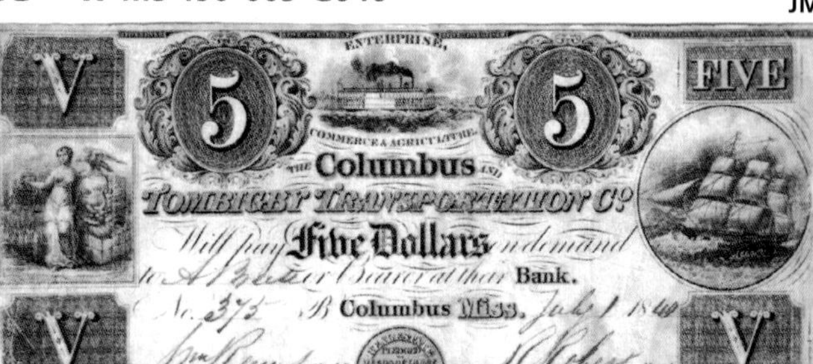

Engraver: Rawdon, Wright & Hatch. ***Comments:*** H-MS-45-G2, Kraus-14170. 18__. 1830s–1840s.

Rarity: URS-8
F $125

$10 • W-MS-190-010-G050
Left: Wharf scene with train and ships. ***Center:*** Riverboat. ***Right:*** Clipper ship. ***Engraver:*** Rawdon, Wright & Hatch. ***Comments:*** H-MS-45-G4, Kraus-14171. 18__. 1830s–1840s.

Rarity: URS-5
F $175

$20 • W-MS-190-020-G060
Left: Wharf scene. ***Center:*** Clipper ships. ***Right:*** 20 / Riverboat / 20. ***Engraver:*** Rawdon, Wright & Hatch. ***Comments:*** H-MS-45-G6, Kraus-14172. 18__. 1830s–1840s.

Rarity: URS-5
F $175

$50 • W-MS-190-050-G070
CC

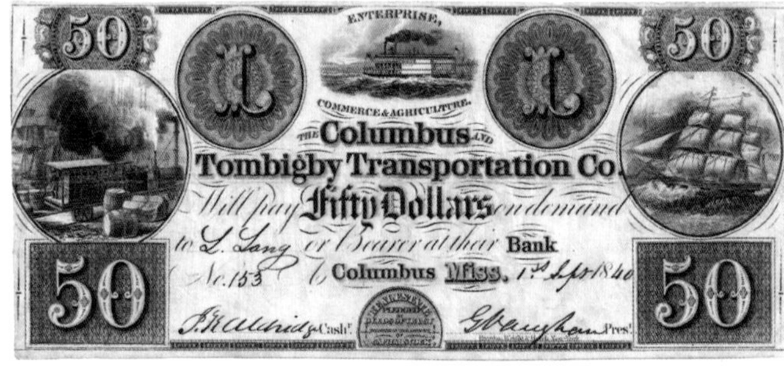

Engraver: Rawdon, Wright & Hatch. ***Comments:*** H-MS-45-G8, Kraus-14173. 18__. 1830s–1840s.

Rarity: URS-8
VF $200

$100 • W-MS-190-100-G080
SI

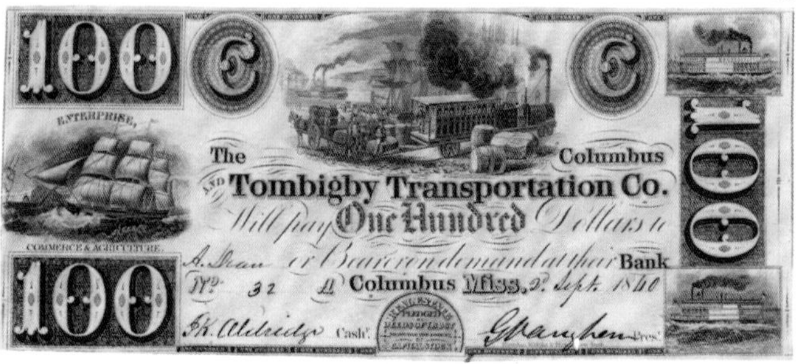

Engraver: Rawdon, Wright & Hatch. ***Comments:*** H-MS-45-G10, Kraus-14174. 18__. 1830s–1840s.

Rarity: URS-8
VF $250

Post Notes

$10 • W-MS-190-010-G090 JM

Comments: H-Unlisted, Kraus-14171a. 1830s–1840s.

Rarity: URS-5

VF $250

$20 • W-MS-190-020-G100 JM

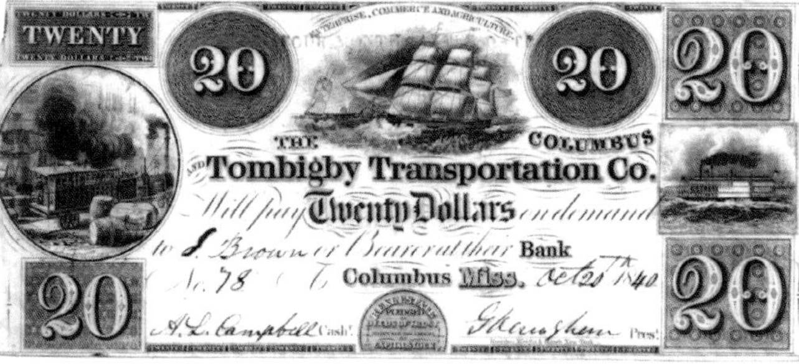

Comments: H-Unlisted, Kraus-14172a. 1830s–1840s.

Rarity: URS-5

VF $250

Columbus Life and General Insurance Company

1852–1860s

W-MS-200

History: The Columbus Life and General Insurance Company was incorporated in 1852 with an authorized capital of $100,000. It was initially barred from banking privileges, but in 1862 it was authorized to issue certificates for circulation. On December 9, 1863, the charter was again amended to further allow the bank to issue bills. The paid-in capital at this time was $300,000.

Sometime during the Civil War, the bank closed for business. It was succeeded in certain interests by the First Columbus National Bank.

Numismatic Commentary: Notes issued in the 1850s are excessively rare.

Valid Issues

25¢ • W-MS-200-00.25-G010 JM

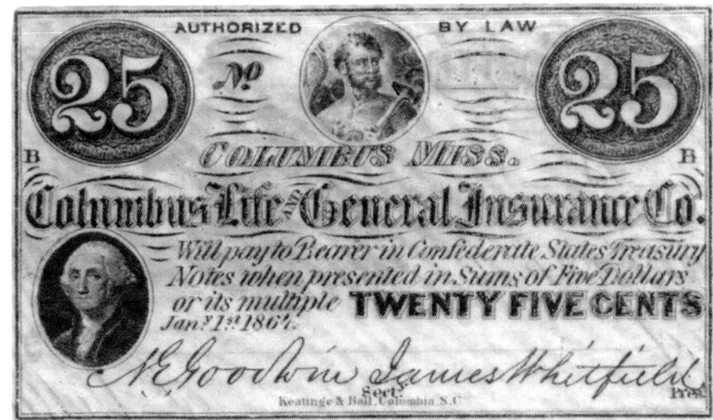

Engraver: Keatinge & Ball. ***Comments:*** H-Unlisted, Kraus-51540. Jany. 1st, 1864.

Rarity: URS-10

EF $60

50¢ • W-MS-200-00.50-G020 JM

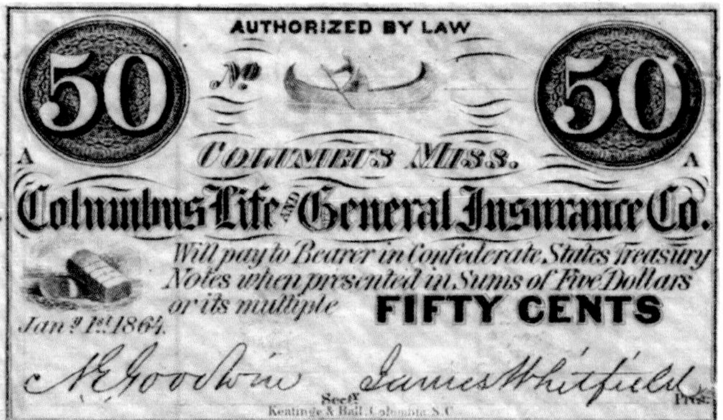

Engraver: Keatinge & Ball. ***Comments:*** H-Unlisted, Kraus-51541. Jany. 1st, 1864.

Rarity: URS-10

EF $60

How to Read the Whitman Numbering System

$1 • W-AL-020-001-G010a

Denomination: Face value of the note shown.

W: Whitman number. This number is a sortable code unique to each bank and note.

AL: Abbreviation for the state under study.

020: Numerical designation specific to each bank.

001: The denomination in dollars.

G010a: G indicates a good or valid note. Other categories are indicated thus: C (counterfeit); R (raised); S (spurious); N (not-attributed); A (altered). Numbers are assigned starting with 010, 020, et seq. Terminal letters following the number indicate variations of a note: a series of different colored overprints, tints, payees, etc., all on the same design of note. For more information, see the "How to Use This Book" section at the front of the volume, page xiv.

50¢ • **W-MS-200-00.50-G025**

Left: Woman standing. ***Center:*** Train. ***Right:*** FIFTY CENTS vertically. ***Comments:*** H-Unlisted, Kraus-51521r. 1860s

Rarity: URS-3
F $300

75¢ • **W-MS-200-00.75-G030**

JM

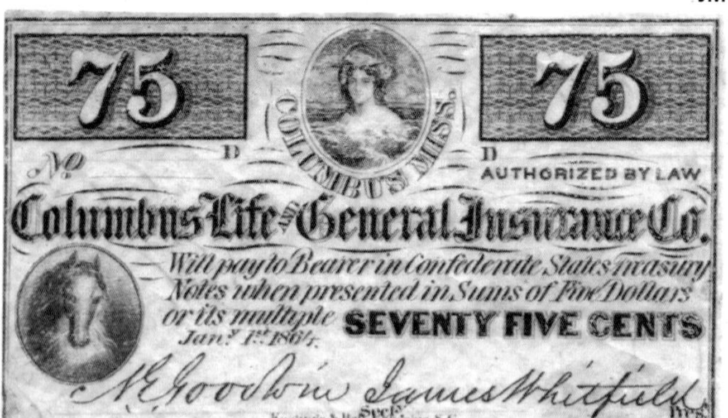

Engraver: Keatinge & Ball. ***Comments:*** H-Unlisted, Kraus-51542. Jany. 1st, 1864.

Rarity: URS-10
EF $75

$1 • **W-MS-200-001-G040**

JM

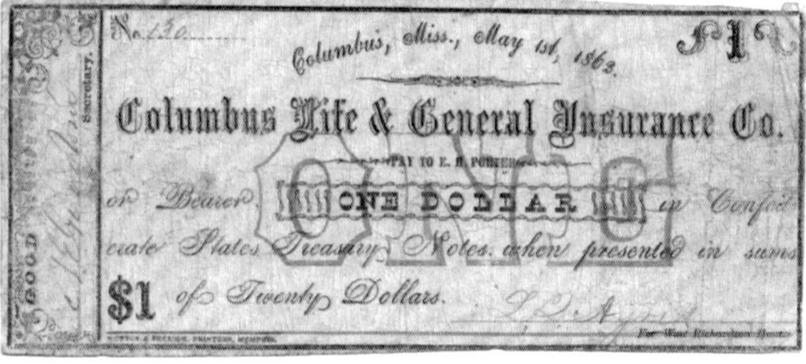

Overprint: Red outlining white ONE. ***Comments:*** H-Unlisted, Kraus-51510. May 1st, 1862.

Rarity: URS-10
F $100

$1 • **W-MS-200-001-G040a**

JM

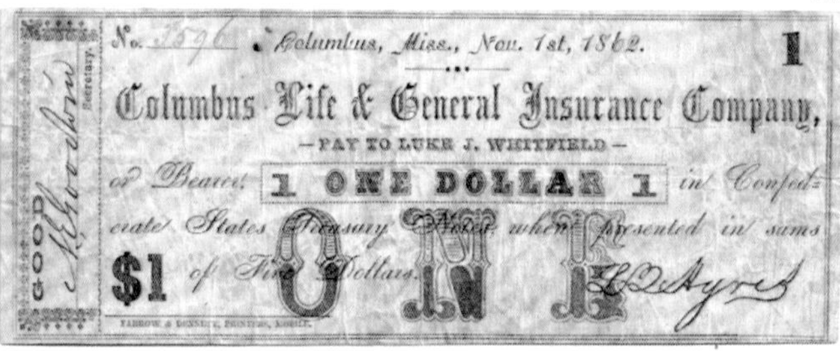

Overprint: Blue ONE. ***Comments:*** H-Unlisted, Kraus-51530. Similar to W-MS-200-001-G040 but with different date. Nov. 1st, 1862.

Rarity: URS-10
F $100

$1 • **W-MS-200-001-G050**

JM

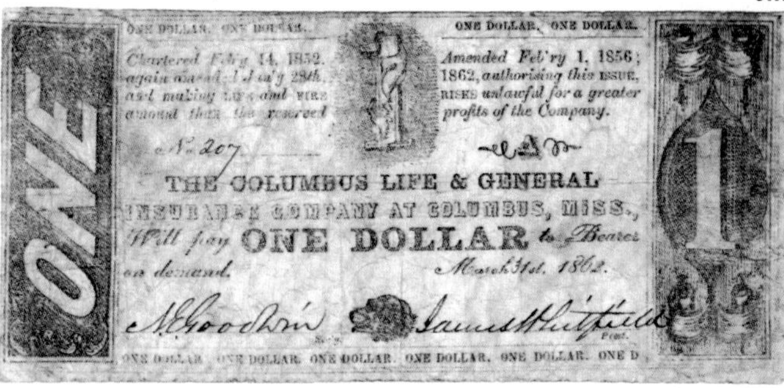

Comments: H-Unlisted, Kraus-51500. March 1st, 1862.

Rarity: URS-8
F $125

$1 • **W-MS-200-001-G060**

JM

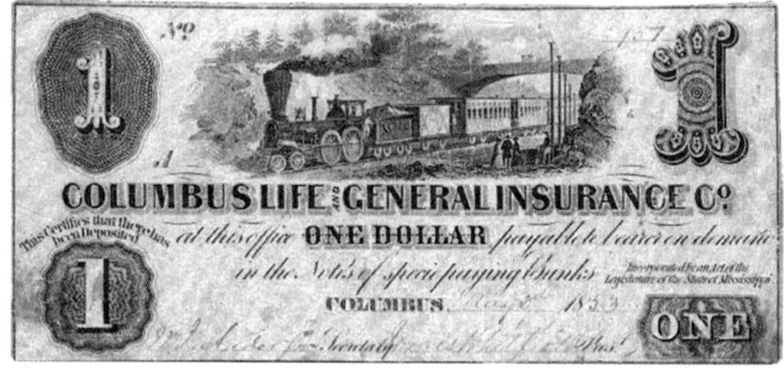

Comments: H-Unlisted, Kraus-46940. 18__. 1850s.

Rarity: URS-2
F $500

$1.50 • **W-MS-200-001.50-G070**

JM

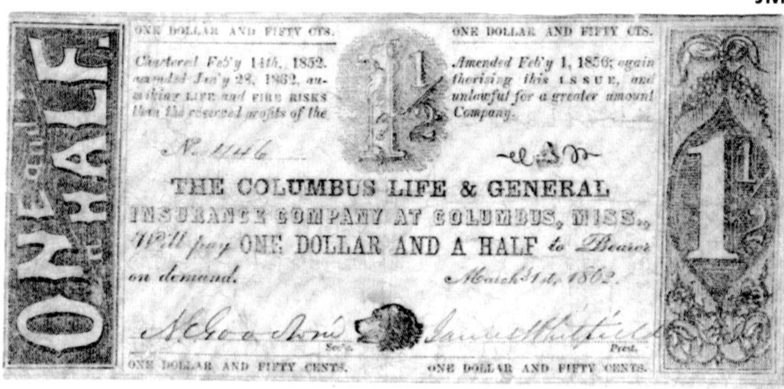

Comments: H-Unlisted, Kraus-51501. March 1st, 1862.

Rarity: URS-4
F $300

$2 • **W-MS-200-002-G080**

JM

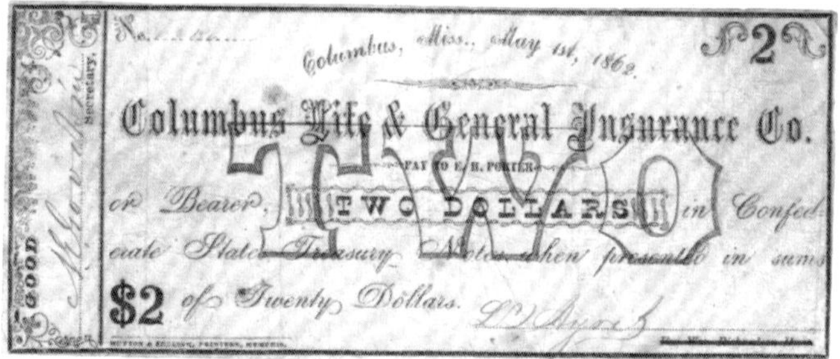

Overprint: Red outlining white TWO. ***Comments:*** H-Unlisted, Kraus-51512. May 1st, 1862.

Rarity: URS-10
F $100

$2 • **W-MS-200-002-G080a** JM

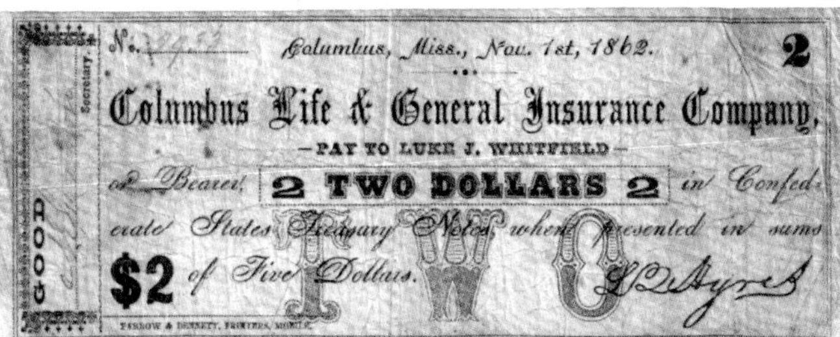

Overprint: Blue TWO. ***Comments:*** H-Unlisted, Kraus-51532. Similar to W-MS-200-002-G080 but with different date. Nov. 1st, 1862.

Rarity: URS-10
F $100

$2 • **W-MS-200-002-G090** JM

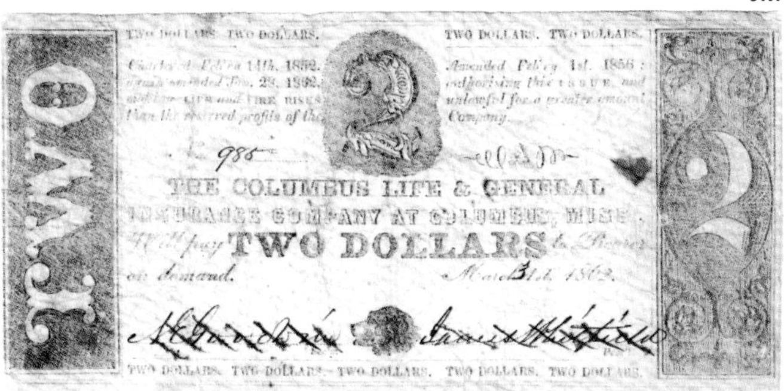

Comments: H-Unlisted, Kraus-51502. March 1st, 1862.

Rarity: URS-4
F $350

$2.50 • **W-MS-200-002.50-G100** JM

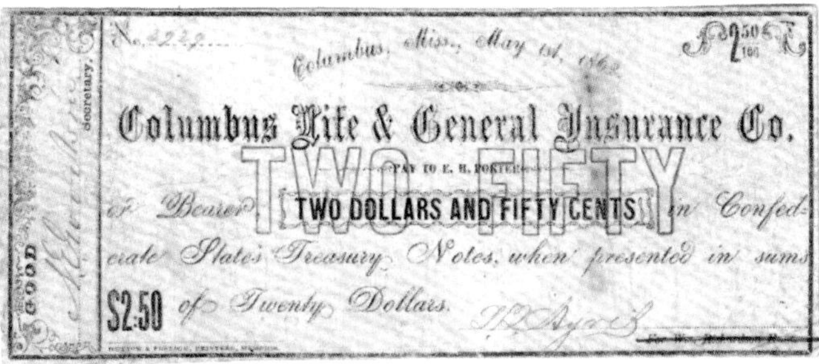

Overprint: Red outlining white TWO FIFTY. ***Comments:*** H-Unlisted, Kraus-51510. May 1st, 1862.

Rarity: URS-8
F $125

$3 • **W-MS-200-003-G110** JM

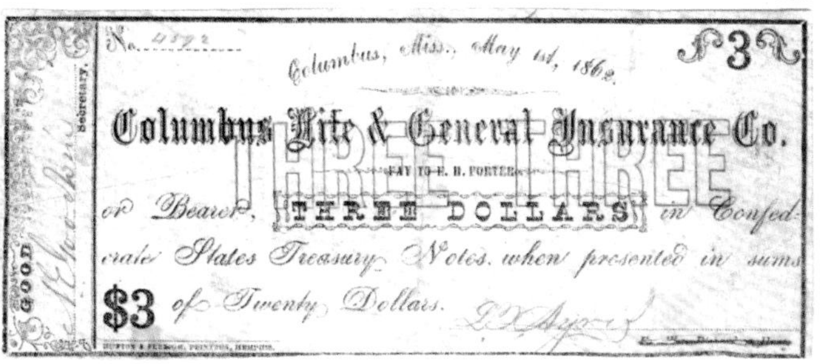

Overprint: Red outlining white THREE THREE. ***Comments:*** H-Unlisted, Kraus-51514. May 1st, 1862.

Rarity: URS-8
F $125

$3 • **W-MS-200-003-G120** JM

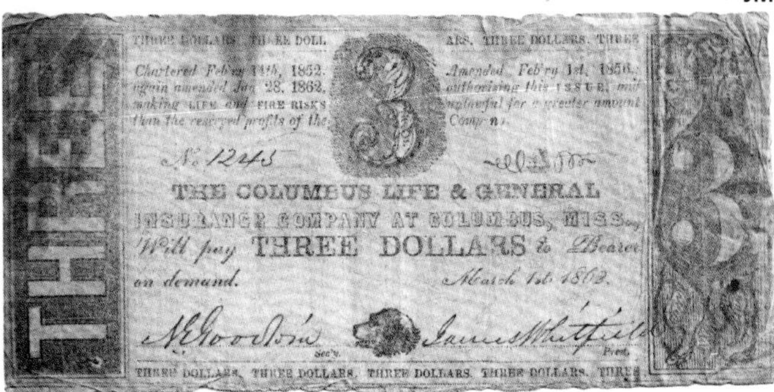

Comments: H-Unlisted, Kraus-51503. March 1st, 1862.

Rarity: URS-4
F $350

$3 • **W-MS-200-003-G125**

Left: Woman standing. ***Center:*** Train. ***Right:*** THREE vertically. ***Comments:*** H-Unlisted, Kraus-51524r. 1860s.

Rarity: URS-3
F $400

$5 • **W-MS-200-005-G130** JM

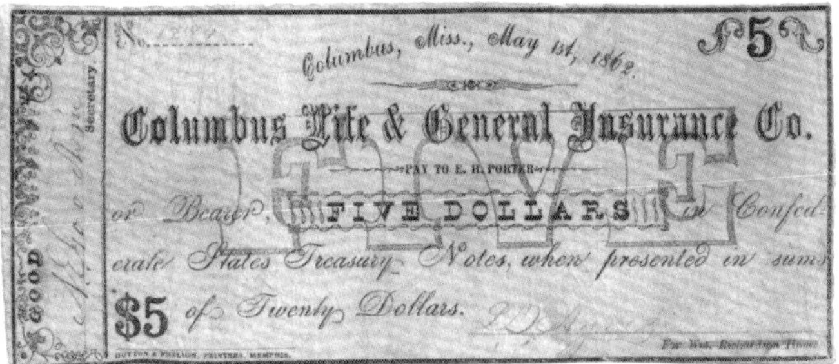

Overprint: Red outlining white FIVE. ***Comments:*** H-Unlisted, Kraus-51515. May 1st, 1862.

Rarity: URS-8
F $125

Commercial Bank of Columbus

1836–1841

W-MS-210

History: The Commercial Bank of Columbus was incorporated on February 26, 1836, with an authorized capital of $1,000,000. It was located on St. John's Street. *Niles' National Register* of February 24, 1838, reported that the bank had a positive net worth of $45,114.19.

On January 5, 1841, it was said that the Commercial Bank of Columbus was thought to have failed in its duty to comply with banking law. At that time no full evidence had been gathered, and so the charter could not be forfeited, but the bank closed soon after.

Numismatic Commentary: Validly issued notes of this bank are very scarce.

Valid Issues

$5 • W-MS-210-005-G010

Left: FIVE vertically. ***Center:*** Wharf scene, Train and steamships. ***Right:*** FIVE vertically. ***Engraver:*** Rawdon, Wright & Hatch. ***Comments:*** H-MS-50-G8, Kraus-3371. 18__. 1830s.

Rarity: URS-3

$10 • W-MS-210-010-G020

Engraver: Rawdon, Wright & Hatch. ***Comments:*** H-MS-50-G14, Kraus-3372. No description available. 18__. 1830s.

Rarity: *None known*

$20 • W-MS-210-020-G030 JM

Engraver: Rawdon, Wright & Hatch. ***Comments:*** H-MS-50-G16, Kraus-3373. 18__. 1830s.

Rarity: URS-4
F $750

$50 • W-MS-210-050-G040

Left: FIFTY vertically. ***Center:*** L / Riverboat, Cotton wagon pulled by mule / L. ***Right:*** 50 / Cotton boll / 50. ***Engraver:*** Rawdon, Wright & Hatch. ***Comments:*** H-MS-50-G18, Kraus-3374. 18__. 1830s.

Rarity: URS-3
F $600

Post Notes

$5 • W-MS-210-005-G050

Left: FIVE vertically. ***Center:*** Wharf scene, Train and steamships. ***Right:*** FIVE vertically. ***Engraver:*** Rawdon, Wright & Hatch. ***Comments:*** H-MS-50-G22, Kraus-3385. 18__. 1830s.

Rarity: URS-3
F $600

$10 • W-MS-210-010-G060

Left: 10. ***Center:*** X / Train and steamboat / X. ***Bottom center:*** Eagle and shield. ***Right:*** 10. ***Engraver:*** Rawdon, Wright & Hatch. ***Comments:*** H-MS-50-G24, Kraus-3386. 18__. 1830s.

Rarity: URS-4
F $750

$20 • W-MS-210-020-G070 JM

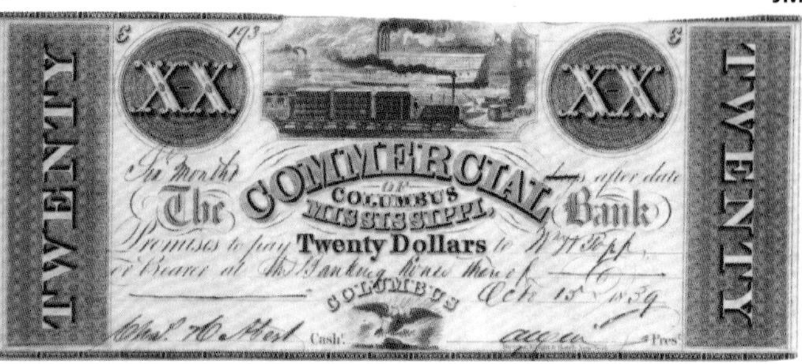

Engraver: Rawdon, Wright & Hatch. ***Comments:*** H-MS-50-G26, Kraus-3387. 18__. 1830s.

Rarity: URS-3
VF $2,000

$50 • W-MS-210-050-G080

Left: FIFTY vertically. ***Center:*** L / Riverboat, Cotton wagon pulled by mule / L. ***Right:*** 50 / Cotton boll / 50. ***Engraver:*** Rawdon, Wright & Hatch. ***Comments:*** H-MS-50-G28, Kraus-3388. 18__. 1830s.

Rarity: URS-3
VF $2,000

Post Notes Payable at the Planters and Merchants Bank, Mobile, Alabama

$5 • W-MS-210-005-G090

Left: FIVE vertically. ***Center:*** Wharf scene, Train and steamships. ***Right:*** FIVE vertically. ***Engraver:*** Rawdon, Wright & Hatch. ***Comments:*** H-MS-50-G32. 18__. 1830s.

Rarity: URS-3
VF $2,000

$10 • W-MS-210-010-G100 JM

Engraver: Rawdon, Wright & Hatch. ***Comments:*** H-MS-50-G34, Kraus-3386d. 18__. 1830s.

Rarity: URS-3
VF $1,800
Selected auction price: Heritage Auctions, October 21, 2015, Lot 18442, VF $1,762

$20 • W-MS-210-020-G110

Left: TWENTY vertically. ***Center:*** XX / Riverboat, Cotton wagon pulled by mule / XX. ***Right:*** XX. ***Engraver:*** Rawdon, Wright & Hatch. ***Comments:*** H-MS-50-G36, Kraus-3387d. 18__. 1830s.

Rarity: URS-3

$50 • W-MS-210-050-G120

JM

Engraver: Rawdon, Wright & Hatch. ***Comments:*** H-MS-50-G38, Kraus-3388d. 18__. 1830s.

Rarity: URS-3
F $2,500
Selected auction price: Heritage Auctions, October 21, 2015, Lot 18443, VF $2,115

$100 • W-MS-210-100-G130

Left: 100 / Minerva with shield. ***Center:*** Medallion head bearing 100 / Woman with chest, Ship, Horse / Medallion head bearing 100. ***Right:*** 100 / Minerva with shield. ***Engraver:*** Rawdon, Wright & Hatch. ***Comments:*** H-Unlisted, Kraus-3389. This note was not issued. 18__. 1830s.

Rarity: *None known*

Post Notes Payable at the Bank of the United States, Philadelphia

$5 • W-MS-210-005-G140

JM

Engraver: Underwood, Bald, Spencer & Hufty. ***Comments:*** H-MS-50-G42. This note was not issued. 18__. 1830s.

Rarity: URS-3
F $1,200

$10 • W-MS-210-010-G150

JM

Engraver: Underwood, Bald, Spencer & Hufty. ***Comments:*** H-MS-50-G44. This note was not issued. 18__. 1830s.

Rarity: URS-4
F $750

$20 • W-MS-210-020-G160

JM

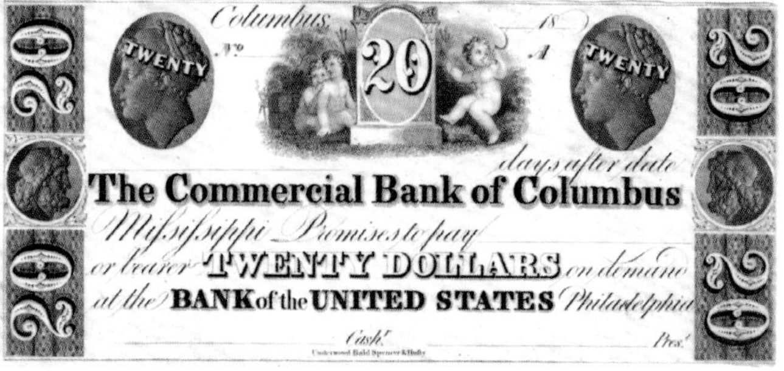

Engraver: Underwood, Bald, Spencer & Hufty. ***Comments:*** H-MS-50-G46, Kraus-3415. This note was not issued. 18__. 1830s.

Rarity: URS-3
Proof $1,000

$50 • W-MS-210-050-G170

CC

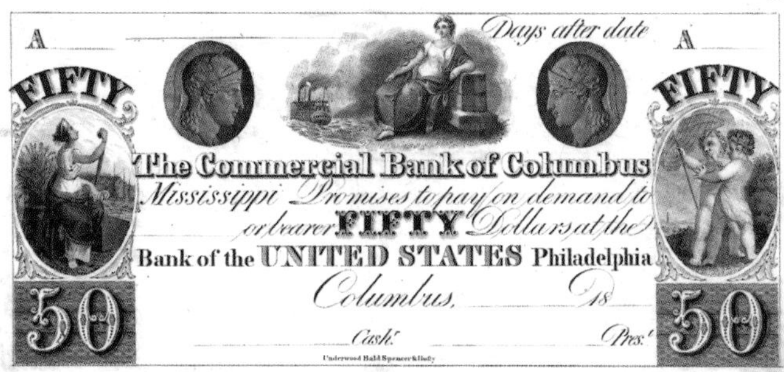

Engraver: Underwood, Bald, Spencer & Hufty. ***Comments:*** H-Unlisted, Kraus-3416. This note was not issued. 18__. 1830s.

Rarity: URS-3
Proof $1,250

$100 • W-MS-210-100-G180

Left: 100 / Minerva with shield. ***Center:*** Medallion head bearing 100 / Woman with chest, Ship, Horse / Medallion head bearing 100. ***Right:*** 100 / Minerva with shield. ***Engraver:*** Underwood, Bald, Spencer & Hufty. ***Comments:*** H-MS-50-G48, Kraus-3417. This note was not issued. 18__. 1830s.

Rarity: URS-3
Proof $1,750

Uncut Post-Note Sheet Payable at the Bank of the United States, Philadelphia

$5-$5-$5-$5 •
W-MS-210-005.005.005.005-US010

RG

Engraver: Underwood, Bald, Spencer & Hufty. ***Comments:*** H-MS-50-G42, G42, G42, G42. All four notes identical. 18__. 1830s.

Rarity: URS-2
F $2,500

Exchange Bank of Columbus

1830s

W-MS-220

History: This is believed to have been an exchange house that issued notes that circulated regionally. No record has been found of a state charter for this bank, and it is presumed it was a private enterprise. It is listed here for collector continuity.

Numismatic Commentary: The 75¢ note has appeared only once at auction.

VALID ISSUES

25¢ • W-MS-220-00.25-G010

Comments: H-Unlisted, Kraus-20510. No description available. 1830s.

Rarity: *None known*

50¢ • W-MS-220-00.50-G020

Comments: H-Unlisted, Kraus-20511. No description available. 1830s.

Rarity: *None known*

75¢ • W-MS-220-00.75-G030

Left: Portrait of Benjamin Franklin / Train. ***Center:*** Cattle with plow. ***Right:*** Coins. ***Comments:*** H-Unlisted, Kraus-20512. 1830s.

Rarity: URS-1
VF $1,000

$1 • W-MS-220-001-G040

Comments: H-Unlisted, Kraus-20513. No description available. 1830s.

Rarity: *None known*

Peoples Change Bank of Columbus

1830s

W-MS-230

History: This is believed to have been an exchange house that issued notes that circulated regionally. No record has been found of a state charter for this bank, and it is presumed it was a private enterprise. It is listed here for collector continuity.

Numismatic Commentary: Notes for this bank are excessively rare.

VALID ISSUES

12-1/2¢ • W-MS-230-00.12.50-G010

Left: Panel. ***Center:*** Riverboat *Safe*. ***Right:*** Panel. ***Comments:*** H-Unlisted, Kraus-20530. 1830s.

Rarity: URS-1
F $1,500

25¢ • W-MS-230-00.25-G020

Comments: H-Unlisted, Kraus-20531. No description available. 1830s.

Rarity: *None known*

50¢ • W-MS-230-00.50-G030

JM

Comments: H-Unlisted, Kraus-20532. 1837.

Rarity: URS-2
F $1,000

$1 • **W-MS-230-001-G040**

Comments: H-Unlisted, Kraus-20534. No description available. 1830s.

Rarity: *None known*

Planters Bank of the State of Mississippi (branch)

1830–1844

W-MS-240

History: The Planters Bank of the State of Mississippi was the second bank to be chartered in the state. It was incorporated on February 10, 1830, with an authorized capital of $3,000,000, $2,000,000 of which was provided from the state through the sale of bonds. In 1830 circulation was $2,207,730, and the capital was worth $1,998,590. The Panic of 1837 struck the bank hard. The state's bonds were repudiated, and the bank failed thereafter. On February 23, 1844, the bank was put into liquidation.

The Planters Bank of the State of Mississippi had its parent bank located in Natchez, W-MS-670, and branch banks located in Jackson, W-MS-470, Manchester, W-MS-555, Monticello, W-MS-580, Port Gibson, W-MS-780, Vicksburg, W-MS-920, Woodville, W-MS-1020, and Yazoo City, W-MS-1070.

Numismatic Commentary: Notes from this branch have Columbus handwritten.

VALID ISSUES

$5 • **W-MS-240-005-G010**

Left: 5 / FIVE vertically / 5. ***Center:*** 5 / Mercury in flight spreading coins from cornucopia / 5. ***Right:*** FIVE vertically. ***Engraver:*** Rawdon, Wright & Co. ***Comments:*** H-MS-175-G40, Kraus-4060. 18__. 1830s.

Rarity: URS-5
F $500

$10 • **W-MS-240-010-G020**

Left: 10 / Aquarius pouring water from amphora / 10. ***Center:*** 10 / Justice and Liberty flanking shield bearing cotton plant and surmounted by eagle / 10. ***Right:*** 10 / Aquarius pouring water from amphora / 10. ***Engraver:*** Rawdon, Wright & Co. ***Comments:*** H-MS-175-G42, Kraus-4061. 18__. 1830s.

Rarity: URS-5
F $500

$20 • **W-MS-240-020-G030**

Left: Woman seated with globe. ***Center:*** 20 / Cotton bales, Hope standing with anchor, Ship / 20. ***Right:*** Group of Indians. ***Engraver:*** Rawdon, Wright & Co. ***Comments:*** H-MS-175-G44, Kraus-4062. 18__. 1830s.

Rarity: URS-5
F $500

$20 • **W-MS-240-020-G040**

JM

Back: Red-brown. ***Engraver:*** Rawdon, Wright, Hatch & Co. ***Comments:*** H-MS-175-G46, Kraus-4075b. 18__. 1830s.

Rarity: URS-5
F $750

$50 • **W-MS-240-050-G050**

Left: Justice standing with eagle bearing portrait of George Washington. ***Center:*** 50 / Woman standing with cotton bales and shield bearing cotton plant surmounted by eagle, Train / 50. ***Right:*** Two women standing. ***Engraver:*** Rawdon, Wright & Co. ***Comments:*** H-MS-175-G48. 18__. 1830s.

Rarity: URS-5
F $750

$50 • **W-MS-240-050-G060**

JM

Back: Red-brown. ***Engraver:*** Rawdon, Wright, Hatch & Co. ***Comments:*** H-MS-175-G50. 18__. 1830s.

Rarity: URS-5
F $500

$50 • **W-MS-240-050-G070**

Left: Athena. ***Center:*** Muse. ***Right:*** Athena. ***Engraver:*** Rawdon, Wright & Co. ***Comments:*** H-Unlisted, Kraus-4063. 18__. 1830s.

Rarity: URS-5
F $500

$100 • **W-MS-240-100-G080**

Left: ONE HUNDRED vertically. ***Center:*** 100 / Group of settlers and Indians / 100. ***Right:*** ONE HUNDRED vertically. ***Engraver:*** Rawdon, Wright & Co. ***Comments:*** H-MS-175-G52, Kraus-4064. 18__. 1830s.

Rarity: URS-5
F $500

$100 • **W-MS-240-100-G090** JM

Back: Red-brown. ***Engraver:*** Rawdon, Wright, Hatch & Co. ***Comments:*** H-MS-175-G54. 18__. 1830s.

Rarity: URS-6
F $250

Real Estate Banking Company of Columbus

Circa 1837

W-MS-250

History: This was an exchange house that issued notes based on real estate holdings. No record has been found of a state charter for this bank, and it was considered a fraud. It is listed here for collector continuity.

Numismatic Commentary: Local Argus Print notes are exceedingly rare.

Valid Issues

$1 • **W-MS-250-001-G010** JM

Engraver: Southern Argus Print. ***Comments:*** H-Unlisted, Kraus-14230. 183_. Circa 1837.

Rarity: URS-3
F $1,500
Selected auction price: Heritage Auctions, April 18, 2012, Lot 15251, F $1,495

$1 • **W-MS-250-001-G020** JM

Engraver: Southern Argus Print. ***Comments:*** H-Unlisted. 183_. Circa 1837.

Rarity: URS-3
F $1,500

$1 • **W-MS-250-001-G030** SI

Comments: H-Unlisted. 183_. Circa 1837.

Rarity: URS-4
F $1,500

$1 • **W-MS-250-001-G040** JM

Engraver: Rawdon, Wright, Hatch & Edson / Rawdon, Wright & Hatch. ***Comments:*** H-MS-55-G4, Kraus-14260r. 18__. Circa 1837.

Rarity: URS-4
F $750

Collectors and Researchers:

If you have new information about any banks or notes listed in this volume, contact Whitman Publishing, Attn: Obsolete Paper Money, 3101 Clairmont Road, Suite G, Atlanta, GA 30329.

$2 • W-MS-250-002-G050 JM

Engraver: Rawdon, Wright, Hatch & Edson / Rawdon, Wright & Hatch. ***Comments:*** H-MS-55-G8, Kraus-14261r. 18__. Circa 1837.

Rarity: URS-4
F $750

$5 • W-MS-250-005-G060

Engraver: Southern Argus Print. ***Comments:*** H-MS-55-G12, Kraus-14233. No description available. 18__. Circa 1837.

Rarity: *None known*

$5 • W-MS-250-005-G070 JM

Engraver: Rawdon, Wright, Hatch & Edson. ***Comments:*** H-Unlisted, Kraus-14262r. 18__. Circa 1837.

Rarity: URS-4
F $450

$5 • W-MS-250-005-G080 JM

Engraver: Western Bank Note Co. / Woodruff & Mason. ***Comments:*** H-Unlisted, Kraus-14270. 18__. Circa 1837.

Rarity: URS-4
F $450

$10 • W-MS-250-010-G090 JM

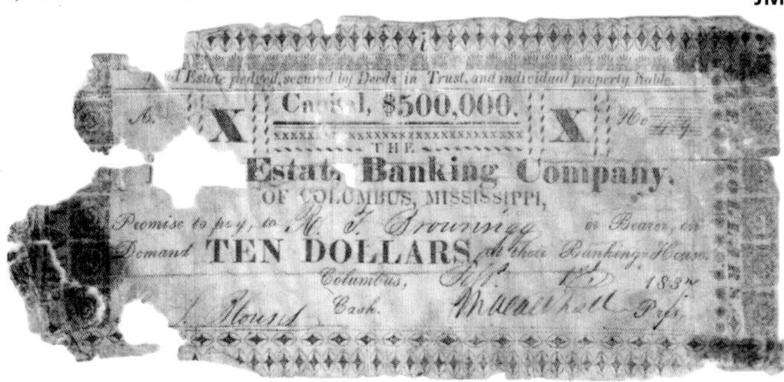

Engraver: Southern Argus Print. ***Comments:*** H-MS-55-G16, Kraus-14234. 18__. Circa 1837.

Rarity: URS-3
Fair $300

$10 • W-MS-250-010-G100

Engraver: Rawdon, Wright, Hatch & Edson. ***Comments:*** H-Unlisted, Kraus-14263. No description available. 18__. Circa 1837.

Rarity: *None known*

$10 • W-MS-250-010-G110 JM

Engraver: Western Bank Note Co. / Woodruff & Mason. ***Comments:*** H-MS-55-G20, Kraus-14271. 18__. Circa 1837.

Rarity: URS-4
F $500

$20 • W-MS-250-020-G120 JM

Comments: H-MS-55-G24, Kraus-14272. 18__. Circa 1837.

Rarity: URS-5
F $450

$50 • W-MS-250-050-G130

JM

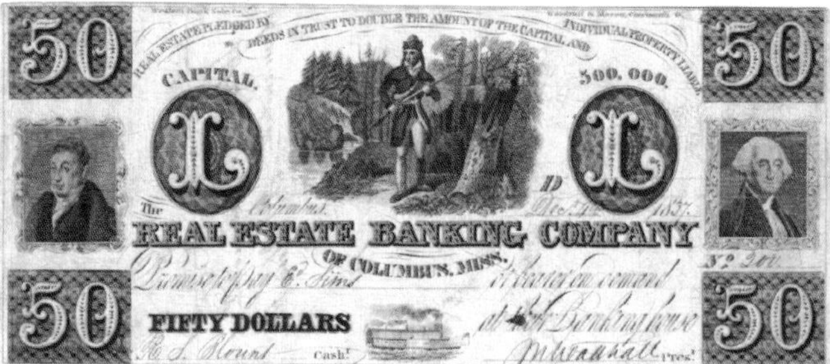

Engraver: Western Bank Note Co. / Woodruff & Mason. ***Comments:*** H-MS-55-G28, Kraus-14273. 18__. Circa 1837.

Rarity: URS-5

F $450

$100 • W-MS-250-100-G140

JM

Comments: H-MS-55-G32, Kraus-14274. 18__. Circa 1837.

Rarity: URS-5

F $750

Tombigby Rail Road and Banking Company

1836–1841

W-MS-260

History: The Tombigby Rail Road and Banking Company (also seen as the Tombigby Rail Road Company on notes) was chartered on February 27, 1836. It was reported to have a positive net worth of $2,403.67 in February 1838. In March 1841 the company, along with several other banking businesses, had its charter revoked for failure to redeem its notes at par for coins.

See also listing under Vicksburg, W-MS-930.

Numismatic Commentary: This bank issued demand notes payable at their office in Columbus as well as post notes payable at the Commercial and Rail Road Bank in Vicksburg.

Valid Issues

$5 • W-MS-260-005-G010

CC

Engraver: Rawdon, Wright & Hatch. ***Comments:*** H-MS-60-G8, Kraus-10246. 18__. 1830s.

Rarity: URS-5

F $550

$10 • W-MS-260-010-G020

CC

Engraver: Rawdon, Wright & Hatch. ***Comments:*** H-MS-60-G10, Kraus-10247. 18__. 1830s.

Rarity: URS-5

F $550

$20 • W-MS-260-020-G030

JM

Engraver: Rawdon, Wright & Hatch. ***Comments:*** H-MS-60-G12, Kraus-10248. 18__. 1830s.

Rarity: URS-4

F $1,000

$50 • **W-MS-260-050-G040**

JM

Engraver: Rawdon, Wright & Hatch. ***Comments:*** H-MS-60-G14, Kraus-10249. 18__. 1830s.

Rarity: URS-4
F $1,500

$100 • **W-MS-260-100-G050**

JM

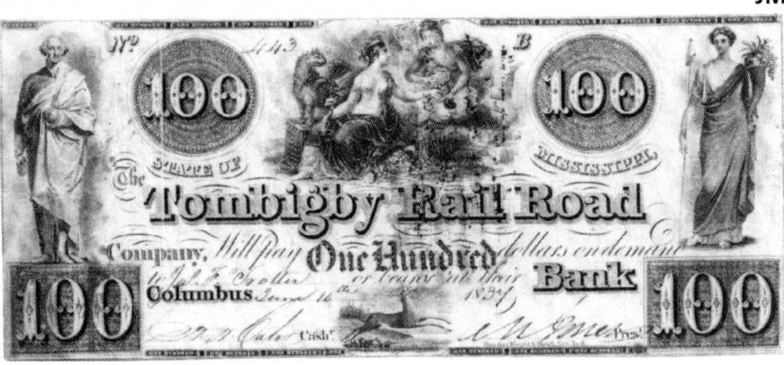

Engraver: Rawdon, Wright & Hatch. ***Comments:*** H-MS-60-G16, Kraus-10250. 18__. 1830s.

Rarity: URS-4
F $2,000

$500 • **W-MS-260-500-G060**

Left: 500 vertically. ***Center:*** 500 / Griffin on strongbox, Moneta receiving cornucopia of coins from flying Mercury / 500. ***Right:*** 500 / Steamboat / 500. ***Engraver:*** Rawdon, Wright & Hatch. ***Comments:*** H-MS-60-G18, Kraus-10251p. Known only as Proofs. 18__. 1830s.

Rarity: URS-1
Proof $3,000

$1,000 • **W-MS-260-1000-G070**

Left: 1000 vertically. ***Center:*** 1000 / Griffin on strongbox, Moneta receiving cornucopia of coins from flying Mercury / 1000. ***Right:*** 1000 vertically. ***Engraver:*** Rawdon, Wright & Hatch. ***Comments:*** H-MS-60-G20, Kraus-10252p. Known only as Proofs. 18__. 1830s.

Rarity: URS-1
Proof $3,500

Post Notes

$5 • **W-MS-260-005-G080**

Left: FIVE vertically. ***Center:*** 5 / Steamboat / 5 / Griffin on strongbox, Moneta receiving cornucopia of coins from flying Mercury. ***Right:*** 5. ***Engraver:*** Rawdon, Wright & Hatch. ***Comments:*** H-MS-60-G22. Likely the same note as W-MS-260-005-G120. 18__. 1830s.

Rarity: *None known*

$10 • **W-MS-260-010-G090**

Left: 10 / Ships / 10. ***Center:*** X / Cherub flying / X / Griffin on strongbox, Moneta receiving cornucopia of coins from flying Mercury. ***Right:*** 10. ***Engraver:*** Rawdon, Wright & Hatch. ***Comments:*** H-MS-60-G24. Likely the same note as W-MS-260-010-G130. 18__. 1830s.

Rarity: *None known*

$20 • **W-MS-260-020-G100**

Engraver: Rawdon, Wright & Hatch. ***Comments:*** H-MS-60-G26. No description available. Likely the same note as W-MS-260-020-G140. 18__. 1830s.

Rarity: *None known*

$50 • **W-MS-260-050-G110**

Engraver: Rawdon, Wright & Hatch. ***Comments:*** H-MS-60-G28. No description available. Likely the same note as W-MS-260-050-G150. 18__. 1830s.

Rarity: *None known*

Post Notes Payable "at the Commercial & Rail Road Bank of Vicksburg"

$5 • **W-MS-260-005-G120**

JM

Engraver: Rawdon, Wright & Hatch. ***Comments:*** H-MS-60-G34, Kraus-10262a. 18__. 1830s.

Rarity: URS-4
F $750

$10 • **W-MS-260-010-G130**

JM

Engraver: Rawdon, Wright & Hatch. ***Comments:*** H-MS-60-G36, Kraus-Unlisted. 18__. 1830s.

Rarity: URS-3
F $950

$20 • **W-MS-260-020-G140**

Engraver: Rawdon, Wright & Hatch. ***Comments:*** H-MS-60-G38, Kraus-10264b. No description available. 18__. 1830s.

Rarity: *None known*

$50 • **W-MS-260-050-G150**

Engraver: Rawdon, Wright & Hatch. ***Comments:*** H-MS-60-G40. No description available. 18__. 1830s.

Rarity: *None known*

Commerce, Mississippi

The area that became Commerce was settled by Thomas Fletcher, who called it Commerce in the hopes that it would one day become a large city. It was founded in 1834 and became the county seat in 1836. By 1839 it was incorporated as the first town in Tunica County. At the time it had a larger population than Memphis, Tennessee.

In 1840 the construction of a railroad through Commerce had almost been completed when Governor Alexander McNutt revoked the charter of the Hernando Rail Road and Banking Company, W-MS-380. This caused the business to go bankrupt, and the construction ceased. Three years later, the Mississippi River changed course, and part of Commerce was submerged. Levees were built in an effort to rescue the town. The county seat was transferred temporarily to Peyton, but in six months it had been returned to Commerce. It was moved officially to Austin not long after.

From that point on most of the land in Commerce was sold to a wealthy cotton planter.

Western Bank of Mississippi
1830s
W-MS-270

History: This is believed to have been an exchange house or office that issued notes to be circulated regionally. No record has been found of a state charter for this bank, and it is presumed it was a private enterprise. It is listed here for collector continuity.

Numismatic Commentary: Only one note is known from this bank in addition to two private merchant-scrip issues from Commerce. The 25¢ and 50¢ notes are speculative listings.

Valid Issues

25¢ • W-MS-270-00.25-G010

Comments: H-Unlisted, Kraus-20555. No description available. 1830s.

Rarity: *None known*

50¢ • W-MS-270-00.50-G020

Comments: H-Unlisted, Kraus-20556. No description available. 1830s.

Rarity: *None known*

$1 • W-MS-270-001-G030 JM

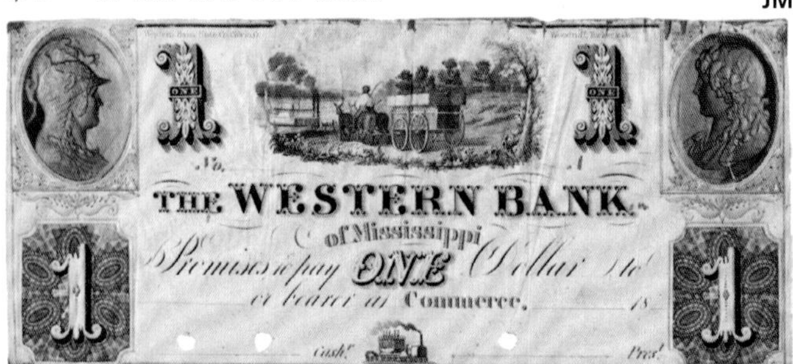

Comments: H-Unlisted, Kraus-20558. 1830s.

Rarity: URS-1

Proof $2,500

Selected auction price: Heritage Auctions, April 23, 2015, Lot 19199, Proof $2,115

Decatur, Mississippi

Decatur, formed in February 1836 out of Neshoba County, became the county seat of Newton. The courthouse and jail were laid out, lots were auctioned for homes and businesses, and the name Decatur was selected after Commodore Stephen Decatur. A liquor shop was one of the earliest businesses. The courthouse served as court in the daytime, and after nightfall it was a bank. The town was considered a rough place, with horse racing, gambling, dog fights, and a dancing school being the regular social activities. The first church did not arrive until 1851, and the second appeared in 1855. An academic school did not follow until 1886.

Much of Decatur was destroyed during the Civil War, but the inhabitants determined to rebuild anyway.

Exchange Banking Company
1830s
W-MS-280

History: This is believed to have been an exchange house or office that had notes circulating regionally. No record has been found of a state charter for this bank, and it is presumed it was a private enterprise. It is listed here for collector continuity.

Numismatic Commentary: Only one note of this bank is known.

Valid Issues

$2 • W-MS-280-002-G010 JM

Comments: H-Unlisted, Kraus-14301. 183_. 1830s.

Rarity: URS-1

G $2,000

Mississippi and Alabama Real Estate Banking Company
1838 and 1839
W-MS-290

History: This was an exchange house that issued notes based on real estate holdings. No record has been found of a state charter for this bank, and it is presumed it was a private enterprise. It is listed here for collector continuity.

In 1839 *Niles' Register* reported the destruction of the "Real Estate Bank at Decatur," stating that:

> . . . the Real Estate Bank at that place was set on fire by a mob, and burned, together with all the books and papers. Nothing was saved . . . So much for mob law in Mississippi.

Numismatic Commentary: The locally produced woodcuts notes are exceedingly rare. With the exception of the $1 and $2 notes, the Burton & Gurley / Childs notes are common.

Valid Issues

$1 • W-MS-290-001-G010

JM

Engraver: Burton & Gurley / Childs. ***Comments:*** H-MS-65-G4, Kraus-14360. 18__. 1839.

Rarity: URS-4
F $350

$2 • W-MS-290-002-G020

JM

Engraver: Burton & Gurley / Childs. ***Comments:*** H-MS-65-G6, Kraus-Unlisted. 18__. 1839.

Rarity: URS-4
F $350

$5 • W-MS-290-005-G030

JM

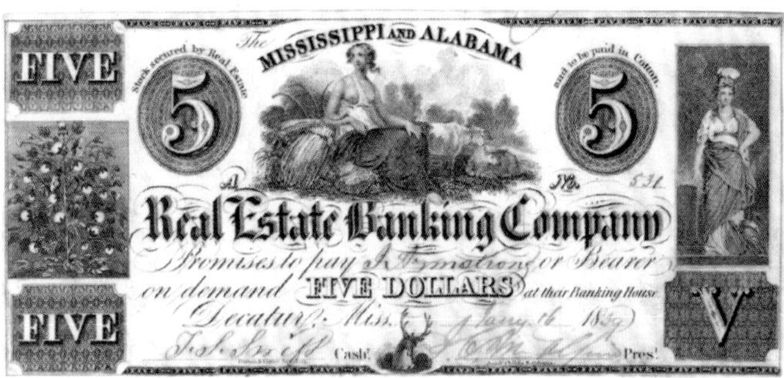

Engraver: Burton & Gurley / Childs. ***Comments:*** H-MS-65-G12, Kraus-Unlisted. 18__. 1839.

Rarity: URS-8
F $150

$10 • W-MS-290-010-G040

Engraver: Burton & Gurley / Childs. ***Comments:*** H-MS-65-G16, Kraus-14363. 18__. 1839.

Rarity: URS-7
F $200

$20 • W-MS-290-020-G050

Left: 20 / Cotton plant / 20. ***Center:*** XX / Three women seated / XX. ***Right:*** Woman standing in niche. ***Engraver:*** Burton & Gurley / Childs. ***Comments:*** H-MS-65-G20, Kraus-Unlisted. 18__. 1839.

Rarity: —

$50 • W-MS-290-050-G060

Left: 50 / Cotton plant / 50. ***Center:*** L / Three cherubs in clouds with 50 on tablet / L. ***Right:*** 50 / Cotton plant / 50. ***Engraver:*** Burton & Gurley / Childs. ***Comments:*** H-MS-65-G22, Kraus-Unlisted. 18__. 1839.

Rarity: *None known*

Locally Printed Woodcut Notes

$5 • W-MS-290-005-G070

JM

Comments: H-MS-65-G10, Kraus-14330. 18__. 1838.

Rarity: URS-3
F $1,000

$10 • W-MS-290-010-G080

JM

Engraver: Burton & Gurley / Childs. ***Comments:*** H-Unlisted. 18__. 1838.

Rarity: URS-3
F $2,000

$20 • **W-MS-290-020-G090**

JM

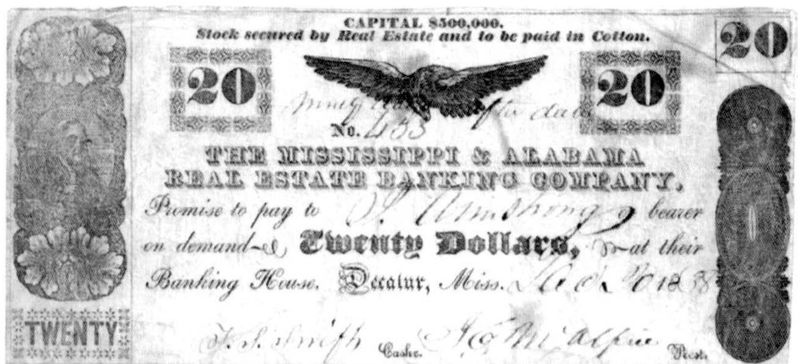

Comments: H-MS-65-G18, Kraus-14332. 18__. 1838.

Rarity: URS-3

F $2,000

Post Notes

$20 • **W-MS-290-020-G100**

JM

Engraver: Burton & Gurley / Childs. ***Comments:*** H-MS-65-G30, Kraus-14364a. 18__. 1839.

Rarity: URS-8

F $200; **Proof** $600

$50 • **W-MS-290-050-G110**

JM

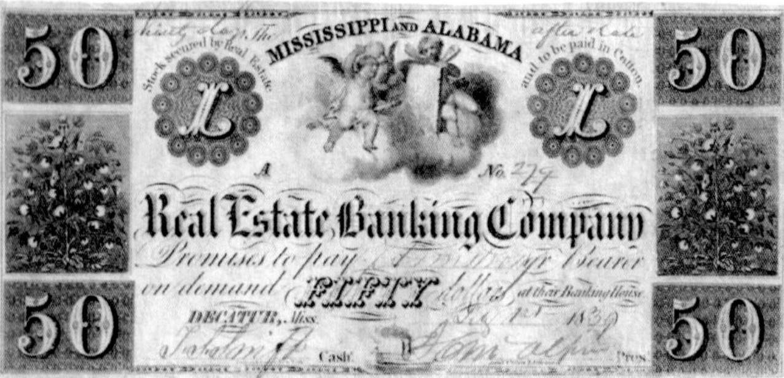

Engraver: Burton & Gurley / Childs. ***Comments:*** H-MS-65-G32, Kraus-14365. 18__. 1839.

Rarity: URS-7

F $300

Enterprise, Mississippi

The town of Enterprise started out as a trading post in east Mississippi. By 1780 the first settlers had arrived, living peacefully with the Choctaw Indians for a while. In 1830 a treaty was signed handing over the Choctaw lands to settlers, and the Native Americans left for the West.

In 1834 Enterprise was officially founded by John J. McRae, who afterwards became governor of Mississippi. The town became the county seat of Clarke, only to be replaced by Quitman later. In 1839 Enterprise was incorporated, and the streets were laid out and named. Soon the town became a prosperous and busy river city, trading in cotton and other necessities. Supplies for neighboring towns including Pascagoula and Hattiesburg were purchased in Enterprise.

Churches and a school followed the commercial entities, and soon sawmills and cotton wagons bolstered Enterprise into becoming the largest city in Mississippi. Horse-drawn street cars ran through the streets on tracks. In 1851 there was a devastating yellow-fever epidemic which decimated the town. The year previously, the Mobile and Ohio Railroad had come through Enterprise, and there had been plans for the Southern Railroad to intersect the M&O. However, the town did not give the railroad any financial assistance, and the intersection went to nearby Meridian instead. Bypassed by the secondary railway, Enterprise began to decline, and Meridian took its place as the biggest trading center in the state. The town served as a supply depot and recruitment center during the Civil War.

Bank of Enterprise
1862
W-MS-300

History: The Bank of Enterprise was authorized on January 17, 1862, with a capital of $500,000.[8] It is unknown if this bank ever opened for business.

Commercial Bank of Enterprise
Circa 1839
W-MS-310

History: This was a fraudulent institution. In 1839 it was reported that the "Southern and Western papers notice appearance of notes of the 'Commercial Bank of Enterprise,' a pretend institution which has neither reality or locality."[9]

Issues

$5 • **W-MS-310-005-G010**

JM

Engraver: Rawdon, Wright, Hatch & Edson / Rawdon, Wright & Hatch. ***Comments:*** H-MS-70-G8, Kraus-3470. 18__. 1830s.

Rarity: URS-4

F $750

$5 • **W-MS-310-005-G010a**

Engraver: Rawdon, Wright, Hatch & Edson / Rawdon, Wright & Hatch. ***Comments:*** H-Unlisted, Kraus-3470c. Similar to W-MS-310-005-G010. 18__. 1830s.

Rarity: URS-3

F $850

$10 • W-MS-310-010-G020 JM

Engraver: Rawdon, Wright, Hatch & Edson / Rawdon, Wright & Hatch. ***Comments:*** H-MS-70-G10, Kraus-3471. 18__. 1830s.

Rarity: URS-3
F $1,000

$20 • W-MS-310-020-G030 JM

Engraver: Rawdon, Wright, Hatch & Edson / Rawdon, Wright & Hatch. ***Comments:*** H-MS-70-G12, Kraus-3472. 18__. 1830s.

Rarity: URS-3
F $1,000

$50 • W-MS-310-050-G040

Left: Hebe / 50. ***Center:*** FIFTY. ***Right:*** Vulcan and Commerce / 50. ***Engraver:*** Rawdon, Wright, Hatch & Edson / Rawdon, Wright & Hatch. ***Comments:*** H-MS-70-G14, Kraus-3473. 18__. 1830s.

Rarity: *None known*

Post Notes

$20 • W-MS-310-020-G050

Left: TWENTY vertically. ***Center:*** 20 / Spread eagle / 20. ***Right:*** TWENTY vertically. ***Engraver:*** Rawdon, Wright, Hatch & Edson / Rawdon, Wright & Hatch. ***Comments:*** H-MS-70-G20, Kraus-3472a. 18__. 1839.

Rarity: URS-3
F $1,000

$50 • W-MS-310-050-G060

Left: Hebe watering eagle / 50. ***Center:*** FIFTY. ***Right:*** Vulcan and Commerce / 50. ***Engraver:*** Rawdon, Wright, Hatch & Edson / Rawdon, Wright & Hatch. ***Comments:*** H-MS-70-G22, Kraus-3473a. 18__. 1839.

Rarity: *None known*

$50 • W-MS-310-050-G060a JM

Engraver: Rawdon, Wright, Hatch & Edson / Rawdon, Wright & Hatch. ***Comments:*** H-Unlisted, Kraus-3473b. Similar to W-MS-310-050-G060. 18__. 1839.

Rarity: URS-3
F $2,000

Gallatin, Mississippi

Gallatin was first settled by two lawyers from Gallatin, Tennessee, who arrived in 1819 and named the new area after their hometown. By 1829 the town had been incorporated. The economy was based primarily on agriculture as a result of slave labor. After the Civil War, as the nearby town of Hazlehurst grew, Gallatin went into decline.

Mississippi Rail Road and Banking Company (branch)

1836–1841

W-MS-320

History: The Mississippi Rail Road and Banking Company (also seen as the Mississippi Rail Road Company on notes) was chartered on February 26, 1836. The bank had a positive net worth of $116,668.06 as of February 24, 1838. In 1840 it was reported that the bank could not redeem its notes, and in March 1841 this issuer, along with several others, had its charter revoked for this reason.

How to Read the Whitman Numbering System

$1 • W-AL-020-001-G010a

Denomination: Face value of the note shown.

W: Whitman number. This number is a sortable code unique to each bank and note.

AL: Abbreviation for the state under study.

020: Numerical designation specific to each bank.

001: The denomination in dollars.

G010a: G indicates a good or valid note. Other categories are indicated thus: C (counterfeit); R (raised); S (spurious); N (not-attributed); A (altered). Numbers are assigned starting with 010, 020, et seq. Terminal letters following the number indicate variations of a note: a series of different colored overprints, tints, payees, etc., all on the same design of note. For more information, see the "How to Use This Book" section at the front of the volume, page xiv.

The Mississippi Rail Road and Banking Company had its parent bank located in Natchez, W-MS-650, and branches located in Canton, W-MS-110, and Raymond, W-MS-810.

Numismatic Commentary: Branch-bank notes stamped with either the Gallatin or Raymond overprints are rare.

Valid Issues

$5 • W-MS-320-005-G010

JM

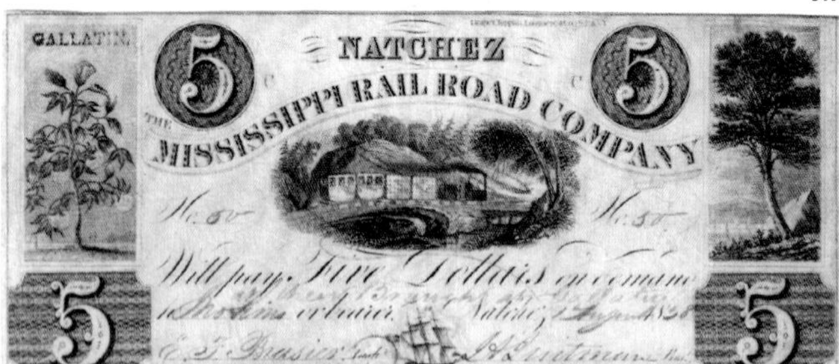

Overprint: Black GALLATIN stamp. ***Engraver:*** Draper, Toppan, Longacre & Co. ***Comments:*** H-MS-170-G36, Kraus-10450a. 18__. 1838.

Rarity: URS-4
F $350

$10 • W-MS-320-010-G020

Left: Cotton plant / 10. ***Center:*** 10 / Train / 10. ***Right:*** Tree / 10. ***Overprint:*** Black GALLATIN stamp. ***Engraver:*** Draper, Toppan, Longacre & Co. ***Comments:*** H-MS-170-G38, Kraus-10451a. 18__. 1838.

Rarity: URS-4
F $350

Post Notes

$5 • W-MS-320-005-G030

JM

Overprint: Black GALLATIN and POST NOTE stamp. ***Engraver:*** Draper, Toppan, Longacre & Co. ***Comments:*** H-Unlisted. 18__. 1838.

Rarity: URS-4
F $350

$10 • W-MS-320-010-G035

Left: Cotton plant / 10. ***Center:*** 10 / Train / 10. ***Right:*** Tree / 10. ***Overprint:*** Black GALLATIN and POST NOTE stamp. ***Engraver:*** Draper, Toppan, Longacre & Co. ***Comments:*** H-Unlisted, Kraus-Unlisted. 18__. 1838.

Rarity: —

$20 • W-MS-320-020-G040

JM

Overprint: Black GALLATIN and POST NOTE stamp. ***Engraver:*** Draper, Toppan, Longacre & Co. ***Comments:*** H-MS-170-G50a, Kraus-10452a. 18__. 1838.

Rarity: URS-4
F $350

Grand Gulf, Mississippi

The French and Spanish governments traded control of the land that would become Mississippi from 1680 to 1803, including the area of Grand Gulf. Land grants were issued to settlers in 1792, allowing the White, Smith, and Marble families to establish a settlement next to the Mississippi River. It was considered a haven in a large, surrounding wilderness, boasting a hotel in 1828 as well as a court house. In 1833 the town was officially incorporated.

Cotton, as was the case in many southern towns, was the primary means of industry in Grand Gulf. It was shipped out on the Mississippi River in vast quantities, totaling an exportation of over 37,000 bales in a decade. A large hospital was built, followed by many stores and a theater, giving rise to a population of 1,000.

In 1843 the beginning of the end started—a yellow-fever epidemic struck the town, catching the attention of even Northern newspapers with its severity. A steamboat explosion nine years later destroyed most of Grand Gulf's docks. In 1853 a tornado razed the area, followed by flooding as the Mississippi River changed its course. By 1860 there were 52 submerged blocks, and by the time of the Civil War, the town was little more than abandoned buildings.

Grand Gulf Rail Road and Banking Company

1833–1840

W-MS-330

History: The Grand Gulf Rail Road and Banking Company was incorporated on December 23, 1833, with an authorized capital of $150,000. The company was granted banking privileges for the purpose of constructing a railroad from Grand Gulf to Port Gibson. In 1836 a further act was passed, raising the capital to $1,150,000 and requiring the bank to redeem its notes in specie. In February 1840 an act was passed forfeiting the charter of the company for failing to do that. Only seven miles of railway had been completed.[10]

Numismatic Commentary: These notes are elusive, with the originally issued notes being very hard to find. The reissued notes are more common but still difficult to locate.

VALID ISSUES

$5 • W-MS-330-005-G010

JM

Engraver: Draper, Toppan, Longacre & Co. ***Comments:*** H-MS-75-G8, Kraus-10290. 18__. 1830s.

Rarity: URS-3
F $2,000; **Proof** $1,500

$10 • W-MS-330-010-G020

JM

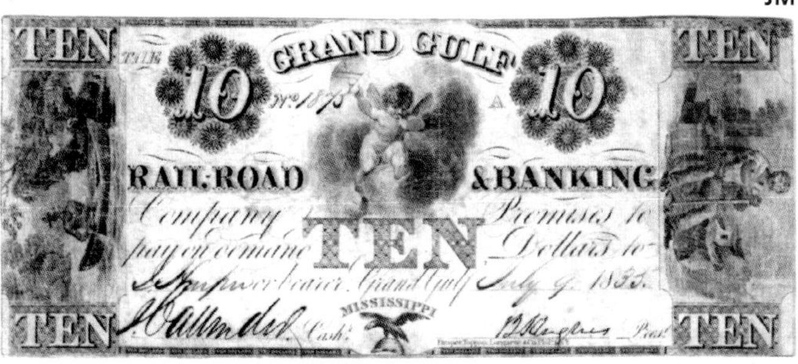

Engraver: Draper, Toppan, Longacre & Co. ***Comments:*** H-MS-75-G10, Kraus-10291. 18__. 1830s.

Rarity: URS-3
F $2,000; **Proof** $2,000

$10 • W-MS-330-010-G020a

JM

Overprint: Blue REISSUED stamp. ***Engraver:*** Draper, Toppan, Longacre & Co. ***Comments:*** H-MS-75-G10a, Kraus-10291a. Similar to W-MS-330-010-G020. 18__. 1830s.

Rarity: URS-3
F $2,000

$20 • W-MS-330-020-G030

Left: 20 / Ship / 20. ***Center:*** Aurora with three horses pulling chariot, Cupid, attendants / Train. ***Right:*** 20 / Ship / 20. ***Engraver:*** Draper, Toppan, Longacre & Co. ***Comments:*** H-MS-75-G12, Kraus-10292. 18__. 1830s.

Rarity: URS-3

$20 • W-MS-330-020-G030a

JM

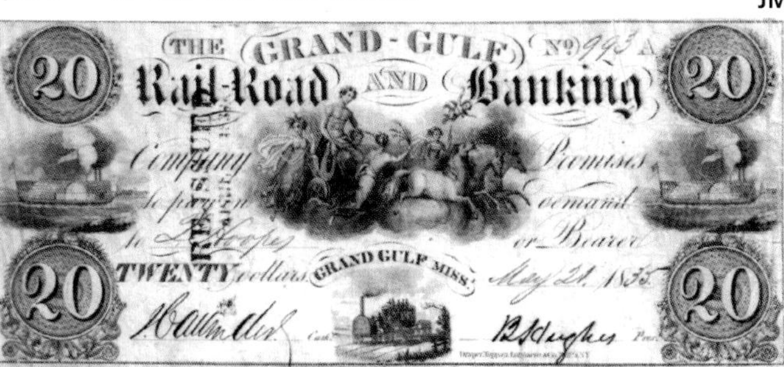

Overprint: Blue REISSUED stamp. ***Engraver:*** Draper, Toppan, Longacre & Co. ***Comments:*** H-MS-75-G12a, Kraus-10292a. Similar to W-MS-330-020-G030.18__. 1830s.

Rarity: URS-3
F $2,000; **Proof** $2,000

$50 • W-MS-330-050-G040

Left: George Washington seated with tablet / 50. ***Center:*** 50 / Riverboats / 50. ***Right:*** George Washington seated with tablet / 50. ***Engraver:*** Draper, Toppan, Longacre & Co. ***Comments:*** H-MS-75-G14, Kraus-10294. 18__. 1830s.

Rarity: URS-3
F $2,500

$50 • W-MS-330-050-G040a

JM

Overprint: Blue REISSUED stamp. ***Engraver:*** Draper, Toppan, Longacre & Co. ***Comments:*** H-MS-75-G14a, Kraus-10294a. Similar to W-MS-330-050-G040.18__. 1830s.

Rarity: URS-3
G $1,500

$100 • W-MS-330-100-G050

Left: Indian with hatchet and bow / 100. ***Center:*** 100 / Train, Mountain scene / 100. ***Right:*** Statue of George Washington / 100. ***Engraver:*** Draper, Toppan, Longacre & Co. ***Comments:*** H-MS-75-G16, Kraus-10295. 18__. 1830s.

Rarity: URS-3
F $2,500

$100 • **W-MS-330-100-G050a**

JM

Overprint: Blue REISSUED stamp. ***Engraver:*** Draper, Toppan, Longacre & Co. ***Comments:*** H-MS-75-G16a, Kraus-10295a. Similar to W-MS-330-100-G050. 18__. 1830s.

Rarity: URS-3
F $3,000

GRENADA, MISSISSIPPI

When Pittsburg and Tulahoma merged in 1836, the town of Grenada was formed. In 1851 a junior college for women was founded. During the Civil War, Confederate troops camped at Grenada, and in December 1862 they departed under command of General Earl Van Dorn to advance on the Union supply depot at Holly Springs. They were successful and destroyed most of the goods.

Bank of Grenada Mississippi {1st}
1837 and 1838
W-MS-340

History: The first Bank of Grenada Mississippi was chartered on May 9, 1837, with an authorized capital of $1,000,000. The president was G.E. Plummer, and the cashier was C.J.F. Wharton. The institution did not last long and was closed the following year. Its charter was officially revoked on January 5, 1841.

Numismatic Commentary: Valid issues and remainders are exceedingly rare.

VALID ISSUES

$5 • **W-MS-340-005-G010**

JM

Engraver: Underwood, Bald, Spencer & Hufty. ***Comments:*** H-MS-80-G8, Kraus-3520. 18__. 1830s.

Rarity: URS-4
Proof $750

$6 • **W-MS-340-006-G020**

Left: 6 / Blacksmith / SIX. ***Center:*** Boy with shovel walking to field. ***Right:*** 6 / Woman seated / SIX. ***Engraver:*** Underwood, Bald, Spencer & Hufty. ***Comments:*** H-MS-80-G10, Kraus-3522. 18__. 1830s.

Rarity: URS-2
Proof $3,500

$7 • **W-MS-340-007-G030**

Left: 7 / Medallion head vertically / 7. ***Center:*** VII / Indian seated at river / VII. ***Right:*** 7 / Medallion head vertically / 7. ***Engraver:*** Underwood, Bald, Spencer & Hufty. ***Comments:*** H-MS-80-G11, Kraus-3523. 18__. 1830s.

Rarity: URS-2
Proof $3,500

$8 • **W-MS-340-008-G040**

Left: Justice with portrait of George Washington. ***Center:*** VIII / Woman with pitchfork in hay field, Men loading wagon / VIII. ***Right:*** 8 / Athena, Eagle, anchor. ***Engraver:*** Underwood, Bald, Spencer & Hufty. ***Comments:*** H-MS-80-G12, Kraus-3524. 18__. 1830s.

Rarity: URS-2
Proof $3,500

$9 • **W-MS-340-009-G050**

Left: 9 / Medallion head vertically / 9. ***Center:*** IX / Zeus and Minerva, Scales / IX. ***Right:*** 9 / Medallion head vertically / 9. ***Engraver:*** Underwood, Bald, Spencer & Hufty. ***Comments:*** H-MS-80-G13, Kraus-3525. 18__. 1830s.

Rarity: URS-2
Proof $3,500

$10 • **W-MS-340-010-G060**

JM

Engraver: Underwood, Bald, Spencer & Hufty. ***Comments:*** H-MS-80-G14, Kraus-3521. 18__. 1830s.

Rarity: URS-4
F $500; **Proof** $750

$20 • **W-MS-340-020-G070**

JM

Engraver: Underwood, Bald, Spencer & Hufty. ***Comments:*** H-MS-80-G16, Kraus-3527. 18__. 1830s.

Rarity: URS-4
VF $600; **Proof** $750

$50 • **W-MS-340-050-G080**

Left: 50 / Medallion head / 50. ***Center:*** Four cherubs, one as Ceres carrying wheat, three with baskets of grapes. ***Right:*** 50 / Medallion head / 50. ***Engraver:*** Underwood, Bald, Spencer & Hufty. ***Comments:*** H-MS-80-G18, Kraus-3528. 18__. 1830s.

Rarity: URS-2
Proof $1,500

$100 • **W-MS-340-100-G090** CC

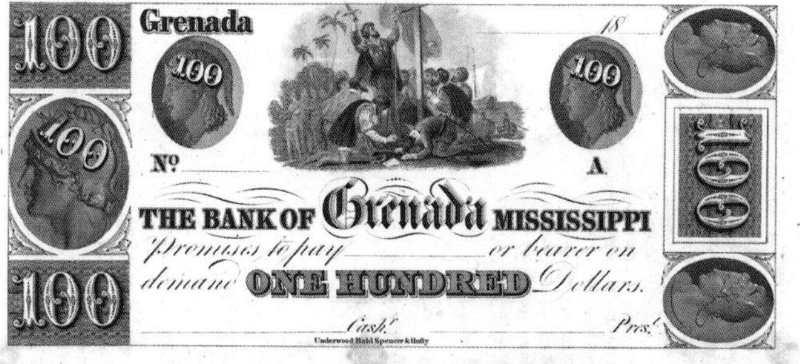

Engraver: Underwood, Bald, Spencer & Hufty. ***Comments:*** H-MS-80-G20, Kraus-3529. 18__. 1830s.

Rarity: URS-2
Proof $4,200

Bank of Grenada Mississippi {2nd}

1862

W-MS-350

History: The second Bank of Grenada Mississippi was authorized on January 17, 1862, with a capital of $500,000.[11] It is unknown if this bank ever went into operation.

Numismatic Commentary: No notes for this bank are known.

Paulding and Pontotoc Rail Road Company

1838–1840

W-MS-360

History: The Paulding and Pontotoc Rail Road Company was incorporated on February 16, 1838, with an authorized capital of $6,000,000. It issued paper money as a convenience to those doing business with it, for a time redeeming bills on demand. On January 6, 1840, the banking privileges of the company were repealed.

Numismatic Commentary: Notes from this bank are exceedingly rare. The $2, $3, and $4 issues are speculative listings and listed for collector continuity. No notes have been seen of the $20, $50, and $100 issues.

Valid Issues

12-1/2¢ • **W-MS-360-00.12.50-G010**

Left: 12-1/2 / 12-1/2. ***Center:*** 1-real coin / Train / 1-real coin. ***Right:*** 12-1/2 / 12-1/2. ***Engraver:*** Rawdon, Wright, & Hatch. ***Comments:*** H-MS-85-G2, Kraus-10310. 18__. 1830s–1840s.

Rarity: URS-1
F $1,500

25¢ • **W-MS-360-00.25-G020**

Engraver: Rawdon, Wright, & Hatch. ***Comments:*** H-MS-85-G4, Kraus-10311. No description available. 18__. 1830s–1840s.

Rarity: *None known*

50¢ • **W-MS-360-00.50-G030**

Engraver: Rawdon, Wright, & Hatch. ***Comments:*** H-MS-85-G6, Kraus-10312. No description available. 18__. 1830s–1840s.

Rarity: *None known*

$1 • **W-MS-360-001-G040**

Left: U.S. silver dollar / ONE. ***Center:*** Riverboat / 1 / Eagle with shield. ***Right:*** ONE / Train / ONE. ***Engraver:*** Rawdon, Wright, & Hatch. ***Comments:*** H-MS-85-G8, Kraus-10313. 18__. 1830s–1840s.

Rarity: URS-1
F $1,500

$2 • **W-MS-360-002-G050**

Engraver: Rawdon, Wright, & Hatch. ***Comments:*** H-MS-85-G10, Kraus-10314. No description available. 18__. 1830s–1840s.

Rarity: *None known*

$3 • **W-MS-360-003-G060**

Engraver: Rawdon, Wright, & Hatch. ***Comments:*** H-MS-85-G12, Kraus-10315. No description available. 18__. 1830s–1840s.

Rarity: *None known*

$4 • **W-MS-360-004-G070**

Engraver: Rawdon, Wright, & Hatch. ***Comments:*** H-MS-85-G14, Kraus-10316. No description available. 18__. 1830s–1840s.

Rarity: *None known*

$5 • **W-MS-360-005-G080** JM

Engraver: Rawdon, Wright, & Hatch. ***Comments:*** H-MS-85-G16, Kraus-10317. 18__. 1830s–1840s.

Rarity: URS-3
F $2,500

$10 • W-MS-360-010-G090
Left: TEN vertically. ***Center:*** X / Train with river traffic / X. ***Right:*** 10 / Train / 10. ***Engraver:*** Rawdon, Wright, & Hatch. ***Comments:*** H-MS-85-G18, Kraus-10318. 18__. 1830s–1840s.
Rarity: URS-3
F $2,500

$20 • W-MS-360-020-G100
Engraver: Rawdon, Wright, & Hatch. ***Comments:*** H-MS-85-G20, Kraus-10319. No description available. 18__. 1830s–1840s.
Rarity: *None known*

$50 • W-MS-360-050-G110
Engraver: Rawdon, Wright, & Hatch. ***Comments:*** H-MS-85-G22, Kraus-10320. No description available. 18__. 1830s–1840s.
Rarity: *None known*

$100 • W-MS-360-100-G120
Engraver: Rawdon, Wright, & Hatch. ***Comments:*** H-MS-85-G24, Kraus-10321. No description available. 18__. 1830s–1840s.
Rarity: *None known*

Post Notes

$10 • W-MS-360-010-G130

JM

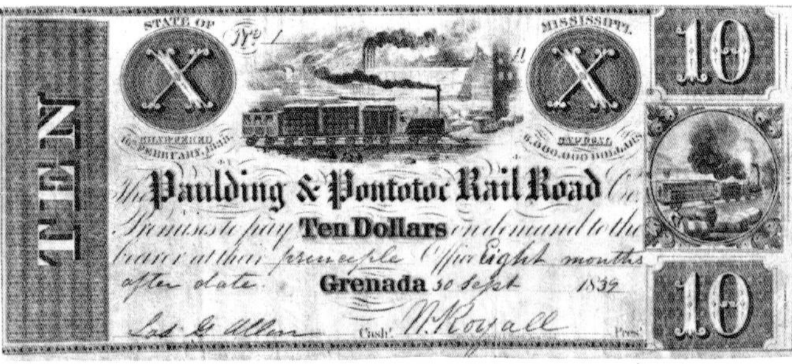

Engraver: Rawdon, Wright, & Hatch. ***Comments:*** H-Unlisted, Kraus-10318b. 18__. 1830s–1840s.
Rarity: URS-1
F $2,000

Planters and Merchants Bank of Mississippi

Circa 1838

W-MS-370

History: This is believed to have been an exchange house or related business that issued notes that circulated regionally. No record has been found of a state charter for this bank, and it is presumed it was a private enterprise. It is listed here for collector continuity.

Numismatic Commentary: Notes from this entity are exceedingly rare.

Valid Issues

25¢ • W-MS-370-00.25-G010

JM

Engraver: Rawdon, Wright & Hatch. ***Comments:*** H-Unlisted, Kraus-3571. 1st Septr. 1838.
Rarity: URS-2
VF $1,500

50¢ • W-MS-370-00.50-G020

JM

Engraver: Rawdon, Wright & Hatch. ***Comments:*** H-Unlisted, Kraus-3572. 1st Septr. 1838.
Rarity: URS-2
VF $1,500

75¢ • W-MS-370-00.75-G030

JM

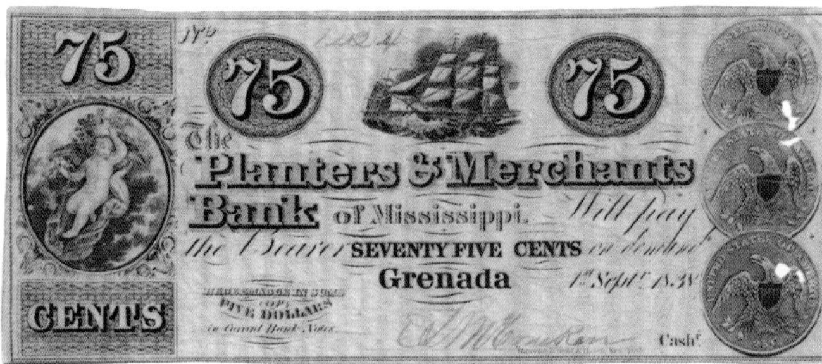

Engraver: Rawdon, Wright & Hatch. ***Comments:*** H-Unlisted, Kraus-3573. 18__. 1830s. 1st Septr. 1838.
Rarity: URS-2
F $1,000

$1 • **W-MS-370-001-G040** JM

Engraver: Rawdon, Wright & Hatch. ***Comments:*** H-MS-90-G2, Kraus-3550. 18__. 1830s.

Rarity: URS-2
VF $2,000

$2 • **W-MS-370-002-G050** JM

Engraver: Rawdon, Wright & Hatch. ***Comments:*** H-MS-90-G4, Kraus-3581. 18__. 1830s.

Rarity: URS-3
F $1,200

$5 • **W-MS-370-005-G060** JM

Engraver: Rawdon, Wright & Hatch. ***Comments:*** H-Unlisted, Kraus-3583r. 18__. 1830s.

Rarity: URS-3
VF $1,500

$10 • **W-MS-370-010-G070** JM

Engraver: Rawdon, Wright & Hatch. ***Comments:*** H-MS-90-G10, Kraus-3584r. 18__. 1830s.

Rarity: URS-3
VF $1,500

$20 • **W-MS-370-020-G080**

Engraver: Rawdon, Wright & Hatch. ***Comments:*** H-MS-90-G12, Kraus-3585. No description available. 18__. 1830s.

Rarity: *None known*

$50 • **W-MS-370-050-G090**

Engraver: Rawdon, Wright & Hatch. ***Comments:*** H-MS-90-G14, Kraus-3586. No description available. 18__. 1830s.

Rarity: *None known*

Post Notes

$3 • **W-MS-370-003-G100** JM

Engraver: Woodruff, Tucker & Co. ***Comments:*** H-MS-90-G24, Kraus-3552. 18__. 1830s.

Rarity: URS-2
F $2,500

$5 • **W-MS-370-005-G110** JM

Engraver: Rawdon, Wright & Hatch. ***Comments:*** H-MS-90-G8, Kraus-3560. 18__. 1830s.

Rarity: URS-3

Hernando, Mississippi

The town of Hernando is named after Hernando de Soto, the discoverer of the Mississippi River.

Hernando Rail Road and Banking Company

1837–1840

W-MS-380

History: The Hernando Rail Road and Banking Company was chartered on May 13, 1837, for the purpose of constructing a railroad spanning from Jefferson to Norfolk. On February 9, 1838, the act was amended, authorizing the company to build a road from Peyton to Hernando.

In 1840 the construction of a railroad through Commerce had almost been completed when Governor Alexander McNutt revoked the charter of the Hernando Rail Road and Banking Company. This caused the railroad to go bankrupt. The bank had ceased paying out specie upon presentation of its notes and thus was in violation of its banking privileges.

Numismatic Commentary: The post notes printed with Mississippi River Currency are very rare.

Remaining at the American Bank Note Co. archives as of 2003 was a $5-$10 face plate and a $50-$100 face plate.

Valid Issues

$5 • W-MS-380-005-G010

Left: FIVE vertically. ***Center:*** Liberty with shield bearing Agriculture, River scene / 5. ***Right:*** Train. ***Engraver:*** Rawdon, Wright & Hatch. ***Comments:*** H-MS-95-G2, Kraus-10350. 18__. 1830s.

Rarity: URS-6
F $325

$10 • W-MS-380-010-G020

CC

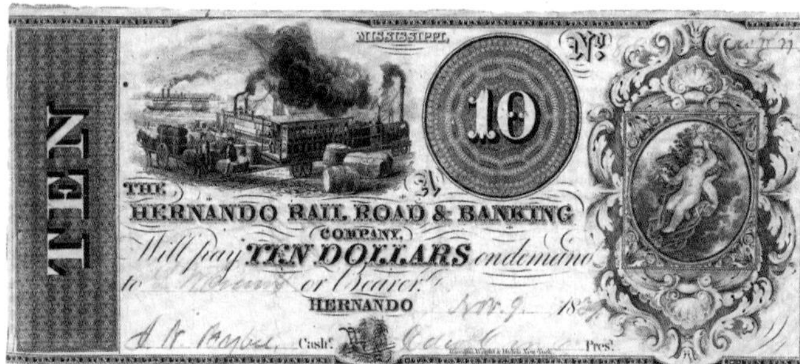

Engraver: Rawdon, Wright & Hatch. ***Comments:*** H-MS-95-G4, Kraus-10351. 18__. 1830s.

Rarity: URS-6
F $325

$20 • W-MS-380-020-G030

Left: TWENTY vertically. ***Center:*** Commerce and Agriculture seated at wharf, Cornucopia, Ships / XX. ***Right:*** Shield bearing train. ***Engraver:*** Rawdon, Wright & Hatch. ***Comments:*** H-MS-95-G6, Kraus-10352. 18__. 1830s.

Rarity: URS-6
F $325

$50 • W-MS-380-050-G040

Comments: H-Unlisted. No description available. 18__. 1830s.

Rarity: *None known*

$100 • W-MS-380-100-G050

Comments: H-Unlisted. No description available. 18__. 1830s.

Rarity: *None known*

Post Notes

$5 • W-MS-380-005-G060

HA, QDB

Back: Red. ***Engraver:*** Western Bank Note Co. / Woodruff, Tucker & Co. ***Comments:*** H-MS-95-G12, Kraus-10360. 18__. 1839.

Rarity: URS-4
F $750

Selected auction price: Heritage Auctions, October 24, 2015, Lot 19632, EF $763

$5 • W-MS-380-005-G070

JM

Engraver: Rawdon, Wright & Hatch. ***Comments:*** H-MS-95-G14. 18__. 1839.

Rarity: URS-7
F $300

$10 • W-MS-380-010-G080 JM

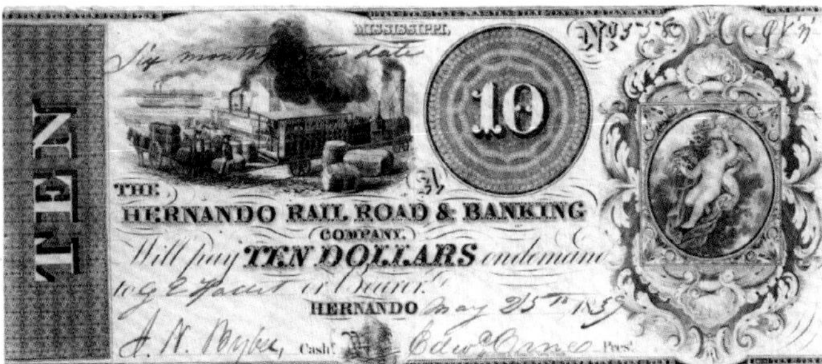

Engraver: Rawdon, Wright & Hatch. ***Comments:*** H-MS-95-G16. 18__. 1839.

Rarity: URS-7
F $300

$20 • W-MS-380-020-G090 JM

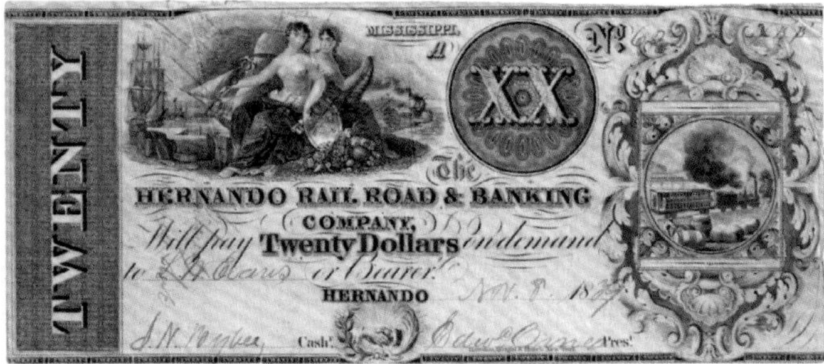

Engraver: Rawdon, Wright & Hatch. ***Comments:*** H-MS-95-G18. 18__. 1839.

Rarity: URS-6
F $350

Post Notes Payable at the Mechanics and Traders Bank, Cincinnati

$20 • W-MS-380-020-G100 JM

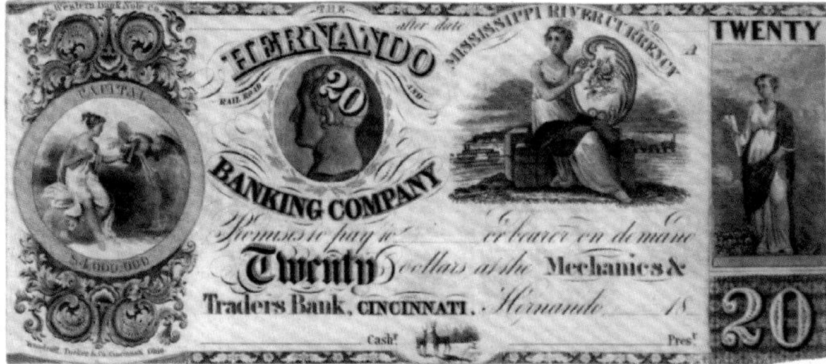

Back: Red. ***Engraver:*** Western Bank Note Co. / Woodruff, Tucker & Co. ***Comments:*** H-MS-95-G26a, Kraus-10380. 18__. 1839.

Rarity: URS-2
F $2,000

Holly Springs, Mississippi

In 1836 Holly Springs (sometimes seen Holley Springs) was settled as a trading center for the surrounding cotton plantations. In a year it had become the seat of Marshall County, and in 1855 it greeted the Mississippi Central Railway, which connected to the Grand Junction, Tennessee.

Holly Springs was used as a supply depot by General Ulysses S. Grant during the Civil War. Most of the supplies were destroyed in a raid in December 1862.

McEwen, King and Company
1837
W-MS-390

History: McEwen, King and Company was an unchartered entity that operated under two names located in Holly Springs—the Exchange Office and McEwen, King and Company Banking House. Both issued large amounts of promissory notes and failed in financial ruin. In time the property was given up to creditors. The amended charter of the Northern Bank of Mississippi, W-MS-400, required the Northern Bank to absorb McEwan, King and Company as well as the Real Estate Bank of Holly Springs, W-MS-410, and honor their notes. Its paper-money issues were unofficial but are listed here in view of numismatic interest in them.

Numismatic Commentary: Both "Exchange Office" and "McEwen, King and Company Banking House" imprints are found on different notes of this company.

Valid Issues

Notes Payable at the Exchange Office

12-1/2¢ • W-MS-390-00.12.50-G010 JM

Engraver: Rawdon, Wright & Hatch. ***Comments:*** H-Unlisted, Kraus-14510. 18__. 1837 and 1838.

Rarity: URS-5
F $350

25¢ • W-MS-390-00.25-G020 JM

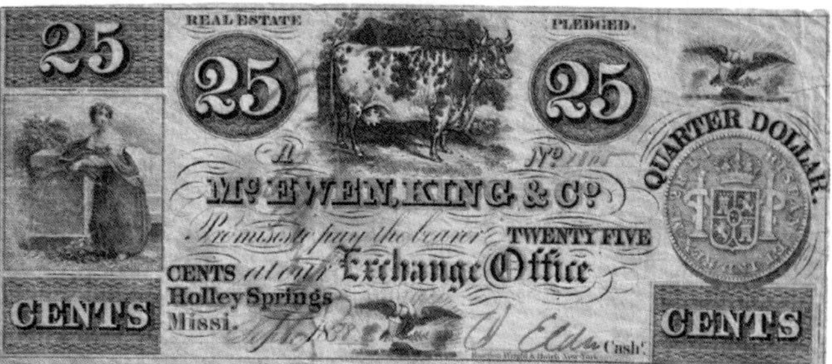

Engraver: Rawdon, Wright & Hatch. ***Comments:*** H-Unlisted, Kraus-14511. 18__. 1837 and 1838.

Rarity: URS-5
F $350

50¢ • **W-MS-390-00.50-G030** JM

Engraver: Rawdon, Wright & Hatch. ***Comments:*** H-Unlisted, Kraus-14512. 1837 and 1838.

Rarity: URS-5
F $350

$1 • **W-MS-390-001-G040** JM

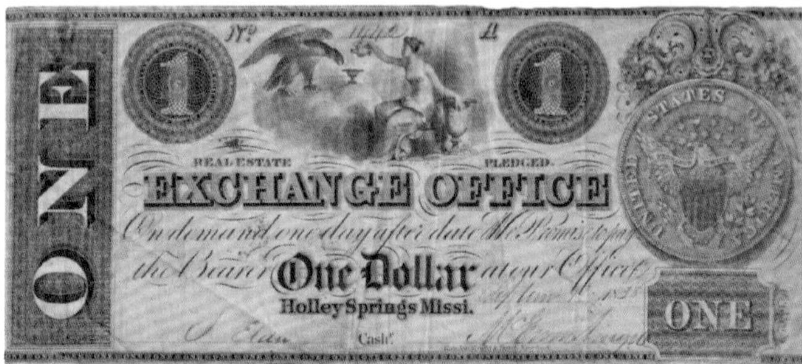

Engraver: Rawdon, Wright & Hatch. ***Comments:*** H-Unlisted, Kraus-14520. 18__. 1837 and 1838.

Rarity: URS-7
F $200

$2 • **W-MS-390-002-G050** JM

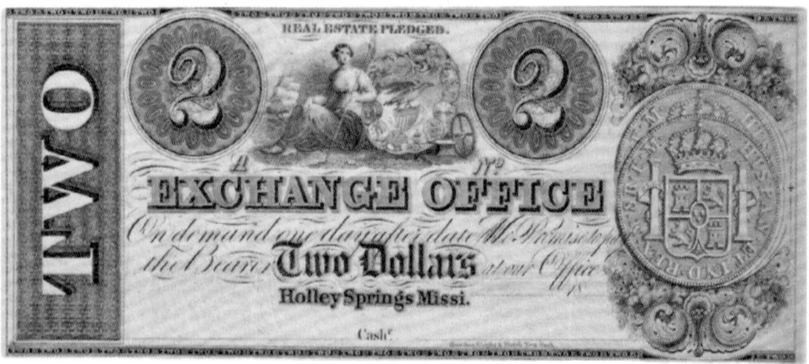

Engraver: Rawdon, Wright & Hatch. ***Comments:*** H-Unlisted, Kraus-14521. 18__. 1837 and 1838.

Rarity: URS-6
F $200

$3 • **W-MS-390-003-G060** JM

Engraver: Rawdon, Wright & Hatch. ***Comments:*** H-Unlisted, Kraus-14522. 18__. 1837 and 1838.

Rarity: URS-6
F $250

$5 • **W-MS-390-005-G070** JM

Engraver: Rawdon, Wright & Hatch. ***Comments:*** H-Unlisted, Kraus-14530. Payable at a merchant in New Orleans. 18__. 1837 and 1838.

Rarity: URS-4
F $400

$5 • **W-MS-390-005-G070a** HA

Engraver: Rawdon, Wright & Hatch. ***Comments:*** H-Unlisted. Similar to W-MS-390-005-G070 but printed in blue ink. 18__. 1837 and 1838.

Rarity: URS-8
Unc-Rem $150

$5 • **W-MS-390-005-G070b** HA

Engraver: Rawdon, Wright & Hatch. ***Comments:*** H-Unlisted. Similar to W-MS-390-005-G070 but printed in blue ink with location spelled "Holley." 18__. 1837 and 1838.

Rarity: URS-8
Unc-Rem $150

$10 • **W-MS-390-010-G080**

JM

Engraver: Rawdon, Wright & Hatch. ***Comments:*** H-Unlisted, Kraus-14531. Payable at a merchant in New Orleans. 18__. 1837 and 1838.

Rarity: URS-4
F $350

$10 • **W-MS-390-010-G080a**

HA

Engraver: Rawdon, Wright & Hatch. ***Comments:*** H-Unlisted. Similar to W-MS-390-010-G080 but printed in blue ink. 18__. 1837 and 1838.

Rarity: URS-8
Unc-Rem $150

$10 • **W-MS-390-010-G080b**

Engraver: Rawdon, Wright & Hatch. ***Comments:*** H-Unlisted. Similar to W-MS-390-010-G080 but printed in blue ink with location spelled "Holley." 18__. 1837 and 1838.

Rarity: URS-3
F $450

$20 • **W-MS-390-020-G090**

JM

Engraver: Rawdon, Wright & Hatch. ***Comments:*** H-Unlisted, Kraus-14532. Payable at a merchant in New Orleans. 18__. 1837 and 1838.

Rarity: URS-3
F $500

$20 • **W-MS-390-020-G090a**

HA

Engraver: Rawdon, Wright & Hatch. ***Comments:*** H-Unlisted. Similar to W-MS-390-020-G090 but printed in blue ink. 18__. 1837 and 1838.

Rarity: URS-8
Unc-Rem $150

$20 • **W-MS-390-020-G090b**

HA

Engraver: Rawdon, Wright & Hatch. ***Comments:*** H-Unlisted. Similar to W-MS-390-020-G090 but printed in blue ink with location spelled "Holley." 18__. 1837 and 1838.

Rarity: URS-8
Unc-Rem $150

Notes Payable at the Banking House

25¢ • **W-MS-390-00.25-G100**

JM

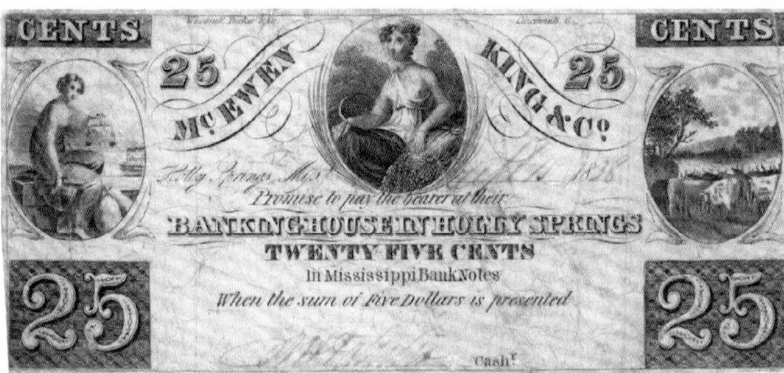

Engraver: Woodruff, Tucker & Co. ***Comments:*** H-Unlisted, Kraus-14590. 18__. 1837 and 1838.

Rarity: URS-4
F $500

25¢ • **W-MS-390-00.25-G100a**

Engraver: Woodruff, Tucker & Co. ***Comments:*** H-Unlisted, Kraus-14580. Similar to W-MS-390-00.25-G100 but with curved presentation statement. 18__. 1837 and 1838.

Rarity: URS-4
F $500

25¢ • **W-MS-390-00.25-G100b**

Engraver: Woodruff, Tucker & Co. ***Comments:*** H-Unlisted. Similar to W-MS-390-00.25-G100 but with curved presentation statement with different floral embellishments. 18__. 1837 and 1838.

Rarity: URS-4
F $500

50¢ • **W-MS-390-00.50-G110**

JM

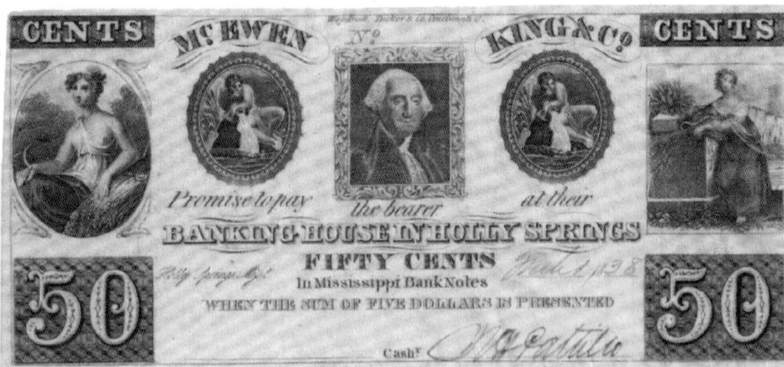

Engraver: Woodruff, Tucker & Co. ***Comments:*** H-Unlisted, Kraus-14591. 18__. 1837 and 1838.

Rarity: URS-4
F $500

50¢ • **W-MS-390-00.50-G110a**

Engraver: Woodruff, Tucker & Co. ***Comments:*** H-Unlisted, Kraus-14581. Similar to W-MS-390-00.50-G110 but with curved presentation statement. 18__. 1837 and 1838.

Rarity: URS-4
F $500

$1 • **W-MS-390-001-G120**

JM

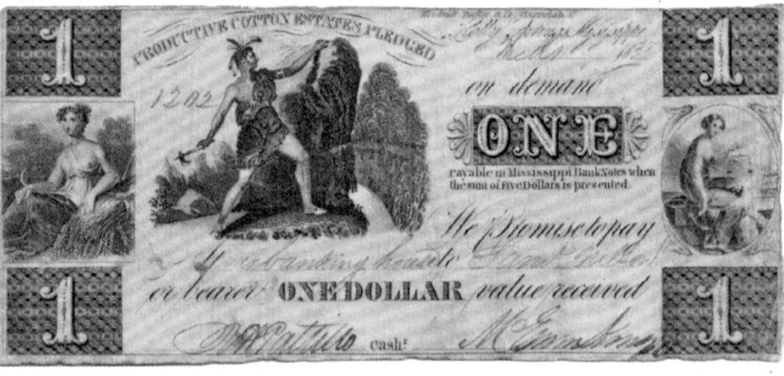

Engraver: Woodruff, Tucker & Co. ***Comments:*** H-Unlisted, Kraus-14600. 18__. 1837 and 1838.

Rarity: URS-4
F $500

$5 • **W-MS-390-005-G125**

Left: 5 / Cows / 5. ***Center:*** Woman seated with shield bearing cotton / 5. ***Right:*** Indian man / 5. ***Engraver:*** Woodruff, Tucker & Co. ***Comments:*** H-Unlisted, Kraus-Unlisted. 18__. 1837 and 1838.

Rarity: —

Post Notes

$1 • **W-MS-390-001-G127**

Left: 1 / Ceres with sickle / 1. ***Center:*** Indian man with hatchet / ONE. ***Right:*** 1 / Justice seated / 1. ***Engraver:*** Woodruff, Tucker & Co. ***Comments:*** H-Unlisted, Kraus-Unlisted. 18__. 1837 and 1838.

Rarity: —

$2 • **W-MS-390-002-G130**

JM

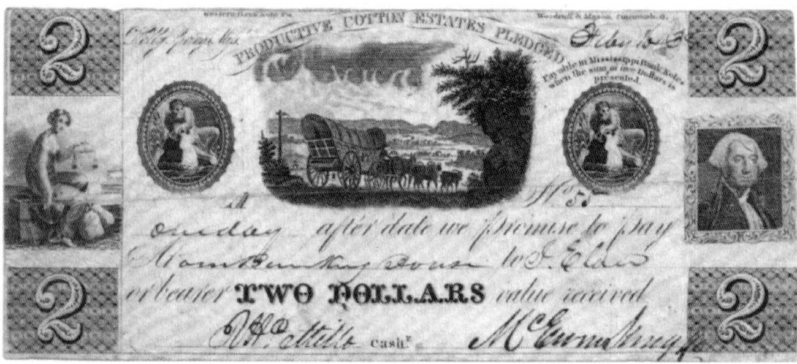

Engraver: Woodruff, Tucker & Co. ***Comments:*** H-Unlisted, Kraus-14511e. 18__. 1837 and 1838.

Rarity: URS-4
F $600

$5 • **W-MS-390-005-G140**

JM

Engraver: Woodruff, Tucker & Co. ***Comments:*** H-Unlisted, Kraus-14614. 18__. 1837 and 1838.

Rarity: URS-5
F $350

$10 • **W-MS-390-010-G150**

JM

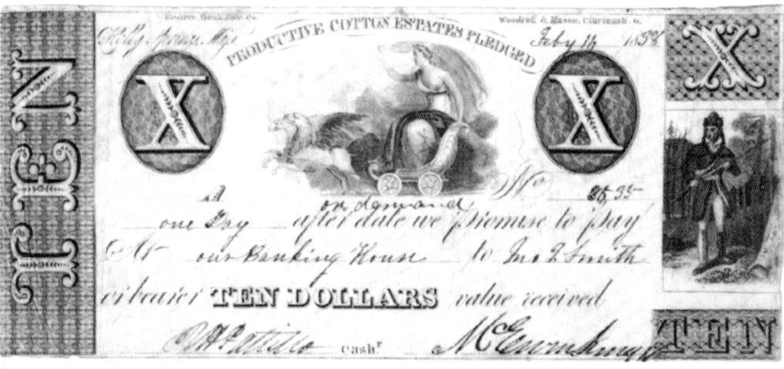

Engraver: Woodruff, Tucker & Co. ***Comments:*** H-Unlisted, Kraus-14615d. 18__. 1837 and 1838.

Rarity: URS-4
F $500

Collectors and Researchers:

If you have new information about any banks or notes listed in this volume, contact Whitman Publishing, Attn: Obsolete Paper Money, 3101 Clairmont Road, Suite G, Atlanta, GA 30329.

$20 • **W-MS-390-020-G160** JM

Engraver: Woodruff & Mason / Western Bank Note Co. ***Comments:*** H-Unlisted, Kraus-14616. 18__. 1837 and 1838.

Rarity: URS-3

F $750

$50 • **W-MS-390-050-G170** JM

Engraver: Western Bank Note Co. / Woodruff & Mason. ***Comments:*** H-Unlisted, Kraus-14617. 18__. 1837 and 1838.

Rarity: URS-3

F $750

$100 • **W-MS-390-100-G180** JM

Engraver: Western Bank Note Co. / Woodruff & Mason. ***Comments:*** H-Unlisted, Kraus-14606. 18__. 1837 and 1838.

Rarity: URS-3

F $1,500

Northern Bank of Mississippi

1837–1860s

W-MS-400

History: The Northern Bank of Mississippi was incorporated on April 28, 1837, with an authorized capital of $2,000,000. The bank was allowed to go into operation when $250,000 had been subscribed to.

The amended charter of the Northern Bank of Mississippi required the Northern Bank to absorb McEwan, King and Company, W-MS-390, as well as the Real Estate Bank of Holly Springs, W-MS-410, and honor their notes. The bank was considered to be of unstable nature, suspending specie payment in 1839. Conditions improved, and the bank continued in operation. In 1852 the cashier was W.E. Chittenden, and the president was J.C. Alderson. Capital was valued at $100,000 in 1855. In 1857 the president was F.W. Lucas, and the cashier was George West. In April 1858 it was reported that the bank had been "brought into operation with the express intent of circulating its notes at a distance. Few of them were seen in Mississippi; but some of them found their way into Arkansas, and the endorsement of them by a commercial firm at Galveston, gave them wide circulation in Texas."[12]

By 1860 the capital had increased to $200,000, but sometime after that the bank failed.

See also listing under Galveston, Texas, W-TX-060.

Numismatic Commentary: Validly issued notes from the 1830s are very rare. W. Goodman, who served as cashier in 1839, had probably also served as cashier at the Agricultural Bank branch in Pontotoc, W-MS-720.

Valid Issues

$5 • **W-MS-400-005-G010** HA

Engraver: Rawdon, Wright & Hatch. ***Comments:*** H-MS-100-G8, Kraus-3631r. 18__. 1830s.

Rarity: URS-5

F $200; **Unc-Rem** $200

$5 • **W-MS-400-005-G020** JM

Engraver: Rawdon, Wright & Hatch. ***Comments:*** H-Unlisted, Kraus-3650. "To the Cashier of the Bank of New-Orleans." 18__. 1850s.

Rarity: URS-5

F $400

$5 • W-MS-400-005-G020a

JM

Overprint: Red die outlining white 5. ***Engraver:*** Rawdon, Wright & Hatch. ***Comments:*** H-Unlisted, Kraus-3660. Similar to W-MS-400-005-G020 but with "To ____ New-Orleans." 18__. 1850s.

Rarity: URS-4
F $750

$10 • W-MS-400-010-G030

Engraver: Rawdon, Wright & Hatch. ***Comments:*** H-MS-100-G10, Kraus-3632. No description available. 18__. 1830s.

Rarity: *None known*

$10 • W-MS-400-010-G040

Engraver: Rawdon, Wright & Hatch. ***Comments:*** H-Unlisted, Kraus-3651. No description available. 18__. 1850s.

Rarity: *None known*

$10 • W-MS-400-010-G050

Left: Female portrait. ***Center:*** Minerva with shield bearing Prosperity. ***Right:*** 10. ***Engraver:*** Rawdon, Wright & Hatch. ***Comments:*** H-Unlisted, Kraus-3661. "To the Cashier of the Bank of New-Orleans." 18__. 1850s.

Rarity: URS-3
F $750

$10 • W-MS-400-010-G050a

Overprint: Red die outlining white 10. ***Engraver:*** Rawdon, Wright & Hatch. ***Comments:*** H-Unlisted, Kraus-3660. Similar to W-MS-400-010-G050 but with "To ____ New-Orleans." 18__. 1850s.

Rarity: *None known*

$20 • W-MS-400-020-G060

HA

Engraver: Rawdon, Wright & Hatch. ***Comments:*** H-MS-100-G12, Kraus-3633. 18__. 1830s.

Rarity: URS-4
F $500

$20 • W-MS-400-020-G070

Engraver: Rawdon, Wright & Hatch. ***Comments:*** H-Unlisted, Kraus-3652. No description available. 18__. 1830s.

Rarity: *None known*

$20 • W-MS-400-020-G075

Engraver: Rawdon, Wright & Hatch. ***Comments:*** H-Unlisted, Kraus-Unlisted. 18__. 1850s.

Rarity: URS-1

$50 • W-MS-400-050-G080

JM

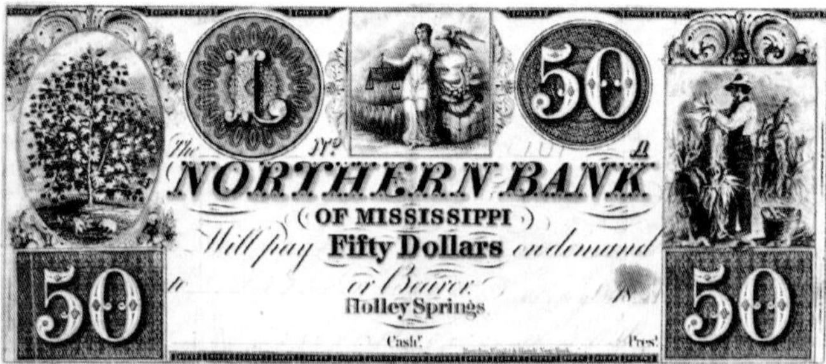

Engraver: Rawdon, Wright & Hatch. ***Comments:*** H-MS-100-G14, Kraus-3634. 18__. 1830s.

Rarity: URS-4
F $750

$50 • W-MS-400-050-G085

Engraver: Rawdon, Wright & Hatch. ***Comments:*** H-Unlisted, Kraus-Unlisted. 18__. 1850s.

Rarity: URS-1

$100 • W-MS-400-100-G090

JM

Engraver: Rawdon, Wright & Hatch. ***Comments:*** H-MS-100-G16, Kraus-3635. 18__. 1830s.

Rarity: URS-4
F $750

Uncut Sheets

$5-$5-$5-$5 •
W-MS-400-005.005.005.005-US010 RG

Engraver: Rawdon, Wright & Hatch. ***Comments:*** H-MS-100-G8, G8, G8, G8. All four notes identical. 18__. 1830s.

Rarity: URS-3
F $1,500

Non-Valid Issues

$100 • W-MS-400-100-N010

Comments: H-Unlisted, Kraus-3635c. Fraudulently issued. Filled-in remainder. 18__. 1830s.

Rarity: —

Real Estate Banking Company of Holly Springs

1837 and 1838

W-MS-410

History: In 1837 this office was formed for the purpose of issuing promissory notes founded on real estate holdings. The president was Sam McCorkle. Financial ruin took place, and McCorkle surrendered his property to creditors.[13] The amended charter of the Northern Bank of Mississippi, W-MS-400, required the Northern Bank to absorb McEwan, King and Company, W-MS-390, as well as the Real Estate Bank of Holly Springs and honor their notes. No record has been found of a state charter for this bank, and it is presumed it was a private enterprise. It is listed here for collector continuity.

Numismatic Commentary: There are two different printers for this bank: the Western Bank Note Co. (under the name Woodruff & Mason) and Underwood, Bald, Spencer & Hufty. Notes from this bank are generally very scarce.

Valid Issues

25¢ • W-MS-410-00.25-G010 JM

Engraver: Woodruff & Co. ***Comments:*** H-MS-105-G4, Kraus-14680. 18__. Circa 1837.

Rarity: URS-4
F $300

50¢ • W-MS-410-00.50-G020 JM

Engraver: Woodruff & Co. ***Comments:*** H-MS-105-G6, Kraus-14681. 18__. Circa 1837.

Rarity: URS-4
F $300

$1 • W-MS-410-001-G030

CC

Engraver: Underwood, Bald, Spencer & Hufty. ***Comments:*** H-MS-105-G10, Kraus-14650. 18__. Circa 1837.

Rarity: URS-5
F $350; **Proof** $1,100

$2 • W-MS-410-002-G040

CC

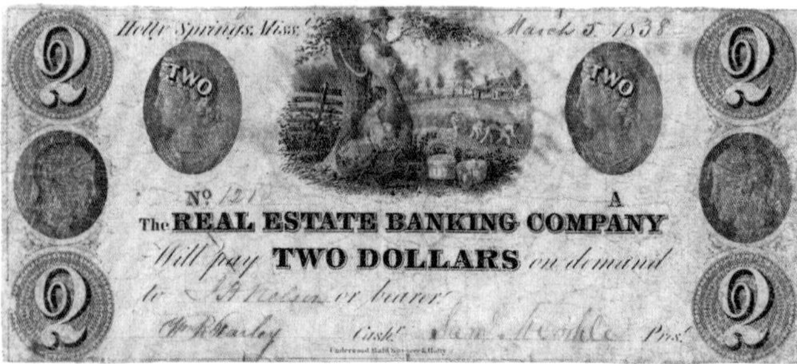

Engraver: Underwood, Bald, Spencer & Hufty. ***Comments:*** H-MS-105-G12, Kraus-14651. 18__. Circa 1837.

Rarity: URS-5
F $350; **Proof** $1,100

$3 • W-MS-410-003-G050

Left: 3 / Ceres seated holding sickle / 3. ***Center:*** Ceres seated by wheat. ***Right:*** 3 / Eagle on rock / THREE. ***Engraver:*** Woodruff & Co. ***Comments:*** H-MS-105-G14, Kraus-14652. Likely the same note as W-MS-410-003-G120. 18__. Circa 1837.

Rarity: URS-3
F $550

$10 • W-MS-410-010-G060

Left: 10 / Medallion head / 10. ***Center:*** "Pat Lyon at the Forge." ***Right:*** Medallion heads bearing 10 vertically. ***Comments:*** H-Unlisted, Kraus-14654. 18__. Circa 1837.

Rarity: URS-3
F $550

$20 • W-MS-410-020-G070

Left: Farmer and family, Tree. ***Center:*** Medallion head / Mercury with caduceus seated on cargo, River / Medallion head. ***Right:*** XX / "Pat Lyon at the Forge." ***Comments:*** H-Unlisted, Kraus-14655. 18__. Circa 1837.

Rarity: URS-3
F $550

$50 • W-MS-410-050-G080

Left: 50 / Medallion heads / 50. ***Center:*** Medallion head / Indian child in canoe with paddle / Medallion head. ***Right:*** 50 / Medallion heads / 50. ***Comments:*** H-Unlisted, Kraus-14656. 18__. Circa 1837.

Rarity: URS-3
F $550

$100 • W-MS-410-100-G090

Left: Medallion head / Cherub as Ceres vertically / Medallion head. ***Center:*** 100 / Four cherubs, one as Ceres carrying sickle and wheat, two carrying basket of grapes, one sitting and working at basket / 100. ***Right:*** Medallion head / Cherub as Ceres vertically / Medallion head. ***Comments:*** H-Unlisted, Kraus-14657. 18__. Circa 1837.

Rarity: URS-3
F $600

Post Notes

$1 • W-MS-410-001-G100

Left: 1 / Hebe in chariot / 1. ***Center:*** 1 / Ceres standing at altar. ***Right:*** 1 / Portrait of Marquis de Lafayette / 1. ***Comments:*** H-Unlisted, Kraus-14690. 18__. Circa 1837.

Rarity: URS-2
F $1,500

$2 • W-MS-410-002-G110

Comments: H-Unlisted, Kraus-14691. No description available. 18__. Circa 1837.

Rarity: *None known*

$3 • W-MS-410-003-G120

JM

Comments: H-Unlisted, Kraus-14692. 18__. Circa 1837.

Rarity: URS-4
F $750

$5 • W-MS-410-005-G130

JM

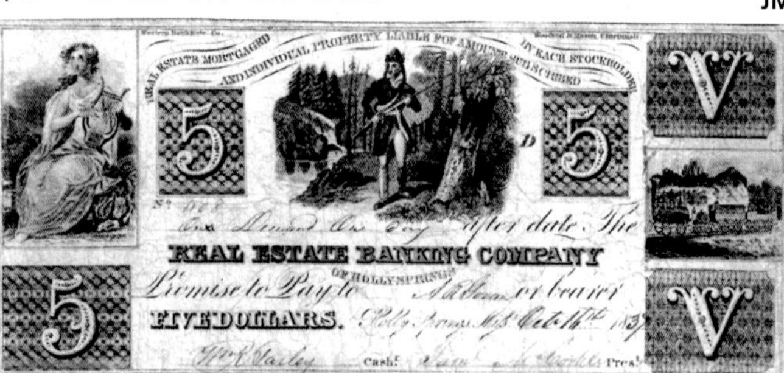

Engraver: Western Bank Note Co. / Woodruff & Mason. ***Comments:*** H-MS-105-G30, Kraus-14693. 18__. Circa 1837.

Rarity: URS-4
F $550

$5 • W-MS-410-005-G140

CC

Engraver: Underwood, Bald, Spencer & Hufty. ***Comments:*** H-MS-105-G32, Kraus-14653. 18__. Circa 1837.

Rarity: URS-5

F $400; **Proof** $1,200

$10 • W-MS-410-010-G150

HA

Engraver: Western Bank Note Co. / Woodruff & Mason. ***Comments:*** H-MS-105-G34, Kraus-14694. 18__. Circa 1837.

Rarity: URS-4

F $750

$20 • W-MS-410-020-G160

HA

Engraver: Western Bank Note Co. / Woodruff & Mason. ***Comments:*** H-MS-105-G38, Kraus-14695. 18__. Circa 1837.

Rarity: URS-4

F $750

$50 • W-MS-410-050-G170

JM

Engraver: Western Bank Note Co. / Woodruff & Mason. ***Comments:*** H-MS-105-G42, Kraus-14696. 18__. Circa 1837.

Rarity: URS-4

F $1,000

$100 • W-MS-410-100-G180

Comments: H-Unlisted, Kraus-14697. No description available. 18__. Circa 1837.

Rarity: *None known*

HOLMESVILLE, MISSISSIPPI

On December 11, 1816, Holmesville was established and named in honor of Major Andrew Hunter Holmes. It became the center for trade and business of Pike County. The Illinois Central Railroad was built in 1857, bypassing Holmesville and connecting Magnolia, Summit, and Osyka. As a result, most of the residents of Holmesville relocated to these towns. Holmesville became a resort town, with many seeking respite during the summer months away from the present dangers of cholera and yellow fever that remained in the bigger cities.

Commercial Bank of Natchez (branch)

1836–1856

W-MS-420

History: The Commercial Bank of Natchez was incorporated on February 27, 1836, with an authorized capital of $3,000,000. The bank was forbidden to distribute notes of a denomination lower than $5. The bank did not last long, and on February 6, 1841, an act was passed to close the branch banks and wind up the affairs of the parent bank. The closing of the bank was extended due to a battle with creditors that went all the way to the U.S. Supreme Court. Finally the bank went into liquidation in 1856.

The Commercial Bank of Natchez had its parent bank located in Natchez, W-MS-640, and branch banks located in Brandon, W-MS-060, Canton, W-MS-100, and Shieldsboro, W-MS-830.

Numismatic Commentary: No validly issued branch notes are known.

VALID ISSUES

$5 • W-MS-420-005-G010

Left: FIVE vertically. ***Center:*** Two cherubs with U.S. flag as Liberty and Commerce, Ship. ***Right:*** FIVE vertically. ***Engraver:*** Underwood, Bald, Spencer & Hufty. ***Comments:*** H-MS-160-G120, Kraus-4020p. 18__. 1830s.

Rarity: *None known*

$10 • W-MS-420-010-G020

Left: TEN vertically. ***Center:*** 10 / Ships / 10. ***Right:*** TEN vertically. ***Engraver:*** Underwood, Bald, Spencer & Hufty. ***Comments:*** H-MS-160-G126, Kraus-4021p. 18__. 1830s.

Rarity: *None known*

$20 • W-MS-420-020-G030

Left: TWENTY vertically. ***Center:*** Medallion head bearing TWENTY / Mercury seated at river / Medallion head bearing TWENTY. ***Right:*** TWENTY vertically. ***Engraver:*** Underwood, Bald, Spencer & Hufty. ***Comments:*** H-MS-160-G128, Kraus-4022p. 18__. 1830s.

Rarity: *None known*

$50 • W-MS-420-050-G040

Left: Athena as Liberty with U.S. shield and spear / FIFTY. ***Center:*** Medallion head bearing FIFTY / Neptune seated on sea / Medallion head bearing FIFTY. ***Right:*** Athena as Liberty with U.S. shield and spear / FIFTY. ***Engraver:*** Underwood, Bald, Spencer & Hufty. ***Comments:*** H-MS-160-G130, Kraus-4023p. 18__. 1830s.

Rarity: *None known*

$100 • W-MS-420-100-G050

Left: Woman standing with medallion head and caduceus / 100. ***Center:*** Medallion head bearing 100 / Indian in canoe / Medallion head bearing 100. ***Right:*** Woman standing with medallion head and caduceus / 100. ***Engraver:*** Underwood, Bald, Spencer & Hufty. ***Comments:*** H-MS-160-G132, Kraus-4024p. 18__. 1830s.

Rarity: *None known*

JACKSON, MISSISSIPPI

Jackson was originally a trade station on the Natchez Trace route. At that early time it was known as Parkerville. It was settled by French-Canadian trader Louis LeFleur. The first village in the area was called LeFleur's Bluff after the original settler, and the trading post rose up around the village during the turn of the century. The post developed quickly after it was selected to be the state's capital due to its central location. On November 28, 1821, the act was passed to authorize the site as the seat of government.

The capital was named after General Andrew Jackson in honor of his January 1815 victory in the Battle of New Orleans. In April 1822 the first plans for the town were laid out as a checkerboard design, allowing for parks and open spaces to alternate with city blocks. The railway connected to Jackson in 1840, and by 1844 there was an east-west line connecting the city with Vicksburg, Raymond, and Brandon.

Jackson was a manufacturing center during the Civil War. In 1863 Union forces captured the city over the course of two battles.

Bank of Jackson
1862
W-MS-430

History: The Bank of Jackson was authorized on January 17, 1862, with a capital of $1,000,000.[14] It is unknown if this bank ever opened for business.

Greens Exchange and Banking Office
1860s
W-MS-440

History: This is believed to have been an exchange house or office that had notes circulating regionally. No record has been found of a state charter for this bank, and it is presumed it was a private enterprise.

Numismatic Commentary: Since the city of Jackson was burned during the Civil War, private-bank notes such as these are extremely rare. Most were printed locally and have minor design variations.

VALID ISSUES

25¢ • W-MS-440-00.25-G010

JM

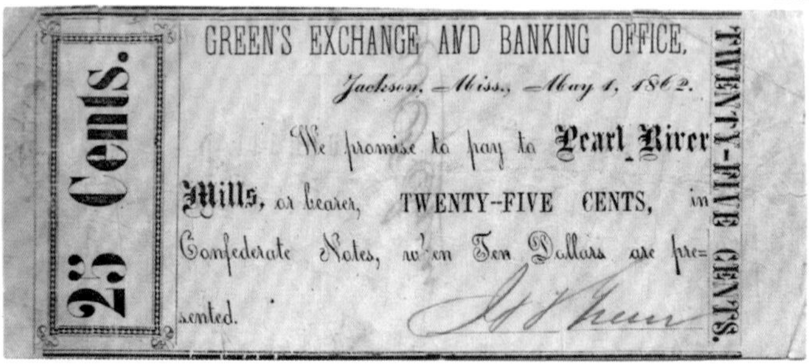

Comments: H-Unlisted, Kraus-53760. May 1, 1862.

Rarity: URS-3

F $1,200

50¢ • W-MS-440-00.50-G020

JM

Comments: H-Unlisted, Kraus-53761. May 1, 1862.

Rarity: URS-3

VG $900

Selected auction price: Heritage Auctions, September 25, 2013, Lot 15984, F $2,350

50¢ • W-MS-440-00.50-G030 JM

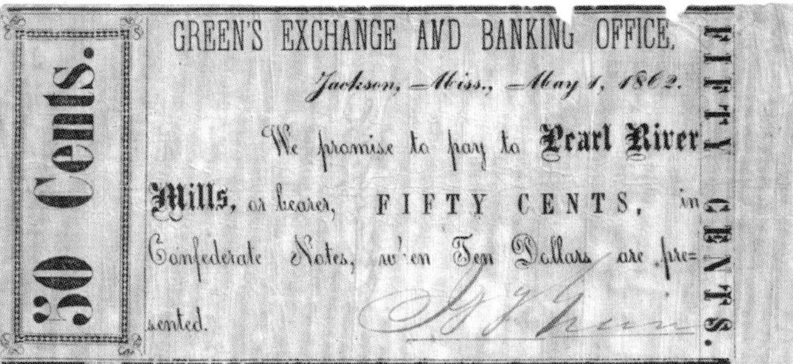

Comments: H-Unlisted. May 1, 1862.

Rarity: URS-3

VG $900

50¢ • W-MS-440-00.50-G040 JM

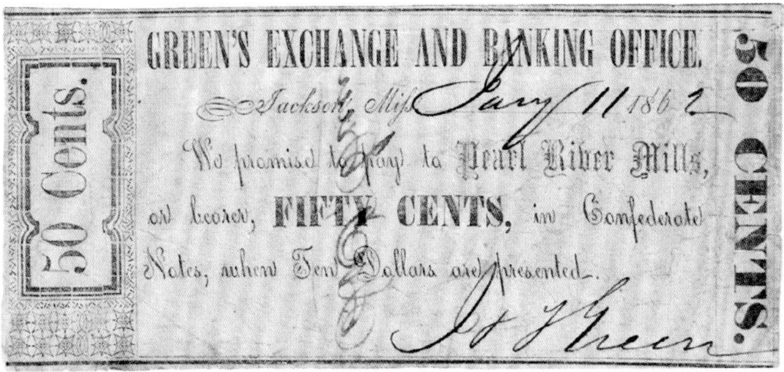

Comments: H-Unlisted. 186_. 1862.

Rarity: URS-3

VG $900

$1 • W-MS-440-001-G050 JM

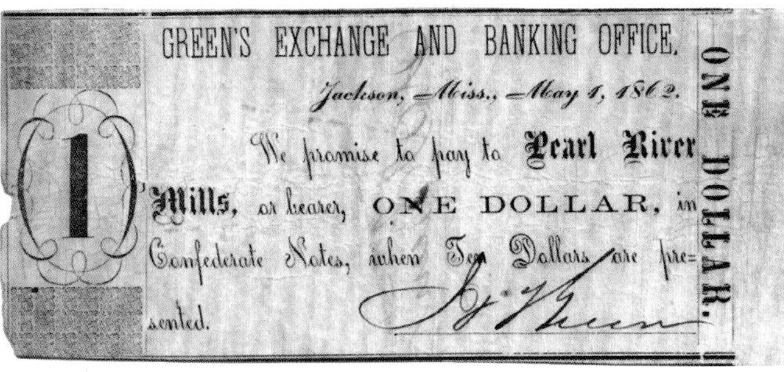

Comments: H-Unlisted. May 1, 1862.

Rarity: URS-3

VG $900

$3 • W-MS-440-003-G060 HA

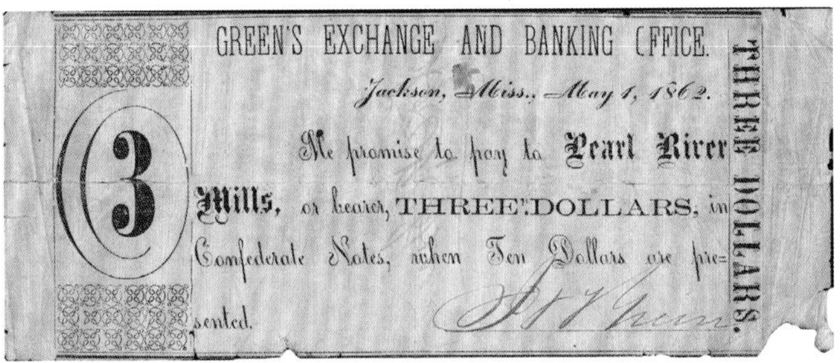

Comments: H-Unlisted. May 1, 1862.

Rarity: URS-3

VG $900

Selected auction price: Heritage Auctions, January 7, 2015, Lot 18669, F $1,410

$3 • W-MS-440-003-G070 JM

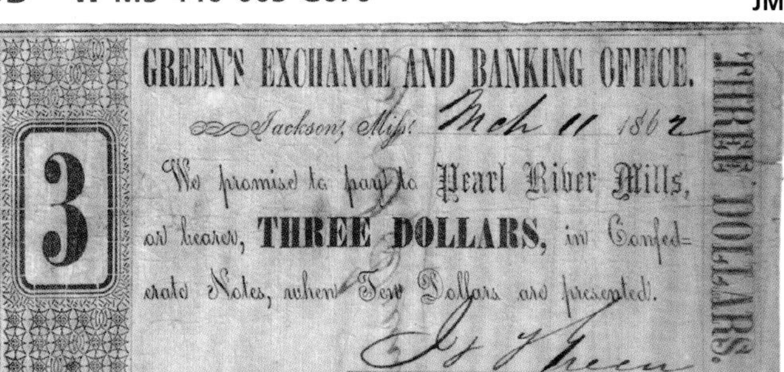

Comments: H-Unlisted. 186_. 1862.

Rarity: URS-3

F $1,100

Griffith and Stewarts Bank

1830s

W-MS-450

History: This is believed to have been an exchange house or office that issued notes to be circulated regionally. No record has been found of a state charter for this bank, and it is presumed it was a private enterprise.

Numismatic Commentary: No notes of this bank are known.

Mississippi Union Bank

1837–1840

W-MS-460

History: The Mississippi Union Bank was incorporated on January 21, 1837, with an authorized capital of $15,500,000. In 1838 the charter was revived under approval of Governor McNutt (the original charter had been approved by Governor Lynch). Nicholas Biddle and the Bank of the United States of Pennsylvania assisted in the distribution and furnished guarantees. The state purchased 50,000 shares of the bank using state bonds, which later came into question and were repudiated.

In 1840 the Mississippi Union Bank was closed and its charter revoked due to its inability to pay out specie. By that time Biddle's bank was insolvent.

Numismatic Commentary: Demand notes from this bank are exceedingly rare. It is likely that the $5 note does not exist, as none are known. William P. Grayson, cashier, was formerly cashier of the West Feliciana Rail Road Bank in Woodville, W-MS-1030.

Valid Issues

$5 • W-MS-460-005-G010

Engraver: Draper, Toppan, Longacre & Co. ***Comments:*** H-MS-110-G8, Kraus-3690. No description available. 18__. 1830s.

Rarity: *None known*

$10 • W-MS-460-010-G020

Left: Portrait of George Washington. ***Center:*** 10 / Men and buildings. ***Right:*** 10. ***Engraver:*** Draper, Toppan, Longacre & Co. ***Comments:*** H-MS-110-G10, Kraus-3691. 18__. 1830s.

Rarity: URS-3
F $550

$20 • W-MS-460-020-G030

JM

Engraver: Draper, Toppan, Longacre & Co. ***Comments:*** H-MS-110-G12, Kraus-3712a. 18__. 1830s.

Rarity: URS-3
F $550

$50 • W-MS-460-050-G040

Engraver: Draper, Toppan, Longacre & Co. ***Comments:*** H-MS-110-G14, Kraus-3693. No description available. 18__. 1830s.

Rarity: *None known*

$50 • W-MS-460-050-G050

Left: Eagle with shield. ***Center:*** Female portrait. ***Right:*** Farmer and wife sitting with dog. ***Comments:*** H-Unlisted, Kraus-3713. 18__. 1830s.

Rarity: URS-1
VF $1,500

$100 • W-MS-460-100-G060

Engraver: Draper, Toppan, Longacre & Co. ***Comments:*** H-MS-110-G16, Kraus-3694. No description available. 18__. 1830s.

Rarity: *None known*

$100 • W-MS-460-100-G070

Left: Farmer harvesting corn. ***Center:*** Maiden with trident. ***Right:*** Train. ***Comments:*** H-Unlisted, Kraus-3714. 18__. 1830s.

Rarity: URS-1
VF $1,500

$500 • W-MS-460-500-G080

Left: 500 / Man seated / 500. ***Center:*** Female portrait. ***Right:*** 500 / Ship / 500. ***Engraver:*** Draper, Toppan, Longacre & Co. ***Comments:*** H-MS-110-G18, Kraus-3695. 18__. 1830s.

Rarity: —

$1,000 • W-MS-460-1000-G090

Left: 1000 / Eagle / 1000. ***Center:*** Two women flanking female portrait. ***Right:*** 1000 / Eagle / 1000. ***Engraver:*** Draper, Toppan, Longacre & Co. ***Comments:*** H-MS-110-G20, Kraus-3696. 18__. 1830s.

Rarity: —

Post Notes

$10 • W-MS-460-010-G100

CC

Engraver: Draper, Toppan, Longacre & Co. ***Comments:*** H-MS-110-G24, Kraus-3711b. 18__. 1830s.

Rarity: URS-5
F $250

$10 • W-MS-460-010-G110

JM

Engraver: Draper, Toppan, Longacre & Co. ***Comments:*** H-MS-110-G26, Kraus-3725. Six months handwritten, interest bearing. 18__. 1830s.

Rarity: URS-5
F $350

$10 • W-MS-460-010-G110a

JM

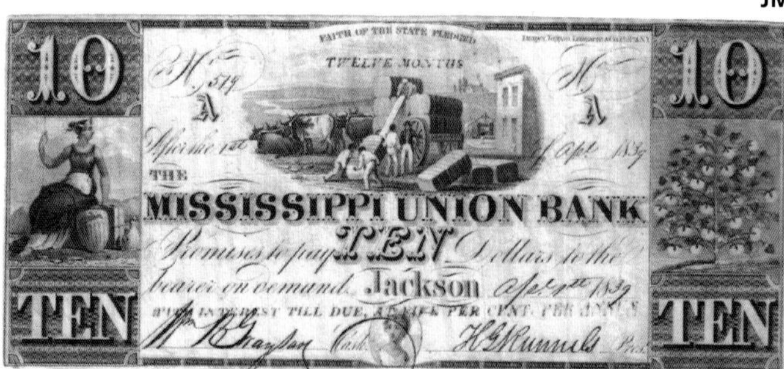

Overprint: Black TWELVE MONTHS. ***Engraver:*** Draper, Toppan, Longacre & Co. ***Comments:*** H-MS-110-G26a, Kraus-3725i. Similar to W-MS-460-010-G110. Twelve months stamped, interest bearing. 18__. 1830s.

Rarity: URS-8
F $200

$20 • W-MS-460-020-G120

JM

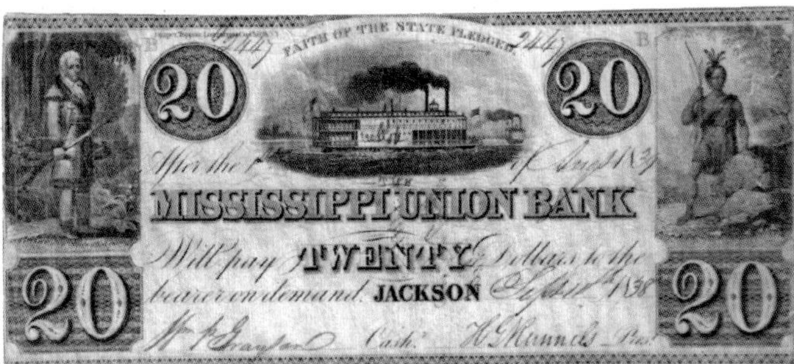

Engraver: Draper, Toppan, Longacre & Co. ***Comments:*** H-Unlisted. 18__. 1830s.

Rarity: URS-3
F $550

$20 • W-MS-460-020-G130

Left: 20 / Train / XX. ***Center:*** XX / Clipper ships / XX. ***Right:*** 20 / Portrait of Marquis de Lafayette / XX. ***Engraver:*** Rawdon, Wright, Hatch & Edson / Rawdon, Wright & Hatch. ***Comments:*** H-MS-110-G30. 18__. 1830s.

Rarity: URS-8
F $200

$20 • W-MS-460-020-G130a

CC, CC

Back: Red-orange. ***Engraver:*** Rawdon, Wright, Hatch & Edson / Rawdon, Wright & Hatch. ***Comments:*** H-MS-110-G30a, Kraus-3755. Similar to W-MS-460-020-G130. 18__. 1830s.

Rarity: URS-8
F $175

$20 • W-MS-460-020-G130b

Overprint: Black POST NOTE stamp. ***Back:*** Red-orange. ***Engraver:*** Rawdon, Wright, Hatch & Edson / Rawdon, Wright & Hatch. ***Comments:*** H-MS-110-G30b. Similar to W-MS-460-020-G130. 18__. 1830s.

Rarity: URS-5
F $350

$50 • W-MS-460-050-G140

JM

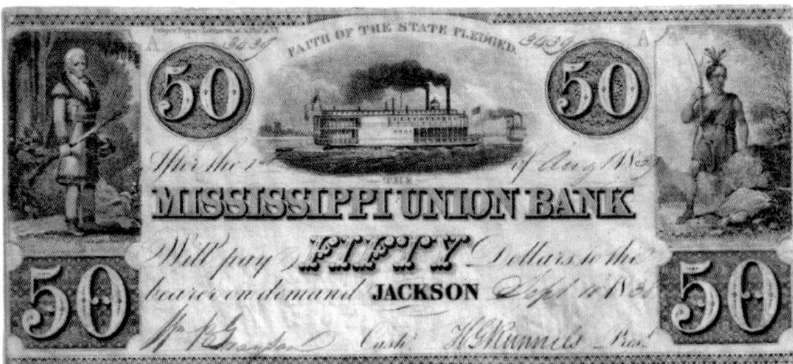

Engraver: Draper, Toppan, Longacre & Co. ***Comments:*** H-Unlisted. 18__. 1830s.

Rarity: URS-4
F $300

$50 • W-MS-460-050-G150

Left: 50 / Clipper ship / 50. ***Center:*** Portrait of George Washington / Neptune reclining with fountain from amphora. ***Right:*** 50 / Riverboat / 50. ***Engraver:*** Rawdon, Wright, Hatch & Edson / Rawdon, Wright & Hatch. ***Comments:*** H-MS-110-G34. 18__. 1830s.

Rarity: URS-3
F $550

$50 • W-MS-460-050-G150a

CC

Back: Red-orange. ***Engraver:*** Rawdon, Wright, Hatch & Edson / Rawdon, Wright & Hatch. ***Comments:*** H-MS-110-G34a, Kraus-3756. Similar to W-MS-460-050-G150. 18__. 1830s.

Rarity: URS-8
F $150

$50 • W-MS-460-050-G150b

Overprint: Black POST NOTE stamp. ***Back:*** Red-orange. ***Engraver:*** Rawdon, Wright, Hatch & Edson / Rawdon, Wright & Hatch. ***Comments:*** H-MS-110-G34b. Similar to W-MS-460-050-G150. 18__. 1830s.

Rarity: —

$100 • **W-MS-460-100-G160** JM

Engraver: Draper, Toppan, Longacre & Co. ***Comments:*** H-MS-110-G36, Kraus-3742. 18__. 1830s.

Rarity: URS-4
F $350

$100 • **W-MS-460-100-G160a**

Overprint: Black WITH INTEREST stamp. ***Engraver:*** Draper, Toppan, Longacre & Co. ***Comments:*** H-MS-110-G36a. Similar to W-MS-460-100-G160. 18__. 1830s.

Rarity: —

$100 • **W-MS-460-100-G170**

Left: 100 / Clipper ships / 100. ***Center:*** Mercury seated / Portrait of Benjamin Franklin. ***Right:*** 100 / Seated goddess / 100. ***Engraver:*** Rawdon, Wright, Hatch & Edson / Rawdon, Wright & Hatch. ***Comments:*** H-MS-110-G38. 18__. 1830s.

Rarity: URS-3
F $550

$100 • **W-MS-460-100-G170a** CC, CC

Back: Red-orange. ***Engraver:*** Rawdon, Wright, Hatch & Edson / Rawdon, Wright & Hatch. ***Comments:*** H-MS-110-G38a, Kraus-3757. Similar to W-MS-460-100-G170. 18__. 1830s.

Rarity: URS-8
F $200; **EF** $350

$100 • **W-MS-460-100-G170b**

Overprint: Black POST NOTE stamp. ***Back:*** Red-orange. ***Engraver:*** Rawdon, Wright, Hatch & Edson / Rawdon, Wright & Hatch. ***Comments:*** H-MS-110-G38b, Kraus-3757q. Similar to W-MS-460-100-G170. 18__. 1830s.

Rarity: —

$500 • **W-MS-460-500-G180**

Left: Woodsman standing with rifle / 500. ***Center:*** 500 / Riverboat / 500. ***Right:*** Indian standing / 500. ***Engraver:*** Draper, Toppan, Longacre & Co. ***Comments:*** H-MS-110-G40. 18__. 1830s.

Rarity: URS-5
F $700

$500 • **W-MS-460-500-G180a** CC

Overprint: Black WITH INTEREST stamp. ***Engraver:*** Draper, Toppan, Longacre & Co. ***Comments:*** H-MS-110-G40a, Kraus-3715o. Similar to W-MS-460-500-G180. 18__. 1830s.

Rarity: URS-4
F $500

$500 • **W-MS-460-500-G190** CC

Engraver: Draper, Toppan, Longacre & Co. ***Comments:*** H-MS-110-G42, Kraus-3744. 18__. 1830s.

Rarity: URS-8
F $400

$1,000 • **W-MS-460-1000-G200** CC

Engraver: Draper, Toppan, Longacre & Co. ***Comments:*** H-MS-110-G46, Kraus-3716g. 18__. 1830s.

Rarity: URS-5
F $750

Notes on Which the Place Payable is Blank

$5 • W-MS-460-005-G210

Engraver: Draper, Toppan, Longacre & Co. ***Comments:*** H-MS-110-G48, Kraus-Unlisted. No description available. 18__. 1830s.

Rarity: *None known*

$10 • W-MS-460-010-G220

Left: Portrait of George Washington. ***Center:*** 10 / Men and buildings. ***Right:*** 10. ***Engraver:*** Draper, Toppan, Longacre & Co. ***Comments:*** H-MS-110-G50, Kraus-Unlisted. 18__. 1830s.

Rarity: —

$20 • W-MS-460-020-G230

Left: Man picking cotton / 20. ***Center:*** 20 / Horse rearing / 20. ***Right:*** Woman standing / 20. ***Engraver:*** Draper, Toppan, Longacre & Co. ***Comments:*** H-MS-110-G52, Kraus-Unlisted. 18__. 1830s.

Rarity: —

$50 • W-MS-460-050-G240

Engraver: Draper, Toppan, Longacre & Co. ***Comments:*** H-MS-110-G54, Kraus-Unlisted. No description available. 18__. 1830s.

Rarity: *None known*

$100 • W-MS-460-100-G250

Engraver: Draper, Toppan, Longacre & Co. ***Comments:*** H-MS-110-G56, Kraus-Unlisted. No description available. 18__. 1830s.

Rarity: *None known*

$500 • W-MS-460-500-G260

Left: 500 / Man seated / 500. ***Center:*** Female portrait. ***Right:*** 500 / Ship / 500. ***Engraver:*** Draper, Toppan, Longacre & Co. ***Comments:*** H-MS-110-G58, Kraus-Unlisted. 18__. 1830s.

Rarity: —

$1,000 • W-MS-460-1000-G270

Left: 1000 / Eagle / 1000. ***Center:*** Two women flanking female portrait. ***Right:*** 1000 / Eagle / 1000. ***Engraver:*** Draper, Toppan, Longacre & Co. ***Comments:*** H-MS-110-G60, Kraus-Unlisted. 18__. 1830s.

Rarity: —

Planters Bank of the State of Mississippi (branch)

1830–1844

W-MS-470

History: The Planters Bank of the State of Mississippi was the second bank to be chartered in the state. It was incorporated on February 10, 1830, with an authorized capital of $3,000,000, $2,000,000 of which was provided from the state through the sale of bonds. The Panic of 1837 struck the bank hard. The state's bonds were repudiated, and the bank failed thereafter. On February 23, 1844, the bank was put into liquidation.

The Planters Bank of the State of Mississippi had its parent bank located in Natchez, W-MS-670, and branch banks located in Columbus, W-MS-240, Manchester, W-MS-555, Monticello, W-MS-580, Port Gibson, W-MS-780, Vicksburg, W-MS-920, Woodville, W-MS-1020, and Yazoo City, W-MS-1070.

Numismatic Commentary: Notes with the Jackson location written in have not been found.

Valid Issues

$5 • W-MS-470-005-G010

Left: 5 / FIVE vertically / 5. ***Center:*** 5 / Mercury in flight spreading coins from cornucopia / 5. ***Right:*** FIVE vertically. ***Engraver:*** Rawdon, Wright & Co. ***Comments:*** H-MS-175-G60, Kraus-4060. 18__. 1830s.

Rarity: *None known*

$10 • W-MS-470-010-G020

Left: 10 / Aquarius pouring water from amphora / 10. ***Center:*** 10 / Justice and Liberty flanking shield bearing cotton plant and surmounted by eagle / 10. ***Right:*** 10 / Aquarius pouring water from amphora / 10. ***Engraver:*** Rawdon, Wright & Co. ***Comments:*** H-MS-175-G62, Kraus-4061. 18__. 1830s.

Rarity: *None known*

$20 • W-MS-470-020-G030

Left: Woman seated with globe. ***Center:*** 20 / Cotton bales, Hope standing with anchor, Ship / 20. ***Right:*** Group of Indians. ***Engraver:*** Rawdon, Wright & Co. ***Comments:*** H-MS-175-G64, Kraus-4062. 18__. 1830s.

Rarity: *None known*

$20 • W-MS-470-020-G040

Left: Woman standing in niche / XX. ***Center:*** 20 / Two women flanking shield surmounted by eagle / 20. ***Right:*** Woman standing in niche / XX. ***Back:*** Red-brown. ***Engraver:*** Rawdon, Wright, Hatch & Co. ***Comments:*** H-MS-175-G66. 18__. 1830s.

Rarity: *None known*

$50 • W-MS-470-050-G050

Left: Justice standing with eagle bearing portrait of George Washington. ***Center:*** 50 / Woman standing with cotton bales and shield bearing cotton plant surmounted by eagle, Train / 50. ***Right:*** Two women standing. ***Engraver:*** Rawdon, Wright & Co. ***Comments:*** H-MS-175-G68. 18__. 1830s.

Rarity: *None known*

$50 • W-MS-470-050-G060

Left: Indian standing with bow / 50. ***Center:*** 50 / Ships / 50. ***Right:*** Indian standing with bow / 50. ***Back:*** Red-brown. ***Engraver:*** Rawdon, Wright, Hatch & Co. ***Comments:*** H-MS-175-G70. 18__. 1830s.

Rarity: *None known*

$50 • W-MS-470-050-G070

Left: Athena. ***Center:*** Muse. ***Right:*** Athena. ***Engraver:*** Rawdon, Wright & Co. ***Comments:*** H-Unlisted, Kraus-4063. 18__. 1830s.

Rarity: *None known*

$100 • W-MS-470-100-G080

Left: ONE HUNDRED vertically. ***Center:*** 100 / Group of settlers and Indians / 100. ***Right:*** ONE HUNDRED vertically. ***Engraver:*** Rawdon, Wright & Co. ***Comments:*** H-MS-175-G72, Kraus-4064. 18__. 1830s.

Rarity: *None known*

$100 • W-MS-470-100-G090

Left: 100 / Men with cattle / 100. ***Center:*** Portrait of George Washington / Woman seated in clouds with eagle bearing portrait of George Washington / Portrait of Benjamin Franklin. ***Right:*** 100 / Men with cattle / 100. ***Back:*** Red-brown. ***Engraver:*** Rawdon, Wright, Hatch & Co. ***Comments:*** H-MS-175-G74. 18__. 1830s.

Rarity: *None known*

Lexington, Mississippi

Lexington began as a trading post in the 1820s and was officially incorporated in 1836. It thereafter became the seat of Holmes County.

Bank of Lexington
1837–1841
W-MS-480

History: The Bank of Lexington was chartered on May 11, 1837, with an authorized capital of $800,000. On March 3, 1841, it was reported that the bank had failed to comply with the bank laws set forth in its charter, which was thereby forfeited.

Numismatic Commentary: Validly issued notes are extremely rare. No $2 issues have ever been seen.

Valid Issues

$1 • W-MS-480-001-G010 CC

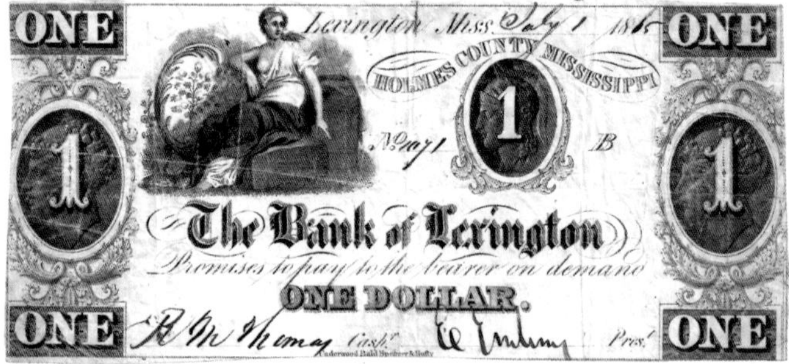

Engraver: Underwood, Bald, Spencer & Hufty. ***Comments:*** H-MS-120-G2, Kraus-3798. Filled-in remainder. 18__. 1830s.

Rarity: URS-4
F $700

How to Read the Whitman Numbering System

$1 • W-AL-020-001-G010a

Denomination: Face value of the note shown.

W: Whitman number. This number is a sortable code unique to each bank and note.

AL: Abbreviation for the state under study.

020: Numerical designation specific to each bank.

001: The denomination in dollars.

G010a: G indicates a good or valid note. Other categories are indicated thus: C (counterfeit); R (raised); S (spurious); N (not-attributed); A (altered). Numbers are assigned starting with 010, 020, et seq. Terminal letters following the number indicate variations of a note: a series of different colored overprints, tints, payees, etc., all on the same design of note. For more information, see the "How to Use This Book" section at the front of the volume, page xiv.

$1 • W-MS-480-001-G010a JM

Engraver: Underwood, Bald, Spencer & Hufty. ***Comments:*** H-MS-120-G2a, Kraus-3798. Similar to W-MS-480-001-G010 but with different date. Jany. 1st, 1839.

Rarity: URS-5
F $350

$2 • W-MS-480-002-G020

Engraver: Underwood, Bald, Spencer & Hufty. ***Comments:*** H-MS-120-G4. No description available. 18__. 1830s.

Rarity: *None known*

$2 • W-MS-480-002-G020a

Engraver: Underwood, Bald, Spencer & Hufty. ***Comments:*** H-MS-120-G4a. Similar to W-MS-480-002-G020 but with different date. Jan. 1, 1839.

Rarity: *None known*

$3 • W-MS-480-003-G030 JM

Engraver: Underwood, Bald, Spencer & Hufty. ***Comments:*** H-MS-120-G6, Kraus-3787r. Filled-in remainder. 18__. 1830s.

Rarity: URS-4
F $750

$3 • W-MS-480-003-G030a

Engraver: Underwood, Bald, Spencer & Hufty. ***Comments:*** H-MS-120-G6a, Kraus-3799. Similar to W-MS-480-003-G030 but with different date. Jan. 1, 1839.

Rarity: —

$5 • W-MS-480-005-G040

JM

Engraver: Underwood, Bald, Spencer & Hufty. ***Comments:*** H-MS-120-G8, Kraus-3788. 18__. 1830s.

Rarity: URS-4
F $300; **Proof** $1,100

$6 • W-MS-480-006-G050

Left: Medallion head / 6 vertically / Medallion head. ***Center:*** 6 / Indian in canoe with paddle / 6. ***Right:*** Medallion head / 6 vertically / Medallion head. ***Engraver:*** Underwood, Bald, Spencer & Hufty. ***Comments:*** H-MS-120-G10, Kraus-3790p. 18__. 1830s.

Rarity: URS-3
Proof $2,500

$7 • W-MS-480-007-G060

JM

Engraver: Underwood, Bald, Spencer & Hufty. ***Comments:*** H-MS-120-G11, Kraus-3791. 18__. 1830s.

Rarity: URS-4
F $1,500; **Proof** $2,500

$8 • W-MS-480-008-G070

JM

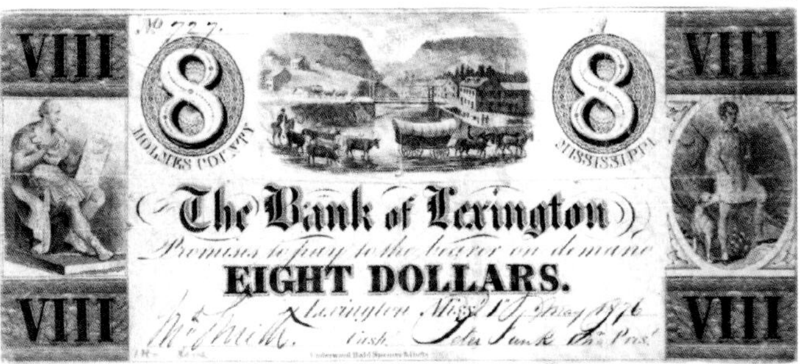

Engraver: Underwood, Bald, Spencer & Hufty. ***Comments:*** H-MS-120-G12, Kraus-3792. 18__. 1830s.

Rarity: URS-4
F $1,500; **Proof** $2,500

$9 • W-MS-480-009-G080

CC

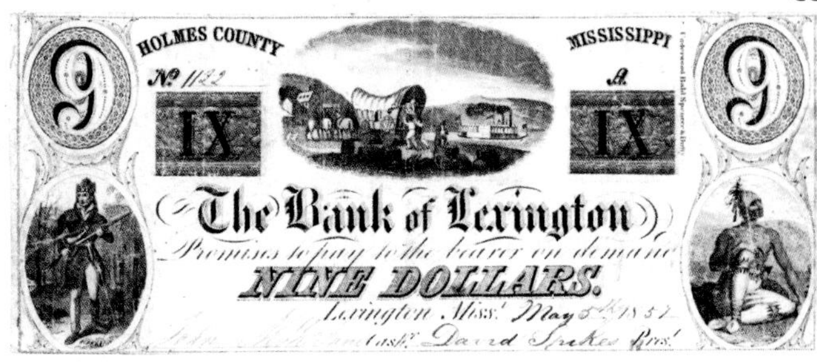

Engraver: Underwood, Bald, Spencer & Hufty. ***Comments:*** H-MS-120-G13, Kraus-3793. 18__. 1830s.

Rarity: URS-4
F $1,500; **Proof** $2,500

$10 • W-MS-480-010-G090

JM

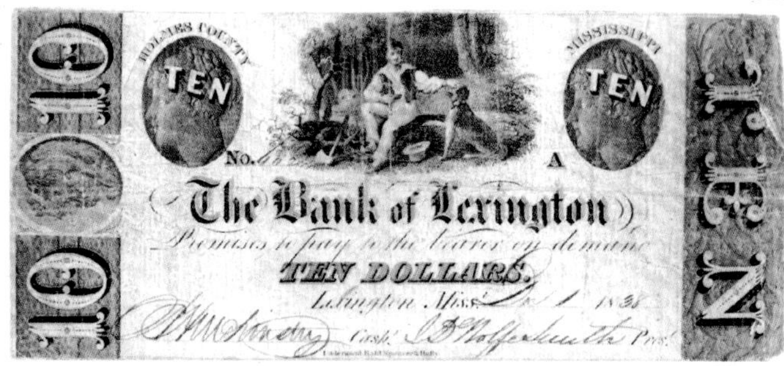

Engraver: Underwood, Bald, Spencer & Hufty. ***Comments:*** H-MS-120-G14, Kraus-3789. 18__. 1830s.

Rarity: URS-3
F $550

$20 • W-MS-480-020-G100

Left: 20 / Farmer leaning against tree, Wife / 20. ***Center:*** Milkmaid with cows, Farmhouse. ***Right:*** XX / Boy with shovel / XX. ***Engraver:*** Underwood, Bald, Spencer & Hufty. ***Comments:*** H-MS-120-G16, Kraus-3795p. 18__. 1830s.

Rarity: URS-3
F $550

$50 • W-MS-480-050-G110

Left: 50 / Cherub as Ceres with sickle / 50. ***Center:*** Commerce seated on cargo, Dock, Riverboat / Medallion head bearing MISSISSIPPI. ***Right:*** 50 / Two cherubs / 50. ***Engraver:*** Underwood, Bald, Spencer & Hufty. ***Comments:*** H-MS-120-G18, Kraus-3796p. 18__. 1830s.

Rarity: URS-3
F $550

$100 • **W-MS-480-100-G120** HA

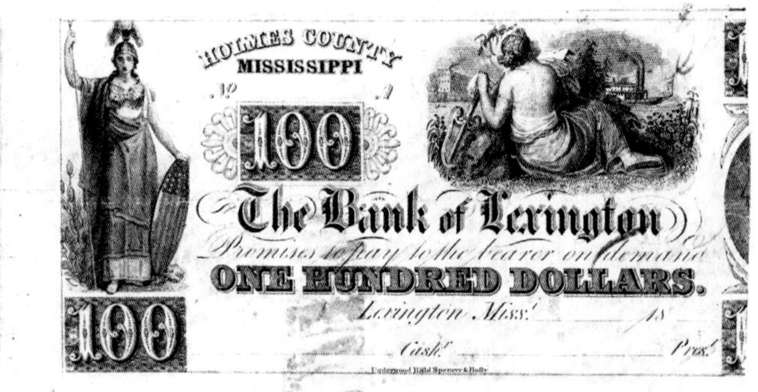

Engraver: Underwood, Bald, Spencer & Hufty. ***Comments:*** H-MS-120-G20, Kraus-3797p. Damaged note. 18__. 1830s.

Rarity: URS-3
VF $1,300
Selected auction price: Heritage Auctions, January 6, 2016, Lot 18603, VF $1,292

Post Notes

$5 • **W-MS-480-005-G130**

Left: FIVE / Medallion head bearing 5 / FIVE. ***Center:*** Medallion head bearing 5 / Indian sitting / Medallion head bearing 5. ***Right:*** FIVE / Medallion head bearing 5 / FIVE. ***Engraver:*** Underwood, Bald, Spencer & Hufty. ***Comments:*** H-MS-120-G26, Kraus-3810r. 18__. 1830s.

Rarity: —

$5 • **W-MS-480-005-G130a** JM

Engraver: Underwood, Bald, Spencer & Hufty. ***Comments:*** H-Unlisted, Kraus-Unlisted. Similar to W-MS-480-005-G130. Post note stamped. 18__. 1830s.

Rarity: URS-4
F $400

$10 • **W-MS-480-010-G140**

Left: 10 / Medallion head vertically / 10. ***Center:*** Boy seated with dog. ***Right:*** TEN vertically. ***Engraver:*** Underwood, Bald, Spencer & Hufty. ***Comments:*** H-MS-120-G28, Kraus-3816. 18__. 1830s.

Rarity: URS-3
F $550

$20 • **W-MS-480-020-G150**

Left: 20 / Farmer leaning against tree, Wife / 20. ***Center:*** Milkmaid with cows, Farmhouse. ***Right:*** XX / Boy with shovel / XX. ***Engraver:*** Underwood, Bald, Spencer & Hufty. ***Comments:*** H-MS-120-G30, Kraus-3817. 18__. 1830s.

Rarity: URS-3
F $550

$20 • **W-MS-480-020-G160** CC

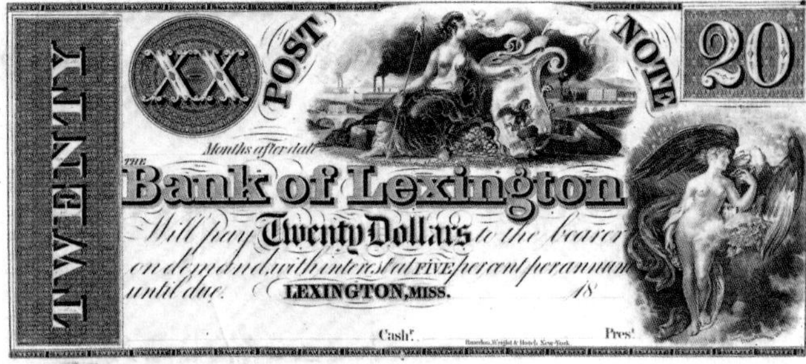

Engraver: Rawdon, Wright & Hatch. ***Comments:*** H-MS-120-G32, Kraus-3840p. 18__. 1830s.

Rarity: URS-6
Unc-Rem $350

$50 • **W-MS-480-050-G170**

Left: 50 / Cherub as Ceres with sickle / 50. ***Center:*** Commerce seated on cargo, Dock, Riverboat / Medallion head bearing MISSISSIPPI. ***Right:*** 50 / Two cherubs / 50. ***Comments:*** H-MS-120-G34, Kraus-3818. 18__. 1830s.

Rarity: URS-3
F $650

$50 • **W-MS-480-050-G180**

Engraver: Rawdon, Wright & Hatch. ***Comments:*** H-MS-120-G36. No description available. 18__. 1830s.

Rarity: *None known*

$100 • **W-MS-480-100-G190**

Left: Minerva with U.S. shield and spear / 100. ***Center:*** Muse with lyre, Riverboat. ***Right:*** 100 / Medallion head / 100. ***Comments:*** H-MS-120-G38, Kraus-3841. 18__. 1830s.

Rarity: URS-3
F $750

$100 • **W-MS-480-100-G200**

Comments: H-MS-120-G40, Kraus-3842. No description available. 18__. 1830s.

Rarity: *None known*

Non-Valid Issues

$1 • **W-MS-480-001-N010**

Comments: H-Unlisted, Kraus-3798f. Fraudulently issued. Filled-in remainder. 18__. 1830s.

Rarity: —

Consolidated Banking Company of Holmes County

1830s

W-MS-490

History: This is believed to have been an exchange house or office that issued notes to be circulated regionally. No record has been found of a state charter for this bank, and it is presumed it was a private enterprise. It is listed here for collector continuity.

Numismatic Commentary: There are few notes known today that were validly issued.

Valid Issues

12-1/2¢ • W-MS-490-00.12.50-G010

Left: 12-1/2 / Man standing with dog. ***Center:*** 12-1/2 / Hebe watering eagle / 12-1/2. ***Right:*** 12-1/2 / Two women seated. ***Engraver:*** Rawdon, Wright & Hatch. ***Comments:*** H-Unlisted, Kraus-20645. 18__. 1830s.

Rarity: URS-1
F $1,500

25¢ • W-MS-490-00.25-G020

Engraver: Rawdon, Wright & Hatch. ***Comments:*** H-Unlisted, Kraus-20646. No description available. 18__. 1830s.

Rarity: *None known*

50¢ • W-MS-490-00.50-G030

Left: Justice holding scales, caduceus, Shield bearing portrait of George Washington. ***Center:*** Commerce seated with cargo. ***Right:*** Ceres. ***Engraver:*** Rawdon, Wright & Hatch. ***Comments:*** H-Unlisted, Kraus-20647. 18__. 1830s.

Rarity: URS-1
F $1,500

$1 • W-MS-490-001-G040 JM

Engraver: Rawdon, Wright & Hatch. ***Comments:*** H-MS-115-G4, Kraus-20660. 18__. 1830s.

Rarity: URS-4
F $500

$2 • W-MS-490-002-G050

Comments: H-MS-115-G6, Kraus-20661. No description available. 18__. 1830s.

Rarity: *None known*

$5 • W-MS-490-005-G060 JM

Engraver: Rawdon, Wright & Hatch. ***Comments:*** H-MS-115-G8, Kraus-20663r. 18__. 1830s.

Rarity: URS-4
F $500

$10 • W-MS-490-010-G070 JM

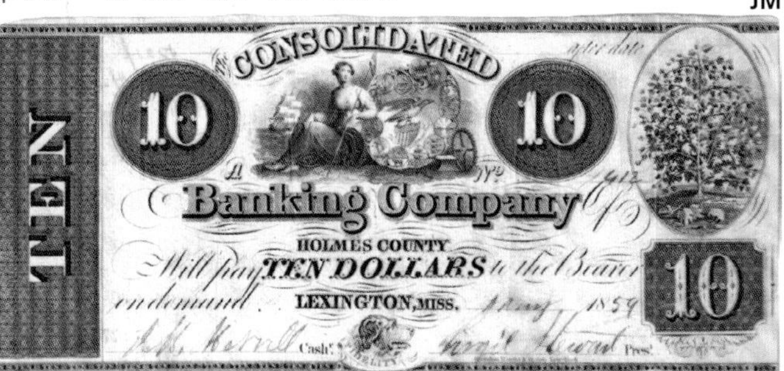

Engraver: Rawdon, Wright & Hatch. ***Comments:*** H-MS-115-G10, Kraus-20664r. 18__. 1830s.

Rarity: URS-4
F $750

Post Notes

$20 • W-MS-490-020-G080 CC

Engraver: Rawdon, Wright & Hatch. ***Comments:*** H-MS-115-G20, Kraus-206. 18__. 1830s.

Rarity: URS-5
F $750

Livingston, Mississippi

Livingston became the county seat in 1829, replacing the town of Beatties Bluff. By 1833 a courthouse and a jail had been built, and in 1836 the town was incorporated. Canton became the county seat that same year, although Livingston remained the seat unofficially until 1858, when the courthouse went out of use.

Livingston was an integral trading center for the surrounding plantations. During the 1850s, railways were spreading across the country, but Livingston was bypassed, and the inhabitants moved to more prosperous towns. From there the town declined, and many businesses shut down.

Citizens Bank of Madison County (branch)

1837–1840

W-MS-500

History: The Citizens Bank of Madison County was incorporated on May 3, 1837, with an authorized capital of $1,000,000. In 1840 an act was passed forcing the bank to forfeit its charter due to its failure to pay specie when its notes were presented for redemption.

The Citizens Bank of Madison County had its parent bank located in Canton, W-MS-090, and a branch bank located in Utica, W-MS-850.

Numismatic Commentary: No notes of Livingston are known.

Louisville, Mississippi

Louisville was named after Colonel Louis Winston and chartered in 1836. From the 1840s to the 1850s Louisville rose to prominence, enjoying prosperity due to its status as a commercial center. The Civil War did not directly touch the area, although men from the county went to fight for the Confederacy. On April 22, 1863, Union colonel Benjamin H. Grierson marched through Louisville, but there was no fighting. Due to this, the town was able to recover much more quickly than other areas in the South.

Planters Real Estate Bank

1837–1839

W-MS-510

History: This was an exchange house that issued notes based on real estate holdings. No record has been found of a state charter for this bank, and it is presumed it was a private enterprise. It is listed here for collector continuity.

Numismatic Commentary: Validly issued notes from this bank are extremely rare.

Valid Issues

$5 • W-MS-510-005-G010

Comments: H-Unlisted, Kraus-14730. No description available. 18__. 1830s.

Rarity: *None known*

$10 • W-MS-510-010-G020

Comments: H-Unlisted, Kraus-14731. No description available. 18__. 1830s.

Rarity: *None known*

$20 • W-MS-510-020-G030

JM

Comments: H-MS-125-G16, Kraus-14732. 183_. 1830s.

Rarity: URS-3

F $1,000

$50 • W-MS-510-050-G040

JM

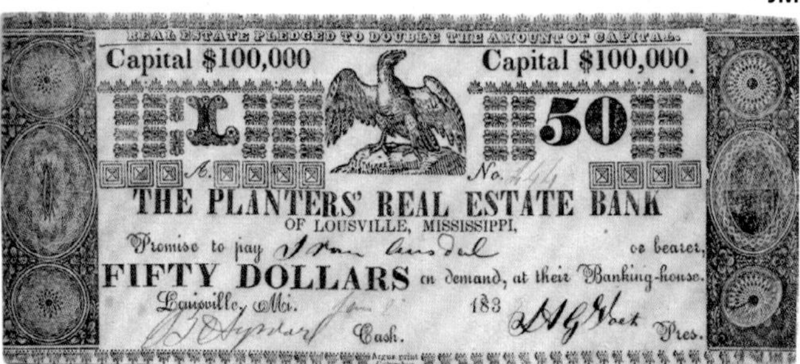

Comments: H-MS-125-G18, Kraus-14740. 183_. 1830s.

Rarity: URS-3

F $1,000

$50 • W-MS-510-050-G040a

Comments: H-Unlisted, Kraus-14741. Similar to W-MS-510-050-G040 but with PLANTERS' misspelled PLANTRES. 18__. 1830s.

Rarity: URS-3

F $1,000

Real Estate Banking Company of Louisville

Circa 1838

W-MS-520

History: This was an exchange house that issued notes based on real estate holdings. No record has been found of a state charter for this bank, and it is presumed it was a private enterprise. It is listed here for collector continuity.

Numismatic Commentary: Notes that were issued validly are exceptionally rare.

Valid Issues

25¢ • W-MS-520-00.25-G010

Comments: H-Unlisted, Kraus-14770. No description available. Circa 1838.

Rarity: *None known*

50¢ • W-MS-520-00.50-G020

Left: Panel. ***Center:*** Train with engineer and passengers. ***Right:*** Panel. ***Comments:*** H-Unlisted, Kraus-14771. Circa 1838.

Rarity: URS-3

F $1,000

$1 • W-MS-520-001-G030

Comments: H-Unlisted, Kraus-14772. No description available. Circa 1838.

Rarity: *None known*

$2 • W-MS-520-002-G040

Left: Panel. ***Center:*** 2 / Train / 2. ***Right:*** Panel. ***Comments:*** H-MS-130-G4, Kraus-14773. Circa 1838.

Rarity: URS-3

F $1,000

$5 • W-MS-520-005-G050

JM

Comments: H-MS-130-G8, Kraus-14774. 183_. Circa 1838.

Rarity: URS-3

F $1,500

$10 • W-MS-520-010-G060

Comments: H-Unlisted, Kraus-14775. No description available. Circa 1838.

Rarity: *None known*

$20 • W-MS-520-020-G070

Left: Panel. ***Center:*** Spread eagle on rock. ***Right:*** Panel. ***Comments:*** H-MS-130-G12, Kraus-14776. Circa 1838.

Rarity: URS-3
F $1,200

$50 • W-MS-520-050-G080

Comments: H-Unlisted, Kraus-1477. No description available. Circa 1838.

Rarity: *None known*

Madisonville, Mississippi

The town of Madison was named after James Madison and was located next to a previously established railroad track. It was settled in 1856 as Madison Station, a stop for the Illinois Central Railroad. The neighboring town of *Madisonville* was settled along a stagecoach route and became the seat of Madison County in 1828. However, its residents transferred to Madison Station to be a part of the railroad community, and Madisonville faded.

Bank of Madison County, Mississippi

1830s

W-MS-530

History: This is believed to have been an exchange house or office that issued notes based on real estate holdings. No record has been found of a state charter for this bank, and it is presumed it was a private enterprise. It is listed here for collector continuity.

Valid Issues

12-1/2¢ • W-MS-530-00.12.50-G010 JM

Engraver: Draper, Toppan, Longacre & Co. ***Comments:*** H-Unlisted, Kraus-14810. 183_. 1830s.

Rarity: URS-4
F $500

12-1/2¢ • W-MS-530-00.12.50-G020 JM

Engraver: Draper, Toppan, Longacre & Co. ***Comments:*** H-Unlisted, Kraus-14811r. 183_. 1830s.

Rarity: URS-4
F $500

12-1/2¢ • W-MS-530-00.12.50-G030 JM

Engraver: Draper, Toppan, Longacre & Co. ***Comments:*** H-Unlisted, Kraus-14812r. 183_. 1830s.

Rarity: URS-4
F $500

25¢ • W-MS-530-00.25-G040 CC

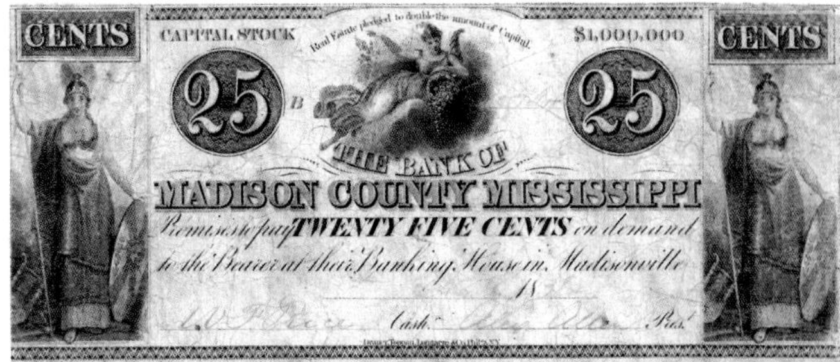

Engraver: Draper, Toppan, Longacre & Co. ***Comments:*** H-MS-135-G4, Kraus-14813. 18__. 1830s.

Rarity: URS-5
F $350

50¢ • W-MS-530-00.50-G050 JM

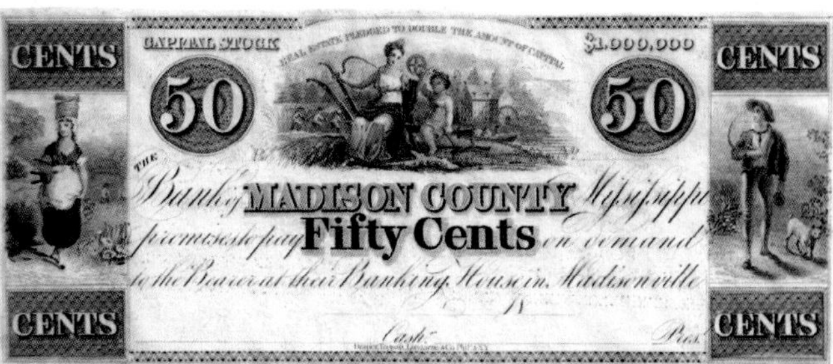

Engraver: Draper, Toppan, Longacre & Co. ***Comments:*** H-MS-135-G6, Kraus-14814. 18__. 1830s.

Rarity: URS-5
F $550

$1 • W-MS-530-001-G060

Engraver: Draper, Toppan, Longacre & Co. ***Comments:*** H-MS-135-G8, Kraus-14815. No description available. 18__. 1830s.

Rarity: *None known*

$2 • W-MS-530-002-G070

Engraver: Draper, Toppan, Longacre & Co. ***Comments:*** H-MS-135-G10, Kraus-14816. 18__. 1830s.

Rarity: URS-5
F $400

$10 • W-MS-530-010-G080

Engraver: Draper, Toppan, Longacre & Co. ***Comments:*** H-MS-135-G14, Kraus-14818. 18__. 1838.

Rarity: URS-3
F $550; **Proof** $750

$20 • W-MS-530-020-G090

Engraver: Draper, Toppan, Longacre & Co. ***Comments:*** H-MS-135-G16, Kraus-14818. 18__. 1838.

Rarity: URS-6
F $250

$20 • W-MS-530-020-G100

Comments: H-Unlisted, Kraus-14820a. No description available. 18__. 1838.

Rarity: *None known*

$50 • W-MS-530-050-G110

Engraver: Draper, Toppan, Longacre & Co. ***Comments:*** H-MS-135-G18, Kraus-14821a. 18__. 1838.

Rarity: URS-4
F $750

$100 • W-MS-530-100-G120

Engraver: Draper, Toppan, Longacre & Co. ***Comments:*** H-Unlisted, Kraus-14822a. 18__. 1838.

Rarity: URS-4
F $750

Post Notes

$5 • W-MS-530-005-G130

CC

Engraver: Draper, Toppan, Longacre & Co. ***Comments:*** H-MS-135-G12, Kraus-14817. 18__. 1838.

Rarity: URS-7
F $200

$5 • W-MS-530-005-G140

Left: FIVE / Farmer with pitchfork / FIVE. ***Center:*** 5 / Indian standing / 5. ***Right:*** FIVE / Female portrait / FIVE. ***Engraver:*** Draper, Toppan, Longacre & Co. ***Comments:*** H-MS-135-G22, Kraus-14817a. Post note handwritten. 18__. 1838.

Rarity: URS-6
F $400

$10 • W-MS-530-010-G150

Left: Female portrait / X. ***Center:*** Justice with Commerce, scales, sword, cornucopia, and fasces. ***Right:*** Female portrait / X. ***Engraver:*** Draper, Toppan, Longacre & Co. ***Comments:*** H-MS-135-G24, Kraus-14818a. Post note handwritten. 18__. 1838.

Rarity: URS-6
F $400

$20 • W-MS-530-020-G160

Left: Justice standing / 20. ***Center:*** Muse playing instrument, Two women seated. ***Right:*** Liberty with U.S. shield / 20. ***Engraver:*** Draper, Toppan, Longacre & Co. ***Comments:*** H-MS-135-G26, Kraus-Unlisted. Post note handwritten. 18__. 1838.

Rarity: URS-5
F $450

Uncut Sheets

12-1/2¢-12-1/2¢-12-1/2¢ •
W-MS-530-00.12.50.00.12.50.00.12.50-US010 JM

Engraver: Draper, Toppan, Longacre & Co. ***Comments:*** All unlisted in Haxby. Likely a partial sheet. 183_. 1830s.

Rarity: URS-3
F $1,500

$5-$5-$5-$20 • W-MS-530-005.005.005.020-US020

Vignette(s): ($5) Farmer with pitchfork / Indian standing / Female portrait. ***($20)*** Justice standing / Muse playing instrument, Two women seated / Liberty with U.S. shield. ***Engraver:*** Draper, Toppan, Longacre & Co. ***Comments:*** H-MS-135-G12, G12, G12, G16. First three notes identical.18__. 1838.

Rarity: —

Non-Valid Issues

$50 • W-MS-530-050-N010

Comments: H-Unlisted, Kraus-14821b. Fraudulently issued. Filled-in remainder. 18__. 1838.

Rarity: —

$100 • W-MS-530-100-N020

Comments: H-Unlisted, Kraus-3349d. Fraudulently issued note during the Confederate period. Filled-in remainder. 18__. 1838.

Rarity: —

Madisonville and Pearl River Turnpike Company

1836–circa 1839

W-MS-535

History: The Madisonville and Pearl River Turnpike Company was incorporated on February 27, 1836, for the purpose of building a turnpike road from Madisonville through Pearl River swamp. The authorized capital was $30,000. Sometime in 1839, the entity closed.

Numismatic Commentary: Kraus lists this company as scrip. It is listed here for collector continuity.

Valid Issues

25¢ • W-MS-535-00.25-G010 JM

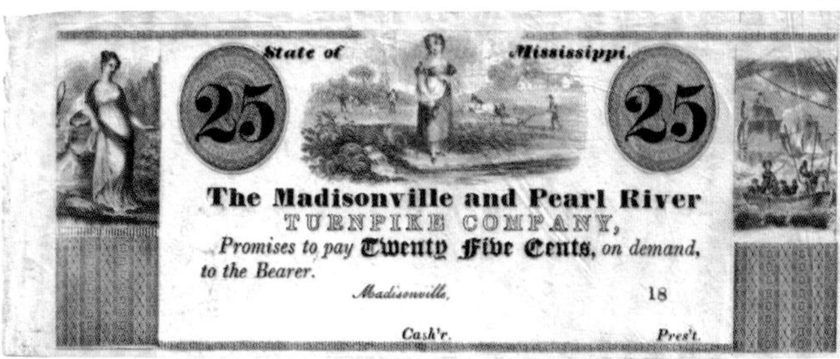

Comments: H-MS-140-G2. 18__. 1830s.

Rarity: URS-3
F $200

50¢ • W-MS-535-00.50-G020 JM

Comments: H-MS-140-G4. 18__. 1830s.

Rarity: URS-3
F $225

75¢ • **W-MS-535-00.75-G030** JM

Comments: H-MS-140-G6. 18__. 1830s.

Rarity: URS-3
F $275

$1 • **W-MS-535-001-G040** JM

Engraver: Draper, Toppan, Longacre & Co. ***Comments:*** H-MS-140-G8. 18__. 1830s.

Rarity: URS-3
F $300

$2 • **W-MS-535-002-G050** JM

Engraver: Draper, Toppan, Longacre & Co. ***Comments:*** H-MS-140-G10. 18__. 1830s.

Rarity: URS-3
VF $400

$3 • **W-MS-535-003-G060** JM

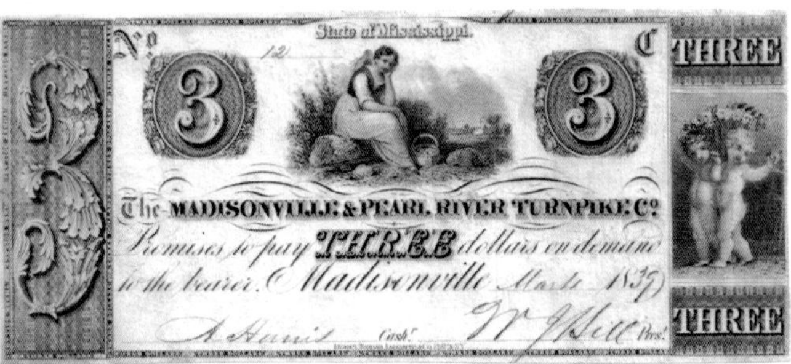

Engraver: Draper, Toppan, Longacre & Co. ***Comments:*** H-MS-140-G12. 18__. 1830s.

Rarity: URS-3
F $500

$5 • **W-MS-535-005-G070** JM

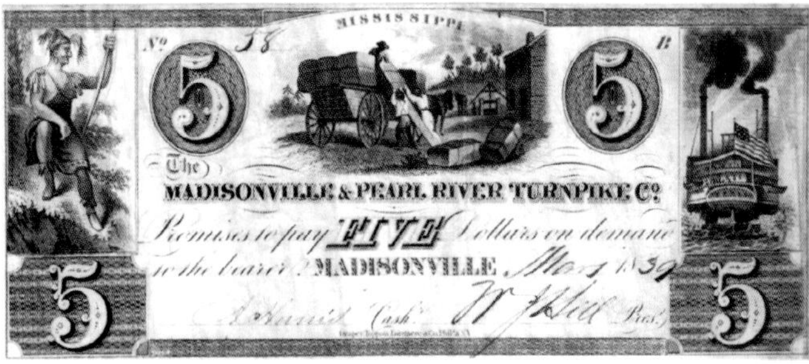

Engraver: Draper, Toppan, Longacre & Co. ***Comments:*** H-MS-140-G14. 18__. 1830s.

Rarity: URS-3
F $500

$10 • **W-MS-535-010-G080** JM

Engraver: Draper, Toppan, Longacre & Co. ***Comments:*** H-MS-140-G16. 18__. 1830s.

Rarity: URS-3
F $500

$20 • **W-MS-535-020-G090** JM

Engraver: Draper, Toppan, Longacre & Co. ***Comments:*** H-MS-140-G18. 18__. 1830s.

Rarity: URS-3
F $500

$50 • **W-MS-535-050-G100** JM

Engraver: Draper, Toppan, Longacre & Co. ***Comments:*** H-MS-140-G20. 18__. 1830s.

Rarity: URS-2
F $750

$100 • W-MS-535-100-G110

JM

Engraver: Draper, Toppan, Longacre & Co. ***Comments:*** H-MS-140-G22. 18__. 1830s.

Rarity: URS-2
VF $1,000

Uncut Sheets

25¢-50¢-75¢ •
W-MS-535-00.25.00.50.00.75-US010

JM

Comments: H-MS-140-G2, G4, G6. 18__. 1830s.

Rarity: —

MANCHESTER, MISSISSIPPI

Manchester began in 1824 as Hannan's Bluff. It was renamed Manchester before being called Yazoo City in 1841.

See also Yazoo City, Mississippi.

Commercial Bank of Manchester

1836–1860

W-MS-540

History: The Commercial Bank of Manchester was chartered on February 26, 1836, with an authorized capital of no more than $2,000,000. The president of the bank was M.B. Hamer, and J.J. Hughes was the cashier. Notes with a denomination less than $5 were not permitted. On February 15, 1838, an act was passed reducing the capital to $1,000,000. *Niles' National Register* of February 24, 1838, reported that the bank had a positive net worth of $32,633.64. In 1840 many banks had their charters suspended due to an inability to pay specie, but this bank survived. In 1860 it finally failed.

After the name of the town changed from Manchester to Yazoo City in 1841, the parent bank became located in Yazoo City, W-MS-1060, without actually moving.

Numismatic Commentary: Validly issued notes from this bank are extremely rare.

VALID ISSUES

$5 • W-MS-540-005-G010

Left: FIVE vertically. ***Center:*** 5 / Commerce seated on dock, cargo, Mercury with coins, Eagle / 5. ***Right:*** Statue of George Washington / V. ***Engraver:*** Rawdon, Wright, & Hatch. ***Comments:*** H-Unlisted, Kraus-3871. 18__. 1830s.

Rarity: *None known*

$10 • W-MS-540-010-G020

Left: TEN vertically. ***Center:*** X / Woman seated / X. ***Right:*** Hope standing with anchor / 10. ***Engraver:*** Rawdon, Wright, & Hatch. ***Comments:*** H-Unlisted, Kraus-3872. 18__. 1830s.

Rarity: *None known*

$20 • W-MS-540-020-G030

Engraver: Rawdon, Wright, Hatch & Edson. ***Comments:*** H-Unlisted, Kraus-3873. No description available. 18__. 1830s.

Rarity: *None known*

$50 • W-MS-540-050-G040

CC

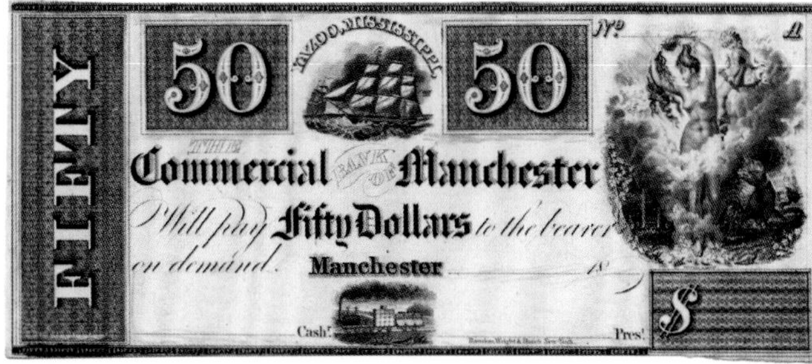

Engraver: Rawdon, Wright, & Hatch. ***Comments:*** H-Unlisted, Kraus-3874. 18__. 1830s.

Rarity: URS-1
Proof $4,000
Selected auction price: Heritage Auctions, April 23, 2015, Lot 19204, Proof $3,995

$100 • **W-MS-540-100-G050**
Engraver: Rawdon, Wright, Hatch & Edson. ***Comments:*** H-Unlisted, Kraus-3875. No description available. 18__. 1830s.

Rarity: *None known*

Post Notes

$5 • **W-MS-540-005-G060**

JM

Overprint: Blue TEN MONTHS / POST NOTE stamp. ***Engraver:*** Rawdon, Wright, & Hatch. ***Comments:*** H-Unlisted, Kraus-3871. 18__. 1830s.

Rarity: URS-2
F $1,500

$10 • **W-MS-540-010-G070**

JM

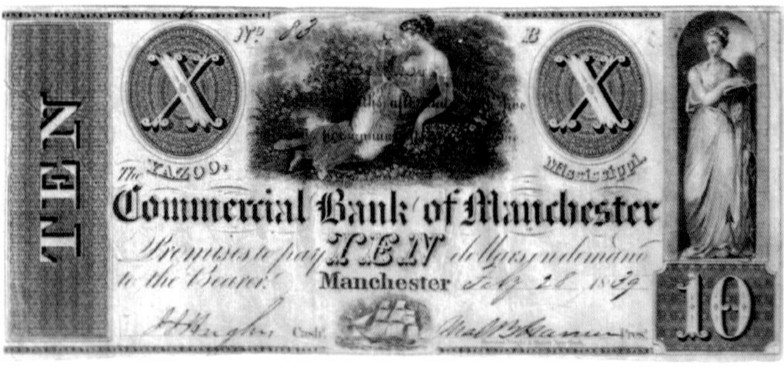

Overprint: Black POST NOTE stamp. ***Engraver:*** Rawdon, Wright, & Hatch. ***Comments:*** H-Unlisted, Kraus-3872. 18__. 1830s.

Rarity: URS-2
F $1,500

Planters Bank of the State of Mississippi (branch)

1830–1844

W-MS-555

History: The Planters Bank of the State of Mississippi was the second bank to be chartered in the state. It was incorporated on February 10, 1830, with an authorized capital of $3,000,000, $2,000,000 of which was provided from the state through the sale of bonds. The Panic of 1837 struck the bank hard. The state's bonds were repudiated, and the bank failed thereafter. On February 23, 1844, the bank was put into liquidation.

The Planters Bank of the State of Mississippi had its parent bank located in Natchez, W-MS-670, and branch banks located in Columbus, W-MS-240, Jackson, W-MS-470, Monticello, W-MS-580, Port Gibson, W-MS-780, Vicksburg, W-MS-920, Woodville, W-MS-1020, and Yazoo City, W-MS-1070.

Numismatic Commentary: Notes from this branch have Manchester handwritten.

Valid Issues

$5 • **W-MS-555-005-G010**

JM

Engraver: Rawdon, Wright & Co. ***Comments:*** H-MS-175-G80. 18__. 1830s.

Rarity: URS-5
F $200

$10 • **W-MS-555-010-G020**
Left: 10 / Neptune pouring water from amphora / 10. ***Center:*** 10 / Justice and Liberty flanking shield bearing cotton plant and surmounted by eagle / 10. ***Right:*** 10 / Neptune pouring water from amphora / 10. ***Engraver:*** Rawdon, Wright & Co. ***Comments:*** H-MS-175-G82. 18__. 1830s.

Rarity: URS-4
F $350

$20 • **W-MS-555-020-G030**
Left: Woman seated with globe. ***Center:*** 20 / Cotton bales, Hope standing with anchor, Ship / 20. ***Right:*** Group of Indians. ***Engraver:*** Rawdon, Wright & Co. ***Comments:*** H-MS-175-G84. 18__. 1830s.

Rarity: URS-4
F $350

$20 • **W-MS-555-020-G040**
Left: Woman standing in niche / XX. ***Center:*** 20 / Two women flanking shield surmounted by eagle / 20. ***Right:*** Woman standing in niche / XX. ***Back:*** Red-brown. ***Engraver:*** Rawdon, Wright, Hatch & Co. ***Comments:*** H-MS-175-G86. 18__. 1830s.

Rarity: URS-4
F $350

$50 • **W-MS-555-050-G050**
Left: Justice standing with eagle bearing portrait of George Washington. ***Center:*** 50 / Woman standing with cotton bales and shield bearing cotton plant surmounted by eagle, Train / 50. ***Right:*** Two women standing. ***Engraver:*** Rawdon, Wright & Co. ***Comments:*** H-MS-175-G88. 18__. 1830s.

Rarity: URS-4
F $350

$50 • **W-MS-555-050-G060** JM

Back: Red-brown. ***Engraver:*** Rawdon, Wright, Hatch & Co. ***Comments:*** H-MS-175-G90. 18__. 1830s.

Rarity: URS-5
F $200

$100 • **W-MS-555-100-G070**

Left: ONE HUNDRED vertically. ***Center:*** 100 / Group of settlers and Indians / 100. ***Right:*** ONE HUNDRED vertically. ***Engraver:*** Rawdon, Wright & Co. ***Comments:*** H-MS-175-G92. 18__. 1830s.

Rarity: URS-4
F $350

$100 • **W-MS-555-100-G080**

Left: 100 / Men with cattle / 100. ***Center:*** Portrait of George Washington / Woman seated in clouds with eagle bearing portrait of George Washington / Portrait of Benjamin Franklin. ***Right:*** 100 / Men with cattle / 100. ***Back:*** Red-brown. ***Engraver:*** Rawdon, Wright, Hatch & Co. ***Comments:*** H-MS-175-G94. 18__. 1830s.

Rarity: URS-4
F $350

Mississippi Springs, Mississippi

Mississippi Springs was envisioned as a community to be laid out by the railroad of the same name. H.R. Austin, who owned the land, was the developer. Dimensions of the project, located near Jackson in Yazoo and Hinds counties, were outlined in the document of incorporation referenced below.

Mississippi Springs Railroad Company

1836–1839

W-MS-570

History: The Mississippi Springs Railroad Company was incorporated on February 19, 1836. The company was to build a railroad from Mississippi Springs to Clinton. This was a state-chartered institution that did not have banking privileges, but it did issue notes. It is listed here for collector continuity.

Valid Issues

12-1/2¢ • **W-MS-570-00.12.50-G010**

Left: Liberty. ***Center:*** Riverboat and clipper ships. ***Right:*** Sailor leaning on anchor. ***Comments:*** H-Unlisted, Kraus-10410. 18__. 1830s.

Rarity: URS-1
F $1,500

12-1/2¢ • **W-MS-570-00.12.50-G020**

Left: Riverboat. ***Center:*** 12-1/2 / Sailor / 12-1/2. ***Right:*** Justice. ***Comments:*** H-MS-150-G4, Kraus-10411. 18__. 1830s.

Rarity: URS-1
F $1,500

25¢ • **W-MS-570-00.25-G030**

Left: Agriculture seated. ***Center:*** Train. ***Right:*** Riverboat. ***Comments:*** H-MS-150-G8, Kraus-10412. 18__. 1830s.

Rarity: URS-1
F $1,500

50¢ • **W-MS-570-00.50-G040**

Comments: H-Unlisted, Kraus-10413. No description available. 18__. 1830s.

Rarity: *None known*

$1 • **W-MS-570-001-G050** JM

Comments: H-Unlisted, Kraus-10414. 183_. 1830s.

Rarity: URS-3
F $1,500

$5 • **W-MS-570-005-G060** JM

Engraver: Draper, Toppan, Longacre & Co. ***Comments:*** H-MS-150-G14, Kraus-10415. 18__. 1830s.

Rarity: URS-3
Proof $2,000

$10 • **W-MS-570-010-G070**

Left: TEN / Train / X. ***Center:*** 10 / Justice with Ceres / 10. ***Right:*** TEN / Riverboat / X. ***Engraver:*** Draper, Toppan, Longacre & Co. ***Comments:*** H-MS-150-G16, Kraus-10416. 18__. 1830s.

Rarity: —

$20 • **W-MS-570-020-G080**

Comments: H-Unlisted, Kraus-10417. No description available. 18__. 1830s.

Rarity: *None known*

$50 • **W-MS-570-050-G090**

Comments: H-Unlisted, Kraus-10418. No description available. 18__. 1830s.

Rarity: *None known*

$100 • **W-MS-570-100-G100**

Comments: H-Unlisted, Kraus-10419. No description available. 18__. 1830s.

Rarity: *None known*

Post Notes Dated at the Girard Bank, Philadelphia

$5 • **W-MS-570-005-G110**

Left: 5 / Riverboat / 5. ***Center:*** Muse with harp and Hope with anchor. ***Right:*** 5 / Trains / 5. ***Engraver:*** Draper, Toppan, Longacre & Co. ***Comments:*** H-MS-150-G24, Kraus-10415a. 18__. 1830s.

Rarity: URS-4
F $350

$10 • **W-MS-570-010-G120**

JM

Engraver: Draper, Toppan, Longacre & Co. ***Comments:*** H-MS-150-G26, Kraus-10416a. 18__. 1830s.

Rarity: URS-3
F $2,000

Monticello, Mississippi

Monticello was settled in Lawrence County and grew up next to the Pearl River. The river brought prosperity to the town in the form of shipping and other transportation.

Planters Bank of the State of Mississippi (branch)

1830–1844

W-MS-580

History: The Planters Bank of the State of Mississippi was the second bank to be chartered in the state. It was incorporated on February 10, 1830, with an authorized capital of $3,000,000, $2,000,000 of which was provided from the state through the sale of bonds. The Panic of 1837 struck the bank hard. The state's bonds were repudiated, and the bank failed thereafter. On February 23, 1844, the bank was put into liquidation.

The Planters Bank of the State of Mississippi had its parent bank located in Natchez, W-MS-670, and branch banks located in Columbus, W-MS-240, Jackson, W-MS-470, Manchester, W-MS-555, Port Gibson, W-MS-780, Vicksburg, W-MS-920, Woodville, W-MS-1020, and Yazoo City, W-MS-1070.

Numismatic Commentary: The Monticello-branch notes appear to be the most common of the branch issues for this bank. Notes from this branch have Monticello handwritten.

Valid Issues

$5 • **W-MS-580-005-G010**

Left: 5 / FIVE vertically / 5. ***Center:*** 5 / Mercury in flight spreading coins from cornucopia / 5. ***Right:*** FIVE vertically. ***Engraver:*** Rawdon, Wright & Co. ***Comments:*** H-MS-175-G100. 18__. 1830s.

Rarity: URS-6
F $150

$10 • **W-MS-580-010-G020**

JM

Engraver: Rawdon, Wright & Co. ***Comments:*** H-MS-175-G102. 18__. 1830s.

Rarity: URS-7
F $75

$20 • **W-MS-580-020-G030**

JM

Engraver: Rawdon, Wright & Co. ***Comments:*** H-MS-175-G104. 18__. 1830s.

Rarity: URS-6
F $175

$20 • **W-MS-580-020-G040**

Left: Woman standing in niche / XX. ***Center:*** 20 / Two women flanking shield surmounted by eagle / 20. ***Right:*** Woman standing in niche / XX. ***Back:*** Red-brown. ***Engraver:*** Rawdon, Wright, Hatch & Co. ***Comments:*** H-MS-175-G106. 18__. 1830s.

Rarity: URS-6
F $175

$50 • W-MS-580-050-G050 JM

Engraver: Rawdon, Wright & Co. ***Comments:*** H-MS-175-G108. 18__. 1830s.

Rarity: URS-6
F $175

$50 • W-MS-580-050-G060 JM

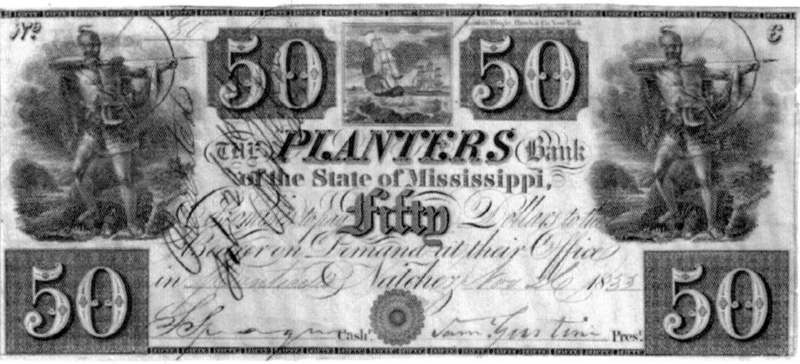

Back: Red-brown. ***Engraver:*** Rawdon, Wright, Hatch & Co. ***Comments:*** H-MS-175-G110. 18__. 1830s.

Rarity: URS-6
F $175

$100 • W-MS-580-100-G070 JM

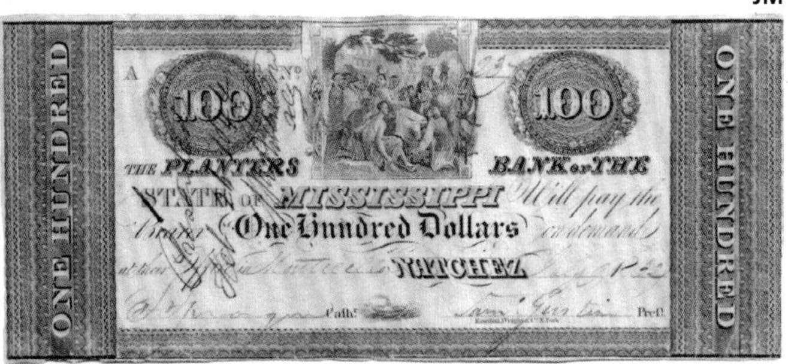

Engraver: Rawdon, Wright & Co. ***Comments:*** H-MS-175-G112. 18__. 1830s.

Rarity: URS-6
F $175

$100 • W-MS-580-100-G080 JM

Back: Red-brown. ***Engraver:*** Rawdon, Wright, Hatch & Co. ***Comments:*** H-MS-175-G114. 18__. 1830s.

Rarity: URS-6
F $200

Natchez, Mississippi

Natchez was the origin point of the Natchez Trace, a popular transportation route which ran from Natchez to Nashville. The Mississippi River brought produce and goods by flat boat to Natchez, and the town grew to prominence as a commercial center. It served as the first capital of the Mississippi Territory for several years until it was replaced by Washington. In 1817 the capital was returned to Natchez, and Mississippi became a state. After statehood, the capital was yet again transferred to Washington.

Natchez became a bustling port with plantation owners shipping out their cotton on steamboats to be transported to New Orleans, Saint Louis, and Cincinnati. The cotton boom attracted new settlers to the state, and the area grew drastically. On May 7, 1840, a tornado hit Natchez, killing hundreds. In 1845 the Natchez Institute was founded, offering free education.

Natchez was left mostly unharmed during the Civil War. The town surrendered in May 1862 after the repatriation of New Orleans by the Union.

Agricultural Bank of Mississippi

1833–1841

W-MS-590

History: The Agricultural Bank of Mississippi was chartered on February 27, 1833, as the third bank to be established in Mississippi. It was given an authorized capital of $2,000,000. Many prior shareholders of the Bank of the State of Mississippi, W-MS-620, took part in the new corporation.[15] Thus it was that the Agricultural Bank of Mississippi took the place of the old entity.

In 1837 the capital of the bank was $1,999,750. In 1838 the bank suspended specie payments, “along with some others, amounting to a total of $2,345,535 in unavailable public funds.”[16] In 1841 its charter was revoked due to its inability to abide by bank law.

The Agricultural Bank of Mississippi had a branch bank located in Pontotoc, W-MS-720.

Numismatic Commentary: The $100 demand note is the rarest note from this bank.

Collectors and Researchers:

If you have new information about any banks or notes listed in this volume, contact Whitman Publishing, Attn: Obsolete Paper Money, 3101 Clairmont Road, Suite G, Atlanta, GA 30329.

VALID ISSUES

$1 • W-MS-590-001-G010

JM

Engraver: Rawdon, Wright & Hatch. ***Comments:*** H-MS-155-G2, Kraus-3911. 18__. 1830s.

Rarity: URS-5
F $200

$2 • W-MS-590-002-G020

Left: TWO / Cotton wagon pulled by oxen / 2. ***Center:*** 2 / Horse / 2. ***Right:*** TWO / Cotton wagon pulled by oxen / 2. ***Engraver:*** Rawdon, Wright & Hatch. ***Comments:*** H-MS-155-G4, Kraus-3912. 18__. 1830s.

Rarity: —

$2 • W-MS-590-002-G020a

JM

Back: Red-orange. ***Engraver:*** Rawdon, Wright & Hatch. ***Comments:*** H-MS-155-G4a, Kraus-3912b. Similar to W-MS-590-002-G020. 18__. 1830s.

Rarity: URS-5
F $200

$3 • W-MS-590-003-G030

Left: 3 / Portrait of George Washington / 3 vertically. ***Center:*** Cotton wagon pulled by oxen / Boy with cattle / Cotton wagon pulled by oxen. ***Right:*** 3 vertically / Ceres at altar / 3 vertically. ***Engraver:*** Rawdon, Wright & Hatch. ***Comments:*** H-MS-155-G6. Possibly made only as Proofs. 18__. 1830s.

Rarity: URS-3
F $450

$3 • W-MS-590-003-G030a

JM

Back: Red-orange. ***Engraver:*** Rawdon, Wright & Hatch. ***Comments:*** H-MS-155-G6a, Kraus-3913. Similar to W-MS-590-003-G030. 18__. 1830s.

Rarity: URS-5
F $500

$5 • W-MS-590-005-G040

CC

Engraver: Rawdon, Wright & Hatch. ***Comments:*** H-MS-155-G8, Kraus-3914p. Possibly made only as Proofs. 18__. 1830s.

Rarity: URS-5
F $500; **Proof** $1,100

$5 • W-MS-590-005-G040a

CC, CC

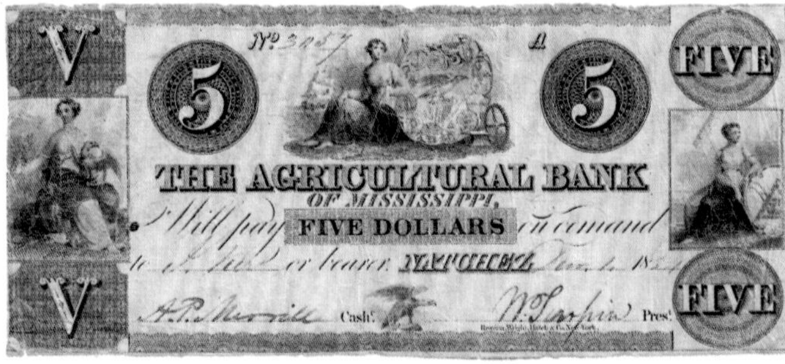

Back: Red-orange. ***Engraver:*** Rawdon, Wright & Hatch. ***Comments:*** H-MS-155-G8a, Kraus-3914. Similar to W-MS-590-005-G040. 18__. 1830s.

Rarity: URS-6
F $300

$10 • W-MS-590-010-G050

Left: X / Ceres with sickle, sheaf, and plow / 10. ***Center:*** TEN / Ship / TEN. ***Right:*** X / Man holding rifle, Dog / 10. ***Engraver:*** Rawdon, Wright & Hatch. ***Comments:*** H-MS-155-G14, Kraus-3915p. Possibly made only as Proofs. 18__. 1830s.

Rarity: URS-3
F $550

$10 • W-MS-590-010-G050a JM

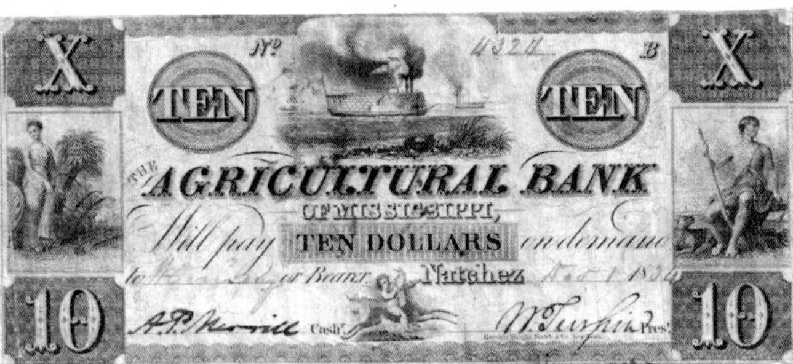

Back: Red-orange. ***Engraver:*** Rawdon, Wright & Hatch. ***Comments:*** H-MS-155-G14a, Kraus-3915. Similar to W-MS-590-010-G050. 18__. 1830s.

Rarity: URS-6
F $300

$20 • W-MS-590-020-G060

Left: 20 / Wheat / 20. ***Center:*** XX / Archimedes lifting world with lever / 20. ***Right:*** TWENTY vertically. ***Engraver:*** Rawdon, Wright & Hatch. ***Comments:*** H-MS-155-G16, Kraus-3916p. Possibly made only as Proofs. 18__. 1830s.

Rarity: URS-3
F $550

$20 • W-MS-590-020-G060a CC

Back: Red-orange. ***Engraver:*** Rawdon, Wright & Hatch. ***Comments:*** H-MS-155-G16a, Kraus-3916. Similar to W-MS-590-020-G060. 18__. 1830s.

Rarity: URS-6
F $250

$50 • W-MS-590-050-G070

Left: FIFTY vertically. ***Center:*** 50 / Ceres seated with wheat, Cattle / 50. ***Right:*** FIFTY vertically. ***Engraver:*** Rawdon, Wright & Hatch. ***Comments:*** H-MS-155-G18, Kraus-3917p. Possibly made only as Proofs. 18__. 1830s.

Rarity: URS-3

$50 • W-MS-590-050-G070a CC, JM

Back: Red-orange. ***Engraver:*** Rawdon, Wright & Hatch. ***Comments:*** H-MS-155-G18a, Kraus-3917. Similar to W-MS-590-050-G070. 18__. 1830s.

Rarity: URS-6
F $300

$100 • W-MS-590-100-G080

Left: Statue of George Washington / 100. ***Center:*** Commerce holding branch, Eagle, Ships. ***Right:*** Woman leaning against column. ***Engraver:*** Rawdon, Wright & Hatch. ***Comments:*** H-MS-155-G20, Kraus-3918p. Possibly made only as Proofs. 18__. 1830s.

Rarity: *None known*

$100 • W-MS-590-100-G080a

Back: Red-orange. ***Engraver:*** Rawdon, Wright & Hatch. ***Comments:*** H-MS-155-G20a, Kraus-3918. Similar to W-MS-590-100-G080. 18__. 1830s.

Rarity: URS-1

Post Notes

$__ • W-MS-590-__-G090 JM

Engraver: Rawdon, Wright & Hatch. ***Comments:*** H-Unlisted, Kraus-3940b. "500" written in. 18__. 1839 and 1840.

Rarity: URS-4
F $500

$__ • W-MS-590-__-G090a

JM

Engraver: Rawdon, Wright & Hatch. *Comments:* H-Unlisted, Kraus-3940b. Similar to W-MS-590-__-G090. "1,000" written in. 18__. 1839 and 1840.

Rarity: URS-4
F $750

$5 • W-MS-590-005-G100

Engraver: Rawdon, Wright, Hatch & Edson / Rawdon, Wright & Hatch. *Comments:* H-Unlisted, Kraus-3930. 18__. 1839 and 1840.

Rarity: *None known*

$10 • W-MS-590-010-G110

JM, SI

Back: Red-orange. *Engraver:* Rawdon, Wright, Hatch & Edson / Rawdon, Wright & Hatch. *Comments:* H-MS-155-G24, Kraus-3931. 18__. 1839 and 1840.

Rarity: URS-6
F $150

$20 • W-MS-590-020-G120

JM

Engraver: Rawdon, Wright, Hatch & Edson / Rawdon, Wright & Hatch. *Comments:* H-MS-155-G28, Kraus-3932. 18__. 1839 and 1840.

Rarity: URS-6
F $150

$50 • W-MS-590-050-G130

CC

Engraver: Rawdon, Wright, Hatch & Edson / Rawdon, Wright & Hatch. *Comments:* H-MS-155-G32, Kraus-3933. 18__. 1839 and 1840.

Rarity: URS-7
F $250

$100 • W-MS-590-100-G140

CC

Engraver: Rawdon, Wright, Hatch & Edson / Rawdon, Wright & Hatch. *Comments:* H-MS-155-G36, Kraus-3934. 18__. 1839 and 1840.

Rarity: URS-7
F $300

Bank of the Mississippi

1809–1818

W-MS-600

History: The Bank of the Mississippi was chartered as a private corporation on December 23, 1809, with an authorized capital of $100,000. The charter was to continue for 25 years, and the directors were responsible for bills in excess of $300,000. The bank officially opened for business on June 10, 1811, after $21,655 had been collected in specie for subscriptions of stock.[17] "From the outset the bank was wisely and judiciously conducted and its bills were never dishonored," states John J. Knox in his *History of Banking*.

On February 14, 1818, the Bank of the Mississippi was reorganized to become the Bank of the State of Mississippi, W-MS-620.

Numismatic Commentary: Handwritten and typeset checks from the early years of the bank's existence exist for collectors. However, no notes are known to exist from this territorial issuer. If ever found, a note from this bank would be the Holy Grail of Mississippi notes.

Valid Issues

$5 • W-MS-600-005-G010

Comments: H-Unlisted, Kraus-636. No description available. 18__. 1810s.

Rarity: *None known*

$10 • W-MS-600-010-G020

Comments: H-MS-165-G4, Kraus-637. No description available. 18__. 1810s.

Rarity: *None known*

$20 • W-MS-600-020-G030

Comments: H-MS-165-G8, Kraus-638. No description available. 18__. 1810s.

Rarity: *None known*

$50 • W-MS-600-050-G040

Comments: H-MS-165-G12, Kraus-639. No description available. 18__. 1810s.

Rarity: *None known*

$100 • W-MS-600-100-G050

Comments: H-MS-165-G16, Kraus-640. No description available. 18__. 1810s.

Rarity: *None known*

Bank of Natchez
1862
W-MS-610

History: The Bank of Natchez was authorized on January 17, 1862, with a capital of $1,000,000.[18] It is unknown if this bank ever opened for business.

Numismatic Commentary: No notes for this bank are known.

Bank of the State of Mississippi
1818–1831
W-MS-620

History: On February 14, 1818, the Bank of the Mississippi, W-MS-600, was reorganized to become the Bank of the State of Mississippi, earning it "a monopoly on all of Mississippi's banking activities."[19] In 1820 the bank made application to become a depository of public money of the state, and, under certain conditions, the application was approved. In 1830 the Planters Bank of the State of Mississippi, W-MS-670, was chartered in direct violation of a pledge made by the legislature to charter no other bank in the state. The managers of the Bank of the State of Mississippi wound up their institute as a result.

The Bank of the State of Mississippi had branch banks located in Port Gibson, W-MS-760, Vicksburg, W-MS-880, and Woodville, W-MS-1000.

Numismatic Commentary: All notes of this bank are extremely rare, with just one or two examples known for each denomination.

Valid Issues

$5 • W-MS-620-005-G010

Left: 5 / 5 vertically. ***Center:*** River scene, Boat, Deer. ***Right:*** NATCHEZ vertically. ***Engraver:*** Murray, Draper, Fairman & Co. ***Comments:*** H-MS-180-G8, Kraus-1070. 18__. 1818–1820s.

Rarity: URS-2
F $1,500

$10 • W-MS-620-010-G020

Left: TEN vertically. ***Center:*** River scene, Boat, Deer. ***Right:*** NATCHEZ vertically. ***Comments:*** H-MS-180-G12, Kraus-1071. 18__. 1818–1820s.

Rarity: URS-2
F $1,500

$20 • W-MS-620-020-G030

Left: TWENTY vertically. ***Center:*** River scene, Boat, Deer. ***Right:*** NATCHEZ vertically. ***Engraver:*** Murray, Draper, Fairman & Co. ***Comments:*** H-MS-180-G16, Kraus-1072. 18__. 1818–1820s.

Rarity: URS-2
F $1,500

$50 • W-MS-620-050-G040

JM

Engraver: Murray, Draper, Fairman & Co. ***Comments:*** H-MS-180-G24, Kraus-1073. 18__. 1818–1820s.

Rarity: URS-2
F $2,500

$100 • W-MS-620-100-G050

Comments: H-Unlisted, Kraus-1074. No description available. 18__. 1818–1820s.

Rarity: *None known*

Bank of the United States {2nd} (branch)
1831–1835
W-MS-630

History: The second Bank of the United States was chartered in 1816 for a duration of 20 years. Its capital was $35,000,000, of which the United States owned $7,000,000. Branch banks in several large cities were opened during 1816 and 1817 in direct competition with state banks.

In 1832 President Andrew Jackson vetoed the 1836 renewal of the Bank of the United States which had been brought up before Congress. This instituted a period of great debate and political turmoil. In late 1833 and early 1834 there was a depression in some areas of business which only served to strengthen the bank, as it was backed by the government. The branches began closing and selling their buildings.

Numismatic Commentary: The vast majority of notes offered on the marketplace from the various branches of the second Bank of the United States are contemporary counterfeits, rarely described as such due to lack of information concerning the genuine. Notes from Natchez are extremely rare.

Valid Issues

$5 • W-MS-630-005-G010

Left: FIVE vertically. *Center:* 5 / Eagle / V. *Right:* FIVE vertically. *Engraver:* Fairman, Draper, Underwood & Co. *Comments:* H-US-2-G556, Kraus-417. 18__. 1830s.

Rarity: *None known*

$5 • W-MS-630-005-G020

Left: FIVE vertically. *Center:* 5 / Eagle / V. *Right:* FIVE vertically. *Engraver:* Fairman, Draper, Underwood & Co. *Comments:* H-US-2-G558. 18__. 1830s.

Rarity: *None known*

$10 • W-MS-630-010-G030

Left: Female portraits. *Center:* 10 / Eagle with shield / 10. *Right:* Female portraits. *Engraver:* Fairman, Draper, Underwood & Co. *Comments:* H-US-2-G562. 18__. 1830s.

Rarity: *None known*

$20 • W-MS-630-020-G040

Left: Eagle / Portrait of George Washington / Medallion head. *Center:* 20 / Eagle with shield / 20. *Right:* Eagle / Portrait of Benjamin Franklin / Medallion head. *Engraver:* Fairman, Draper, Underwood & Co. *Comments:* H-US-2-G566. 18__. 1830s.

Rarity: *None known*

$20 • W-MS-630-020-G050

Left: 20 vertically. *Center:* 20 / Eagle with shield / 20. *Right:* XX vertically. *Engraver:* Danforth, Underwood, Bald & Spencer. *Comments:* H-US-2-G568. 18__. 1830s.

Rarity: *None known*

$50 • W-MS-630-050-G060

Left: Eagle / Portrait of George Washington / Medallion head. *Center:* 50 / Eagle with shield / 50. *Right:* Eagle / Portrait of Benjamin Franklin / Medallion head. *Engraver:* Fairman, Draper, Underwood & Co. *Comments:* H-US-2-G572. 18__. 1830s.

Rarity: *None known*

$50 • W-MS-630-050-G070

Left: L / Medallion head / 50. *Center:* FIFTY / 50 / Eagle with shield / FIFTY / L. *Right:* 50 / Medallion head / L. *Engraver:* Danforth, Underwood, Bald & Spencer. *Comments:* H-US-2-G574. 18__. 1830s.

Rarity: *None known*

$100 • W-MS-630-100-G080

Left: Eagle / Portrait of George Washington / Medallion head. *Center:* 100 / Eagle with shield / 100. *Right:* Eagle / Portrait of Benjamin Franklin / Medallion head. *Engraver:* Fairman, Draper, Underwood & Co. *Comments:* H-US-2-G578. 18__. 1830s.

Rarity: *None known*

$100 • W-MS-630-100-G090

Left: 100 / Medallion head / C. *Center:* 100 / Eagle with shield / 100. *Right:* C / Medallion head / 100. *Engraver:* Danforth, Underwood, Bald & Spencer. *Comments:* H-US-2-G580. 18__. 1830s.

Rarity: *None known*

Non-Valid Issues

$50 • W-MS-630-050-C060

Engraver: Fairman, Draper, Underwood & Co. *Comments:* H-US-2-C572. Counterfeit of W-MS-630-050-G060. 18__. 1830s.

Rarity: *None known*

$100 • W-MS-630-100-C080

Engraver: Danforth, Underwood, Bald & Spencer. *Comments:* H-US-2-C578. Counterfeit of W-MS-630-100-G080. 18__. 1830s.

Rarity: *None known*

Commercial Bank of Natchez

1836–1856

W-MS-640

History: The Commercial Bank of Natchez was incorporated on February 27, 1836, with an authorized capital of $3,000,000. The bank was forbidden to distribute notes of a denomination lower than $5. *Niles' National Register* of February 24, 1838, reported that the bank had a positive net worth of $206,806.94.

The bank did not last long, and on February 6, 1841, an act was passed to close the branch banks and wind up the affairs of the parent bank. The closing of the bank was extended due to a battle with creditors that went all the way to the U.S. Supreme Court. Finally the bank went into liquidation in 1856.

The Commercial Bank of Natchez had branch banks located in Brandon, W-MS-060, Canton, W-MS-100, Holmesville, W-MS-420, and Shieldsboro, W-MS-830.

Numismatic Commentary: Validly issued notes are extremely rare. No validly issued branch notes are known. Since the bank continued in operation for a long time, most of its validly issued notes were redeemed. There are a few Proof notes known. Recent auction prices indicate that notes of this bank are highly sought after by collectors.

Valid Issues

$5 • W-MS-640-005-G010

CC

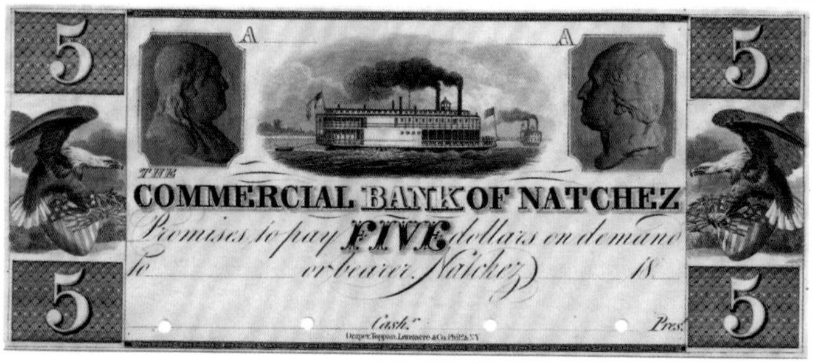

Engraver: Underwood, Bald, Spencer & Hufty. *Comments:* H-MS-160-G8, Kraus-3990p. 18__. 1830s.

Rarity: URS-3

Proof $2,900

Selected auction price: Heritage Auctions, October 17, 2012, Lot 15242, Proof $2,820

$10 • **W-MS-640-010-G020**

Engraver: Unverified, but likely Underwood, Bald, Spencer & Hufty. ***Comments:*** H-MS-160-G14, Kraus-3991. No description available. 18__. 1830s.

Rarity: *None known*

$20 • **W-MS-640-020-G030**

Left: 20 / Ship / 20. ***Center:*** XX / Woman seated, Man in water / XX. ***Right:*** 20 / Ship / 20. ***Engraver:*** Unverified, but likely Underwood, Bald, Spencer & Hufty. ***Comments:*** H-MS-160-G16, Kraus-3992. 18__. 1830s.

Rarity: *None known*

$50 • **W-MS-640-050-G040**

CC

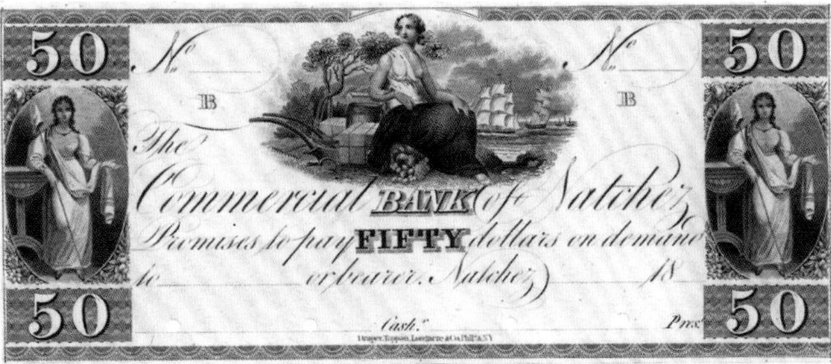

Engraver: Draper, Toppan, Longacre & Co. ***Comments:*** H-MS-160-G18, Kraus-3993p. 18__. 1830s.

Rarity: URS-2
Proof $3,000

$100 • **W-MS-640-100-G050**

CC

Engraver: Draper, Toppan, Longacre & Co. ***Comments:*** H-MS-160-G20, Kraus-3994p. 18__. 1830s.

Rarity: URS-2
Proof $3,500

$500 • **W-MS-640-500-G060**

Left: FIVE HUNDRED vertically. ***Center:*** Liberty with eagle and shield. ***Right:*** FIVE HUNDRED vertically. ***Engraver:*** Underwood, Bald, Spencer & Hufty. ***Comments:*** H-MS-160-G22, Kraus-4010p. 18__. 1830s.

Rarity: URS-1
Proof $4,000

$1,000 • **W-MS-640-1000-G070**

JM

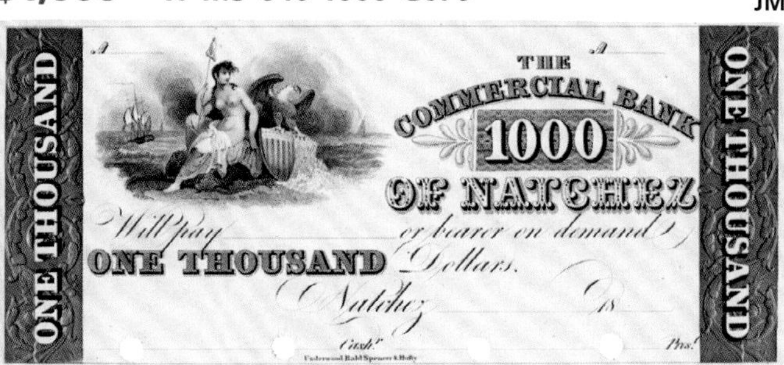

Engraver: Underwood, Bald, Spencer & Hufty. ***Comments:*** H-MS-160-G24, Kraus-4011p. 18__. 1830s.

Rarity: URS-2
Proof $2,500
Selected auction price: Heritage Auctions, October 21, 2015, Lot 18453, Proof $5,405

Post Notes

$20 • **W-MS-640-020-G080**

JM

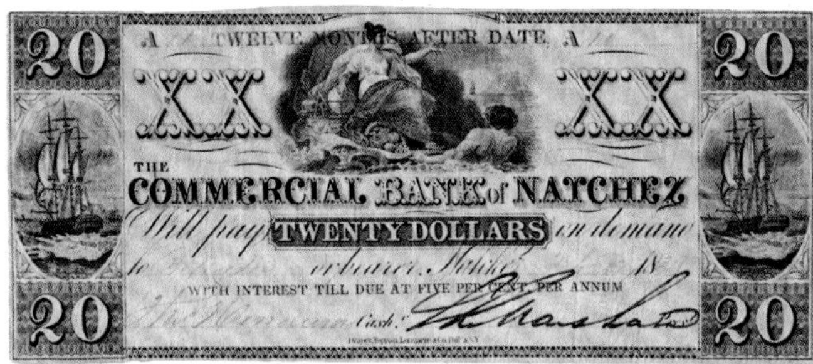

Overprint: Black TWELVE MONTHS AFTER DATE stamp. ***Engraver:*** Draper, Toppan, Longacre & Co. ***Comments:*** H-Unlisted. 18__. 1830s.

Rarity: URS-2
F $150
Selected auction price: Heritage Auctions, April 23, 2015, Lot 19207, VF $3,760

How to Read the Whitman Numbering System

$1 • **W-AL-020-001-G010a**

Denomination: Face value of the note shown.

W: Whitman number. This number is a sortable code unique to each bank and note.

AL: Abbreviation for the state under study.

020: Numerical designation specific to each bank.

001: The denomination in dollars.

G010a: G indicates a good or valid note. Other categories are indicated thus: C (counterfeit); R (raised); S (spurious); N (not-attributed); A (altered). Numbers are assigned starting with 010, 020, et seq. Terminal letters following the number indicate variations of a note: a series of different colored overprints, tints, payees, etc., all on the same design of note. For more information, see the "How to Use This Book" section at the front of the volume, page xiv.

New Orleans Interbank Issues

$5 • W-MS-640-005-G090

JM, JM

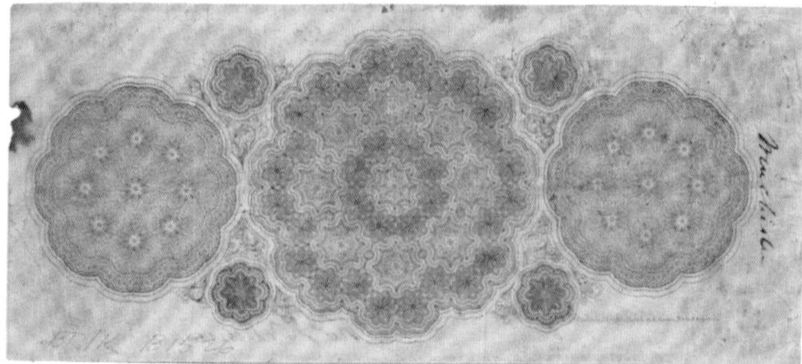

Back: Blue. ***Engraver:*** Rawdon, Wright, Hatch & Edson. ***Comments:*** H-Unlisted, Kraus-4030. 18__. 1830s.

Rarity: URS-3
F $2,500

$10 • W-MS-640-010-G100

Comments: H-Unlisted, Kraus-4031. No description available. 18__. 1830s.

Rarity: *None known*

$20 • W-MS-640-020-G110

RH, RH

Engraver: Rawdon, Wright, Hatch & Edson. ***Comments:*** H-Unlisted, Kraus-4032. 18__. 1830s.

Rarity: URS-2
F $3,000

Notes on Which the Place Payable is Blank

$5 • W-MS-640-005-G120

CC

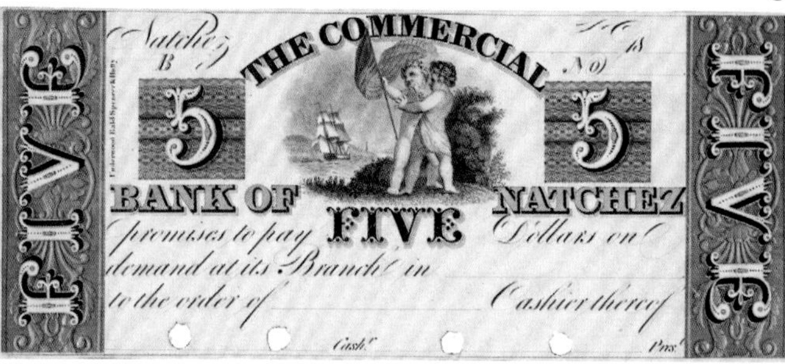

Engraver: Underwood, Bald, Spencer & Hufty. ***Comments:*** H-MS-160-G150. 18__. 1830s.

Rarity: URS-3
Proof $2,400
Selected auction price: Heritage Auctions, October 21, 2015, Lot 18452, Proof $1,410; Heritage Auctions, October 17, 2012, Lot 15243, Proof $2,232

$10 • W-MS-640-010-G130

CC

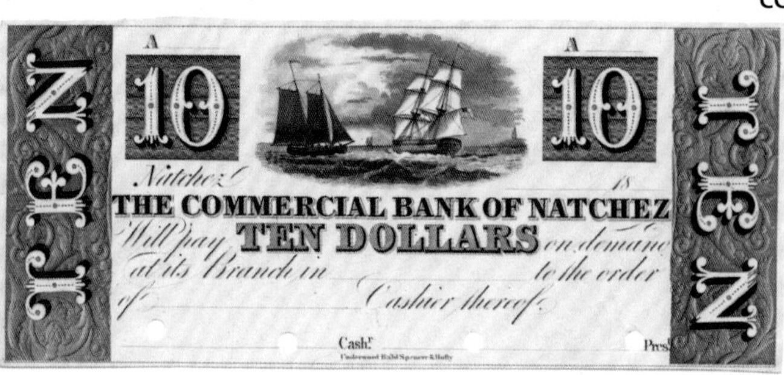

Engraver: Underwood, Bald, Spencer & Hufty. ***Comments:*** H-MS-160-G156. 18__. 1830s.

Rarity: URS-4
Proof $1,600
Selected auction price: Heritage Auctions, April 23, 2015, Lot 19205, Proof $1,527

$20 • W-MS-640-020-G140

JM

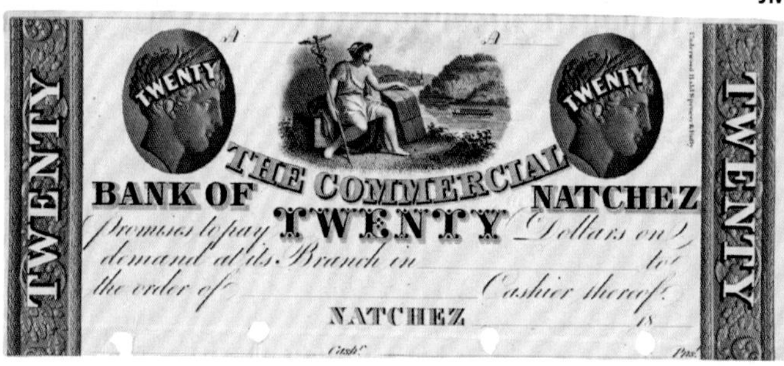

Engraver: Underwood, Bald, Spencer & Hufty. ***Comments:*** H-MS-160-G158. 18__. 1830s.

Rarity: URS-4
Proof $1,600
Selected auction price: Heritage Auctions, April 23, 2015, Lot 19206, Proof $2,467

$50 • **W-MS-640-050-G150** JM

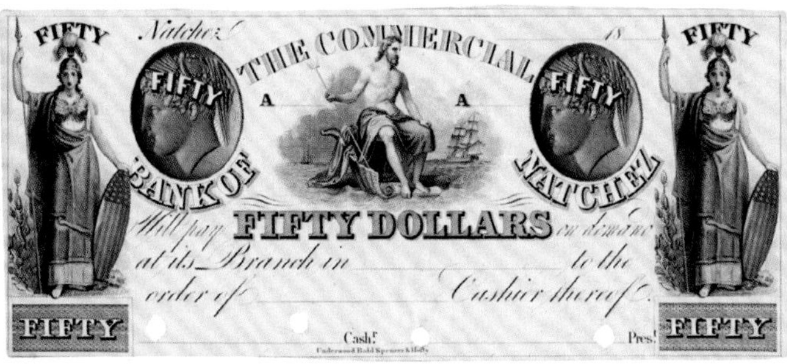

Engraver: Underwood, Bald, Spencer & Hufty. ***Comments:*** H-MS-160-G160. 18__. 1830s.

Rarity: URS-3

Proof $3,200

Selected auction price: Heritage Auctions, April 23, 2015, Lot 19208, Proof $3,055

$100 • **W-MS-640-100-G160**

Left: Woman standing with medallion head and caduceus / 100. ***Center:*** Medallion head bearing 100 / Indian in canoe / Medallion head bearing 100. ***Right:*** Woman standing with medallion head and caduceus / 100. ***Engraver:*** Underwood, Bald, Spencer & Hufty. ***Comments:*** H-MS-160-G162. 18__. 1830s.

Rarity: URS-3

Proof $4,500

Non-Valid Issues

$5 • **W-MS-640-005-A010** JM

Engraver: Underwood, Bald, Spencer & Hufty. ***Comments:*** H-MS-160-A5. Altered from $5 Commercial Bank of Enterprise, Enterprise, Mississippi. 18__. 1830s.

Rarity: URS-3

F $500

Mississippi Rail Road and Banking Company

1836–1841

W-MS-650

History: The Mississippi Rail Road and Banking Company (also seen as the Mississippi Rail Road Company on notes) was chartered on February 26, 1836. The bank had a positive net worth of $116,668.06 as of February 24, 1838. In 1840 it was reported that the bank could not redeem its notes, and in March 1841 this issuer, along with several others, had its charter revoked for this reason.

The Mississippi Rail Road and Banking Company had branches located in Canton, W-MS-110, Gallatin, W-MS-320, and Raymond, W-MS-810.

Numismatic Commentary: Post notes from the parent bank in Natchez are very common. Branch-bank notes stamped with either the Gallatin or Raymond overprints are rare. No notes are known with a Canton overprint.

Valid Issues

$5 • **W-MS-650-005-G010**

Left: Cotton plant / 5. ***Center:*** 5 / Train / 5. ***Right:*** Tree / 5. ***Engraver:*** Draper, Toppan, Longacre & Co. ***Comments:*** H-MS-170-G2, Kraus-10450. 18__. 1830s.

Rarity: *None known*

$10 • **W-MS-650-010-G020**

Left: Cotton plant / 10. ***Center:*** 10 / Train / 10. ***Right:*** Tree / 10. ***Engraver:*** Draper, Toppan, Longacre & Co. ***Comments:*** H-MS-170-G4. 18__. 1830s.

Rarity: *None known*

$20 • **W-MS-650-020-G030**

Left: Cotton plant / 20. ***Center:*** 20 / Train / 20. ***Right:*** Tree / 20. ***Engraver:*** Draper, Toppan, Longacre & Co. ***Comments:*** H-MS-170-G6, Kraus-10452. 18__. 1830s.

Rarity: *None known*

$50 • **W-MS-650-050-G040**

Left: Cotton plant / 50. ***Center:*** 50 / Train / 50. ***Right:*** Tree / 50. ***Engraver:*** Draper, Toppan, Longacre & Co. ***Comments:*** H-MS-170-G8, Kraus-10453. 18__. 1830s.

Rarity: *None known*

$100 • **W-MS-650-100-G050**

Left: Cotton plant / 100. ***Center:*** 100 / Train / 100. ***Right:*** Tree / 100. ***Engraver:*** Draper, Toppan, Longacre & Co. ***Comments:*** H-MS-170-G10, Kraus-10454. 18__. 1830s.

Rarity: *None known*

Post Notes

$5 • **W-MS-650-005-G060** CC

Overprint: Black POST NOTE stamp. ***Engraver:*** Draper, Toppan, Longacre & Co. ***Comments:*** H-MS-170-G12, Kraus-10450d. 18__. 1839.

Rarity: URS-8

F $200

$10 • W-MS-650-010-G070

CC

Overprint: Black POST NOTE stamp. ***Engraver:*** Draper, Toppan, Longacre & Co. ***Comments:*** H-MS-170-G14, Kraus-10451d. 18__. 1839.

Rarity: URS-8
F $200

$20 • W-MS-650-020-G080

JM

Overprint: Black POST NOTE stamp. ***Engraver:*** Draper, Toppan, Longacre & Co. ***Comments:*** H-MS-170-G16, Kraus-10452d. 18__. 1839.

Rarity: URS-8
F $200

$50 • W-MS-650-050-G090

JM

Overprint: Black POST NOTE stamp. ***Engraver:*** Draper, Toppan, Longacre & Co. ***Comments:*** H-MS-170-G18, Kraus-10453d. 18__. 1839.

Rarity: URS-8
F $200

$50 • W-MS-650-050-G090a

Overprint: Black POST NOTE stamp. ***Engraver:*** Draper, Toppan, Longacre & Co. ***Comments:*** H-Unlisted, Kraus-10460. Similar to W-MS-650-050-G090 but with no bottom-center ship vignette. 18__. 1839.

Rarity: URS-8
F $200

$100 • W-MS-650-100-G100

Left: Cotton plant / 100. ***Center:*** 100 / Train / 100. ***Right:*** Tree / 100. ***Overprint:*** Black POST NOTE stamp. ***Engraver:*** Draper, Toppan, Longacre & Co. ***Comments:*** H-MS-170-G20, Kraus-10454d. 18__. 1839.

Rarity: URS-8
F $200; **EF** $300

$100 • W-MS-650-100-G100a

CC

Overprint: Black POST NOTE stamp. ***Engraver:*** Draper, Toppan, Longacre & Co. ***Comments:*** H-Unlisted, Kraus-10461. Similar to W-MS-650-100-G100 but with no bottom-center ship vignette. 18__. 1839.

Rarity: URS-8
F $200; **EF** $300

Mississippi Shipping Company
1833–1840s
W-MS-660

History: The Mississippi Shipping Company was incorporated on December 23, 1833, with an authorized capital of $500,000. It issued paper money as a convenience to its patrons. Presumably, such bills had a limited circulation. In the 1840s it was reported that notes of the bank were at a discount.

Numismatic Commentary: Validly issued notes are fairly common, including the fractional currency and the $1, $3, and $5 notes. The $10, $20, $50, and $100 notes are known only as Proofs. Every note from this issuer is payable "one day after date."

Valid Issues
Post Notes

12-1/2¢ • W-MS-660-00.12.50-G010

JM

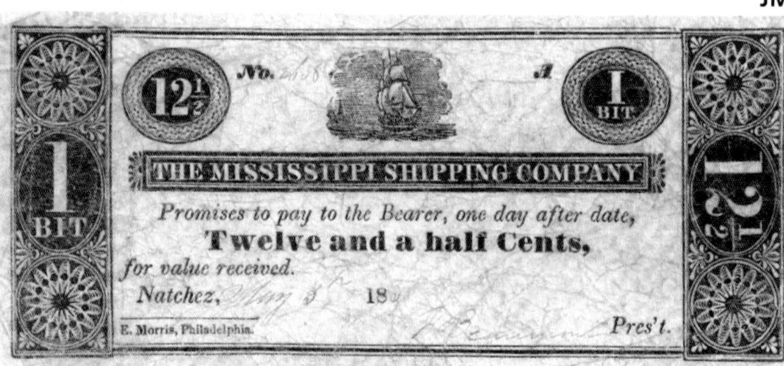

Comments: H-Unlisted, Kraus-30250. 18__. 1830s–1840s.

Rarity: URS-7
F $200

25¢ • W-MS-660-00.25-G020 JM

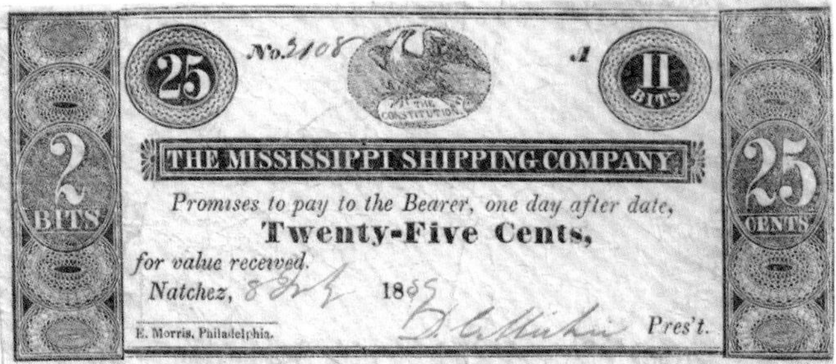

Comments: H-Unlisted, Kraus-30251. 18__. 1830s–1840s.

Rarity: URS-6
F $200

50¢ • W-MS-660-00.50-G030 CC

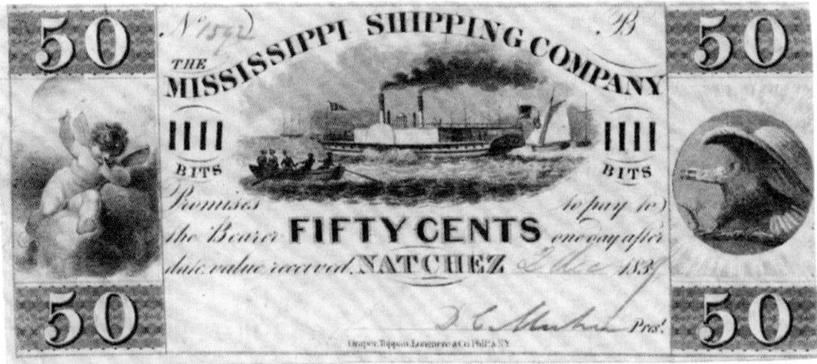

Engraver: Draper, Toppan, Longacre & Co. ***Comments:*** H-Unlisted, Kraus-30253. 183_. 1830s–1840s.

Rarity: URS-7
F $175

$1 • W-MS-660-001-G040 JM

Engraver: Draper, Toppan, Longacre & Co. ***Comments:*** H-Unlisted, Kraus-30254. 18__. 1830s–1840s.

Rarity: URS-7
F $150

$3 • W-MS-660-003-G050 ANS

Engraver: Draper, Toppan, Longacre & Co. ***Comments:*** H-Unlisted. 18__. 1830s–1840s.

Rarity: URS-6
F $250

$5 • W-MS-660-005-G060 CC

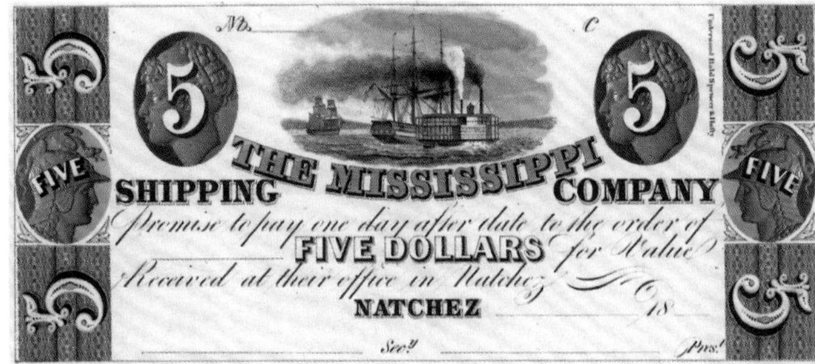

Engraver: Underwood, Bald, Spencer & Hufty. ***Comments:*** H-Unlisted. 18__. 1830s–1840s.

Rarity: URS-6
Proof $1,000

$10 • W-MS-660-010-G070 JM

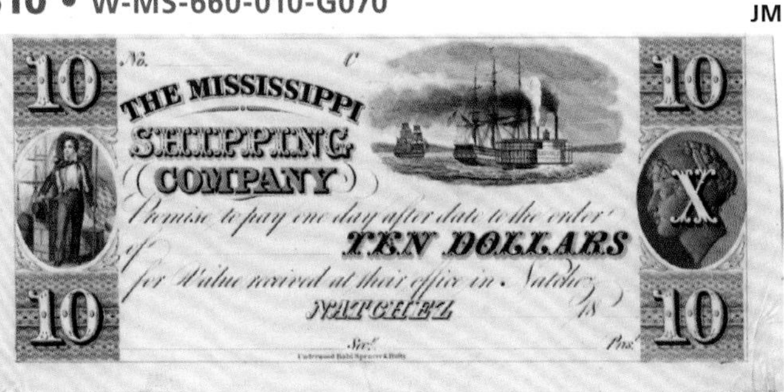

Engraver: Underwood, Bald, Spencer & Hufty. ***Comments:*** H-Unlisted. 18__. 1830s–1840s.

Rarity: URS-6
Proof $1,000

$20 • W-MS-660-020-G080 JM

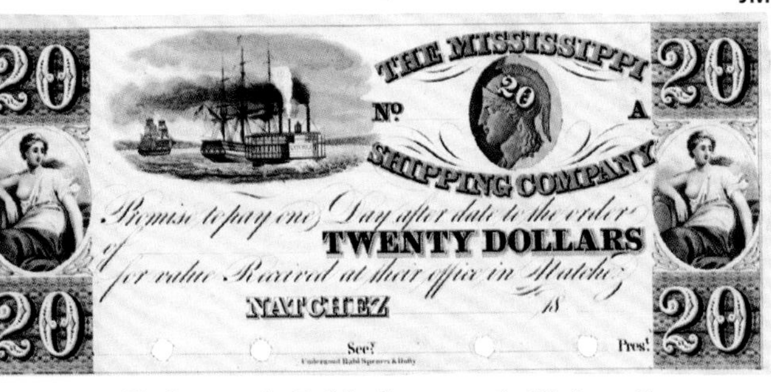

Engraver: Underwood, Bald, Spencer & Hufty. ***Comments:*** H-Unlisted. 18__. 1830s–1840s.

Rarity: URS-5
Proof $1,000

$50 • W-MS-660-050-G090

Left: Medallion head / 50 / Medallion head. ***Center:*** Medallion head / Natchez riverboat, Ships / Medallion head. ***Right:*** Medallion head / 50 / Medallion head. ***Engraver:*** Underwood, Bald, Spencer & Hufty. ***Comments:*** H-Unlisted, Kraus-30272p. 18__. 1830s–1840s.

Rarity: URS-3
Proof $2,000

$100 • W-MS-660-100-G100

Left: 100 / Ship / 100. ***Center:*** Medallion head / Natchez riverboat, Ships / Medallion head. ***Right:*** 100 / Ship / 100. ***Engraver:*** Underwood, Bald, Spencer & Hufty. ***Comments:*** H-Unlisted, Kraus-30273p. 18__. 1830s–1840s.

Rarity: URS-3
Proof $2,000

Planters Bank of the State of Mississippi

1830–1844

W-MS-670

History: The Planters Bank of the State of Mississippi was the second bank to be chartered in the state. It was incorporated on February 10, 1830, with an authorized capital of $3,000,000, $2,000,000 of which was provided from the state through the sale of bonds. This made the Planters Bank of the State of Mississippi the fiscal agent of the state of Mississippi.[20] The directors of the bank were not legally allowed to borrow more than $6,000 of bank funds at any one time. Loans were made by securities in real estate and mortgages. In 1835 the president of the bank was Joseph Perkins. The capital was $4,080,882, and bills in circulation totaled $1,607,572.

The Panic of 1837 struck the bank hard, and it was reported in *Niles' National Register* that "the notes of the Mississippi Planters Bank to the amount of three or four hundred thousand dollars, payable at the Bank of America, are now running to maturity, but there are no faults to meet them, and they are of course protested." The state's bonds were repudiated, and the bank failed thereafter. On February 23, 1844, the bank was put into liquidation.

The Planters Bank of the State of Mississippi had branch banks located in Columbus, W-MS-240, Jackson, W-MS-470, Manchester, W-MS-555, Monticello, W-MS-580, Port Gibson, W-MS-780, Vicksburg, W-MS-920, Woodville, W-MS-1020, and Yazoo City, W-MS-1070.

Numismatic Commentary: Demand notes and post notes have "Payable at Natchez" handwritten in.

Valid Issues

$5 • W-MS-670-005-G010 CC

Engraver: Rawdon, Wright & Co. ***Comments:*** H-MS-175-G2, Kraus-4060. 18__. 1830s.

Rarity: URS-5
Proof $1,000

$10 • W-MS-670-010-G020 CC

Engraver: Rawdon, Wright & Co. ***Comments:*** H-MS-175-G6, Kraus-4061. 18__. 1830s.

Rarity: URS-5
Proof $1,100

$20 • W-MS-670-020-G030 CC

Engraver: Rawdon, Wright & Co. ***Comments:*** H-MS-175-G12, Kraus-4062. 18__. 1830s.

Rarity: URS-5
Proof $1,800

$20 • W-MS-670-020-G040 CC

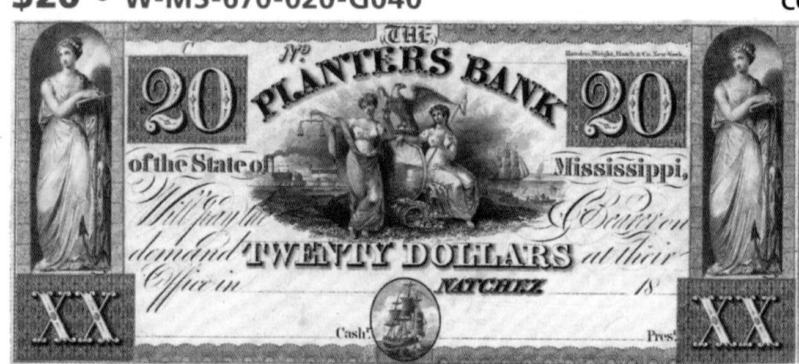

Engraver: Rawdon, Wright, Hatch & Co. ***Comments:*** H-Unlisted. 18__. 1830s.

Rarity: URS-4
Proof $1,200

$20 • W-MS-670-020-G040a JM

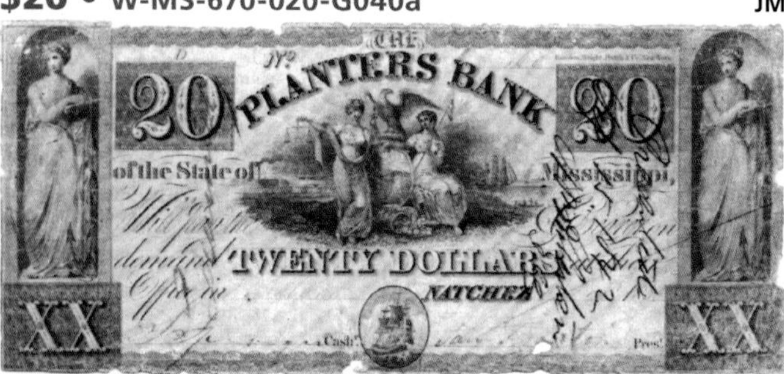

Back: Red-brown. ***Engraver:*** Rawdon, Wright, Hatch & Co. ***Comments:*** H-MS-175-G14a, Kraus-4075. Similar to W-MS-670-020-G040. 18__. 1830s.

Rarity: URS-6
VG $150; **F** $200

$50 • **W-MS-670-050-G050** CC

Engraver: Rawdon, Wright & Co. ***Comments:*** H-MS-175-G16, Kraus-4063. 18__. 1830s.

Rarity: URS-5
F $250; **Proof** $1,900

$50 • **W-MS-670-050-G060** JM

Back: Red-brown. ***Engraver:*** Rawdon, Wright, Hatch & Co. ***Comments:*** H-MS-175-G18a, Kraus-4076. 18__. 1830s.

Rarity: URS-6
F $175

$100 • **W-MS-670-100-G070** CC

Engraver: Rawdon, Wright & Co. ***Comments:*** H-MS-175-G20, Kraus-4064. 18__. 1830s.

Rarity: URS-4
Proof $1,700

$100 • **W-MS-670-100-G080** JM, JM

Back: Red-brown woman in niche / Woman in niche. ***Engraver:*** Rawdon, Wright, Hatch & Co. ***Comments:*** H-MS-175-G22a, Kraus-4077. 18__. 1830s.

Rarity: URS-6
F $250; **Proof** $1,000

Interest-Bearing Post Notes

$5 • **W-MS-670-005-G090** JM

Overprint: Black TWELVE MONTHS stamp. ***Engraver:*** Rawdon, Wright & Co. ***Comments:*** H-MS-175-G30, Kraus-4060ei. 18__. 1839.

Rarity: URS-3
F $450

$10 • **W-MS-670-010-G095**

Left: 10 / Aquarius pouring water from amphora / 10. ***Center:*** 10 / Justice and Liberty flanking shield bearing cotton plant and surmounted by eagle / 10. ***Right:*** 10 / Aquarius pouring water from amphora / 10. ***Overprint:*** Black TWELVE MONTHS stamp. ***Engraver:*** Rawdon, Wright, Hatch & Co. ***Comments:*** H-Unlisted. 18__. 1830s.

Rarity: URS-3
F $450

$20 • **W-MS-670-020-G100**

Left: Woman standing in niche / XX. ***Center:*** 20 / Two women flanking shield surmounted by eagle / 20. ***Right:*** Woman standing in niche / XX. ***Overprint:*** Black TWELVE MONTHS stamp. ***Engraver:*** Rawdon, Wright, Hatch & Co. ***Comments:*** H-Unlisted. 18__. 1839.

Rarity: URS-3
F $450

$20 • W-MS-670-020-G100a JM

Overprint: Black TWELVE MONTHS stamp. ***Back:*** Red-brown. ***Engraver:*** Rawdon, Wright, Hatch & Co. ***Comments:*** H-MS-175-G34a. Similar to W-MS-670-020-G100. 18__. 1839.

Rarity: URS-3
F $250

$20 • W-MS-670-020-G105

Left: Woman seated with globe. ***Center:*** 20 / Cotton bales, Hope standing with anchor, Ship / 20. ***Right:*** Group of Indians. ***Overprint:*** Black TWELVE MONTHS stamp. ***Engraver:*** Rawdon, Wright, Hatch & Co. ***Comments:*** H-Unlisted, Kraus-Unlisted. 18__. 1830s.

Rarity: —

$50 • W-MS-670-050-G110

Left: Indian standing with bow / 50. ***Center:*** 50 / Ships / 50. ***Right:*** Indian standing with bow / 50. ***Overprint:*** Black TWELVE MONTHS stamp. ***Engraver:*** Rawdon, Wright, Hatch & Co. ***Comments:*** H-Unlisted. 18__. 1830s.

Rarity: URS-3
F $350

$50 • W-MS-670-050-G110a CC

Overprint: Black TWELVE MONTHS stamp. ***Back:*** Red-brown. ***Engraver:*** Rawdon, Wright, Hatch & Co. ***Comments:*** H-Unlisted. Similar to W-MS-670-050-G110. 18__. 1830s.

Rarity: URS-3
F $250

$50 • W-MS-670-050-G115

Left: Justice standing with eagle bearing portrait of George Washington. ***Center:*** 50 / Woman standing with cotton bales and shield bearing cotton plant surmounted by eagle, Train / 50. ***Right:*** Two women standing. ***Overprint:*** Black TWELVE MONTHS stamp. ***Engraver:*** Rawdon, Wright, Hatch & Co. ***Comments:*** H-Unlisted, Kraus-Unlisted. 18__. 1830s.

Rarity: —

$100 • W-MS-670-100-G117

Left: ONE HUNDRED vertically. ***Center:*** 100 / Group of settlers and Indians / 100. ***Right:*** ONE HUNDRED vertically. ***Overprint:*** Black TWELVE MONTHS stamp. ***Engraver:*** Rawdon, Wright, Hatch & Co. ***Comments:*** H-Unlisted. 18__. 1830s.

Rarity: URS-3
F $400

$100 • W-MS-670-100-G117a

Overprint: Black TWELVE MONTHS stamp. ***Back:*** Red-brown. ***Engraver:*** Rawdon, Wright, Hatch & Co. ***Comments:*** H-Unlisted. Similar to W-MS-670-100-G115. 18__. 1830s.

Rarity: URS-3
F $400

Notes on Which the Place Payable is Blank

$5 • W-MS-670-005-G120

Left: 5 / FIVE vertically / 5. ***Center:*** 5 / Mercury in flight spreading coins from cornucopia / 5. ***Right:*** FIVE vertically. ***Engraver:*** Rawdon, Wright & Co. ***Comments:*** H-MS-175-G180. 18__. 1830s.

Rarity: —

$10 • W-MS-670-010-G130

Left: 10 / Neptune pouring water from amphora / 10. ***Center:*** 10 / Justice and Liberty flanking shield bearing cotton plant and surmounted by eagle / 10. ***Right:*** 10 / Neptune pouring water from amphora / 10. ***Engraver:*** Rawdon, Wright & Co. ***Comments:*** H-MS-175-G182. 18__. 1830s.

Rarity: *None known*

$20 • W-MS-670-020-G140

Left: Woman seated with globe. ***Center:*** 20 / Cotton bales, Hope standing with anchor, Ship / 20. ***Right:*** Group of Indians. ***Engraver:*** Rawdon, Wright & Co. ***Comments:*** H-MS-175-G184. 18__. 1830s.

Rarity: *None known*

$20 • W-MS-670-020-G150

Left: Woman standing in niche / XX. ***Center:*** 20 / Two women flanking shield surmounted by eagle / 20. ***Right:*** Woman standing in niche / XX. ***Back:*** Red-brown. ***Engraver:*** Rawdon, Wright, Hatch & Co. ***Comments:*** H-MS-175-G186. 18__. 1830s.

Rarity: *None known*

$50 • W-MS-670-050-G160

Left: Justice standing with eagle bearing portrait of George Washington. ***Center:*** 50 / Woman standing with cotton bales and shield bearing cotton plant surmounted by eagle, Train / 50. ***Right:*** Two women standing. ***Engraver:*** Rawdon, Wright & Co. ***Comments:*** H-MS-175-G188. 18__. 1830s.

Rarity: *None known*

$50 • W-MS-670-050-G170

Left: Indian standing with bow / 50. ***Center:*** 50 / Ships / 50. ***Right:*** Indian standing with bow / 50. ***Back:*** Red-brown. ***Engraver:*** Rawdon, Wright, Hatch & Co. ***Comments:*** H-MS-175-G190. 18__. 1830s.

Rarity: *None known*

$100 • **W-MS-670-100-G180**

Left: ONE HUNDRED vertically. ***Center:*** 100 / Group of settlers and Indians / 100. ***Right:*** ONE HUNDRED vertically. ***Engraver:*** Rawdon, Wright & Co. ***Comments:*** H-MS-175-G192. 18__. 1830s.

Rarity: *None known*

$100 • **W-MS-670-100-G190**

Left: 100 / Men with cattle / 100. ***Center:*** Portrait of George Washington / Woman seated in clouds with eagle bearing portrait of George Washington / Portrait of Benjamin Franklin. ***Right:*** 100 / Men with cattle / 100. ***Back:*** Red-brown. ***Engraver:*** Rawdon, Wright, Hatch & Co. ***Comments:*** H-MS-175-G194. 18__. 1830s.

Rarity: *None known*

Notes Payable at an Unknown Bank in New York

$10 • **W-MS-670-010-G200**

Left: 10 / Cherub writing on panel / 10. ***Center:*** 10 / Hercules wrestling lion / 10. ***Right:*** Indian standing with bow / 10. ***Engraver:*** Rawdon, Wright, Hatch & Co. ***Comments:*** H-MS-175-G198. 18__. 1830s.

Rarity: URS-3
F $350

$20 • **W-MS-670-020-G210**

Left: Hebe standing with eagle / 20. ***Center:*** XX / Portrait of George Washington / XX. ***Right:*** Hebe standing with eagle / 20. ***Engraver:*** Rawdon, Wright, Hatch & Co. ***Comments:*** H-MS-175-G200, Kraus-4091. 18__. 1830s.

Rarity: URS-3
F $350

$50 • **W-MS-670-050-G220**

Left: 50 / Hebe watering eagle / 50. ***Center:*** Woman flying through air / 50 / Woman flying through air. ***Right:*** Woman flying through air / 50. ***Engraver:*** Rawdon, Wright, Hatch & Co. ***Comments:*** H-MS-175-G202, Kraus-4092. 18__. 1830s.

Rarity: URS-3
F $350

$100 • **W-MS-670-100-G230**

Left: Liberty, eagle, Sun in mirror. ***Center:*** Indian standing with bow. ***Right:*** Woman riding dolphins. ***Engraver:*** Rawdon, Wright, Hatch & Co. ***Comments:*** H-Unlisted, Kraus-4093. 18__. 1830s.

Rarity: URS-3
F $350

Notes Payable at an Unknown Bank in Philadelphia

$10 • **W-MS-670-010-G240**

Left: 10 / Cherub writing on panel / 10. ***Center:*** 10 / Hercules wrestling lion / 10. ***Right:*** Indian standing with bow / 10. ***Engraver:*** Rawdon, Wright, Hatch & Co. ***Comments:*** H-MS-175-G208, Kraus-4090. 18__. 1830s.

Rarity: URS-3
F $350

$20 • **W-MS-670-020-G250**

Left: Hebe standing with eagle / 20. ***Center:*** XX / Portrait of George Washington / XX. ***Right:*** Hebe standing with eagle / 20. ***Engraver:*** Rawdon, Wright, Hatch & Co. ***Comments:*** H-MS-175-G210. 18__. 1830s.

Rarity: URS-3
F $350

$50 • **W-MS-670-050-G260**

Left: 50 / Hebe watering eagle / 50. ***Center:*** Woman flying through air / 50 / Woman flying through air. ***Right:*** Woman flying through air / 50. ***Engraver:*** Rawdon, Wright, Hatch & Co. ***Comments:*** H-MS-175-G212. 18__. 1830s.

Rarity: URS-3
F $350

Notes Payable at a New York or Philadelphia Bank on Which the Place Payable is Blank

$10 • **W-MS-670-010-G270**

Left: 10 / Cherub writing on panel / 10. ***Center:*** 10 / Hercules wrestling lion / 10. ***Right:*** Indian standing with bow / 10. ***Engraver:*** Rawdon, Wright, Hatch & Co. ***Comments:*** H-MS-175-G220, Kraus-4110. 18__. 1830s.

Rarity: *None known*

$10 • **W-MS-670-010-G270a**

Engraver: Rawdon, Wright, Hatch & Co. ***Comments:*** H-MS-175-G220a, Kraus-4110. Similar to W-MS-670-010-G270. 18__. 1830s.

Rarity: *None known*

$20 • **W-MS-670-020-G280**

Left: Hebe standing with eagle / 20. ***Center:*** XX / Portrait of George Washington / XX. ***Right:*** Hebe standing with eagle / 20. ***Engraver:*** Rawdon, Wright, Hatch & Co. ***Comments:*** H-MS-175-G224, Kraus-4111. 18__. 1830s.

Rarity: *None known*

$20 • **W-MS-670-020-G280a**

Engraver: Rawdon, Wright, Hatch & Co. ***Comments:*** H-MS-175-G224a. Similar to W-MS-670-020-G280. 18__. 1830s.

Rarity: *None known*

$50 • **W-MS-670-050-G290** JM

Engraver: Rawdon, Wright, Hatch & Co. ***Comments:*** H-MS-175-G228, Kraus-4112. 18__. 1830s.

Rarity: URS-3
Proof $1,500

$50 • **W-MS-670-050-G290a**
Engraver: Rawdon, Wright, Hatch & Co. ***Comments:*** H-MS-175-G228a. Similar to W-MS-670-050-G290. 18__. 1830s.
Rarity: *None known*

$100 • **W-MS-670-100-G300**
Left: Liberty, eagle, Sun in mirror. ***Center:*** Indian standing with bow. ***Right:*** Woman riding dolphins. ***Engraver:*** Rawdon, Wright, Hatch & Co. ***Comments:*** H-Unlisted, Kraus-4113. 18__. 1830s.
Rarity: *None known*

W.A. Britton and Company Banking House
1835–1860s
W-MS-680

History: The W.A. Britton and Company Banking House was actually a brokerage and exchange business, not chartered as a bank of issue. It closed down during the Civil War.

See also listing under New Orleans, Louisiana, W-LA-430.

Valid Issues

$1 • **W-MS-680-001-G010** JM

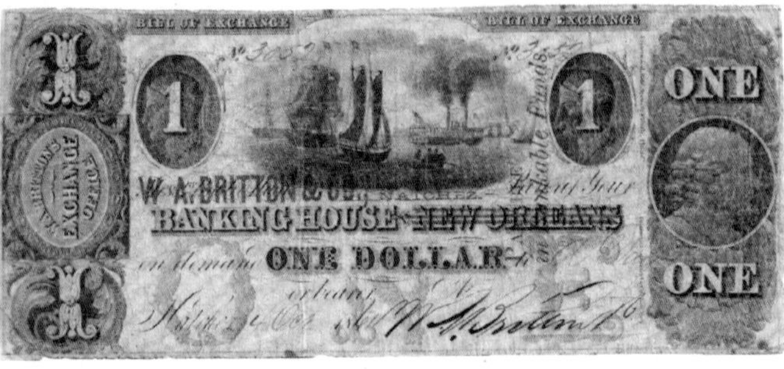

Overprint: Black W.A. BRITTON & CO. stamped over crossed out NEW ORLEANS. ***Engraver:*** Underwood, Bald, Spencer & Hufty / Danforth, Underwood & Co. ***Comments:*** H-Unlisted, Kraus-51303. 184_. 1840s.
Rarity: URS-4
G $750

$2 • **W-MS-680-002-G020** JM

Overprint: Black W.A. BRITTON & CO. stamped over crossed out NEW ORLEANS. ***Engraver:*** Underwood, Bald, Spencer & Hufty / Danforth, Underwood & Co. ***Comments:*** H-Unlisted, Kraus-51304. 184_. 1840s.
Rarity: URS-4
G $750

$3 • **W-MS-680-003-G030** JM

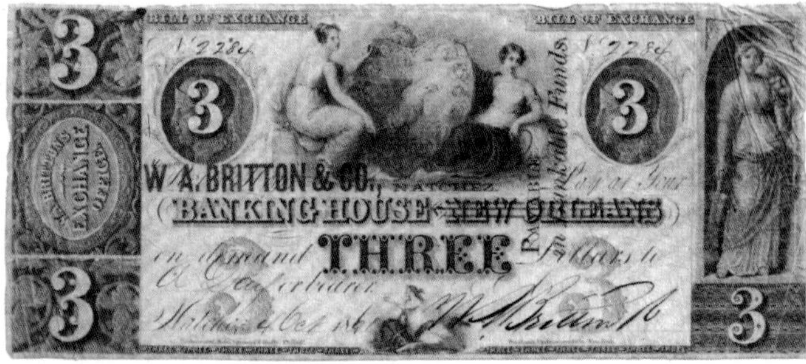

Overprint: Black W.A. BRITTON & CO. stamped over crossed out NEW ORLEANS. ***Engraver:*** Underwood, Bald, Spencer & Hufty / Danforth, Underwood & Co. ***Comments:*** H-Unlisted, Kraus-51305. 184_. 1840s.
Rarity: URS-3
VG $1,000

Oakland, Mississippi

The town of Oakland was chartered in 1848 on land that had originally been settled in 1798 by John Henderson.

Farmers Real Estate Bank of Mississippi
1830s
W-MS-690

History: This is believed to have been an exchange house or office that issued notes based on real estate holdings. No record has been found of a state charter for this bank, and it is presumed it was a private enterprise. It is listed here for collector continuity.

In 1838 the *Farmer's Register* noted this:

> The unchartered or real estate banks seem to be more infamous than those that swindle under the forms of law. We have been informed that the "Oakland Bank" [Farmers Real Estate Bank of Mississippi located at Oakland]—one of the machines for making money—has dispatched a pair of saddle bags full of their notes to Texas in order to obtain the property of these people for their worthless trash.

Numismatic Commentary: Only the $3 note is currently known.

Valid Issues

$1 • **W-MS-690-001-G010**
Comments: H-Unlisted, Kraus-14850. No description available. 1830s.
Rarity: *None known*

$2 • **W-MS-690-002-G020**
Comments: H-Unlisted, Kraus-14851. No description available. 1830s.
Rarity: *None known*

$3 • **W-MS-690-003-G030** JM

Engraver: Western Bank Note Co. / Woodruff & Mason. ***Comments:*** H-Unlisted, Kraus-14852. 18__. 1830s.

Rarity: URS-3
F $2,000

$5 • **W-MS-690-005-G040**

Comments: H-Unlisted, Kraus-14853. No description available. 1830s.

Rarity: *None known*

$10 • **W-MS-690-010-G050**

Comments: H-Unlisted, Kraus-14854. No description available. 1830s.

Rarity: *None known*

Oswego, Mississippi

Oswego was historically known as Oswego Landing and was located in Holmes County, bordered by the Yazoo and Big Black rivers. Cotton and timber were primary industries. The town no longer exists today.

Bank of Vicksburg {1st} (branch)

1837–1840

W-MS-700

History: On May 3, 1837, the Bank of Vicksburg was incorporated with an authorized capital of $2,000,000. This amount was to be divided into shares of $100 apiece, with $500,000 in subscriptions being required before the bank could open. In 1840 an act was passed declaring the charter of the Bank of Vicksburg forfeit for a lack of paying out specie on notes presented for redemption.

The Bank of Vicksburg had its parent bank located in Vicksburg, W-MS-890, and a branch bank located in Woodville, W-MS-1010.

Numismatic Commentary: No validly issued notes are known for this branch. Notes with Oswego written in are filled-in remainders and not valid issues.

Issues

$5 • **W-MS-700-005-G010**

Left: FIVE vertically. ***Center:*** V / Liberty seated with eagle and shield / V. ***Right:*** FIVE vertically. ***Engraver:*** Underwood, Bald, Spencer & Hufty. ***Comments:*** H-Unlisted, Kraus-4400. 18__. 1830s.

Rarity: *None known*

$10 • **W-MS-700-010-G020**

Left: TEN vertically. ***Center:*** Mercury and Ceres seated at riverbank. ***Right:*** TEN vertically. ***Engraver:*** Underwood, Bald, Spencer & Hufty. ***Comments:*** H-Unlisted, Kraus-4401. 18__. 1830s.

Rarity: *None known*

$10 • **W-MS-700-010-G030**

Left: TEN vertically. ***Center:*** Woman seated by architectural building / 10 / Instruments / 10. ***Right:*** TENS vertically. ***Engraver:*** Underwood, Bald, Spencer & Hufty. ***Comments:*** H-Unlisted, Kraus-4420. 18__. 1830s.

Rarity: *None known*

$15 • **W-MS-700-015-G040**

Left: FIFTEEN / Cherub as Ceres / 15. ***Center:*** Medallion head / Commerce and Industry seated with amphora / Medallion head. ***Right:*** FIFTEEN / Cherub as Ceres / 15. ***Engraver:*** Underwood, Bald, Spencer & Hufty. ***Comments:*** H-MS-210-G36, Kraus-4421. 18__. 1830s.

Rarity: *None known*

$20 • **W-MS-700-020-G050**

Left: 20 / Man relaxing after harvest / 20. ***Center:*** Ceres and Proserpina flying. ***Right:*** XX / Indian seated / XX. ***Engraver:*** Underwood, Bald, Spencer & Hufty. ***Comments:*** H-MS-210-G38, Kraus-4422. 18__. 1830s.

Rarity: *None known*

$20 • **W-MS-700-020-G060**

Left: Liberty as Athena with shield. ***Center:*** Ceres seated on cotton bale with shield bearing cotton plant. ***Right:*** Liberty as Athena with shield. ***Engraver:*** Underwood, Bald, Spencer & Hufty. ***Comments:*** H-Unlisted, Kraus-4402. 18__. 1830s.

Rarity: *None known*

$20 • **W-MS-700-020-G070**

Left: Justice standing with sword / 20. ***Center:*** Ships. ***Right:*** Muse, Ship / 20. ***Engraver:*** Underwood, Bald, Spencer & Hufty. ***Comments:*** H-Unlisted, Kraus-4430. 18__. 1830s.

Rarity: *None known*

$25 • **W-MS-700-025-G080**

Left: 25 / Woman standing / 25. ***Center:*** Ceres, Commerce, and Industry seated / Medallion head / 25 / Medallion head. ***Right:*** 25 / Cherubs as Liberty and Ceres / 25. ***Engraver:*** Underwood, Bald, Spencer & Hufty. ***Comments:*** H-MS-210-G40, Kraus-4423. 18__. 1830s.

Rarity: *None known*

$50 • **W-MS-700-050-G090**

Left: Justice / 50. ***Center:*** Medallion head / Woman seated with tablet / Medallion head. ***Right:*** Justice / 50. ***Engraver:*** Underwood, Bald, Spencer & Hufty. ***Comments:*** H-Unlisted, Kraus-4403. 18__. 1830s.

Rarity: *None known*

$50 • **W-MS-700-050-G100**

Left: Ships. ***Center:*** Commerce seated at dock, Ships. ***Right:*** Ships. ***Engraver:*** Underwood, Bald, Spencer & Hufty. ***Comments:*** H-Unlisted, Kraus-4431. 18__. 1830s.

Rarity: *None known*

$100 • W-MS-700-100-G110

Left: Medallion head / 100 vertically / Medallion head. ***Center:*** 100 / Mercury seated at river holding caduceus / 100. ***Right:*** Medallion head / Cherub as Ceres / Medallion head. ***Engraver:*** Underwood, Bald, Spencer & Hufty. ***Comments:*** H-Unlisted, Kraus-4404. 18__. 1830s.

Rarity: *None known*

$500 • W-MS-700-500-G120

Left: Woman standing with caduceus and shield / 500 vertically. ***Center:*** Shield bearing cotton plant, Three cherubs, one as Ceres. ***Right:*** FIVE HUNDRED vertically. ***Engraver:*** Underwood, Bald, Spencer & Hufty. ***Comments:*** H-Unlisted, Kraus-4405. 18__. 1830s.

Rarity: *None known*

Non-Valid Issues

$20 • W-MS-700-020-N010

Comments: H-Unlisted, Kraus-4430e. Fraudulently issued. Filled-in remainder. 18__. 1830s.

Rarity: *None known*

Paulding, Mississippi

Paulding was named after Revolutionary War hero John Paulding. It is an unincorporated community in Jasper County. Settled in 1833, Paulding was for a time called the "Queen City of the East," but when the railway was planned, Paulding refused to pay for it. Thus the railway went through the western part of the county, and Paulding stagnated in growth.

Mississippi and Alabama Rail Road Company (branch)

1837–1841

W-MS-710

History: The Mississippi and Alabama Rail Road Company was chartered on February 9, 1836. The company was to lay a road from Brandon to Mobile. In 1838, with its circulation in need of redemption, the bank issued 70-day post notes payable in Philadelphia. It seemed the company was speculating in cotton, and by 1840 it was in trouble. The company evolved to become a bankrupt, fraudulent enterprise that ended poorly. Later certain elements became a part of the Southern Railroad Company.

The Mississippi and Alabama Rail Road Company had its parent bank located in Brandon, W-MS-070.

Valid Issues

$5 • W-MS-710-005-G010

JM

Back: Plain. ***Engraver:*** Draper, Toppan, Longacre & Co. ***Comments:*** H-MS-25-G70, Kraus-10140k. Handwritten "at" written over engraved "to" and handwritten "Paulding" in space for payee's name. 18__. 1838.

Rarity: —

$5 • W-MS-710-005-G010a

Back: Orange. ***Engraver:*** Draper, Toppan, Longacre & Co. ***Comments:*** H-MS-25-G70b, Kraus-Unlisted. Similar to W-MS-710-005-G010. 18__. 1838.

Rarity: URS-3
F $350

$5 • W-MS-710-005-G015

Left: 5 / Portrait of Stephen Girard / 5. ***Center:*** Moneta seated with treasure chest. ***Right:*** 5 / Portrait of Stephen Girard / 5. ***Engraver:*** Draper, Toppan, Longacre & Co. ***Comments:*** H-Unlisted, Kraus-Unlisted. 18__. 1830s.

Rarity: URS-3

$10 • W-MS-710-010-G020

Left: 10 / Train / 10. ***Center:*** Portrait of George Washington. ***Right:*** 10 / Train / 10. ***Back:*** Plain. ***Engraver:*** Draper, Toppan, Longacre & Co. ***Comments:*** H-MS-25-G72, Kraus-Unlisted. Handwritten "at" written over engraved "to" and handwritten "Paulding" in space for payee's name. 18__. 1838.

Rarity: —

$10 • W-MS-710-010-G020a

Back: Orange. ***Engraver:*** Draper, Toppan, Longacre & Co. ***Comments:*** H-MS-25-G72b, Kraus-Unlisted. Similar to W-MS-710-010-G020. 18__. 1838.

Rarity: URS-3
F $350

$10 • W-MS-710-010-G020b

Overprint: Black REISSUED stamp. ***Back:*** Orange. ***Engraver:*** Draper, Toppan, Longacre & Co. ***Comments:*** H-Unlisted, Kraus-Unlisted. Similar to W-MS-710-010-G020. 18__. 1838.

Rarity: —

$10 • W-MS-710-010-G025

Left: 10 / Portrait of George Washington / 10. ***Center:*** Spread eagle. ***Right:*** 10 / Portrait of Marquis de Lafayette / 10. ***Engraver:*** Draper, Toppan, Longacre & Co. ***Comments:*** H-Unlisted, Kraus-Unlisted. 18__. 1830s.

Rarity: URS-3

$20 • W-MS-710-020-G030

JM

Back: Plain. ***Engraver:*** Draper, Toppan, Longacre & Co. ***Comments:*** H-MS-25-G74, Kraus-10142k. Handwritten "at" written over engraved "to" and handwritten "Paulding" in space for payee's name. 18__. 1838.

Rarity: URS-5
F $125

$20 • W-MS-710-020-G030a

Overprint: Black REISSUED stamp. ***Back:*** Plain. ***Engraver:*** Draper, Toppan, Longacre & Co. ***Comments:*** H-MS-25-G74a, Kraus-Unlisted. Similar to W-MS-710-020-G030. 18__. 1838.

Rarity: URS-5
F $125

$20 • W-MS-710-020-G030b

Back: Orange. ***Engraver:*** Draper, Toppan, Longacre & Co. ***Comments:*** H-MS-25-G74b, Kraus-Unlisted. Similar to W-MS-710-020-G030. 18__. 1838.

Rarity: URS-4
F $150

$20 • W-MS-710-020-G030c

JM

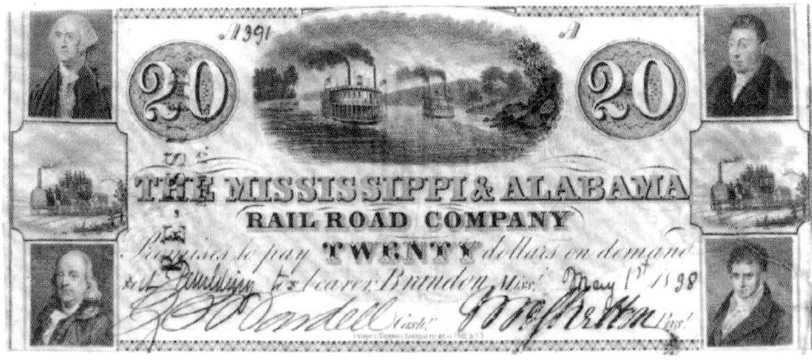

Overprint: Black REISSUED stamp. ***Back:*** Orange. ***Engraver:*** Draper, Toppan, Longacre & Co. ***Comments:*** H-Unlisted, Kraus-Unlisted. Similar to W-MS-710-020-G030. 18__. 1830s.

Rarity: URS-3
F $250

$20 • W-MS-710-020-G035

Left: Portrait of George Washington / 20 / Portrait of John Marshall. ***Center:*** 20 / Woman seated with child and plow / 20. ***Right:*** Portrait of Marquis de Lafayette / 20 / Portrait of Robert Fulton. ***Engraver:*** Draper, Toppan, Longacre & Co. ***Comments:*** H-Unlisted, Kraus-Unlisted. 18__. 1830s.

Rarity: URS-3

$25 • W-MS-710-025-G040

Left: Portrait of George Washington / Train / Portrait of Benjamin Franklin. ***Center:*** 25 / Three women seated / 25. ***Right:*** Portrait of Marquis de Lafayette / Train / Portrait of Robert Fulton. ***Back:*** Plain. ***Engraver:*** Draper, Toppan, Longacre & Co. ***Comments:*** H-MS-25-G76, Kraus-10123l. Handwritten "at" written over engraved "to" and handwritten "Paulding" in space for payee's name. 18__. 1838.

Rarity: —

$25 • W-MS-710-025-G040a

JM

Overprint: Black REISSUED stamp. ***Back:*** Plain. ***Engraver:*** Draper, Toppan, Longacre & Co. ***Comments:*** H-MS-25-G76a, Kraus-Unlisted. Similar to W-MS-710-025-G040. 18__. 1838.

Rarity: —

$25 • W-MS-710-025-G040b

JM

Back: Orange. ***Engraver:*** Draper, Toppan, Longacre & Co. ***Comments:*** H-MS-25-G76b, Kraus-Unlisted. Similar to W-MS-710-025-G040. 18__. 1838.

Rarity: —

$25 • W-MS-710-025-G040c

Overprint: Black REISSUED stamp. ***Back:*** Orange. ***Engraver:*** Draper, Toppan, Longacre & Co. ***Comments:*** H-Unlisted, Kraus-Unlisted. Similar to W-MS-710-025-G040. 18__. 1830s.

Rarity: —

$25 • W-MS-710-025-G045

Left: Portrait of George Washington / 25 / Portrait of John Marshall. ***Center:*** 25 / Train / 25. ***Right:*** Portrait of Marquis de Lafayette / 25 / Portrait of Robert Fulton. ***Engraver:*** Draper, Toppan, Longacre & Co. ***Comments:*** H-Unlisted, Kraus-Unlisted. 18__. 1830s.

Rarity: URS-3

$50 • **W-MS-710-050-G050**

JM

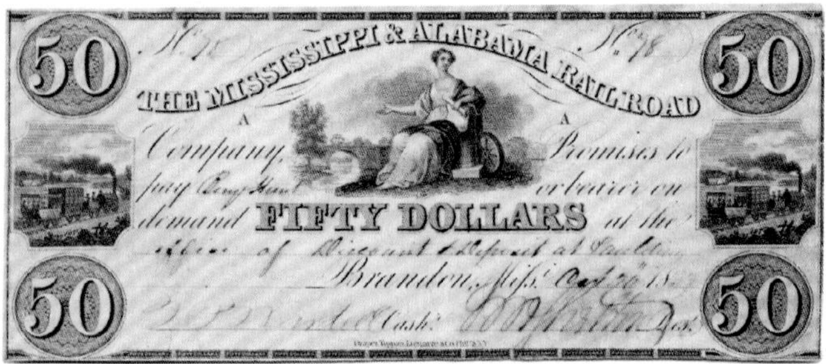

Engraver: Draper, Toppan, Longacre & Co. ***Comments:*** H-MS-25-G78, Kraus-Unlisted. Handwritten "at the office of Discount & Deposit at Paulding." 18__. 1837.

Rarity: URS-3
F $450

$50 • **W-MS-710-050-G060**

Left: 50 / Portrait of Robert Fulton / 50. ***Center:*** Portrait of Benjamin Franklin / Woman seated / Portrait of Benjamin Franklin. ***Right:*** 50 / Portrait of Robert Fulton / 50. ***Back:*** Plain. ***Engraver:*** Draper, Toppan, Longacre & Co. ***Comments:*** H-MS-25-G80, Kraus-10145k. Handwritten "at" written over engraved "to" and handwritten "Paulding" in space for payee's name. 18__. 1838.

Rarity: —

$50 • **W-MS-710-050-G060a**

Overprint: Black REISSUED stamp. ***Back:*** Plain. ***Engraver:*** Draper, Toppan, Longacre & Co. ***Comments:*** H-MS-25-G80a, Kraus-Unlisted. Similar to W-MS-710-050-G060. 18__. 1838.

Rarity: —

$50 • **W-MS-710-050-G060b**

JM

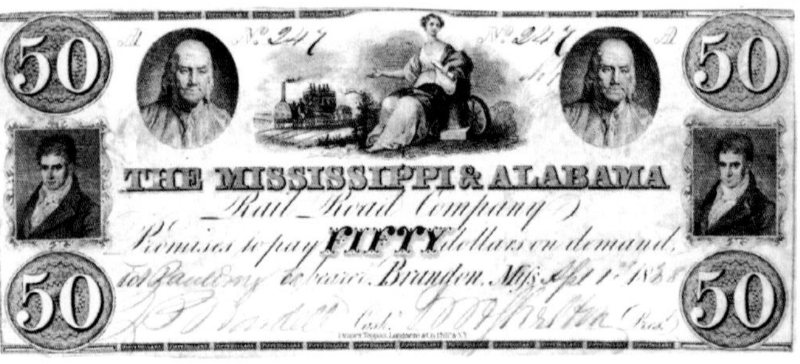

Back: Orange. ***Engraver:*** Draper, Toppan, Longacre & Co. ***Comments:*** H-MS-25-G80b, Kraus-Unlisted. Similar to W-MS-710-050-G060. 18__. 1838.

Rarity: URS-3
F $450

$50 • **W-MS-710-050-G060c**

Overprint: Black REISSUED stamp. ***Back:*** Orange. ***Engraver:*** Draper, Toppan, Longacre & Co. ***Comments:*** H-Unlisted, Kraus-Unlisted. Similar to W-MS-710-050-G060. 18__. 1830s.

Rarity: URS-3

$100 • **W-MS-710-100-G070**

CC

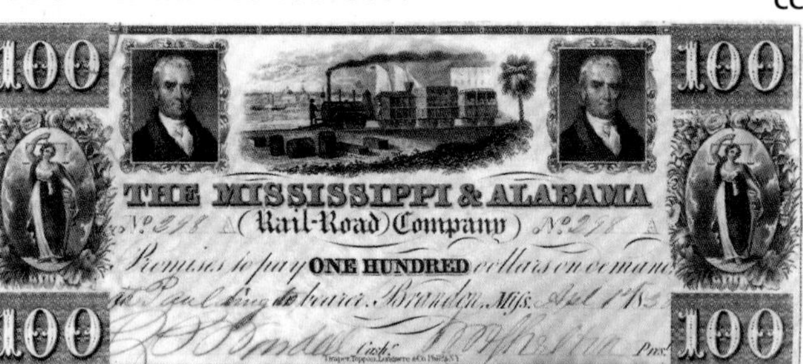

Back: Orange. ***Engraver:*** Draper, Toppan, Longacre & Co. ***Comments:*** H-MS-25-G82, Kraus-10146k. Handwritten "at" written over engraved "to" and handwritten "Paulding" in space for payee's name. 18__. 1838.

Rarity: URS-4
F $450

$100 • **W-MS-710-100-G070a**

JM

Overprint: Black REISSUED stamp. ***Back:*** Orange. ***Engraver:*** Draper, Toppan, Longacre & Co. ***Comments:*** H-Unlisted, Kraus-Unlisted. Similar to W-MS-710-100-G070. 18__. 1838.

Rarity: URS-4
F $450

$100 • **W-MS-710-100-G080**

Left: Justice standing / 100. ***Center:*** 100 / Commerce seated, Dog lying down, Train, Building / 100. ***Right:*** Justice standing / 100. ***Engraver:*** Draper, Toppan, Longacre & Co. ***Comments:*** H-Unlisted, Kraus-Unlisted. 18__. 1837.

Rarity: URS-3

Collectors and Researchers:

If you have new information about any banks or notes listed in this volume, contact Whitman Publishing, Attn: Obsolete Paper Money, 3101 Clairmont Road, Suite G, Atlanta, GA 30329.

Pontotoc, Mississippi

On February 9, 1836, Pontotoc was created from lands ceded to the United States as part of the departure of the Chickasaw Indians. The name of the town comes from a Chickasaw word for "land of hanging grapes." The Natchez Trace passed through Pontotoc, bringing trade and commerce to the town.

Agricultural Bank of Mississippi (branch)

1833–1840

W-MS-720

History: The Agricultural Bank of Mississippi was chartered on February 27, 1833, as the third bank to be established in Mississippi. It was authorized a capital of $2,000,000. In 1838 the bank suspended specie payments. In 1840 its charter was revoked due to its inability to abide by bank law.

The Agricultural Bank of Mississippi had its parent bank located in Natchez, W-MS-590.

Valid Issues

50¢ • W-MS-720-00.50-G005 JM

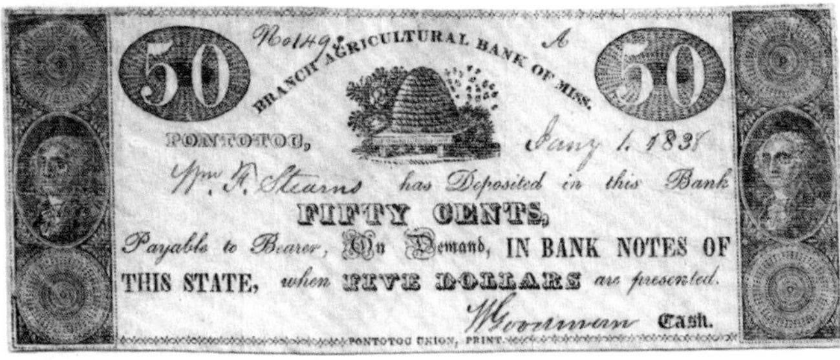

Engraver: Pontotoc Union Print. ***Comments:*** H-Unlisted. 183_. 1830s.

Rarity: —

$1 • W-MS-720-001-G010

Left: 1. ***Center:*** 1 / Cherub / 1. ***Right:*** U.S. silver dollar / ONE. ***Engraver:*** Rawdon, Wright & Hatch. ***Comments:*** H-Unlisted. 18__. 1830s.

Rarity: *None known*

$2 • W-MS-720-002-G020

Left: TWO / Cotton wagon pulled by oxen / 2. ***Center:*** 2 / Female portrait / Horse / 2. ***Right:*** TWO / Cotton wagon pulled by oxen / 2. ***Engraver:*** Rawdon, Wright & Hatch. ***Comments:*** H-Unlisted. 18__. 1830s.

Rarity: *None known*

$2 • W-MS-720-002-G020a

Back: Red-orange. ***Engraver:*** Rawdon, Wright & Hatch. ***Comments:*** H-Unlisted. Similar to W-MS-720-002-G020. 18__. 1830s.

Rarity: *None known*

$3 • W-MS-720-003-G030

Left: 3 / Portrait of George Washington / 3 vertically. ***Center:*** Boy with cattle and cotton wagon pulled by oxen. ***Right:*** 3 / Ceres at altar / 3 vertically. ***Engraver:*** Rawdon, Wright & Hatch. ***Comments:*** H-Unlisted. 18__. 1830s.

Rarity: *None known*

$3 • W-MS-720-003-G030a

Back: Red-orange. ***Engraver:*** Rawdon, Wright & Hatch. ***Comments:*** H-Unlisted. Similar to W-MS-720-003-G030. 18__. 1830s.

Rarity: *None known*

$5 • W-MS-720-005-G040

Left: V / Ceres seated with eagle / V. ***Center:*** 5 / Liberty holding pole and cap, Shield / 5. ***Right:*** FIVE / Industry seated with rake and shield / FIVE. ***Engraver:*** Rawdon, Wright & Hatch. ***Comments:*** H-Unlisted. 18__. 1830s.

Rarity: *None known*

$5 • W-MS-720-005-G040a

Back: Red-orange. ***Engraver:*** Rawdon, Wright & Hatch. ***Comments:*** H-Unlisted. Similar to W-MS-720-005-G040. 18__. 1830s.

Rarity: *None known*

$10 • W-MS-720-010-G050

Left: X / Ceres as Agriculture / 10. ***Center:*** TEN / Ship / TEN. ***Right:*** X / Man holding rifle, Dog / 10. ***Engraver:*** Rawdon, Wright & Hatch. ***Comments:*** H-Unlisted. 18__. 1830s.

Rarity: *None known*

$10 • W-MS-720-010-G050a

Back: Red-orange. ***Engraver:*** Rawdon, Wright & Hatch. ***Comments:*** H-Unlisted. Similar to W-MS-720-010-G050. 18__. 1830s.

Rarity: *None known*

$20 • W-MS-720-020-G060

Left: Wheat. ***Center:*** Archimedes lifting world with lever. ***Right:*** TWENTY vertically. ***Engraver:*** Rawdon, Wright & Hatch. ***Comments:*** H-Unlisted. Possibly made only as Proofs. 18__. 1830s.

Rarity: *None known*

$20 • W-MS-720-020-G060a

Back: Red-orange. ***Engraver:*** Rawdon, Wright & Hatch. ***Comments:*** H-Unlisted. Similar to W-MS-720-020-G060. 18__. 1830s.

Rarity: *None known*

$50 • W-MS-720-050-G070

Left: FIFTY vertically. ***Center:*** 50 / Ceres seated with wheat, Cattle / 50. ***Right:*** FIFTY vertically. ***Engraver:*** Rawdon, Wright & Hatch. ***Comments:*** H-Unlisted. Possibly made only as Proofs. 18__. 1830s.

Rarity: *None known*

$50 • W-MS-720-050-G070a

Back: Red-orange. ***Engraver:*** Rawdon, Wright & Hatch. ***Comments:*** H-Unlisted. Similar to W-MS-720-050-G070. 18__. 1830s.

Rarity: *None known*

$100 • W-MS-720-100-G080

Left: Statue of George Washington / 100. ***Center:*** Commerce holding branch, Eagle, Ships. ***Right:*** Woman leaning against column. ***Engraver:*** Rawdon, Wright & Hatch. ***Comments:*** H-Unlisted. 18__. 1830s.

Rarity: *None known*

$100 • W-MS-720-100-G080a

Back: Red-orange. ***Engraver:*** Rawdon, Wright & Hatch. ***Comments:*** H-Unlisted. Similar to W-MS-720-100-G080. 18__. 1830s.

Rarity: *None known*

Post Notes

$__ • W-MS-720-__-G090

Engraver: Rawdon, Wright, Hatch & Edson / Rawdon, Wright & Hatch. ***Comments:*** H-Unlisted. "500" or "1,000" written in. 18__. 1839 and 1840.

Rarity: *None known*

$5 • W-MS-720-005-G100

Engraver: Rawdon, Wright, Hatch & Edson / Rawdon, Wright & Hatch. ***Comments:*** H-Unlisted. 18__. 1839 and 1840.

Rarity: *None known*

$10 • W-MS-720-010-G110

Left: TEN vertically. ***Center:*** 10 / Ceres seated / 10. ***Right:*** Two cherubs as Liberty and Ceres, Mercury. ***Engraver:*** Rawdon, Wright, Hatch & Edson / Rawdon, Wright & Hatch. ***Comments:*** H-Unlisted. 18__. 1839 and 1840.

Rarity: *None known*

$20 • W-MS-720-020-G120

Left: TWENTY vertically. ***Center:*** 20 / Horse trotting / 20. ***Right:*** Commerce standing on shore, Eagle, Shield. ***Engraver:*** Rawdon, Wright, Hatch & Edson / Rawdon, Wright & Hatch. ***Comments:*** H-Unlisted. 18__. 1839 and 1840.

Rarity: *None known*

$50 • W-MS-720-050-G130

Left: FIFTY vertically. ***Center:*** 50 / Liberty reclining at river, Shield, Eagle / 50. ***Right:*** Riverboat, Cotton plants. ***Engraver:*** Rawdon, Wright, Hatch & Edson / Rawdon, Wright & Hatch. ***Comments:*** H-Unlisted. 18__. 1839 and 1840.

Rarity: *None known*

$100 • W-MS-720-100-G140

Left: ONE HUNDRED vertically. ***Center:*** 100 / Two farmers seated, Woman pouring water / 100. ***Bottom center:*** Dog and strongbox. ***Right:*** Farmer harvesting corn / 100. ***Engraver:*** Rawdon, Wright, Hatch & Edson / Rawdon, Wright & Hatch. ***Comments:*** H-Unlisted. 18__. 1839 and 1840.

Rarity: *None known*

Chickasaw Land Bank
1830s
W-MS-730

History: This is believed to have been an exchange house or office that issued notes based on real estate holdings. No record has been found of a state charter for this bank, and it is presumed it was a private enterprise. It is listed here for collector continuity.

Numismatic Commentary: Only the 25¢ and the 50¢ notes appear to be validly issued. The $1, $2, and $3 notes are known only as Proofs or remainders.

Valid Issues

25¢ • W-MS-730-00.25-G010

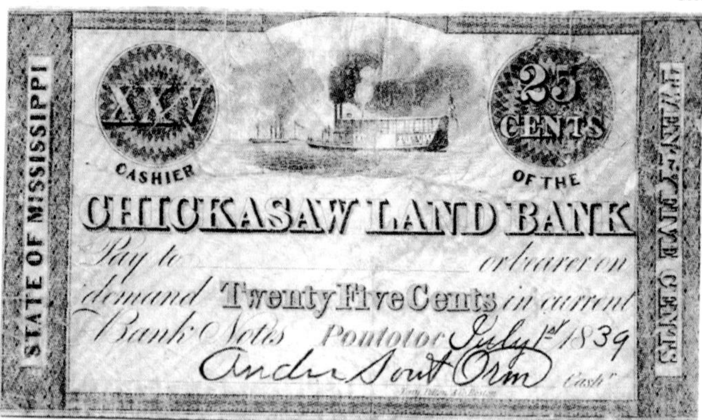

Engraver: Terry, Pelton & Co. ***Comments:*** H-Unlisted, Kraus-14880. 18__. 1830s.

Rarity: URS-3
F $2,500

50¢ • W-MS-730-00.50-G020

JM

Engraver: Terry, Pelton & Co. ***Comments:*** H-Unlisted, Kraus-14881. 18__. 1830s.

Rarity: URS-3
F $2,500

$1 • W-MS-730-001-G030

JM

Engraver: Terry, Pelton & Co. ***Comments:*** H-Unlisted, Kraus-14893. 18__. 1830s.

Rarity: URS-3
VF $2,400
Selected auction price: Heritage Auctions, April 23, 2015, Lot 19209, VF $2,350

$2 • W-MS-730-002-G040

JM

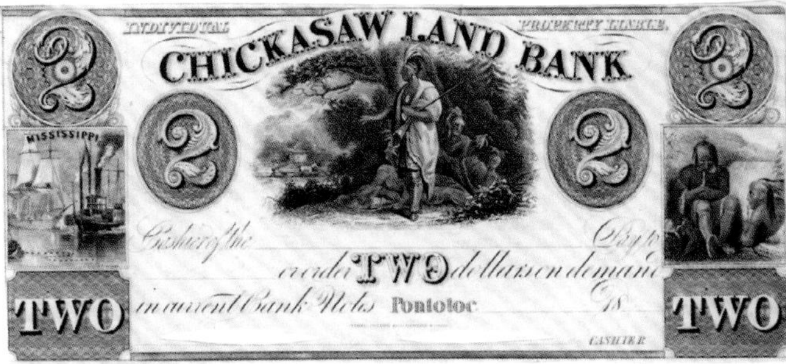

Engraver: Terry, Pelton & Co. ***Comments:*** H-Unlisted, Kraus-14894. 18__. 1830s.

Rarity: URS-2
F $3,000

$3 • W-MS-730-003-G050

JM

Engraver: Terry, Pelton & Co. ***Comments:*** H-Unlisted, Kraus-14895. 18__. 1830s.

Rarity: URS-2
F $2,000

Port Gibson, Mississippi

Port Gibson was chartered on March 12, 1803. It was originally settled in 1729 by French colonists. In 1843 the Port Gibson Female College was established, and the city rose in prosperity, with an economy strong in cotton and resulting industries. The wealth of the area saved it from destruction in the Civil War, as it was considered by General Ulysses S. Grant to be "too beautiful to burn."

Bank of Port Gibson

1837–1840s

W-MS-745

History: The Bank of Port Gibson was incorporated on May 11, 1837, with an authorized capital of $1,000,000. Large amounts of paper-money sheets were printed. The bank was located in a large stone building of Corinthian design, which is still standing today. The fate of the bank is unknown.

Numismatic Commentary: Valid, issued notes bearing the signatures of C.W. Mancaster (cashier) and N.N. Spencer (president) are very rare. Mancaster was cashier at the Lake Washington and Deer Creek Rail Road in Princeton, W-MS-800.

Uncut sheets of the Bank of Port Gibson were recycled during the Civil War—the plain backs of these notes were used to print other issues. This makes the $1-$2-$3-$5 sheet and issues very rare.

Valid Issues

$1 • W-MS-745-001-G010

JM

Engraver: Draper, Toppan, Longacre & Co. ***Comments:*** H-MS-185-G8, Kraus-4275. 18__. 1830s.

Rarity: URS-5
F $200

$2 • W-MS-745-002-G020

Left: TWO / Portrait of Henry Clay / 2. ***Center:*** Hope reclining on shore, Ship. ***Right:*** TWO / Portrait of Daniel Webster / 2. ***Engraver:*** Draper, Toppan, Longacre & Co. ***Comments:*** H-MS-185-G16, Kraus-4276. 18__. 1830s.

Rarity: *None known*

$3 • W-MS-745-003-G030

Left: THREE / Portrait of Henry Clay / 3. ***Center:*** Hope reclining on shore, Ship. ***Right:*** THREE / Portrait of Daniel Webster / 3. ***Engraver:*** Draper, Toppan, Longacre & Co. ***Comments:*** H-Unlisted, Kraus-4277. 18__. 1830s.

Rarity: *None known*

$5 • W-MS-745-005-G040

JM

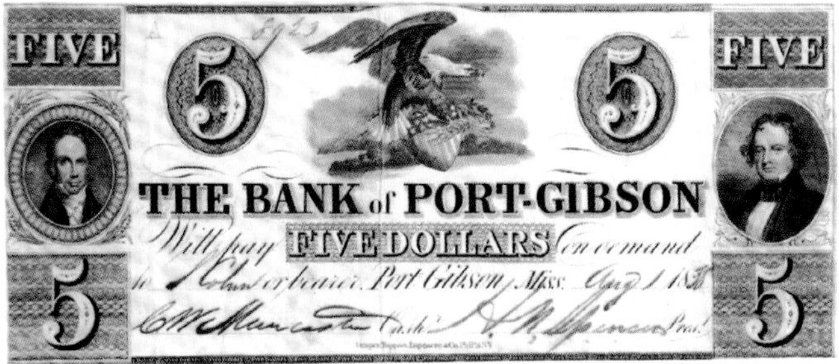

Engraver: Draper, Toppan, Longacre & Co. ***Comments:*** H-MS-185-G20, Kraus-4278. 18__. 1830s.

Rarity: URS-4
F $250

$10 • W-MS-745-010-G050

CC

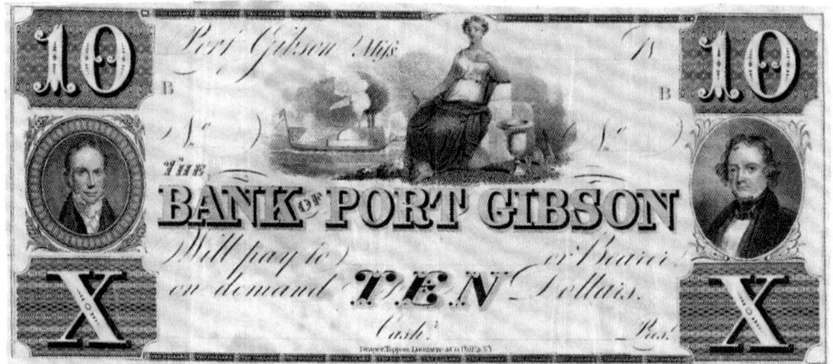

Engraver: Draper, Toppan, Longacre & Co. ***Comments:*** H-MS-185-G22, Kraus-4279r. 18__. 1830s.

Rarity: URS-7
F $250; **Unc-Rem** $250

$20 • W-MS-745-020-G060

CC

Engraver: Draper, Toppan, Longacre & Co. ***Comments:*** H-MS-185-G24, Kraus-4280. 18__. 1830s.

Rarity: URS-3
VF $475; **Unc-Rem** $250

Post Notes

$10 • W-MS-745-010-G070

JM

Overprint: Black POST NOTE stamp. ***Engraver:*** Draper, Toppan, Longacre & Co. ***Comments:*** H-Unlisted, Kraus-4279a. 18__. 1830s.

Rarity: URS-4
F $350

$20 • W-MS-745-020-G080

CC

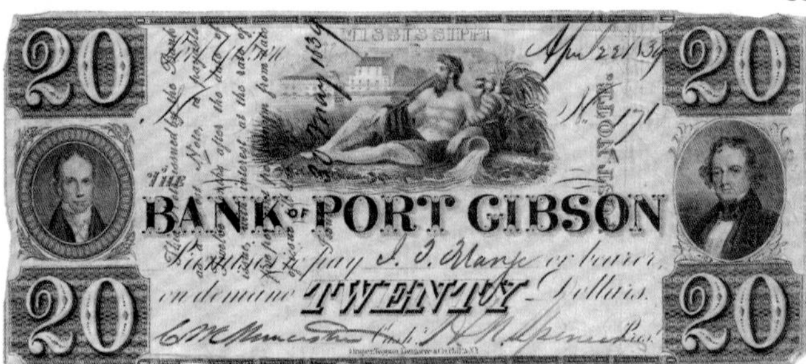

Overprint: Black POST NOTE stamp. ***Engraver:*** Draper, Toppan, Longacre & Co. ***Comments:*** H-Unlisted, Kraus-4280a. 18__. 1830s.

Rarity: URS-4
F $550

$50 • W-MS-745-050-G090

Left: 50 / Portrait of Henry Clay / 50. ***Center:*** 50 / Woman seated / 50. ***Right:*** 50 / Portrait of Daniel Webster / 50. ***Engraver:*** Draper, Toppan, Longacre & Co. ***Comments:*** H-MS-185-G26, Kraus-4281. 18__. 1830s.

Rarity: URS-3
F $350

$100 • W-MS-745-100-G100

Left: 100 / Portrait of Henry Clay / 100. ***Center:*** 100 / Eagle / 100. ***Right:*** 100 / Portrait of Daniel Webster / 100. ***Engraver:*** Draper, Toppan, Longacre & Co. ***Comments:*** H-MS-185-G28, Kraus-4282. 18__. 1830s.

Rarity: URS-3
F $350

Non-Valid Issues

$10 • W-MS-745-010-N010

Comments: H-Unlisted, Kraus-4279c. Fraudulently issued. Filled-in remainder. 18__. 1830s.

Rarity: —

$20 • W-MS-745-020-N020

Comments: H-Unlisted, Kraus-4280c. Fraudulently issued. Filled-in remainder. 18__. 1830s.

Rarity: —

Bank of the State of Mississippi (branch)

1818–1831

W-MS-760

History: On February 14, 1818, the Bank of the Mississippi, W-MS-600, was reorganized to become the Bank of the State of Mississippi. In 1830 the Planters Bank of the State of Mississippi, W-MS-670, was chartered in direct violation of a pledge made by the legislature to charter no other bank in the state. The managers of the Bank of the State of Mississippi wound up their institute as a result.

The Bank of the State of Mississippi had its parent bank located in Natchez, W-MS-620, and branch banks located in Vicksburg, W-MS-880, and Woodville, W-MS-1000.

Valid Issues

$5 • W-MS-760-005-G010

Left: 5 / 5 vertically. ***Center:*** River scene, Boat, Deer. ***Right:*** NATCHEZ vertically. ***Engraver:*** Murray, Draper, Fairman & Co. ***Comments:*** H-Unlisted. 18__. 1818–1820s.

Rarity: *None known*

$10 • W-MS-760-010-G020

Left: TEN vertically. ***Center:*** River scene, Boat, Deer. ***Right:*** NATCHEZ vertically. ***Comments:*** H-Unlisted. 18__. 1818–1820s.

Rarity: *None known*

$20 • W-MS-760-020-G030

Left: TWENTY vertically. ***Center:*** River scene, Boat, Deer. ***Right:*** NATCHEZ vertically. ***Engraver:*** Murray, Draper, Fairman & Co. ***Comments:*** H-Unlisted. 18__. 1818–1820s.

Rarity: *None known*

$50 • W-MS-760-050-G040

Left: FIFTY vertically. ***Center:*** River scene, Boat, Deer. ***Right:*** NATCHEZ vertically. ***Engraver:*** Murray, Draper, Fairman & Co. ***Comments:*** H-Unlisted. 18__. 1818–1820s.

Rarity: *None known*

$100 • W-MS-760-100-G050

Engraver: Murray, Draper, Fairman & Co. ***Comments:*** H-Unlisted, Kraus-1074. No description available. 18__. 1818–1820s.

Rarity: *None known*

Grand Gulf and Port Gibson Rail Road Company

1852–1862

W-MS-770

History: The Grand Gulf and Port Gibson Rail Road Company was incorporated on October 16, 1852, with an authorized capital of $100,000. The president was H.M. Spencer, who was also the president of the Bank of Port Gibson, W-MS-745, some 20 years earlier.

Valid Issues

10¢ • W-MS-770-00.10-G010 JM

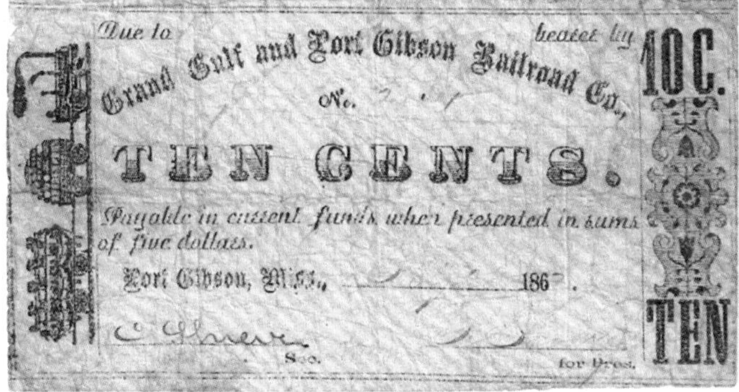

Comments: H-Unlisted, Kraus-52310. Printed in blue. 186_. 1830s–1840s.

Rarity: URS-5
F $250

25¢ • W-MS-770-00.25-G020 JM

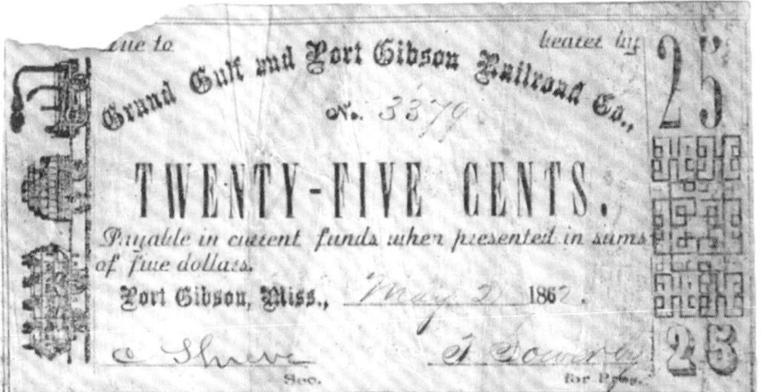

Comments: H-Unlisted, Kraus-52301. Printed in red. 186_. 1830s–1840s.

Rarity: URS-4
F $175

50¢ • W-MS-770-00.50-G030 JM

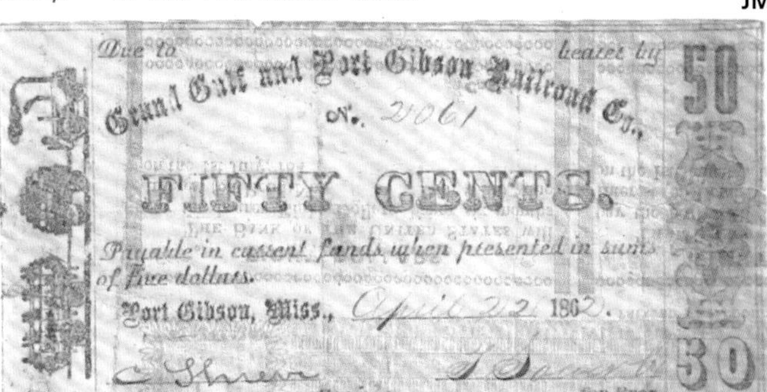

Comments: H-Unlisted, Kraus-52302. Printed in red. 186_. 1830s–1840s.

Rarity: URS-4
F $175

$1 • W-MS-770-001-G040 JM

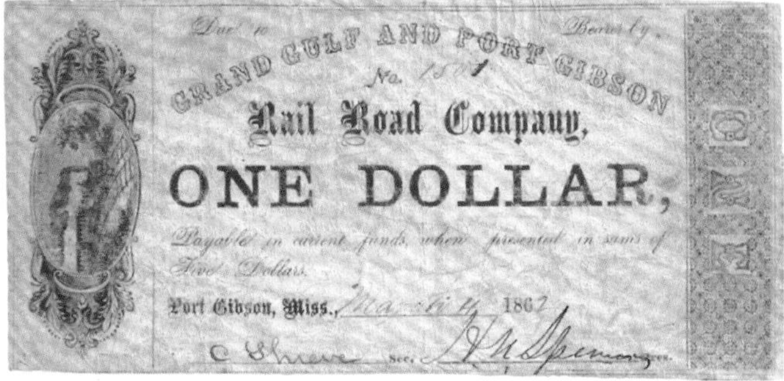

Comments: H-Unlisted, Kraus-52303. 186_. Printed in red. 1830s–1840s.

Rarity: URS-5
F $125

$1.25 • W-MS-770-001.25-G050 JM

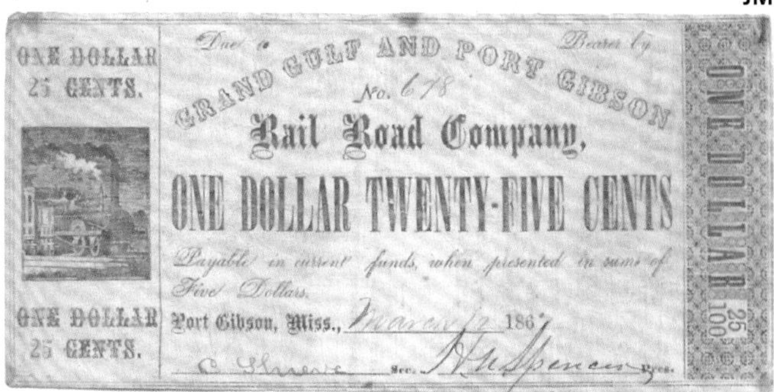

Comments: H-Unlisted, Kraus-52304. Printed in red. 186_. 1830s–1840s.

Rarity: URS-5
F $250

$2 • W-MS-770-002-G060

JM

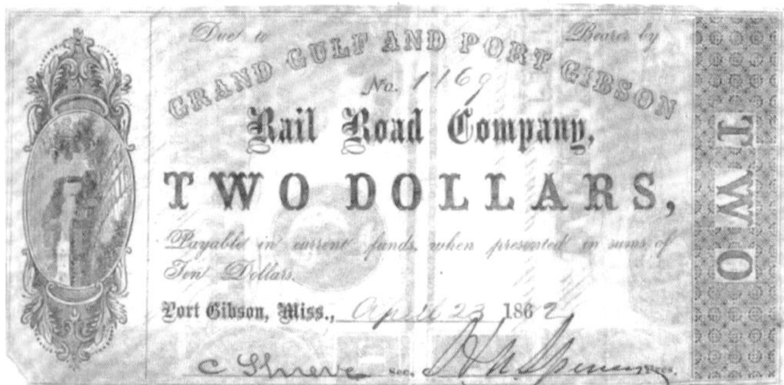

Comments: H-Unlisted, Kraus-52305. Printed in red. 186_. 1830s–1840s.

Rarity: URS-5
F $250

$2.50 • W-MS-770-002.50-G070

JM

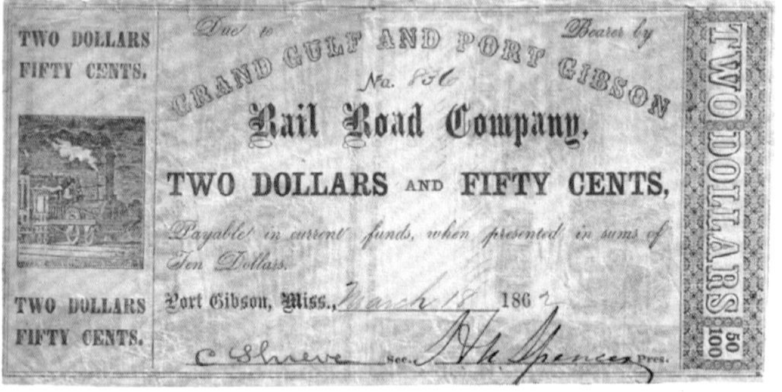

Comments: H-Unlisted, Kraus-52306. Printed in red. 186_. 1830s–1840s.

Rarity: URS-5
F $250

Planters Bank of the State of Mississippi (branch)

1830–1844

W-MS-780

History: The Planters Bank of the State of Mississippi was the second bank to be chartered in the state. It was incorporated on February 10, 1830, with an authorized capital of $3,000,000, $2,000,000 of which was provided from the state through the sale of bonds. The Panic of 1837 struck the bank hard. The state's bonds were repudiated, and the bank failed thereafter. On February 23, 1844, the bank was put into liquidation.

The Planters Bank of the State of Mississippi had its parent bank located in Natchez, W-MS-670, and branch banks located in Columbus, W-MS-240, Jackson, W-MS-470, Manchester, W-MS-555, Monticello, W-MS-580, Vicksburg, W-MS-920, Woodville, W-MS-1020, and Yazoo City, W-MS-1070.

Numismatic Commentary: Port Gibson is handwritten in on all notes from this branch.

Valid Issues

$5 • W-MS-780-005-G010

Left: 5 / FIVE vertically / 5. ***Center:*** 5 / Mercury in flight spreading coins from cornucopia / 5. ***Right:*** FIVE vertically. ***Engraver:*** Rawdon, Wright & Co. ***Comments:*** H-MS-175-G120, Kraus-4060. 18__. 1830s.

Rarity: URS-4
F $250

$10 • W-MS-780-010-G020

Left: 10 / Neptune pouring water from amphora / 10. ***Center:*** 10 / Justice and Liberty flanking shield bearing cotton plant and surmounted by eagle / 10. ***Right:*** 10 / Neptune pouring water from amphora / 10. ***Engraver:*** Rawdon, Wright & Co. ***Comments:*** H-MS-175-G122, Kraus-4061. 18__. 1830s.

Rarity: URS-4
F $250

$20 • W-MS-780-020-G030

JM

Engraver: Rawdon, Wright & Co. ***Comments:*** H-MS-175-G124, Kraus-4062. 18__. 1830s.

Rarity: URS-4
F $250

$20 • W-MS-780-020-G040

Left: Woman standing in niche / XX. ***Center:*** 20 / Two women flanking shield surmounted by eagle / 20. ***Right:*** Woman standing in niche / XX. ***Back:*** Red-brown. ***Engraver:*** Rawdon, Wright, Hatch & Co. ***Comments:*** H-MS-175-G126. 18__. 1830s.

Rarity: URS-4
F $250

$50 • W-MS-780-050-G050

Left: Justice standing with eagle bearing portrait of George Washington. ***Center:*** 50 / Woman standing with cotton bales and shield bearing cotton plant surmounted by eagle, Train / 50. ***Right:*** Two women standing. ***Engraver:*** Rawdon, Wright & Co. ***Comments:*** H-MS-175-G128, Kraus-4063. 18__. 1830s.

Rarity: URS-4
F $275

$50 • W-MS-780-050-G060

Left: Indian standing with bow / 50. ***Center:*** 50 / Ships / 50. ***Right:*** Indian standing with bow / 50. ***Back:*** Red-brown. ***Engraver:*** Rawdon, Wright, Hatch & Co. ***Comments:*** H-MS-175-G130. 18__. 1830s.

Rarity: URS-4
F $275

$100 • **W-MS-780-100-G070** JM

Engraver: Rawdon, Wright & Co. ***Comments:*** H-MS-175-G132, Kraus-4064. 18__. 1830s.

Rarity: URS-4
F $350

$100 • **W-MS-780-100-G080**

Left: 100 / Men with cattle / 100. ***Center:*** Portrait of George Washington / Woman seated in clouds with eagle bearing portrait of George Washington / Portrait of Benjamin Franklin. ***Right:*** 100 / Men with cattle / 100. ***Back:*** Red-brown. ***Engraver:*** Rawdon, Wright, Hatch & Co. ***Comments:*** H-MS-175-G134. 18__. 1830s.

Rarity: URS-4
F $350

PRINCETON, MISSISSIPPI

In the 1820s William Prince settled the area that would later become Princeton, his namesake. By 1830 the town was Washington County's seat, replacing New Mexico, which had fallen to the flooding of the Mississippi River. The town had a landing on the river, and in 1838 a steamboat exploded there, killing over 100 passengers. This and another explosion the same week pressed the government to legislate measures to be taken for the protection of passengers.

Princeton had a population of 600, as well as 12 stores, a bank, a school, a stable, and an inn. In 1844 the county seat was moved to Greenville, and the town began to decline. The Mississippi River slowly ate away at the town, and soon most of the area had caved in to the water.

Bank of Mississippi

1838–1860

W-MS-790

History: The Lake Washington and Deer Creek Rail Road and Banking Company, W-MS-800, was reorganized after being released of its obligation to construct a railroad, and its name was changed by an act approved on February 16, 1838, to become the Bank of Mississippi.

The Mississippi River began to change its course, disrupting the town of Princeton. On February 10, 1860, the Bank of Mississippi moved to Greenville, although it issued no notes there.

Numismatic Commentary: The $5, $10, and $20 notes are known only as remainders. The valid $50 and $100 notes are very rare. The $5-$5-$5-$5 and the $10-$10-$10-$20 sheets with plain backs were recycled to print other issues during the Civil War. This makes these sheets and the corresponding issues very rare.

VALID ISSUES

$5 • **W-MS-790-005-G010**

Left: Medallion head bearing 5 / FIVEs / Medallion head bearing 5 vertically. ***Center:*** Two women seated by urn, Sailing ship and factory. ***Right:*** Medallion head bearing 5 / FIVEs / Medallion head bearing 5 vertically. ***Engraver:*** Underwood, Bald, Spencer & Hufty. ***Comments:*** H-MS-195-G8, Kraus-4310. 18__. 1830s.

Rarity: URS-4
F $350

$10 • **W-MS-790-010-G020** CC

Engraver: Underwood, Bald, Spencer & Hufty. ***Comments:*** H-MS-195-G12, Kraus-4311. 1830s.

Rarity: URS-6
Unc-Rem $350

$20 • **W-MS-790-020-G030** JM

Engraver: Underwood, Bald, Spencer & Hufty. ***Comments:*** H-MS-195-G16, Kraus-4312. 1830s.

Rarity: URS-5
Unc-Rem $400

$50 • **W-MS-790-050-G040** CC

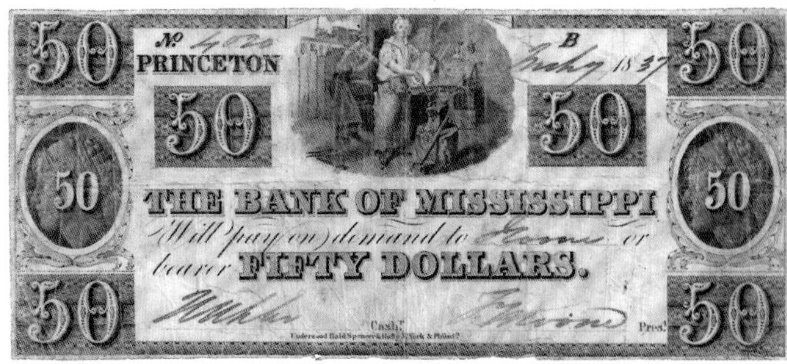

Engraver: Underwood, Bald, Spencer & Hufty. ***Comments:*** H-MS-195-G20, Kraus-4313. 1830s.

Rarity: URS-4
F $900; **Unc-Rem** $500

$100 • W-MS-790-100-G050 JM

Engraver: Underwood, Bald, Spencer & Hufty. ***Comments:*** H-MS-195-G24, Kraus-4314. 1830s.

Rarity: URS-3
G $250

Lake Washington and Deer Creek Rail Road and Banking Company

1836–1838

W-MS-800

History: The Lake Washington and Deer Creek Rail Road and Banking Company was incorporated on February 26, 1836, with an authorized capital of $600,000. Of this, $200,000 had to be subscribed to before the bank could open for business. The purpose of the company was to raise funds to lay a railway line from Lake Washington to Deer Creek. Using this railway, cotton would be moved from Princeton to shipping ports along the Mississippi River.

The Lake Washington and Deer Creek Rail Road and Banking Company was reorganized after being released of its obligation to construct a railroad, and its name was changed by an act approved on February 16, 1838, to become the Bank of Mississippi, W-MS-790. Unfortunately, only part of the railway was completed before the charter was repealed in 1839.[21]

How to Read the Whitman Numbering System

$1 • W-AL-020-001-G010a

Denomination: Face value of the note shown.

W: Whitman number. This number is a sortable code unique to each bank and note.

AL: Abbreviation for the state under study.

020: Numerical designation specific to each bank.

001: The denomination in dollars.

G010a: G indicates a good or valid note. Other categories are indicated thus: C (counterfeit); R (raised); S (spurious); N (not-attributed); A (altered). Numbers are assigned starting with 010, 020, et seq. Terminal letters following the number indicate variations of a note: a series of different colored overprints, tints, payees, etc., all on the same design of note. For more information, see the "How to Use This Book" section at the front of the volume, page xiv.

Numismatic Commentary: C.W. Mancaster, the cashier, became the cashier of the Bank of Port Gibson, W-MS-745.

Valid Issues

$5 • W-MS-800-005-G010 CC

Engraver: Underwood, Bald, Spencer & Hufty. ***Comments:*** H-MS-190-G4, Kraus-10490r. 18__. 1830s.

Rarity: URS-7
F $200; **Proof** $1,000

$10 • W-MS-800-010-G020 JM

Engraver: Underwood, Bald, Spencer & Hufty. ***Comments:*** H-MS-190-G6, Kraus-10491. 18__. 1830s.

Rarity: URS-7
F $250

$20 • W-MS-800-020-G030 CC

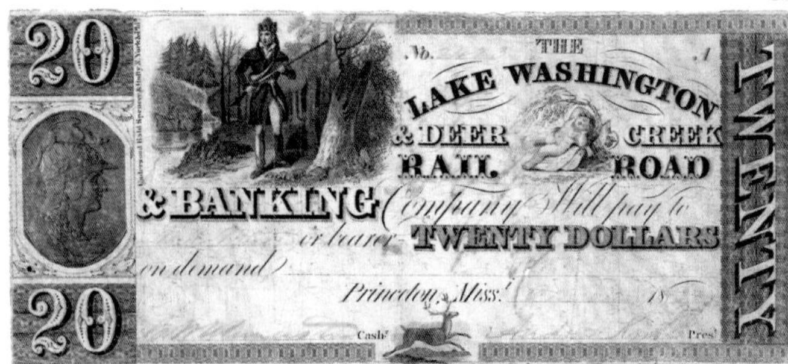

Engraver: Underwood, Bald, Spencer & Hufty. ***Comments:*** H-MS-190-G8, Kraus-10492. 18__. 1830s.

Rarity: URS-7
F $350

$50 • W-MS-800-050-G040 CC

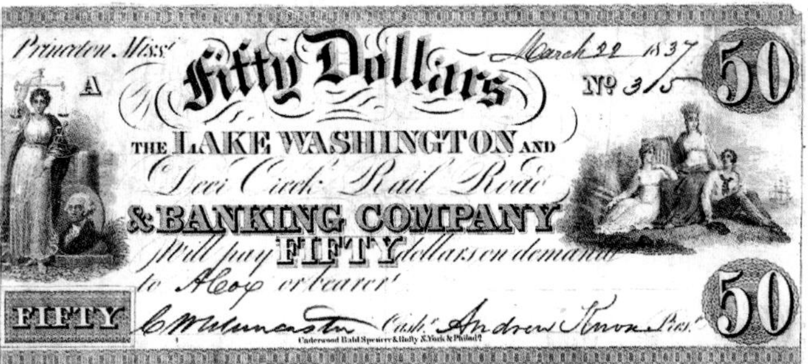

Engraver: Underwood, Bald, Spencer & Hufty. ***Comments:*** H-MS-190-G10, Kraus-10493. 18__. 1830s.

Rarity: URS-5
VF $600

$100 • W-MS-800-100-G050 CC

Engraver: Underwood, Bald, Spencer & Hufty. ***Comments:*** H-MS-190-G12, Kraus-10494. 18__. 1830s.

Rarity: URS-4
F $950

RAYMOND, MISSISSIPPI

The town of Raymond was settled to be the seat of Hinds County. It was selected in 1829 due to the fact that the original seat of the county was prone to flooding, and in 1830 the town received its charter. With a close proximity to the Natchez Trace, bringing trade and travel, Raymond prospered. During the 1840s a spring provided water that was sought by travelers for its healthful qualities, and in 1859 a new courthouse was built.

Mississippi Rail Road and Banking Company (branch)

1836–1841

W-MS-810

History: The Mississippi Rail Road and Banking Company (also seen as the Mississippi Rail Road Company on notes) was chartered on February 26, 1836. The bank had a positive net worth of $116,668.06 as of February 24, 1838. In 1840 it was reported that the bank could not redeem its notes, and in March 1841 this issuer, along with several others, had its charter revoked for this reason.

The Mississippi Rail Road and Banking Company had its parent bank located in Natchez, W-MS-650, and branches located in Canton, W-MS-110, and Gallatin, W-MS-320.

Numismatic Commentary: Notes that were issued validly are very rare.

VALID ISSUES

$5 • W-MS-810-005-G010

Left: Cotton plant / 5. ***Center:*** 5 / Train / 5. ***Right:*** Tree / 5. ***Overprint:*** Black RAYMOND stamp. ***Engraver:*** Draper, Toppan, Longacre & Co. ***Comments:*** H-MS-170-G52. 18__. 1838.

Rarity: URS-3
F $550

$10 • W-MS-810-010-G020

Left: Cotton plant / 10. ***Center:*** 10 / Train / 10. ***Right:*** Tree / 10. ***Overprint:*** Black RAYMOND stamp. ***Engraver:*** Draper, Toppan, Longacre & Co. ***Comments:*** H-MS-170-G54. 18__. 1838.

Rarity: URS-3
F $550

$20 • W-MS-810-020-G030 JM

Overprint: Black RAYMOND stamp. ***Engraver:*** Draper, Toppan, Longacre & Co. ***Comments:*** H-MS-170-G56, Kraus-10452g. 18__. 1838.

Rarity: URS-3
F $550

RODNEY, MISSISSIPPI

In January 1763 the area that would become Rodney was settled by the French. It was known at that time as Petit Gouffre, or "Little Gulf." Over the years it passed through British and Spanish control, until finally it was sold to Thomas Calvit in 1798. The town was settled, expanded, and finally renamed Rodney in 1828 in honor of Judge Thomas Rodney.

During the Civil War, some excitement took place in Rodney, and the local Presbyterian church was fired upon by a Union gunboat. However, Confederate forces regained control of the town, and the rest of the area received little damage.

Commercial Bank of Rodney

1836–1840

W-MS-820

History: The Commercial Bank of Rodney was incorporated on February 27, 1836, with an authorized capital of $800,000. *Niles' National Register* of February 24, 1838, reported that the bank had a positive net worth of $19,791.01. On February 22, 1840, the bank was forced to surrender its charter and banking privileges, on account of not paying specie to note holders.

Numismatic Commentary: Validly issued notes are very rare.

Valid Issues

$1 • W-MS-820-001-G010

JM

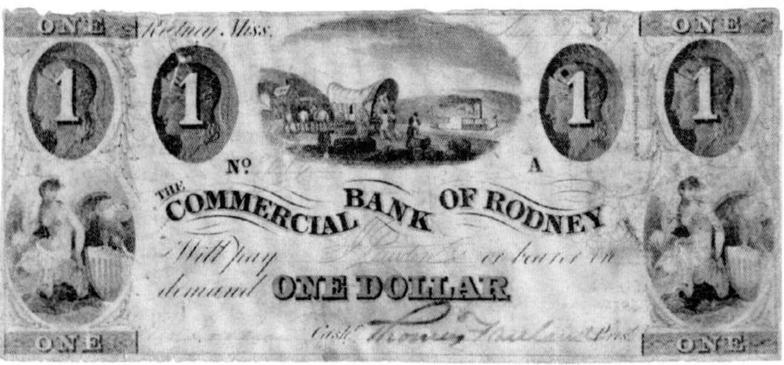

Engraver: Underwood, Bald, Spencer & Hufty. ***Comments:*** H-Unlisted, Kraus-4350. 18__. 1830s.

Rarity: URS-2
F $1,000

$2 • W-MS-820-002-G020

Left: Medallion head bearing TWO / Ceres seated in 2 / Medallion head bearing TWO. ***Center:*** Medallion head / Mercury sitting with Ceres at dock, Cargo / Medallion head. ***Right:*** Medallion head bearing TWO / Ceres seated in 2 / Medallion head bearing TWO. ***Engraver:*** Underwood, Bald, Spencer & Hufty. ***Comments:*** H-Unlisted, Kraus-4351. 18__. 1830s.

Rarity: URS-3
F $650

$3 • W-MS-820-003-G030

Left: THREE / Medallion head / Man with sickle, Ceres / THREE. ***Center:*** Medallion head / Riverboat / Medallion head. ***Right:*** THREE / Medallion head / "Pat Lyon at the Forge" / THREE. ***Engraver:*** Underwood, Bald, Spencer & Hufty. ***Comments:*** H-Unlisted, Kraus-4352. 18__. 1830s.

Rarity: URS-3
F $650

$5 • W-MS-820-005-G040

CC

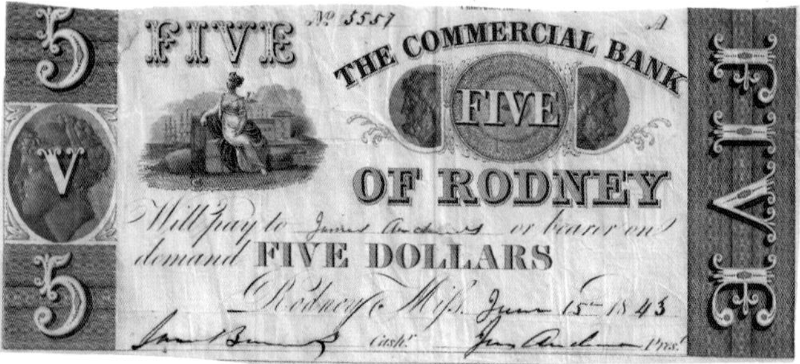

Engraver: Underwood, Bald, Spencer & Hufty. ***Comments:*** H-MS-200-G10, Kraus-4354. 18__. 1830s.

Rarity: URS-3
F $1,000

$10 • W-MS-820-010-G050

JM

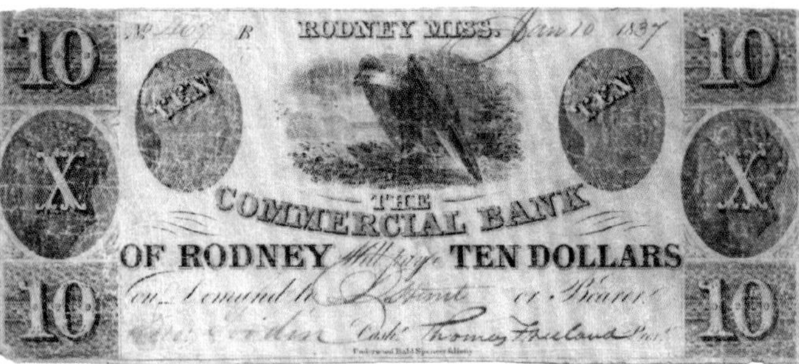

Engraver: Underwood, Bald, Spencer & Hufty. ***Comments:*** H-MS-200-G16, Kraus-4355. 18__. 1830s.

Rarity: URS-3
F $1,000

$20 • W-MS-820-020-G060

JM

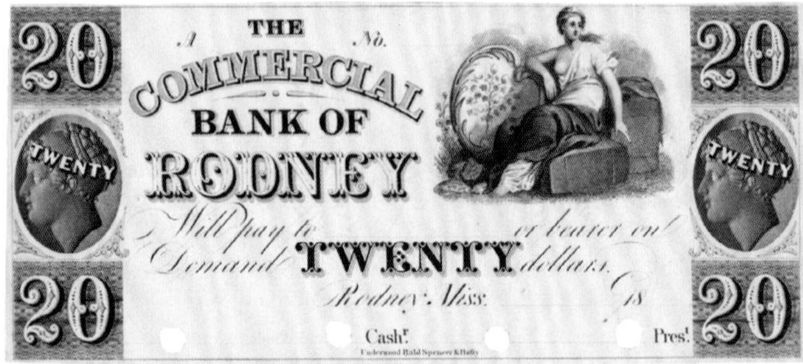

Engraver: Underwood, Bald, Spencer & Hufty. ***Comments:*** H-MS-200-G18, Kraus-4356. 18__. 1830s.

Rarity: URS-3
F $1,000; **Proof** $2,000
Selected auction price: Heritage Auctions, April 23, 2015, Lot 19210, Proof $2,585

$50 • W-MS-820-050-G070

JM

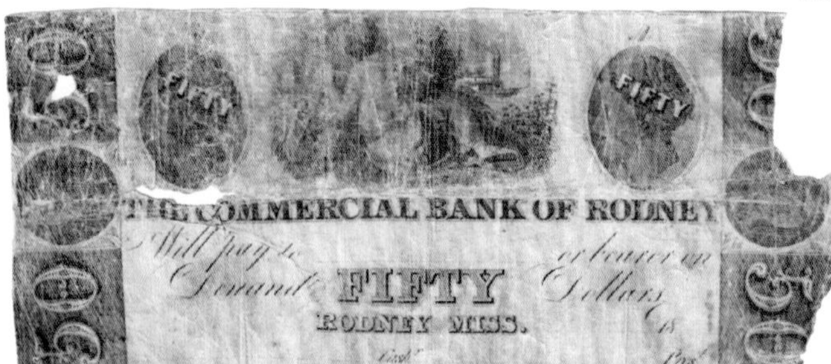

Engraver: Underwood, Bald, Spencer & Hufty. ***Comments:*** H-MS-200-G20, Kraus-4357. 18__. 1830s.

Rarity: URS-3
F $1,000

$100 • W-MS-820-100-G080 JM

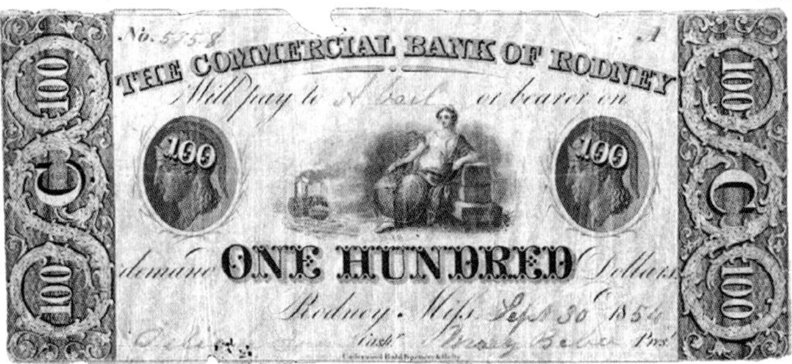

Engraver: Underwood, Bald, Spencer & Hufty. ***Comments:*** H-MS-200-G22, Kraus-4358. 18__. 1830s.

Rarity: URS-3
F $2,500; **Proof** $2,600

Post Notes

$__ • W-MS-820-__-G090 JM

Engraver: Underwood, Bald, Spencer & Hufty. ***Comments:*** H-Unlisted, Kraus-4353. "500" handwritten. 18__. 1830s.

Rarity: URS-3
F $1,000

$5 • W-MS-820-005-G100

Left: 5 / Medallion head bearing V / 5. ***Center:*** FIVE / Commerce sitting on bales of cotton, Ships and building / Medallion head / FIVE / Medallion head. ***Right:*** FIVE vertically. ***Engraver:*** Underwood, Bald, Spencer & Hufty. ***Comments:*** H-Unlisted, Kraus-4354b. 18__. 1830s.

Rarity: URS-3
F $1,000

Uncut Sheets

$10-$20-$50-$100 •
W-MS-820-010.020.050.100-US010

Vignette(s): ($10) Medallion head bearing X / Medallion heads / Eagle on log / Medallion heads/ Medallion head bearing X. ***($20)*** Medallion head bearing TWENTY / Commerce seated on cargo with shield bearing cotton plant / Medallion head bearing TWENTY. ***($50)*** Medallion head / Medallion head bearing FIFTY / Muse with lyre, River, steamboat, and building / Medallion head bearing FIFTY / Medallion head. ***($100)*** Medallion head bearing 100 / Commerce seated on cargo holding caduceus, Riverboat and building / Medallion head bearing 100. ***Engraver:*** Underwood, Bald, Spencer & Hufty. ***Comments:*** H-MS-200-G16, G18, G20, G22. 18__. 1830s.

Rarity: URS-3
EF $3,500

Non-Valid Issues

$100 • W-MS-820-100-R010

Center: Covered wagon at river. ***Engraver:*** Underwood, Bald, Spencer & Hufty. ***Comments:*** H-MS-200-R5, Kraus-4350b. Raised from $1. 18__. 1830s.

Rarity: URS-3
F $900

Shieldsboro, Mississippi

The area that would later become Bay Saint Louis was originally and formally known as Shieldsboro. A post office was established on October 11, 1819, under the Shieldsboro name. On April 27, 1875, the name was changed to Bay Saint Louis. The town overlooks the Bay of Saint Louis, its namesake, as well as the Mississippi Sound and the Gulf of Mexico.

For a long time the area was sparsely inhabited, but between 1813 and 1816 the territory was opened to potential settlers. There was an explosion of growth, and 3,300 families were reported to have moved from Virginia, Georgia, Tennessee, North Carolina, and South Carolina.

Commercial Bank of Natchez (branch)

1836–1856

W-MS-830

History: The Commercial Bank of Natchez was incorporated on February 27, 1836, with an authorized capital of $3,000,000. The bank was forbidden to distribute notes of a denomination lower than $5. The bank did not last long, and on February 6, 1841, an act was passed to close the branch banks and wind up the affairs of the parent bank. The closing of the bank was extended due to a battle with creditors that went all the way to the U.S. Supreme Court. Finally the bank went into liquidation in 1856.

The Commercial Bank of Natchez had its parent bank located in Natchez, W-MS-640, and branch banks located in Brandon, W-MS-060, Canton, W-MS-100, and Holmesville, W-MS-420.

Numismatic Commentary: No notes with the Shieldsboro location are known today. The following are speculative listings based on the parent bank.

Valid Issues

$5 • W-MS-830-005-G010

Left: FIVE vertically. ***Center:*** Two cherubs with U.S. flag as Liberty and Commerce, Ship. ***Right:*** FIVE vertically. ***Engraver:*** Underwood, Bald, Spencer & Hufty. ***Comments:*** H-Unlisted, Kraus-4020p. 18__. 1830s.

Rarity: *None known*

$10 • W-MS-830-010-G020

Left: TEN vertically. ***Center:*** 10 / Ships / 10. ***Right:*** TEN vertically. ***Engraver:*** Underwood, Bald, Spencer & Hufty. ***Comments:*** H-Unlisted, Kraus-4021p. 18__. 1830s.

Rarity: *None known*

$20 • W-MS-830-020-G030

Left: TWENTY vertically. ***Center:*** Medallion head bearing TWENTY / Mercury seated at river / Medallion head bearing TWENTY. ***Right:*** TWENTY vertically. ***Engraver:*** Underwood, Bald, Spencer & Hufty. ***Comments:*** H-Unlisted, Kraus-4022p. 18__. 1830s.

Rarity: *None known*

$50 • W-MS-830-050-G040

Left: Athena as Liberty with U.S. shield and spear / FIFTY. ***Center:*** Medallion head bearing FIFTY / Neptune seated on sea / Medallion head bearing FIFTY. ***Right:*** Athena as Liberty with U.S. shield and spear / FIFTY. ***Engraver:*** Underwood, Bald, Spencer & Hufty. ***Comments:*** H-Unlisted, Kraus-4023p. 18__. 1830s.

Rarity: *None known*

$100 • W-MS-830-100-G050

Left: Woman standing with medallion head and caduceus / 100. ***Center:*** Medallion head bearing 100 / Indian in canoe / Medallion head bearing 100. ***Right:*** Woman standing with medallion head and caduceus / 100. ***Engraver:*** Underwood, Bald, Spencer & Hufty. ***Comments:*** H-Unlisted, Kraus-4024p. 18__. 1830s.

Rarity: *None known*

STARKVILLE, MISSISSIPPI

The first inhabitants of the land that later made up Starkville were the Choccuma Indians. Later the Choctaw and Chickasaw allied together and drove out the tribe, only to be displaced themselves in the 1830s with the Indian Removal Act and the various land treaties that were affecting Native Americans all across the South.

Settlers started arriving in the area, attracted by two springs which provided a place for mills. One of these mills produced clapboards, after which the town was known as Boardtown. In 1835 its name was changed to honor General John Stark when it became the county seat of Oktibbeha.

Real Estate Banking Company of Starkville

1830s–1860s

W-MS-840

History: This was an exchange house that issued notes based on real estate holdings. No record has been found of a state charter for this bank, and it is presumed it was a private enterprise. It is listed here for collector continuity.

Numismatic Commentary: Validly issued notes are very rare.

VALID ISSUES

$5 • W-MS-840-005-G010 JM

Engraver: Argus Print. ***Comments:*** H-Unlisted, Kraus-14930. 183_. 1830s.

Rarity: URS-3
F $550

$10 • W-MS-840-010-G020 JM

Engraver: Argus Print. ***Comments:*** H-Unlisted, Kraus-14931. 183_. 1830s.

Rarity: URS-4
F $750

$20 • W-MS-840-020-G030

Comments: H-Unlisted, Kraus-14932. No description available. 18__. 1862.

Rarity: *None known*

$20 • W-MS-840-020-G040

Comments: H-Unlisted, Kraus-14952. No description available. 18__. 1862.

Rarity: *None known*

$25 • W-MS-840-025-G050 JM

Engraver: Argus Print. ***Comments:*** H-Unlisted, Kraus-14933. 183_. 1830s.

Rarity: URS-4
F $750

$50 • **W-MS-840-050-G060** JM

Engraver: Argus Print. ***Comments:*** H-Unlisted, Kraus-14934. 183_. 1830s.

Rarity: URS-3
F $1,000

$50 • **W-MS-840-050-G070**

Comments: H-Unlisted, Kraus-14953. No description available. 18__. 1862.

Rarity: *None known*

$100 • **W-MS-840-100-G080**

Comments: H-Unlisted, Kraus-14935. No description available. 18__. 1862.

Rarity: *None known*

$100 • **W-MS-840-100-G090**

Comments: H-Unlisted, Kraus-14954. No description available. 18__. 1862.

Rarity: *None known*

Post Notes

$5 • **W-MS-840-005-G100** JM

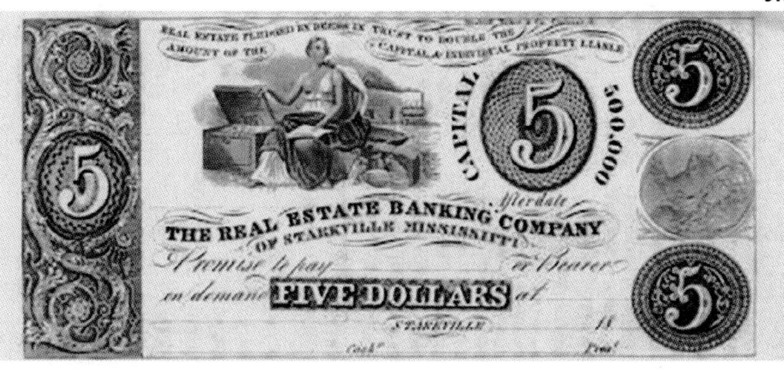

Engraver: Woodruff, Tucker & Co. ***Comments:*** H-Unlisted, Kraus-14950r. 18__. 1860s.

Rarity: URS-4
Proof $1,000

$10 • **W-MS-840-010-G110** JM

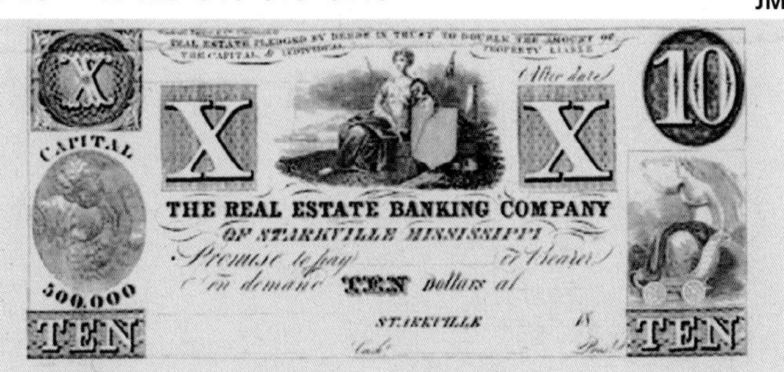

Engraver: Woodruff, Tucker & Co. ***Comments:*** H-Unlisted, Kraus-14951. 18__. 1862.

Rarity: URS-4
Proof $1,000

Non-Valid Issues

$10 • **W-MS-840-010-N010**

Comments: H-Unlisted, Kraus-14951b. Fraudulently issued. Filled-in remainder. 1830s.

Rarity: —

Utica, Mississippi

That land that made up Utica was settled in 1809. It was originally known as Cane Ridge because of the number of canebrakes in the area. By 1835 the name was changed to Utica, after Utica, New York. It had a post office and was surrounded by farmlands which produced fruits and vegetables and hardwood timber. Cotton was a profitable export. There were two banks, two hotels, a school, an industrial college, three churches, and various mills.

Citizens Bank of Madison County (branch)

1837–1840

W-MS-850

History: The Citizens Bank of Madison County was incorporated on May 3, 1837, with an authorized capital of $1,000,000. In 1840 an act was passed forcing the bank to forfeit its charter due to its failure to pay specie when its notes were presented for redemption.

The Citizens Bank of Madison County had its parent bank located in Canton, W-MS-090, and a branch bank located in Livingston, W-MS-500.

Numismatic Commentary: The notes listed below are speculative based on the parent bank. No notes with this branch imprint are known today.

Valid Issues

25¢ • **W-MS-850-00.25-G010**

Left: CENTS / 2-reales coin / 25. ***Center:*** 25 / Riverboat / 25. ***Right:*** Venus rising from the sea. ***Engraver:*** Rawdon, Wright & Hatch. ***Comments:*** H-Unlisted, Kraus-3341r. 18__. 1838.

Rarity: *None known*

50¢ • **W-MS-850-00.50-G020**

Left: CENTS / Cherub / 50. ***Center:*** 50 / Farmer plowing with two horses / 50. ***Right:*** FIFTY CENTS / HALF A DOLLAR / 4-reales coin / 50. ***Engraver:*** Rawdon, Wright & Hatch. ***Comments:*** H-Unlisted, Kraus-3342r. 18__. 1838.

Rarity: *None known*

$1 • **W-MS-850-001-G030**

Left: Justice and Liberty with eagle flanking state arms. ***Center:*** Liberty with pole and cap, Shield and eagle. ***Right:*** ONE / U.S. dollar coin / ONE. ***Engraver:*** Rawdon, Wright & Hatch. ***Comments:*** H-Unlisted, Kraus-3343. 18__. 1838.

Rarity: *None known*

$2 • W-MS-850-002-G040

Left: U.S. silver dollar. ***Center:*** Riverboat, Mule wagon. ***Right:*** Woman with wheat at altar. ***Engraver:*** Rawdon, Wright & Hatch. ***Comments:*** H-Unlisted, Kraus-3344. 18__. 1838.

Rarity: *None known*

$5 • W-MS-850-005-G050

Left: 5. ***Center:*** Commerce seated with eagle. ***Right:*** 5. ***Engraver:*** Rawdon, Wright & Hatch. ***Comments:*** H-Unlisted, Kraus-3345. 18__. 1838.

Rarity: *None known*

$10 • W-MS-850-010-G060

Left: 10. ***Center:*** Mercury, goddess, and warrior in clouds. ***Right:*** 10. ***Engraver:*** Rawdon, Wright & Hatch. ***Comments:*** H-Unlisted, Kraus-3346. 18__. 1838.

Rarity: *None known*

$20 • W-MS-850-020-G070

Left: TWENTY vertically. ***Center:*** Steamboat. ***Right:*** Vulcan, Mercury, and Ceres sitting / XX. ***Engraver:*** Rawdon, Wright & Hatch. ***Comments:*** H-Unlisted, Kraus-3347. 18__. 1838.

Rarity: *None known*

$50 • W-MS-850-050-G080

Left: Mercury and Commerce with griffin / 50. ***Center:*** L / Steamboat / L. ***Right:*** 50 / Steam and sailing ships / 50. ***Engraver:*** Rawdon, Wright & Hatch. ***Comments:*** H-Unlisted, Kraus-3348. 18__. 1838.

Rarity: *None known*

$100 • W-MS-850-100-G090

Left: 100 / Vulcan, Commerce, Trade, and eagle / 100. ***Center:*** C / Commerce and Ceres seated with mirror, Cornucopia and ships. ***Right:*** C / 100. ***Engraver:*** Rawdon, Wright & Hatch. ***Comments:*** H-Unlisted, Kraus-3349. 18__. 1838.

Rarity: *None known*

Non-Valid Issues

$100 • W-MS-850-100-N010

Comments: H-Unlisted, Kraus-3349d. Fraudulently issued note during the Confederate period. 18__. 1838.

Rarity: *None known*

Commercial and Rail Road Bank of Vicksburg (branch)

1831–1840

W-MS-860

History: The Commercial and Rail Road Bank of Vicksburg (also seen in print as the Commercial Railroad and Banking Company) was incorporated on December 19, 1831, under the name of the Clinton and Vicksburg Rail Road Company. It had an authorized capital of $4,000,000. On January 28, 1836, it was reincorporated with the name of Commercial and Rail Road Bank of Vicksburg. It was to lay a railway from Vicksburg to Clinton, and of the three other railroad and banking companies in the state and decade, it was the only one to complete its task. By 1840 there were 54 miles of railroad completed.[22] In the year before the railway's completion, the company began winding up its banking affairs. In 1839 it was reported that the bank had suspended specie payments and that the stock held in New York and Philadelphia had been running down.[23] With the railroad finished, the bank finalized its affairs and closed.

The Commercial and Rail Road Bank of Vicksburg had its parent bank located in Vicksburg, W-MS-910, and branch banks located in Clinton, W-MS-150, and Vernon, W-MS-870.

Vernon, Mississippi

Vernon, located west of Livingston, was incorporated in 1833. It was inhabited by wealthy planters and slave owners.

Commercial and Rail Road Bank of Vicksburg (branch)

1831–1840

W-MS-870

History: The Commercial and Rail Road Bank of Vicksburg (also seen in print as the Commercial Railroad and Banking Company) was incorporated on December 19, 1831, under the name of the Clinton and Vicksburg Rail Road Company. It had an authorized capital of $4,000,000. On January 28, 1836, it was reincorporated with the name of Commercial and Rail Road Bank of Vicksburg. It was to lay a railway from Vicksburg to Clinton, and of the three other railroad and banking companies in the state and decade, it was the only one to complete its task. By 1840 there were 54 miles of railroad completed.[24] In the year before the railway's completion, the company began winding up its banking affairs. In 1839 it was reported that the bank had suspended specie payments and that the stock held in New York and Philadelphia had been running down.[25] With the railroad finished, the bank finalized its affairs and closed.

The Commercial and Rail Road Bank of Vicksburg had its parent bank located in Vicksburg, W-MS-910, and branch banks located in Clinton, W-MS-150, and Utica, W-MS-860.

Numismatic Commentary: Validly issued notes from this branch are extremely rare.

Valid Issues

$5 • W-MS-870-005-G010

JM

Engraver: Underwood, Bald, Spencer & Hufty. ***Comments:*** H-MS-205-G44, Kraus-10584b. 18__. 1830s.

Rarity: URS-4

F $750

$10 • W-MS-870-010-G020

Left: 10 / Medallion head / 10. ***Center:*** 10 / Neptune seated, Ship / X. ***Right:*** X / Medallion head / X. ***Engraver:*** Underwood, Bald, Spencer & Hufty. ***Comments:*** H-MS-205-G46, Kraus-10585b. 18__. 1830s.

Rarity: *None known*

$20 • W-MS-870-020-G030

Left: 20 / Medallion head / 20. ***Center:*** 20 / Sailor standing on dock holding flag / 20. ***Right:*** 20 / Medallion head / 20. ***Engraver:*** Underwood, Bald, Spencer & Hufty. ***Comments:*** H-MS-205-G48, Kraus-10586b. 18__. 1830s.

Rarity: *None known*

$50 • W-MS-870-050-G040

Left: 50 / Portrait of Dewitt Clinton / 50. ***Center:*** Train, Riverboat, Alligator / 50. ***Right:*** FIFTY vertically. ***Engraver:*** Rawdon, Wright, Hatch & Edson. ***Comments:*** H-MS-205-G50, Kraus-10595b. 18__. 1830s.

Rarity: *None known*

$100 • W-MS-870-100-G050

Left: ONE HUNDRED vertically. ***Center:*** 100 / Liberty seated with shield, Ship / 100. ***Right:*** ONE HUNDRED vertically. ***Engraver:*** Rawdon, Wright, Hatch & Edson. ***Comments:*** H-MS-205-G52, Kraus-10596b. 18__. 1830s.

Rarity: *None known*

VICKSBURG, MISSISSIPPI

First settled by French colonists, the area that later became Vicksburg was inhabited by Native Americans for many decades after the original colony was attacked and destroyed. In 1801 much of the land was ceded to the United States, and in 1825 the village of Walnut Hills was incorporated as Vicksburg. Its name was in honor of Newitt Vick, a missionary of the area. In 1835 there was a mob as inhabitants of the city tried to force out all gamblers. In the end five men were hanged for shooting and killing a doctor.

After an extended siege, Vicksburg surrendered during the Civil War, allowing the Union army to control the Mississippi River. This surrender and the defeat of Confederate general Robert E. Lee at Gettysburg is considered to be the turning point of the Civil War.

Bank of the State of Mississippi (branch)

1818–1831

W-MS-880

History: On February 14, 1818, the Bank of the Mississippi, W-MS-600, was reorganized to become the Bank of the State of Mississippi. In 1830 the Planters Bank of the State of Mississippi, W-MS-670, was chartered in direct violation of a pledge made by the legislature to charter no other bank in the state. The managers of the Bank of the State of Mississippi wound up their institute as a result.

The Bank of the State of Mississippi had its parent bank located in Natchez, W-MS-620, and branch banks located in Port Gibson, W-MS-760, and Woodville, W-MS-1000.

Numismatic Commentary: No issued notes are known. The following listings are speculative based on the parent bank.

VALID ISSUES

$5 • W-MS-880-005-G010

Left: 5 / 5 vertically. ***Center:*** River scene, Boat, Deer. ***Right:*** NATCHEZ vertically. ***Engraver:*** Murray, Draper, Fairman & Co. ***Comments:*** H-Unlisted. 18__. 1818–1820s.

Rarity: *None known*

$10 • W-MS-880-010-G020

Left: TEN vertically. ***Center:*** River scene, Boat, Deer. ***Right:*** NATCHEZ vertically. ***Comments:*** H-Unlisted. 18__. 1818–1820s.

Rarity: *None known*

$20 • W-MS-880-020-G030

Left: TWENTY vertically. ***Center:*** River scene, Boat, Deer. ***Right:*** NATCHEZ vertically. ***Engraver:*** Murray, Draper, Fairman & Co. ***Comments:*** H-Unlisted. 18__. 1818–1820s.

Rarity: *None known*

$50 • W-MS-880-050-G040

Left: FIFTY vertically. ***Center:*** River scene, Boat, Deer. ***Right:*** NATCHEZ vertically. ***Engraver:*** Murray, Draper, Fairman & Co. ***Comments:*** H-Unlisted. 18__. 1818–1820s.

Rarity: *None known*

$100 • W-MS-880-100-G050

Engraver: Murray, Draper, Fairman & Co. ***Comments:*** H-Unlisted, Kraus-1074. No description available. 18__. 1818–1820s.

Rarity: *None known*

Bank of Vicksburg {1st}

1837–1840

W-MS-890

History: On May 3, 1837, the first Bank of Vicksburg was incorporated with an authorized capital of $2,000,000. This amount was to be divided into shares of $100 apiece, with $500,000 in subscriptions being required before the bank could open. In 1840 an act was passed declaring the charter of the Bank of Vicksburg forfeit for failing to redeem its notes in specie when presented.

The Bank of Vicksburg had branch banks located in Oswego, W-MS-700, and Woodville, W-MS-1010.

Valid Issues

$5 • W-MS-890-005-G010

CC

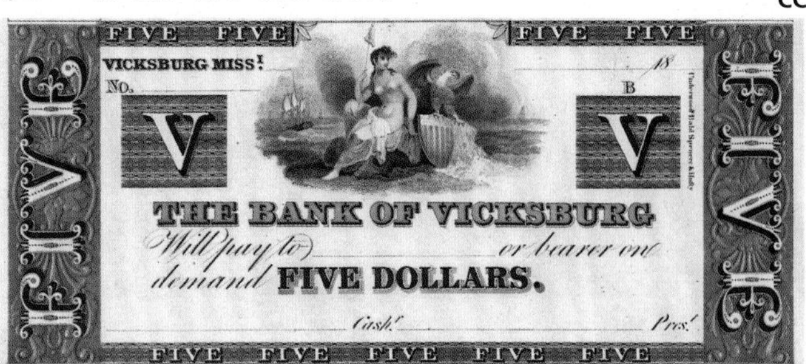

Engraver: Underwood, Bald, Spencer & Hufty. ***Comments:*** H-MS-210-G8, Kraus-4400. 18__. 1830s.

Rarity: URS-3
Proof $1,500

$10 • W-MS-890-010-G020

CC

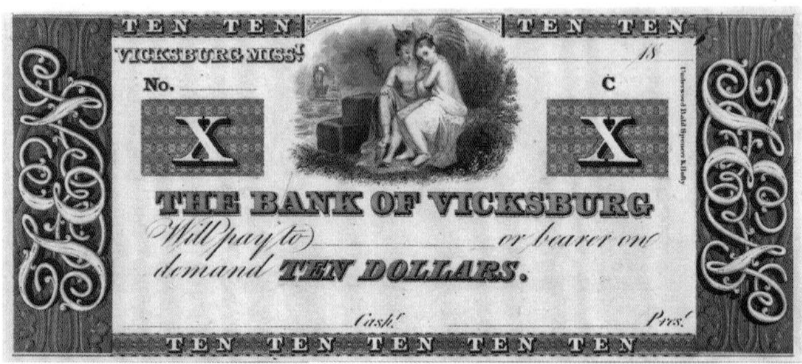

Engraver: Underwood, Bald, Spencer & Hufty. ***Comments:*** H-MS-210-G10, Kraus-4401. 18__. 1830s.

Rarity: URS-3
Proof $1,250

$10 • W-MS-890-010-G030

CC

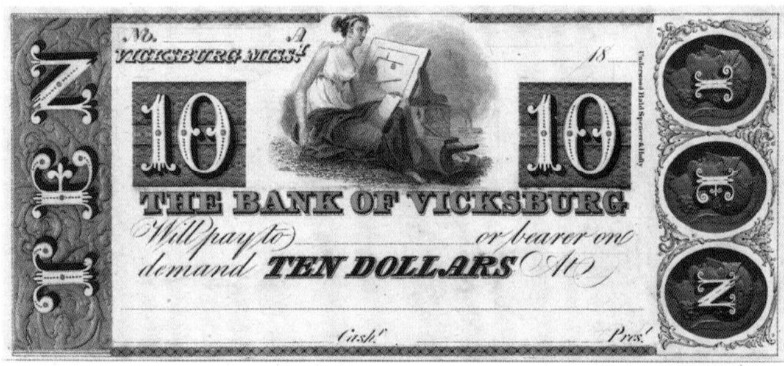

Engraver: Underwood, Bald, Spencer & Hufty. ***Comments:*** H-Unlisted, Kraus-4420. 18__. 1830s.

Rarity: URS-3
Proof $3,400
Selected auction price: Heritage Auctions, October 21, 2015, Lot 18456, Remainder $1,880

$20 • W-MS-890-020-G040

CC

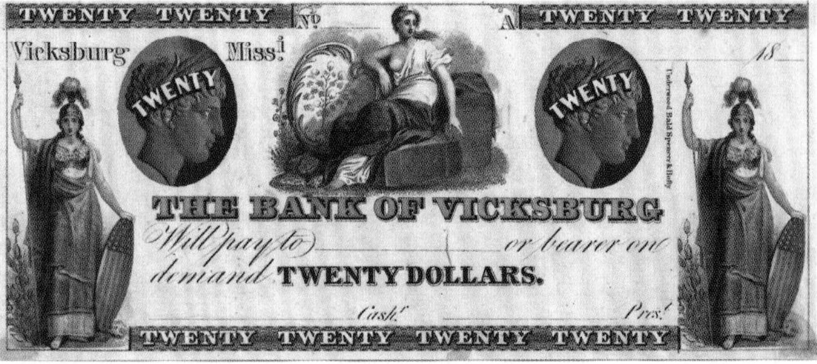

Engraver: Underwood, Bald, Spencer & Hufty. ***Comments:*** H-Unlisted, Kraus-4402. 18__. 1830s.

Rarity: URS-3
Proof $1,800

$50 • W-MS-890-050-G050

CC

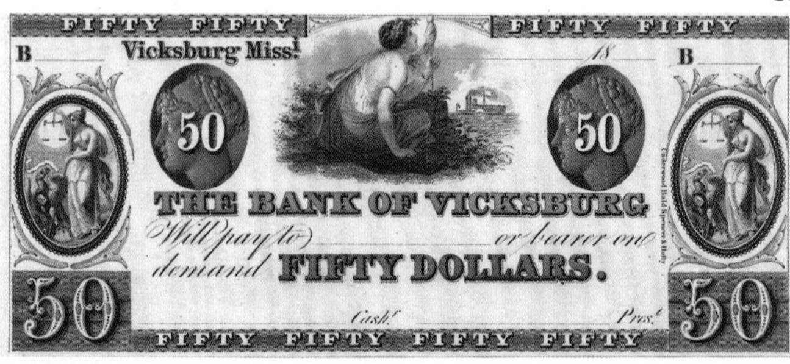

Engraver: Underwood, Bald, Spencer & Hufty. ***Comments:*** H-MS-210-G14, Kraus-4403. 18__. 1830s.

Rarity: URS-2
Proof $2,000

$100 • W-MS-890-100-G060

CC

Engraver: Underwood, Bald, Spencer & Hufty. ***Comments:*** H-MS-210-G16, Kraus-4404. 18__. 1830s.

Rarity: URS-2
Proof $2,500

$500 • W-MS-890-500-G070

CC

Engraver: Underwood, Bald, Spencer & Hufty. ***Comments:*** H-Unlisted, Kraus-4405. 18__. 1830s.

Rarity: URS-2
Proof $6,000

Post Notes

$5 • W-MS-890-005-G080

JM

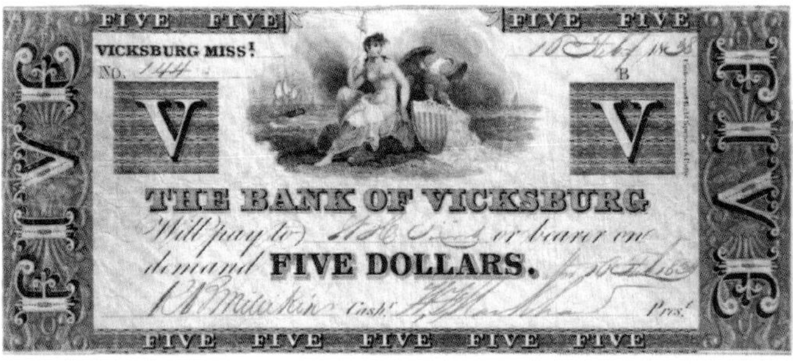

Engraver: Underwood, Bald, Spencer & Hufty. ***Comments:*** H-MS-210-G20, Kraus-4400d. 18__. 1838.

Rarity: URS-4
F $500

$10 • W-MS-890-010-G090

JM

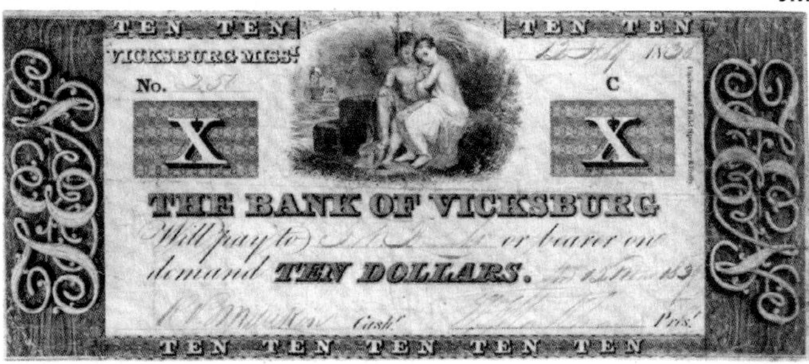

Engraver: Underwood, Bald, Spencer & Hufty. ***Comments:*** H-MS-210-G22, Kraus-4401c. 18__. 1838.

Rarity: URS-4
F $500

$20 • W-MS-890-020-G095

Left: Liberty as Athena with shield. ***Center:*** Ceres seated on cotton bale with shield bearing cotton plant. ***Right:*** Liberty as Athena with shield. ***Engraver:*** Underwood, Bald, Spencer & Hufty. ***Comments:*** H-Unlisted, Kraus-4402d. 18__. 1830s.

Rarity: URS-4
F $500

$20 • W-MS-890-020-G100

JM

Engraver: W.E. Tucker. ***Comments:*** H-MS-210-G24, Kraus-4430. 18__. 1830s.

Rarity: URS-3
F $1,500

$50 • W-MS-890-050-G110

JM

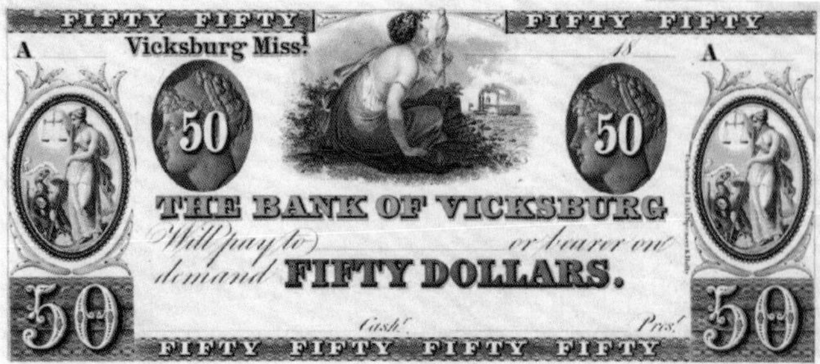

Engraver: Underwood, Bald, Spencer & Hufty. ***Comments:*** H-MS-210-G26, Kraus-4403c. 18__. 1838.

Rarity: URS-3
F $2,000

$50 • W-MS-890-050-G120

JM

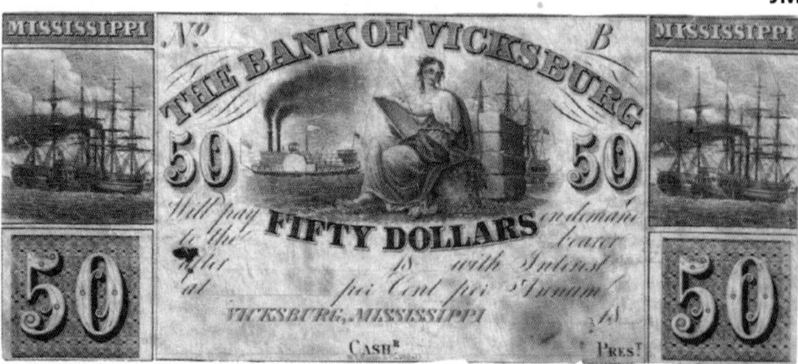

Engraver: Tucker. ***Comments:*** H-MS-210-G28, Kraus-4431. 18__. 1830s.

Rarity: URS-3
F $1,500

$100 • W-MS-890-100-G130

JM

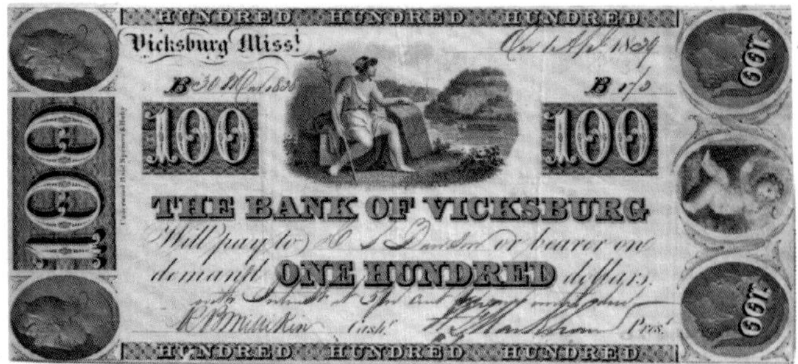

Engraver: Underwood, Bald, Spencer & Hufty. ***Comments:*** H-MS-210-G30, Kraus-4404c. 18__. 1838.

Rarity: URS-4
VG $1,000; **F** $1,500

Notes on Which the Place Payable is Blank

$15 • W-MS-890-015-G140 CC

Engraver: Underwood, Bald, Spencer & Hufty. ***Comments:*** H-MS-210-G56, Kraus-4421. 18__. 1830s.

Rarity: URS-3
Proof $6,750
Selected auction price: Heritage Auctions, April 23, 2015, Lot 19211, VF $3,995

$20 • W-MS-890-020-G150 CC

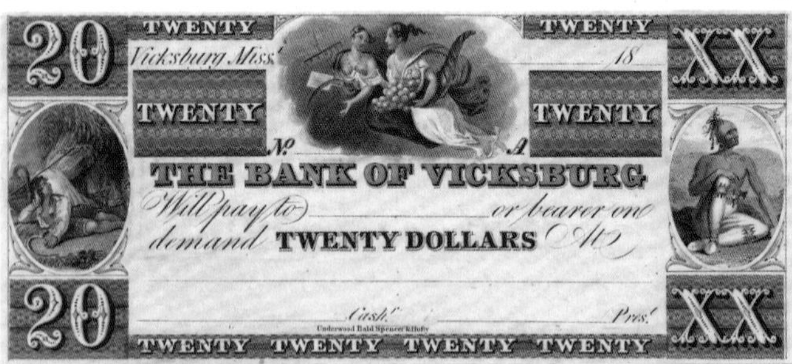

Engraver: Underwood, Bald, Spencer & Hufty. ***Comments:*** H-MS-210-G58, Kraus-4422.18__. 1830s.

Rarity: URS-3
Proof $3,250

$25 • W-MS-890-025-G160 CC

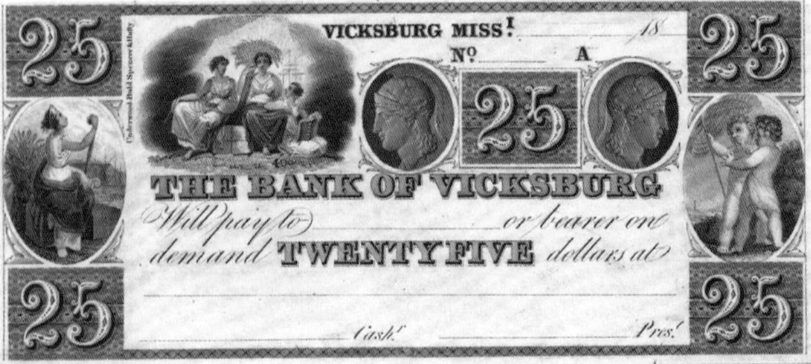

Engraver: Underwood, Bald, Spencer & Hufty. ***Comments:*** H-MS-210-G60, Kraus-4423.18__. 1830s.

Rarity: URS-3
Proof $6,750

Non-Valid Issues

$20 • W-MS-890-020-N010

Comments: H-Unlisted, Kraus-4430e. Fraudulently issued. Filled-in remainder. 18__. 1830s.

Rarity: —

Bank of Vicksburg {2nd}

1862

W-MS-900

History: The second Bank of Vicksburg was authorized on January 17, 1862, with a capital of $1,000,000.[26] It is unknown if this bank ever opened for business.

Numismatic Commentary: No notes are known.

Commercial and Rail Road Bank of Vicksburg

1831–1840

W-MS-910

History: The Commercial and Rail Road Bank of Vicksburg (also seen in print as the Commercial Railroad and Banking Company) was incorporated on December 19, 1831, under the name of the Clinton and Vicksburg Rail Road Company. It had an authorized capital of $4,000,000. On January 28, 1836, it was reincorporated with the name of Commercial and Rail Road Bank of Vicksburg. It was to lay a railway from Vicksburg to Clinton, and of the three other railroad and banking companies in the state and decade, it was the only one to complete its task. By 1840 there were 54 miles of railroad completed.[27] In the year leading up to the railway's completion, the company began winding up its banking affairs. In 1839 it was reported that the bank had suspended specie payments and that the stock held in New York and Philadelphia had been running down.[28] With the railroad finished, the bank finalized its affairs and closed.

The Commercial and Rail Road Bank of Vicksburg had its branch banks located in Clinton, W-MS-150, Utica, W-MS-860, and Vernon, W-MS-870.

Numismatic Commentary: This bank issued demand notes payable at the parent bank in Vicksburg as well as demand notes payable at branches. Notes are known to exist from the office in Clinton and the office in Vernon.

Valid Issues

$4 • W-MS-910-004-G010

Left: Medallion heads. ***Center:*** Woman seated with easel, paint brush, and canvas. ***Engraver:*** Underwood, Bald, & Spencer. ***Comments:*** H-MS-205-G6, Kraus-10550. 18__. 1830s.

Rarity: URS-1
F $2,500

$5 • W-MS-910-005-G020

JM

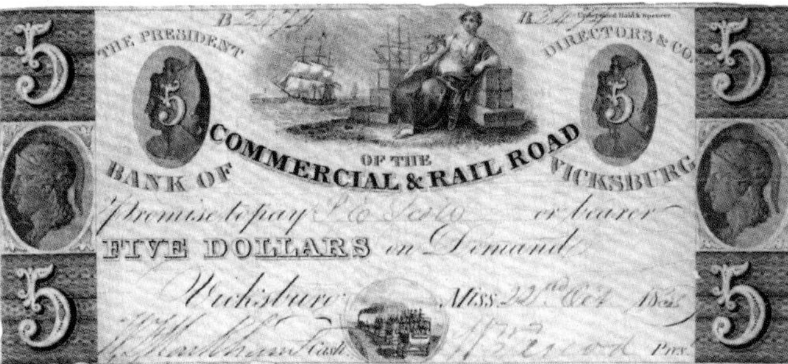

Engraver: Underwood, Bald, Spencer & Hufty. ***Comments:*** H-MS-205-G8, Kraus-10560. 18__. 1830s.

Rarity: URS-5
F $500; **Proof** $1,500

$10 • W-MS-910-010-G030

JM

Engraver: Underwood, Bald, Spencer & Hufty. ***Comments:*** H-MS-205-G12, Kraus-10561. 18__. 1830s.

Rarity: URS-5
F $500; **Proof** $1,500

$20 • W-MS-910-020-G040

JM

Engraver: Underwood, Bald, Spencer & Hufty. ***Comments:*** H-MS-205-G16, Kraus-10562. 18__. 1830s.

Rarity: URS-8
F $750; **Proof** $1,800

$50 • W-MS-910-050-G050

JM

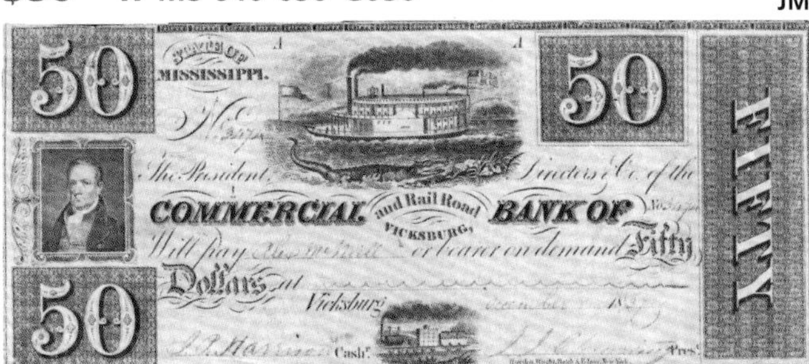

Engraver: Rawdon, Wright, Hatch & Edson. ***Comments:*** H-MS-205-G18, Kraus-10563. 18__. 1830s.

Rarity: URS-4
F $1,000; **Proof** $3,000

$100 • W-MS-910-100-G060

JM

Engraver: Rawdon, Wright, Hatch & Edson. ***Comments:*** H-MS-205-G20, Kraus-10564. 18__. 1830s.

Rarity: URS-3
F $1,250
Selected auction price: Heritage Auctions, September 16, 2015, Lot 18447, VF $1,410

$500 • W-MS-910-500-G070

CC

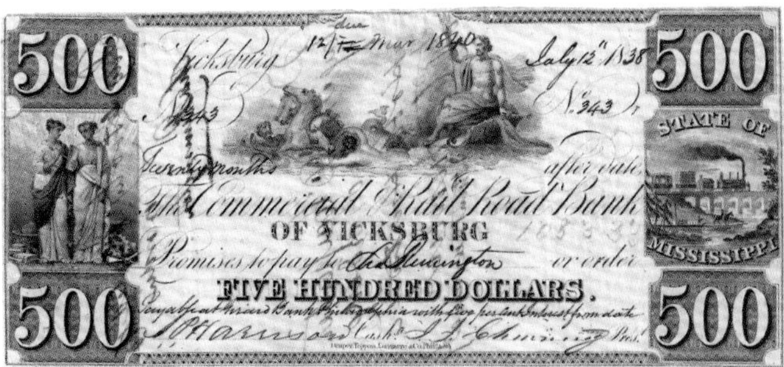

Engraver: Rawdon, Wright, Hatch & Edson. ***Comments:*** H-Unlisted, Kraus-10631. 18__. 1830s.

Rarity: URS-3
F $2,800

Collectors and Researchers:

If you have new information about any banks or notes listed in this volume, contact Whitman Publishing, Attn: Obsolete Paper Money, 3101 Clairmont Road, Suite G, Atlanta, GA 30329.

Notes Payable at the Phenix Bank, New York

$__ • W-MS-910-__-G080 JM

Engraver: Underwood, Bald & Spencer. ***Comments:*** H-Unlisted, Kraus-10597. "500" handwritten. 18__. 1830s.

Rarity: URS-2
F $2,000

$5 • W-MS-910-005-G090 JM

Engraver: Draper, Toppan, Longacre & Co. ***Comments:*** H-MS-205-G58, Kraus-10610. 18__. 1830s.

Rarity: URS-3
F $1,500

Notes Payable at the Union Bank of Louisiana, New Orleans

$5 • W-MS-910-005-G100

Left: 5 / Medallion head / 5 ***Center:*** Medallion head bearing 5 / Ship, Woman seated with bales on dock / Medallion head bearing 5. ***Right:*** 5 / Medallion head / 5. ***Engraver:*** Underwood, Bald, Spencer & Hufty. ***Comments:*** H-MS-205-G64. 18__. 1830s.

Rarity: *None known*

$10 • W-MS-910-010-G110

Left: 10 / Medallion head / 10. ***Center:*** 10 / Neptune seated, Ship / X. ***Right:*** X / Medallion head / X. ***Engraver:*** Underwood, Bald, Spencer & Hufty. ***Comments:*** H-MS-205-G66, Kraus-10561d. 18__. 1830s.

Rarity: URS-3
F $550

$20 • W-MS-910-020-G120

Left: 20 / Medallion head / 20. ***Center:*** 20 / Sailor standing on dock holding flag / 20. ***Right:*** 20 / Medallion head / 20. ***Engraver:*** Underwood, Bald, Spencer & Hufty. ***Comments:*** H-MS-205-G68. 18__. 1830s.

Rarity: URS-3
F $550

$50 • W-MS-910-050-G130

Left: 50 / Portrait of Dewitt Clinton / 50. ***Center:*** Riverboat, Alligator / 50. ***Right:*** FIFTY vertically. ***Engraver:*** Rawdon, Wright, Hatch & Edson. ***Comments:*** H-MS-205-G70. 18__. 1830s.

Rarity: *None known*

$100 • W-MS-910-100-G140

Left: ONE HUNDRED vertically. ***Center:*** 100 / Liberty seated with shield, Ship / 100. ***Right:*** ONE HUNDRED vertically. ***Engraver:*** Rawdon, Wright, Hatch & Edson. ***Comments:*** H-MS-205-G72. 18__. 1830s.

Rarity: *None known*

Post Notes Dated at the Girard Bank, Philadelphia

$50 • W-MS-910-050-G150 CC

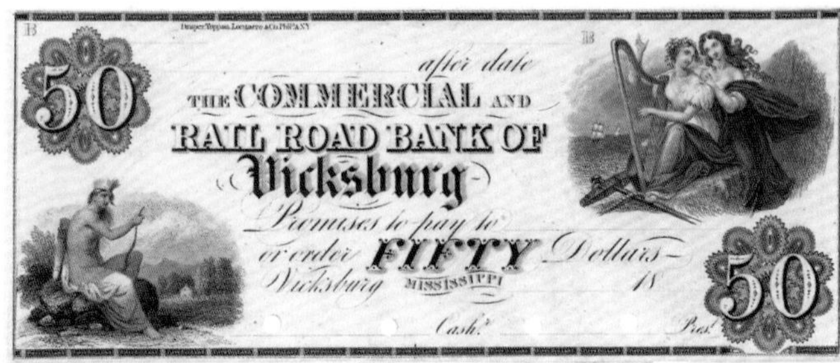

Engraver: Draper, Toppan, Longacre & Co. ***Comments:*** H-Unlisted, Kraus-10620. 18__. 1830s.

Rarity: URS-2
Proof $2,800

$100 • W-MS-910-100-G160 JM

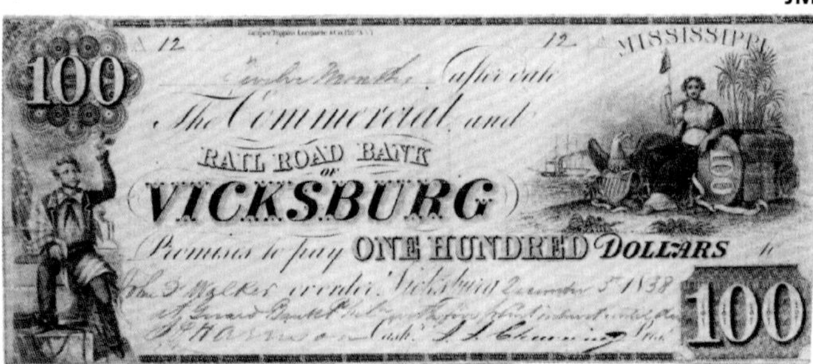

Engraver: Rawdon, Wright, Hatch & Edson. ***Comments:*** H-Unlisted, Kraus-10621. 18__. 1830s.

Rarity: URS-3
F $1,200

Selected auction price: Heritage Auctions, October 21, 2015, Lot 18455, VF $1,645; Heritage Auctions, April 23, 2014, Lot 15208, VF $2,820

Notes on Which the Place Payable is Blank

$5 • **W-MS-910-005-G170** CC

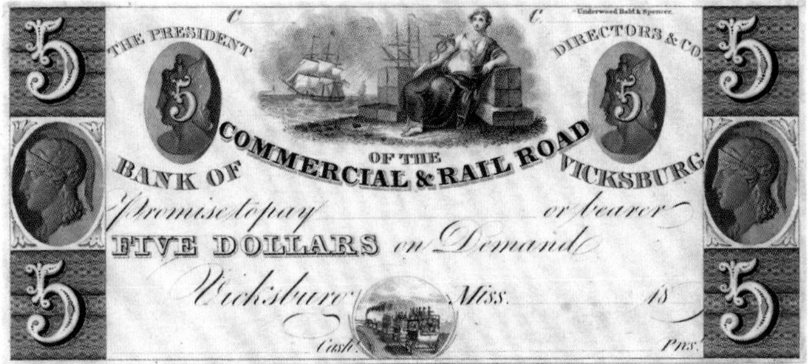

Engraver: Underwood, Bald, Spencer & Hufty. ***Comments:*** H-MS-205-G78. 18__. 1830s.

Rarity: URS-4
Proof $750

$10 • **W-MS-910-010-G180** CC

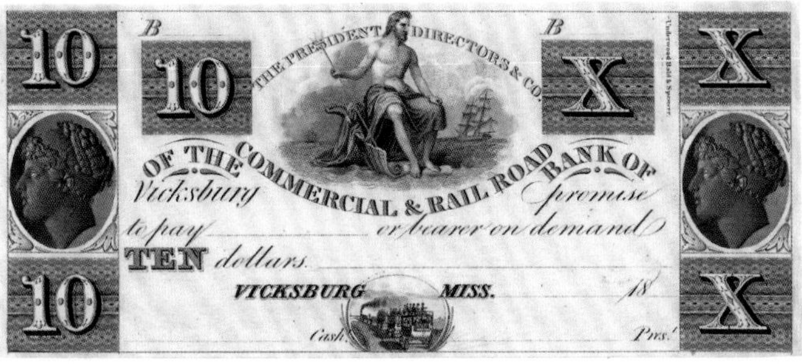

Engraver: Underwood, Bald, Spencer & Hufty. ***Comments:*** H-MS-205-G80. 18__. 1830s.

Rarity: URS-4
Proof $750

$20 • **W-MS-910-020-G190** CC

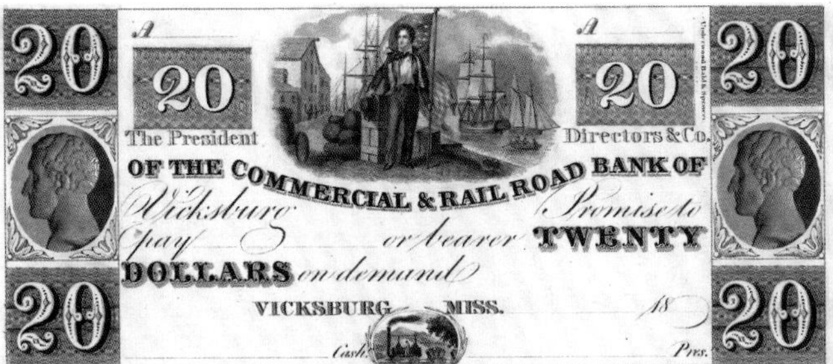

Engraver: Underwood, Bald, Spencer & Hufty. ***Comments:*** H-MS-205-G82. 18__. 1830s.

Rarity: URS-3
Proof $1,200

$50 • **W-MS-910-050-G200**

Left: 50 / Portrait of Dewitt Clinton / 50. ***Center:*** Riverboat, Alligator / 50. ***Right:*** FIFTY vertically. ***Engraver:*** Rawdon, Wright, Hatch & Edson. ***Comments:*** H-MS-205-G84. 18__. 1830s.

Rarity: URS-3
F $1,000

$100 • **W-MS-910-100-G210**

Left: ONE HUNDRED vertically. ***Center:*** 100 / Liberty seated with shield, Ship / 100. ***Right:*** ONE HUNDRED vertically. ***Engraver:*** Rawdon, Wright, Hatch & Edson. ***Comments:*** H-MS-205-G86. 18__. 1830s.

Rarity: URS-3
F $1,000

Planters Bank of the State of Mississippi (branch)

1830–1844

W-MS-920

History: The Planters Bank of the State of Mississippi was the second bank to be chartered in the state. It was incorporated on February 10, 1830, with an authorized capital of $3,000,000, $2,000,000 of which was provided from the state through the sale of bonds. The Panic of 1837 struck the bank hard. The state's bonds were repudiated, and the bank failed thereafter. On February 23, 1844, the bank was put into liquidation.

The Planters Bank of the State of Mississippi had its parent bank located in Natchez, W-MS-670, and branch banks located in Columbus, W-MS-240, Jackson, W-MS-470, Manchester, W-MS-555, Monticello, W-MS-580, Port Gibson, W-MS-780, Woodville, W-MS-1020, and Yazoo City, W-MS-1070.

Valid Issues

$5 • **W-MS-920-005-G010**

Left: 5 / FIVE vertically / 5. ***Center:*** 5 / Mercury in flight spreading coins from cornucopia / 5. ***Right:*** FIVE vertically. ***Engraver:*** Rawdon, Wright & Co. ***Comments:*** H-MS-175-G140, Kraus-4060. 18__. 1830s.

Rarity: URS-3
F $650

$10 • **W-MS-920-010-G020**

Left: 10 / Neptune pouring water from amphora / 10. ***Center:*** 10 / Justice and Liberty flanking shield bearing cotton plant and surmounted by eagle / 10. ***Right:*** 10 / Neptune pouring water from amphora / 10. ***Engraver:*** Rawdon, Wright & Co. ***Comments:*** H-MS-175-G142, Kraus-4061. 18__. 1830s.

Rarity: URS-3
F $650

$20 • **W-MS-920-020-G030**

Left: Woman seated with globe. ***Center:*** 20 / Cotton bales, Hope standing with anchor, Ship / 20. ***Right:*** Group of Indians. ***Engraver:*** Rawdon, Wright & Co. ***Comments:*** H-MS-175-G144, Kraus-4062. 18__. 1830s.

Rarity: URS-3
F $650

$20 • **W-MS-920-020-G040**

Left: Woman standing in niche / XX. ***Center:*** 20 / Two women flanking shield surmounted by eagle / 20. ***Right:*** Woman standing in niche / XX. ***Back:*** Red-brown. ***Engraver:*** Rawdon, Wright, Hatch & Co. ***Comments:*** H-MS-175-G146. 18__. 1830s.

Rarity: URS-3
F $650

$50 • W-MS-920-050-G050

Left: Justice standing with eagle bearing portrait of George Washington. ***Center:*** 50 / Woman standing with cotton bales and shield bearing cotton plant surmounted by eagle, Train / 50. ***Right:*** Two women standing. ***Engraver:*** Rawdon, Wright & Co. ***Comments:*** H-MS-175-G148, Kraus-4063. 18__. 1830s.

Rarity: URS-3
F $650

$50 • W-MS-920-050-G060

Left: Indian standing with bow / 50. ***Center:*** 50 / Ships / 50. ***Right:*** Indian standing with bow / 50. ***Back:*** Red-brown. ***Engraver:*** Rawdon, Wright, Hatch & Co. ***Comments:*** H-MS-175-G150. 18__. 1830s.

Rarity: URS-3
F $650

$100 • W-MS-920-100-G070

Left: ONE HUNDRED vertically. ***Center:*** 100 / Group of settlers and Indians / 100. ***Right:*** ONE HUNDRED vertically. ***Engraver:*** Rawdon, Wright & Co. ***Comments:*** H-MS-175-G152, Kraus-4064. 18__. 1830s.

Rarity: URS-3
F $650

$100 • W-MS-920-100-G080

Left: 100 / Men with cattle / 100. ***Center:*** Portrait of George Washington / Woman seated in clouds with eagle bearing portrait of George Washington / Portrait of Benjamin Franklin. ***Right:*** 100 / Men with cattle / 100. ***Back:*** Red-brown. ***Engraver:*** Rawdon, Wright, Hatch & Co. ***Comments:*** H-MS-175-G154. 18__. 1830s.

Rarity: URS-3
F $650

Tombigby Rail Road and Banking Company

1836–1841

W-MS-930

History: The Tombigby Rail Road and Banking Company (also seen as the Tombigby Rail Road Company on notes) was chartered on February 27, 1836. It was reported to have a positive net worth of $2,403.67 in February 1838. In March 1841 the Tombigby Rail Road and Banking Company, along with several other banks, had its charter revoked for failing to redeem its notes in specie.

See also listing under Columbus, W-MS-260.

Vicksburg Bank

1861

W-MS-940

History: In November 1861 the Vicksburg Bank was chartered, but it is uncertain whether the bank ever went into operation. Little else has been found about its history.

Numismatic Commentary: No notes are known today.

Vicksburg Exchange and Banking Company

1830s

W-MS-950

History: This is believed to have been an exchange house or related business that issued notes for regional circulation. No record has been found of a state charter for this bank, and it is presumed it was a private enterprise. It is listed here for collector continuity.

Numismatic Commentary: Only one remainder note is known of this bank.

Valid Issues

$1 • W-MS-950-001-G010

Comments: H-Unlisted, Kraus-20775. No description available. 18__. 1830s.

Rarity: *None known*

$5 • W-MS-950-005-G020

Comments: H-Unlisted, Kraus-20778. No description available. 18__. 1830s.

Rarity: *None known*

$10 • W-MS-950-010-G030

JM

Engraver: Western Bank Note Co. / Woodruff & Mason. ***Comments:*** H-MS-215-G8, Kraus-20779. 18__. 1830s.

Rarity: URS-1
VF $4,300
Selected auction price: Heritage Auctions, October 21, 2015, Lot 18457, VF $4,230

Vicksburg Water Works and Banking Company

1837–1839

W-MS-960

History: The Vicksburg Water Works and Banking Company was chartered on May 13, 1837, with an authorized capital of $500,000. In 1839 the bank was reorganized and its officers joined with the Mississippi Union Bank, W-MS-460. A state report of January 5, 1841, stated that the Vicksburg Water Works and Banking Company was under injunction but had failed to comply with the order.

Valid Issues

$2 • W-MS-960-002-G010

Engraver: Draper, Toppan, Longacre & Co. ***Comments:*** H-Unlisted, Kraus-4460. No description available. 18__. 1830s.

Rarity: *None known*

$5 • W-MS-960-005-G020

CC

Engraver: Draper, Toppan, Longacre & Co. ***Comments:*** H-MS-220-G8, Kraus-4465. 18__. 1830s.

Rarity: URS-4
F $500
Selected auction price: Heritage Auctions, October 24, 2015, Lot 19666, VF $940

$10 • W-MS-960-010-G030

HA

Engraver: Draper, Toppan, Longacre & Co. ***Comments:*** H-MS-220-G10, Kraus-4466. 18__. 1830s.

Rarity: URS-5
F $450
Selected auction price: Heritage Auctions, October 24, 2015, Lot 19667, VF $822

$20 • W-MS-960-020-G040

CC

Engraver: Draper, Toppan, Longacre & Co. ***Comments:*** H-MS-220-G12, Kraus-4467. 18__. 1830s.

Rarity: URS-4
F $775
Selected auction price: Heritage Auctions, January 5, 2012, Lot 15951, VF $1,092

$50 • W-MS-960-050-G050

JM

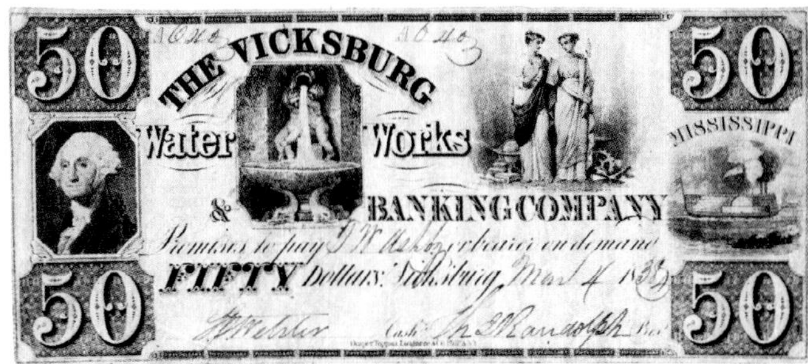

Engraver: Draper, Toppan, Longacre & Co. ***Comments:*** H-MS-220-G14, Kraus-4468. 18__. 1830s.

Rarity: URS-4
F $900
Selected auction price: Heritage Auctions, April 23, 2015, Lot 19212, VF $2,585

$100 • W-MS-960-100-G060

CC

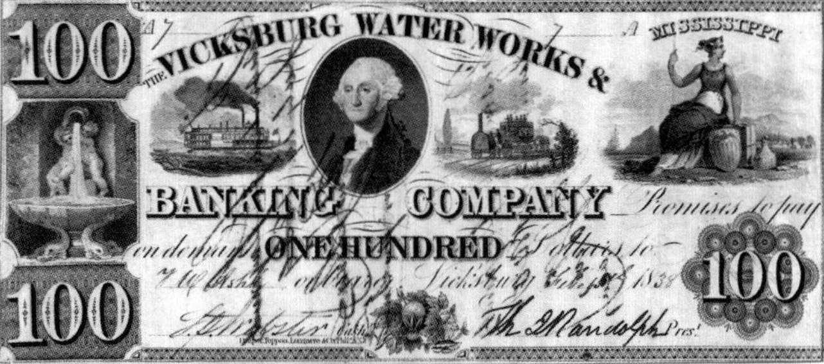

Engraver: Draper, Toppan, Longacre & Co. ***Comments:*** H-MS-220-G16, Kraus-4469. 18__. 1830s.

Rarity: URS-4
VF $2,450
Selected auction price: Heritage Auctions, April 18, 2012, Lot 15253, VF $2,415

Wahalak, Mississippi

In 1837 Wahalak was settled on the Wahalak Creek by Victor Welsh. The creek was attached to the Noxubee River. With access to river transportation, the town quickly grew, and soon there were three churches, two schools, two doctors, and several businesses. It was considered an educational center, but with the oncoming of the Mobile and Ohio Railroad, which bypassed the town, it settled into a swift decline.

Kemper and Noxubee Navigation and Real Estate Banking Company

1830s

W-MS-970

History: This is believed to have been an exchange house or office that issued notes based on real estate holdings. No record has been found of a state charter for this bank, and it is presumed it was a private enterprise. It is listed here for collector continuity.

Numismatic Commentary: Validly issued notes are very rare.

Valid Issues

$1 • W-MS-970-001-G010

Left: 1 / Medallion head bearing 1 / 1. ***Center:*** Portrait of Marquis de Lafayette / Indian seated near river with rifle / Male portrait. ***Right:*** 1 / Medallion head bearing 1 / 1. ***Engraver:*** Underwood, Bald, Spencer & Hufty. ***Comments:*** H-MS-225-G2, Kraus-14980. 18__. 1830s.

Rarity: URS-3
F $600

$2 • W-MS-970-002-G020

Left: Indian. ***Center:*** Portrait of George Washington / Eagle at river bank, Steamboat / Portrait of Benjamin Franklin. ***Right:*** 2 / Medallion head / 2. ***Engraver:*** Underwood, Bald, Spencer & Hufty. ***Comments:*** H-MS-225-G4, Kraus-14981. 18__. 1830s.

Rarity: URS-3
F $600

$5 • W-MS-970-005-G030

Left: 5 / Indian seated / 5. ***Center:*** Portrait of Daniel Webster / Mercury with cargo, River / Portrait of Andrew Jackson. ***Right:*** 5 / Indian seated / 5. ***Engraver:*** Underwood, Bald, Spencer & Hufty. ***Comments:*** H-MS-225-G8, Kraus-14982. 18__. 1830s.

Rarity: URS-3
F $600

$10 • W-MS-970-010-G040

JM

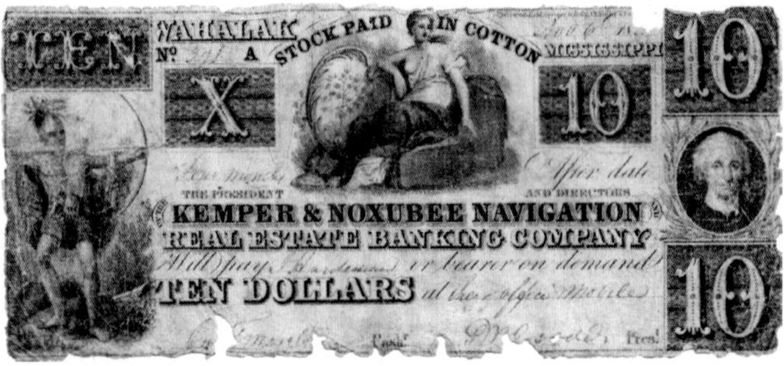

Engraver: Underwood, Bald, Spencer & Hufty. ***Comments:*** H-Unlisted, Kraus-14990b. 18__. 1830s.

Rarity: URS-3
G $2,000

$20 • W-MS-970-020-G050

Left: 20 / Male portrait / XX. ***Center:*** Indian seated with bow and arrows, Valley. ***Right:*** 20 / Male portrait / XX. ***Engraver:*** Underwood, Bald, Spencer & Hufty. ***Comments:*** H-Unlisted, Kraus-14991. May have been made only as Proofs. 18__. 1830s.

Rarity: URS-3
F $1,000

$50 • W-MS-970-050-G055

Engraver: Underwood, Bald, Spencer & Hufty. ***Comments:*** H-Unlisted, Kraus-Unlisted. No description available. 18__. 1830s.

Rarity: *None known*

$100 • W-MS-970-100-G060

Left: 100 / Indian seated / 100. ***Center:*** Medallion head / Muse, River and riverboat / Medallion head. ***Right:*** 100 / Portrait of George Washington / 100. ***Engraver:*** Underwood, Bald, Spencer & Hufty. ***Comments:*** H-Unlisted, Kraus-14992. May have been made only as Proofs. 18__. 1830s.

Rarity: —

Warrenton, Mississippi

In 1805 a church and a cemetery were established in the town of Warrenton, followed in 1809 by a courthouse. The same year Warrenton became the county seat. A post office was opened in 1811, and the town was incorporated in 1820. This made Warrenton the economic and commercial center of the area.

The neighboring town of Vicksburg prospered during this time, and soon the county seat was transferred to the better-situated location. Despite this, Warrenton continued to thrive in the 1830s due to cotton exportation. The prosperity was not to last, and the swampy location of the community led to yellow-fever, cholera, and small-pox outbreaks. The Civil War brought further destruction when Union forces damaged the town.

Exchange Bank

1830s

W-MS-980

History: This is believed to have been an exchange house or office that issued notes for regional circulation. No record has been found of a state charter for this bank, and it is presumed it was a private enterprise. It is listed here for collector continuity.

Valid Issues

$5 • W-MS-980-005-G010

Comments: H-Unlisted, Kraus-20810. No description available. 1830s.

Rarity: *None known*

$10 • W-MS-980-010-G020

Left: Sailor with flag / 10. ***Center:*** Harbor scene, Dock, cargo, Schooner. ***Right:*** Portrait of George Washington / 10. ***Comments:*** H-Unlisted, Kraus-20811r. 1830s.

Rarity: URS-1
F $2,500

Warrenton Change Banking Association

1830s

W-MS-990

History: This is believed to have been an exchange house or office that issued notes for regional circulation. No record has been found of a state charter for this bank, and it is presumed it was a private enterprise. It is listed here for collector continuity.

Valid Issues

12-1/2¢ • W-MS-990-00.12.50-G010

JM

Comments: H-Unlisted, Kraus-20830. 183_. 1830s.

Rarity: URS-2

F $2,000

25¢ • W-MS-990-00.25-G020

Comments: H-Unlisted, Kraus-20831. No description available. 1830s.

Rarity: *None known*

50¢ • W-MS-990-00.50-G030

JM

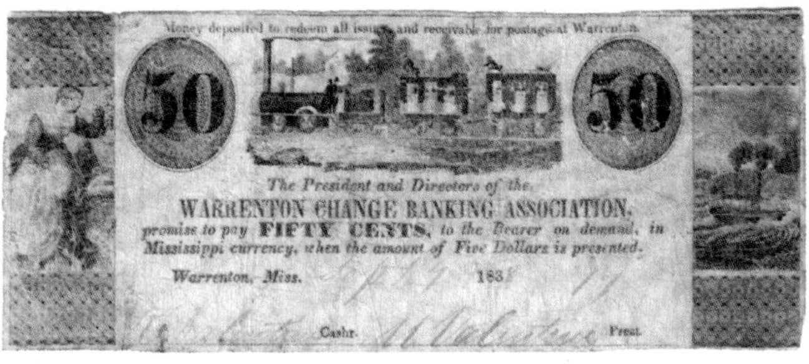

Comments: H-Unlisted, Kraus-20832. 183_. 1830s.

Rarity: URS-2

F $1,500

$1 • W-MS-990-001-G040

Comments: H-Unlisted, Kraus-20833. No description available. 1830s.

Rarity: *None known*

Woodville, Mississippi

Woodville was incorporated in 1811. The main sources of commerce in the area were cotton and timber. Plantations were established all around the town. The West Feliciana Rail Road and Banking Company was formed just for the purpose of shipping the cotton to marketplaces across the country. This plantation community enjoyed prosperity until the Civil War.

Bank of the State of Mississippi (branch)

1818–1831

W-MS-1000

History: On February 14, 1818, the Bank of the Mississippi, W-MS-600, was reorganized to become the Bank of the State of Mississippi. In 1830 the Planters Bank of the State of Mississippi, W-MS-670, was chartered in direct violation of a pledge made by the legislature to charter no other bank in the state. The managers of the Bank of the State of Mississippi wound up their institute as a result.

The Bank of the State of Mississippi had its parent bank located in Natchez, W-MS-620, and branch banks located in Port Gibson, W-MS-760, and Vicksburg, W-MS-880.

Valid Issues

$5 • W-MS-1000-005-G010

Left: 5 / 5 vertically. ***Center:*** River scene, Boat, Deer. ***Right:*** NATCHEZ vertically. ***Engraver:*** Murray, Draper, Fairman & Co. ***Comments:*** H-Unlisted. 18__. 1818–1820s.

Rarity: *None known*

$10 • W-MS-1000-010-G020

Left: TEN vertically. ***Center:*** River scene, Boat, Deer. ***Right:*** NATCHEZ vertically. ***Comments:*** H-Unlisted. 18__. 1818–1820s.

Rarity: *None known*

$20 • W-MS-1000-020-G030

Left: TWENTY vertically. ***Center:*** River scene, Boat, Deer. ***Right:*** NATCHEZ vertically. ***Engraver:*** Murray, Draper, Fairman & Co. ***Comments:*** H-Unlisted. 18__. 1818–1820s.

Rarity: *None known*

$50 • W-MS-1000-050-G040

Left: FIFTY vertically. ***Center:*** River scene, Boat, Deer. ***Right:*** NATCHEZ vertically. ***Engraver:*** Murray, Draper, Fairman & Co. ***Comments:*** H-Unlisted. 18__. 1818–1820s.

Rarity: *None known*

$100 • W-MS-1000-100-G050

Engraver: Murray, Draper, Fairman & Co. ***Comments:*** H-Unlisted, Kraus-1074. No description available. 18__. 1818–1820s.

Rarity: *None known*

Bank of Vicksburg {1st} (branch)

1837–1840

W-MS-1010

History: On May 3, 1837, the Bank of Vicksburg was incorporated with an authorized capital of $2,000,000. This amount was to be divided into shares of $100 apiece, with $500,000 in subscriptions being required before the bank could open. In 1840 an act was passed declaring the charter of the Bank of Vicksburg forfeit for a lack of paying out specie on notes presented for redemption.

The Bank of Vicksburg had its parent bank located in Vicksburg, W-MS-890, and a branch bank located in Oswego, W-MS-700.

Valid Issues

$15 • W-MS-1010-015-G010

Left: FIFTEEN / Cherub as Ceres / 15. ***Center:*** Medallion head / Commerce and Industry seated with amphora / Medallion head. ***Right:*** FIFTEEN / Cherub as Ceres / 15. ***Engraver:*** Underwood, Bald, Spencer & Hufty. ***Comments:*** H-MS-210-G46. 18__. 1830s.

Rarity: *None known*

$25 • W-MS-1010-025-G020

Left: 25 / Woman standing / 25. ***Center:*** Ceres, Commerce, and Industry seated / Medallion head / 25 / Medallion head. ***Right:*** 25 / Cherubs as Liberty and Ceres / 25. ***Engraver:*** Underwood, Bald, Spencer & Hufty. ***Comments:*** H-MS-210-G50. 18__. 1830s.

Rarity: *None known*

Non-Valid Issues

$20 • W-MS-1010-020-N010

JM

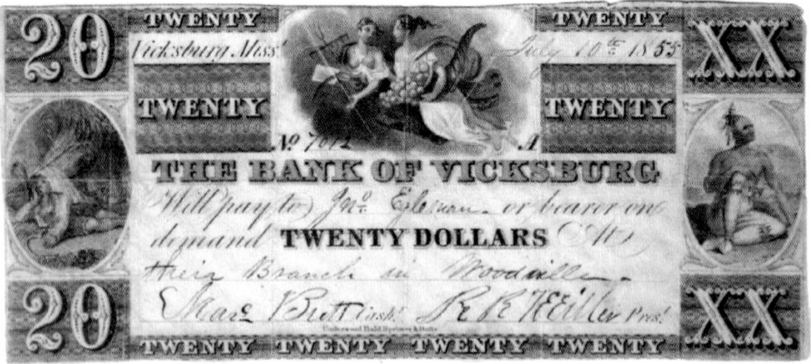

Engraver: Underwood, Bald, Spencer & Hufty. ***Comments:*** H-MS-210-G48. Falsely filled-in remainder. 18__. 1830s.

Rarity: URS-3
F $1,500

Planters Bank of the State of Mississippi (branch)

1830–1844

W-MS-1020

History: The Planters Bank of the State of Mississippi was the second bank to be chartered in the state. It was incorporated on February 10, 1830, with an authorized capital of $3,000,000, $2,000,000 of which was provided from the state through the sale of bonds. The Panic of 1837 struck the bank hard. The state's bonds were repudiated, and the bank failed thereafter. On February 23, 1844, the bank was put into liquidation.

The Planters Bank of the State of Mississippi had its parent bank located in Natchez, W-MS-670, and branch banks located in Columbus, W-MS-240, Jackson, W-MS-470, Manchester, W-MS-555, Monticello, W-MS-580, Port Gibson, W-MS-780, Vicksburg, W-MS-920, and Yazoo City, W-MS-1070.

Valid Issues

25¢ • W-MS-1020-00.25-G010

JM

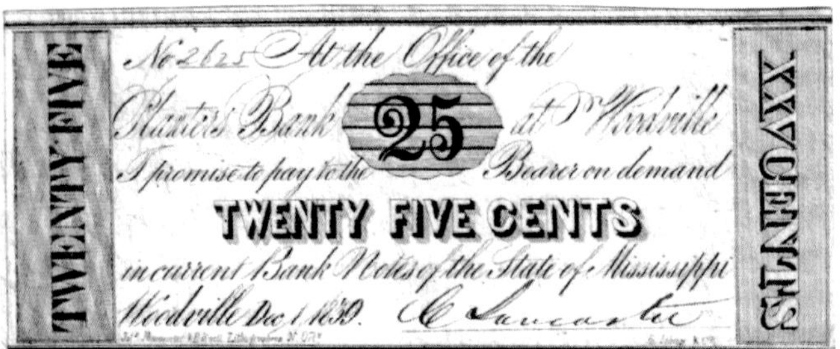

Comments: H-Unlisted, Kraus-32090-1. Branch location engraved. Dec. 1, 1839.

Rarity: URS-4
F $500

50¢ • W-MS-1020-00.50-G020

JM

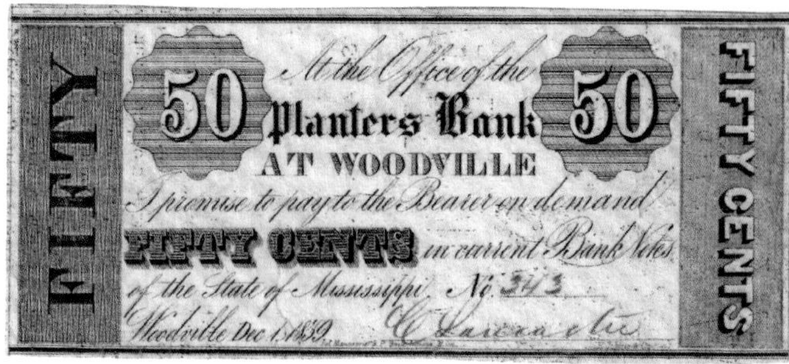

Comments: H-Unlisted, Kraus-32091-1. Branch location engraved. Dec. 1, 1839.

Rarity: URS-3
F $1,000

$5 • W-MS-1020-005-G030

Left: 5 / FIVE vertically / 5. ***Center:*** 5 / Mercury in flight spreading coins from cornucopia / 5. ***Right:*** FIVE vertically. ***Engraver:*** Rawdon, Wright & Co. ***Comments:*** H-MS-175-G160. Branch location handwritten. 18__. 1830s.

Rarity: URS-4
F $450

$10 • W-MS-1020-010-G040

Left: 10 / Neptune pouring water from amphora / 10. ***Center:*** 10 / Justice and Liberty flanking shield bearing cotton plant and surmounted by eagle / 10. ***Right:*** 10 / Neptune pouring water from amphora / 10. ***Engraver:*** Rawdon, Wright & Co. ***Comments:*** H-MS-175-G162. Branch location handwritten. 18__. 1830s.

Rarity: URS-4
F $450

$20 • W-MS-1020-020-G050

Left: Woman seated with globe. ***Center:*** 20 / Cotton bales, Hope standing with anchor, Ship / 20. ***Right:*** Group of Indians. ***Engraver:*** Rawdon, Wright & Co. ***Comments:*** H-MS-175-G164. Branch location handwritten. 18__. 1830s.

Rarity: URS-4
F $450

$20 • W-MS-1020-020-G060

Left: Woman standing in niche / XX. ***Center:*** 20 / Two women flanking shield surmounted by eagle / 20. ***Right:*** Woman standing in niche / XX. ***Back:*** Red-brown. ***Engraver:*** Rawdon, Wright, Hatch & Co. ***Comments:*** H-MS-175-G166. Branch location handwritten. 18__. 1830s.

Rarity: URS-4
F $450

$50 • W-MS-1020-050-G070

Left: Justice standing with eagle bearing portrait of George Washington. ***Center:*** 50 / Woman standing with cotton bales and shield bearing cotton plant surmounted by eagle, Train / 50. ***Right:*** Two women standing. ***Engraver:*** Rawdon, Wright & Co. ***Comments:*** H-MS-175-G168. Branch location handwritten. 18__. 1830s.

Rarity: URS-4
F $450

$50 • **W-MS-1020-050-G080**

Left: Indian standing with bow / 50. ***Center:*** 50 / Ships / 50. ***Right:*** Indian standing with bow / 50. ***Back:*** Red-brown. ***Engraver:*** Rawdon, Wright, Hatch & Co. ***Comments:*** H-MS-175-G170. Branch location handwritten. 18__. 1830s.

Rarity: URS-4
F $450

$100 • **W-MS-1020-100-G090**

Left: ONE HUNDRED vertically. ***Center:*** 100 / Group of settlers and Indians / 100. ***Right:*** ONE HUNDRED vertically. ***Engraver:*** Rawdon, Wright & Co. ***Comments:*** H-MS-175-G172. Branch location handwritten. 18__. 1830s.

Rarity: URS-4
F $500

$100 • **W-MS-1020-100-G100**

Left: 100 / Men with cattle / 100. ***Center:*** Portrait of George Washington / Woman seated in clouds with eagle bearing portrait of George Washington / Portrait of Benjamin Franklin. ***Right:*** 100 / Men with cattle / 100. ***Back:*** Red-brown. ***Engraver:*** Rawdon, Wright, Hatch & Co. ***Comments:*** H-MS-175-G174. Branch location handwritten. 18__. 1830s.

Rarity: URS-4
F $500

West Feliciana Rail Road Company

1835–1860s

W-MS-1030

History: The West Feliciana Rail Road Company (sometimes seen on notes as the W.F. Rail Road Bank) was conceived in 1828 by several planters and bankers. Due to the wealth of the area and a need to keep pace with the thriving economy, the railroad was chartered on March 25, 1831, by the Louisiana legislature. In January 1835 the West Feliciana Rail Road Company was invested with banking privileges for the purpose of shipping cotton to marketplaces across the country. On February 24, 1838, *Niles' National Register* reported that the bank had a positive net worth of $24,023.78. Despite setbacks and some opposition, the railroad succeeded, and in 1842 the rails reached Woodville. The company continued into the Civil War but closed sometime after.

Numismatic Commentary: Validly issued notes from this entity are excessively rare.

Valid Issues

12-1/2¢ • **W-MS-1030-00.12.50-G005**

Left: 12-1/2 CENTS vertically. ***Center:*** Train. ***Right:*** 12-1/2 CENTS vertically. ***Comments:*** H-Unlisted. Signed by William P. Grayson, who was cashier of the West Feliciana Rail Road Company. He subsequently became the cashier of the Mississippi Union Bank in Jackson 18__. 1830s.

Rarity: —

$5 • **W-MS-1030-005-G010**

JM

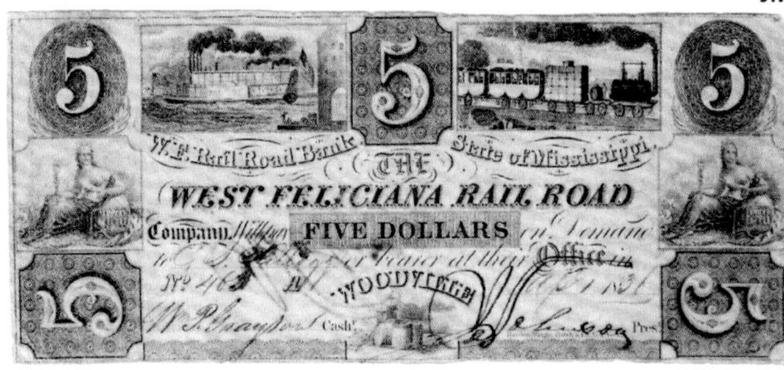

Engraver: Rawdon, Wright, Hatch & Co. ***Comments:*** H-MS-230-G8, Kraus-10672. 18__. 1830s.

Rarity: URS-3
F $1,000

$5 • **W-MS-1030-005-G020**

JM

Engraver: Rawdon, Wright, Hatch & Edson. ***Comments:*** H-MS-230-G10, Kraus-10686. 18__. 1830s.

Rarity: URS-3
Proof $2,500

$5 • **W-MS-1030-005-G030**

Comments: H-Unlisted, Kraus-10700. No description available. 18__. 1830s–1850s.

Rarity: *None known*

$10 • **W-MS-1030-010-G040**

CC

Engraver: Rawdon, Wright, Hatch & Co. ***Comments:*** H-MS-230-G12, Kraus-10673. 18__. 1830s.

Rarity: URS-3
Proof $2,500

$10 • **W-MS-1030-010-G050**

Left: TEN vertically. ***Center:*** Train. ***Right:*** Commerce leaning on column. ***Engraver:*** Rawdon, Wright, Hatch & Edson. ***Comments:*** H-MS-230-G14, Kraus-10687. 18__. 1830s.

Rarity: *None known*

$10 • W-MS-1030-010-G060

Comments: H-Unlisted, Kraus-10701. No description available. 18__. 1830s–1850s.

Rarity: *None known*

$20 • W-MS-1030-020-G070

JM

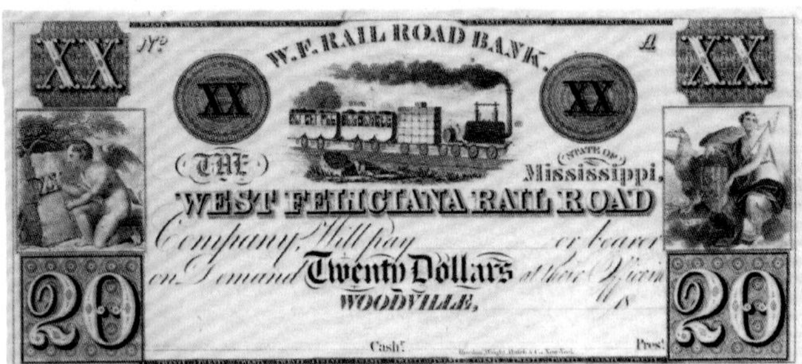

Engraver: Rawdon, Wright, Hatch & Co. ***Comments:*** H-MS-230-G16, Kraus-10674. 18__. 1830s.

Rarity: URS-3

Unc-Rem $1,000

$20 • W-MS-1030-020-G080

Left: Liberty seated with eagle. ***Center:*** Train. ***Right:*** Woman standing with staff. ***Engraver:*** Rawdon, Wright, Hatch & Edson. ***Comments:*** H-MS-230-G18, Kraus-10688. 18__. 1830s.

Rarity: URS-3

$50 • W-MS-1030-050-G090

RG

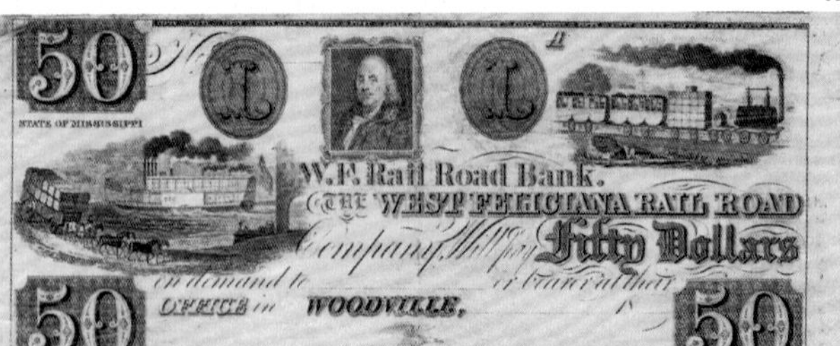

Engraver: Rawdon, Wright, Hatch & Co. ***Comments:*** H-MS-230-G20, Kraus-10675. 18__. 1830s.

Rarity: URS-2

Unc-Rem $2,000

How to Read the Whitman Numbering System

$1 • W-AL-020-001-G010a

Denomination: Face value of the note shown.

W: Whitman number. This number is a sortable code unique to each bank and note.

AL: Abbreviation for the state under study.

020: Numerical designation specific to each bank.

001: The denomination in dollars.

G010a: G indicates a good or valid note. Other categories are indicated thus: C (counterfeit); R (raised); S (spurious); N (not-attributed); A (altered). Numbers are assigned starting with 010, 020, et seq. Terminal letters following the number indicate variations of a note: a series of different colored overprints, tints, payees, etc., all on the same design of note. For more information, see the "How to Use This Book" section at the front of the volume, page xiv.

$50 • W-MS-1030-050-G100

Left: FIFTY vertically. ***Center:*** Train. ***Right:*** Liberty holding cornucopia. ***Engraver:*** Rawdon, Wright, Hatch & Edson. ***Comments:*** H-MS-230-G22, Kraus-10689. 18__. 1840s–1850s.

Rarity: URS-3

$100 • W-MS-1030-100-G110

RG

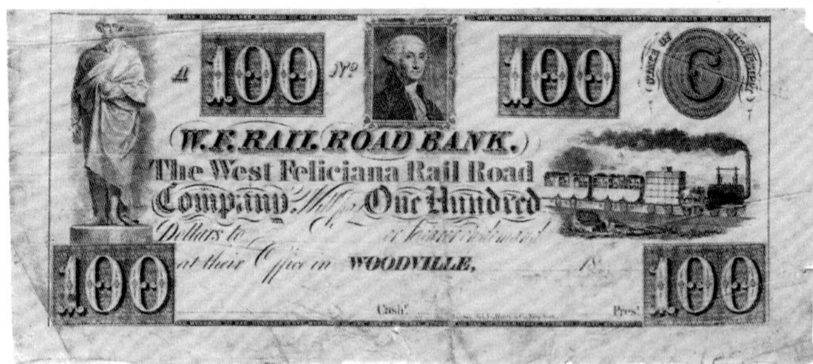

Engraver: Rawdon, Wright, Hatch & Co. ***Comments:*** H-MS-230-G24, Kraus-10676. 18__. 1830s.

Rarity: URS-2

Unc-Rem $2,000

$100 • W-MS-1030-100-G120

Left: 100. ***Center:*** Train. ***Right:*** ONE HUNDRED vertically. ***Engraver:*** Rawdon, Wright, Hatch & Edson. ***Comments:*** H-MS-230-G26, Kraus-106900. 18__. 1840s–1850s.

Rarity: URS-3

Unc-Rem $1,500

Payable at the Fulton Bank in New York

$20 • W-MS-1030-020-G130

Left: 20 / Liberty seated with eagle / 20. ***Center:*** Train. ***Right:*** XX / Bull / 20. ***Comments:*** H-Unlisted, Kraus-10702. 18__. 1830s.

Rarity: URS-3

F $600

$50 • W-MS-1030-050-G140

Left: FIFTY vertically. ***Center:*** Train. ***Right:*** Liberty holding cornucopia / 50. ***Comments:*** H-Unlisted, Kraus-10703. 18__. 1830s.

Rarity: URS-3

F $600

$100 • W-MS-1030-100-G150

Left: 100. ***Center:*** Train. ***Right:*** ONE HUNDRED vertically. ***Comments:*** H-Unlisted, Kraus-10704. 18__. 1840s–1850s.

Rarity: URS-3

F $600

Post Notes

$__ • W-MS-1030-__-G160

Left: POST NOTE vertically. ***Center:*** Train. ***Right:*** POST NOTE vertically. ***Engraver:*** Rawdon, Wright, Hatch & Edson. ***Comments:*** H-MS-230-G30, Kraus-10705. 18__. 1830s.

Rarity: URS-3

F $600

Civil War Emergency Issues

10¢ • W-MS-1030-00.10-G170

JM

Overprint: Red 10 / CENTS vertically. ***Comments:*** H-MS-230-G40a, Kraus-52453. 186_. 1860s.

Rarity: URS-3
F $500

25¢ • W-MS-1030-00.25-G180

JM

Overprint: Green 25 / CENTS vertically. ***Comments:*** H-MS-230-G42a, Kraus-52454. 186_. 1860s.

Rarity: URS-3
F $500

50¢ • W-MS-1030-00.50-G190

JM

Overprint: Blue 50 / CENTS vertically. ***Comments:*** H-MS-230-G44a, Kraus-52455. 186_. 1860s.

Rarity: URS-3
F $550

$1 • W-MS-1030-001-G200

JM

Overprint: Green ONE on micro-ONEs. ***Comments:*** H-MS-230-G46a, Kraus-52450. 186_. 1860s.

Rarity: URS-6
F $250

$2 • W-MS-1030-002-G210

JM

Overprint: Blue TWO. ***Comments:*** H-MS-230-G48a, Kraus-52451. 186_. 1860s.

Rarity: URS-6
F $300

$3 • W-MS-1030-003-G220

JM

Overprint: Yellow THREE. ***Comments:*** H-MS-230-G50a, Kraus-52452. 186_. 1860s.

Rarity: URS-6
F $350

Civil War Emergency Issues Payable in Confederate States Notes

$1 • W-MS-1030-001-G230

JM

Overprint: Green ONE on micro-ONEs. ***Comments:*** H-Unlisted, Kraus-52456. 186_. 1860s.

Rarity: URS-6
F $350

$2 • W-MS-1030-002-G240

JM

Overprint: Blue TWO. ***Comments:*** H-Unlisted, Kraus-52457. 186_. 1860s.

Rarity: URS-6
F $350

$3 • W-MS-1030-003-G250

HA

Overprint: Yellow THREE. ***Comments:*** H-Unlisted, Kraus-52458. 186_. 1860s.

Rarity: URS-6
F $400

Uncut Sheets

$20-$20-$50-$100 •

W-MS-1030-020.020.050.100-US010

RG

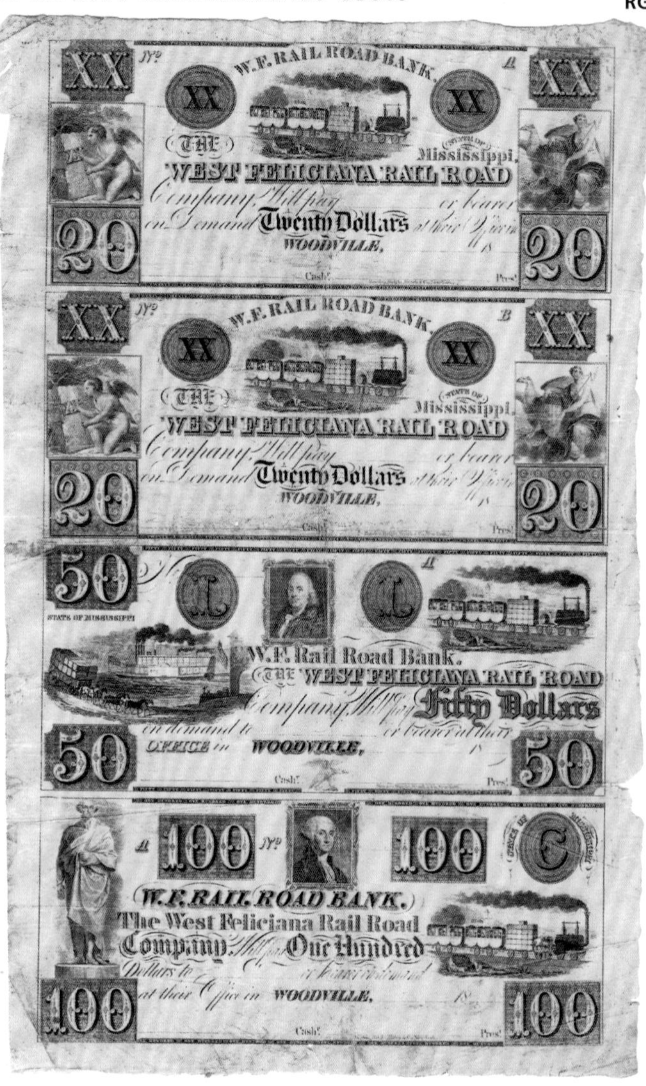

Engraver: Rawdon, Wright, Hatch & Co. ***Comments:*** H-MS-230-G16, G16, G20, G24. First two notes identical. 18__. 1830s.

Rarity: URS-1
F $7,500

Non-Valid Issues

$1 • W-MS-1030-001-C200

Overprint: None. ***Comments:*** H-MS-230-G46b, Kraus-52450a. Counterfeit of W-MS-1030-001-G200. 186_. 1860s.

Rarity: URS-3
F $300

Wyatt, Mississippi

Extinct today, Wyatt was situated in Lafayette County on the Tallahatchie River. It was settled long before Oxford or Holly Springs—what would be near neighbors today—and was incorporated in 1838. The name was originally Mitchell's Bluff, but was changed in honor of Wyatt Mitchell. Wyatt was a large shipping port, and residents hoped it would eclipse all other towns in the area. A gin factory, a hotel, and many mercantile houses were located here. After the Panic of 1837, the town began to decline. A single, small battle during the Civil War is designated as the "Battle of Wyatt."

What was the town of Wyatt now lies beneath the waters of Sardis Lake.

Tallahatchie Bridge and Turnpike Company

1838

W-MS-1040

History: The Tallahatchie Bridge and Turnpike Company was a real estate banking company run by A. Gillis and Thomas H. Allen, who flooded the county with fractional currency. It was considered to be a sound and solid company, at least for a time.

Numismatic Commentary: Issued notes are excessively rare. Most notes are known from recycled remainder sheets that were used to print notes from other issuers during the Civil War.

Valid Issues

12-1/2¢ • W-MS-1040-00.12.50-G010

Left: Justice seated with scales and sword. ***Center:*** 12-1/2. ***Comments:*** H-Unlisted, Kraus-15020. 1838.

Rarity: —

25¢ • W-MS-1040-00.25-G020

JM

Comments: H-Unlisted, Kraus-15021. 18__. 1838.

Rarity: URS-2

F $1,500

50¢ • W-MS-1040-00.50-G030

Left: Muse holding Euterpe. ***Center:*** Ceres holding sheaf. ***Right:*** Ceres seated holding sheaf. ***Comments:*** H-Unlisted, Kraus-15022. 1838.

Rarity: —

$1 • W-MS-1040-001-G040

JM

Comments: H-Unlisted, Kraus-15024. 18__. 1838.

Rarity: URS-3

F $1,500

$1 • W-MS-1040-001-G050

Comments: H-Unlisted, Kraus-15040. No description available. 1838.

Rarity: *None known*

$5 • W-MS-1040-005-G060

Comments: H-Unlisted, Kraus-15025. No description available. 1838.

Rarity: *None known*

$10 • W-MS-1040-010-G070

Comments: H-Unlisted, Kraus-15026. No description available. 1838.

Rarity: *None known*

$20 • W-MS-1040-020-G080

Comments: H-Unlisted, Kraus-15027. No description available. 1838.

Rarity: *None known*

Post Notes

$5 • W-MS-1040-005-G090

JM

Comments: H-Unlisted, Kraus-15041a. 18__. 1838.

Rarity: URS-2

Fair $750

$10 • W-MS-1040-010-G100

Comments: H-Unlisted, Kraus-15042. No description available. 1838.

Rarity: *None known*

$20 • W-MS-1040-020-G110

Center: Neptune pouring water / Indian with tomahawk / Neptune pouring water. ***Comments:*** H-Unlisted, Kraus-15043. 1838.

Rarity: *None known*

$50 • **W-MS-1040-050-G120**

Comments: H-Unlisted, Kraus-15044. No description available. 1838.

Rarity: *None known*

$100 • **W-MS-1040-100-G130**

Comments: H-Unlisted, Kraus-15045. No description available. 1838.

Rarity: *None known*

YAZOO CITY, MISSISSIPPI

Yazoo City was founded in 1824 under the name of Hannan's Bluff. It was briefly known as Manchester before it was designated as Yazoo City in 1841. The town became the county seat in 1849, just before being struck by a yellow-fever epidemic in 1853. The Civil War brought more turmoil to the town, as a shipyard was set up on the Yazoo River in the city. This became a prime target for Union forces, and it was destroyed in 1863. The Confederate army quickly took back control of the area. In the second attack the city was almost wholly burned down. After the war the city was rebuilt, but another strike of yellow fever reduced the population.

See also Manchester, Mississippi.

Bank of Yazoo City

1862

W-MS-1050

History: The Bank of Yazoo City was authorized on January 17, 1862, with a capital of $500,000.[29] It is unknown if this bank ever went into operation.

Numismatic Commentary: No notes from this bank are known.

Commercial Bank of Manchester

1836–1860

W-MS-1060

History: The Commercial Bank of Manchester was chartered on February 26, 1836, with an authorized capital of no more than $2,000,000. The president of the bank was M.B. Hamer, and J.J. Hughes was the cashier. Notes with a denomination less than $5 were not permitted. On February 15, 1838, an act was passed reducing the capital to $1,000,000. In 1840 many banks had their charters suspended due to an inability to pay specie, but this bank survived. In 1860 it finally failed.

After the name of the town changed from Manchester to Yazoo City in 1841, the parent bank, W-MS-540, became located in Yazoo City without actually moving.

Numismatic Commentary: Notes issued by the Commercial Bank of Manchester in Yazoo City were issued in the late 1850s and are very scarce.

VALID ISSUES

$5 • **W-MS-1060-005-G010**

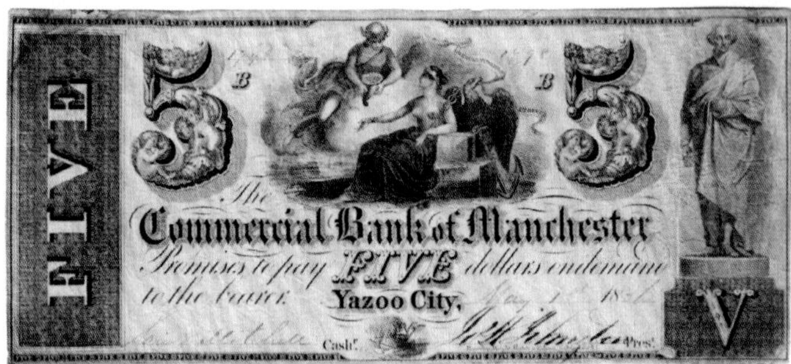

Engraver: Rawdon, Wright, Hatch & Edson. ***Comments:*** H-MS-235-G2, Kraus-4490. 18__. 1850s.

Rarity: URS-3
F $1,000

$5 • **W-MS-1060-005-G020**

Engraver: Rawdon, Wright, Hatch & Edson. ***Comments:*** H-Unlisted, Kraus-4500. No description available. 18__. 1830s.

Rarity: *None known*

$10 • **W-MS-1060-010-G030**

Left: Minerva with spear. ***Center:*** Commerce reclining in garden of flowers / Steamship. ***Right:*** X bearing cherub. ***Engraver:*** Rawdon, Wright, Hatch & Edson. ***Comments:*** H-MS-235-G4, Kraus-4501. 18__. 1830s.

Rarity: *None known*

$20 • **W-MS-1060-020-G040**

Engraver: Rawdon, Wright, Hatch & Edson. ***Comments:*** H-MS-235-G6, Kraus-4502. No description available. 18__. 1830s.

Rarity: *None known*

$50 • **W-MS-1060-050-G050**

Engraver: Rawdon, Wright, Hatch & Edson. ***Comments:*** H-MS-235-G8, Kraus-4503. No description available. 18__. 1830s.

Rarity: *None known*

$100 • **W-MS-1060-100-G060**

Engraver: Rawdon, Wright, Hatch & Edson. ***Comments:*** H-MS-235-G10, Kraus-4504. No description available. 18__. 1830s.

Rarity: *None known*

Notes on Which the Place Payable is Blank

$10 • **W-MS-1060-010-G070**

JM

Back: Plain. ***Engraver:*** Rawdon, Wright, Hatch & Edson. ***Comments:*** H-MS-235-G34, Kraus-4501a. 18__. 1830s.

Rarity: URS-3
F $950

$20 • W-MS-1060-020-G080

Back: Plain. ***Engraver:*** Rawdon, Wright, Hatch & Edson. ***Comments:*** H-MS-235-G36. No description available. 18__. 1830s.

Rarity: *None known*

$50 • W-MS-1060-050-G090

Back: Plain. ***Engraver:*** Rawdon, Wright, Hatch & Edson. ***Comments:*** H-MS-235-G38. No description available. 18__. 1830s.

Rarity: *None known*

$50 • W-MS-1060-050-G090a

Back: Red-orange. ***Engraver:*** Rawdon, Wright, Hatch & Edson. ***Comments:*** H-MS-235-G38a. Similar to W-MS-1060-050-G090. 18__. 1830s.

Rarity: *None known*

$100 • W-MS-1060-100-G100

Left: ONE HUNDRED vertically. ***Center:*** 100 / Commerce reclining. ***Right:*** 100 / Liberty sitting on wharf / 100. ***Back:*** Plain. ***Engraver:*** Rawdon, Wright, Hatch & Edson. ***Comments:*** H-MS-235-G40, Kraus-4519b. 18__. 1830s.

Rarity: *None known*

$100 • W-MS-1060-100-G100a

Back: Red-orange. ***Engraver:*** Rawdon, Wright, Hatch & Edson. ***Comments:*** H-MS-235-G40a. Similar to W-MS-1060-100-G100. 18__. 1830s.

Rarity: URS-3
F $650

Post Notes Payable at an Unknown Bank in New York

$5 • W-MS-1060-005-G110

Engraver: Rawdon, Wright, Hatch & Edson. ***Comments:*** H-Unlisted, Kraus-4515. No description available. 18__. 1830s.

Rarity: *None known*

$10 • W-MS-1060-010-G120

Engraver: Rawdon, Wright, Hatch & Edson. ***Comments:*** H-Unlisted, Kraus-4516. No description available. 18__. 1830s.

Rarity: *None known*

$20 • W-MS-1060-020-G130

Engraver: Rawdon, Wright, Hatch & Edson. ***Comments:*** H-Unlisted, Kraus-4517. No description available. 18__. 1830s.

Rarity: *None known*

$50 • W-MS-1060-050-G140

Engraver: Rawdon, Wright, Hatch & Edson. ***Comments:*** H-Unlisted, Kraus-4518. No description available. 18__. 1830s.

Rarity: *None known*

Planters Bank of the State of Mississippi (branch)

1830–1844

W-MS-1070

History: The Planters Bank of the State of Mississippi was the second bank to be chartered in the state. It was incorporated on February 10, 1830, with an authorized capital of $3,000,000, $2,000,000 of which was provided from the state through the sale of bonds. The Panic of 1837 struck the bank hard. The state's bonds were repudiated, and the bank failed thereafter. On February 23, 1844, the bank was put into liquidation.

The Planters Bank of the State of Mississippi had its parent bank located in Natchez, W-MS-670, and branch banks located in Columbus, W-MS-240, Jackson, W-MS-470, Manchester, W-MS-555, Monticello, W-MS-580, Port Gibson, W-MS-780, Vicksburg, W-MS-920, and Woodville, W-MS-1020.

Numismatic Commentary: As Yazoo City was known as Manchester during the 1830s, there are no known notes with the Yazoo City imprint.

The Obsolete Bank Notes of Tennessee

State Banking in Tennessee

The Early Years

Tennessee joined the Union as a state in 1796. The first bank chartered afterward was the Nashville Bank in November 1807, capitalized at $200,000. In 1817 the legislature provided for banks to be established in Gallatin, Murfreesboro, Rogersville, Shelbyville, and Winchester. Before they were fully organized they became branches of the Nashville Bank, now with a capital of $2,400,000. It is recorded that on March 31, 1823, over $250,000 in older bills was burned. The bank continued in business with one or two suspensions of specie payments until it was liquidated in 1827. Those who redeemed their notes received face value for them. Stockholders sustained a small loss on their shares.

The first Bank of the State of Tennessee was chartered on November 20, 1811, with headquarters in Knoxville. Branches were set up at Clarksville, Columbia, and Jonesboro, followed by offices in Carthage, Franklin, Kingston, Maryville, and Nashville. The state was a shareholder. Capital was set for the branches at $200,000 to $400,000 each. Most branches operated independently of the Knoxville home office, an exception being the Nashville branch which was also the most profitable in the system. The bank wound down its operations in the 1820s in a transition in which the second bank of the same name conducted business.

In 1817 the Farmers and Mechanics Bank of Nashville was chartered. On June 18, 1819, in an era of difficult economic times nationwide, this bank was the first in the state to suspend specie payments after having paid out more than $30,000 in coin in the preceding two months to redeem bills as presented. Continuing well into the 1820s, this action and the depreciated value of notes of other banks cast a pall on bills of Tennessee. They were viewed with particular disfavor and traded at deep discounts in relation to silver coins, even deeper discounts in gold, and in some quarters were refused at any price.

Into the 1820s

Economic t imes continued to be difficult, and the circulation of currency slowed dramatically. On September 23, 1820, *Niles' Weekly Register* reported that at exchange offices in Baltimore there had been no transactions in Tennessee bills in recent times.

On July 26, 1820, the second Bank of the State of Tennessee was chartered with an expiration year of 1843, with the thought that it would do what other banks had not or could not: promptly pay specie and issue bills that were worth par in commerce. This was the brainchild of Governor Joseph McMinn, who had convened a special session of the legislature to consider and enact the law of authorization. Headquartered in Nashville, the bank had branches in Columbia, Franklin, and Knoxville. However, reality proved to be different from theory. The bank did not operate ideally but did play a part in business and trade. Its bills flooded commerce with $1,000,000 in face value and became so depreciated that two other large banks in the state resolved not to accept them at all. In 1830 the cashier of the bank was found to have secretly run $100,000 in overdrafts through the bank. He had not posted accounts for 18 months, and he was the only one who knew who owed money. Curiously, he was allowed to settle the account in a manner which was said to have been satisfactory to certain people who held high offices in the state government. The system shut down in 1832 by order of Governor William Carroll with a great loss to the state. The next year in his message to the state legislature, Carroll gave this poignant comment: "The establishment of banks for the purpose of relieving the people from pecuniary distress is, in most cases, ruinous to those who avail themselves of such relief."

The second Bank of the United States, chartered by Congress in 1816, proposed to open a branch in Nashville. Upon learning of this, the legislature levied a yearly tax of $50,000 per office on any out-of-state bank proposing to do business in Tennessee, an action similar to that taken in Ohio. As was the case with the Ohio tax, this was later ruled unconstitutional by the U.S. Supreme Court. Afterward, in August 1827, the branch of the Bank of the United States began business. The branch was discontinued in the 1830s, as were all others due to the fact that the charter was set to expire in 1836.

Banking in the 1830s

State deposits and much other business were transferred to the new Union Bank of Tennessee, chartered on October 18, 1832, with a capital authorized up to $3,000,000. The state requested the option to buy up to a third of the stock, and eventually paid in $500,000—financed by the sale of bonds. Opening for business in 1835, the bank operated successfully with several branches. Most business was done in Memphis.[1]

The Farmers and Merchants Bank of Memphis was chartered in November 1833 with an authorized capital of $600,000. Large quantities of bills were issued. Controls were lax, and the bank collapsed, or almost did, in 1847. Control was obtained by fraudsters who thereafter issued large quantities of worthless notes. The Planters Bank, chartered on November 11, 1833, began business the following February, became important in the state, and had branches in Athens, Clarksville, Franklin, Memphis, Pulaski, and Winchester.

The Panic of 1837, which carried through to early 1843, was difficult for all banks, and specie payments were suspended, then resumed, then by some banks suspended again. Currency was plentiful in circulation, but gold and silver coins were scarce.

The Bank of the State of Tennessee, the third effort at a state-run bank, was chartered on January 19, 1839, capitalized at $5,000,000, and financed by the state. Economic times remained sluggish, and the sale of bonds did not meet expectations. After many difficulties it went into operation in Nashville, and branches were opened in Athens, Clarksville, Columbia, Knoxville, Memphis, Murfreesboro, Rogersville, Shelbyville, Somerville, and Trenton, followed later by one in Sparta. This bank lasted through the Civil War, but barely. During the conflict, certain officers took assets of the bank and spirited them off to Atlanta, where they were only partially recovered after the war.

Later Years

During the Panic of 1837 the banks in Tennessee stopped paying coins in exchange for their currency. In 1842 it was announced that specie payments would be resumed statewide on July 1, but some banks were not ready, and resumption did not take place until August 1.

In 1843 the Bank of East Tennessee, capitalized at $800,000 and with private stockholders, was set up in Knoxville and issued much paper money. In 1848 the Bank of Lawrenceburg was capitalized for $100,000.

Bankers' Magazine reported this in January 1850:

> The Joint Committee on Banks in the Tennessee Legislature has reported in favor of a general free banking law, with a bill carrying out that system. The minimum capital is $100,000. The outline of the system is stated as follows:
>
> An association of persons, or a single one, purchases $100,000 or more of State stock. This is deposited with a Commissioner or Comptroller, appointed for the purpose, who shall cause to be engraved and printed, at the expense of the party applying, notes of the nature of bank notes to the amount of said stock, (in some projects only 90 per cent. of such stock,) countersigned by himself, and to be signed by the officers of the bank where the same are payable. Then follow various provisions of security.
>
> The advantage to the banker is as follows: He draws the interest of his State stock deposited, say 5 per cent., and loans out the notes based on this stock at 6 or 7 per cent.,—sufficient to bear expenses of banking house, officers, &c. The security to the note holder is, that the Comptroller will be always able to pay the whole issue in State or U.S. stock, the law so guarding it as to prevent a greater issue than is provided for by it. This system, while it is the most safe of any yet devised for the note holder, is more profitable to the banker, and more beneficial to the country, by making the State stock a safe circulating currency capital for the business of the people. The Tennessee bill provides a payment of 25 cents on every $100, for school purposes in lieu of every other State tax.

Free banking was taking hold across the country and in time resulted in the establishment of many new institutions. The legislative session of 1851 and 1852 passed the Free Banking Law, essentially patterned on the New York state legislation. "Quite a number of banks were organized under this law on fictitious capital, and 'wildcat' banks were as plentiful as grasshoppers," historian John Jay Knox commented. Further:

> The issuance of bank notes of a high order of engraving seemed to be the order of the day. The rule of $3 in capital to $1 in specie seemed to be obsolete, and the redundancy of currency was enormous. In 1853 Governor Andrew Johnson, in his message to the General Assembly, did not hesitate to condemn the wretched system of banking the state had gradually fallen into, and he suggested the liquidation of the State Bank, and again in 1855 and in 1857. This ridiculous system of banking which pervaded every state in the Union, had its weight in producing the Panic of 1857.

A writer in *Bankers' Magazine*, August 1856, stated this concerning free banks:

> They are decidedly injurious to the trading interests of the community. They discount very little business paper, if any; they gather up all the circulation of the stock banks, which have hitherto been doing a regular banking business, by exchanging their . . . notes therefore, then run upon those banks for specie or eastern exchange, and thereby cramp them so that they are unable to discount scarcely anything for their customers. These free banks are in fact nothing but broker concerns—they add nothing. . . .

By the end of 1856 there were 46 banks operating in the state, the quality of which varied from poor to solid. After the Panic of 1857, banking was quiet. Then came the Civil War. The effects on state banking in Tennessee were not as harmful as for other states in the South.

Numismatic Comments

As might be expected from the checkered reputations of many banks in Tennessee, ranging from failed early institutions to rampant "wildcats" of the 1850s, a large trail of paper was left behind. As a result, a general representation of bills of this state are easily collected today. Those of the 1850s and early 1860s are ornate and colorful. The numismatic landscape is also sprinkled with rarities and unconfirmed notes, especially among early issues and those bearing the imprints of branch offices.

Due to the enthusiasm and effort of the late Paul Garland, notes of this state were very popular decades ago, before the currency of certain other states moved into the mainstream. For many, this enthusiasm continues today.

The standard reference on Tennessee paper money is *The History of Early Tennessee Banks and their Issues*, by Paul E. Garland and published in 1983. For any scholar of Tennessee's complex banking history, this is a great book to have.

Athens, Tennessee

The Athens area was inhabited by Cherokee when the first Europeans arrived. In 1819 a treaty was signed selling the land to the United States, and in 1822 Athens was laid out to be the county seat. The name of the town is thought to have come from Athens, Greece.

In 1834 the population of Athens was over 500 residents. An iron forge was in operation, as were several other construction and mechanical businesses. In the 1830s the Hiwassee Railroad connected Knoxville, Tennessee, to Dalton, Georgia. It did not connect to Athens until 1851. There was a hotel and a courthouse, and dairy farms were run by Jesse Mayfield.

During the Civil War the town was divided nearly in half on the subject of secession. In 1861 the movement was voted down, although soldiers from the area went to fight on both sides of the war—truly a case of neighbor fighting against neighbor. In preparation for his infamous "March to the Sea" in 1864, General William Tecumseh Sherman was headquartered at the local Bridges Hotel.

Bank of the State of Tennessee {3rd} (branch)

1838–1866

W-TN-010

History: The third Bank of the State of Tennessee (also seen in print as the Bank of Tennessee) was chartered on January 19, 1838, with an authorized capital of $5,000,000. The bank opened for business in February.

On May 15, 1838, the branch in Athens was opened with a capital of $400,000. The president was William H. Ballew, and the cashier was A. Blizard. The bank suspended specie payments a couple of times in 1838 and 1839, due to the panic of that time, but afterward it resumed and had a profitable and successful career. During the Civil War, the Union army entered the state, and some officers of the Bank of the State of Tennessee fled south with the bank's specie. After the war, the bank's assets were returned to Governor William G. Brownlow in Nashville. Half of the bank's funds had been transferred into state bonds. In 1864 the branch's capital was $164,000. W.C. Witt was the cashier.

By February 1866 the Bank of the State of Tennessee was authorized to go into liquidation.

The third Bank of the State of Tennessee had its parent bank located in Nashville, W-TN-690, and branch banks located in Clarksville, W-TN-120, Columbia, W-TN-190, Knoxville, W-TN-365, Memphis, W-TN-490, Murfreesboro, W-TN-610, Rogersville, W-TN-890, Shelbyville, W-TN-920, Somerville, W-TN-960, Sparta, W-TN-980, and Trenton, W-TN-1030.

Numismatic Commentary: Signed and issued notes redeemable in Athens are considered to be quite scarce, with surviving-note estimates ranging from fewer than 5 to about 25. The listed $5 and $100 notes were unknown to Garland. Fractional notes of 5¢, 10¢, 25¢, and 50¢ denominations exist (listed under the parent bank, W-TN-690), printed by J. Manouvrier, New Orleans, and dated 1861.

Valid Issues

$1 • W-TN-010-001-G010

Left: Woman seated with farmer / Female portrait. ***Center:*** 1 / Man plowing with horses / 1. ***Right:*** ONE / Medallion head / ONE. ***Engraver:*** Draper, Toppan & Co. ***Comments:*** H-TN-195-G70. Mar. 1, 1842.

Rarity: —

$1 • W-TN-010-001-G010a

Engraver: Toppan, Carpenter & Co. ***Comments:*** H-TN-195-G70a. Similar to W-TN-010-001-G010 but with different date and engraver imprint. Mar. 1, ____. 1840s, 1861.

Rarity: —

$1 • W-TN-010-001-G020 CC

Engraver: Toppan, Carpenter, Casilear & Co. ***Comments:*** H-TN-195-G72. 18__. 1850s–1860s.

Rarity: URS-5
F $275

$1 • W-TN-010-001-G030

Left: 1 / Portrait of boy. ***Center:*** Indian on horseback hunting buffalo. ***Right:*** 1 / Female portrait. ***Tint:*** Red-orange. ***Back:*** Red-orange. ***Engraver:*** Toppan, Carpenter & Co. ***Comments:*** H-TN-195-G74a. 18__. 1850s.

Rarity: URS-4
F $375

$2 • W-TN-010-002-G040

Left: TWO / Woman seated in 2 / 2. ***Center:*** 2 / Woman seated on bales / 2. ***Right:*** 2 / Ship / 2. ***Engraver:*** Draper, Toppan & Co. ***Comments:*** H-TN-195-G76. Mar. 1, 1842.

Rarity: —

$2 • W-TN-010-002-G040a

Engraver: Toppan, Carpenter & Co. ***Comments:*** H-TN-195-G76a. Similar to W-TN-010-002-G040 but with different date and engraver imprint. Mar. 1, ____. 1840s, 1861.

Rarity: —

$2 • **W-TN-010-002-G050** CC

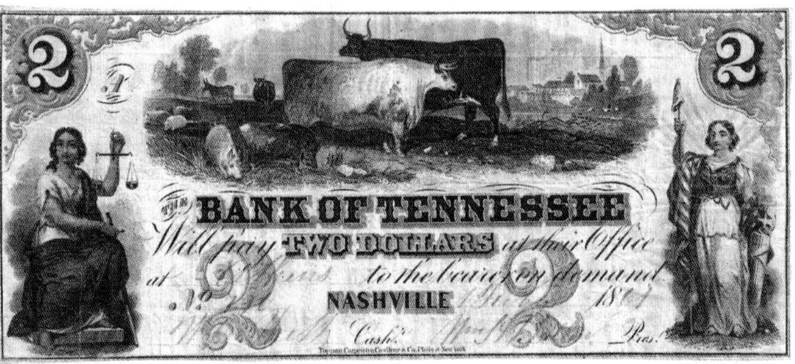

Engraver: Toppan, Carpenter, Casilear & Co. ***Comments:*** H-TN-195-G78. 18__. 1850s–1860s.

Rarity: URS-5
F $325

$2 • **W-TN-010-002-G060**

Left: 2 / Female portrait. ***Center:*** Soldier, Woman, and two Indians looking at bust of George Washington. ***Right:*** 2 / Portrait of Charles Carroll. ***Tint:*** Red-orange. ***Back:*** Red-orange. ***Engraver:*** Toppan, Carpenter & Co. ***Comments:*** H-TN-195-G80a. 18__. 1850s.

Rarity: URS-5
F $325

$3 • **W-TN-010-003-G070**

Left: THREE / Woman standing / THREE. ***Center:*** 3 / Men on horses, sheep / 3. ***Right:*** THREE / Cherubs in 3 / THREE. ***Engraver:*** Draper, Toppan & Co. ***Comments:*** H-TN-195-G82. Mar. 1, 1842.

Rarity: *None known*

$3 • **W-TN-010-003-G070a**

Engraver: Toppan, Carpenter & Co. ***Comments:*** H-TN-195-G82a. Similar to W-TN-010-003-G070 but with different date and engraver imprint. Mar. 1, ____. 1840s, 1861.

Rarity: *None known*

$5 • **W-TN-010-005-G080**

Left: 5 / Woman leaning on column / V. ***Center:*** Woman seated with shield. ***Right:*** 5 / Justice standing with scales and eagle / V. ***Engraver:*** Rawdon, Wright, Hatch & Edson / Rawdon, Wright & Hatch. ***Comments:*** H-TN-195-G84. 18__. 1838–1840s.

Rarity: *None known*

$5 • **W-TN-010-005-G090**

Left: Three men / 5. ***Center:*** Portrait of James Madison. ***Right:*** 5 / Medallion head. ***Engraver:*** Danforth, Bald & Co. ***Comments:*** H-TN-195-G86. 18__. 1861.

Rarity: URS-2
F $650

$5 • **W-TN-010-005-G090a**

Back: Red-orange. ***Engraver:*** Danforth, Bald & Co. ***Comments:*** H-TN-195-G86a. Similar to W-TN-010-005-G090. 18__. 1850s.

Rarity: URS-5
F $300

$5 • **W-TN-010-005-G090b**

Tint: Red-orange outlining white V / 5 / V. ***Back:*** Red-orange. ***Engraver:*** Danforth, Bald & Co. ***Comments:*** H-TN-195-G86b. Similar to W-TN-010-005-G090. 18__. 1850s.

Rarity: URS-5
F $300

$10 • **W-TN-010-010-G100**

Left: 10 / Eagle with shield / X. ***Center:*** Woman with children seated among parcels, Factories and farmhouse. ***Right:*** 10 / Shield / X. ***Engraver:*** Draper, Toppan, Longacre & Co. ***Comments:*** H-TN-195-G92. 18__. 1838–1840s.

Rarity: —

$10 • **W-TN-010-010-G110**

Left: 10 / Portrait of James K. Polk. ***Center:*** Portrait of Andrew Jackson. ***Right:*** 10 / Portrait of Cave Johnson. ***Tint:*** Red-orange outlining white 10 / 10. ***Back:*** Blue. ***Engraver:*** Toppan, Carpenter & Co. ***Comments:*** H-TN-195-G94a. 18__. 1850s–1861.

Rarity: URS-4
F $400

$20 • **W-TN-010-020-G120**

Left: 20 / Man writing on tablet / 20. ***Center:*** Woman standing with eagle and shield. ***Right:*** 20 / Shield / 20. ***Engraver:*** Draper, Toppan, Longacre & Co. ***Comments:*** H-TN-195-G96. 18__. 1838–1840s.

Rarity: —

$20 • **W-TN-010-020-G120a**

Engraver: Toppan, Carpenter & Co. ***Comments:*** H-TN-195-G96a. Similar to W-TN-010-020-G120 but with different engraver imprint. 18__. 1840s–1850s

Rarity: —

$20 • **W-TN-010-020-G130**

Left: 20 / Portrait of Zachary Taylor / 20. ***Center:*** Three women reclining, Ship / 20. ***Right:*** Justice seated with sword and scales / TWENTY. ***Engraver:*** Toppan, Carpenter, Casilear & Co. ***Comments:*** H-TN-195-G98. 18__. 1850s.

Rarity: URS-4
F $400

$20 • **W-TN-010-020-G130a**

Back: Red-orange. ***Engraver:*** Toppan, Carpenter, Casilear & Co. ***Comments:*** H-TN-195-G98a. Similar to W-TN-010-020-G130. 18__. 1850s.

Rarity: URS-4
F $400

$20 • **W-TN-010-020-G130b**

Tint: Red-orange outlining white TWENTY. ***Back:*** Red-orange. ***Engraver:*** Toppan, Carpenter, Casilear & Co. ***Comments:*** H-TN-195-G98b. Similar to W-TN-010-020-G130. 18__. 1850s.

Rarity: URS-4
F $400

$50 • **W-TN-010-050-G140**

Left: 50 / Shield / 50. ***Center:*** Liberty with eagle and shield. ***Right:*** 50 / Portrait of George Washington / 50. ***Engraver:*** Draper, Toppan, Longacre & Co. ***Comments:*** H-TN-195-G100. 18__. 1838–1840s.

Rarity: —

$100 • **W-TN-010-100-G150**

Left: Atlas lifting world on shoulders / 100. ***Center:*** 100 / Justice with eagle and shield / 100. ***Right:*** Atlas lifting world on shoulders / 100. ***Engraver:*** Draper, Toppan, Longacre & Co. ***Comments:*** H-TN-195-G102. 18__. 1838–1850s.

Rarity: —

Non-Valid Issues

$10 • W-TN-010-010-C100

Engraver: Draper, Toppan, Longacre & Co. ***Comments:*** H-TN-195-C92. Counterfeit of W-TN-010-010-G100. 18__. 1830s.

Rarity: —

$20 • W-TN-010-020-C120a

Engraver: Toppan, Carpenter & Co. ***Comments:*** H-TN-195-C96a. Counterfeit of W-TN-010-020-G120a. 18__. 1850s.

Rarity: —

$20 • W-TN-010-020-C130

Engraver: Toppan, Carpenter, Casilear & Co. ***Comments:*** H-TN-195-C98. Counterfeit of W-TN-010-020-G130. 18__. 1850s.

Rarity: URS-2
F $750

$20 • W-TN-010-020-C130a

Back: Red-orange. ***Engraver:*** Toppan, Carpenter, Casilear & Co. ***Comments:*** H-TN-195-C98a. Counterfeit of W-TN-010-020-G130a. 18__. 1850s.

Rarity: *None known*

$20 • W-TN-010-020-C130b

Tint: Red-orange outlining white TWENTY. ***Back:*** Red-orange. ***Engraver:*** Toppan, Carpenter, Casilear & Co. ***Comments:*** H-TN-195-C98b. Counterfeit of W-TN-010-020-G130b. 18__. 1850s.

Rarity: *None known*

$50 • W-TN-010-050-C140

Engraver: Draper, Toppan, Longacre & Co. ***Comments:*** H-TN-195-C100. Counterfeit of W-TN-010-050-G140. 18__. 1850s.

Rarity: *None known*

Planters Bank of Tennessee (branch)

1834–1865

W-TN-020

History: The Planters Bank of Tennessee was chartered on November 11, 1833, with an authorized capital of $2,000,000. The Athens branch was opened in 1834. In 1848 the president was James H. Regan, and David Cleage was the cashier. Capital was stated to be $249,150. In 1855 this dropped to $150,000. In 1865 the bank was forced to liquidate and close its affairs.

The Planters Bank of Tennessee had its parent bank located in Nashville, W-TN-810, and branch banks located in Clarksville, W-TN-140, Columbia, W-TN-210, Franklin, W-TN-300, LaGrange, W-TN-410, Memphis, W-TN-570, Murfreesboro, W-TN-630, Pulaski, W-TN-870, Rogersville, W-TN-910, Shelbyville, W-TN-940, Somerville, W-TN-970, Sparta, W-TN-990, Trenton, W-TN-1050, and Winchester, W-TN-1070.

Numismatic Commentary: Current collectors feel that signed and issued notes of the Planters Bank of Tennessee, Athens, are on par with the Athens notes issued by the third Bank of the State of Tennessee, W-TN-010. Fractional notes of 10¢, 25¢, 30¢, 50¢, and 80¢ notes are considered to be scarce to very scarce, while the dollar-denominated notes are slightly less so. The $50 and $100 were unknown to Garland.

Valid Issues

$1 • W-TN-020-001-G010

Left: 1 / Medallion head bearing ONE / 1. ***Center:*** 1 with cherub / Woman seated with boxes. ***Right:*** Woman standing in 1. ***Engraver:*** Rawdon, Wright, Hatch & Edson. ***Comments:*** H-TN-185-G46. 18__. 1840s.

Rarity: *None known*

$2 • W-TN-020-002-G020

Left: 2 / Woman with sheaf / 2. ***Center:*** 2 with cherubs / Woman seated with boxes. ***Right:*** Woman standing in 2. ***Engraver:*** Rawdon, Wright, Hatch & Edson. ***Comments:*** H-TN-185-G48. Dec. 1, 1860.

Rarity: *None known*

$3 • W-TN-020-003-G030

Left: 3 / Medallion head / 3. ***Center:*** 3 with cherubs / Two men flanking shield bearing cow surmounted by beehive. ***Right:*** Woman standing in 3. ***Engraver:*** Rawdon, Wright, Hatch & Edson. ***Comments:*** H-TN-185-G50. Dec. 1, 1860.

Rarity: *None known*

$5 • W-TN-020-005-G040

Left: FIVE / Woman with cog wheel / 5 vertically. ***Center:*** 5 / Horse / 5. ***Right:*** FIVE / Man seated / 5 vertically. ***Engraver:*** Rawdon, Wright, & Hatch. ***Comments:*** H-TN-185-G52. 18__. 1830s.

Rarity: *None known*

$5 • W-TN-020-005-G050

Left: Medallion head / FIVE / Medallion head. ***Center:*** FIVE / Man standing with dog / FIVE. ***Right:*** Medallion head / FIVE / Medallion head. ***Engraver:*** Underwood, Bald & Spencer. ***Comments:*** H-TN-185-G54. 18__. 1830s–1840s.

Rarity: URS-5
F $300

$5 • W-TN-020-005-G050a

Engraver: Underwood, Bald & Spencer. ***Comments:*** H-TN-185-G54a. Similar to W-TN-020-005-G050. 18__. 1830s–1840s.

Rarity: *None known*

$10 • W-TN-020-010-G060

Left: X / Ten gold dollars / 10. ***Center:*** 10 / Mechanic seated with cogwheel, Steamboat / 10. ***Right:*** TEN / Woman standing with anchor / TEN. ***Engraver:*** Rawdon, Wright, & Hatch. ***Comments:*** H-TN-185-G56. 18__. 1830s.

Rarity: *None known*

$10 • W-TN-020-010-G070

Left: Medallion head / TEN / Medallion head. ***Center:*** 10 / Farm scene, Harvest / X. ***Right:*** Medallion head / TEN / Medallion head. ***Engraver:*** Underwood, Bald & Spencer. ***Comments:*** H-TN-185-G58. 18__. 1830s–1840s.

Rarity: URS-4
F $400

$10 • W-TN-020-010-G070a

Engraver: Underwood, Bald & Spencer. ***Comments:*** H-TN-185-G58a. Similar to W-TN-020-010-G070. 18__. 1830s–1840s.

Rarity: *None known*

$20 • W-TN-020-020-G080
Engraver: Rawdon, Wright, & Hatch. ***Comments:*** H-TN-185-G60. No description available. 18__. 1830s.
Rarity: *None known*

$20 • W-TN-020-020-G090
Left: 20 / Medallion head / 20. ***Center:*** 20 / Medallion head / 20. ***Right:*** 20 / Medallion head / 20. ***Engraver:*** Underwood, Bald & Spencer. ***Comments:*** H-TN-185-G62. 18__. 1830s–1840s.
Rarity: URS-4
F $400

$20 • W-TN-020-020-G090a
Engraver: Underwood, Bald & Spencer. ***Comments:*** H-TN-185-G62a. Similar to W-TN-020-020-G090. 18__. 1830s–1840s.
Rarity: —

$50 • W-TN-020-050-G100
Left: 50 / Medallion head / 50. ***Center:*** Medallion heads / Woman seated, Ship / Medallion heads. ***Right:*** 50 / Medallion head / 50. ***Engraver:*** Underwood, Bald, Spencer & Hufty. ***Comments:*** H-TN-185-G64. 18__. 1830s–1850s.
Rarity: —

$100 • W-TN-020-100-G110
Left: 100 / Three women seated vertically / 100. ***Center:*** Medallion head / Boy reclining under corn, Plow / Medallion head. ***Right:*** 100 / Three women seated vertically / 100. ***Engraver:*** Underwood, Bald, Spencer & Hufty. ***Comments:*** H-TN-185-G66. 18__. 1830s–1850s.
Rarity: —

Civil War Fractional Notes

5¢ • W-TN-020-00.05-G120
Center: FIVE CENTS. ***Right:*** 5. ***Engraver:*** Adams. ***Comments:*** H-TN-185-G70. Jan. 1, 1862.
Rarity: —

10¢ • W-TN-020-00.10-G130
Center: TEN CENTS. ***Right:*** 10. ***Engraver:*** Adams. ***Comments:*** H-TN-185-G72. Jan. 1, 1862.
Rarity: —

25¢ • W-TN-020-00.25-G140
Center: TWENTY FIVE CENTS. ***Right:*** 25. ***Engraver:*** Adams. ***Comments:*** H-TN-185-G74. Jan. 1, 1862.
Rarity: —

30¢ • W-TN-020-00.30-G150
Center: THIRTY CENTS. ***Right:*** 30. ***Engraver:*** Adams. ***Comments:*** H-TN-185-G76. Jan. 1, 1862.
Rarity: —

50¢ • W-TN-020-00.50-G160
Center: FIFTY CENTS. ***Right:*** 50. ***Back:*** Red. ***Engraver:*** Adams. ***Comments:*** H-TN-185-G78. Jan. 1, 1862.
Rarity: —

80¢ • W-TN-020-00.80-G170
Center: EIGHTY CENTS. ***Right:*** 80. ***Back:*** Red. ***Engraver:*** Adams. ***Comments:*** H-TN-185-G80. Jan. 1, 1862.
Rarity: —

Non-Valid Issues

$10 • W-TN-020-010-S010
Left: Woman. ***Center:*** Woman, Train, Steamboat. ***Right:*** Ceres. ***Comments:*** H-TN-185-S20. 18__. 1840s.
Rarity: —

$10 • W-TN-020-010-S020
Left: 10 / Justice with scales. ***Center:*** X with cherubs / Two women seated. ***Right:*** 10 / Justice with scales. ***Engraver:*** Rawdon, Wright & Hatch. ***Comments:*** H-TN-185-S22. From a genuine plate of the Planters Bank of Alabama, Wetumpka, Alabama. 18__. 1840s.
Rarity: —

$20 • W-TN-020-020-S030
Center: Eagle. ***Comments:*** H-TN-185-S24. 18__. 1840s.
Rarity: —

$20 • W-TN-020-020-S040
Left: 20 / Female portrait / XX. ***Center:*** Woman seated near ocean with shield. ***Right:*** 20 / Female portrait / XX. ***Engraver:*** Rawdon, Wright & Hatch. ***Comments:*** H-TN-185-S26. From a genuine plate of the Planters Bank of Alabama, Wetumpka, Alabama. 18__. 1840s.
Rarity: —

$50 • W-TN-020-050-S050
Left: FIFTY DOLLARS vertically. ***Center:*** 50 / Eagle on bale / 50. ***Right:*** STATE OF TENNESSEE vertically. ***Engraver:*** Rawdon, Wright & Hatch. ***Comments:*** H-TN-185-S28. From a genuine plate of the Planters Bank of Alabama, Wetumpka, Alabama. 18__. 1840s.
Rarity: —

$100 • W-TN-020-100-S060
Left: HUNDRED vertically. ***Center:*** Deer, River. ***Right:*** Portrait of George Washington. ***Engraver:*** Rawdon, Wright & Hatch. ***Comments:*** H-TN-185-S30. From a genuine plate of the Planters Bank of Alabama, Wetumpka, Alabama. 18__. 1840s.
Rarity: —

$100 • W-TN-020-100-S070
Left: Medallion head. ***Center:*** C / Factory / C. ***Right:*** 100 diagonally. ***Engraver:*** Rawdon, Wright & Hatch. ***Comments:*** H-TN-185-S32. 18__. 1840s.
Rarity: —

Bolivar, Tennessee

The first settlers arrived in the land that became Bolivar in 1819. The town was established in 1823 under the name of Hatchie Town. It became the county seat of Hardeman and was renamed Bolivar on October 18, 1825, in honor of General Simon Bolivar.

Collectors and Researchers:

If you have new information about any banks or notes listed in this volume, contact Whitman Publishing, Attn: Obsolete Paper Money, 3101 Clairmont Road, Suite G, Atlanta, GA 30329.

Farmers and Merchants Bank (branch)

1833–1854

W-TN-030

History: The Farmers and Merchants Bank was chartered in 1833 with an authorized capital of $600,000. In 1835 it opened for business. After more than a decade of operation, the bank finally failed, although notes dated 1854 were issued in an attempt to revive the bank:

> For a brief period it enjoyed a high credit, transacted too large a business, and in the heyday of its career it fell . . . in the spring of 1847, the bill-holders having sustained heavy losses thereby. The wreck of the bank fell into the hands of some adventurous speculators who tried every scheme their ingenuity could devise to resuscitate its existence, and its notes of circulation were briefly foisted upon the public. . . .[2]

The Farmers and Merchants Bank had its parent bank located in Memphis, W-TN-530, and a branch bank located in Nashville, W-TN-780.

Numismatic Commentary: Notes issued in Bolivar were unknown to Garland.

Remaining at the American Bank Note Co. archives as of 2003 was a $10-$10-$20-$50 face plate, a $1-$1-$2-$3 face plate, and a $5-$5-$5-$5 face plate.

Valid Issues

$1 • W-TN-030-001-G010

Comments: H-Unlisted. No description available. 18__. 1830s.

Rarity: *None known*

$2 • W-TN-030-002-G020

Comments: H-Unlisted. No description available. 18__. 1830s.

Rarity: *None known*

$3 • W-TN-030-003-G030

Comments: H-Unlisted. No description available. 18__. 1830s.

Rarity: *None known*

$5 • W-TN-030-005-G040

Left: 5 / Indian with gun in trees. ***Center:*** Ship. ***Right:*** Woman flying in clouds / 5. ***Engraver:*** Draper, Toppan, Longacre & Co. ***Comments:*** H-TN-100-G26. 18__. 1830s–1840s.

Rarity: —

$10 • W-TN-030-010-G050

Left: 10 / Woman with basket and pole. ***Center:*** Cart with bales, Farmhouse. ***Right:*** Indian with bow / 10. ***Engraver:*** Draper, Toppan, Longacre & Co. ***Comments:*** H-TN-100-G28. 18__. 1830s.

Rarity: —

$20 • W-TN-030-020-G060

Left: 20 / Cherub in clouds holding medallion bearing XX. ***Center:*** Angel flying, Bust of George Washington, Eagle. ***Right:*** 20 / Cherub in clouds holding medallion bearing XX. ***Engraver:*** Draper, Toppan, Longacre & Co. ***Comments:*** H-TN-100-G30. 18__. 1830s.

Rarity: —

$50 • W-TN-030-050-G070

Comments: H-Unlisted. No description available. 18__. 1830s.

Rarity: *None known*

Brownsville, Tennessee

Brownsville was an agricultural town surrounded by farms and prosperous plantation homes. Soon after the town was founded, the Tabernacle Campground was established in 1826. Today the descendants of the Reverend Howell Taylor gather at the yearly "camp-meeting."

Agricultural Bank of Tennessee

1854–1858

W-TN-040

History: On March 4, 1854, the Agricultural Bank of Tennessee was chartered with an authorized capital of $100,000. John D. Ware was elected president, and Martin Gridley was the cashier. By 1858 the bank had closed.

Numismatic Commentary: Garland noted that the assets of this bank were purchased by A.J. Stevens & Co. of Des Moines, Iowa, and moved to that city, where the notes were overstamped with the name of the new owners and reissued. Known notes were also made payable at Racine and LaCrosse, Wisconsin. W-TN-040-001-G010, W-TN-040-002-G030, and W-TN-040-005-G050 are among the most common. All notes seen to date have overprints of LaCrosse or Racine.

Remaining at the American Bank Note Co. archives as of 2003 was a $1-$2-$5-$5 face plate and an altered, unfinished $1-$2-$5-$5 face plate.

Valid Issues

$1 • W-TN-040-001-G010 CC

Engraver: Wellstood, Hanks, Hay & Whiting. ***Comments:*** H-TN-5-G2, Garland-30. 185_. 1850s.

Rarity: URS-9

F $100

$1 • W-TN-040-001-G020

Left: 1 / Haymakers, Dog. ***Center:*** Indians, Train. ***Right:*** 1 / Scene. ***Comments:*** H-TN-5-G4, Garland-29. 18__. 1850s.

Rarity: URS-3

F $600

$2 • **W-TN-040-002-G030** CC

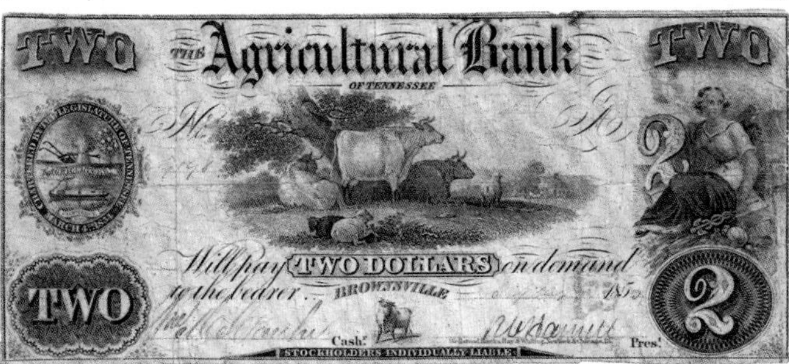

Engraver: Wellstood, Hanks, Hay & Whiting. ***Comments:*** H-TN-5-G6, Garland-32. 185_. 1850s.

Rarity: URS-9
F $100

$2 • **W-TN-040-002-G040**

Left: TWO / 2 / Ships. ***Center:*** Indians hunting buffalo. ***Right:*** 2 / Two women reaping. ***Comments:*** H-TN-5-G8, Garland-31. 18__. 1850s.

Rarity: URS-2
F $600

$5 • **W-TN-040-005-G050** CC

Engraver: Wellstood, Hanks, Hay & Whiting. ***Comments:*** H-TN-5-G10, Garland-34. 185_. 1850s.

Rarity: URS-9
F $100

$10 • **W-TN-040-010-G060**

Left: V / Two Indians. ***Center:*** Portrait of George Washington / Women, Train, Steamship. ***Right:*** 2 / 5 / Women, Two men, Building. ***Comments:*** H-TN-5-G12. 18__. 1850s.

Rarity: URS-2
F $600

Bank of America (branch)

1856–1858

W-TN-050

History: In 1856 the Bank of America was chartered. By 1858 the bank had closed.

The Bank of America had its parent bank located in Clarksville, W-TN-100, and branch banks located in Dresden, W-TN-260, and Rogersville, W-TN-880.

Numismatic Commentary: A number of unsigned remainder notes are known for the parent bank in Clarkville, but genuine, signed and issued notes of the Brownsville branch are very scarce to rare—if they exist at all.

Valid Issues

$5 • **W-TN-050-005-G010**

Left: V / Portrait of Andrew Jackson. ***Center:*** Two women flanking shield. ***Right:*** 5 / Portrait of General Ambrose Davie. ***Overprint:*** Red FIVE. ***Engraver:*** Bald, Cousland & Co. / Baldwin, Bald & Cousland. ***Comments:*** H-TN-15-G20a, Garland-36. 18__. 1850s.

Rarity: URS-2
F $600

$10 • **W-TN-050-010-G020**

Left: X / Portrait of Winston Jones Davie. ***Center:*** Woman and man flanking shield bearing wheat. ***Right:*** 10 / Portrait of Elizabeth Phillips. ***Overprint:*** Red TEN. ***Engraver:*** Bald, Cousland & Co. / Baldwin, Bald & Cousland. ***Comments:*** H-TN-15-G22a, Garland-37. 18__. 1850s.

Rarity: URS-2
F $600

$20 • **W-TN-050-020-G030**

Left: 20 / Portrait of Winston Jones Davie. ***Center:*** Family playing with bear cub, Horse. ***Right:*** 20 / Female portrait. ***Overprint:*** Red XX. ***Engraver:*** Bald, Cousland & Co. / Baldwin, Bald & Cousland. ***Comments:*** H-TN-15-G24a, Garland-38. 18__. 1850s.

Rarity: URS-2
F $600

Carthage, Tennessee

William Walton arrived in the 1780s to the land that would become Carthage. In 1800 he helped construct Walton Road, connecting Knoxville with the rest of Tennessee. A ferry and a tavern were along the road, and by 1804 the community was chosen to be the seat of Smith County. Carthage was laid out as a town soon afterwards.

The Cumberland and Caney Fork rivers brought economic affluence to Carthage, and soon there was a shipping and steamboat port located here. The Civil War saw Carthage as a route for the Confederate army.

Bank of the State of Tennessee {1st} (branch)

1817–1820

W-TN-060

History: The first Bank of the State of Tennessee was chartered on November 20, 1811, with an authorized capital of $400,000. The capital was to be divided into shares of $50 apiece. The state subscribed to $20,000, on the provision that the state reserved the right to withdraw its funds after ten years. Hugh Lawson White was the president. No notes under $5 were allowed to be issued. In 1817 the branch in Carthage was opened.

The Bank of the State of Tennessee discontinued business in 1820, at which time the stated capital was $371,107. The branches failed at the same time with a combined capital of $573,915.

The first Bank of the State of Tennessee had its parent bank located in Knoxville, W-TN-355, and branch banks located in Clarksville, W-TN-110, Columbia, W-TN-170, Franklin, W-TN-280, Jonesboro, W-TN-335, Kingston, W-TN-340, Maryville, W-TN-440, and Nashville, W-TN-670.

Numismatic Commentary: Garland pictured the $50 note from his collection and felt it may be unique—the serial number was 350, payable to a Robert Allen.

Valid Issues

$5 • W-TN-060-005-G010

Left: FIVE vertically. ***Center:*** Man plowing with horses / 5. ***Right:*** TENNESSEE vertically. ***Engraver:*** Murray, Draper, Fairman & Co. ***Comments:*** H-TN-75-G24. 18__. 1810s.

Rarity: —

$10 • W-TN-060-010-G020

Left: TEN vertically. ***Center:*** Men harvesting corn / 10. ***Right:*** TENNESSEE vertically. ***Engraver:*** Murray, Draper, Fairman & Co. ***Comments:*** H-TN-75-G26. 18__. 1810s.

Rarity: —

$20 • W-TN-060-020-G030

Left: TWENTY vertically. ***Center:*** XX / Justice seated / XX. ***Right:*** TENNESSEE vertically. ***Engraver:*** Murray, Draper, Fairman & Co. ***Comments:*** H-TN-75-G28. 18__. 1810s.

Rarity: —

$50 • W-TN-060-050-G040

Left: FIFTY vertically. ***Center:*** 50 / Ships / 50. ***Right:*** TENNESSEE vertically. ***Engraver:*** Murray, Draper, Fairman & Co. ***Comments:*** H-TN-75-G30. 181_. 1810s.

Rarity: URS-1
F $3,000

$100 • W-TN-060-100-G050

Left: HUNDRED vertically. ***Center:*** Scene. ***Right:*** TENNESSEE vertically. ***Engraver:*** Murray, Draper, Fairman & Co. ***Comments:*** H-TN-75-G32. 18__. 1810s.

Rarity: —

Non-Valid Issues

$3 • W-TN-060-003-N010

Left: THREE DOLLARS vertically. ***Center:*** 3 / 3. ***Right:*** THREE DOLLARS vertically. ***Engraver:*** Murray, Draper, Fairman & Co. ***Comments:*** H-TN-75-N5. 18__. 1810s.

Rarity: —

$50 • W-TN-060-050-N020

Left: FIFTY vertically. ***Center:*** 50 / Ship / L. ***Right:*** FIFTY DOLLARS vertically. ***Engraver:*** Murray, Draper, Fairman & Co. ***Comments:*** H-TN-75-N6. 18__. 1810s.

Rarity: —

Chattanooga, Tennessee

Chattanooga was originally a small Native American settlement located on Chattanooga Creek. The name means "to draw fish out of water." When settlers arrived in the area, the name was adopted for the new town. It was originally known as Ross's Landing and occupied what is modern-day Broad Street. In 1839 the town was incorporated as Chattanooga.

River commerce brought great prosperity to the area, and in 1850 the railway brought a boom of commercial growth with it. Cotton from the South and corn from the North were brought to the marketplace and shipped out all across the country.

Chattanooga saw much action during the Civil War. The town was besieged, bombarded, saw battle in and around it boundaries, and finally became fully under Union control on September 9, 1863, after the Battle of Missionary Ridge forced the Confederate army out of the area. After the war, Chattanooga became a railroad, industrial, and manufacturing hub.

Bank of Chattanooga

1854–1866

W-TN-070

History: On February 2, 1854, the Bank of Chattanooga was chartered with an authorized capital of $100,000, not to exceed $500,000. There was great confidence placed in the bank by the community, as "gentlemen of ample responsibility are the principal stockholders, and notes of tens and twenties will be put into circulation, at the commencement."[3]

In 1854 W.D. Fulton was elected cashier, and William Williams was named as president. In 1857 these values were given: capital $421,400; bills in circulation $671,630; specie $102,297; real estate $6,775. In 1860 it was realized by the public that the stockholders of the Bank of Chattanooga and the Bank of Memphis, W-TN-480, were the same. On February 8 of that year, the Bank of Memphis surrendered its charter and transformed into a branch of the Bank of Chattanooga. In 1861 John Overton, former president of the Bank of Memphis, W-TN-480, replaced Williams as president. In 1866 the Bank of Chattanooga was closed up.

The Bank of Chattanooga had a branch located in Memphis, W-TN-470.

Numismatic Commentary: The Bank of Chattanooga is one of the most prolific issuers in the state of Tennessee. Fractional and dollar-denominated notes from 1862 or 1863 are readily available. Notes redeemable at the Bank of Memphis, W-TN-480, are also reasonably common, and the train cars on the various notes bear different inscriptions (Memphis, Little Rock, etc.). Many of those notes were printed by the American Bank Note Co., and as such it is assumed that the parent bank closed as Civil War hostilities consumed the Chattanooga area, and the Memphis branch operated in the Union-occupied city until closing in 1866.

Remaining at the American Bank Note Co. archives as of 2003 was a $10-$10-$10-$10 back plate and a $50-$100 face plate. The 1990 Christie's sale of the American Bank Note Co. archives produced a $1-$1-$2-$3 sheet, a $5-$5-$10-$20 sheet, a $50-$100 sheet, and a partial $5-$5 sheet.

Valid Issues

$5 • W-TN-070-005-G010

CC

Engraver: Danforth, Wright & Co. ***Comments:*** H-TN-10-G2, Garland-89. 18__. 1850s.

Rarity: URS-10
F $100

$5 • W-TN-070-005-G010a

CC

Overprint: Red FIVE. ***Engraver:*** Danforth, Wright & Co. ***Comments:*** H-TN-10-G2a, Garland-91. Similar to W-TN-070-005-G010. 18__. 1850s–1861.

Rarity: URS-10
F $100

$10 • W-TN-070-010-G020

CC

Engraver: Danforth, Wright & Co. ***Comments:*** H-TN-10-G4, Garland-93. 18__. 1850s.

Rarity: URS-7
F $100

$10 • W-TN-070-010-G020a

CC

Overprint: Red TEN. ***Engraver:*** Danforth, Wright & Co. ***Comments:*** H-TN-10-G4a, Garland-95. Similar to W-TN-070-010-G020. 18__. 1850s–1861.

Rarity: URS-8
F $125

$20 • W-TN-070-020-G030

CC

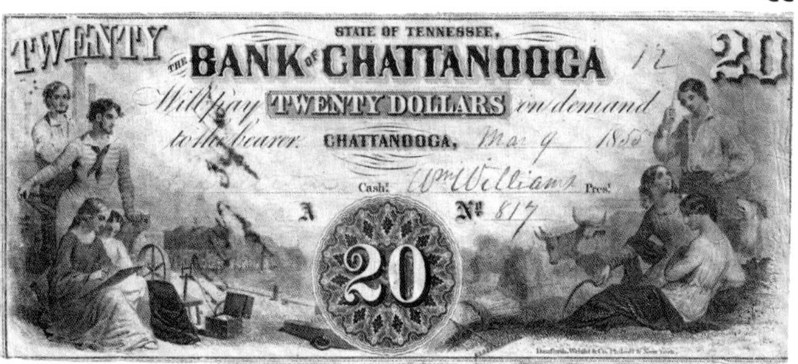

Engraver: Danforth, Wright & Co. ***Comments:*** H-TN-10-G6, Garland-101. 18__. 1850s.

Rarity: URS-6
F $275

$20 • W-TN-070-020-G030a

Left: TWENTY / Men and women seated, Loom. ***Center:*** 20. ***Right:*** 20 / Men and women seated, Cattle. ***Overprint:*** Red TWENTY. ***Engraver:*** Danforth, Wright & Co. ***Comments:*** H-TN-10-G6a, Garland-104. Similar to W-TN-070-020-G030. 18__. 1850s–1861.

Rarity: URS-6
F $225

$50 • W-TN-070-050-G040

CC

Tint: Red-orange lathework and dies outlining white 50 / 50. ***Engraver:*** Danforth, Wright & Co. ***Comments:*** H-TN-10-G8a, Garland-109. 18__. 1850s–1861.

Rarity: URS-5
VF $750; **Proof** $3,000
Selected auction price: Heritage Auctions, April 18, 2012, Lot 15349, VF $2,185

$100 • **W-TN-070-100-G050**

Left: 100 / Woman with shield, Eagle. ***Center:*** 100. ***Right:*** 100 / Female portrait. ***Tint:*** Red-orange outlining white 100. ***Engraver:*** Danforth, Wright & Co. ***Comments:*** H-TN-10-G10a, Garland-114. 18__. 1850s–1861.

Rarity: URS-5
VF $1,100; **Proof** $4,000

Civil War Emergency Issues

$1 • **W-TN-070-001-G060**

Left: ONE vertically. ***Center:*** 1 / ONE DOLLAR / 1. ***Right:*** ONE / 1 / ONE. ***Engraver:*** Manouvrier. ***Comments:*** H-TN-10-G14. 28 August 1861.

Rarity: URS-7
F $150

$1 • **W-TN-070-001-G060a** CC

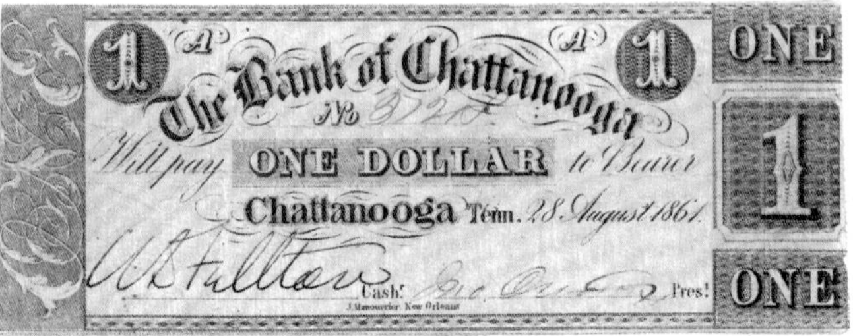

Engraver: Manouvrier. ***Comments:*** H-TN-10-G14a. Similar to W-TN-070-001-G060 but with serial number. 28 August 1861.

Rarity: URS-7
F $150

$1 • **W-TN-070-001-G060b**

Overprint: Green ONE. ***Engraver:*** Manouvrier. ***Comments:*** H-TN-10-G14b. Similar to W-TN-070-001-G060 but with serial number. 28 August 1861.

Rarity: —

$1 • **W-TN-070-001-G060c** CC

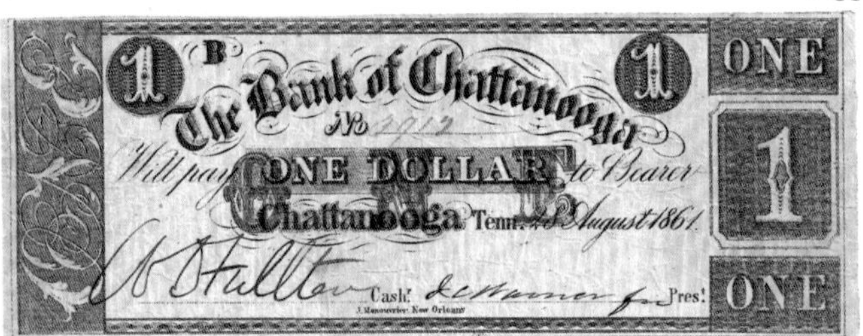

Overprint: Blue ONE. ***Engraver:*** Manouvrier. ***Comments:*** H-Unlisted. Similar to W-TN-070-001-G060 but with serial number. 28 August 1861.

Rarity: URS-7
F $175

$2 • **W-TN-070-002-G070**

Left: TWO vertically. ***Center:*** 2 / Woman reclining, Ship / 2. ***Right:*** TWO DOLLARS vertically. ***Engraver:*** Manouvrier. ***Comments:*** H-TN-10-G16. 28 August 1861.

Rarity: —

$2 • **W-TN-070-002-G070a** CC

Engraver: Manouvrier. ***Comments:*** H-TN-10-G16a. Similar to W-TN-070-002-G070 but with serial number. 28 August 1861.

Rarity: URS-8
F $125

$2 • **W-TN-070-002-G070b** CC

Overprint: Green TWO. ***Engraver:*** Manouvrier. ***Comments:*** H-TN-10-G16b. Similar to W-TN-070-002-G070 but with serial number. 28 August 1861.

Rarity: URS-8
F $125

$3 • **W-TN-070-003-G080** CC

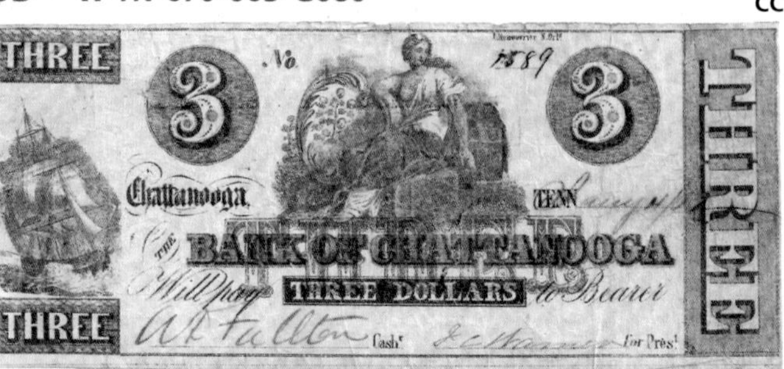

Overprint: Red THREE. ***Engraver:*** Manouvrier. ***Comments:*** H-TN-10-G18b. 1860s.

Rarity: URS-8
F $175

Notes Payable in Confederate Treasury Notes

25¢ • W-TN-070-00.25-G090

ANS

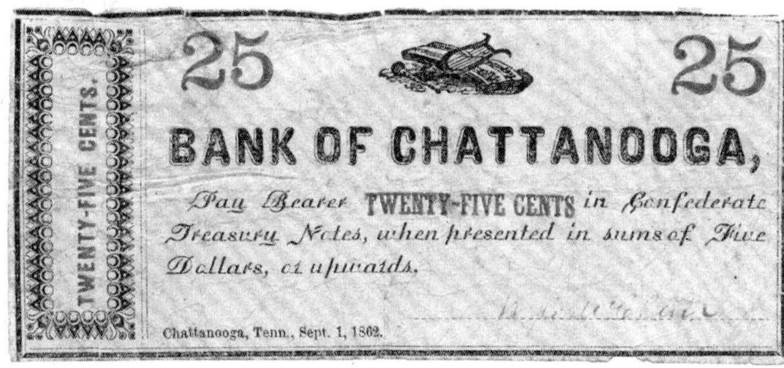

Comments: H-TN-10-G20, Garland-41. Printed in red and black. Sept. 1, 1862.

Rarity: URS-8
F $75

25¢ • W-TN-070-00.25-G100

CC

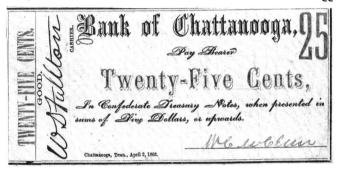

Comments: H-TN-10-G22, Garland-43. Printed in red and black. April 2, 1863.

Rarity: URS-8
F $75

50¢ • W-TN-070-00.50-G110

Left: FIFTY CENTS vertically. ***Center:*** FIFTY CENTS / 50. ***Comments:*** H-TN-10-G24, Garland-46. Printed in red and black. Sept. 1, 1862.

Rarity: URS-8
F $100

50¢ • W-TN-070-00.50-G110a

CC

Comments: H-Unlisted. Printed in red and black. Similar to W-TN-070-00.50-G110 but with different date. April 2, 1863.

Rarity: URS-8
F $75

50¢ • W-TN-070-00.50-G120

ANS

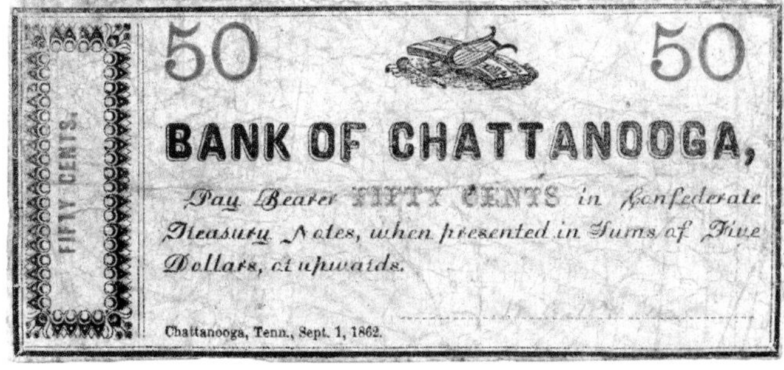

Comments: H-Unlisted. Printed in red and black. Sept. 1, 1862.

Rarity: URS-8
F $75

50¢ • W-TN-070-00.50-G120a

CC

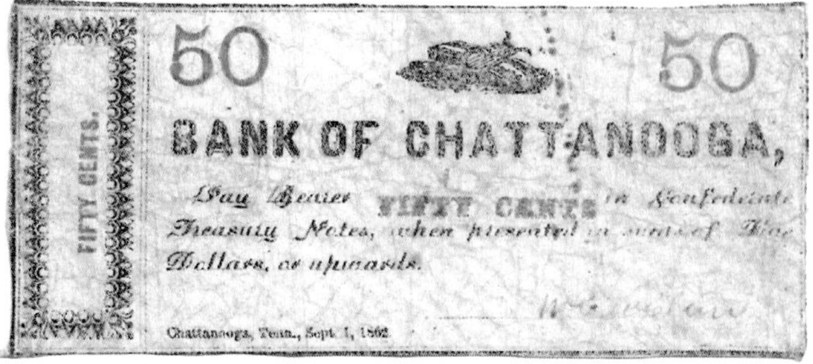

Comments: H-Unlisted. Similar to W-TN-070-00.50-G120 but with left panel text printed further right. Printed in red and black. Sept. 1, 1862.

Rarity: URS-8
F $75

50¢ • W-TN-070-00.50-G120b

Comments: H-TN-10-G26, Garland-44. Printed in red and black. Similar to W-TN-070-00.50-G120 but with different date. April 2, 1863.

Rarity: —

50¢ • W-TN-070-00.50-G120c

Comments: H-TN-10-G26a, Garland-45. Printed in red and black. Similar to W-TN-070-00.50-G120 but with different date. April 2, 1863.

Rarity: —

75¢ • W-TN-070-00.75-G130

Left: SEVENTY-FIVE CENTS vertically. ***Center:*** 75 / Harp and musical implements / 75. ***Comments:*** H-TN-10-G28. Printed in red and black. Sept. 1, 1862.

Rarity: URS-6
F $150

75¢ • W-TN-070-00.75-G140

Left: SEVENTY-FIVE CENTS vertically. ***Center:*** SEVENTY-FIVE CENTS / 75. ***Comments:*** H-TN-10-G30, Garland-48. Printed in red and black. April 2, 1863.

Rarity: URS-6
F $125

$1 • **W-TN-070-001-G150** CC

Comments: H-TN-10-G32, Garland-52. Printed on the backs of uncut sheets. August, 1862.

Rarity: URS-9
F $75

$1 • **W-TN-070-001-G160** ANS

Comments: H-TN-10-G32a, Garland-53. Similar to W-TN-070-001-G160. Printed on the backs of uncut sheets. August, 1862.

Rarity: URS-9
F $75

$1 • **W-TN-070-001-G160a** CC

Comments: H-TN-10-G32b, Garland-54. Similar to W-TN-070-001-G160. Printed in red and black. Printed on the backs of uncut sheets. August, 1862.

Rarity: URS-9
F $75

$1 • **W-TN-070-001-G160b** CC

Comments: H-TN-10-G32c, Garland-55. Similar to W-TN-070-001-G160. Printed in red and black. Printed on the backs of uncut sheets. August, 1862.

Rarity: URS-9
F $75

$1 • **W-TN-070-001-G160c**

Left: ONE DOLLAR vertically. ***Center:*** Train / 1. ***Right:*** ONE DOLLAR vertically. ***Comments:*** H-TN-10-G32d, Garland-56. Similar to W-TN-070-001-G160. Printed on the backs of uncut sheets. August, 1862.

Rarity: URS-6
F $200

$1 • **W-TN-070-001-G170** CC

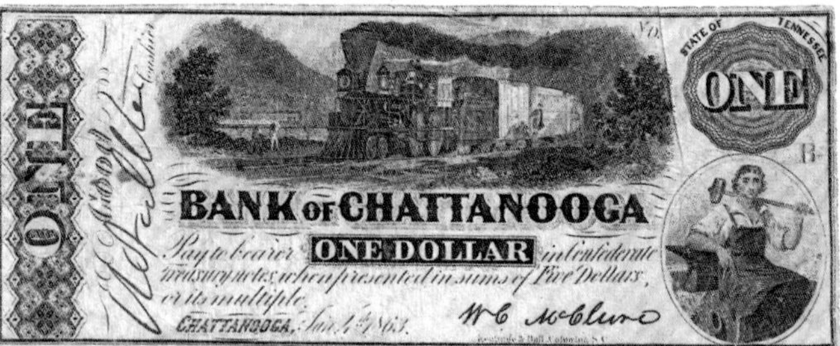

Engraver: Keatinge & Ball. ***Comments:*** H-TN-10-G34, Garland-58. Jan. 4th, 1863.

Rarity: URS-8
F $125

$1 • **W-TN-070-001-G170a** ANS

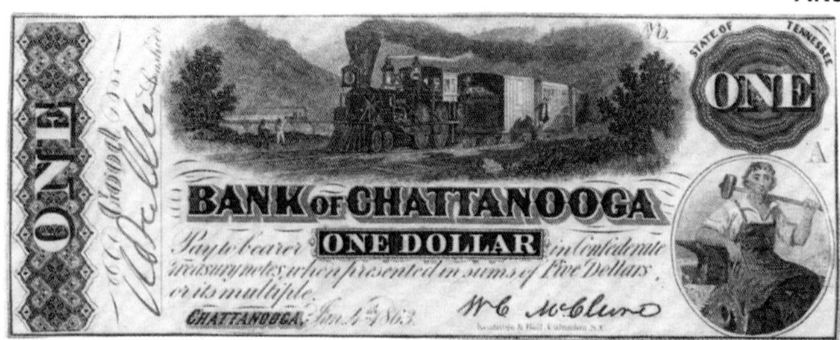

Engraver: Keatinge & Ball. ***Comments:*** H-TN-10-G34a, Garland-59. Similar to W-TN-070-001-G170. Jan. 4th, 1863.

Rarity: URS-9
F $135

$1 • **W-TN-070-001-G170b**

Left: ONE vertically. ***Center:*** Train. ***Right:*** ONE / Mechanic with hammer. ***Engraver:*** Keatinge & Ball. ***Comments:*** H-TN-10-G34b, Garland-60. Similar to W-TN-070-001-G170. Jan. 4th, 1863.

Rarity: URS-6
F $200

$1 • **W-TN-070-001-G170c**

Engraver: Keatinge & Ball. ***Comments:*** H-TN-10-G34c. Similar to W-TN-070-001-G170. Jan. 4th, 1863.

Rarity: URS-8
F $150

$2 • W-TN-070-002-G180

ANS

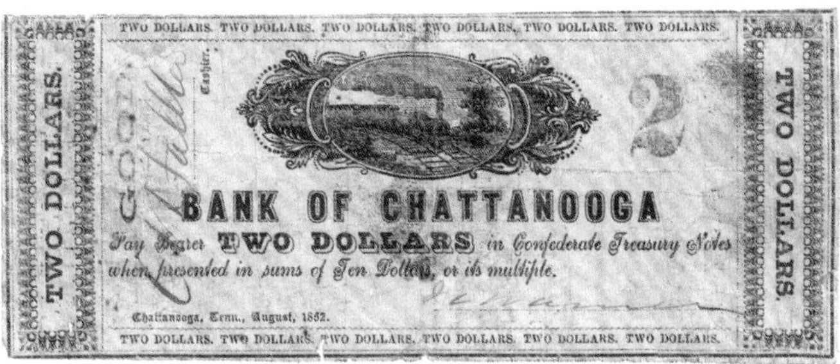

Engraver: Keatinge & Ball. ***Comments:*** H-TN-10-G36, Garland-66. Printed in red and black. Printed on the backs of uncut sheets. August, 1862.

Rarity: URS-9
F $125

$2 • W-TN-070-002-G180a

CC

Engraver: Keatinge & Ball. ***Comments:*** H-TN-10-G36a, Garland-67. Similar to W-TN-070-002-G180. Printed on the backs of uncut sheets. August, 1862.

Rarity: URS-10
F $75

$2 • W-TN-070-002-G180b

CC

Engraver: Keatinge & Ball. ***Comments:*** H-Unlisted. Similar to W-TN-070-002-G180. Printed on the backs of uncut sheets. August, 1862.

Rarity: URS-9
F $125

$2 • W-TN-070-002-G180c

Left: TWO DOLLARS vertically. ***Center:*** Train / 2. ***Right:*** TWO DOLLARS vertically. ***Engraver:*** Keatinge & Ball. ***Comments:*** H-TN-10-G36b, Garland-68. Similar to W-TN-070-002-G180. Printed on the backs of uncut sheets. August, 1862.

Rarity: —

$2 • W-TN-070-002-G180d

CC

Engraver: Keatinge & Ball. ***Comments:*** H-TN-10-G36c, Garland-69. Similar to W-TN-070-002-G180. Printed in red and black. Printed on the backs of uncut sheets. August, 1862.

Rarity: URS-11
F $75

$2 • W-TN-070-002-G180e

Engraver: Keatinge & Ball. ***Comments:*** H-TN-10-G36d, Garland-70. Similar to W-TN-070-002-G180. Printed in red and black. Printed on the backs of uncut sheets. August, 1862.

Rarity: URS-6
F $175

$2 • W-TN-070-002-G180f

CC

Engraver: Keatinge & Ball. ***Comments:*** H-TN-10-G36e, Garland-71. Similar to W-TN-070-002-G180. Printed in red and black. Printed on the backs of uncut sheets. August, 1862.

Rarity: URS-10
F $60; **EF** $125

$2 • W-TN-070-002-G190

Left: TWO vertically. ***Center:*** TWO / Woman seated with shield. ***Right:*** TWO / 2. ***Engraver:*** Keatinge & Ball. ***Comments:*** H-TN-10-G38, Garland-72. Jan. 4th, 1863.

Rarity: URS-7
F $150

$2 • W-TN-070-002-G190a

Engraver: Keatinge & Ball. ***Comments:*** H-TN-10-G38a, Garland-73. Similar to W-TN-070-002-G190. Jan. 4th, 1863.

Rarity: URS-7
F $150

$2 • W-TN-070-002-G190b

CC

Engraver: Keatinge & Ball. ***Comments:*** H-TN-10-G38b, Garland-74. Similar to W-TN-070-002-G190. Jan. 4th, 1863.

Rarity: URS-10
F $60

$2 • W-TN-070-002-G190c

Engraver: Keatinge & Ball. ***Comments:*** H-TN-10-G38c. Similar to W-TN-070-002-G190. Jan. 4th, 1863.

Rarity: URS-7
F $150

$3 • W-TN-070-003-G200

CC

Comments: H-TN-10-G40, Garland-76. Printed on the backs of uncut sheets. August, 1862.

Rarity: URS-10
F $75

$3 • W-TN-070-003-G210

CC

Comments: H-TN-10-G42, Garland-80. Printed in red and black. Printed on the backs of uncut sheets. August, 1862.

Rarity: URS-10
F $75

$3 • W-TN-070-003-G210a

CC

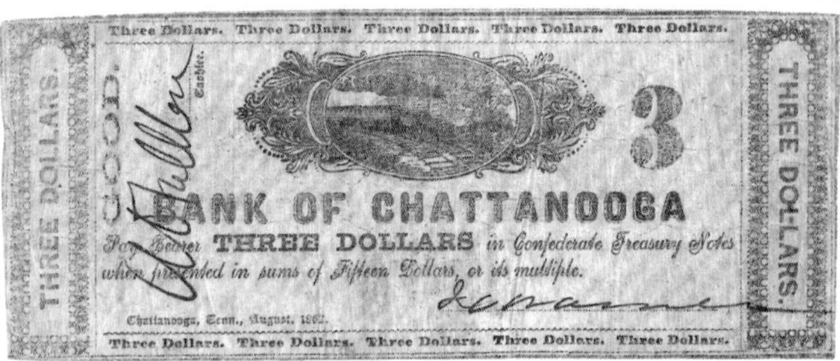

Comments: H-TN-10-G42a, Garland-81. Similar to W-TN-070-003-G210. Printed in red and black. Printed on the backs of uncut sheets. August, 1862.

Rarity: URS-10
F $75

$3 • W-TN-070-003-G210b

CC

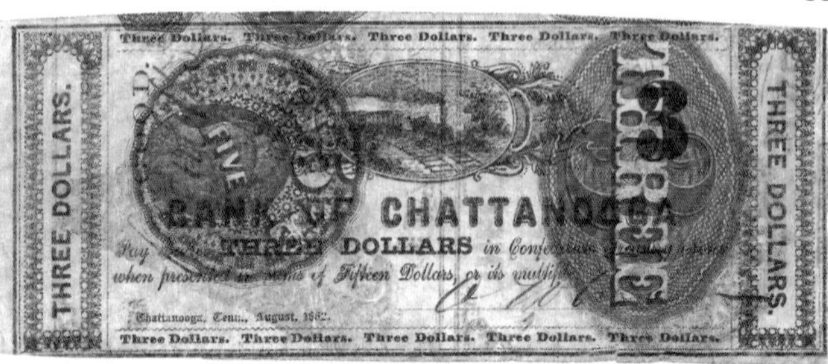

Comments: H-Unlisted. Similar to W-TN-070-003-G210. Printed on the backs of uncut sheets. August, 1862.

Rarity: URS-10
F $75

$3 • W-TN-070-003-G210c

ANS

Comments: H-TN-10-G42b, Garland-82. Similar to W-TN-070-003-G210. Printed in red and black. Printed on the backs of uncut sheets. August, 1862.

Rarity: URS-10
F $75

$3 • W-TN-070-003-G210d

Left: THREE DOLLARS vertically. ***Center:*** Train / 3. ***Right:*** THREE DOLLARS vertically. ***Comments:*** H-TN-10-G42c, Garland-83. Similar to W-TN-070-003-G210. Printed in red and black. Printed on the backs of uncut sheets. August, 1862.

Rarity: —

$3 • W-TN-070-003-G210e CC

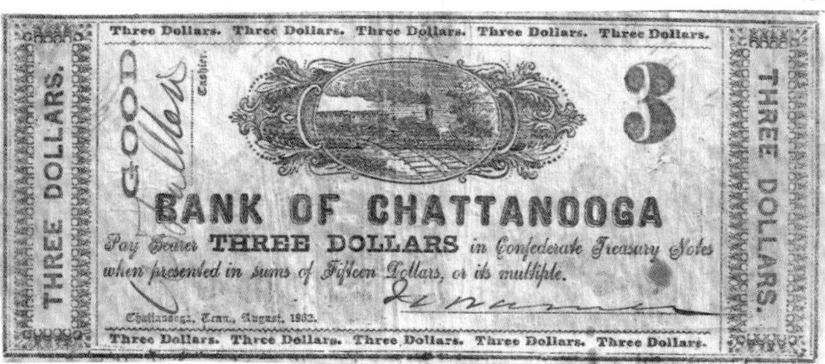

Comments: H-TN-10-G42d, Garland-84. Similar to W-TN-070-003-G210. Printed in red and black. Printed on the backs of uncut sheets. August, 1862.

Rarity: URS-10
F $100

$3 • W-TN-070-003-G210f CC

Comments: H-TN-10-G42e, Garland-85. Similar to W-TN-070-003-G210. Printed in red and black. Printed on the backs of uncut sheets. August, 1862.

Rarity: URS-10
F $75

$3 • W-TN-070-003-G220

Left: THREE vertically. ***Center:*** THREE DOLLARS. ***Right:*** 3 / Man holding basket of cotton, Harvest. ***Engraver:*** Keatinge & Ball. ***Comments:*** H-TN-10-G44, Garland-86. Jan. 4th, 1863.

Rarity: URS-7
F $100

$3 • W-TN-070-003-G220a

Engraver: Keatinge & Ball. ***Comments:*** H-TN-10-G44a, Garland-87. Similar to W-TN-070-003-G220. Jan. 4th, 1863.

Rarity: URS-7
F $100

$3 • W-TN-070-003-G220b CC

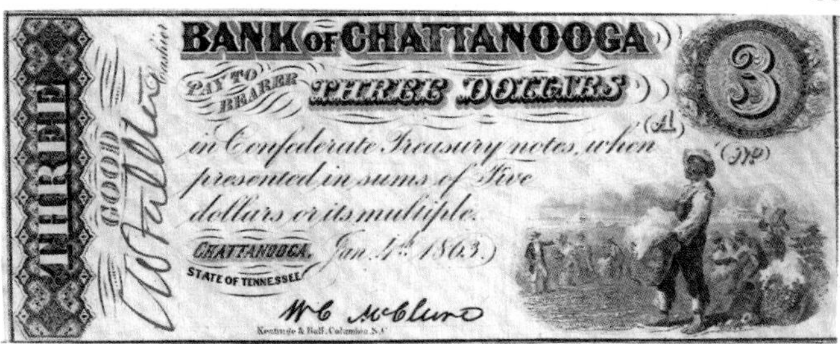

Engraver: Keatinge & Ball. ***Comments:*** H-TN-10-G44b, Garland-88. Similar to W-TN-070-003-G220. Jan. 4th, 1863.

Rarity: URS-9
F $100

$3 • W-TN-070-003-G220c CC

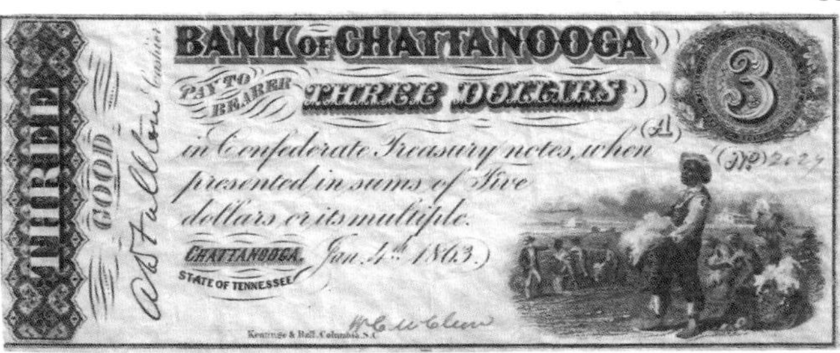

Engraver: Keatinge & Ball. ***Comments:*** H-TN-10-G44c. Similar to W-TN-070-003-G220but with serial number. Jan. 4th, 1863.

Rarity: URS-8
F $125

Notes Payable at the Bank of Memphis

$5 • W-TN-070-005-G230

Left: Woman standing with medallion head / 5. ***Center:*** Two women reaching out to angel. ***Right:*** 5. ***Overprint:*** Blue stamp. ***Engraver:*** Danforth, Wright & Co. ***Comments:*** H-TN-10-G46, Garland-528. 18__. 1850s.

Rarity: URS-6
F $150

$5 • W-TN-070-005-G230a CC

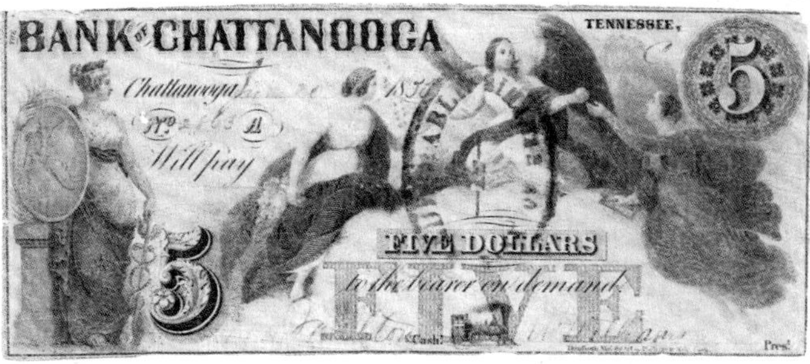

Overprint: Red FIVE / Blue stamp. ***Engraver:*** Danforth, Wright & Co. ***Comments:*** H-TN-10-G46a, Garland-529. Similar to W-TN-070-005-G230. 18__. 1850s–1861.

Rarity: URS-8
F $125

$10 • W-TN-070-010-G240 CC

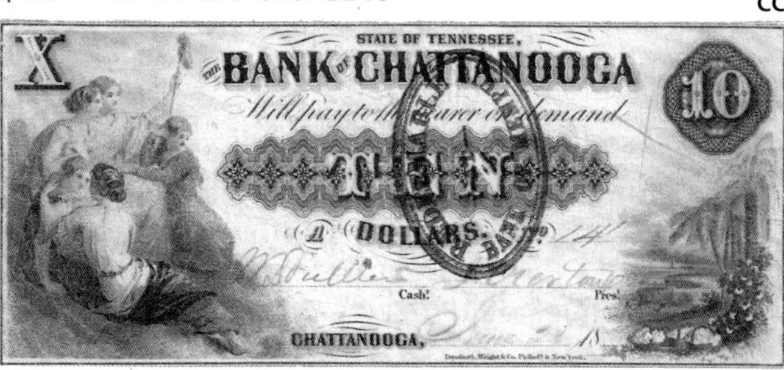

Overprint: Blue stamp. ***Engraver:*** Danforth, Wright & Co. ***Comments:*** H-TN-10-G48, Garland-530. 18__. 1850s.

Rarity: URS-5
F $250

$10 • **W-TN-070-010-G240a** CC

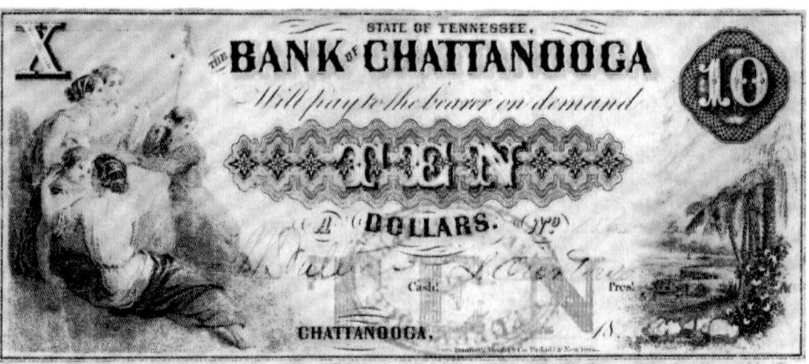

Overprint: Red TEN / Blue stamp. ***Engraver:*** Danforth, Wright & Co. ***Comments:*** H-TN-10-G48a, Garland-531. Similar to W-TN-070-010-G240. 18__. 1850s.

Rarity: URS-7
F $175

$10 • **W-TN-070-010-G250** CC, CC

Tint: Red-orange. ***Back:*** Red-orange portrait of George Washington. ***Engraver:*** American Bank Note Co. ***Comments:*** H-TN-10-G50a, Garland-532. Train car reads "Memphis & Ohio." 18__. 1860.

Rarity: URS-6
F $325

$10 • **W-TN-070-010-G250a**

Left: 10 / X. ***Center:*** Train. ***Right:*** 10. ***Tint:*** Red-orange. ***Back:*** Red-orange. ***Engraver:*** American Bank Note Co. ***Comments:*** H-TN-10-G50c, Garland-533. Similar to W-TN-070-010-G250. 18__. 1860.

Rarity: URS-6
F $325

$10 • **W-TN-070-010-G250b** GB, GB

Tint: Red-orange. ***Back:*** Red-orange portrait of George Washington. ***Engraver:*** American Bank Note Co. ***Comments:*** H-TN-10-G50e, Garland-534. Similar to W-TN-070-010-G250 but train car reads "Memphis & Little Rock." 18__. 1860.

Rarity: URS-7
F $225

$10 • **W-TN-070-010-G250c** GB, GB

Tint: Red-orange. ***Back:*** Red-orange portrait of George Washington. ***Engraver:*** American Bank Note Co. ***Comments:*** H-TN-10-G50g, Garland-535. Similar to W-TN-070-010-G250 but train car reads "Mississippi & Tennessee." 18__. 1860.

Rarity: URS-6
F $300

$20 • W-TN-070-020-G260 CC

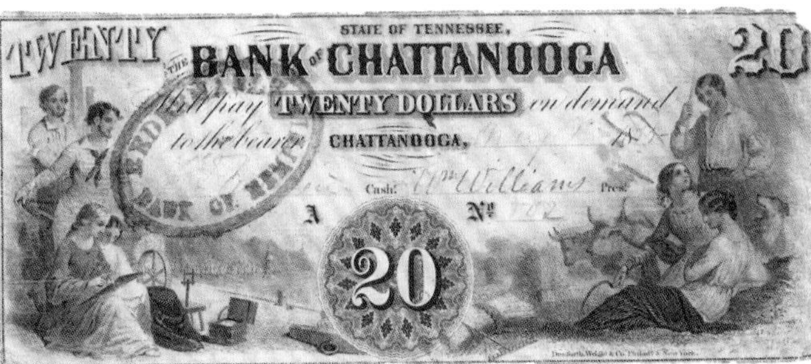

Overprint: Blue stamp. ***Engraver:*** Danforth, Wright & Co. ***Comments:*** H-TN-10-G52, Garland-536. 18__. 1850s.

Rarity: URS-4
F $250

$20 • W-TN-070-020-G260a

Left: TWENTY / Men and women seated, Loom. ***Center:*** 20. ***Right:*** 20 / Men and women seated, Cattle. ***Overprint:*** Blue stamp. ***Engraver:*** Danforth, Wright & Co. ***Comments:*** H-TN-10-G52a, Garland-537. Similar to W-TN-070-020-G260. 18__. 1850s.

Rarity: URS-4
F $250

$20 • W-TN-070-020-G260b CC

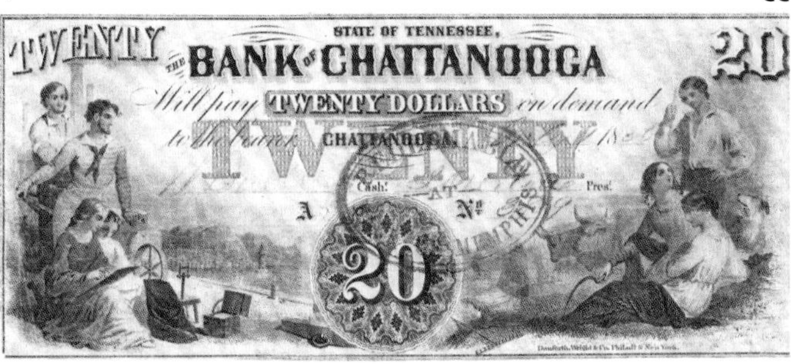

Overprint: Red TWENTY / Blue stamp. ***Engraver:*** Danforth, Wright & Co. ***Comments:*** H-TN-10-G52b, Garland-538. Similar to W-TN-070-020-G260. 18__. 1850s–1861.

Rarity: URS-8
F $140

$20 • W-TN-070-020-G260c CC

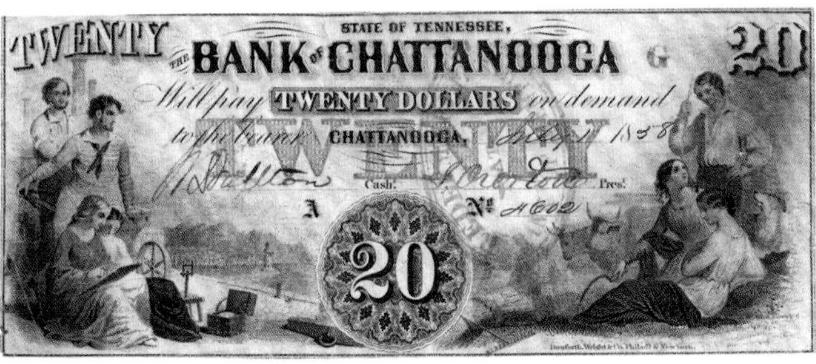

Overprint: Red TWENTY / Red stamp. ***Engraver:*** Danforth, Wright & Co. ***Comments:*** H-Unlisted. Similar to W-TN-070-020-G260. 18__. 1850s–1861.

Rarity: URS-8
F $125

$20 • W-TN-070-020-G270 CC, CC

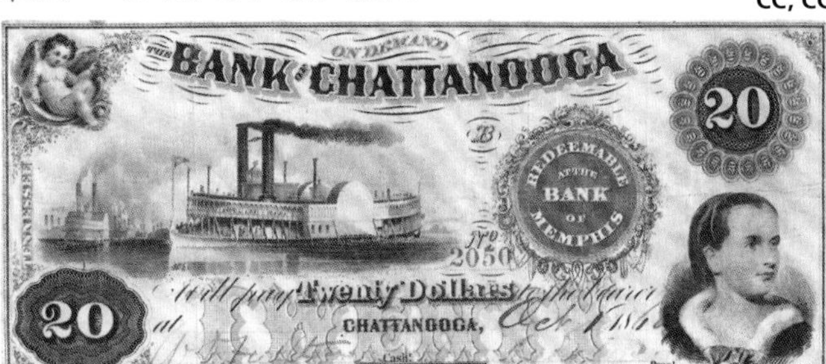

Tint: Red-orange. ***Back:*** Red-orange. ***Engraver:*** American Bank Note Co. ***Comments:*** H-TN-10-G54a, Garland-540. 18__. 1859 and 1860.

Rarity: URS-7
F $250

$50 • W-TN-070-050-G280

Left: Woman with wheat / 50. ***Center:*** 50 / Woman with dove / 50. ***Right:*** 50 / Woman with cornucopia. ***Overprint:*** Blue stamp. ***Tint:*** Red-orange. ***Engraver:*** Danforth, Wright & Co. ***Comments:*** H-TN-10-G56, Garland-542. 18__. 1850s–1861.

Rarity: URS-6
F $350

$50 • W-TN-070-050-G290 CC, CC

Tint: Red-orange pledge, die bearing white 50, and FIFTY / L / FIFTY. ***Back:*** Red-orange. ***Engraver:*** American Bank Note Co. ***Comments:*** H-TN-10-G58a, Garland-543. 18__. 1859 and 1860.

Rarity: URS-6
F $450; **VF** $650

$100 • W-TN-070-100-G300

CC

Overprint: Blue stamp. ***Tint:*** Red-orange lathework and die outlining white 100. ***Engraver:*** Danforth, Wright & Co. ***Comments:*** H-TN-10-G60, Garland-545. 18__. 1850s–1861.

Rarity: URS-5
VF $1,900
Selected auction price: Heritage Auctions, October 24, 2015, Lot 20016, VF $1,880

$100 • W-TN-070-100-G310

CC, CC

Tint: Red-orange. ***Back:*** Red-orange portrait of Benjamin Franklin / Portrait of George Washington / Medallion heads. ***Engraver:*** American Bank Note Co. ***Comments:*** H-TN-10-G62a, Garland-546. 18__. 1859 and 1860.

Rarity: URS-6
F $500

Non-Valid Issues

$20 • W-TN-070-020-R010

Engraver: Danforth, Wright & Co. ***Comments:*** H-TN-10-R10. Raised from W-TN-070-005-G010. 18__. 1850s.

Rarity: —

$50 • W-TN-070-050-R020

Engraver: Danforth, Wright & Co. ***Comments:*** H-TN-10-R15. Raised from W-TN-070-005-G010. 18__. 1850s.

Rarity: —

Bank of East Tennessee (branch)

1843–1858

W-TN-080

History: In 1843 the Bank of East Tennessee was chartered with an authorized capital of $800,000. In 1853 it was reported that the bank had suspended specie payments, but it was still considered to be in good credit. The capital of the branch located at Chattanooga was $100,000 in 1857. W.F. Ragsdale was the cashier, and B. Chandler was the president. By 1858, however, the bank had closed.

The Bank of East Tennessee had its parent bank located in Knoxville, W-TN-345, and a branch bank located in Jonesboro, W-TN-330.

Numismatic Commentary: Notes payable at the Chattanooga branch are readily available.

Valid Issues

$1 • W-TN-080-001-G010

Left: 1 on shield / ONE / 1. ***Center:*** Portrait of Andrew Jackson. ***Right:*** 1 / Women standing and sitting. ***Back:*** Red-orange portrait of Rachel Jackson. ***Engraver:*** Danforth, Wright & Co. ***Comments:*** H-TN-55-G60a, Garland-118. 18__. 1850s.

Rarity: URS-7
F $100

$2 • W-TN-080-002-G020

Left: TWO / 2 / TWO / Portrait of Dolley Madison. ***Center:*** Liberty seated with shield. ***Right:*** TWO / 2 / TWO / Portrait of Kate Sevier. ***Back:*** Red-orange medallion head bearing TWO. ***Engraver:*** Danforth, Wright & Co. ***Comments:*** H-TN-55-G62a, Garland-119. 18__. 1850s.

Rarity: URS-7
F $100

How to Read the Whitman Numbering System

$1 • W-AL-020-001-G010a

Denomination: Face value of the note shown.

W: Whitman number. This number is a sortable code unique to each bank and note.

AL: Abbreviation for the state under study.

020: Numerical designation specific to each bank.

001: The denomination in dollars.

G010a: G indicates a good or valid note. Other categories are indicated thus: C (counterfeit); R (raised); S (spurious); N (not-attributed); A (altered). Numbers are assigned starting with 010, 020, et seq. Terminal letters following the number indicate variations of a note: a series of different colored overprints, tints, payees, etc., all on the same design of note. For more information, see the "How to Use This Book" section at the front of the volume, page xiv.

$3 • W-TN-080-003-G030 SI, SI

Back: Red-orange. ***Engraver:*** Danforth, Wright & Co. ***Comments:*** H-TN-55-G64a, Garland-120. 18__. 1850s.

Rarity: URS-7
F $125

$5 • W-TN-080-005-G040

Left: FIVE vertically. ***Center:*** V / Man seated / 5. ***Right:*** V / Portrait of Henry Clay / V. ***Engraver:*** Wellstood, Hanks, Hay & Whiting. ***Comments:*** H-TN-55-G66, Garland-121. Oct. 1, 185_. 1854.

Rarity: URS-7
F $175

$5 • W-TN-080-005-G050 QDB, QDB

Back: Red-orange. ***Engraver:*** Danforth, Wright & Co. ***Comments:*** H-TN-55-G68a, Garland-122. 18__. 1850s.

Rarity: URS-8
F $125

$5 • W-TN-080-005-G060 CC, CC

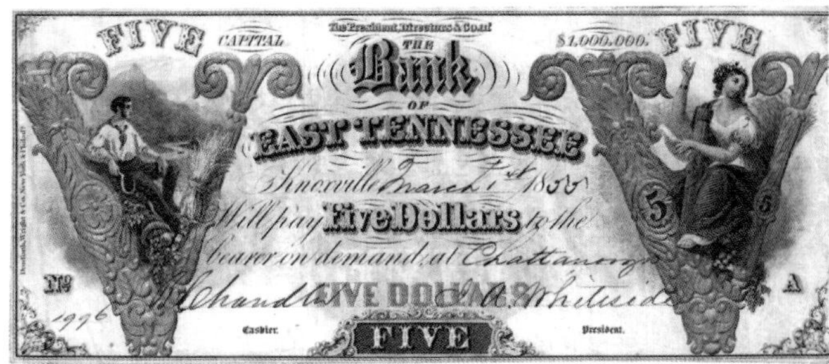

Back: Red-orange medallion head bearing FIVE / Medallion head bearing FIVE. ***Engraver:*** Danforth, Wright & Co. ***Comments:*** H-TN-55-G70a, Garland-123. 18__. 1850s.

Rarity: URS-8
F $100; **VF** $175

$10 • W-TN-080-010-G070

Left: TEN vertically. ***Center:*** 10 / Man and woman seated / X. ***Right:*** 10 / Portrait of George Washington / TEN. ***Engraver:*** Wellstood, Hanks, Hay & Whiting. ***Comments:*** H-TN-55-G72, Garland-124. Oct. 1, 185_. 1854.

Rarity: URS-6
F $200

$10 • W-TN-080-010-G080

Left: 10 / Medallion head / Portrait of John C. Calhoun / Medallion head / X. ***Right:*** 10 / Medallion head / Portrait of James K. Polk / Medallion head / X. ***Back:*** Red-orange. ***Engraver:*** Danforth, Wright & Co. ***Comments:*** H-TN-55-G74a, Garland-125. 18__. 1850s.

Rarity: URS-7
F $150

$20 • W-TN-080-020-G090

Left: XX / Portrait of Benjamin Franklin / 20. ***Center:*** 20 / Steamship / 20. ***Right:*** XX / Portrait of Henry Clay / 20. ***Engraver:*** Wellstood, Hanks, Hay & Whiting. ***Comments:*** H-TN-55-G76, Garland-126. Oct. 1, 185_. 1854.

Rarity: URS-4
F $350

$20 • W-TN-080-020-G100

Left: 20 / Medallion head of William Shakespeare / XX. ***Center:*** TWENTY / 20. ***Right:*** 20 / Medallion head / XX. ***Back:*** Red-orange. ***Engraver:*** Danforth, Wright & Co. ***Comments:*** H-TN-55-G78a, Garland-127. 18__. 1850s.

Rarity: URS-7
F $175

Union Bank of Tennessee (branch)

1832–1865

W-TN-090

History: On October 18, 1832, the Union Bank of Tennessee (also sometimes seen as the Union Bank of the State of Tennessee on notes) was chartered with an authorized capital of $3,000,000. The bank also absorbed the assets of the failed second Bank of the State of Tennessee, W-TN-680, which had been abolished that year. The state subscribed to $500,000 of the bank's capital, to be financed by bonds.

In 1855 the branch in Chattanooga had a capital of $200,000. E.G. Pearl was the cashier, and J.A. Whiteside was the president. By 1860 J.P. McMillin had taken the position of cashier, and J.B. Johnson was the president. In 1865 the Union Bank of Tennessee went into liquidation.

The Union Bank of Tennessee had its parent bank located in Nashville, W-TN-840, and branch banks located in Columbia, W-TN-220, Jackson, W-TN-325, Knoxville, W-TN-400, and Memphis, W-TN-600.

Numismatic Commentary: All signed and issued notes of this branch are scarce, with only an obvious counterfeit $20 being somewhat available.

Valid Issues

$5 • W-TN-090-005-G010

Center: Portrait of Napoleon Bonaparte. ***Engraver:*** Underwood, Bald, Spencer & Hufty. ***Comments:*** H-TN-210-G40, Garland-131. 18__. 1840s–1850s.

Rarity: URS-3
F $900

$10 • W-TN-090-010-G020

Left: Medallion head / TEN / Medallion head. ***Center:*** 10 / Hebe watering eagle / 10. ***Right:*** Medallion head / TEN / Medallion head. ***Engraver:*** Draper, Underwood, Bald & Spencer. ***Comments:*** H-TN-210-G42, Garland-132. 18__. 1830s.

Rarity: URS-3
F $900

$20 • W-TN-090-020-G030

Left: 20 / Woman seated / 20. ***Center:*** Ship / Two women flanking shield bearing eagle, surmounted by eagle / Ship. ***Right:*** 20 / Woman seated / 20. ***Engraver:*** Chas. Toppan. ***Comments:*** H-TN-210-G44, Garland-133. 18__. 1830s–1840s.

Rarity: URS-3
F $900

$20 • W-TN-090-020-G040

Center: Portrait of Benjamin Franklin / Portrait of Napoleon Bonaparte / Portrait of Benjamin Franklin. ***Engraver:*** Underwood, Bald, Spencer & Hufty. ***Comments:*** H-TN-210-G46. 18__. 1830s.

Rarity: URS-3
F $900

$50 • W-TN-090-050-G050

Left: 50 / Ship / 50. ***Center:*** Portrait of Indian / Woman seated / Portrait of Indian. ***Right:*** 50 / Ship / 50. ***Engraver:*** Chas. Toppan. ***Comments:*** H-TN-210-G48a. 18__. 1830s–1840s.

Rarity: *None known*

$100 • W-TN-090-100-G060

Left: 100 / Justice / 100. ***Center:*** Steamboat, Woman reclining with globe, Cherub / Steamboat. ***Right:*** 100 / Justice / 100. ***Engraver:*** Chas. Toppan. ***Comments:*** H-TN-210-G50a. 18__. 1830s–1840s.

Rarity: *None known*

Non-Valid Issues

$20 • W-TN-090-020-C030

Engraver: Chas. Toppan. ***Comments:*** H-TN-210-C44, Garland-134. Counterfeit of W-TN-090-020-G030. 18__. 1830s–1840s.

Rarity: URS-6
F $375

Clarksville, Tennessee

The area that made up Clarksville was given in the form of land grants to soldiers after the Revolutionary War. The plots were to act as repayment for time served, as the federal government lacked the funds to do so during the war. In 1790 the land was sectioned off and distributed.

By 1806 Clarksville had grown substantially, and the Rural Academy was established. Later Mount Pleasant Academy took its place, and by 1819 there were 22 stores, a silversmith, a bakery, and steamboats that navigated the Cumberland River to trade hardware, sugar, glass, fabric, and coffee. Surrounding plantations and farms brought flour, tobacco, cotton, and corn to Clarksville for transportation out to markets in New Orleans and Pittsburgh.

The rivers were not the only means of trade available to the town, however, and four roads allowed further commerce to occur. In 1829 a bridge was built connecting New Providence and Clarksville, spanning the Red River. A turnpike was built nine years later, and in 1855 Clarksville was officially incorporated as a city. On October 1, 1859, the railway arrived in the area, and the Memphis, Clarksville and Louisville Railroad was formed.

Due to its large population of farmers and planters who depended on slavery for the tobacco industry, the Clarksville area almost unanimously voted to secede and join the Confederacy in the Civil War. The city changed hands during the early months of the war, but by early 1862 it was firmly in Union control. The town became a haven for escaped and freed slaves.

Bank of America

1856–1858

W-TN-100

History: In 1856 the Bank of America was chartered. M.D. Davies was elected president, and J.F. Barnes was the cashier. In 1857 Charles M. Hiter was elected to replace Barnes, who had resigned. The capital in that year was $250,000. By 1858 the bank had closed.

The Bank of America had branch banks located in Brownsville, W-TN-050, Dresden, W-TN-260, and Rogersville, W-TN-880.

Numismatic Commentary: The $5 and $10 remainder notes of this bank can generally be found with patience. The higher-denomination notes are scarce and known from remainders. The 1990 Christie's sale signed and issued notes should command a substantial premium.

The 1990 Christie's sale of the American Bank Note Co. archives produced 4 sheets of 4 different combinations for 16 sheets in total. This is thought to be the source of most of the remainder notes available to collectors today. Included were two $5-$5-$5-$10 sheets and two $20-$20-$50-$100 sheets.

Valid Issues

$5 • W-TN-100-005-G010

Left: V / Portrait of Andrew Jackson. ***Center:*** Two women flanking shield. ***Right:*** 5 / Portrait of General Ambrose Davie. ***Overprint:*** Red FIVE. ***Engraver:*** Bald, Cousland & Co. / Baldwin, Bald & Cousland. ***Comments:*** H-TN-15-G8a. 18__. 1850s.

Rarity: URS-4
F $350

$5 • W-TN-100-005-G010a

Tint: Red-orange lathework and microlettering outlining white FIVE. ***Engraver:*** American Bank Note Co. ***Comments:*** H-TN-15-G8b. Similar to W-TN-100-005-G010 but with different engraver imprint. 18__. 1858.

Rarity: URS-7
F $150

$10 • W-TN-100-010-G020

Left: X / Portrait of Winston Jones Davie. ***Center:*** Woman and man flanking shield bearing wheat. ***Right:*** 10 / Portrait of Elizabeth Phillips. ***Overprint:*** Red TEN. ***Engraver:*** Bald, Cousland & Co. / Baldwin, Bald & Cousland. ***Comments:*** H-TN-15-G10a. 18__. 1850s.

Rarity: URS-4
F $350

$10 • W-TN-100-010-G020a

Tint: Red-orange lathework and microlettering outlining white TEN. ***Engraver:*** American Bank Note Co. ***Comments:*** H-TN-15-G10b. Similar to W-TN-100-010-G020 but with different engraver imprint. 18__. 1858.

Rarity: URS-7
F $350

$20 • W-TN-100-020-G030

Left: 20 / Portrait of Winston Jones Davie. ***Center:*** Family playing with bear cub, Horse. ***Right:*** 20 / Female portrait. ***Overprint:*** Red XX. ***Engraver:*** Bald, Cousland & Co. / Baldwin, Bald & Cousland. ***Comments:*** H-TN-15-G12a. 18__. 1850s.

Rarity: URS-4
F $350

$50 • W-TN-100-050-G040

Left: 50 / Male portrait. ***Center:*** Eagle with arrows and shield, Globe, Flags. ***Right:*** 50 / Male portrait. ***Engraver:*** Bald, Cousland & Co. / Baldwin, Bald & Cousland. ***Comments:*** H-TN-15-G14. 18__. 1850s.

Rarity: URS-4
F $450

$100 • W-TN-100-100-G050

Left: 100 / Male portrait. ***Center:*** Woman and Indian man flanking male portrait. ***Right:*** C / 100 / C. ***Engraver:*** Bald, Cousland & Co. / Baldwin, Bald & Cousland. ***Comments:*** H-TN-15-G16. 18__. 1850s.

Rarity: URS-4
F $550

Notes on Which the Place Payable is Blank

$5 • W-TN-100-005-G060

Left: V / Portrait of Andrew Jackson. ***Center:*** Two women flanking shield. ***Right:*** 5 / Portrait of General Ambrose Davie. ***Engraver:*** Bald, Cousland & Co. / Baldwin, Bald & Cousland. ***Comments:*** H-TN-15-G60, Garland-135. 18__. 1850s.

Rarity: —

$5 • W-TN-100-005-G060a

CC

Overprint: Red FIVE. ***Engraver:*** Bald, Cousland & Co. / Baldwin, Bald & Cousland. ***Comments:*** H-TN-15-G60a, Garland-136. Similar to W-TN-100-005-G060. 18__. 1850s.

Rarity: URS-10
Unc-Rem $125; **Proof** $350

$5 • W-TN-100-005-G060b

CC

Overprint: Red large FIVE. ***Engraver:*** Bald, Cousland & Co. / Baldwin, Bald & Cousland. ***Comments:*** H-Unlisted. Similar to W-TN-100-005-G060. 18__. 1850s.

Rarity: URS-10
Proof $300

$5 • **W-TN-100-005-G060c**

CC

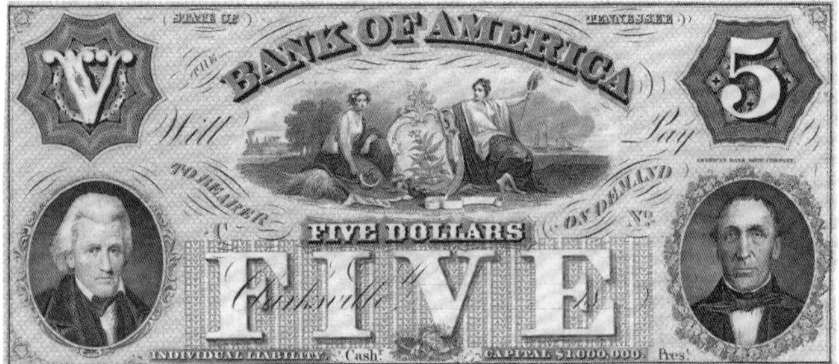

Tint: Red-orange lathework and panel of microlettering outlining white FIVE. ***Engraver:*** American Bank Note Co. ***Comments:*** H-TN-15-G60b, Garland-137. Similar to W-TN-100-005-G060 but with different engraver imprint. 18__. 1858.

Rarity: URS-7
Unc-Rem $275

$10 • **W-TN-100-010-G070**

Left: X / Portrait of Winston Jones Davie. ***Center:*** Woman and man flanking shield bearing wheat. ***Right:*** 10 / Portrait of Elizabeth Phillips. ***Engraver:*** Bald, Cousland & Co. / Baldwin, Bald & Cousland. ***Comments:*** H-TN-15-G62, Garland-138. 18__. 1850s.

Rarity: —

$10 • **W-TN-100-010-G070a**

CC

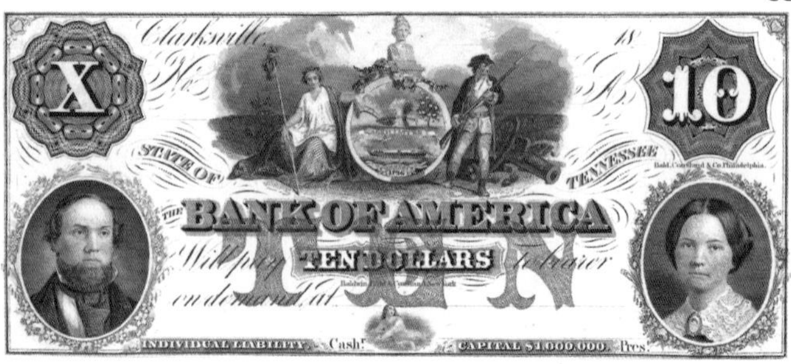

Overprint: Red TEN. ***Engraver:*** Bald, Cousland & Co. / Baldwin, Bald & Cousland. ***Comments:*** H-TN-15-G62a, Garland-139. Similar to W-TN-100-010-G070. 18__. 1850s.

Rarity: URS-8
Unc-Rem $275

$10 • **W-TN-100-010-G070b**

CC

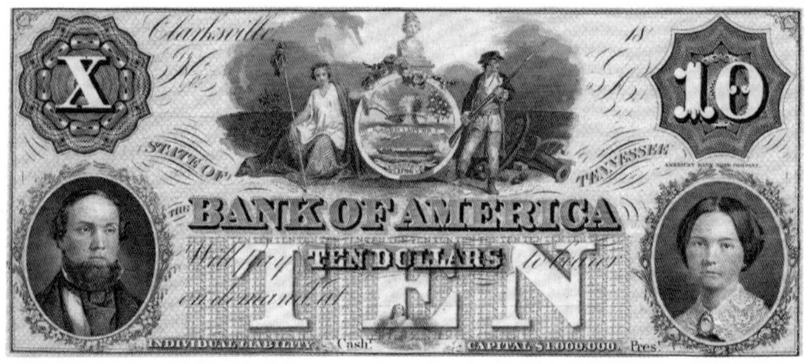

Tint: Red-orange lathework and panel of microlettering outlining white TEN. ***Engraver:*** American Bank Note Co. ***Comments:*** H-TN-15-G62b, Garland-140. Similar to W-TN-100-010-G070 but with different engraver imprint. 18__. 1858.

Rarity: URS-7
Unc-Rem $350

$20 • **W-TN-100-020-G080**

CC

Overprint: Red XX. ***Engraver:*** Bald, Cousland & Co. / Baldwin, Bald & Cousland. ***Comments:*** H-TN-15-G64a, Garland-141. 18__. 1850s.

Rarity: URS-7
Unc-Rem $300; **Proof** $800

$50 • **W-TN-100-050-G090**

SBG

Engraver: Bald, Cousland & Co. / Baldwin, Bald & Cousland. ***Comments:*** H-TN-15-G66, Garland-142. 18__. 1850s.

Rarity: URS-5
Proof $650

$50 • **W-TN-100-050-G090a**

CC

Overprint: Red FIFTY. ***Engraver:*** Bald, Cousland & Co. / Baldwin, Bald & Cousland. ***Comments:*** H-Unlisted. Similar to W-TN-100-050-G090. 18__. 1850s.

Rarity: URS-5
Proof $650

$100 • **W-TN-100-100-G100**

Left: 100 / Male portrait. ***Center:*** Woman and Indian man flanking male portrait. ***Right:*** C / 100 / C. ***Engraver:*** Bald, Cousland & Co. / Baldwin, Bald & Cousland. ***Comments:*** H-TN-15-G68, Garland-143. 18__. 1850s.

Rarity: —

$100 • W-TN-100-100-G100a CC

Overprint: Red 100. ***Engraver:*** Bald, Cousland & Co. / Baldwin, Bald & Cousland. ***Comments:*** H-Unlisted. Similar to W-TN-100-100-G100. 18__. 1850s.

Rarity: URS-4
Proof $1,000
Selected auction price: Heritage Auctions, September 7, 2011, Lot 15806, Proof $805

Bank of the State of Tennessee {1st} (branch)

1817–1820
W-TN-110

History: The first Bank of the State of Tennessee was chartered on November 20, 1811, with an authorized capital of $400,000. The capital was to be divided into shares of $50 apiece. The state subscribed to $20,000, on the provision that the state reserved the right to withdraw its funds after ten years. Hugh Lawson White was the president. No notes under $5 were allowed to be issued. In 1817 the branch bank in Clarksville was opened.

The Bank of the State of Tennessee discontinued business in 1820, at which time the stated capital was $371,107. The branches failed at the same time with a combined capital of $573,915.

The first Bank of the State of Tennessee had its parent bank located in Knoxville, W-TN-355, and branch banks located in Carthage, W-TN-060, Columbia, W-TN-170, Franklin, W-TN-280, Jonesboro, W-TN-335, Kingston, W-TN-340, Maryville, W-TN-440, and Nashville, W-TN-670.

Numismatic Commentary: No notes for this branch bank have been seen.

Valid Issues

$5 • W-TN-110-005-G010
Left: FIVE vertically. ***Center:*** Man plowing with horses / 5. ***Right:*** TENNESSEE vertically. ***Engraver:*** Murray, Draper, Fairman & Co. ***Comments:*** H-TN-75-G40. 18__. 1810s.
Rarity: *None known*

$10 • W-TN-110-010-G020
Left: TEN vertically. ***Center:*** Men harvesting corn / 10. ***Right:*** TENNESSEE vertically. ***Engraver:*** Murray, Draper, Fairman & Co. ***Comments:*** H-TN-75-G42. 18__. 1810s.
Rarity: *None known*

$20 • W-TN-110-020-G030
Left: TWENTY vertically. ***Center:*** XX / Justice seated / XX. ***Right:*** TENNESSEE vertically. ***Engraver:*** Murray, Draper, Fairman & Co. ***Comments:*** H-TN-75-G44. 18__. 1810s.
Rarity: *None known*

$50 • W-TN-110-050-G040
Left: FIFTY vertically. ***Center:*** 50 / Ships / 50. ***Right:*** TENNESSEE vertically. ***Engraver:*** Murray, Draper, Fairman & Co. ***Comments:*** H-TN-75-G46. 18__. 1810s.
Rarity: *None known*

$100 • W-TN-110-100-G050
Left: HUNDRED vertically. ***Center:*** Scene. ***Right:*** TENNESSEE vertically. ***Engraver:*** Murray, Draper, Fairman & Co. ***Comments:*** H-TN-75-G48. 18__. 1810s.
Rarity: *None known*

Non-Valid Issues

$3 • W-TN-110-003-N010
Left: THREE DOLLARS vertically. ***Center:*** 3 / 3. ***Right:*** THREE DOLLARS vertically. ***Engraver:*** Murray, Draper, Fairman & Co. ***Comments:*** H-TN-75-N9. 18__. 1810s.
Rarity: *None known*

$50 • W-TN-110-050-N020
Left: FIFTY vertically. ***Center:*** 50 / Ship / L. ***Right:*** FIFTY DOLLARS vertically. ***Engraver:*** Murray, Draper, Fairman & Co. ***Comments:*** H-TN-75-N12. 18__. 1810s.
Rarity: *None known*

Bank of the State of Tennessee {3rd} (branch)

1838–1866
W-TN-120

History: The third Bank of the State of Tennessee (also seen in print as the Bank of Tennessee) was chartered on January 19, 1838, with an authorized capital of $5,000,000. The bank opened for business in February.

The branch in Clarksville operated very successfully. The bank suspended specie payments a couple of times in 1838 and 1839, due to the panic of that time, but afterward it resumed and had a profitable and successful career. In 1854 D.N. Kennedy, cashier of the branch, resigned to go into the private-banking business. B.H. Wisdom took his place, and R.W. Humphreys was the cashier. In 1857 the capital was $223,000.

The Union army entered the state in early 1862, and some officers of the Bank of the State of Tennessee fled south with the bank's specie. After the war, the bank's assets were returned to Governor William G. Brownlow in Nashville. Half of the bank's funds had been transferred into state bonds.

By February 1866 the Bank of the State of Tennessee was authorized to go into liquidation.

The third Bank of the State of Tennessee had its parent bank located in Nashville, W-TN-690, and branch banks located in Athens, W-TN-010, Columbia, W-TN-190, Knoxville, W-TN-365, Memphis, W-TN-490, Murfreesboro, W-TN-610, Rogersville, W-TN-890, Shelbyville, W-TN-920, Somerville, W-TN-960, Sparta, W-TN-980, and Trenton, W-TN-1030.

Numismatic Commentary: Clarksville branch notes are all scarce to rare. Denominations of $50 and $100 were unknown to Garland and may not exist.

Valid Issues

$1 • W-TN-120-001-G010

Left: Woman seated with farmer / Female portrait. ***Center:*** 1 / Man plowing with horses / 1. ***Right:*** ONE / Medallion head / ONE. ***Engraver:*** Draper, Toppan & Co. ***Comments:*** H-TN-195-G106. Mar. 1, 1842.

Rarity: —

$1 • W-TN-120-001-G010a

Engraver: Toppan, Carpenter & Co. ***Comments:*** H-TN-195-G106a. Similar to W-TN-120-001-G010 but with different date and engraver imprint. Mar. 1, ____. 1840s, 1861.

Rarity: —

$1 • W-TN-120-001-G020

CC

Engraver: Toppan, Carpenter, Casilear & Co. ***Comments:*** H-TN-195-G108. 18__. 1850s.

Rarity: URS-4
F $240

$1 • W-TN-120-001-G030

Left: 1 / Portrait of boy. ***Center:*** Indian on horseback hunting buffalo. ***Right:*** 1 / Female portrait. ***Tint:*** Red-orange. ***Back:*** Red-orange. ***Engraver:*** Toppan, Carpenter & Co. ***Comments:*** H-TN-195-G110a. 18__. 1850s.

Rarity: URS-4
F $250

$2 • W-TN-120-002-G040

Left: TWO / Woman seated in 2 / 2. ***Center:*** 2 / Woman seated on bales / 2. ***Right:*** 2 / Ship / 2. ***Engraver:*** Draper, Toppan & Co. ***Comments:*** H-TN-195-G112. Mar. 1, 1842.

Rarity: *None known*

$2 • W-TN-120-002-G040a

Engraver: Toppan, Carpenter & Co. ***Comments:*** H-TN-195-G112a. Similar to W-TN-120-002-G040 but with different date and engraver imprint. Mar. 1, ____. 1840s, 1861.

Rarity: *None known*

$2 • W-TN-120-002-G050

Left: 2 / Justice seated with scales. ***Center:*** Cattle / 2 / 2. ***Right:*** 2 / Liberty with pole, cap, and flag. ***Engraver:*** Toppan, Carpenter, Casilear & Co. ***Comments:*** H-TN-195-G114. 18__. 1850s.

Rarity: URS-3
F $450

$2 • W-TN-120-002-G060

Left: 2 / Female portrait. ***Center:*** Soldier, Woman, and two Indians looking at bust of George Washington. ***Right:*** 2 / Portrait of Charles Carroll. ***Tint:*** Red-orange. ***Back:*** Red-orange. ***Engraver:*** Toppan, Carpenter & Co. ***Comments:*** H-TN-195-G116a. 18__. 1850s.

Rarity: URS-3
F $500

$3 • W-TN-120-003-G070

Left: THREE / Woman standing / THREE. ***Center:*** 3 / Men on horses, sheep / 3. ***Right:*** THREE / Cherubs in 3 / THREE. ***Engraver:*** Draper, Toppan & Co. ***Comments:*** H-TN-195-G118. Mar. 1, 1842.

Rarity: —

$3 • W-TN-120-003-G070a

Engraver: Toppan, Carpenter & Co. ***Comments:*** H-TN-195-G118a. Similar to W-TN-120-003-G070 but with different date and engraver imprint. Mar. 1, ____. 1840s, 1861.

Rarity: —

$5 • W-TN-120-005-G080

Left: 5 / Woman leaning on column / V. ***Center:*** Woman seated with shield. ***Right:*** 5 / Justice standing with scales and eagle / V. ***Engraver:*** Rawdon, Wright, Hatch & Edson / Rawdon, Wright & Hatch. ***Comments:*** H-TN-195-G120. 18__. 1838–1840s.

Rarity: —

$5 • W-TN-120-005-G090

Left: Three men / 5. ***Center:*** Portrait of James Madison. ***Right:*** 5 / Medallion head. ***Back:*** Red-orange. ***Engraver:*** Danforth, Bald & Co. ***Comments:*** H-TN-195-G122a. 18__. 1850s.

Rarity: URS-3
F $500

$5 • W-TN-120-005-G090a

Tint: Red-orange outlining white V / 5 / V. ***Back:*** Red-orange. ***Engraver:*** Danforth, Bald & Co. ***Comments:*** H-TN-195-G122b. Similar to W-TN-120-005-G090. 18__. 1850s.

Rarity: URS-6
F $200

$10 • W-TN-120-010-G100

Left: 10 / Eagle with shield / X. ***Center:*** Woman with children seated among parcels, Factories and farmhouse. ***Right:*** 10 / Shield / X. ***Engraver:*** Draper, Toppan, Longacre & Co. ***Comments:*** H-TN-195-G128. 18__. 1838–1840s.

Rarity: URS-3
F $450

$10 • W-TN-120-010-G110

Left: 10 / Portrait of James K. Polk. ***Center:*** Portrait of Andrew Jackson. ***Right:*** 10 / Portrait of Cave Johnson. ***Tint:*** Red-orange outlining white 10 / 10. ***Back:*** Blue. ***Engraver:*** Toppan, Carpenter & Co. ***Comments:*** H-TN-195-G132a. 18__. 1850s–1861.

Rarity: URS-3
F $500

$20 • **W-TN-120-020-G120**

Left: 20 / Man writing on tablet / 20. ***Center:*** Woman standing with eagle and shield. ***Right:*** 20 / Shield / 20. ***Engraver:*** Draper, Toppan, Longacre & Co. ***Comments:*** H-TN-195-G134. 18__. 1838–1840s.

Rarity: *None known*

$20 • **W-TN-120-020-G120a**

Engraver: Toppan, Carpenter & Co. ***Comments:*** H-TN-195-G134a. Similar to W-TN-120-020-G120 but with different engraver imprint. 18__. 1840s–1850s

Rarity: *None known*

$20 • **W-TN-120-020-G130**

Left: 20 / Portrait of Zachary Taylor / 20. ***Center:*** Three women reclining, Ship / 20. ***Right:*** Justice seated with sword and scales / TWENTY. ***Engraver:*** Toppan, Carpenter, Casilear & Co. ***Comments:*** H-TN-195-G136. 18__. 1850s.

Rarity: URS-4

F $350

$20 • **W-TN-120-020-G130a**

Back: Red-orange. ***Engraver:*** Toppan, Carpenter, Casilear & Co. ***Comments:*** H-TN-195-G136a. Similar to W-TN-120-020-G130. 18__. 1850s.

Rarity: *None known*

$20 • **W-TN-120-020-G130b**

Tint: Red-orange outlining white TWENTY. ***Back:*** Red-orange. ***Engraver:*** Toppan, Carpenter, Casilear & Co. ***Comments:*** H-TN-195-G136b. Similar to W-TN-120-020-G130. 18__. 1850s.

Rarity: URS-5

F $300

$50 • **W-TN-120-050-G140**

Left: 50 / Shield / 50. ***Center:*** Liberty with eagle and shield. ***Right:*** 50 / Portrait of George Washington / 50. ***Engraver:*** Draper, Toppan, Longacre & Co. ***Comments:*** H-TN-195-G138. 18__. 1838–1840s.

Rarity: *None known*

$100 • **W-TN-120-100-G150**

Left: Atlas lifting world on shoulders / 100. ***Center:*** 100 / Justice with eagle and shield / 100. ***Right:*** Atlas lifting world on shoulders / 100. ***Engraver:*** Draper, Toppan, Longacre & Co. ***Comments:*** H-TN-195-G140. 18__. 1838–1850s.

Rarity: *None known*

Non-Valid Issues

$10 • **W-TN-120-010-C100**

Engraver: Draper, Toppan, Longacre & Co. ***Comments:*** H-TN-195-C128. Counterfeit of W-TN-120-010-G100. 18__. 1853.

Rarity: *None known*

$20 • **W-TN-120-020-C120a**

Engraver: Toppan, Carpenter & Co. ***Comments:*** H-TN-195-C134a. Counterfeit of W-TN-120-020-G120a. 18__. 1853.

Rarity: *None known*

$20 • **W-TN-120-020-C130**

Engraver: Toppan, Carpenter, Casilear & Co. ***Comments:*** H-TN-195-C136. Counterfeit of W-TN-120-020-G130. 18__. 1853.

Rarity: URS-5

F $300

$20 • **W-TN-120-020-C130a**

Back: Red-orange. ***Engraver:*** Toppan, Carpenter, Casilear & Co. ***Comments:*** H-TN-195-C136a. Counterfeit of W-TN-120-020-G130a. 18__. 1853.

Rarity: *None known*

$20 • **W-TN-120-020-C130b**

Tint: Red-orange outlining white TWENTY. ***Back:*** Red-orange. ***Engraver:*** Toppan, Carpenter, Casilear & Co. ***Comments:*** H-TN-195-C136b. Counterfeit of W-TN-120-020-G130b. 18__. 1853.

Rarity: *None known*

Northern Bank of Tennessee

1854–1860s

W-TN-130

History: The Northern Bank of Tennessee was chartered in 1854 with an authorized capital of $100,000. In 1857 these values were given: capital $60,000; bills in circulation $40,351; specie $13,455. The president at this time was D.N. Kennedy, and James L. Glenn was the cashier. By 1863 the capital had risen to $100,000.

The Northern Bank of Tennessee did a long and prosperous business, well beyond the bank-note–issuing era under study. John J. Knox, in his *History of Banking*, reports that:

> The Northern Bank of Tennessee . . . never suspended specie payment. As long as gold could be obtained its notes were redeemed in gold, and when the greenback was declared legal tender, the notes of this bank were redeemed in that currency. . . . the old institution is beginning its 46th year with new stockholders and officers, with every prospect of continued success. It is believed this bank is the only ante-bellum bank of this State now in existence.

Numismatic Commentary: Proof notes are very rare. Signed and issued notes have not been recorded.

The 1990 Christie's sale of the American Bank Note Co. archives produced a $1-$1-$2-$5 sheet.

Valid Issues

$1 • **W-TN-130-001-G010**

Left: 1 on ONE / Woman holding child. ***Center:*** Woman with bale and shield, Ship / 1. ***Right:*** ONE on 1 / Liberty with eagle and shield / ONE. ***Engraver:*** Danforth, Wright & Co. ***Comments:*** H-TN-20-G2, Garland-172. Nov. 1, 1855.

Rarity: URS-3

Proof $950

$2 • **W-TN-130-002-G020**

Left: 2 / TWO / 2. ***Center:*** Men in foundry. ***Right:*** 2 / Woman with sheaf. ***Engraver:*** Danforth, Wright & Co. ***Comments:*** H-TN-20-G4, Garland-173. Nov. 1, 1855.

Rarity: URS-2

Proof $1,500

$5 • **W-TN-130-005-G030**
Left: 5 / Portrait of Millard Fillmore. ***Center:*** V / Cherubs with pole and cap / V. ***Right:*** 5 / Portrait of Felix Grundy. ***Engraver:*** Danforth, Wright & Co. ***Comments:*** H-TN-20-G6, Garland-174. Nov. 1, 1855.

Rarity: URS-3
Proof $1,000

Planters Bank of Tennessee (branch)

1834–1865

W-TN-140

History: The Planters Bank of Tennessee was chartered on November 11, 1833, with an authorized capital of $2,000,000. In 1834 the branch located in Clarksville was opened. In 1848 Thomas W. Barksdale was the cashier. Capital at that time was $23,932, but by 1855 this had risen to $150,000. William P. Hume became the cashier, and H.F. Beaumont was the president. In 1860 the capital was as high as $500,000. In 1865 the bank was forced to liquidate and close its affairs.

The Planters Bank of Tennessee had its parent bank located in Nashville, W-TN-810, and branch banks located in Athens, W-TN-020, Columbia, W-TN-210, Franklin, W-TN-300, LaGrange, W-TN-410, Memphis, W-TN-570, Murfreesboro, W-TN-630, Pulaski, W-TN-870, Rogersville, W-TN-910, Shelbyville, W-TN-940, Somerville, W-TN-970, Sparta, W-TN-990, Trenton, W-TN-1050, and Winchester, W-TN-1070.

Numismatic Commentary: All signed and issued notes are scarce to very scarce. Denominations above $20 were unknown to Garland.

Valid Issues

$1 • **W-TN-140-001-G010**
Left: 1 / Medallion head bearing ONE / 1. ***Center:*** 1 with cherub / Woman seated with boxes. ***Right:*** Woman standing in 1. ***Engraver:*** Rawdon, Wright, Hatch & Edson. ***Comments:*** H-TN-185-G86. 18__. 1840s.

Rarity: *None known*

$2 • **W-TN-140-002-G020**
Left: 2 / Woman with sheaf / 2. ***Center:*** 2 with cherubs / Woman seated with boxes. ***Right:*** Woman standing in 2. ***Engraver:*** Rawdon, Wright, Hatch & Edson. ***Comments:*** H-TN-185-G88. Dec. 1, 1860.

Rarity: *None known*

$3 • **W-TN-140-003-G030**
Left: 3 / Medallion head / 3. ***Center:*** 3 with cherubs / Two men flanking shield bearing cow surmounted by beehive. ***Right:*** Woman standing in 3. ***Engraver:*** Rawdon, Wright, Hatch & Edson. ***Comments:*** H-TN-185-G90. Dec. 1, 1860.

Rarity: *None known*

$5 • **W-TN-140-005-G040**
Left: FIVE / Woman with cog wheel / 5 vertically. ***Center:*** 5 / Horse / 5. ***Right:*** FIVE / Man seated / 5 vertically. ***Engraver:*** Rawdon, Wright, & Hatch. ***Comments:*** H-TN-185-G92. 18__. 1830s.

Rarity: *None known*

$5 • **W-TN-140-005-G050**
Left: Medallion head / FIVE / Medallion head. ***Center:*** FIVE / Man standing with dog / FIVE. ***Right:*** Medallion head / FIVE / Medallion head. ***Engraver:*** Underwood, Bald & Spencer. ***Comments:*** H-TN-185-G94, Garland-194. 18__. 1830s–1840s.

Rarity: URS-6
F $100

$5 • **W-TN-140-005-G050a**
Engraver: Underwood, Bald & Spencer. ***Comments:*** H-TN-185-G94a. Similar to W-TN-140-005-G050. 18__. 1830s–1840s.

Rarity: *None known*

$10 • **W-TN-140-010-G060**
Left: X / Ten gold dollars / 10. ***Center:*** 10 / Mechanic seated with cogwheel, Steamboat / 10. ***Right:*** TEN / Woman standing with anchor / TEN. ***Engraver:*** Rawdon, Wright, & Hatch. ***Comments:*** H-TN-185-G96. 18__. 1830s.

Rarity: *None known*

$10 • **W-TN-140-010-G070**
Left: Medallion head / TEN / Medallion head. ***Center:*** 10 / Farm scene, Harvest / X. ***Right:*** Medallion head / TEN / Medallion head. ***Engraver:*** Underwood, Bald & Spencer. ***Comments:*** H-TN-185-G98, Garland-195. 18__. 1830s–1840s.

Rarity: URS-5
F $300

$10 • **W-TN-140-010-G070a**
Engraver: Underwood, Bald & Spencer. ***Comments:*** H-TN-185-G98a. Similar to W-TN-140-010-G070. 18__. 1830s–1840s.

Rarity: *None known*

$20 • **W-TN-140-020-G080**
Engraver: Rawdon, Wright, & Hatch. ***Comments:*** H-TN-185-G100. No description available. 18__. 1830s.

Rarity: *None known*

$20 • **W-TN-140-020-G090**
Left: 20 / Medallion head / 20. ***Center:*** 20 / Medallion head / 20. ***Right:*** 20 / Medallion head / 20. ***Engraver:*** Underwood, Bald & Spencer. ***Comments:*** H-TN-185-G102, Garland-196. 18__. 1830s–1840s.

Rarity: URS-5
F $300

$20 • **W-TN-140-020-G090a**
Engraver: Underwood, Bald & Spencer. ***Comments:*** H-TN-185-G102a. Similar to W-TN-140-020-G090. 18__. 1830s–1840s.

Rarity: *None known*

$50 • **W-TN-140-050-G100**
Left: 50 / Medallion head / 50. ***Center:*** Medallion heads / Woman seated, Ship / Medallion heads. ***Right:*** 50 / Medallion head / 50. ***Engraver:*** Underwood, Bald, Spencer & Hufty. ***Comments:*** H-TN-185-G104. 18__. 1830s–1850s.

Rarity: *None known*

$100 • **W-TN-140-100-G110**
Left: 100 / Three women seated vertically / 100. ***Center:*** Medallion head / Boy reclining under corn, Plow / Medallion head. ***Right:*** 100 / Three women seated vertically / 100. ***Engraver:*** Underwood, Bald, Spencer & Hufty. ***Comments:*** H-TN-185-G106. 18__. 1830s–1850s.

Rarity: *None known*

Civil War Fractional Notes

5¢ • W-TN-140-00.05-G120

Center: FIVE CENTS. ***Right:*** 5. ***Engraver:*** Adams. ***Comments:*** H-TN-185-G110, Garland-188. Jany. 1st, 1862.

Rarity: URS-5
F $250

10¢ • W-TN-140-00.10-G130

Center: TEN CENTS. ***Right:*** 10. ***Engraver:*** Adams. ***Comments:*** H-TN-185-G112, Garland-189. Jany. 1st, 1862.

Rarity: URS-5
F $250

25¢ • W-TN-140-00.25-G140

Center: TWENTY FIVE CENTS. ***Right:*** 25. ***Engraver:*** Adams. ***Comments:*** H-TN-185-G114, Garland-190. Jany. 1st, 1862.

Rarity: URS-5
F $250

30¢ • W-TN-140-00.30-G150 CC

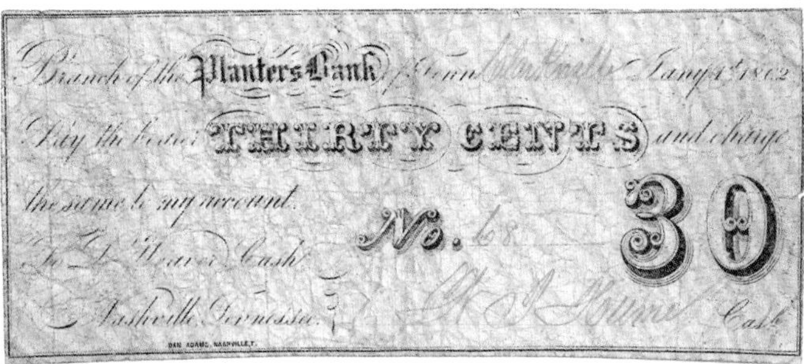

Engraver: Adams. ***Comments:*** H-TN-185-G116, Garland-191. Jany. 1st, 1862.

Rarity: URS-5
F $250

50¢ • W-TN-140-00.50-G160

Center: FIFTY CENTS. ***Right:*** 50. ***Back:*** Red. ***Engraver:*** Adams. ***Comments:*** H-TN-185-G118, Garland-192. Jany. 1st, 1862.

Rarity: URS-5
F $250

80¢ • W-TN-140-00.80-G170

Center: EIGHTY CENTS. ***Right:*** 80. ***Back:*** Red. ***Engraver:*** Adams. ***Comments:*** H-TN-185-G120, Garland-193. Jany. 1st, 1862.

Rarity: URS-5
F $250

Non-Valid Issues

$10 • W-TN-140-010-S010

Left: Woman. ***Center:*** Woman, Train, Steamboat. ***Right:*** Ceres. ***Comments:*** H-TN-185-S36. 18__. 1840s.

Rarity: *None known*

$10 • W-TN-140-010-S020

Left: 10 / Justice with scales. ***Center:*** X with cherubs / Two women seated. ***Right:*** 10 / Justice with scales. ***Engraver:*** Rawdon, Wright & Hatch. ***Comments:*** H-TN-185-S38. From a genuine plate of the Planters Bank of Alabama, Wetumpka, Alabama. 18__. 1840s.

Rarity: *None known*

$20 • W-TN-140-020-S030

Center: Eagle. ***Comments:*** H-TN-185-S40. 18__. 1840s.

Rarity: *None known*

$20 • W-TN-140-020-S040

Left: 20 / Female portrait / XX. ***Center:*** Woman seated near ocean with shield. ***Right:*** 20 / Female portrait / XX. ***Engraver:*** Rawdon, Wright & Hatch. ***Comments:*** H-TN-185-S42. From a genuine plate of the Planters Bank of Alabama, Wetumpka, Alabama. 18__. 1840s.

Rarity: *None known*

$50 • W-TN-140-050-S050

Left: FIFTY DOLLARS vertically. ***Center:*** 50 / Eagle on bale / 50. ***Right:*** STATE OF TENNESSEE vertically. ***Engraver:*** Rawdon, Wright & Hatch. ***Comments:*** H-TN-185-S44. From a genuine plate of the Planters Bank of Alabama, Wetumpka, Alabama. 18__. 1840s.

Rarity: *None known*

$100 • W-TN-140-100-S060

Left: HUNDRED vertically. ***Center:*** Deer, River. ***Right:*** Portrait of George Washington. ***Engraver:*** Rawdon, Wright & Hatch. ***Comments:*** H-TN-185-S46. From a genuine plate of the Planters Bank of Alabama, Wetumpka, Alabama. 18__. 1840s.

Rarity: *None known*

$100 • W-TN-140-100-S070

Left: Medallion head. ***Center:*** C / Factory / C. ***Right:*** 100 diagonally. ***Engraver:*** Rawdon, Wright & Hatch. ***Comments:*** H-TN-185-S48. 18__. 1840s.

Rarity: *None known*

Cleveland, Tennessee

Bradley County was established in 1836, and Cleveland was settled to be its county seat. It was named after Colonel Benjamin Cleveland, a commander during the American Revolution. The area was originally known as Taylor's Place and was home to Andrew Taylor.

The water sources surrounding Cleveland fed directly into its growth, and by 1838 the population was 400 strong. Two churches and an academy were established, and on February 4, 1842, the city was incorporated. The railway arrived in the 1850s.

The town was divided about the matter of secession as war loomed, but in the end Cleveland voted against it in June 1861. The following November the railroad bridge was destroyed, and Cleveland was occupied by Confederate fxxorces until 1863.

Ocoee Bank
1854–1862
W-TN-150

History: On February 25, 1854, the Ocoee Bank was chartered with an authorized capital of $100,000. By 1857 the bank had $96,580 of bills in circulation, and $22,633 in specie was in the vault. Thomas H. Callaway was the president, and Thomas J. Campbell was the cashier. In 1860 the capital had risen to $130,000. W.A. Branner became the cashier, and George A. Branner took the presidency. By 1862 the bank had closed its affairs.

The Ocoee Bank had a branch bank located in Knoxville, W-TN-385.

Numismatic Commentary: Notes from this bank have a wide appeal due to the 1996 Summer Olympics that took place in Atlanta with events on the Ocoee River, which still holds ongoing summertime popularity as a whitewater-rafting destination. Within the series are easy-to-find and attractive $1, $2, $5, and $10 notes. There are also notes that are thought to be very scarce to rare. Proofs are known of W-TN-150-001-G010 and W-TN-150-020-G080, the latter thought to be unique.

The 1990 Christie's sale of the American Bank Note Co. archives produced at least 23 sheets of remainder notes to the marketplace, including a $5-$5-$10-$20 sheet.

Valid Issues

$1 • W-TN-150-001-G010

LK

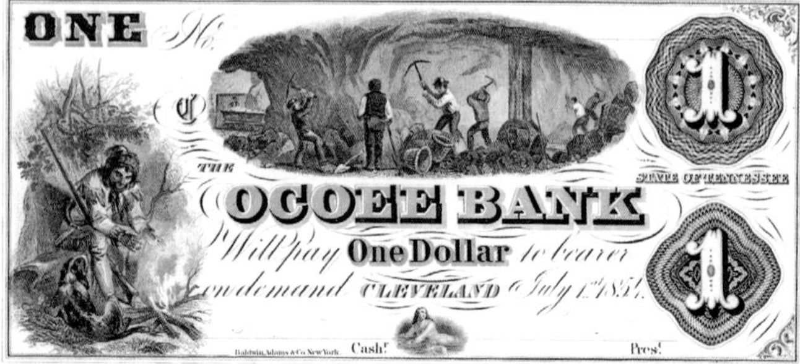

Engraver: Baldwin, Adams & Co. ***Comments:*** H-TN-25-G2, Garland-197. July 1st, 1854.

Rarity: URS-3

Proof $600

Selected auction price: Stack's Bowers Galleries, May 2010, Proof $525

$1 • W-TN-150-001-G010a

CC

Overprint: Red ONE. ***Engraver:*** Baldwin, Adams & Co. ***Comments:*** H-TN-25-G2a, Garland-198. Similar to W-TN-150-001-G010. July 1st, 1854.

Rarity: URS-3

Proof $1,050

$1 • W-TN-150-001-G020

CC

Engraver: Bald, Adams & Co. / Bald, Cousland & Co. ***Comments:*** H-TN-25-G4, Garland-199. Jan. 1, 1855.

Rarity: URS-1

Proof $3,000

$1 • W-TN-150-001-G020a

ANS

Overprint: Red ONE. ***Engraver:*** American Bank Note Co. ***Comments:*** H-TN-25-G4a, Garland-200. Similar to W-TN-150-001-G020 but with different date and engraver imprint. 1st Novr. 1859.

Rarity: URS-8

Unc-Rem $150; **Proof** $350

$1 • W-TN-150-001-G020b

CC

Overprint: Red ONE. ***Engraver:*** American Bank Note Co. ***Comments:*** H-TN-25-G4b, Garland-201. Similar to W-TN-150-001-G020 but with different date and engraver imprint. 1st Novr. 1860.

Rarity: URS-7

F $200

$2 • W-TN-150-002-G030

CC

Engraver: Baldwin, Adams & Co. ***Comments:*** H-TN-25-G6, Garland-202. July 1st, 1854.

Rarity: URS-2

Proof $1,250

$2 • W-TN-150-002-G030a

Left: TWO / Portrait of Euclid Waterhouse. ***Center:*** Indian and family in canoe. ***Right:*** 2 / Portrait of Thomas H. Callaway. ***Overprint:*** Red TWO. ***Engraver:*** Baldwin, Adams & Co. ***Comments:*** H-TN-25-G6a, Garland-204. Similar to W-TN-150-002-G030. July 1st, 1854.

Rarity: URS-2
Proof $1,250

$2 • W-TN-150-002-G030b

Engraver: Bald, Adams & Co. / Bald, Cousland & Co. ***Comments:*** H-TN-25-G6b, Garland-203. Similar to W-TN-150-002-G030 but with different date and engraver imprint. Jan. 1, 1855.

Rarity: URS-1
Proof $4,000

$2 • W-TN-150-002-G030c

SI

Overprint: Red TWO. ***Engraver:*** American Bank Note Co. ***Comments:*** H-TN-25-G6c, Garland-205. Similar to W-TN-150-002-G030 but with different date and engraver imprint. 1st Novr. 1859.

Rarity: URS-8
F $250

$2 • W-TN-150-002-G030d

CC

Overprint: Red TWO. ***Engraver:*** American Bank Note Co. ***Comments:*** H-TN-25-G6d, Garland-206. Similar to W-TN-150-002-G030 but with different date and engraver imprint. 1st Novr. 1860.

Rarity: URS-8
F $200

Collectors and Researchers:

If you have new information about any banks or notes listed in this volume, contact Whitman Publishing, Attn: Obsolete Paper Money, 3101 Clairmont Road, Suite G, Atlanta, GA 30329.

$5 • W-TN-150-005-G040

CC

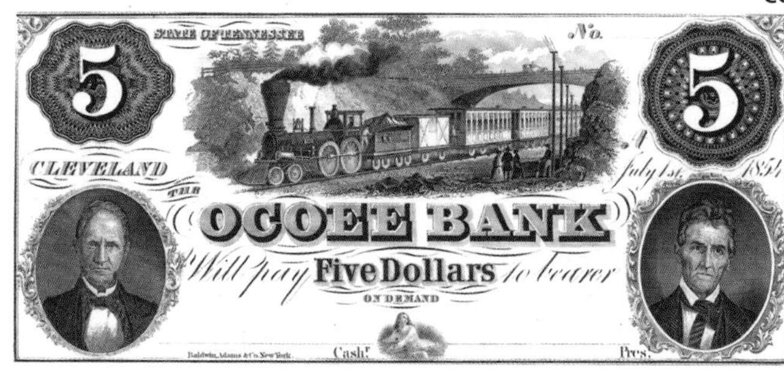

Engraver: Baldwin, Adams & Co. ***Comments:*** H-TN-25-G8, Garland-207. July 1st, 1854.

Rarity: URS-3
F $500

$5 • W-TN-150-005-G040a

Left: 5 / Portrait of Thomas H. Callaway. ***Center:*** Train. ***Right:*** 5 / Portrait of Euclid Waterhouse. ***Overprint:*** Red FIVE. ***Engraver:*** Baldwin, Adams & Co. ***Comments:*** H-TN-25-G8a. Similar to W-TN-150-005-G040. July 1st, 1854.

Rarity: —

$5 • W-TN-150-005-G050

CC

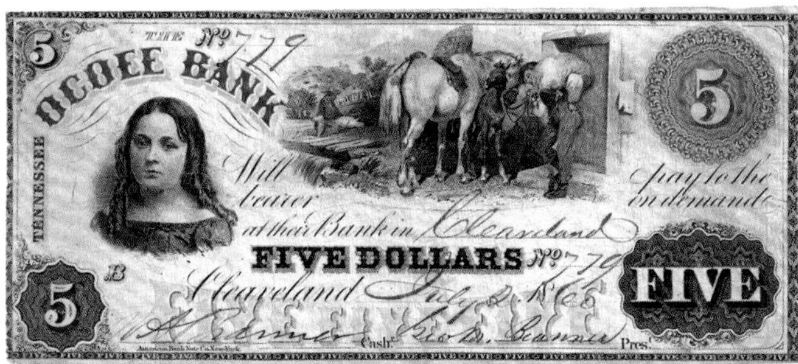

Tint: Red-orange bank title, FIVE / FIVE / FIVE, and die outlining white 5. ***Engraver:*** American Bank Note Co. ***Comments:*** H-TN-25-G10c, Garland-208. 18__. 1860.

Rarity: URS-5
F $250

$10 • W-TN-150-010-G060

CC

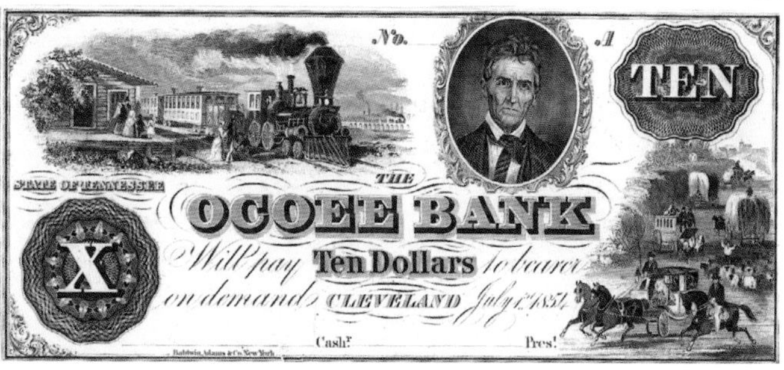

Engraver: Baldwin, Adams & Co. ***Comments:*** H-TN-25-G12, Garland-210. July 1st, 1854.

Rarity: URS-4
Proof $350

$10 • W-TN-150-010-G060a

Left: Train / X. ***Center:*** Portrait of Euclid Waterhouse. ***Right:*** TEN / Street scene with horses and carriages. ***Overprint:*** Red TEN. ***Engraver:*** Baldwin, Adams & Co. ***Comments:*** H-TN-25-G12a. Similar to W-TN-150-010-G060. July 1st, 1854.

Rarity: —

$10 • W-TN-150-010-G070

CC

Tint: Red-orange TEN, bank title, 10 / 10, and die outlining white 10. ***Engraver:*** American Bank Note Co. ***Comments:*** H-TN-25-G14c, Garland-211. 18__. 1860.

Rarity: URS-8
F $200

$20 • W-TN-150-020-G080

CC

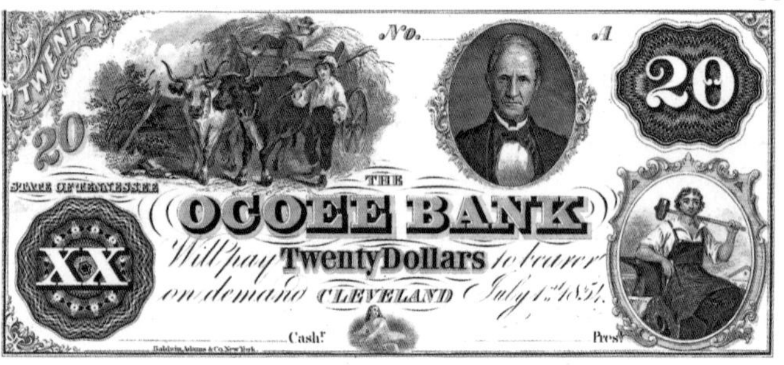

Engraver: Baldwin, Adams & Co. ***Comments:*** H-TN-25-G16, Garland-213. July 1st, 1854.

Rarity: URS-4
Proof $475

$20 • W-TN-150-020-G080a

Left: TWENTY / 20 / Boys with oxen and hay wagon / XX. ***Center:*** Portrait of Thomas H. Calloway. ***Right:*** 20 / Mechanic with hammer. ***Overprint:*** Red XX. ***Engraver:*** Baldwin, Adams & Co. ***Comments:*** H-TN-25-G16a. Similar to W-TN-150-020-G080. July 1st, 1854.

Rarity: —

Notes on Which the Place Payable is Blank

$1 • W-TN-150-001-G090

RG

Overprint: Red ONE. ***Engraver:*** American Bank Note Co. ***Comments:*** H-TN-25-G36a. 1st Novr. 1859.

Rarity: URS-6
F $200

$2 • W-TN-150-002-G100

QDB

Overprint: Red TWO. ***Engraver:*** American Bank Note Co. ***Comments:*** H-TN-25-G38a. 1st Novr. 1859.

Rarity: URS-5
F $300

Uncut Sheets

$1-$1-$1-$2 • W-TN-150-001.001.001.002-US010

Vignette(s): ($1) Forester in front of fire / Men mining. ***($2)*** Portrait of Euclid Waterhouse / Indian and family in canoe / Portrait of Thomas H. Callaway. ***Overprint(s):*** Red. ***Engraver:*** Baldwin, Adams & Co. ***Comments:*** H-TN-25-G2, G2, G2, G6. First three notes identical. July 1st, 1854.

Rarity: URS-3
Proof $1,500

Uncut Sheet on Which the Place Payable is Blank

$1-$1-$1-$2 • W-TN-150-001.001.001.002-US020 RG

Overprint(s): Red. ***Engraver:*** American Bank Note Co. ***Comments:*** H-TN-25-G36a, G36a, G36a, G38a. First three notes identical. 1st Novr. 1859.

Rarity: URS-3
Unc-Rem $1,400
Selected auction price: Heritage Auctions, January 8, 2014, Lot 15439, EF $1,175

Columbia, Tennessee

Maury County was laid out in 1807, and Columbia followed the same year to be its seat. The town was incorporated in 1817 and was surrounded by wealthy plantations that cultivated tobacco, hemp, and livestock. Many farms were dedicated to the breeding of thoroughbred race horses.

Agricultural Bank

Circa 1839

W-TN-160

History: A non-existent bank represented only by fraudulent notes.

Numismatic Commentary: In decades of searching around the world for Tennessee bank notes, Paul Garland was able to find only one $20 note from this bank. He considered it to be unique.

Issues

$20 • W-TN-160-020-S010

Left: XX / Portrait of George Washington / XX. ***Center:*** 20 / Ships. ***Right:*** 20 / Farming implements, Wheat / 20. ***Comments:*** H-TN-30-S10, Garland-226. 18__. 1830s.

Rarity: URS-1
Proof $4,000

Bank of the State of Tennessee {1st} (branch)

1817–1820

W-TN-170

History: The first Bank of the State of Tennessee was chartered on November 20, 1811, with an authorized capital of $400,000. The capital was to be divided into shares of $50 apiece. The state subscribed to $20,000, on the provision that the state reserved the right to withdraw its funds after ten years. Hugh Lawson White was the president. No notes under $5 were allowed to be issued. The branch in Columbia opened in 1817.

The Bank of the State of Tennessee discontinued business in 1820, at which time the stated capital was $371,107. The branches failed at the same time with a combined capital of $573,915.

The first Bank of the State of Tennessee had its parent bank located in Knoxville, W-TN-355, and branch banks located in Carthage, W-TN-060, Clarksville, W-TN-110, Franklin, W-TN-280, Jonesboro, W-TN-335, Kingston, W-TN-340, Maryville, W-TN-440, and Nashville, W-TN-670.

Numismatic Commentary: No notes of this branch bank are known.

Valid Issues

$5 • W-TN-170-005-G010

Left: FIVE vertically. ***Center:*** Man plowing with horses / 5. ***Right:*** TENNESSEE vertically. ***Engraver:*** Murray, Draper, Fairman & Co. ***Comments:*** H-TN-75-G56. 18__. 1810s.

Rarity: *None known*

$10 • W-TN-170-010-G020

Left: TEN vertically. ***Center:*** Men harvesting corn / 10. ***Right:*** TENNESSEE vertically. ***Engraver:*** Murray, Draper, Fairman & Co. ***Comments:*** H-TN-75-G58. 18__. 1810s.

Rarity: *None known*

$20 • W-TN-170-020-G030
Left: TWENTY vertically. *Center:* XX / Justice seated / XX. *Right:* TENNESSEE vertically. *Engraver:* Murray, Draper, Fairman & Co. *Comments:* H-TN-75-G60. 18__. 1810s.
Rarity: *None known*

$50 • W-TN-170-050-G040
Left: FIFTY vertically. *Center:* 50 / Ships / 50. *Right:* TENNESSEE vertically. *Engraver:* Murray, Draper, Fairman & Co. *Comments:* H-TN-75-G62. 18__. 1810s.
Rarity: *None known*

$100 • W-TN-170-100-G050
Left: HUNDRED vertically. *Center:* Scene. *Right:* TENNESSEE vertically. *Engraver:* Murray, Draper, Fairman & Co. *Comments:* H-TN-75-G64. 18__. 1810s.
Rarity: *None known*

Non-Valid Issues

$3 • W-TN-170-003-N010
Left: THREE DOLLARS vertically. *Center:* 3 / 3. *Right:* THREE DOLLARS vertically. *Engraver:* Murray, Draper, Fairman & Co. *Comments:* H-TN-75-N15. 18__. 1810s.
Rarity: *None known*

$50 • W-TN-170-050-N020
Left: FIFTY vertically. *Center:* 50 / Ship / L. *Right:* FIFTY DOLLARS vertically. *Engraver:* Murray, Draper, Fairman & Co. *Comments:* H-TN-75-N18. 18__. 1810s.
Rarity: *None known*

Bank of the State of Tennessee {2nd} (branch)
1820–1832
W-TN-180

History: The second Bank of the State of Tennessee was chartered on July 26, 1820, during the first financial panic of that state, with a capital of $1,000,000.

Unfortunately, the Bank of the State of Tennessee became a negative example of what happens when banks are established for the purpose of solving financial problems. In 1832 the Bank of the State of Tennessee ceased operations, and its funds and assets were placed with the Union Bank of Tennessee, W-TN-840.

The second Bank of the State of Tennessee had its parent bank located in Nashville, W-TN-680, and branch banks located in Franklin, W-TN-290, and Knoxville, W-TN-360.

Numismatic Commentary: No notes of this bank are known. Private checks were issued from this branch, as stated by Garland. The following listings are speculative based on the parent bank.

Valid Issues

$1 • W-TN-180-001-G010
Comments: H-TN-190-G40. No description available. 18__. 1820s.
Rarity: *None known*

$2 • W-TN-180-002-G020
Comments: H-TN-190-G42. No description available. 18__. 1820s.
Rarity: *None known*

$5 • W-TN-180-005-G030
Comments: H-TN-190-G44. No description available. 18__. 1820s.
Rarity: *None known*

$10 • W-TN-180-010-G040
Comments: H-TN-190-G46. No description available. 18__. 1820s.
Rarity: *None known*

$20 • W-TN-180-020-G050
Comments: H-TN-190-G48. No description available. 18__. 1820s.
Rarity: *None known*

$50 • W-TN-180-050-G060
Comments: H-TN-190-G50. No description available. 18__. 1820s.
Rarity: *None known*

$100 • W-TN-180-100-G070
Comments: H-TN-190-G52. No description available. 18__. 1820s.
Rarity: *None known*

Bank of the State of Tennessee {3rd} (branch)
1838–1866
W-TN-190

History: The third Bank of the State of Tennessee (also seen in print as the Bank of Tennessee) was chartered on January 19, 1838, with an authorized capital of $5,000,000. The bank opened for business in February. The bank suspended specie payments a couple of times in 1838 and 1839, due to the panic of that time, but afterward it resumed and had a profitable and successful career. The branch in Columbia had a capital of $190,130 in 1855. R.H. Hill was the cashier, and John B. Grovers was the president. In 1863 J.C. Rye was the cashier, with L.D. Myers in the position of president.

During the Civil War, the Union army entered the state, and some officers of the Bank of the State of Tennessee fled south with the bank's specie. After the war, the bank's assets were returned to Governor William G. Brownlow in Nashville. Half of the bank's funds had been transferred into state bonds.

By February 1866 the Bank of the State of Tennessee was authorized to go into liquidation.

The third Bank of the State of Tennessee had its parent bank located in Nashville, W-TN-690, and branch banks located in Athens, W-TN-010, Clarksville, W-TN-120, Knoxville, W-TN-365, Memphis, W-TN-490, Murfreesboro, W-TN-610, Rogersville, W-TN-890, Shelbyville, W-TN-920, Somerville, W-TN-960, Sparta, W-TN-980, and Trenton, W-TN-1030.

Numismatic Commentary: Columbia branch notes are available with searching, although all must be considered scarce to rare. Denominations above $20 were unknown to Garland and have not been seen. It is believed that a majority of the surviving examples are cancelled in some form. Uncancelled, signed and issued notes command a premium.

Valid Issues

$1 • W-TN-190-001-G010

Left: Woman seated with farmer / Female portrait. ***Center:*** 1 / Man plowing with horses / 1. ***Right:*** ONE / Medallion head / ONE. ***Engraver:*** Draper, Toppan & Co. ***Comments:*** H-TN-195-G144. Mar. 1, 1842.

Rarity: *None known*

$1 • W-TN-190-001-G010a

Engraver: Toppan, Carpenter & Co. ***Comments:*** H-TN-195-G144a. Similar to W-TN-190-001-G010 but with different date and engraver imprint. Mar. 1, ____. 1840s, 1861.

Rarity: *None known*

$1 • W-TN-190-001-G020 CC

Engraver: Toppan, Carpenter, Casilear & Co. ***Comments:*** H-TN-195-G146. 18__. 1850s.

Rarity: URS-5
F $300

$1 • W-TN-190-001-G030

Left: 1 / Portrait of boy. ***Center:*** Indian on horseback hunting buffalo. ***Right:*** 1 / Female portrait. ***Tint:*** Red-orange. ***Back:*** Red-orange. ***Engraver:*** Toppan, Carpenter & Co. ***Comments:*** H-TN-195-G148a, Garland-238. 18__. 1850s.

Rarity: URS-5
F $250

$2 • W-TN-190-002-G040

Left: TWO / Woman seated in 2 / 2. ***Center:*** 2 / Woman seated on bales / 2. ***Right:*** 2 / Ship / 2. ***Engraver:*** Draper, Toppan & Co. ***Comments:*** H-TN-195-G150. Mar. 1, 1842.

Rarity: *None known*

$2 • W-TN-190-002-G040a

Engraver: Toppan, Carpenter & Co. ***Comments:*** H-TN-195-G150a. Similar to W-TN-190-002-G040 but with different date and engraver imprint. Mar. 1, ____. 1840s, 1861.

Rarity: *None known*

$2 • W-TN-190-002-G050

Left: 2 / Justice seated with scales. ***Center:*** Cattle / 2 / 2. ***Right:*** 2 / Liberty with pole, cap, and flag. ***Engraver:*** Toppan, Carpenter, Casilear & Co. ***Comments:*** H-TN-195-G152. 18__. 1850s.

Rarity: URS-4
F $300

$2 • W-TN-190-002-G060

Left: 2 / Female portrait. ***Center:*** Soldier, Woman, and two Indians looking at bust of George Washington. ***Right:*** 2 / Portrait of Charles Carroll. ***Tint:*** Red-orange. ***Back:*** Red-orange. ***Engraver:*** Toppan, Carpenter & Co. ***Comments:*** H-TN-195-G154a. 18__. 1850s.

Rarity: URS-6
F $250

$3 • W-TN-190-003-G070

Left: THREE / Woman standing / THREE. ***Center:*** 3 / Men on horses, sheep / 3. ***Right:*** THREE / Cherubs in 3 / THREE. ***Engraver:*** Draper, Toppan & Co. ***Comments:*** H-TN-195-G156. Mar. 1, 1842.

Rarity: *None known*

$3 • W-TN-190-003-G070a

Engraver: Toppan, Carpenter & Co. ***Comments:*** H-TN-195-G156a. Similar to W-TN-190-003-G070 but with different date and engraver imprint. Mar. 1, ____. 1840s, 1861.

Rarity: *None known*

$5 • W-TN-190-005-G080

Left: 5 / Woman leaning on column / V. ***Center:*** Woman seated with shield. ***Right:*** 5 / Justice standing with scales and eagle / V. ***Engraver:*** Rawdon, Wright, Hatch & Edson / Rawdon, Wright & Hatch. ***Comments:*** H-TN-195-G158. 18__. 1838–1840s.

Rarity: URS-1
VF $2,500

$5 • W-TN-190-005-G090

Left: Three men / 5. ***Center:*** Portrait of James Madison. ***Right:*** 5 / Medallion head. ***Back:*** Red-orange. ***Engraver:*** Danforth, Bald & Co. ***Comments:*** H-TN-195-G160a. 18__. 1850s.

Rarity: URS-6
F $250

$5 • W-TN-190-005-G090a

Tint: Red-orange outlining white V / 5 / V. ***Back:*** Red-orange. ***Engraver:*** Danforth, Bald & Co. ***Comments:*** H-TN-195-G160b. Similar to W-TN-190-005-G090. 18__. 1850s.

Rarity: URS-5
F $275

$10 • W-TN-190-010-G100

Left: 10 / Eagle with shield / X. ***Center:*** Woman with children seated among parcels, Factories and farmhouse. ***Right:*** 10 / Shield / X. ***Engraver:*** Draper, Toppan, Longacre & Co. ***Comments:*** H-TN-195-G166. 18__. 1838–1840s.

Rarity: URS-5
F $295

$10 • W-TN-190-010-G110

Left: 10 / Portrait of James K. Polk. ***Center:*** Portrait of Andrew Jackson. ***Right:*** 10 / Portrait of Cave Johnson. ***Tint:*** Red-orange outlining white 10 / 10. ***Back:*** Blue. ***Engraver:*** Toppan, Carpenter & Co. ***Comments:*** H-TN-195-G170a. 18__. 1850s–1861.

Rarity: URS-6
F $250

$20 • W-TN-190-020-G120

Left: 20 / Man writing on tablet / 20. ***Center:*** Woman standing with eagle and shield. ***Right:*** 20 / Shield / 20. ***Engraver:*** Draper, Toppan, Longacre & Co. ***Comments:*** H-TN-195-G172. 18__. 1838–1840s.

Rarity: *None known*

$20 • W-TN-190-020-G120a

Engraver: Toppan, Carpenter & Co. ***Comments:*** H-TN-195-G172a. Similar to W-TN-190-020-G120 but with different engraver imprint. 18__. 1840s–1850s

Rarity: *None known*

$20 • W-TN-190-020-G130

Left: 20 / Portrait of Zachary Taylor / 20. ***Center:*** Three women reclining, Ship / 20. ***Right:*** Justice seated with sword and scales / TWENTY. ***Engraver:*** Toppan, Carpenter, Casilear & Co. ***Comments:*** H-TN-195-G174. 18__. 1850s.

Rarity: URS-5
F $325

$20 • W-TN-190-020-G130a

Back: Red-orange. ***Engraver:*** Toppan, Carpenter, Casilear & Co. ***Comments:*** H-TN-195-G174a. Similar to W-TN-190-020-G130. 18__. 1850s.

Rarity: URS-5
F $325

$20 • W-TN-190-020-G130b

Tint: Red-orange outlining white TWENTY. ***Back:*** Red-orange. ***Engraver:*** Toppan, Carpenter, Casilear & Co. ***Comments:*** H-TN-195-G174b. Similar to W-TN-190-020-G130. 18__. 1850s.

Rarity: URS-5
F $325

$50 • W-TN-190-050-G140

Left: 50 / Shield / 50. ***Center:*** Liberty with eagle and shield. ***Right:*** 50 / Portrait of George Washington / 50. ***Engraver:*** Draper, Toppan, Longacre & Co. ***Comments:*** H-TN-195-G176. 18__. 1838–1840s.

Rarity: *None known*

$100 • W-TN-190-100-G150

Left: Atlas lifting world on shoulders / 100. ***Center:*** 100 / Justice with eagle and shield / 100. ***Right:*** Atlas lifting world on shoulders / 100. ***Engraver:*** Draper, Toppan, Longacre & Co. ***Comments:*** H-TN-195-G178. 18__. 1838–1850s.

Rarity: *None known*

Non-Valid Issues

$10 • W-TN-190-010-C100

Engraver: Draper, Toppan, Longacre & Co. ***Comments:*** H-TN-195-C166. Counterfeit of W-TN-190-010-G100. 18__. 1853.

Rarity: —

$20 • W-TN-190-020-C120a

Engraver: Toppan, Carpenter & Co. ***Comments:*** H-TN-195-C172a. Counterfeit of W-TN-190-020-G120a. 18__. 1853.

Rarity: —

$20 • W-TN-190-020-C130

Engraver: Toppan, Carpenter, Casilear & Co. ***Comments:*** H-TN-195-C174. Counterfeit of W-TN-190-020-G130. 18__. 1853.

Rarity: —

$20 • W-TN-190-020-C130a

Back: Red-orange. ***Engraver:*** Toppan, Carpenter, Casilear & Co. ***Comments:*** H-TN-195-C174a. Counterfeit of W-TN-190-020-G130a. 18__. 1853.

Rarity: —

$20 • W-TN-190-020-C130b

Tint: Red-orange outlining white TWENTY. ***Back:*** Red-orange. ***Engraver:*** Toppan, Carpenter, Casilear & Co. ***Comments:*** H-TN-195-C174b. Counterfeit of W-TN-190-020-G130b. 18__. 1853.

Rarity: —

Bank of the United States of Pennsylvania

1838–1841

W-TN-200

History: The Bank of the United States of Pennsylvania was chartered by the Pennsylvania legislature and had no connection with the first Bank of the United States (1791–1811) or the second Bank of the United States (1816–1836). These two entities, headquartered in Philadelphia, were chartered by Congress and had many branches. Nicholas Biddle, earlier the president of the second Bank of the United States, supervised the formation of the Bank of the United States of Pennsylvania. He neglected to put "of Pennsylvania" on his notes in an attempt to deceive holders of the notes, who would then pass them at a distance. The bank failed in 1841. Biddle, a scion of Philadelphia society, died in disgrace not long after.

Issues

Post Notes Payable at Columbia, Tennessee

$20 • W-TN-200-020-N010

Left: TWENTY / Mercury flying / DOLLARS. ***Center:*** 20 / Eagle with shield, Farmer plowing, Ship / 20. ***Right:*** POST / Mercury flying / NOTE. ***Engraver:*** Draper, Toppan, Longacre & Co. ***Comments:*** H-Unlisted, Garland-253. 18__. 1830s.

Rarity: URS-1
Proof $4,500

$500 • W-TN-200-500-N020 CC

Engraver: Draper, Toppan, Longacre & Co. ***Comments:*** H-Unlisted, Garland-254. 18__. 1830s.

Rarity: URS-3
Proof $2,500

Planters Bank of Tennessee (branch)

1834–1865

W-TN-210

History: The Planters Bank of Tennessee was chartered on November 11, 1833, with an authorized capital of $2,000,000. The branch located in Columbia opened in 1834 in an effort to compete with the opening of the second Bank of the State of Tennessee branch, W-TN-180. It had a capital of $190,130 in 1848. F.G. Roche was the cashier. In 1865 the bank was forced to liquidate and close its affairs.

The Planters Bank of Tennessee had its parent bank located in Nashville, W-TN-810, and branch banks located in Athens, W-TN-020, Clarksville, W-TN-140, Franklin, W-TN-300, LaGrange, W-TN-410, Memphis, W-TN-570, Murfreesboro, W-TN-630, Pulaski, W-TN-870, Rogersville, W-TN-910, Shelbyville, W-TN-940, Somerville, W-TN-970, Sparta, W-TN-990, Trenton, W-TN-1050, and Winchester, W-TN-1070.

Numismatic Commentary: The only note from this branch known to Garland, and thought to be unique, was the note printed from a fraudulently obtained plate for the Planters Bank of Alabama in Wetumpka.

VALID ISSUES

$1 • W-TN-210-001-G010
Left: 1 / Medallion head bearing ONE / 1. ***Center:*** 1 with cherub / Woman seated with boxes. ***Right:*** Woman standing in 1. ***Engraver:*** Rawdon, Wright, Hatch & Edson. ***Comments:*** H-TN-185-G126. 18__. 1840s.

Rarity: *None known*

$2 • W-TN-210-002-G020
Left: 2 / Woman with sheaf / 2. ***Center:*** 2 with cherubs / Woman seated with boxes. ***Right:*** Woman standing in 2. ***Engraver:*** Rawdon, Wright, Hatch & Edson. ***Comments:*** H-TN-185-G128. Dec. 1, 1860.

Rarity: *None known*

$3 • W-TN-210-003-G030
Left: 3 / Medallion head / 3. ***Center:*** 3 with cherubs / Two men flanking shield bearing cow surmounted by beehive. ***Right:*** Woman standing in 3. ***Engraver:*** Rawdon, Wright, Hatch & Edson. ***Comments:*** H-TN-185-G130. Dec. 1, 1860.

Rarity: *None known*

$5 • W-TN-210-005-G040
Left: Medallion head / FIVE / Medallion head. ***Center:*** FIVE / Man standing with dog / FIVE. ***Right:*** Medallion head / FIVE / Medallion head. ***Engraver:*** Underwood, Bald & Spencer. ***Comments:*** H-TN-185-G132, Garland-250. 18__. 1830s–1840s.

Rarity: *None known*

$10 • W-TN-210-010-G050
Left: Medallion head / TEN / Medallion head. ***Center:*** 10 / Farm scene, Harvest / X. ***Right:*** Medallion head / TEN / Medallion head. ***Engraver:*** Underwood, Bald & Spencer. ***Comments:*** H-TN-185-G134, Garland-251. 18__. 1830s–1840s.

Rarity: *None known*

$20 • W-TN-210-020-G060
Left: 20 / Medallion head / 20. ***Center:*** 20 / Medallion head / 20. ***Right:*** 20 / Medallion head / 20. ***Engraver:*** Underwood, Bald & Spencer. ***Comments:*** H-TN-185-G136, Garland-252. 18__. 1830s–1840s.

Rarity: *None known*

$50 • W-TN-210-050-G070
Left: 50 / Medallion head / 50. ***Center:*** Medallion heads / Woman seated, Ship / Medallion heads. ***Right:*** 50 / Medallion head / 50. ***Engraver:*** Underwood, Bald, Spencer & Hufty. ***Comments:*** H-TN-185-G138. 18__. 1830s–1850s.

Rarity: *None known*

$100 • W-TN-210-100-G080
Left: 100 / Three women seated vertically / 100. ***Center:*** Medallion head / Boy reclining under corn, Plow / Medallion head. ***Right:*** 100 / Three women seated vertically / 100. ***Engraver:*** Underwood, Bald, Spencer & Hufty. ***Comments:*** H-TN-185-G140. 18__. 1830s–1850s.

Rarity: *None known*

NON-VALID ISSUES

$10 • W-TN-210-010-S010
Left: Woman. ***Center:*** Woman, Train, Steamboat. ***Right:*** Ceres. ***Comments:*** H-TN-185-S52. 18__. 1840s.

Rarity: *None known*

$10 • W-TN-210-010-S020
Left: 10 / Justice with scales. ***Center:*** X with cherubs / Two women seated. ***Right:*** 10 / Justice with scales. ***Engraver:*** Rawdon, Wright & Hatch. ***Comments:*** H-TN-185-S54, Garland-251. From a genuine plate of the Planters Bank of Alabama, Wetumpka, Alabama. 18__. 1840s.

Rarity: URS-1
F $550

$20 • W-TN-210-020-S030
Center: Eagle. ***Comments:*** H-TN-185-S56. 18__. 1840s.

Rarity: *None known*

$20 • W-TN-210-020-S040
Left: 20 / Female portrait / XX. ***Center:*** Woman seated near ocean with shield. ***Right:*** 20 / Female portrait / XX. ***Engraver:*** Rawdon, Wright & Hatch. ***Comments:*** H-TN-185-S58. From a genuine plate of the Planters Bank of Alabama, Wetumpka, Alabama. 18__. 1840s.

Rarity: *None known*

How to Read the Whitman Numbering System

$1 • W-AL-020-001-G010a

Denomination: Face value of the note shown.

W: Whitman number. This number is a sortable code unique to each bank and note.

AL: Abbreviation for the state under study.

020: Numerical designation specific to each bank.

001: The denomination in dollars.

G010a: G indicates a good or valid note. Other categories are indicated thus: C (counterfeit); R (raised); S (spurious); N (not-attributed); A (altered). Numbers are assigned starting with 010, 020, et seq. Terminal letters following the number indicate variations of a note: a series of different colored overprints, tints, payees, etc., all on the same design of note. For more information, see the "How to Use This Book" section at the front of the volume, page xiv.

$50 • **W-TN-210-050-S050**
Left: FIFTY DOLLARS vertically. ***Center:*** 50 / Eagle on bale / 50. ***Right:*** STATE OF TENNESSEE vertically. ***Engraver:*** Rawdon, Wright & Hatch. ***Comments:*** H-TN-185-S60. From a genuine plate of the Planters Bank of Alabama, Wetumpka, Alabama. 18__. 1840s.

Rarity: *None known*

$100 • **W-TN-210-100-S060**
Left: HUNDRED vertically. ***Center:*** Deer, River. ***Right:*** Portrait of George Washington. ***Engraver:*** Rawdon, Wright & Hatch. ***Comments:*** H-TN-185-S62. From a genuine plate of the Planters Bank of Alabama, Wetumpka, Alabama. 18__. 1840s.

Rarity: *None known*

$100 • **W-TN-210-100-S070**
Left: Medallion head. ***Center:*** C / Factory / C. ***Right:*** 100 diagonally. ***Engraver:*** Rawdon, Wright & Hatch. ***Comments:*** H-TN-185-S64. 18__. 1840s.

Rarity: *None known*

Union Bank of Tennessee (branch)

1832–1865

W-TN-220

History: On October 18, 1832, the Union Bank of Tennessee (also sometimes seen as the Union Bank of the State of Tennessee on notes) was chartered with an authorized capital of $3,000,000. The bank also absorbed the assets of the failed second Bank of the State of Tennessee, W-TN-680, which had been abolished that year. The state subscribed to $500,000 of the bank's capital, to be financed by bonds.

In 1848 the president of the branch in Columbia was Evan Young. S.A. Hamner was the cashier, and capital was $150,000. In 1855 S.D. Frierson took over the presidency, followed by William Park in 1857. In 1860 George W. Seay took the cashiership.

In 1865 the Union Bank of Tennessee went into liquidation.

The Union Bank of Tennessee had its parent bank located in Nashville, W-TN-840, and branch banks located in Chattanooga, W-TN-090, Jackson, W-TN-325, Knoxville, W-TN-400, and Memphis, W-TN-600.

Numismatic Commentary: Actual notes from this bank remain unknown. Fractional checks drawn on this bank by the office of Chaffin, Kirk & Co. are known to exist in denominations of 6-1/4¢, 25¢, 50¢, $1, $2, $3, and $4 payable in "Tennessee or Alabama bank notes when the sum of Five Dollars is presented." Fewer than ten examples of any of these notes are thought to exist.

Dandridge, Tennessee

European settlers arrived in Dandridge in 1783. The town was declared the county seat of Jefferson in 1793, when it was named after Martha Dandridge Washington. During the Civil War, a battle took place at Dandridge in the struggle to control Knoxville.

Bank of Jefferson

1856–1858

W-TN-230

History: In 1856 the Bank of Jefferson was chartered with an authorized capital of $100,000. W.H. Inman was the president, and W.P. Inman was the cashier. The bank did not operate for very long, and by 1858 it had closed.

Numismatic Commentary: Few notes are known to exist—Garland estimated two to four examples of each denomination. As often seen with other banks, two varieties of each denomination exist—one with a red overprint, and one without.

Remaining at the American Bank Note Co. archives as of 2003 was a $5-$5-$10-$20 face plate. The 1990 Christie's sale of the American Bank Note Co. archives produced seven $5-$5-$10-$20 sheets.

Valid Issues

$5 • **W-TN-230-005-G010**
Left: 5 / Portrait of girl. ***Center:*** Woman with cattle. ***Right:*** 5 / FIVE / 5. ***Engraver:*** Bald, Cousland & Co. / Baldwin, Bald & Cousland. ***Comments:*** H-TN-40-G2, Garland-267. June 2nd, 1856.

Rarity: —

$5 • **W-TN-230-005-G010a**

CC

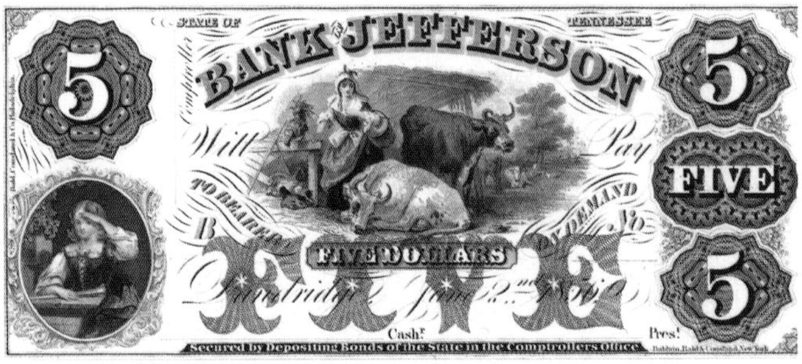

Overprint: Red FIVE. ***Engraver:*** Bald, Cousland & Co. / Baldwin, Bald & Cousland. ***Comments:*** H-TN-40-G2a, Garland-268. Similar to W-TN-230-005-G010. June 2nd, 1856.

Rarity: URS-4
Proof $500

$10 • **W-TN-230-010-G020**
Left: X / TEN / X. ***Center:*** State arms / Woman reclining with mirror. ***Right:*** 10 / Male portrait. ***Engraver:*** Bald, Cousland & Co. / Baldwin, Bald & Cousland. ***Comments:*** H-TN-40-G4, Garland-269. June 2nd, 1856.

Rarity: URS-3
F $500

$10 • W-TN-230-010-G020a CC

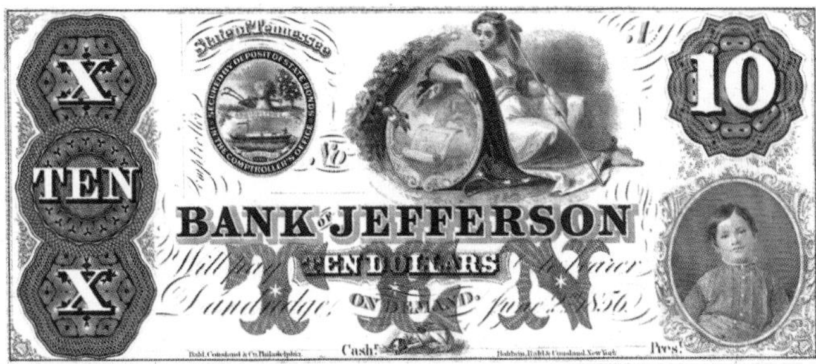

Overprint: Red TEN. ***Engraver:*** Bald, Cousland & Co. / Baldwin, Bald & Cousland. ***Comments:*** H-TN-40-G4a, Garland-270. Similar to W-TN-230-010-G020. June 2nd, 1856.

Rarity: URS-3
Proof $1,200
Selected auction price: Heritage Auctions, September 2008, Lot 12721, Proof $1,150

$20 • W-TN-230-020-G030

Left: Haying scene / XX. ***Center:*** State arms. ***Right:*** 20 / Female portrait. ***Engraver:*** Bald, Cousland & Co. / Baldwin, Bald & Cousland. ***Comments:*** H-TN-40-G6, Garland-271. June 2nd, 1856.

Rarity: URS-3
Proof $900

$20 • W-TN-230-020-G030a CC

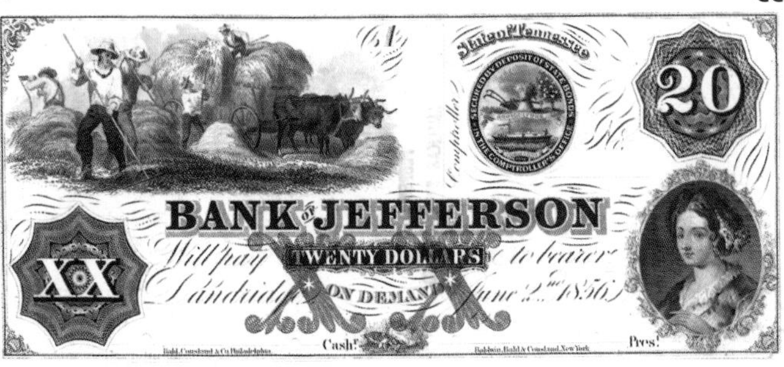

Overprint: Red XX. ***Engraver:*** Bald, Cousland & Co. / Baldwin, Bald & Cousland. ***Comments:*** H-TN-40-G6a, Garland-272. Similar to W-TN-230-020-G030. June 2nd, 1856.

Rarity: URS-4
Proof $500

Central Bank of Tennessee (branch)

1856 and 1857

W-TN-240

History: In 1856 it was reported that "there never was any such corporation as the Central Bank of Tennessee, and that Belknap, Tremain & Haven, merely took upon themselves that name under which to carry on their banking business—without any charter or act of incorporation."[4] By 1857 the enterprise, along with its branches, had failed.

The Central Bank of Tennessee had its parent bank located in Nashville, W-TN-720, and a branch bank located in Paris, W-TN-860.

Numismatic Commentary: Notes of this bank are intriguing and readily available, more often than not found with overprinted letters. Whether these were endorsements or markings of spurious notes is unknown.

Valid Issues

$5 • W-TN-240-005-G010 SI

Overprint: Red FIVE. ***Engraver:*** Toppan, Carpenter & Co. ***Comments:*** H-TN-140-G30a, Garland-273. 18__. 1850s.

Rarity: URS-9
F $150; **EF** $275

$10 • W-TN-240-010-G020 ANS

Overprint: Red TEN. ***Engraver:*** Toppan, Carpenter & Co. ***Comments:*** H-TN-140-G34a, Garland-274. 18__. 1850s.

Rarity: URS-8
F $150; **EF** $300

Dandridge Bank

1854–1858

W-TN-250

History: In 1854 the Dandridge Bank was chartered with an authorized capital of $100,000. S.N. Inman was elected cashier, and John Roper was president. In 1857 William A. Branner replaced Inman as cashier, and the capital fell to $50,000. By 1858 the bank had closed.

Numismatic Commentary: Examples are scarce to very scarce but not totally impossible to find. These notes are among the more attractive and visually appealing in the state of Tennessee, especially the $20.

Remaining at the American Bank Note Co. archives as of 2003 was a $10-$20 face plate and a $10-$20 tint plate. The 1990 Christie's sale of the American Bank Note Co. archives produced a $1-$1-$2-$5 sheet and two partial $10-$20 sheets.

Valid Issues

$1 • W-TN-250-001-G010

Left: ONE on 1 / Train. ***Center:*** Cattle, sheep, houses, wagons. ***Right:*** 1 / Woman standing on bale, Ships. ***Engraver:*** Danforth, Wright & Co. ***Comments:*** H-TN-35-G2, Garland-275. May 1st, 1854.

Rarity: URS-4
F $350

$2 • W-TN-250-002-G020

Left: 2 / Milkmaid. ***Center:*** Farmers working. ***Right:*** 2 / Woman seated. ***Engraver:*** Danforth, Wright & Co. ***Comments:*** H-TN-35-G4, Garland-277. May 1st, 1854.

Rarity: URS-4
F $350

$5 • W-TN-250-005-G030

CC

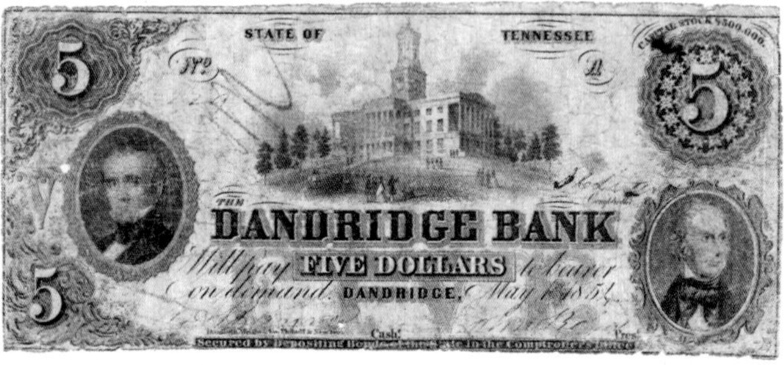

Engraver: Danforth, Wright & Co. ***Comments:*** H-TN-35-G6, Garland-279. May 1st, 1854.

Rarity: URS-4
F $350

$10 • W-TN-250-010-G040

Left: 10 / Liberty seated with shield. ***Center:*** Two women seated. ***Right:*** 10 / X. ***Engraver:*** Danforth, Wright & Co. ***Comments:*** H-TN-35-G8, Garland-281. July 1st, 1854.

Rarity: URS-4
F $350

$10 • W-TN-250-010-G040a

Engraver: Danforth, Wright & Co. / ABNCo. monogram. ***Comments:*** H-TN-35-G8b, Garland-282. Similar to W-TN-250-010-G040 but with additional engraver imprint. July 1st, 1854.

Rarity: URS-4
Unc-Rem $350

$20 • W-TN-250-020-G050

Left: 20 / Woman seated with sheaf, plow, Train. ***Center:*** XX / Woman reclining with cornucopia. ***Right:*** Woman holding up 20. ***Engraver:*** Danforth, Wright & Co. ***Comments:*** H-TN-35-G10, Garland-283. July 1st, 1854.

Rarity: URS-5
F $300

$20 • W-TN-250-020-G050a

CC

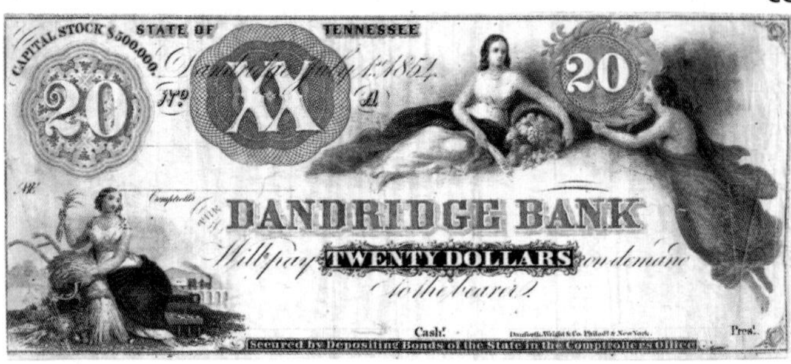

Tint: Red-orange die outlining white 20, bank title, and die outlining white 20. ***Engraver:*** Danforth, Wright & Co. / ABNCo. monogram. ***Comments:*** H-TN-35-G10b, Garland-284. Similar to W-TN-250-020-G050 but with additional engraver imprint. July 1st, 1854.

Rarity: URS-5
VF $700

Dresden, Tennessee

The county seat of Weakley, Dresden was named after Dresden, Germany, the hometown of the commissioner who laid out the town. In April 1825 the lots were put up for sale, including 90 for commercial and residential use and a central block designated for the courthouse.

Bank of America (branch)

1856–1858

W-TN-260

History: In 1856 the Bank of America was chartered. In 1857 the cashier was R.Y. Johnson, and capital was $100,000. By 1858 the bank had closed.

The Bank of America had its parent bank located in Clarksville, W-TN-100, and branch banks located in Brownsville, W-TN-050, and Rogersville, W-TN-880.

Numismatic Commentary: Signed notes do exist but are very scarce to rare.

Valid Issues

$5 • W-TN-260-005-G010

Left: V / Portrait of Andrew Jackson. ***Center:*** Two women flanking shield. ***Right:*** 5 / Portrait of General Ambrose Davie. ***Overprint:*** Red FIVE. ***Engraver:*** Bald, Cousland & Co. / Baldwin, Bald & Cousland. ***Comments:*** H-TN-15-G32a, Garland-285. 18__. 1850s.

Rarity: URS-4
F $400

$10 • W-TN-260-010-G020

Left: X / Portrait of Winston Jones Davie. ***Center:*** Woman and man flanking shield bearing wheat. ***Right:*** 10 / Portrait of Elizabeth Phillips. ***Overprint:*** Red TEN. ***Engraver:*** Bald, Cousland & Co. / Baldwin, Bald & Cousland. ***Comments:*** H-TN-15-G34a, Garland-286. 18__. 1850s.

Rarity: URS-3
F $750

$20 • W-TN-260-020-G030

Left: 20 / Portrait of Winston Jones Davie. ***Center:*** Family playing with bear cub, Horse. ***Right:*** 20 / Female portrait. ***Overprint:*** Red XX. ***Engraver:*** Bald, Cousland & Co. / Baldwin, Bald & Cousland. ***Comments:*** H-TN-15-G36a, Garland-287. 18__. 1850s.

Rarity: URS-3
F $750

Fayetteville, Tennessee

Fayetteville was established in 1809 after being ceded to the United States in 1806 by the Cherokee Indians. The town was named after Fayetteville, North Carolina, the origin of many residents. The first settler to arrive was Ezekiel Norris, followed by Alexander and Andrew Greer, Matthew Buchanan, and William Edmonson.

Fayetteville Tennessee Bank

1815–1819

W-TN-270

History: In 1815 the Fayetteville Tennessee Bank was chartered with an authorized capital of $200,000. By 1817 the same was valued at $110,000. In 1819 the bank failed.

Numismatic Commentary: Notes from this bank are extremely scarce to rare. The pictured $5 and $10 notes are thought to have no more than five survivors.

Valid Issues

$1 • W-TN-270-001-G010

Left: ONE vertically. ***Center:*** 1 / 1. ***Right:*** ONE DOLLAR vertically. ***Engraver:*** Murray, Draper, Fairman & Co. ***Comments:*** H-TN-45-G2, Garland-288. 18__. 1810s.

Rarity: URS-4
F $350

$2 • W-TN-270-002-G020

Left: TWO vertically. ***Center:*** 2 / 2. ***Right:*** TWO DOLLARS vertically. ***Engraver:*** Murray, Draper, Fairman & Co. ***Comments:*** H-TN-45-G4, Garland-289. 18__. 1810s.

Rarity: URS-3
F $650

$3 • W-TN-270-003-G030 NJW

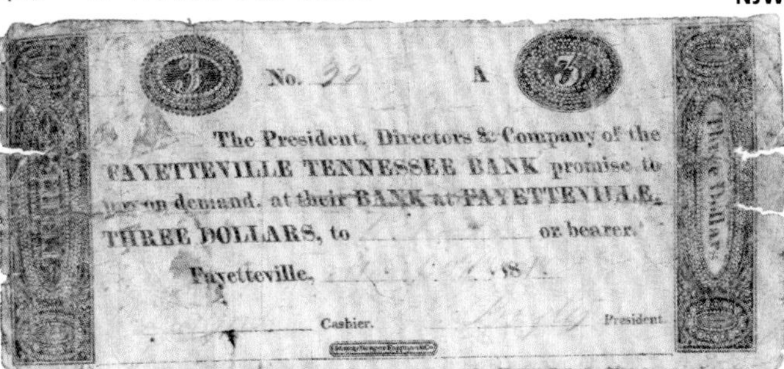

Engraver: Murray, Draper, Fairman & Co. ***Comments:*** H-TN-45-G6, Garland-290. 18__. 1810s.

Rarity: URS-3
F $600

$4 • W-TN-270-004-G035 HA

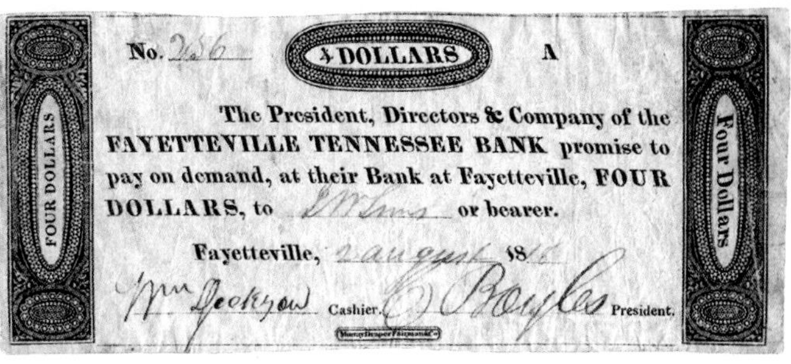

Engraver: Murray, Draper, Fairman & Co. ***Comments:*** H-Unlisted, Garland-Unlisted. 18__. 1810s.

Rarity: —

$5 • W-TN-270-005-G040 CC

Engraver: Murray, Draper, Fairman & Co. ***Comments:*** H-TN-45-G8, Garland-291. 18__. 1810s.

Rarity: URS-4
F $500

$10 • W-TN-270-010-G050 HA

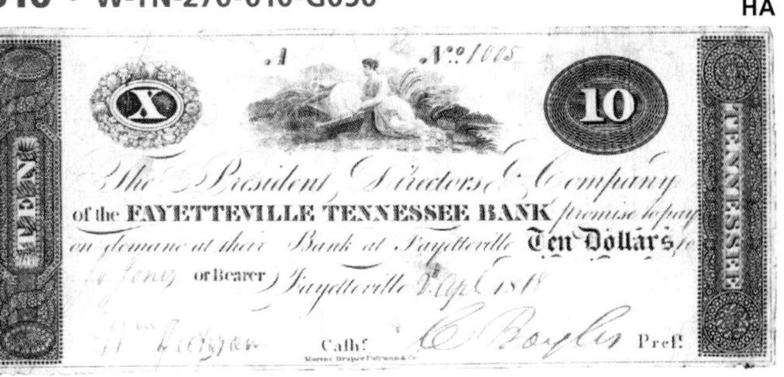

Engraver: Murray, Draper, Fairman & Co. ***Comments:*** H-TN-45-G12, Garland-292. 18__. 1810s.

Rarity: URS-4
F $600

$20 • W-TN-270-020-G060

Left: TWENTY vertically. ***Center:*** XX / Woman seated / 20. ***Right:*** TENNESSEE vertically. ***Engraver:*** Murray, Draper, Fairman & Co. ***Comments:*** H-TN-45-G16, Garland-293. 18__. 1810s.

Rarity: URS-1
F $1,000

Post Notes

$__ • W-TN-270-__-G070

CC

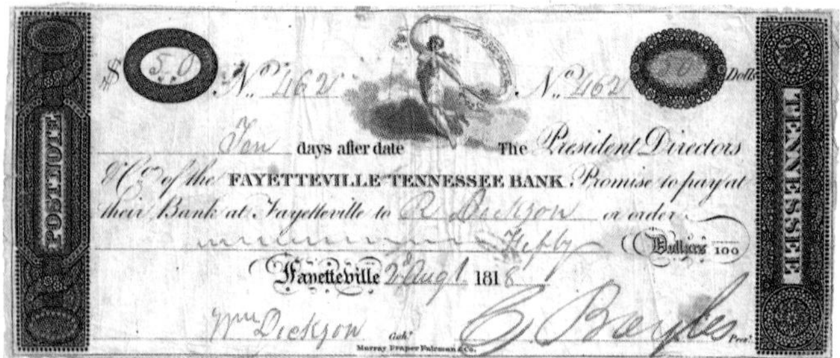

Engraver: Murray, Draper, Fairman & Co. ***Comments:*** H-TN-45-G20, Garland-294. 181_. 1810s.

Rarity: URS-2
VF $1,500

Franklin, Tennessee

Franklin was founded on October 26, 1799, by Abram Maury Jr. The town was named after Benjamin Franklin. The first house was built by a Scottish immigrant named Ewen Cameron—his descendants remain in Franklin.

The Battle of Franklin took place on November 30, 1864. Almost 10,000 men were killed, wounded, captured, or declared missing. Over 40 buildings were seized to be used as hospitals for Confederate soldiers as the victorious Union army moved on.

Bank of the State of Tennessee {1st} (branch)

1817–1820

W-TN-280

History: The first Bank of the State of Tennessee was chartered on November 20, 1811, with an authorized capital of $400,000. The capital was to be divided into shares of $50 apiece. The state subscribed to $20,000, on the provision that the state reserved the right to withdraw its funds after ten years. Hugh Lawson White was the president. No notes under $5 were allowed to be issued. In 1817 a branch in Franklin was opened.

The Bank of the State of Tennessee discontinued business in 1820, at which time the stated capital was $371,107. The branches failed at the same time with a combined capital of $573,915.

The first Bank of the State of Tennessee had its parent bank located in Knoxville, W-TN-355, and branch banks located in Carthage, W-TN-060, Clarksville, W-TN-110, Columbia, W-TN-170, Jonesboro, W-TN-335, Kingston, W-TN-340, Maryville, W-TN-440, and Nashville, W-TN-670.

Numismatic Commentary: The only surviving note known of this bank is the $50 imaged below.

Valid Issues

$5 • W-TN-280-005-G010

Left: FIVE vertically. ***Center:*** Man plowing with horses / 5. ***Right:*** TENNESSEE vertically. ***Engraver:*** Murray, Draper, Fairman & Co. ***Comments:*** H-TN-75-G72. 18__. 1810s.

Rarity: *None known*

$10 • W-TN-280-010-G020

Left: TEN vertically. ***Center:*** Men harvesting corn / 10. ***Right:*** TENNESSEE vertically. ***Engraver:*** Murray, Draper, Fairman & Co. ***Comments:*** H-TN-75-G74. 18__. 1810s.

Rarity: *None known*

$20 • W-TN-280-020-G030

Left: TWENTY vertically. ***Center:*** XX / Justice seated / XX. ***Right:*** TENNESSEE vertically. ***Engraver:*** Murray, Draper, Fairman & Co. ***Comments:*** H-TN-75-G76. 18__. 1810s.

Rarity: *None known*

$50 • W-TN-280-050-G040

CC

Engraver: Murray, Draper, Fairman & Co. ***Comments:*** H-TN-75-G78, Garland-297. 181_. 1810s.

Rarity: URS-2
F $1,500

$100 • W-TN-280-100-G050

Left: HUNDRED vertically. ***Center:*** Scene. ***Right:*** TENNESSEE vertically. ***Engraver:*** Murray, Draper, Fairman & Co. ***Comments:*** H-TN-75-G80. 18__. 1810s.

Rarity: *None known*

Non-Valid Issues

$3 • W-TN-280-003-N010

Left: THREE DOLLARS vertically. ***Center:*** 3 / 3. ***Right:*** THREE DOLLARS vertically. ***Engraver:*** Murray, Draper, Fairman & Co. ***Comments:*** H-TN-75-N21. 18__. 1810s.

Rarity: *None known*

$50 • W-TN-280-050-N020

Left: FIFTY vertically. ***Center:*** 50 / Ship / L. ***Right:*** FIFTY DOLLARS vertically. ***Engraver:*** Murray, Draper, Fairman & Co. ***Comments:*** H-TN-75-N24. 18__. 1810s.

Rarity: *None known*

Bank of the State of Tennessee {2nd} (branch)

1820–1832

W-TN-290

History: The second Bank of the State of Tennessee was chartered on July 26, 1820, during the first financial panic of that state, with a capital of $1,000,000.

Unfortunately, the Bank of the State of Tennessee became a negative example of what happens when banks are established for the purpose of solving financial problems. In 1832 the Bank of the State of Tennessee ceased operations, and its funds and assets were placed with the Union Bank of Tennessee, W-TN-840.

The second Bank of the State of Tennessee had its parent bank located in Nashville, W-TN-680, and branch banks located in Columbia, W-TN-180, and Knoxville, W-TN-360.

Numismatic Commentary: There are currently no known notes payable at this branch. The notes listed below are speculative based on the parent bank's issues.

Valid Issues

$1 • W-TN-290-001-G010

Comments: H-TN-190-G60. No description available. 18__. 1820s.

Rarity: *None known*

$2 • W-TN-290-002-G020

Comments: H-TN-190-G62. No description available. 18__. 1820s.

Rarity: *None known*

$5 • W-TN-290-005-G030

Comments: H-TN-190-G64. No description available. 18__. 1820s.

Rarity: *None known*

$10 • W-TN-290-010-G040

Comments: H-TN-190-G66. No description available. 18__. 1820s.

Rarity: *None known*

$20 • W-TN-290-020-G050

Comments: H-TN-190-G68. No description available. 18__. 1820s.

Rarity: *None known*

$50 • W-TN-290-050-G060

Comments: H-TN-190-G70. No description available. 18__. 1820s.

Rarity: *None known*

$100 • W-TN-290-100-G070

Comments: H-TN-190-G72. No description available. 18__. 1820s.

Rarity: *None known*

Planters Bank of Tennessee (branch)

1834–1865

W-TN-300

History: The Planters Bank of Tennessee was chartered on November 11, 1833, with an authorized capital of $2,000,000. The branch in Franklin was opened in 1834 and had a capital of $150,000 in 1855. William S. Campbell was the cashier, and J.H. Otey was the president. In 1865 the bank was forced to liquidate and close its affairs.

The Planters Bank of Tennessee had its parent bank located in Nashville, W-TN-810, and branch banks located in Athens, W-TN-020, Clarksville, W-TN-140, Columbia, W-TN-210, LaGrange, W-TN-410, Memphis, W-TN-570, Murfreesboro, W-TN-630, Pulaski, W-TN-870, Rogersville, W-TN-910, Shelbyville, W-TN-940, Somerville, W-TN-970, Sparta, W-TN-990, Trenton, W-TN-1050, and Winchester, W-TN-1070.

Numismatic Commentary: There are no currently known signed and issued notes payable at this branch, although it is thought some could have existed. Speculative listings based on the parent bank are listed below. All signed and issued fractional notes are dated Jan. 1st, 1862, and are considered to be scarce.

Valid Issues

$1 • W-TN-300-001-G010

Left: 1 / Medallion head bearing ONE / 1. ***Center:*** 1 with cherub / Woman seated with boxes. ***Right:*** Woman standing in 1. ***Engraver:*** Rawdon, Wright, Hatch & Edson. ***Comments:*** H-TN-185-G146. 18__. 1840s.

Rarity: *None known*

$2 • W-TN-300-002-G020

Left: 2 / Woman with sheaf / 2. ***Center:*** 2 with cherubs / Woman seated with boxes. ***Right:*** Woman standing in 2. ***Engraver:*** Rawdon, Wright, Hatch & Edson. ***Comments:*** H-TN-185-G148. Dec. 1, 1860.

Rarity: *None known*

$3 • W-TN-300-003-G030

Left: 3 / Medallion head / 3. ***Center:*** 3 with cherubs / Two men flanking shield bearing cow surmounted by beehive. ***Right:*** Woman standing in 3. ***Engraver:*** Rawdon, Wright, Hatch & Edson. ***Comments:*** H-TN-185-G150. Dec. 1, 1860.

Rarity: *None known*

$5 • W-TN-300-005-G040

Left: Medallion head / FIVE / Medallion head. ***Center:*** FIVE / Man standing with dog / FIVE. ***Right:*** Medallion head / FIVE / Medallion head. ***Engraver:*** Underwood, Bald & Spencer. ***Comments:*** H-TN-185-G152. 18__. 1830s–1840s.

Rarity: *None known*

$5 • W-TN-300-005-G040a

Engraver: Underwood, Bald & Spencer. ***Comments:*** H-TN-185-G152a. Similar to W-TN-300-005-G040. 18__. 1830s–1840s.

Rarity: *None known*

$10 • W-TN-300-010-G050

Left: Medallion head / TEN / Medallion head. ***Center:*** 10 / Farm scene, Harvest / X. ***Right:*** Medallion head / TEN / Medallion head. ***Engraver:*** Underwood, Bald & Spencer. ***Comments:*** H-TN-185-G154. 18__. 1830s–1840s.

Rarity: *None known*

$10 • W-TN-300-010-G050a

Engraver: Underwood, Bald & Spencer. ***Comments:*** H-TN-185-G154a. Similar to W-TN-300-010-G050. 18__. 1830s–1840s.

Rarity: *None known*

$20 • W-TN-300-020-G060

Left: 20 / Medallion head / 20. ***Center:*** 20 / Medallion head / 20. ***Right:*** 20 / Medallion head / 20. ***Engraver:*** Underwood, Bald & Spencer. ***Comments:*** H-TN-185-G156. 18__. 1830s–1840s.

Rarity: *None known*

$20 • W-TN-300-020-G060a

Engraver: Underwood, Bald & Spencer. ***Comments:*** H-TN-185-G156a. Similar to W-TN-300-020-G060. 18__. 1830s–1840s.

Rarity: *None known*

$50 • **W-TN-300-050-G070**

Left: 50 / Medallion head / 50. ***Center:*** Medallion heads / Woman seated, Ship / Medallion heads. ***Right:*** 50 / Medallion head / 50. ***Engraver:*** Underwood, Bald, Spencer & Hufty. ***Comments:*** H-TN-185-G158. 18__. 1830s–1850s.

Rarity: *None known*

$100 • **W-TN-300-100-G080**

Left: 100 / Three women seated vertically / 100. ***Center:*** Medallion head / Boy reclining under corn, Plow / Medallion head. ***Right:*** 100 / Three women seated vertically / 100. ***Engraver:*** Underwood, Bald, Spencer & Hufty. ***Comments:*** H-TN-185-G160. 18__. 1830s–1850s.

Rarity: *None known*

Civil War Fractional Notes

5¢ • **W-TN-300-00.05-G090**

Center: FIVE CENTS. ***Right:*** 5. ***Engraver:*** Adams. ***Comments:*** H-TN-185-G164. Jan. 1st, 1862.

Rarity: URS-5
F $300

10¢ • **W-TN-300-00.10-G100**

Center: TEN CENTS. ***Right:*** 10. ***Engraver:*** Adams. ***Comments:*** H-TN-185-G166. Jan. 1st, 1862.

Rarity: URS-5
F $300

25¢ • **W-TN-300-00.25-G110**

Center: TWENTY FIVE CENTS. ***Right:*** 25. ***Engraver:*** Adams. ***Comments:*** H-TN-185-G168. Jan. 1st, 1862.

Rarity: URS-5
F $300

30¢ • **W-TN-300-00.30-G120**

Center: THIRTY CENTS. ***Right:*** 30. ***Engraver:*** Adams. ***Comments:*** H-TN-185-G170. Jan. 1st, 1862.

Rarity: URS-5
F $300

50¢ • **W-TN-300-00.50-G130**

Center: FIFTY CENTS. ***Right:*** 50. ***Back:*** Red. ***Engraver:*** Adams. ***Comments:*** H-TN-185-G172. Jan. 1st, 1862.

Rarity: URS-5
F $300

80¢ • **W-TN-300-00.80-G140**

Center: EIGHTY CENTS. ***Right:*** 80. ***Back:*** Red. ***Engraver:*** Adams. ***Comments:*** H-TN-185-G174. Jan. 1st, 1862.

Rarity: URS-5
F $300

Non-Valid Issues

$10 • **W-TN-300-010-S010**

Left: Woman. ***Center:*** Woman, Train, Steamboat. ***Right:*** Ceres. ***Comments:*** H-TN-185-S68. 18__. 1840s.

Rarity: —

$10 • **W-TN-300-010-S020**

Left: 10 / Justice with scales. ***Center:*** X with cherubs / Two women seated. ***Right:*** 10 / Justice with scales. ***Engraver:*** Rawdon, Wright & Hatch. ***Comments:*** H-TN-185-S70. From a genuine plate of the Planters Bank of Alabama, Wetumpka, Alabama. 18__. 1840s.

Rarity: —

$20 • **W-TN-300-020-S030**

Center: Eagle. ***Comments:*** H-TN-185-S72. 18__. 1840s.

Rarity: —

$20 • **W-TN-300-020-S040**

Left: 20 / Female portrait / XX. ***Center:*** Woman seated near ocean with shield. ***Right:*** 20 / Female portrait / XX. ***Engraver:*** Rawdon, Wright & Hatch. ***Comments:*** H-TN-185-S74. From a genuine plate of the Planters Bank of Alabama, Wetumpka, Alabama. 18__. 1840s.

Rarity: —

$50 • **W-TN-300-050-S050**

Left: FIFTY DOLLARS vertically. ***Center:*** 50 / Eagle on bale / 50. ***Right:*** STATE OF TENNESSEE vertically. ***Engraver:*** Rawdon, Wright & Hatch. ***Comments:*** H-TN-185-S76. From a genuine plate of the Planters Bank of Alabama, Wetumpka, Alabama. 18__. 1840s.

Rarity: —

$100 • **W-TN-300-100-S060**

Left: HUNDRED vertically. ***Center:*** Deer, River. ***Right:*** Portrait of George Washington. ***Engraver:*** Rawdon, Wright & Hatch. ***Comments:*** H-TN-185-S78. From a genuine plate of the Planters Bank of Alabama, Wetumpka, Alabama. 18__. 1840s.

Rarity: —

$100 • **W-TN-300-100-S070**

Left: Medallion head. ***Center:*** C / Factory / C. ***Right:*** 100 diagonally. ***Engraver:*** Rawdon, Wright & Hatch. ***Comments:*** H-TN-185-S80. 18__. 1840s.

Rarity: —

Gallatin, Tennessee

In 1802 Gallatin was selected and established to be the permanent seat of Sumner County. It was named after Albert Gallatin, who had been the Secretary of the Treasury to Thomas Jefferson and James Madison during their presidencies. Andrew Jackson was one of the first purchasers of a town lot when the land was sectioned in 1803. Jackson also established the first general store in the town. The first courthouse and jail were built in 1803, and in 1815 the town was officially incorporated.

Prior to the Civil War, Gallatin desired to remain neutral and opposed secession. However, once the war broke out in earnest, the citizens gave support to the Confederacy in defense of their home state. The town was seized by the Union army in 1862, as it was considered a strategic location due to its placement on the railroad and the Cumberland River. The city was reoccupied by Confederate forces for a brief time, but in November 1862 it was taken again by Union troops.

Nashville Bank (branch)

1817–1827

W-TN-310

History: In 1807 the Nashville Bank was chartered with an authorized capital of $200,000, to be divided into shares of $50 apiece. In 1817 several banks were chartered across the state—in the towns of Gallatin, Murfreesboro, Rogersville, Shelbyville, and Winchester—and were given the option of either joining the first Bank of the State of Tennessee, W-TN-355, or of joining with the Nashville Bank. The corporations chose the Nashville Bank and became branches forthwith.

On March 31, 1823, the Nashville Bank, along with its branches, burned a total of $250,000 worth of bank notes in order to increase the value of its circulation. In 1827 the bank was liquidated.

The Nashville Bank had its parent bank located in Nashville, W-TN-800, and branch banks located in Murfreesboro, W-TN-640, Rogersville, W-TN-900, Shelbyville, W-TN-930, and Winchester, W-TN-1060.

Numismatic Commentary: Surviving notes are very scarce and only the $5 and $10 notes were known to Garland.

Valid Issues

$1 • W-TN-310-001-G010

Left: ONE vertically. ***Center:*** 1 / Woman seated / 1. ***Right:*** TENNESSEE vertically. ***Engraver:*** Tanner, Kearny & Tiebout. ***Comments:*** H-TN-180-G64. 18__. 1810s.

Rarity: *None known*

$2 • W-TN-310-002-G020

Left: TWO vertically. ***Center:*** 2 / Woman seated / 2. ***Right:*** TENNESSEE vertically. ***Engraver:*** Tanner, Kearny & Tiebout. ***Comments:*** H-TN-180-G66. 18__. 1810s.

Rarity: *None known*

$5 • W-TN-310-005-G030

Left: FIVE vertically. ***Center:*** 5 / Woman seated / 5. ***Right:*** NASHVILLE vertically. ***Engraver:*** Murray, Draper, Fairman & Co. ***Comments:*** H-TN-180-G70, Garland-319. 18__. 1810s.

Rarity: URS-4
F $450

$5 • W-TN-310-005-G040

Left: FIVE vertically. ***Center:*** 5 / Woman seated / 5. ***Right:*** TENNESSEE vertically. ***Engraver:*** Tanner, Kearny & Tiebout. ***Comments:*** H-TN-180-G72. 18__. 1810s–1820s.

Rarity: *None known*

$10 • W-TN-310-010-G050

Left: TEN vertically. ***Center:*** 10 / Woman seated / 10. ***Right:*** NASHVILLE vertically. ***Engraver:*** Murray, Draper, Fairman & Co. ***Comments:*** H-TN-180-G74. 18__. 1810s.

Rarity: *None known*

$10 • W-TN-310-010-G060

Left: TEN vertically. ***Center:*** 10 / Woman seated / 10. ***Right:*** TENNESSEE vertically. ***Engraver:*** Tanner, Kearny & Tiebout. ***Comments:*** H-TN-180-G76, Garland-320. 18__. 1810s–1820s.

Rarity: URS-3
F $750

$20 • W-TN-310-020-G070

Left: TWENTY vertically. ***Center:*** 20 / Woman seated / 20. ***Right:*** NASHVILLE vertically. ***Engraver:*** Murray, Draper, Fairman & Co. ***Comments:*** H-TN-180-G78. 18__. 1810s.

Rarity: *None known*

$20 • W-TN-310-020-G080

Left: TWENTY vertically. ***Center:*** 20 / Woman seated / 20. ***Right:*** TENNESSEE vertically. ***Engraver:*** Tanner, Kearny & Tiebout. ***Comments:*** H-TN-180-G80. 18__. 1810s–1820s.

Rarity: *None known*

Non-Valid Issues

$10 • W-TN-310-010-C060

Engraver: Tanner, Kearny & Tiebout. ***Comments:*** H-TN-180-C76, Garland-321. Counterfeit of W-TN-310-010-G060. 18__. 1810s–1820s.

Rarity: URS-4
F $400

Greeneville, Tennessee

In 1784 North Carolina ceded the lands including Greeneville to the U.S. Congress as a means of paying its debts. Afterwards, with the lands belonging to the federal government as opposed to any particular state, the inhabitants of Greene and neighboring counties decided to try and form an independent state. The first-draft constitution for the state of Franklin (after Benjamin Franklin) was rejected. The next attempt was approved at the first state legislature in December 1785, in a log house in Greeneville. The constitution was based on and similar to the North Carolina state constitution. The state of Franklin, however, was transitory and collapsed. The land was then absorbed by Tennessee.

Prior to the Civil War, Greeneville was home to a very strong abolitionist mindset. After Tennessee seceded from the Union, 30 counties around and including Greeneville met together to discuss the formation of a separate state—the state of East Tennessee—which would remain with the United States. The state government of Tennessee rejected the idea and sent Confederate forces to occupy the area.

Two conspirators in East Tennessee bridge burnings were executed in Greeneville on November 30, 1861. The Confederate army occupied Greeneville in 1863 under orders of James Longstreet. The following year there was a raid by Union soldiers which caused the death of Confederate general John Hunt Morgan.

State Stock Bank

Circa 1857

W-TN-320

History: The State Stock Bank was chartered in 1857. However, it was reported that "the notes issued by it are not secured by State Stocks, or at least they show no indication of it upon their face. They are considered doubtful."[5]

The State Stock Bank had a branch bank located in Tazewell, W-TN-1020.

Numismatic Commentary: Signed and issued notes are very scarce to rare. This bank is known mostly through Proofs.

The 1990 Christie's sale of the American Bank Note Co. archives produced a $5-$5-$10-$20 sheet.

VALID ISSUES

$5 • W-TN-320-005-G010

Left: V / 5. ***Center:*** Hunter shooting deer. ***Right:*** 5 / Woman with cornucopia. ***Engraver:*** Danforth, Wright & Co. ***Comments:*** H-Unlisted, Garland-322. Jany. 1st, 1857.

Rarity: URS-3
Proof $3,500

$5 • W-TN-320-005-G020 SBG

Tint: Red-orange lathework and dies outlining white 5 on FIVE. ***Engraver:*** Danforth, Wright & Co. ***Comments:*** H-TN-50-G2a, Garland-323. Jany. 1st, 1857.

Rarity: URS-3
Proof $9,200
Selected auction price: Heritage Auctions, March 2011, Proof $9,200

$10 • W-TN-320-010-G030 HA

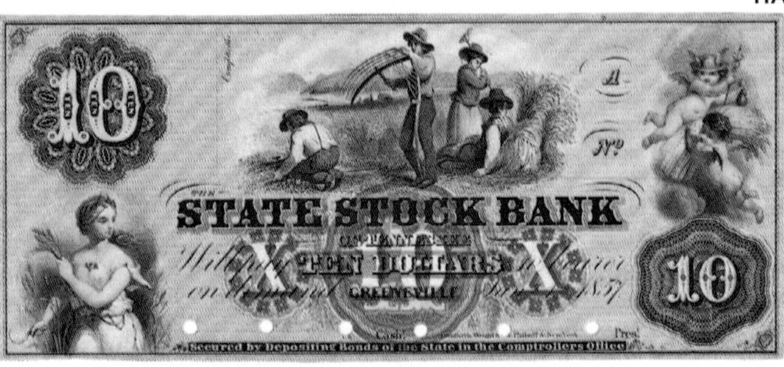

Tint: Red-orange lathework and dies outlining white X / 10 on X on TEN / X. ***Engraver:*** Danforth, Wright & Co. ***Comments:*** H-TN-50-G4a, Garland-324. Jany. 1st, 1857.

Rarity: URS-3
Proof $5,000
Selected auction price: Heritage Auctions, October 21, 2015, Lot 18578, Proof $4,935

$20 • W-TN-320-020-G040 RS

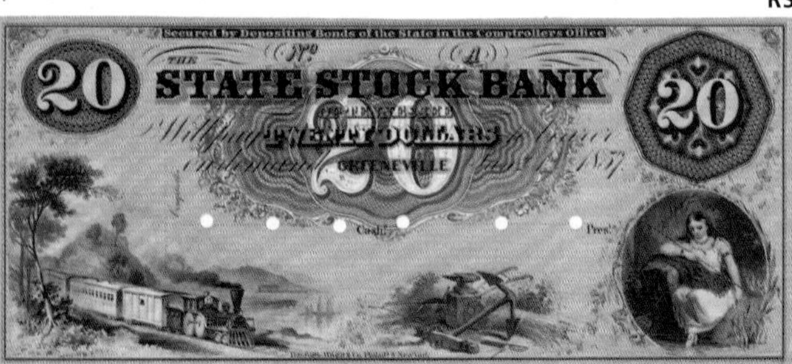

Tint: Red-orange lathework and dies outlining white 20. ***Engraver:*** Danforth, Wright & Co. ***Comments:*** H-TN-50-G6a, Garland-326. Jany. 1st, 1857.

Rarity: URS-1
Proof $5,000

JACKSON, TENNESSEE

Jackson was settled along the Forked Deer River prior to 1820. It was first called Alexandria, but in 1822 the town received its new name in honor of General Andrew Jackson.

Agricultural pursuits were the primary form of commerce. These brought about the rise of a large trading and retail center which served the surrounding farming areas.

Jackson was occupied by Union forces from 1862 until the end of the war. A skirmish occurred here during the winter of 1862 when General Nathan Bedford Forrest attempted to derail trains on the supply line to Ulysses S. Grant.

Union Bank of Tennessee (branch)

1832–1865

W-TN-325

History: On October 18, 1832, the Union Bank of Tennessee (also sometimes seen as the Union Bank of the State of Tennessee on notes) was chartered with an authorized capital of $3,000,000.

In 1848 the president of the branch at Jackson was James Caruthers. John W. Campbell was the cashier, and the capital was $200,000. In 1856 a total reorganization of the branch took place, and E.F. McKnight was elected cashier, accompanied by W.H. Stephens as president. On February 9, 1859, the *Worcester Palladium* reported that the branch of the Union Bank of Tennessee "was robbed of a large amount of specie and paper money on the night of the 3d inst., and the clerk murdered. At last accounts no clue to the perpetrators had been discovered."

In 1865 the Union Bank of Tennessee went into liquidation.

The Union Bank of Tennessee had its parent bank located in Nashville, W-TN-840, and branch banks located in Chattanooga, W-TN-090, Columbia, W-TN-220, Knoxville, W-TN-400, and Memphis, W-TN-600.

Numismatic Commentary: Known signed and issued notes payable at this branch are very scarce. Just the $1 and $5 examples were known to Garland. Denominations higher than $10 are unknown for this branch.

VALID ISSUES

50¢ • W-TN-325-00.50-G005 CC

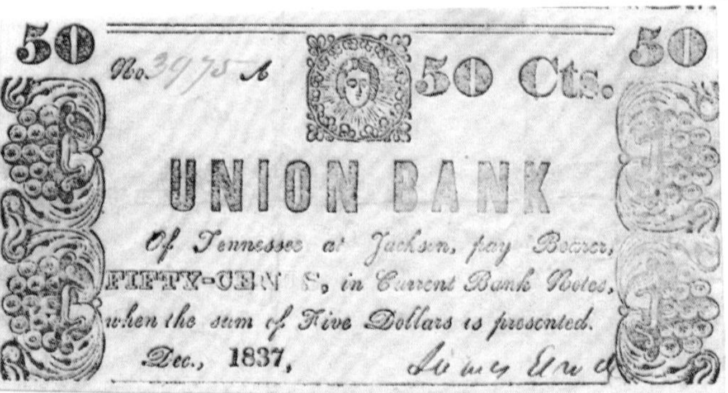

Comments: H-Unlisted, Garland-Unlisted. Dec., 1837.

Rarity: URS-2
EF $650

$1 • W-TN-325-001-G010

Left: 1 / Portrait of Andrew Jackson / 1. ***Center:*** ONE DOLLAR. ***Right:*** ONE / Angel seated in clouds with 1. ***Engraver:*** Draper, Toppan & Co. ***Comments:*** H-TN-210-G54, Garland-331. Jan. 2, 1843.

Rarity: URS-2
F $900

$2 • W-TN-325-002-G020

Left: 2 / Portrait of George Washington / II. ***Center:*** TWO DOLLARS. ***Right:*** 2 / Woman seated with bales and sickle. ***Engraver:*** Draper, Toppan & Co. ***Comments:*** H-TN-210-G56. Jan. 2, 1843.

Rarity: *None known*

$3 • W-TN-325-003-G030

Left: 3 / Portrait of Benjamin Franklin / III. ***Center:*** Ships, Two women flanking shield bearing cotton plant and plow, Train. ***Right:*** 3 / Female portrait / III. ***Engraver:*** Draper, Toppan & Co. ***Comments:*** H-TN-210-G58. Jan. 2, 1843.

Rarity: *None known*

$5 • W-TN-325-005-G040

Left: Eagle. ***Center:*** Portrait of George Washington / Steamboat / Portrait of Marquis de Lafayette. ***Right:*** Eagle. ***Engraver:*** Unverified, but likely Chas. Toppan. ***Comments:*** H-TN-210-G60. 18__. 1830s–1840s.

Rarity: *None known*

$5 • W-TN-325-005-G050 CC

Engraver: Underwood, Bald, Spencer & Hufty. ***Comments:*** H-TN-210-G64, Garland-332. 18__. 1840s–1850s.

Rarity: URS-4
F $300

$10 • W-TN-325-010-G060

Left: Medallion head / TEN / Medallion head. ***Center:*** 10 / Haying scene, Woman and man, Men harvesting. ***Right:*** Medallion head / TEN / Medallion head. ***Engraver:*** Unverified, but likely Chas. Toppan. ***Comments:*** H-TN-210-G66. 18__. 1830s–1840s.

Rarity: —

Collectors and Researchers:

If you have new information about any banks or notes listed in this volume, contact Whitman Publishing, Attn: Obsolete Paper Money, 3101 Clairmont Road, Suite G, Atlanta, GA 30329.

$10 • W-TN-325-010-G070 CC

Engraver: Draper, Underwood, Bald & Spencer. ***Comments:*** H-TN-210-G68. 18__. 1830s.

Rarity: URS-3
F $600

$20 • W-TN-325-020-G080

Left: 20 / Woman seated / 20. ***Center:*** Ship / Two women flanking shield bearing eagle, surmounted by eagle / Ship. ***Right:*** 20 / Woman seated / 20. ***Engraver:*** Chas. Toppan. ***Comments:*** H-TN-210-G70. 18__. 1830s–1840s.

Rarity: —

$20 • W-TN-325-020-G090

Center: Portrait of Benjamin Franklin / Portrait of Napoleon Bonaparte / Portrait of Benjamin Franklin. ***Engraver:*** Underwood, Bald, Spencer & Hufty. ***Comments:*** H-TN-210-G72. 18__. 1830s.

Rarity: —

$50 • W-TN-325-050-G100

Left: 50 / Ship / 50. ***Center:*** Portrait of Indian / Woman seated / Portrait of Indian. ***Right:*** 50 / Ship / 50. ***Engraver:*** Chas. Toppan. ***Comments:*** H-TN-210-G74. 18__. 1830s–1840s.

Rarity: —

$50 • W-TN-325-050-G100a

Engraver: Chas. Toppan / Toppan, Carpenter & Co. ***Comments:*** H-TN-210-G74a. Similar to W-TN-325-050-G100 but with additional engraver imprint. 18__. 1840s–1850s.

Rarity: —

$100 • W-TN-325-100-G110

Left: 100 / Justice / 100. ***Center:*** Steamboat, Woman reclining with globe, Cherub / Steamboat. ***Right:*** 100 / Justice / 100. ***Engraver:*** Chas. Toppan. ***Comments:*** H-TN-210-G76. 18__. 1830s–1840s.

Rarity: —

$100 • W-TN-325-100-G110a

Engraver: Chas. Toppan / Toppan, Carpenter & Co. ***Comments:*** H-TN-210-G76a. Similar to W-TN-325-100-G110 but with additional engraver imprint. 18__. 1840s–1850s.

Rarity: —

$500 • W-TN-325-500-G120

Left: 500 / Medallion head of George Washington / 500. ***Center:*** Eagle with shield and cornucopia. ***Right:*** 500 / Medallion head of Benjamin Franklin / 500. ***Engraver:*** Draper, Toppan, Longacre & Co. ***Comments:*** H-TN-210-G78. 18__. 1830s–1840s.

Rarity: —

$1,000 • **W-TN-325-1000-G130**

Left: 1000 / Medallion head of Benjamin Franklin / 1000. ***Center:*** Eagle with shield and cornucopia. ***Right:*** 1000 / Medallion head of George Washington / 1000. ***Engraver:*** Draper, Toppan, Longacre & Co. ***Comments:*** H-TN-210-G80. 18__. 1830s–1840s.

Rarity: —

Post Notes

$5 • **W-TN-325-005-G140**

Left: Medallion head / FIVE / Medallion head. ***Center:*** Medallion head / 5. ***Right:*** Medallion head / FIVE / Medallion head. ***Engraver:*** Underwood, Bald, Spencer & Hufty. ***Comments:*** H-TN-210-G84. 18__. 1830s.

Rarity: —

$10 • **W-TN-325-010-G150**

Left: Medallion head / TEN / Medallion head. ***Center:*** 10 / Hebe watering eagle / 10. ***Right:*** Medallion head / TEN / Medallion head. ***Engraver:*** Draper, Underwood, Bald & Spencer. ***Comments:*** H-TN-210-G86. 18__. 1830s.

Rarity: —

$20 • **W-TN-325-020-G160**

Center: Portrait of Benjamin Franklin / Portrait of Napoleon Bonaparte / Portrait of Benjamin Franklin. ***Engraver:*** Underwood, Bald, Spencer & Hufty. ***Comments:*** H-TN-210-G88. 18__. 1830s.

Rarity: —

Non-Valid Issues

$1 • **W-TN-325-001-S010** CC

Engraver: Underwood, Bald, Spencer & Hufty. ***Comments:*** H-TN-210-S6. 18__. 1840s.

Rarity: URS-3
F $450

$4 • **W-TN-325-004-N010** CC

Engraver: Woodruff, Tucker & Co. ***Comments:*** H-Unlisted. 18__. 1840s.

Rarity: URS-2
F $1,100

$10 • **W-TN-325-010-S020**

Left: TEN vertically. ***Center:*** Woman seated / Woman with sword seated with shield bearing 10 / Woman seated. ***Right:*** 10 / Woman standing / TEN. ***Engraver:*** Underwood, Bald, Spencer & Hufty. ***Comments:*** H-TN-210-S8. 18__. 1840s.

Rarity: *None known*

$20 • **W-TN-325-020-C080**

Engraver: Chas. Toppan. ***Comments:*** H-TN-210-C70. Counterfeit of W-TN-325-020-G080. 18__. 1830s–1840s.

Rarity: *None known*

Jonesboro, Tennessee

Jonesborough (later shortened to Jonesboro) was founded in 1779 when the area still belonged to North Carolina. It was thus named after a North Carolina legislator, Willie Jones. In 1784 Jonesboro became the capital of the brief state of Franklin, which never was officially recognized and was later absorbed by Tennessee.

The largest concentration of abolitionist movement outside of the states that joined the Confederacy was found in Jonesboro. In 1820 Elihu Embree began publishing *The Emancipator*, the first American periodical that focused wholly on the abolition of slavery. Upper East Tennessee was home to a fervent abolitionist movement, voted against secession twice, and sent a goodly portion of its fathers and sons to fight for the Union.

Bank of East Tennessee (branch)

1843–1858

W-TN-330

History: In 1843 the Bank of East Tennessee was chartered with an authorized capital of $800,000. In 1853 it was reported that the bank had suspended specie payments, but it was still considered to be in good credit. By 1858, however, it had closed.

The Bank of East Tennessee had its parent bank located in Knoxville, W-TN-345, and a branch bank located in Chattanooga, W-TN-080.

Numismatic Commentary: Notes from this bank are quite artistic, with visually dramatic vignettes, color, and—in many cases—two-sided printing. All denominations are reasonably available. As Garland noted, signatories of the notes can be different, sometimes affecting the scarcity and value. Scarcer than notes signed by the cashier and president of the parent bank are notes signed by William G. Gammon, first an exchange agent in Jonesboro and then cashier of the Jonesboro branch. Sometimes Gammon's signature appears on the back of notes, possibly prior to him assuming the position of cashier.

Valid Issues

$1 • **W-TN-330-001-G010**

Left: Woman standing with 1 / ONE. ***Center:*** Train. ***Right:*** 1 on shield / Portrait of Hugh Lawson White. ***Engraver:*** Wellstood, Hanks, Hay & Whiting. ***Comments:*** H-TN-55-G80, Garland-344. Oct. 1, 185_. 1854.

Rarity: URS-7
F $150

$1 • W-TN-330-001-G020 CC, CC

Back: Red-orange portrait of Rachel Jackson. ***Engraver:*** Danforth, Wright & Co. ***Comments:*** H-TN-55-G82a, Garland-345. 18__. 1850s.

Rarity: URS-9
F $120

$2 • W-TN-330-002-G030 CC

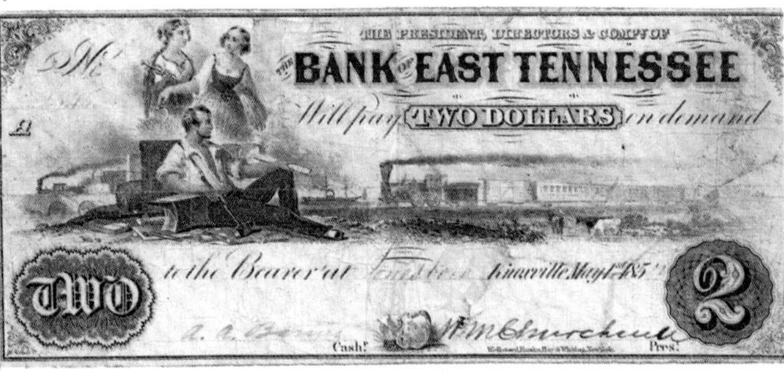

Engraver: Wellstood, Hanks, Hay & Whiting. ***Comments:*** H-TN-55-G84, Garland-346. May 1st, 185_. 1854.

Rarity: URS-9
F $125

$2 • W-TN-330-002-G040 CC, CC

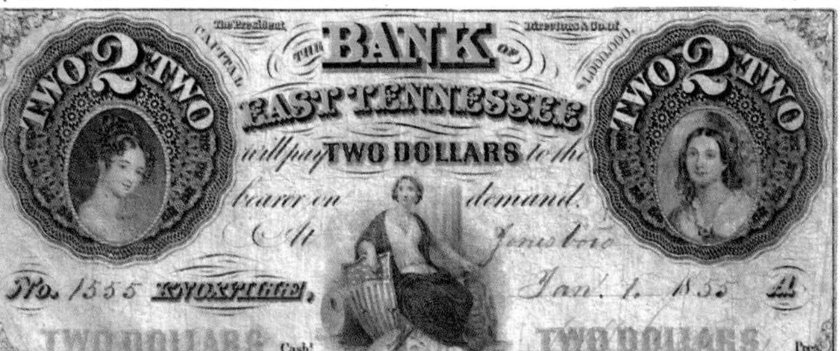

Back: Red-orange medallion head bearing TWO. ***Engraver:*** Danforth, Wright & Co. ***Comments:*** H-TN-55-G86a, Garland-347. 18__. 1850s.

Rarity: URS-8
F $150

$3 • W-TN-330-003-G050 CC

Engraver: Wellstood, Hanks, Hay & Whiting. ***Comments:*** H-TN-55-G88, Garland-348. May 1st, 185_. 1854.

Rarity: URS-7
F $175

$3 • W-TN-330-003-G060 CC, CC

Back: Red-orange. ***Engraver:*** Danforth, Wright & Co. ***Comments:*** H-TN-55-G90a, Garland-349. 18__. 1850s.

Rarity: URS-8
F $125

$5 • W-TN-330-005-G070 CC

Engraver: Wellstood, Benson & Hanks. ***Comments:*** H-TN-55-G92, Garland-352. Oct. 1st, 185_. 1854.

Rarity: URS-8
F $135

$5 • **W-TN-330-005-G080** CC

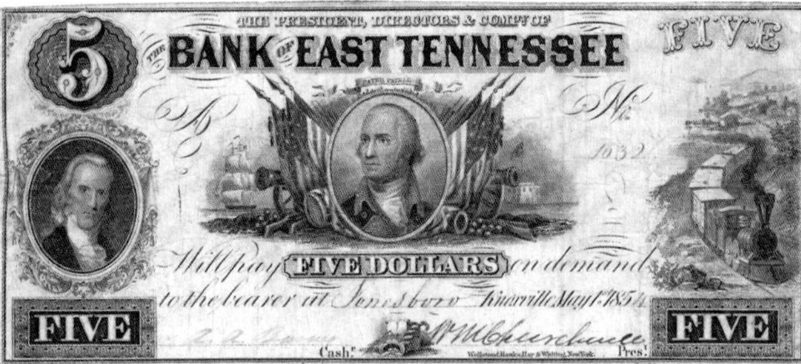

Engraver: Wellstood, Hanks, Hay & Whiting. ***Comments:*** H-TN-55-G94, Garland-351. May 1st, 185_. 1854.

Rarity: URS-8
F $150

$5 • **W-TN-330-005-G090** CC

Back: Red-orange. ***Engraver:*** Danforth, Wright & Co. ***Comments:*** H-TN-55-G96a, Garland-353. 18__. 1850s.

Rarity: URS-9
F $125

$5 • **W-TN-330-005-G100** SI, SI

Back: Red-orange medallion head bearing FIVE / Medallion head bearing FIVE. ***Engraver:*** Danforth, Wright & Co. ***Comments:*** H-TN-55-G98a, Garland-350. 18__. 1850s.

Rarity: URS-9
F $125

$10 • **W-TN-330-010-G110** CC

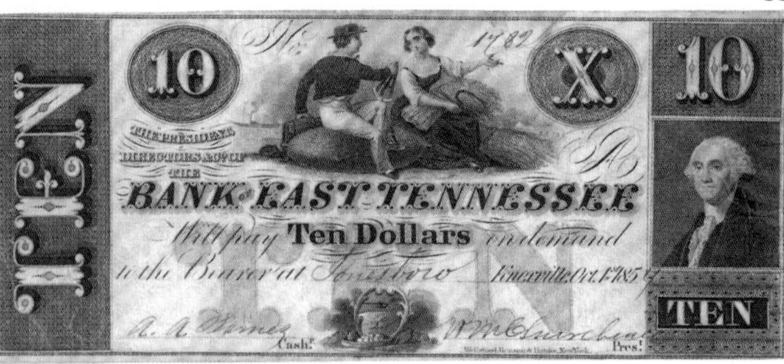

Engraver: Wellstood, Benson & Hanks. ***Comments:*** H-TN-55-G100, Garland-354. Oct. 1st, 185_. 1854.

Rarity: URS-8
F $125; **VF** $175

$10 • **W-TN-330-010-G120** CC, CC

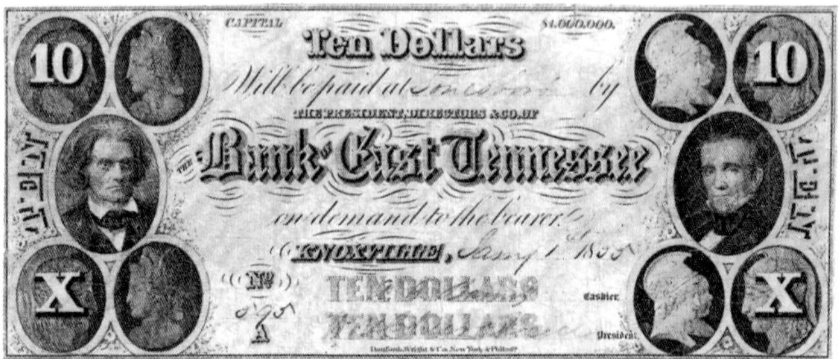

Back: Red-orange. ***Engraver:*** Danforth, Wright & Co. ***Comments:*** H-TN-55-G100a, Garland-355. 18__. 1850s.

Rarity: URS-7
F $150

$20 • **W-TN-330-020-G130** CC

Engraver: Wellstood, Benson & Hanks. ***Comments:*** H-TN-55-G102, Garland-356. Oct. 1st, 185_. 1854.

Rarity: URS-7
F $150; **VF** $200

$20 • **W-TN-330-020-G140** CC, CC

Back: Red-orange. ***Engraver:*** Danforth, Wright & Co. ***Comments:*** H-TN-55-G104a, Garland-357. 18__. 1850s.

Rarity: URS-8
F $125

Bank of the State of Tennessee {1st} (branch)

1817–1820

W-TN-335

History: The first Bank of the State of Tennessee was chartered on November 20, 1811, with an authorized capital of $400,000. The capital was to be divided into shares of $50 apiece. The state subscribed to $20,000, on the provision that the state reserved the right to withdraw its funds after ten years. Hugh Lawson White was the president. No notes under $5 were allowed to be issued. The branch in Jonesboro opened in 1817.

The Bank of the State of Tennessee discontinued business in 1820, at which time the stated capital was $371,107. The branches failed at the same time with a combined capital of $573,915.

The first Bank of the State of Tennessee had its parent bank located in Knoxville, W-TN-355, and branch banks located in Carthage, W-TN-060, Clarksville, W-TN-110, Columbia, W-TN-170, Franklin, W-TN-280, Kingston, W-TN-340, Maryville, W-TN-440, and Nashville, W-TN-670.

Numismatic Commentary: No notes of this branch, genuine or otherwise, are currently known. Garland and Haxby each listed W-TN-335-050-N020, although Garland considered it to be both unique and genuine. The note bore the correct signatures of both the cashier, Luke Lea, and the president, Hugh Lawson White.

Valid Issues

$5 • **W-TN-335-005-G010**

Left: FIVE vertically. ***Center:*** Man plowing with horses / 5. ***Right:*** TENNESSEE vertically. ***Engraver:*** Murray, Draper, Fairman & Co. ***Comments:*** H-TN-75-G88. 18__. 1810s.

Rarity: *None known*

$10 • **W-TN-335-010-G020**

Left: TEN vertically. ***Center:*** Men harvesting corn / 10. ***Right:*** TENNESSEE vertically. ***Engraver:*** Murray, Draper, Fairman & Co. ***Comments:*** H-TN-75-G90. 18__. 1810s.

Rarity: *None known*

$20 • **W-TN-335-020-G030**

Left: TWENTY vertically. ***Center:*** XX / Justice seated / XX. ***Right:*** TENNESSEE vertically. ***Engraver:*** Murray, Draper, Fairman & Co. ***Comments:*** H-TN-75-G92. 18__. 1810s.

Rarity: *None known*

$50 • **W-TN-335-050-G040**

Left: FIFTY vertically. ***Center:*** 50 / Ships / 50. ***Right:*** TENNESSEE vertically. ***Engraver:*** Murray, Draper, Fairman & Co. ***Comments:*** H-TN-75-G94. 18__. 1810s.

Rarity: *None known*

$100 • **W-TN-335-100-G050**

Left: HUNDRED vertically. ***Center:*** Scene. ***Right:*** TENNESSEE vertically. ***Engraver:*** Murray, Draper, Fairman & Co. ***Comments:*** H-TN-75-G96. 18__. 1810s.

Rarity: *None known*

Non-Valid Issues

$3 • **W-TN-335-003-N010**

Left: THREE DOLLARS vertically. ***Center:*** 3 / 3. ***Right:*** THREE DOLLARS vertically. ***Engraver:*** Murray, Draper, Fairman & Co. ***Comments:*** H-TN-75-N27. 18__. 1810s.

Rarity: *None known*

$50 • **W-TN-335-050-N020**

Left: FIFTY vertically. ***Center:*** 50 / Ship / L. ***Right:*** FIFTY DOLLARS vertically. ***Engraver:*** Murray, Draper, Fairman & Co. ***Comments:*** H-TN-75-N30, Garland-358. 18__. 1810s.

Rarity: *None known*

Kingston, Tennessee

Kingston was settled on October 23, 1799, and was named after Major Robert King. The town became the capital of Tennessee for a single day, September 21, 1807, when the General Assembly joined to honor a deal with the Cherokee Indians, who had agreed to cede the land to the state if the capital would be moved to the new town. This was done, for the day, and then the capital was returned to Knoxville.

Bank of the State of Tennessee {1st} (branch)

1817–1820

W-TN-340

History: The first Bank of the State of Tennessee was chartered on November 20, 1811, with an authorized capital of $400,000. The capital was to be divided into shares of $50 apiece. The state subscribed to $20,000, on the provision that the state reserved the right to withdraw its funds after ten years. Hugh Lawson White was the president. No notes under $5 were allowed to be issued. The branch in Kingston opened in 1817.

The Bank of the State of Tennessee discontinued business in 1820, at which time the stated capital was $371,107. The branches failed at the same time with a combined capital of $573,915.

The first Bank of the State of Tennessee had its parent bank located in Knoxville, W-TN-355, and branch banks located in Carthage, W-TN-060, Clarksville, W-TN-110, Columbia, W-TN-170, Franklin, W-TN-280, Jonesboro, W-TN-335, Maryville, W-TN-440, and Nashville, W-TN-670.

Numismatic Commentary: No notes of this branch are known to exist today.

Valid Issues

$5 • W-TN-340-005-G010

Left: FIVE vertically. ***Center:*** Man plowing with horses / 5. ***Right:*** TENNESSEE vertically. ***Engraver:*** Murray, Draper, Fairman & Co. ***Comments:*** H-TN-75-G104. 18__. 1810s.

Rarity: *None known*

$10 • W-TN-340-010-G020

Left: TEN vertically. ***Center:*** Men harvesting corn / 10. ***Right:*** TENNESSEE vertically. ***Engraver:*** Murray, Draper, Fairman & Co. ***Comments:*** H-TN-75-G106. 18__. 1810s.

Rarity: *None known*

$20 • W-TN-340-020-G030

Left: TWENTY vertically. ***Center:*** XX / Justice seated / XX. ***Right:*** TENNESSEE vertically. ***Engraver:*** Murray, Draper, Fairman & Co. ***Comments:*** H-TN-75-G108. 18__. 1810s.

Rarity: *None known*

$50 • W-TN-340-050-G040

Left: FIFTY vertically. ***Center:*** 50 / Ships / 50. ***Right:*** TENNESSEE vertically. ***Engraver:*** Murray, Draper, Fairman & Co. ***Comments:*** H-TN-75-G110. 18__. 1810s.

Rarity: *None known*

$100 • W-TN-340-100-G050

Left: HUNDRED vertically. ***Center:*** Scene. ***Right:*** TENNESSEE vertically. ***Engraver:*** Murray, Draper, Fairman & Co. ***Comments:*** H-TN-75-G112. 18__. 1810s.

Rarity: *None known*

Non-Valid Issues

$3 • W-TN-340-003-N010

Left: THREE DOLLARS vertically. ***Center:*** 3 / 3. ***Right:*** THREE DOLLARS vertically. ***Engraver:*** Murray, Draper, Fairman & Co. ***Comments:*** H-TN-75-N33. 18__. 1810s.

Rarity: *None known*

$50 • W-TN-340-050-N020

Left: FIFTY vertically. ***Center:*** 50 / Ship / L. ***Right:*** FIFTY DOLLARS vertically. ***Engraver:*** Murray, Draper, Fairman & Co. ***Comments:*** H-TN-75-N36. 18__. 1810s.

Rarity: *None known*

Knoxville, Tennessee

In 1786 the first settlers arrived in what would become Knoxville. James White and James Connor built White's Fort on the land, and in 1790 Charles McClung surveyed the area. Lots were set aside for a town common, a church, a graveyard, and a school. The town was selected to be the capital of the Territory south of the Ohio River and was named Knoxville after Henry Knox.

Several years of turmoil followed, with great conflict between settlers and the native Cherokees. Finally peace was negotiated in 1794. When Tennessee became a state in 1796, Knoxville became the capital. In 1817 the capital was transferred to Murfreesboro.

For a time Knoxville was considered a rowdy river town, with seven taverns and no church. It became a stopping point for travelers and migrants on their journey west. Flatboat and steamboat traffic became a large source of both visitors and trade, as Knoxville lay on the junction of three rivers. Soon Knoxville was the regional center of commerce, with tobacco, corn, whiskey, and cotton travelling through the town out to distant markets. During the 1850s the population doubled as the East Tennessee and Georgia Railroad made its appearance.

Knoxville was placed under martial law in the summer of 1861 after Union sympathizers burned city bridges. Until 1863 the town remained under Confederate control, but that year Ambrose Burnside pushed the Confederate army out of the area.

Bank of East Tennessee

1843–1858

W-TN-345

History: In 1843 the Bank of East Tennessee was chartered with an authorized capital of $800,000. According to *Bankers' Magazine*, this "was not affiliated with the state but was the property of private shareholders."[6] In 1850 the bank officially opened. In 1854 W.M. Churchwell was elected to be the president, replacing J.W.J. Niles who had resigned. A.A. Barnes was the cashier at this time.

In 1853 it was reported that the bank had suspended specie payments, but it was still considered to be in good credit. By 1858, however, it had closed. The winding up of its affairs lasted until 1863.

The Bank of East Tennessee had branch banks located in Chattanooga, W-TN-080, and Jonesboro, W-TN-330.

Numismatic Commentary: Notes from this bank are quite artistic, with dramatic vignettes and color. Two-sided printing is also common. But unlike the notes payable at the Jonesboro branch, notes payable in Knoxville are more elusive, but in most cases should be acquirable.

Remaining at the American Bank Note Co. archives as of 2003 was a $10-$20 face plate, a $1-$1-$1-$2 face plate, a $1-$1-$2-$3 face plate, a $1-$2-$3-$5 back plate, a $1-$2-$5-$5 face plate, and three $5-$5-$10-$20 face plates. The 1990 Christie's sale of the American Bank Note Co. archives produced a $1-$2-$3-$5 sheet and a $5-$5-$10-$20 sheet, as well as two back sheet Proofs from these notes.

VALID ISSUES

$1 • W-TN-345-001-G010

Left: 1 / Portrait of Hugh Lawson White / ONE. ***Center:*** Woman seated / 1. ***Right:*** Eagle, Two women seated / ONE. ***Engraver:*** Toppan, Carpenter & C0. ***Comments:*** H-TN-55-G2, Garland-360. 18__. 1850s.

Rarity: —

$1 • W-TN-345-001-G020

CC

Engraver: Wellstood, Benson & Hanks. ***Comments:*** H-TN-55-G4, Garland-363. 18__. 1850s.

Rarity: URS-7
VF $250

$1 • W-TN-345-001-G030

HA

Overprint: Red ONE. ***Engraver:*** Wellstood, Hanks, Hay & Whiting. ***Comments:*** H-TN-55-G6a, Garland-361. 18__. 1852.

Rarity: URS-4
EF $450

$1 • W-TN-345-001-G030a

Left: Woman standing with 1 / ONE. ***Center:*** Train. ***Right:*** 1 on shield / Portrait of Hugh Lawson White. ***Overprint:*** Red ONE. ***Engraver:*** Wellstood, Hanks, Hay & Whiting. ***Comments:*** H-TN-55-G6b, Garland-362. Similar to W-TN-345-001-G030 but with different date. Oct. 1, 1852.

Rarity: URS-1
VF $950

$1 • W-TN-345-001-G030b

Engraver: Wellstood, Hanks, Hay & Whiting. ***Comments:*** H-TN-55-G6d. Similar to W-TN-345-001-G030 but with different date. May 1, 185_. 1854.

Rarity: *None known*

$1 • W-TN-345-001-G040

Left: 1 on shield / ONE / 1. ***Center:*** Portrait of Andrew Jackson. ***Right:*** 1 / Women standing and sitting. ***Back:*** Red-orange portrait of Rachel Jackson. ***Engraver:*** Danforth, Wright & Co. ***Comments:*** H-TN-55-G8a, Garland-364. 18__. 1850s.

Rarity: URS-6
F $350

$2 • W-TN-345-002-G050

Left: Indian reclining / 2. ***Center:*** Ship. ***Right:*** Woman seated / 2. ***Engraver:*** Toppan, Carpenter & Co. ***Comments:*** H-TN-55-G10, Garland-365. 18__. 1850s.

Rarity: —

$2 • W-TN-345-002-G060

CC

Engraver: Wellstood, Benson & Hanks. ***Comments:*** H-TN-55-G12, Garland-366. 18__. 1850s.

Rarity: URS-7
F $150

$2 • W-TN-345-002-G070

Left: TWO. ***Center:*** Two women and man reclining, Trains. ***Right:*** 2. ***Overprint:*** Red TWO. ***Engraver:*** Wellstood, Hanks, Hay & Whiting. ***Comments:*** H-TN-55-G14a. 18__. 1852.

Rarity: —

$2 • W-TN-345-002-G070a

Overprint: Red TWO. ***Engraver:*** Wellstood, Hanks, Hay & Whiting. ***Comments:*** H-TN-55-G14b. Similar to W-TN-345-002-G070 but with different date. Oct. 1, 1852.

Rarity: —

$2 • W-TN-345-002-G070b

Engraver: Wellstood, Hanks, Hay & Whiting. ***Comments:*** H-TN-55-G14d. Similar to W-TN-345-002-G070 but with different date. May 1, 185_. 1854.

Rarity: —

$2 • W-TN-345-002-G080

SBG, SBG

Back: Red-orange medallion head bearing TWO. ***Engraver:*** Danforth, Wright & Co. ***Comments:*** H-TN-55-G16a, Garland-368. 18__. 1850s.

Rarity: URS-2
Proof $2,600
Selected auction price: Stack's Bowers Galleries, March 2013, Proof $2,600

$3 • W-TN-345-003-G090

CC

Engraver: Toppan, Carpenter & Co. ***Comments:*** H-TN-55-G18, Garland-369. 18__. 1850s.

Rarity: URS-2
F $900

$3 • W-TN-345-003-G100

CC

Engraver: Wellstood, Benson & Hanks. ***Comments:*** H-TN-55-G20, Garland-371. 18__. 1850s.

Rarity: URS-6
F $250

$3 • W-TN-345-003-G110

Left: Woman with shield bearing III vertically. ***Center:*** 3 / Woman seated writing / 3. ***Right:*** Portrait of Hugh Lawson White / 3. ***Overprint:*** Red THREE. ***Engraver:*** Wellstood, Hanks, Hay & Whiting. ***Comments:*** H-TN-55-G22a, Garland-370. 18__. 1852

Rarity: URS-1
Proof $6,000

$3 • W-TN-345-003-G110a

Engraver: Wellstood, Hanks, Hay & Whiting. ***Comments:*** H-TN-55-G24a. Similar to W-TN-345-003-G110 but with different date. May 1, 185_. 1854.

Rarity: —

$3 • W-TN-345-003-G120

CC, CC

Back: Red-orange. ***Engraver:*** Danforth, Wright & Co. ***Comments:*** H-TN-55-G26a, Garland-372. 18__. 1850s.

Rarity: URS-6
F $450; **Proof** $3,900
Selected auction price: Stack's Bowers Galleries, March 2013, Lot 2354, Proof $3,900

How to Read the Whitman Numbering System

$1 • W-AL-020-001-G010a

Denomination: Face value of the note shown.

W: Whitman number. This number is a sortable code unique to each bank and note.

AL: Abbreviation for the state under study.

020: Numerical designation specific to each bank.

001: The denomination in dollars.

G010a: G indicates a good or valid note. Other categories are indicated thus: C (counterfeit); R (raised); S (spurious); N (not-attributed); A (altered). Numbers are assigned starting with 010, 020, et seq. Terminal letters following the number indicate variations of a note: a series of different colored overprints, tints, payees, etc., all on the same design of note. For more information, see the "How to Use This Book" section at the front of the volume, page xiv.

$4 • W-TN-345-004-G130

Left: 4 / Portrait of Benjamin Franklin / 4. ***Center:*** Man and woman flanking shield bearing cotton plant. ***Right:*** 4 / Portrait of Rachel Jackson / 4. ***Engraver:*** Toppan, Carpenter & Co. ***Comments:*** H-TN-55-G28, Garland-373. 18__. 1850s.

Rarity: URS-1
Proof $4,000

$5 • W-TN-345-005-G140

CC

Engraver: Toppan, Carpenter & Co. ***Comments:*** H-TN-55-G30, Garland-374. 18__. 1850s.

Rarity: URS-2
F $900

$5 • W-TN-345-005-G150

Left: FIVE vertically. ***Center:*** V / Man seated / 5. ***Right:*** V / Portrait of Henry Clay / V. ***Engraver:*** Wellstood, Benson & Hanks. ***Comments:*** H-TN-55-G32, Garland-377. 18__. 1850s.

Rarity: URS-6
F $150

$5 • W-TN-345-005-G160

CC

Overprint: Red FIVE. ***Engraver:*** Wellstood, Hanks, Hay & Whiting. ***Comments:*** H-TN-55-G34a, Garland-376. 18__. 1852.

Rarity: URS-6
F $350

$5 • W-TN-345-005-G170

Left: FIVE vertically. ***Center:*** V / Man seated / 5. ***Right:*** V / Portrait of Henry Clay / V. ***Engraver:*** Wellstood, Hanks, Hay & Whiting. ***Comments:*** H-TN-55-G34d. May 1, 185_. 1854.

Rarity: —

$5 • W-TN-345-005-G180

SBG, SBG

Back: Red-orange. ***Engraver:*** Danforth, Wright & Co. ***Comments:*** H-TN-55-G36a, Garland-378. 18__. 1855.

Rarity: URS-3
Proof $1,500

$5 • W-TN-345-005-G190

CC, SBG

Back: Red-orange medallion head bearing FIVE / Medallion head bearing FIVE. ***Engraver:*** Danforth, Wright & Co. ***Comments:*** H-TN-55-G38a, Garland-379. 18__. 1855.

Rarity: URS-4
F $275; **Proof** $1,700

$10 • **W-TN-345-010-G200**

CC

Engraver: Toppan, Carpenter & Co. ***Comments:*** H-TN-55-G40, Garland-380. 18__. 1850s.

Rarity: URS-1
F $950

$10 • **W-TN-345-010-G210**

Left: TEN vertically. ***Center:*** Portrait of George Washington. ***Right:*** 10 / Portrait of George Washington / X. ***Engraver:*** Wellstood, Benson & Hanks. ***Comments:*** H-TN-55-G42, Garland-382. 18__. 1850s.

Rarity: URS-3
F $650

$10 • **W-TN-345-010-G220**

Left: Woman reclining with shield bearing arm and hammer / 10 / Sailor seated with shield. ***Center:*** Cherubs flanking portrait of Hugh Lawson White. ***Right:*** 10 / Liberty standing with X. ***Overprint:*** Red TEN. ***Engraver:*** Wellstood, Hanks, Hay & Whiting. ***Comments:*** H-TN-55-G44a, Garland-381. Oct. 18, 1852.

Rarity: URS-1
Proof $3,000

$10 • **W-TN-345-010-G230**

CC

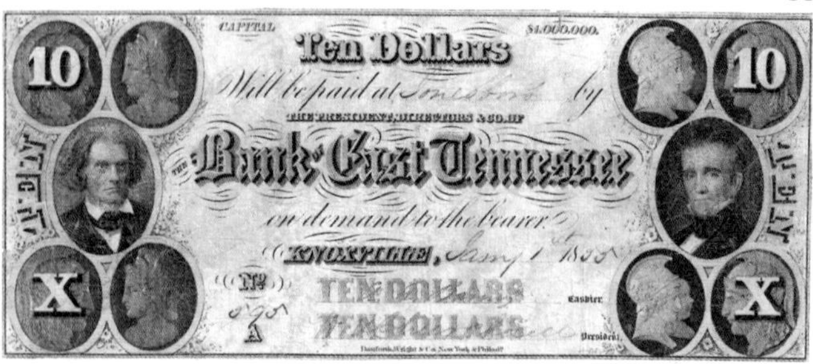

Engraver: Danforth, Wright & Co. ***Comments:*** H-TN-55-G46, Garland-383. 18__. 1855.

Rarity: URS-6
F $175; **Proof** $3,100

$20 • **W-TN-345-020-G240**

Left: Portrait of Benjamin Franklin. ***Center:*** TWENTY / 20. ***Right:*** Portrait of Henry Clay. ***Engraver:*** Wellstood, Benson & Hanks. ***Comments:*** H-TN-55-G48, Garland-384. 18__. 1850s.

Rarity: URS-3
F $650

$20 • **W-TN-345-020-G250**

SBG, SBG

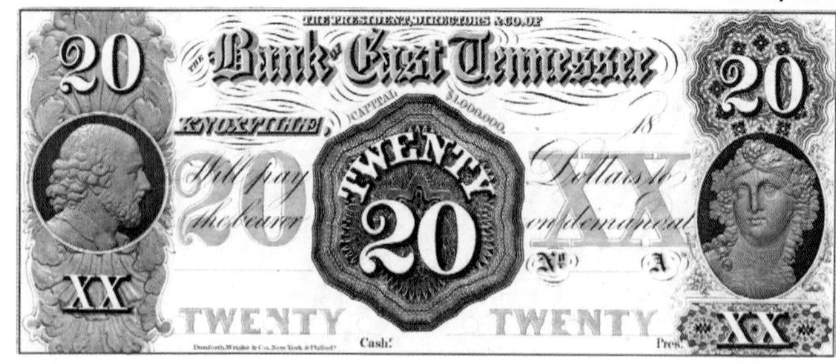

Back: Red-orange. ***Engraver:*** Danforth, Wright & Co. ***Comments:*** H-TN-55-G50, Garland-385. 18__. 1855.

Rarity: URS-3
F $750; **Proof** $2,600
Selected auction price: Stack's Bowers Galleries, March 2013, Lot 5328, Proof $2,600

$50 • **W-TN-345-050-G260**

Left: FIFTY / Woman seated / Train. ***Center:*** 50 / Woman seated and woman reclining with shield and eagle. ***Right:*** 50 / Portrait of Hugh Lawson White / L. ***Engraver:*** Wellstood, Benson & Hanks. ***Comments:*** H-TN-55-G52, Garland-386. 18__. 1850s.

Rarity: URS-1
Proof $5,000

$50 • **W-TN-345-050-G260a**

ANS, ANS

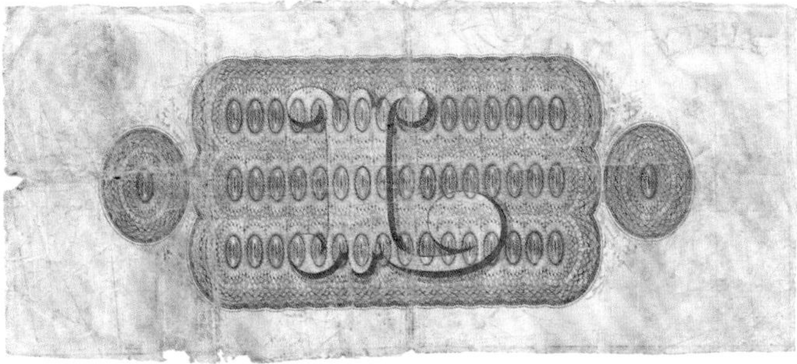

Back: Red-brown. ***Engraver:*** Wellstood, Benson & Hanks. ***Comments:*** H-TN-55-G52a. Similar to W-TN-345-050-G260. 18__. 1850s.

Rarity: URS-3
F $1,100

$100 • **W-TN-345-100-G270**

CC

Engraver: Wellstood, Benson & Hanks. ***Comments:*** H-TN-55-G54, Garland-387. 18__. 1850s.

Rarity: URS-3
VF $1,200; **Proof** $2,800
Selected auction price: Heritage Auctions, April 18, 2012, Lot 15354, VF $1,207

$100 • **W-TN-345-100-G270a**

Back: Red-brown. ***Engraver:*** Wellstood, Benson & Hanks. ***Comments:*** H-TN-55-G54a. Similar to W-TN-345-100-G270. 18__. 1850s.

Rarity: *None known*

Uncut Sheets

$5-$5-$10-$20 •
W-TN-345-005.005.010.020-US010

RG

Back(s): Red-orange. ***Engraver:*** Danforth, Wright & Co. ***Comments:*** H-TN-55-G36a, G36a, G46, G50. First two notes identical. 18__. 1855.

Rarity: URS-5
F $1,200

Bank of Knoxville

1853–1860

W-TN-350

History: In 1853 the Bank of Knoxville was chartered with an authorized capital of $100,000. William M. Churchwell was the president, and Samuel Morrow was the cashier. In 1855 John L. Moses took the position of cashier, and H.A.M. White became the president.

In 1857 the bank had a circulation of $41,400. That year the president became Dyer Pearl, and E.G. Pearl became the cashier. The capital was $50,000.

On March 20, 1860, an act was passed uniting the Bank of Knoxville with the City Bank, W-TN-740, to be known from that point on as a single entity under the title of the City Bank. The outstanding circulation of the Bank of Knoxville was to be redeemed by the City Bank, and no further circulation with the Bank of Knoxville name was to be issued.

Numismatic Commentary: The redemption of Bank of Knoxville notes was seemingly quite successful, and today, surviving notes are very scarce to rare. It is possible that less than a dozen signed and issued notes of the $1, $2, and $3 denominations survive. Today, Proofs are known of the $5, $10, and $20 denominations.

Remaining at the American Bank Note Co. archives as of 2003 were two $1-$1-$2-$3 face plates. The 1990 Christie's sale of the American Bank Note Co. archives produced 14 sheets of demand notes (in denominations of $1-$1-$2-$3 and $5-$5-$10-$20) and 1 sheet of certificates of deposit.

Valid Issues

$1 • W-TN-350-001-G010

NJW

Overprint: Red ONE. ***Engraver:*** Danforth, Bald & Co. ***Comments:*** H-TN-65-G2a, Garland-389. 18__. 1850s.

Rarity: URS-4

VF $1,000

Selected auction price: Heritage Auctions, January 8, 2014, Lot 15440, VF $1,057

$2 • W-TN-350-002-G020

CC

Overprint: Red TWO. ***Engraver:*** Danforth, Bald & Co. ***Comments:*** H-TN-65-G4a, Garland-391. 18__. 1850s.

Rarity: URS-4

F $525

$3 • W-TN-350-003-G030

NJW

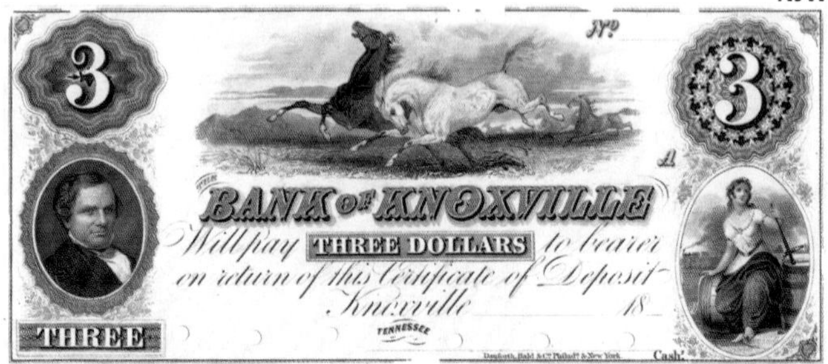

Engraver: Danforth, Bald & Co. ***Comments:*** H-Unlisted. 18__. 1850s.

Rarity: URS-3

Proof $1,750

$3 • W-TN-350-003-G030a

CC

Overprint: Red THREE. ***Engraver:*** Danforth, Bald & Co. ***Comments:*** H-TN-65-G6a, Garland-393. Similar to W-TN-350-003-G030. 18__. 1850s.

Rarity: URS-4

F $275

$5 • W-TN-350-005-G040

NJW

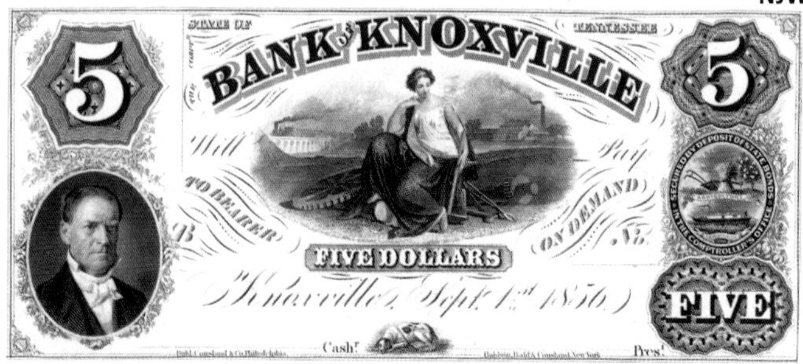

Engraver: Bald, Cousland & Co. / Baldwin, Bald & Cousland. ***Comments:*** H-TN-65-G8, Garland-395. Sept. 1st, 1856.

Rarity: URS-4

Proof $450

$5 • W-TN-350-005-G040a

CC

Overprint: Red FIVE. ***Engraver:*** Bald, Cousland & Co. / Baldwin, Bald & Cousland. ***Comments:*** H-TN-65-G8a, Garland-396. Similar to W-TN-350-005-G040. Sept. 1st, 1856.

Rarity: URS-4
Proof $450

$10 • W-TN-350-010-G050

NJW

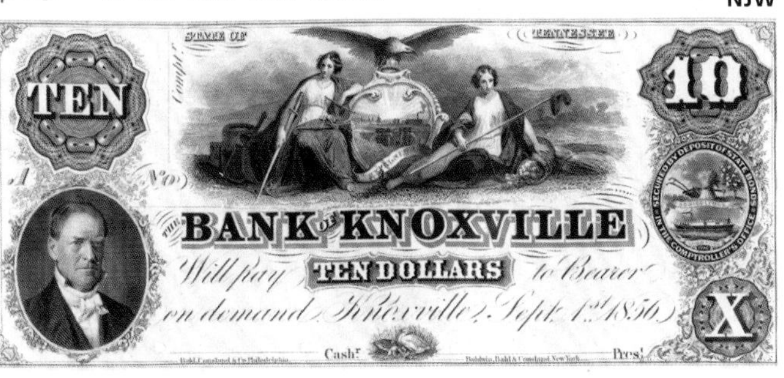

Engraver: Bald, Cousland & Co. / Baldwin, Bald & Cousland. ***Comments:*** H-TN-65-G10, Garland-397. Sept. 1st, 1856.

Rarity: URS-2
Proof $2,000

$10 • W-TN-350-010-G050a

CC

Overprint: Red TEN. ***Engraver:*** Bald, Cousland & Co. / Baldwin, Bald & Cousland. ***Comments:*** H-TN-65-G10a, Garland-398. Similar to W-TN-350-010-G050. Sept. 1st, 1856.

Rarity: URS-2
Proof $1,300

$20 • W-TN-350-020-G060

NJW

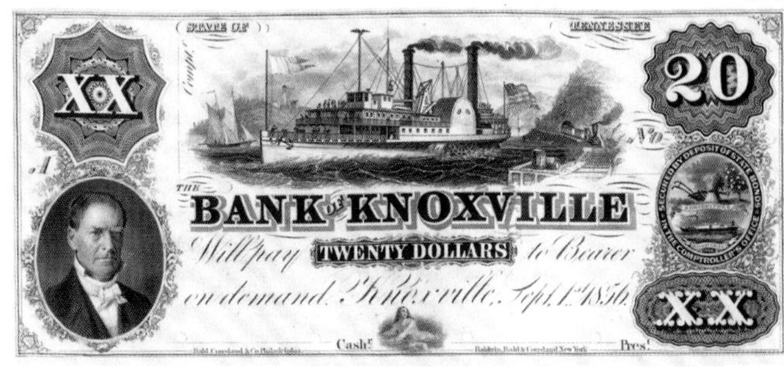

Engraver: Bald, Cousland & Co. / Baldwin, Bald & Cousland. ***Comments:*** H-TN-65-G12, Garland-399. Sept. 1st, 1856.

Rarity: URS-2
Proof $1,400

$20 • W-TN-350-020-G060a

CC

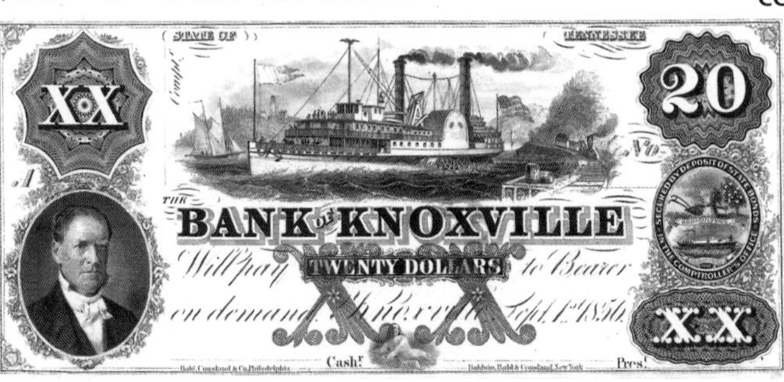

Overprint: Red XX. ***Engraver:*** Bald, Cousland & Co. / Baldwin, Bald & Cousland. ***Comments:*** H-TN-65-G12a, Garland-400. Similar to W-TN-350-020-G060. Sept. 1st, 1856.

Rarity: URS-2
Proof $1,400

Bank of the State of Tennessee {1st}

1811–1820

W-TN-355

History: The first Bank of the State of Tennessee was chartered on November 20, 1811, with an authorized capital of $400,000. The capital was to be divided into shares of $50 apiece. The state subscribed to $20,000, on the provision that the state reserved the right to withdraw its funds after ten years. Hugh Lawson White was the president. No notes under $5 were allowed to be issued.

The Bank of the State of Tennessee discontinued business in 1820, at which time the stated capital was $371,107.

The first Bank of the State of Tennessee had branch banks located in Carthage, W-TN-060, Clarksville, W-TN-110, Columbia, W-TN-170, Franklin, W-TN-280, Jonesboro, W-TN-335, Kingston, W-TN-340, Maryville, W-TN-440, and Nashville, W-TN-670.

Numismatic Commentary: Few notes remain from the first incarnation of the Bank of the State of Tennessee. All are considered rare to possibly unique.

Valid Issues

$5 • W-TN-355-005-G010
Left: FIVE vertically. ***Center:*** Man plowing with horses / 5. ***Right:*** TENNESSEE vertically. ***Engraver:*** Murray, Draper, Fairman & Co. ***Comments:*** H-TN-75-G8. 18__. 1810s.

Rarity: —

$10 • W-TN-355-010-G020 CC

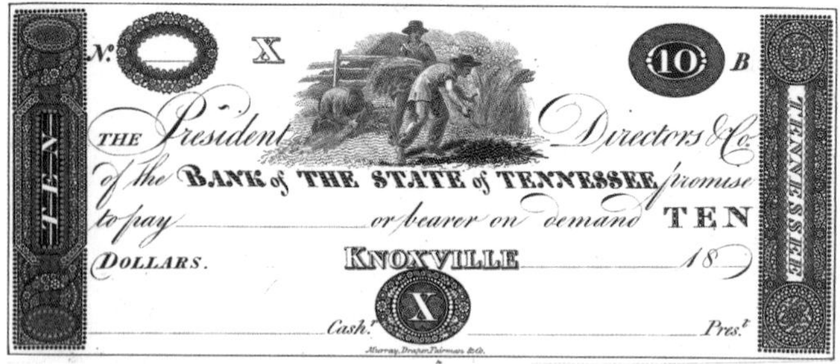

Engraver: Murray, Draper, Fairman & Co. ***Comments:*** H-TN-75-G10, Garland-405. 18__. 1810s.

Rarity: URS-3
Proof $1,400

$20 • W-TN-355-020-G030
Left: TWENTY vertically. ***Center:*** XX / Justice seated / XX. ***Right:*** TENNESSEE vertically. ***Engraver:*** Murray, Draper, Fairman & Co. ***Comments:*** H-TN-75-G12, Garland-406. 18__. 1810s.

Rarity: URS-1
Proof $3,500

$50 • W-TN-355-050-G040
Left: FIFTY vertically. ***Center:*** 50 / Ships / 50. ***Right:*** TENNESSEE vertically. ***Engraver:*** Murray, Draper, Fairman & Co. ***Comments:*** H-TN-75-G14, Garland-407. 18__. 1810s.

Rarity: URS-1
Proof $5,000

$100 • W-TN-355-100-G050
Left: HUNDRED vertically. ***Center:*** Scene. ***Right:*** TENNESSEE vertically. ***Engraver:*** Murray, Draper, Fairman & Co. ***Comments:*** H-TN-75-G16, Garland-408. 18__. 1810s.

Rarity: *None known*

Bank of the State of Tennessee {2nd} (branch)
1820–1832
W-TN-360

History: The second Bank of the State of Tennessee was chartered on July 26, 1820, during the first financial panic of that state, with a capital of $1,000,000.

Unfortunately, the Bank of the State of Tennessee became a negative example of what happens when banks are established for the purpose of solving financial problems. In 1832 the Bank of the State of Tennessee ceased operations, and its funds and assets were placed with the Union Bank of Tennessee, W-TN-840.

The second Bank of the State of Tennessee had its parent bank located in Nashville, W-TN-680, and branch banks located in Columbia, W-TN-180, and Franklin, W-TN-290.

Numismatic Commentary: No notes are currently known today.

Valid Issues

$1 • W-TN-360-001-G010
Comments: H-TN-190-G80. No description available. 18__. 1820s.

Rarity: *None known*

$2 • W-TN-360-002-G020
Comments: H-TN-190-G82. No description available. 18__. 1820s.

Rarity: *None known*

$5 • W-TN-360-005-G030
Comments: H-TN-190-G84. No description available. 18__. 1820s.

Rarity: *None known*

$10 • W-TN-360-010-G040
Comments: H-TN-190-G86. No description available. 18__. 1820s.

Rarity: *None known*

$20 • W-TN-360-020-G050
Comments: H-TN-190-G88. No description available. 18__. 1820s.

Rarity: *None known*

$50 • W-TN-360-050-G060
Comments: H-TN-190-G90. No description available. 18__. 1820s.

Rarity: *None known*

$100 • W-TN-360-100-G070
Comments: H-TN-190-G92. No description available. 18__. 1820s.

Rarity: *None known*

Bank of the State of Tennessee {3rd} (branch)
1838–1866
W-TN-365

History: The third Bank of the State of Tennessee (also seen in print as the Bank of Tennessee) was chartered on January 19, 1838, with an authorized capital of $5,000,000. The bank opened for business in February. The bank suspended specie payments a couple of times in 1838 and 1839, due to the panic of that time, but afterward it resumed and had a profitable and successful career. During the Civil War, the Union army entered the state, and some officers of the Bank of the State of Tennessee fled south with the bank's specie. After the war, the bank's assets were returned to Governor William G. Brownlow in Nashville. Half of the bank's funds had been transferred into state bonds.

By February 1866 the Bank of the State of Tennessee was authorized to go into liquidation.

The third Bank of the State of Tennessee had its parent bank located in Nashville, W-TN-690, and branch banks located in Athens, W-TN-010, Clarksville, W-TN-120, Columbia, W-TN-190, Memphis, W-TN-490, Murfreesboro, W-TN-610, Rogersville, W-TN-890, Shelbyville, W-TN-920, Somerville, W-TN-960, Sparta, W-TN-980, and Trenton, W-TN-1030.

Numismatic Commentary: During the Civil War, Tennessee was truly a house divided. The president of this branch, Dr. J.M.G. Ramsey, was appointed a Confederate depository. He moved the assets of this branch to Maryville, Louden, Athens, Cleveland, and Dalton, Georgia, and then to Atlanta. With Sherman advancing, the specie fled to Augusta, Georgia, and then to Charlotte, North Carolina, and back to Augusta. The city fell to Union forces, and the bank's assets were captured. That the funds were returned to the new state government is amazing.

With this background, issues payable in Knoxville are an interesting addition for any Civil War buff or collector. While most of the notes have survival rates estimated to several dozen, this branch presents a challenge.

Valid Issues

$1 • W-TN-365-001-G010

CC

Tint: Red-orange lathework and panel of microlettering outlining white ONE. ***Back:*** Red-orange. ***Engraver:*** Toppan, Carpenter & Co. ***Comments:*** H-TN-195-G190a, Garland-432. 18__. 1850s.

Rarity: URS-6
F $225

$2 • W-TN-365-002-G020

CC

Tint: Red-orange lathework and panel of microlettering outlining white TWO. ***Back:*** Red-orange. ***Engraver:*** Toppan, Carpenter & Co. ***Comments:*** H-TN-195-G192a, Garland-433. 18__. 1850s.

Rarity: URS-6
F $250

$5 • W-TN-365-005-G030

Left: Three men / 5. ***Center:*** Portrait of James Madison. ***Right:*** 5 / Medallion head. ***Back:*** Red-orange. ***Engraver:*** Danforth, Bald & Co. ***Comments:*** H-TN-195-G194a, Garland-434. 18__. 1850s.

Rarity: *None known*

$5 • W-TN-365-005-G030a

HA, HA

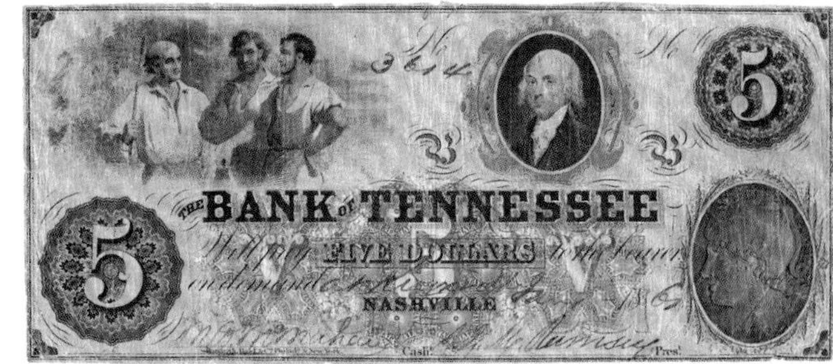

Tint: Red-orange lathework and dies outlining white V / 5 / V. ***Back:*** Red-orange. ***Engraver:*** Danforth, Bald & Co. ***Comments:*** H-TN-195-G194b. Similar to W-TN-365-005-G030. 18__. 1850s.

Rarity: URS-6
F $300

$10 • W-TN-365-010-G040

Left: 10 / Portrait of James K. Polk. ***Center:*** Portrait of Andrew Jackson. ***Right:*** 10 / Portrait of Cave Johnson. ***Tint:*** Red-orange outlining white 10 / 10. ***Back:*** Blue. ***Engraver:*** Toppan, Carpenter & Co. ***Comments:*** H-TN-195-G196a, Garland-435. 18__. 1850s–1861.

Rarity: URS-5
F $400

$20 • W-TN-365-020-G050

Left: 20 / Portrait of Zachary Taylor / 20. ***Center:*** Three women reclining, Ship / 20. ***Right:*** Justice seated with sword and scales / TWENTY. ***Tint:*** Red-orange lathework and panel of microlettering outlining white TWENTY. ***Back:*** Red-orange. ***Engraver:*** Toppan, Carpenter, Casilear & Co. ***Comments:*** H-TN-195-G198c, Garland-436. 18__. 1850s.

Rarity: URS-4
F $500

$50 • W-TN-365-050-G060

Left: 50 / Shield / 50. ***Center:*** Liberty with eagle and shield. ***Right:*** 50 / Portrait of George Washington / 50. ***Tint:*** Red-orange lathework and panel of microlettering outlining white FIFTY. ***Back:*** Blue. ***Engraver:*** Toppan, Carpenter, Casilear & Co / ABNCo. monogram. ***Comments:*** H-TN-195-G200c, Garland-437. 18__. 1859–1861.

Rarity: URS-1
Proof $5,000

$100 • **W-TN-365-100-G070**

Left: Atlas lifting world on shoulders / 100. ***Center:*** 100 / Justice with eagle and shield / 100. ***Right:*** Atlas lifting world on shoulders / 100. ***Tint:*** Red-orange outlining white HUNDRED. ***Back:*** Red-orange. ***Engraver:*** Toppan, Carpenter, Casilear & Co / ABNCo. monogram. ***Comments:*** H-TN-195-G202c, Garland-438. 18__. 1838–1850s.

Rarity: URS-1
Proof $6,000

Civil War Issues Payable in Confederate Treasury Notes

5¢ • **W-TN-365-00.05-G080**

HA

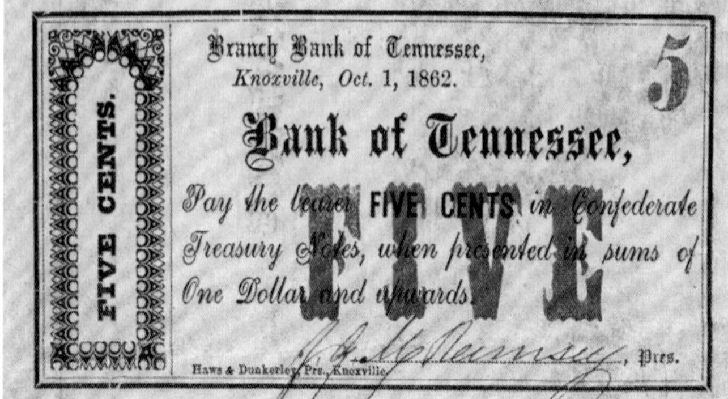

Overprint: Red bold FIVE / 5. ***Engraver:*** Haws & Dunkerley. ***Comments:*** H-TN-195-G210. Signature line for president. Printed on the back of a remainder check of the Bank of East Tennessee, Knoxville. Oct. 1, 1862.

Rarity: URS-7
F $125

5¢ • **W-TN-365-00.05-G080a**

CC

Overprint: Red ornate FIVE / 5. ***Engraver:*** Haws & Dunkerley. ***Comments:*** H-TN-195-G210a. Similar to W-TN-365-00.05-G080 but with signature line for cashier. Printed on the back of a remainder check of the Bank of East Tennessee, Knoxville. Oct. 1, 1862.

Rarity: URS-7
F $125

10¢ • **W-TN-365-00.10-G090**

CC

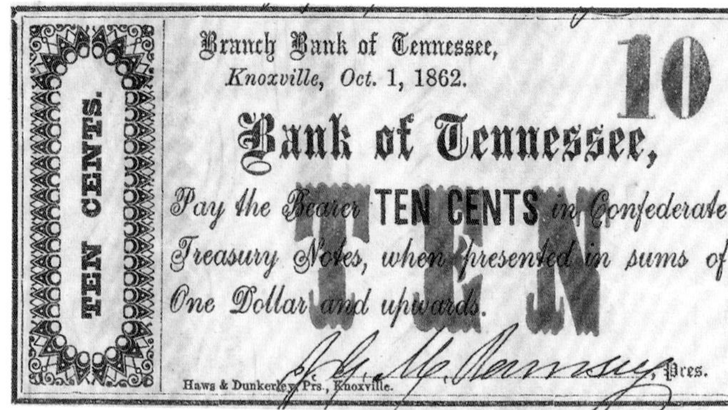

Overprint: Red bold TEN / 10. ***Engraver:*** Haws & Dunkerley. ***Comments:*** H-TN-195-G212, Garland-416. Signature line for president. Printed on the back of a remainder check of the Bank of East Tennessee, Knoxville. Oct. 1, 1862.

Rarity: URS-7
F $100; **Unc-Rem** $275

10¢ • **W-TN-365-00.10-G090a**

Left: TEN CENTS vertically. ***Center:*** TEN CENTS. ***Right:*** 10. ***Overprint:*** Red bold TEN / 10. ***Engraver:*** Haws & Dunkerley. ***Comments:*** H-TN-195-G212a, Garland-417. Similar to W-TN-365-00.10-G090 but with signature line for cashier. Printed on the back of a remainder check of the Bank of East Tennessee, Knoxville. Oct. 1, 1862.

Rarity: URS-6
F $125

10¢ • **W-TN-365-00.10-G090b**

Overprint: Red ornate TEN / 10. ***Engraver:*** Haws & Dunkerley. ***Comments:*** H-TN-195-G212c, Garland-418. Similar to W-TN-365-00.10-G090. Signature line for president. Printed on the back of a remainder check of the Bank of East Tennessee, Knoxville. Oct. 1, 1862.

Rarity: URS-6
F $125

10¢ • **W-TN-365-00.10-G090c**

CC

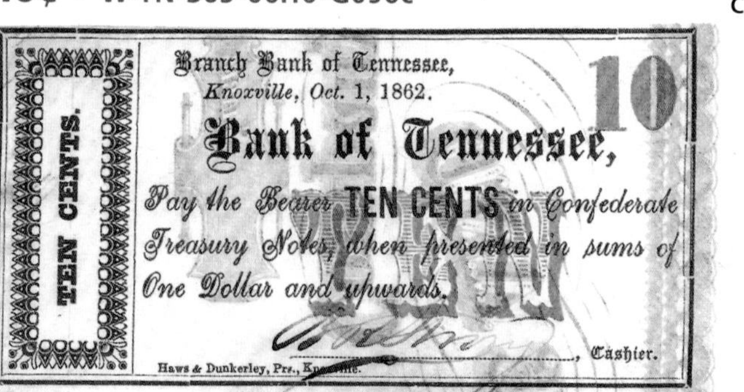

Overprint: Red ornate TEN / 10. ***Engraver:*** Haws & Dunkerley. ***Comments:*** H-TN-195-G212d, Garland-419. Similar to W-TN-365-00.10-G090 but with signature line for cashier. Printed on the back of a remainder check of the Bank of East Tennessee, Knoxville. Oct. 1, 1862.

Rarity: URS-7
F $75; **Unc-Rem** $275

25¢ • W-TN-365-00.25-G100

CC

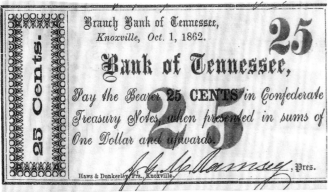

Overprint: Red bold 25 / 25. ***Engraver:*** Haws & Dunkerley. ***Comments:*** H-TN-195-G214c, Garland-421. Signature line for president. Printed on the back of a remainder check of the Bank of East Tennessee, Knoxville. Oct. 1, 1862.

Rarity: URS-7
F $100; **Unc-Rem** $275

25¢ • W-TN-365-00.25-G100a

Left: 25 Cents vertically. ***Center:*** 25 CENTS. ***Right:*** 25. ***Overprint:*** Red bold 25 / 25. ***Engraver:*** Haws & Dunkerley. ***Comments:*** H-TN-195-G214d, Garland-422. Similar to W-TN-365-00.25-G100 but with signature line for cashier. Printed on the back of a remainder check of the Bank of East Tennessee, Knoxville. Oct. 1, 1862.

Rarity: URS-10
F $150; **Unc-Rem** $350

25¢ • W-TN-365-00.25-G100b

Overprint: Red thin 25 / 25. ***Engraver:*** Haws & Dunkerley. ***Comments:*** H-TN-195-G214, Garland-423. Similar to W-TN-365-00.25-G100. Signature line for president. Printed on the back of a remainder check of the Bank of East Tennessee, Knoxville. Oct. 1, 1862.

Rarity: URS-6
F $125

25¢ • W-TN-365-00.25-G100c

CC

Overprint: Red thin 25 / 25. ***Engraver:*** Haws & Dunkerley. ***Comments:*** H-TN-195-G214a, Garland-424. Similar to W-TN-365-00.25-G100 but with signature line for cashier. Printed on the back of a remainder check of the Bank of East Tennessee, Knoxville. Oct. 1, 1862.

Rarity: URS-7
F $75; **EF** $150

50¢ • W-TN-365-00.50-G110

CC

Overprint: Red bold 50 / 50. ***Engraver:*** Haws & Dunkerley. ***Comments:*** H-TN-195-G216c, Garland-426. Signature line for president. Oct. 1, 1862.

Rarity: URS-8
F $100; **Unc-Rem** $325

50¢ • W-TN-365-00.50-G110a

Left: FIFTY CENTS vertically. ***Center:*** FIFTY CENTS. ***Right:*** 50. ***Overprint:*** Red bold 50 / 50. ***Engraver:*** Haws & Dunkerley. ***Comments:*** H-TN-195-G216d, Garland-427. Similar to W-TN-365-00.50-G110 but with signature line for cashier. Oct. 1, 1862.

Rarity: —

50¢ • W-TN-365-00.50-G110b

ANS

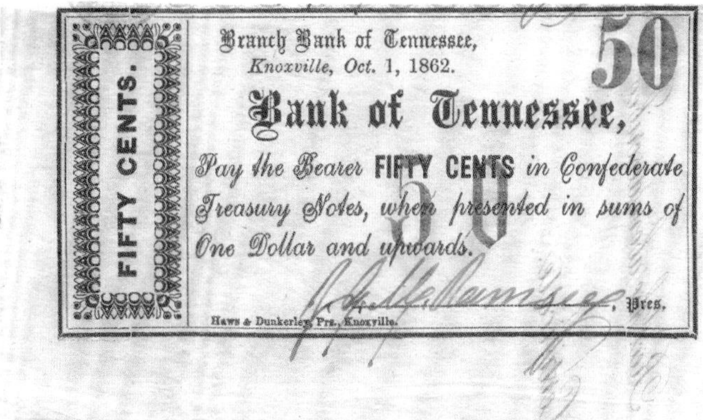

Overprint: Red thin 50 / 50. ***Engraver:*** Haws & Dunkerley. ***Comments:*** H-TN-195-G216, Garland-428. Signature line for president. Oct. 1, 1862.

Rarity: URS-8
F $125

Collectors and Researchers:

If you have new information about any banks or notes listed in this volume, contact Whitman Publishing, Attn: Obsolete Paper Money, 3101 Clairmont Road, Suite G, Atlanta, GA 30329.

50¢ • W-TN-365-00.50-G110c

CC

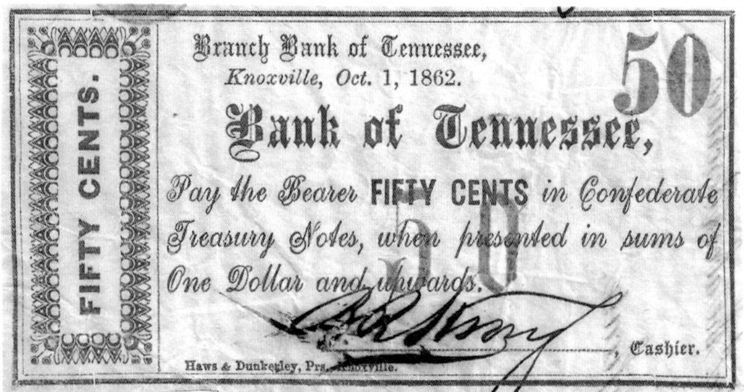

Overprint: Red thin 50 / 50. ***Engraver:*** Haws & Dunkerley. ***Comments:*** H-TN-195-G216a, Garland-429. Similar to W-TN-365-00.50-G110 but with signature line for cashier. Oct. 1, 1862.

Rarity: URS-6
F $150

Non-Valid Issues

$20 • W-TN-365-020-C050

SI, SI

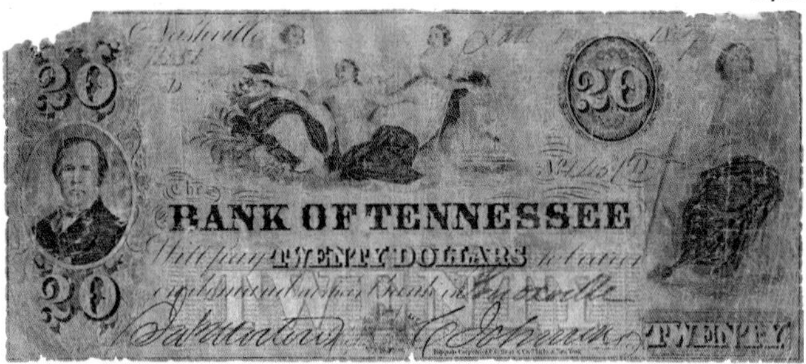

Tint: Red-orange lathework and panel of microlettering outlining white TWENTY. ***Back:*** Red-orange. ***Engraver:*** Toppan, Carpenter, Casilear & Co. ***Comments:*** H-Unlisted. Counterfeit of W-TN-365-020-G050. 18__. 1850s.

Rarity: URS-4
G $225

Citizens Bank of Nashville and Memphis (branch)

1852–1858

W-TN-370

History: On February 25, 1852, the Citizens Bank of Nashville and Memphis was chartered with an authorized capital of $200,000, limited to $500,000. The doors opened for business in 1854. Immediately the bank was held to be in good standing. By 1858, however, the bank had closed its affairs.

The Citizens Bank of Nashville and Memphis had its parent banks located at Memphis, W-TN-510, and Nashville, W-TN-730.

Numismatic Commentary: Notes from this branch are relatively scarce and harder to find than the estimated survival rates would suggest. Most available will be the $1, $2, and $5 notes, but the $3, $10, $20, $50, and $100 notes are decidedly rare. The overall challenge to this bank is likely due to pressure from collectors of Memphis, Nashville, and/or Knoxville notes and city memorabilia.

Valid Issues

Notes Dated at Nashville

$1 • W-TN-370-001-G010

Left: Portrait of Andrew Jackson / 1. ***Center:*** Ship. ***Right:*** 1 / Female portrait / 1. ***Engraver:*** Toppan, Carpenter, Casilear & Co. ***Comments:*** H-TN-145-G18, Garland-439. 185_. 1850s.

Rarity: —

$2 • W-TN-370-002-G020

Left: 2 / Portrait of Governor Aaron V. Brown. ***Center:*** Oxen drawing cart, Farmer. ***Right:*** 2 / Indian reclining. ***Engraver:*** Toppan, Carpenter, Casilear & Co. ***Comments:*** H-TN-145-G20, Garland-442. 185_. 1850s.

Rarity: —

$3 • W-TN-370-003-G030

CC

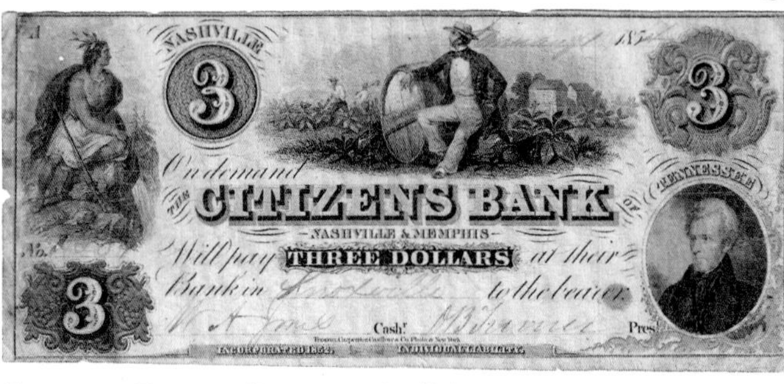

Engraver: Toppan, Carpenter, Casilear & Co. ***Comments:*** H-TN-145-G22. 185_. 1850s.

Rarity: URS-3
F $350

$5 • W-TN-370-005-G040

CC

Engraver: Toppan, Carpenter, Casilear & Co. ***Comments:*** H-TN-145-G24, Garland-446. 185_. 1850s.

Rarity: URS-4
F $250

$10 • **W-TN-370-010-G050**

Left: 10 / Portrait of Andrew Jackson. ***Center:*** Soldiers on horseback, Battle. ***Right:*** 10 / Cotton plant. ***Engraver:*** Toppan, Carpenter, Casilear & Co. ***Comments:*** H-TN-145-G26, Garland-448. 185_. 1850s.

Rarity: URS-3
F $350

$20 • **W-TN-370-020-G060**

Left: Portrait of Andrew Jackson / 20. ***Center:*** Woman seated with bale, sheaf, shield, barrel. ***Right:*** 20 / Portrait of Judge John Catron. ***Engraver:*** Toppan, Carpenter, Casilear & Co. ***Comments:*** H-TN-145-G28, Garland-450. 185_. 1850s.

Rarity: URS-3
F $350

$50 • **W-TN-370-050-G070**

CC

Engraver: Toppan, Carpenter, Casilear & Co. ***Comments:*** H-TN-145-G30, Garland-452. 185_. 1850s.

Rarity: URS-1
F $1,400

$100 • **W-TN-370-100-G080**

Left: Three women holding shield aloft / 100. ***Center:*** 100 / Eagle with shield. ***Right:*** Portrait of Andrew Jackson / C. ***Engraver:*** Toppan, Carpenter, Casilear & Co. ***Comments:*** H-TN-145-G32. 185_. 1850s.

Rarity: —

Notes Dated at Memphis

$1 • **W-TN-370-001-G090**

CC

Engraver: Toppan, Carpenter, Casilear & Co. ***Comments:*** H-TN-145-G66, Garland-440. 185_. 1850s.

Rarity: URS-7
F $250

$1 • **W-TN-370-001-G090a**

SI

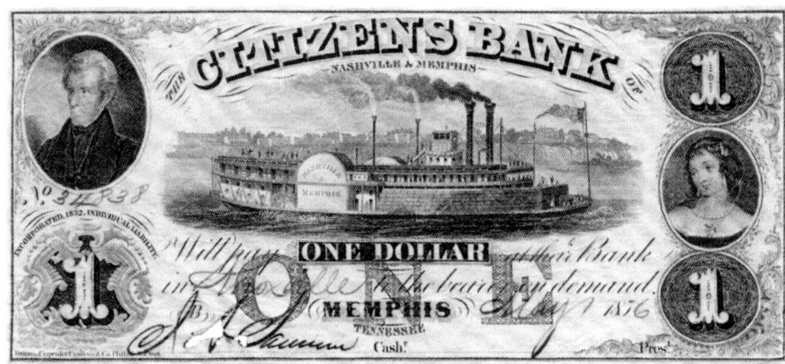

Overprint: Red ONE. ***Engraver:*** Toppan, Carpenter, Casilear & Co. ***Comments:*** H-TN-145-G66a, Garland-441. Similar to W-TN-370-001-G090. 185_. 1850s.

Rarity: URS-7
F $175; **EF** $400

$2 • **W-TN-370-002-G100**

Left: 2 / Portrait of Governor Aaron V. Brown. ***Center:*** Oxen drawing cart, Farmer. ***Right:*** 2 / Indian reclining. ***Engraver:*** Toppan, Carpenter, Casilear & Co. ***Comments:*** H-TN-145-G68, Garland-443. 185_. 1850s.

Rarity: —

$2 • **W-TN-370-002-G100a**

GB

Overprint: Red TWO. ***Engraver:*** Toppan, Carpenter, Casilear & Co. ***Comments:*** H-TN-145-G68a, Garland-444. Similar to W-TN-370-002-G100. 185_. 1850s.

Rarity: URS-6
VF $300; **EF** $400

$3 • **W-TN-370-003-G110**

GB

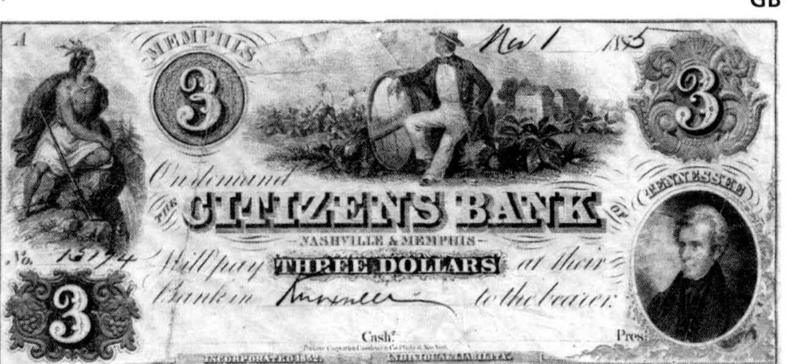

Engraver: Toppan, Carpenter, Casilear & Co. ***Comments:*** H-TN-145-G70, Garland-445. 185_. 1850s.

Rarity: URS-5
F $300

$5 • **W-TN-370-005-G120** CC

Engraver: Toppan, Carpenter, Casilear & Co. ***Comments:*** H-TN-145-G72, Garland-447. 185_. 1850s.

Rarity: URS-6
F $275

$10 • **W-TN-370-010-G130** CC

Engraver: Toppan, Carpenter, Casilear & Co. ***Comments:*** H-TN-145-G74, Garland-449. 18__. 1850s.

Rarity: URS-5
F $350

$20 • **W-TN-370-020-G140** CC

Engraver: Toppan, Carpenter, Casilear & Co. ***Comments:*** H-TN-145-G78, Garland-451. 18__. 1850s.

Rarity: URS-5
F $350

$50 • **W-TN-370-050-G150** ANS

Engraver: Toppan, Carpenter, Casilear & Co. ***Comments:*** H-TN-145-G80, Garland-453. 185_. 1850s.

Rarity: URS-2
F $650

$100 • **W-TN-370-100-G160** CC

Engraver: Toppan, Carpenter, Casilear & Co. ***Comments:*** H-TN-145-G82, Garland-454. 185_. 1850s.

Rarity: URS-3
F $1,300; **VF** $1,600
Selected auction price(s): Heritage Auctions, January 20, 2015, Lot 83263, Choice About New $1,292; Heritage Auctions, April 27, 2011, Lot 15322, Choice About New $1,038

Non-Valid Issues

$10 • **W-TN-370-010-R010**

Engraver: Toppan, Carpenter, Casilear & Co. ***Comments:*** H-TN-145-R5. Raised from W-TN-370-001-G010. 185_. 1850s.

Rarity: —

Farmers Bank

1854–1858

W-TN-375

History: The Farmers Bank was chartered in 1854 with an authorized capital of $50,000. It commenced operations on January 3, 1855. H.L. McClung was elected president, and A. McClung became the cashier. In 1857 W.B. Shapard took the position of president, and William T. Wheless replaced McClung as cashier. In 1858 the bank was liquidated.

Numismatic Commentary: Notes from this bank are very scarce. Garland knew of signed and issued $1, $2, and $5 notes. Higher denominations are known only as Proofs.

The 1990 Christie's sale of the American Bank Note Co. archives produced two $1-$1-$1-$2 sheets and a partial $5-$5 sheet.

Valid Issues

$1 • **W-TN-375-001-G010**

Left: Farmer on horse with sheep / ONE. ***Center:*** Portrait of Hugh Lawson White. ***Right:*** 1 / Woman seated with shield. ***Overprint:*** Red ONE. ***Engraver:*** Danforth, Wright & Co. ***Comments:*** H-TN-60-G2a. November 1st, 1853.

Rarity: URS-4
F $300

$1 • W-TN-375-001-G010a

CC

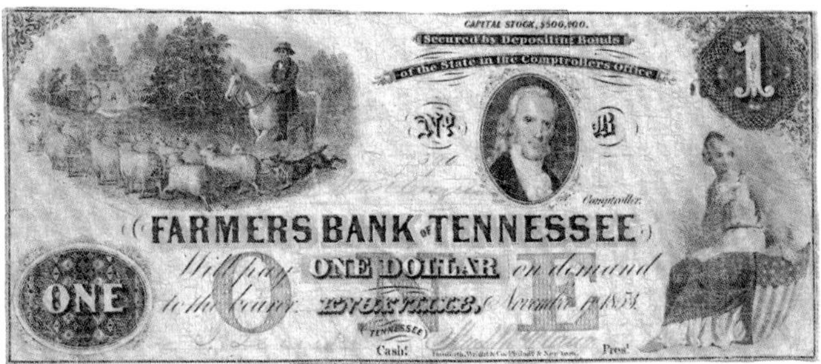

Overprint: Green ONE. ***Engraver:*** Danforth, Wright & Co. ***Comments:*** H-Unlisted, Garland-455. Similar to W-TN-375-001-G010. November 1st, 1853.

Rarity: URS-4
F $1,400; **Proof** $1,250
Selected auction price: Heritage Auctions, September 25, 2013, Lot 16087, Proof $940

$2 • W-TN-375-002-G020

Left: 2 / Male portrait / TWO. ***Center:*** Man on horse, boy, livestock. ***Right:*** 2 / Cattle on road, Bridge. ***Overprint:*** Red TWO. ***Engraver:*** Danforth, Wright & Co. ***Comments:*** H-TN-60-G4a, Garland-456. November 1st, 1853.

Rarity: URS-4
F $300

$5 • W-TN-375-005-G030

Left: Woman with flowers / 5. ***Center:*** Farmer with scythe and sailor flanking shield. ***Right:*** 5 / FIVE / FIVE / 5 over V. ***Overprint:*** Red. ***Engraver:*** Danforth, Wright & Co. ***Comments:*** H-TN-60-G6, Garland-457. November 1st, 1853.

Rarity: URS-3
F $375

$5 • W-TN-375-005-G030a

CC

Overprint: None. ***Engraver:*** Danforth, Wright & Co. ***Comments:*** H-Unlisted. Similar to W-TN-375-005-G030 but with different date. June 1st, 1856.

Rarity: URS-3
G $250; **F** $400

$10 • W-TN-375-010-G040

Comments: H-TN-60-G8, Garland-458. No description available. 18__. 1850s.

Rarity: *None known*

$20 • W-TN-375-020-G050

Comments: H-TN-60-G10, Garland-459. No description available. 18__. 1850s.

Rarity: *None known*

$50 • W-TN-375-050-G060

Comments: H-TN-60-G12, Garland-460. No description available. 18__. 1850s.

Rarity: *None known*

Miners and Manufacturers Bank

1854–1859

W-TN-380

History: The Miners and Manufacturers Bank was chartered in 1854 with an authorized capital of $2,000,000. Joseph L. King was elected president, and H.L. McClung, former president of the Farmers Bank, W-TN-375, was to be the cashier. In 1855 the capital was $500,000. By 1859 the bank had liquidated and closed its business.

Numismatic Commentary: This is one of the rarest issuing banks in the state of Tennessee. The $5, W-TN-380-005-G010, is reasonably collectible. All other notes are prohibitively rare or available so seldom as to be a rare opportunity. Proofs are known of $1, $5, and $10 notes.

Remaining at the American Bank Note Co. archives as of 2003 was a $1-$1-$2-$3 face plate. The 1990 Christie's sale of the American Bank Note Co. archives produced a $5-$5-$10-$10 sheet.

Valid Issues

$5 • W-TN-380-005-G010

CC

Overprint: Red-orange FIVE. ***Engraver:*** Draper, Welsh & Co. ***Comments:*** H-TN-70-G6a, Garland-464. 18__. 1850s.

Rarity: URS-5
F $500

$10 • W-TN-380-010-G020

CC

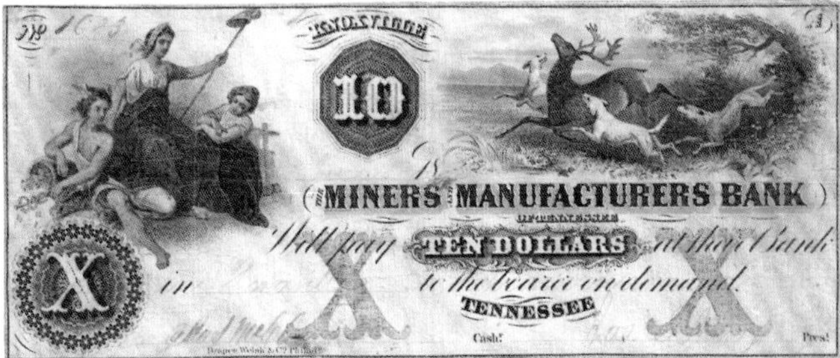

Overprint: Red-orange X / X. ***Engraver:*** Draper, Welsh & Co. ***Comments:*** H-TN-70-G8a, Garland-466. 18__. 1850s.

Rarity: URS-5
F $650

Notes on Which the Place Payable is Blank

$1 • W-TN-380-001-G030

Left: Bales / 1 / Parcels. ***Center:*** Cherub rolling Liberty Seated dollar. ***Right:*** 1 / Woman standing with corn and 1. ***Engraver:*** Rawdon, Wright, Hatch & Edson. ***Comments:*** H-TN-70-G16, Garland-461. May have been made only as Proofs. 18__. 1850s.

Rarity: URS-3
F $500

$2 • W-TN-380-002-G040

Engraver: Rawdon, Wright, Hatch & Edson. ***Comments:*** H-TN-70-G18, Garland-462. No description available. May have been made only as Proofs. 18__. 1850s.

Rarity: *None known*

$3 • W-TN-380-003-G050

Comments: H-Unlisted. No description available. 18__. 1850s.

Rarity: *None known*

$5 • W-TN-380-005-G060

Left: FIVE / Farmer harvesting / 5. ***Center:*** 5 / Horse-drawn cart, Men walking. ***Right:*** 5 / Female portrait. ***Engraver:*** Rawdon, Wright, Hatch & Edson. ***Comments:*** H-TN-70-G20, Garland-463. May have been made only as Proofs. 18__. 1850s.

Rarity: URS-1
F $2,000

$10 • W-TN-380-010-G070

Left: Three women seated / X. ***Center:*** 10. ***Right:*** Dogs pulling down deer. ***Engraver:*** Rawdon, Wright, Hatch & Edson. ***Comments:*** H-TN-70-G22, Garland-465. May have been made only as Proofs. 18__. 1850s.

Rarity: URS-1
F $2,000

$20 • W-TN-380-020-G080

Left: TWENTY / Portrait. ***Center:*** Three men on horseback, Cattle. ***Right:*** 20. ***Engraver:*** Rawdon, Wright, Hatch & Edson. ***Comments:*** H-TN-70-G24, Garland-467. May have been made only as Proofs. 18__. 1850s.

Rarity: URS-1
F $2,000

$50 • W-TN-380-050-G090

Left: Mechanic, Factory. ***Center:*** 50 / Child with rabbits / 50. ***Right:*** Three cherubs with globe, hammer, anvil, sheaf. ***Engraver:*** Rawdon, Wright, Hatch & Edson. ***Comments:*** H-TN-70-G26, Garland-468. May have been made only as Proofs. 18__. 1850s.

Rarity: URS-1
F $2,000

Ocoee Bank (branch)

1854–1862

W-TN-385

History: On February 25, 1854, the Ocoee Bank was chartered with an authorized capital of $100,000. By 1857 the bank had $96,580 of bills in circulation, and $22,633 in specie was in the vault. Thomas H. Callaway was the president, and Thomas J. Campbell was the cashier. In 1860 the capital had risen to $130,000. W.A. Branner became the cashier, and George A. Branner took the presidency. By 1862 the bank had closed its affairs.

The Ocoee Bank had its parent bank located in Cleveland, W-TN-150.

Numismatic Commentary: Estimates are that as many as two-dozen notes of each denomination survive from this branch, yet notes with the American Bank Note Co. imprint are decidedly scarcer than that.

Valid Issues

$1 • W-TN-385-001-G010

Left: ONE / Forester in front of fire. ***Center:*** Indians in teepee overlooking city. ***Right:*** 1 / 1. ***Overprint:*** Red ONE. ***Engraver:*** American Bank Note Co. ***Comments:*** H-TN-25-G20a, Garland-469. Nov. 1, 1859.

Rarity: URS-7
F $150

$2 • W-TN-385-002-G020

Left: TWO / Portrait of Euclid Waterhouse. ***Center:*** Indian and family in canoe. ***Right:*** 2 / Portrait of Thomas H. Callaway. ***Overprint:*** Red TWO. ***Engraver:*** American Bank Note Co. ***Comments:*** H-TN-25-G22a, Garland-471. Nov. 1, 1859.

Rarity: URS-7
F $200

$5 • W-TN-385-005-G030

Left: 5 / 5. ***Center:*** Female portrait / Man with horses. ***Right:*** 5 / FIVE. ***Tint:*** Red-orange outlining FIVE / FIVE / FIVE. ***Engraver:*** Toppan, Carpenter & Co. / ABNCo. monogram. ***Comments:*** H-TN-25-G24c, Garland-473. 18__. 1850s.

Rarity: URS-8
VF $200

$5 • W-TN-385-005-G030a

Tint: Red-orange outlining FIVE / FIVE / FIVE. ***Engraver:*** American Bank Note Co. ***Comments:*** H-TN-25-G24d, Garland-474. Similar to W-TN-385-005-G030 but with different engraver imprint. 18__. 1860s.

Rarity: URS-5
F $300

$10 • W-TN-385-010-G040

CC

Tint: Red-orange TEN, bank title, 10 / 10, and die outlining white 10. ***Engraver:*** Toppan, Carpenter & Co. / ABNCo. monogram. ***Comments:*** H-TN-25-G26c, Garland-475. 18__. 1850s.

Rarity: URS-7
F $175; **VF** $300

$10 • **W-TN-385-010-G040a**

Engraver: American Bank Note Co. ***Comments:*** H-TN-25-G26d, Garland-476. Similar to W-TN-385-010-G040 but with different engraver imprint. 18__. 1860s.

Rarity: URS-4
F $350

Civil War Emergency Issues

$1 • **W-TN-385-001-G050** SI

Tint: Green. ***Comments:*** H-TN-25-G30a. Jan. 8, 1862.

Rarity: URS-9
F $100

$2 • **W-TN-385-002-G060**

Left: TWO DOLLARS vertically. ***Center:*** TWO / Train / 2. ***Right:*** TENNESSEE vertically. ***Tint:*** Green. ***Comments:*** H-TN-25-G32a, Garland-472. Jan. 8, 1862.

Rarity: URS-6
F $150

South Western Rail Road Bank (branch)

1836–1855

W-TN-390

History: The South Western Rail Road Bank (also sometimes seen as the Southwestern Railroad Bank) was an adjunct to the Louisville, Cincinnati and Charleston Railroad. It was planned to finance the connection of the railroad between Charleston and Ohio, and therefore the bank was chartered to open branches in South Carolina, North Carolina, and Tennessee. There was a branch planned in Kentucky, but the state prohibited banking activities on the part of the institution, and it never came to be in that state. The bank was capitalized at an authorized amount of $6,000,000.

In December 1838 an act was passed to establish branches for the bank, one of which was located in Knoxville, Tennessee. No record of the branch in North Carolina has been found.

See also listing under Charleston, South Carolina.

Numismatic Commentary: Notes of the Knoxville branch of the South Western Rail Road Bank had "Tennessee" handwritten but were printed in South Carolina. All notes are extremely rare.

Valid Issues

Notes Payable in Knoxville, Tennessee

$5 • **W-SC-150-005-G060**

Left: Woman with shield bearing palmetto tree / 5 in die / Two men standing. ***Center:*** 5 in die / Train / 5 in die. ***Bottom center:*** Ship. ***Right:*** Two women / 5 in die / Shield. ***Engraver:*** Draper, Toppan, Longacre & Co. ***Comments:*** H-SC-35-G14a, Sheheen-400. "Tennessee" handwritten. Dec. 1, 1838.

Rarity: *None known*

$10 • **W-SC-150-010-G070**

Left: Woman with shield bearing palmetto tree / 10 in die / Two men standing. ***Center:*** 10 in die / Train / 10 in die. ***Bottom center:*** Ship. ***Right:*** Two women / 10 in die / Shield. ***Engraver:*** Draper, Toppan, Longacre & Co. ***Comments:*** H-SC-35-G16a, Sheheen-Unlisted. "Tennessee" handwritten. Dec. 1, 1838.

Rarity: —

$20 • **W-SC-150-020-G080**

Left: Woman with shield bearing palmetto tree / 20 in die / Two men standing. ***Center:*** 20 in die / Ship / 20 in die. ***Bottom center:*** Ship. ***Right:*** Two women / 20 in die / Shield. ***Engraver:*** Draper, Toppan, Longacre & Co. ***Comments:*** H-SC-35-G18a, Sheheen-Unlisted. "Tennessee" handwritten. Dec. 1, 1838.

Rarity: —

Union Bank of Tennessee (branch)

1832–1865

W-TN-400

History: On October 18, 1832, the Union Bank of Tennessee (also sometimes seen as the Union Bank of the State of Tennessee on notes) was chartered with an authorized capital of $3,000,000. The bank also absorbed the assets of the failed second Bank of the State of Tennessee, W-TN-680, which had been abolished that year. The state subscribed to $500,000 of the bank's capital, to be financed by bonds.

In 1848 James H. Cowan was the president of the branch located in Knoxville. H.A.M. White was the cashier, and the capital was $150,000. In 1865 the Union Bank of Tennessee went into liquidation.

The Union Bank of Tennessee had its parent bank located in Nashville, W-TN-840, and branch banks located in Chattanooga, W-TN-090, Columbia, W-TN-220, Jackson, W-TN-325, and Memphis, W-TN-600.

Numismatic Commentary: All notes from this branch are rare but for the contemporary counterfeit $20, W-TN-400-020-C070. No denomination above $20 was known to Garland.

Valid Issues

$1 • **W-TN-400-001-G010**

Left: 1 / Portrait of Andrew Jackson / 1. ***Center:*** ONE DOLLAR. ***Right:*** ONE / Angel seated in clouds with 1. ***Engraver:*** Draper, Toppan & Co. ***Comments:*** H-TN-210-G94. Jan. 2, 1843.

Rarity: —

$2 • W-TN-400-002-G020

Left: 2 / Portrait of George Washington / II. ***Center:*** TWO DOLLARS. ***Right:*** 2 / Woman seated with bales and sickle. ***Engraver:*** Draper, Toppan & Co. ***Comments:*** H-TN-210-G96. Jan. 2, 1843.

Rarity: *None known*

$3 • W-TN-400-003-G030

Left: 3 / Portrait of Benjamin Franklin / III. ***Center:*** Ships, Two women flanking shield bearing cotton plant and plow, Train. ***Right:*** 3 / Female portrait / III. ***Engraver:*** Draper, Toppan & Co. ***Comments:*** H-TN-210-G98. Jan. 2, 1843.

Rarity: —

$5 • W-TN-400-005-G035

Left: Eagle. ***Center:*** Portrait of George Washington / Steamboat / Portrait of Marquis de Lafayette. ***Right:*** Eagle. ***Engraver:*** Unverified, but likely Chas. Toppan. ***Comments:*** H-TN-210-G100. 18__. 1830s–1840s.

Rarity: —

$5 • W-TN-400-005-G040

Center: Portrait of Napoleon Bonaparte. ***Engraver:*** Underwood, Bald, Spencer & Hufty. ***Comments:*** H-TN-210-G104. 18__. 1840s–1850s.

Rarity: —

$10 • W-TN-400-010-G050

Left: Medallion head / TEN / Medallion head. ***Center:*** 10 / Haying scene, Woman and man, Men harvesting. ***Right:*** Medallion head / TEN / Medallion head. ***Engraver:*** Unverified, but likely Chas. Toppan. ***Comments:*** H-TN-210-G106. 18__. 1830s–1840s.

Rarity: —

$10 • W-TN-400-010-G060

Left: Medallion head / TEN / Medallion head. ***Center:*** 10 / Hebe watering eagle / 10. ***Right:*** Medallion head / TEN / Medallion head. ***Engraver:*** Draper, Underwood, Bald & Spencer. ***Comments:*** H-TN-210-G108. 18__. 1830s.

Rarity: —

$20 • W-TN-400-020-G070

Left: 20 / Woman seated / 20. ***Center:*** Ship / Two women flanking shield bearing eagle, surmounted by eagle / Ship. ***Right:*** 20 / Woman seated / 20. ***Engraver:*** Chas. Toppan. ***Comments:*** H-TN-210-G110. 18__. 1830s–1840s.

Rarity: —

$20 • W-TN-400-020-G080

Center: Portrait of Benjamin Franklin / Portrait of Napoleon Bonaparte / Portrait of Benjamin Franklin. ***Engraver:*** Underwood, Bald, Spencer & Hufty. ***Comments:*** H-TN-210-G112. 18__. 1830s.

Rarity: —

$50 • W-TN-400-050-G090

Left: 50 / Ship / 50. ***Center:*** Portrait of Indian / Woman seated / Portrait of Indian. ***Right:*** 50 / Ship / 50. ***Engraver:*** Chas. Toppan. ***Comments:*** H-TN-210-G114. 18__. 1830s–1840s.

Rarity: —

$50 • W-TN-400-050-G090a

Engraver: Chas. Toppan / Toppan, Carpenter & Co. ***Comments:*** H-TN-210-G114a. Similar to W-TN-400-050-G090 but with additional engraver imprint. 18__. 1840s–1850s.

Rarity: —

$100 • W-TN-400-100-G100

Left: 100 / Justice / 100. ***Center:*** Steamboat, Woman reclining with globe, Cherub / Steamboat. ***Right:*** 100 / Justice / 100. ***Engraver:*** Chas. Toppan. ***Comments:*** H-TN-210-G116. 18__. 1830s–1840s.

Rarity: —

$100 • W-TN-400-100-G100a

Engraver: Chas. Toppan / Toppan, Carpenter & Co. ***Comments:*** H-TN-210-G116a. Similar to W-TN-400-100-G100 but with additional engraver imprint. 18__. 1840s–1850s.

Rarity: —

$500 • W-TN-400-500-G110

Left: 500 / Medallion head of George Washington / 500. ***Center:*** Eagle with shield and cornucopia. ***Right:*** 500 / Medallion head of Benjamin Franklin / 500. ***Engraver:*** Draper, Toppan, Longacre & Co. ***Comments:*** H-TN-210-G118. 18__. 1830s–1840s.

Rarity: —

$1,000 • W-TN-400-1000-G120

Left: 1000 / Medallion head of Benjamin Franklin / 1000. ***Center:*** Eagle with shield and cornucopia. ***Right:*** 1000 / Medallion head of George Washington / 1000. ***Engraver:*** Draper, Toppan, Longacre & Co. ***Comments:*** H-TN-210-G120. 18__. 1830s–1840s.

Rarity: —

Post Notes

$5 • W-TN-400-005-G130

Left: Medallion head / FIVE / Medallion head. ***Center:*** Medallion head / 5 / FIVEs around border. ***Right:*** Medallion head / FIVE / Medallion head. ***Engraver:*** Underwood, Bald, Spencer & Hufty. ***Comments:*** H-TN-210-G124. 18__. 1830s.

Rarity: —

$10 • W-TN-400-010-G140

Left: Medallion head / TEN / Medallion head. ***Center:*** 10 / Hebe watering eagle / 10. ***Right:*** Medallion head / TEN / Medallion head. ***Engraver:*** Draper, Underwood, Bald & Spencer. ***Comments:*** H-TN-210-G126. 18__. 1830s.

Rarity: —

$20 • W-TN-400-020-G150

Center: Portrait of Benjamin Franklin / Portrait of Napoleon Bonaparte / Portrait of Benjamin Franklin. ***Engraver:*** Underwood, Bald, Spencer & Hufty. ***Comments:*** H-TN-210-G128. 18__. 1830s.

Rarity: —

Non-Valid Issues

$1 • W-TN-400-001-S010

Left: ONE vertically. ***Center:*** Woman seated / Woman with sword seated with shield bearing 1 / Woman seated. ***Right:*** 1 / Woman standing / ONE. ***Engraver:*** Underwood, Bald, Spencer & Hufty. ***Comments:*** H-TN-210-S10. 18__. 1840s.

Rarity: URS-3

F $350

$10 • W-TN-400-010-S020

Left: TEN vertically. ***Center:*** Woman seated / Woman with sword seated with shield bearing 10 / Woman seated. ***Right:*** 10 / Woman standing / TEN. ***Engraver:*** Underwood, Bald, Spencer & Hufty. ***Comments:*** H-TN-210-S12. 18__. 1840s.

Rarity: —

$20 • **W-TN-400-020-C070** CC

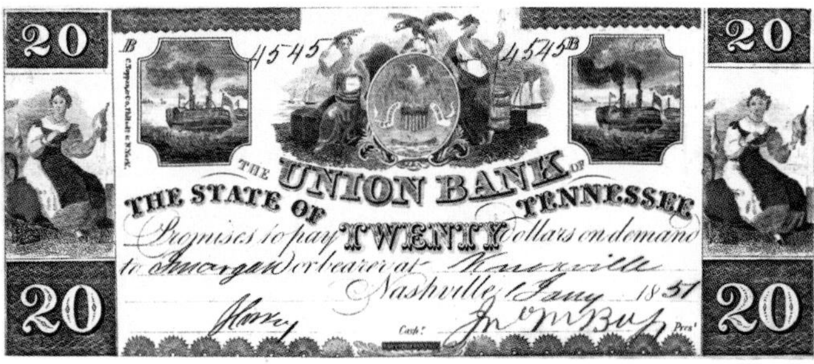

Engraver: Chas. Toppan. ***Comments:*** H-TN-210-C110. Counterfeit of W-TN-400-020-G070. 18__. 1830s–1840s.

Rarity: URS-5
Unc-Rem $450

LaGrange, Tennessee

The land that later included LaGrange was surveyed in 1822 on behalf of the Rains family. The area was divided out, and Samuel B. Harper came into possession of 167 acres in the southern tract. He is credited with laying out the town, which was built on his land.

In 1828 the post office was established, and in 1829 the town was chartered. A store was opened in 1827 by George Gray, and merchants flocked to the area between 1830 and 1840. By the time of the Civil War, LaGrange boasted a population of 2,000 inhabitants in its bustling community. Its location over the Wolf River made it a prime point for wealthy town dwellers who wished to escape the cities in the summer. This same feature also made the town strategically vital to Union and Confederate forces, who alternately vied for the tactical position throughout the war.

Planters Bank of Tennessee (branch)

1834–1865

W-TN-410

History: The Planters Bank of Tennessee was chartered on November 11, 1833, with an authorized capital of $2,000,000. The LaGrange branch opened in 1834. In 1848 the president was R.C. Brinkley. James Penn was elected the cashier, and the capital was $150,000. In 1864 D.A. Shepherd was the cashier, and E. McDavitt was the president. In 1865 the bank was forced to liquidate and close its affairs.

The Planters Bank of Tennessee had its parent bank located in Nashville, W-TN-810, and branch banks located in Athens, W-TN-020, Clarksville, W-TN-140, Columbia, W-TN-210, Franklin, W-TN-300, Memphis, W-TN-570, Murfreesboro, W-TN-630, Pulaski, W-TN-870, Rogersville, W-TN-910, Shelbyville, W-TN-940, Somerville, W-TN-970, Sparta, W-TN-990, Trenton, W-TN-1050, and Winchester, W-TN-1070.

Numismatic Commentary: No notes have been confirmed to exist.

Valid Issues

$1 • **W-TN-410-001-G010**

Left: 1 / Medallion head bearing ONE / 1. ***Center:*** 1 with cherub / Woman seated with boxes. ***Right:*** Woman standing in 1. ***Engraver:*** Rawdon, Wright, Hatch & Edson. ***Comments:*** H-TN-185-G180. 18__. 1840s.

Rarity: *None known*

$2 • **W-TN-410-002-G020**

Left: 2 / Woman with sheaf / 2. ***Center:*** 2 with cherubs / Woman seated with boxes. ***Right:*** Woman standing in 2. ***Engraver:*** Rawdon, Wright, Hatch & Edson. ***Comments:*** H-TN-185-G182. Dec. 1, 1860.

Rarity: *None known*

$3 • **W-TN-410-003-G030**

Left: 3 / Medallion head / 3. ***Center:*** 3 with cherubs / Two men flanking shield bearing cow surmounted by beehive. ***Right:*** Woman standing in 3. ***Engraver:*** Rawdon, Wright, Hatch & Edson. ***Comments:*** H-TN-185-G184. Dec. 1, 1860.

Rarity: *None known*

$5 • **W-TN-410-005-G040**

Left: Medallion head / FIVE / Medallion head. ***Center:*** FIVE / Man standing with dog / FIVE. ***Right:*** Medallion head / FIVE / Medallion head. ***Engraver:*** Underwood, Bald & Spencer. ***Comments:*** H-TN-185-G186. 18__. 1830s–1840s.

Rarity: *None known*

$10 • **W-TN-410-010-G050**

Left: Medallion head / TEN / Medallion head. ***Center:*** 10 / Farm scene, Harvest / X. ***Right:*** Medallion head / TEN / Medallion head. ***Engraver:*** Underwood, Bald & Spencer. ***Comments:*** H-TN-185-G188. 18__. 1830s–1840s.

Rarity: *None known*

$20 • **W-TN-410-020-G060**

Left: 20 / Medallion head / 20. ***Center:*** 20 / Medallion head / 20. ***Right:*** 20 / Medallion head / 20. ***Engraver:*** Underwood, Bald & Spencer. ***Comments:*** H-TN-185-G190. 18__. 1830s–1840s.

Rarity: *None known*

$50 • **W-TN-410-050-G070**

Left: 50 / Medallion head / 50. ***Center:*** Medallion heads / Woman seated, Ship / Medallion heads. ***Right:*** 50 / Medallion head / 50. ***Engraver:*** Underwood, Bald, Spencer & Hufty. ***Comments:*** H-TN-185-G192. 18__. 1830s–1850s.

Rarity: *None known*

$100 • **W-TN-410-100-G080**

Left: 100 / Three women seated vertically / 100. ***Center:*** Medallion head / Boy reclining under corn, Plow / Medallion head. ***Right:*** 100 / Three women seated vertically / 100. ***Engraver:*** Underwood, Bald, Spencer & Hufty. ***Comments:*** H-TN-185-G194. 18__. 1830s–1850s.

Rarity: *None known*

Non-Valid Issues

$10 • **W-TN-410-010-S010**

Left: Woman. ***Center:*** Woman, Train, Steamboat. ***Right:*** Ceres. ***Comments:*** H-TN-185-S84. 18__. 1840s.

Rarity: *None known*

$10 • W-TN-410-010-S020

Left: 10 / Justice with scales. ***Center:*** X with cherubs / Two women seated. ***Right:*** 10 / Justice with scales. ***Engraver:*** Rawdon, Wright & Hatch. ***Comments:*** H-TN-185-S86. From a genuine plate of the Planters Bank of Alabama, Wetumpka, Alabama. 18__. 1840s.

Rarity: *None known*

$20 • W-TN-410-020-S030

Center: Eagle. ***Comments:*** H-TN-185-S88. 18__. 1840s.

Rarity: *None known*

$20 • W-TN-410-020-S040

Left: 20 / Female portrait / XX. ***Center:*** Woman seated near ocean with shield. ***Right:*** 20 / Female portrait / XX. ***Engraver:*** Rawdon, Wright & Hatch. ***Comments:*** H-TN-185-S90. From a genuine plate of the Planters Bank of Alabama, Wetumpka, Alabama. 18__. 1840s.

Rarity: *None known*

$50 • W-TN-410-050-S050

Left: FIFTY DOLLARS vertically. ***Center:*** 50 / Eagle on bale / 50. ***Right:*** STATE OF TENNESSEE vertically. ***Engraver:*** Rawdon, Wright & Hatch. ***Comments:*** H-TN-185-S92. From a genuine plate of the Planters Bank of Alabama, Wetumpka, Alabama. 18__. 1840s.

Rarity: *None known*

$100 • W-TN-410-100-S060

Left: HUNDRED vertically. ***Center:*** Deer, River. ***Right:*** Portrait of George Washington. ***Engraver:*** Rawdon, Wright & Hatch. ***Comments:*** H-TN-185-S94. From a genuine plate of the Planters Bank of Alabama, Wetumpka, Alabama. 18__. 1840s.

Rarity: *None known*

$100 • W-TN-410-100-S070

Left: Medallion head. ***Center:*** C / Factory / C. ***Right:*** 100 diagonally. ***Engraver:*** Rawdon, Wright & Hatch. ***Comments:*** H-TN-185-S96. 18__. 1840s.

Rarity: *None known*

LAWRENCEBURG, TENNESSEE

In 1806 the Cherokee Indians sold the land that would become Lawrenceburg to the United States. In 1817 David Crockett established a powder mill at Shoal Creek. He then helped to select the location for the county seat of Lawrence. At first Crockett was concerned about flooding, with the town being so close to the river, but his opposition was overridden, and Lawrenceburg was established. Ironically, Crockett and his family moved after a flood destroyed his mill.

Lawrenceburg Bank of Tennessee

1848–1860

W-TN-420

History: The Lawrenceburg Bank of Tennessee was chartered in 1848 with an authorized capital of $100,000. In 1849 the capital was $47,348, and circulation was $71,596. S.E. Rose was elected president, and William Simonton was the cashier. In 1857 these values were given: capital $50,000; bills in circulation $56,741; specie $20,266; real estate $3,600.

In 1860 the bank was liquidated. Its assets were sold to W.H. Slover & Company of Memphis, where it became a part of the Gayoso Savings Institution.

Numismatic Commentary: Signed and issued notes are rare and most desirable. Remainder notes are attractive and colorful, with many overstamped "Redeemed by the Gayoso Savings Institution."

VALID ISSUES

$1 • W-TN-420-001-G010

Left: 1 / Woman seated. ***Center:*** Men and women seated, Harvest. ***Right:*** 1 / Indian woman as Liberty seated with shield. ***Engraver:*** Toppan, Carpenter & Co. ***Comments:*** H-TN-80-G2, Garland-498. 18__. 1848–1850s.

Rarity: URS-8
F $200

$2 • W-TN-420-002-G020

Left: Woman holding up 2 / TWO. ***Center:*** Man reclining, Cattle. ***Right:*** TWO / Woman with sheaf / 2. ***Engraver:*** Toppan, Carpenter & Co. ***Comments:*** H-TN-80-G4, Garland-499. 18__. 1848–1850s.

Rarity: URS-7
F $225

$5 • W-TN-420-005-G030

Left: 5 / Farmer with corn / 5. ***Center:*** 5 / Men and women resting under tree, Horses. ***Right:*** 5 / Woman seated in 5 / 5. ***Engraver:*** Toppan, Carpenter & Co. ***Comments:*** H-TN-80-G6, Garland-500. 18__. 1848–1850s.

Rarity: URS-7
F $225

$5 • W-TN-420-005-G040 HW

Engraver: Toppan, Carpenter, Casilear & Co. ***Comments:*** H-TN-80-G8, Garland-501. 18__. 1850s.

Rarity: URS-4
F $300

$5 • **W-TN-420-005-G040a** SI

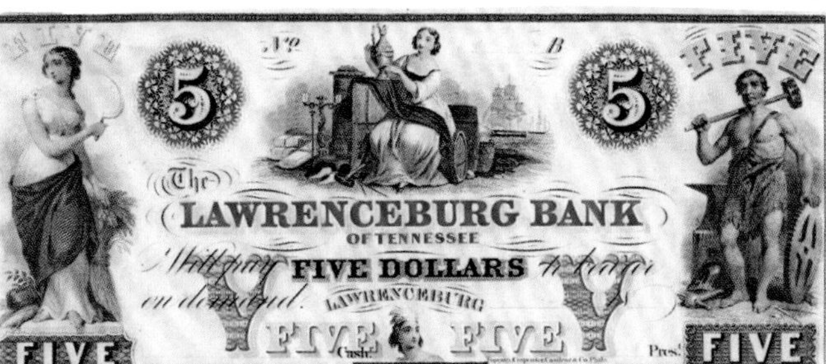

Tint: Red-orange dies bearing white 5 / 5, bank title, and V / FIVE / FIVE / V. ***Engraver:*** Toppan, Carpenter, Casilear & Co. / American Bank Note Co. ***Comments:*** H-TN-80-G8a, Garland-502. Similar to W-TN-420-005-G040 but with additional engraver imprint. 18__. 1850s.

Rarity: URS-6
Unc-Rem $400

$10 • **W-TN-420-010-G050** HW

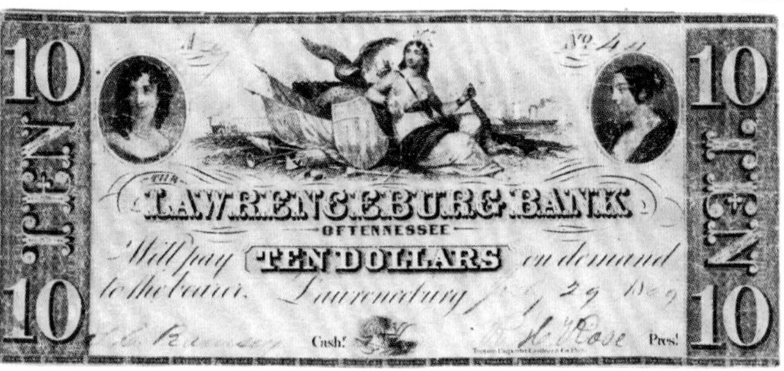

Engraver: Toppan, Carpenter, Casilear & Co. ***Comments:*** H-TN-80-G10, Garland-503. 18__. 1850s.

Rarity: URS-3
F $450

$10 • **W-TN-420-010-G050a** SI

Tint: Red-orange end panels, bank title, and TEN / TEN. ***Engraver:*** Toppan, Carpenter, Casilear & Co. / American Bank Note Co. ***Comments:*** H-TN-80-G10a, Garland-504. Similar to W-TN-420-010-G050 but with additional engraver imprint. 18__. 1850s.

Rarity: URS-6
Unc-Rem $300

$20 • **W-TN-420-020-G060** HW

Engraver: Toppan, Carpenter, Casilear & Co. ***Comments:*** H-TN-80-G12, Garland-505. 18__. 1850s.

Rarity: URS-1
VF $3,500

$20 • **W-TN-420-020-G060a** CC

Tint: Red-orange dies bearing white 20 / 20, bank title, and TWENTY. ***Engraver:*** Toppan, Carpenter, Casilear & Co. / American Bank Note Co. ***Comments:*** H-TN-80-G12a, Garland-506. Similar to W-TN-420-020-G060 but with additional engraver imprint. 18__. 1850s.

Rarity: URS-6
Unc-Rem $350

Notes Payable in Confederate Treasury Notes at the Gayoso Savings Institution

$1 • **W-TN-420-001-G070** ANS

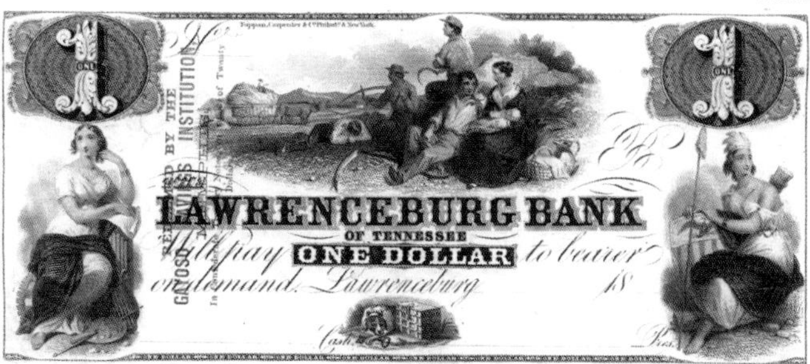

Overprint: Red stamp. ***Engraver:*** Toppan, Carpenter & Co. ***Comments:*** H-TN-80-G14, Garland-666. 18__. 1862.

Rarity: URS-8
F $150

$2 • W-TN-420-002-G080 CC

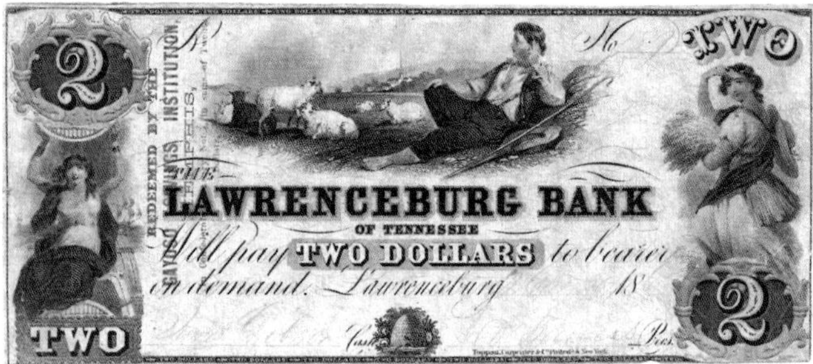

Overprint: Red stamp. ***Engraver:*** Toppan, Carpenter & Co. ***Comments:*** H-TN-80-G16, Garland-667. 18__. 1862.

Rarity: URS-8

F $175

$5 • W-TN-420-005-G090 CC

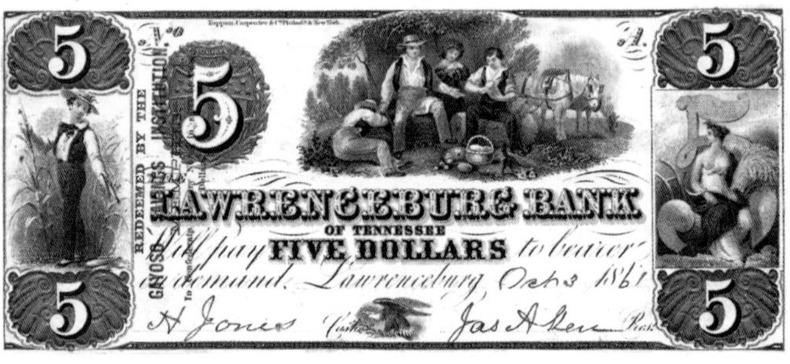

Overprint: Red stamp. ***Engraver:*** Toppan, Carpenter & Co. ***Comments:*** H-TN-80-G18, Garland-668. 18__. 1862.

Rarity: URS-7

F $175; **EF** $300

Uncut Sheets

$1-$1-$2-$5 • W-TN-420-001.001.002.005-US010 RG

Overprint(s): Red stamp. ***Engraver:*** Toppan, Carpenter & Co. ***Comments:*** H-TN-80-G14, G14, G16, G18. First two notes identical. 18__. 1862.

Rarity: URS-3

F $2,000

LEBANON, TENNESSEE

The city of Lebanon was incorporated in 1801. It received its name after the Cedars of Lebanon mentioned in the Bible and also due to the large number of cedar trees that flourished in the area.

Bank of Middle Tennessee

1854–1865

W-TN-430

History: The Bank of Middle Tennessee was chartered in 1854 with an authorized capital of $100,000. The cashier was C.W. Jackson, and the president was S.T. Mottley. In 1857 these values were given: capital $83,509; bills in circulation $80,222; specie $16,352; real estate $3,000.

On June 8, 1865, an act was passed accepting the surrender of the charter for the Bank of Middle Tennessee, allowing the bank to liquidate its affairs and close down.

Numismatic Commentary: A very rare bank to collect. Garland estimated a survival number of two to four notes of each denomination.

The 1990 Christie's sale of the American Bank Note Co. archives produced a $1-$2-$3-$5 sheet and a $5-$10-$10-$20 sheet, as well as two back sheet Proofs in the same denominations.

VALID ISSUES

Free-Bank Issues

$1 • W-TN-430-001-G010

Left: State arms / ONE DOLLAR / 1. ***Center:*** Woman reclining, Shield bearing factory, Sheep. ***Right:*** 1 / ONE / Woman standing with shield and pillar. ***Back:*** Red. ***Comments:*** H-TN-85-G2. 18__. 1850s.

Rarity: URS-2
Proof $1,500

$2 • W-TN-430-002-G020

Left: State arms / 2. ***Center:*** Indian man reclining, Shield surmounted by eagle, Sailor standing. ***Right:*** 2 / Portrait of George Washington. ***Back:*** Red. ***Comments:*** H-TN-85-G4. 18__. 1850s.

Rarity: URS-2
Proof $1,500

$3 • W-TN-430-003-G030

Left: State arms / Male portrait. ***Center:*** 3 / Eagle on shield, Ship. ***Right:*** 3 / Male portrait. ***Back:*** Red. ***Comments:*** H-TN-85-G6. 18__. 1850s.

Rarity: URS-1
Proof $4,000

$5 • W-TN-430-005-G040

Left: FIVE / Woman with sheaf. ***Center:*** Portrait of Henry Clay / Eagle, Ships. ***Right:*** 5 / State arms. ***Tint:*** Red. ***Back:*** Red. ***Comments:*** H-TN-85-G8a, Garland-511. 18__. 1850s.

Rarity: URS-2
Proof $1,500

$10 • W-TN-430-010-G050

CC

Back: Red. ***Comments:*** H-Unlisted. 18__. 1850s.

Rarity: URS-3
Proof $3,500

$10 • W-TN-430-010-G050a

Tint: Red. ***Back:*** Red. ***Comments:*** H-TN-85-G10a, Garland-512. Similar to W-TN-430-010-G050. 18__. 1850s.

Rarity: —

$20 • W-TN-430-020-G060

Left: 20 / Man standing with scythe. ***Center:*** Two men in field, Tobacco, barrels. ***Right:*** 20 / State arms. ***Tint:*** Red. ***Back:*** Red. ***Comments:*** H-TN-85-G12a, Garland-515. 18__. 1850s.

Rarity: URS-2
Proof $4,000

Chartered-Bank Issues

$1 • W-TN-430-001-G070

Left: ONE DOLLAR / 1. ***Center:*** Woman reclining, Shield bearing factory, Sheep. ***Right:*** 1 / ONE / Woman standing with shield and pillar. ***Engraver:*** American Bank Note Co. ***Comments:*** H-TN-85-G20, Garland-507. 186_. 1860s.

Rarity: —

$2 • W-TN-430-002-G080

Left: 2. ***Center:*** Indian man reclining, Shield surmounted by eagle, Sailor standing. ***Right:*** 2 / Portrait of George Washington. ***Engraver:*** American Bank Note Co. ***Comments:*** H-TN-85-G22, Garland-508. 186_. 1860s.

Rarity: —

$3 • W-TN-430-003-G090

Left: Male portrait. ***Center:*** 3 / Eagle on shield, Ship. ***Right:*** 3 / Male portrait. ***Engraver:*** American Bank Note Co. ***Comments:*** H-TN-85-G24, Garland-509. 186_. 1860s.

Rarity: —

$5 • W-TN-430-005-G100

CC

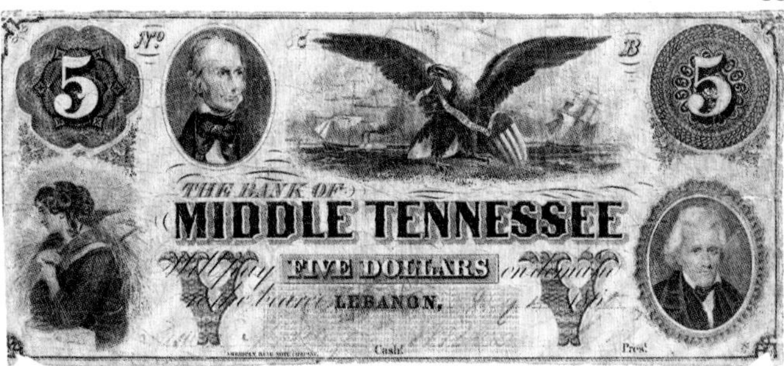

Tint: Red V / V, panel of microlettering, and dies bearing white 5 / 5. ***Back:*** Red-orange. ***Engraver:*** American Bank Note Co. ***Comments:*** H-TN-85-G26b, Garland-510. 186_. 1860s.

Rarity: URS-3
F $1,050

$10 • W-TN-430-010-G110

Left: 10 / Pledge. ***Center:*** Man watering horses beside well, Sheep, goats, house. ***Right:*** 10 / Male portrait. ***Tint:*** Red. ***Back:*** Red-orange. ***Engraver:*** American Bank Note Co. ***Comments:*** H-TN-85-G28b, Garland-513. 186_. 1860s.

Rarity: URS-3
F $1,000

$20 • **W-TN-430-020-G120** CC

Tint: Red TWENTY and dies bearing white 20 / 20. ***Back:*** Red-orange. ***Engraver:*** American Bank Note Co. ***Comments:*** H-TN-85-G30b, Garland-514. 186_. 1860s.

Rarity: URS-3
G $400; **F** $600

MARYVILLE, TENNESSEE

Maryville started out as Fort Craig, settled in 1785 by John Craig. The town was incorporated on July 11, 1795, and it was renamed in honor of Mary Grainger Blount.

Bank of the State of Tennessee {1st} (branch)

1817–1820

W-TN-440

History: The first Bank of the State of Tennessee was chartered on November 20, 1811, with an authorized capital of $400,000. The capital was to be divided into shares of $50 apiece. The state subscribed to $20,000, on the provision that the state reserved the right to withdraw its funds after ten years. Hugh Lawson White was the president. No notes under $5 were allowed to be issued. In 1817 the Maryville branch was opened.

The Bank of the State of Tennessee discontinued business in 1820, at which time the stated capital was $371,107. The branches failed at the same time with a combined capital of $573,915.

The first Bank of the State of Tennessee had its parent bank located in Knoxville, W-TN-355, and branch banks located in Carthage, W-TN-060, Clarksville, W-TN-110, Columbia, W-TN-170, Franklin, W-TN-280, Jonesboro, W-TN-335, Kingston, W-TN-340, and Nashville, W-TN-670.

Numismatic Commentary: No genuine notes are known.

VALID ISSUES

$5 • **W-TN-440-005-G010**

Left: FIVE vertically. ***Center:*** Man plowing with horses / 5. ***Right:*** TENNESSEE vertically. ***Engraver:*** Murray, Draper, Fairman & Co. ***Comments:*** H-TN-75-G120. 18__. 1810s.

Rarity: *None known*

$10 • **W-TN-440-010-G020**

Left: TEN vertically. ***Center:*** Men harvesting corn / 10. ***Right:*** TENNESSEE vertically. ***Engraver:*** Murray, Draper, Fairman & Co. ***Comments:*** H-TN-75-G122. 18__. 1810s.

Rarity: *None known*

$20 • **W-TN-440-020-G030**

Left: TWENTY vertically. ***Center:*** XX / Justice seated / XX. ***Right:*** TENNESSEE vertically. ***Engraver:*** Murray, Draper, Fairman & Co. ***Comments:*** H-TN-75-G124. 18__. 1810s.

Rarity: *None known*

$50 • **W-TN-440-050-G040**

Left: FIFTY vertically. ***Center:*** 50 / Ships / 50. ***Right:*** TENNESSEE vertically. ***Engraver:*** Murray, Draper, Fairman & Co. ***Comments:*** H-TN-75-G126. 18__. 1810s.

Rarity: *None known*

$100 • **W-TN-440-100-G050**

Left: HUNDRED vertically. ***Center:*** Scene. ***Right:*** TENNESSEE vertically. ***Engraver:*** Murray, Draper, Fairman & Co. ***Comments:*** H-TN-75-G128. 18__. 1810s.

Rarity: *None known*

NON-VALID ISSUES

$3 • **W-TN-440-003-N010** CC

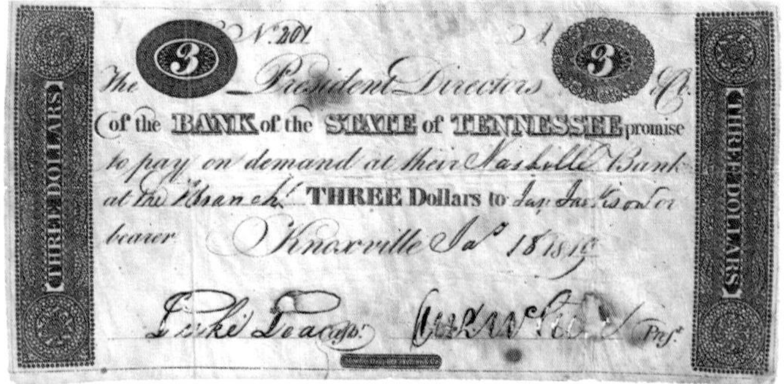

Engraver: Murray, Draper, Fairman & Co. ***Comments:*** H-TN-75-N39. 181_. 1810s.

Rarity: URS-3
F $500

$50 • **W-TN-440-050-N020**

Left: FIFTY vertically. ***Center:*** 50 / Ship / L. ***Right:*** FIFTY DOLLARS vertically. ***Engraver:*** Murray, Draper, Fairman & Co. ***Comments:*** H-TN-75-N42. 18__. 1810s.

Rarity: *None known*

MCMINNVILLE, TENNESSEE

From its settlement, McMinnville was a thriving center of agriculture. It was considered to be the most prosperous village in the area, with a population of 300. There were also five stores, two wagon shops, a silversmith, three blacksmith shops, a shoe shop, two churches, a flour mill, two doctors, and no taverns. Years later, in 1876, the town was officially incorporated.

Bucks Bank

1856–1862

W-TN-450

History: The Bucks Bank was chartered in 1856 with an authorized capital of $50,000. In 1857 these values were given: capital $50,000; bills in circulation $31,465; specie $25,912. The president was William White, and the cashier was Benjamin F. Paine. In 1860 Samuel L. Colville replaced Paine as cashier. In 1862 the bank was liquidated and closed its affairs.

Numismatic Commentary: Remainders exist of "Bucks Bank" notes. Signed and issued notes are extremely rare. Issues with "The Bucks Bank" are possibly unique.

The 1990 Christie's sale of the American Bank Note Co. archives produced two \$5-\$5-\$5-\$5 sheets.

Valid Issues

\$5 • W-TN-450-005-G010

Left: FIVE / Farmer and family. ***Center:*** Indian standing with gun. ***Right:*** 5 / Portrait of Andrew Jackson. ***Engraver:*** Danforth, Wright & Co. ***Comments:*** H-TN-90-G2, Garland-518. Title reads "THE BUCK'S BANK." 18__. 1850s.

Rarity: URS-2
F \$400; **Proof** \$1,000

\$5 • W-TN-450-005-G010a CC

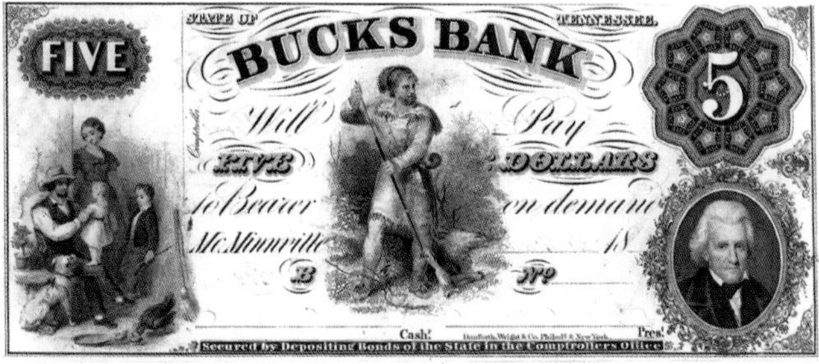

Engraver: Danforth, Wright & Co. ***Comments:*** H-TN-90-G2a, Garland-517. Similar to W-TN-450-005-G010 but title reads "BUCKS BANK." 18__. 1850s.

Rarity: URS-6
EF \$350; **Proof** \$800

Memphis, Tennessee

Memphis was founded on May 22, 1819, and incorporated on December 19, 1826. The first settlers were John Overton, James Winchester, and Andrew Jackson. The town received its name from the capital of Egypt, located on the Nile River.

Memphis soon became a trade and transportation hub due to its location on the Mississippi River. Built on the Chickasaw Bluffs, the town was elevated enough from the river that it could avoid flooding, which was a serious problem and the downfall of many cities that lay along the massive waterway. Cotton plantations were developed in the area, and soon the city was home to a huge cotton market. Hand in hand with the cotton production was a large slave market, providing labor to work the plantations.

The Memphis and Charleston Railroad connected the Atlantic coast of South Carolina and Memphis in 1857, making it the only railway to cross the southern states from east to west prior to the Civil War. The 1840s, 1850s, and 1860s saw a massive wave of immigration as Irish fled the Great Famine occurring in their homeland. German immigrants also made an appearance.

In June 1861 Tennessee seceded from the Union. Memphis was chosen to be a Confederate base, but Union forces quickly captured the town on June 6, 1862. The Union army then used Memphis as a supply base, which allowed the city to continue prospering economically.

Banking House of John S. Dye, Cincinnati

1846–1850s

W-TN-460

History: The Banking House of John S. Dye was chartered by the state of Tennessee on January 26, 1846. Dye was a prolific publisher but a fraudster who bore credentials that many found to be satisfactory, allowing him to produce many publications on bank notes and counterfeit detectors.

Numismatic Commentary: Although unlisted in Haxby, these notes are appealing to many collectors, as the central vignette is the Heraldic Eagle reverse from a Draped Bust silver dollar. All notes are rare with only two of the \$1 imaged below known. The \$5 was unknown to Garland and may be unique.

Valid Issues

Notes Redeemable at the City Exchange Company of Memphis

\$1 • W-TN-460-001-G010 GB

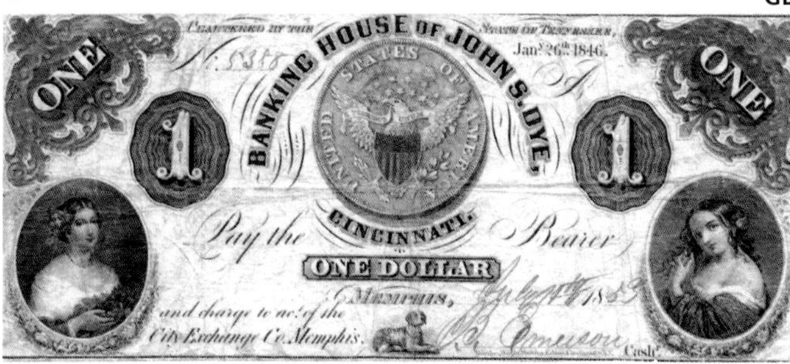

Engraver: Rawdon, Wright, Hatch & Edson. ***Comments:*** H-Unlisted, Garland-594. Jany. 26th, 1846. 1840s–1850s.

Rarity: URS-6
F \$350

\$5 • W-TN-460-005-G020 SBG

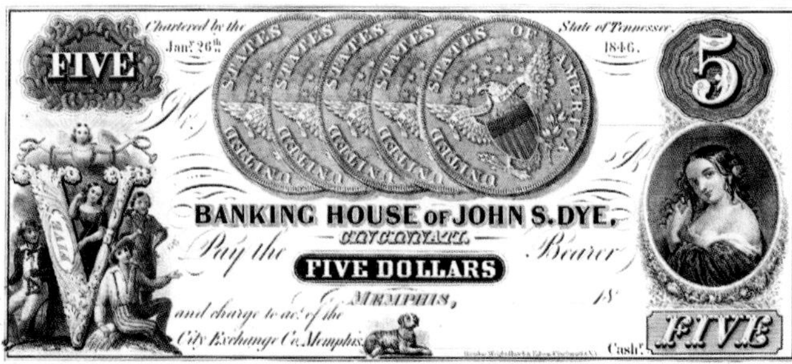

Engraver: Rawdon, Wright, Hatch & Edson. ***Comments:*** H-Unlisted. Jany. 26th, 1846. 1840s–1850s.

Rarity: —
Proof \$300

Bank of Chattanooga (branch)
1860–1860s
W-TN-470

History: On February 2, 1854, the Bank of Chattanooga was chartered with an authorized capital of $100,000, not to exceed $500,000. In 1860 it was realized by the public that the stockholders of the Bank of Chattanooga and the Bank of Memphis, W-TN-480, were the same. On February 8 of that year, the Bank of Memphis surrendered its charter and transformed into a branch of the Bank of Chattanooga. Sometime in the 1860s, the Bank of Chattanooga was closed.

The Bank of Chattanooga had its parent bank located in Chattanooga, W-TN-070.

Bank of Memphis
1854–1860
W-TN-480

History: In 1854 the Bank of Memphis was chartered with an authorized capital of $100,000. W.F. Barry was elected to be cashier, and R.C. Brinkley was the president. In 1857 there was a change in organization and John Overton became the president, with F.G. Roche as cashier. In that year capital had dropped to $50,000.

In 1860 it was realized by the public that the stockholders of the Bank of Chattanooga, W-TN-070, and the Bank of Memphis were the same. On February 8 of that year, the Bank of Memphis surrendered its charter and transformed into a branch of the Bank of Chattanooga.

Numismatic Commentary: Signed and issued notes of the Bank of Memphis are rare, with Garland estimating that perhaps two to four signed notes existed of each denomination.

The 1990 Christie's sale of the American Bank Note Co. archives produced two $1-$1-$1-$2 sheets and a $5-$5-$10-$20 sheet.

Valid Issues
Free-Bank Issues
$1 • W-TN-480-001-G010

SBG

SBG

Back: Red-orange. ***Engraver:*** Danforth, Wright & Co. ***Comments:*** H-TN-110-G2a, Garland-548. Septr. 1st, 1853.

Rarity: URS-3
Proof $1,500

$2 • W-TN-480-002-G020

SBG

Back: Red-orange. ***Engraver:*** Danforth, Wright & Co. ***Comments:*** H-TN-110-G4a, Garland-549. Back of note shown. June 1st, 1854.

Rarity: URS-3
Proof $1,500

$5 • W-TN-480-005-G030

SBG, SBG

Back: Red-orange. ***Engraver:*** Danforth, Wright & Co. ***Comments:*** H-TN-110-G6a, Garland-550. June 1st, 1854.

Rarity: URS-3
Proof $2,000

$10 • W-TN-480-010-G040 SBG

Back: Red-orange. ***Engraver:*** Danforth, Wright & Co. ***Comments:*** H-TN-110-G8a, Garland-552. Back of note shown. June 1st, 1854.

Rarity: URS-3
Proof $2,000

$20 • W-TN-480-020-G050 SBG, SBG

Back: Red-orange. ***Engraver:*** Danforth, Wright & Co. ***Comments:*** H-TN-110-G10a, Garland-554. June 1st, 1854.

Rarity: URS-3
Proof $2,500

Unregistered Civil War Issues

$1 • W-TN-480-001-G060

Left: 1 / ONE / Male portrait. ***Center:*** Three women in clouds with compass, sickle, sextant, anchor, cornucopia. ***Right:*** 1 on shield / Woman standing with shield. ***Back:*** Red-orange. ***Comments:*** H-TN-110-G16. 18__. 1860s.

Rarity: —

$2 • W-TN-480-002-G070

Left: TWO. ***Center:*** Train, trees, factories. ***Right:*** 2 / Woman standing with globe, eagle, spear. ***Back:*** Red-orange. ***Comments:*** H-TN-110-G18. 18__. 1860s.

Rarity: —

$5 • W-TN-480-005-G080

Left: Girl with dog. ***Center:*** 5 on V on FIVE / Hebe watering eagle. ***Right:*** 5 / FIVE. ***Back:*** Red-orange. ***Comments:*** H-TN-110-G20, Garland-551. 18__. 1860s.

Rarity: —

$10 • W-TN-480-010-G090

Left: 10. ***Center:*** Woman reclining, Eagle, Train on bridge. ***Right:*** X / Male portrait. ***Back:*** Red-orange. ***Comments:*** H-TN-110-G22, Garland-553. 18__. 1860s.

Rarity: —

$20 • W-TN-480-020-G100

Left: Male portrait. ***Center:*** 20 / State House. ***Right:*** 20 / Eagle on shield. ***Back:*** Red-orange. ***Comments:*** H-TN-110-G24, Garland-555. 18__. 1860s.

Rarity: —

Bank of the State of Tennessee {3rd} (branch)

1838–1866

W-TN-490

History: The third Bank of the State of Tennessee (also seen in print as the Bank of Tennessee) was chartered on January 19, 1838, with an authorized capital of $5,000,000. The bank opened for business in February. The bank suspended specie payments a couple of times in 1838 and 1839, due to the panic of that time, but afterward it resumed and had a profitable and successful career. The branch in Memphis had a capital of $300,000 in 1861. The cashier was Charles H. Haile, and the president was Joseph Lenow.

During the Civil War, the Union army entered the state, and some officers of the Bank of the State of Tennessee fled south with the bank's specie. After the war, the bank's assets were returned to Governor William G. Brownlow in Nashville. Half of the bank's funds had been transferred into state bonds.

By February 1866 the Bank of the State of Tennessee was authorized to go into liquidation.

The third Bank of the State of Tennessee had its parent bank located in Nashville, W-TN-690, and branch banks located in Athens, W-TN-010, Clarksville, W-TN-120, Columbia, W-TN-190, Knoxville, W-TN-365, Murfreesboro, W-TN-610, Rogersville, W-TN-890, Shelbyville, W-TN-920, Somerville, W-TN-960, Sparta, W-TN-980, and Trenton, W-TN-1030.

Numismatic Commentary: Notes payable in Memphis are relatively scarce with survival estimates of perhaps a dozen or so for each variety. The $3 is the rarest denomination. Notes that are punch-cancelled, "PAID," and signed by a member of the Funding Board are especially desirable.

Valid Issues

$1 • W-TN-490-001-G010

Left: Woman seated with farmer / Female portrait. ***Center:*** 1 / Man plowing with horses / 1. ***Right:*** ONE / Medallion head / ONE. ***Engraver:*** Draper, Toppan & Co. ***Comments:*** H-TN-195-G220a. Mar. 1, ____. 1861.

Rarity: URS-5
F $250

$1 • W-TN-490-001-G020

GB, GB

Tint: Red-orange lathework and panel of microlettering outlining white ONE. ***Back:*** Red-orange. ***Engraver:*** Toppan, Carpenter & Co. ***Comments:*** H-TN-195-G222a, Garland-559. 18__. 1850s.

Rarity: URS-5
F $250

$2 • W-TN-490-002-G030

Left: TWO / Woman seated in 2 / 2. ***Center:*** 2 / Woman seated on bales / 2. ***Right:*** 2 / Ship / 2. ***Engraver:*** Draper, Toppan & Co. ***Comments:*** H-TN-195-G224a. Mar. 1, ____. 1861

Rarity: —

$2 • W-TN-490-002-G040

GB, GB

Tint: Red-orange lathework and panel of microlettering outlining white TWO. ***Back:*** Red-orange. ***Engraver:*** Toppan, Carpenter & Co. ***Comments:*** H-TN-195-G226a, Garland-560. 18__. 1860s.

Rarity: URS-5
F $250

$3 • W-TN-490-003-G050

GB

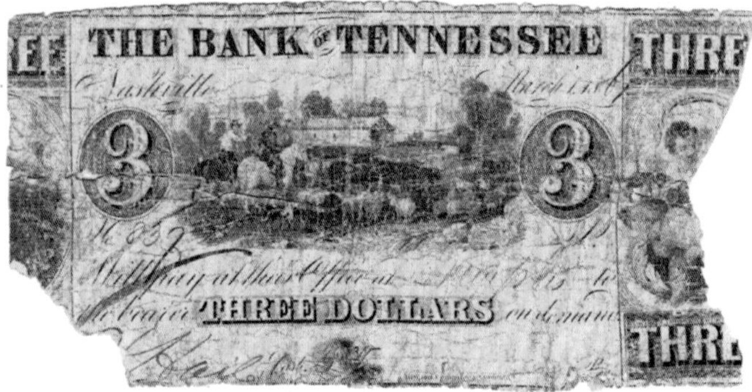

Engraver: Draper, Toppan & Co. ***Comments:*** H-TN-195-G228a, Garland-561. Mar. 1, 1842.

Rarity: URS-2
Poor $275

$5 • W-TN-490-005-G060

Left: Three men / 5. ***Center:*** Portrait of James Madison. ***Right:*** 5 / Medallion head. ***Engraver:*** Danforth, Bald & Co. ***Comments:*** H-TN-195-G230, Garland-562. Aug. 1, 1861.

Rarity: URS-5
F $300

$5 • W-TN-490-005-G060a

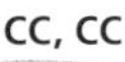
CC, CC

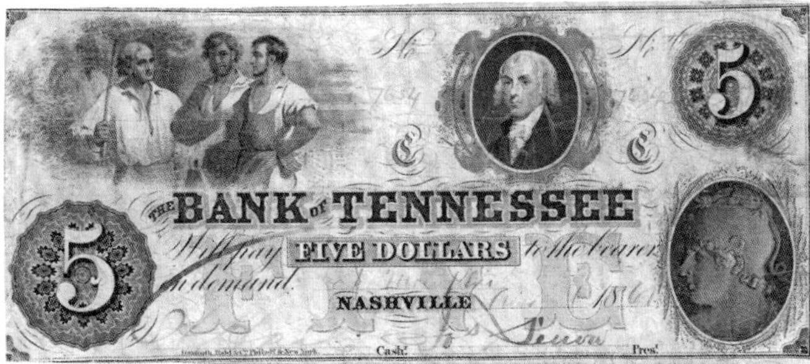

Back: Red-orange. ***Engraver:*** Danforth, Bald & Co. ***Comments:*** H-TN-195-G230a, Garland-563. Similar to W-TN-490-005-G060. 18__. 1850s.

Rarity: URS-5
VF $225

$5 • W-TN-490-005-G060b

Tint: Red-orange outlining white V / 5 / V. ***Back:*** Red-orange. ***Engraver:*** Danforth, Bald & Co. ***Comments:*** H-TN-195-G230b, Garland-564. Similar to W-TN-490-005-G060. 18__. 1850s.

Rarity: URS-5
VF $225

$10 • W-TN-490-010-G070

GB, GB

Tint: Red-orange outlining white 10 / 10. ***Back:*** Blue. ***Engraver:*** Toppan, Carpenter & Co. ***Comments:*** H-TN-195-G232a, Garland-566. 18__. 1850s–1861.

Rarity: URS-5
VF $225

$20 • W-TN-490-020-G080

GB, GB

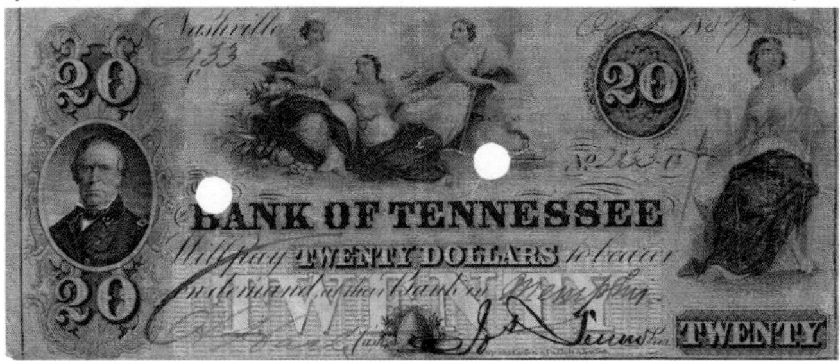

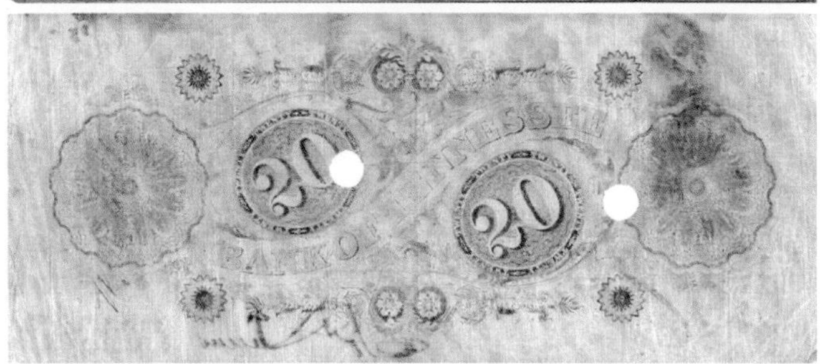

Tint: Red-orange lathework and panel of microlettering outlining white TWENTY. ***Back:*** Red-orange. ***Engraver:*** Toppan, Carpenter, Casilear & Co. ***Comments:*** H-TN-195-G234a, Garland-567. 18__. 1850s.

Rarity: URS-4
VF $300

NON-VALID ISSUES

$1 • W-TN-490-001-S010

GB

Engraver: Toppan, Carpenter, Casilear & Co. ***Comments:*** H-Unlisted, Garland-237. 18__. 1850s.

Rarity: URS-6
F $150

Bank of West Tennessee

1854–1860s

W-TN-500

History: On February 2, 1854, the Bank of West Tennessee was chartered with an authorized capital of $150,000. In 1857 these values were given: capital $85,000; bills in circulation $81,400; specie $25,945. The president at the time was W.O. Lofland, and the cashier was C.D. Smith. In 1860 Ben May took the place of cashier, and T.A. Nelson became the president. During the 1860s the Bank of West Tennessee was liquidated and closed its business.

Numismatic Commentary: Paul Garland recounted that this was an unknown bank until a hoard was brought to a convention in Toronto, Ontario, where the notes were purchased by a dealer from Cleveland, Ohio, and himself. $2 and $5 notes are readily available. $10 and $20 notes are a bit scarcer. $50 and $100 notes are very scarce.

Valid Issues

$1 • W-TN-500-001-G010

CC

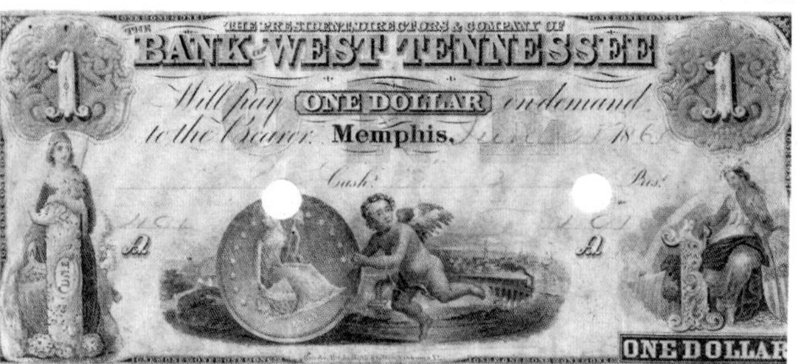

Engraver: Rawdon, Wright, Hatch & Edson. ***Comments:*** H-TN-130-G2, Garland-569. 18__. 1850s–1860s.

Rarity: URS-5
F $150; **VF** $200

$2 • W-TN-500-002-G020

CC

Engraver: Rawdon, Wright, Hatch & Edson. ***Comments:*** H-TN-130-G4, Garland-570. 18__. 1850s–1860s.

Rarity: URS-7
VF $150

$5 • W-TN-500-005-G030

GB, SI

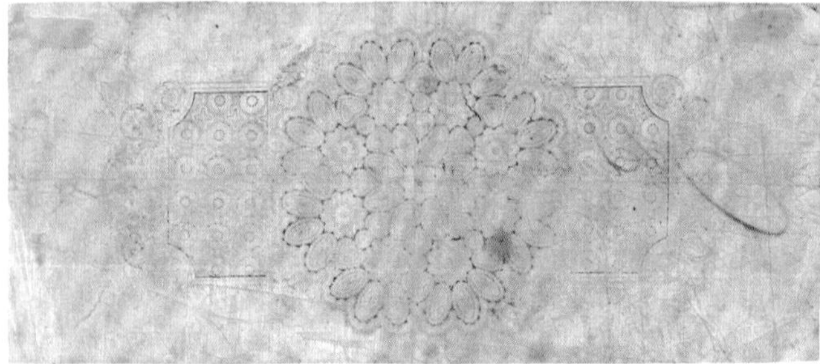

Back: Red-orange. ***Engraver:*** Rawdon, Wright, Hatch & Edson. ***Comments:*** H-TN-130-G6a, Garland-571. 18__. 1850s.

Rarity: URS-8
F $70; **VF** $90

$5 • W-TN-500-005-G030a

SI, SI

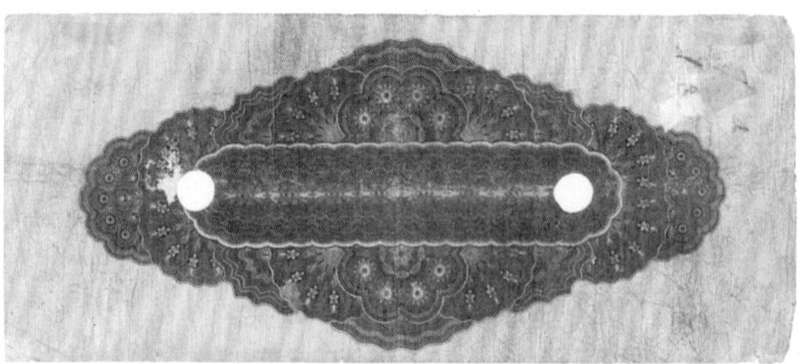

Back: Blue. ***Engraver:*** Rawdon, Wright, Hatch & Edson / ABNCo. monogram. ***Comments:*** H-TN-130-G6b, Garland-572. Similar to W-TN-500-005-G030 but with additional engraver imprint. 18__. 1861.

Rarity: URS-8
VF $75; **EF** $100; **AU** $175

$10 • W-TN-500-010-G040

Left: 10 / Dog, Hunter leaning on gun. ***Center:*** Woman seated against bales, Ships. ***Right:*** 10 / Woman standing with corn and X / TEN DOL. ***Back:*** Red-orange. ***Engraver:*** Rawdon, Wright, Hatch & Edson. ***Comments:*** H-TN-130-G8a, Garland-573. 18__. 1850s.

Rarity: URS-8
F $100

How to Read the Whitman Numbering System

$1 • W-AL-020-001-G010a

Denomination: Face value of the note shown.

W: Whitman number. This number is a sortable code unique to each bank and note.

AL: Abbreviation for the state under study.

020: Numerical designation specific to each bank.

001: The denomination in dollars.

G010a: G indicates a good or valid note. Other categories are indicated thus: C (counterfeit); R (raised); S (spurious); N (not-attributed); A (altered). Numbers are assigned starting with 010, 020, et seq. Terminal letters following the number indicate variations of a note: a series of different colored overprints, tints, payees, etc., all on the same design of note. For more information, see the "How to Use This Book" section at the front of the volume, page xiv.

$10 • W-TN-500-010-G040a

CC, CC

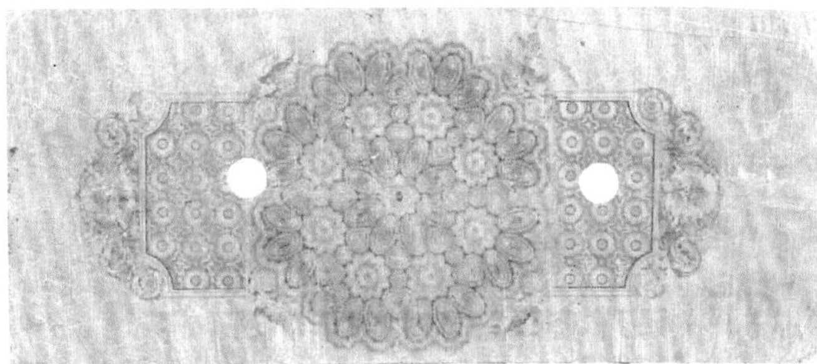

Back: Red-orange. ***Engraver:*** Rawdon, Wright, Hatch & Edson / ABNCo. monogram. ***Comments:*** H-Unlisted, Garland-Unlisted. Similar to W-TN-500-010-G040 but with additional engraver imprint. 18__. 1861.

Rarity: URS-8
F $100

$10 • W-TN-500-010-G040b

CC, CC

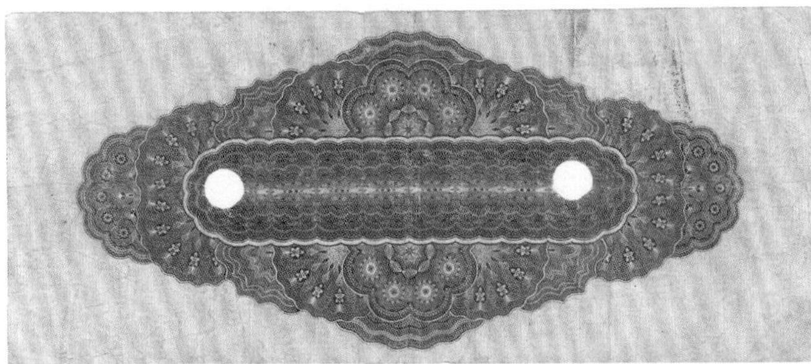

Back: Blue. ***Engraver:*** Rawdon, Wright, Hatch & Edson / ABNCo. monogram. ***Comments:*** H-TN-130-G8b, Garland-574. Similar to W-TN-500-010-G040 but with additional engraver imprint. 18__. 1861.

Rarity: URS-7
VF $125

$20 • W-TN-500-020-G050

CC

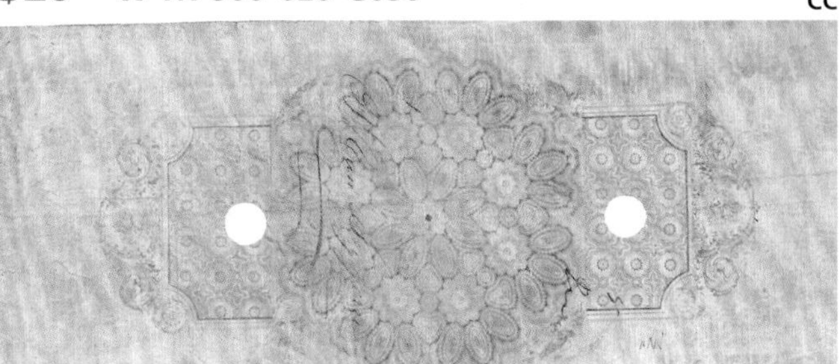

Back: Red-orange. ***Engraver:*** Rawdon, Wright, Hatch & Edson. ***Comments:*** H-TN-130-G10a, Garland-575. Back of note shown. 18__. 1850s.

Rarity: URS-8
VF $125; **EF** $150; **AU** $175

$20 • W-TN-500-020-G050a

CC, CC

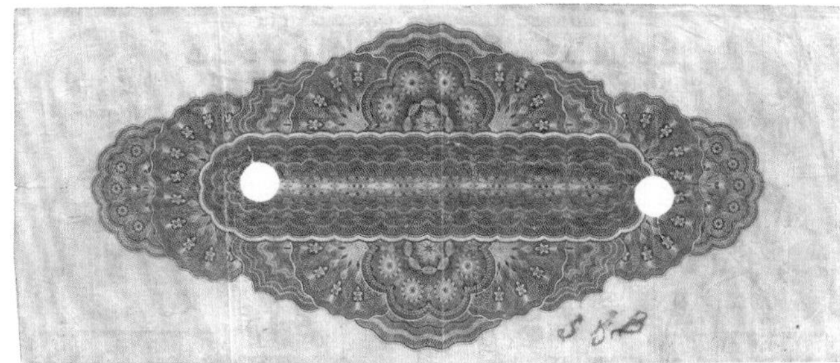

Back: Blue. ***Engraver:*** Rawdon, Wright, Hatch & Edson / ABNCo. monogram. ***Comments:*** H-TN-130-G10b, Garland-576. Similar to W-TN-500-020-G050 but with additional engraver imprint. 18__. 1861.

Rarity: URS-7
F $75; **VF** $100

$50 • W-TN-500-050-G060

Left: 50 / Mermaid and merman / Ship / FIFTY DOL. ***Center:*** Woman seated with bales, spinning wheel, cotton plant. ***Right:*** 50 / Woman standing / 50. ***Back:*** Red-orange. ***Engraver:*** Rawdon, Wright, Hatch & Edson. ***Comments:*** H-TN-130-G12a, Garland-Unlisted. 18__. 1850s.

Rarity: *None known*

$50 • **W-TN-500-050-G060a**

CC, CC

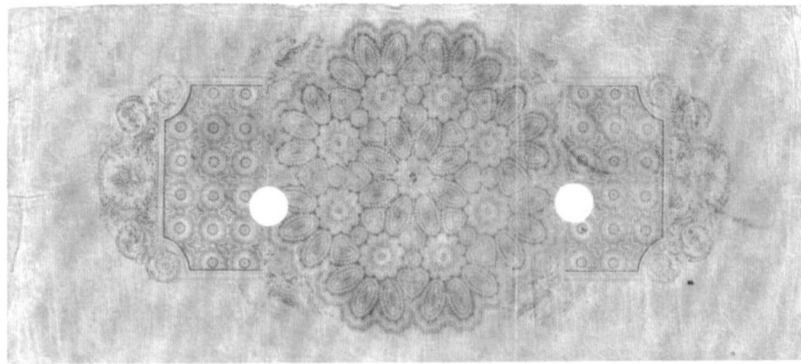

Back: Green. ***Engraver:*** Rawdon, Wright, Hatch & Edson. ***Comments:*** H-Unlisted, Garland-577. Similar to W-TN-500-050-G060. 18__. 1850s.

Rarity: URS-3
VG $150; **F** $290

$50 • **W-TN-500-050-G060b**

CC, CC

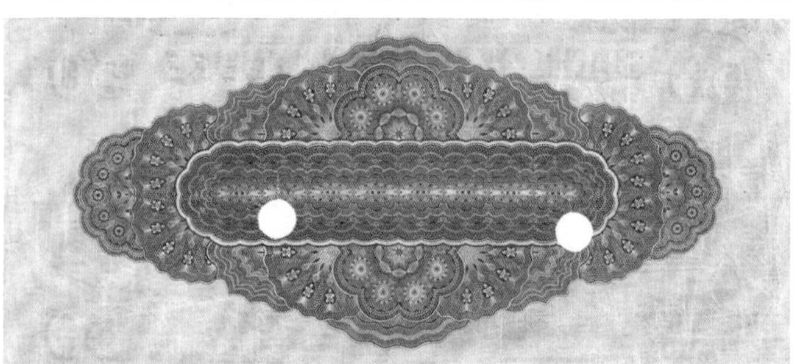

Back: Blue. ***Engraver:*** Rawdon, Wright, Hatch & Edson / ABNCo. monogram. ***Comments:*** H-TN-130-G12b, Garland-578. Similar to W-TN-500-050-G060 but with additional engraver imprint. 18__. 1861.

Rarity: URS-6
F $150; **VF** $200

$100 • **W-TN-500-100-G070**

Left: 100 / Portrait of George Washington / ONE HUNDRED. ***Center:*** U.S. Capitol. ***Right:*** 100 / Liberty seated with globe and shield / ONE HUNDRED. ***Back:*** Red-orange. ***Engraver:*** Rawdon, Wright, Hatch & Edson. ***Comments:*** H-TN-130-G14a. 18__. 1850s.

Rarity: —

$100 • **W-TN-500-100-G070a**

CC, CC

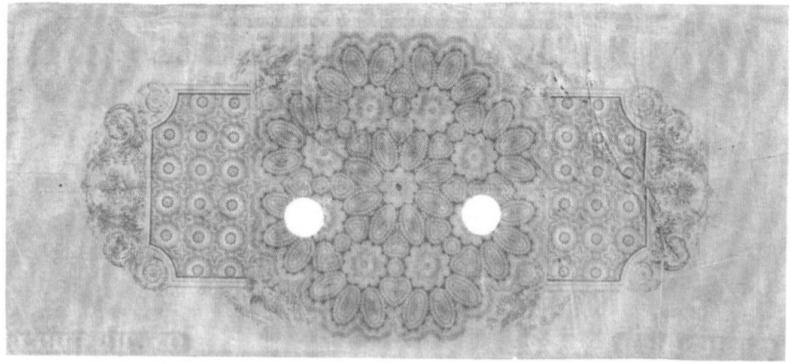

Back: Green. ***Engraver:*** Rawdon, Wright, Hatch & Edson. ***Comments:*** H-Unlisted, Garland-579. Similar to W-TN-500-100-G070. 18__. 1850s.

Rarity: URS-5
VF $350

$100 • **W-TN-500-100-G070b**

CC, CC

Back: Blue. ***Engraver:*** Rawdon, Wright, Hatch & Edson / ABNCo. monogram. ***Comments:*** H-TN-130-G14b, Garland-580. Similar to W-TN-500-100-G070 but with additional engraver imprint. 18__. 1861.

Rarity: URS-6
F $150; **VF** $250

Citizens Bank of Nashville and Memphis

1852–1858

W-TN-510

History: On February 25, 1852, the Citizens Bank of Nashville and Memphis was chartered with an authorized capital of $200,000, limited to $500,000. The doors opened for business in 1854. Immediately the bank was held to be in good standing, with a report in *Bankers' Magazine* stating that:

> The gentlemen concerned in obtaining this charter are of established commercial and financial means and credit, and furnish to the community the fullest guarantees, while their business capacity holds out the assurance that the institution will also be made profitable to the stockholders. We learn that all the stock in this bank was subscribed yesterday, and the first two installments were paid in. This is certainly doing business in quick time, and shows the soundness of the basis upon which the application for this charter was granted.[7]

In 1857 the president of the bank was S.P. Walker, with John A. Sannoner elected as cashier. By 1858, however, the bank had closed its affairs.

See also listing under Nashville, W-TN-730.

The Citizens Bank of Nashville and Memphis had a branch bank located in Knoxville, W-TN-370.

Numismatic Commentary: The Citizens Bank of Nashville and Memphis appears, after the fact, to have been insolvent from opening to closing, with the Committee to Investigate the Citizen's Bank concluding, ". . . are further of the opinion that most of the time from the day of organization at Memphis to the day it closed its doors that it carried on its operation without any actual cash." Lower-denomination notes are reasonably scarce, with survival estimates in the five- to ten-note range. The $100 note is by far the rarest.

Remaining at the American Bank Note Co. archives as of 2003 was a $1-$1-$2-$2 face plate.

Valid Issues

$1 • W-TN-510-001-G010

GB

Engraver: Toppan, Carpenter, Casilear & Co. ***Comments:*** H-TN-145-G50, Garland-585. 185_. 1850s.

Rarity: URS-7

VG $125; **F** $200

$2 • W-TN-510-002-G020

CC

Engraver: Toppan, Carpenter, Casilear & Co. ***Comments:*** H-TN-145-G52, Garland-586. 185_. 1850s.

Rarity: URS-4

VF $325; **Unc-Rem** $300

$3 • W-TN-510-003-G030

Left: Indian woman seated / 3. ***Center:*** 3 / Farmer seated with shield. ***Right:*** 3 / Portrait of Andrew Jackson. ***Engraver:*** Toppan, Carpenter, Casilear & Co. ***Comments:*** H-TN-145-G54, Garland-587. 185_. 1850s.

Rarity: —

$5 • W-TN-510-005-G040

Left: 5 / Train / FIVE. ***Center:*** Liberty seated with eagle and shield. ***Right:*** 5 / Portrait of Andrew Jackson. ***Engraver:*** Toppan, Carpenter, Casilear & Co. ***Comments:*** H-TN-145-G56, Garland-588. 185_. 1850s.

Rarity: URS-5

VF $275

$10 • W-TN-510-010-G050

Left: 10 / Portrait of Andrew Jackson. ***Center:*** Soldiers on horseback, Battle. ***Right:*** 10 / Cotton plant. ***Engraver:*** Toppan, Carpenter, Casilear & Co. ***Comments:*** H-TN-145-G58, Garland-589. 185_. 1850s.

Rarity: —

$20 • W-TN-510-020-G060

Left: Portrait of Andrew Jackson / 20. ***Center:*** Woman seated with bale, sheaf, shield, barrel. ***Right:*** 20 / Portrait of Judge John Catron. ***Engraver:*** Toppan, Carpenter, Casilear & Co. ***Comments:*** H-TN-145-G60, Garland-590. 185_. 1850s.

Rarity: —

$50 • W-TN-510-050-G070

Left: 50 / Portrait of George Washington / L. ***Center:*** Indian woman reclining with eagle, flags, shield. ***Right:*** 50 / Portrait of Andrew Jackson / L. ***Engraver:*** Toppan, Carpenter, Casilear & Co. ***Comments:*** H-TN-145-G62, Garland-591. 185_. 1850s.

Rarity: —

$100 • W-TN-510-100-G080

Left: Three women holding shield aloft / 100. ***Center:*** 100 / Eagle with shield. ***Right:*** Portrait of Andrew Jackson / C. ***Engraver:*** Toppan, Carpenter, Casilear & Co. ***Comments:*** H-TN-145-G64, Garland-592. 185_. 1850s.

Rarity: —

Commercial Bank
1854–1868
W-TN-520

History: The Commercial Bank was chartered on March 1, 1854, with an authorized capital of $100,000. G.W. Lincoln was elected to be the cashier, and E.H. Skaggs became the president. In 1857 these values were given: capital $50,000; bills in circulation $35,650; specie $18,427.

In 1860 J.W. Page became the cashier, and W.M. Folwell was elected president. In 1864 there was a reorganization of officers, and John Ainslie became cashier. J.W. Page Jr. took his father's place as president. In 1868 the bank was liquidated.

Numismatic Commentary: Of all the notes from Memphis banks, Commercial Bank notes stand out for the most complex engraving, visual eye appeal, and extraordinary color. As such, this bank has been a target of accumulators over the years. Small groups of various notes exist but are simply off the market, making the notes seem scarcer than they really are. The $20, $50, and $100 denominations are much rarer than the lower-denomination notes.

The 1990 Christie's sale of the American Bank Note Co. archives produced a $1-$2-$5-$10 sheet.

Valid Issues
Free-Bank Issues

$1 • W-TN-520-001-G010

Left: 1 / Two women reaching to angel. ***Center:*** State arms. ***Right:*** 1 / Panel bearing ONE. ***Engraver:*** Danforth, Wright & Co. ***Comments:*** H-TN-95-G2, Garland-595. Feby. 1st, 1854.

Rarity: URS-3
Proof $1,500

$2 • W-TN-520-002-G020

Left: 2 / State arms. ***Center:*** Two women seated. ***Right:*** 2 / Panel bearing 2. ***Engraver:*** Danforth, Wright & Co. ***Comments:*** H-TN-95-G4, Garland-596. Feby. 1st, 1854.

Rarity: URS-3
Proof $1,500

$5 • W-TN-520-005-G030

CC

Engraver: Danforth, Wright & Co. ***Comments:*** H-TN-95-G6, Garland-597. Feby. 1st, 1854.

Rarity: URS-3
F $550; **Proof** $1,500

$5 • W-TN-520-005-G040

CC

Tint: Red-orange. ***Engraver:*** National Bank Note Co. ***Comments:*** H-TN-95-G8a, Garland-598. 186_. 1860s.

Rarity: URS-5; URS-1
F $350; **VF** $500
Proof $5,400
Selected auction price: Stack's Bowers Galleries, August 2013, Lot 3082, Proof $5,400

$10 • W-TN-520-010-G050

Left: Panel bearing TEN. ***Center:*** X / Man coming home to family. ***Right:*** 10 / State arms. ***Back:*** Blue. ***Engraver:*** Danforth, Wright & Co. ***Comments:*** H-TN-95-G10a, Garland-600. Feby. 1st, 1854.

Rarity: URS-4
F $350; **VF** $500; **Proof** $1,500

$10 • W-TN-520-010-G050a

CC

Back: Blue. ***Engraver:*** Danforth, Wright & Co. / ABNCo. monogram. ***Comments:*** H-TN-95-G10b. Similar to W-TN-520-010-G050 but with additional engraver imprint. Feby. 1st, 1854.

Rarity: URS-3
F $1,000

$10 • W-TN-520-010-G060

GB

Tint: Red-orange. ***Engraver:*** National Bank Note Co. ***Comments:*** H-TN-95-G12a, Garland-601. 186_. 1860s.

Rarity: URS-5; URS-1
VF $500; **EF** $750
Proof $6,600
Selected auction price: Stack's Bowers Galleries, August 2013, Lot 3083, Proof $6,600

$20 • **W-TN-520-020-G070** CC

Tint: Red-orange. ***Back:*** Blue. ***Engraver:*** American Bank Note Co. ***Comments:*** H-TN-95-G14b, Garland-602. 18__. 1860s.

Rarity: URS-3
F $1,000

$50 • **W-TN-520-050-G080**

Left: Cotton harvest scene, Cart. ***Center:*** Female portrait. ***Right:*** 50 / Cotton plant. ***Engraver:*** American Bank Note Co. ***Comments:*** H-TN-95-G16b, Garland-604. 18__. 1860s.

Rarity: URS-2
VF $1,750

$100 • **W-TN-520-100-G090**

Left: Portrait of child / 100. ***Center:*** Steamboat, Wagon loaded with cotton. ***Right:*** 100 / Woman and child. ***Engraver:*** American Bank Note Co. ***Comments:*** H-TN-95-G18b, Garland-605. 18__. 1860s.

Rarity: URS-3; URS-1
F $2,000
Proof $3,000

Unregistered Civil War Issues

$5 • **W-TN-520-005-G100** RG

Tint: Red-orange. ***Engraver:*** National Bank Note Co. ***Comments:*** H-TN-95-G26a. 186_. 1860s.

Rarity: URS-3
VF $600

$10 • **W-TN-520-010-G110**

Left: Panel bearing TEN. ***Center:*** X / Man coming home to family. ***Right:*** 10 / State arms. ***Back:*** Blue. ***Engraver:*** Danforth, Wright & Co. / ABNCo. monogram. ***Comments:*** H-TN-95-G28b. Feby. 1st, 1854.

Rarity: —

$10 • **W-TN-520-010-G120** ANS

Tint: Red-orange. ***Engraver:*** National Bank Note Co. ***Comments:*** H-TN-95-G30a. 186_. 1860s.

Rarity: URS-5
F $400

Uncut Sheets

$5-$10 • **W-TN-520-005.010-US010** RG

Tint(s): Red-orange. ***Engraver:*** National Bank Note Co. ***Comments:*** H-TN-95-G26a, G30a. 186_. 1860s.

Rarity: URS-3
F $750

Non-Valid Issues

$10 • **W-TN-520-010-R010**

Engraver: Danforth, Wright & Co. ***Comments:*** H-TN-95-R5. Raised from W-TN-520-001-G010. Feby. 1st, 1854.

Rarity: —

Farmers and Merchants Bank

1833–1854

W-TN-530

History: The first bank to be established in Memphis and the first bank in West Tennessee, the Farmers and Merchants Bank was chartered on November 27, 1833, with an authorized capital of $600,000. In 1835 it opened for business. In 1837 the capital was $503,940, and circulation was $189,835. The president was S. Wheatley, and the cashier was Charles Lofland. The bank was located on Main and Winchester streets before moving to Jefferson and Front streets.

After more than a decade of operation, the bank finally failed, although notes dated 1854 were issued in an attempt to revive the bank:

> For a brief period it enjoyed a high credit, transacted too large a business, and in the heyday of its career it fell . . . in the spring of 1847, the bill-holders having sustained heavy losses thereby. The wreck of the bank fell into the hands of some adventurous speculators who tried every scheme their ingenuity could devise to resuscitate its existence, and its notes of circulation were briefly foisted upon the public. . . .[8]

The Farmers and Merchants Bank had branch banks located in Bolivar, W-TN-030, and Nashville, W-TN-780.

Numismatic Commentary: Notes issued prior to 1847 are most desirable and very scarce to rare. After protracted litigation, an attempt to reestablish the bank was undertaken with the issuance of numerous notes dated 1854. The issues were prolific. Given the variety of denominations and diversity of designs, this popular bank is fairly easy to collect. Notes of the $3 denomination are the scarcest. The $500 and $1,000 denominations are the rarest.

Remaining at the American Bank Note Co. archives as of 2003 was a $10-$10-$20-$50 face plate, a $1-$1-$2-$3 face plate, and a $5-$5-$5-$5 face plate. The 1990 Christie's sale of the American Bank Note Co. archives produced a $5-$5-$5-$5 sheet, a $10-$10-$10-$20 sheet, two $50-$100 sheets, and a partial $5-$5 sheet. There was also a single $10 note mounted on a card.

Valid Issues

Early Issues

$1 • W-TN-530-001-G010

RG

Engraver: Draper, Toppan & Co. ***Comments:*** H-TN-100-G2, Garland-612. January 2, 1843.

Rarity: URS-4
VF $200; **EF** $250; **AU** $400

$2 • W-TN-530-002-G020

RG

Engraver: Draper, Toppan & Co. ***Comments:*** H-TN-100-G4, Garland-620. January 2, 1843.

Rarity: URS-4
VF $275; **AU** $450

$3 • W-TN-530-003-G030

RG

Engraver: Draper, Toppan & Co. ***Comments:*** H-TN-100-G6, Garland-628. January 2, 1843.

Rarity: URS-4
Prog. Proof $1,900
Selected auction price: Heritage Auctions, September 7, 2011, Lot 15807, Prog. Proof $1,840

$3 • W-TN-530-003-G030a

CC, CC

Back: Red. ***Engraver:*** Draper, Toppan & Co. ***Comments:*** H-Unlisted, Garland-629. Similar to W-TN-530-003-G030. January 2, 1843.

Rarity: URS-4
VG $300; **F** $350; **VF** $400

$5 • **W-TN-530-005-G040** CC

Engraver: Draper, Toppan, Longacre & Co. ***Comments:*** H-TN-100-G8, Garland-635. 18__. 1830s–1840s.

Rarity: URS-4
F $250; **VF** $400

$5 • **W-TN-530-005-G050** GB

Engraver: Draper, Toppan, Longacre & Co. ***Comments:*** H-TN-100-G10, Garland-636. 18__. 1830s.

Rarity: URS-3
VG $300; **F** $350

$5 • **W-TN-530-005-G050a** GB

Engraver: Draper, Toppan, Longacre & Co. ***Comments:*** H-TN-100-G10a, Garland-637. Similar to W-TN-530-005-G050 but with "STATE OF TENNESSEE." 18__. 1830s–1840s.

Rarity: URS-6
F $150; **Unc-Rem** $250

$5 • **W-TN-530-005-G050b** GB

Engraver: Toppan, Carpenter & Co. ***Comments:*** H-TN-100-G10b, Garland-638. Similar to W-TN-530-005-G050 but with different engraver imprint and "STATE OF TENNESSEE." 18__. 1840s.

Rarity: URS-6
F $90; **VF** $150; **AU** $250

$5 • **W-TN-530-005-G050c**

Back: Red. ***Engraver:*** Toppan, Carpenter & Co. ***Comments:*** H-Unlisted, Garland-639. Similar to W-TN-530-005-G050 but with different engraver imprint and "STATE OF TENNESSEE." 18__. 1830s.

Rarity: URS-6
F $100; **EF** $150; **AU** $250

$10 • **W-TN-530-010-G060** GB

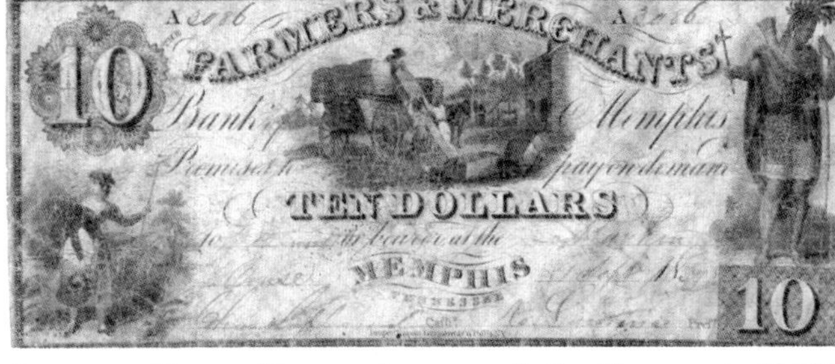

Engraver: Draper, Toppan, Longacre & Co. ***Comments:*** H-TN-100-G12, Garland-648. 18__. 1830s.

Rarity: URS-4
VG $275; **F** $350

$10 • **W-TN-530-010-G070**

Left: TEN / Woman reclining / TEN. ***Center:*** 10 / Indian standing / 10. ***Right:*** 10 / Train / 10. ***Engraver:*** Draper, Toppan, Longacre & Co. ***Comments:*** H-TN-100-G14, Garland-649. 18__. 1830s–1840s.

Rarity: URS-3
F $350; **EF** $450

Collectors and Researchers:

If you have new information about any banks or notes listed in this volume, contact Whitman Publishing, Attn: Obsolete Paper Money, 3101 Clairmont Road, Suite G, Atlanta, GA 30329.

$10 • **W-TN-530-010-G070a** GB

Engraver: Draper, Toppan, Longacre & Co. ***Comments:*** H-TN-100-G14a, Garland-650. Similar to W-TN-530-010-G070 but with "TENNESSEE." 18__. 1840s.

Rarity: URS-6
F $100; **EF** $250

$10 • **W-TN-530-010-G070b** SI, CC

Back: Red. ***Engraver:*** Toppan, Carpenter & Co. ***Comments:*** H-TN-100-G14b, Garland-651. Similar to W-TN-530-010-G070 but with different engraver imprint. 18__. 1840s.

Rarity: URS-6
VF $175; **EF** $250; **Unc-Rem** $400

$20 • **W-TN-530-020-G080** SBG

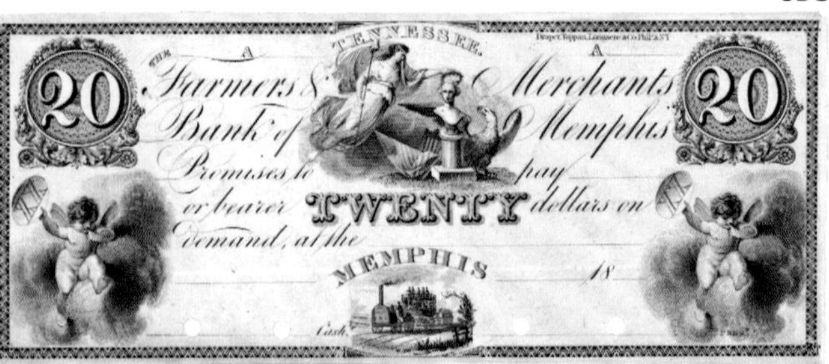

Engraver: Draper, Toppan, Longacre & Co. ***Comments:*** H-TN-100-G16, Garland-654. 18__. 1830s.

Rarity: URS-3
F $300; **VF** $450; **Proof** $1,000

$20 • **W-TN-530-020-G090** SI

Engraver: Draper, Toppan, Longacre & Co. ***Comments:*** H-TN-100-G18a, Garland-655. 18__. 1830s–1840s.

Rarity: URS-7
F $100; **VF** $120 **EF** $200; **AU** $250

$20 • **W-TN-530-020-G090a**

Back: Red. ***Engraver:*** Draper, Toppan, Longacre & Co. ***Comments:*** H-Unlisted, Garland-656. Similar to W-TN-530-020-G090. 18__. 1830s–1840s.

Rarity: URS-7
F $50; **VF** $75; **EF** $125; **AU** $250

$50 • **W-TN-530-050-G100** SBG

Engraver: Draper, Toppan, Longacre & Co. ***Comments:*** H-TN-100-G20a, Garland-657. 18__. 1830s–1840s.

Rarity: URS-6
F $100; **VF** $150; **EF** $200; **AU** $350; **Proof** $1,000

$50 • **W-TN-530-050-G100a**

Back: Red. ***Engraver:*** Draper, Toppan, Longacre & Co. ***Comments:*** H-Unlisted, Garland-658. Similar to W-TN-530-050-G100. 18__. 1830s–1840s.

Rarity: URS-4
F $250

$100 • **W-TN-530-100-G110** GB

Engraver: Chas. Toppan / Draper, Toppan, Longacre & Co. ***Comments:*** H-TN-100-G22a, Garland-659. 18__. 1830s–1840s.

Rarity: URS-6
F $150; **VF** $250

Revived-Bank Issues

$1 • W-TN-530-001-G120

Left: ONE / Eagle / ONE. ***Center:*** 1 / Two women flanking shield surmounted by eagle. ***Right:*** 1. ***Back:*** Red-orange. ***Engraver:*** Draper, Toppan & Co. ***Comments:*** H-TN-100-G40a, Garland-613. 18__. 1850s.

Rarity: URS-3
F $250

$1 • W-TN-530-001-G130 GB

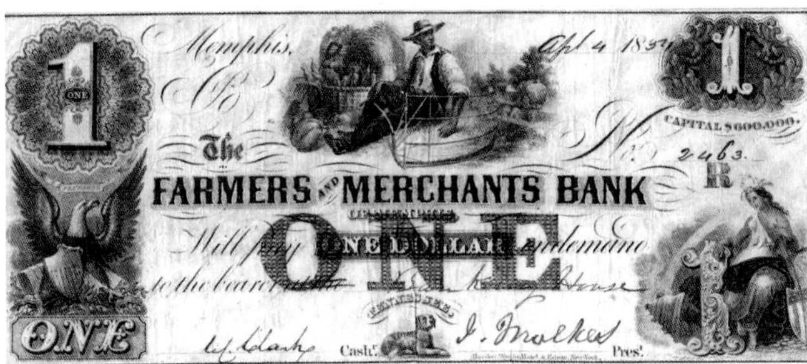

Overprint: Blue ONE. ***Engraver:*** Rawdon, Wright, Hatch & Edson. ***Comments:*** H-TN-100-G42, Garland-614. 18__. 1850s.

Rarity: URS-5
F $75; **VF** $100

$1 • W-TN-530-001-G130a

Overprint: Red ONE. ***Engraver:*** Rawdon, Wright, Hatch & Edson. ***Comments:*** H-TN-100-G42a. Similar to W-TN-530-001-G130. Handwritten "Banking House." 18__. 1854.

Rarity: URS-8
F $50; **VF** $75; **EF** $100

$1 • W-TN-530-001-G130b CC

Overprint: Blue ONE. ***Engraver:*** Rawdon, Wright, Hatch & Edson. ***Comments:*** H-TN-100-G42b, Garland-615. Similar to W-TN-530-001-G130. Handwritten "Banking House." 18__. 1854.

Rarity: URS-8
F $50; **VF** $75; **EF** $100; **AU** $175

$1 • W-TN-530-001-G130c ANS

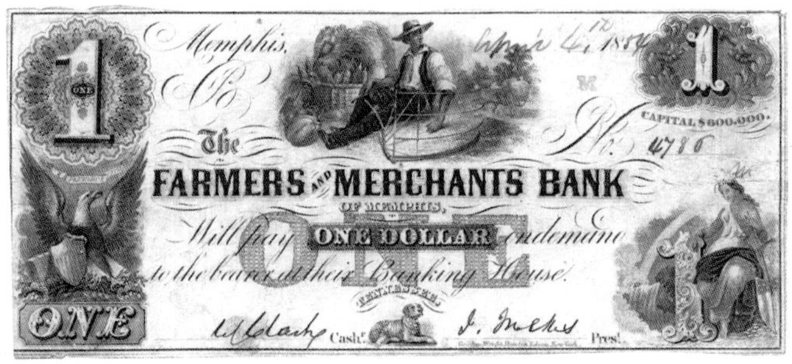

Overprint: Red ONE. ***Engraver:*** Rawdon, Wright, Hatch & Edson. ***Comments:*** H-TN-100-G42c, Garland-616. Similar to W-TN-530-001-G130. Engraved "Banking House." 18__. 1854.

Rarity: URS-8
F $40; **VF** $75; **EF** $100

$1 • W-TN-530-001-G130d

Overprint: Blue ONE. ***Engraver:*** Rawdon, Wright, Hatch & Edson. ***Comments:*** H-TN-100-G42d. Similar to W-TN-530-001-G130. Engraved "Banking House." 18__. 1854.

Rarity: —

$1 • W-TN-530-001-G130e GB

Overprint: Red ONE. ***Engraver:*** Rawdon, Wright, Hatch & Edson. ***Comments:*** H-Unlisted, Garland-617. Similar to W-TN-530-001-G130 but with different date. Engraved "Banking House." 18__. May 1, 1854.

Rarity: URS-8
F $50; **VF** $75; **EF** $100

$1 • W-TN-530-001-G130f

Overprint: Red ONE. ***Engraver:*** Rawdon, Wright, Hatch & Edson. ***Comments:*** H-TN-100-G42e, Garland-618. Similar to W-TN-530-001-G130 but with different date. Engraved "Banking House." Aug. 1, 1854.

Rarity: URS-8
F $50; **VF** $75; **EF** $100

$1 • W-TN-530-001-G130g

Overprint: Red ONE. ***Engraver:*** Rawdon, Wright, Hatch & Edson. ***Comments:*** H-Unlisted, Garland-619. Similar to W-TN-530-001-G130 but with different date. Engraved "Banking House." Stamped "WORTHLESS." Aug. 1, 1854.

Rarity: URS-5
VG $75; **F** $125

$2 • W-TN-530-002-G140

Left: 2 / Cherubs in 2. ***Center:*** Two women flanking shield bearing cotton plant. ***Right:*** 2 / Female portrait / 2. ***Back:*** Red-orange. ***Engraver:*** Draper, Toppan & Co. ***Comments:*** H-TN-100-G44a, Garland-621. 18__. 1850s.

Rarity: URS-5
F $100; **VF** $150

$2 • W-TN-530-002-G150

Left: 2 / Portrait of Benjamin Franklin / TWO. ***Center:*** Train. ***Right:*** 2 / Woman seated with 2 / TWO. ***Engraver:*** Rawdon, Wright, Hatch & Edson. ***Comments:*** H-TN-100-G46, Garland-622. 18__. 1854.

Rarity: URS-5
F $75; **VF** $125

$2 • **W-TN-530-002-G150a**

Overprint: Red TWO. ***Engraver:*** Rawdon, Wright, Hatch & Edson. ***Comments:*** H-TN-100-G46a. Similar to W-TN-530-002-G150. Handwritten "Banking House." 18__. 1854.

Rarity: —

$2 • **W-TN-530-002-G150b** ANS

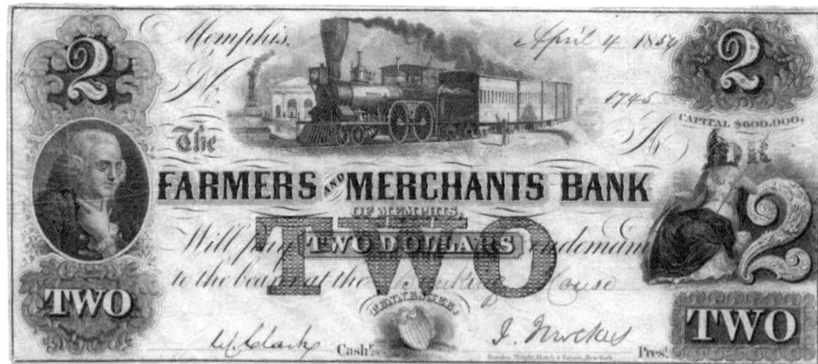

Overprint: Blue TWO. ***Engraver:*** Rawdon, Wright, Hatch & Edson. ***Comments:*** H-TN-100-G46b, Garland-623. Similar to W-TN-530-002-G150. Handwritten "Banking House." 18__. 1854.

Rarity: URS-7
F $100; **VF** $125

$2 • **W-TN-530-002-G150c** 

Overprint: Red TWO. ***Engraver:*** Rawdon, Wright, Hatch & Edson. ***Comments:*** H-TN-100-G46c, Garland-624. Similar to W-TN-530-002-G150. Engraved "Banking House." 18__. 1854.

Rarity: URS-7
F $100; **EF** $150

$2 • **W-TN-530-002-G150d**

Overprint: Blue TWO. ***Engraver:*** Rawdon, Wright, Hatch & Edson. ***Comments:*** H-TN-100-G46d. Similar to W-TN-530-002-G150. Engraved "Banking House." 18__. 1854.

Rarity: —

$2 • **W-TN-530-002-G150e** 

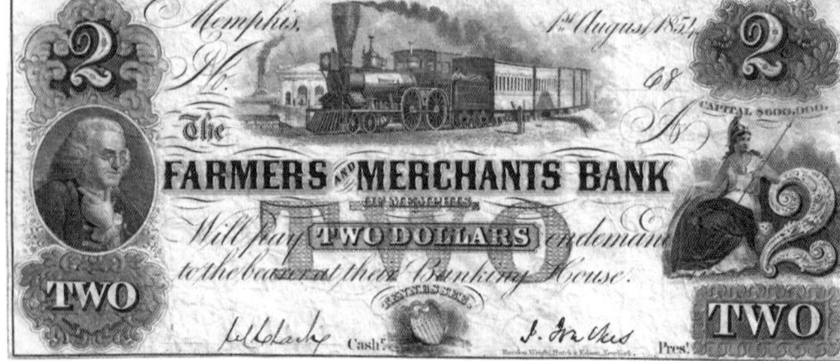

Overprint: Red TWO. ***Engraver:*** Rawdon, Wright, Hatch & Edson. ***Comments:*** H-TN-100-G46e, Garland-626. Similar to W-TN-530-002-G150 but with different date. Engraved "Banking House." 1st August 1854.

Rarity: URS-7
F $100; **VF** $125

$3 • **W-TN-530-003-G160**

Left: Medallion head of Benjamin Franklin. ***Center:*** 3 / Women seated, Ship. ***Right:*** 3 / Three cherubs in and around 3. ***Back:*** Red-orange. ***Engraver:*** Draper, Toppan & Co. ***Comments:*** H-TN-100-G48a, Garland-629. 18__. 1850s.

Rarity: URS-4
VG $150; **F** $200; **VF** $250

$3 • **W-TN-530-003-G170**

Left: 3 / Portrait of George Washington / THREE. ***Center:*** Woman seated, Ship. ***Right:*** 3 / Three men in and around 3. ***Engraver:*** Rawdon, Wright, Hatch & Edson. ***Comments:*** H-TN-100-G50, Garland-630. 18__. 1854.

Rarity: URS-3
F $350

$3 • **W-TN-530-003-G170a**

Overprint: Red THREE. ***Engraver:*** Rawdon, Wright, Hatch & Edson. ***Comments:*** H-TN-100-G50a. Similar to W-TN-530-003-G170. Handwritten "Banking House." 18__. 1854.

Rarity: *None known*

$3 • **W-TN-530-003-G170b** CC

Overprint: Blue THREE. ***Engraver:*** Rawdon, Wright, Hatch & Edson. ***Comments:*** H-TN-100-G50b, Garland-631. Similar to W-TN-530-003-G170. Handwritten "Banking House." 18__. 1854.

Rarity: URS-7
F $100; **VF** $125; **EF** $200

$3 • **W-TN-530-003-G170c** ANS

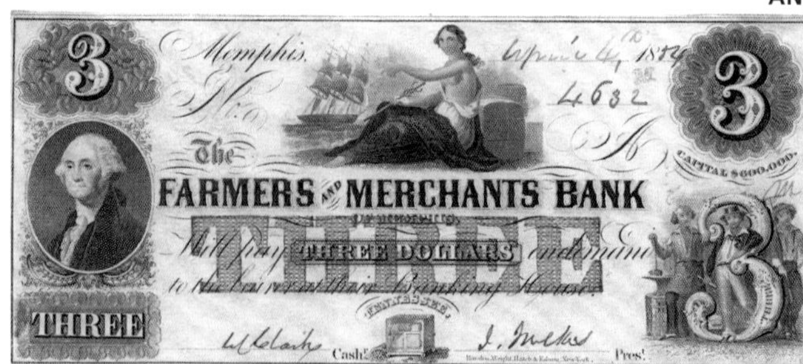

Overprint: Red THREE. ***Engraver:*** Rawdon, Wright, Hatch & Edson. ***Comments:*** H-TN-100-G50c, Garland-632. Similar to W-TN-530-003-G170. Engraved "Banking House." 18__. 1854.

Rarity: URS-7
F $100; **VF** $125; **EF** $200

$3 • W-TN-530-003-G170d

GB

Overprint: Red THREE. ***Engraver:*** Rawdon, Wright, Hatch & Edson. ***Comments:*** H-Unlisted, Garland-633. Similar to W-TN-530-003-G170. Engraved "Banking House." 18__. 1854.

Rarity: URS-7
VF $100; **EF** $150

$3 • W-TN-530-003-G170e

Overprint: Blue THREE. ***Engraver:*** Rawdon, Wright, Hatch & Edson. ***Comments:*** H-TN-100-G50d. Similar to W-TN-530-003-G170. Engraved "Banking House." 18__. 1854.

Rarity: —

$3 • W-TN-530-003-G170f

GB

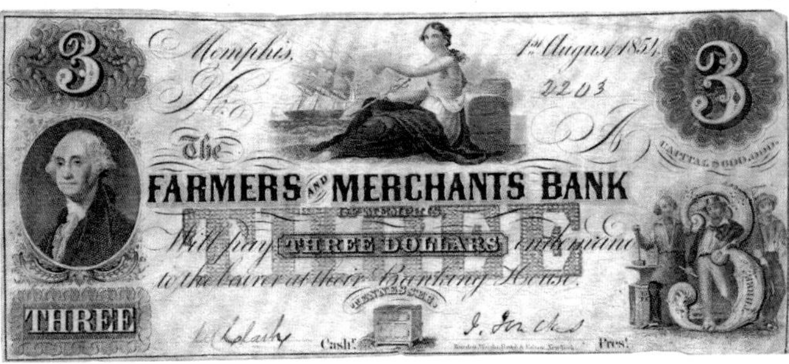

Overprint: Red THREE. ***Engraver:*** Rawdon, Wright, Hatch & Edson. ***Comments:*** H-TN-100-G50e, Garland-634. Similar to W-TN-530-003-G170 but with different date. Engraved "Banking House." 1st August 1854.

Rarity: URS-7
VF $100; **EF** $150

$5 • W-TN-530-005-G180

CC

Back: Red-orange. ***Engraver:*** Toppan, Carpenter & Co. ***Comments:*** H-TN-100-G52a. 18__. 1850s.

Rarity: URS-8
F $150

$5 • W-TN-530-005-G190

Left: 5 / FIVE / FIVE. ***Center:*** Indian woman, hunter, and three cherubs with five coins. ***Right:*** 5 / Female portrait / FIVE. ***Engraver:*** Rawdon, Wright, Hatch & Edson. ***Comments:*** H-TN-100-G54. 18__. 1854.

Rarity: —

$5 • W-TN-530-005-G190a

SI

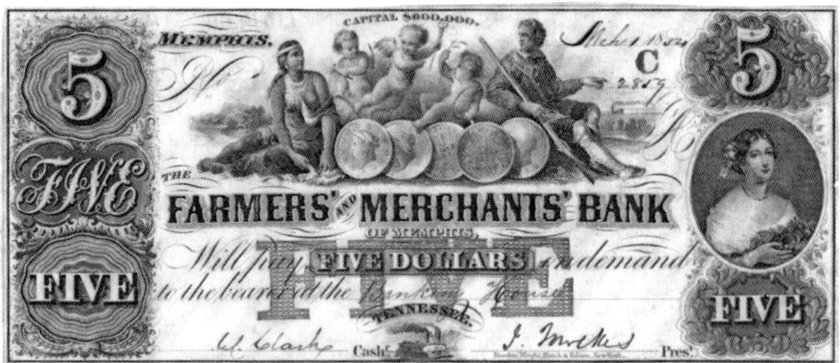

Overprint: Red FIVE. ***Engraver:*** Rawdon, Wright, Hatch & Edson. ***Comments:*** H-TN-100-G54a, Garland-641. Similar to W-TN-530-005-G190. Handwritten "Banking House." 18__. 1854.

Rarity: URS-8
F $50; **VF** $75; **EF** $125; **AU** $175

$5 • W-TN-530-005-G190b

LK

Overprint: Blue FIVE. ***Engraver:*** Rawdon, Wright, Hatch & Edson. ***Comments:*** H-TN-100-G54b, Garland-644. Similar to W-TN-530-005-G190. Handwritten "Banking House." 18__. 1854.

Rarity: URS-7
F $100; **EF** $175

$5 • W-TN-530-005-G190c

CC

Overprint: Red FIVE. ***Engraver:*** Rawdon, Wright, Hatch & Edson. ***Comments:*** H-TN-100-G54c, Garland-643. Similar to W-TN-530-005-G190. Engraved "Banking House." 18__. 1854.

Rarity: URS-7
F $50; **VF** $75; **EF** $125; **AU** $175

$5 • **W-TN-530-005-G190d**

CC

Overprint: Blue FIVE. ***Engraver:*** Rawdon, Wright, Hatch & Edson. ***Comments:*** H-TN-100-G54d, Garland-646. Similar to W-TN-530-005-G190. Engraved "Banking House." 18__. 1854.

Rarity: URS-7
F $50; **VF** $75; **EF** $125; **AU** $175

$5 • **W-TN-530-005-G190e**

Overprint: Green FIVE. ***Engraver:*** Rawdon, Wright, Hatch & Edson. ***Comments:*** H-TN-100-G54e. Similar to W-TN-530-005-G190. Handwritten "Banking House." 18__. 1854.

Rarity: *None known*

$5 • **W-TN-530-005-G190f**

Overprint: Green FIVE. ***Engraver:*** Rawdon, Wright, Hatch & Edson. ***Comments:*** H-TN-100-G54f. Similar to W-TN-530-005-G190 but with different date. Engraved "Banking House." Aug. 1, 1854.

Rarity: *None known*

$10 • **W-TN-530-010-G200**

Left: TEN / Woman reclining / TEN. ***Center:*** 10 / Indian standing / 10. ***Right:*** 10 / Train / 10. ***Back:*** Red-orange. ***Engraver:*** Toppan, Carpenter & Co. ***Comments:*** H-TN-100-G56a, Garland-652. 18__. 1850s.

Rarity: URS-6
F $150; **AU** $250

$10 • **W-TN-530-010-G210**

Left: 10 / Hebe watering eagle. ***Center:*** Ship. ***Right:*** 10 / Female portrait / TEN. ***Engraver:*** Rawdon, Wright, Hatch & Edson. ***Comments:*** H-TN-100-G58. 18__. 1854.

Rarity: —

$10 • **W-TN-530-010-G210a**

Overprint: Red TEN. ***Engraver:*** Rawdon, Wright, Hatch & Edson. ***Comments:*** H-TN-100-G58b. Similar to W-TN-530-010-G210. Engraved "Banking House." 18__. 1854.

Rarity: —

$10 • **W-TN-530-010-G210b**

QDB

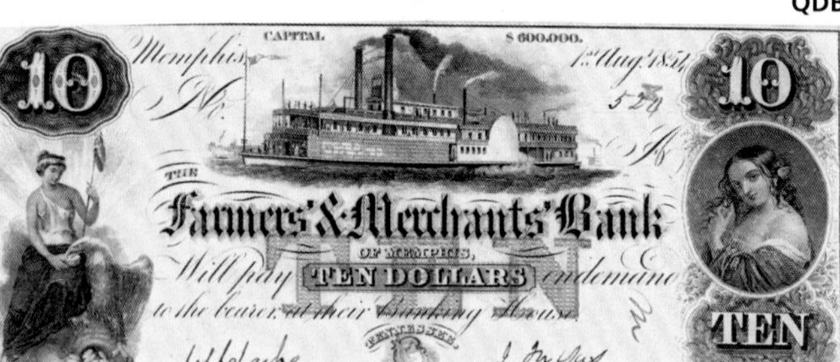

Overprint: Red TEN. ***Engraver:*** Rawdon, Wright, Hatch & Edson. ***Comments:*** H-TN-100-G58c, Garland-653. Similar to W-TN-530-010-G210 but with different date. Engraved "Banking House." 1st Augt, 1854.

Rarity: URS-4
AU $400; **Unc-Rem** $500

$20 • **W-TN-530-020-G220**

CC

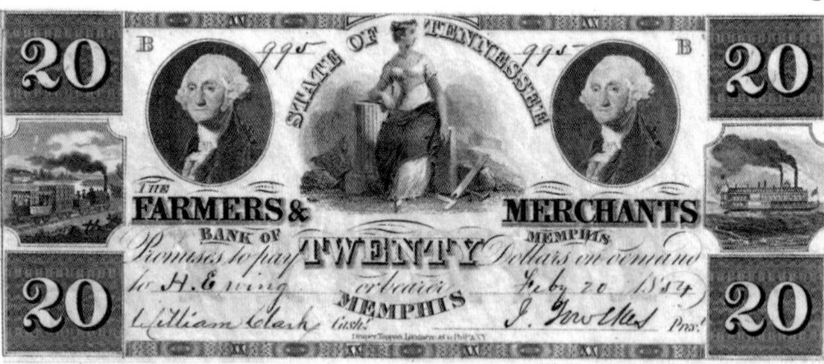

Back: Red. ***Engraver:*** Draper, Toppan, Longacre & Co. ***Comments:*** H-TN-100-G60a, Garland-656. 18__. 1854.

Rarity: URS-7
F $150

$50 • **W-TN-530-050-G230**

LK

Back: Red. ***Engraver:*** Draper, Toppan, Longacre & Co. ***Comments:*** H-TN-100-G62a, Garland-658. 18__. 1854.

Rarity: URS-7
F $200; **Unc-Rem** $300

How to Read the Whitman Numbering System

$1 • **W-AL-020-001-G010a**

Denomination: Face value of the note shown.

W: Whitman number. This number is a sortable code unique to each bank and note.

AL: Abbreviation for the state under study.

020: Numerical designation specific to each bank.

001: The denomination in dollars.

G010a: G indicates a good or valid note. Other categories are indicated thus: C (counterfeit); R (raised); S (spurious); N (not-attributed); A (altered). Numbers are assigned starting with 010, 020, et seq. Terminal letters following the number indicate variations of a note: a series of different colored overprints, tints, payees, etc., all on the same design of note. For more information, see the "How to Use This Book" section at the front of the volume, page xiv.

$100 • W-TN-530-100-G240 CC

Back: Red. ***Engraver:*** Draper, Toppan, Longacre & Co. ***Comments:*** H-TN-100-G64a, Garland-660. 18__. 1854.

Rarity: URS-7
F $200; **EF** $300

$500 • W-TN-530-500-G250 CC

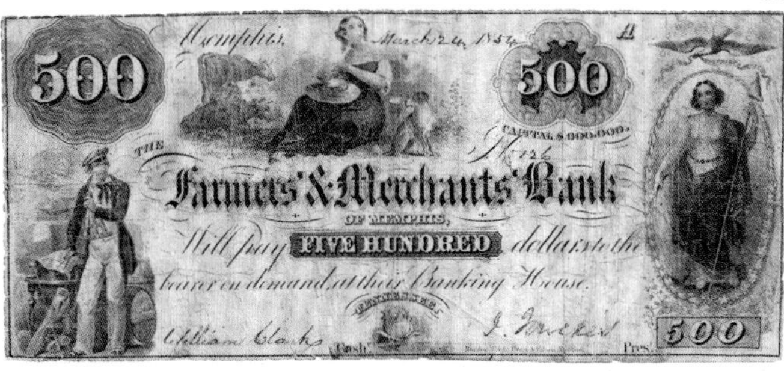

Engraver: Rawdon, Wright, Hatch & Edson. ***Comments:*** H-TN-100-G66a, Garland-660a. 18__. 1850s.

Rarity: URS-3
VG $1,500; **F** $1,750; **VF** $2,000

$1,000 • W-TN-530-1000-G260 CC

Engraver: Rawdon, Wright, Hatch & Edson. ***Comments:*** H-TN-100-G68a, Garland-661. 18__. 1850s.

Rarity: URS-2
VF $2,500

Uncut Sheets

$1-$1-$2-$3 • W-TN-530-001.001.002.003-US010 RG

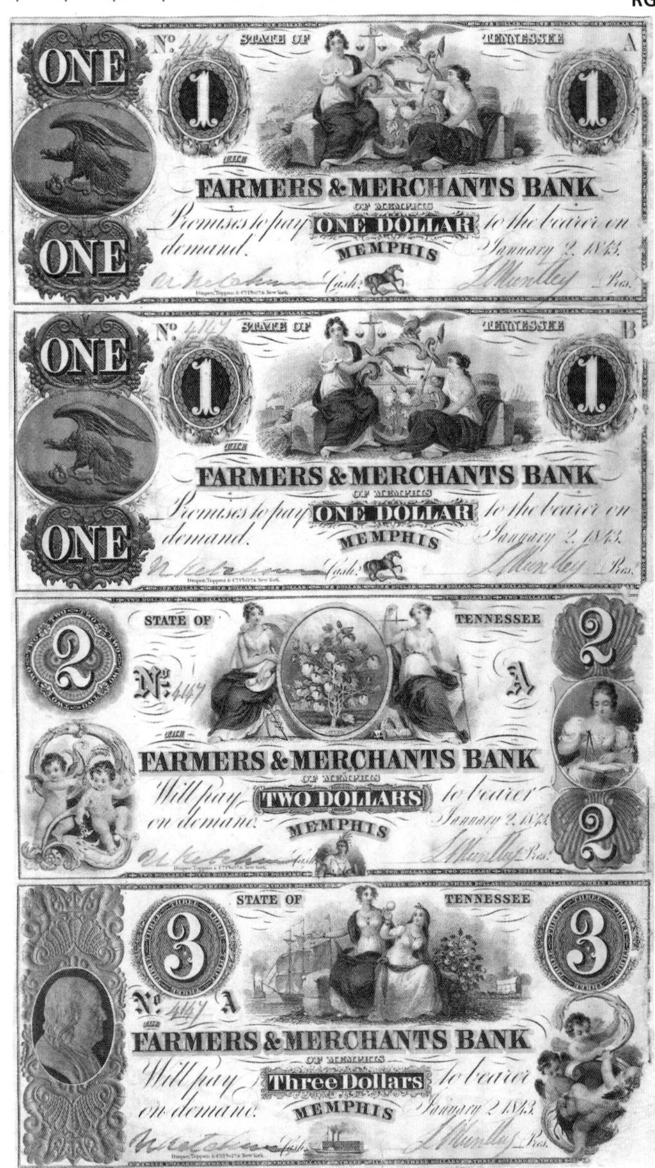

Engraver: Draper, Toppan & Co. ***Comments:*** H-TN-100-G2, G2, G4, G6. First two notes identical. January 2, 1843.

Rarity: URS-3
F $1,100
Selected auction price: Heritage Auctions, January 5, 2012, Lot 16126, About New Apparent $920

Non-Valid Issues

Early Issues

$100 • W-TN-530-100-R010

Engraver: Draper, Toppan, Longacre & Co. ***Comments:*** H-TN-100-R5. Raised from W-TN-530-005-G040. 18__. 1830s.

Rarity: —

Revived-Bank Issues

$5 • W-TN-530-005-R020

Engraver: Rawdon, Wright, Hatch & Edson. ***Comments:*** H-TN-100-R5. Raised from W-TN-530-001-G130.18__. 1854.

Rarity: —

$5 • W-TN-530-005-N010

GB, GB

Back: Red. ***Engraver:*** Toppan, Carpenter & Co. ***Comments:*** H-Unlisted. Fraudulently filled-in remainder. 18__. 1860s.

Rarity: URS-6

F $100; **EF** $150; **AU** $250

Mechanics Bank

1854–1858

W-TN-540

History: In 1854 the Mechanics Bank was chartered with an authorized capital of $100,000. The president was E.W.M. King, and Henry R. Push was the cashier. In November 1854 it was reported that a robbery had occurred on the Mechanics Bank. Some $20,000 in $10 bills had been stolen, and it was declared by the president that none of the bills would be redeemed. Eventually, $12,000 of the stolen bills were recovered. By 1858 the bank had closed its doors.

Numismatic Commentary: This bank was a prolific issuer of notes, making it easily collectible today with numerous notes readily available. For the most part, the designs are complex, if a bit cluttered looking. They lack color other than the various overprints, making them a bit dull. Of all the denominations, the $1 varieties are the scarcest.

The 1990 Christie's sale of the American Bank Note Co. archives produced a $1-$1-$3-$5 sheet and a partial $10-$10 sheet.

Valid Issues

$1 • W-TN-540-001-G010

SI

Engraver: Danforth, Wright & Co. ***Comments:*** H-TN-105-G2, Garland-670. May 1st, 1854.

Rarity: URS-7

VF $100; **EF** $150; **AU** $200

$1 • W-TN-540-001-G010a

Left: ONE / Woman seated with U.S. shield. ***Center:*** Train. ***Right:*** ONE on 1 / Portrait of Andrew Jackson. ***Overprint:*** Red 1. ***Engraver:*** Danforth, Wright & Co. ***Comments:*** H-TN-105-G2a. Similar to W-TN-540-001-G010. May 1st, 1854.

Rarity: —

$1 • W-TN-540-001-G010b

CC

Overprint: Blue 1. ***Engraver:*** Danforth, Wright & Co. ***Comments:*** H-TN-105-G2b, Garland-671. Similar to W-TN-540-001-G010. May 1st, 1854.

Rarity: URS-5

VF $200; **EF** $250

$1 • W-TN-540-001-G010c

CC

Overprint: Red serifed 1. ***Engraver:*** Danforth, Wright & Co. ***Comments:*** H-TN-105-G2c, Garland-674. Similar to W-TN-540-001-G010. May 1st, 1854.

Rarity: URS-5

VF $225; **EF** $275

$1 • W-TN-540-001-G010d

CC

Overprint: Blue serifed 1. ***Engraver:*** Danforth, Wright & Co. ***Comments:*** H-TN-105-G2d, Garland-672. Similar to W-TN-540-001-G010. May 1st, 1854.

Rarity: URS-5
VF $200; **EF** $250

$3 • W-TN-540-003-G020

CC

Engraver: Danforth, Wright & Co. ***Comments:*** H-TN-105-G4, Garland-675. May 1st, 1854.

Rarity: URS-7
VF $200; **EF** $250

$3 • W-TN-540-003-G020a

GB

Overprint: Red 3. ***Engraver:*** Danforth, Wright & Co. ***Comments:*** H-TN-105-G4a, Garland-678. Similar to W-TN-540-003-G020. May 1st, 1854.

Rarity: URS-6
F $250; **VF** $300; **EF** $450

$3 • W-TN-540-003-G020b

GB

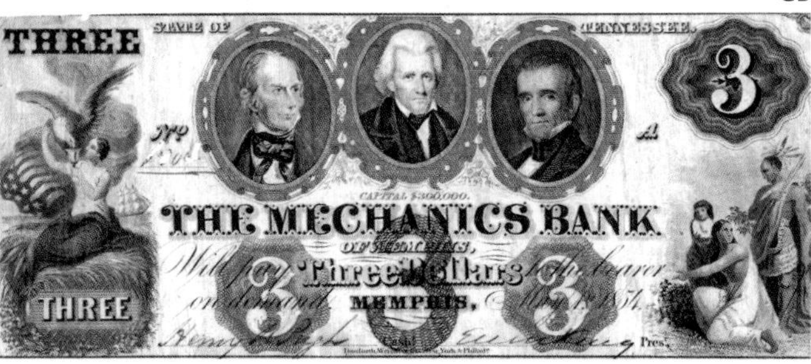

Overprint: Blue 3. ***Engraver:*** Danforth, Wright & Co. ***Comments:*** H-TN-105-G4b, Garland-676. Similar to W-TN-540-003-G020. May 1st, 1854.

Rarity: URS-6
F $250; **VF** $300; **EF** $450

$3 • W-TN-540-003-G020c

Overprint: Red scalloped 3. ***Engraver:*** Danforth, Wright & Co. ***Comments:*** H-TN-105-G4c, Garland-679. Similar to W-TN-540-003-G020. May 1st, 1854.

Rarity: URS-6
F $150; **VF** $200; **EF** $250

$3 • W-TN-540-003-G020d

Overprint: Blue scalloped 3. ***Engraver:*** Danforth, Wright & Co. ***Comments:*** H-TN-105-G4d, Garland-677. Similar to W-TN-540-003-G020. May 1st, 1854.

Rarity: URS-6
F $150; **VF** $200; **EF** $250

$5 • W-TN-540-005-G030

ANS

Engraver: Danforth, Wright & Co. ***Comments:*** H-TN-105-G6, Garland-680. May 1st, 1854.

Rarity: URS-8
VG $40; **F** $75; **VF** $100; **EF** $200

$5 • W-TN-540-005-G030a

Left: FIVE / Portrait of Benjamin Franklin / FIVE. ***Center:*** Three women seated / Portrait of George Washington / Two women seated. ***Right:*** 5 / Portrait of Andrew Jackson / 5. ***Overprint:*** Red knobbed 5 / 5. ***Engraver:*** Danforth, Wright & Co. ***Comments:*** H-TN-105-G6a, Garland-687. Similar to W-TN-540-005-G030. May 1st, 1854.

Rarity: URS-6
VF $100; **EF** $125

$5 • W-TN-540-005-G030b

ANS

Overprint: Blue 5 / 5. ***Engraver:*** Danforth, Wright & Co. ***Comments:*** H-TN-105-G6b, Garland-684. Similar to W-TN-540-005-G030. May 1st, 1854.

Rarity: URS-8
VF $125; **Unc-Rem** $200

$5 • W-TN-540-005-G030c

CC

Overprint: Green 5 / 5. ***Engraver:*** Danforth, Wright & Co. ***Comments:*** H-TN-105-G6c, Garland-681. Similar to W-TN-540-005-G030. May 1st, 1854.

Rarity: URS-6

VF $150; **EF** $225

$5 • W-TN-540-005-G030d

ANS

Overprint: Red scalloped 5 / 5. ***Engraver:*** Danforth, Wright & Co. ***Comments:*** H-TN-105-G6d, Garland-689. Similar to W-TN-540-005-G030. May 1st, 1854.

Rarity: URS-6

F $150; **AU** $200; **Unc-Rem** $250

$5 • W-TN-540-005-G030e

SI

Overprint: Blue scalloped 5 / 5. ***Engraver:*** Danforth, Wright & Co. ***Comments:*** H-TN-105-G6e, Garland-686. Similar to W-TN-540-005-G030. Scallops have two points on top bell of 5. May 1st, 1854.

Rarity: URS-7

VF $120; **AU** $175; **Unc-Rem** $200

$5 • W-TN-540-005-G030f

GB

Overprint: Blue scalloped 5 / 5. ***Engraver:*** Danforth, Wright & Co. ***Comments:*** H-Unlisted, Garland-685. Similar to W-TN-540-005-G030. Scallops have three points on top bell of 5. May 1st, 1854.

Rarity: URS-7

EF $150; **AU** $175; **Unc-Rem** $200

$5 • W-TN-540-005-G030g

CC

Overprint: Green scalloped 5 / 5. ***Engraver:*** Danforth, Wright & Co. ***Comments:*** H-TN-105-G6f, Garland-682. Similar to W-TN-540-005-G030. May 1st, 1854.

Rarity: URS-6

VF $125; **EF** $150; **Unc-Rem** $250

$5 • W-TN-540-005-G030h

GB

Overprint: Red knobbed 5 / 5. ***Engraver:*** Danforth, Wright & Co. ***Comments:*** H-Unlisted, Garland-Unlisted. Similar to W-TN-540-005-G030. May 1st, 1854.

Rarity: —

$10 • W-TN-540-010-G040

CC

Engraver: Danforth, Wright & Co. ***Comments:*** H-TN-105-G8, Garland-690. 185_. 1854.

Rarity: URS-7

F $100; **AU** $200

$10 • **W-TN-540-010-G040a**

GB

Engraver: Danforth, Wright & Co. ***Comments:*** H-TN-105-G8a, Garland-691. Similar to W-TN-540-010-G040 but with different date. July __, 1854.

Rarity: URS-7
F $100; **AU** $200

$10 • **W-TN-540-010-G040b**

CC

Overprint: Red X. ***Engraver:*** Danforth, Wright & Co. ***Comments:*** H-TN-105-G8b, Garland-706. Similar to W-TN-540-010-G040. 185_. 1854.

Rarity: URS-6
F $150

$10 • **W-TN-540-010-G040c**

GB

Overprint: Red X. ***Engraver:*** Danforth, Wright & Co. ***Comments:*** H-TN-105-G8c, Garland-707. Similar to W-TN-540-010-G040 but with different date. July __, 1854.

Rarity: URS-6
AU $250

$10 • **W-TN-540-010-G040d**

Overprint: Blue X. ***Engraver:*** Danforth, Wright & Co. ***Comments:*** H-TN-105-G8d, Garland-700. Similar to W-TN-540-010-G040. 185_. 1854.

Rarity: URS-5
VF $250

$10 • **W-TN-540-010-G040e**

Overprint: Blue X. ***Engraver:*** Danforth, Wright & Co. ***Comments:*** H-TN-105-G8e. Similar to W-TN-540-010-G040 but with different date. July __, 1854.

Rarity: URS-4
VF $350

$10 • **W-TN-540-010-G040f**

GB

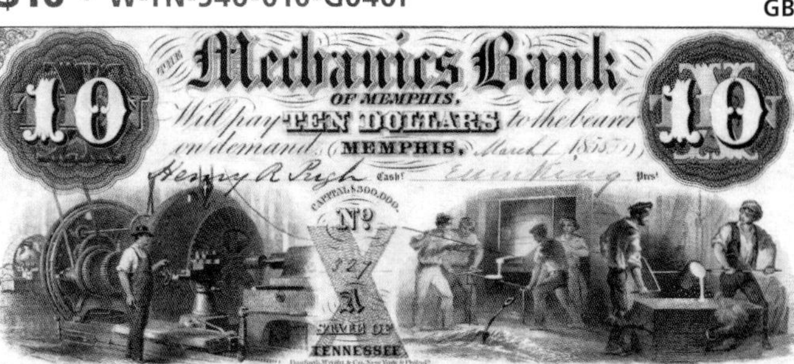

Overprint: Green X. ***Engraver:*** Danforth, Wright & Co. ***Comments:*** H-TN-105-G8f, Garland-694. Similar to W-TN-540-010-G040. 185_. 1854.

Rarity: URS-7
AU $200

$10 • **W-TN-540-010-G040g**

CC

Overprint: Green X. ***Engraver:*** Danforth, Wright & Co. ***Comments:*** H-TN-105-G8g, Garland-695. Similar to W-TN-540-010-G040 but with different date. July __, 1854.

Rarity: URS-7
AU $200

$10 • **W-TN-540-010-G040h**

Overprint: Red scalloped X. ***Engraver:*** Danforth, Wright & Co. ***Comments:*** H-TN-105-G8h, Garland-708. Similar to W-TN-540-010-G040. 185_. 1854.

Rarity: URS-5
VF $350

$10 • **W-TN-540-010-G040i**

GB

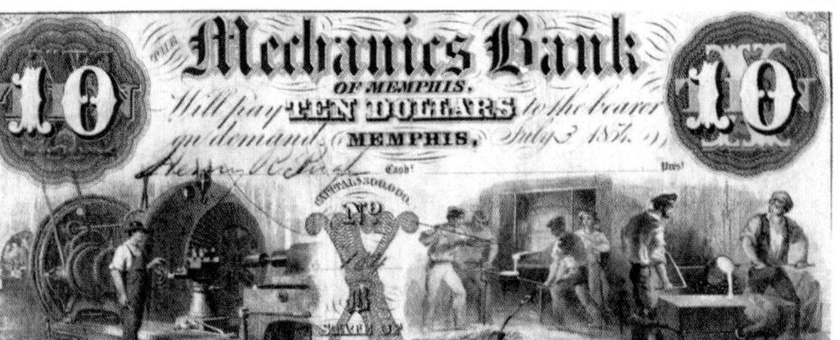

Overprint: Red scalloped X. ***Engraver:*** Danforth, Wright & Co. ***Comments:*** H-TN-105-G8i, Garland-709. Similar to W-TN-540-010-G040 but with different date. July __, 1854.

Rarity: URS-6
EF $200

$10 • W-TN-540-010-G040j

GB

Overprint: Blue scalloped X. ***Engraver:*** Danforth, Wright & Co. ***Comments:*** H-TN-105-G8j, Garland-702. Similar to W-TN-540-010-G040. 185_. 1854.

Rarity: URS-6
EF $250; **Unc-Rem** $400

$10 • W-TN-540-010-G040k

Overprint: Blue scalloped X. ***Engraver:*** Danforth, Wright & Co. ***Comments:*** H-TN-105-G8k. Similar to W-TN-540-010-G040 but with different date. July __, 1854.

Rarity: *None known*

$10 • W-TN-540-010-G040l

GB

Overprint: Green scalloped X. ***Engraver:*** Danforth, Wright & Co. ***Comments:*** H-TN-105-G8l, Garland-696. Similar to W-TN-540-010-G040. 185_. 1854.

Rarity: URS-7
AU $200

$10 • W-TN-540-010-G040m

GB

Overprint: Green scalloped X. ***Engraver:*** Danforth, Wright & Co. ***Comments:*** H-TN-105-G8m, Garland-697. Similar to W-TN-540-010-G040 but with different date. July __, 1854.

Rarity: URS-7
EF $150; **AU** $200

$10 • W-TN-540-010-G040n

Overprint: Red serifed X. ***Engraver:*** Danforth, Wright & Co. ***Comments:*** H-TN-105-G8n, Garland-704. Similar to W-TN-540-010-G040. 185_. 1854.

Rarity: URS-5
VF $200; **EF** $275

$10 • W-TN-540-010-G040o

CC

Overprint: Red serifed X. ***Engraver:*** Danforth, Wright & Co. ***Comments:*** H-TN-105-G8o. Similar to W-TN-540-010-G040 but with different date. July __, 1854.

Rarity: URS-8
VF $200

$10 • W-TN-540-010-G040p

CC

Overprint: Blue scalloped X. ***Engraver:*** Danforth, Wright & Co. ***Comments:*** H-TN-105-G8p, Garland-698. Similar to W-TN-540-010-G040. 185_. 1854.

Rarity: URS-7
AU $250

$10 • W-TN-540-010-G040q

CC

Overprint: Blue serifed X. ***Engraver:*** Danforth, Wright & Co. ***Comments:*** H-TN-105-G8q, Garland-699. Similar to W-TN-540-010-G040 but with different date. July __, 1854.

Rarity: URS-7
EF $200; **AU** $250

$10 • W-TN-540-010-G040r

CC

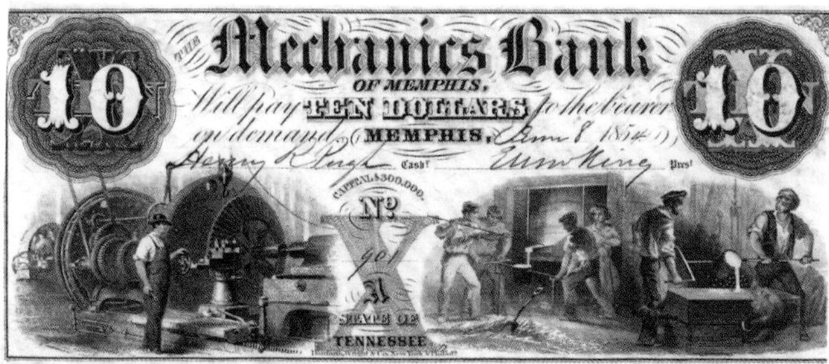

Overprint: Green serifed X. ***Engraver:*** Danforth, Wright & Co. ***Comments:*** H-TN-105-G8r, Garland-692. Similar to W-TN-540-010-G040. 185_. 1854.

Rarity: URS-7
EF $125; **AU** $175

$10 • W-TN-540-010-G040s

GB

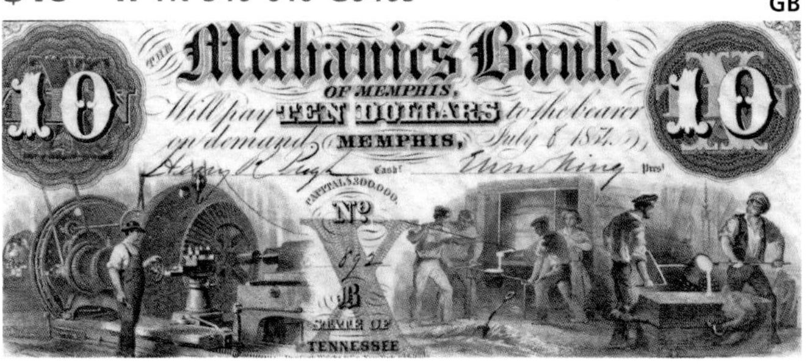

Overprint: Green serifed X. ***Engraver:*** Danforth, Wright & Co. ***Comments:*** H-TN-105-G8s, Garland-693. Similar to W-TN-540-010-G040 but with different date. July __, 1854.

Rarity: URS-7
AU $200

Memphis Banking Company

Circa 1837

W-TN-550

History: No information has been found concerning this bank.

Valid Issues

$4 • W-TN-550-004-G010

Left: Woman standing. ***Center:*** Farm tools and implements. ***Right:*** Portrait of Benjamin Franklin / Portrait of Andrew Jackson / Portrait of Benjamin Franklin. ***Comments:*** H-TN-115-G8, Garland-721. 183_. 1830s.

Rarity: URS-1
Proof $3,500

Memphis Savings Institution

1852–1870

W-TN-560

History: The Memphis Savings Institution (also known as the Memphis City Savings Institution and the Savings Institution of Memphis) was incorporated on February 4, 1852, with an authorized capital of $100,000. E. Snyder was the president, and J.R.S. Oliver was the cashier. In 1870 the bank's name was changed to the City Bank, after the bank-note–issuing era under study.

Numismatic Commentary: The most common notes to be found from this bank are the $5 and $10 denominations. Others are scarce to rare.

The 1990 Christie's sale of the American Bank Note Co. archives produced a $1-$2 sheet of certificates of deposit.

Valid Issues

$1 • W-TN-560-001-G010

Left: Three figures watching ship / Medallion head. ***Center:*** 1 / ONE DOLLAR. ***Right:*** Justice and Industry seated with shield / Woman with rake. ***Comments:*** H-Unlisted, Garland-723. 18__. 1850s.

Rarity: URS-6
VF $150

$1 • W-TN-560-001-G020

GB

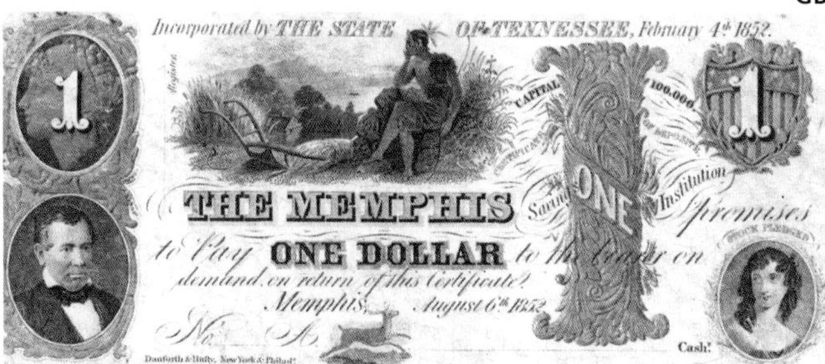

Engraver: Danforth & Hufty. ***Comments:*** H-Unlisted, Garland-724. August 6th, 1852.

Rarity: URS-3
VF $500

$1 • W-TN-560-001-G020a

CC, CC

Back: Red. ***Engraver:*** Danforth & Hufty. ***Comments:*** H-Unlisted, Garland-725. Similar to W-TN-560-001-G020. August 6th, 1852.

Rarity: URS-3
VG $250

$1 • **W-TN-560-001-G030** CC

Engraver: Cincinnati Bank Note Co. ***Comments:*** H-Unlisted, Garland-726. August 6th, 1855.

Rarity: URS-5

G $150; **EF** $425; **AU** $500

$2 • **W-TN-560-002-G040** SI

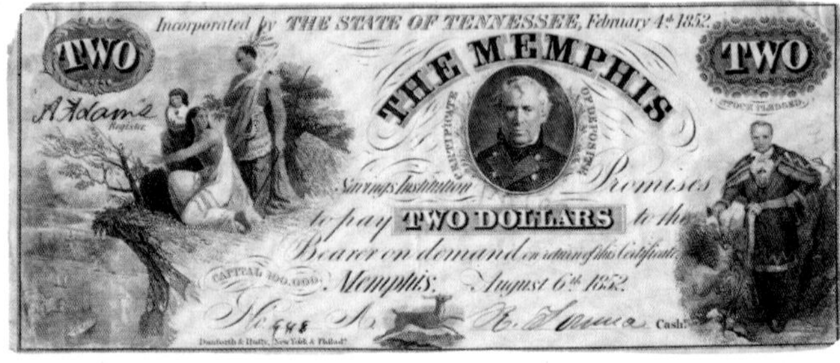

Engraver: Danforth & Hufty. ***Comments:*** H-Unlisted, Garland-727. August 6th, 1855.

Rarity: URS-4

F $350; **VF** $450

$2 • **W-TN-560-002-G040a**

Left: TWO / Indian family looking over port. ***Center:*** Male portrait. ***Right:*** TWO / Man standing. ***Overprint:*** Stamp. ***Engraver:*** Danforth & Hufty. ***Comments:*** H-Unlisted, Garland-728. Similar to W-TN-560-002-G040. August 6th, 1855.

Rarity: URS-1

F $3,500

$5 • **W-TN-560-005-G050** CC

Engraver: Danforth, Bald & Co. ***Comments:*** H-Unlisted, Garland-729. August 6th, 1855.

Rarity: URS-7

AU $350

$10 • **W-TN-560-010-G060** JF

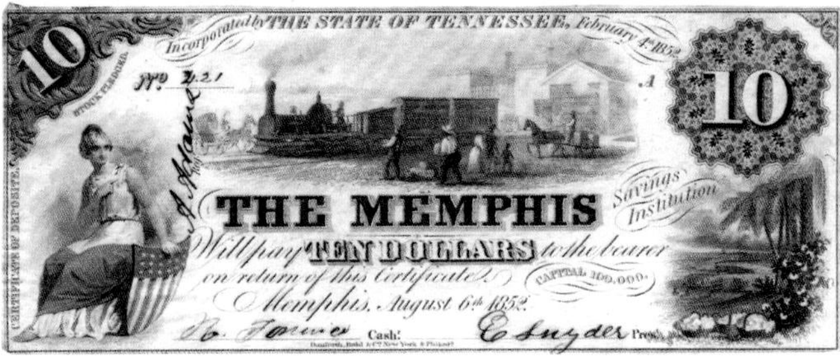

Engraver: Danforth, Bald & Co. ***Comments:*** H-Unlisted, Garland-730. August 6th, 1855.

Rarity: URS-7

EF $350

Planters Bank of Tennessee (branch)

1834–1865

W-TN-570

History: The Planters Bank of Tennessee was chartered on November 11, 1833, with an authorized capital of $2,000,000. In 1834 the branch in Memphis was opened. The holders of the books and assets of this branch fled the city in advance of the Union occupation in 1862. In 1865 the bank was forced to liquidate and close its affairs.

The Planters Bank of Tennessee had its parent bank located in Nashville, W-TN-810, and branch banks located in Athens, W-TN-020, Clarksville, W-TN-140, Columbia, W-TN-210, Franklin, W-TN-300, LaGrange, W-TN-410, Murfreesboro, W-TN-630, Pulaski, W-TN-870, Rogersville, W-TN-910, Shelbyville, W-TN-940, Somerville, W-TN-970, Sparta, W-TN-990, Trenton, W-TN-1050, and Winchester, W-TN-1070.

Numismatic Commentary: This branch is generally quite scarce, if not rare. No accumulations are known.

Valid Issues

$1 • **W-TN-570-001-G010**

Left: 1 / Medallion head bearing ONE / 1. ***Center:*** 1 with cherub / Woman seated with boxes. ***Right:*** Woman standing in 1. ***Engraver:*** Rawdon, Wright, Hatch & Edson. ***Comments:*** H-TN-185-G200. 18__. 1840s.

Rarity: *None known*

$2 • **W-TN-570-002-G020**

Left: 2 / Woman with sheaf / 2. ***Center:*** 2 with cherubs / Woman seated with boxes. ***Right:*** Woman standing in 2. ***Engraver:*** Rawdon, Wright, Hatch & Edson. ***Comments:*** H-TN-185-G202. Dec. 1, 1860.

Rarity: *None known*

$3 • **W-TN-570-003-G030**
Left: 3 / Medallion head / 3. ***Center:*** 3 with cherubs / Two men flanking shield bearing cow surmounted by beehive. ***Right:*** Woman standing in 3. ***Engraver:*** Rawdon, Wright, Hatch & Edson. ***Comments:*** H-TN-185-G204. Dec. 1, 1860.

Rarity: *None known*

$5 • **W-TN-570-005-G040**
Left: Medallion head / FIVE / Medallion head. ***Center:*** FIVE / Man standing with dog / FIVE. ***Right:*** Medallion head / FIVE / Medallion head. ***Engraver:*** Underwood, Bald & Spencer. ***Comments:*** H-TN-185-G206. 18__. 1830s–1840s.

Rarity: *None known*

$5 • **W-TN-570-005-G040a**
Engraver: Underwood, Bald & Spencer. ***Comments:*** H-TN-185-G206a. Similar to W-TN-570-005-G040. 18__. 1830s–1840s.

Rarity: *None known*

$5 • **W-TN-570-005-G050**
Left: 5 / V. ***Center:*** Three women with tablet and harp. ***Right:*** 5 over V / Justice seated. ***Back:*** Red-orange. ***Engraver:*** Danforth, Wright & Co. ***Comments:*** H-TN-185-G208a. 18__. 1850s–1861.

Rarity: *None known*

$10 • **W-TN-570-010-G060**
Left: Medallion head / TEN / Medallion head. ***Center:*** 10 / Farm scene, Harvest / X. ***Right:*** Medallion head / TEN / Medallion head. ***Engraver:*** Underwood, Bald & Spencer. ***Comments:*** H-TN-185-G210. 18__. 1830s–1840s.

Rarity: *None known*

$10 • **W-TN-570-010-G060a**
Engraver: Underwood, Bald & Spencer. ***Comments:*** H-TN-185-G210a. Similar to W-TN-570-010-G060. 18__. 1830s–1840s.

Rarity: *None known*

$10 • **W-TN-570-010-G070** GB, GB

Back: Red-orange. ***Engraver:*** Danforth, Wright & Co. ***Comments:*** H-TN-185-G212, Garland-744. "Redeemable at Memphis" stamped. 18__. 1850s.

Rarity: URS-3
G $225

$20 • **W-TN-570-020-G080**
Left: 20 / Medallion head / 20. ***Center:*** 20 / Medallion head / 20. ***Right:*** 20 / Medallion head / 20. ***Engraver:*** Underwood, Bald & Spencer. ***Comments:*** H-TN-185-G214. 18__. 1830s–1840s.

Rarity: *None known*

$20 • **W-TN-570-020-G080a**
Engraver: Underwood, Bald & Spencer. ***Comments:*** H-TN-185-G214a. Similar to W-TN-570-020-G080. 18__. 1830s–1840s.

Rarity: *None known*

$50 • **W-TN-570-050-G090**
Left: 50 / Medallion head / 50. ***Center:*** Medallion heads / Woman seated, Ship / Medallion heads. ***Right:*** 50 / Medallion head / 50. ***Engraver:*** Underwood, Bald, Spencer & Hufty. ***Comments:*** H-TN-185-G216. 18__. 1830s–1850s.

Rarity: *None known*

$50 • **W-TN-570-050-G095** GB

Engraver: Danforth, Wright & Co. ***Comments:*** H-Unlisted, Garland-746. "Redeemable at Memphis" stamped. 18__. 1830s–1850s.

Rarity: URS-2
AG $500

$100 • **W-TN-570-100-G100**
Left: 100 / Three women seated vertically / 100. ***Center:*** Medallion head / Boy reclining under corn, Plow / Medallion head. ***Right:*** 100 / Three women seated vertically / 100. ***Engraver:*** Underwood, Bald, Spencer & Hufty. ***Comments:*** H-TN-185-G218. 18__. 1830s–1850s.

Rarity: *None known*

Civil War Fractional Notes

5¢ • **W-TN-570-00.05-G110**
Center: FIVE CENTS. ***Right:*** 5. ***Engraver:*** Adams. ***Comments:*** H-TN-185-G222. Jany. 1st, 1862.

Rarity: URS-5
F $250

10¢ • **W-TN-570-00.10-G120**
Center: TEN CENTS. ***Right:*** 10. ***Engraver:*** Adams. ***Comments:*** H-TN-185-G224. Jany. 1st, 1862.

Rarity: URS-5
F $250

25¢ • W-TN-570-00.25-G130 GB

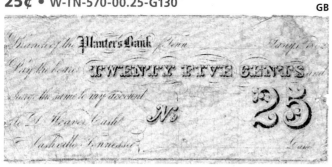

Engraver: Adams. ***Comments:*** H-TN-185-G226, Garland-739. Jany. 1st, 1862.

Rarity: URS-6
G $100; **VG** $125

30¢ • W-TN-570-00.30-G140

Center: THIRTY CENTS. ***Right:*** 30. ***Engraver:*** Adams. ***Comments:*** H-TN-185-G228. Jany. 1st, 1862.

Rarity: URS-5
F $250

50¢ • W-TN-570-00.50-G150

Center: FIFTY CENTS. ***Right:*** 50. ***Back:*** Red. ***Engraver:*** Adams. ***Comments:*** H-TN-185-G230. Jany. 1st, 1862.

Rarity: URS-5
F $250

80¢ • W-TN-570-00.80-G160

Center: EIGHTY CENTS. ***Right:*** 80. ***Back:*** Red. ***Engraver:*** Adams. ***Comments:*** H-TN-185-G232. Jany. 1st, 1862.

Rarity: URS-5
F $250

Non-Valid Issues

$10 • W-TN-570-010-S010

Left: Woman. ***Center:*** Woman, Train, Steamboat. ***Right:*** Ceres. ***Comments:*** H-TN-185-S100. 18__. 1840s.

Rarity: —

$10 • W-TN-570-010-S020

Left: 10 / Justice with scales. ***Center:*** X with cherubs / Two women seated. ***Right:*** 10 / Justice with scales. ***Engraver:*** Rawdon, Wright & Hatch. ***Comments:*** H-TN-185-S102. From a genuine plate of the Planters Bank of Alabama, Wetumpka, Alabama. 18__. 1840s.

Rarity: URS-2
F $450

$20 • W-TN-570-020-S030

Center: Eagle. ***Comments:*** H-TN-185-S104. 18__. 1840s.

Rarity: —

$20 • W-TN-570-020-S040

Left: 20 / Female portrait / XX. ***Center:*** Woman seated near ocean with shield. ***Right:*** 20 / Female portrait / XX. ***Engraver:*** Rawdon, Wright & Hatch. ***Comments:*** H-TN-185-S106. From a genuine plate of the Planters Bank of Alabama, Wetumpka, Alabama. 18__. 1840s.

Rarity: —

$50 • W-TN-570-050-S050

Left: FIFTY DOLLARS vertically. ***Center:*** 50 / Eagle on bale / 50. ***Right:*** STATE OF TENNESSEE vertically. ***Engraver:*** Rawdon, Wright & Hatch. ***Comments:*** H-TN-185-S108. From a genuine plate of the Planters Bank of Alabama, Wetumpka, Alabama. 18__. 1840s.

Rarity: —

$100 • W-TN-570-100-S060

Left: HUNDRED vertically. ***Center:*** Deer, River. ***Right:*** Portrait of George Washington. ***Engraver:*** Rawdon, Wright & Hatch. ***Comments:*** H-TN-185-S110. From a genuine plate of the Planters Bank of Alabama, Wetumpka, Alabama. 18__. 1840s.

Rarity: —

$100 • W-TN-570-100-S070

Left: Medallion head. ***Center:*** C / Factory / C. ***Right:*** 100 diagonally. ***Engraver:*** Rawdon, Wright & Hatch. ***Comments:*** H-TN-185-S112. 18__. 1840s.

Rarity: —

River Bank

1858–1862

W-TN-580

History: The River Bank was organized after the Commercial Bank, W-TN-520, but was in business for only a short time. It was established in 1858 as a free bank with an authorized capital of $100,000. It closed sometime in 1862, when it went into voluntary liquidation.

Numismatic Commentary: Even though the Garland reference estimated that two to four notes of each denomination existed, the only note known to him was a $10 Proof. A signed and issued note of this bank has not been seen.

The 1990 Christie's sale of the American Bank Note Co. archives produced a $5-$5-$10-$20 sheet.

Valid Issues

$5 • W-TN-580-005-G010 CC

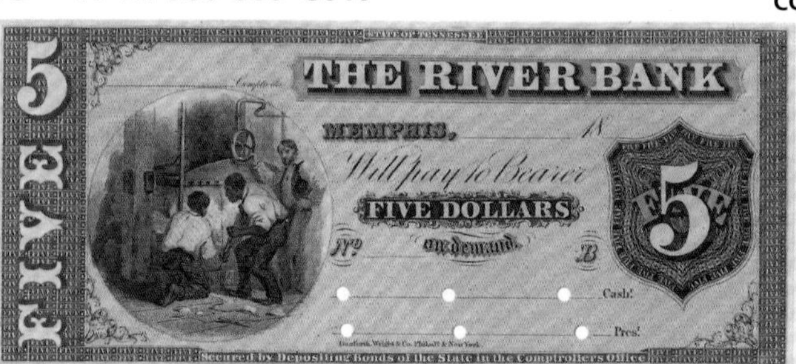

Tint: Red-brown lathework and frame outlining white 5 / FIVE vertically / and microlettering. ***Engraver:*** Danforth, Wright & Co. ***Comments:*** H-TN-120-G2a, Garland-749. 18__. 1850s.

Rarity: URS-2
Proof $5,900
Selected auction price: Stack's Bowers Galleries, June 2010, Lot 5757, Proof $5,900

$10 • W-TN-580-010-G020

Left: Hunter shooting deer / 10. ***Center:*** 10. ***Right:*** X / TEN vertically. ***Tint:*** Red-brown lathework. ***Engraver:*** Danforth, Wright & Co. ***Comments:*** H-TN-120-G4a, Garland-751. 18__. 1850s.

Rarity: URS-2
Proof $5,500

$20 • W-TN-580-020-G030

Left: 20 / Female portrait. ***Center:*** 20. ***Right:*** 20 / Two cherubs flying. ***Tint:*** Red-brown lathework. ***Engraver:*** Danforth, Wright & Co. ***Comments:*** H-TN-120-G6a, Garland-753. 18__. 1850s.

Rarity: URS-1
Proof $6,500

Southern Bank of Tennessee

1854–1858

W-TN-590

History: In 1854 the Southern Bank of Tennessee was chartered with an authorized capital of $100,000. Winston J. Davie was elected president, and W.S. Macrae became the cashier.

On September 7, 1858, it was reported that the Southern Bank of Tennessee had been suspended. It was quickly liquidated after that.

Numismatic Commentary: Of the denominations available, the scarcest are the $1, $2, and $3. Nevertheless they should be found with diligence. The $5 and $10 are more readily acquired.

The 1990 Christie's sale of the American Bank Note Co. archives produced a $1-$1-$2-$3 sheet and a $5-$5-$5-$10 sheet.

Valid Issues

$1 • W-TN-590-001-G010 CC

Engraver: Danforth, Wright & Co. ***Comments:*** H-TN-125-G2, Garland-755. Decr. 1st, 1853.

Rarity: URS-5
Unc-Rem $350

$2 • W-TN-590-002-G020 CC

Engraver: Danforth, Wright & Co. ***Comments:*** H-TN-125-G4, Garland-756. Decr. 1st, 1853.

Rarity: URS-4
EF $350; **Unc-Rem** $500

$3 • W-TN-590-003-G030 GB

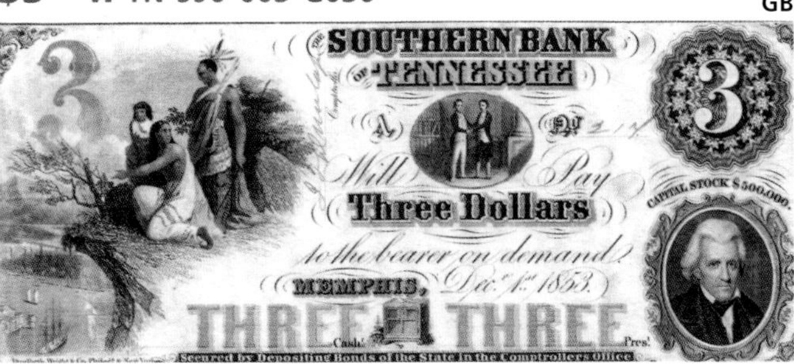

Engraver: Danforth, Wright & Co. ***Comments:*** H-TN-125-G6, Garland-757. Decr. 1st, 1853.

Rarity: URS-4
VF $350; **Unc-Rem** $500; **Unc-S&D** $700

$5 • W-TN-590-005-G040 GB, GB

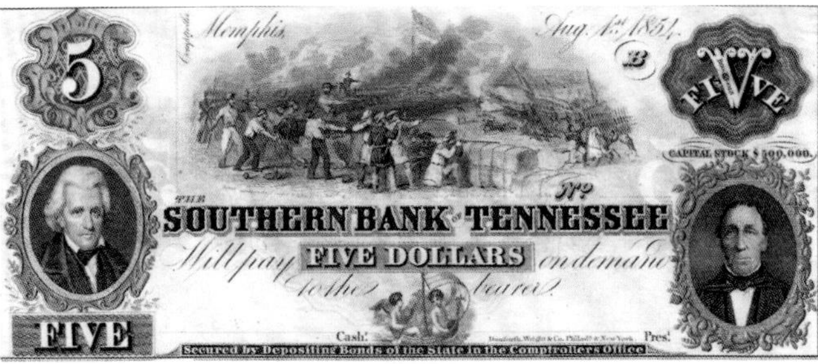

Back: Red-orange. ***Engraver:*** Danforth, Wright & Co. ***Comments:*** H-TN-125-G8, Garland-759. Aug. 1st, 1854.

Rarity: URS-7
F $300; **Unc-Rem** $400

$5 • **W-TN-590-005-G040a** GB

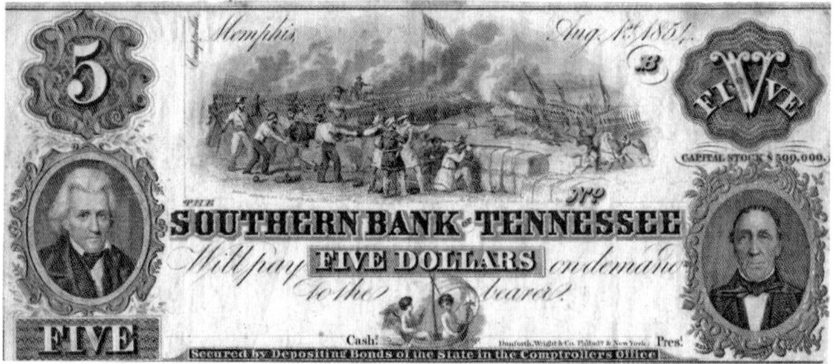

Back: Plain. ***Engraver:*** Danforth, Wright & Co. ***Comments:*** H-TN-125-G8a, Garland-758. Similar to W-TN-590-005-G040. Aug. 1st, 1854.

Rarity: URS-7
F $200; **Unc-Rem** $250

$10 • **W-TN-590-010-G050** CC, GB

Back: Red-orange. ***Engraver:*** Danforth, Wright & Co. ***Comments:*** H-TN-125-G10, Garland-761. August 1st, 1854.

Rarity: URS-6
Unc-Rem $350; **Unc-S&D** $350

$10 • **W-TN-590-010-G050a** GB

Back: Plain. ***Engraver:*** Danforth, Wright & Co. ***Comments:*** H-TN-125-G10a, Garland-760. Similar to W-TN-590-010-G050. August 1st, 1854.

Rarity: URS-6
F $225; **Unc-Rem** $250

Uncut Sheets

$5-$5-$5-$10 • **W-TN-590-005.005.005.010-US010**

Vignette(s): ***($5)*** Portrait of Andrew Jackson / "Battle of New Orleans" / Portrait of Ambrose Davie. ***($10)*** Minerva standing with shield and spear / Woman reclining with cherub painting, Ship / Male portrait. ***Back(s):*** Plain. ***Engraver:*** Danforth, Wright & Co. ***Comments:*** H-TN-125-G8a, G8a, G8a, G10a. First three notes identical. Aug. 1, 1854.

Rarity: —

Union Bank of Tennessee (branch)

1832–1865

W-TN-600

History: On October 18, 1832, the Union Bank of Tennessee (also sometimes seen as the Union Bank of the State of Tennessee on notes) was chartered with an authorized capital of $3,000,000. The bank also absorbed the assets of the failed second Bank of the State of Tennessee, W-TN-680, which had been abolished that year. The state subscribed to $500,000 of the bank's capital, to be financed by bonds.

John Pope was the president of the Memphis branch, accompanied by H.C. Walker. The capital was $150,000. In 1864 the cashier of the bank was Frederick W. Smith, and the president was W.B. Waldran. In 1865 the Union Bank of Tennessee went into liquidation.

The Union Bank of Tennessee had its parent bank located in Nashville, W-TN-840, and branch banks located in Chattanooga, W-TN-090, Columbia, W-TN-220, Jackson, W-TN-325, and Knoxville, W-TN-400.

Numismatic Commentary: The Memphis-branch notes are very scarce.

Valid Issues

$1 • **W-TN-600-001-G010**

Left: 1 / Portrait of Andrew Jackson / 1. ***Center:*** ONE DOLLAR. ***Right:*** ONE / Angel seated in clouds with 1. ***Engraver:*** Draper, Toppan & Co. ***Comments:*** H-TN-210-G134, Garland-762. Jan. 2, 1843.

Rarity: *None known*

$2 • **W-TN-600-002-G020**

Left: 2 / Portrait of George Washington / II. ***Center:*** TWO DOLLARS. ***Right:*** 2 / Woman seated with bales and sickle. ***Engraver:*** Draper, Toppan & Co. ***Comments:*** H-TN-210-G136, Garland-763. Jan. 2, 1843.

Rarity: *None known*

$3 • **W-TN-600-003-G030**

Left: 3 / Portrait of Benjamin Franklin / III. ***Center:*** Ships, Two women flanking shield bearing cotton plant and plow, Train. ***Right:*** 3 / Female portrait / III. ***Engraver:*** Draper, Toppan & Co. ***Comments:*** H-TN-210-G138, Garland-764. Jan. 2, 1843.

Rarity: URS-3
F $750

$5 • **W-TN-600-005-G040**

Left: Eagle. ***Center:*** Portrait of George Washington / Steamboat / Portrait of Marquis de Lafayette. ***Right:*** Eagle. ***Engraver:*** Unverified, but likely Chas. Toppan. ***Comments:*** H-TN-210-G140. 18__. 1830s–1840s.

Rarity: —

$5 • **W-TN-600-005-G050**

Left: Medallion head / FIVE / Medallion head. ***Center:*** Medallion head of Napoleon Bonaparte / 5. ***Right:*** Medallion head / FIVE / Medallion head. ***Engraver:*** Underwood, Bald, Spencer & Hufty. ***Comments:*** H-TN-210-G144, Garland-766. 18__. 1840s–1850s.

Rarity: URS-5
F $250

$5 • **W-TN-600-005-G050a** GB

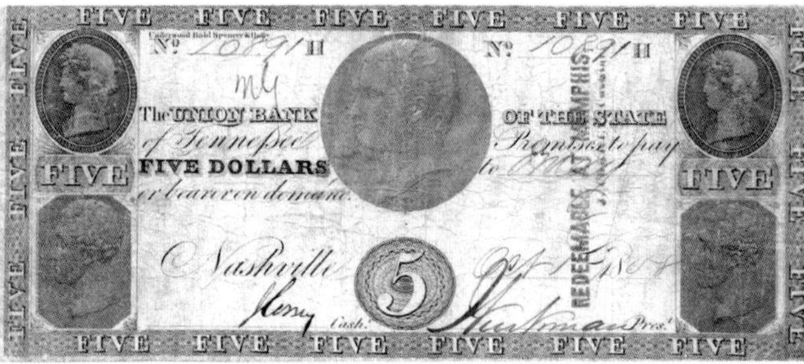

Overprint: Red stamp. ***Engraver:*** Underwood, Bald, Spencer & Hufty. ***Comments:*** H-TN-210-G144a. Similar to W-TN-600-005-G050. 18__. 1840s–1850s.

Rarity: URS-5
F $300

$10 • **W-TN-600-010-G060**

Left: Medallion head / TEN / Medallion head. ***Center:*** 10 / Haying scene, Woman and man, Men harvesting. ***Right:*** Medallion head / TEN / Medallion head. ***Engraver:*** Unverified, but likely Chas. Toppan. ***Comments:*** H-TN-210-G146. 18__. 1830s–1840s.

Rarity: —

$10 • **W-TN-600-010-G070**

Left: Medallion head / TEN / Medallion head. ***Center:*** 10 / Hebe watering eagle / 10. ***Right:*** Medallion head / TEN / Medallion head. ***Engraver:*** Draper, Underwood, Bald & Spencer. ***Comments:*** H-TN-210-G148, Garland-767. 18__. 1830s.

Rarity: URS-4
F $350

$10 • **W-TN-600-010-G070a** CC

Overprint: Red stamp. ***Engraver:*** Draper, Underwood, Bald & Spencer. ***Comments:*** H-TN-210-G148a. Similar to W-TN-600-010-G070. 18__. 1830s.

Rarity: URS-4
VG $350; **F** $450

$20 • **W-TN-600-020-G080**

Left: 20 / Woman seated / 20. ***Center:*** Ship / Two women flanking shield bearing eagle, surmounted by eagle / Ship. ***Right:*** 20 / Woman seated / 20. ***Engraver:*** Chas. Toppan. ***Comments:*** H-TN-210-G150. 18__. 1830s–1840s.

Rarity: —

$20 • **W-TN-600-020-G090**

Center: Portrait of Benjamin Franklin / Portrait of Napoleon Bonaparte / Portrait of Benjamin Franklin. ***Engraver:*** Underwood, Bald, Spencer & Hufty. ***Comments:*** H-TN-210-G152. 18__. 1830s.

Rarity: —

$20 • **W-TN-600-020-G090a**

Overprint: Red stamp. ***Engraver:*** Underwood, Bald, Spencer & Hufty. ***Comments:*** H-TN-210-G152a. Similar to W-TN-600-020-G090. 18__. 1830s.

Rarity: —

$50 • **W-TN-600-050-G100**

Left: 50 / Ship / 50. ***Center:*** Portrait of Indian / Woman seated / Portrait of Indian. ***Right:*** 50 / Ship / 50. ***Engraver:*** Chas. Toppan. ***Comments:*** H-TN-210-G154, Garland-769. 18__. 1830s–1840s.

Rarity: —

$50 • **W-TN-600-050-G100a**

Engraver: Chas. Toppan / Toppan, Carpenter & Co. ***Comments:*** H-TN-210-G154a. Similar to W-TN-600-050-G100 but with additional engraver imprint. 18__. 1840s–1850s.

Rarity: —

$50 • **W-TN-600-050-G100b** CC

Overprint: Red stamp. ***Engraver:*** Chas. Toppan / Toppan, Carpenter & Co. ***Comments:*** H-TN-210-G154b, Garland-770. Similar to W-TN-600-050-G100 but with additional engraver imprint. 18__. 1840s–1850s.

Rarity: URS-1
F $1,500

$100 • **W-TN-600-100-G110**

Left: 100 / Justice / 100. ***Center:*** Steamboat, Woman reclining with globe, Cherub / Steamboat. ***Right:*** 100 / Justice / 100. ***Engraver:*** Chas. Toppan. ***Comments:*** H-TN-210-G156. 18__. 1830s–1840s.

Rarity: *None known*

$100 • **W-TN-600-100-G110a**

Engraver: Chas. Toppan / Toppan, Carpenter & Co. ***Comments:*** H-TN-210-G156a. Similar to W-TN-600-100-G110 but with additional engraver imprint. 18__. 1840s–1850s.

Rarity: *None known*

$100 • **W-TN-600-100-G110b**

Engraver: Chas. Toppan / Toppan, Carpenter & Co. ***Comments:*** H-TN-210-G156b. Similar to W-TN-600-100-G110 but with additional engraver imprint. 18__. 1840s–1850s.

Rarity: *None known*

$500 • **W-TN-600-500-G120**

Left: 500 / Medallion head of George Washington / 500. ***Center:*** Eagle with shield and cornucopia. ***Right:*** 500 / Medallion head of Benjamin Franklin / 500. ***Engraver:*** Draper, Toppan, Longacre & Co. ***Comments:*** H-TN-210-G158. 18__. 1830s–1840s.

Rarity: *None known*

$1,000 • **W-TN-600-1000-G130**

Left: 1000 / Medallion head of Benjamin Franklin / 1000. ***Center:*** Eagle with shield and cornucopia. ***Right:*** 1000 / Medallion head of George Washington / 1000. ***Engraver:*** Draper, Toppan, Longacre & Co. ***Comments:*** H-TN-210-G160. 18__. 1830s–1840s.

Rarity: *None known*

Non-Valid Issues

$1 • **W-TN-600-001-S010**

Left: ONE vertically. ***Center:*** Woman seated / Woman with sword seated with shield bearing 1 / Woman seated. ***Right:*** 1 / Woman standing / ONE. ***Engraver:*** Underwood, Bald, Spencer & Hufty. ***Comments:*** H-TN-210-S14. 18__. 1840s.

Rarity: *None known*

$10 • **W-TN-600-010-S020**

Left: TEN vertically. ***Center:*** Woman seated / Woman with sword seated with shield bearing 10 / Woman seated. ***Right:*** 10 / Woman standing / TEN. ***Engraver:*** Underwood, Bald, Spencer & Hufty. ***Comments:*** H-TN-210-S16. 18__. 1840s.

Rarity: —

$20 • **W-TN-600-020-C080**

Engraver: Chas. Toppan. ***Comments:*** H-TN-210-C150. Counterfeit of W-TN-600-020-G080. 18__. 1830s–1840s.

Rarity: —

Murfreesboro, Tennessee

A county seat for Rutherford was established in 1811 and called Cannonsburgh. Soon the town was renamed Murfreesboro after Colonel Hardy Murfree. In 1818 it became the state capital, replacing Knoxville, which had become inconveniently located as the state expanded its boundaries to the west. In 1826 the capital moved on to Nashville.

The Battle of Murfreesboro (Battle of Stones River) was fought on December 31, 1862. In the following few days there were over 23,000 casualties, making this the bloodiest battle in the Civil War by percentage of its combatants. Murfreesboro became a supply depot for the Union army.

Bank of the State of Tennessee {3rd} (branch)

1838–1866

W-TN-610

History: The third Bank of the State of Tennessee (also seen in print as the Bank of Tennessee) was chartered on January 19, 1838, with an authorized capital of $5,000,000. The bank opened for business in February. The bank suspended specie payments a couple of times in 1838 and 1839, due to the panic of that time, but afterward it resumed and had a profitable and successful career. During the Civil War, the Union army entered the state, and some officers of the Bank of the State of Tennessee fled south with the bank's specie. After the war, the bank's assets were returned to Governor William G. Brownlow in Nashville. Half of the bank's funds had been transferred into state bonds.

By February 1866 the Bank of the State of Tennessee was authorized to go into liquidation.

The third Bank of the State of Tennessee had its parent bank located in Nashville, W-TN-690, and branch banks located in Athens, W-TN-010, Clarksville, W-TN-120, Columbia, W-TN-190, Knoxville, W-TN-365, Memphis, W-TN-490, Rogersville, W-TN-890, Shelbyville, W-TN-920, Somerville, W-TN-960, Sparta, W-TN-980, and Trenton, W-TN-1030.

Numismatic Commentary: Garland expressed the opinion that ". . . regardless of statements in previous lists, that no branch of this bank ever existed in Murphreesboro. There could have been an agent." As no notes have been identified, this is probably correct.

Exchange Bank

1852–1858

W-TN-620

History: In 1852 the Exchange Bank was chartered. By 1855 the capital was $250,000. James Spence was the cashier, and William Spence became the president. In 1857 the capital had dropped to $100,000. By 1858 the bank had closed its affairs.

Numismatic Commentary: A fairly prolific issuer of $1, $2, $3, $5, and $10 denominations, this bank has notes that are generally easy to locate. The scarcest seem to be the $2 issues with a printed date of Nov. 1st, 1852.

Remaining at the American Bank Note Co. archives as of 2003 was a $1-$1-$2-$3 face plate. The 1990 Christie's sale of the American Bank Note Co. archives produced a $1-$1-$1-$5 sheet and a $5-$5-$5-$10 sheet.

Valid Issues

$1 • **W-TN-620-001-G010**

Left: ONE / Portrait of Hugh Lawson White / ONE. ***Center:*** Two women flanking shield surmounted by eagle. ***Right:*** ONE / State arms / Cherubs flanking 1. ***Overprint:*** Red ONE. ***Engraver:*** Wellstood, Hanks, Hay & Whiting. ***Comments:*** H-TN-135-G2a, Garland-772. Novr. 1st, 1852.

Rarity: URS-4

F $350

$1 • W-TN-620-001-G010a

SI

Overprint: Red ONE. ***Engraver:*** Wellstood, Hanks, Hay & Whiting. ***Comments:*** H-TN-135-G2b, Garland-773. Similar to W-TN-620-001-G010 but with different date. Nov. 1, 185_. 1853.

Rarity: URS-6
F $300

$1 • W-TN-620-001-G020

SI

Engraver: Danforth, Wright & Co. ***Comments:*** H-TN-135-G4, Garland-776. 18__. 1850s.

Rarity: URS-7
F $150

$2 • W-TN-620-002-G030

Left: 2 on shield / 2. ***Center:*** Two women flanking shield surmounted by eagle / State arms. ***Right:*** Train / 2. ***Overprint:*** Red TWO. ***Engraver:*** Wellstood, Hanks, Hay & Whiting. ***Comments:*** H-TN-135-G8, Garland-778. Nov. 1, 1852.

Rarity: URS-4
F $350

$2 • W-TN-620-002-G030a

Overprint: Red TWO. ***Engraver:*** Wellstood, Hanks, Hay & Whiting. ***Comments:*** H-TN-135-G8c, Garland-779. Similar to W-TN-620-002-G030 but with different date. Nov. 1, 185_. 1850s.

Rarity: URS-7
F $250

$3 • W-TN-620-003-G040

Left: III. ***Center:*** Two women flanking shield surmounted by eagle / State arms. ***Right:*** 3 / Female portrait. ***Overprint:*** Red THREE. ***Engraver:*** Wellstood, Hanks, Hay & Whiting. ***Comments:*** H-TN-135-G12a, Garland-783. Nov. 1, 1852.

Rarity: URS-4
F $350

$3 • W-TN-620-003-G040a

CC

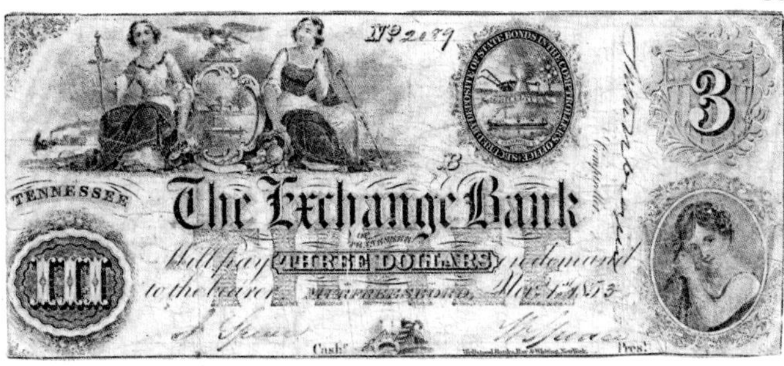

Overprint: Red THREE. ***Engraver:*** Wellstood, Hanks, Hay & Whiting. ***Comments:*** H-TN-135-G12c, Garland-784. Similar to W-TN-620-003-G040 but with different date. Novr. 1st, 185_. 1850s.

Rarity: URS-7
F $150

$5 • W-TN-620-005-G050

CC

Engraver: Danforth, Wright & Co. ***Comments:*** H-TN-135-G16, Garland-787. 18__. 1850s.

Rarity: URS-7
F $250

$5 • W-TN-620-005-G060

CC, CC

Back: Red-orange. ***Engraver:*** Danforth, Wright & Co. ***Comments:*** H-TN-135-G18a, Garland-789. 18__. 1850s.

Rarity: URS-7
F $150; **EF** $250; **Proof** $1,500

$10 • **W-TN-620-010-G070**

CC, CC

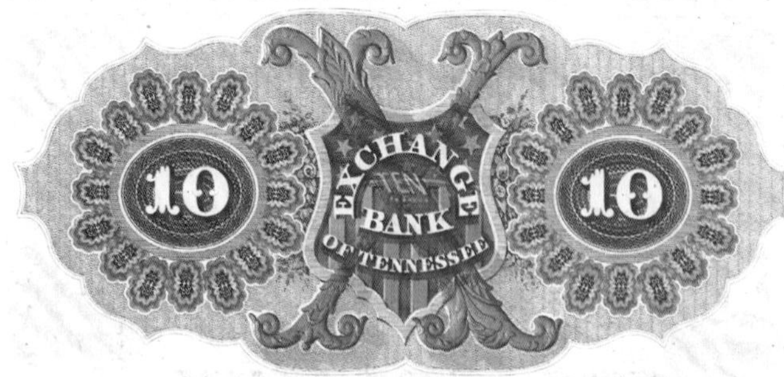

Back: Red-orange. ***Engraver:*** Danforth, Wright & Co. ***Comments:*** H-TN-135-G20a, Garland-791. 18__. 1850s.

Rarity: URS-7

F $150; **Proof** $1,500

Non-Valid Issues

$1 • **W-TN-620-001-S010**

CC

Engraver: Danforth, Underwood & Co. ***Comments:*** H-TN-135-S5, Garland-771. Novr. 1st, 1852.

Rarity: URS-4

F $250

$2 • **W-TN-620-002-S020**

Left: 2 / Portrait of Benjamin Franklin / TWO. ***Center:*** Man plowing. ***Right:*** 2 / Portrait of George Washington / TWO. ***Engraver:*** Danforth, Underwood & Co. ***Comments:*** H-TN-135-S10, Garland-782. Nov. 1, 1852.

Rarity: URS-3

F $350

Planters Bank of Tennessee (branch)

1834–1865

W-TN-630

History: The Planters Bank of Tennessee was chartered on November 11, 1833, with an authorized capital of $2,000,000. In 1834 the branch in Murfreesboro was opened. William Ledbetter was the cashier in 1863. John W. Childress was the president. In 1865 the bank was forced to liquidate and close its affairs.

The Planters Bank of Tennessee had its parent bank located in Nashville, W-TN-810, and branch banks located in Athens, W-TN-020, Clarksville, W-TN-140, Columbia, W-TN-210, Franklin, W-TN-300, LaGrange, W-TN-410, Memphis, W-TN-570, Pulaski, W-TN-870, Rogersville, W-TN-910, Shelbyville, W-TN-940, Somerville, W-TN-970, Sparta, W-TN-990, Trenton, W-TN-1050, and Winchester, W-TN-1070.

Numismatic Commentary: It is likely that the fractional Civil War notes of this branch are scarcer than previously thought, and that the listed $5, $10, and $20 denominations do not exist.

Valid Issues

$5 • **W-TN-630-005-G010**

Comments: H-TN-185-G238, Garland-800. No description available. 18__. 1860s.

Rarity: *None known*

$10 • **W-TN-630-010-G020**

Comments: H-TN-185-G240, Garland-801. No description available. 18__. 1860s.

Rarity: *None known*

$20 • **W-TN-630-020-G030**

Comments: H-TN-185-G242, Garland-802. No description available. 18__. 1860s.

Rarity: *None known*

Civil War Fractional Notes

5¢ • **W-TN-630-00.05-G040**

CC

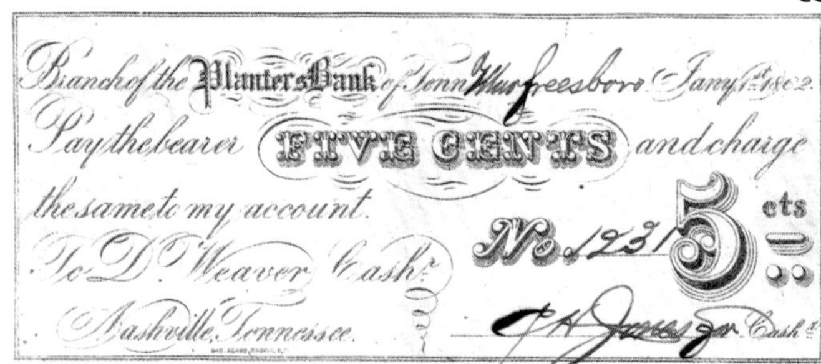

Engraver: Adams. ***Comments:*** H-TN-185-G248. Jany. 1st, 1862.

Rarity: URS-5

VF $300

Collectors and Researchers:

If you have new information about any banks or notes listed in this volume, contact Whitman Publishing, Attn: Obsolete Paper Money, 3101 Clairmont Road, Suite G, Atlanta, GA 30329.

10¢ • **W-TN-630-00.10-G050**

Center: TEN CENTS. ***Right:*** 10. ***Engraver:*** Adams. ***Comments:*** H-TN-185-G248. Jany. 1st, 1862.

Rarity: URS-5
F $250

25¢ • **W-TN-630-00.25-G060**

Center: TWENTY FIVE CENTS. ***Right:*** 25. ***Engraver:*** Adams. ***Comments:*** H-TN-185-G250. Jany. 1st, 1862.

Rarity: URS-5
F $250

30¢ • **W-TN-630-00.30-G070** CC

Engraver: Adams. ***Comments:*** H-TN-185-G252. Jany. 1st, 1862.

Rarity: URS-5
F $350

50¢ • **W-TN-630-00.50-G080**

Center: FIFTY CENTS. ***Right:*** 50. ***Back:*** Red. ***Engraver:*** Adams. ***Comments:*** H-TN-185-G254. Jany. 1st, 1862.

Rarity: URS-5
F $350

80¢ • **W-TN-630-00.80-G090** CC

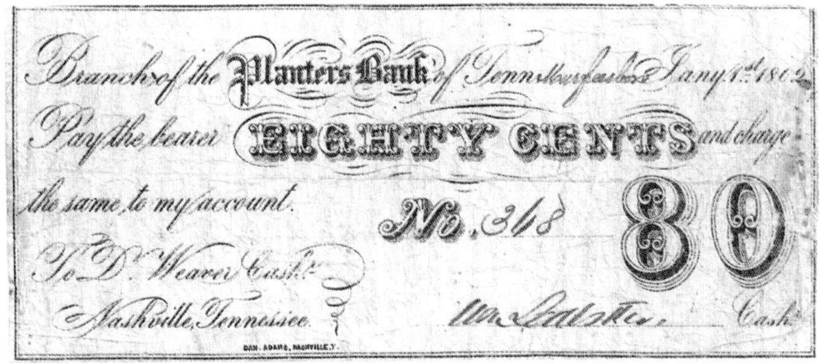

Back: Red. ***Engraver:*** Adams. ***Comments:*** H-TN-185-G256. Jany. 1st, 1862.

Rarity: URS-5
F $350

Nashville Bank (branch)

1817–1827

W-TN-640

History: In 1807 the Nashville Bank was chartered with an authorized capital of $200,000, to be divided into shares of $50 apiece. In 1817 several banks were chartered across the state—in the towns of Gallatin, Murfreesboro, Rogersville, Shelbyville, and Winchester—and were given the option of either joining the first Bank of the State of Tennessee, W-TN-355, or of joining with the Nashville Bank. The corporations chose the Nashville Bank and became branches forthwith.

On March 31, 1823, the Nashville Bank, along with its branches, burned a total of $250,000 worth of bank notes in order to increase the value of its circulation. In 1827 the bank was liquidated.

The Nashville Bank had its parent bank located in Nashville, W-TN-800, and branch banks located in Gallatin, W-TN-310, Rogersville, W-TN-900, Shelbyville, W-TN-930, and Winchester, W-TN-1060.

Numismatic Commentary: Notes from this branch are unknown to the collecting community today.

VALID ISSUES

$1 • **W-TN-640-001-G010**

Left: ONE vertically. ***Center:*** 1 / Woman seated / 1. ***Right:*** TENNESSEE vertically. ***Engraver:*** Tanner, Kearny & Tiebout. ***Comments:*** H-TN-180-G84. 18__. 1810s.

Rarity: *None known*

$2 • **W-TN-640-002-G020**

Left: TWO vertically. ***Center:*** 2 / Woman seated / 2. ***Right:*** TENNESSEE vertically. ***Engraver:*** Tanner, Kearny & Tiebout. ***Comments:*** H-TN-180-G86. 18__. 1810s.

Rarity: *None known*

$5 • **W-TN-640-005-G030**

Left: FIVE vertically. ***Center:*** 5 / Woman seated / 5. ***Right:*** NASHVILLE vertically. ***Engraver:*** Murray, Draper, Fairman & Co. ***Comments:*** H-TN-180-G90. 18__. 1810s.

Rarity: *None known*

$5 • **W-TN-640-005-G040**

Left: FIVE vertically. ***Center:*** 5 / Woman seated / 5. ***Right:*** TENNESSEE vertically. ***Engraver:*** Tanner, Kearny & Tiebout. ***Comments:*** H-TN-180-G92. 18__. 1810s–1820s.

Rarity: *None known*

$10 • **W-TN-640-010-G050**

Left: TEN vertically. ***Center:*** 10 / Woman seated / 10. ***Right:*** NASHVILLE vertically. ***Engraver:*** Murray, Draper, Fairman & Co. ***Comments:*** H-TN-180-G94. 18__. 1810s.

Rarity: *None known*

$10 • **W-TN-640-010-G060**

Left: TEN vertically. ***Center:*** 10 / Woman seated / 10. ***Right:*** TENNESSEE vertically. ***Engraver:*** Tanner, Kearny & Tiebout. ***Comments:*** H-TN-180-G96. 18__. 1810s–1820s.

Rarity: *None known*

$20 • **W-TN-640-020-G070**

Left: TWENTY vertically. ***Center:*** 20 / Woman seated with 20 / 20. ***Right:*** NASHVILLE vertically. ***Engraver:*** Murray, Draper, Fairman & Co. ***Comments:*** H-TN-180-G98. 18__. 1810s.

Rarity: *None known*

$20 • **W-TN-640-020-G080**

Left: TWENTY vertically. ***Center:*** 20 / Woman seated with 20 / 20. ***Right:*** TENNESSEE vertically. ***Engraver:*** Tanner, Kearny & Tiebout. ***Comments:*** H-TN-180-G100. 18__. 1810s–1820s.

Rarity: *None known*

Nashville, Tennessee

Nashville was settled in 1779 by James Robertson, John Donelson, and others. They picked a location close to the old Fort Nashborough and named the town, similarly, after Francis Nash. With a strategic location on the Cumberland River, Nashville quickly became a thriving port town. Eventually it became a significant railway hub as well.

By 1800 the city had a population of 345. Nashville was incorporated in 1806, and the same year it became the county seat of Davidson. In 1843 it became the permanent capital of Tennessee.

Nashville was the first state capital to be taken by the Union army—it was considered a prime target with its port and prosperity, and it remained occupied by Union troops for the duration of the war. The Battle of Nashville in December 1864 was fought here and is considered to be the most decisive tactical victory for the Union army.

Bank of Commerce
1855–1858
W-TN-650

History: In 1855 the Bank of Commerce was chartered. J.D. James was the president, and D.D. James was the cashier. By 1857 the capital was $50,000. In 1858 the bank closed its affairs.

Numismatic Commentary: This bank is one of the rarest issuers in the state of Tennessee.

The 1990 Christie's sale of the American Bank Note Co. archives produced a three-note sheet of $5-$5-$5.

Valid Issues

$5 • W-TN-650-005-G010

Left: Woman with fruit / 5. ***Center:*** Sailor reclining, Ship. ***Right:*** 5 / Steamboat *Pacific*. ***Overprint:*** Red. ***Comments:*** H-TN-155-G12, Garland-803. 18__. 1850s.

Rarity: URS-4
Proof $2,500

Non-Valid Issues

$1 • W-TN-650-001-N010

Center: Man pointing to ship. ***Comments:*** H-TN-155-N5, Garland-Unlisted. 18__. 1850s

Rarity: —

$5 • W-TN-650-005-S010 ANS

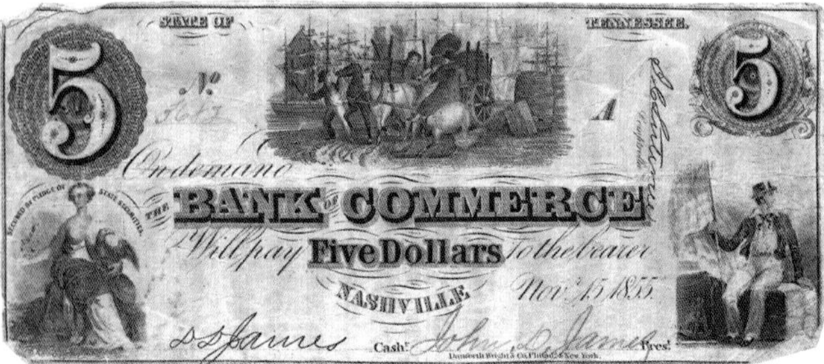

Engraver: Danforth, Wright & Co. ***Comments:*** H-TN-155-S10, Garland-804. Novr. 15, 1855.

Rarity: URS-5
F $175

$20 • W-TN-650-020-N020

Center: Spread eagle. ***Comments:*** H-TN-155-N10, Garland-Unlisted. 18__. 1850s

Rarity: —

Bank of Nashville
1807–1826
W-TN-660

History: In 1807 the Bank of Nashville was chartered with an authorized capital of $500,000. In 1815 the bank was forced to suspend specie payments, causing the capital to drop to $400,000 in 1817. In an effort to keep the bank solvent, five branches were established, and the capital was raised to $1,031,705.[9] Nevertheless the bank was suffering, and its notes were at a 60-percent discount.

In July 1826 the bank finally began to pay out specie again. Not two months had passed before the bank was in suspension once more, after $260,000 in specie had been drawn from the bank.[10] The bank failed shortly after that.

The locations of the Bank of Nashville branches are unknown.

Numismatic Commentary: It is believed that the $1, $2, and $3 denominations are scarcer than the $5 and $10 notes.

Remaining at the American Bank Note Co. archives as of 2003 was a $1-$1-$2-$3 face plate and a $5-$5-$5-$10 face plate. The 1990 Christie's sale of the American Bank Note Co. archives produced a $1-$1-$2-$3 sheet and a $5-$5-$5-$10 sheet.

Valid Issues

$1 • W-TN-660-001-G010 CC

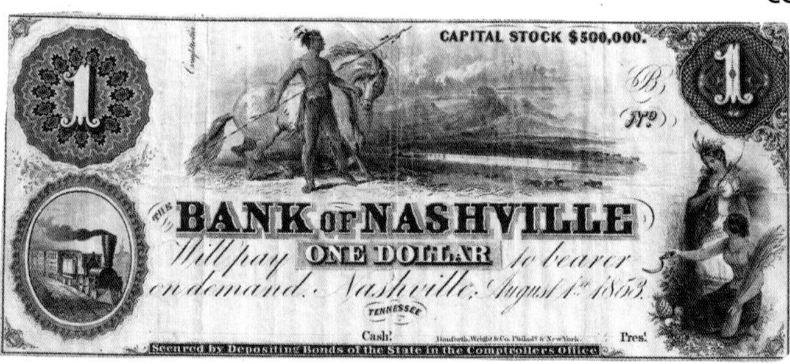

Engraver: Danforth, Wright & Co. ***Comments:*** H-TN-175-G2, Garland-805. August 1st, 1853.

Rarity: URS-6
F $250

$2 • **W-TN-660-002-G020** CC

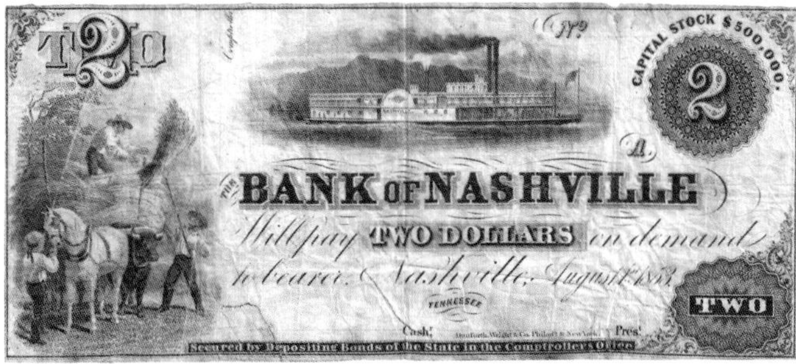

Engraver: Danforth, Wright & Co. ***Comments:*** H-TN-175-G4, Garland-806. August 1st, 1853.

Rarity: URS-6
F $250

$3 • **W-TN-660-003-G030**

Left: Bridge over water, Ships / 3. ***Center:*** 3. ***Right:*** 3 / Justice with scales, Woman kneeling. ***Engraver:*** Danforth, Wright & Co. ***Comments:*** H-TN-175-G6, Garland-807. Aug. 1, 1853.

Rarity: URS-5
F $350

$5 • **W-TN-660-005-G040** CC

Engraver: Danforth, Wright & Co. ***Comments:*** H-TN-175-G8, Garland-808. 18__. 1850s.

Rarity: URS-7
F $200; **VF** $300

$5 • **W-TN-660-005-G040a**

Left: 5 / Farmer and family. ***Center:*** Woman seated with shield bearing 5. ***Right:*** 5 / State arms. ***Tint:*** Red-orange. ***Engraver:*** Danforth, Wright & Co. ***Comments:*** H-TN-175-G8a, Garland-809. Similar to W-TN-660-005-G040. 18__. 1850s.

Rarity: URS-5
F $250

$10 • **W-TN-660-010-G050** CC

Engraver: Danforth, Wright & Co. ***Comments:*** H-TN-175-G10, Garland-810. 18__. 1850s.

Rarity: URS-7
F $300

$10 • **W-TN-660-010-G050a**

Left: Two women. ***Center:*** X / Eagle with shield / 10. ***Right:*** Woman seated with globe and spear. ***Tint:*** Red-orange. ***Engraver:*** Danforth, Wright & Co. ***Comments:*** H-TN-175-G10a, Garland-811. Similar to W-TN-660-010-G050. 18__. 1850s.

Rarity: URS-3
F $550

Non-Valid Issues

$10 • **W-TN-660-010-R010**

Engraver: Danforth, Wright & Co. ***Comments:*** H-TN-175-R5. Raised from W-TN-660-001-G010. Aug. 1, 1853.

Rarity: —

Bank of the State of Tennessee {1st} (branch)

1817–1820

W-TN-670

History: The first Bank of the State of Tennessee was chartered on November 20, 1811, with an authorized capital of $400,000. The capital was to be divided into shares of $50 apiece. The state subscribed to $20,000, on the provision that the state reserved the right to withdraw its funds after ten years. Hugh Lawson White was the president. No notes under $5 were allowed to be issued. In 1817 the branch in Nashville was opened.

The Bank of the State of Tennessee discontinued business in 1820, at which time the stated capital was $371,107. The branches failed at the same time with a combined capital of $573,915.

The first Bank of the State of Tennessee had its parent bank located in Knoxville, W-TN-355, and branch banks located in Carthage, W-TN-060, Clarksville, W-TN-110, Columbia, W-TN-170, Franklin, W-TN-280, Jonesboro, W-TN-335, Kingston, W-TN-340, and Maryville, W-TN-440.

Numismatic Commentary: Any note of this branch bank is extremely rare.

Valid Issues

$5 • **W-TN-670-005-G010**

Left: FIVE vertically. ***Center:*** Man plowing with horses / 5. ***Right:*** TENNESSEE vertically. ***Engraver:*** Murray, Draper, Fairman & Co. ***Comments:*** H-TN-75-G136. 18__. 1810s.

Rarity: URS-3
F $750

$10 • **W-TN-670-010-G020**

Left: TEN vertically. ***Center:*** Men harvesting corn / 10. ***Right:*** TENNESSEE vertically. ***Engraver:*** Murray, Draper, Fairman & Co. ***Comments:*** H-TN-75-G138. 18__. 1810s.

Rarity: URS-1
F $1,500

$20 • **W-TN-670-020-G030**

Left: TWENTY vertically. ***Center:*** XX / Justice seated / XX. ***Right:*** TENNESSEE vertically. ***Engraver:*** Murray, Draper, Fairman & Co. ***Comments:*** H-TN-75-G140. 18__. 1810s.

Rarity: URS-1
F $1,500

$50 • **W-TN-670-050-G040**

Left: FIFTY vertically. ***Center:*** 50 / Ships / 50. ***Right:*** TENNESSEE vertically. ***Engraver:*** Murray, Draper, Fairman & Co. ***Comments:*** H-TN-75-G142. 18__. 1810s.

Rarity: URS-1
F $1,500

$100 • **W-TN-670-100-G050**

Left: HUNDRED vertically. ***Center:*** Scene. ***Right:*** TENNESSEE vertically. ***Engraver:*** Murray, Draper, Fairman & Co. ***Comments:*** H-TN-75-G144. 18__. 1810s.

Rarity: —

NON-VALID ISSUES

$3 • **W-TN-670-003-N010**

CC

Engraver: Murray, Draper, Fairman & Co. ***Comments:*** H-TN-75-N45, Garland-818. 181_. 1810s.

Rarity: URS-1
F $1,200

$50 • **W-TN-670-050-N020**

Left: FIFTY vertically. ***Center:*** 50 / Ship / L. ***Right:*** FIFTY DOLLARS vertically. ***Engraver:*** Murray, Draper, Fairman & Co. ***Comments:*** H-TN-75-N48. 18__. 1810s.

Rarity: —

Bank of the State of Tennessee {2nd}

1820–1832

W-TN-680

History: The second Bank of the State of Tennessee was chartered on July 26, 1820, during the first financial panic of that state, with a capital of $1,000,000, "for the purpose of relieving the distress of the country and improving the revenue of the State."[11] The capital was to be supplemented by funds of the state and the sales of public lands.

Unfortunately, the Bank of the State of Tennessee became a negative example of what happens when banks are established for the purpose of solving financial problems. Andrew Jackson took a strong stand against the bank, declaring that it was "a violation of . . . the Constitution of the United States."[12] Nevertheless, the bill was passed authorizing the bank, and notes were quickly at a discount thereafter. Other banks in the state refused to accept them, overdrafts were committed, the cashier defaulted in the amount of $67,695, and bookkeeping was neglected.

In 1832 the Bank of the State of Tennessee ceased operations, and its funds and assets were placed with the Union Bank of Tennessee, W-TN-840.

The second Bank of the State of Tennessee had branch banks located in Columbia, W-TN-180, Franklin, W-TN-290, and Knoxville, W-TN-360.

Numismatic Commentary: Signed and issued notes from this bank are excessively rare, if not unknown.

Remaining at the American Bank Note Co. archives as of 2003 was a $50-$20-$10-$5 face plate and a $5-$5-$10-$3 face plate.

VALID ISSUES

6-1/4¢ • **W-TN-680-00.06.25-G010**

Engraver: Murray, Draper, Fairman & Co. ***Comments:*** H-TN-190-G2. No description available. 18__. 1820s.

Rarity: *None known*

12-1/2¢ • **W-TN-680-00.12.50-G020**

Engraver: Murray, Draper, Fairman & Co. ***Comments:*** H-TN-190-G4. No description available. June 20, 1824.

Rarity: *None known*

12-1/2¢ • **W-TN-680-00.12.50-G030**

CC

Engraver: Murray, Draper, Fairman & Co. ***Comments:*** H-TN-190-G6, Garland-826. 18__. 1820s.

Rarity: URS-1
F $1,200

12-1/2¢ • **W-TN-680-00.12.50-G040**

CC

Comments: H-TN-190-G10, Garland-825. June 20th, 1824.

Rarity: URS-1
F $1,000

12-1/2¢ • **W-TN-680-00.12.50-G050** CC

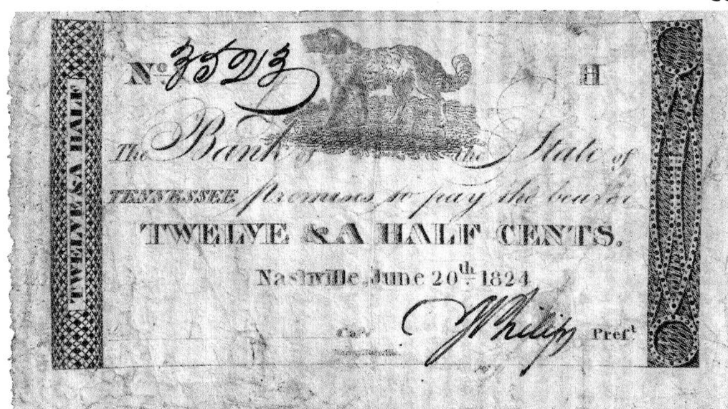

Comments: H-Unlisted, Garland-Unlisted. June 20th, 1824.

Rarity: URS-1
F $1,000

25¢ • **W-TN-680-00.25-G060** CC

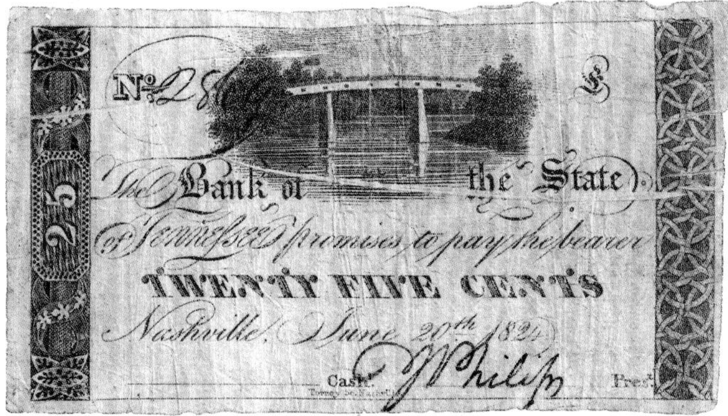

Engraver: Torrey. ***Comments:*** H-TN-190-G14, Garland-827. June 20th, 1824.

Rarity: URS-1
F $1,000

50¢ • **W-TN-680-00.50-G070**

Comments: H-TN-190-G18, Garland-831. No description available. 18__. 1820s.

Rarity: *None known*

$1 • **W-TN-680-001-G080**

Comments: H-TN-190-G20, Garland-832. No description available. 18__. 1820s.

Rarity: *None known*

$2 • **W-TN-680-002-G090**

Comments: H-TN-190-G22, Garland-833. No description available. 18__. 1820s.

Rarity: *None known*

$3 • **W-TN-680-003-G100**

Comments: H-Unlisted, Garland-Unlisted. No description available. 18__. 1820s.

Rarity: *None known*

$5 • **W-TN-680-005-G110**

Comments: H-TN-190-G24, Garland-834. No description available. 18__. 1820s.

Rarity: *None known*

$10 • **W-TN-680-010-G120**

Comments: H-TN-190-G26, Garland-835. No description available. 18__. 1820s.

Rarity: *None known*

$20 • **W-TN-680-020-G130**

Comments: H-TN-190-G28, Garland-836. No description available. 18__. 1820s.

Rarity: *None known*

$50 • **W-TN-680-050-G140**

Comments: H-TN-190-G30, Garland-837. No description available. 18__. 1820s.

Rarity: *None known*

$100 • **W-TN-680-100-G150**

Comments: H-TN-190-G32, Garland-838. No description available. 18__. 1820s.

Rarity: *None known*

Non-Valid Issues

25¢ • **W-TN-680-00.25-C060** CC

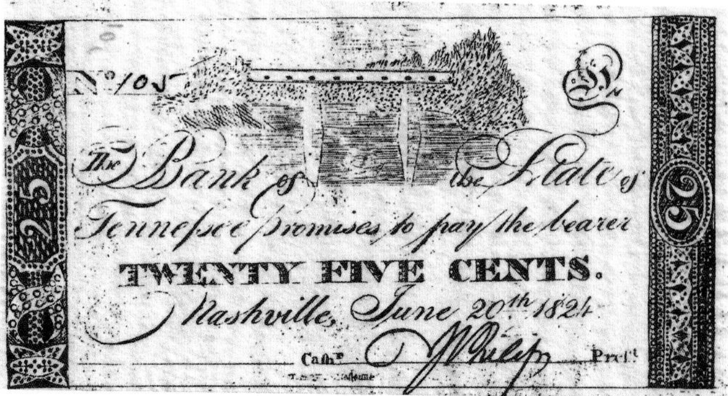

Engraver: Torrey. ***Comments:*** H-TN-190-C14, Garland-828. Counterfeit of W-TN-680-00.25-G060. June 20th, 1824.

Rarity: URS-5
F $300

Bank of the State of Tennessee {3rd}

1838–1866

W-TN-690

History: The third Bank of the State of Tennessee (also seen in print as the Bank of Tennessee) was chartered on January 19, 1838, with an authorized capital of $5,000,000. This amount was to be supplemented by the common school fund, as well as revenue from the state and sales of Ocoee land. Any balance would be filled in by state bonds. Only $1,000,000 of these bonds were actually purchased by the American Life Insurance and Trust Company of New York. The other $1,500,000 had to be cancelled.[13] By the time the bank was ready to go into operation, the paid-in capital was $3,226,796.

The bank opened for business in February. William Nichol was the president, and Henry Ewing was the cashier. Willoughby Williams became the president later. When he resigned in 1843, he was succeeded in turn by Felix Robertson, A.O.P. Nicholson, Cave Johnson, Granville P. Smith, and G.C. Torbitt. The bank suspended specie payments a couple of times in 1838 and 1839, due to the panic of that time, but afterward it resumed and had a profitable and successful career. In 1842 the capital of the bank was $3,130,646, and circulation was $1,384,078. In 1849 the capital was reduced to $2,500,000. By 1855 the capital had dropped still further to $1,325,916. James Morton was the cashier at the time. In 1857 these values were given: capital $3,679,668; bills in circulation $1,468,851; specie $940,023; real estate $231,491.

During the Civil War, the Union army entered the state, and some officers of the Bank of the State of Tennessee fled south with the bank's specie. After the war, the bank's assets were returned to Governor William G. Brownlow in Nashville. Half of the bank's funds had been transferred into state bonds.

On February 16, 1866, the Bank of the State of Tennessee was authorized to go into liquidation.

The third Bank of the State of Tennessee had branch banks located in Athens, W-TN-010, Clarksville, W-TN-120, Columbia, W-TN-190, Knoxville, W-TN-365, Memphis, W-TN-490, Murfreesboro, W-TN-610, Rogersville, W-TN-890, Shelbyville, W-TN-920, Somerville, W-TN-960, Sparta, W-TN-980, and Trenton, W-TN-1030.

Numismatic Commentary: It is interesting to learn that it took until 1933—more than half a century—for litigation to sort out the state of Tennessee's liability to redeem notes issued by this bank. Fractional notes from the Civil War years are available, although rare varieties do exist. The $1 and $5 notes are readily available, while the higher denominations are very scarce to rare. Many notes are cancelled, as a Funding Board oversaw the redemption of the notes. Non-cancelled notes command a premium.

The 1990 Christie's sale of the American Bank Note Co. archives produced a $5-$5-$5-$5 sheet.

Valid Issues

$1 • W-TN-690-001-G010

Left: Woman seated with farmer / Female portrait. ***Center:*** 1 / Man plowing with horses / 1. ***Right:*** ONE / Medallion head / ONE. ***Engraver:*** Draper, Toppan & Co. ***Comments:*** H-TN-195-G2, Garland-862. Mar. 1, 1842.

Rarity: URS-3
F $550

$1 • W-TN-690-001-G010a

Engraver: Toppan, Carpenter & Co. ***Comments:*** H-TN-195-G2a, Garland-863. Similar to W-TN-690-001-G010 but with different date and engraver imprint. Mar. 1, ____. 1840s, 1861.

Rarity: URS-3
F $550

$1 • W-TN-690-001-G020

Left: 1 / Sailor standing with flag. ***Center:*** 1 / Two women seated with cog wheel / 1. ***Right:*** 1 / Woman with sheaf on back. ***Engraver:*** Toppan, Carpenter, Casilear & Co. ***Comments:*** H-TN-195-G4, Garland-864. 18__. 1850s.

Rarity: URS-7
F $125

$1 • W-TN-690-001-G030

Left: 1 / Portrait of boy. ***Center:*** Indian on horseback hunting buffalo. ***Right:*** 1 / Female portrait. ***Tint:*** Red-orange. ***Back:*** Red-orange. ***Engraver:*** Toppan, Carpenter & Co. ***Comments:*** H-TN-195-G6a, Garland-867. 18__. 1850s.

Rarity: URS-4
F $250

$2 • W-TN-690-002-G040

Left: TWO / Woman seated in 2 / 2. ***Center:*** 2 / Woman seated on bales / 2. ***Right:*** 2 / Ship / 2. ***Engraver:*** Draper, Toppan & Co. ***Comments:*** H-TN-195-G8, Garland-873. Mar. 1, 1842.

Rarity: URS-3
F $550

$2 • W-TN-690-002-G040a

Engraver: Toppan, Carpenter & Co. ***Comments:*** H-TN-195-G8a, Garland-874. Similar to W-TN-690-002-G040 but with different date and engraver imprint. Mar. 1, ____. 1840s, 1861.

Rarity: URS-3
F $550

$2 • W-TN-690-002-G050

SBG

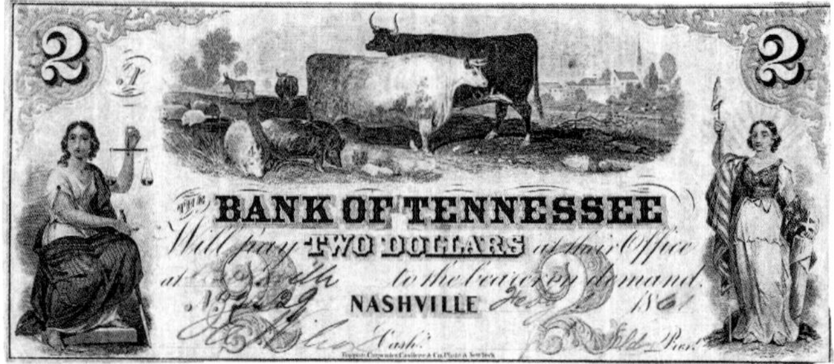

Engraver: Toppan, Carpenter, Casilear & Co. ***Comments:*** H-TN-195-G10, Garland-869. 18__. 1850s.

Rarity: URS-7
F $250

$2 • W-TN-690-002-G060

Left: 2 / Female portrait. ***Center:*** Soldier, Woman, and two Indians looking at bust of George Washington. ***Right:*** 2 / Portrait of Charles Carroll. ***Tint:*** Red-orange. ***Back:*** Red-orange. ***Engraver:*** Toppan, Carpenter & Co. ***Comments:*** H-TN-195-G12a, Garland-872. 18__. 1850s.

Rarity: URS-7
F $250

$3 • W-TN-690-003-G070

Left: THREE / Woman standing / THREE. ***Center:*** 3 / Men on horses, sheep / 3. ***Right:*** THREE / Cherubs in 3 / THREE. ***Engraver:*** Draper, Toppan & Co. ***Comments:*** H-TN-195-G14, Garland-875. Mar. 1, 1842.

Rarity: URS-3
F $550

$3 • W-TN-690-003-G070a

Engraver: Toppan, Carpenter & Co. ***Comments:*** H-TN-195-G14a, Garland-875. Similar to W-TN-690-003-G070 but with different date and engraver imprint. Mar. 1, ____. 1840s, 1861.

Rarity: URS-3
F $550

$5 • W-TN-690-005-G080

Left: 5 / Woman leaning on column / V. ***Center:*** Woman seated with shield. ***Right:*** 5 / Justice standing with scales and eagle / V. ***Engraver:*** Rawdon, Wright, Hatch & Edson / Rawdon, Wright & Hatch. ***Comments:*** H-TN-195-G16, Garland-876. 18__. 1838–1840s.

Rarity: URS-1
F $3,000

$5 • W-TN-690-005-G090 CC

Back: Plain. ***Engraver:*** Danforth, Bald & Co. ***Comments:*** H-Unlisted, Garland-877. 18__. 1850s.

Rarity: URS-7
F $175; **Proof** $1,500

$5 • W-TN-690-005-G090a CC

Back: Red-orange. ***Engraver:*** Danforth, Bald & Co. ***Comments:*** H-TN-195-G18a. Similar to W-TN-690-005-G090. Back of note shown. 18__. 1850s.

Rarity: URS-7
F $175

$5 • W-TN-690-005-G090b

Tint: Red-orange outlining white V / 5 / V. ***Back:*** Red-orange. ***Engraver:*** Danforth, Bald & Co. ***Comments:*** H-TN-195-G18b, Garland-878. Similar to W-TN-690-005-G090. 18__. 1850s.

Rarity: URS-7
F $175

$10 • W-TN-690-010-G100 SI

Engraver: Draper, Toppan, Longacre & Co. ***Comments:*** H-TN-195-G24, Garland-886. 18__. 1838–1840s.

Rarity: URS-3
F $550

$10 • W-TN-690-010-G110

Left: 10 / Portrait of James K. Polk. ***Center:*** Portrait of Andrew Jackson. ***Right:*** 10 / Portrait of Cave Johnson. ***Tint:*** Red-orange lathework outlining white 10 / 10. ***Back:*** Blue. ***Engraver:*** Toppan, Carpenter & Co. ***Comments:*** H-TN-195-G26a, Garland-882. 18__. 1850s–1861.

Rarity: URS-3
F $550

$20 • W-TN-690-020-G120

Left: 20 / Man writing on tablet / 20. ***Center:*** Woman standing with eagle and shield. ***Right:*** 20 / Shield / 20. ***Engraver:*** Draper, Toppan, Longacre & Co. ***Comments:*** H-TN-195-G28. 18__. 1838–1840s.

Rarity: —

$20 • W-TN-690-020-G120a

Engraver: Toppan, Carpenter & Co. ***Comments:*** H-TN-195-G28a, Garland-888. Similar to W-TN-690-020-G120 but with different engraver imprint. 18__. 1840s–1850s

Rarity: URS-3
F $500

$20 • W-TN-690-020-G130

Left: 20 / Portrait of Zachary Taylor / 20. ***Center:*** Three women reclining, Ship / 20. ***Right:*** Justice seated with sword and scales / TWENTY. ***Engraver:*** Toppan, Carpenter, Casilear & Co. ***Comments:*** H-TN-195-G30, Garland-890. 18__. 1850s.

Rarity: —

$20 • W-TN-690-020-G130a

Back: Red-orange. ***Engraver:*** Toppan, Carpenter, Casilear & Co. ***Comments:*** H-TN-195-G30a. Similar to W-TN-690-020-G130. 18__. 1850s.

Rarity: —

$20 • W-TN-690-020-G130b

Tint: Red-orange outlining white TWENTY. ***Back:*** Red-orange. ***Engraver:*** Toppan, Carpenter, Casilear & Co. ***Comments:*** H-TN-195-G30b, Garland-892. Similar to W-TN-690-020-G130. 18__. 1850s.

Rarity: —

$50 • W-TN-690-050-G140

Left: 50 / Shield / 50. ***Center:*** Hebe watering eagle. ***Right:*** 50 / Portrait of George Washington / 50. ***Engraver:*** Draper, Toppan, Longacre & Co. ***Comments:*** H-TN-195-G32. 18__. 1838–1840s.

Rarity: —

$50 • W-TN-690-050-G140a CC

Back: Red-orange. ***Engraver:*** Toppan, Carpenter, Casilear & Co. ***Comments:*** H-TN-195-G32a, Garland-896. Similar to W-TN-690-050-G140 but with different engraver imprint. 18__. 1850s.

Rarity: URS-2
F $600

$100 • **W-TN-690-100-G150**

Left: Atlas lifting world on shoulders / 100. ***Center:*** 100 / Justice with eagle and shield / 100. ***Right:*** Atlas lifting world on shoulders / 100. ***Engraver:*** Draper, Toppan, Longacre & Co. ***Comments:*** H-TN-195-G34. 18__. 1838–1850s.

Rarity: —

$100 • **W-TN-690-100-G150a**

Back: Red-orange. ***Engraver:*** Toppan, Carpenter, Casilear & Co. ***Comments:*** H-TN-195-G34a, Garland-899. Similar to W-TN-690-100-G150 but with different engraver imprint. 18__. 1850s.

Rarity: URS-1
F $5,000

Post Notes

$10 • **W-TN-690-010-G160**

Left: 10 / Eagle with shield / X. ***Center:*** Woman with children seated among parcels, Factories and farmhouse. ***Right:*** 10 / Shield / X. ***Engraver:*** Draper, Toppan, Longacre & Co. ***Comments:*** H-TN-195-G38. 18__. 1830s.

Rarity: —

$20 • **W-TN-690-020-G170**

Left: 20 / Man writing on tablet / 20. ***Center:*** Woman standing with eagle and shield. ***Right:*** 20 / Shield / 20. ***Engraver:*** Draper, Toppan, Longacre & Co. ***Comments:*** H-TN-195-G40. 18__. 1830s.

Rarity: —

$500 • **W-TN-690-500-G180** CC

Engraver: Rawdon, Wright & Hatch. ***Comments:*** H-Unlisted, Garland-901. 18__. 1860s.

Rarity: URS-1
F $4,000

Notes on Which the Place Payable is Blank

$1 • **W-TN-690-001-G190**

Left: Woman seated with farmer / Female portrait. ***Center:*** 1 / Man plowing with horses / 1. ***Right:*** ONE / Medallion head / ONE. ***Engraver:*** Draper, Toppan & Co. ***Comments:*** H-TN-195-G470. Mar. 1, 1842.

Rarity: —

$1 • **W-TN-690-001-G200**

Left: 1 / Sailor standing with flag. ***Center:*** 1 / Two women seated with cog wheel / 1. ***Right:*** 1 / Woman with sheaf on back. ***Engraver:*** Toppan, Carpenter, Casilear & Co. ***Comments:*** H-TN-195-G472. 18__. 1850s.

Rarity: —

$1 • **W-TN-690-001-G200a**

Back: Red-orange. ***Engraver:*** Toppan, Carpenter, Casilear & Co. ***Comments:*** H-TN-195-G472a. Similar to W-TN-690-001-G200. 18__. 1850s.

Rarity: —

$1 • **W-TN-690-001-G210**

Left: 1 / Portrait of boy. ***Center:*** Indian on horseback hunting buffalo. ***Right:*** 1 / Female portrait. ***Tint:*** Red-orange. ***Back:*** Red-orange. ***Engraver:*** Toppan, Carpenter & Co. ***Comments:*** H-TN-195-G474a. 18__. 1850s.

Rarity: —

$2 • **W-TN-690-002-G220**

Left: TWO / Woman seated in 2 / 2. ***Center:*** 2 / Woman seated on bales / 2. ***Right:*** 2 / Ship / 2. ***Engraver:*** Draper, Toppan & Co. ***Comments:*** H-TN-195-G476. Mar. 1, 1842.

Rarity: —

$2 • **W-TN-690-002-G230**

Left: 2 / Justice seated with scales. ***Center:*** Cattle / 2 / 2. ***Right:*** 2 / Liberty with pole, cap, and flag. ***Engraver:*** Toppan, Carpenter, Casilear & Co. ***Comments:*** H-TN-195-G478. 18__. 1850s.

Rarity: —

$2 • **W-TN-690-002-G230a**

Back: Red-orange. ***Engraver:*** Toppan, Carpenter, Casilear & Co. ***Comments:*** H-TN-195-G478a. Similar to W-TN-690-002-G230. 18__. 1850s.

Rarity: —

$2 • **W-TN-690-002-G240**

Left: 2 / Female portrait. ***Center:*** Soldier, Woman, and two Indians looking at bust of George Washington. ***Right:*** 2 / Portrait of Charles Carroll. ***Tint:*** Red-orange. ***Back:*** Red-orange. ***Engraver:*** Toppan, Carpenter & Co. ***Comments:*** H-TN-195-G480a. 18__. 1850s.

Rarity: —

$3 • **W-TN-690-003-G250**

Left: THREE / Woman standing / THREE. ***Center:*** 3 / Men on horses, sheep / 3. ***Right:*** THREE / Cherubs in 3 / THREE. ***Engraver:*** Draper, Toppan & Co. ***Comments:*** H-TN-195-G482. Mar. 1, 1842.

Rarity: —

How to Read the Whitman Numbering System

$1 • **W-AL-020-001-G010a**

Denomination: Face value of the note shown.

W: Whitman number. This number is a sortable code unique to each bank and note.

AL: Abbreviation for the state under study.

020: Numerical designation specific to each bank.

001: The denomination in dollars.

G010a: G indicates a good or valid note. Other categories are indicated thus: C (counterfeit); R (raised); S (spurious); N (not-attributed); A (altered). Numbers are assigned starting with 010, 020, et seq. Terminal letters following the number indicate variations of a note: a series of different colored overprints, tints, payees, etc., all on the same design of note. For more information, see the "How to Use This Book" section at the front of the volume, page xiv.

$5 • **W-TN-690-005-G260**

Left: 5 / Woman leaning on column / V. ***Center:*** Woman seated with shield. ***Right:*** 5 / Justice standing with scales and eagle / V. ***Engraver:*** Rawdon, Wright, Hatch & Edson / Rawdon, Wright & Hatch. ***Comments:*** H-TN-195-G484. 18__. 1838–1840s.

Rarity: —

$5 • **W-TN-690-005-G270** RG

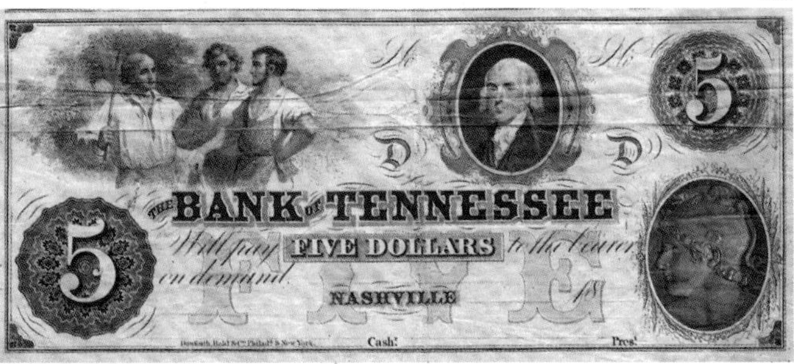

Engraver: Danforth, Bald & Co. ***Comments:*** H-TN-195-G486. 18__. 1850s.

Rarity: URS-7
F $200

$5 • **W-TN-690-005-G270a**

Tint: Red-orange outlining white V / 5 / V. ***Back:*** Red-orange. ***Engraver:*** Danforth, Bald & Co. ***Comments:*** H-TN-195-G486a. Similar to W-TN-690-005-G270. 18__. 1850s.

Rarity: —

$6 • **W-TN-690-006-G280**

Left: VI / Men harvesting cotton / VI. ***Center:*** 6 / Woman seated with shield / 6. ***Right:*** VI / Cow / VI. ***Engraver:*** Rawdon, Wright & Hatch. ***Comments:*** H-TN-195-G488. 18__. 1850s.

Rarity: —

$7 • **W-TN-690-007-G290**

Engraver: Rawdon, Wright & Hatch. ***Comments:*** H-TN-195-G489. No description available. 18__. 1850s.

Rarity: *None known*

$8 • **W-TN-690-008-G300**

Engraver: Rawdon, Wright & Hatch. ***Comments:*** H-TN-195-G490. No description available. 18__. 1850s.

Rarity: *None known*

$9 • **W-TN-690-009-G310**

Engraver: Rawdon, Wright & Hatch. ***Comments:*** H-TN-195-G491. No description available. 18__. 1850s.

Rarity: *None known*

$10 • **W-TN-690-010-G320**

Left: 10 / Eagle with shield / X. ***Center:*** Woman with children seated among parcels, Factories and farmhouse. ***Right:*** 10 / Shield / X. ***Engraver:*** Draper, Toppan, Longacre & Co. ***Comments:*** H-TN-195-G492. 18__. 1838–1840s.

Rarity: —

$10 • **W-TN-690-010-G330**

Left: Three women with anchor / TEN. ***Center:*** 10 / Woman seated with plow and shield, Train. ***Right:*** X / TEN / 10. ***Engraver:*** Toppan, Carpenter, Casilear & Co. ***Comments:*** H-TN-195-G494, Garland-885. Probably made only as Proofs. 18__. 1830s–1840s.

Rarity: —

$10 • **W-TN-690-010-G340**

Left: 10 / Portrait of James K. Polk. ***Center:*** Portrait of Andrew Jackson. ***Right:*** 10 / Portrait of Cave Johnson. ***Tint:*** Red-orange outlining white 10 / 10. ***Engraver:*** Toppan, Carpenter & Co. ***Comments:*** H-TN-195-G496a. 18__. 1850s–1861.

Rarity: —

$20 • **W-TN-690-020-G350**

Left: 20 / Man writing on tablet / 20. ***Center:*** Woman standing with eagle and shield. ***Right:*** 20 / Shield / 20. ***Engraver:*** Draper, Toppan, Longacre & Co. ***Comments:*** H-TN-195-G498. 18__. 1838–1840s.

Rarity: —

$20 • **W-TN-690-020-G360**

Left: 20 / Portrait of Zachary Taylor / 20. ***Center:*** Three women reclining, Ship / 20. ***Right:*** Justice seated with sword and scales / TWENTY. ***Engraver:*** Toppan, Carpenter, Casilear & Co. ***Comments:*** H-TN-195-G500. 18__. 1850s.

Rarity: —

$20 • **W-TN-690-020-G360a**

Back: Red-orange. ***Engraver:*** Toppan, Carpenter, Casilear & Co. ***Comments:*** H-TN-195-G500a. Similar to W-TN-690-020-G360. 18__. 1850s.

Rarity: —

$20 • **W-TN-690-020-G360b**

Tint: Red-orange outlining white TWENTY. ***Back:*** Red-orange. ***Engraver:*** Toppan, Carpenter, Casilear & Co. ***Comments:*** H-TN-195-G500b. Similar to W-TN-690-020-G360. 18__. 1850s.

Rarity: —

$20 • **W-TN-690-020-G360c** CC, CC

Tint: Red-orange lathework and panel of microlettering outlining white TWENTY. ***Back:*** Blue. ***Engraver:*** American Bank Note Co. / ABNCo. monogram. ***Comments:*** H-TN-195-G500c, Garland-894. Similar to W-TN-690-020-G360 but with different engraver imprint. 18__. 1850s.

Rarity: URS-6
F $200

$50 • W-TN-690-050-G370

Left: 50 / Shield / 50. ***Center:*** Hebe watering eagle. ***Right:*** 50 / Portrait of George Washington / 50. ***Engraver:*** Draper, Toppan, Longacre & Co. ***Comments:*** H-TN-195-G502. 18__. 1838–1840s.

Rarity: —

$50 • W-TN-690-050-G370a

Back: Red-orange. ***Engraver:*** Toppan, Carpenter, Casilear & Co. ***Comments:*** H-TN-195-G502a, Garland-896. Similar to W-TN-690-050-G370 but with different engraver imprint. 18__. 1850s.

Rarity: URS-1
F $2,000

$50 • W-TN-690-050-G370b

CC

Tint: Red-orange lathework and panel of microlettering outlining white FIFTY. ***Back:*** Blue. ***Engraver:*** Toppan, Carpenter, Casilear & Co / ABNCo. monogram. ***Comments:*** H-TN-195-G502b, Garland-898. Similar to W-TN-690-050-G370 but with different engraver imprint. 18__. 1859–1861.

Rarity: URS-4
F $875

$100 • W-TN-690-100-G380

Left: Atlas lifting world on shoulders / 100. ***Center:*** 100 / Hebe watering eagle / 100. ***Right:*** Atlas lifting world on shoulders / 100. ***Engraver:*** Draper, Toppan, Longacre & Co. ***Comments:*** H-TN-195-G504. 18__. 1838–1850s.

Rarity: —

$100 • W-TN-690-100-G380a

Back: Red-orange. ***Engraver:*** Toppan, Carpenter, Casilear & Co. ***Comments:*** H-TN-195-G504a, Garland-899. Similar to W-TN-690-100-G380 but with different engraver imprint. 18__. 1850s.

Rarity: URS-1
F $3,580

$100 • W-TN-690-100-G380b

CC

CC

Tint: Red-orange lathework and panel of microlettering outlining white HUNDRED. ***Back:*** Blue medallion head of George Washington / Medallion head of George Washington. ***Engraver:*** Toppan, Carpenter, Casilear & Co / ABNCo. monogram. ***Comments:*** H-TN-195-G504c, Garland-Unlisted. Similar to W-TN-690-100-G380 but with different engraver imprint. 18__. 1838–1850s.

Rarity: URS-2
F $250

$500 • W-TN-690-500-G390

HA

Tint: Red-orange. ***Engraver:*** American Bank Note Co. ***Comments:*** H-TN-195-G506a, Garland-902. 18__. 1860s.

Rarity: URS-3
VF $8,700; **Proof** $6,500
Selected auction price: Heritage Auctions, April 2014, Lot 3513, VF $8,700

$500 • W-TN-690-500-G400

Left: Portrait of girl. ***Center:*** 500. ***Right:*** Portrait of girl. ***Tint:*** Red-orange. ***Engraver:*** American Bank Note Co. ***Comments:*** H-TN-195-G508a. 18__. 1860s.

Rarity: —

$1,000 • W-TN-690-1000-G405

Left: Woman holding dove. ***Center:*** 1000 / ONE THOUSAND. ***Right:*** Female portrait. ***Tint:*** Red-orange die and M / 1000 / M. ***Engraver:*** American Bank Note Co. ***Comments:*** H-Unlisted, Garland-903. 18__. 1860s.

Rarity: URS-3
VF $9,000; **Proof** $6,500

Civil War Issues

5¢ • W-TN-690-00.05-G410

Left: FIVE CENTS vertically. ***Center:*** Spanish-American coin / Ship / Spanish-American coin. ***Right:*** FIVE CENTS vertically. ***Overprint:*** Red HALF DIME. ***Engraver:*** Manouvrier. ***Comments:*** H-TN-195-G50, Garland-840. December 1st, 1861.

Rarity: URS-5
F $250

5¢ • W-TN-690-00.05-G410a

SI

Overprint: None. ***Engraver:*** Manouvrier. ***Comments:*** H-TN-195-G50a, Garland-839. Similar to W-TN-690-00.05-G410. December 1st, 1861.

Rarity: URS-7
VF $75

5¢ • W-TN-690-00.05-G420

CC

Engraver: Manouvrier. ***Comments:*** H-TN-195-G52, Garland-841. December 1st, 1861.

Rarity: URS-7
F $75

10¢ • W-TN-690-00.10-G430

Left: TEN CENTS vertically. ***Center:*** 2-reales coin / Train / 2-reales coin. ***Right:*** TEN CENTS vertically. ***Overprint:*** Red ONE DIME. ***Engraver:*** Manouvrier. ***Comments:*** H-TN-195-G54, Garland-843. December 1st, 1861.

Rarity: URS-5
F $150

10¢ • W-TN-690-00.10-G430a

Engraver: Manouvrier. ***Comments:*** H-TN-195-G54a. Similar to W-TN-690-00.10-G430. December 1st, 1861.

Rarity: —

10¢ • W-TN-690-00.10-G430b

SI

Overprint: None. ***Engraver:*** Manouvrier. ***Comments:*** H-TN-195-G54b, Garland-Unlisted. Similar to W-TN-690-00.10-G430. December 1st, 1861.

Rarity: URS-9
F $75

10¢ • W-TN-690-00.10-G430c

CC

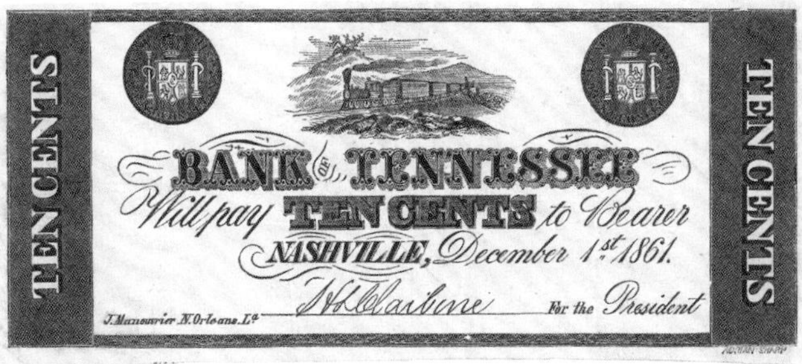

Overprint: None. ***Engraver:*** Manouvrier. ***Comments:*** H-TN-195-G54c, Garland-842. Similar to W-TN-690-00.10-G430. December 1st, 1861.

Rarity: URS-7
F $125

10¢ • W-TN-690-00.10-G440

CC

Engraver: Manouvrier. ***Comments:*** H-TN-195-G56, Garland-844. December 1st, 1861.

Rarity: URS-7
EF $125

10¢ • W-TN-690-00.10-G450

Left: TEN CENTS vertically. ***Center:*** 2-reales coin / Train / 10. ***Right:*** TEN CENTS vertically. ***Engraver:*** Manouvrier. ***Comments:*** H-TN-195-G58. Handwritten “FIVE CENTS” across right end. December 1st, 1861.

Rarity: —

10¢ • W-TN-690-00.10-G450a

Engraver: Manouvrier. ***Comments:*** H-TN-195-G58a, Garland-846. Handwritten “FIVE CENTS” across right end has been trimmed off. Similar to W-TN-690-00.10-G450. December 1st, 1861.

Rarity: URS-6
F $150

25¢ • W-TN-690-00.25-G460

ANS

Engraver: Manouvrier. ***Comments:*** H-TN-195-G60, Garland-851. December 1st, 1861.

Rarity: URS-7
F $75

25¢ • W-TN-690-00.25-G460a CC

Overprint: Red QUARTER DOLL. ***Engraver:*** Manouvrier. ***Comments:*** H-TN-195-G60a, Garland-852. Similar to W-TN-690-00.25-G460. December 1st, 1861.

Rarity: URS-4
F $300

25¢ • W-TN-690-00.25-G460b SI

Overprint: None. ***Engraver:*** Manouvrier. ***Comments:*** H-TN-195-G60b. Similar to W-TN-690-00.25-G460. December 1st, 1861.

Rarity: URS-8
F $75

50¢ • W-TN-690-00.50-G470 SI

Engraver: Manouvrier. ***Comments:*** H-TN-195-G62, Garland-856. December 1st, 1861.

Rarity: URS-6
F $100

50¢ • W-TN-690-00.50-G470a

Left: 2-reales coin / 50. ***Center:*** Train. ***Right:*** 2-reales coin / 50. ***Overprint:*** Red HALF DOLL. ***Engraver:*** Manouvrier. ***Comments:*** H-TN-195-G62a, Garland-855. Similar to W-TN-690-00.50-G470. December 1st, 1861.

Rarity: URS-4
F $300

50¢ • W-TN-690-00.50-G470b CC

Overprint: None. ***Engraver:*** Manouvrier. ***Comments:*** H-TN-195-G62b, Garland-854. Similar to W-TN-690-00.50-G470. December 1st, 1861.

Rarity: URS-7
F $125

$1 • W-TN-690-001-G480

Left: 2-reales coin / 1. ***Center:*** Barrels, Plow, Farm implements. ***Right:*** 2-reales coin / 1. ***Overprint:*** Red ONE DOLLAR. ***Engraver:*** Manouvrier. ***Comments:*** H-TN-195-G64, Garland-858. December 1st, 1861.

Rarity: URS-5
F $250

$1 • W-TN-690-001-G480a SI

Overprint: None. ***Engraver:*** Manouvrier. ***Comments:*** H-TN-195-G64a. Similar to W-TN-690-001-G480. December 1st, 1861.

Rarity: URS-9
F $75

Uncut Sheets

5¢-10¢-10¢-25¢-50¢-50¢ •

W-TN-690-00.05.00.10.00.10.00.25.00.50.00.50-US010 ANS

Engraver: Manouvrier. ***Comments:*** H-TN-195-G52, G56, G56, G60, G62, G62. This is likely a half sheet with the right side cut off. December 1st, 1861.

Rarity: URS-3
F $750

$5-$5-$5-$5 •

W-TN-690-005.005.005.005-US020 RG

Engraver: Danforth, Bald & Co. ***Comments:*** H-TN-195-G486, G486, G486, G486. All four notes identical. 18__. 1850s.

Rarity: URS-4
F $800

Non-Valid Issues

$10 • W-TN-690-010-C100

Engraver: Draper, Toppan, Longacre & Co. ***Comments:*** H-TN-195-C24. Counterfeit of W-TN-690-010-G100. 18__. 1853.

Rarity: URS-3
F $450

$20 • W-TN-690-020-C120a

Engraver: Toppan, Carpenter & Co. ***Comments:*** H-TN-195-C28a. Counterfeit of W-TN-690-020-G120a. 18__. 1853.

Rarity: —

$20 • W-TN-690-020-C130

Engraver: Toppan, Carpenter, Casilear & Co. ***Comments:*** H-TN-195-C30. Counterfeit of W-TN-690-020-G130. 18__. 1853.

Rarity: URS-3
F $400

$20 • W-TN-690-020-C130a

Back: Red-orange. ***Engraver:*** Toppan, Carpenter, Casilear & Co. ***Comments:*** H-TN-195-C30a. Counterfeit of W-TN-690-020-G130a. 18__. 1853.

Rarity: —

$20 • W-TN-690-020-C130b

Tint: Red-orange outlining white TWENTY. ***Back:*** Red-orange. ***Engraver:*** Toppan, Carpenter, Casilear & Co. ***Comments:*** H-TN-195-C30b. Counterfeit of W-TN-690-020-G130b. 18__. 1853.

Rarity: —

$50 • W-TN-690-050-C140

Engraver: Draper, Toppan, Longacre & Co. ***Comments:*** H-TN-195-C32. Counterfeit of W-TN-690-050-G140. 18__. 1853.

Rarity: URS-3
F $500

Post Notes

$10 • W-TN-690-010-C160

Engraver: Draper, Toppan, Longacre & Co. ***Comments:*** H-TN-195-C38. Counterfeit of W-TN-690-010-G160. 18__. 1830s.

Rarity: —

Notes on Which the Place Payable is Blank

$20 • W-TN-690-020-C350

Engraver: Draper, Toppan, Longacre & Co. ***Comments:*** H-TN-195-C498a. Counterfeit of W-TN-690-020-G350. 18__. 1838–1840s.

Rarity: —

$20 • W-TN-690-020-C350a

Engraver: Draper, Toppan, Longacre & Co. ***Comments:*** H-Unlisted. Similar to W-TN-690-020-C350. 18__. 1838–1840s.

Rarity: —

$50 • W-TN-690-050-C370

Engraver: Draper, Toppan, Longacre & Co. ***Comments:*** H-TN-195-C502. Counterfeit of W-TN-690-050-G370. 18__. 1838–1840s.

Rarity: —

Bank of the Union

1850s–1860s

W-TN-700

History: A different institution from the Union Bank of Tennessee, W-TN-840, in the same city, the Bank of the Union was located at 24 Cedar Street and was very active in its time. In 1857 these values were given: capital $88,180; bills in circulation $15,643; specie $4,632. Daniel F. Carter was the president at the time, and G.H. Slaughter was the cashier. In 1861 John Herriford took the place of cashier, and the capital rose to $100,000.

Numismatic Commentary: Generally a scarcer issuer, but notes should be obtainable with diligent hunting.

Remaining at the American Bank Note Co. archives as of 2003 was a $10-$20 face plate, a $10-$20 tint plate, and a $1-$1-$1-$5 face plate. The 1990 Christie's sale of the American Bank Note Co. archives produced a $1-$1-$1-$5 sheet.

Valid Issues

$1 • W-TN-700-001-G010 CC

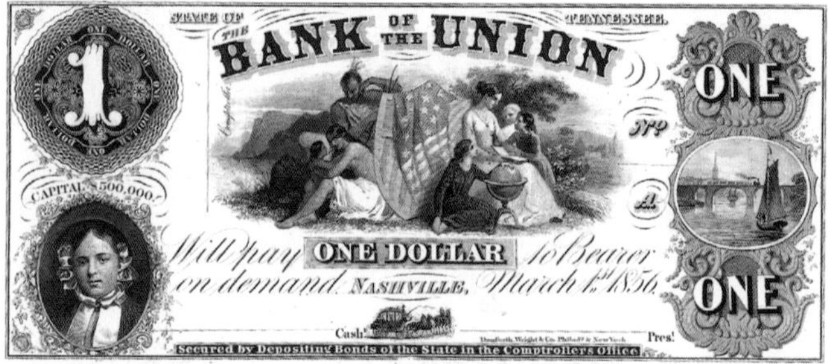

Engraver: Danforth, Wright & Co. ***Comments:*** H-TN-205-G2, Garland-904. March 1st, 1856.

Rarity: URS-5
Proof $1,250

$1 • W-TN-700-001-G010a CC

Overprint: Red ONE. ***Engraver:*** Danforth, Wright & Co. ***Comments:*** H-TN-205-G2a, Garland-905. Similar to W-TN-700-001-G010. March 1st, 1856.

Rarity: URS-5
F $250; **Proof** $1,050
Selected auction price: Heritage Auctions, April 18, 2012, Lot 15358, Proof $1,035

$5 • W-TN-700-005-G020

Left: Woman with U.S. shield seated in 5 / FIVE. ***Center:*** Portrait of Andrew Jackson surrounded by flags and cannons. ***Right:*** 5 / Hebe watering eagle, Flag, Ship / FIVE. ***Engraver:*** Danforth, Wright & Co. ***Comments:*** H-TN-205-G4, Garland-906. March 1st, 1856.

Rarity: URS-6
F $225

$5 • W-TN-700-005-G020a CC

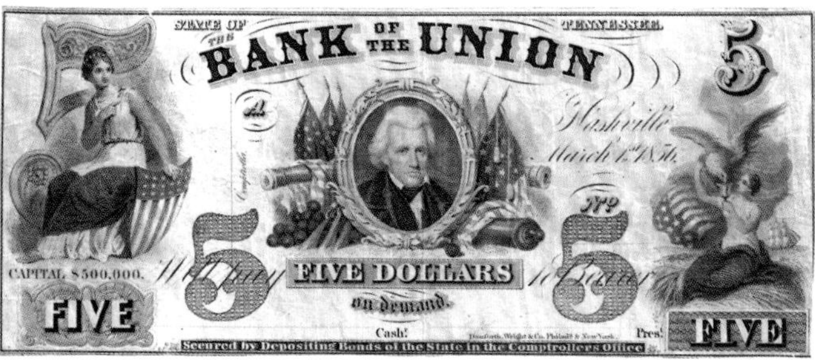

Overprint: Red 5 / 5. ***Engraver:*** Danforth, Wright & Co. ***Comments:*** H-TN-205-G4a, Garland-907. Similar to W-TN-700-005-G020. March 1st, 1856.

Rarity: URS-6
F $250; **VF** $325

$10 • W-TN-700-010-G030

Left: X / X. ***Center:*** Man plowing with horses / Female portrait. ***Right:*** 10 / Portrait of James K. Polk. ***Engraver:*** Danforth, Wright & Co. ***Comments:*** H-Unlisted, Garland-908. Mar. 1, 1865.

Rarity: URS-4
F $350

$10 • W-TN-700-010-G030a

Engraver: American Bank Note Co. ***Comments:*** H-TN-205-G6a, Garland-909. Similar to W-TN-700-010-G030 but with different date and engraver imprint. Printed in red and black. 18__. 1860s.

Rarity: URS-5
F $275

$20 • W-TN-700-020-G040

Left: 20 / Portrait of Henry Clay. ***Center:*** Woman seated with eagle and shield, Farm scene, Train. ***Right:*** 20 / Female portrait. ***Engraver:*** Danforth, Wright & Co. ***Comments:*** H-Unlisted, Garland-910. Mar. 1, 1865.

Rarity: URS-4
F $350

$20 • W-TN-700-020-G040a

Engraver: American Bank Note Co. ***Comments:*** H-TN-205-G8a, Garland-911. Similar to W-TN-700-020-G040 but with different date and engraver imprint. Printed in red and black. 18__. 1860s.

Rarity: URS-4
F $350

Bank of the United States {2nd} (branch)

1817–1836

W-TN-710

History: The second Bank of the United States was chartered in 1816 for a duration of 20 years. Its capital was $35,000,000, of which the United States owned $7,000,000. Branch banks in several large cities were opened during 1816 and 1817 in direct competition with state banks.

The Nashville branch of the second Bank of the United States was approved in 1817. The bank subscribed to a capital of $53,463. However, an act was passed imposing a tax of $50,000 a year on any out-of-state bank, and it was not until the act was repealed that the branch could finally be established. In August 1827 the bank opened in a building at the corner of College Street and Public Square. John Somerville was chosen to be the cashier, and Josiah Nichol became the president.[14]

In 1832 President Andrew Jackson vetoed the 1836 renewal of the Bank of the United States which had been brought up before Congress. This instituted a period of great debate and political turmoil. In late 1833 and early 1834 there was a depression in some areas of business which only served to strengthen the bank, as it was backed by the government. With the Jackson veto standing, the branches began closing and selling their buildings. By March 1836, only the Boston, New York City, Savannah, Nashville, and main Philadelphia facilities remained unsold.

Numismatic Commentary: Any note payable at Nashville from the Bank of the United States is very rare, if they exist at all. Garland opined that each and every note he had seen in his long life of studying and collecting Tennessee notes was a contemporary counterfeit. This opinion holds today.

Valid Issues

$5 • W-TN-710-005-G010 CC

Engraver: Fairman, Draper, Underwood & Co. ***Comments:*** H-US-2-G516, Garland-912. 18__. 1810s–1820s.

Rarity: URS-6
VF $600

$5 • W-TN-710-005-G020

Left: FIVE vertically. ***Center:*** 5 / Eagle / V. ***Right:*** FIVE vertically. ***Engraver:*** Fairman, Draper, Underwood & Co. ***Comments:*** H-US-2-G518. 18__. 1820s–1830s.

Rarity: —

$10 • W-TN-710-010-G030

Left: Portrait / Portrait. ***Center:*** 10 / Eagle / 10. ***Right:*** Portrait / Portrait. ***Engraver:*** Fairman, Draper, Underwood & Co. ***Comments:*** H-US-2-G522, Garland-913. 18__. 1810s–1820s.

Rarity: URS-4
VF $800

$10 • W-TN-710-010-G040

Left: TEN vertically. ***Center:*** 10 / Eagle / X. ***Right:*** TEN vertically. ***Engraver:*** Fairman, Draper, Underwood & Co. ***Comments:*** H-US-2-G524. 18__. 1820s–1830s.

Rarity: —

$20 • **W-TN-710-020-G050**
Left: Portrait / Portrait. ***Center:*** 20 / Eagle / 20. ***Right:*** Portrait / Portrait. ***Engraver:*** Murray, Draper, Fairman & Co. ***Comments:*** H-US-2-G528, Garland-914. 18__. 1810s–1820s.

Rarity: URS-4
VF $800

$20 • **W-TN-710-020-G060**
Left: Eagle / Portrait of George Washington / Medallion head. ***Center:*** 20 / Eagle / 20. ***Right:*** Eagle / Portrait of Benjamin Franklin / Medallion head. ***Engraver:*** Fairman, Draper, Underwood & Co. ***Comments:*** H-US-2-G530. 18__. 1820s–1830s.

Rarity: —

$20 • **W-TN-710-020-G070**
Left: 20 vertically. ***Center:*** 20 / Eagle / 20. ***Right:*** XX vertically. ***Engraver:*** Danforth, Underwood, Bald & Spencer. ***Comments:*** H-US-2-G532. 18__. 1830s.

Rarity: —

$50 • **W-TN-710-050-G080**
Left: Portrait / Portrait. ***Center:*** 50 / Eagle / 50. ***Right:*** Portrait / Portrait. ***Engraver:*** Murray, Draper, Fairman & Co. ***Comments:*** H-US-2-G536. 18__. 1810s–1820s.

Rarity: —

$50 • **W-TN-710-050-G090**
Left: Eagle / Portrait of George Washington / Medallion head. ***Center:*** 50 / Eagle / 50. ***Right:*** Eagle / Portrait of Benjamin Franklin / Medallion head. ***Engraver:*** Fairman, Draper, Underwood & Co. ***Comments:*** H-US-2-G538, Garland-915. 18__. 1830s.

Rarity: URS-4
VF $900

$50 • **W-TN-710-050-G100**
Left: L / Medallion head / 50. ***Center:*** FIFTY / 50 / Eagle / FIFTY / L. ***Right:*** 50 / Medallion head / L. ***Engraver:*** Danforth, Underwood, Bald & Spencer. ***Comments:*** H-US-2-G540. 18__. 1830s.

Rarity: —

$100 • **W-TN-710-100-G110**
Left: Portrait / Portrait. ***Center:*** 100 / Eagle / 100. ***Right:*** Portrait / Portrait. ***Engraver:*** Murray, Draper, Fairman & Co. ***Comments:*** H-US-2-G544. 18__. 1810s–1820s.

Rarity: —

$100 • **W-TN-710-100-G120**
Left: Eagle / Portrait of George Washington / Medallion head. ***Center:*** 100 / Eagle / 100. ***Right:*** Eagle / Portrait of Benjamin Franklin / Medallion head. ***Engraver:*** Fairman, Draper, Underwood & Co. ***Comments:*** H-US-2-G546, Garland-916. 18__. 1820s–1830s.

Rarity: —

$100 • **W-TN-710-100-G130**
Left: 100 / Medallion head / C. ***Center:*** 100 / Eagle / 100. ***Right:*** C / Medallion head / 100. ***Engraver:*** Danforth, Underwood, Bald & Spencer. ***Comments:*** H-US-2-G548. 18__. 1830s.

Rarity: —

Non-Valid Issues

$5 • **W-TN-710-005-C010**

ANS

Engraver: Murray, Draper, Fairman & Co. ***Comments:*** H-US-2-C516. Counterfeit of W-TN-710-005-G010. 18__. 1820s.

Rarity: URS-7
F $150

$10 • **W-TN-710-010-C030**

CC

Engraver: Murray, Draper, Fairman & Co. ***Comments:*** H-US-2-C522. Counterfeit of W-TN-710-010-G030. 18__. 1820s.

Rarity: URS-7
F $200

$20 • **W-TN-710-020-C050**
Engraver: Murray, Draper, Fairman & Co. ***Comments:*** H-US-2-C528. Counterfeit of W-TN-710-020-G050. 18__. 1820s.

Rarity: —

$20 • **W-TN-710-020-N010**

HA

Engraver: Draper, Underwood, Bald & Spencer. ***Comments:*** H-Unlisted. 18__. 1830s.

Rarity: URS-5
VF $750

$50 • **W-TN-710-050-C090**
Engraver: Fairman, Draper, Underwood & Co. ***Comments:*** H-US-2-C538. Counterfeit of W-TN-710-050-G090. 18__. 1830s.

Rarity: —

$100 • **W-TN-710-100-C110**

Engraver: Murray, Draper, Fairman & Co. ***Comments:*** H-US-2-C544. Counterfeit of W-TN-710-100-G110. 18__. 1820s.

Rarity: —

$100 • **W-TN-710-100-C120**

CC

Engraver: Danforth, Underwood, Bald & Spencer. ***Comments:*** H-US-2-C546. Counterfeit of W-TN-710-100-G120. 18__. 1830s.

Rarity: URS-5

F $800

Central Bank of Tennessee

1856 and 1857

W-TN-720

History: In 1856 it was reported that "there never was any such corporation as the Central Bank of Tennessee, and that Belknap, Tremain & Haven, merely took upon themselves that name under which to carry on their banking business—without any charter or act of incorporation."[15] By 1857 the enterprise, along with its branches, had failed.

The Central Bank of Tennessee had branch banks located in Dandridge, W-TN-240, and Paris, W-TN-860.

Numismatic Commentary: Most denominations are available to a beginning collector today, although some scarcer varieties do exist. Overstamps of birds were used by this bank to deter counterfeiters.

Valid Issues

$1 • **W-TN-720-001-G010**

ANS

Engraver: Danforth, Wright & Co. ***Comments:*** H-TN-140-G2, Garland-917. June 25th, 1855.

Rarity: URS-7

F $150; **Unc-Rem** $1,100

Selected auction price: Heritage Auctions, January 7, 2015, Lot 18786, Unc $1,116

$1 • **W-TN-720-001-G010a**

CC

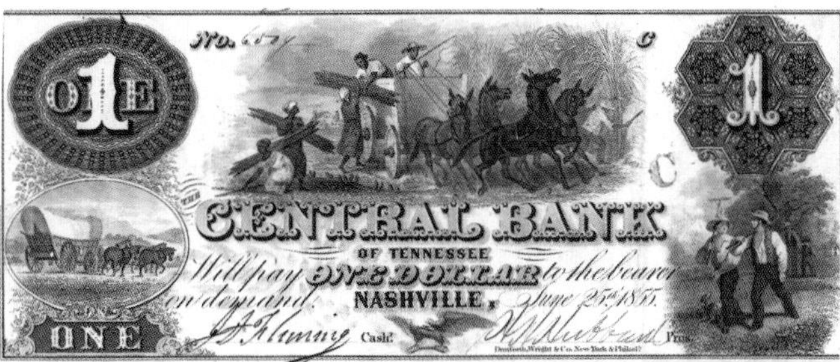

Back: Red bird. ***Engraver:*** Danforth, Wright & Co. ***Comments:*** H-TN-140-G2a, Garland-918. Similar to W-TN-720-001-G010. June 25th, 1855.

Rarity: URS-6

F $250; **VF** $350

$2 • **W-TN-720-002-G020**

CC

Engraver: Danforth, Wright & Co. ***Comments:*** H-TN-140-G4, Garland-920. June 25th, 1855.

Rarity: URS-7

F $150; **EF** $350

$2 • **W-TN-720-002-G020a**

Left: 2 on TWO / Horses plowing. ***Center:*** Horse-drawn wagons, Road. ***Right:*** 2 / Portrait of sailor. ***Back:*** Red bird. ***Engraver:*** Danforth, Wright & Co. ***Comments:*** H-TN-140-G4a, Garland-921. Similar to W-TN-720-002-G020. June 25th, 1855.

Rarity: URS-5

F $250

$5 • **W-TN-720-005-G030**

CC

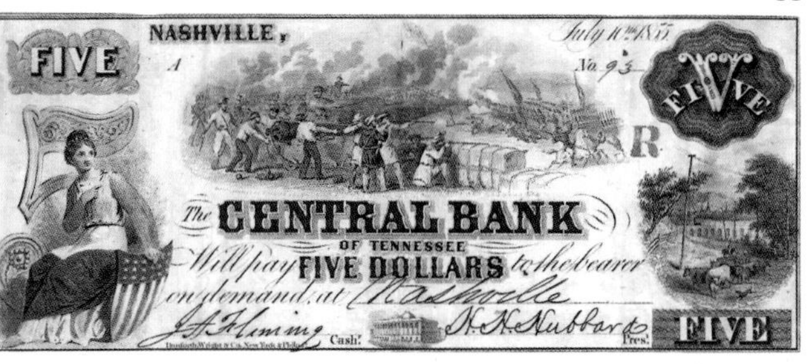

Engraver: Danforth, Wright & Co. ***Comments:*** H-TN-140-G12, Garland-925. June 25th, 1855.

Rarity: URS-6

F $200; **VF** $250

$5 • **W-TN-720-005-G030a**

Back: Red bird. ***Engraver:*** Danforth, Wright & Co. ***Comments:*** H-TN-140-G12a. Similar to W-TN-720-005-G030. June 25th, 1855.

Rarity: URS-6

F $250; **VF** $300

$10 • **W-TN-720-010-G040** CC

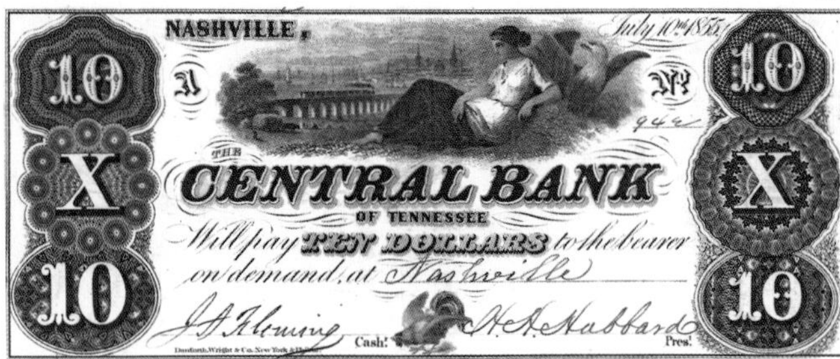

Engraver: Danforth, Wright & Co. ***Comments:*** H-TN-140-G18, Garland-926. June 25th, 1855.

Rarity: URS-6
F $200; **VF** $275

$10 • **W-TN-720-010-G040a**

Left: 10 / X / 10. ***Center:*** Woman reclining with eagle, Train on bridge. ***Right:*** 10 / X / 10. ***Back:*** Red bird. ***Engraver:*** Danforth, Wright & Co. ***Comments:*** H-TN-140-G18a, Garland-927. Similar to W-TN-720-010-G040. June 25th, 1855.

Rarity: URS-5
F $300

$20 • **W-TN-720-020-G050** CC

Engraver: Danforth, Wright & Co. ***Comments:*** H-TN-140-G20, Garland-928. June 25th, 1855.

Rarity: URS-6
F $250; **Unc-Rem** $500

$20 • **W-TN-720-020-G050a**

Back: Red bird. ***Engraver:*** Danforth, Wright & Co. ***Comments:*** H-TN-140-G20a. Similar to W-TN-720-020-G050. June 25th, 1855.

Rarity: URS-6
F $300

Notes on Which the Place Payable is Blank

$1 • **W-TN-720-001-G060**

Left: 1 on ONE / Horses drawing covered wagon / ONE. ***Center:*** Harvest scene, Men loading horse-drawn wagon. ***Right:*** 1 / Two farmers walking. ***Engraver:*** Danforth, Wright & Co. ***Comments:*** H-TN-140-G50, Garland-919. August 1st, 1855.

Rarity: URS-7
F $150

$2 • **W-TN-720-002-G070**

Left: 2 on TWO / Horses plowing. ***Center:*** Horse-drawn wagons, Road. ***Right:*** 2 / Portrait of sailor. ***Engraver:*** Danforth, Wright & Co. ***Comments:*** H-TN-140-G52, Garland-923. August 1st, 1855.

Rarity: URS-7
F $150

$5 • **W-TN-720-005-G080**

Left: FIVE / Liberty with U.S. shield seated in 5. ***Center:*** "Battle of New Orleans." ***Right:*** V on FIVE / Cattle, Bridge / FIVE. ***Engraver:*** Danforth, Wright & Co. ***Comments:*** H-TN-140-G54, Garland-925. July 10th, 1855.

Rarity: —

$10 • **W-TN-720-010-G090**

Left: 10 / X / 10. ***Center:*** Woman reclining with eagle, Train on bridge. ***Right:*** 10 / X / 10. ***Engraver:*** Danforth, Wright & Co. ***Comments:*** H-TN-140-G56, Garland-926. July 10th, 1855.

Rarity: —

$20 • **W-TN-720-020-G100**

Left: 20 / Liberty seated with shield. ***Center:*** XX / Woman reclining with eagle. ***Right:*** 20 / Train. ***Engraver:*** Danforth, Wright & Co. ***Comments:*** H-TN-140-G58, Garland-928. July 10th, 1855.

Rarity: —

Citizens Bank of Nashville and Memphis

1852–1858

W-TN-730

History: On February 25, 1852, the Citizens Bank of Nashville and Memphis was chartered with an authorized capital of $200,000, limited to $500,000. The doors opened for business in 1854. Immediately the bank was held to be in good standing, with a report in *Bankers' Magazine* stating that:

> The gentlemen concerned in obtaining this charter are of established commercial and financial means and credit, and furnish to the community the fullest guarantees, while their business capacity holds out the assurance that the institution will also be made profitable to the stockholders. We learn that all the stock in this bank was subscribed yesterday, and the first two installments were paid in. This is certainly doing business in quick time, and shows the soundness of the basis upon which the application for this charter was granted.[16]

In 1857 the president of the bank was S.P. Walker, with John A. Sannoner elected as cashier. By 1858, however, the bank had closed its affairs.

See also listing under Memphis, W-TN-510.

The Citizens Bank of Nashville and Memphis had a branch bank located in Knoxville, W-TN-370.

Numismatic Commentary: Although chartered in Nashville, control of this bank was taken by citizens of Memphis, where the bank actually opened.

Valid Issues

$1 • W-TN-730-001-G010

SI

Engraver: Toppan, Carpenter, Casilear & Co. ***Comments:*** H-TN-145-G2, Garland-585. 185_. 1850s.

Rarity: URS-4
F $300

$2 • W-TN-730-002-G020

Left: 2 / Portrait of Governor Aaron V. Brown. ***Center:*** Oxen drawing cart, Farmer. ***Right:*** 2 / Indian reclining. ***Engraver:*** Toppan, Carpenter, Casilear & Co. ***Comments:*** H-TN-145-G4, Garland-586. 185_. 1850s.

Rarity: URS-4
F $300

Notes on Which the Place Payable is Blank

$1 • W-TN-730-001-G030

Left: Portrait of Andrew Jackson / 1. ***Center:*** Ship. ***Right:*** 1 / Female portrait / 1. ***Engraver:*** Toppan, Carpenter, Casilear & Co. ***Comments:*** H-TN-145-G34, Garland-585. 185_. 1850s.

Rarity: URS-4
F $300

$2 • W-TN-730-002-G040

Left: 2 / Portrait of Governor Aaron V. Brown. ***Center:*** Oxen drawing cart, Farmer. ***Right:*** 2 / Indian reclining. ***Engraver:*** Toppan, Carpenter, Casilear & Co. ***Comments:*** H-TN-145-G36, Garland-586. 185_. 1850s.

Rarity: URS-4
F $300

$5 • W-TN-730-005-G050

Left: 5 / Train / FIVE. ***Center:*** Liberty seated with eagle and shield. ***Right:*** 5 / Portrait of Andrew Jackson. ***Engraver:*** Toppan, Carpenter, Casilear & Co. ***Comments:*** H-TN-145-G40, Garland-588. 185_. 1850s.

Rarity: URS-4
F $300

City Bank

1856–1864

W-TN-740

History: In 1856 the City Bank was chartered with an authorized capital of $50,000. In 1857 these values were given: capital $50,000; bills in circulation $45,000; specie $5,231.

On March 20, 1860, an act was passed uniting the Bank of Knoxville, W-TN-350, with the City Bank, to be known from that point on as a single entity under the title of the City Bank. The outstanding circulation of the Bank of Knoxville was to be redeemed by the City Bank, but no further circulation with the Bank of Knoxville name was to be issued. In 1864 the bank wrapped up its business and closed.

Numismatic Commentary: Surviving notes are scarce but should be obtainable. The easiest to locate are the two $5 varieties of the American Bank Note Co.

The 1990 Christie's sale of the American Bank Note Co. archives produced a $1-$1-$1-$5 sheet.

Valid Issues

$1 • W-TN-740-001-G010

Left: 1 / Portrait of John Bell. ***Center:*** Two women flanking shield bearing eagle. ***Right:*** 1 / Portrait of Felix Grundy. ***Engraver:*** Danforth, Wright & Co. ***Comments:*** H-TN-150-G2, Garland-929. Novr. 1st, 1855.

Rarity: URS-3
Proof $1,000

$1 • W-TN-740-001-G010a

CC

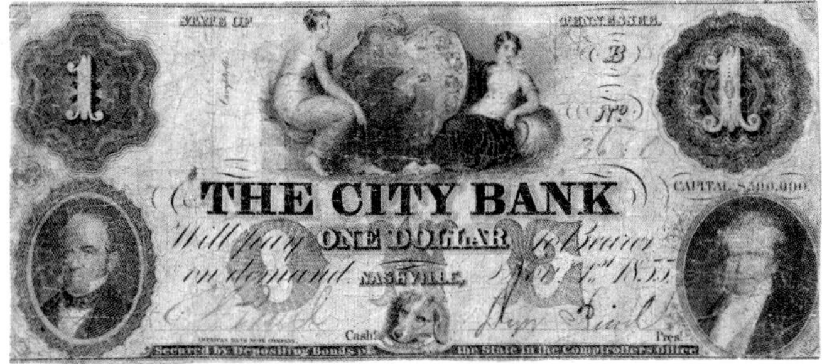

Overprint: Red ONE. ***Engraver:*** American Bank Note Co. ***Comments:*** H-TN-150-G2c, Garland-930. Similar to W-TN-740-001-G010 but with different engraver imprint. Novr. 1st, 1855.

Rarity: URS-5
F $300

Collectors and Researchers:

If you have new information about any banks or notes listed in this volume, contact Whitman Publishing, Attn: Obsolete Paper Money, 3101 Clairmont Road, Suite G, Atlanta, GA 30329.

$5 • **W-TN-740-005-G020**

Left: V / Portrait of Hugh Lawson White. ***Center:*** Woman reclining with eagle / FIVE. ***Right:*** 5 / Portrait of James K. Polk / 5. ***Engraver:*** Danforth, Wright & Co. ***Comments:*** H-TN-150-G4, Garland-931. Novr. 1st, 1855.

Rarity: —

$5 • **W-TN-740-005-G020a**

CC

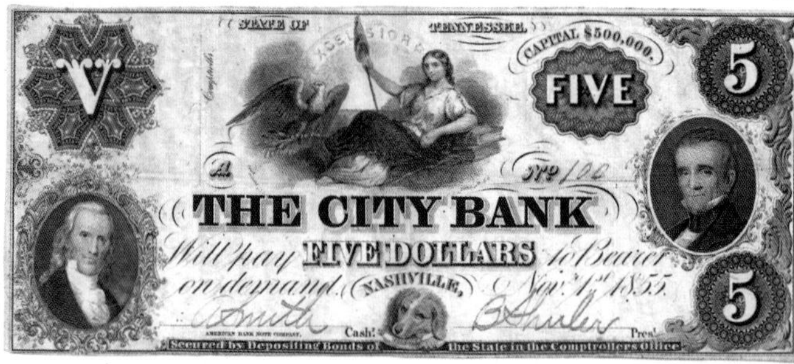

Engraver: American Bank Note Co. ***Comments:*** H-TN-150-G4b, Garland-932. Similar to W-TN-740-005-G020 but with different engraver imprint. Novr. 1st, 1855.

Rarity: URS-6
F $350; **Proof** $1,500

$5 • **W-TN-740-005-G020b**

CC

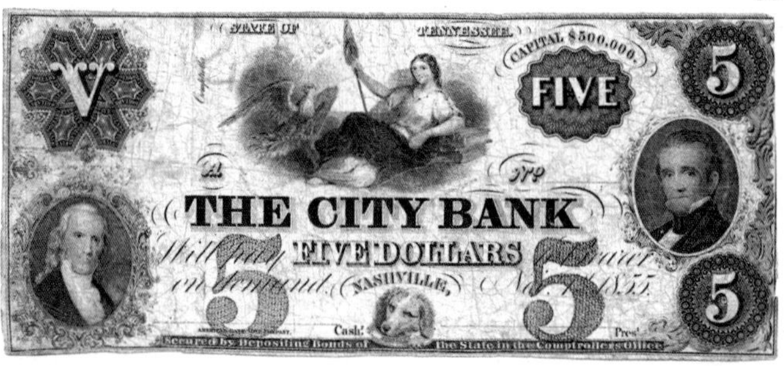

Overprint: Red 5 / 5. ***Engraver:*** American Bank Note Co. ***Comments:*** H-TN-150-G4c, Garland-933. Similar to W-TN-740-005-G020 but with different engraver imprint. Novr. 1st, 1855.

Rarity: URS-6
F $350

$10 • **W-TN-740-010-G030**

CC

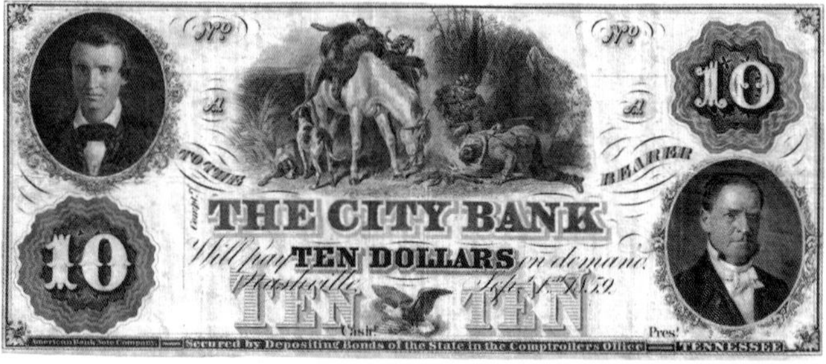

Tint: Red-orange bank title, TEN / TEN, and dies bearing white 10 / 10. ***Engraver:*** American Bank Note Co. ***Comments:*** H-TN-150-G6a, Garland-934. Sept. 1st, 1859.

Rarity: URS-4
VF $575; **Proof** $1,050
Selected auction price: Heritage Auctions, April 22, 2015, Lot 18490, About New $1,057

$20 • **W-TN-740-020-G040**

CC

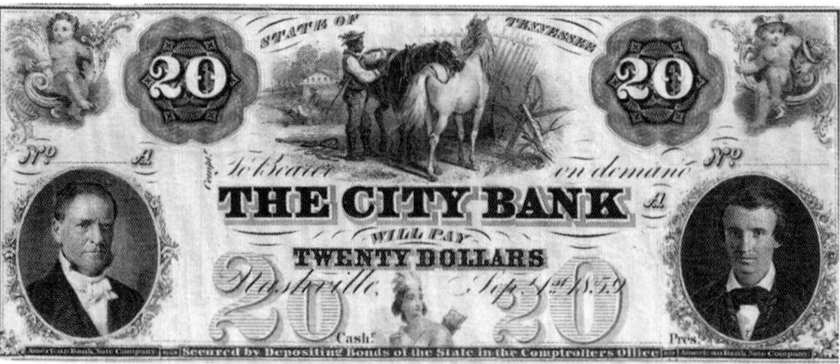

Tint: Red-orange 20 / 20 and dies bearing white 20s. ***Engraver:*** American Bank Note Co. ***Comments:*** H-TN-150-G8a, Garland-935. Sept. 1st, 1859.

Rarity: URS-3
EF $850; **Proof** $1,900
Selected auction price: Heritage Auctions, January 7, 2015, Lot 18787, Proof $1,880

$50 • **W-TN-740-050-G050**

CC

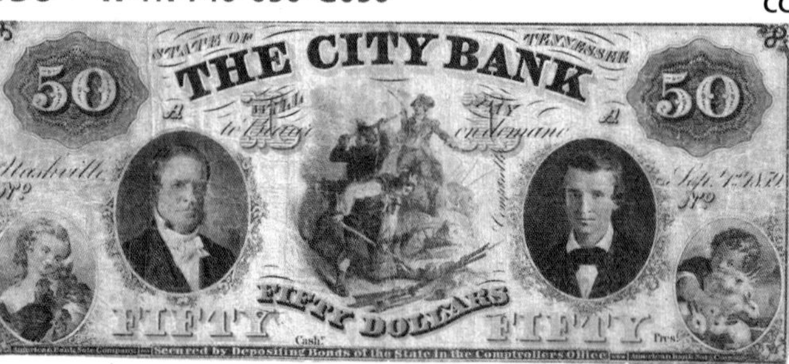

Tint: Red-orange L / L, FIFTY / FIFTY, and dies bearing white 50 / 50. ***Engraver:*** American Bank Note Co. ***Comments:*** H-TN-150-G10a, Garland-936. Sept. 1st, 1859.

Rarity: URS-5
F $775

Non-Valid Issues

$5 • **W-TN-740-005-AR010**

Left: Portrait of Andrew Jackson. ***Center:*** Steamboat. ***Right:*** Female portrait. ***Engraver:*** Toppan, Carpenter, Casilear & Co. ***Comments:*** H-TN-150-A5. Possibly altered and raised from W-TN-230-005-G010. 18__. 1850s.

Rarity: —

$10 • **W-TN-740-010-AR020**

Left: Portrait of Andrew Jackson. ***Center:*** Steamboat. ***Right:*** Female portrait. ***Engraver:*** Toppan, Carpenter, Casilear & Co. ***Comments:*** H-TN-150-A10. Possibly altered and raised from W-TN-230-005-G010. 18__. 1850s.

Rarity: —

Exchange Bank of Cincinnati

1837–1840

W-TN-750

History: No record has been discovered of this bank but for the spurious notes that were issued. Possibly connected to the Kentucky bank of the same name, W-KY-910.

Issues

$2 • W-TN-750-002-G010

CC

Engraver: Rawdon, Wright & Hatch. ***Comments:*** H-Unlisted, Garland-969. 18__. 1840.

Rarity: URS-3
F $450

Exchange Bank of Louisville

Circa 1840

W-TN-760

History: This appears to have been a short-lived enterprise.

Numismatic Commentary: No proof that this bank ever existed has been found, beyond the note listed below. It is thought that the entire issue was fraudulent.

Valid Issues

$1 • W-TN-760-001-G010

CC

Comments: H-TN-160-G2, Garland-938. 184_. 1840s.

Rarity: URS-4
F $300; **Proof** $1,000

Farmers and Mechanics Bank

1817–1819

W-TN-770

History: The Farmers and Mechanics Bank was chartered in 1817 with an authorized capital of $400,000. Trouble struck almost immediately, and on June 18, 1819, the bank was forced to suspend specie payments. It was the first in the state to do so, and the bank failed as a result.

Numismatic Commentary: The $5 denomination is the only note that might be obtainable over time. All other denominations issued by this bank are rare.

Valid Issues

$1 • W-TN-770-001-G010

Left: TENNESSEE vertically. ***Center:*** 1 / Woman reclining / 1. ***Right:*** ONE / 1 vertically. ***Engraver:*** Murray, Draper, Fairman & Co. ***Comments:*** H-TN-165-G4, Garland-939. 18__. 1810s.

Rarity: URS-3
F $400

$2 • W-TN-770-002-G020

Left: TENNESSEE vertically. ***Center:*** 2 / Woman reclining / 2. ***Right:*** 2 vertically / TWO. ***Engraver:*** Murray, Draper, Fairman & Co. ***Comments:*** H-TN-165-G6, Garland-940. 18__. 1810s.

Rarity: URS-2
F $475

$5 • W-TN-770-005-G030

CC

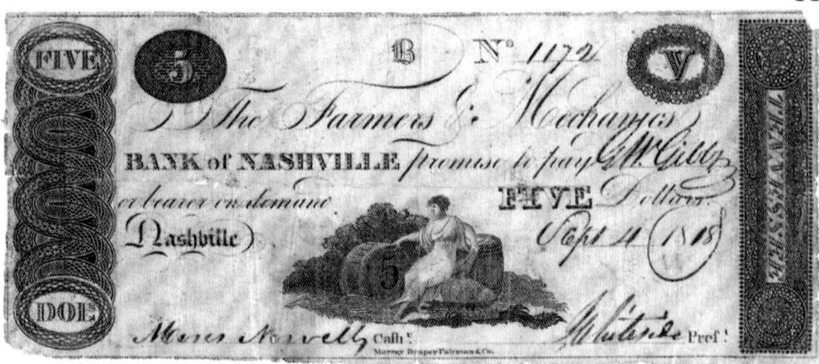

Engraver: Murray, Draper, Fairman & Co. ***Comments:*** H-TN-165-G8, Garland-941. 18__. 1810s.

Rarity: URS-4
F $350

$10 • W-TN-770-010-G040

CC

Engraver: Murray, Draper, Fairman & Co. ***Comments:*** H-TN-165-G12, Garland-942. 18__. 1810s.

Rarity: URS-4
F $350; **VF** $475

Farmers and Merchants Bank (branch)

1833–1854

W-TN-780

History: The Farmers and Merchants Bank was chartered in 1833 with an authorized capital of $600,000. In 1835 it opened for business. After more than a decade of operation, the bank finally failed, although notes dated 1854 were issued in an attempt to revive the bank:

> For a brief period it enjoyed a high credit, transacted too large a business, and in the heyday of its career it fell . . . in the spring of 1847, the bill-holders having sustained heavy losses thereby. The wreck of the bank fell into the hands of some adventurous speculators who tried every scheme their ingenuity could devise to resuscitate its existence, and its notes of circulation were briefly foisted upon the public. . . .[17]

The Farmers and Merchants Bank had its parent bank located in Memphis, W-TN-530, and a branch bank located in Bolivar, W-TN-030.

Numismatic Commentary: No notes of this branch are known.

Valid Issues

$5 • W-TN-780-005-G010

Comments: H-Unlisted, Garland-943. No description available. 18__. 1830s–1840s.

Rarity: *None known*

$10 • W-TN-780-010-G020

Comments: H-Unlisted, Garland-944. No description available. 18__. 1830s–1840s.

Rarity: *None known*

Merchants Bank of Nashville

1855–1861

W-TN-790

History: In 1855 the Merchants Bank of Nashville was chartered with an authorized capital of $100,000. In 1857 these values were given: bills in circulation $39,464; specie $14,500; real estate $12,000. W.B. Shapard was the president, and J. Porterfield was the cashier. By 1861 the bank had closed.

Numismatic Commentary: These notes are among the most eye-catching of issues, but all notes from this bank are very scarce.

Remaining at the American Bank Note Co. archives as of 2003 was a $1-$1-$1-$5 face plate. The 1990 Christie's sale of the American Bank Note Co. archives produced $1-$1-$1-$5 sheet.

Valid Issues

$1 • W-TN-790-001-G010

CC

Overprint: Red ONE. ***Engraver:*** Danforth, Wright & Co. ***Comments:*** H-TN-170-G2a, Garland-946. Novr. 1st, 1855.

Rarity: URS-3

F $650; **Proof** $1,000

$2 • W-TN-790-002-G020

Overprint: Red. ***Engraver:*** Danforth, Wright & Co. ***Comments:*** H-TN-170-G4a, Garland-947. No description available. Novr. 1st, 1855.

Rarity: *None known*

$5 • W-TN-790-005-G030

CC

Overprint: Red 5 / 5. ***Engraver:*** Danforth, Wright & Co. ***Comments:*** H-TN-170-G6a, Garland-948. Novr. 1st, 1855.

Rarity: URS-4

F $500

$10 • W-TN-790-010-G040

Left: 10 / Indian. ***Center:*** Sailor holding flag, Ships. ***Right:*** X / Liberty with shield. ***Overprint:*** Red TEN. ***Engraver:*** Rawdon, Wright & Hatch. ***Comments:*** H-Unlisted, Garland-949. 18__. 1850s–1860s.

Rarity: —

$20 • W-TN-790-020-G050

SI

Tint: Red-orange. ***Engraver:*** American Bank Note Co. ***Comments:*** H-TN-170-G10a, Garland-950. 18__. 1860s.

Rarity: URS-4

VF $900; **EF** $1,000

Selected auction price: Heritage Auctions, April 23, 2014, Lot 15414, VF $881

Uncut Sheets

$1-$1-$1-$5 • W-TN-790-001.001.001.005-US010

Vignette(s): ($1) Ships. ***($5)*** Portrait of Andrew Jackson / Cattle. ***Overprint(s):*** Red. ***Engraver:*** Danforth, Wright & Co. ***Comments:*** H-TN-170-G2a, G2a, G2a, G6a. First three notes identical. Novr. 1st, 1855.

Rarity: —

VF $2,000

Non-Valid Issues

$1 • W-TN-790-001-S010

Center: Wild steer, Horse and trees. ***Comments:*** H-TN-170-S5. 18__. 1850s.

Rarity: —

$5 • **W-TN-790-005-S020**

Left: 5 / Indian man with dog, slain deer. ***Center:*** Sailor with bale and flag. ***Right:*** 5 / Woman standing with shield. ***Engraver:*** Rawdon, Wright & Hatch. ***Comments:*** H-TN-170-S10. 18__. 1850s.

Rarity: —

$10 • **W-TN-790-010-S030** CC

Engraver: Rawdon, Wright & Hatch. ***Comments:*** H-TN-170-S15, Garland-949. 18__. 1850s.

Rarity: URS-3
F $600

Nashville Bank
1807–1827
W-TN-800

History: In 1807 the Nashville Bank was chartered with an authorized capital of $200,000, to be divided into shares of $50 apiece. This was later increased to $400,000 when the charter of the bank was extended to last until 1838. In 1818 Stephen Cantrell was elected president, replacing Josiah Nichol. At this time Wilkins Tannehill was the cashier.

In 1817 several banks were chartered across the state—in the towns of Gallatin, Murfreesboro, Rogersville, Shelbyville, and Winchester—and were given the option of either joining the first Bank of the State of Tennessee, W-TN-355, or of joining with the Nashville Bank. The corporations chose the Nashville Bank and became branches forthwith.

On March 31, 1823, the Nashville Bank, along with its branches, burned a total of $250,000 worth of bank notes in order to increase the value of its circulation. In 1827 the bank was liquidated. At the time the bank and its branches had a combined capital of $994,560.[18]

The Nashville Bank had branch banks located in Gallatin, W-TN-310, Murfreesboro, W-TN-640, Rogersville, W-TN-900, Shelbyville, W-TN-930, and Winchester, W-TN-1060.

Numismatic Commentary: These notes are possibly the earliest issues from the "frontier." All are considered to be rare, if not unique. Known notes are likely from the 1990 Christie's sale of the American Bank Note Co. archives.

The 1990 Christie's sale of the American Bank Note Co. archives produced a $1-$1-$2-$3 sheet, a $5-$5-$10-$10 sheet, and a $100-$50-$20-$20 sheet. This lot brought forward numerous Haxby entries that had previously been listed as unconfirmed, as well as added three new notes that had never been seen before.

Valid Issues

$1 • **W-TN-800-001-G010**

Left: ONE DOLLAR vertically. ***Center:*** ONE / ONE. ***Right:*** ONE DOLLAR vertically. ***Comments:*** H-TN-180-G10, Garland-952. 181_. 1810s.

Rarity: URS-1
Proof $1,000

$1 • **W-TN-800-001-G020** CC

Engraver: Tanner, Kearny & Tiebout. ***Comments:*** H-TN-180-G12. 18__. 1810s.

Rarity: URS-2
Proof $950

$2 • **W-TN-800-002-G030** CC

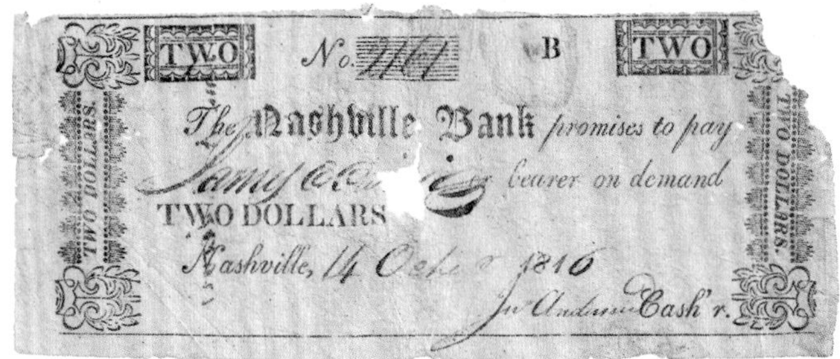

Comments: H-TN-180-G16, Garland-Unlisted. 181_. 1810s.

Rarity: URS-3
VG $350

$2 • **W-TN-800-002-G040** CC

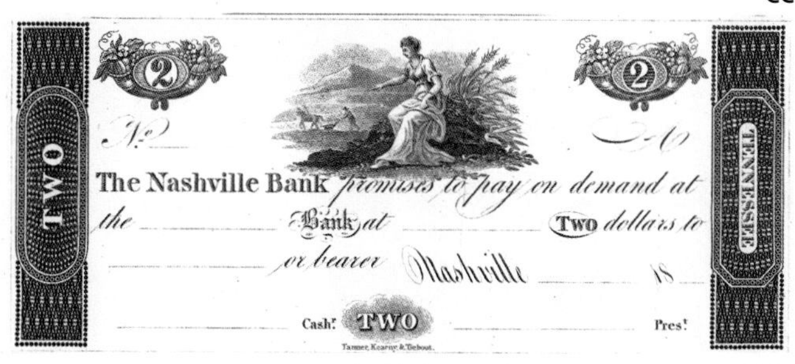

Engraver: Tanner, Kearny & Tiebout. ***Comments:*** H-TN-180-G18, Garland-953. 18__. 1810s.

Rarity: URS-3
Proof $1,750

$3 • W-TN-800-003-G050

CC

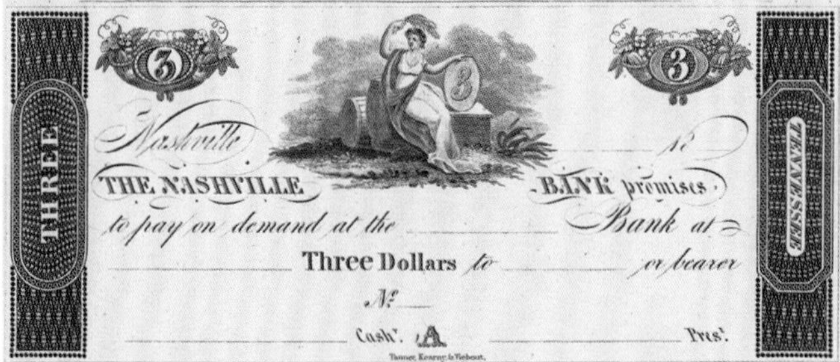

Engraver: Tanner, Kearny & Tiebout. ***Comments:*** H-TN-180-G22, Garland-954. 18__. 1810s.

Rarity: URS-2
Proof $1,975

$5 • W-TN-800-005-G060

Left: FIVE vertically. ***Center:*** 5 / FIVE / Beehive, cotton bale, plow. ***Right:*** 5. ***Engraver:*** Harrison. ***Comments:*** H-TN-180-G26, Garland-955. 18__. 1810s.

Rarity: URS-4
F $550

$5 • W-TN-800-005-G070

Left: FIVE vertically. ***Center:*** 5. ***Right:*** FIVE / Bale, plow. ***Engraver:*** Harrison. ***Comments:*** H-TN-180-G28. 18__. 1810s.

Rarity: —

$5 • W-TN-800-005-G080

ANS

Engraver: Murray, Draper, Fairman & Co. ***Comments:*** H-TN-180-G30, Garland-Unlisted. 18__. 1810s.

Rarity: URS-2
F $750

$5 • W-TN-800-005-G090

CC

Engraver: Tanner, Kearny & Tiebout. ***Comments:*** H-TN-180-G32. 18__. 1810s–1820s.

Rarity: URS-3
Proof $1,250

$10 • W-TN-800-010-G100

Left: TEN vertically. ***Center:*** 10 / TEN / Plow, bale. ***Right:*** 10. ***Engraver:*** W. Harrison. ***Comments:*** H-TN-180-G36, Garland-956. 18__. 1810s.

Rarity: URS-3
Proof $1,250

$10 • W-TN-800-010-G110

Left: TEN vertically. ***Center:*** 10 / Woman seated / 10. ***Right:*** NASHVILLE vertically. ***Engraver:*** Murray, Draper, Fairman & Co. ***Comments:*** H-TN-180-G38. 18__. 1810s.

Rarity: URS-3
Proof $1,250

$10 • W-TN-800-010-G120

CC

Engraver: Tanner, Kearny & Tiebout. ***Comments:*** H-TN-180-G40. 18__. 1810s–1820s.

Rarity: URS-2
Proof $1,250

$20 • W-TN-800-020-G130

Left: TWENTY vertically. ***Center:*** Plow, bale / 20. ***Right:*** TWENTY. ***Engraver:*** Harrison. ***Comments:*** H-TN-180-G44. 18__. 1810s.

Rarity: —

$20 • W-TN-800-020-G140

Left: TWENTY vertically. ***Center:*** 20 / Woman seated / 20. ***Right:*** NASHVILLE vertically. ***Engraver:*** Murray, Draper, Fairman & Co. ***Comments:*** H-TN-180-G46. 18__. 1810s.

Rarity: —

$20 • W-TN-800-020-G150

CC

Engraver: Tanner, Kearny & Tiebout. ***Comments:*** H-TN-180-G48, Garland-957. 18__. 1810s–1820s.

Rarity: URS-2
EF $1,000; **Proof** $1,250
Selected auction price: Spink & Smythe, June 2009, Lot 486, EF $1,100

$50 • **W-TN-800-050-G160**
Left: FIFTY vertically. ***Center:*** Plow, bale / 50. ***Right:*** FIFTY. ***Engraver:*** Harrison. ***Comments:*** H-TN-180-G52, Garland-958. 18__. 1810s.
Rarity: URS-2
Proof $1,750

$50 • **W-TN-800-050-G170**
Left: FIFTY vertically. ***Center:*** 50 / Woman seated / 50. ***Right:*** NASHVILLE vertically. ***Engraver:*** Murray, Draper, Fairman & Co. ***Comments:*** H-TN-180-G54. 18__. 1810s.
Rarity: —

$50 • **W-TN-800-050-G180**
CC

Engraver: Tanner, Kearny & Tiebout. ***Comments:*** H-Unlisted. 18__. 1810s.
Rarity: URS-1
Proof $1,750

$100 • **W-TN-800-100-G190**
MR

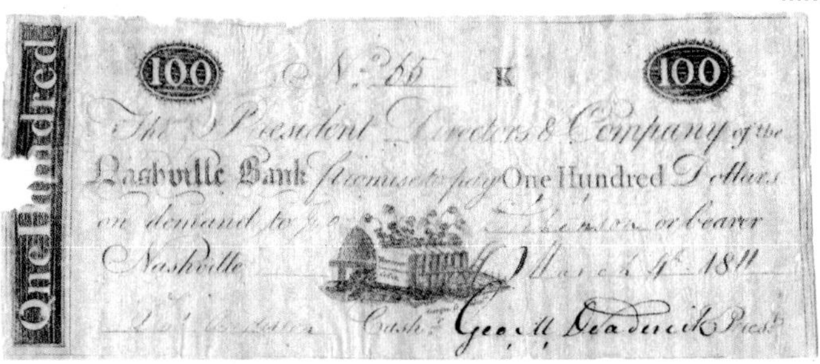

Engraver: Harrison. ***Comments:*** H-TN-180-G58, Garland-959. 18__. 1810s.
Rarity: URS-3
F $1,000

$100 • **W-TN-800-100-G200**
Left: HUNDRED vertically. ***Center:*** 100 / Woman seated / 100. ***Right:*** NASHVILLE vertically. ***Engraver:*** Tanner, Kearney & Tiebout. ***Comments:*** H-TN-180-G60. 18__. 1810s.
Rarity: URS-1
F $1,500

Non-Valid Issues

$2 • **W-TN-800-002-C040**
Engraver: Tanner, Kearny & Tiebout. ***Comments:*** H-TN-180-C18. Counterfeit of W-TN-800-002-G040. 18__. 1810s.
Rarity: —

$3 • **W-TN-800-003-C050**
Comments: H-TN-180-C22. Counterfeit of W-TN-800-003-G050. 18__. 1810s.
Rarity: —

$5 • **W-TN-800-005-C070**
Engraver: Harrison. ***Comments:*** H-TN-180-C28. Counterfeit of W-TN-800-005-G070. 18__. 1810s.
Rarity: —

$10 • **W-TN-800-010-C100**
CC

Engraver: W. Harrison. ***Comments:*** H-TN-180-C36. Counterfeit of W-TN-800-010-G100. 18__. 1810s.
Rarity: URS-6
VF $500

$20 • **W-TN-800-020-C150**
Engraver: Tanner, Kearny & Tiebout. ***Comments:*** H-TN-180-C48. Counterfeit of W-TN-800-020-G150. 18__. 1810s–1820s.
Rarity: —

$50 • **W-TN-800-050-C160**
Engraver: Harrison. ***Comments:*** H-TN-180-C52. Counterfeit of W-TN-800-050-G160. 18__. 1810s.
Rarity: —

$100 • **W-TN-800-100-C190**
Engraver: Harrison. ***Comments:*** H-TN-180-C58. Counterfeit of W-TN-800-100-G190. 18__. 1810s.
Rarity: —

$100 • **W-TN-800-100-C200**
Engraver: Murray, Draper, Fairman & Co. ***Comments:*** H-TN-180-C60. Counterfeit of W-TN-800-100-G200. 18__. 1810s.
Rarity: —

Planters Bank of Tennessee
1833–1865
W-TN-810

History: The Planters Bank of Tennessee was chartered on November 11, 1833, with an authorized capital of $2,000,000. Edward B. Litchfield was the first president, and Nicholas Hobson was elected as cashier.

In 1837 Matthew Watson became president. In 1842 the capital of the bank was $2,242,800, and bills in circulation totaled $818,560. In 1854 Dempsey Weaver became the cashier. These values were given in 1857: capital $1,355,600; bills in circulation $1,291,238; specie $479,116; real estate $42,697. In 1865 the bank was forced to liquidate and close its affairs.

The Planters Bank of Tennessee had branch banks located in Athens, W-TN-020, Clarksville, W-TN-140, Columbia, W-TN-210, Franklin, W-TN-300, LaGrange, W-TN-410, Memphis, W-TN-570, Murfreesboro, W-TN-630, Pulaski, W-TN-870, Rogersville, W-TN-910, Shelbyville, W-TN-940, Somerville, W-TN-970, Sparta, W-TN-990, Trenton, W-TN-1050, and Winchester, W-TN-1070.

Numismatic Commentary: Within the issues of this bank are both readily attainable notes and outright rarities. Some examples likely exist only as Proofs.

Remaining at the American Bank Note Co. archives as of 2003 was a $1-$1-$1-$2 face plate and a $1-$1-$1-$2 tint plate. The 1990 Christie's sale of the American Bank Note Co. archives produced one sheet of post notes and five sheets of demand notes, along with four sheets of corresponding back Proofs. The demand-note sheets were denominated $5-$5-$10-$20, $5-$5-$5-$5, $10-$10-$10-$10, $20-$20-$20-$20, and $50-$50-$100-$100.

Valid Issues

$1 • W-TN-810-001-G010

Left: 1 / Medallion head bearing ONE / 1. ***Center:*** 1 with cherub / Woman seated with boxes. ***Right:*** Woman standing in 1. ***Engraver:*** Rawdon, Wright, Hatch & Edson. ***Comments:*** H-TN-185-G2. 18__. 1840s.

Rarity: —

$1 • W-TN-810-001-G010a

CC

Back: Red-orange. ***Engraver:*** Rawdon, Wright, Hatch & Edson. ***Comments:*** H-TN-185-G2a, Garland-981. Similar to W-TN-810-001-G010 but with different date. December 1st, 1860.

Rarity: URS-6
F $250

$1 • W-TN-810-001-G010b

Engraver: Rawdon, Wright, Hatch & Edson. ***Comments:*** H-TN-185-G2b. Similar to W-TN-810-001-G010 but with different date. December 1st, 1860.

Rarity: URS-6
F $250

$1 • W-TN-810-001-G020

Left: ONE over 1 / Two women. ***Center:*** Ship. ***Right:*** ONE over 1 / Female portrait. ***Tint:*** Green. ***Engraver:*** American Bank Note Co. ***Comments:*** H-TN-185-G4a, Garland-983. September 1st, 1862.

Rarity: URS-5
F $350

$2 • W-TN-810-002-G030

Left: 2 / Woman with sheaf / 2. ***Center:*** 2 with cherubs / Woman seated with boxes. ***Right:*** Woman standing in 2. ***Engraver:*** Rawdon, Wright, Hatch & Edson. ***Comments:*** H-TN-185-G6, Garland-985. 18__. 1840s.

Rarity: URS-5
F $350

$2 • W-TN-810-002-G030a

CC

Back: Red-orange. ***Engraver:*** Rawdon, Wright, Hatch & Edson. ***Comments:*** H-TN-185-G6a, Garland-984. Similar to W-TN-810-002-G030 but with different date. December 1st, 1860.

Rarity: URS-5
F $550

$2 • W-TN-810-002-G030b

Engraver: Rawdon, Wright, Hatch & Edson. ***Comments:*** H-TN-185-G6b. Similar to W-TN-810-002-G030 but with different date. December 1st, 1860.

Rarity: —

$2 • W-TN-810-002-G040

HA

Tint: Green 2 / 2 and dies outlining white 2. ***Engraver:*** American Bank Note Co. ***Comments:*** H-TN-185-G8a, Garland-986. September 1st, 1862.

Rarity: URS-4
F $750

Selected auction price: Heritage Auctions, October 24, 2015, Lot 20021, F $1,410

$3 • W-TN-810-003-G050

Left: 3 / Medallion head / 3. ***Center:*** 3 with cherubs / Two men flanking shield bearing cow surmounted by beehive. ***Right:*** Woman standing in 3. ***Engraver:*** Rawdon, Wright, Hatch & Edson. ***Comments:*** H-TN-185-G10, Garland-988. December 1st, 1860.

Rarity: URS-5
F $500

$3 • W-TN-810-003-G050a

CC

Back: Red-orange. ***Engraver:*** Rawdon, Wright, Hatch & Edson. ***Comments:*** H-TN-185-G10a, Garland-987. Similar to W-TN-810-003-G050 but with different date. December 1st, 1860.

Rarity: URS-5
F $750

$3 • W-TN-810-003-G050b

Engraver: Rawdon, Wright, Hatch & Edson. ***Comments:*** H-TN-185-G10b. Similar to W-TN-810-003-G050 but with different date. December 1st, 1860.

Rarity: —

$5 • W-TN-810-005-G060

CC

Engraver: Rawdon, Wright, & Hatch. ***Comments:*** H-TN-185-G12, Garland-989. 18__. 1830s.

Rarity: URS-1
Proof $3,500

$5 • W-TN-810-005-G070

CC

Engraver: Underwood, Bald & Spencer. ***Comments:*** H-TN-185-G14a, Garland-991. 18__. 1830s–1840s.

Rarity: URS-5
Proof $850

$5 • W-TN-810-005-G080

Left: Three women flanking shield surmounted by eagle / 5. ***Center:*** FIVE. ***Right:*** 5 / Medallion head. ***Engraver:*** Danforth, Bald & Co. ***Comments:*** H-TN-185-G16, Garland-993. 18__. 1850s.

Rarity: URS-5
Proof $750

$5 • W-TN-810-005-G090

CC

Left: 5 / V. ***Center:*** Three women with tablet and harp. ***Right:*** 5 over V over FIVE / Justice seated. ***Engraver:*** Danforth, Wright & Co. ***Comments:*** H-TN-185-G18. 18__. 1850s–1861.

Rarity: URS-3
Proof $1,000

$5 • W-TN-810-005-G090a

CC

Back: Red-orange. ***Engraver:*** Danforth, Wright & Co. ***Comments:*** H-TN-185-G18a, Garland-990. Similar to W-TN-810-005-G090. 18__. 1850s–1861.

Rarity: URS-5
F $250

$10 • W-TN-810-010-G100

CC

Engraver: Rawdon, Wright, & Hatch. ***Comments:*** H-TN-185-G20, Garland-996. 18__. 1830s.

Rarity: URS-3
Proof $1,600
Selected auction price: Stack's Bowers Galleries, August 2013, Lot 24417, Proof $1,600

$10 • W-TN-810-010-G110

CC

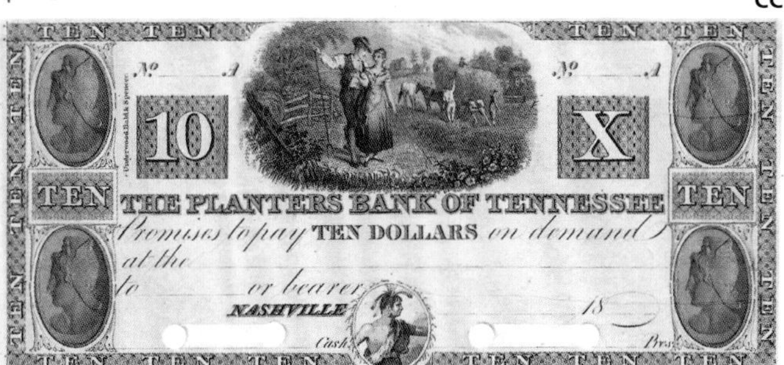

Engraver: Underwood, Bald & Spencer. ***Comments:*** H-TN-185-G22a, Garland-997. 18__. 1830s–1840s.

Rarity: URS-3
Proof $1,000

$10 • **W-TN-810-010-G120**

Left: 10. ***Center:*** Woman and Indian reclining with shield bearing X / Medallion head. ***Right:*** 10. ***Engraver:*** Danforth, Bald & Co. ***Comments:*** H-TN-185-G24, Garland-995. 18__. 1850s.

Rarity: URS-3
Proof $1,000

$10 • **W-TN-810-010-G130**

Left: Two women. ***Center:*** 10 / Milkmaid seated. ***Right:*** 10 / Cotton plant. ***Engraver:*** Danforth, Wright & Co. ***Comments:*** H-TN-185-G26, Garland-994. May have been made only as Proofs. 18__. 1850s.

Rarity: URS-3
Proof $1,000

$10 • **W-TN-810-010-G130a** CC, CC

Back: Red-orange. ***Engraver:*** Danforth, Wright & Co. ***Comments:*** H-TN-185-G26a, Garland-994. Similar to W-TN-810-010-G130. 18__. 1850s–1861.

Rarity: URS-3
F $650

$20 • **W-TN-810-020-G140**

Engraver: Rawdon, Wright, & Hatch. ***Comments:*** H-TN-185-G28, Garland-Unlisted. No description available. 18__. 1830s.

Rarity: *None known*

$20 • **W-TN-810-020-G150**

Left: 20 / Medallion head / 20. ***Center:*** 20 / Medallion head / 20. ***Right:*** 20 / Medallion head / 20. ***Engraver:*** Underwood, Bald & Spencer. ***Comments:*** H-TN-185-G30a, Garland-1000. 18__. 1830s–1840s.

Rarity: URS-5
Proof $850

$20 • **W-TN-810-020-G160**

Left: Two men and two women with spinning wheel, boxes, and factory. ***Center:*** 20 / Medallion head. ***Right:*** 20. ***Engraver:*** Danforth, Bald & Co. ***Comments:*** H-TN-185-G32, Garland-998. 18__. 1850s.

Rarity: URS-1
Proof $3,500

$20 • **W-TN-810-020-G170**

Left: 20 / Portrait of Dolley Madison / XX. ***Center:*** Three women reclining. ***Right:*** 20 / Train. ***Engraver:*** Danforth, Wright & Co. ***Comments:*** H-TN-185-G34, Garland-999. May have been made only as Proofs. 18__. 1850s.

Rarity: URS-3
Proof $1,250

$20 • **W-TN-810-020-G170a** CC, CC

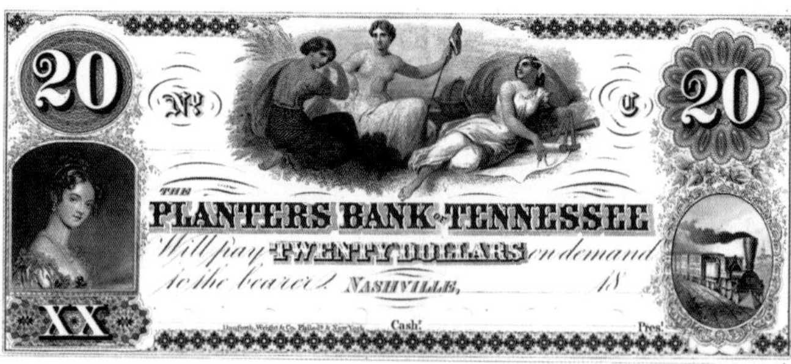

Back: Red-orange. ***Engraver:*** Danforth, Wright & Co. ***Comments:*** H-TN-185-G34a, Garland-999. Similar to W-TN-810-020-G170. 18__. 1850s–1861.

Rarity: URS-3
Proof $2,000

$50 • **W-TN-810-050-G180** CC

Engraver: Underwood, Bald, Spencer & Hufty. ***Comments:*** H-TN-185-G36, Garland-1003. 18__. 1830s–1850s.

Rarity: URS-3
Proof $1,500

$50 • **W-TN-810-050-G190**

Left: 50 / Three men standing. ***Center:*** Portrait of Andrew Jackson. ***Right:*** L / 50 / FIFTY. ***Engraver:*** Danforth, Wright & Co. ***Comments:*** H-TN-185-G38. 18__. 1850s.

Rarity: URS-4
G $400

$50 • **W-TN-810-050-G190a**

Back: Red-orange. ***Engraver:*** Danforth, Wright & Co. ***Comments:*** H-TN-185-G38a, Garland-1002. Similar to W-TN-810-050-G190. 18__. 1850s–1861.

Rarity: URS-4
Proof $2,500

$50 • **W-TN-810-050-G190b** cc, cc

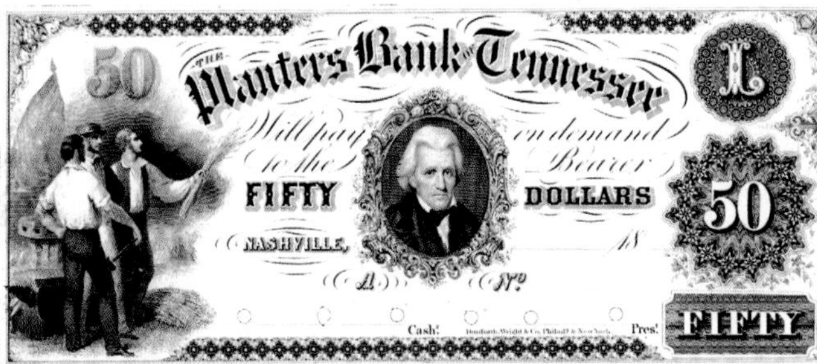

Back: Blue. ***Engraver:*** Danforth, Wright & Co. ***Comments:*** H-Unlisted, Garland-Unlisted. Similar to W-TN-810-050-G190. 18__. 1850s–1861.

Rarity: URS-1
Proof $5,000

$100 • **W-TN-810-100-G200**

Left: 100 / Three women seated vertically / 100. ***Center:*** Medallion head / Boy reclining under corn, Plow / Medallion head. ***Right:*** 100 / Three women seated vertically / 100. ***Engraver:*** Underwood, Bald, Spencer & Hufty. ***Comments:*** H-TN-185-G40, Garland-1005. 18__. 1830s–1850s.

Rarity: URS-3
Proof $3,000

$100 • **W-TN-810-100-G210**

Left: 100 / Portrait of George Washington. ***Center:*** C / Two women seated with shield bearing wheat / 100. ***Right:*** ONE HUNDRED vertically. ***Engraver:*** Danforth, Wright & Co. ***Comments:*** H-TN-185-G42, Garland-1004. 18__. 1850s.

Rarity: URS-3
Proof $3,000

$100 • **W-TN-810-100-G210a**

Back: Red-orange. ***Engraver:*** Danforth, Wright & Co. ***Comments:*** H-TN-185-G42a. Similar to W-TN-810-100-G210. 18__. 1850s–1861.

Rarity: —

$100 • **W-TN-810-100-G210b** cc, cc

Back: Blue. ***Engraver:*** Danforth, Wright & Co. ***Comments:*** H-Unlisted. Similar to W-TN-810-100-G210. 18__. 1850s–1861.

Rarity: URS-1
Proof $5,500

Post Notes

$__ • **W-TN-810-__-G220** cc

Engraver: Underwood, Bald, Spencer & Hufty. ***Comments:*** H-Unlisted, Garland-Unlisted. 18__. 1840s.

Rarity: URS-3
Proof $750

How to Read the Whitman Numbering System

$1 • **W-AL-020-001-G010a**

Denomination: Face value of the note shown.

W: Whitman number. This number is a sortable code unique to each bank and note.

AL: Abbreviation for the state under study.

020: Numerical designation specific to each bank.

001: The denomination in dollars.

G010a: G indicates a good or valid note. Other categories are indicated thus: C (counterfeit); R (raised); S (spurious); N (not-attributed); A (altered). Numbers are assigned starting with 010, 020, et seq. Terminal letters following the number indicate variations of a note: a series of different colored overprints, tints, payees, etc., all on the same design of note. For more information, see the "How to Use This Book" section at the front of the volume, page xiv.

Notes on Which the Place Payable is Blank

$1 • W-TN-810-001-G230

Center: Vessels, Farmer with two horses, Farmhouse. ***Comments:*** H-TN-185-G330. 18__. 1840s.

Rarity: —

$5 • W-TN-810-005-G240

Left: FIVE / Woman with cog wheel / 5 vertically. ***Center:*** 5 / Horse / 5. ***Right:*** FIVE / Man seated / 5 vertically. ***Engraver:*** Rawdon, Wright, & Hatch. ***Comments:*** H-TN-185-G334. 18__. 1830s.

Rarity: —

$5 • W-TN-810-005-G250

Left: Medallion head / FIVE / Medallion head. ***Center:*** FIVE / Man standing with dog / FIVE. ***Right:*** Medallion head / FIVE / Medallion head. ***Engraver:*** Underwood, Bald & Spencer. ***Comments:*** H-TN-185-G336. 18__. 1830s–1840s.

Rarity: URS-5
Proof $850

$10 • W-TN-810-010-G260

CC

Engraver: Underwood, Bald & Spencer. ***Comments:*** H-TN-185-G340. 18__. 1830s–1840s.

Rarity: URS-4
Proof $1,000

$20 • W-TN-810-020-G270

CC

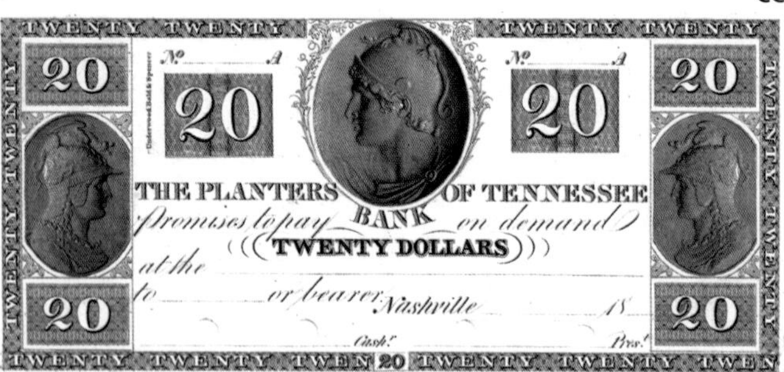

Engraver: Underwood, Bald & Spencer. ***Comments:*** H-TN-185-G344. 18__. 1830s–1840s.

Rarity: URS-4
Proof $1,000

$50 • W-TN-810-050-G280

Left: 50 / Medallion head / 50. ***Center:*** Medallion heads / Woman seated, Ship / Medallion heads. ***Right:*** 50 / Medallion head / 50. ***Engraver:*** Underwood, Bald, Spencer & Hufty. ***Comments:*** H-TN-185-G348. 18__. 1830s–1850s.

Rarity: URS-4
Proof $1,000

$100 • W-TN-810-100-G290

Left: 100 / Three women seated vertically / 100. ***Center:*** Medallion head / Boy reclining under corn, Plow / Medallion head. ***Right:*** 100 / Three women seated vertically / 100. ***Engraver:*** Underwood, Bald, Spencer & Hufty. ***Comments:*** H-TN-185-G352. 18__. 1830s–1850s.

Rarity: URS-4
Proof $1,000

Non-Valid Issues

$10 • W-TN-810-010-S010

Left: Woman. ***Center:*** Woman, Train, Steamboat. ***Right:*** Ceres. ***Comments:*** H-TN-185-S4. 18__. 1840s.

Rarity: —

$10 • W-TN-810-010-S020

CC

Engraver: Rawdon, Wright & Hatch. ***Comments:*** H-TN-185-S6. From a genuine plate of the Planters Bank of Alabama, Wetumpka, Alabama. 18__. 1840s.

Rarity: URS-3
F $800

$20 • W-TN-810-020-C160

CC

Engraver: Danforth, Bald & Co. ***Comments:*** H-TN-185-C32. Counterfeit of the W-TN-810-020-G160. 18__. 1850s.

Rarity: URS-4
F $300

$20 • W-TN-810-020-S030

Center: Eagle. ***Comments:*** H-TN-185-S8. 18__. 1840s.

Rarity: —

$20 • W-TN-810-020-S040

Left: 20 / Female portrait / XX. ***Center:*** Woman seated near ocean with shield. ***Right:*** 20 / Female portrait / XX. ***Engraver:*** Rawdon, Wright & Hatch. ***Comments:*** H-TN-185-S10. From a genuine plate of the Planters Bank of Alabama, Wetumpka, Alabama. 18__. 1840s.

Rarity: —

$50 • W-TN-810-050-S050
Left: FIFTY DOLLARS vertically. ***Center:*** 50 / Eagle on bale / 50. ***Right:*** STATE OF TENNESSEE vertically. ***Engraver:*** Rawdon, Wright & Hatch. ***Comments:*** H-TN-185-S12. From a genuine plate of the Planters Bank of Alabama, Wetumpka, Alabama. 18__. 1840s.

Rarity: —

$100 • W-TN-810-100-S060
Left: HUNDRED vertically. ***Center:*** Deer, River. ***Right:*** Portrait of George Washington. ***Engraver:*** Rawdon, Wright & Hatch. ***Comments:*** H-TN-185-S14. From a genuine plate of the Planters Bank of Alabama, Wetumpka, Alabama. 18__. 1840s.

Rarity: —

$100 • W-TN-810-100-S070 CC

Engraver: Rawdon, Wright, Hatch & Edson. ***Comments:*** H-TN-185-S16. 18__. 1840s.

Rarity: URS-4
F $750

Notes on Which the Place Payable is Blank

$2 • W-TN-810-002-R010
Comments: H-TN-185-R5. Raised from $1. 18__. 1830s–1840s.

Rarity: —

$3 • W-TN-810-003-R020
Comments: H-TN-185-G10. Raised from $1. 18__. 1830s–1840s.

Rarity: —

$5 • W-TN-810-005-R030
Comments: H-TN-185-R15. Raised from $1. 18__. 1830s–1840s.

Rarity: —

$10 • W-TN-810-010-N010
Bottom center: Mechanic arm and hammer. ***Comments:*** H-TN-185-N10. 18__. 1830s–1840s.

Rarity: —

$100 • W-TN-810-100-A010
Comments: H-TN-185-A10. No description available. Altered from $100 Planters Bank of Alabama, Florence, Alabama. 18__. 1830s–1840s.

Rarity: *None known*

Savings Bank of Louisville
1837 and 1838
W-TN-820

History: This entity was operated by an agent of Otis, Arnold & Co., out of Cincinnati, Ohio. The firm is listed as an illegal note issuer in the 1839 Ohio *Bank Commissioners' Report*. It was involved with the Exchange Bank of Cincinnati, W-KY-910, which seemed to be the redemption partner for several banks in Ohio and other states, including Tennessee.

Numismatic Commentary: Notes from this bank are scarce, with probably fewer than a dozen of any denomination and variety surviving. A patient collector should still be able to obtain an example.

Valid Issues
Notes Payable in Current Bank Notes

$1 • W-TN-820-001-G010 SI

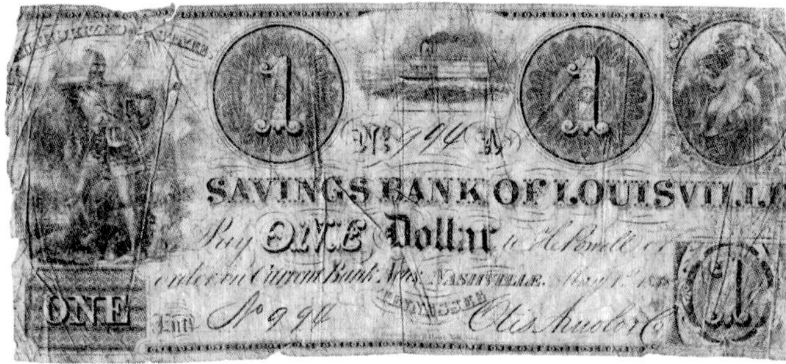

Engraver: Rawdon, Wright & Hatch. ***Comments:*** H-Unlisted, Garland-971. May 1st, 1838.

Rarity: URS-4
F $300

$2 • W-TN-820-002-G020 CC

Engraver: Rawdon, Wright & Hatch. ***Comments:*** H-Unlisted, Garland-973. May 1st, 1838.

Rarity: URS-4
F $250

$2 • W-TN-820-002-G030 CC

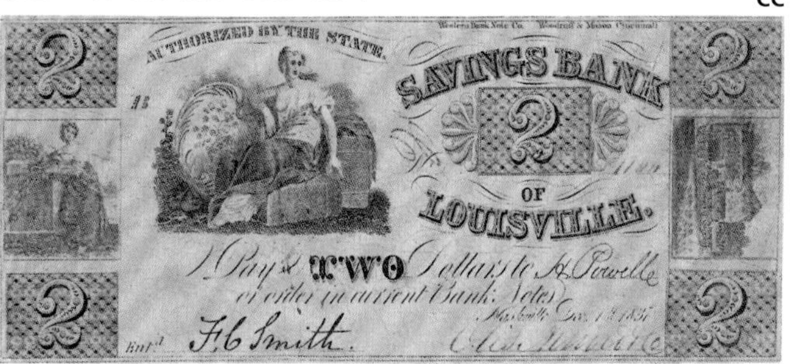

Engraver: Western Bank Note Co. / Woodruff & Mason. ***Comments:*** H-Unlisted. Dec. 1st, 1837.

Rarity: URS-3
F $400

Traders Bank

1855–1862

W-TN-830

History: The Traders Bank was chartered in 1855 under the Free Banking Act with an authorized capital of $50,000. W.B. Shapard Jr. was the cashier, and John Porterfield was the president. It was located at the corner of Cherry and Union streets. In 1862 the bank was liquidated.

Numismatic Commentary: The fractional Civil War issues are rare. Patience will be required, but other notes can be obtained.

Valid Issues

Free-Bank Issues

$1 • W-TN-830-001-G010

CC

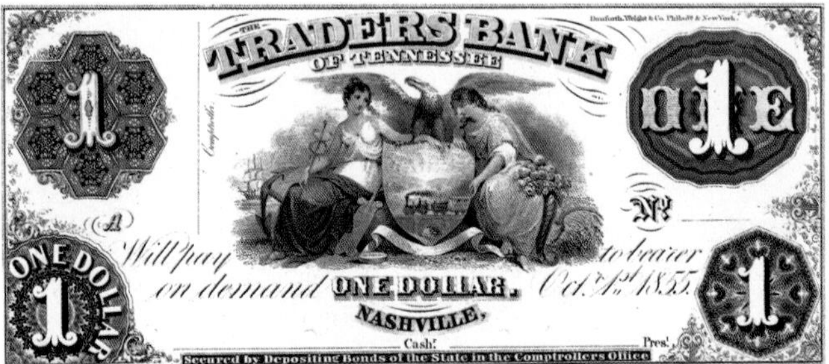

Engraver: Danforth, Wright & Co. ***Comments:*** H-TN-200-G2, Garland-1018. Octr. 1st, 1855.

Rarity: URS-4

Proof $1,200

$1 • W-TN-830-001-G010a

CC

Overprint: Red ONE. ***Engraver:*** American Bank Note Co. ***Comments:*** H-TN-200-G2b, Garland-1019. Similar to W-TN-830-001-G010 but with different engraver imprint. Octr. 1st, 1855.

Rarity: URS-6

F $200

$5 • W-TN-830-005-G020

Left: 5 / Man standing. ***Center:*** Men on horseback, Cattle. ***Right:*** 5 / V / 5. ***Engraver:*** Danforth, Wright & Co. ***Comments:*** H-TN-200-G4, Garland-1020. October 1st, 1855.

Rarity: URS-4

F $400

$5 • W-TN-830-005-G020a

HA

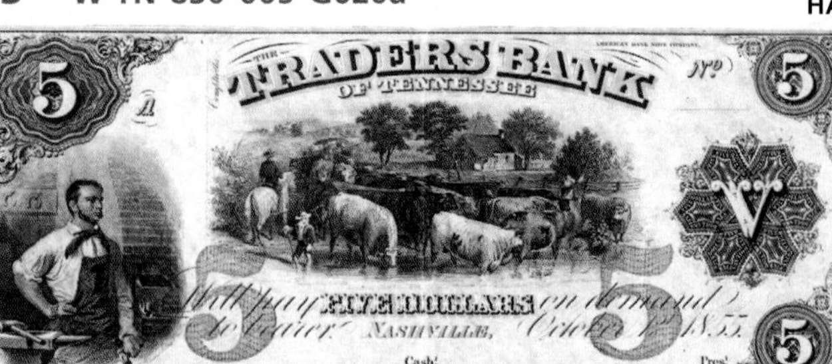

Overprint: Red 5 / 5. ***Engraver:*** American Bank Note Co. ***Comments:*** H-TN-200-G4b, Garland-1021. Similar to W-TN-830-005-G020 but with different engraver imprint. October 1st, 1855.

Rarity: URS-4

EF $750; **Proof** $1,250

$10 • W-TN-830-010-G030

CC

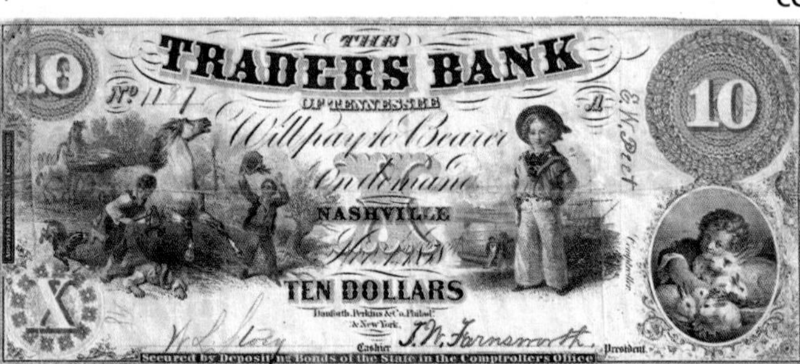

Tint: Red-brown X and dies outlining white 10 / X / 10. ***Engraver:*** Danforth, Perkins & Co. / American Bank Note Co. ***Comments:*** H-TN-200-G6a, Garland-1022. Novr. 1st, 1858.

Rarity: URS-3

F $1,500; **Proof** $1,050

Selected auction price: Heritage Auctions, April 22, 2015, Lot 18489, Apparent About New $1,057

Unregistered Civil War Issues

25¢ • W-TN-830-00.25-G040

CC

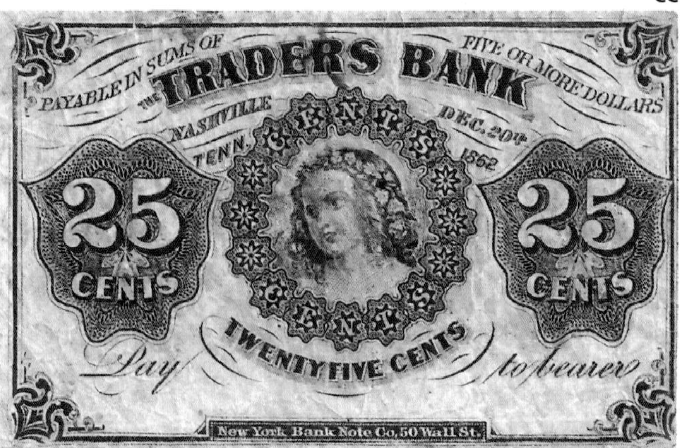

Back: Red-brown. ***Engraver:*** New York Bank Note Co. ***Comments:*** H-TN-200-G10a, Garland-1016. Dec. 20th, 1862.

Rarity: URS-3

F $350

50¢ • W-TN-830-00.50-G050

Center: 50 / Female portrait / 50. ***Engraver:*** New York Bank Note Co. ***Comments:*** H-TN-200-G12, Garland-1017. Dec. 20, 1862.

Rarity: URS-2
F $500

50¢ • W-TN-830-00.50-G050a

Back: Green. ***Engraver:*** New York Bank Note Co. ***Comments:*** H-TN-200-G12a, Garland-Unlisted. Similar to W-TN-830-00.50-G050. Dec. 20, 1862.

Rarity: *None known*

Uncut Sheets

$10 • W-TN-830-010-US010 RG

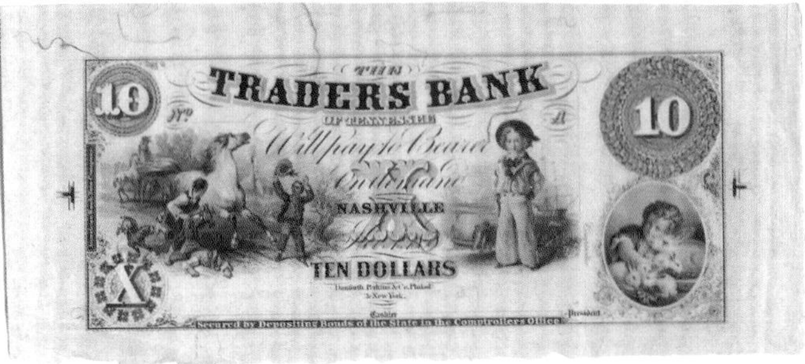

Tint: Red-brown X and dies outlining white 10 / X / 10. ***Engraver:*** Danforth, Perkins & Co. / American Bank Note Co. ***Comments:*** H-TN-200-G6a. Sheet of one note. Novr. 1st, 1858.

Rarity: URS-2
F $2,000; **Proof** $4,500

Non-Valid Issues
Free-Bank Issues

$10 • W-TN-830-010-R010

Engraver: Danforth, Wright & Co. ***Comments:*** H-TN-200-R5. Raised from W-TN-830-001-G010 series. Oct., 1, 1855.

Rarity: —

$20 • W-TN-830-020-R020

Engraver: Danforth, Wright & Co. ***Comments:*** H-TN-200-R10. Raised from W-TN-830-001-G010 series. Oct., 1, 1855.

Rarity: —

Union Bank of Tennessee
1832–1865
W-TN-840

History: On October 18, 1832, the Union Bank of Tennessee (also sometimes seen as the Union Bank of the State of Tennessee on notes) was chartered with an authorized capital of $3,000,000. The bank also absorbed the assets of the failed second Bank of the State of Tennessee, W-TN-680, which had been abolished that year. The state subscribed to $500,000 of the bank's capital, to be financed by bonds.

In 1837 these values were given: capital $2,553,179; circulation $89,240; post notes $598,336. The president was John M. Bass, and the cashier was J. Correy. In 1842 circulation was as high as $857,550, dropping again to $287,950 the following year. In 1854 John Kirkman took the place of John M. Bass, who had resigned two years previously. By 1863 the capital was $2,000,000.

In 1865 the Union Bank of Tennessee went into liquidation.

The Union Bank of Tennessee had branch banks located in Chattanooga, W-TN-090, Columbia, W-TN-220, Jackson, W-TN-325, Knoxville, W-TN-400, and Memphis, W-TN-600.

Numismatic Commentary: On early notes the title of this bank is listed as "The Union Bank of the State of Tennessee." All notes are very scarce to rare, with only the $1 being seen more frequently. It takes a patient, ambitious collector with means to tackle the Union Bank of Tennessee. There are a number of checks from Thomas B. Coleman drawn on this bank, in addition to "Stationery Store Notes" as described by Garland. Both signed and remainder notes are unknown. The Christie's American Bank Note Co. auction contained a good number of sheets.

Remaining at the American Bank Note Co. archives as of 2003 were two $10-$10-$10-$20 face plates, a $10-$10-$10-$20 tint plate, a $1-$1-$1-$2 face plate, a $1-$1-$1-$2 tint plate, a $500-$1,000 face plate, a $500-$1,000 tint plate, a $50-$50-$100-$100 face plate, a $50-$50-$100-$100 tint plate, a $5-$5-$5-$5 face plate, and a $5-$5-$5-$5 tint plate. The 1990 Christie's sale of the American Bank Note Co. archives produced three $5-$5-$5-$5 sheets, one $10-$10-$10-$10 sheet, two $20-$20-$50-$100 sheets, and one $500-$1,000 sheet.

Valid Issues

$1 • W-TN-840-001-G010 CC

Engraver: Draper, Toppan & Co. ***Comments:*** H-TN-210-G2, Garland-1023. Handwritten 61 over engraved 43 in date. January 2, 1843.

Rarity: URS-4
F $400

$2 • W-TN-840-002-G020

CC

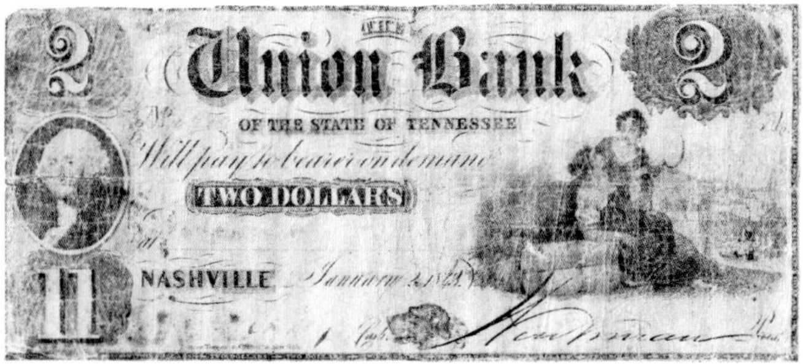

Engraver: Draper, Toppan & Co. ***Comments:*** H-TN-210-G4, Garland-1025. Handwritten 61 over engraved 43 in date. January 2, 1843.

Rarity: URS-3
F $550; **VF** $880
Selected auction price: Heritage Auctions, October 24, 2015, Lot 20025, VF $881

$3 • W-TN-840-003-G030

Left: 3 / Portrait of Benjamin Franklin / III. ***Center:*** Ships, Two women flanking shield bearing cotton plant and plow, Train. ***Right:*** 3 / Female portrait / III. ***Engraver:*** Draper, Toppan & Co. ***Comments:*** H-TN-210-G6, Garland-1027. January 2, 1843.

Rarity: URS-3
F $650

$5 • W-TN-840-005-G040

Engraver: Chas. Toppan & Co. ***Comments:*** H-TN-210-G8. No description available. 18__. 1830s–1840s.

Rarity: *None known*

$5 • W-TN-840-005-G050

Left: Medallion head / FIVE / Medallion head. ***Center:*** Medallion head / 5 / FIVEs around border. ***Right:*** Medallion head / FIVE / Medallion head. ***Engraver:*** Underwood, Bald, Spencer & Hufty. ***Comments:*** H-TN-210-G10. 18__. 1840s–1850s.

Rarity: URS-3
F $600

$10 • W-TN-840-010-G060

CC

Engraver: Draper, Underwood, Bald & Spencer. ***Comments:*** H-TN-210-G12, Garland-1033. 18__. 1830s–1840s.

Rarity: URS-3
Proof $600

$10 • W-TN-840-010-G070

Left: Medallion head / TEN / Medallion head. ***Center:*** 10 / Hebe watering eagle / 10. ***Right:*** Medallion head / TEN / Medallion head. ***Engraver:*** Draper, Underwood, Bald & Spencer. ***Comments:*** H-TN-210-G14, Garland-1032. 18__. 1830s.

Rarity: URS-3
Proof $750

$20 • W-TN-840-020-G080

Left: 20 / Woman seated / 20. ***Center:*** Ship / Two women flanking shield bearing eagle, surmounted by eagle / Ship. ***Right:*** 20 / Woman seated / 20. ***Engraver:*** Chas. Toppan. ***Comments:*** H-TN-210-G16, Garland-1037. 18__. 1830s–1840s.

Rarity: URS-3
Proof $750

$20 • W-TN-840-020-G090

Center: Portrait of Benjamin Franklin / Portrait of Napoleon Bonaparte / Portrait of Benjamin Franklin. ***Engraver:*** Underwood, Bald, Spencer & Hufty. ***Comments:*** H-TN-210-G18, Garland-1036. 18__. 1830s.

Rarity: URS-3
Proof $750

$50 • W-TN-840-050-G100

Left: 50 / Ship / 50. ***Center:*** Portrait of Indian / Woman seated / Portrait of Indian. ***Right:*** 50 / Ship / 50. ***Engraver:*** Chas. Toppan. ***Comments:*** H-TN-210-G20, Garland-1040. 18__. 1830s–1840s.

Rarity: URS-3
Proof $850

$50 • W-TN-840-050-G100a

Engraver: Chas. Toppan / Toppan, Carpenter & Co. ***Comments:*** H-TN-210-G20a. Similar to W-TN-840-050-G100 but with additional engraver imprint. 18__. 1840s–1850s.

Rarity: URS-3
Proof $850

$100 • W-TN-840-100-G110

Left: 100 / Justice / 100. ***Center:*** Steamboat / Woman reclining with globe, Cherub / Steamboat. ***Right:*** 100 / Justice / 100. ***Engraver:*** Chas. Toppan. ***Comments:*** H-TN-210-G22. 18__. 1830s–1840s.

Rarity: URS-3
Proof $900

$100 • W-TN-840-100-G110a

Engraver: Chas. Toppan / Toppan, Carpenter & Co. ***Comments:*** H-TN-210-G22a. Similar to W-TN-840-100-G110 but with additional engraver imprint. 18__. 1840s–1850s.

Rarity: URS-3
Proof $900

$500 • W-TN-840-500-G120

Left: 500 / Medallion head of George Washington / 500. ***Center:*** Eagle with shield and cornucopia. ***Right:*** 500 / Medallion head of Benjamin Franklin / 500. ***Engraver:*** Draper, Toppan, Longacre & Co. ***Comments:*** H-TN-210-G24. 18__. 1830s–1840s.

Rarity: URS-3
Proof $1,200

$1,000 • W-TN-840-1000-G130

Left: 1000 / Medallion head of Benjamin Franklin / 1000. ***Center:*** Eagle with shield and cornucopia. ***Right:*** 1000 / Medallion head of George Washington / 1000. ***Engraver:*** Draper, Toppan, Longacre & Co. ***Comments:*** H-TN-210-G26. 18__. 1830s–1840s.

Rarity: URS-3
Proof $1,500

Post Notes

$__ • W-TN-840-__-G140

Left: POST NOTE vertically. ***Center:*** __ / Roman senator seated / __. ***Right:*** POST / Medallion head / NOTE vertically. ***Engraver:*** Underwood, Bald, Spencer & Hufty. ***Comments:*** H-Unlisted, Garland-1051. 18__. 1830s.

Rarity: URS-1
Proof $3,500

$5 • W-TN-840-005-G150 CC

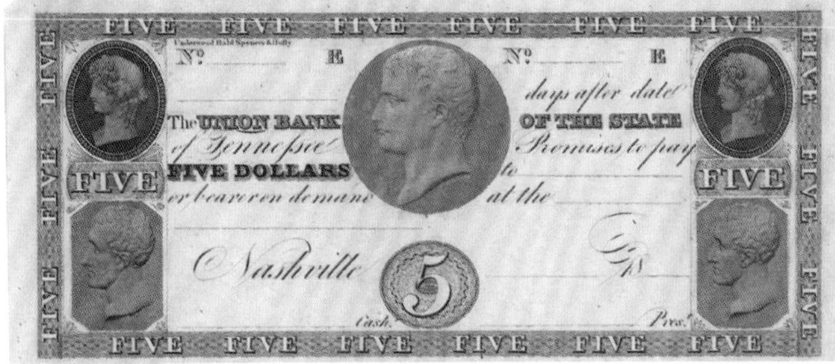

Engraver: Underwood, Bald, Spencer & Hufty. ***Comments:*** H-TN-210-G30. 18__. 1830s.

Rarity: URS-4
Proof $1,100

$10 • W-TN-840-010-G160 CC

Engraver: Draper, Underwood, Bald & Spencer. ***Comments:*** H-TN-210-G34. 18__. 1830s.

Rarity: URS-2
F $700

$20 • W-TN-840-020-G170

Center: Portrait of Benjamin Franklin / Portrait of Napoleon Bonaparte / Portrait of Benjamin Franklin. ***Engraver:*** Underwood, Bald, Spencer & Hufty. ***Comments:*** H-TN-210-G38. 18__. 1830s.

Rarity: —

Post Notes Payable at the Bank of Maryland, Baltimore

$5 • W-TN-840-005-G180 CC

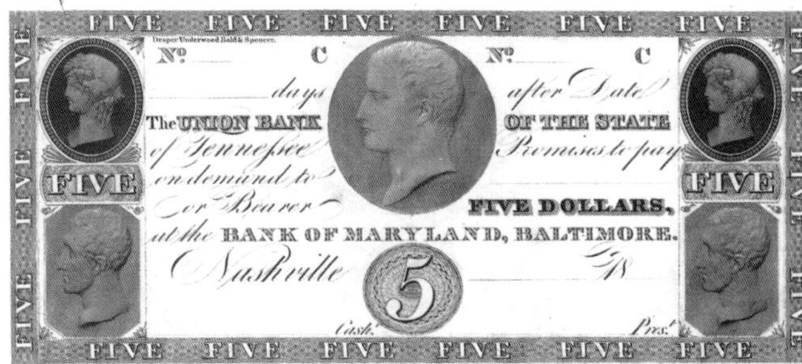

Engraver: Draper, Underwood, Bald & Spencer. ***Comments:*** H-TN-210-G190. 18__. 1830s.

Rarity: URS-4
Proof $650

$20 • W-TN-840-020-G190

Center: Portrait of Benjamin Franklin / Portrait of Napoleon Bonaparte / Portrait of Benjamin Franklin. ***Engraver:*** Underwood, Bald, Spencer & Hufty. ***Comments:*** H-TN-210-G194. 18__. 1830s.

Rarity: —

Notes Payable in Tennessee Bank Notes

12-1/2¢ • W-TN-840-00.12.50-G200 CC

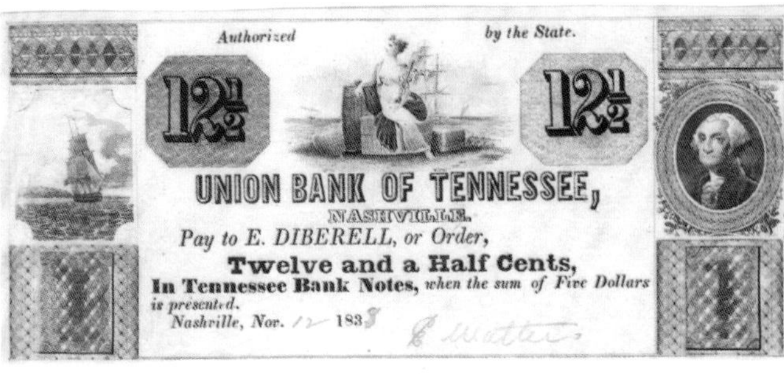

Comments: H-Unlisted, Garland-1052. Nov. 183_. 1830s.

Rarity: URS-5
EF $400; **AU** $650

$1 • W-TN-840-001-G215 CC

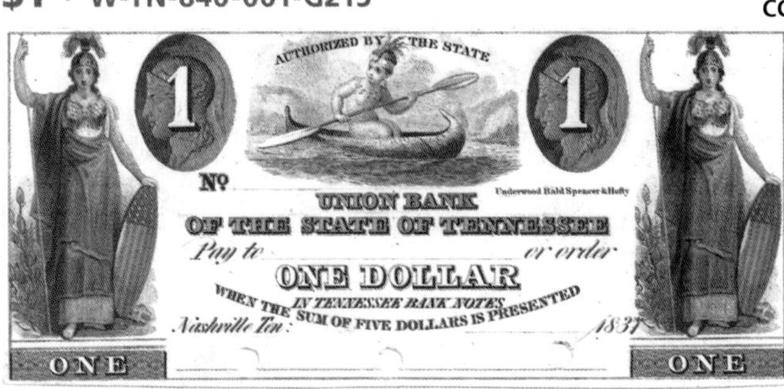

Engraver: Underwood, Bald, Spencer & Hufty. ***Comments:*** H-Unlisted. 1837.

Rarity: URS-4
Proof $700

$2 • **W-TN-840-002-G230**

CC

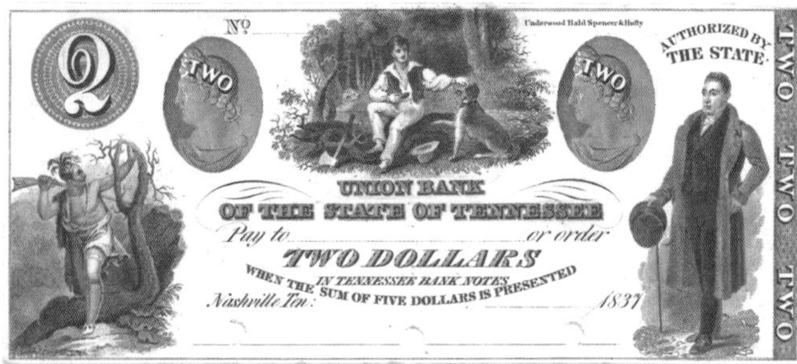

Engraver: Underwood, Bald, Spencer & Hufty. ***Comments:*** H-Unlisted, Garland-Unlisted. 1837.

Rarity: URS-2
Proof $1,200

Notes on Which the Place Payable is Blank

$1 • **W-TN-840-001-G240**

SBG

Engraver: Draper, Toppan & Co. ***Comments:*** H-TN-210-G200, Garland-1023. January 2, 1843.

Rarity: URS-2
Proof $1,200

$1 • **W-TN-840-001-G250**

CC

Tint: Red-orange frame, 1 / 1, and dies bearing white ONE. ***Engraver:*** American Bank Note Co. ***Comments:*** H-TN-210-G202a, Garland-1024. 186_. 1862.

Rarity: URS-5
F $650; **Proof** $3,300
Selected auction price: Heritage Auctions, October 21, 2015, Lot 18580, Proof $3,290

$2 • **W-TN-840-002-G260**

CC

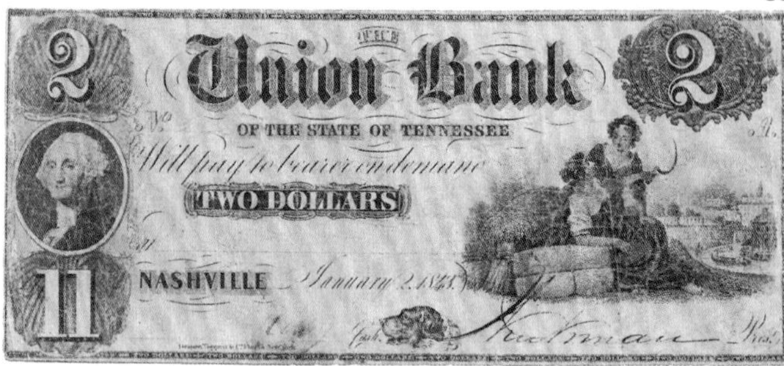

Engraver: Draper, Toppan & Co. ***Comments:*** H-TN-210-G204, Garland-1025. January 2, 1843.

Rarity: URS-3
F $400

$2 • **W-TN-840-002-G270**

CC

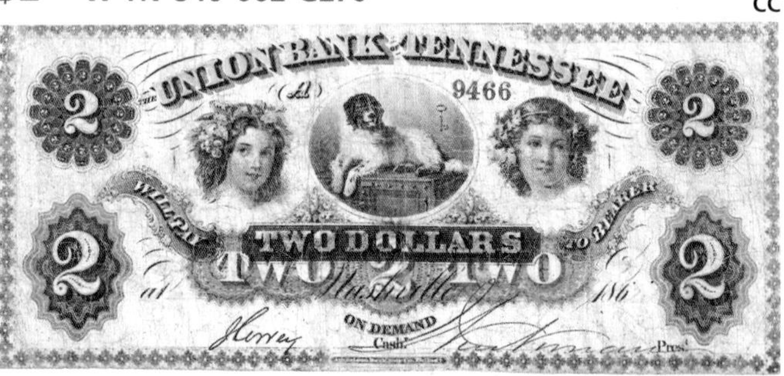

Tint: Red-orange frame, dies bearing white 2 / 2, and dies outlining white TWO / 2 / TWO. ***Engraver:*** American Bank Note Co. ***Comments:*** H-TN-210-G206a, Garland-1026. 186_. 1862.

Rarity: URS-4
F $950; **VF** $1,600
Selected auction price: Spink & Smythe, January 2009, Lot 1033, VF $1,600

$3 • **W-TN-840-003-G280**

CC

Engraver: Draper, Toppan & Co. ***Comments:*** H-TN-210-G208, Garland-1027. Handwritten 61 over engraved 43 in date. January 2, 1843.

Rarity: URS-3
F $500; **Proof** $1,600

$5 • **W-TN-840-005-G290** CC

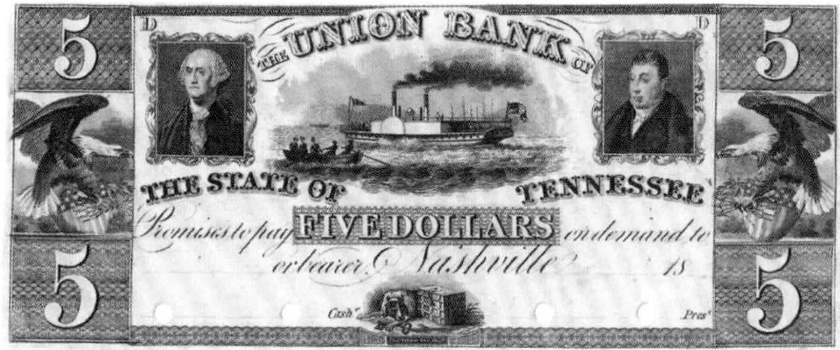

Engraver: Unverified, but likely Chas. Toppan. ***Comments:*** H-TN-210-G210, Garland-1029. 18__. 1830s–1840s.

Rarity: URS-3
Proof $1,000

$5 • **W-TN-840-005-G300** CC

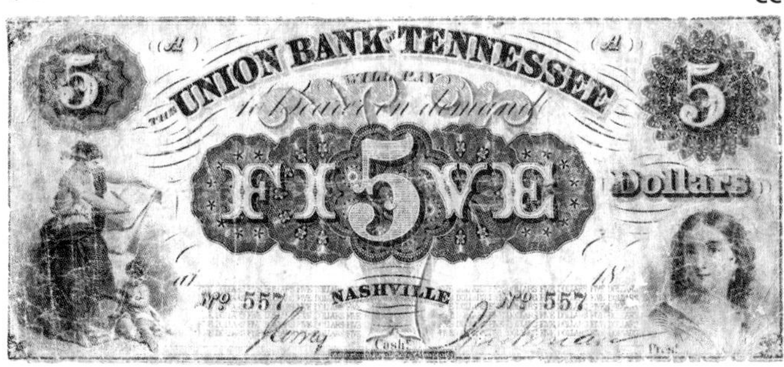

Tint: Red-orange V, panel of microlettering, and dies bearing white 5 / 5. ***Engraver:*** American Bank Note Co. ***Comments:*** H-TN-210-G214a, Garland-1030. 18__. 1861.

Rarity: URS-4
F $650
Selected auction price: Heritage Auctions, January 8, 2014, Lot 15443, F $881

$5 • **W-TN-840-005-G300a**

Engraver: American Bank Note Co. ***Comments:*** H-Unlisted, Garland-1031. Similar to W-TN-840-005-G300, Garland-1031. Printed in red and black. 18__. 1861.

Rarity: URS-4
F $650

$10 • **W-TN-840-010-G310**

Left: Medallion head / TEN / Medallion head. ***Center:*** 10 / Haying scene, Woman and man, Men harvesting. ***Right:*** Medallion head / TEN / Medallion head. ***Engraver:*** Unverified, but likely Chas. Toppan. ***Comments:*** H-TN-210-G216, Garland-1034. 18__. 1830s–1840s.

Rarity: URS-3
Proof $2,500

$10 • **W-TN-840-010-G320** CC

Tint: Red-orange frame, TEN / TEN, and 10 / 10. ***Engraver:*** American Bank Note Co. ***Comments:*** H-TN-210-G220a, Garland-1035. 18__. 1850s–1860s.

Rarity: URS-4
VF $2,800; **Proof** $12,000
Selected auction price: Heritage Auctions, January 7, 2015, Lot 18788, VF $2,820; Stack's Bowers Galleries, August 2011, Lot 5303, Proof $12,650

$20 • **W-TN-840-020-G330**

Left: 20 / Woman seated / 20. ***Center:*** Ship / Two women flanking shield bearing eagle, surmounted by eagle / Ship. ***Right:*** 20 / Woman seated / 20. ***Engraver:*** Chas. Toppan. ***Comments:*** H-TN-210-G222. 18__. 1830s–1840s.

Rarity: —

$20 • **W-TN-840-020-G340**

Left: TWENTY vertically. ***Center:*** 20 / Female portrait / 20. ***Right:*** TWENTY vertically. ***Tint:*** Red-orange. ***Engraver:*** American Bank Note Co. ***Comments:*** H-TN-210-G224a, Garland-1038. 18__. 1850s–1860s.

Rarity: URS-3
Proof $2,500

$50 • **W-TN-840-050-G350**

Left: 50 / Ship / 50. ***Center:*** Portrait of Indian / Woman seated / Portrait of Indian. ***Right:*** 50 / Ship / 50. ***Engraver:*** Chas. Toppan. ***Comments:*** H-TN-210-G226, Garland-1040. 18__. 1830s–1840s.

Rarity: URS-3
Proof $2,500

$50 • **W-TN-840-050-G360** CC

Tint: Red-orange L / L, FIFTY / FIFTY, and dies bearing white 50 / 50. ***Engraver:*** American Bank Note Co. ***Comments:*** H-TN-210-G228a, Garland-1041. 18__. 1850s–1860s.

Rarity: URS-3
Prop. Proof $750; **Proof** $5,000

$100 • **W-TN-840-100-G370**
Left: 100 / Justice / 100. ***Center:*** Steamboat / Woman reclining with globe, Cherub / Steamboat. ***Right:*** 100 / Justice / 100. ***Engraver:*** Chas. Toppan. ***Comments:*** H-TN-210-G230, Garland-1043. 18__. 1830s–1840s.

Rarity: URS-3
Proof $3,500

$100 • **W-TN-840-100-G380**
Left: 100 / Justice / 100. ***Center:*** Eagle / Woman reclining with globe, Cherub / Eagle. ***Right:*** 100 / Justice / 100. ***Engraver:*** Chas. Toppan. ***Comments:*** H-Unlisted, Garland-1044. 18__. 1830s–1840s.

Rarity: URS-4
Proof $3,000

$100 • **W-TN-840-100-G390**
Left: 100 / Female portrait. ***Center:*** Mule-drawn wagon, Cotton fields. ***Right:*** 100 / Portrait of child. ***Tint:*** Red-orange. ***Engraver:*** American Bank Note Co. ***Comments:*** H-TN-210-G232a, Garland-1045. 18__. 1850s–1860s.

Rarity: URS-3
Prop. Proof $750

$500 • **W-TN-840-500-G400**
Left: 500 / Medallion head of George Washington / 500. ***Center:*** Eagle with shield and cornucopia. ***Right:*** 500 / Medallion head of Benjamin Franklin / 500. ***Engraver:*** Draper, Toppan, Longacre & Co. ***Comments:*** H-TN-210-G234, Garland-1047. 18__. 1830s–1840s.

Rarity: URS-3
Proof $3,000

$500 • **W-TN-840-500-G410**
Left: 500 / Cotton plant. ***Center:*** Train. ***Right:*** 500 / Female portrait. ***Tint:*** Red-orange. ***Engraver:*** American Bank Note Co. ***Comments:*** H-TN-210-G236a, Garland-1048. 18__. 1850s–1860s.

Rarity: URS-3
Proof $3,000

$500 • **W-TN-840-500-G410a** CC

Tint: Green FIVE HUNDRED and dies bearing white 500 / 500. ***Engraver:*** American Bank Note Co. ***Comments:*** H-Unlisted, Garland-Unlisted. Similar to W-TN-840-500-G410. 18__. 1850s–1860s.

Rarity: URS-1
Prop. Proof $700

$1,000 • **W-TN-840-1000-G420** SBG

Engraver: Draper, Toppan, Longacre & Co. ***Comments:*** H-TN-210-G238, Garland-1049. 18__. 1830s–1840s.

Rarity: URS-3
Proof $3,200

$1,000 • **W-TN-840-1000-G430**
Left: Cotton plant / 1000. ***Center:*** Portrait of child. ***Right:*** 1000 / Steamboat. ***Tint:*** Red-orange. ***Engraver:*** American Bank Note Co. ***Comments:*** H-TN-210-G240a, Garland-1050. 18__. 1850s–1860s.

Rarity: URS-3
Prop. Proof $800

$1,000 • **W-TN-840-1000-G430a** HA

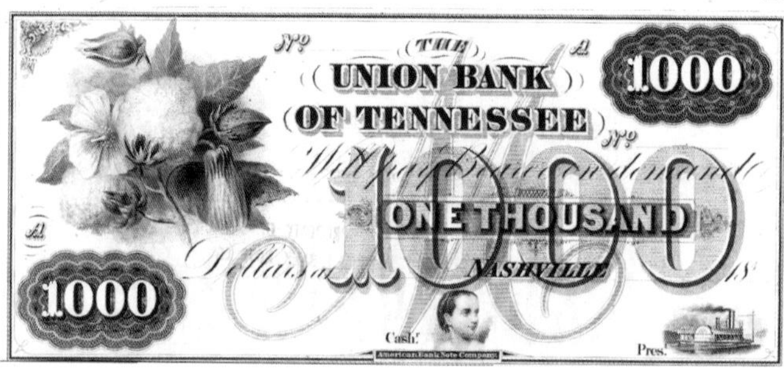

Tint: Green 1000 and die bearing white 1000. ***Engraver:*** American Bank Note Co. ***Comments:*** H-Unlisted. Similar to W-TN-840-1000-G430. 18__. 1850s–1860s.

Rarity: —
Selected auction price: Heritage Auctions, January 13, 2014, Lot 19488, Choice New $881

Non-Valid Issues

$1 • **W-TN-840-001-S010**
Left: ONE vertically. ***Center:*** Woman seated / Woman with sword seated with shield bearing 1 / Woman seated. ***Right:*** 1 / Woman standing / ONE. ***Engraver:*** Underwood, Bald, Spencer & Hufty. ***Comments:*** H-TN-210-S2. 18__. 1840s.

Rarity: —

$10 • **W-TN-840-010-S020**
Left: TEN vertically. ***Center:*** Woman seated / Woman with sword seated with shield bearing 10 / Woman seated. ***Right:*** 10 / Woman standing / TEN. ***Engraver:*** Underwood, Bald, Spencer & Hufty. ***Comments:*** H-TN-210-S4. 18__. 1840s.

Rarity: —

$20 • **W-TN-840-020-C080**
Engraver: Chas. Toppan. ***Comments:*** H-TN-210-C16. Counterfeit of the W-TN-840-020-G080. 18__. 1830s–1840s.

Rarity: —

Paris, Tennessee

Paris was established in December 1822. It was laid out in 104 lots to be sold at auction the following year. On September 30, 1823, it was incorporated, making it the first official town in West Tennessee. The town was named after Paris, France, to honor the Marquis de Lafayette.

Bank of Paris

1855–1858

W-TN-850

History: The Bank of Paris was chartered in 1855 with an authorized capital of $50,000. W.B. Dortch was the president, and H.C. West was the cashier. By 1858 the bank had closed.

Numismatic Commentary: No issued notes of this bank have been seen. Proofs are known.

The 1990 Christie's sale of the American Bank Note Co. archives produced a sheet of $1-$1-$1-$5.

Valid Issues

$1 • W-TN-850-001-G010

Left: 1 / Farmer seated under tree. ***Center:*** Covered wagons, horses, carts. ***Right:*** 1 / Female portrait. ***Engraver:*** Danforth, Wright & Co. ***Comments:*** H-TN-215-G2, Garland-1090. Dec. 1, 1855.

Rarity: URS-4
Proof $1,500

$5 • W-TN-850-005-G020

Left: 5 / Man plowing with two horses. ***Center:*** V / Indian woman seated with shield, bow and arrows, Steamship. ***Right:*** FIVE vertically. ***Engraver:*** Danforth, Wright & Co. ***Comments:*** H-TN-215-G4, Garland-1091. Dec. 1, 1855.

Rarity: URS-4
Proof $1,500

Central Bank of Tennessee (branch)

1856 and 1857

W-TN-860

History: In 1856 it was reported that "there never was any such corporation as the Central Bank of Tennessee, and that Belknap, Tremain & Haven, merely took upon themselves that name under which to carry on their banking business—without any charter or act of incorporation."[19] By 1857 the enterprise, along with all its branches, had failed.

The Central Bank of Tennessee had its parent bank located in Nashville, W-TN-720, and a branch bank located in Dandridge, W-TN-240.

Numismatic Commentary: As the only collectible bank from this town, most notes appear to be held in collections. Enough notes are thought to survive that collectors should be able to acquire an example if desired.

Valid Issues

$1 • W-TN-860-001-G010

Left: 1 on ONE / Horses drawing covered wagon / ONE. ***Center:*** Harvest scene, Men loading horse-drawn wagon. ***Right:*** 1 / Two farmers walking. ***Engraver:*** Danforth, Wright & Co. ***Comments:*** H-TN-140-G40, Garland-1092. Aug. 1, 1855.

Rarity: URS-6
F $250

$2 • W-TN-860-002-G020

Left: 2 on TWO / Horses plowing. ***Center:*** Horse-drawn wagons, Road. ***Right:*** 2 / Portrait of sailor. ***Engraver:*** Danforth, Wright & Co. ***Comments:*** H-TN-140-G42, Garland-1093. Aug. 1, 1855.

Rarity: URS-6
F $250

$5 • W-TN-860-005-G030 CC

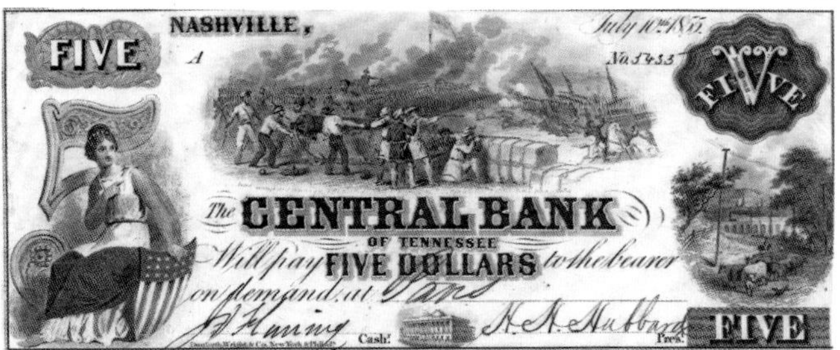

Engraver: Danforth, Wright & Co. ***Comments:*** H-TN-140-G46, Garland-1094. July 10th, 1855.

Rarity: URS-6
F $250

$10 • W-TN-860-010-G040 HA

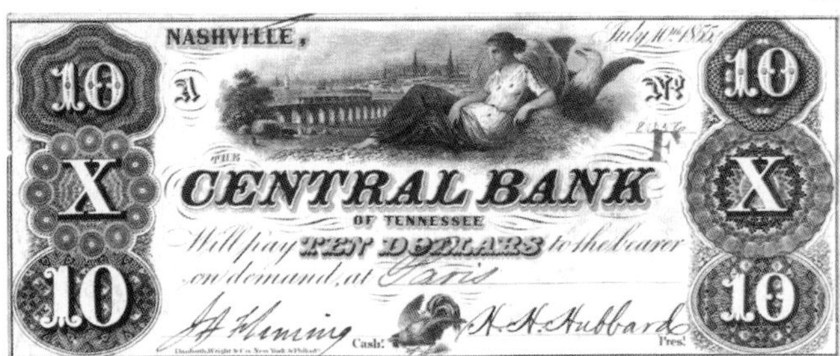

Engraver: Danforth, Wright & Co. ***Comments:*** H-TN-140-G48, Garland-1095. July 10th, 1855.

Rarity: URS-5
F $350

$20 • W-TN-860-020-G050

Left: 20 / Liberty seated with shield. ***Center:*** XX / Woman reclining with eagle. ***Right:*** 20 / Train. ***Engraver:*** Danforth, Wright & Co. ***Comments:*** H-TN-140-G50, Garland-1096. July 10th, 1855.

Rarity: URS-5
F $350

Collectors and Researchers:

If you have new information about any banks or notes listed in this volume, contact Whitman Publishing, Attn: Obsolete Paper Money, 3101 Clairmont Road, Suite G, Atlanta, GA 30329.

Pulaski, Tennessee

In 1809 Pulaski was founded and settled. The area became the site of several battles during the Civil War. There was even a hanging in 1863 when Sam Davis, a Confederate courier, was sentenced to death for suspected espionage.

Planters Bank of Tennessee (branch)

1834–1865

W-TN-870

History: The Planters Bank of Tennessee was chartered on November 11, 1833, with an authorized capital of $2,000,000. In 1834 the branch in Pulaski was opened. In 1848 the president was A.M. Ballentine. E.B. Smith was the cashier. In 1854 Smith passed away, and he was succeeded by G.W. Petway. The capital was $150,000. In 1865 the bank was forced to liquidate and close its affairs.

The Planters Bank of Tennessee had its parent bank located in Nashville, W-TN-810, and branch banks located in Athens, W-TN-020, Clarksville, W-TN-140, Columbia, W-TN-210, Franklin, W-TN-300, LaGrange, W-TN-410, Memphis, W-TN-570, Murfreesboro, W-TN-630, Rogersville, W-TN-910, Shelbyville, W-TN-940, Somerville, W-TN-970, Sparta, W-TN-990, Trenton, W-TN-1050, and Winchester, W-TN-1070.

Numismatic Commentary: Given the paucity of Pulaski notes found in museum holdings, auction archives, and collections, notes from this bank appear to be rarer than previously thought. It is thought that the dollar-denominated notes may have been issued by the parent bank but not by this branch.

Valid Issues

$1 • W-TN-870-001-G010

Left: 1 / Medallion head bearing ONE / 1. ***Center:*** 1 with cherub / Woman seated with boxes. ***Right:*** Woman standing in 1. ***Engraver:*** Rawdon, Wright, Hatch & Edson. ***Comments:*** H-TN-185-G262. 18__. 1840s.

Rarity: —

$2 • W-TN-870-002-G020

Left: 2 / Woman with sheaf / 2. ***Center:*** 2 with cherubs / Woman seated with boxes. ***Right:*** Woman standing in 2. ***Engraver:*** Rawdon, Wright, Hatch & Edson. ***Comments:*** H-TN-185-G264. Dec. 1, 1860.

Rarity: —

$3 • W-TN-870-003-G030

Left: 3 / Medallion head / 3. ***Center:*** 3 with cherubs / Two men flanking shield bearing cow surmounted by beehive. ***Right:*** Woman standing in 3. ***Engraver:*** Rawdon, Wright, Hatch & Edson. ***Comments:*** H-TN-185-G266. Dec. 1, 1860.

Rarity: —

$5 • W-TN-870-005-G040

Left: FIVE / Woman with cog wheel / 5 vertically. ***Center:*** 5 / Horse / 5. ***Right:*** FIVE / Man seated / 5 vertically. ***Engraver:*** Rawdon, Wright, & Hatch. ***Comments:*** H-TN-185-G268. 18__. 1830s.

Rarity: —

$5 • W-TN-870-005-G050

Left: Medallion head / FIVE / Medallion head. ***Center:*** FIVE / Man standing with dog / FIVE. ***Right:*** Medallion head / FIVE / Medallion head. ***Engraver:*** Underwood, Bald & Spencer. ***Comments:*** H-TN-185-G270. 18__. 1830s–1840s.

Rarity: URS-5

F $350

$5 • W-TN-870-005-G050a

Engraver: Underwood, Bald & Spencer. ***Comments:*** H-TN-185-G270a. Similar to W-TN-870-005-G050. 18__. 1830s–1840s.

Rarity: —

$10 • W-TN-870-010-G060

Left: X / Ten gold dollars / 10. ***Center:*** 10 / Mechanic seated with cogwheel, Steamboat / 10. ***Right:*** TEN / Woman standing with anchor / TEN. ***Engraver:*** Rawdon, Wright, & Hatch. ***Comments:*** H-TN-185-G272. 18__. 1830s.

Rarity: —

$10 • W-TN-870-010-G070

Left: Medallion head / TEN / Medallion head. ***Center:*** 10 / Farm scene, Harvest / X. ***Right:*** Medallion head / TEN / Medallion head. ***Engraver:*** Underwood, Bald & Spencer. ***Comments:*** H-TN-185-G274. 18__. 1830s–1840s.

Rarity: URS-5

F $350

$10 • W-TN-870-010-G070a

Engraver: Underwood, Bald & Spencer. ***Comments:*** H-TN-185-G274a. Similar to W-TN-870-010-G070. 18__. 1830s–1840s.

Rarity: —

$20 • W-TN-870-020-G080

Engraver: Rawdon, Wright, & Hatch. ***Comments:*** H-TN-185-G276. No description available. 18__. 1830s.

Rarity: *None known*

$20 • W-TN-870-020-G090

Left: 20 / Medallion head / 20. ***Center:*** 20 / Medallion head / 20. ***Right:*** 20 / Medallion head / 20. ***Engraver:*** Underwood, Bald & Spencer. ***Comments:*** H-TN-185-G278. 18__. 1830s–1840s.

Rarity: URS-4

F $300

$20 • W-TN-870-020-G090a

Engraver: Underwood, Bald & Spencer. ***Comments:*** H-TN-185-G278a. Similar to W-TN-870-020-G090. 18__. 1830s–1840s.

Rarity: —

$50 • W-TN-870-050-G100

Left: 50 / Medallion head / 50. ***Center:*** Medallion heads / Woman seated, Ship / Medallion heads. ***Right:*** 50 / Medallion head / 50. ***Engraver:*** Underwood, Bald, Spencer & Hufty. ***Comments:*** H-TN-185-G280. 18__. 1830s–1850s.

Rarity: —

$100 • W-TN-870-100-G110

Left: 100 / Three women seated vertically / 100. ***Center:*** Medallion head / Boy reclining under corn, Plow / Medallion head. ***Right:*** 100 / Three women seated vertically / 100. ***Engraver:*** Underwood, Bald, Spencer & Hufty. ***Comments:*** H-TN-185-G282. 18__. 1830s–1850s.

Rarity: —

Civil War Fractional Notes

5¢ • W-TN-870-00.05-G120

Center: FIVE CENTS. ***Right:*** 5. ***Engraver:*** Adams. ***Comments:*** H-TN-185-G286, Garland-1098. Jan. 1, 1862.

Rarity: URS-3
F $350

10¢ • W-TN-870-00.10-G130

Center: TEN CENTS. ***Right:*** 10. ***Engraver:*** Adams. ***Comments:*** H-TN-185-G288, Garland-1099. Jan. 1, 1862.

Rarity: URS-3
F $350

25¢ • W-TN-870-00.25-G140

Center: TWENTY FIVE CENTS. ***Right:*** 25. ***Engraver:*** Adams. ***Comments:*** H-TN-185-G290, Garland-1100. Jan. 1, 1862.

Rarity: URS-3
F $350

30¢ • W-TN-870-00.30-G150

Center: THIRTY CENTS. ***Right:*** 30. ***Engraver:*** Adams. ***Comments:*** H-TN-185-G292, Garland-1101. Jan. 1, 1862.

Rarity: URS-3
F $375

50¢ • W-TN-870-00.50-G160

Center: FIFTY CENTS. ***Right:*** 50. ***Back:*** Red. ***Engraver:*** Adams. ***Comments:*** H-TN-185-G294, Garland-1102. Jan. 1, 1862.

Rarity: URS-3
F $375

80¢ • W-TN-870-00.80-G170

Center: EIGHTY CENTS. ***Right:*** 80. ***Back:*** Red. ***Engraver:*** Adams. ***Comments:*** H-TN-185-G296, Garland-1103. Jan. 1, 1862.

Rarity: URS-3
F $375

Non-Valid Issues

$10 • W-TN-870-010-S010

Left: Woman. ***Center:*** Woman, Train, Steamboat. ***Right:*** Ceres. ***Comments:*** H-TN-185-S116. 18__. 1840s.

Rarity: —

$10 • W-TN-870-010-S020

Left: 10 / Justice with scales. ***Center:*** X with cherubs / Two women seated. ***Right:*** 10 / Justice with scales. ***Engraver:*** Rawdon, Wright & Hatch. ***Comments:*** H-TN-185-S118. From a genuine plate of the Planters Bank of Alabama, Wetumpka, Alabama. 18__. 1840s.

Rarity: —

$20 • W-TN-870-020-S030

Center: Eagle. ***Comments:*** H-TN-185-S120. 18__. 1840s.

Rarity: —

$20 • W-TN-870-020-S040

Left: 20 / Female portrait / XX. ***Center:*** Woman seated near ocean with shield. ***Right:*** 20 / Female portrait / XX. ***Engraver:*** Rawdon, Wright & Hatch. ***Comments:*** H-TN-185-S122. From a genuine plate of the Planters Bank of Alabama, Wetumpka, Alabama. 18__. 1840s.

Rarity: —

$50 • W-TN-870-050-S050

Left: FIFTY DOLLARS vertically. ***Center:*** 50 / Eagle on bale / 50. ***Right:*** STATE OF TENNESSEE vertically. ***Engraver:*** Rawdon, Wright & Hatch. ***Comments:*** H-TN-185-S124. From a genuine plate of the Planters Bank of Alabama, Wetumpka, Alabama. 18__. 1840s.

Rarity: —

$100 • W-TN-870-100-S060

Left: HUNDRED vertically. ***Center:*** Deer, River. ***Right:*** Portrait of George Washington. ***Engraver:*** Rawdon, Wright & Hatch. ***Comments:*** H-TN-185-S126. From a genuine plate of the Planters Bank of Alabama, Wetumpka, Alabama. 18__. 1840s.

Rarity: —

$100 • W-TN-870-100-S070

Left: Medallion head. ***Center:*** C / Factory / C. ***Right:*** 100 diagonally. ***Engraver:*** Rawdon, Wright & Hatch. ***Comments:*** H-TN-185-S128. 18__. 1840s.

Rarity: —

Rogersville, Tennessee

Rogersville was originally settled in 1775. The land was sold after a Native American attack, and Colonel Thomas Amis built a fort at Big Creek. A store, a blacksmith shop, and a distillery followed the building of a fortified stone house for Amis to live in, and eventually a sawmill and gristmill followed.

In 1785 the brief state of Franklin established Spencer County and declared Rogersville to be the county seat. Eventually this area was transferred to Tennessee.

During the Civil War, there was much activity in Rogersville. After a surprise attack by Confederate forces, the Union army was driven away from the area, and Rogersville remained in Confederate control for the remainder of the war. For the most part, the town was spared much damage.

Bank of America (branch)

1856–1858

W-TN-880

History: In 1856 the Bank of America was chartered. J.E. Wilcox was elected cashier. The capital was $100,000. By 1858 the bank had closed.

The Bank of America had its parent bank located in Clarksville, W-TN-100, and branch banks located in Brownsville, W-TN-050, and Dresden, W-TN-260.

Numismatic Commentary: A bank owned by the enterprising Davie family, this entity was a long, long way from the center of operations in rural West Tennessee. Signed and issued notes are extremely rare. Unsigned notes are readily available.

Valid Issues

$5 • W-TN-880-005-G010

Left: V / Portrait of Andrew Jackson. ***Center:*** Two women flanking shield. ***Right:*** 5 / Portrait of General Ambrose Davie. ***Overprint:*** Red FIVE. ***Engraver:*** Bald, Cousland & Co. / Baldwin, Bald & Cousland. ***Comments:*** H-TN-15-G44a, Garland-1119. 18__. 1850s.

Rarity: URS-4
F $400

$10 • W-TN-880-010-G020

Left: X / Portrait of Winston Jones Davie. ***Center:*** Woman and man flanking shield bearing wheat. ***Right:*** 10 / Portrait of Elizabeth Phillips. ***Overprint:*** Red TEN. ***Engraver:*** Bald, Cousland & Co. / Baldwin, Bald & Cousland. ***Comments:*** H-TN-15-G46a, Garland-1120. 18__. 1850s.

Rarity: URS-3
F $500

$20 • W-TN-880-020-G030

Left: 20 / Portrait of Winston Jones Davie. ***Center:*** Family playing with bear cub, Horse. ***Right:*** 20 / Female portrait. ***Overprint:*** Red XX. ***Engraver:*** Bald, Cousland & Co. / Baldwin, Bald & Cousland. ***Comments:*** H-TN-15-G48a, Garland-1121. 18__. 1850s.

Rarity: URS-2
F $1,200

Bank of the State of Tennessee {3rd} (branch)

1838–1866

W-TN-890

History: The third Bank of the State of Tennessee (also seen in print as the Bank of Tennessee) was chartered on January 19, 1838, with an authorized capital of $5,000,000. The bank opened for business in February. The bank suspended specie payments a couple of times in 1838 and 1839, due to the panic of that time, but afterward it resumed and had a profitable and successful career. In 1855 the cashier of the Rogersville branch was H. Fain, and the president was William Hutcheson. In 1863 George R. Powell took the cashiership, and Jacob Miller was the president.

During the Civil War, the Union army entered the state, and some officers of the Bank of the State of Tennessee fled south with the bank's specie. After the war, the bank's assets were returned to Governor William G. Brownlow in Nashville. Half of the bank's funds had been transferred into state bonds.

By February 1866 the Bank of the State of Tennessee was authorized to go into liquidation.

The third Bank of the State of Tennessee had its parent bank located in Nashville, W-TN-690, and branch banks located in Athens, W-TN-010, Clarksville, W-TN-120, Columbia, W-TN-190, Knoxville, W-TN-365, Memphis, W-TN-490, Murfreesboro, W-TN-610, Shelbyville, W-TN-920, Somerville, W-TN-960, Sparta, W-TN-980, and Trenton, W-TN-1030.

Numismatic Commentary: Given the number of surviving notes, the operations of this branch must have been successful. All denominations can be located. The collecting of notes with "Decreed To Be Spurious" overstamps can be a challenge, as several seek out and hold such notes.

Valid Issues

$1 • W-TN-890-001-G010

Left: Woman seated with farmer / Female portrait. ***Center:*** 1 / Man plowing with horses / 1. ***Right:*** ONE / Medallion head / ONE. ***Engraver:*** Draper, Toppan & Co. ***Comments:*** H-TN-195-G240. Mar. 1, 1842.

Rarity: —

$1 • W-TN-890-001-G010a

Engraver: Toppan, Carpenter & Co. ***Comments:*** H-TN-195-G240a. Similar to W-TN-890-001-G010 but with different date and engraver imprint. Mar. 1, ____. 1840s, 1861.

Rarity: —

$1 • W-TN-890-001-G020

CC

Engraver: Toppan, Carpenter, Casilear & Co. ***Comments:*** H-TN-195-G242, Garland-1129. 18__. 1850s.

Rarity: URS-6
F $200

$1 • W-TN-890-001-G030

SI, SI

Tint: Red-orange lathework and panel of microlettering outlining white ONE. ***Back:*** Red-orange. ***Engraver:*** Toppan, Carpenter & Co. ***Comments:*** H-TN-195-G244a, Garland-1132. 18__. 1850s.

Rarity: URS-5
F $300

$2 • W-TN-890-002-G040

Left: TWO / Woman seated in 2 / 2. ***Center:*** 2 / Woman seated on bales / 2. ***Right:*** 2 / Ship / 2. ***Engraver:*** Draper, Toppan & Co. ***Comments:*** H-TN-195-G246. Mar. 1, 1842.

Rarity: —

$2 • W-TN-890-002-G040a

Engraver: Toppan, Carpenter & Co. ***Comments:*** H-TN-195-G246a. Similar to W-TN-890-002-G040 but with different date and engraver imprint. Mar. 1, ____. 1840s, 1861.

Rarity: —

$2 • **W-TN-890-002-G050** CC

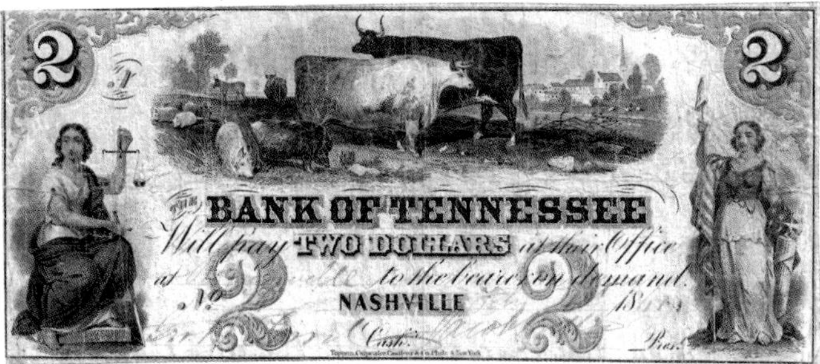

Engraver: Toppan, Carpenter, Casilear & Co. ***Comments:*** H-TN-195-G248, Garland-1133. 18__. 1850s.

Rarity: URS-5
F $300

$2 • **W-TN-890-002-G060**

Left: 2 / Female portrait. ***Center:*** Soldier, Woman, and two Indians looking at bust of George Washington. ***Right:*** 2 / Portrait of Charles Carroll. ***Tint:*** Red-orange. ***Back:*** Red-orange. ***Engraver:*** Toppan, Carpenter & Co. ***Comments:*** H-TN-195-G250a, Garland-1135. 18__. 1850s.

Rarity: URS-4
F $350

$3 • **W-TN-890-003-G070**

Left: THREE / Woman standing / THREE. ***Center:*** 3 / Men on horses, sheep / 3. ***Right:*** THREE / Cherubs in 3 / THREE. ***Engraver:*** Draper, Toppan & Co. ***Comments:*** H-TN-195-G252, Garland-Unlisted. Mar. 1, 1842.

Rarity: *None known*

$3 • **W-TN-890-003-G070a**

Engraver: Toppan, Carpenter & Co. ***Comments:*** H-TN-195-G252a, Garland-Unlisted. Similar to W-TN-890-003-G070 but with different date and engraver imprint. Mar. 1, ____. 1840s, 1861.

Rarity: *None known*

$5 • **W-TN-890-005-G080**

Left: 5 / Woman leaning on column / V. ***Center:*** Woman seated with shield. ***Right:*** 5 / Justice standing with scales and eagle / V. ***Engraver:*** Rawdon, Wright, Hatch & Edson / Rawdon, Wright & Hatch. ***Comments:*** H-TN-195-G254, Garland-Unlisted. 18__. 1838–1840s.

Rarity: *None known*

$5 • **W-TN-890-005-G090**

Left: Three men / 5. ***Center:*** Portrait of James Madison. ***Right:*** 5 / Medallion head. ***Back:*** Red-orange. ***Engraver:*** Danforth, Bald & Co. ***Comments:*** H-TN-195-G256a, Garland-1136. 18__. 1850s.

Rarity: *None known*

$5 • **W-TN-890-005-G090a**

Tint: Red-orange outlining white V / 5 / V. ***Back:*** Red-orange. ***Engraver:*** Danforth, Bald & Co. ***Comments:*** H-TN-195-G256b, Garland-Unlisted. Similar to W-TN-890-005-G090. 18__. 1850s.

Rarity: *None known*

$10 • **W-TN-890-010-G100**

Left: 10 / Eagle with shield / X. ***Center:*** Woman with children seated among parcels, Factories and farmhouse. ***Right:*** 10 / Shield / X. ***Engraver:*** Draper, Toppan, Longacre & Co. ***Comments:*** H-TN-195-G262, Garland-Unlisted. 18__. 1838–1840s.

Rarity: *None known*

$10 • **W-TN-890-010-G110**

Left: 10 / Portrait of James K. Polk. ***Center:*** Portrait of Andrew Jackson. ***Right:*** 10 / Portrait of Cave Johnson. ***Tint:*** Red-orange outlining white 10 / 10. ***Back:*** Blue. ***Engraver:*** Toppan, Carpenter & Co. ***Comments:*** H-TN-195-G266a, Garland-1139. 18__. 1850s–1861.

Rarity: URS-4
F $400

$20 • **W-TN-890-020-G120**

Left: 20 / Man writing on tablet / 20. ***Center:*** Woman standing with eagle and shield. ***Right:*** 20 / Shield / 20. ***Engraver:*** Draper, Toppan, Longacre & Co. ***Comments:*** H-TN-195-G268. 18__. 1838–1840s.

Rarity: *None known*

$20 • **W-TN-890-020-G120a**

Engraver: Toppan, Carpenter & Co. ***Comments:*** H-TN-195-G268a, Garland-Unlisted. Similar to W-TN-890-020-G120 but with different engraver imprint. 18__. 1840s–1850s

Rarity: *None known*

$20 • **W-TN-890-020-G130**

Left: 20 / Portrait of Zachary Taylor / 20. ***Center:*** Three women reclining, Ship / 20. ***Right:*** Justice seated with sword and scales / TWENTY. ***Engraver:*** Toppan, Carpenter, Casilear & Co. ***Comments:*** H-TN-195-G270, Garland-1140. 18__. 1850s.

Rarity: URS-4
F $350

$20 • **W-TN-890-020-G130a**

Back: Red-orange. ***Engraver:*** Toppan, Carpenter, Casilear & Co. ***Comments:*** H-TN-195-G270a, Garland-Unlisted. Similar to W-TN-890-020-G130. 18__. 1850s.

Rarity: *None known*

$20 • **W-TN-890-020-G130b**

Tint: Red-orange outlining white TWENTY. ***Back:*** Red-orange. ***Engraver:*** Toppan, Carpenter, Casilear & Co. ***Comments:*** H-TN-195-G270b, Garland-Unlisted. Similar to W-TN-890-020-G130. 18__. 1850s.

Rarity: *None known*

$50 • **W-TN-890-050-G140**

Left: 50 / Shield / 50. ***Center:*** Liberty with eagle and shield. ***Right:*** 50 / Portrait of George Washington / 50. ***Engraver:*** Draper, Toppan, Longacre & Co. ***Comments:*** H-TN-195-G272, Garland-Unlisted. 18__. 1838–1840s.

Rarity: *None known*

$100 • **W-TN-890-100-G150**

Left: Atlas lifting world on shoulders / 100. ***Center:*** 100 / Justice with eagle and shield / 100. ***Right:*** Atlas lifting world on shoulders / 100. ***Engraver:*** Draper, Toppan, Longacre & Co. ***Comments:*** H-TN-195-G274, Garland-Unlisted. 18__. 1838–1850s.

Rarity: *None known*

Non-Valid Issues

$10 • W-TN-890-010-C100

Engraver: Draper, Toppan, Longacre & Co. ***Comments:*** H-TN-195-C262. Counterfeit of W-TN-890-010-G100. 18__. 1853.

Rarity: —

$20 • W-TN-890-020-C130

Engraver: Toppan, Carpenter & Co. ***Comments:*** H-TN-195-C270. Counterfeit of W-TN-890-020-G130. 18__. 1853.

Rarity: —

$20 • W-TN-890-020-C130a

Engraver: Toppan, Carpenter, Casilear & Co. ***Comments:*** H-TN-195-C270a. Counterfeit of W-TN-890-020-G130a. 18__. 1853.

Rarity: —

$20 • W-TN-890-020-C130b

Back: Red-orange. ***Engraver:*** Toppan, Carpenter, Casilear & Co. ***Comments:*** H-TN-195-C270b. Counterfeit of W-TN-890-020-G130b. 18__. 1853.

Rarity: —

$50 • W-TN-890-050-C140

Engraver: Draper, Toppan, Longacre & Co. ***Comments:*** H-TN-195-C272. Counterfeit of W-TN-890-050-G140. 18__. 1853.

Rarity: —

Nashville Bank (branch)

1817–1827

W-TN-900

History: In 1807 the Nashville Bank was chartered with an authorized capital of $200,000, to be divided into shares of $50 apiece. In 1817 several banks were chartered across the state—in the towns of Gallatin, Murfreesboro, Rogersville, Shelbyville, and Winchester—and were given the option of either joining the first Bank of the State of Tennessee, W-TN-355, or of joining with the Nashville Bank. The corporations chose the Nashville Bank and became branches forthwith.

On March 31, 1823, the Nashville Bank, along with its branches, burned a total of $250,000 worth of bank notes in order to increase the value of its circulation. In 1827 the bank was liquidated.

The Nashville Bank had its parent bank located in Nashville, W-TN-800, and branch banks located in Gallatin, W-TN-310, Murfreesboro, W-TN-640, Shelbyville, W-TN-930, and Winchester, W-TN-1060.

Numismatic Commentary: Any note from this bank is very rare and possibly unique.

Valid Issues

$1 • W-TN-900-001-G010

Left: ONE vertically. ***Center:*** 1 / Woman seated / 1. ***Right:*** TENNESSEE vertically. ***Engraver:*** Tanner, Kearny & Tiebout. ***Comments:*** H-TN-180-G104. 18__. 1810s.

Rarity: —

$2 • W-TN-900-002-G020

Left: TWO vertically. ***Center:*** 2 / Woman seated / 2. ***Right:*** TENNESSEE vertically. ***Engraver:*** Tanner, Kearny & Tiebout. ***Comments:*** H-TN-180-G106. 18__. 1810s.

Rarity: —

$5 • W-TN-900-005-G030

CC

Engraver: Murray, Draper, Fairman & Co. ***Comments:*** H-TN-180-G110. 18__. 1810s.

Rarity: URS-2
VF $750

$5 • W-TN-900-005-G040

Left: FIVE vertically. ***Center:*** 5 / Woman seated / 5. ***Right:*** TENNESSEE vertically. ***Engraver:*** Tanner, Kearny & Tiebout. ***Comments:*** H-TN-180-G112, Garland-1141. 18__. 1810s–1820s.

Rarity: URS-1
F $1,400

$10 • W-TN-900-010-G050

Left: TEN vertically. ***Center:*** 10 / Woman seated / 10. ***Right:*** NASHVILLE vertically. ***Engraver:*** Murray, Draper, Fairman & Co. ***Comments:*** H-TN-180-G114. 18__. 1810s.

Rarity: —

$10 • W-TN-900-010-G060

Left: TEN vertically. ***Center:*** 10 / Woman seated / 10. ***Right:*** TENNESSEE vertically. ***Engraver:*** Tanner, Kearny & Tiebout. ***Comments:*** H-TN-180-G116, Garland-1142. 18__. 1810s–1820s.

Rarity: URS-1
F $1,400

$20 • W-TN-900-020-G070

Left: TWENTY vertically. ***Center:*** 20 / Woman seated / 20. ***Right:*** NASHVILLE vertically. ***Engraver:*** Murray, Draper, Fairman & Co. ***Comments:*** H-TN-180-G118. 18__. 1810s.

Rarity: —

$20 • W-TN-900-020-G080

CC

Engraver: Tanner, Kearny & Tiebout. ***Comments:*** H-TN-180-G120, Garland-1143. 18__. 1810s–1820s.

Rarity: URS-2
F $1,200

Non-Valid Issues

$20 • W-TN-900-020-C080

Engraver: Tanner, Kearny & Tiebout. ***Comments:*** H-TN-180-C120. Counterfeit of W-TN-900-020-G080. 18__. 1810s–1820s.

Rarity: —

Planters Bank of Tennessee (branch)

1834–1865

W-TN-910

History: The Planters Bank of Tennessee was chartered on November 11, 1833, with an authorized capital of $2,000,000. In 1834 the Rogersville branch was opened. The president was Hugh Walker, and the cashier was Hiram Fain. In 1865 the bank was forced to liquidate and close its affairs.

The Planters Bank of Tennessee had its parent bank located in Nashville, W-TN-810, and branch banks located in Athens, W-TN-020, Clarksville, W-TN-140, Columbia, W-TN-210, Franklin, W-TN-300, LaGrange, W-TN-410, Memphis, W-TN-570, Murfreesboro, W-TN-630, Pulaski, W-TN-870, Shelbyville, W-TN-940, Somerville, W-TN-970, Sparta, W-TN-990, Trenton, W-TN-1050, and Winchester, W-TN-1070.

Numismatic Commentary: There are no notes from this branch known.

SHELBYVILLE, TENNESSEE

Shelbyville is the seat of Bedford County. It was laid out for settlement in 1810 and was officially incorporated in 1819. The Tennessee Walking–horse industry found its home here.

Bank of the State of Tennessee {3rd} (branch)

1838–1866

W-TN-920

History: The third Bank of the State of Tennessee (also seen in print as the Bank of Tennessee) was chartered on January 19, 1838, with an authorized capital of $5,000,000. The bank opened for business in February. The bank suspended specie payments a couple of times in 1838 and 1839, due to the panic of that time, but afterward it resumed and had a profitable and successful career. The branch located in Shelbyville had a capital of $223,931 in 1855. R.N. Wallace was the cashier, and Robert Mathews was the president. In 1860 the capital had risen to $240,000, and Thomas Lipscomb had taken the position of president.

During the Civil War, the Union army entered the state, and some officers of the Bank of the State of Tennessee fled south with the bank's specie. After the war, the bank's assets were returned to Governor William G. Brownlow in Nashville. Half of the bank's funds had been transferred into state bonds.

By February 1866 the Bank of the State of Tennessee was authorized to go into liquidation.

The third Bank of the State of Tennessee had its parent bank located in Nashville, W-TN-690, and branch banks located in Athens, W-TN-010, Clarksville, W-TN-120, Columbia, W-TN-190, Knoxville, W-TN-365, Memphis, W-TN-490, Murfreesboro, W-TN-610, Rogersville, W-TN-890, Somerville, W-TN-960, Sparta, W-TN-980, and Trenton, W-TN-1030.

Numismatic Commentary: Notes from this branch are collectible, although it may require patience and searching. Cancelled notes appear to be more common than uncancelled notes. The $20 denomination seems to be the scarcest issue.

VALID ISSUES

$1 • W-TN-920-001-G010

Left: Woman seated with farmer / Female portrait. ***Center:*** 1 / Man plowing with horses / 1. ***Right:*** ONE / Medallion head / ONE. ***Engraver:*** Draper, Toppan & Co. ***Comments:*** H-TN-195-G280. Mar. 1, 1842.

Rarity: —

$1 • W-TN-920-001-G010a

Engraver: Toppan, Carpenter & Co. ***Comments:*** H-TN-195-G280a. Similar to W-TN-920-001-G010 but with different date and engraver imprint. Mar. 1, ____. 1840s, 1861.

Rarity: —

$1 • W-TN-920-001-G020

CC

Engraver: Toppan, Carpenter, Casilear & Co. ***Comments:*** H-TN-195-G282, Garland-1151. 18__. 1850s.

Rarity: URS-6
F $275

$1 • W-TN-920-001-G030

Left: 1 / Portrait of boy. ***Center:*** Indian on horseback hunting buffalo. ***Right:*** 1 / Female portrait. ***Tint:*** Red-orange. ***Back:*** Red-orange. ***Engraver:*** Toppan, Carpenter & Co. ***Comments:*** H-TN-195-G284a. 18__. 1850s.

Rarity: URS-6
F $275

$2 • W-TN-920-002-G040

Left: TWO / Woman seated in 2 / 2. ***Center:*** 2 / Woman seated on bales / 2. ***Right:*** 2 / Ship / 2. ***Engraver:*** Draper, Toppan & Co. ***Comments:*** H-TN-195-G286. Mar. 1, 1842.

Rarity: —

$2 • W-TN-920-002-G040a

Engraver: Toppan, Carpenter & Co. ***Comments:*** H-TN-195-G286a. Similar to W-TN-920-002-G040 but with different date and engraver imprint. Mar. 1, ____. 1840s, 1861.

Rarity: —

$2 • W-TN-920-002-G050

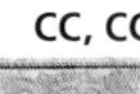

Back: Red-orange. ***Engraver:*** Toppan, Carpenter, Casilear & Co. ***Comments:*** H-TN-195-G288, Garland-1153. 18__. 1850s.

Rarity: URS-4
F $350

$2 • W-TN-920-002-G060

Left: 2 / Female portrait. ***Center:*** Soldier, Woman, and two Indians looking at bust of George Washington. ***Right:*** 2 / Portrait of Charles Carroll. ***Tint:*** Red-orange. ***Back:*** Red-orange. ***Engraver:*** Toppan, Carpenter & Co. ***Comments:*** H-TN-195-G290a, Garland-1154. 18__. 1850s.

Rarity: URS-5
F $300

$3 • W-TN-920-003-G070

Left: THREE / Woman standing / THREE. ***Center:*** 3 / Men on horses, sheep / 3. ***Right:*** THREE / Cherubs in 3 / THREE. ***Engraver:*** Draper, Toppan & Co. ***Comments:*** H-TN-195-G292. Mar. 1, 1842.

Rarity: —

$3 • W-TN-920-003-G070a

Engraver: Toppan, Carpenter & Co. ***Comments:*** H-TN-195-G292a. Similar to W-TN-920-003-G070 but with different date and engraver imprint. Mar. 1, ____. 1840s, 1861.

Rarity: —

$5 • W-TN-920-005-G080

Left: 5 / Woman leaning on column / V. ***Center:*** Woman seated with shield. ***Right:*** 5 / Justice standing with scales and eagle / V. ***Engraver:*** Rawdon, Wright, Hatch & Edson / Rawdon, Wright & Hatch. ***Comments:*** H-TN-195-G294. 18__. 1838–1840s.

Rarity: —

$5 • W-TN-920-005-G090

Left: Three men / 5. ***Center:*** Portrait of James Madison. ***Right:*** 5 / Medallion head. ***Back:*** Red-orange. ***Engraver:*** Danforth, Bald & Co. ***Comments:*** H-TN-195-G296a, Garland-1155. 18__. 1850s.

Rarity: URS-5
F $250

$5 • W-TN-920-005-G090a

Tint: Red-orange outlining white V / 5 / V. ***Back:*** Red-orange. ***Engraver:*** Danforth, Bald & Co. ***Comments:*** H-TN-195-G296b. Similar to W-TN-920-005-G090. 18__. 1850s.

Rarity: —

$10 • W-TN-920-010-G100

Left: 10 / Eagle with shield / X. ***Center:*** Woman with children seated among parcels, Factories and farmhouse. ***Right:*** 10 / Shield / X. ***Engraver:*** Draper, Toppan, Longacre & Co. ***Comments:*** H-TN-195-G302. 18__. 1838–1840s.

Rarity: —

$10 • W-TN-920-010-G110

Left: 10 / Portrait of James K. Polk. ***Center:*** Portrait of Andrew Jackson. ***Right:*** 10 / Portrait of Cave Johnson. ***Tint:*** Red-orange outlining white 10 / 10. ***Back:*** Blue. ***Engraver:*** Toppan, Carpenter & Co. ***Comments:*** H-TN-195-G306a, Garland-1156. 18__. 1850s–1861.

Rarity: URS-5
F $300

$20 • W-TN-920-020-G120

Left: 20 / Man writing on tablet / 20. ***Center:*** Woman standing with eagle and shield. ***Right:*** 20 / Shield / 20. ***Engraver:*** Draper, Toppan, Longacre & Co. ***Comments:*** H-TN-195-G308. 18__. 1838–1840s.

Rarity: —

$20 • W-TN-920-020-G120a

Engraver: Toppan, Carpenter & Co. ***Comments:*** H-TN-195-G308a, Garland-1157. Similar to W-TN-920-020-G120 but with different engraver imprint. 18__. 1840s–1850s

Rarity: URS-1
F $1,500

$20 • W-TN-920-020-G130

Left: 20 / Portrait of Zachary Taylor / 20. ***Center:*** Three women reclining, Ship / 20. ***Right:*** Justice seated with sword and scales / TWENTY. ***Engraver:*** Toppan, Carpenter, Casilear & Co. ***Comments:*** H-TN-195-G310, Garland-1158. 18__. 1850s.

Rarity: URS-4
F $450

$20 • W-TN-920-020-G130a

Back: Red-orange. ***Engraver:*** Toppan, Carpenter, Casilear & Co. ***Comments:*** H-TN-195-G310a. Similar to W-TN-920-020-G130. 18__. 1850s.

Rarity: —

$20 • W-TN-920-020-G130b

Tint: Red-orange outlining white TWENTY. ***Back:*** Red-orange. ***Engraver:*** Toppan, Carpenter, Casilear & Co. ***Comments:*** H-TN-195-G310b, Garland-1159. Similar to W-TN-920-020-G130. 18__. 1850s.

Rarity: URS-4
F $450

$50 • W-TN-920-050-G140

Left: 50 / Shield / 50. ***Center:*** Liberty with eagle and shield. ***Right:*** 50 / Portrait of George Washington / 50. ***Engraver:*** Draper, Toppan, Longacre & Co. ***Comments:*** H-TN-195-G312, Garland-Unlisted. 18__. 1838–1840s.

Rarity: —

$100 • W-TN-920-100-G150
Left: Atlas lifting world on shoulders / 100. *Center:* 100 / Justice with eagle and shield / 100. *Right:* Atlas lifting world on shoulders / 100. *Engraver:* Draper, Toppan, Longacre & Co. *Comments:* H-TN-195-G314. 18__. 1838–1850s.
Rarity: —

Non-Valid Issues

$10 • W-TN-920-010-C100
Engraver: Draper, Toppan, Longacre & Co. *Comments:* H-TN-195-C302. Counterfeit of W-TN-920-010-G100. 18__. 1853.
Rarity: —

$20 • W-TN-920-020-C120a
Engraver: Toppan, Carpenter & Co. *Comments:* H-TN-195-C308a. Counterfeit of W-TN-920-020-G120a. 18__. 1853.
Rarity: —

$20 • W-TN-920-020-C130
Engraver: Toppan, Carpenter, Casilear & Co. *Comments:* H-TN-195-C310. Counterfeit of W-TN-920-020-G130. 18__. 1853.
Rarity: —

$20 • W-TN-920-020-C130a
Back: Red-orange. *Engraver:* Toppan, Carpenter, Casilear & Co. *Comments:* H-TN-195-C310a. Counterfeit of W-TN-920-020-G130a. 18__. 1853.
Rarity: —

$20 • W-TN-920-020-C130b
Tint: Red-orange outlining white TWENTY. *Back:* Red-orange. *Engraver:* Toppan, Carpenter, Casilear & Co. *Comments:* H-TN-195-C310b. Counterfeit of W-TN-920-020-G130b. 18__. 1853.
Rarity: —

$50 • W-TN-920-050-C140
Engraver: Draper, Toppan, Longacre & Co. *Comments:* H-TN-195-C312. Counterfeit of W-TN-920-050-G140. 18__. 1853.
Rarity: —

Nashville Bank (branch)
1817–1827
W-TN-930

History: In 1807 the Nashville Bank was chartered with an authorized capital of $200,000, to be divided into shares of $50 apiece. In 1817 several banks were chartered across the state—in the towns of Gallatin, Murfreesboro, Rogersville, Shelbyville, and Winchester—and were given the option of either joining the first Bank of the State of Tennessee, W-TN-355, or of joining with the Nashville Bank. The corporations chose the Nashville Bank and became branches forthwith.

On March 31, 1823, the Nashville Bank, along with its branches, burned a total of $250,000 worth of bank notes in order to increase the value of its circulation. In 1827 the bank was liquidated.

The Nashville Bank had its parent bank located in Nashville, W-TN-800, and branch banks located in Gallatin, W-TN-310, Murfreesboro, W-TN-640, Rogersville, W-TN-900, and Winchester, W-TN-1060.

Numismatic Commentary: Garland lists a $20 note that he believed to be unique. Haxby lists the same note, but as a counterfeit. No other notes of this branch are currently known.

Valid Issues

$1 • W-TN-930-001-G010
Left: ONE vertically. *Center:* 1 / Woman seated / 1. *Right:* TENNESSEE vertically. *Engraver:* Tanner, Kearny & Tiebout. *Comments:* H-TN-180-G124. 18__. 1810s.
Rarity: *None known*

$2 • W-TN-930-002-G020
Left: TWO vertically. *Center:* 2 / Woman seated / 2. *Right:* TENNESSEE vertically. *Engraver:* Tanner, Kearny & Tiebout. *Comments:* H-TN-180-G126. 18__. 1810s.
Rarity: *None known*

$5 • W-TN-930-005-G030
Left: FIVE vertically. *Center:* 5 / Woman seated / 5. *Right:* NASHVILLE vertically. *Engraver:* Murray, Draper, Fairman & Co. *Comments:* H-TN-180-G130. 18__. 1810s.
Rarity: *None known*

$5 • W-TN-930-005-G040
Left: FIVE vertically. *Center:* 5 / Woman seated / 5. *Right:* TENNESSEE vertically. *Engraver:* Tanner, Kearny & Tiebout. *Comments:* H-TN-180-G132, Garland-1160. 18__. 1810s–1820s.
Rarity: *None known*

$10 • W-TN-930-010-G050
Left: TEN vertically. *Center:* 10 / Woman seated / 10. *Right:* NASHVILLE vertically. *Engraver:* Murray, Draper, Fairman & Co. *Comments:* H-TN-180-G134. 18__. 1810s.
Rarity: *None known*

$10 • W-TN-930-010-G060
Left: TEN vertically. *Center:* 10 / Woman seated / 10. *Right:* TENNESSEE vertically. *Engraver:* Tanner, Kearny & Tiebout. *Comments:* H-TN-180-G136, Garland-1161. 18__. 1810s–1820s.
Rarity: *None known*

$20 • W-TN-930-020-G070
Left: TWENTY vertically. *Center:* 20 / Woman seated / 20. *Right:* NASHVILLE vertically. *Engraver:* Murray, Draper, Fairman & Co. *Comments:* H-TN-180-G138. 18__. 1810s.
Rarity: *None known*

$20 • W-TN-930-020-G080
Left: TWENTY vertically. *Center:* 20 / Woman seated / 20. *Right:* TENNESSEE vertically. *Engraver:* Tanner, Kearny & Tiebout. *Comments:* H-TN-180-G140, Garland-1162. 18__. 1810s–1820s.
Rarity: URS-1
F $1,500

Non-Valid Issues

$20 • W-TN-930-020-C080
Engraver: Tanner, Kearny & Tiebout. *Comments:* H-TN-180-C140. Counterfeit of W-TN-930-020-G080. 18__. 1810s–1820s.
Rarity: URS-1
F $450

Planters Bank of Tennessee (branch)

1834–1865

W-TN-940

History: The Planters Bank of Tennessee was chartered on November 11, 1833, with an authorized capital of $2,000,000. The Shelbyville branch was opened in 1834 and had a capital of $223,932 in 1848. Robert Matthews was the president, and William S. Jett was the cashier. In 1865 the bank was forced to liquidate and close its affairs.

The Planters Bank of Tennessee had its parent bank located in Nashville, W-TN-810, and branch banks located in Athens, W-TN-020, Clarksville, W-TN-140, Columbia, W-TN-210, Franklin, W-TN-300, LaGrange, W-TN-410, Memphis, W-TN-570, Murfreesboro, W-TN-630, Pulaski, W-TN-870, Rogersville, W-TN-910, Somerville, W-TN-970, Sparta, W-TN-990, Trenton, W-TN-1050, and Winchester, W-TN-1070.

Numismatic Commentary: No notes are known for this branch.

Shelbyville Bank of Tennessee

1854–1862

W-TN-950

History: On March 4, 1854, the Shelbyville Bank of Tennessee was chartered with an authorized capital of $100,000. In 1857 these values were given: capital $118,863; bills in circulation $133,955; specie $35,662; real estate $2,853. The president was Edward Cooper, and W.S. Jett was the cashier. By 1862 the bank had been liquidated.

Numismatic Commentary: The notes of this bank all display bold and attractive designs. $1 notes are readily attainable, $2 less so, and the other denominations are all very scarce to rare. Proofs are known for $2, $5, $10, and $20 issues.

The 1990 Christie's sale of the American Bank Note Co. archives produced a $1-$1-$1-$2 sheet, and nine $5-$5-$10-$20 sheets.

VALID ISSUES

$1 • W-TN-950-001-G010 CC

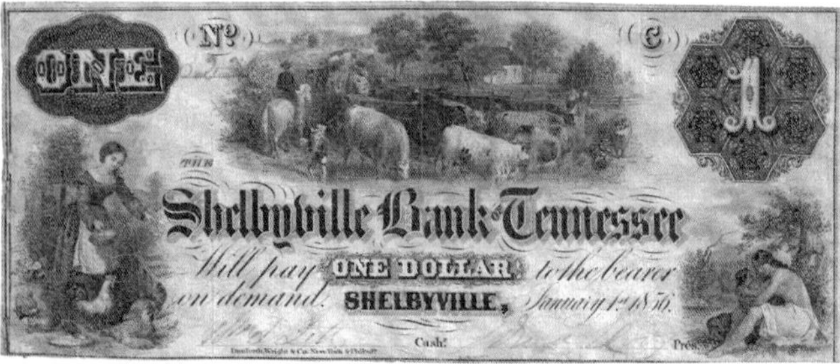

Engraver: Danforth, Wright & Co. ***Comments:*** H-TN-220-G2, Garland-1163. January 1st, 1856.

Rarity: URS-7
F $200; **Proof** $750

$1 • W-TN-950-001-G020

Left: ONE vertically. ***Center:*** ONE DOLLAR / 1. ***Right:*** 1 / 1. ***Engraver:*** Dan Adams. ***Comments:*** H-Unlisted, Garland-1164. Nov. 21, 1861.

Rarity: URS-7
F $300

$2 • W-TN-950-002-G030

Left: 2 / Farmer with family. ***Center:*** Train. ***Right:*** 2 / Three women. ***Engraver:*** Danforth, Wright & Co. ***Comments:*** H-TN-220-G4, Garland-1166. Jan. 1, 1856.

Rarity: URS-6
F $350; **Proof** $1,200

$5 • W-TN-950-005-G040

Left: V / Ceres with sheaf. ***Center:*** Portrait of Governor Neil S. Brown / Indian stalking deer. ***Right:*** 5 / Man carrying wheat. ***Engraver:*** Bald, Cousland & Co. / Baldwin, Bald & Cousland. ***Comments:*** H-TN-220-G6, Garland-1167. 18__. 1850s–1860s.

Rarity: URS-3
F $750

$5 • W-TN-950-005-G040a CC

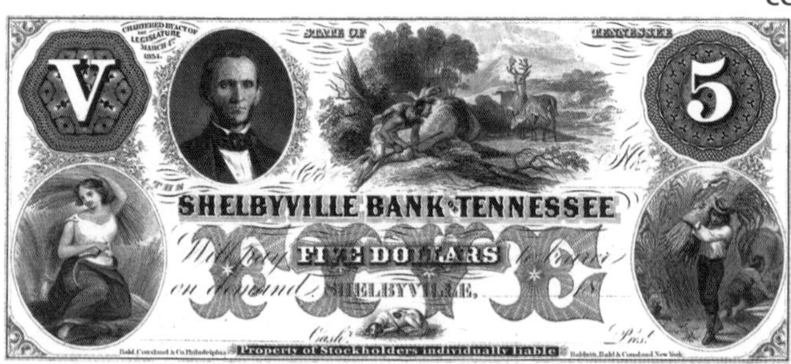

Overprint: Red FIVE. ***Engraver:*** Bald, Cousland & Co. / Baldwin, Bald & Cousland. ***Comments:*** H-TN-220-G6a, Garland-1168. Similar to W-TN-950-005-G040. 18__. 1850s–1860s.

Rarity: URS-4
Proof $750

$10 • W-TN-950-010-G050

Left: TEN / Man on horseback. ***Center:*** Portrait of Judge John Catron / Woman with cattle. ***Right:*** 10 / Portrait of George Washington. ***Engraver:*** Bald, Cousland & Co. / Baldwin, Bald & Cousland. ***Comments:*** H-TN-220-G8, Garland-1169. 18__. 1850s–1860s.

Rarity: URS-3
F $650

$10 • W-TN-950-010-G050a CC

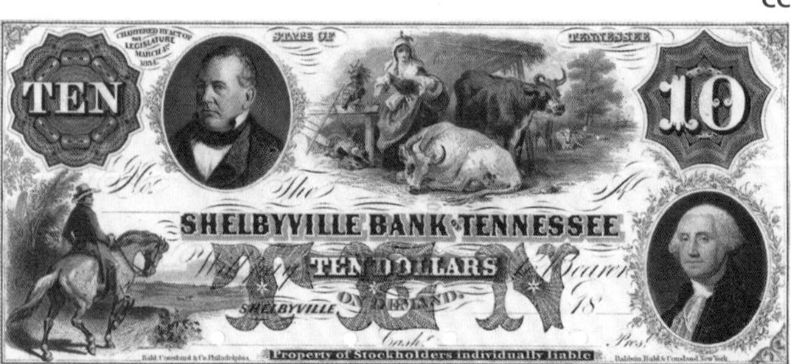

Overprint: Red TEN. ***Engraver:*** Bald, Cousland & Co. / Baldwin, Bald & Cousland. ***Comments:*** H-TN-220-G8a, Garland-1170. Similar to W-TN-950-010-G050. 18__. 1850s–1860s.

Rarity: URS-3
Proof $1,000

$20 • W-TN-950-020-G060

Left: Woman seated / XX. ***Center:*** Cattle. ***Right:*** 20 / Portrait of Andrew Jackson. ***Engraver:*** Bald, Cousland & Co. / Baldwin, Bald & Cousland. ***Comments:*** H-TN-220-G10, Garland-1171. 18__. 1850s–1860s.

Rarity: URS-3
Proof $1,000

$20 • W-TN-950-020-G060a

CC

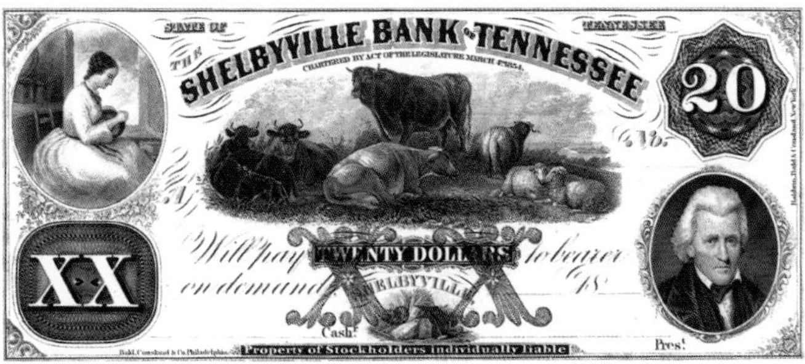

Overprint: Red XX. ***Engraver:*** Bald, Cousland & Co. / Baldwin, Bald & Cousland. ***Comments:*** H-TN-220-G10a, Garland-1172. Similar to W-TN-950-020-G060. 18__. 1850s–1860s.

Rarity: URS-2
Proof $1,200

Civil War Emergency Issues

$1 • W-TN-950-001-G070

CC

Engraver: Dan Adams. ***Comments:*** H-TN-220-G16, Garland-Unlisted. Novr. 21, 1861.

Rarity: URS-6
VF $250

Non-Valid Issues

$1 • W-TN-950-001-C020

Engraver: Dan Adams. ***Comments:*** H-Unlisted, Garland-1165. Counterfeit of W-TN-950-001-G020. Nov. 21, 1861.

Rarity: —

Civil War Emergency Issues

$1 • W-TN-950-001-C070

Comments: H-TN-220-C16. Counterfeit of W-TN-950-001-G070. Nov. 21, 1861.

Rarity: —

Somerville, Tennessee

Somerville was incorporated in 1836 and named after Lieutenant Robert Somerville. He was killed in 1814 at the Battle of Horseshoe Bend.

Bank of the State of Tennessee {3rd} (branch)

1838–1866

W-TN-960

History: The third Bank of the State of Tennessee (also seen in print as the Bank of Tennessee) was chartered on January 19, 1838, with an authorized capital of $5,000,000. The bank opened for business in February. The bank suspended specie payments a couple of times in 1838 and 1839, due to the panic of that time, but afterward it resumed and had a profitable and successful career. In 1857 the president of the Somerville branch was Alexander Williamson. James Pettit was the cashier, and the capital was $250,000. In 1860 N. Rhodes became the cashier.

During the Civil War, the Union army entered the state, and some officers of the Bank of the State of Tennessee fled south with the bank's specie. After the war, the bank's assets were returned to Governor William G. Brownlow in Nashville. Half of the bank's funds had been transferred into state bonds.

By February 1866 the Bank of the State of Tennessee was authorized to go into liquidation.

The third Bank of the State of Tennessee had its parent bank located in Nashville, W-TN-690, and branch banks located in Athens, W-TN-010, Clarksville, W-TN-120, Columbia, W-TN-190, Knoxville, W-TN-365, Memphis, W-TN-490, Murfreesboro, W-TN-610, Rogersville, W-TN-890, Shelbyville, W-TN-920, Sparta, W-TN-980, and Trenton, W-TN-1030.

Numismatic Commentary: Notes from Somerville appear to be scarcer than previously believed. All of the dollar-denominated notes are considered scarce to very scarce. The area surrounding Somerville during the Civil War was often a no man's land. With Union troops occupying Memphis, the outlying rural area was only patrolled. Confederate raiders harassed the patrols, and opportunistic outlaws preyed on the general population. Trusted paper currency was used heavily, and so it appears that much of the Somerville-branch issues were.

Valid Issues

$1 • W-TN-960-001-G010

Left: Woman seated with farmer / Female portrait. ***Center:*** 1 / Man plowing with horses / 1. ***Right:*** ONE / Medallion head / ONE. ***Engraver:*** Draper, Toppan & Co. ***Comments:*** H-TN-195-G320. Mar. 1, 1842.

Rarity: —

$1 • W-TN-960-001-G010a

Engraver: Toppan, Carpenter & Co. ***Comments:*** H-TN-195-G320a. Similar to W-TN-960-001-G010 but with different date and engraver imprint. Mar. 1, ____. 1840s, 1861.

Rarity: —

$1 • **W-TN-960-001-G020**

Left: 1 / Sailor standing with flag. ***Center:*** 1 / Two women seated with cog wheel / 1. ***Right:*** 1 / Woman with sheaf on back. ***Engraver:*** Toppan, Carpenter, Casilear & Co. ***Comments:*** H-TN-195-G322. 18__. 1850s.

Rarity: URS-5
F $200

$1 • **W-TN-960-001-G030** CC, CC

Tint: Red-orange lathework and panel of microlettering outlining white ONE. ***Back:*** Red-orange. ***Engraver:*** Toppan, Carpenter & Co. ***Comments:*** H-TN-195-G324a. 18__. 1850s.

Rarity: URS-4
F $250

$2 • **W-TN-960-002-G040**

Left: TWO / Woman seated in 2 / 2. ***Center:*** 2 / Woman seated on bales / 2. ***Right:*** 2 / Ship / 2. ***Engraver:*** Draper, Toppan & Co. ***Comments:*** H-TN-195-G326. Mar. 1, 1842.

Rarity: —

$2 • **W-TN-960-002-G040a**

Engraver: Toppan, Carpenter & Co. ***Comments:*** H-TN-195-G326a. Similar to W-TN-960-002-G040 but with different date and engraver imprint. Mar. 1, ____. 1840s, 1861.

Rarity: —

$2 • **W-TN-960-002-G050**

Left: 2 / Justice seated with scales. ***Center:*** Cattle / 2 / 2. ***Right:*** 2 / Liberty with pole, cap, and flag. ***Engraver:*** Toppan, Carpenter, Casilear & Co. ***Comments:*** H-TN-195-G328. 18__. 1850s.

Rarity: URS-5
F $300

$2 • **W-TN-960-002-G060**

Left: 2 / Female portrait. ***Center:*** Soldier, Woman, and two Indians looking at bust of George Washington. ***Right:*** 2 / Portrait of Charles Carroll. ***Tint:*** Red-orange. ***Back:*** Red-orange. ***Engraver:*** Toppan, Carpenter & Co. ***Comments:*** H-TN-195-G330a. 18__. 1850s.

Rarity: URS-4
F $350

$3 • **W-TN-960-003-G070**

Left: THREE / Woman standing / THREE. ***Center:*** 3 / Men on horses, sheep / 3. ***Right:*** THREE / Cherubs in 3 / THREE. ***Engraver:*** Draper, Toppan & Co. ***Comments:*** H-TN-195-G332. Mar. 1, 1842.

Rarity: —

$3 • **W-TN-960-003-G070a**

Engraver: Toppan, Carpenter & Co. ***Comments:*** H-TN-195-G332a. Similar to W-TN-960-003-G070 but with different date and engraver imprint. Mar. 1, ____. 1840s, 1861.

Rarity: —

$5 • **W-TN-960-005-G080**

Left: 5 / Woman leaning on column / V. ***Center:*** Woman seated with shield. ***Right:*** 5 / Justice standing with scales and eagle / V. ***Engraver:*** Rawdon, Wright, Hatch & Edson / Rawdon, Wright & Hatch. ***Comments:*** H-TN-195-G334. 18__. 1838–1840s.

Rarity: —

$5 • **W-TN-960-005-G090**

Left: Three men / 5. ***Center:*** Portrait of James Madison. ***Right:*** 5 / Medallion head. ***Back:*** Red-orange. ***Engraver:*** Danforth, Bald & Co. ***Comments:*** H-TN-195-G336a, Garland-1188. 18__. 1850s.

Rarity: URS-4
F $350

$5 • **W-TN-960-005-G090a**

Tint: Red-orange outlining white V / 5 / V. ***Back:*** Red-orange. ***Engraver:*** Danforth, Bald & Co. ***Comments:*** H-TN-195-G336b. Similar to W-TN-960-005-G090. 18__. 1850s.

Rarity: —

$10 • **W-TN-960-010-G100**

Left: 10 / Eagle with shield / X. ***Center:*** Woman with children seated among parcels, Factories and farmhouse. ***Right:*** 10 / Shield / X. ***Engraver:*** Draper, Toppan, Longacre & Co. ***Comments:*** H-TN-195-G342. 18__. 1838–1840s.

Rarity: —

$10 • **W-TN-960-010-G110**

Left: 10 / Portrait of James K. Polk. ***Center:*** Portrait of Andrew Jackson. ***Right:*** 10 / Portrait of Cave Johnson. ***Tint:*** Red-orange outlining white 10 / 10. ***Back:*** Blue. ***Engraver:*** Toppan, Carpenter & Co. ***Comments:*** H-TN-195-G346a. 18__. 1850s–1861.

Rarity: URS-5
F $300

$20 • **W-TN-960-020-G120**

Left: 20 / Man writing on tablet / 20. ***Center:*** Hebe watering eagle. ***Right:*** 20 / Shield / 20. ***Engraver:*** Draper, Toppan, Longacre & Co. ***Comments:*** H-TN-195-G348. 18__. 1838–1840s.

Rarity: —

$20 • W-TN-960-020-G120a

CC

Engraver: Toppan, Carpenter & Co. ***Comments:*** H-TN-195-G348a, Garland-1191. Similar to W-TN-960-020-G120 but with different engraver imprint. 18__. 1840s–1850s

Rarity: URS-1
F $1,250

$20 • W-TN-960-020-G130

CC

Back: Plain. ***Engraver:*** Toppan, Carpenter, Casilear & Co. ***Comments:*** H-TN-195-G350, Garland-1192a. 18__. 1850s.

Rarity: URS-4
VF $350

$20 • W-TN-960-020-G130a

CC, CC

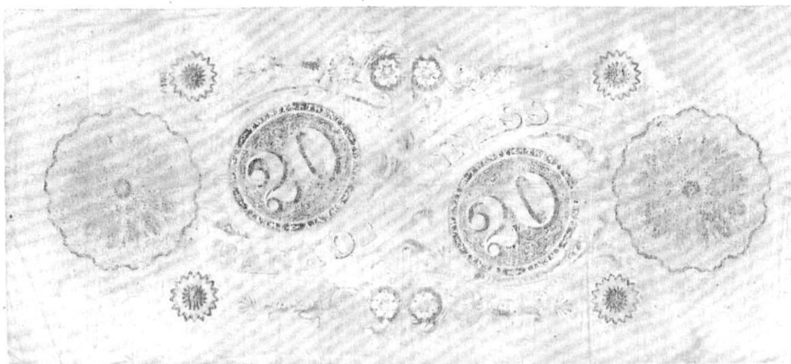

Back: Red-orange. ***Engraver:*** Toppan, Carpenter, Casilear & Co. ***Comments:*** H-TN-195-G350a, Garland-1192. Similar to W-TN-960-020-G130. 18__. 1850s.

Rarity: URS-4
F $350

$20 • W-TN-960-020-G130b

Tint: Red-orange outlining white TWENTY. ***Back:*** Red-orange. ***Engraver:*** Toppan, Carpenter, Casilear & Co. ***Comments:*** H-TN-195-G350b. Similar to W-TN-960-020-G130. 18__. 1850s.

Rarity: —

$50 • W-TN-960-050-G140

Left: 50 / Shield / 50. ***Center:*** Liberty with eagle and shield. ***Right:*** 50 / Portrait of George Washington / 50. ***Engraver:*** Draper, Toppan, Longacre & Co. ***Comments:*** H-TN-195-G352. 18__. 1838–1840s.

Rarity: —

$100 • W-TN-960-100-G150

Left: Atlas lifting world on shoulders / 100. ***Center:*** 100 / Justice with eagle and shield / 100. ***Right:*** Atlas lifting world on shoulders / 100. ***Engraver:*** Draper, Toppan, Longacre & Co. ***Comments:*** H-TN-195-G354. 18__. 1838–1850s.

Rarity: —

NON-VALID ISSUES

$5 • W-TN-960-005-S010

CC

Engraver: Danforth, Bald & Co. ***Comments:*** H-Unlisted, Garland-1189. 18__. 1850s.

Rarity: URS-4
F $350

$10 • W-TN-960-010-C100

Engraver: Draper, Toppan, Longacre & Co. ***Comments:*** H-TN-195-C342. Counterfeit of W-TN-960-010-G100. 18__. 1853.

Rarity: —

How to Read the Whitman Numbering System

$1 • W-AL-020-001-G010a

Denomination: Face value of the note shown.

W: Whitman number. This number is a sortable code unique to each bank and note.

AL: Abbreviation for the state under study.

020: Numerical designation specific to each bank.

001: The denomination in dollars.

G010a: G indicates a good or valid note. Other categories are indicated thus: C (counterfeit); R (raised); S (spurious); N (not-attributed); A (altered). Numbers are assigned starting with 010, 020, et seq. Terminal letters following the number indicate variations of a note: a series of different colored overprints, tints, payees, etc., all on the same design of note. For more information, see the "How to Use This Book" section at the front of the volume, page xiv.

$20 • W-TN-960-020-C120a

Engraver: Toppan, Carpenter & Co. ***Comments:*** H-TN-195-C348a. Counterfeit of W-TN-960-020-G120a. 18__. 1850.

Rarity: —

$20 • W-TN-960-020-C130

Engraver: Toppan, Carpenter, Casilear & Co. ***Comments:*** H-TN-195-C350. Counterfeit of W-TN-960-020-G130. 18__. 1853.

Rarity: —

$20 • W-TN-960-020-C130a

Back: Red-orange. ***Engraver:*** Toppan, Carpenter, Casilear & Co. ***Comments:*** H-TN-195-C350a. Counterfeit of W-TN-960-020-G130a. 18__. 1853.

Rarity: —

$20 • W-TN-960-020-C130b

Tint: Red-orange outlining white TWENTY. ***Back:*** Red-orange. ***Engraver:*** Toppan, Carpenter, Casilear & Co. ***Comments:*** H-TN-195-C350b. Counterfeit of W-TN-960-020-G130b. 18__. 1853.

Rarity: —

$50 • W-TN-960-050-C140

Engraver: Draper, Toppan, Longacre & Co. ***Comments:*** H-TN-195-C352. Counterfeit of W-TN-960-050-G140. 18__. 1853.

Rarity: —

Planters Bank of Tennessee (branch)

1834–1865

W-TN-970

History: The Planters Bank of Tennessee was chartered on November 11, 1833, with an authorized capital of $2,000,000. The branch in Somerville was opened in 1834. James Pettit was the cashier, and H. Owen was the president. In 1865 the bank was forced to liquidate and close its affairs.

The Planters Bank of Tennessee had its parent bank located in Nashville, W-TN-810, and branch banks located in Athens, W-TN-020, Clarksville, W-TN-140, Columbia, W-TN-210, Franklin, W-TN-300, LaGrange, W-TN-410, Memphis, W-TN-570, Murfreesboro, W-TN-630, Pulaski, W-TN-870, Rogersville, W-TN-910, Shelbyville, W-TN-940, Sparta, W-TN-990, Trenton, W-TN-1050, and Winchester, W-TN-1070.

Numismatic Commentary: There are no known notes from this branch.

Sparta, Tennessee

In 1806 White County was created, and in 1809 the town of Sparta was established to be its county seat. It was named after the city of Sparta from ancient Greece. When the state legislature of Tennessee was voting to choose a spot for the permanent capital, Sparta was in the running and was even tied with Nashville. In the end, Sparta lost by a single vote, and Nashville took the honor.

Nevertheless, Sparta was ideally located on a stage-coach road between the two major cities of Knoxville and Nashville, and thus it grew substantially. The Sparta Rock House inn was built in the 1830s for the purpose of providing a place of respite for coach travelers, and many important figures rested here on their journeys.

Bank of the State of Tennessee {3rd} (branch)

1838–1866

W-TN-980

History: The third Bank of the State of Tennessee (also seen in print as the Bank of Tennessee) was chartered on January 19, 1838, with an authorized capital of $5,000,000. The bank opened for business in February. The bank suspended specie payments a couple of times in 1838 and 1839, due to the panic of that time, but afterward it resumed and had a profitable and successful career. In 1855 the branch located in Sparta had a capital of $223,931. William M. Young was the cashier, and J.G. Mitchell was the president. As of 1857 William P. Goodbare had become president, and J.G. Mitchell had taken the role of cashier.

During the Civil War, the Union army entered the state, and some officers of the Bank of the State of Tennessee fled south with the bank's specie. After the war, the bank's assets were returned to Governor William G. Brownlow in Nashville. Half of the bank's funds had been transferred into state bonds.

By February 1866 the Bank of the State of Tennessee was authorized to go into liquidation.

The third Bank of the State of Tennessee had its parent bank located in Nashville, W-TN-690, and branch banks located in Athens, W-TN-010, Clarksville, W-TN-120, Columbia, W-TN-190, Knoxville, W-TN-365, Memphis, W-TN-490, Murfreesboro, W-TN-610, Rogersville, W-TN-890, Shelbyville, W-TN-920, Somerville, W-TN-960, and Trenton, W-TN-1030.

Numismatic Commentary: Notes payable at the Sparta branch are scarcer than perceived, but should be available. Only the $20 denomination is considered very scarce to rare.

Valid Issues

$1 • W-TN-980-001-G010

Left: Woman seated with farmer / Female portrait. ***Center:*** 1 / Man plowing with horses / 1. ***Right:*** ONE / Medallion head / ONE. ***Engraver:*** Draper, Toppan & Co. ***Comments:*** H-TN-195-G360. Mar. 1, 1842.

Rarity: —

$1 • W-TN-980-001-G010a

Engraver: Toppan, Carpenter & Co. ***Comments:*** H-TN-195-G360a. Similar to W-TN-980-001-G010 but with different date and engraver imprint. Mar. 1, ____. 1840s, 1861.

Rarity: —

$1 • W-TN-980-001-G020

Left: 1 / Sailor standing with flag. ***Center:*** 1 / Two women seated with cog wheel / 1. ***Right:*** 1 / Woman with sheaf on back. ***Engraver:*** Toppan, Carpenter, Casilear & Co. ***Comments:*** H-TN-195-G362. 18__. 1850s.

Rarity: URS-4
F $300

$1 • W-TN-980-001-G030

Left: 1 / Portrait of boy. ***Center:*** Indian on horseback hunting buffalo. ***Right:*** 1 / Female portrait. ***Tint:*** Red-orange. ***Back:*** Red-orange. ***Engraver:*** Toppan, Carpenter & Co. ***Comments:*** H-TN-195-G364a, Garland-1201. 18__. 1850s.

Rarity: URS-4
F $350

$2 • W-TN-980-002-G040

Left: TWO / Woman seated in 2 / 2. ***Center:*** 2 / Woman seated on bales / 2. ***Right:*** 2 / Ship / 2. ***Engraver:*** Draper, Toppan & Co. ***Comments:*** H-TN-195-G366. Mar. 1, 1842.

Rarity: —

$2 • W-TN-980-002-G040a

Engraver: Toppan, Carpenter & Co. ***Comments:*** H-TN-195-G366a. Similar to W-TN-980-002-G040 but with different date and engraver imprint. Mar. 1, ____. 1840s, 1861.

Rarity: —

$2 • W-TN-980-002-G050

Left: 2 / Justice seated with scales. ***Center:*** Cattle / 2 / 2. ***Right:*** 2 / Liberty with pole, cap, and flag. ***Engraver:*** Toppan, Carpenter, Casilear & Co. ***Comments:*** H-TN-195-G368. 18__. 1850s.

Rarity: URS-5
F $300

$2 • W-TN-980-002-G060

Left: 2 / Female portrait. ***Center:*** Soldier, Woman, and two Indians looking at bust of George Washington. ***Right:*** 2 / Portrait of Charles Carroll. ***Tint:*** Red-orange. ***Back:*** Red-orange. ***Engraver:*** Toppan, Carpenter & Co. ***Comments:*** H-TN-195-G370a, Garland-1203. 18__. 1850s.

Rarity: URS-5
F $300

$3 • W-TN-980-003-G070

Left: THREE / Woman standing / THREE. ***Center:*** 3 / Men on horses, sheep / 3. ***Right:*** THREE / Cherubs in 3 / THREE. ***Engraver:*** Draper, Toppan & Co. ***Comments:*** H-TN-195-G372. Mar. 1, 1842.

Rarity: —

$3 • W-TN-980-003-G070a

Engraver: Toppan, Carpenter & Co. ***Comments:*** H-TN-195-G372a. Similar to W-TN-980-003-G070 but with different date and engraver imprint. Mar. 1, ____. 1840s, 1861.

Rarity: —

$5 • W-TN-980-005-G080

Left: 5 / Woman leaning on column / V. ***Center:*** Woman seated with shield. ***Right:*** 5 / Justice standing with scales and eagle / V. ***Engraver:*** Rawdon, Wright, Hatch & Edson / Rawdon, Wright & Hatch. ***Comments:*** H-TN-195-G374. 18__. 1838–1840s.

Rarity: —

$5 • W-TN-980-005-G090

Left: Three men / 5. ***Center:*** Portrait of James Madison. ***Right:*** 5 / Medallion head. ***Back:*** Red-orange. ***Engraver:*** Danforth, Bald & Co. ***Comments:*** H-TN-195-G376a, Garland-1204. 18__. 1850s.

Rarity: URS-4
F $400

$5 • W-TN-980-005-G090a

Tint: Red-orange outlining white V / 5 / V. ***Back:*** Red-orange. ***Engraver:*** Danforth, Bald & Co. ***Comments:*** H-TN-195-G376b. Similar to W-TN-980-005-G090. 18__. 1850s.

Rarity: URS-5
F $350

$10 • W-TN-980-010-G100

Left: 10 / Eagle with shield / X. ***Center:*** Woman with children seated among parcels, Factories and farmhouse. ***Right:*** 10 / Shield / X. ***Engraver:*** Draper, Toppan, Longacre & Co. ***Comments:*** H-TN-195-G382. 18__. 1838–1840s.

Rarity: —

$10 • W-TN-980-010-G110

Left: 10 / Portrait of James K. Polk. ***Center:*** Portrait of Andrew Jackson. ***Right:*** 10 / Portrait of Cave Johnson. ***Tint:*** Red-orange outlining white 10 / 10. ***Back:*** Blue. ***Engraver:*** Toppan, Carpenter & Co. ***Comments:*** H-TN-195-G386a, Garland-1206. 18__. 1850s–1861.

Rarity: URS-4
F $450

$20 • W-TN-980-020-G120

Left: 20 / Man writing on tablet / 20. ***Center:*** Woman standing with eagle and shield. ***Right:*** 20 / Shield / 20. ***Engraver:*** Draper, Toppan, Longacre & Co. ***Comments:*** H-TN-195-G388, Garland-1207. 18__. 1838–1840s.

Rarity: URS-1
F $1,250

$20 • W-TN-980-020-G120a

Engraver: Toppan, Carpenter & Co. ***Comments:*** H-TN-195-G388a. Similar to W-TN-980-020-G120 but with different engraver imprint. 18__. 1840s–1850s

Rarity: —

$20 • W-TN-980-020-G130

Left: 20 / Portrait of Zachary Taylor / 20. ***Center:*** Three women reclining, Ship / 20. ***Right:*** Justice seated with sword and scales / TWENTY. ***Engraver:*** Toppan, Carpenter, Casilear & Co. ***Comments:*** H-TN-195-G390, Garland-1208. 18__. 1850s.

Rarity: URS-4
F $450

$20 • W-TN-980-020-G130a

Back: Red-orange. ***Engraver:*** Toppan, Carpenter, Casilear & Co. ***Comments:*** H-TN-195-G390a. Similar to W-TN-980-020-G130. 18__. 1850s.

Rarity: —

$20 • W-TN-980-020-G130b

Tint: Red-orange outlining white TWENTY. ***Back:*** Red-orange. ***Engraver:*** Toppan, Carpenter, Casilear & Co. ***Comments:*** H-TN-195-G390b, Garland-1209. Similar to W-TN-980-020-G130. 18__. 1850s.

Rarity: URS-4
F $500

$50 • W-TN-980-050-G140

Left: 50 / Shield / 50. ***Center:*** Liberty with eagle and shield. ***Right:*** 50 / Portrait of George Washington / 50. ***Engraver:*** Draper, Toppan, Longacre & Co. ***Comments:*** H-TN-195-G392. 18__. 1838–1840s.

Rarity: —

$100 • **W-TN-980-100-G150**

Left: Atlas lifting world on shoulders / 100. ***Center:*** 100 / Justice with eagle and shield / 100. ***Right:*** Atlas lifting world on shoulders / 100. ***Engraver:*** Draper, Toppan, Longacre & Co. ***Comments:*** H-TN-195-G394. 18__. 1838–1850s.

Rarity: —

Non-Valid Issues

$10 • **W-TN-980-010-C100**

Engraver: Draper, Toppan, Longacre & Co. ***Comments:*** H-TN-195-C382. Counterfeit of W-TN-980-010-G100. 18__. 1853.

Rarity: —

$20 • **W-TN-980-020-C120a**

Engraver: Toppan, Carpenter & Co. ***Comments:*** H-TN-195-C388a. Counterfeit of W-TN-980-020-G120a. 18__. 1853.

Rarity: —

$20 • **W-TN-980-020-C130**

Engraver: Toppan, Carpenter, Casilear & Co. ***Comments:*** H-TN-195-C390. Counterfeit of W-TN-980-020-G130. 18__. 1853.

Rarity: —

$20 • **W-TN-980-020-C130a**

Back: Red-orange. ***Engraver:*** Toppan, Carpenter, Casilear & Co. ***Comments:*** H-TN-195-C390a. Counterfeit of W-TN-980-020-G130a. 18__. 1853.

Rarity: —

$20 • **W-TN-980-020-C130b**

Tint: Red-orange outlining white TWENTY. ***Back:*** Red-orange. ***Engraver:*** Toppan, Carpenter, Casilear & Co. ***Comments:*** H-TN-195-C390b, Garland-1210. Counterfeit of W-TN-980-020-G130b. 18__. 1853.

Rarity: URS-3
F $550

$50 • **W-TN-980-050-C140**

Engraver: Draper, Toppan, Longacre & Co. ***Comments:*** H-TN-195-C392. Counterfeit of W-TN-980-050-G140. 18__. 1853.

Rarity: —

Planters Bank of Tennessee (branch)

1834–1865

W-TN-990

History: The Planters Bank of Tennessee was chartered on November 11, 1833, with an authorized capital of $2,000,000. The Sparta branch was opened in 1834 and had a capital of $227,028 in 1848. S.J. Walling was the president, and W.M. Young was the cashier. In 1865 the bank was forced to liquidate and close its affairs.

The Planters Bank of Tennessee had its parent bank located in Nashville, W-TN-810, and branch banks located in Athens, W-TN-020, Clarksville, W-TN-140, Columbia, W-TN-210, Franklin, W-TN-300, LaGrange, W-TN-410, Memphis, W-TN-570, Murfreesboro, W-TN-630, Pulaski, W-TN-870, Rogersville, W-TN-910, Shelbyville, W-TN-940, Somerville, W-TN-970, Trenton, W-TN-1050, and Winchester, W-TN-1070.

Numismatic Commentary: No notes from this branch are known.

Tazewell, Tennessee

John Hunt was one of the first settlers of Tazewell. In 1804 the town became the county seat of Claiborne at Hunt's urging. An amusing local legend also states that the rival town for the position, Springdale, failed in the running due to the fact that its inhabitants were too inebriated to vote on the day of the selection. Hunt became the sheriff, with the county government gathering at his private home until a courthouse could be built.

During the Civil War, Tazewell was occupied by Confederate troops. The city was evacuated in November, and most of the city was destroyed by fire.

Bank of Claiborne

1854–1858

W-TN-1000

History: In 1854 the Bank of Claiborne was chartered with an authorized capital of $100,000. The cashier was I.L. Evans, and the president was R.J. Foster. By 1858 the bank had failed. On February 4, 1860, an act was passed appointing a comptroller to redeem notes of the bank using its assets for 12 months.

Numismatic Commentary: Only the $5 denominations are known as signed and issued. $1 and $2 notes are known only through Proofs.

The 1990 Christie's sale of the American Bank Note Co. archives produced a $2-$3-$5-$5 sheet.

Valid Issues

$2 • **W-TN-1000-002-G010**

Left: 2 / TWO / 2. ***Center:*** Woman in 2, Farm. ***Right:*** 2 / Two farmers walking, Dog, Boy, Wagon. ***Engraver:*** Danforth, Wright & Co. ***Comments:*** H-TN-225-G2, Garland-1215. Nov. 1st, 1854.

Rarity: URS-1
Proof $2,500

$3 • **W-TN-1000-003-G020**

Left: 3 / Text / THREE. ***Center:*** Woman, Deer and shield, Grain, Sheep. ***Right:*** THREE / Cherubs in 3. ***Engraver:*** Danforth, Wright & Co. ***Comments:*** H-TN-225-G4, Garland-1216. Nov. 1st, 1854.

Rarity: URS-1
Proof $2,500

$5 • **W-TN-1000-005-G030**

CC

Engraver: Danforth, Wright & Co. ***Comments:*** H-TN-225-G6, Garland-1217. Nov. 1st, 1854.

Rarity: URS-4
F $1,000; **Proof** $1,200

$5 • W-TN-1000-005-G030a

NJW, NJW

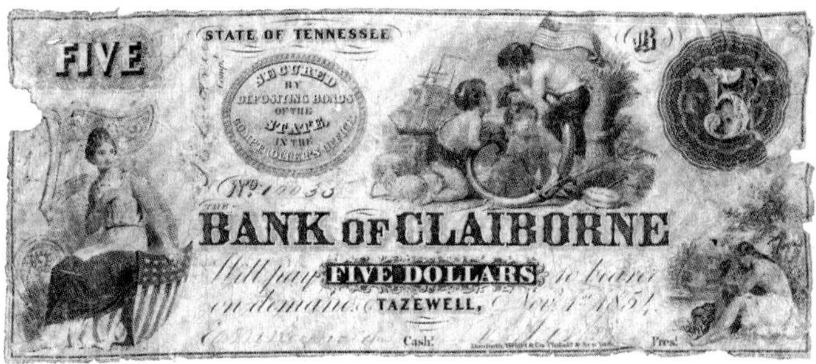

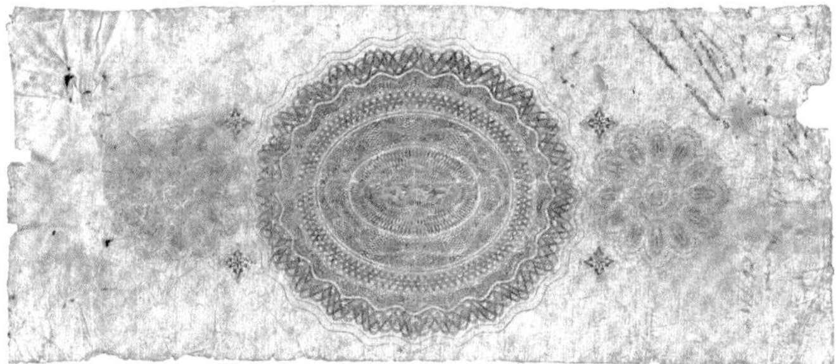

Back: Red-orange. ***Engraver:*** Danforth, Wright & Co. ***Comments:*** H-TN-225-G6a, Garland-1218. Similar to W-TN-1000-005-G030. Nov. 1st, 1854.

Rarity: URS-4
G $750

Uncut Sheets

$2-$2-$3-$5 • W-TN-1000-002.002.003.005-US010

Vignette(s): ($2) Woman, Farm / Farmers walking, Dog, Boy, Wagon. ***($3)*** Woman, Deer and shield, Grain, Sheep / Cherubs. ***($5)*** Woman seated in 5 with shield / Cherubs / Woman seated with child. ***Engraver:*** Danforth, Wright & Co. ***Comments:*** H-TN-225-G2, G2, G4, G6. First two notes identical. Nov. 1st, 1854.

Rarity: —

Bank of Tazewell

1854–1858

W-TN-1010

History: The Bank of Tazewell was chartered in 1854 with an authorized capital of $100,000. The president was E.H. Skaggs, and the cashier was C. Hitchings. By 1858 the bank had failed.

Numismatic Commentary: All notes are very scarce to rare.

The 1990 Christie's sale of the American Bank Note Co. archives produced a $5-$10-$20-$50 sheet.

Valid Issues

$5 • W-TN-1010-005-G010

Left: 5 on V / Farmers, House. ***Center:*** 5. ***Right:*** 5 / Men with horses in smith's shop. ***Engraver:*** Danforth, Wright & Co. ***Comments:*** H-TN-230-G2. May 1, 1854.

Rarity: URS-3
Proof $1,500

$5 • W-TN-1010-005-G010a

Back: Red-orange. ***Engraver:*** Danforth, Wright & Co. ***Comments:*** H-TN-230-G2a, Garland-1219. Similar to W-TN-1010-005-G010. May 1, 1854.

Rarity: URS-3
Proof $1,500

$5 • W-TN-1010-005-G010b

Back: Red-orange. ***Engraver:*** Danforth, Wright & Co. ***Comments:*** H-TN-230-G2b, Garland-1220. Similar to W-TN-1010-005-G010 but with different date. Oct. 1, 1854.

Rarity: URS-4
Proof $1,200

$10 • W-TN-1010-010-G020

Left: 10 / Portrait of Franklin Pierce. ***Center:*** U.S. Capitol. ***Right:*** X / Hebe watering eagle, Flag, Ship. ***Engraver:*** Danforth, Wright & Co. ***Comments:*** H-TN-230-G10, Garland-1221. May 1, 1854.

Rarity: URS-4
Proof $1,500

$10 • W-TN-1010-010-G020a

Back: Red-orange. ***Engraver:*** Danforth, Wright & Co. ***Comments:*** H-TN-230-G10a. Similar to W-TN-1010-010-G020. May 1, 1854.

Rarity: URS-3
Proof $2,500

$20 • W-TN-1010-020-G030

Left: Men and women standing and sitting. ***Center:*** 20 / Milkmaid with cows. ***Right:*** 20. ***Engraver:*** Danforth, Wright & Co. ***Comments:*** H-TN-230-G12, Garland-1222. May 1, 1854.

Rarity: URS-3
Proof $2,000

$20 • W-TN-1010-020-G030a

Back: Red-orange. ***Engraver:*** Danforth, Wright & Co. ***Comments:*** H-TN-230-G12a, Garland-1223. Similar to W-TN-1010-020-G030. May 1, 1854.

Rarity: URS-3
Proof $2,500

$50 • W-TN-1010-050-G040

Left: L / 50 / L. ***Center:*** State House. ***Right:*** 50. ***Engraver:*** Danforth, Wright & Co. ***Comments:*** H-TN-230-G14, Garland-1224. May 1, 1854.

Rarity: URS-2
Proof $5,000

$50 • W-TN-1010-050-G040a

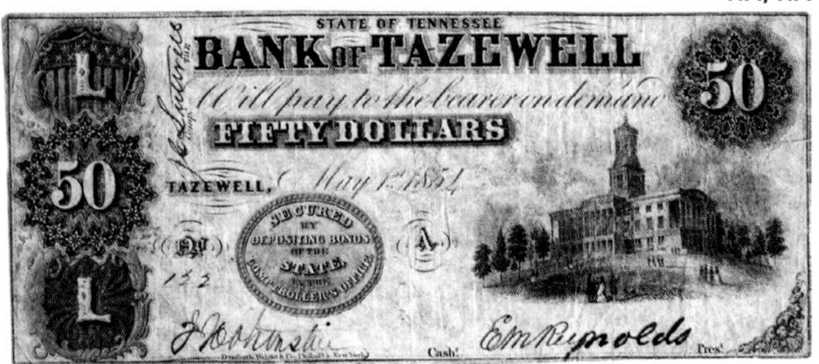

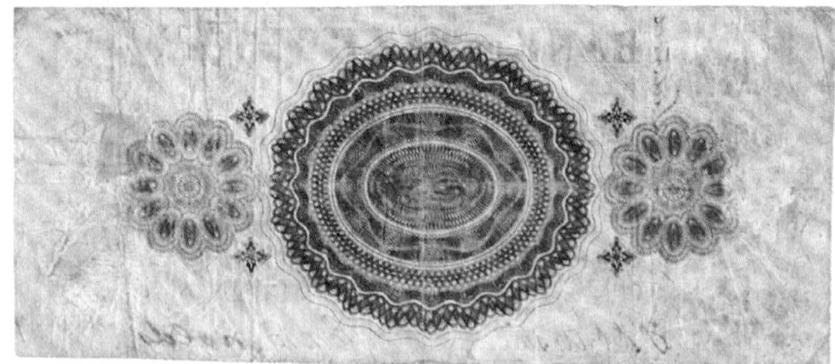

Back: Red-orange. ***Engraver:*** Danforth, Wright & Co. ***Comments:*** H-TN-230-G14a. Similar to W-TN-1010-050-G040. May 1, 1854.

Rarity: URS-2
Proof $4,000

State Stock Bank (branch)

Circa 1857

W-TN-1020

History: The State Stock Bank was chartered in 1857. However, it was reported that "the notes issued by it are not secured by State Stocks, or at least they show no indication of it upon their face. They are considered doubtful."[20]

The State Stock Bank had its parent bank located in Greeneville, W-TN-320.

Numismatic Commentary: It is thought that no notes from this branch survive today.

Valid Issues

$5 • W-TN-1020-005-G010

Left: V / 5. ***Center:*** Indian shooting deer. ***Right:*** 5 / Woman with cornucopia. ***Tint:*** Red-orange. ***Engraver:*** Danforth, Wright & Co. ***Comments:*** H-Unlisted, Garland-1225. Jan. 1, 1857.

Rarity: —

$10 • W-TN-1020-010-G020

Left: 10 / Female portrait. ***Center:*** Harvest scene. ***Right:*** Two cherubs with sheaf. ***Tint:*** Red-orange. ***Engraver:*** Danforth, Wright & Co. ***Comments:*** H-Unlisted, Garland-1226. Jan. 1, 1857.

Rarity: —

$20 • W-TN-1020-020-G030

Left: 20 / Train. ***Center:*** 20 / Anchor. ***Right:*** 20 / Woman seated. ***Tint:*** Red-orange. ***Engraver:*** Danforth, Wright & Co. ***Comments:*** H-Unlisted, Garland-1227. Jan. 1, 1857.

Rarity: —

Trenton, Tennessee

Even before its incorporation, Trenton was the seat for Gibson County and was originally known as Gibson Port. The first court was held on January 5, 1824, and the following year the local post office was moved to Trenton. On December 14, 1847, Trenton was incorporated.

Bank of the State of Tennessee {3rd} (branch)

1838–1866

W-TN-1030

History: The third Bank of the State of Tennessee (also seen in print as the Bank of Tennessee) was chartered on January 19, 1838, with an authorized capital of $5,000,000. John A. Taliaferro was the cashier, and John S. Davis was the president of the Trenton branch in 1855. In 1857 R.W. Hubbard became the president, and O.B. Caldwell became the cashier.

By February 1866 the Bank of the State of Tennessee was authorized to go into liquidation.

The third Bank of the State of Tennessee had its parent bank located in Nashville, W-TN-690, and branch banks located in Athens, W-TN-010, Clarksville, W-TN-120, Columbia, W-TN-190, Knoxville, W-TN-365, Memphis, W-TN-490, Murfreesboro, W-TN-610, Rogersville, W-TN-890, Shelbyville, W-TN-920, Somerville, W-TN-960, and Sparta, W-TN-980.

Numismatic Commentary: For some reason there are no known Civil War fractionals from this branch. All dollar-denominated notes are scarce—perhaps scarcer than previously estimated—given the paucity of notes in collections and archives.

Valid Issues

$1 • W-TN-1030-001-G010

Left: Woman seated with farmer / Female portrait. ***Center:*** 1 / Man plowing with horses / 1. ***Right:*** ONE / Medallion head / ONE. ***Engraver:*** Draper, Toppan & Co. ***Comments:*** H-TN-195-G400. Mar. 1, 1842.

Rarity: —

$1 • W-TN-1030-001-G010a

Engraver: Toppan, Carpenter & Co. ***Comments:*** H-TN-195-G400a. Similar to W-TN-1030-001-G010 but with different date and engraver imprint. Mar. 1, ____. 1840s, 1861.

Rarity: —

$1 • W-TN-1030-001-G020

Left: 1 / Sailor standing with flag. ***Center:*** 1 / Two women seated with cog wheel / 1. ***Right:*** 1 / Woman with sheaf on back. ***Engraver:*** Toppan, Carpenter, Casilear & Co. ***Comments:*** H-TN-195-G402. 18__. 1850s.

Rarity: URS-4
F $300

$1 • **W-TN-1030-001-G030** CC, CC

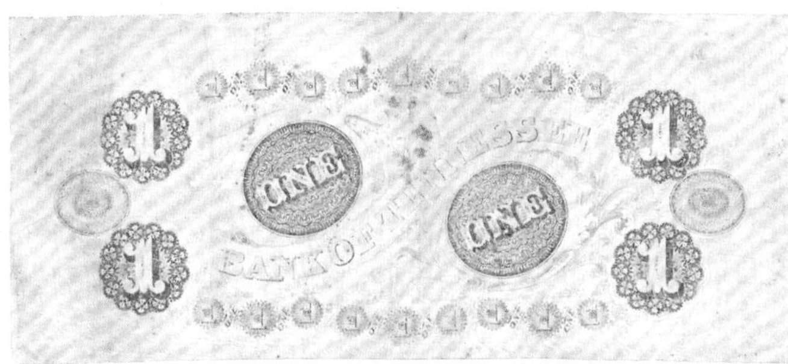

Tint: Red-orange lathework and panel of microlettering outlining white ONE. ***Back:*** Red-orange. ***Engraver:*** Toppan, Carpenter & Co. ***Comments:*** H-TN-195-G404a, Garland-1231. 18__. 1850s.

Rarity: URS-4
F $200

$2 • **W-TN-1030-002-G040**
Left: TWO / Woman seated in 2 / 2. ***Center:*** 2 / Woman seated on bales / 2. ***Right:*** 2 / Ship / 2. ***Engraver:*** Draper, Toppan & Co. ***Comments:*** H-TN-195-G406. Mar. 1, 1842.

Rarity: —

$2 • **W-TN-1030-002-G040a**
Engraver: Toppan, Carpenter & Co. ***Comments:*** H-TN-195-G406a. Similar to W-TN-1030-002-G040 but with different date and engraver imprint. Mar. 1, ____. 1840s, 1861.

Rarity: —

$2 • **W-TN-1030-002-G050**
Left: 2 / Justice seated with scales. ***Center:*** Cattle / 2 / 2. ***Right:*** 2 / Liberty with pole, cap, and flag. ***Engraver:*** Toppan, Carpenter, Casilear & Co. ***Comments:*** H-TN-195-G408, Garland-1232. 18__. 1850s.

Rarity: URS-3
F $550

$2 • **W-TN-1030-002-G060**
Left: 2 / Female portrait. ***Center:*** Soldier, Woman, and two Indians looking at bust of George Washington. ***Right:*** 2 / Portrait of Charles Carroll. ***Tint:*** Red-orange. ***Back:*** Red-orange. ***Engraver:*** Toppan, Carpenter & Co. ***Comments:*** H-TN-195-G410a, Garland-1233. 18__. 1850s.

Rarity: URS-3
F $550

$3 • **W-TN-1030-003-G070**
Left: THREE / Woman standing / THREE. ***Center:*** 3 / Men on horses, sheep / 3. ***Right:*** THREE / Cherubs in 3 / THREE. ***Engraver:*** Draper, Toppan & Co. ***Comments:*** H-TN-195-G412. Mar. 1, 1842.

Rarity: —

$3 • **W-TN-1030-003-G070a**
Engraver: Toppan, Carpenter & Co. ***Comments:*** H-TN-195-G412a. Similar to W-TN-1030-003-G070 but with different date and engraver imprint. Mar. 1, ____. 1840s, 1861.

Rarity: —

$5 • **W-TN-1030-005-G080**
Left: 5 / Woman leaning on column / V. ***Center:*** Woman seated with shield. ***Right:*** 5 / Justice standing with scales and eagle / V. ***Engraver:*** Rawdon, Wright, Hatch & Edson / Rawdon, Wright & Hatch. ***Comments:*** H-TN-195-G414. 18__. 1838–1840s.

Rarity: —

$5 • **W-TN-1030-005-G090**
Left: Three men / 5. ***Center:*** Portrait of James Madison. ***Right:*** 5 / Medallion head. ***Back:*** Red-orange. ***Engraver:*** Danforth, Bald & Co. ***Comments:*** H-TN-195-G416a, Garland-1236. 18__. 1850s.

Rarity: URS-4
F $350

$5 • **W-TN-1030-005-G090a**
Tint: Red-orange outlining white V / 5 / V. ***Back:*** Red-orange. ***Engraver:*** Danforth, Bald & Co. ***Comments:*** H-TN-195-G416b. Similar to W-TN-1030-005-G090. 18__. 1850s.

Rarity: —

$10 • **W-TN-1030-010-G100**
Left: 10 / Eagle with shield / X. ***Center:*** Woman with children seated among parcels, Factories and farmhouse. ***Right:*** 10 / Shield / X. ***Engraver:*** Draper, Toppan, Longacre & Co. ***Comments:*** H-TN-195-G422. 18__. 1838–1840s.

Rarity: —

$10 • **W-TN-1030-010-G110**
Left: 10 / Portrait of James K. Polk. ***Center:*** Portrait of Andrew Jackson. ***Right:*** 10 / Portrait of Cave Johnson. ***Tint:*** Red-orange outlining white 10 / 10. ***Back:*** Blue. ***Engraver:*** Toppan, Carpenter & Co. ***Comments:*** H-TN-195-G426a, Garland-1237. 18__. 1850s–1861.

Rarity: URS-4
F $350

$20 • **W-TN-1030-020-G120**
Left: 20 / Man writing on tablet / 20. ***Center:*** Woman standing with eagle and shield. ***Right:*** 20 / Shield / 20. ***Engraver:*** Draper, Toppan, Longacre & Co. ***Comments:*** H-TN-195-G428. 18__. 1838–1840s.

Rarity: —

$20 • **W-TN-1030-020-G120a**
Engraver: Toppan, Carpenter & Co. ***Comments:*** H-TN-195-G428a. Similar to W-TN-1030-020-G120 but with different engraver imprint. 18__. 1840s–1850s

Rarity: —

$20 • **W-TN-1030-020-G130**
Left: 20 / Portrait of Zachary Taylor / 20. ***Center:*** Three women reclining, Ship / 20. ***Right:*** Justice seated with sword and scales / TWENTY. ***Engraver:*** Toppan, Carpenter, Casilear & Co. ***Comments:*** H-TN-195-G430, Garland-1238. 18__. 1850s.

Rarity: URS-3
F $550

$20 • W-TN-1030-020-G130a

Back: Red-orange. ***Engraver:*** Toppan, Carpenter, Casilear & Co. ***Comments:*** H-TN-195-G430a. Similar to W-TN-1030-020-G130. 18__. 1850s.

Rarity: —

$20 • W-TN-1030-020-G130b

Tint: Red-orange outlining white TWENTY. ***Back:*** Red-orange. ***Engraver:*** Toppan, Carpenter, Casilear & Co. ***Comments:*** H-TN-195-G430b, Garland-1240. Similar to W-TN-1030-020-G130. 18__. 1850s.

Rarity: URS-3
F $550

$50 • W-TN-1030-050-G140

Left: 50 / Shield / 50. ***Center:*** Liberty with eagle and shield. ***Right:*** 50 / Portrait of George Washington / 50. ***Engraver:*** Draper, Toppan, Longacre & Co. ***Comments:*** H-TN-195-G432. 18__. 1838–1840s.

Rarity: —

$100 • W-TN-1030-100-G150

Left: Atlas lifting world on shoulders / 100. ***Center:*** 100 / Justice with eagle and shield / 100. ***Right:*** Atlas lifting world on shoulders / 100. ***Engraver:*** Draper, Toppan, Longacre & Co. ***Comments:*** H-TN-195-G436. 18__. 1838–1850s.

Rarity: —

Civil War Issue

$1 • W-TN-1030-001-G160

CC

Comments: H-TN-195-G440, Garland-1228. 1862.

Rarity: URS-4
F $300

Bank of Trenton

1856–1859

W-TN-1040

History: The Bank of Trenton was chartered in 1856. The president was R.W. Hubbard, and O.B. Caldwell was the cashier. By 1859 the bank had closed.

Numismatic Commentary: Garland thought signed and issued notes from this bank to be the rarest of all.

The 1990 Christie's sale of the American Bank Note Co. archives produced two $1-$2-$5-$5 sheets.

Valid Issues

$1 • W-TN-1040-001-G010

CC

Engraver: Danforth, Wright & Co. ***Comments:*** H-TN-235-G2, Garland-1245. January 1st, 1856.

Rarity: URS-3
F $750; **Proof** $1,200

$2 • W-TN-1040-002-G020

Left: Ceres standing / TWO. ***Center:*** Bridge, Steamboats. ***Right:*** 2 / State arms. ***Engraver:*** Danforth, Wright & Co. ***Comments:*** H-TN-235-G4, Garland-1246. January 1st, 1856.

Rarity: URS-2
Proof $1,500

$5 • W-TN-1040-005-G030

CC

Engraver: Danforth, Wright & Co. ***Comments:*** H-TN-235-G6, Garland-1247. January 1st, 1856.

Rarity: URS-3
F $750; **Proof** $1,500

$5 • W-TN-1040-005-G040

CC

Tint: Red-brown lathework, V, panel of microlettering outlining white 5 / 5, and die outlining white 5. ***Engraver:*** Danforth, Wright & Co. ***Comments:*** H-TN-235-G8a, Garland-1248. 18__. 1850s.

Rarity: URS-2
Proof $7,000
Selected auction price: Stack's Bowers Galleries, August 2011, Lot 5306, Proof $7,000

$10 • W-TN-1040-010-G050

Left: X / Portrait of Henry Clay. ***Center:*** X / Portrait of Lucretia Hart Clay / X. ***Right:*** 10 / State arms. ***Tint:*** Red-brown lathework. ***Engraver:*** Danforth, Wright & Co. ***Comments:*** H-TN-235-G10a, Garland-1249. 18__. 1850s.

Rarity: URS-2
Proof $6,000

$20 • W-TN-1040-020-G060

Left: XX / Male portrait. ***Center:*** 20. ***Right:*** 20 / Portrait of Lucretia Hart Clay. ***Tint:*** Red-brown lathework. ***Engraver:*** Danforth, Wright & Co. ***Comments:*** H-TN-235-G12a, Garland-1250. 18__. 1850s.

Rarity: URS-2
Proof $6,000

Planters Bank of Tennessee (branch)

1834–1865

W-TN-1050

History: The Planters Bank of Tennessee was chartered on November 11, 1833, with an authorized capital of $2,000,000. The Trenton branch was opened in 1834. In 1848 N.J. Hess was the president. John A. Taliaferro was the cashier. In 1865 the bank was forced to liquidate and close its affairs.

The Planters Bank of Tennessee had its parent bank located in Nashville, W-TN-810, and branch banks located in Athens, W-TN-020, Clarksville, W-TN-140, Columbia, W-TN-210, Franklin, W-TN-300, LaGrange, W-TN-410, Memphis, W-TN-570, Murfreesboro, W-TN-630, Pulaski, W-TN-870, Rogersville, W-TN-910, Shelbyville, W-TN-940, Somerville, W-TN-970, Sparta, W-TN-990, and Winchester, W-TN-1070.

Numismatic Commentary: There are no known notes of the Trenton branch.

Winchester, Tennessee

On November 22, 1809, Winchester was established to be the county seat of Franklin. It was laid out the following year and named for James Winchester. The Tennessee and Alabama Female Institute was founded in 1851. Later it was renamed after Mary Corn Sharp to become the Mary Sharp College. The college boasted a curriculum that matched Amherst College and University of Virginia. Winchester soon became an educational hub with the college's influence, and other schools rose after it, including Carrick Academy, Winchester Female Academy, and Winchester Normal College.

Confederate troops occupied the city first during the Civil War, only to be rebuffed by Union forces. It was located in a strategic position for the Confederate army, who retreated through Winchester in 1863.

Nashville Bank (branch)

1817–1827

W-TN-1060

History: In 1807 the Nashville Bank was chartered with an authorized capital of $200,000, to be divided into shares of $50 apiece. In 1817 several banks were chartered across the state—in the towns of Gallatin, Murfreesboro, Rogersville, Shelbyville, and Winchester—and were given the option of either joining the first Bank of the State of Tennessee, W-TN-355, or of joining with the Nashville Bank. The corporations chose the Nashville Bank and became branches forthwith.

On March 31, 1823, the Nashville Bank, along with its branches, burned a total of $250,000 worth of bank notes in order to increase the value of its circulation. In 1827 the bank was liquidated.

The Nashville Bank had its parent bank located in Nashville, W-TN-800, and branch banks located in Gallatin, W-TN-310, Murfreesboro, W-TN-640, Rogersville, W-TN-900, and Shelbyville, W-TN-930.

Numismatic Commentary: The only known note from this branch is the $20. Garland thought it was unique. Haxby implies there is more than one.

Valid Issues

$1 • W-TN-1060-001-G010

Left: ONE vertically. ***Center:*** 1 / Woman seated / 1. ***Right:*** TENNESSEE vertically. ***Engraver:*** Tanner, Kearny & Tiebout. ***Comments:*** H-TN-180-G144. 18__. 1810s.

Rarity: *None known*

$2 • W-TN-1060-002-G020

Left: TWO vertically. ***Center:*** 2 / Woman seated / 2. ***Right:*** TENNESSEE vertically. ***Engraver:*** Tanner, Kearny & Tiebout. ***Comments:*** H-TN-180-G146. 18__. 1810s.

Rarity: *None known*

$5 • W-TN-1060-005-G030

Left: FIVE vertically. ***Center:*** 5 / Woman seated / 5. ***Right:*** NASHVILLE vertically. ***Engraver:*** Murray, Draper, Fairman & Co. ***Comments:*** H-TN-180-G150. 18__. 1810s.

Rarity: *None known*

$5 • W-TN-1060-005-G040

Left: FIVE vertically. ***Center:*** 5 / Woman seated / 5. ***Right:*** TENNESSEE vertically. ***Engraver:*** Tanner, Kearny & Tiebout. ***Comments:*** H-TN-180-G152, Garland-1251. 18__. 1810s–1820s.

Rarity: *None known*

Collectors and Researchers:

If you have new information about any banks or notes listed in this volume, contact Whitman Publishing, Attn: Obsolete Paper Money, 3101 Clairmont Road, Suite G, Atlanta, GA 30329.

$10 • W-TN-1060-010-G050
Left: TEN vertically. *Center:* 10 / Woman seated / 10. *Right:* NASHVILLE vertically. *Engraver:* Murray, Draper, Fairman & Co. *Comments:* H-TN-180-G154. 18__. 1810s.
Rarity: *None known*

$10 • W-TN-1060-010-G060
Left: TEN vertically. *Center:* 10 / Woman seated / 10. *Right:* TENNESSEE vertically. *Engraver:* Tanner, Kearny & Tiebout. *Comments:* H-TN-180-G156, Garland-1252. 18__. 1810s–1820s.
Rarity: *None known*

$20 • W-TN-1060-020-G070
Left: TWENTY vertically. *Center:* 20 / Woman seated / 20. *Right:* NASHVILLE vertically. *Engraver:* Murray, Draper, Fairman & Co. *Comments:* H-TN-180-G158. 18__. 1810s.
Rarity: *None known*

$20 • W-TN-1060-020-G080
Left: TWENTY vertically. *Center:* 20 / Woman seated / 20. *Right:* TENNESSEE vertically. *Engraver:* Tanner, Kearny & Tiebout. *Comments:* H-TN-180-G160, Garland-1253. 18__. 1810s–1820s.
Rarity: URS-2
F $1,000

Non-Valid Issues

$20 • W-TN-1060-020-C080
Engraver: Tanner, Kearny & Tiebout. *Comments:* H-TN-180-C160. Counterfeit of W-TN-1060-020-G080. 18__. 1810s–1820s.
Rarity: —

Planters Bank of Tennessee (branch)
1834–1865
W-TN-1070

History: The Planters Bank of Tennessee was chartered on November 11, 1833, with an authorized capital of $2,000,000. In 1834 the branch in Winchester was opened. In 1865 the bank was forced to liquidate and close its affairs.

The Planters Bank of Tennessee had its parent bank located in Nashville, W-TN-810, and branch banks located in Athens, W-TN-020, Clarksville, W-TN-140, Columbia, W-TN-210, Franklin, W-TN-300, LaGrange, W-TN-410, Memphis, W-TN-570, Murfreesboro, W-TN-630, Pulaski, W-TN-870, Rogersville, W-TN-910, Shelbyville, W-TN-940, Somerville, W-TN-970, Sparta, W-TN-990, and Trenton, W-TN-1050.

Numismatic Commentary: No notes of this branch are known today.

Valid Issues

$1 • W-TN-1070-001-G010
Left: 1 / Medallion head bearing ONE / 1. *Center:* 1 with cherub / Woman seated with boxes. *Right:* Woman standing in 1. *Engraver:* Rawdon, Wright, Hatch & Edson. *Comments:* H-TN-185-G302. 18__. 1840s.
Rarity: *None known*

$2 • W-TN-1070-002-G020
Left: 2 / Woman with sheaf / 2. *Center:* 2 with cherubs / Woman seated with boxes. *Right:* Woman standing in 2. *Engraver:* Rawdon, Wright, Hatch & Edson. *Comments:* H-TN-185-G304. Dec. 1, 1860.
Rarity: *None known*

$3 • W-TN-1070-003-G030
Left: 3 / Medallion head / 3. *Center:* 3 with cherubs / Two men flanking shield bearing cow surmounted by beehive. *Right:* Woman standing in 3. *Engraver:* Rawdon, Wright, Hatch & Edson. *Comments:* H-TN-185-G306. Dec. 1, 1860.
Rarity: *None known*

$5 • W-TN-1070-005-G040
Left: Medallion head / FIVE / Medallion head. *Center:* FIVE / Man standing with dog / FIVE. *Right:* Medallion head / FIVE / Medallion head. *Engraver:* Underwood, Bald & Spencer. *Comments:* H-TN-185-G308, Garland-1254. 18__. 1830s–1840s.
Rarity: *None known*

$10 • W-TN-1070-010-G050
Left: Medallion head / TEN / Medallion head. *Center:* 10 / Farm scene, Harvest / X. *Right:* Medallion head / TEN / Medallion head. *Engraver:* Underwood, Bald & Spencer. *Comments:* H-TN-185-G310, Garland-1255. 18__. 1830s–1840s.
Rarity: *None known*

$20 • W-TN-1070-020-G060
Left: 20 / Medallion head / 20. *Center:* 20 / Medallion head / 20. *Right:* 20 / Medallion head / 20. *Engraver:* Underwood, Bald & Spencer. *Comments:* H-TN-185-G312, Garland-1256. 18__. 1830s–1840s.
Rarity: *None known*

$50 • W-TN-1070-050-G070
Left: 50 / Medallion head / 50. *Center:* Medallion heads / Woman seated, Ship / Medallion heads. *Right:* 50 / Medallion head / 50. *Engraver:* Underwood, Bald, Spencer & Hufty. *Comments:* H-TN-185-G314. 18__. 1830s–1850s.
Rarity: *None known*

$100 • W-TN-1070-100-G080
Left: 100 / Three women seated vertically / 100. *Center:* Medallion head / Boy reclining under corn, Plow / Medallion head. *Right:* 100 / Three women seated vertically / 100. *Engraver:* Underwood, Bald, Spencer & Hufty. *Comments:* H-TN-185-G316. 18__. 1830s–1850s.
Rarity: *None known*

Non-Valid Issues

$10 • W-TN-1070-010-S010
Left: Woman. *Center:* Woman, Train, Steamboat. *Right:* Ceres. *Comments:* H-TN-185-S132. 18__. 1840s.
Rarity: *None known*

$10 • W-TN-1070-010-S020
Left: 10 / Justice with scales. *Center:* X with cherubs / Two women seated. *Right:* 10 / Justice with scales. *Engraver:* Rawdon, Wright & Hatch. *Comments:* H-TN-185-S134. From a genuine plate of the Planters Bank of Alabama, Wetumpka, Alabama. 18__. 1840s.
Rarity: *None known*

$20 • W-TN-1070-020-S030

Center: Eagle. ***Comments:*** H-TN-185-S136. 18__. 1840s.

Rarity: *None known*

$20 • W-TN-1070-020-S040

Left: 20 / Female portrait / XX. ***Center:*** Woman seated near ocean with shield. ***Right:*** 20 / Female portrait / XX. ***Engraver:*** Rawdon, Wright & Hatch. ***Comments:*** H-TN-185-S138. From a genuine plate of the Planters Bank of Alabama, Wetumpka, Alabama. 18__. 1840s.

Rarity: *None known*

$50 • W-TN-1070-050-S050

Left: FIFTY DOLLARS vertically. ***Center:*** 50 / Eagle on bale / 50. ***Right:*** STATE OF TENNESSEE vertically. ***Engraver:*** Rawdon, Wright & Hatch. ***Comments:*** H-TN-185-S140. From a genuine plate of the Planters Bank of Alabama, Wetumpka, Alabama. 18__. 1840s.

Rarity: *None known*

$100 • W-TN-1070-100-S060

Left: HUNDRED vertically. ***Center:*** Deer, River. ***Right:*** Portrait of George Washington. ***Engraver:*** Rawdon, Wright & Hatch. ***Comments:*** H-TN-185-S142. From a genuine plate of the Planters Bank of Alabama, Wetumpka, Alabama. 18__. 1840s.

Rarity: *None known*

$100 • W-TN-1070-100-S070

Left: Medallion head. ***Center:*** C / Factory / C. ***Right:*** 100 diagonally. ***Engraver:*** Rawdon, Wright & Hatch. ***Comments:*** H-TN-185-S144. 18__. 1840s.

Rarity: *None known*

The Obsolete Bank Notes of Texas

State Banking in Texas

Currency of Texas

The history of paper money issued by state-chartered banks in Texas is necessarily brief, as just three banks were involved. In earlier times the Republic of Texas, an independent entity, issued its own government paper, but this is not studied here.

In December 1856 *Bankers' Magazine* stated that "there is one bank in the state, at Galveston, having a capital of $322,000." This bank, the Commercial and Agricultural Bank of Texas, also had a branch in Brownsville at that time.

The bank was first authorized by the Republic of Texas (before Texas joined the Union in 1845) in April 1835, to be headquartered in the town of Columbia. The bank did not open at this time, as the war with Mexico started in late 1835. The capital was set at a maximum of $1,000,000, and the bank was allowed to establish branches wherever it wanted to. One was approved for Brazos. Nevertheless, on December 14, 1837, the Congress of the Republic passed an act prohibiting any person or entity to issue paper money. On February 3, 1841, the Congress authorized McKinney & Williams, proprietors of the Commercial and Agricultural Bank of Texas, to issue $30,000 worth of bills, as the partnership had provided financial aid to the Texas government at an earlier time. Notes were printed in anticipation before the bank was again prohibited from opening, although it was reorganized under the original charter in 1847 (when it was located in Galveston, as mentioned above).

The second entry in the bank lineup was the Bank of Vernon, a fraudulent entity which operated in the 1840s. Even the town was fictitious![1] Bills of the Northern Bank of Mississippi (see under Mississippi) circulated extensively in Texas, accounting for the third bank which circulated notes in the state. In the absence of currency from other Texas-based banks, these were well received by the public.

Numismatic Comments

Collectors of obsolete currency can revel in the issues of Texas, but not in those paid out by state-chartered banks. Instead, it is notes of the Republic of Texas, an entity not studied here, that provide much of the action, in addition to bills of more than 200 issuers of scrip.

Within the purview of the present text, bills of the Commercial and Agricultural Bank of Texas are rare today with the exception of some remainders of the $1 denomination. Those of the Commercial and Agricultural Bank located in Galveston are generally uncollectible, although certain $10 counterfeits dated January 1, 1848, are seen now and then. Bills of the Bank of Vernon, again essentially uncollectible, exist when found in the form of alterations to represent *Ohio* banks. On the whole, remainders provide most of the supply of bills of these banks. Dated, signed, and issued notes are very rare.

The standard reference on Texas paper money is *Texas Obsolete Notes and Scrip*, by Bob Medlar and published in 1968. For any scholar of Texas' complex banking history, this is a great book to have. Most notes are also pictured on the Internet, courtesy of the Rowe-Barr Collection at the DeGolyer Library of Southern Methodist University (www.digitalcollections.smu.edu).

Brazos, Texas

In 1837 what later became Brazos County was part of the much larger Washington County. The area was split down the middle by the Brazos River and was progressively called Brazos, Washington, and Washington on the Brazos throughout the 1840s, 1850s, and 1860s.

Brazos was an influential center for commerce and politics in the early history of Texas. It was strategically located near the confluence of the Brazos and Navasota rivers; close to the La Bahía Road; 70 miles north of Houston; and 200 miles from the coast. In 1821 the first settlers, led by Andrew Robinson and his family, settled the area that would later become the town. The next year a ferry across the Brazos was established. In December 1833 the town was laid out. Captain John Hall bought the grant from the Robinson family and began to sell town lots. The town became a supply point, attracting merchants and tradesmen with its location on the river, and settlers from neighboring communities flocked to what became a commercially flourishing hub. Agricultural development increased, and because the town was elevated on bluffs above the river, flooding was a lesser threat. The area was briefly evacuated during the Texas Revolution.

New settlers came to the town after the conflict had been settled, and soon timber lots, brickyards, sawmills, and a post office were established. On June 5, 1837, the town was officially incorporated. A period of decadence followed, with gambling and lawlessness posing problems, but soon the excitement was settled by the establishment of organized religion and several churches. From there the town became a center of education as well as journalism and commerce. Steamboats traveled up and down the Brazos River to transport cotton and other goods. The city was even the capital of Texas for a brief time. However, when the railroad came through Texas, it bypassed the area, and as a result the town declined. During the 1860s most residents made the transition to the cities of Brenham and Navasota.

Commercial and Agricultural Bank of Texas (branch)

1835–1837

W-TX-010

History: On April 30, 1835, the Commercial and Agricultural Bank of Texas was established. On December 14, 1837, the issuance or circulation of promissory notes was prohibited by the Congress of the Republic. However, the Commercial and Agricultural Bank of Texas was authorized to issue notes to the amount of $30,000. Another act followed stating that "all laws granting to any individual, individuals or corporations the authority to issue either bills or promissory notes to pass or circulate as money, are hereby repealed." Thus the bank was yet again deprived of its ability to circulate funds, and the charter lapsed.[2]

Notes were printed in anticipation for a parent-bank address at Columbia, W-TX-040. The bank officially re-opened later in Galveston, W-TX-050, with a branch located in Brownsville, W-TX-030.

Numismatic Commentary: Although notes were printed in anticipation for the parent bank in Columbia, no notes have been found with the Brazos imprint on them.

Texas Railroad, Navigation and Banking Company

1836

W-TX-020

History: On December 16, 1836, the Texas Railroad, Navigation and Banking Company was incorporated with an authorized capital of $5,000,000. This was increasable to $10,000,000, and the institution was granted the privilege of building an international canal connecting the Rio Grande and Sabine rivers. The canal and railroad branches were authorized to an unlimited amount.

The bank was not allowed to go into operation until $1,000,000 had been paid in specie. Further, a $25,000 "good faith bonus" was to be paid in gold and silver within 18 months of the bank becoming operational, or the charter would lapse. The $5,000,000 stock was subscribed to, and the $25,000 was provided in Republic of Texas Treasury notes. These notes were receivable for all dues by law. However, the treasurer of the Republic refused to receive the notes, although a written acknowledgement was given that the funds had been presented. As a result, the bank's charter was forfeited.[3] The entity was uncovered as a speculation scheme, and thus the citizens were presumed "saved."

Brownsville, Texas

A fort located on the Mexican border of Texas was commissioned in 1845 due to the instability of the region which heralded the onset of the Mexican-American War. After the conflict, the fort was renamed after Major Jacob Brown, who had been killed in battle.

The town of Brownsville rose up around the fort and was established in 1848 by Charles Stillman. It became the county seat of Cameron on January 13, 1849. The town was incorporated on January 24, 1850, but the act was repealed on April 1, 1852, due to land disputes between Stillman and the former land owners. The city was reincorporated on February 7, 1853.

Commercial and Agricultural Bank of Texas (branch)

1847–1858

W-TX-030

History: On April 30, 1835, the Commercial and Agricultural Bank of Texas was established. However, the bank did not officially open. Notes were printed in anticipation for a parent-bank address at Columbia, W-TX-040. At the time a branch was located in Brazos, W-TX-010.

On December 30, 1847, Samuel M. Williams reorganized the bank under the original charter to become the only banking institution in the state of Texas. It went into operation on January 1, 1848. In 1858 Samuel Williams passed away, and the affairs of the bank were wound up by B.A. Shepherd, one of the stockholders.

The Commercial and Agricultural Bank of Texas had its parent bank located in Galveston, W-TX-050.

Numismatic Commentary: Bills of the Commercial and Agricultural Bank of Texas are rare today, with none seen bearing the Brownsville imprint. An uncut sheet of the $5 listed below has been seen with the Brownsville imprint.

Valid Issues

$5 • W-TX-030-005-G010

Left: 5 / Cotton plant, barrel, implements / FIVE. ***Center:*** Portrait of George Washington flanked by Ceres and woman. ***Bottom center:*** Bales and barrels. ***Right:*** 5 / Portrait of Rachel Jackson. ***Engraver:*** Danforth & Hufty. ***Comments:*** H-TX-6-G24a, Medlar-Unlisted. January 1st, 1848.

Rarity: URS-3

$10 • W-TX-030-010-G020

Left: X / Cotton plant, barrel, implements / TEN. ***Center:*** Portrait of George Washington flanked by Ceres and woman. ***Bottom center:*** Bales and barrels. ***Right:*** X / Portrait of Rachel Jackson. ***Engraver:*** Danforth & Hufty. ***Comments:*** H-TX-6-G26a, Medlar-Unlisted. January 1st, 1848.

Rarity: *None known*

Uncut Sheets

$5-$5-$5-$5 • W-TX-030-005.005.005.005-US010

Vignette(s): ($5) Cotton plant, barrel, implements / Portrait of George Washington flanked by Ceres and woman / Bales and barrels / Portrait of Rachel Jackson. ***Engraver:*** Danforth & Hufty. ***Comments:*** H-TX-6-G24a, G24a, G24a, G24a. All four notes identical. January 1st, 1848.

Rarity: URS-1
Proof $20,000

COLUMBIA, TEXAS

The area that was known as Columbia (today West Columbia) was incorporated in 1826 by Josiah Hughes Bell. He laid out the town west of Marian (today East Columbia) and between the Brazos and San Bernard rivers. The history of the town is extremely brief. Columbia became the capital of the Republic of Texas in September 1836 and experienced a short burst of economic expansion. In April 1837, however, the seat of government was transferred to Houston, and the commerce of Columbia declined.

Commercial and Agricultural Bank of Texas

1835–1837

W-TX-040

History: On April 30, 1835, the Commercial and Agricultural Bank of Texas (the *Banco de Agricultura*) was established by the state of Coahuila and Texas, when Texas was still a province of Mexico. The authorized capital was not to exceed $1,000,000 and was to be divided into 10,000 shares. The charter was granted to Samuel M. Williams, and notes were printed in anticipation.

On December 14, 1837, after Texas became independent, the issuance or circulation of promissory notes was prohibited by the Congress of the Republic. However, the Commercial and Agricultural Bank of Texas was authorized to issue notes to the amount of $30,000. Another act followed stating that "all laws granting to any individual, individuals or corporations the authority to issue either bills or promissory notes to pass or circulate as money, are hereby repealed." Thus the bank was yet again deprived of its ability to circulate funds, and the charter lapsed.[4]

At the time a branch was located in Brazos, W-TX-010. The bank officially re-opened later in Galveston, W-TX-050, with a branch located in Brownsville, W-TX-030.

Numismatic Commentary: A few remainders from the Commercial and Agricultural Bank of Texas exist, but all are scarce. Dated, signed, and issued notes are very rare.

Valid Issues

$1 • W-TX-040-001-G010

CC

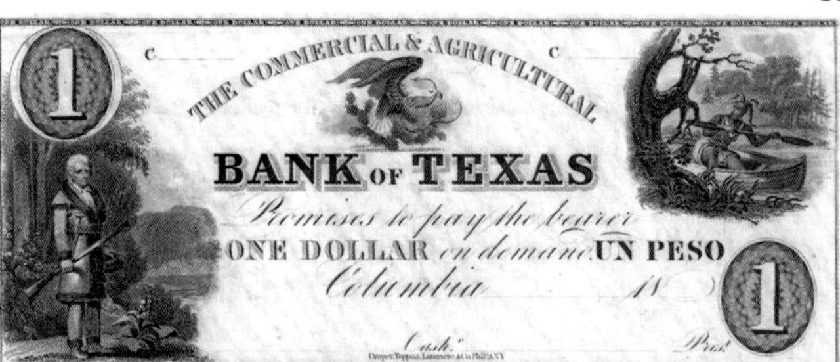

Engraver: Draper, Toppan, Longacre & Co. ***Comments:*** H-TX-5-G2, Medlar-18. Also payable "Un Peso." 18__. 1830s.

Rarity: URS-8
Unc-Rem $400

$2 • W-TX-040-002-G020

CC

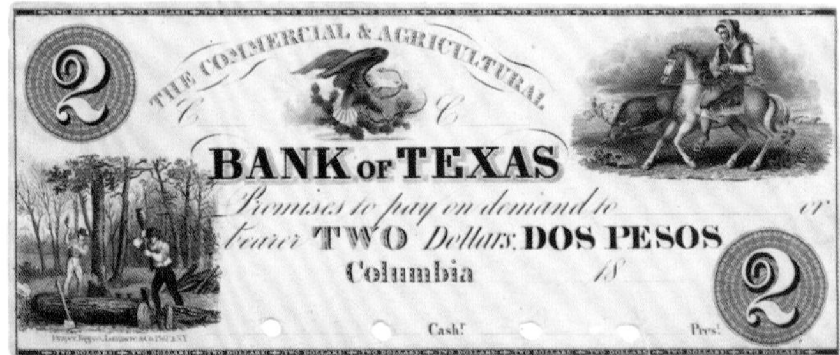

Engraver: Draper, Toppan, Longacre & Co. ***Comments:*** H-TX-5-G4, Medlar-19. Also payable "Dos Pesos." 18__. 1830s.

Rarity: URS-3
Unc-Rem $4,000; **Proof** $7,700
Selected auction price: Heritage Auctions, April 2015, Lot 19326, About New $7,637

$3 • W-TX-040-003-G030

CC

Engraver: Draper, Toppan, Longacre & Co. ***Comments:*** H-TX-5-G6, Medlar-20. Also payable "Tres Pesos." 18__. 1830s.

Rarity: URS-3
Proof $5,000

$5 • W-TX-040-005-G040

DG

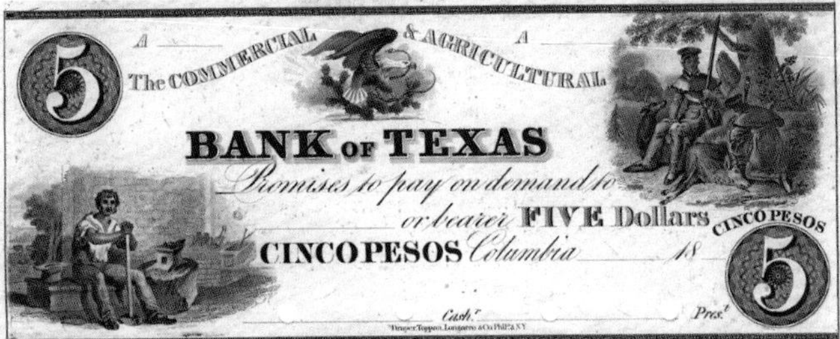

Engraver: Draper, Toppan, Longacre & Co. ***Comments:*** H-TX-5-G8, Medlar-21. Also payable "Cinco Pesos." 18__. 1830s.

Rarity: URS-4

Proof $4,000

$10 • W-TX-040-010-G050

HA

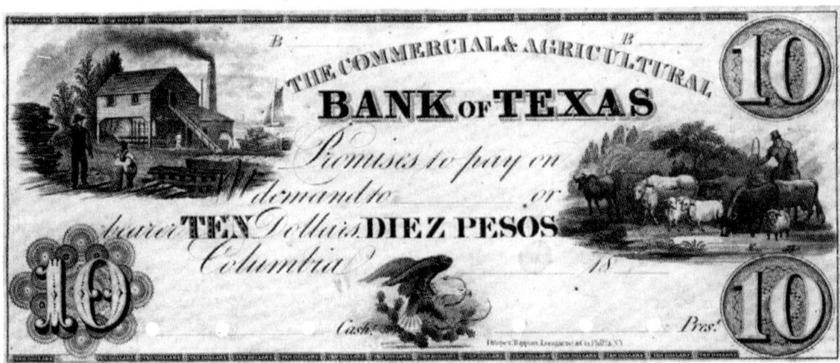

Engraver: Draper, Toppan, Longacre & Co. ***Comments:*** H-TX-5-G10, Medlar-22. Also payable "Diez Pesos." 18__. 1830s.

Rarity: URS-1

Proof $14,000

Selected auction price: Heritage Auctions, April 2015, Lot 19327, Proof $14,100

$20 • W-TX-040-020-G060

DG

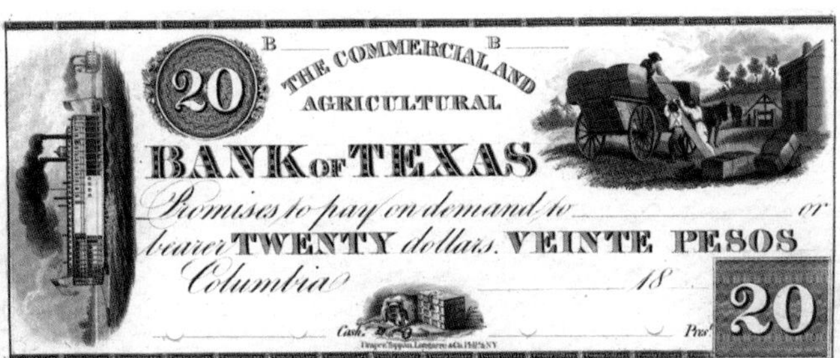

Engraver: Draper, Toppan, Longacre & Co. ***Comments:*** H-TX-5-G12, Medlar-23. Also payable "Veinte Pesos." 18__. 1830s.

Rarity: URS-1

Proof $7,500

$50 • W-TX-040-050-G070

DG

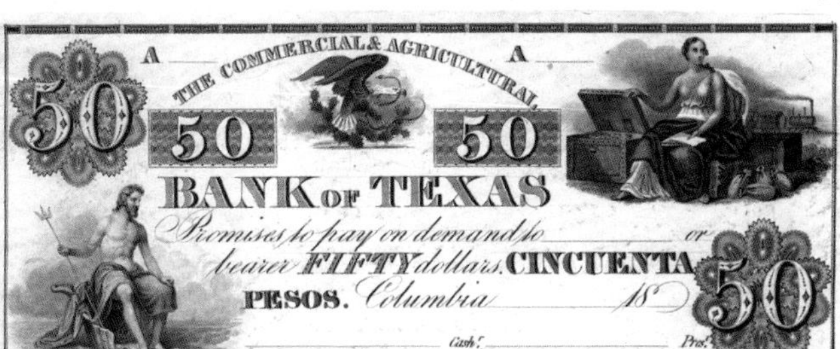

Engraver: Draper, Toppan, Longacre & Co. ***Comments:*** H-Unlisted, Medlar-Unlisted. Also payable "Cincuenta Pesos." 18__. 1830s.

Rarity: URS-1

Proof $8,500

$100 • W-TX-040-100-G080

DG

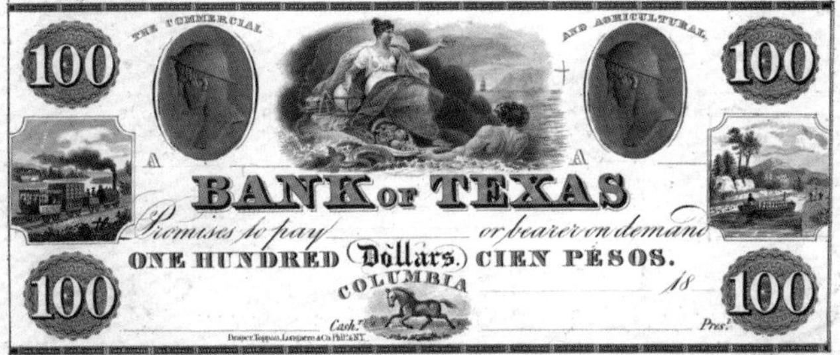

Engraver: Draper, Toppan, Longacre & Co. ***Comments:*** H-TX-5-G14, Medlar-Unlisted. Also payable "Cien Pesos." 18__. 1830s.

Rarity: URS-1

Proof $9,500

How to Read the Whitman Numbering System

$1 • W-AL-020-001-G010a

Denomination: Face value of the note shown.

W: Whitman number. This number is a sortable code unique to each bank and note.

AL: Abbreviation for the state under study.

020: Numerical designation specific to each bank.

001: The denomination in dollars.

G010a: G indicates a good or valid note. Other categories are indicated thus: C (counterfeit); R (raised); S (spurious); N (not-attributed); A (altered). Numbers are assigned starting with 010, 020, et seq. Terminal letters following the number indicate variations of a note: a series of different colored overprints, tints, payees, etc., all on the same design of note. For more information, see the "How to Use This Book" section at the front of the volume, page xiv.

Uncut Sheets

$1-$1-$1-$1 • W-TX-040-001.001.001.001-US010 RG

Engraver: Draper, Toppan, Longacre & Co. ***Comments:*** H-TX-5-G2, G2, G2, G2. All four notes identical. 18__. 1830s.

Rarity: URS-6

Unc-Rem $1,750; **Proof** $10,000

Selected auction price: Heritage Auctions, April 2015, Lot 19325, Proof $10,575

$3-$2-$2-$2 • W-TX-040-003.002.002.002-US020 DG

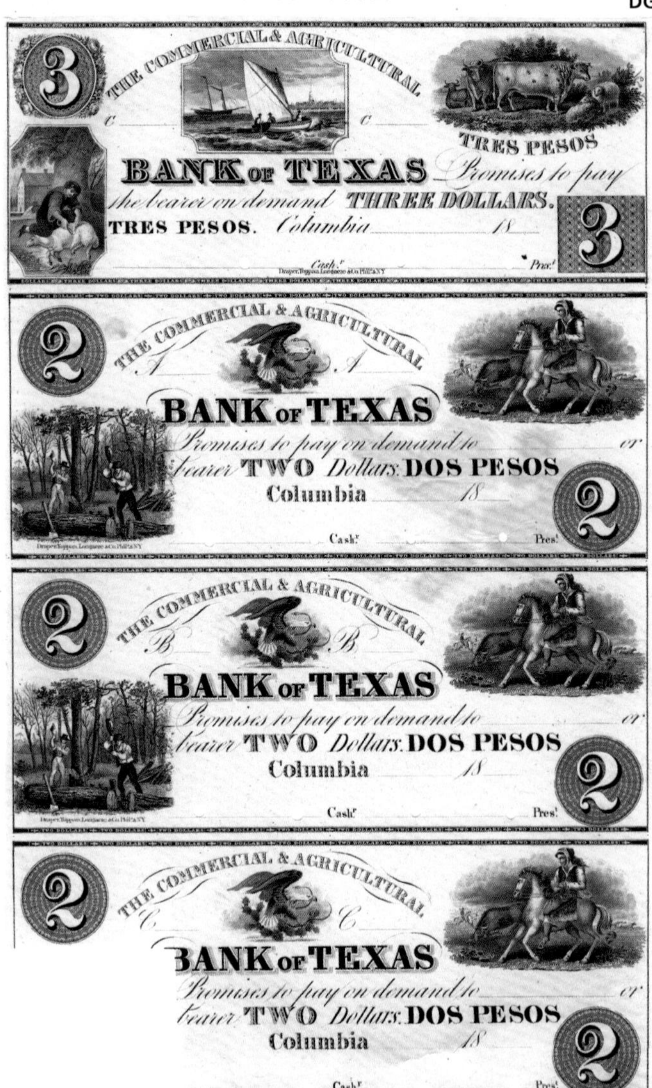

Engraver: Draper, Toppan, Longacre & Co. ***Comments:*** H-TX-5-G6, G4, G4, G4. Last three notes identical. Bottom corner cut. 18__. 1830s.

Rarity: URS-1

Proof $12,500

$3-$3-$5-$5 •

W-TX-040-003.003.005.005-US030 DG

Engraver: Draper, Toppan, Longacre & Co. ***Comments:*** H-TX-5-G6, G6, G8, G8. First two notes identical; last two notes identical. 18__. 1830s.

Rarity: URS-1
Proof $18,000

$10-$10-$20-$20 •

W-TX-040-010.010.020.020-US040 DG

Engraver: Draper, Toppan, Longacre & Co. ***Comments:*** H-TX-5-G10, G10, G12, G12. First two notes identical; last two notes identical. 18__. 1830s.

Rarity: URS-1
Proof $25,000

$50-$100 • W-TX-040-050.100-US050 DG

Engraver: Draper, Toppan, Longacre & Co. ***Comments:*** H-Unlisted, H-TX-5-G14. 18__. 1830s.

Rarity: URS-1
Proof $17,500

Galveston, Texas

Galveston (or Galveston Island) was originally inhabited by the Karankawa and Akokisa Native Americans. At that time the land was called Auia. In 1528 Spanish explorer Álvar Núñez Cabeza de Vaca (literally "Head of a Cow") was shipwrecked on the island but did not remain. José de Evia arrived in 1785 and called the island Gálveztown in honor of Bernardo de Gálvez y Madrid (the Count of Galvez). The first permanent settlement was built in 1816 by Louis-Michel Aury, a pirate in support of Mexico's rebellion against Spain. The following year the pirate Jean Lafitte took over and made the island his kingdom, calling it Campeche and establishing himself as the head of government. The U.S. Navy forced the pirates off of the island in 1821.

In 1825 the Port of Galveston was established by the General Congress of the United Mexican States. In 1830 a customs house was built. The city was officially incorporated by the Republic of Texas in 1839 and became a strong port of entry to Texas. New settlers arrived during the 1840s, including a flood of German immigrants and Jewish merchants.

For Texas, Galveston was the home of the first post office and naval base in 1836; the first cotton compress in 1842; the first insurance company in 1854; and the first gas lights in 1856. The inhabitants of Galveston opposed slavery and supported the Union during the Civil War. In January 1863 Union troops were forced from the city in the Battle of Galveston. After the war ended, the city suffered, attacked by a yellow-fever epidemic. Waterfront cities across the nation experienced these epidemics, along with bouts of cholera.

Commercial and Agricultural Bank of Texas

1847–1858

W-TX-050

History: On April 30, 1835, the Commercial and Agricultural Bank of Texas was established. However, the bank did not officially open. Notes were printed in anticipation for a parent-bank address at Columbia, W-TX-040. At the time a branch was located in Brazos, W-TX-010.

On December 30, 1847, Samuel M. Williams reorganized the bank under the original charter to become the only banking institution in the state of Texas. It went into operation on January 1, 1848. Williams and a Mr. McMillan were elected president and cashier, respectively. The bank was considered to be established under honorable conditions. The paid-in capital was $300,000.

In June 1855 the capital was valued at $322,000, where it remained through May 1857. A contemporary reporter wrote that:

> since the establishment of this bank the mercantile interest of this portion of Texas has been much benefited as it has introduced a system of promptness in taking up promissory notes on the day on which they are due, which was far from being the custom in olden times; besides which, this establishment does a good business in exchange and has been a great convenience to the merchants of Galveston.[5]

In 1858 Samuel Williams passed away, and the affairs of the bank were wound up by B.A. Shepherd, one of the stockholders. In 1859 *Bankers' Magazine* reported that the bank was "in the process of liquidation, and no other can be established in that state without a change in the constitution."[6]

The Commercial and Agricultural Bank of Texas had a branch bank located in Brownsville, W-TX-030.

Numismatic Commentary: Notes of the Commercial and Agricultural Bank located in Galveston are generally uncollectible, although certain $10 counterfeits dated January 1, 1848, are seen now and then.

Remaining at the American Bank Note Co. archives as of 2003 was a $10-$20-$50-$100 back plate, a $1-$1-$1-$3 back plate, a $1-$1-$1-$3 face plate, and a $5-$5-$5-$10 back plate.

Valid Issues

$1 • W-TX-050-001-G010 HA

Engraver: Danforth & Hufty. ***Comments:*** H-TX-6-G2, Medlar-Unlisted. 184_. 1848.

Rarity: URS-2
VF $5,000

$1 • **W-TX-050-001-G010a** DG, DG

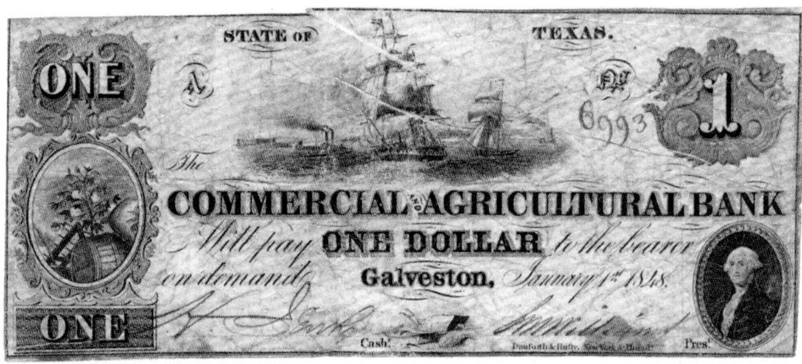

Back: Blue outlining white 1 / TEXAS / 1. ***Engraver:*** Danforth & Hufty. ***Comments:*** H-TX-6-G2a, Medlar-3. Similar to W-TX-050-001-G010 but with different date. January 1st, 1848.

Rarity: URS-2

VF $5,000

$2 • **W-TX-050-002-G020**

Engraver: Danforth & Hufty. ***Comments:*** H-Unlisted, Medlar-4. No description available. January 1, 1848.

Rarity: *None known*

$3 • **W-TX-050-003-G030** DG

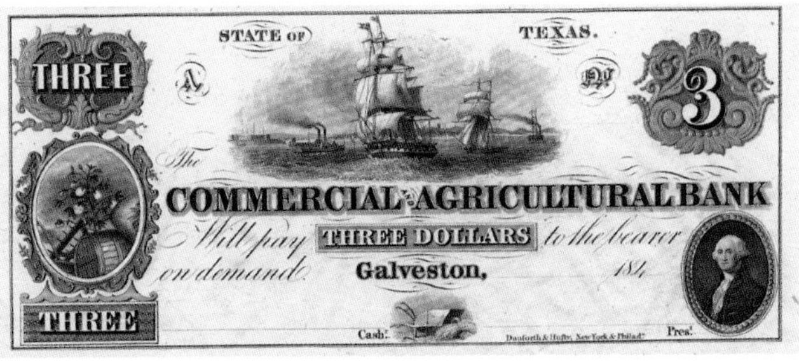

Engraver: Danforth & Hufty. ***Comments:*** H-TX-6-G4, Medlar-Unlisted. Likely made only as Proofs. 184_. 1848.

Rarity: URS-1

Proof $5,000

$3 • **W-TX-050-003-G030a** DG, DG

Back: Blue outlining white 3 / TEXAS / 3. ***Engraver:*** Danforth & Hufty. ***Comments:*** H-TX-6-G4a, Medlar-5. Similar to W-TX-050-003-G030 but with different date. January 1st, 1848.

Rarity: URS-1

VG $5,000; **Proof** $6,000

$5 • **W-TX-050-005-G040** DG

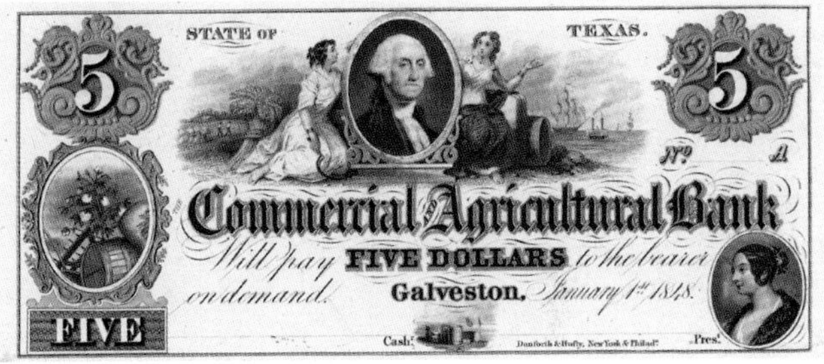

Engraver: Danforth & Hufty. ***Comments:*** H-Unlisted, Medlar-6. January 1st, 1848.

Rarity: URS-1

Proof $6,000

$10 • **W-TX-050-010-G050** DG

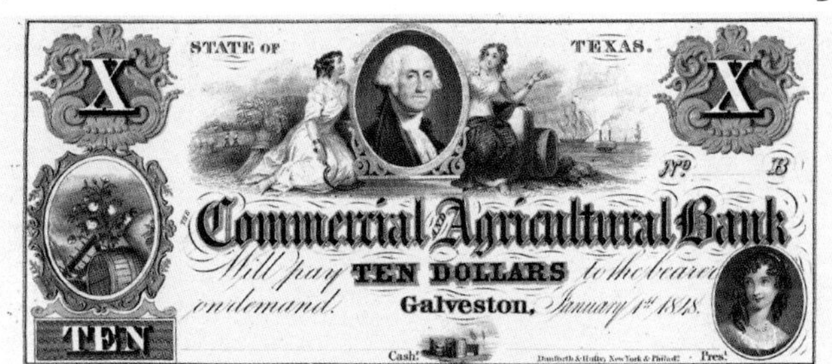

Engraver: Danforth & Hufty. ***Comments:*** H-TX-6-G8, Medlar-Unlisted. Likely made only as Proofs. January 1st, 1848.

Rarity: URS-1

Proof $6,000

$10 • **W-TX-050-010-G050a** DG, DG

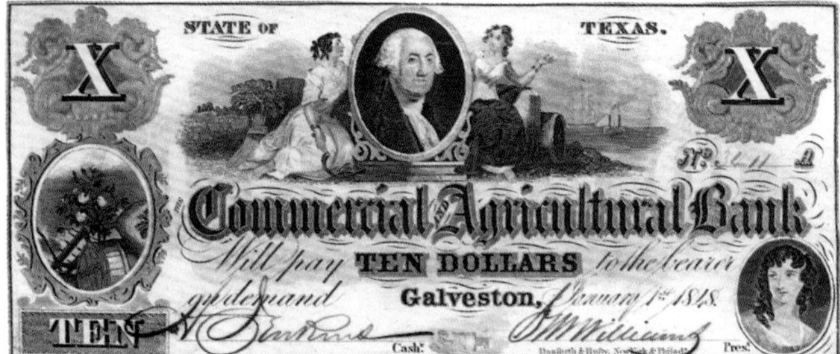

Back: Blue outlining white 10 / TEXAS / 10. ***Engraver:*** Danforth & Hufty. ***Comments:*** H-TX-6-G8a, Medlar-7. Similar to W-TX-050-010-G050. January 1st, 1848.

Rarity: URS-2
VF $5,500

$20 • **W-TX-050-020-G060** DG

Engraver: Danforth & Hufty. ***Comments:*** H-TX-6-G10, Medlar-Unlisted. Likely made only as Proofs. 18__. 1848.

Rarity: URS-1
Proof $7,500

$20 • **W-TX-050-020-G060a**

Back: Blue outlining white 20 / TEXAS / 20. ***Engraver:*** Danforth & Hufty. ***Comments:*** H-TX-6-G10a, Medlar-8. Similar to W-TX-050-020-G060 but with different date. January 1, 1848.

Rarity: *None known*

$50 • **W-TX-050-050-G070** DG

Engraver: Danforth & Hufty. ***Comments:*** H-TX-6-G12, Medlar-9. Likely made only as Proofs. 18__. 1848.

Rarity: URS-1
Proof $7,500

$50 • **W-TX-050-050-G070a**

Back: Blue outlining white 50 / TEXAS / 50. ***Engraver:*** Danforth & Hufty. ***Comments:*** H-TX-6-G12a, Medlar-Unlisted. Similar to W-TX-050-050-G070 but with different date. January 1, 1848.

Rarity: *None known*

$100 • **W-TX-050-100-G080** DG

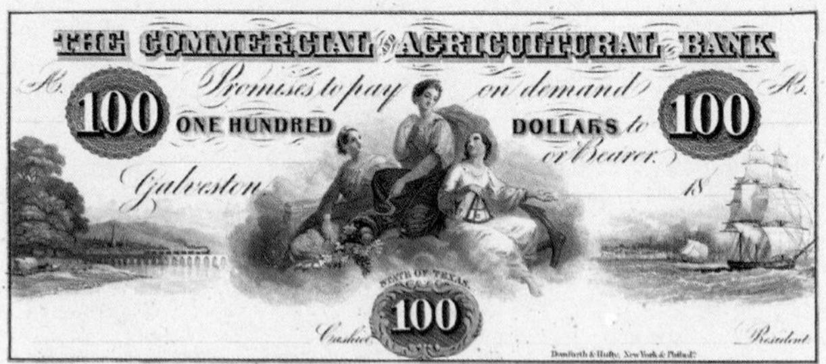

Engraver: Danforth & Hufty. ***Comments:*** H-TX-6-G14, Medlar-Unlisted. Likely made only as Proofs. 18__. 1848.

Rarity: URS-1
Proof $10,000

$100 • **W-TX-050-100-G080a** DG, DG

Back: Blue outlining white 100 / TEXAS vertically / C / TEXAS vertically / 100. ***Engraver:*** Danforth & Hufty. ***Comments:*** H-TX-6-G14a, Medlar-10. Similar to W-TX-050-100-G080 but with different date. 18__. 1848.

Rarity: URS-1
VF $12,500

Notes on Which the Place Payable is Blank

$5 • **W-TX-050-005-G090**

Engraver: Danforth & Hufty. ***Comments:*** H-TX-6-G36, Medlar-Unlisted. No description available. Likely made only as Proofs. January 1, 1848.

Rarity: *None known*

$5 • **W-TX-050-005-G090a**

Back: Blue. ***Engraver:*** Danforth & Hufty. ***Comments:*** H-TX-6-G36a, Medlar-Unlisted. No description available. Similar to W-TX-050-005-G090. January 1, 1848.

Rarity: *None known*

$10 • **W-TX-050-010-G100**

Left: X / Cotton plant, barrel, implements / TEN. ***Center:*** Portrait of George Washington flanked by Ceres and woman. ***Bottom center:*** Bales and barrels. ***Right:*** X / Portrait of Rachel Jackson. ***Engraver:*** Danforth & Hufty. ***Comments:*** H-TX-6-G38, Medlar-Unlisted. Likely made only as Proofs. January 1, 1848.

Rarity: *None known*

$10 • **W-TX-050-010-G100a**

Back: Blue outlining white 10 / TEXAS / 10. ***Engraver:*** Danforth & Hufty. ***Comments:*** H-TX-6-G38a, Medlar-Unlisted. Similar to W-TX-050-010-G100. January 1, 1848.

Rarity: *None known*

Uncut Sheets

$1-$1-$1-$3 • **W-TX-050-001.001.001.003-US010** DG

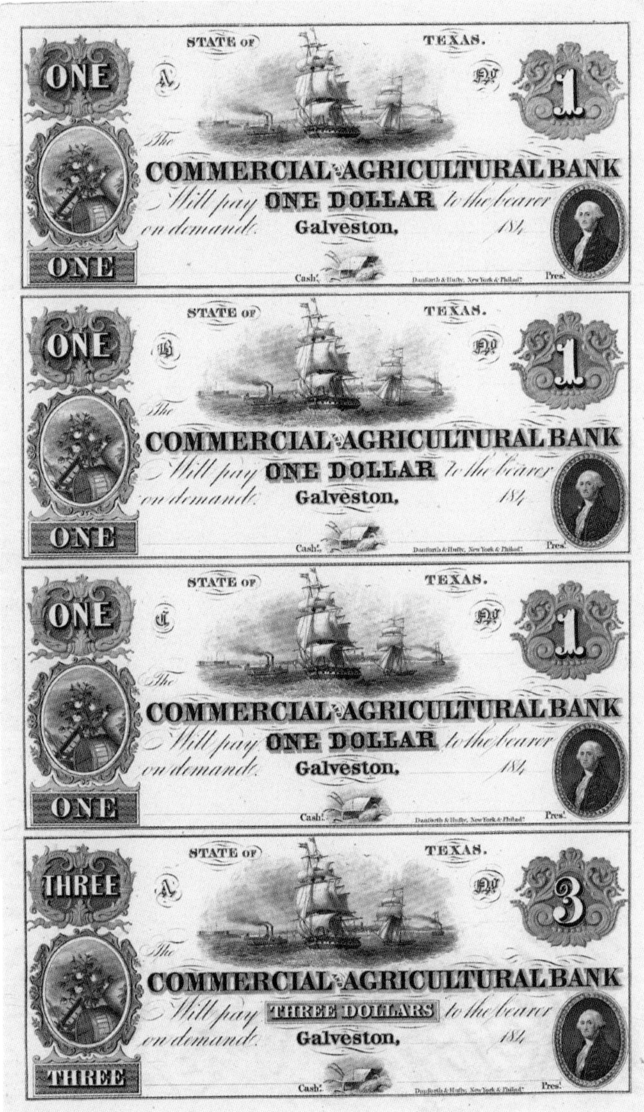

Engraver: Danforth & Hufty. ***Comments:*** H-TX-6-G2, G2, G2, G4. First three notes identical. 184_. 1848.

Rarity: URS-1
Proof $22,500

$5-$5-$5-$10 • **W-TX-050-005.005.005.010-US020** DG

Engraver: Danforth & Hufty. ***Comments:*** H-Unlisted, H-Unlisted, H-Unlisted, H-TX-5-G8. First three notes identical. January 1st, 1848.

Rarity: URS-1
Proof $22,500

$100-$50-$20-$10 •
W-TX-050-100.050.020.010-US030

DG

Engraver: Danforth & Hufty. ***Comments:*** H-TX-6-G14, G12, G10, G8. Variously dated 18__, 18__, 18__, January 1st, 1848. 1848.

Rarity: URS-1
Proof $30,500

Non-Valid Issues

$10 • W-TX-050-010-C050a

DG, DG

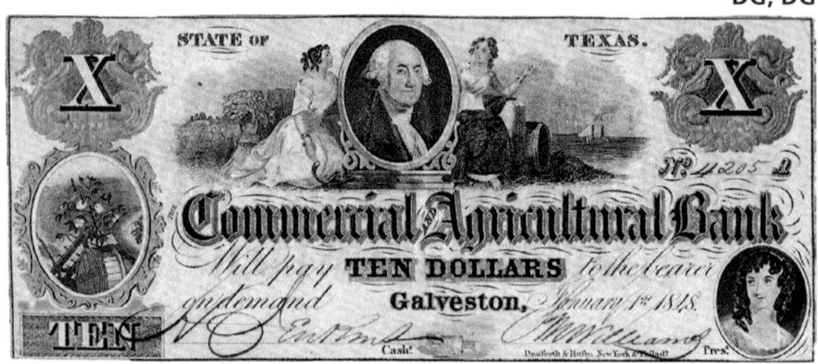

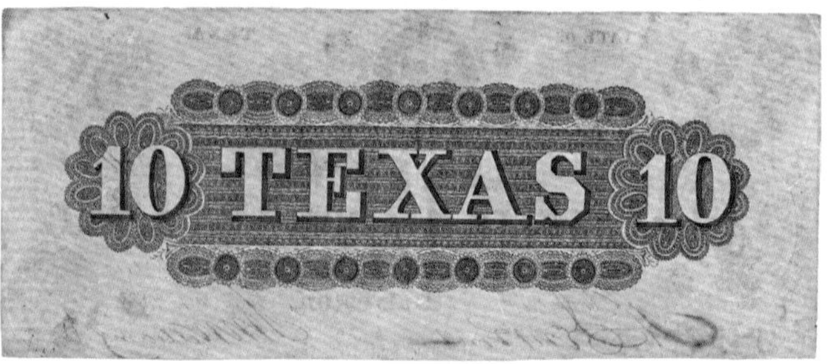

Back: Blue outlining white 10 / TEXAS / 10. ***Engraver:*** Danforth & Hufty. ***Comments:*** H-TX-6-C8a, Medlar-Unlisted. Counterfeit of W-TX-050-010-G050a. January 1st, 1848.

Rarity: URS-5
VF $3,500

Selected auction price(s): Heritage Auctions, January 2015, Lot 18824, Choice About Uncirculated $3,290; Heritage Auctions, April 2015, Lot 18508, Choice About New $1,938; Heritage Auctions, April 2015, Lot 18509, EF $2,820; Heritage Auctions, September 2015, Lot 18344, Unc $2,350; Heritage Auctions, April 2014, Lot 15417, VF $3,525

Northern Bank of Mississippi
1850s–1860s
W-TX-060

History: The Northern Bank of Mississippi was incorporated on April 28, 1837, at Holly Springs, Mississippi, with an authorized capital of $2,000,000. In April 1858 it was reported that the bank had been "brought into operation with the express intent of circulating its notes at a distance. Few of them were seen in Mississippi; but some of them found their way into Arkansas, and the endorsement of them by a commercial firm at Galveston, gave them wide circulation in Texas."[7]

Between 1846 and 1852, Texas law held staunch reservations against the issuance of bank notes. Nevertheless, R. & D.G. Mills, a commercial house located in Galveston, put the notes of the Northern Bank of Mississippi into circulation under their own endorsement and backing. Being the richest commercial house in Texas and "regarded with unshaken confidence," R. & D.G. Mills gave the notes the stability they needed in order to be recognize as viable currency. The notes were known as "Mills' money" and had a circulation between $40,000 and $300,000.[8] The locals considered the money to be of good standing, despite their own inhibitions about the source bank, which was held to be unsound. The Mississippi and Alabama Rail Road notes also carry their endorsement on the backs of the issues.

On February 7, 1862, it was reported by the *State Gazette* in Austin that the Mills house had been suspended. Panic gripped the public, but the resolution was better than thought, and though Mills had losses to report, it bounced back swiftly. By the time of the Civil War it was operating successfully once more.

See also listing under Holly Springs, Mississippi, W-MS-400.

Numismatic Commentary: While notes of the Northern Bank of Mississippi circulated extensively in Texas, none have been found bearing any Texas imprint on them.

Vernon, Texas

A fraudulent bank circulated notes with a Vernon imprint long before there was ever a Vernon, Texas. A town called Eagle Springs was incorporated as Vernon in 1880, named after George Washington's home of Mount Vernon.

Bank of Vernon

1840s

W-TX-070

History: A fraudulent bank represented only by spurious notes that were then altered to other banks around the country. In 1842 it was reported that the Bank of Wooster, Wooster, Ohio, had $10 notes altered from the Bank of Vernon circulating.[9]

Issues

$5 • W-TX-070-005-G010

Center: Two Indians pointing to ship and steamboat. ***Engraver:*** Boston Bank Note Co. ***Comments:*** H-TX-10-G8, Medlar-Unlisted. 18__. 1840s.

Rarity: *None known*

$10 • W-TX-070-010-G020

Left: TEN / Woman wearing hat and holding sickle / 10. ***Center:*** X / Two eagles flanking shield bearing anchor / X. ***Right:*** 10 / Ship and steamboat / TEN. ***Engraver:*** Boston Bank Note Co. ***Comments:*** H-TX-10-G10, Medlar-Unlisted. 18__. 1840s.

Rarity: *None known*

$20 • W-TX-070-020-G030

Center: Reaper seated on stone holding sickle, Wheat field and farmhouse. ***Engraver:*** Boston Bank Note Co. ***Comments:*** H-TX-10-G12, Medlar-Unlisted. 18__. 1840s.

Rarity: *None known*

$50 • W-TX-070-050-G040

Center: Sailor seated on bales holding U.S. flag, Vessels. ***Engraver:*** Boston Bank Note Co. ***Comments:*** H-TX-10-G14, Medlar-Unlisted. 18__. 1840s.

Rarity: *None known*

Waco, Texas

The Wichita Native American tribe (also called the Waco Indians) occupied present-day Waco for many years before Spanish settlers arrived. In 1825 Stephen F. Austin made a treaty with the inhabitants, and the land was transferred to pioneers. Neil McLennan arrived in 1838; Jacob de Cordova bought his property and hired George B. Erath to survey the land. In 1849 the first block of the city was laid out.

The name Lamartine was initially considered for the city, but Erath convinced landowners to name the area Waco in honor of the original inhabitants. In March 1849 the first house was built. In 1866 entrepreneurs decided to build the first bridge spanning the Brazos River. This effort spawned the Waco Bridge Company, which built the Waco Suspension Bridge, completed in 1870, that spanned 475 feet of river.

Bank of the Republic of Texas

1839 and 1840

W-TX-080

History: On January 21, 1839, a bill to incorporate the Bank of the Republic of Texas was voted upon. The desire was to establish a national bank with the credit and resources of the Republic. It would be a government-controlled entity, both in terms of capital and in terms of officers. It would serve as the government's fiscal agent and a bank of deposit. Branches were to be established as needed throughout Texas. In 1840 a loan was sought to establish the bank, but it was never finalized.[10]

Endnotes

Alabama

1. John J. Knox, *The History of Banking*, New York, Bradford Rhodes & Company, 1900.

2. Walter Rosene Jr., *Alabama Obsolete Notes and Scrip*, Society of Paper Money Collectors, Inc., 1984.

3. Walter Rosene Jr., *Alabama Obsolete Notes and Scrip*, Society of Paper Money Collectors, Inc., 1984.

4. Walter Rosene Jr., *Alabama Obsolete Notes and Scrip*, Society of Paper Money Collectors, Inc., 1984.

5. Walter Rosene Jr., *Alabama Obsolete Notes and Scrip*, Society of Paper Money Collectors, Inc., 1984.

6. Walter Rosene Jr., *Alabama Obsolete Notes and Scrip*, Society of Paper Money Collectors, Inc., 1984.

7. *Bankers' Magazine*, June 1848.

8. Walter Rosene Jr., *Alabama Obsolete Notes and Scrip*, Society of Paper Money Collectors, Inc., 1984.

Arkansas

1. John J. Knox, *The History of Banking*, New York, Bradford Rhodes & Company, 1900.

2. John J. Knox, *The History of Banking*, New York, Bradford Rhodes & Company, 1900.

3. Matt Rothert Sr., NLG, *Arkansas Obsolete Notes and Scrip*, Society of Paper Money Collectors, Inc., 1985.

4. John J. Knox, *The History of Banking*, New York, Bradford Rhodes & Company, 1900.

5. Davis R. Dewey, *State Banking Before the Civil War*, 1910, p. 160.

6. John J. Knox, *The History of Banking*, New York, Bradford Rhodes & Company, 1900.

Kentucky

1. *Niles' Weekly Register*, March 9, 1816. The Haxby text does not list bills of the $50 and $100 denomination.

2. *Niles' Weekly Register*, April 24, 1819.

3. *Niles' Weekly Register*, April 17, 1819.

4. *Bankers' Magazine*, October 1846.

5. William M. Gouge, *The Curse of Paper-Money and Banking*, 1833, p. 88.

6. Earl Hughes, *Kentucky Obsolete Notes and Scrip*, 1998.

7. Davis R. Dewey, *State Banking Before the Civil War*, 1910, p. 21.

8. Basil Wilson Duke, *History of Bank of Kentucky, 1792–1895*, 1980, p. 38.

9. Basil Wilson Duke, *History of Bank of Kentucky, 1792–1895*, 1980, p. 49.

10. *Bankers' Magazine*, November 1849.

11. *Bankers' Magazine*, September 1870.

12. Journal of the House of Representatives of the Commonwealth of Kentucky, 1853, p. 458.

Louisiana

1. S.A. Trufant, *Review of Banking in New Orleans, 1830–1840*, p. 13.

2. *N.O. Picayune,* October 3.

3. *Bankers' Magazine*, April 1848.

4. Davis R. Dewey, *State Banking Before the Civil War*, 1910, p. 40.

5. S.A. Trufant, *Review of Banking in New Orleans, 1830–1840*, p. 8

6. *Hunt's Merchant's Magazine and Commercial Review*, April 1850, p. 451.

7. *Hunt's Merchant's Magazine and Commercial Review*, April 1850, p. 451.

8. *Bankers' Magazine*, May 1850.

9. S.A. Trufant, *Review of Banking in New Orleans, 1830–1840*, p. 13.

10. Norman Walter, *Standard History of New Orleans*, Louisiana, Municipal Government; Henry Rightor, editor, *Municipal and Military History*, The Lewis Publishing Company, Chicago, 1900.

11. Google's *Journal of Banking* reports a statement from the New Orleans Bank for May 1841 which gives the amount of real estate loans separate from other loans. The amount was $37,793,798.

12. *Bankers' Magazine*, February 1848.

13. Condy Raguet, *The Financial Register of the United States*, Vol. 2, p. 29.

14. *Niles' Register,* Oct. 8, 1832, Vol. 43, p. 87.

15. John J. Knox, *The History of Banking*, New York, Bradford Rhodes & Company, 1900.

16. S.A. Trufant, *Review of Banking in New Orleans, 1830–1840*, p. 13.

17. S.A. Trufant, *Review of Banking in New Orleans, 1830–1840*, p. 13.

Mississippi

1. *Farmers' Register*, 1841, pg. 186.

2. L. Chandler Leggett, *Mississippi Obsolete Paper Money and Scrip*, Society of Paper Money Collectors, Inc., 1975.

3. The reference is to Nicholas Biddle, earlier associated with the second Bank of the United States (charter expired in 1836). Biddle later set up the Bank of the United States of Pennsylvania. He omitted "of Pennsylvania" on his notes, misleading the public. The new bank failed and Biddle, a scion of Philadelphia society, died in disgrace.

4. *Laws of the State of Mississippi*, 1862, p. 162.

5. L. Chandler Leggett, *Mississippi Obsolete Paper Money and Scrip*, Society of Paper Money Collectors, Inc., 1975.

6. *Niles' National Register,* April 6, 1839.

7. *Laws of the State of Mississippi*, 1862, p. 162.

8. *Laws of the State of Mississippi*, 1862, p. 162.

9. Francis Preston Blair, *The Extra Globe*, Washington, D.C., 1839, pg. 231.

10. L. Chandler Leggett, *Mississippi Obsolete Paper Money and Scrip*, Society of Paper Money Collectors, Inc., 1975.

11. *Laws of the State of Mississippi*, 1862, p. 161.

12. *Bankers' Magazine and Statistical Register*, Vol. 14, Part 1, pg. 6.

13. L. Chandler Leggett, *Mississippi Obsolete Paper Money and Scrip*, Society of Paper Money Collectors, Inc., 1975.

14. *Laws of the State of Mississippi*, 1862, pp. 147–162.

15. L. Chandler Leggett, *Mississippi Obsolete Paper Money and Scrip*, Society of Paper Money Collectors, Inc., 1975.

16. John J. Knox, *The History of Banking*, New York, Bradford Rhodes & Company, 1900, p. 325.

17. L. Chandler Leggett, *Mississippi Obsolete Paper Money and Scrip*, Society of Paper Money Collectors, Inc., 1975.

18. *Laws of the State of Mississippi*, 1862, p. 161.

19. L. Chandler Leggett, *Mississippi Obsolete Paper Money and Scrip*, Society of Paper Money Collectors, Inc., 1975.

20. L. Chandler Leggett, *Mississippi Obsolete Paper Money and Scrip*, Society of Paper Money Collectors, Inc., 1975.

21. Troy Woods. *Delta Plantations: The Beginning*. Published by the author, 2010.

22. L. Chandler Leggett, *Mississippi Obsolete Paper Money and Scrip*, Society of Paper Money Collectors, Inc., 1975.

23. *Niles' National Register,* April 6, 1839.

24. L. Chandler Leggett, *Mississippi Obsolete Paper Money and Scrip*, Society of Paper Money Collectors, Inc., 1975.

25. *Niles' National Register,* April 6, 1839.

26. *Laws of the State of Mississippi*, 1862, p. 161.

27. L. Chandler Leggett, *Mississippi Obsolete Paper Money and Scrip*, Society of Paper Money Collectors, Inc., 1975.

28. *Niles' National Register,* April 6, 1839.

29. *Laws of the State of Mississippi*, 1862, p. 162.

Tennessee

1. *Bankers' Magazine*, August 1856, p. 84.

2. *Bankers' Magazine*, August 1856, p. 84.

3. *Bankers' Magazine*, June 1854.

4. Reports of Cases Argued and Determined in the Supreme Court of Tennessee, Vol. 39.

5. *Weekly Racine Advocate*, Wednesday, July 22, 1857, Racine, Wisconsin, pg. 3.

6. *Bankers' Magazine*, August 1856, p. 87.

7. *Bankers' Magazine*, June 1852.

8. *Bankers' Magazine*, August 1856, p. 84.

9. William M. Gouge, *The Curse of Paper-Money and Banking*, 1833, p. 95.

10. William M. Gouge, *The Curse of Paper-Money and Banking*, 1833, p. 95.

11. John J. Knox, *The History of Banking*, New York, Bradford Rhodes & Company, 1900.

12. John J. Knox, *The History of Banking*, New York, Bradford Rhodes & Company, 1900.

13. John J. Knox, *The History of Banking*, New York, Bradford Rhodes & Company, 1900.

14. John J. Knox, *The History of Banking*, New York, Bradford Rhodes & Company, 1900.

15. Reports of Cases Argued and Determined in the Supreme Court of Tennessee, Vol. 39.

16. *Bankers' Magazine*, June 1852.

17. *Bankers' Magazine*, August 1856, p. 84.

18. John J. Knox, *The History of Banking*, New York, Bradford Rhodes & Company, 1900.

19. Reports of Cases Argued and Determined in the Supreme Court of Tennessee, Vol. 39.

20. *Weekly Racine Advocate*, Wednesday, July 22, 1857, Racine, Wisconsin, pg. 3.

Texas

1. There was no town named Vernon in Texas at the time. Years later in 1880 a community was named Vernon, but there was no connection to earlier currency bearing that imprint.

2. *Bankers' Magazine*, February 1853, p. 616 (from *History of Banking*).

3. John J. Knox, *The History of Banking*, New York, Bradford Rhodes & Company, 1900.

4. *Bankers' Magazine*, February 1853, p. 616 (from *History of Banking*).

5. *The Book of Texas*, p. 284.

6. *Bankers' Magazine*, Volume 13, p. 411.

7. *Bankers' Magazine and Statistical Register*, Volume 14, Part 1, pg 6.

8. John J. Knox, *The History of Banking*, New York, Bradford Rhodes & Company, 1900.

9. *Journal of Banking from July 1841 to July 1842*, p. 140.

10. John J. Knox, *The History of Banking*, New York, Bradford Rhodes & Company, 1900.

Glossary

back—the paper-money equivalent of "reverse" used for coins. The front side of a note is called the face.

bank—in the present context, a business set up under a state or federal (e.g. Bank of the United States) charter to engage in the business of receiving and disbursing funds, making loans, issuing paper money, and engaging in related activities.

bank note—a small, rectangular piece of paper money $1 face value or higher issued by a state-chartered bank. Imprinted with a denomination or value and the name/location of the issuing bank. Intended for use in commercial transactions. *Synonyms*: bill, note, bank bill.

bank-note reporter—commercial booklet or publication sold at a premium to bankers, merchants, etc., listing whether banks were solvent or not, descriptions of their notes, and the discounts at which their paper currency traded with exchange brokers and in commerce. *Synonym*: counterfeit detector.

bill—see *bank note.*

blue pup—nickname for a bank that later became insolvent or a circulating note issued by a bank that would not redeem their bills at par. *Synonyms*: owl, red dog.

burin—small, sharp, steel tool, often with a wooden handle, used to carefully engrave on a copper or steel plate.

Canada green—see *Patent green tint.*

capital of a bank—the amount of money authorized by a state charter to be paid in by shareholders and provide funds for a bank's operation.

cashier—in a small bank, the chief operating officer, sometimes the only employee, who opened and closed the bank, signed and supervised the issuance of currency, made loans (often subject to the approval of others), and conducted the business of the bank. The highest-salaried employee. In a large bank, the officer in charge of funds, receipts, and payments, the keeper of bank records.

certified note—a note graded and placed in a sealed holder by a commercial grading service.

charter—operating authorization given by a state legislature to permit a company to engage in banking.

charter expiration—charters were sometimes given to banks for a specific term, such as 20 years, after which a renewal could be applied for. In other instances, a corporation was dissolved and the same people obtained a new charter to continue in business.

circulation of a bank—the total face-value of a given bank's bills in commercial circulation (not including notes held in the bank's vault or not yet issued).

clearing house—a bank or organization that took in bills from various sources and sent them to member banks for exchange or redemption.

counter—technical name for the part of a note showing the denomination in a separate vignette, such as 5, 10, 20, etc., or as a Roman numeral, V, X, M, etc. Some counters are very ornate.

counterfeit—a bill in imitation of an original design but printed from false plates by someone not authorized to do so.

counterfeit detector—see *bank-note reporter*. Often spelled "detecter" in the mid-19th century.

country bank—a bank located in a town or village, not a city or metropolitan area. Sometimes bills of country banks traded at a discount in comparison to banks with large capital located in cities.

cycloidal configuration—latticework, usually printed in color, with arcs and inscriptions said to deter counterfeiting. Also referred to as the "cycloidal" or "kaleidograph counter." Term used by the National Bank Note Company, which utilized James McDonough's patent of March 23, 1860, in which an engraving combined the name of the issuer, the denomination, and geometric, cycloidal, rosette work into a product to prevent alteration or counterfeiting of bank notes.

cylinder die—see *transfer roll.*

date on a note—the time that a note or series of notes was issued. Sometimes a partial date such as 18__ was given, after which the year, month, and day would be added in ink. In other instances a full date was given, such as Jany. 1, 1853, representing the date of a certain series or design. Months were usually abbreviated. Notes with such a printed date could be used for a long time afterward.

denomination—the face or stated value printed on a bill, this being the amount for which the bill could be redeemed in specie or exchanged for other bills. Popular denominations of bills in use in commerce included $1, $2, $3, $5, $10, $20, $50, and $100. Other denominations were occasionally used.

deposit bank—a bank into which the Treasury Department placed federal funds. During the 1830s these were nicknamed "pet banks." Also spelled "deposite."

deuce—numismatic nickname for a $2 bill.

engraver—a skilled artist who, with a burin and other tools, hand-engraves lettering, motifs, and other elements into a printing plate or design element matrix. Various mechanical devices are sometimes used as well.

engraving—intaglio or recessed design elements and lettering engraved by hand or added by the siderographic process to a printing plate. A motif, print, or other reproduction on paper made from an engraved printing plate.

essay—an experimental impression of a partial or completed note printed to test the design or evaluate a concept. The paper-money equivalent of a pattern or trial-piece coin. French: *essai.*

exchange broker, broker—a person or business specializing in buying and selling current and obsolete paper money and gold and silver coins.

face—the paper-money equivalent of "obverse" used for coins. The reverse side of a note is called the back.

free bank—a bank set up under one or another of the state laws enacted from the late 1830s onward whereby any group of people could form a bank providing that assurances were made that sufficient capital would be raised.

geometric lathe—machine that uses gears and linkages to create rosettes, spirals, and other decorative elements on a soft metal plate, which is then hardened and reproduced through siderography for use in creating bank-note printing plates.

grade—designation assigned by numismatists to signify the amount of wear or circulation a note has experienced and its condition today (see How-To-Use for more information). Grading can be expressed by adjectives such as Good, Extremely Fine, and Uncirculated or by abbreviations in combination with numbers from 1 to 70, such as EF-40 or Unc-63 (adapted from the American Numismatic Association coin-grading system).

green tint—see *Patent green tint.*

imprint—printed information added to a bank note, especially the name of an engraver or printer.

ink ball—a porous ball of cloth or other absorbent substance that was charged with ink and then wiped across the face of a printing plate. Superseded by the ink roller.

ink roller—a rubber roller that is partly immersed in a pan or other supply of ink, then used to spread the ink across the face of a printing plate.

inked signature—the signature of a bank president or cashier on currency.

launder—often used in a derogatory sense, the cleaning of paper money to enhance its appearance. Careful cleaning, such as to remove grease or grime, can be beneficial but should be done only by experts. In the early 20th century the Treasury Department added several machines to launder soiled paper money, after which the reconditioned notes were again placed into circulation.

legal tender—a bank note that could be used to pay any and all debts except for custom duties. Most notes of state-chartered banks were accepted at par only within the region of issue.

margin—the blank area or white strip beyond the design or printed information at the border of a note. Wide margins are preferred to narrow ones. There are no general rules.

microprint, microprinting—nearly microscopic-size lettering added to a note, such as on Perkins Patent Stereotype Plate notes and related formats.

notaphily—originated by Kenneth R. Lake as a proposal to give a name to the study and appreciation of paper money. Originally found in Yasha Beresiner's "An Introduction to Paper Money," *The Numismatist*, March 1979.

note—see *bank note.*

obverse—see *face.*

overprint—color printing on a note; a design, grill, denomination, or other element intended to defer counterfeiting. Sometimes these were applied before the black section of the note was printed.

owl—nickname for a circulating note issued by a bank that would not redeem them at par or a bank that later became insolvent. Inspired by the worthless bills of the Owl Creek Bank of Mount Vernon, Ohio. *Synonyms*: blue pup, red dog.

panic—an excitement in financial circles caused by unfavorable economic or banking conditions in which holders of bank notes and securities became frightened and rushed to convert paper to gold and silver coins.

par—the value printed on a note.

Patent green tint, green tint, "Canada green"—green imprint, usually called "overprint," of lacy green said to be a deterrent against counterfeiting. Except for paper-money sheets that required bronzing, the adding of a green tint was the first printing operation on a blank sheet as reported by S.M. Clark, *Report to the Secretary of the Treasury*, November 26, 1864. As to whether this priority was always followed is not known. The patent was held by Rawdon, Wright, Hatch & Edson, later the American Bank Note Co., having been acquired from a Canadian inventor.

payee—the first person to receive the note when it was issued. This became a nuisance, and many cashiers simply added a short name and used it over and over again. In other instances a name such as Benjamin Franklin or Henry Clay was added to the printing plate.

pet bank—popular nickname for a bank into which the Treasury Department placed federal funds during the second Andrew Jackson administration.

pinhole—in the 19th century it was common practice to stitch several notes together for safekeeping, hiding within a coat's lining, or storing in a small pile. Today, when certain notes are held to the light, tiny holes can be seen.

plate—a rectangle of copper or hardened steel with engraved or otherwise recessed lettering, motifs, and other elements used to print bank notes. Currency of the period under study was often printed four notes to a plate or, if higher denominations, two notes to a plate.

plate letter—a printed letter, often from A to D, signifying the note's position on a four-subject printing plate. In other instances, single plates with various letters were locked into a frame and plate letters were not in any order. If a plate was slightly altered, the plate letter might be given another letter to accompany it, such as Aa, aA, Ab. If a sheet had more than one denomination, each would start anew with A. As examples, a $1-$1-$1-$2 sheet might use A, B, C, A. A four-subject sheet of $5 notes would use A, B, C, D.

plate position—the position of a note on a printing plate, sometimes determinable by the plate letter.

post note—a bill imprinted with a statement that it was redeemable at par only at a later specified date.

president—the chairman of the board of directors, presided over board meetings, signed currency. Often engaged in other activities, but visited a bank occasionally. Other times a local person who was on the premises often and made decisions beyond the duties of the cashier.

printer—an individual or firm that prints bank notes using a press, plates, paper, and ink. A printer may or may not have engraving skills. Most if not all printers of bank notes also produced other products such as book plates and decorative prints.

Progressive Proof note—a note printed from a plate which was not completely finished and was absent some lettering, ornaments, or other features. Used to inspect a design as it was being created.

Proof note—a Proof (capitalization optional) note is an impression from a complete or partially complete plate for testing or to illustrate its appearance such as showing to prospective bank clients. Proof notes are usually printed on only one side and show either the front or back. Such Proof notes are highly prized today. Specimen notes are related but were not issued for test purposes. Sometimes printed on ordinary bank-note paper, often on India paper, sometimes on light cardboard or mounted on a thin card. *Synonym*: Proof.

protector—a color overprint or underprint on a note; a design, grill, denomination, or other element intended to defer counterfeiting. *Synonym*: overprint.

rag—nickname for a circulating note that either had no value or was worn to the point of tattering.

ragpicker—nickname in the past for a collector of paper money.

red dog—nickname for a circulating note issued by a bank that would not redeem them at par or a bank that later became insolvent. *Synonyms*: blue pup, owl.

reenter, re-enter—engraving or transfer process whereby original information on a bank-note printing plate is removed and new information is entered in its place. This could permit an old plate to be used for a different bank.

reverse—see *back*.

roll, roller die—see *transfer roll*.

rose machine—a geometric lathe.

run on a bank—see *panic*. Sometimes engineered by profiteers who would encourage a run through rumors of insolvency (which would depreciate the value of a bank's bills), buy up discounted notes, and later redeem them at par as a form of speculation.

safety fund, safety fund bank—a bank chartered with the requirement that it deposit certain of its capital into approved bonds and other securities.

scrip, scrip note—a bill issued by an entity other than a chartered bank, such as a canal, railroad, factory, etc. A bill issued by a bank or other entity with a face value below $1.

security features—aspects of the design or printing of a note intended to deter copying and counterfeiting. In early times, this consisted of minute design elements expertly engraved, as well as printing on special paper. Chapter 7 of volume 1 in this series discusses various methods.

selvage—unused space on a sheet of paper money beyond the normal trim borders of the individual notes.

serial number—a number inked or printed by a numbering machine on a note prior to issuing it. Banks sometimes started serial numbers anew with each day or each month. Serial numbers were kept low by keying them to dates, making them faster to write. For this reason most serial numbers are in the hundreds or low thousands.

sheet of notes, uncut sheet—an uncut group of notes, as printed, usually four subjects with denominations from $1 to $20, usually with more than one denomination per sheet. $50, $100, and higher denominations were printed two to a sheet. Many notes were printed singly in earlier times.

shinplaster—derogatory nickname popular in the early 19th century to denote a scrip note or bank note that had no monetary value, such as an issue of the Hard Times era. Derived from the popular practice of mixing paper sheets and hardener to affix to a person's shins to relieve pain.

siderography, siderographic—the process of engraving a motif, lettering, or other elements on a soft steel plate, then hardening it, after which a cylinder die or transfer roll of soft steel is forcibly rolled into its surface under high pressure in a transfer press, picking up a relief image. The cylinder die is then hardened, placed into a transfer press, and rolled with pressure into a soft steel or copper plate. This transfers the design in recessed form. The plate is then hardened and used to print notes. Lettering, emblems, and other design elements can be added to plates in this manner.

signatures on notes—usually with the cashier's signature in ink at the lower left and the president's at the lower right. Legally a note had no value until signed by both officers.

specie—gold or silver coins.

specie payment—the payment of a gold or silver coin by a bank in exchange for a bank note presented for redemption.

specimen note—a Proof note for examination or display, a plate impression not intended for circulation.

spider press—a rectangular printing press used to make bank notes. The name derives from multiple thin arms extending from the press that are slowly turned by hand to press a sheet of dampened paper into the ink-filled recesses of a printing plate.

surcharge—extra printing or information added to a note after the main printing was finished. *Synonym*: overprint.

suspension, suspension of specie payments—when a bank refused to redeem its notes in silver or gold coins. This usually happened when a bank had problems or in times of general financial distress. See *run on a bank*.

transfer roll—a hard steel cylinder with a hole at the center for a shaft, on the outside face of which is a raised design, vignette, counter, or other element used in bank-note printing. Transfer rolls are used to imprint a design into a printing plate by the siderographic process. *Synonyms*: cylinder die, roll, roller die.

Unc-Rem—grade designator signifying that an Uncirculated note is an unsigned, undated remainder.

Unc-S&D—grade designator signifying that an Uncirculated note was signed and dated, but never issued.

vignette—an ornamental or illustrative element of a bank note, such as a portrait, allegorical scene, or motif from history. Pronounced "vinn-yet."

wildcat bank—a bank with or without charter that issued paper money with little or no backing. Such banks were often set up in remote locations.

Bibliography

Baker, W.S. *American Engravers and Their Works*. Philadelphia, Pennsylvania: Gebbie & Barrie, 1875.

Bankers' Magazine. Various issues, 1840–1849, title change to *Bankers' Magazine and Statistical Register*, 1849. Other titles: *Bankers' Magazine and State Financial Register*, *Bankers' Magazine and Journal of the Money Market*. Boston, Massachusetts: Wm. Crosby and H.P. Nicholes.

Ball, Douglas B. Historical information written for and included in the catalog of the *Abner Reed Sale of United States Paper Money*, NASCA, October 31 to November 2, 1983.

Bank Note Reporter. Iola, Wisconsin: 1990s to date. Bathe, Greville and Dorothy. *Jacob Perkins: His Inventions, His Times & His Contemporaries*. The Historical Society of Philadelphia, Pennsylvania, 1943.

Benedict, Harry Yandell, and John Avery Lomax. *The Book of Texas*. Doubleday, Page, 1916.

Berkey, William A. *The Money Question*. The Legal Tender Paper Monetary System of the United States. Grand Rapids, Michigan: Published by the author, 1876.

Blair, Francis Preston. *The Extra Globe*. Washington, D.C.: Printed for the editors, 1839.

Blanchard, Julian. "Cycloidal Configurations," *Essay-Proof Journal*, Vol. 20, No. 2 (1963) through Vol. 21, No. 2 (1964). Reprint of Ormsby's circa 1862 pamphlet, with new introductory remarks.

Blanchard, Julian. "Waterman Lily Ormsby, 1809–1883, Bank Note Engraver," commencing in the *Essay-Proof Journal*, January 1957.

Bodenhorn, Howard. *State Banking in Early America: A New Economic History*. Oxford and New York: Oxford University Press, 2003.

Boggs, Winthrop S. *Ten Decades Ago 1840–1850: A Study of the Work of Rawdon, Wright, Hatch & Edson of New York City*. American Philatelic Society, 1949.

Bowers, Q. David and David M. Sundman. *100 Greatest American Currency Notes*. Atlanta, Georgia: Whitman Publishing, LLC, 2005.

Bowers, Q. David. *Obsolete Paper Money Issued by Banks in the United States, 1782–1866*. Atlanta, Georgia: Whitman Publishing, LLC, 2006.

Chaddock, Robert E. *The Safety Fund Banking System in New York 1829–1866*. Washington, D.C.: Government Printing Office, 1910, for the National Monetary Commission. 61st Congress, 2d Session, Senate, Document No. 581.

Cheap Money. New York City, New York: The Century Co., 1892.

Christie's. "Important Early American Bank Notes, 1810–1874" from the Archives of the American Bank Note Company, catalog of the auction sale held September 14 and 15, 1990.

Davis, Andrew McFarland (introduction by). *Colonial Currency Reprints*. 4 volumes. Boston, Massachusetts: The Prince Society, 1910 and 1911.

Dewey, Davis R. *State Banking Before the Civil War*. Washington, D.C.: Government Printing Office, 1910, for the National Monetary Commission. 61st Congress, 2d Session, Senate, Document No. 581.

Dewey, Davis R. *State Banking before the Civil War; and the Safety Fund Banking System in New York*. Published by the American Economic Association.

Dillistin, William H. *Bank Note Reporters and Counterfeit Detectors, 1826–1866*. Numismatic Notes and Monographs No. 114. New York City, New York: American Numismatic Society, 1949.

Doty, Richard. *Pictures from a Distant Country: Seeing America Through Old Paper Money*. Atlanta, Georgia: Whitman Publishing, LLC, 2013.

Duke, Basil Wilson. *History of the Bank of Kentucky, 1792–1895*. Arno Press, 1980.

Dunbar, Charles F. *Chapters on the Theory and History of Banking*. New York and London: G.P. Putnam's Sons, 1892.

Dunbar, Seymour. *A History of Transportation in America*. 4 volumes. Indianapolis, Indiana: The Bobbs-Merrill Company, 1915.

Duncombe, Charles. *Duncombe's Free Banking: An Essay on Banking, Currency, Finance, Exchanges, and Political Economy*. Cleveland, Ohio: Sanford & Co., 1841.

Durand, Roger H. *Interesting Notes* series: *About Denominations* (1988), *About History* (1990), *About Indians* (1991), *About Territories* (1992), *About Christmas* (1993), *About Allegorical Representations* (1994), *About Vignettes* (1995), *About Portraits* (1996), *About Vignettes II* (1996), *About Portraits II* (1997), *About Vignettes III* (2001), *About Portraits III* (2004).

Durand, Roger H. *Obsolete Notes and Scrip of Rhode Island and the Providence Plantations*, 1981.

Essay-Proof Journal. New York City, New York: The Essay-Proof Society, 1944.

Farmers' Register. Various dates. Petersburg, Virginia: Edmund Ruffin.

Ferguson, John L., and J.H. Atkinson. *Historic Arkansas*. Little Rock, Arkansas: Arkansas History Commission, 1970.

Financial Register of the United States, The. Vol. 1, July 1837 to July 1838. Philadelphia, Pennsylvania: Wirtz & Tatem, 1838.

Garland, Paul E. *The History of Early Tennessee Banks and Their Issues*. Published by the author. 1983.

Glaser, Lynn. *Counterfeiting in America*. New York City, New York: Clarkson N. Potter, Inc., 1968.

Golembe, Carter H. *State Banks and the Development of the West, 1830–1844*. New York City, New York: Arno Press, 1978. Originally presented as the author's thesis, Columbus University, 1952.

Gouge, William M. *The Curse of Paper-Money and Banking; or a Short History of Banking in the United States of America, with an Account of its Ruinous Effects on Landowners, Farmers, Trades, and on All the Illustrious Classes of the Community*. Philadelphia, Pennsylvania, 1833.

Griffiths, William H. *The Story of the American Bank Note Company*. New York City, New York: American Bank Note Company, 1959.

Harris, Elizabeth M. "Sir William Congreve and His Compound-Plate Printing," *United States National Museum Bulletin 252*, Paper 71 in *Contributions from The Museum of History and Technology*, Washington, D.C., Smithsonian Institution Press, 1967.

Haxby, James A. *Standard Catalog of United States Obsolete Bank Notes 1782–1866*. Krause Publications Inc., 1988.

Hessler, Gene. *The Engraver's Line*. Port Clinton, Ohio: BNR Press, 1993.

Hildreth, Richard. *The History of Banks, to Which is Added a Demonstration of the Advantages and Necessity of Free Competition in the World of Banking*. Boston, Massachusetts: Hilliard, Gray & Company, 1837.

Holabird, Fred N. and Al Adams. *Gold! At Pigeon Roost, The Story of America's First Gold Mining Scrip*. Published by the author, 2010.

Homans, Isaac Smith. *Hunt's Merchants' Magazine and Commercial Review*. Volume 22. Harvard University: Freeman Hunt, 1850.

Hughes, Earl. *Kentucky Obsolete Notes and Scrip*. Society of Paper Money Collectors, Inc. 1998.

Hunter, Dard. *Papermaking: The History and Technique of an Ancient Craft*. New York City, New York: Dover Publications, Inc., 1978. Reprint of 1943 edition by Alfred A. Knopf, Inc.

Kleeberg, John M. (editor). *Money of Pre-Federal America*. New York City, New York: American Numismatic Society, 1992 (programs presented at the Coinage of the Americas Conference, 1991).

Knapp, Samuel L. "Memoir of Jacob Perkins." Published in 1835 and 1836 in *Family Magazine*, New York. Reprinted with extensive added numismatic commentary in *The Colonial Newsletter*, Volume 27, No. 3, November 1987, Serial No. 77.

Knox, John Jay Knox. *History of Banking*. New York City, New York: Bradford Rhodes & Company, 1900. Anthology of Knox's articles and speeches published posthumously.

Kraus, Guy. *Mississippi Obsolete Notes and Scrip*. Published by the author, 1996.

Lewis, Lawrence Jr. *A History of the Bank of North America, the First Bank Chartered in the United States*. Philadelphia, Pennsylvania: J.B. Lippincott & Co., 1882.

Leggett, L. Chandler. *Mississippi Obsolete Paper Money and Scrip*. Society of Paper Money Collectors, Inc. 1975.

McCabe, Robert. "Waterman Lilly Ormsby and the Continental Bank Note Co.," *Paper Money*, March–April 2001. Includes much information found in the National Archives by Wayne DeCesar, fully credited by McCabe.

McCulloch, Hugh. *Men and Measures of Half a Century*. New York City, New York: Charles Scribner's Sons, 1889.

McKay, George L. *Early American Currency*. New York City, New York: The Typophiles, 1944.

Medlar, Bob. *Texas Obsolete Notes and Scrip*. Society of Paper Money Collectors, Inc. 1968.

Mossman, Philip L. *Money of the American Colonies and Confederation: A Numismatic, Economic & Historical Correlation*. New York City, New York: American Numismatic Society, 1993. Magisterial study of early money in America, emphasizing coins, but with a chapter on paper money.

Newman, Eric P. *Early Paper Money of America*. 4th edition. Iola, Wisconsin: Krause Publications, 1997.

Niles' Register. Various issues of *Niles' Weekly Register* 1811 to 1837, title change to *Niles' National Register*, September 2, 1837, continuing to 1849. Baltimore, Maryland, briefly Washington, D.C.

Numismatic Scrapbook Magazine. Hewitt Brothers and Sidney Printing and Publishing Co., 1935–1966.

Numismatist, The. Journal of the American Numismatic Association; established by Dr. George F. Heath in 1888.

Ormsby, W.L. *Bank Note Engraving*. New York City, New York: Published by the author, 1852.

Ormsby, W.L. *Cycloidal Configurations, or the Harvest of Counterfeiters, Containing Matter of the Highest Importance concerning Paper Money, also Explaining the Unit System of Bank Note Engraving*. New York City, New York: Published by the author, 1862.

Paper Money. Journal of the Society of Paper Money Collectors: 1960s to date.

Peyton, George, *How to Detect Counterfeit Bank Notes; or, an Illustrated Treatise on the Detection of Counterfeit, Altered, and Spurious Bank Notes, with Original Bank Note Plates and designs, by Rawdon, Wright, Hatch & Edson, Bank Note Engravers, of New-York, the Whole Forming an Unerring Guide, by which Every Person Can, on Examination, Detect Spurious Bank Notes of Every Description, No Matter How Well Executed They May Appear*. New York City, New York: Published for the author, 1856.

Raguet, Condy. *A Treatise on Currency & Banking*. 2nd edition. Philadelphia, Pennsylvania: Grigg & Elliot, 1840.

Raguet, Condy. *The Financial Register of the United States*. Volume 2. Philadelphia, Pennsylvania: Wirtz & Tatem, 1838.

Remarks on the Manufacture of Bank Notes and Other Promises to Pay, Addressed to the Bankers of the Southern Confederacy. Columbia, South Carolina: Keatinge & Ball, 1864. Copy digitized by the UNC-CH digitization project, "Documenting the American South," from call number 2919 Conf. (Rare Book Collection, University of North Carolina at Chapel Hill) 31 p., [1] leaf of plates: ill. Columbia, S.C. Steam Power-press of F.G. DeFontaine & Co., 1864.

Rice, Foster Wild. "Antecedents of the American Bank Note Company of 1858," *The Essay-Proof Journal*, Fall 1961.

Rightor, Henry, ed. *Municipal and Military History*. Chicago, Illinois: The Lewis Publishing Company, 1900.

Rosene Jr., Walter. *Alabama Obsolete Notes and Scrip*. Society of Paper Money Collectors, Inc. 1984.

Rothert Sr., NLG, Matt. *Arkansas Obsolete Notes and Scrip*. Society of Paper Money Collectors, Inc. 1985.

Schweikart, Larry. *Banking in the American South: From the Age of Jackson to Reconstruction*. Southern Literary Studies. Louisiana State University Press, 1987.

Scott, Kenneth. *Counterfeiting in Colonial America*. New York City, New York: Oxford University Press, 1957.

Sears, Louis Martin. *Jefferson and the Embargo*. Durham, North Carolina: Duke University Press, 1927.

Shull, Hugh. *A Guide Book of Southern States Currency*. Atlanta, Georgia: Whitman Publishing LLC, 2007.

Stauffer, David McNelly. *American Engravers Upon Copper and Steel*. New York City, New York: The Grolier Club of the City of New York, 1907.

Stokes, Howard Kemble. *Chartered banking in Rhode Island, 1791–1900*. Providence, Rhode Island: Preston & Rounds Company, 1902.

Tomasko, Mark D. *The Feel of Steel: The Art and History of Bank-Note Engraving in the United States*. 2nd edition. New York City, New York: American Numismatic Society, 2012.

Trufant, S.A. *Review of Banking in New Orleans, 1830–1840*. 1918.

Walter, Norman. *Standard History of New Orleans*, Louisiana, Municipal Government.

White, Horace. *Money and Banking*. Boston and London: Ginn & Company, 1896.

Woods, Troy. *Delta Plantations: The Beginning*. Published by the author, 2010.

Worthen, W.B. *Early Banking in Arkansas*. Prepared at the Request of the Arkansas Bankers' Association for its Meeting in April 1906.

About the Author

Q. David Bowers became a professional numismatist as a teenager in 1953, later (1960) earning a B.A. in Finance from Pennsylvania State University, which in 1976 bestowed its Distinguished Alumnus Award on him. He served as president of the Professional Numismatists Guild from 1977 to 1979 and president of the American Numismatic Association from 1983 to 1985. He is a recipient of the Founders Award and Farran Zerbe Award, the highest honors of the PNG and the ANA. He is the author of more than 50 books, including many on paper money, and has received more honors from the Numismatic Literary Guild than has any other person. His column, "The Joys of Collecting," has been a feature of *Coin World* since 1961 and is the longest-running column by any author in the history of numismatics. He may be contacted at P.O. Box 539, Wolfeboro Falls, NH 03896 or by email at qdbarchive@metrocast.net.

About the Foreword Writer

Randy Shipley's passion for numismatics started with the acquisition of coins from circulation. In the late 1950s he began filling blue Whitman coin folders with cents, nickels, and Mercury dimes. Walking Liberty half dollars and Washington quarters were available, and Barber halves and Barber quarters were also seen from time to time. His passion quickly turned from coins to paper money when he saw and acquired his first 1864 Confederate $10 note. The genuine, brown-ink signatures, serial numbers, and historical scenes took him back in time like nothing else he had seen before. From there Shipley purchased three obsolete bank notes for $3 each. The rest, as they say, is history. Since 1978 Randy Shipley has attended almost every major numismatic event in the United States where obsolete bank notes have been present. He is a life-member of the American Numismatic Association, the Society of Paper Money Collectors, the Professional Currency Dealers Association, and many others.

About the State Editors

Arkansas

Rodney Kelley got into numismatics at an early age: his father had an interest in coins, and Kelley developed an interest in history from listening to his grandfathers on either side of the family. After finding a piece of reproduction Confederate money in the back of an old picture frame, bought at an antique shop with his mother, Kelley was hooked on Confederate paper money. His mother took him to local coin shops and shows. It was at such a show in Pine Bluff, Arkansas, that Kelley met Matt Rothert Sr., who introduced him to Arkansas obsolete paper money. At the same show Kelley became a junior member of the American Numismatic Association (1972). Over the years the two stayed in touch and developed a friendship, and when Rothert decided to write a book on Arkansas obsolete notes and scrip, Kelley assisted him with cataloguing the notes. Later he reviewed the Arkansas section of Hugh Shull's *A Guide Book of Southern States Currency*.

Kelley received a Bachelor of Science degree from Arkansas Tech University in December 1979. From there he attended Clemson University in a graduate program studying Natural Resource Management. As a Regulatory Project Manager he works for the U.S. Army Corps of Engineers evaluating projects that affect waters of the United States. He currently is working on scanning and developing his collection of Arkansas notes to add to the obsolete paper money database of the Society of Paper Money Collectors.

Kentucky

Tony Swicer started collecting U.S. coins in 1959, followed by So-Called Dollars in 1978 and national-bank notes from his home state of Kentucky in 2003. His interest in numismatics began when his father, a 20-years-man in the U.S. Air Force, would take him to the bank and get $10 worth of pennies. Swicer would go through the assortment and fill in his Whitman blue folders. From there he graduated to nickels, all the way through silver dollars and gold. By the late 1970s virtually every series was complete.

Swicer has more than 50 years of numismatic experience, 12 of which have been dedicated to the collection and study of obsolete paper money. As an integral part of Florida United Numismatics, Inc. (FUN), Swicer has served on the board and has been both vice-president and president of the organization. He is currently the FUN Club Liaison and writes a monthly newsletter to all of the FUN member clubs, as well as a newsletter to American Numismatic Association (ANA) clubs in the southeast. His numismatic expertise and accessibility have won him numerous awards, including most recently the ANA Presidential Award in January 2015 and the ANA Medal of Merit in September 2015.

Louisiana

Randy K. Haynie has been a collector of Louisiana currency for more than 50 years. As a Boy Scout, he began collecting Lincoln pennies in order to earn his collection merit badge. His interest grew quickly, and it was not long before he became enthralled with Louisiana obsolete currency. Due to the fact that many Louisiana notes and scrip were readily available in the 1970s, he was able to rapidly grow his collection.

Haynie's collection of Louisiana obsolete currency has expanded over the decades and is widely considered to be the deepest, covering state banks as well as parish, municipal, and merchant notes. Haynie also collects Louisiana lottery tickets and documents issued by the first Louisiana Lottery Company.

Haynie is a lifetime member of the American Numismatist Association and the Society of Paper Money Collectors, and a member of the Fractional Currency Collectors and the Confederate Stamp Alliance. In 1998 Haynie was appointed by Mike Foster, at the time governor of Louisiana, to serve on the Louisiana Commemorative Coin Advisory Commission, which was responsible for designing the Louisiana Commemorative quarter. Additionally, in 2012 Haynie was appointed by then Louisiana governor Bobby Jindal to serve on the state's Bi-Centennial Commission to honor Louisiana's 200 years of statehood. Haynie speaks before various coin clubs and historic organizations throughout the state of Louisiana and is always happy to share his knowledge with other collectors.

Mississippi

Justin McClure became interested in Mississippi history at a very early age and began collecting Mississippi obsolete paper money when he found a small bundle of Confederate and obsolete Mississippi notes in an old barn. He became seriously interested in Mississippi obsolete notes, in particular, in the late 1980s, when Yancey Green, a coin-dealer friend in Memphis, called to see if he had any interest in purchasing a collection of about 100 Mississippi obsolete bank notes. He ended up acquiring the collection and has been active in adding to his Mississippi collection ever since.

Over the last 30 years of collecting, McClure has gotten to know many of the major collectors and dealers of Mississippi obsolete notes and has accumulated an in-depth knowledge about Mississippi obsoletes. He assisted Guy Kraus in compiling a listing of known obsolete notes from Mississippi and in reviewing early drafts of Kraus's book, titled *Mississippi Obsolete Notes & Scrip*. McClure is currently working on a companion book that will provide a more-detailed historical context about the issuers and the banking and political climate from the period when the notes were issued. McClure also collects national-bank notes, bottles, whiskey jugs, Civil War relics, and other historical items of interest from Mississippi.

McClure graduated from the University of Mississippi in 1985, with a BBA in banking and finance, and from the University of Mississippi law school in 1988.

Tennessee

Gary L. Burhop is a collector, investor, and dealer in Tennessee obsolete paper money. He specializes in Memphis obsolete bank notes in particular, as well as in Morgan dollars and the coinage of Canada. Burhop has been involved in numismatics since 1960 and in obsolete paper money since 1985. He is a member of the American Numismatic Association (ANA), the Arkansas Numismatic Society, and the Mississippi Numismatic Association, among others. His quest is to better the understanding and appreciation of Tennessee economics and banking systems, pre- and post-Civil War, for both himself and others.

Texas

Michael E. Marotta is a technical writer who has published over 300 magazine and newspaper articles on a wide range of subjects related to business, technology, and culture. He joined the American Numismatic Association in 1994, and in 1996 the ANA granted him a first-place Heath Literary Award. In 2002 he was awarded second place in this category. He has also been honored for his writing by Women in Computing (2000) and the Michigan State Numismatic Society (2002). He worked as a senior staff writer and international editor for Coin World in 1999 and 2000, and was webmaster of the Michigan State Numismatic Society from 2004 to 2011. From 2004 to 2007 he was the editor of the MSNS *Mich-Matist*.

Marotta has published articles in *The Numismatist* on Coronet Cents, Mercury Dimes, and Proof Double Eagles, among other topics. His most recent work was "Pursuing Paper Artifacts: A Checklist for Syngraphists," about the study of bank checks, drafts, and similar fiduciary instruments (April 2015). He has also written more than a dozen articles for *The Celator* about the coins of Greek cities, including Athens, Colophon, and Cyrene. Currently the secretary of the Capital City Coin Club of Austin, Texas, he also served as secretary and vice president of the Livingston County (Michigan) Coin Club in 1994 and 1996. He was elected twice (2003 and 2005) to serve as a governor of the Michigan State Numismatic Society.

General Index

Index to Banks, by State

Alabama

Planters and Merchants Bank (1818–1825; W-AL-140), 21–22
Planters and Merchants Bank (1836–1842; W-AL-230), 30
Planters and Merchants Bank (branch) (1836–1842; W-AL-030), 8
Planters Bank of Alabama (1830s–1840s; W-AL-060), 15
Planters Bank of Alabama (1840s; W-AL-360), 48–49
Planters Bank of Alabama (1861; W-AL-080), 15
Rail Road Bank (1850s; W-AL-160), 22
Real Estate Banking Company of South Alabama (1838–1841; W-AL-330), 44–45
Real Estate Banking Company of Wetumpka (1838 and 1839; W-AL-370), 49
Southern Bank of Alabama (1850–1866; W-AL-240), 31
Tombeckbe Bank (1818–1827; W-AL-300), 40
Wetumpka Trading Company (1830s–1860s; W-AL-380), 49–50

Arkansas

Bank of the State of Arkansas (1837–1843; W-AR-070), 58–63
Bank of the State of Arkansas (branch) (1838–1843; W-AR-020), 53–54
Bank of the State of Arkansas (branch) (1838–1843; W-AR-040), 55–57
Bank of the State of Arkansas (branch) (1839–1843; W-AR-010), 52–53
Exchange Bank of Helena (1850s–1860s; W-AR-050), 57
Real Estate Bank of the State of Arkansas (1836–1843; W-AR-080), 63–64
Real Estate Bank of the State of Arkansas (branch) (1839–1843; W-AR-030), 54–55
Real Estate Bank of the State of Arkansas (branch) (1839–1843; W-AR-060), 58
Real Estate Bank of the State of Arkansas (branch) (1839–1843; W-AR-100), 64–65
Real Estate Bank of the State of Arkansas (branch) (1840–1843; W-AR-090), 64

Kentucky

Agricultural Deposit Bank (1856–1860s; W-KY-750), 143
Augusta Exporting Company (1818; W-KY-020), 69
Bank of Ashland (1856–1872; W-KY-010), 68–69
Bank of Ashland (branch) (1856–1869; W-KY-1420), 210
Bank of Ashland (branch) (1860–1872; W-KY-1010), 172
Bank of Barbourville (1818–1820; W-KY-030), 69–70
Bank of Burlington (1818–1820; W-KY-170), 82–83
Bank of Columbia (1818–1820; W-KY-210), 86–87
Bank of Cynthiana (1818–1820; W-KY-280), 93–94
Bank of Danville (1818–1820; W-KY-310), 96
Bank of Flemingsburg (1818–1820; W-KY-380), 101–102
Bank of George Town (1818–1820; W-KY-470), 118–119
Bank of Green River (1818–1820; W-KY-490), 121
Bank of Greensburgh (1818–1820; W-KY-530), 123–124
Bank of Greenville (1818–1820; W-KY-560), 126
Bank of Henderson (1818–1820; W-KY-630), 132–133
Bank of Kentucky {1st} (1806–1824; W-KY-420), 105–108
Bank of Kentucky {1st} (branch) (1807–1822; W-KY-1350), 199
Bank of Kentucky {1st} (branch) (1807–1822; W-KY-840), 155–157
Bank of Kentucky {1st} (branch) (1808–1822; W-KY-1380), 202–203
Bank of Kentucky {1st} (branch) (1808–1822; W-KY-760), 143–144
Bank of Kentucky {1st} (branch) (1813–1822; W-KY-1570), 221–222
Bank of Kentucky {1st} (branch) (1815–1822; W-KY-050), 72
Bank of Kentucky {1st} (branch) (1815–1822; W-KY-1260), 192–193
Bank of Kentucky {1st} (branch) (1815–1822; W-KY-320), 96–97
Bank of Kentucky {1st} (branch) (1816–1822; W-KY-1430), 211
Bank of Kentucky {1st} (branch) (1816–1822; W-KY-1580), 222–223
Bank of Kentucky {1st} (branch) (1816–1822; W-KY-660), 136
Bank of Kentucky {1st} (branch) (1817–1822; W-KY-1500), 217–218
Bank of Kentucky {1st} (branch) (1817–1822; W-KY-500), 121
Bank of Kentucky {2nd} (1834–1860s; W-KY-850), 157–162
Bank of Kentucky {2nd} (branch) (1834–1865; W-KY-670), 136–138
Bank of Kentucky {2nd} (branch) (1834–1866; W-KY-080), 73–75
Bank of Kentucky {2nd} (branch) (1834–1866; W-KY-1220), 189
Bank of Kentucky {2nd} (branch) (1834–1866; W-KY-140), 80–81
Bank of Kentucky {2nd} (branch) (1834–1866; W-KY-220), 87–88
Bank of Kentucky {2nd} (branch) (1834–1866; W-KY-770), 144–146
Bank of Kentucky {2nd} (branch) (1834–1882; W-KY-1020), 172–173
Bank of Kentucky {2nd} (branch) (1835–1866; W-KY-540), 124–125
Bank of Kentucky {2nd} (branch) (1835–1871; W-KY-430), 108–110
Bank of Kentucky {2nd} (branch) (1837–1866; W-KY-330), 97–98
Bank of Kentucky {2nd} (branch) (1860s–1866; W-KY-1100), 177–178
Bank of Kentucky {2nd} (branch) (1860s–1866; W-KY-390), 102–103
Bank of Kentucky {2nd} (branch) (1860s–1866; W-KY-510), 122
Bank of Limestone (1818–1827; W-KY-1030), 173–174
Bank of Louisville (1833–1860s; W-KY-860), 162–164
Bank of Louisville (branch) (1833–1860s; W-KY-400), 103–104
Bank of Louisville (branch) (1845–1860s; W-KY-1230), 189–190

Northern Bank of Kentucky (branch) (1835–1860s; W-KY-040), 70–71
Northern Bank of Kentucky (branch) (1835–1860s; W-KY-1280), 193–195
Northern Bank of Kentucky (branch) (1835–1860s; W-KY-1360), 199–202
Northern Bank of Kentucky (branch) (1835–1860s; W-KY-260), 91–93
Northern Bank of Kentucky (branch) (1835–1860s; W-KY-305), 95–96
Northern Bank of Kentucky (branch) (1835–1860s; W-KY-960), 168–170
Northern Bank of Kentucky (branch) (1859 and 1860; W-KY-520), 122–123
Owensboro Deposit Bank (1860s; W-KY-1190), 187
Paris Bank (1818; W-KY-1290), 195
Peoples Bank of Kentucky (1856–1860s; W-KY-100), 76–78
Peoples Bank of Kentucky (1856–1860s; W-KY-970), 170
Peoples Bank of Kentucky (branch) (1856–1860s; W-KY-1250), 192
Peoples Bank of Kentucky (branch) (1856–1860s; W-KY-620), 130–132
Peoples Bank of Kentucky (branch) (1860s; W-KY-110), 78–79
Petersburg Steam Mill Company (1818–1820; W-KY-1310), 196
Planters and Manufacturers Bank (1854; W-KY-980), 170
Real Estate Bank of Covington (1818–1820; W-KY-270), 93
Richmond Bank (1818; W-KY-1370), 202
Sanders Manufacturing Company (1818–1820; W-KY-1410), 210
Savings Bank of Louisville (1854; W-KY-990), 170
South Western Real Estate Bank of Kentucky (Circa 1838; W-KY-370), 100–101
Southern Bank of Kentucky (1818–1820; W-KY-120), 79–80
Southern Bank of Kentucky (1839–1865; W-KY-1400), 205–209
Southern Bank of Kentucky (branch) (1839–1865; W-KY-1000), 170–171
Southern Bank of Kentucky (branch) (1839–1865; W-KY-1200), 187–188
Southern Bank of Kentucky (branch) (1839–1865; W-KY-130), 80
Southern Bank of Kentucky (branch) (1839–1865; W-KY-1460), 213–214
Southern Bank of Kentucky (branch) (1850–1864; W-KY-200), 85–86
Southern Bank of Kentucky (branch) (1852–1865; W-KY-650), 135–136
Southern Bank of Kentucky (branch) (1858–1865; W-KY-740), 141–142
Springfield Deposit Bank (1860s; W-KY-1520), 218
Stanford Bank (1818; W-KY-1530), 218
Stanford Deposit Bank (1854–1860s; W-KY-1540), 219
Traders and Mechanics Bank (1839; W-KY-180), 83
Union Bank of Elizabethtown (1818–1820; W-KY-350), 98–99
Winchester Commercial Bank (1818–1820; W-KY-1600), 224

Louisiana

Atchafalaya Rail Road and Banking Company (1836–1847; W-LA-090), 232–235
Bank of America (1857–1862; W-LA-110), 236–237
Bank of Commerce (1853–1862; W-LA-120), 237–242
Bank of James Robb (1857–1859; W-LA-130), 242–243
Bank of Louisiana (1824–1863; W-LA-140), 243–258
Bank of Louisiana (branch) (1824–1863; W-LA-010), 227
Bank of Louisiana (branch) (1824–1863; W-LA-030), 228
Bank of Louisiana (branch) (1824–1863; W-LA-060), 229
Bank of Louisiana (branch) (1824–1863; W-LA-440), 344
Bank of Louisiana (branch) (1824–1863; W-LA-460), 344
Bank of New Orleans {1st} (1811–1842; W-LA-150), 258
Bank of New Orleans {2nd} (1853–1870; W-LA-160), 259–262
Bank of Orleans (1811–1849; W-LA-170), 262–267
Bank of the United States {1st} (branch) (1791–1811; W-LA-175), 267–268
Bank of the United States {2nd} (branch) (1817–1835; W-LA-180), 268–270
Bank of the United States of Pennsylvania (1838–1841; W-LA-190), 270
Banking House of Gray, Macmurdo and Company (1850s–1860s; W-LA-100), 235
Canal Bank (1831–1870; W-LA-195), 270
Citizens Bank of Louisiana (1833–1874; W-LA-200), 270–281
Citizens Bank of Louisiana (branch) (1860–1874; W-LA-480), 345–348
City Bank of New Orleans (1831–1850; W-LA-210), 282–287
Clinton and Port Hudson Rail Road Company (1833–1842; W-LA-080), 230–231
Commercial Bank (1833–1843; W-LA-220), 287–289
Consolidated Association Bank of the Planters of Louisiana (1827–1842; W-LA-230), 289–291
Crescent City Bank (1857–1862; W-LA-240), 291–293
Exchange and Banking Company (1835–1842; W-LA-255), 294–296
Exchange Bank (1860s; W-LA-250), 293–294
Insurance Bank of W.B. Partee and Company (1847–1851; W-LA-260), 296–297
Louisiana Bank (1804–1819; W-LA-270), 297–298
Louisiana State Bank (1818–1870; W-LA-280), 298–304
Louisiana State Bank (branch) (1818–1825; W-LA-020), 227
Louisiana State Bank (branch) (1818–1825; W-LA-070), 229
Louisiana State Bank (branch) (1818–1825; W-LA-450), 344
Louisiana State Bank (branch) (1818–1870; W-LA-470), 345
Louisiana State Bank (branch) (1836–1852; W-LA-290), 304–306
Louisiana State Bank (branch) (1850–1870; W-LA-040), 228

Louisiana State Bank (branch) (1850–1870; W-LA-490), 348
Mechanics and Traders Bank (1833–1879; W-LA-300), 306–309
Merchants and Traders Bank of New Orleans (1830s–1850; W-LA-330), 313
Merchants Bank of New Orleans {1st} (1836–1845; W-LA-310), 309–310
Merchants Bank of New Orleans {2nd} (1859–1879; W-LA-320), 310–313
New Orleans and Carrollton Rail Road and Banking Company (1835–1844; W-LA-340), 313–314
New Orleans and Carrollton Rail Road and Banking Company (branch) (1835–1844; W-LA-050), 229
New Orleans Canal and Banking Company (1831–1870; W-LA-350), 314–332
New Orleans Gas Light and Banking Company (1835–1845; W-LA-360), 332–333
New Orleans Improvement and Banking Company (1836–1842; W-LA-370), 333–334
New Orleans, Jackson and Great Northern Rail Road Company (1861 and 1862; W-LA-380), 334–335
Planters Bank (1811–1826; W-LA-390), 336
Southern Bank (1854–1879; W-LA-400), 336–338
Union Bank of Louisiana {1st} (1832–1842; W-LA-410), 338–339
Union Bank of Louisiana {1st} (branch) (1832–1842; W-LA-055), 229
Union Bank of Louisiana {2nd} (1854–1871; W-LA-420), 339–342
W.A. Britton and Company Banking House (1835–1860s; W-LA-430), 342–344

Mississippi

Aberdeen and Pontotoc Rail Road and Banking Company (1836–1840; W-MS-010), 351–352
Agricultural Bank of Mississippi (1833–1841; W-MS-590), 431–434
Agricultural Bank of Mississippi (branch) (1833–1840; W-MS-720), 451–452
Bank of Aberdeen (1862; W-MS-020), 352–353
Bank of Brookhaven (1862; W-MS-080), 369
Bank of Columbus (1862; W-MS-180), 380
Bank of Enterprise (1862; W-MS-300), 394
Bank of Grenada Mississippi {1st} (1837 and 1838; W-MS-340), 398–399
Bank of Grenada Mississippi {2nd} (1862; W-MS-350), 399
Bank of Jackson (1862; W-MS-430), 412
Bank of Lexington (1837–1841; W-MS-480), 418–420
Bank of Madison County, Mississippi (1830s; W-MS-530), 423–425
Bank of Mississippi (1838–1860; W-MS-790), 457–458
Bank of Natchez (1862; W-MS-610), 435
Bank of Port Gibson (1837–1840s; W-MS-745), 453–454
Bank of the Mississippi (1809–1818; W-MS-600), 434–435
Bank of the State of Mississippi (1818–1831; W-MS-620), 435
Bank of the State of Mississippi (branch) (1818–1831; W-MS-1000), 475
Bank of the State of Mississippi (branch) (1818–1831; W-MS-760), 454–455
Bank of the State of Mississippi (branch) (1818–1831; W-MS-880), 465
Bank of the United States {2nd} (branch) (1831–1835; W-MS-630), 435–436
Bank of Vicksburg {1st} (1837–1840; W-MS-890), 465–468
Bank of Vicksburg {1st} (branch) (1837–1840; W-MS-1010), 475–476
Bank of Vicksburg {1st} (branch) (1837–1840; W-MS-700), 447–448
Bank of Vicksburg {2nd} (1862; W-MS-900), 468
Bank of Yazoo City (1862; W-MS-1050), 482
Benton and Manchester Rail Road and Banking Company (1836–1840; W-MS-050), 355–356
Chickasaw Land Bank (1830s; W-MS-730), 452–453
Citizens Bank of Madison County (1837–1840; W-MS-090), 369–371
Citizens Bank of Madison County (branch) (1837–1840; W-MS-500), 421
Citizens Bank of Madison County (branch) (1837–1840; W-MS-850), 463–464
Citizens Change Banking Company (1838; W-MS-140), 374–375
Columbus and Tombigby Transportation Company (1839 and 1840; W-MS-190), 380–381
Columbus Life and General Insurance Company (1852–1860s; W-MS-200), 381–383
Commercial and Rail Road Bank of Vicksburg (1831–1840; W-MS-910), 468–471
Commercial and Rail Road Bank of Vicksburg (branch) (1831–1840; W-MS-860), 464
Commercial and Rail Road Bank of Vicksburg (branch) (1831–1840; W-MS-870), 464–465
Commercial and Rail Road Bank of Vicksburg (branch) (1836–1840; W-MS-150), 375
Commercial Bank of Colbert (1830s; W-MS-170), 379
Commercial Bank of Columbus (1836–1841; W-MS-210), 383
Commercial Bank of Enterprise (Circa 1839; W-MS-310), 394–395
Commercial Bank of Manchester (1836–1860; W-MS-1060), 482–483
Commercial Bank of Manchester (1836–1860; W-MS-540), 427–428
Commercial Bank of Natchez (1836–1856; W-MS-640), 436–439
Commercial Bank of Natchez (branch) (1836–1856; W-MS-060), 356–357
Commercial Bank of Natchez (branch) (1836–1856; W-MS-100), 371
Commercial Bank of Natchez (branch) (1836–1856; W-MS-420), 411–412
Commercial Bank of Natchez (branch) (1836–1856; W-MS-830), 461–462
Commercial Bank of Rodney (1836–1840; W-MS-820), 459–461
Consolidated Banking Company of Holmes County (1830s; W-MS-490), 420–421

Tennessee

Nashville Bank (branch) (1817–1827; W-TN-640), 593
Nashville Bank (branch) (1817–1827; W-TN-900), 636
Nashville Bank (branch) (1817–1827; W-TN-930), 639
Northern Bank of Tennessee (1854–1860s; W-TN-130), 509–510
Ocoee Bank (1854–1862; W-TN-150), 511–515
Ocoee Bank (branch) (1854–1862; W-TN-385), 550–551
Planters Bank of Tennessee (1833–1865; W-TN-810), 617–623
Planters Bank of Tennessee (branch) (1834–1865; W-TN-020), 488–489
Planters Bank of Tennessee (branch) (1834–1865; W-TN-1050), 651
Planters Bank of Tennessee (branch) (1834–1865; W-TN-1070), 652–653
Planters Bank of Tennessee (branch) (1834–1865; W-TN-140), 510–511
Planters Bank of Tennessee (branch) (1834–1865; W-TN-210), 518–520
Planters Bank of Tennessee (branch) (1834–1865; W-TN-300), 525–526
Planters Bank of Tennessee (branch) (1834–1865; W-TN-410), 553–554
Planters Bank of Tennessee (branch) (1834–1865; W-TN-570), 584–586
Planters Bank of Tennessee (branch) (1834–1865; W-TN-630), 592–593
Planters Bank of Tennessee (branch) (1834–1865; W-TN-870), 632–633
Planters Bank of Tennessee (branch) (1834–1865; W-TN-910), 637
Planters Bank of Tennessee (branch) (1834–1865; W-TN-940), 640
Planters Bank of Tennessee (branch) (1834–1865; W-TN-970), 644
Planters Bank of Tennessee (branch) (1834–1865; W-TN-990), 646
River Bank (1858–1862; W-TN-580), 586–587
Savings Bank of Louisville (1837 and 1838; W-TN-820), 623
Shelbyville Bank of Tennessee (1854–1862; W-TN-950), 640–641
South Western Rail Road Bank (branch) (1836–1855; W-TN-390), 551
Southern Bank of Tennessee (1854–1858; W-TN-590), 587–588
State Stock Bank (branch) (Circa 1857; W-TN-1020), 648
State Stock Bank (Circa 1857; W-TN-320), 527–528
Traders Bank (1855–1862; W-TN-830), 624–625
Union Bank of Tennessee (1832–1865; W-TN-840), 625–630
Union Bank of Tennessee (branch) (1832–1865; W-TN-090), 504
Union Bank of Tennessee (branch) (1832–1865; W-TN-220), 520
Union Bank of Tennessee (branch) (1832–1865; W-TN-325), 528–530
Union Bank of Tennessee (branch) (1832–1865; W-TN-400), 551–553
Union Bank of Tennessee (branch) (1832–1865; W-TN-600), 588–590

Texas

Bank of the Republic of Texas (1839 and 1840; W-TX-080), 665
Bank of Vernon (1840s; W-TX-070), 665
Commercial and Agricultural Bank of Texas (1835–1837; W-TX-040), 656–660
Commercial and Agricultural Bank of Texas (1847–1858; W-TX-050), 660–664
Commercial and Agricultural Bank of Texas (branch) (1835–1837; W-TX-010), 655
Commercial and Agricultural Bank of Texas (branch) (1847–1858; W-TX-030), 655–656
Northern Bank of Mississippi (1850s–1860s; W-TX-060), 664
Texas Railroad, Navigation and Banking Company (1836; W-TX-020), 655

Haxby-to-Whitman Numbers Cross-Reference and Index

Alabama

Haxby No.	Whitman No.	Page
H-AL-5-G2	W-AL-010-001-G010	3
H-AL-5-G4	W-AL-010-002-G020	4
H-AL-5-G6	W-AL-010-003-G030	4
H-AL-5-G8	W-AL-010-005-G040	4
H-AL-5-G10	W-AL-010-010-G050	4
H-AL-5-G12	W-AL-010-020-G060	4
H-AL-5-G14	W-AL-010-050-G070	4
H-AL-5-G16	W-AL-010-100-G080	4
H-AL-5-C16	W-AL-010-100-C080	4
H-AL-5-G56	W-AL-020-001-G010	5
H-AL-5-G56a	W-AL-020-001-G010a	5
H-AL-5-G58	W-AL-020-002-G020	5
H-AL-5-G58a	W-AL-020-002-G020a	5
H-AL-5-G60	W-AL-020-003-G030	5
H-AL-5-G60a	W-AL-020-003-G030a	5
H-AL-5-G62	W-AL-020-004-G040	5
H-AL-5-G62a	W-AL-020-004-G040a	5
H-AL-5-G64	W-AL-020-005-G050	5
H-AL-5-G66	W-AL-020-010-G060	5
H-AL-5-G68	W-AL-020-020-G070	6
H-AL-5-G70	W-AL-020-050-G080	6
H-AL-5-G72	W-AL-020-100-G090	6
H-AL-5-G76	W-AL-020-005-G100	6
H-AL-5-G78	W-AL-020-010-G110	6
H-AL-5-G80	W-AL-020-020-G120	6
H-AL-5-G82	W-AL-020-050-G130	6
H-AL-5-G84	W-AL-020-100-G140	6
H-AL-5-G90	W-AL-020-005-G150	6
H-AL-5-G92	W-AL-020-010-G160	6
H-AL-5-G94	W-AL-020-020-G170	6
H-AL-5-G96	W-AL-020-050-G180	6
H-AL-5-G98	W-AL-020-100-G190	6
H-AL-5-G100	W-AL-020-005-G200	7
H-AL-5-G102	W-AL-020-010-G210	7
H-AL-5-G104	W-AL-020-020-G220	7
H-AL-5-G106	W-AL-020-050-G230	7
H-AL-5-G108	W-AL-020-100-G240	7
H-AL-5-G110	W-AL-020-005-G250	7
H-AL-5-G112	W-AL-020-010-G260	7
H-AL-5-G114	W-AL-020-020-G270	7

Haxby No.	Whitman No.	Page
H-US-2-G478	W-AL-200-005-G020	27
H-US-2-G482	W-AL-200-010-G030	27
H-US-2-G484	W-AL-200-010-G040	27
H-US-2-G488	W-AL-200-020-G050	27
H-US-2-G490	W-AL-200-020-G060	27
H-US-2-G492	W-AL-200-020-G070	27
H-US-2-G496	W-AL-200-050-G080	27
H-US-2-G498	W-AL-200-050-G090	27
H-US-2-G500	W-AL-200-050-G100	27
H-US-2-G504	W-AL-200-100-G110	27
H-US-2-G506	W-AL-200-100-G120	27
H-US-2-G508	W-AL-200-100-G130	27
H-US-2-C476	W-AL-200-005-C010	28
H-US-2-C482	W-AL-200-010-C030	28
H-US-2-C488	W-AL-200-020-C050	28
H-US-2-C498	W-AL-200-050-C090	28
H-US-2-C504	W-AL-200-100-C110	28
H-US-2-C506	W-AL-200-100-C120	28
	W-AL-210-050-G010	28
	W-AL-220-002-G010	28
	W-AL-220-002-G020	28
	W-AL-220-003-G030	28
	W-AL-220-003-G030a	29
	W-AL-220-003-G040	29
	W-AL-220-005-G050	29
	W-AL-225-00.05-G010	29
	W-AL-225-00.10-G020	29
	W-AL-225-00.50-G030	29
	W-AL-225-001-G040	30
	W-AL-225-002-G050	30
	W-AL-225-003-G060	30
H-AL-50-G2	W-AL-230-001-G010	30
H-AL-50-G4	W-AL-230-002-G020	30
H-AL-50-G6	W-AL-230-003-G030	30
H-AL-50-G8	W-AL-230-005-G040	30
H-AL-50-G10	W-AL-230-010-G050	30
H-AL-50-G12	W-AL-230-020-G060	30
H-AL-50-G14	W-AL-230-050-G070	30
H-AL-50-G16	W-AL-230-100-G080	30
H-AL-60-G2	W-AL-240-005-G010	31
H-AL-60-G2a	W-AL-240-005-G010a	31
H-AL-60-G4	W-AL-240-010-G020	31
H-AL-60-G4a	W-AL-240-010-G020a	31
H-AL-60-G6	W-AL-240-020-G030	31
H-AL-60-G8	W-AL-240-050-G040	31
H-AL-60-G10	W-AL-240-100-G050	31
H-AL-60-G12	W-AL-240-500-G060	31
H-AL-60-N10	W-AL-240-050-N010	31
H-AL-60-N15	W-AL-240-050-N020	31
	W-AL-250-001-G010	32
	W-AL-250-002-G020	32
	W-AL-250-005-G030	32
H-AL-75-G2	W-AL-260-001-G010	32
H-AL-75-G4	W-AL-260-002-G020	32
H-AL-75-G6	W-AL-260-003-G030	32
H-AL-75-G8	W-AL-260-005-G040	33
H-AL-75-G10a	W-AL-260-010-G050	33
H-AL-75-G12a	W-AL-260-020-G060	33
H-AL-75-S5	W-AL-260-002-S010	33
H-AL-75-S5a	W-AL-260-002-S010a	33
H-AL-75-S10	W-AL-260-003-S020	33
H-AL-75-S10a	W-AL-260-003-S020a	33
	W-AL-270-001-G010	33
	W-AL-270-003-G020	33
H-AL-5-G210	W-AL-270-005-G030	34
H-AL-5-G212	W-AL-270-010-G040	34
H-AL-5-G214	W-AL-270-020-G050	34
H-AL-5-G216	W-AL-270-050-G060	34
H-AL-5-G218	W-AL-270-100-G070	34
H-AL-5-G230	W-AL-270-020-G080	34
H-AL-5-G232	W-AL-270-050-G090	34
H-AL-5-G234	W-AL-270-100-G100	34
	W-AL-270-010-G110	34
H-AL-65-G2	W-AL-280-001-G010	35
H-AL-65-G4	W-AL-280-001-G020	35
H-AL-65-G4a	W-AL-280-001-G020a	35
	W-AL-280-001-G030	35
H-AL-65-G6	W-AL-280-002-G040	35
H-AL-65-G8	W-AL-280-002-G050	35
H-AL-65-G8a	W-AL-280-002-G050a	35
	W-AL-280-002-G060	35
	W-AL-280-002-G070	35
H-AL-65-G10	W-AL-280-003-G080	35
H-AL-65-G10a	W-AL-280-003-G080a	36
	W-AL-280-003-G090	36
	W-AL-280-004-G100	36
H-AL-65-G12	W-AL-280-005-G110	36
H-AL-65-G12a	W-AL-280-005-G110a	36
H-AL-65-G12b	W-AL-280-005-G110b	36
	W-AL-280-005-G120	36
H-AL-65-G16	W-AL-280-010-G130	37
H-AL-65-G16a	W-AL-280-010-G130a	37
H-AL-65-G16b	W-AL-280-010-G130b	37
	W-AL-280-010-G140	37
H-AL-65-G18	W-AL-280-020-G150	37
H-AL-65-G18a	W-AL-280-020-G150a	37
H-AL-65-G18b	W-AL-280-020-G150b	37
	W-AL-280-020-G160	37
H-AL-65-G20	W-AL-280-050-G170	37
H-AL-65-G20a	W-AL-280-050-G170a	37
H-AL-65-G20b	W-AL-280-050-G170b	37
H-AL-65-G22	W-AL-280-100-G180	38
H-AL-65-G22a	W-AL-280-100-G180a	38
H-AL-65-G22b	W-AL-280-100-G180b	38
	W-AL-280-500-G190	38
H-AL-65-G28a	W-AL-280-500-G190a	38
H-AL-65-A5	W-AL-280-001-A010	38
H-AL-65-A6	W-AL-280-002-A020	38
H-AL-65-A9	W-AL-280-005-A030	39
H-AL-65-A12	W-AL-280-010-A040	39
H-AL-65-A15	W-AL-280-020-A050	39
H-AL-70-G2a	W-AL-290-001-G010	39
H-AL-70-G8a	W-AL-290-005-G020	39
H-AL-70-G12a	W-AL-290-020-G030	39
H-AL-80-G2	W-AL-300-001-G010	40
H-AL-80-G4	W-AL-300-002-G020	40
H-AL-80-G6	W-AL-300-003-G030	40
H-AL-80-G8	W-AL-300-005-G040	40
H-AL-80-G10	W-AL-300-010-G050	40
H-AL-80-G12	W-AL-300-020-G060	40
H-AL-95-G2a	W-AL-310-005-G010	41
H-AL-95-G4a	W-AL-310-010-G020	41
H-AL-95-G6a	W-AL-310-020-G030	41
H-AL-95-G8a	W-AL-310-050-G040	41
	W-AL-310-050-G040a	41
H-AL-95-G10a	W-AL-310-100-G050	41
	W-AL-310-100-G060	42
	W-AL-310-005-C010	42
	W-AL-310-005-C010a	42
H-AL-85-G2a	W-AL-320-001-G010	42
H-AL-85-G4a	W-AL-320-002-G020	42
H-AL-85-G6a	W-AL-320-003-G030	43
H-AL-85-G8a	W-AL-320-005-G040	43
H-AL-85-G8b	W-AL-320-005-G040a	43
H-AL-85-G10a	W-AL-320-010-G050	43
H-AL-85-G10b	W-AL-320-010-G050a	43
H-AL-85-G12a	W-AL-320-020-G060	43
H-AL-85-G12b	W-AL-320-020-G060a	44
H-AL-85-G14a	W-AL-320-050-G070	44
H-AL-85-G14b	W-AL-320-050-G070a	44
H-AL-85-G16a	W-AL-320-100-G080	44
H-AL-85-G16b	W-AL-320-100-G080a	44
H-AL-90-G2	W-AL-330-001-G010	45
H-AL-90-G4	W-AL-330-002-G020	45
H-AL-90-G6	W-AL-330-003-G030	45
H-AL-90-G8	W-AL-330-005-G040	45
H-AL-90-G10	W-AL-330-010-G050	45
	W-AL-330-020-G060	45

Arkansas

Kentucky

Louisiana

Haxby No.	Whitman No.	Page
	W-LA-260-00.10-G010	296
	W-LA-260-00.25-G020	297
	W-LA-260-00.50-G030	297
	W-LA-260-001-G040	297
	W-LA-260-002-G050	297
H-LA-70-G4	W-LA-270-005-G010	297
H-LA-70-G10	W-LA-270-010-G020	297
H-LA-70-G16	W-LA-270-020-G030	297
H-LA-70-G20	W-LA-270-050-G040	298
H-LA-70-G24	W-LA-270-100-G050	298
H-LA-70-G28	W-LA-270-500-G060	298
H-LA-70-G32	W-LA-270-1000-G070	298
H-LA-70-C4	W-LA-270-005-C010	298
H-LA-80-G2	W-LA-280-001-G010	298
H-LA-80-G2a	W-LA-280-001-G010a	299
H-LA-80-G4	W-LA-280-002-G020	299
H-LA-80-G4a	W-LA-280-002-G020a	299
H-LA-80-G6	W-LA-280-003-G030	299
H-LA-80-G6a	W-LA-280-003-G030a	299
H-LA-80-G8	W-LA-280-005-G040	299
H-LA-80-G12	W-LA-280-005-G050	299
H-LA-80-G14a	W-LA-280-005-G060	300
H-LA-80-G14b	W-LA-280-005-G060a	300
H-LA-80-G16a	W-LA-280-005-G070	300
H-LA-80-G18	W-LA-280-010-G080	300
H-LA-80-G22	W-LA-280-010-G090	300
H-LA-80-G24a	W-LA-280-010-G100	300
H-LA-80-G24b	W-LA-280-010-G100a	300
H-LA-80-G26	W-LA-280-010-G110	301
H-LA-80-G28	W-LA-280-020-G120	301
H-LA-80-G32	W-LA-280-020-G130	301
H-LA-80-G34a	W-LA-280-020-G140	301
H-LA-80-G38	W-LA-280-050-G150	301
H-LA-80-G42	W-LA-280-050-G160	301
H-LA-80-G44a	W-LA-280-050-G170	301
H-LA-80-G44b	W-LA-280-050-G170a	301
H-LA-80-G46a	W-LA-280-050-G180	302
H-LA-80-G48	W-LA-280-100-G190	302
H-LA-80-G52	W-LA-280-100-G200	302
H-LA-80-G54a	W-LA-280-100-G210	302
H-LA-80-G54b	W-LA-280-100-G210a	302
H-LA-80-G56	W-LA-280-100-G220	303
H-LA-80-G60a	W-LA-280-500-G230	303
H-LA-80-G64a	W-LA-280-1000-G240	303
H-LA-80-G2a, G2a, G4a, G6a	W-LA-280-001.001.002.003-US010	303
H-LA-80-C8	W-LA-280-005-C040	303
H-LA-80-C18	W-LA-280-010-C080	303
H-LA-80-C24b	W-LA-280-010-C100a	304
H-LA-80-N5	W-LA-280-010-N010	304
H-LA-80-C34a	W-LA-280-020-C140	304
H-LA-80-R5	W-LA-280-050-R010	304
H-LA-80-S5	W-LA-280-050-S010	304
H-LA-80-C48	W-LA-280-100-C190	304
H-LA-80-C54a	W-LA-280-100-C210	304
H-LA-80-R10	W-LA-280-100-R020	304
H-LA-80-S10	W-LA-280-100-S020	304
H-LA-80-G80a	W-LA-290-005-G010	304
H-LA-80-G82a	W-LA-290-010-G020	305
H-LA-80-G84a	W-LA-290-020-G030	305
H-LA-80-G80a, G80a, G80a, G80a	W-LA-290-005.005.005.005-US010	305
H-LA-80-G82a, G82a, G82a, G82a	W-LA-290-010.010.010.010-US020	306
H-LA-80-C82a	W-LA-290-010-C020	306
H-LA-85-G2	W-LA-300-005-G010	306
H-LA-85-G6	W-LA-300-010-G020	306
H-LA-85-G10	W-LA-300-020-G030	307
H-LA-85-G14	W-LA-300-050-G040	307
H-LA-85-G18	W-LA-300-100-G050	307
H-LA-85-G18a	W-LA-300-005-G060	307
H-LA-85-G18b	W-LA-300-005-G060a	307
H-LA-85-G20a	W-LA-300-010-G070	307
H-LA-85-G20b	W-LA-300-010-G070a	307
H-LA-85-G22a	W-LA-300-020-G080	308
H-LA-85-G22b	W-LA-300-020-G080a	308
H-LA-85-G24a	W-LA-300-050-G090	308
H-LA-85-G24b	W-LA-300-050-G090a	308
H-LA-85-G26a	W-LA-300-100-G100	308
H-LA-85-G26b	W-LA-300-100-G100a	308
	W-LA-300-1000-G110	308
	W-LA-300-001-G120	308
H-LA-85-G30a	W-LA-300-005-G130	308
H-LA-85-G32a	W-LA-300-010-G140	308
H-LA-85-G34a	W-LA-300-020-G150	308
H-LA-85-G36a	W-LA-300-050-G160	309
H-LA-85-G38a	W-LA-300-100-G170	309
H-LA-85-A5	W-LA-300-003-A010	309
H-LA-85-N5	W-LA-300-005-N010	309
H-LA-85-A10	W-LA-300-005-A020	309
H-LA-85-C6	W-LA-300-010-C020	309
H-LA-85-A15	W-LA-300-010-A030	309
H-LA-85-R5	W-LA-300-050-R010	309
H-LA-85-R10	W-LA-300-100-R020	309
H-LA-90-G2	W-LA-310-005-G010	309
H-LA-90-G4	W-LA-310-010-G020	310
H-LA-90-G6	W-LA-310-020-G030	310
H-LA-90-G8	W-LA-310-050-G040	310
H-LA-90-G10	W-LA-310-100-G050	310
H-LA-90-R5	W-LA-310-050-R010	310
H-LA-95-G4a	W-LA-320-005-G010	310
H-LA-95-G6a	W-LA-320-010-G020	311
H-LA-95-G8a	W-LA-320-020-G030	311
H-LA-95-G10a	W-LA-320-050-G040	311
H-LA-95-G12a	W-LA-320-100-G050	311
H-LA-95-G14a	W-LA-320-001-G060	311
H-LA-95-G16a	W-LA-320-001.50-G070	312
	W-LA-320-001.50-G070a	312
	W-LA-320-002-G080	312
H-LA-95-G22a	W-LA-320-005-G090	312
H-LA-95-G24a	W-LA-320-005-G100	312
H-LA-95-G26a	W-LA-320-010-G110	312
H-LA-95-G28a	W-LA-320-020-G120	312
H-LA-95-G30a	W-LA-320-050-G130	312
	W-LA-320-100-G140	313
H-LA-95-G32a	W-LA-320-100-G140a	313
H-LA-95-C8a	W-LA-320-020-C030	313
H-LA-110-G2	W-LA-340-005-G010	313
H-LA-110-G4	W-LA-340-010-G020	313
H-LA-110-G6	W-LA-340-020-G030	313
H-LA-110-G8	W-LA-340-050-G040	313
H-LA-110-G10	W-LA-340-100-G050	313
	W-LA-340-1000-G055	314
H-LA-110-G12	W-LA-340-005-G060	314
H-LA-110-G14	W-LA-340-010-G070	314
H-LA-110-G16	W-LA-340-020-G080	314
H-LA-110-G18	W-LA-340-050-G090	314
H-LA-110-G20	W-LA-340-100-G100	314
H-LA-110-G22	W-LA-340-500-G110	314
H-LA-110-G24	W-LA-340-1000-G120	314
H-LA-105-G6	W-LA-350-005-G010	315
H-LA-105-G10	W-LA-350-005-G020	315
H-LA-105-G12a	W-LA-350-005-G030	315
H-LA-105-G14a	W-LA-350-005-G040	315
	W-LA-350-005-G050	316
H-LA-105-G16	W-LA-350-010-G060	316
H-LA-105-G20	W-LA-350-010-G070	316
H-LA-105-G22a	W-LA-350-010-G080	316
H-LA-105-G24a	W-LA-350-010-G090	316
H-LA-105-G26a	W-LA-350-010-G100	316
H-LA-105-G28	W-LA-350-020-G110	316
H-LA-105-G32	W-LA-350-020-G120	317
H-LA-105-G32a	W-LA-350-020-G120a	317
	W-LA-350-020-G130	317
H-LA-105-G34a	W-LA-350-020-G130a	317
H-LA-105-G36a	W-LA-350-020-G140	317
	W-LA-350-050-G150	318
H-LA-105-G40	W-LA-350-050-G160	318
H-LA-105-G44	W-LA-350-050-G170	318

Mississippi

Haxby No.	Whitman No.	Page
H-MS-10-G8	W-MS-010-005-G010	351
H-MS-10-G14	W-MS-010-010-G020	351
H-MS-10-G16	W-MS-010-020-G030	351
H-MS-10-G18	W-MS-010-050-G040	351
H-MS-10-G20	W-MS-010-100-G050	352
	W-MS-010-005-G060	352
	W-MS-010-010-G070	352
	W-MS-010-020-G080	352
	W-MS-010-050-G090	352
	W-MS-010-100-G100	352
	W-MS-020-001-G010	352
	W-MS-020-002-G020	352
	W-MS-020-003-G030	352
	W-MS-020-005-G040	352
	W-MS-020-005-G050	353
	W-MS-020-005-G050a	353
	W-MS-020-010-G060	353
	W-MS-020-020-G070	353
	W-MS-020-020-G080	353
	W-MS-030-001-G010	354
	W-MS-030-002-G020	354
	W-MS-030-003-G030	354
	W-MS-030-005-G040	354
	W-MS-030-010-G050	354
	W-MS-030-020-G060	354
H-MS-15-G4	W-MS-040-005-G010	355
H-MS-15-G8	W-MS-040-010-G020	355
H-MS-15-G12	W-MS-040-020-G030	355
	W-MS-050-005-G010	355
H-MS-20-G10	W-MS-050-010-G020	355
H-MS-20-G10a	W-MS-050-010-G020a	356
H-MS-20-G12	W-MS-050-020-G030	356
H-MS-20-G12a	W-MS-050-020-G030a	356
	W-MS-050-050-G040	356
	W-MS-050-100-G050	356
	W-MS-050-020-G060	356
	W-MS-060-005-G010	356
	W-MS-060-010-G020	357
	W-MS-060-020-G030	357
	W-MS-060-050-G040	357
	W-MS-060-100-G050	357
H-MS-25-G2	W-MS-070-001-G010	357
	W-MS-070-001-G020	357
H-MS-25-G4	W-MS-070-002-G030	357
H-MS-25-G6	W-MS-070-003-G040	358
H-MS-25-G8	W-MS-070-005-G050	358
H-MS-25-G8b	W-MS-070-005-G050a	358
H-MS-25-G10	W-MS-070-005-G060	358
H-MS-25-G12	W-MS-070-010-G070	358
H-MS-25-G12a	W-MS-070-010-G070a	358
H-MS-25-G12b	W-MS-070-010-G070b	358
H-MS-25-G12c	W-MS-070-010-G070c	359
H-MS-25-G14	W-MS-070-010-G080	359
	W-MS-070-010-G080a	359
H-MS-25-G16	W-MS-070-020-G090	359
H-MS-25-G16a	W-MS-070-020-G090a	359
H-MS-25-G16b	W-MS-070-020-G090b	360
	W-MS-070-020-G090c	360
H-MS-25-G18	W-MS-070-020-G100	360
H-MS-25-G22	W-MS-070-025-G110	360
H-MS-25-G22a	W-MS-070-025-G110a	360
H-MS-25-G22b	W-MS-070-025-G110b	360
	W-MS-070-025-G110c	360
H-MS-25-G24	W-MS-070-025-G120	361
H-MS-25-G26	W-MS-070-050-G130	361
H-MS-25-G26a	W-MS-070-050-G130a	361
H-MS-25-G26b	W-MS-070-050-G130b	361
	W-MS-070-050-G130c	361
H-MS-25-G28	W-MS-070-050-G140	361
H-MS-25-G30	W-MS-070-100-G150	361
H-MS-25-G30a	W-MS-070-100-G150a	362
H-MS-25-G30b	W-MS-070-100-G150b	362
	W-MS-070-100-G150c	362
H-MS-25-G32	W-MS-070-100-G160	362
	W-MS-070-100-G160a	362
H-MS-25-G34	W-MS-070-500-G170	362
H-MS-25-G34a	W-MS-070-500-G170a	362
H-MS-25-G36	W-MS-070-1000-G180	362
H-MS-25-G36a	W-MS-070-1000-G180a	363
H-MS-25-G40	W-MS-070-005-G190	363
H-MS-25-G40a	W-MS-070-005-G190a	363
H-MS-25-G42	W-MS-070-010-G200	363
H-MS-25-G42a	W-MS-070-010-G200a	363
H-MS-25-G44	W-MS-070-010-G210	363
H-MS-25-G48	W-MS-070-020-G220	363
H-MS-25-G50	W-MS-070-020-G230	363
H-MS-25-G54	W-MS-070-050-G240	363
H-MS-25-G56b	W-MS-070-050-G250	364
H-MS-25-G58	W-MS-070-050-G260	364
H-MS-25-G62	W-MS-070-100-G270	364
H-MS-25-G64b	W-MS-070-100-G280	364
H-MS-25-G66	W-MS-070-100-G290	364
H-MS-25-G90	W-MS-070-005-G300	364
	W-MS-070-005-G300a	364
H-MS-25-G92	W-MS-070-010-G310	364
H-MS-25-G92a	W-MS-070-010-G310a	365
H-MS-25-G94	W-MS-070-010-G320	365
H-MS-25-G96	W-MS-070-020-G330	365
	W-MS-070-025-G335	365
H-MS-25-G98	W-MS-070-050-G340	365
H-MS-25-G100	W-MS-070-100-G350	365
H-MS-25-G104	W-MS-070-010-G360	365
H-MS-25-G110	W-MS-070-005-G370	365
H-MS-25-G112	W-MS-070-010-G380	366
H-MS-25-G114	W-MS-070-020-G390	366
	W-MS-070-025-G400	366
H-MS-25-G118	W-MS-070-050-G410	366
H-MS-25-G120	W-MS-070-100-G420	366
H-MS-25-G124	W-MS-070-005-G430	366
	W-MS-070-005-G435	366
H-MS-25-G126	W-MS-070-010-G440	366
	W-MS-070-010-G445	367
H-MS-25-G130	W-MS-070-005-G450	367
H-MS-25-G132	W-MS-070-010-G460	367
H-MS-25-G136	W-MS-070-020-G470	367
H-MS-25-G138	W-MS-070-025-G480	367
	W-MS-070-050-G485	367
	W-MS-070-100-G490	367
H-MS-25-G146	W-MS-070-005-G495	367
H-MS-25-G148	W-MS-070-010-G500	367
H-MS-25-G156	W-MS-070-005-G510	368
H-MS-25-G158	W-MS-070-010-G520	368
H-MS-25-G160	W-MS-070-010-G530	368
H-MS-25-G164	W-MS-070-020-G540	368
H-MS-25-G166	W-MS-070-025-G550	368
	W-MS-070-025-G550a	368
H-MS-25-G170	W-MS-070-050-G560	368
	W-MS-070-050-G560a	368
H-MS-25-G174	W-MS-070-100-G570	369
	W-MS-070-001-N010	369
	W-MS-070-002-N020	369
	W-MS-070-003-N030	369
H-MS-30-G20	W-MS-090-00.25-G010	369
H-MS-30-G22	W-MS-090-00.50-G020	369
H-MS-30-G24	W-MS-090-001-G030	370
H-MS-30-G26	W-MS-090-002-G040	370
H-MS-30-G30	W-MS-090-005-G050	370
H-MS-30-G32	W-MS-090-010-G060	370
H-MS-30-G36	W-MS-090-020-G070	370
H-MS-30-G38	W-MS-090-050-G080	370
H-MS-30-G40	W-MS-090-100-G090	371
H-MS-30-G24, G24, G26	W-MS-090-001.001.002-US010	371
	W-MS-090-100-N010	371
H-MS-160-G100	W-MS-100-005-G010	371

Haxby No.	Whitman No.	Page
H-MS-175-G88	W-MS-555-050-G050	428
H-MS-175-G90	W-MS-555-050-G060	429
H-MS-175-G92	W-MS-555-100-G070	429
H-MS-175-G94	W-MS-555-100-G080	429
	W-MS-570-00.12.50-G010	429
H-MS-150-G4	W-MS-570-00.12.50-G020	429
H-MS-150-G8	W-MS-570-00.25-G030	429
	W-MS-570-00.50-G040	429
	W-MS-570-001-G050	429
H-MS-150-G14	W-MS-570-005-G060	429
H-MS-150-G16	W-MS-570-010-G070	429
	W-MS-570-020-G080	430
	W-MS-570-050-G090	430
	W-MS-570-100-G100	430
H-MS-150-G24	W-MS-570-005-G110	430
H-MS-150-G26	W-MS-570-010-G120	430
H-MS-175-G100	W-MS-580-005-G010	430
H-MS-175-G102	W-MS-580-010-G020	430
H-MS-175-G104	W-MS-580-020-G030	430
H-MS-175-G106	W-MS-580-020-G040	430
H-MS-175-G108	W-MS-580-050-G050	431
H-MS-175-G110	W-MS-580-050-G060	431
H-MS-175-G112	W-MS-580-100-G070	431
H-MS-175-G114	W-MS-580-100-G080	431
H-MS-155-G2	W-MS-590-001-G010	432
H-MS-155-G4	W-MS-590-002-G020	432
H-MS-155-G4a	W-MS-590-002-G020a	432
H-MS-155-G6	W-MS-590-003-G030	432
H-MS-155-G6a	W-MS-590-003-G030a	432
H-MS-155-G8	W-MS-590-005-G040	432
H-MS-155-G8a	W-MS-590-005-G040a	432
H-MS-155-G14	W-MS-590-010-G050	433
H-MS-155-G14a	W-MS-590-010-G050a	433
H-MS-155-G16	W-MS-590-020-G060	433
H-MS-155-G16a	W-MS-590-020-G060a	433
H-MS-155-G18	W-MS-590-050-G070	433
H-MS-155-G18a	W-MS-590-050-G070a	433
H-MS-155-G20	W-MS-590-100-G080	433
H-MS-155-G20a	W-MS-590-100-G080a	433
	W-MS-590-__-G090	433
	W-MS-590-__-G090a	434
	W-MS-590-005-G100	434
H-MS-155-G24	W-MS-590-010-G110	434
H-MS-155-G28	W-MS-590-020-G120	434
H-MS-155-G32	W-MS-590-050-G130	434
H-MS-155-G36	W-MS-590-100-G140	434
	W-MS-600-005-G010	435
H-MS-165-G4	W-MS-600-010-G020	435
H-MS-165-G8	W-MS-600-020-G030	435
H-MS-165-G12	W-MS-600-050-G040	435
H-MS-165-G16	W-MS-600-100-G050	435
H-MS-180-G8	W-MS-620-005-G010	435
H-MS-180-G12	W-MS-620-010-G020	435
H-MS-180-G16	W-MS-620-020-G030	435
H-MS-180-G24	W-MS-620-050-G040	435
	W-MS-620-100-G050	435
H-US-2-G556	W-MS-630-005-G010	436
H-US-2-G558	W-MS-630-005-G020	436
H-US-2-G562	W-MS-630-010-G030	436
H-US-2-G566	W-MS-630-020-G040	436
H-US-2-G568	W-MS-630-020-G050	436
H-US-2-G572	W-MS-630-050-G060	436
H-US-2-G574	W-MS-630-050-G070	436
H-US-2-G578	W-MS-630-100-G080	436
H-US-2-G580	W-MS-630-100-G090	436
H-US-2-C572	W-MS-630-050-C060	436
H-US-2-C578	W-MS-630-100-C080	436
H-MS-160-G8	W-MS-640-005-G010	436
H-MS-160-G14	W-MS-640-010-G020	437
H-MS-160-G16	W-MS-640-020-G030	437
H-MS-160-G18	W-MS-640-050-G040	437
H-MS-160-G20	W-MS-640-100-G050	437
H-MS-160-G22	W-MS-640-500-G060	437
H-MS-160-G24	W-MS-640-1000-G070	437
	W-MS-640-020-G080	437
	W-MS-640-005-G090	438
	W-MS-640-010-G100	438
	W-MS-640-020-G110	438
H-MS-160-G150	W-MS-640-005-G120	438
H-MS-160-G156	W-MS-640-010-G130	438
H-MS-160-G158	W-MS-640-020-G140	438
H-MS-160-G160	W-MS-640-050-G150	439
H-MS-160-G162	W-MS-640-100-G160	439
H-MS-160-A5	W-MS-640-005-A010	439
H-MS-170-G2	W-MS-650-005-G010	439
H-MS-170-G4	W-MS-650-010-G020	439
H-MS-170-G6	W-MS-650-020-G030	439
H-MS-170-G8	W-MS-650-050-G040	439
H-MS-170-G10	W-MS-650-100-G050	439
H-MS-170-G12	W-MS-650-005-G060	439
H-MS-170-G14	W-MS-650-010-G070	440
H-MS-170-G16	W-MS-650-020-G080	440
H-MS-170-G18	W-MS-650-050-G090	440
	W-MS-650-050-G090a	440
H-MS-170-G20	W-MS-650-100-G100	440
	W-MS-650-100-G100a	440
	W-MS-660-00.12.50-G010	440
	W-MS-660-00.25-G020	441
	W-MS-660-00.50-G030	441
	W-MS-660-001-G040	441
	W-MS-660-003-G050	441
	W-MS-660-005-G060	441
	W-MS-660-010-G070	441
	W-MS-660-020-G080	441
	W-MS-660-050-G090	441
	W-MS-660-100-G100	442
H-MS-175-G2	W-MS-670-005-G010	442
H-MS-175-G6	W-MS-670-010-G020	442
H-MS-175-G12	W-MS-670-020-G030	442
	W-MS-670-020-G040	442
H-MS-175-G14a	W-MS-670-020-G040a	442
H-MS-175-G16	W-MS-670-050-G050	443
H-MS-175-G18a	W-MS-670-050-G060	443
H-MS-175-G20	W-MS-670-100-G070	443
H-MS-175-G22a	W-MS-670-100-G080	443
H-MS-175-G30	W-MS-670-005-G090	443
	W-MS-670-010-G095	443
	W-MS-670-020-G100	443
H-MS-175-G34a	W-MS-670-020-G100a	444
	W-MS-670-020-G105	444
	W-MS-670-050-G110	444
	W-MS-670-050-G110a	444
	W-MS-670-050-G115	444
	W-MS-670-100-G117	444
	W-MS-670-100-G117a	444
H-MS-175-G180	W-MS-670-005-G120	444
H-MS-175-G182	W-MS-670-010-G130	444
H-MS-175-G184	W-MS-670-020-G140	444
H-MS-175-G186	W-MS-670-020-G150	444
H-MS-175-G188	W-MS-670-050-G160	444
H-MS-175-G190	W-MS-670-050-G170	444
H-MS-175-G192	W-MS-670-100-G180	445
H-MS-175-G194	W-MS-670-100-G190	445
H-MS-175-G198	W-MS-670-010-G200	445
H-MS-175-G200	W-MS-670-020-G210	445
H-MS-175-G202	W-MS-670-050-G220	445
	W-MS-670-100-G230	445
H-MS-175-G208	W-MS-670-010-G240	445
H-MS-175-G210	W-MS-670-020-G250	445
H-MS-175-G212	W-MS-670-050-G260	445
H-MS-175-G220	W-MS-670-010-G270	445
H-MS-175-G220a	W-MS-670-010-G270a	445
H-MS-175-G224	W-MS-670-020-G280	445
H-MS-175-G224a	W-MS-670-020-G280a	445
H-MS-175-G228	W-MS-670-050-G290	445
H-MS-175-G228a	W-MS-670-050-G290a	446
	W-MS-670-100-G300	446
	W-MS-680-001-G010	446

Tennessee

Haxby No.	Whitman No.	Page
H-TN-210-G68	W-TN-325-010-G070	529
H-TN-210-G70	W-TN-325-020-G080	529
H-TN-210-G72	W-TN-325-020-G090	529
H-TN-210-G74	W-TN-325-050-G100	529
H-TN-210-G74a	W-TN-325-050-G100a	529
H-TN-210-G76	W-TN-325-100-G110	529
H-TN-210-G76a	W-TN-325-100-G110a	529
H-TN-210-G78	W-TN-325-500-G120	529
H-TN-210-G80	W-TN-325-1000-G130	530
H-TN-210-G84	W-TN-325-005-G140	530
H-TN-210-G86	W-TN-325-010-G150	530
H-TN-210-G88	W-TN-325-020-G160	530
H-TN-210-S6	W-TN-325-001-S010	530
	W-TN-325-004-N010	530
H-TN-210-S8	W-TN-325-010-S020	530
H-TN-210-C70	W-TN-325-020-C080	530
H-TN-55-G80	W-TN-330-001-G010	530
H-TN-55-G82a	W-TN-330-001-G020	531
H-TN-55-G84	W-TN-330-002-G030	531
H-TN-55-G86a	W-TN-330-002-G040	531
H-TN-55-G88	W-TN-330-003-G050	531
H-TN-55-G90a	W-TN-330-003-G060	531
H-TN-55-G92	W-TN-330-005-G070	531
H-TN-55-G94	W-TN-330-005-G080	532
H-TN-55-G96a	W-TN-330-005-G090	532
H-TN-55-G98a	W-TN-330-005-G100	532
H-TN-55-G100	W-TN-330-010-G110	532
H-TN-55-G100a	W-TN-330-010-G120	532
H-TN-55-G102	W-TN-330-020-G130	532
H-TN-55-G104a	W-TN-330-020-G140	533
H-TN-75-G88	W-TN-335-005-G010	533
H-TN-75-G90	W-TN-335-010-G020	533
H-TN-75-G92	W-TN-335-020-G030	533
H-TN-75-G94	W-TN-335-050-G040	533
H-TN-75-G96	W-TN-335-100-G050	533
H-TN-75-N27	W-TN-335-003-N010	533
H-TN-75-N30	W-TN-335-050-N020	533
H-TN-75-G104	W-TN-340-005-G010	534
H-TN-75-G106	W-TN-340-010-G020	534
H-TN-75-G108	W-TN-340-020-G030	534
H-TN-75-G110	W-TN-340-050-G040	534
H-TN-75-G112	W-TN-340-100-G050	534
H-TN-75-N33	W-TN-340-003-N010	534
H-TN-75-N36	W-TN-340-050-N020	534
H-TN-55-G2	W-TN-345-001-G010	535
H-TN-55-G4	W-TN-345-001-G020	535
H-TN-55-G6a	W-TN-345-001-G030	535
H-TN-55-G6b	W-TN-345-001-G030a	535
H-TN-55-G6d	W-TN-345-001-G030b	535
H-TN-55-G8a	W-TN-345-001-G040	535
H-TN-55-G10	W-TN-345-002-G050	535
H-TN-55-G12	W-TN-345-002-G060	535
H-TN-55-G14a	W-TN-345-002-G070	535
H-TN-55-G14b	W-TN-345-002-G070a	535
H-TN-55-G14d	W-TN-345-002-G070b	535
H-TN-55-G16a	W-TN-345-002-G080	536
H-TN-55-G18	W-TN-345-003-G090	536
H-TN-55-G20	W-TN-345-003-G100	536
H-TN-55-G22a	W-TN-345-003-G110	536
H-TN-55-G24a	W-TN-345-003-G110a	536
H-TN-55-G26a	W-TN-345-003-G120	536
H-TN-55-G28	W-TN-345-004-G130	537
H-TN-55-G30	W-TN-345-005-G140	537
H-TN-55-G32	W-TN-345-005-G150	537
H-TN-55-G34a	W-TN-345-005-G160	537
H-TN-55-G34d	W-TN-345-005-G170	537
H-TN-55-G36a	W-TN-345-005-G180	537
H-TN-55-G38a	W-TN-345-005-G190	537
H-TN-55-G40	W-TN-345-010-G200	538
H-TN-55-G42	W-TN-345-010-G210	538
H-TN-55-G44a	W-TN-345-010-G220	538
H-TN-55-G46	W-TN-345-010-G230	538
H-TN-55-G48	W-TN-345-020-G240	538
H-TN-55-G50	W-TN-345-020-G250	538
H-TN-55-G52	W-TN-345-050-G260	538
H-TN-55-G52a	W-TN-345-050-G260a	539
H-TN-55-G54	W-TN-345-100-G270	539
H-TN-55-G54a	W-TN-345-100-G270a	539
H-TN-55-G36a, G36a, G46, G50	W-TN-345-005.005.010.020-US010	539
H-TN-65-G2a	W-TN-350-001-G010	540
H-TN-65-G4a	W-TN-350-002-G020	540
	W-TN-350-003-G030	540
H-TN-65-G6a	W-TN-350-003-G030a	540
H-TN-65-G8	W-TN-350-005-G040	540
H-TN-65-G8a	W-TN-350-005-G040a	541
H-TN-65-G10	W-TN-350-010-G050	541
H-TN-65-G10a	W-TN-350-010-G050a	541
H-TN-65-G12	W-TN-350-020-G060	541
H-TN-65-G12a	W-TN-350-020-G060a	541
H-TN-75-G8	W-TN-355-005-G010	542
H-TN-75-G10	W-TN-355-010-G020	542
H-TN-75-G12	W-TN-355-020-G030	542
H-TN-75-G14	W-TN-355-050-G040	542
H-TN-75-G16	W-TN-355-100-G050	542
H-TN-190-G80	W-TN-360-001-G010	542
H-TN-190-G82	W-TN-360-002-G020	542
H-TN-190-G84	W-TN-360-005-G030	542
H-TN-190-G86	W-TN-360-010-G040	542
H-TN-190-G88	W-TN-360-020-G050	542
H-TN-190-G90	W-TN-360-050-G060	542
H-TN-190-G92	W-TN-360-100-G070	542
H-TN-195-G190a	W-TN-365-001-G010	543
H-TN-195-G192a	W-TN-365-002-G020	543
H-TN-195-G194a	W-TN-365-005-G030	543
H-TN-195-G194b	W-TN-365-005-G030a	543
H-TN-195-G196a	W-TN-365-010-G040	543
H-TN-195-G198c	W-TN-365-020-G050	543
H-TN-195-G200c	W-TN-365-050-G060	543
H-TN-195-G202c	W-TN-365-100-G070	544
H-TN-195-G210	W-TN-365-00.05-G080	544
H-TN-195-G210a	W-TN-365-00.05-G080a	544
H-TN-195-G212	W-TN-365-00.10-G090	544
H-TN-195-G212a	W-TN-365-00.10-G090a	544
H-TN-195-G212c	W-TN-365-00.10-G090b	544
H-TN-195-G212d	W-TN-365-00.10-G090c	544
H-TN-195-G214c	W-TN-365-00.25-G100	545
H-TN-195-G214d	W-TN-365-00.25-G100a	545
H-TN-195-G214	W-TN-365-00.25-G100b	545
H-TN-195-G214a	W-TN-365-00.25-G100c	545
H-TN-195-G216c	W-TN-365-00.50-G110	545
H-TN-195-G216d	W-TN-365-00.50-G110a	545
H-TN-195-G216	W-TN-365-00.50-G110b	545
H-TN-195-G216a	W-TN-365-00.50-G110c	546
	W-TN-365-020-C050	546
H-TN-145-G18	W-TN-370-001-G010	546
H-TN-145-G20	W-TN-370-002-G020	546
H-TN-145-G22	W-TN-370-003-G030	546
H-TN-145-G24	W-TN-370-005-G040	546
H-TN-145-G26	W-TN-370-010-G050	547
H-TN-145-G28	W-TN-370-020-G060	547
H-TN-145-G30	W-TN-370-050-G070	547
H-TN-145-G32	W-TN-370-100-G080	547
H-TN-145-G66	W-TN-370-001-G090	547
H-TN-145-G66a	W-TN-370-001-G090a	547
H-TN-145-G68	W-TN-370-002-G100	547
H-TN-145-G68a	W-TN-370-002-G100a	547
H-TN-145-G70	W-TN-370-003-G110	547
H-TN-145-G72	W-TN-370-005-G120	548
H-TN-145-G74	W-TN-370-010-G130	548
H-TN-145-G78	W-TN-370-020-G140	548
H-TN-145-G80	W-TN-370-050-G150	548
H-TN-145-G82	W-TN-370-100-G160	548
H-TN-145-R5	W-TN-370-010-R010	548
H-TN-60-G2a	W-TN-375-001-G010	548
	W-TN-375-001-G010a	549
H-TN-60-G4a	W-TN-375-002-G020	549
H-TN-60-G6	W-TN-375-005-G030	549
	W-TN-375-005-G030a	549

Haxby No.	Whitman No.	Page
H-TN-95-G16b	W-TN-520-050-G080	569
H-TN-95-G18b	W-TN-520-100-G090	569
H-TN-95-G26a	W-TN-520-005-G100	569
H-TN-95-G28b	W-TN-520-010-G110	569
H-TN-95-G30a	W-TN-520-010-G120	569
H-TN-95-G26a, G30a	W-TN-520-005.010-US010	569
H-TN-95-R5	W-TN-520-010-R010	569
H-TN-100-G2	W-TN-530-001-G010	570
H-TN-100-G4	W-TN-530-002-G020	570
H-TN-100-G6	W-TN-530-003-G030	570
	W-TN-530-003-G030a	570
H-TN-100-G8	W-TN-530-005-G040	571
H-TN-100-G10	W-TN-530-005-G050	571
H-TN-100-G10a	W-TN-530-005-G050a	571
H-TN-100-G10b	W-TN-530-005-G050b	571
	W-TN-530-005-G050c	571
H-TN-100-G12	W-TN-530-010-G060	571
H-TN-100-G14	W-TN-530-010-G070	571
H-TN-100-G14a	W-TN-530-010-G070a	572
H-TN-100-G14b	W-TN-530-010-G070b	572
H-TN-100-G16	W-TN-530-020-G080	572
H-TN-100-G18a	W-TN-530-020-G090	572
	W-TN-530-020-G090a	572
H-TN-100-G20a	W-TN-530-050-G100	572
	W-TN-530-050-G100a	572
H-TN-100-G22a	W-TN-530-100-G110	572
H-TN-100-G40a	W-TN-530-001-G120	573
H-TN-100-G42	W-TN-530-001-G130	573
H-TN-100-G42a	W-TN-530-001-G130a	573
H-TN-100-G42b	W-TN-530-001-G130b	573
H-TN-100-G42c	W-TN-530-001-G130c	573
H-TN-100-G42d	W-TN-530-001-G130d	573
	W-TN-530-001-G130e	573
H-TN-100-G42e	W-TN-530-001-G130f	573
	W-TN-530-001-G130g	573
H-TN-100-G44a	W-TN-530-002-G140	573
H-TN-100-G46	W-TN-530-002-G150	573
H-TN-100-G46a	W-TN-530-002-G150a	574
H-TN-100-G46b	W-TN-530-002-G150b	574
H-TN-100-G46c	W-TN-530-002-G150c	574
H-TN-100-G46d	W-TN-530-002-G150d	574
H-TN-100-G46e	W-TN-530-002-G150e	574
H-TN-100-G48a	W-TN-530-003-G160	574
H-TN-100-G50	W-TN-530-003-G170	574
H-TN-100-G50a	W-TN-530-003-G170a	574
H-TN-100-G50b	W-TN-530-003-G170b	574
H-TN-100-G50c	W-TN-530-003-G170c	574
	W-TN-530-003-G170d	575
H-TN-100-G50d	W-TN-530-003-G170e	575
H-TN-100-G50e	W-TN-530-003-G170f	575
H-TN-100-G52a	W-TN-530-005-G180	575
H-TN-100-G54	W-TN-530-005-G190	575
H-TN-100-G54a	W-TN-530-005-G190a	575
H-TN-100-G54b	W-TN-530-005-G190b	575
H-TN-100-G54c	W-TN-530-005-G190c	575
H-TN-100-G54d	W-TN-530-005-G190d	576
H-TN-100-G54e	W-TN-530-005-G190e	576
H-TN-100-G54f	W-TN-530-005-G190f	576
H-TN-100-G56a	W-TN-530-010-G200	576
H-TN-100-G58	W-TN-530-010-G210	576
H-TN-100-G58b	W-TN-530-010-G210a	576
H-TN-100-G58c	W-TN-530-010-G210b	576
H-TN-100-G60a	W-TN-530-020-G220	576
H-TN-100-G62a	W-TN-530-050-G230	576
H-TN-100-G64a	W-TN-530-100-G240	577
H-TN-100-G66a	W-TN-530-500-G250	577
H-TN-100-G68a	W-TN-530-1000-G260	577
H-TN-100-G2, G2, G4, G6	W-TN-530-001.001.002.003-US010	577
H-TN-100-R5	W-TN-530-100-R010	578
H-TN-100-R5	W-TN-530-005-R020	578
	W-TN-530-005-N010	578
H-TN-105-G2	W-TN-540-001-G010	578
H-TN-105-G2a	W-TN-540-001-G010a	578
H-TN-105-G2b	W-TN-540-001-G010b	578
H-TN-105-G2c	W-TN-540-001-G010c	578
H-TN-105-G2d	W-TN-540-001-G010d	579
H-TN-105-G4	W-TN-540-003-G020	579
H-TN-105-G4a	W-TN-540-003-G020a	579
H-TN-105-G4b	W-TN-540-003-G020b	579
H-TN-105-G4c	W-TN-540-003-G020c	579
H-TN-105-G4d	W-TN-540-003-G020d	579
H-TN-105-G6	W-TN-540-005-G030	579
H-TN-105-G6a	W-TN-540-005-G030a	579
H-TN-105-G6b	W-TN-540-005-G030b	579
H-TN-105-G6c	W-TN-540-005-G030c	580
H-TN-105-G6d	W-TN-540-005-G030d	580
H-TN-105-G6e	W-TN-540-005-G030e	580
	W-TN-540-005-G030f	580
H-TN-105-G6f	W-TN-540-005-G030g	580
	W-TN-540-005-G030h	580
H-TN-105-G8	W-TN-540-010-G040	580
H-TN-105-G8a	W-TN-540-010-G040a	581
H-TN-105-G8b	W-TN-540-010-G040b	581
H-TN-105-G8c	W-TN-540-010-G040c	581
H-TN-105-G8d	W-TN-540-010-G040d	581
H-TN-105-G8e	W-TN-540-010-G040e	581
H-TN-105-G8f	W-TN-540-010-G040f	581
H-TN-105-G8g	W-TN-540-010-G040g	581
H-TN-105-G8h	W-TN-540-010-G040h	581
H-TN-105-G8i	W-TN-540-010-G040i	581
H-TN-105-G8j	W-TN-540-010-G040j	582
H-TN-105-G8k	W-TN-540-010-G040k	582
H-TN-105-G8l	W-TN-540-010-G040l	582
H-TN-105-G8m	W-TN-540-010-G040m	582
H-TN-105-G8n	W-TN-540-010-G040n	582
H-TN-105-G8o	W-TN-540-010-G040o	582
H-TN-105-G8p	W-TN-540-010-G040p	582
H-TN-105-G8q	W-TN-540-010-G040q	582
H-TN-105-G8r	W-TN-540-010-G040r	583
H-TN-105-G8s	W-TN-540-010-G040s	583
H-TN-115-G8	W-TN-550-004-G010	583
	W-TN-560-001-G010	583
	W-TN-560-001-G020	583
	W-TN-560-001-G020a	583
	W-TN-560-001-G030	584
	W-TN-560-002-G040	584
	W-TN-560-002-G040a	584
	W-TN-560-005-G050	584
	W-TN-560-010-G060	584
H-TN-185-G200	W-TN-570-001-G010	584
H-TN-185-G202	W-TN-570-002-G020	584
H-TN-185-G204	W-TN-570-003-G030	585
H-TN-185-G206	W-TN-570-005-G040	585
H-TN-185-G206a	W-TN-570-005-G040a	585
H-TN-185-G208a	W-TN-570-005-G050	585
H-TN-185-G210	W-TN-570-010-G060	585
H-TN-185-G210a	W-TN-570-010-G060a	585
H-TN-185-G212	W-TN-570-010-G070	585
H-TN-185-G214	W-TN-570-020-G080	585
H-TN-185-G214a	W-TN-570-020-G080a	585
H-TN-185-G216	W-TN-570-050-G090	585
	W-TN-570-050-G095	585
H-TN-185-G218	W-TN-570-100-G100	585
H-TN-185-G222	W-TN-570-00.05-G110	585
H-TN-185-G224	W-TN-570-00.10-G120	585
H-TN-185-G226	W-TN-570-00.25-G130	586
H-TN-185-G228	W-TN-570-00.30-G140	586
H-TN-185-G230	W-TN-570-00.50-G150	586
H-TN-185-G232	W-TN-570-00.80-G160	586
H-TN-185-S100	W-TN-570-010-S010	586
H-TN-185-S102	W-TN-570-010-S020	586
H-TN-185-S104	W-TN-570-020-S030	586
H-TN-185-S106	W-TN-570-020-S040	586
H-TN-185-S108	W-TN-570-050-S050	586
H-TN-185-S110	W-TN-570-100-S060	586
H-TN-185-S112	W-TN-570-100-S070	586
H-TN-120-G2a	W-TN-580-005-G010	586
H-TN-120-G4a	W-TN-580-010-G020	587

Haxby No.	Whitman No.	Page
H-TN-185-G6	W-TN-810-002-G030	618
H-TN-185-G6a	W-TN-810-002-G030a	618
H-TN-185-G6b	W-TN-810-002-G030b	618
H-TN-185-G8a	W-TN-810-002-G040	618
H-TN-185-G10	W-TN-810-003-G050	618
H-TN-185-G10a	W-TN-810-003-G050a	619
H-TN-185-G10b	W-TN-810-003-G050b	619
H-TN-185-G12	W-TN-810-005-G060	619
H-TN-185-G14a	W-TN-810-005-G070	619
H-TN-185-G16	W-TN-810-005-G080	619
H-TN-185-G18	W-TN-810-005-G090	619
H-TN-185-G18a	W-TN-810-005-G090a	619
H-TN-185-G20	W-TN-810-010-G100	619
H-TN-185-G22a	W-TN-810-010-G110	619
H-TN-185-G24	W-TN-810-010-G120	620
H-TN-185-G26	W-TN-810-010-G130	620
H-TN-185-G26a	W-TN-810-010-G130a	620
H-TN-185-G28	W-TN-810-020-G140	620
H-TN-185-G30a	W-TN-810-020-G150	620
H-TN-185-G32	W-TN-810-020-G160	620
H-TN-185-G34	W-TN-810-020-G170	620
H-TN-185-G34a	W-TN-810-020-G170a	620
H-TN-185-G36	W-TN-810-050-G180	620
H-TN-185-G38	W-TN-810-050-G190	620
H-TN-185-G38a	W-TN-810-050-G190a	620
	W-TN-810-050-G190b	621
H-TN-185-G40	W-TN-810-100-G200	621
H-TN-185-G42	W-TN-810-100-G210	621
H-TN-185-G42a	W-TN-810-100-G210a	621
	W-TN-810-100-G210b	621
	W-TN-810-__-G220	621
H-TN-185-G330	W-TN-810-001-G230	622
H-TN-185-G334	W-TN-810-005-G240	622
H-TN-185-G336	W-TN-810-005-G250	622
H-TN-185-G340	W-TN-810-010-G260	622
H-TN-185-G344	W-TN-810-020-G270	622
H-TN-185-G348	W-TN-810-050-G280	622
H-TN-185-G352	W-TN-810-100-G290	622
H-TN-185-S4	W-TN-810-010-S010	622
H-TN-185-S6	W-TN-810-010-S020	622
H-TN-185-C32	W-TN-810-020-C160	622
H-TN-185-S8	W-TN-810-020-S030	622
H-TN-185-S10	W-TN-810-020-S040	622
H-TN-185-S12	W-TN-810-050-S050	623
H-TN-185-S14	W-TN-810-100-S060	623
H-TN-185-S16	W-TN-810-100-S070	623
H-TN-185-R5	W-TN-810-002-R010	623
H-TN-185-G10	W-TN-810-003-R020	623
H-TN-185-R15	W-TN-810-005-R030	623
H-TN-185-N10	W-TN-810-010-N010	623
H-TN-185-A10	W-TN-810-100-A010	623
	W-TN-820-001-G010	623
	W-TN-820-002-G020	623
	W-TN-820-002-G030	623
H-TN-200-G2	W-TN-830-001-G010	624
H-TN-200-G2b	W-TN-830-001-G010a	624
H-TN-200-G4	W-TN-830-005-G020	624
H-TN-200-G4b	W-TN-830-005-G020a	624
H-TN-200-G6a	W-TN-830-010-G030	624
H-TN-200-G10a	W-TN-830-00.25-G040	624
H-TN-200-G12	W-TN-830-00.50-G050	625
H-TN-200-G12a	W-TN-830-00.50-G050a	625
H-TN-200-G6a	W-TN-830-010-US010	625
H-TN-200-R5	W-TN-830-010-R010	625
H-TN-200-R10	W-TN-830-020-R020	625
H-TN-210-G2	W-TN-840-001-G010	625
H-TN-210-G4	W-TN-840-002-G020	626
H-TN-210-G6	W-TN-840-003-G030	626
H-TN-210-G8	W-TN-840-005-G040	626
H-TN-210-G10	W-TN-840-005-G050	626
H-TN-210-G12	W-TN-840-010-G060	626
H-TN-210-G14	W-TN-840-010-G070	626
H-TN-210-G16	W-TN-840-020-G080	626
H-TN-210-G18	W-TN-840-020-G090	626
H-TN-210-G20	W-TN-840-050-G100	626
H-TN-210-G20a	W-TN-840-050-G100a	626
H-TN-210-G22	W-TN-840-100-G110	626
H-TN-210-G22a	W-TN-840-100-G110a	626
H-TN-210-G24	W-TN-840-500-G120	626
H-TN-210-G26	W-TN-840-1000-G130	627
	W-TN-840-__-G140	627
H-TN-210-G30	W-TN-840-005-G150	627
H-TN-210-G34	W-TN-840-010-G160	627
H-TN-210-G38	W-TN-840-020-G170	627
H-TN-210-G190	W-TN-840-005-G180	627
H-TN-210-G194	W-TN-840-020-G190	627
	W-TN-840-00.12.50-G200	627
	W-TN-840-001-G215	627
	W-TN-840-002-G230	628
H-TN-210-G200	W-TN-840-001-G240	628
H-TN-210-G202a	W-TN-840-001-G250	628
H-TN-210-G204	W-TN-840-002-G260	628
H-TN-210-G206a	W-TN-840-002-G270	628
H-TN-210-G208	W-TN-840-003-G280	628
H-TN-210-G210	W-TN-840-005-G290	629
H-TN-210-G214a	W-TN-840-005-G300	629
	W-TN-840-005-G300a	629
H-TN-210-G216	W-TN-840-010-G310	629
H-TN-210-G220a	W-TN-840-010-G320	629
H-TN-210-G222	W-TN-840-020-G330	629
H-TN-210-G224a	W-TN-840-020-G340	629
H-TN-210-G226	W-TN-840-050-G350	629
H-TN-210-G228a	W-TN-840-050-G360	629
H-TN-210-G230	W-TN-840-100-G370	630
	W-TN-840-100-G380	630
H-TN-210-G232a	W-TN-840-100-G390	630
H-TN-210-G234	W-TN-840-500-G400	630
H-TN-210-G236a	W-TN-840-500-G410	630
	W-TN-840-500-G410a	630
H-TN-210-G238	W-TN-840-1000-G420	630
H-TN-210-G240a	W-TN-840-1000-G430	630
	W-TN-840-1000-G430a	630
H-TN-210-S2	W-TN-840-001-S010	630
H-TN-210-S4	W-TN-840-010-S020	630
H-TN-210-C16	W-TN-840-020-C080	630
H-TN-215-G2	W-TN-850-001-G010	631
H-TN-215-G4	W-TN-850-005-G020	631
H-TN-140-G40	W-TN-860-001-G010	631
H-TN-140-G42	W-TN-860-002-G020	631
H-TN-140-G46	W-TN-860-005-G030	631
H-TN-140-G48	W-TN-860-010-G040	631
H-TN-140-G50	W-TN-860-020-G050	631
H-TN-185-G262	W-TN-870-001-G010	632
H-TN-185-G264	W-TN-870-002-G020	632
H-TN-185-G266	W-TN-870-003-G030	632
H-TN-185-G268	W-TN-870-005-G040	632
H-TN-185-G270	W-TN-870-005-G050	632
H-TN-185-G270a	W-TN-870-005-G050a	632
H-TN-185-G272	W-TN-870-010-G060	632
H-TN-185-G274	W-TN-870-010-G070	632
H-TN-185-G274a	W-TN-870-010-G070a	632
H-TN-185-G276	W-TN-870-020-G080	632
H-TN-185-G278	W-TN-870-020-G090	632
H-TN-185-G278a	W-TN-870-020-G090a	632
H-TN-185-G280	W-TN-870-050-G100	632
H-TN-185-G282	W-TN-870-100-G110	632
H-TN-185-G286	W-TN-870-00.05-G120	633
H-TN-185-G288	W-TN-870-00.10-G130	633
H-TN-185-G290	W-TN-870-00.25-G140	633
H-TN-185-G292	W-TN-870-00.30-G150	633
H-TN-185-G294	W-TN-870-00.50-G160	633
H-TN-185-G296	W-TN-870-00.80-G170	633
H-TN-185-S116	W-TN-870-010-S010	633
H-TN-185-S118	W-TN-870-010-S020	633
H-TN-185-S120	W-TN-870-020-S030	633
H-TN-185-S122	W-TN-870-020-S040	633
H-TN-185-S124	W-TN-870-050-S050	633
H-TN-185-S126	W-TN-870-100-S060	633

Texas